lonely pl

D0019844

Eastern
USA

| | | | | | | | | | |
ND
MN
MI
VT
NH New England p162
ME
SD
WI
NY
MA
CT RI
New York, New Jersey & Pennsylvania p54
IA
Great Lakes p510
NE
IL IN OH
PA
NJ
MD DE
Washington, DC & the Capital Region p246
KS
MO
WV VA
KY
TN
NC
The South p324
AR
SC
OK
MS AL GA
LA
TX
Florida p452
FL

THIS EDITION WRITTEN AND RESEARCHED BY
Karla Zimmerman,
Amy C Balfour, Adam Karlin, Zora O'Neill,
Kevin Raub, Regis St Louis, Mara Vorhees

NEW YORK CITY P55

BAXTER STATE PARK P245, MAINE

Contents

Welcome to Eastern USA

Flanked by megacities New York City and Chicago; landscaped with dune-backed beaches, smoky mountains and gator swamps; and steeped in musical roots, the East rolls out a sweet trip.

Mighty Metropolises

Brimming with 8.4 million people, the megalopolis of New York looms like an alien mother ship over the East, offering a mind-blowing array of culture, cuisine and entertainment. Cloud-poking Chicago, power-brokering Washington, DC and fiery, Latin-fused Miami rise up close on its heels as other one-of-a-kind cityscapes. Look deeper to find the captivating old quarters of New Orleans, reborn from waterlogged ashes, and raw-edged Detroit, where young DIY devotees are flocking to transform the abandoned city.

Beaches & Back Roads

Some of America's best beaches are on the East Coast, from the wild dunes and whale-rich waters of Cape Cod to the taffy-shop-lined boardwalks of Ocean City or the coral reefs of the Florida Keys. Inland, nature puts on a show in the swampy Florida Everglades, wolf-howling Boundary Waters, mist-tipped Appalachian Mountains and New England's forests, which blaze red, orange and yellow each autumn. Slowpoke byways unfurl throughout so you can soak up the landscapes, from historic Civil War battlefields to kitschy roadside attractions.

Chowhounds' Smorgasbord

Good eatin' reaches epic proportions here: hulking steamed lobsters with melted butter in Maine's seafood shacks, bagels and lox in Manhattan's delis, saucy barbecue ribs in Memphis' roadhouses, butter-smothered biscuits in North Carolina's diners, hot-spiced gumbo in New Orleans' cafes...and for dessert, thick slices of berry pie in the Midwest's supper clubs. You'll certainly work up a thirst, which you can slake with the region's sweet white wines, microbrewed beers and home-grown bourbon.

Cultural Cradle

The museums here are the nation's greatest hits: the Smithsonian, housing everything but the kitchen sink; the Metropolitan Museum of Art, a city-state of treasures; and the Art Institute of Chicago, hanging Impressionists by the roomful. Explore the roots of the blues, jazz, and rock and roll at musical meccas such as Memphis' Sun Studio, where Elvis got his groove on; Cleveland's Rock and Roll Hall of Fame, for artifacts like Jimi Hendrix' Stratocaster; and the juke joints of Clarksdale, where blues slide guitar first pierced the air. For sky-high designs, Chicago and New York are drawing boards for the modern era's great architects.

Why I Love Eastern USA

By Karla Zimmerman, Writer

I love the big city/rural mash-up in the eastern part of the country. You can be surrounded by skyscrapers in Chicago for breakfast, then two hours later be driving beside clip-clopping horses and buggies in Indiana's Amish country. You can be in the corridors of power in Washington, DC's Capitol for lunch, then hiking mountains in Virginia's dreamy Shenandoah National Park 90 minutes later. Throughout the region the music rocks, exquisite beers flow, and back-road diners, rib joints and lobster shacks tempt you into yet another slice of pie. Mmm, pie...

For more about our writers, see page 672

Above: Downtown Chicago (p514)

Eastern USA

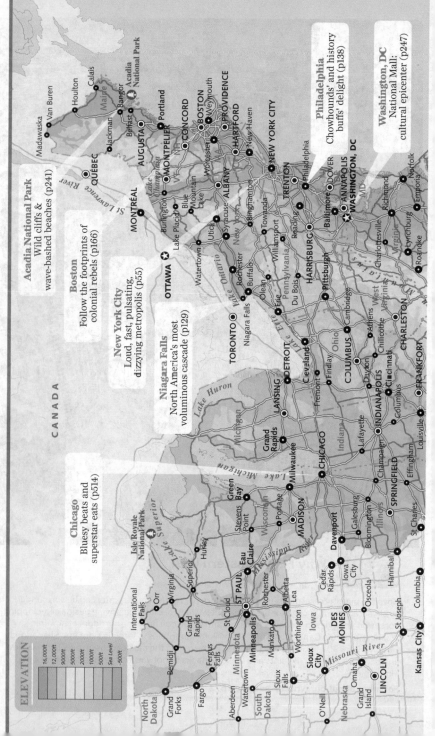

ELEVATION

16,000ft
12,000ft
9000ft
5000ft
2000ft
1000ft
500ft
Sea Level
-500ft

Chicago
Bluesy beats and superstar eats (p514)

Niagara Falls
North America's most voluminous cascade (p129)

New York City
Loud, fast, pulsating, dizzying metropolis (p55)

Boston
Follow the footprints of colonial rebels (p166)

Acadia National Park
Wild cliffs & wave-bashed beaches (p241)

Philadelphia
Chowhounds' and history buffs' delight (p138)

Washington, DC
National Mall: cultural epicenter (p247)

0 ——— 500 km
0 ——— 300 miles

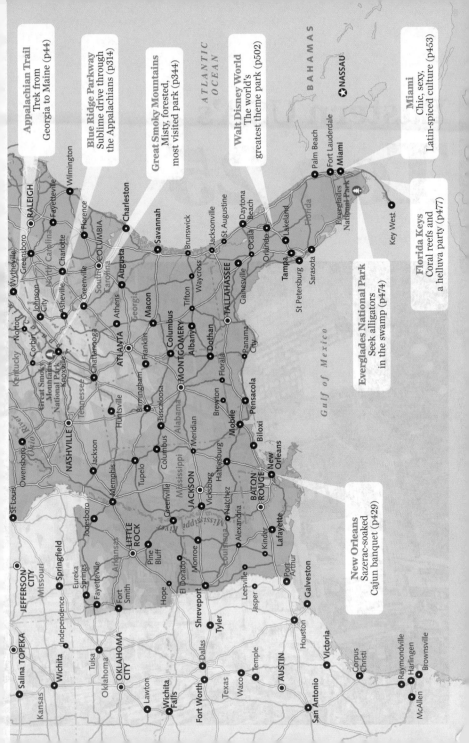

Appalachian Trail
Trek from Georgia to Maine (p44)

Blue Ridge Parkway
Sublime drive through the Appalachians (p314)

Great Smoky Mountains
Misty, forested, most visited park (p344)

Walt Disney World
The world's greatest theme park (p502)

Miami
Chic, sexy, Latin-spiced culture (p453)

Florida Keys
Coral reefs and a helluva party (p477)

Everglades National Park
Seek alligators in the swamp (p474)

New Orleans
Sazerac-soaked Cajun banquet (p429)

ATLANTIC OCEAN

BAHAMAS

◉ NASSAU

Gulf of Mexico

Eastern USA's
Top 25

New York City

1 Home to striving artists, hedge-fund moguls and immigrants from every corner of the globe, New York City (p55) is constantly reinventing itself. It remains one of the world centers of fashion, theater, food, music, publishing, advertising and finance. A staggering number of museums, parks and ethnic neighborhoods are scattered through the five boroughs. Do as every New Yorker does: hit the streets. Every block reflects the character and history of this dizzying kaleidoscope, and on even a short walk you can cross continents. Times Square (p69)

National Mall

2 Nearly 2 miles long and lined with iconic monuments and hallowed marble buildings, the National Mall (p250) is the epicenter of Washington, DC's political and cultural life. In the summer, massive music and food festivals are staged here, while year-round visitors wander the halls of America's finest museums lining the green. For exploring American history, there's no better place to ruminate, whether tracing your hand along the Vietnam War Memorial or ascending the steps of the Lincoln Memorial, where Martin Luther King Jr gave his famous 'I Have a Dream' speech. Lincoln Memorial (p250)

ANDREY BAYDA / SHUTTERSTOCK ©

DANITA DELIMONT / GETTY IMAGES ©

Walt Disney World

3 Want to set the bar high? Call yourself the 'Happiest Place on Earth.' Walt Disney World (p502) does, and then pulls out all the stops to deliver the exhilarating sensation that you are the most important character in the show. Despite all the frantic rides, entertainment and nostalgia, the magic is watching your own child swell with belief after they have made Goofy laugh, been curtsied to by Cinderella, guarded the galaxy with Buzz Lightyear, and battled Darth Maul like your very own Jedi knight. View of Expedition Everest

Chicago

4 The Windy City (p514) will blow you away with its architecture, lakefront beaches and world-class museums. But its true mojo is its blend of high culture and earthy pleasures. Is there another metropolis that dresses its Picasso sculpture in local sports-team gear? Where residents queue for hot dogs in equal measure to North America's top restaurants? Winters are brutal, but come summer, Chicago fetes the warm days with food and music festivals that make fine use of its waterfront.

New England in Fall

5 It's a major event, one approaching epic proportions in New England (p162): watching the leaves change color. You can do it anywhere – all you need is one brilliant tree. But if you're most people, you'll want *lots* of trees. From the Berkshires in Massachusetts and the Litchfield Hills in Connecticut to the Green Mountains in Vermont, entire hillsides blaze in brilliant crimsons, oranges and yellows. Covered bridges and white-steeple churches with abundant maple trees put Vermont and New Hampshire at the forefront of leaf-peeping heaven.

Route 66

6 Known as the Mother Road, this fragile ribbon of concrete was the USA's original road trip, launched in 1926. It begins in Chicago, and the 300-mile stretch onward through Illinois (p539) offers classic, time-warped touring. Fork into thick slabs of pie in small-town diners; snap photos of roadside attractions like the Gemini Giant, a sky-high fiberglass spaceman; and motor on past neon signs, drive-in movie theaters and other Americana. From here it's 2100 miles more to the end of the route in Los Angeles.
Charlie Parker's Diner, Springfield (p540), Illinois

New Orleans

7 Reborn after Hurricane Katrina in 2005, New Orleans (p429) is back. Caribbean-colonial architecture, Creole cuisine and a riotous air of celebration seem more alluring than ever in the Big Easy. Nights are spent catching Dixieland jazz, blues and rock amid bouncing live-music joints, and the city's annual festivals (Mardi Gras, Jazz Fest) are famous the world over. 'Nola' is also a food-loving town that celebrates its myriad culinary influences. Feast on lip-smacking jambalaya, soft-shelled crab and Louisiana *cochon* (pulled pork) before hitting the bar scene on Frenchman St. Preservation Hall (p443), French Quarter

PLAN YOUR TRIP EASTERN USA'S TOP 25

ROSAIRENEBETANCOURT 3 / ALAMY STOCK PHOTO ©

FRANZ MARC FREI / GETTY IMAGES ©

Blue Ridge Parkway

8 In the southern Appalachian Mountains of Virginia and North Carolina, you can take in sublime sunsets, watch for wildlife and lose all sense of the present while staring off at the vast wilderness surrounding this 469-mile roadway (p314). Hikes take you deeper into nature, from easy trails along lakes to challenging scrambles up to eagles'-nest heights. Camp or spend the night at forest lodges, and don't miss the bluegrass- and mountain-music scene of nearby towns such as Asheville, NC and Floyd and Galax in Virginia.

Niagara Falls

9 Crowded? Cheesy? Well, yes. Niagara is short too – it barely cracks the top 500 waterfalls worldwide for height. But c'mon, when those great muscular bands of water arch over the precipice like liquid glass and roar into the void below, and when you sail toward it in a misty little boat, Niagara Falls (p129) impresses big time. In terms of sheer volume, nowhere in North America beats its thundering cascade, with more than one million bathtubs of water plummeting over the edge every second.

DANITA DELIMONT / GETTY IMAGES ©

MARK DAFFEY / GETTY IMAGES ©

C. KURT HOLTER / SHUTTERSTOCK ©

EVGESHAG / GETTY IMAGES ©

DE AGOSTINI / W. BUSS / GETTY IMAGES ©

Civil War Sites

10 Sites are scattered over swaths of the eastern USA, from Pennsylvania to Louisiana. Renowned places to connect with some of America's darkest hours are at Antietam, Maryland (p289), site of the bloodiest day in American history, where 23,000 soldiers died; Gettysburg (p153), Pennsylvania (the battlefield and cemetery, where President Lincoln delivered his 'Four score...' address); and Vicksburg (p417), Mississippi (a must for history buffs, with a 16-mile driving tour through the areas General Grant besieged for 47 days). In summer, many sites host battle re-enactments.
Antietam National Battlefield

Boston

11 From cobbled colonial lanes to crazed sports fans, Boston (p166) brews a colorful scene. It is arguably the USA's most historic city – site of the Boston Tea Party, Paul Revere's ride and the first battle of the Revolutionary War, all of which you can trace on the 2.5-mile, red-brick Freedom Trail. Harvard University's campus lets you be a little rebellious yourself at its edgy music clubs. Boston's oyster houses, cafes and trattorias (especially thick in the Italian North End) fortify you for the evening's exploits. Memorial Hall, Harvard University (p173)

Antebellum South

12 Steeped in history and regional pride, the antebellum South is about grand homes and cotton plantations, moss-draped trees and azalea-choked gardens. Absorb the vibe in Charleston (p346), while strolling, admiring the architecture and lingering over dinners on the verandah. Fall under the spell of Savannah's live oaks, shady boulevards, seafood and humid nights. Or ogle the mansions of genteel Natchez (p419), the oldest town on the Mississippi River – you'd be hard-pressed to see more sweeping staircases per square mile anywhere else. Colonial-style house, Natchez, Mississippi

Florida Keys

13 This island chain drifts as far south as you can get in the continental USA. Except for drinking and partying, people come to the Keys (p477) to fish, snorkel, dive, kayak, hike, cycle, fish some more, snorkel again. North America's best coral reefs percolate under the jade-green water and provide brag-worthy expeditions. Then there's Key West, the gloriously unkempt, bawdy, freak-loving exclamation point at the end of the line. Hippies, fire-jugglers, artists and other free spirits converge on its carnival atmosphere after dark.

Musical Roots

14 Name the genre, and it probably began here. The Mississippi Delta (p415) birthed the blues, while New Orleans opened the door to jazz. Rock and roll arrived the day Elvis Presley walked into Sun Studio (p359) in Memphis. And country made its way from fiddle-and-banjo Appalachian hamlets to Nashville's Grand Ole Opry (p374). The Mississippi River took the music north, where Chicago and Detroit riffed into the electric blues and Motown sound, respectively. It all translates into great live music wherever you are in the region.

STEPHEN FRINK / GETTY IMAGES ©

SUE STOKES / SHUTTERSTOCK ©

COSMO CONDINA / GETTY IMAGES ©

KRAIG LIEB / GETTY IMAGES ©

JOHN COLETTI / GETTY IMAGES ©

Miami

15 How does one city get so lucky? Most content themselves with one or two highlights, but Miami (p453) seems to have it all. Beyond the stunning beaches and Art Deco Historic District, there's culture at every turn. In cigar-filled dance halls, Havana expats dance to *son* and *boleros*; in exclusive nightclubs stiletto-heeled, fiery-eyed Brazilian models shake to Latin hip-hop; and in the park old men clack dominoes. To top it off, street vendors and restaurants dish out flavors from the Caribbean, Cuba, Argentina and Spain.

Boardwalk Empire

16 Strolling along the East Coast's beach boardwalk is a rite of passage, be it in Rehoboth Beach (p291), Delaware; Ocean City, Maryland; Virginia Beach, Virginia; or Atlantic City, New Jersey. It doesn't matter where. The point is to enjoy the all-star roster of summer indulgence that lines the walkway: funnel cakes, go-karts, pizza shacks, glow-in-the-dark minigolf, saltwater-taffy shops. Parents push strollers, tots lick ice-cream cones, and teenagers check each other out. Don't get so caught up you forget to take in the sea views! Rehoboth Beach boardwalk

Mississippi River

17 As Old Man River (p589) traces through the country from its Northwoods beginning in Minnesota to its palmetto-fringed end in Louisiana, it meanders past eagles' nests and juke joints, pine forests and plantations. Covering more than 2000 miles, it churns through major cities like Memphis (p357), Minneapolis and New Orleans. There are still riverboats, as in Mark Twain's heyday, but they're more likely to be casinos or tour vessels now. Road-trippers heed the call of the mythic Great River Road, as it edges the waterway throughout its duration.

KENNAN HARVEY / GETTY IMAGES ©

СЕРГЕЙ УРЯДНИКОВ / GETTY IMAGES ©

Appalachian Trail

18 The country's longest footpath (p44) is over 2100 miles long, crosses six national parks and slices through 14 states from Georgia to Maine. Deep woods, alpine peaks, cow-dotted farms and foraging bears are all part of the landscape. It's estimated that two to three million people trek a portion of the trail every year, inhaling the fresh air and admiring the spectacular scenery. Fewer than 600 hikers persevere all the way through. Got six months and fortitude to spare? The reward is sublime – true for shorter stretches, too.

Everglades National Park

19 The Everglades (p474) unnerve. They don't reach majestically skyward or fill your heart with the aching beauty of a glacier-carved valley. They ooze, flat and watery, a river of grass mottled by hammocks, cypress domes and mangroves. You can't hike them, not really. To properly explore the Everglades – and meet its prehistoric residents, like the snaggle-toothed crocodile – you must leave the safety of land. Push a canoe off a muddy bank, tamp down your fear and explore the waterways on the Everglades' own, unforgettable terms.

New England Beaches

20 Summer in New England can get quite humid, so the region's population flocks to the coast for cool ocean breezes. In Massachusetts, great beaches ring Martha's Vineyard (p196), the area's largest island. At nearby Cape Cod National Seashore, salt marshes and wild dunes dot the landscape, while humpback whales spout offshore. Unspoiled Block Island offers simple pleasures such as rolling farms, uncrowded beaches and quiet hiking and cycling trails – all just a short float from Rhode Island. Aquinnah (Gay Head) Cliffs (p198), Martha's Vineyard

Acadia National Park

21 Acadia National Park (p241) is where the mountains meet the sea. Miles of rocky coastline and even more miles of hiking and biking trails make this wonderland Maine's most popular destination, and deservedly so. The high point (literally) is Cadillac Mountain, the 1530ft peak that can be accessed by foot, bicycle or vehicle; early risers can catch the country's first sunrise from this celebrated summit. Later in the day, after working up an appetite on the trails and beaches, indulge in tea and popovers at Jordan Pond.

Cadillac Mountain (p242)

Great Smoky Mountains

22 Named after the heather-colored mist that hangs over the peaks, the Smokies (p344) comprise a national park that receives more visitors than any other. The pocket of deep Appalachian woods straddles Tennessee and North Carolina, protecting thickly forested ridges where black bears, white-tailed deer, antlered elk, wild turkeys and over 1600 kinds of flowers find sanctuary. Nearly 10 million people a year come to hike, camp, ride horses, cycle, raft and fly fish, though it's easy to lose the crowds if you're willing to walk or paddle. *Little River, Great Smoky Mountains National Park*

Philadelphia

23 Philly (p138) is often overlooked in the pantheon of great American cities, and that's a shame. It's a beautiful place, its streets dotted with gracious squares and linked with cobbled alleys. As the 'birthplace of American government' – where the founding fathers signed the Declaration of Independence in 1776 – history abounds (the Liberty Bell! Ben Franklin's office!). But it's not all about the past: the dining scene has heated up way beyond the famed cheesesteak sandwich. Chowhounds' eateries lurk on every corner, and most are reasonably priced. *Elfreth's Alley (p139), Old City district*

MRRTYXPILOT / GETTY IMAGES ©

FRI.MM JOHN / GETTY IMAGES ©

Great Lakes

24 Together, the five Great Lakes (p510) – Superior, Michigan, Huron, Ontario and Erie – that extend across the region's north possess about 20% of the earth's fresh water and 95% of America's. They offer miles of beaches, dunes, resort towns and lighthouse-dotted scenery. Add in wave-bashed cliffs, islands freckling the shore, and freighters chugging in to busy ports, and you can see how the region earned its 'Third Coast' nickname. Anglers, kayakers and even surfers will find their sweet spot here. Lighthouse on the shore of Lake Huron

Amish Country

25 Life slows way down in the Amish communities of northeast Ohio, southeast Pennsylvania and northern Indiana – the USA's three largest Amish clusters. Little boys in straw hats steer horse-drawn buggies, long-bearded men hand-plow the tidy fields, and demurely dressed women and girls carry shoofly pies to market. The 'Plain People,' as they're known, are a centuries-old sect who live a simple life without electricity, telephones or motorized vehicles. Lancaster (p152) in Pennsylvania, Berlin in Ohio, and Middlebury in Indiana, are good places to see the clock turned back. Lancaster County Amish community

Need to Know

For more information, see Survival Guide (p641)

Currency
US dollar ($)

Language
English

Visas
Visitors from Canada, the UK, Australia, New Zealand, Japan and many EU countries do not need visas for less than 90 days, with ESTA approval. Other nations, see travel.state.gov.

Money
ATMs widely available. Credits cards accepted at most hotels, restaurants and shops.

Cell Phones
Foreign phones operating on tri- or quad-band frequencies will work in the USA. Or purchase inexpensive cell phones with a pay-as-you-go plan here.

Time
Eastern Standard Time (GMT minus five hours) in NYC, New England, Florida; Central Standard Time (GMT minus six hours) in Chicago, Nashville, New Orleans

When to Go

Boston
GO Apr–Oct

New York City
GO May–Sep

Chicago
GO May–Sep

Washington, DC
GO Mar–Apr & Sep–Oct

New Orleans
GO Feb–May

Miami
GO Dec–Apr

Tropical climate
Dry climate
Warm to hot summers, mild winters
Mild to hot summers, cold winters

High Season
(Jun–Aug)

➡ Warm, sunny days across the region.

➡ Accommodations prices peak (30% up on average).

➡ Big outdoor music festivals abound: Milwaukee's Summerfest, Newport's Folk Fest, Chicago's Lollapalooza etc.

Shoulder (Apr–May, Sep–Oct)

➡ Milder temperatures; can be rainy.

➡ Wildflowers bloom, especially in May.

➡ Fall foliage areas (ie New England, Blue Ridge Parkway) remain busy.

Low Season
(Nov–Mar)

➡ Dark, wintry days, with snowfall in the north.

➡ Lowest prices for accommodation (aside from ski resorts and warmer getaway destinations like Florida, for which it's peak season).

➡ Attractions keep shorter hours or close for the winter.

Useful Websites

Lonely Planet (www.lonely planet.com/usa) Destination information, hotel bookings, travel forum, photos, travel news.

National Park Service (www.nps.gov) Gateway to America's greatest natural treasures: its national parks.

Eater (www.eater.com) Foodie insight into two dozen American cities.

Roadside America (www.roadsideamerica.com) For all things weird and wacky.

New York Times Travel (www.nytimes.com/section/travel) Travel news, practical advice and engaging features.

Important Numbers

To call a number within the US, dial 1, followed by the area code and the seven-digit number.

USA country code	✐1
International access code	✐011
Emergency	✐911
Directory assistance	✐411
International directory assistance	✐00

Exchange Rates

Australia	A$1	$0.72
Canada	C$1	$0.75
Europe	€1	$1.06
Japan	¥100	$0.81
New Zealand	NZ$1	$0.65
UK	UK£1	$1.51

For current exchange rates see www.xe.com.

Daily Costs

**Budget:
Less than $100**

➡ Dorm beds: $20–$40; campgrounds: $15–$30; budget motels: $60–$80

➡ Lunch from a cafe or food truck: $5–$9

➡ Travel on public transit: $2–$3

**Midrange:
$150–$250**

➡ Double room in midrange hotel: $100–$250

➡ Popular restaurant dinner per person: $25–$40

➡ Car hire per day: from $30

**Top End:
More than $250**

➡ Room in a top hotel/resort: from $250

➡ Dining in top restaurant per person: $60–$100

➡ Big night out (plays, concerts, clubs): $60–$200

Opening Hours

Opening hours vary throughout the year. We've provided high-season opening hours; hours will generally decrease in the shoulder and low seasons.

Banks 8:30am–4:30pm Monday to Friday

Bars 5pm–midnight Sunday to Thursday, to 2am Friday and Saturday

Clubs 10pm–3am Thursday to Saturday

Shopping malls 9am–9pm

Stores 9am–6pm Monday to Saturday, noon–5pm Sunday

Supermarkets 8am–8pm, some open 24 hours

Arriving in Eastern USA

John F Kennedy International (New York; p111) From JFK take the AirTrain to Jamaica Station and then LIRR to Penn Station, which costs $12 to $15 (45 minutes). A taxi to Manhattan costs $52, plus toll and tip (45 to 90 minutes).

O'Hare International (Chicago; p537) The CTA Blue Line train ($5) runs 24/7. Trains depart every 10 minutes or so; they reach downtown in 40 minutes. Airport Express shuttle vans cost $32 (approximately 60 minutes); taxis cost around $50 (30 minutes or so).

Miami International (p469) SuperShuttle to South Beach for $21 (50 to 90 minutes); taxi to Miami Beach for $35 (40 to 60 minutes); or take the Metrorail to downtown (Government Center) for $2.25 (15 minutes).

Getting Around

Car Driving is the main way to access the region. In big cities (New York, Chicago) it can be a hassle, though, with traffic gridlock and hefty parking fees (upward of $40 per day). Car rentals are available in every town.

Train Outside the Boston-to-Washington, DC corridor train travel is mostly for scenic journeys. **Amtrak** (www.amtrak.com) is the national carrier.

Bus Short-haul carriers such as Megabus (www.megabus.com/us) and Bolt Bus (www.boltbus.com) are popular for getting between main cities (eg New York to DC) – this is typically the cheapest way to travel. Tickets must be purchased online in advance.

For much more on **getting around**, see p653.

If You Like...

Big Cities

New York City You can't get bigger than NYC: 8.4 million people strong; loud, fast, pulsing with energy, symphonic and always evolving. (p55)

Chicago The Midwest's metropolis is a cultural stew of skyscrapers, public art, vast museums, indie clubs and a delirious number of eats. (p514)

Baltimore The gritty port city has morphed into a hip beauty, sporting world-class museums, trendy shops and boutique hotels. (p277)

Philadelphia History is everywhere in the USA's first capital, but Philly's urbane side comes out in its energetic food, music and arts scenes. (p138)

Detroit A case study of how cities rise and fall, and maybe – just maybe – rise again. (p563)

Old-Fashioned Americana

Wellfleet Drive-In Flash back to the 1950s at this movie theater in Cape Cod. (p193)

Arcade Tuck into thick pancakes at the classic Memphis diner that Elvis used to frequent. (p363)

Route 66 Mom-and-pop motels, neon-lit pie shops and oddball roadside attractions – and that's just along Illinois' 300-mile stretch of road. (p539)

Worcester, MA The city that launched the diner has several tucked around town. (p199)

National Parks

Great Smoky Mountains Heather-colored mist clings to the peaks, while black bears, elk and wild turkeys prowl the USA's most visited park. (p344)

Acadia Maine's unspoiled wilderness offers surging coastal mountains, towering sea cliffs, surf-pounded beaches and quiet ponds. (p241)

Shenandoah Spectacular vistas unfurl along the Blue Ridge Mountains, with great hiking and camping, including along the Appalachian Trail. (p309)

Everglades South Florida's watery wonderland is home to snaggle-toothed crocodiles, stealthy panthers, pink flamingos and mellow manatees. (p474)

Isle Royale Floating in Lake Superior's midst, it's devoid of roads, cars and crowds, giving moose and loons room to roam. (p580)

Fabulous Food

Maine lobster, Philly cheesesteaks, Memphis barbecue, Wisconsin cheddar – you'll need to loosen the belt wherever you are in the East.

New Orleans Hot-spiced gumbo, fresh-shucked oysters and bourbon-soaked bread pudding highlight the Creole menu in America's most food-centric city. (p429)

New York City Whether you crave steak frites, sushi, chicken tikka masala or gourmet hot dogs, globe-trotting Gotham has you covered. (p55)

Chicago The Windy City plates an unapologetically rich clash of high gastronomy and comfort food, plus neighborhoods packed with ethnic eats. (p514)

Charleston The well-bred, gardenia-scented city brings on decadent, low-country fare such as shrimp and grits and she-crab soup. (p346)

Minneapolis It has been called 'America's next great food city' for its creative, sustainable, Scandinavian-tinged eateries. (p592)

Architecture

Chicago Birthplace of the sky-scraper, Chicago has magnificent works by many of the great 20th-century architects. (p514)

Fallingwater This Frank Lloyd Wright masterpiece blends into the forested landscape and the waterfall over which the house is built. (p157)

Miami Miami's Art Deco Historic District is a Technicolor dream come to life. (p453)

Taliesin Another one for Frank Lloyd Wright fans: Taliesin was the site of his home and influential school in Spring Green, Wisconsin. (p587)

Columbus Believe it: there's big architecture in small Columbus, Indiana – thanks to the town's forward-thinking industrialists. (p546)

Savannah This Southern belle never fails to turn heads with her striking antebellum buildings. (p402)

Museums

Smithsonian Institution The nation's premier treasure chest is actually a group of 19 museums. Best of all, they're all free. (p259)

Metropolitan Museum of Art The top-draw attraction in NYC is like a cultural city-state, boasting a trove of two million artworks. (p80)

Art Institute of Chicago The nation's second-largest art museum (after the Met) hangs masterpieces aplenty, especially impressionist paintings. (p515)

Rock and Roll Hall of Fame & Museum It has Jimi Hendrix's Stratocaster and John Lennon's Sgt Pepper suit, all in Cleveland. (p550)

Top: Creole-style shrimp and sausage gumbo
Bottom: Birch trees in Acadia National Park (p241)

National Civil Rights Museum Moving exhibits set across the street from where Martin Luther King Jr was assassinated in Memphis. (p357)

Theme Parks

Walt Disney World Plunge into the fairy-tale world of the 'Happiest Place on Earth' and get swept up in miles of nostalgia and thrill rides. (p502)

Dollywood A paean to the much-loved country singer Dolly Parton, with Appalachian-themed rides and attractions in the hills of Tennessee. (p380)

Cedar Point Home to several of the globe's tallest and fastest roller coasters, like the 120mph Top Thrill Dragster. (p554)

Universal Orlando Resort Famed home of Universal Studios and the new Wizarding World of Harry Potter. (p408)

Outdoor Activities

Appalachian Trail Even if you choose not to walk all 2100 miles, hop on for a day hike to experience the sublime scenery; 14 states provide access. (p44)

Boundary Waters Canoe deep into Minnesota's northern wilderness to camp under the stars and perhaps glimpse the aurora borealis. (p606)

New River Gorge National River Legendary white water froths in West Virginia, ripping through a primeval forest gorge that's utterly Eden-like. (p320)

Long Island Surf's up in New York, from Montauk's waves to Nassau County's Long Beach. (p113)

Stowe Mountain Vermont practically invented snowboarding.

The state's premier crag is *the* place to shred. (p220)

Presidential Range Challenging trails, lofty peaks and an excellent hut-to-hut system in New Hampshire's White Mountains. (p231)

History

The north has Colonial and Revolutionary hot spots, while the mid-Atlantic and south hold the majority of Civil War battlefields.

Independence National Historic Park Highlights include the Liberty Bell and Independence Hall, where America's founders signed the Constitution. (p138)

Boston's Freedom Trail Visit Paul Revere's home, an 18th-century graveyard and 14 other Revolutionary War sites along the 2.5-mile path. (p173)

Henry Ford Museum/ Greenfield Village These two museums hold US history's greatest hits: the bus Rosa Parks sat in, the Wright Brothers' airplane workshop and more. (p570)

Washington, DC See the sites where Lincoln was assassinated, Martin Luther King Jr gave his most famous speech and Nixon's presidency was undone. (p246)

Vicksburg The Mississippi bluffs that General Grant besieged for 47 days are ground zero for Civil War enthusiasts. (p417)

Williamsburg Step back into the 1700s in this preserved town, the largest living history museum on the planet. (p302)

Harpers Ferry A fascinating open-air museum of 19th-century village life framed by mountains and rivers. (p318)

Nightlife

New Orleans Go beyond Bourbon St into the neighborhoods where Sazerac swirls in glasses and jazz, Dixieland and zydeco spill from clubs. (p429)

New York City As Sinatra sang, it's the city that doesn't sleep, with bars and clubs throughout town staying open until 4am nightly. (p55)

Athens, Georgia The compact little college town boasts a mighty music scene that launched the B-52s and REM. (p400)

Nashville Everyone strums the guitar here, and there are bars and honky tonks aplenty for boot-stompin' shows into the wee hours. (p366)

Key West A lot of booze goes down the hatch in this raucous, free-spirited, carnival of a town. (p400)

Offbeat America

Foamhenge A magnificent homage to Styrofoam, this Stonehenge redux is done to scale and is appropriately tranquil around sunset. (p313)

NashTrash Tours Nashville's tall-haired 'Jugg Sisters' take visitors on a deliciously tacky journey through the city's spicier side. (p367)

Spam Museum Try your hand at canning the sweet pork magic in Austin, Minnesota, the blue-tinned meat's revered birthplace. (p603)

American Visionary Art Museum Peruse outsider art (including pieces created by the clinically insane) at this Baltimore gem. (p279)

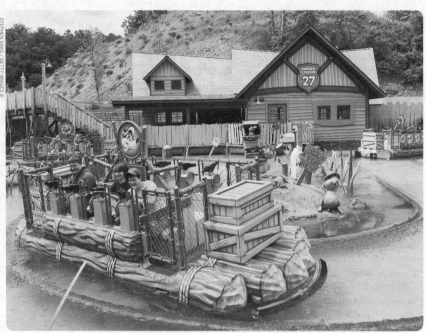

STEPHEN SAKS / GETTY IMAGES ©

Amusement ride at Dollywood (p380), Tennessee

Vent Haven Ventriloquist Museum Some 700 goggle-eyed dummies stare from a house near Cincinnati. (p560)

World's Largest Ball of Twine It's a 17,400lb behemoth sitting in a Minnesota gazebo. (p601)

Theater

New York City and Chicago are the stars, while smaller cities such as Minneapolis give voice to emerging talents.

Broadway Theater District It doesn't get more iconic than the bright lights and glittering marquees along a certain street in Midtown Manhattan. (p69)

Steppenwolf Theatre John Malkovich, Gary Sinise and other now-famous actors launched

Chicago's scene here more than four decades ago. (p534)

Guthrie Theater Minneapolis has so many theaters it's nick-named 'the Mini Apple.' The uber cool Guthrie leads the pack. (p599)

American Players Theatre Stages Shakespeare and other classics outdoors amid the woodlands of Spring Green, Wisconsin. (p589)

Grand Ole Opry There's more than country music under the lights – it's a full-fledged, foot-stompin' variety show. (p374)

Beaches

South Beach The world-famous strand is less about wave-frolicking than taking in the

parade of people on Miami's favorite playground. (p456)

Cape Cod National Seashore Massive sand dunes, pictur-esque lighthouses and cool forests invite endless exploring on the Massachusetts cape. (p191)

Grayton Beach This pristine coastal park on the Florida pan-handle has gorgeous seascapes and arty little villages. (p508)

Michigan's Gold Coast Endless stretches of sand, dunes, winer-ies, orchards and B&B-filled towns blanket the state's western shoreline. (p573)

Outer Banks North Carolina's isolated barrier islands offer everything from popular beach-es to remote strands where wild ponies run free. (p325)

Month by Month

January

The New Year starts off with a shiver as snowfall blankets large swaths of the northern regions. Ski resorts kick into high gear, while sun-lovers seek refuge in warmer climes (especially Florida).

✿ Mummers Parade

Philadelphia's biggest event is this brilliant parade (www.mummers.com) on New Year's Day, for which local clubs spend months creating costumes and mobile scenery in order to win top honors. String bands and clowns add to the general good cheer.

✿ Chinese New Year

In late January or early February, you'll find colorful celebrations and feasting anywhere there's a Chinatown. NYC and Chicago each ring in the occasion with a parade, floats, firecrackers, bands and plenty of merriment.

✿ St Paul Winter Carnival

Is it cold in Minnesota in late January? You betcha. That doesn't stop denizens from bundling up in parkas and snow boots to partake in 10 days of ice sculptures, ice skating and ice fishing (www.wintercarnival.com).

February

Despite indulging in winter mountain getaways, many Americans dread February for its long, dark nights and frozen days. For foreign visitors, this can be the cheapest time to travel, with ultra discount rates for flights and hotels.

✿ Mardi Gras

Held in late February or early March, on the day before Ash Wednesday, Mardi Gras (Fat Tuesday) is the finale of Carnival. New Orleans' celebrations (www.mardigrasneworleans.com) are legendary, as colorful parades, masquerade balls and plenty of feasting rule the day.

March

The first blossoms of spring arrive – at least in the South (the North still shivers in the chill). In New England's mountains, it's still ski season. Meanwhile, the Spring Break masses descend on Florida.

☆ Baseball Spring Training

Throughout March, Florida hosts Major League Baseball's spring training 'Grapefruit League' (www.floridagrapefruitleague.com): 15 pro baseball teams train and play exhibition games, drawing fans to the Orlando, Tampa Bay and southeast areas.

✿ St Patrick's Day

On the 17th, the patron saint of Ireland is honored with brass bands and ever-flowing pints of Guinness. Huge parades occur in New York, Boston and Chicago (which goes all-out by dyeing the Chicago River green).

✿ National Cherry Blossom Festival

The brilliant blooms of Japanese cherry blossoms around DC's Tidal Basin are celebrated with concerts, parades, *taiko* drumming, kite-flying and loads of other events during the three-week fest (www.nationalcherryblossomfestival.org). More than 1.5 million people go each year, so don't forget to book ahead.

✖ Maple Syrup Tasting

Vermont's maple syrup producers invite the public to their 'sugarhouses' to see the sweet stuff being made during the Vermont Maple Open House Weekend (www.vermontmaple.org) in late March. Maine producers do the same on the last Sunday of the month.

April

The weather is warming up, but April can still be unpredictable, with chilly weather mixed with a few teasingly warm days up north. Down south, it's a fine time to travel.

🏃 Boston Marathon

At the country's oldest marathon (www.baa.org), tens of thousands of spectators watch runners cross the finish line at Copley Sq on Patriots' Day, a Massachusetts holiday held on the third Monday of April.

☆ New Orleans Jazz Fest

The Big Easy hosts the country's best jazz jam (www.nojazzfest.com) for 10 days in late April with top-notch horn blowers and ivory ticklers. Almost better than the music is the food: soft-shell crab po' boys, Cajun rice with pork sausage and white-chocolate bread pudding.

☆ Tribeca Film Festival

Robert De Niro co-organizes this NYC soiree (www.tribecafilm.com) showcasing documentaries and narrative features, held during 12 days in late April. It has quickly risen in stature since its 2002 inception.

May

May is true spring and one of the loveliest times to travel in the region, with blooming wildflowers and generally mild sunny weather. Summer crowds and high prices have yet to arrive.

☆ Kentucky Derby

On the first Saturday of the month, a who's who of upper-crust America puts on their pinstripe suits and most flamboyant hats and descends on Louisville for the horse race (www.kentuckyderby.com) known as the 'greatest two minutes in sports.'

☆ Movement Electronic Music Festival

The world's largest electronic music festival (www.movement.us) packs Detroit's Hart Plaza over Memorial Day weekend. You'll find both up-and-comers and the big names in the biz, such as Snoop Dog, Skrillex and Felix da Housecat, at the dance-loving extravaganza.

June

Summer is here. Americans spend more time at outdoor cafes

and restaurants, and head to the shore or to national parks. School is out; vacationers fill the highways and resorts, bringing higher prices.

☆ Chicago Blues Festival

It's the globe's biggest free blues fest (www.chicagobluesfestival.us), with three days of the electrified music that made Chicago famous. More than a half-million people unfurl blankets by the multiple stages that take over Grant Park in early June.

☆ Bonnaroo Music & Arts Fest

Set in Tennessee's heartland on a 700-acre farm, this sprawling music fest (www.bonnaroo.com) showcases big-name rock, soul, country and more over four days in mid-June.

🧜 Mermaid Parade

In Brooklyn, NYC, Coney Island celebrates summer's steamy arrival with a kitsch-loving parade (www.coneyisland.com), complete with skimpily attired mermaids and horn-blowing mermen.

☆ CMA Music Festival

Legions of country-music fans don their cowboy boots and unite in Nashville for the chance to hear the genre's top crooners. Over 400 artists perform at stages in Riverfront Park and Nissan Stadium (www.cmafest.com).

☆ Summerfest

Milwaukee lets loose with a heckuva music fest (www.summerfest.com) for 11 days in late June/early July, with hundreds of big-name rock, blues, jazz, country and alternative bands swarming 10 lakefront stages. Local beer, brats and cheese accompany the proceedings.

July

With summer in full swing, Americans break out the backyard barbecues or head for the beach. The prices are high and the crowds can be fierce, but it's one of the liveliest times to visit.

⭐ Independence Day

The nation celebrates its birthday with a fireworks-filled bang on the 4th. In Philadelphia, descendents of the Declaration of Independence signatories ring the Liberty Bell. Boston, New York and Washington, DC are also great spots to enjoy the fun.

⭐ National Black Arts Festival

Artists converge on Atlanta for this event (www. nbaf.org) celebrating African American music, theater, literature and film. Wynton Marsalis, Spike Lee and Youssou N'Dour are among those who've performed here.

⭐ Newport Folk Festival

Newport, Rhode Island, a summer haunt of the well-heeled, hosts this high-energy music fest (www. newportfolk.org) in late July. Top folk artists take to the storied stage, best remembered as the venue where Bob Dylan went electric.

August

Expect blasting heat in August, with temperatures and humidity less bearable the further south you go. You'll find people-packed beaches, high prices and empty cities on weekends, when residents escape to the nearest waterfront.

⭐ Lollapalooza

This massive rock fest (www.lollapalooza.com) in Chicago is a raucous event, with 130 bands – including many A-listers – spilling off eight stages in Grant Park the first weekend in August.

🍴 Maine Lobster Festival

If you love lobster like Maine loves lobster, indulge in this feeding frenzy (www.mainelobsterfestival. com) held in Rockland in early August. King Neptune and the Sea Goddess oversee a week full of events and, of course, as many crustaceans as you can eat.

September

With the end of summer, cooler days arrive, making for pleasant outings region wide. The kids are back in school, and concert halls, gallery spaces and performing-arts venues kick off a new season.

⭐ New York Film Festival

One of several big film fests in NYC, this one features world premieres from across the globe, plus Q&As with indie and mainstream directors alike. Lincoln Center (www.filmlinc.com) plays host.

October

Temperatures are falling as autumn brings fiery colors to northern climes. It's high season where the leaves are most brilliant (New England); elsewhere expect lower prices and fewer crowds.

⭐ Fantasy Fest

Key West's answer to Mardi Gras brings more than 100,000 revelers to the subtropical enclave during the week leading up to Halloween. Expect parades, colorful floats, costume parties, the selecting of a conch king and queen and plenty of alcohol-fueled merriment (www.fantasyfest.com).

⭐ Halloween

It's not just for kids; adults celebrate Halloween at masquerade parties. In NYC, you can don a costume and join the Halloween parade up Sixth Ave. Chicago does a cultural take with skeleton-rich Day of the Dead events at the National Museum of Mexican Art.

November

No matter where you go, this is generally low season, with cold winds discouraging visitors. Prices are lower (although airfares skyrocket around Thanksgiving). There's much happening culturally in the main cities.

🍴 Thanksgiving

On the fourth Thursday of November, Americans gather with family and friends over daylong feasts of roast turkey, sweet potatoes, cranberry sauce, wine,

pumpkin pie and loads of other dishes. New York City hosts a huge parade, and there's pro football on TV.

December

Winter arrives, though skiing conditions in eastern USA usually aren't ideal until January. Christmas lights and holiday fairs make the region come alive during the festive season.

🎇 Art Basel

This massive arts fest (www.artbasel.com) has four days of cutting-edge art, film, architecture and design. More than 250 major galleries from across the globe come to the event, with works by some 2000 artists, plus much hobnobbing with a glitterati crowd in Miami Beach.

🎇 New Year's Eve

Americans are of two minds when it comes to ringing in the New Year. Some join festive crowds to celebrate; others plot a getaway to escape the mayhem. Whichever you choose, plan well in advance. Expect high prices (especially in NYC).

Top: Newport Folk Festival, Rhode Island
Bottom: Mermaid Parade (p27), Brooklyn, NYC

Itineraries

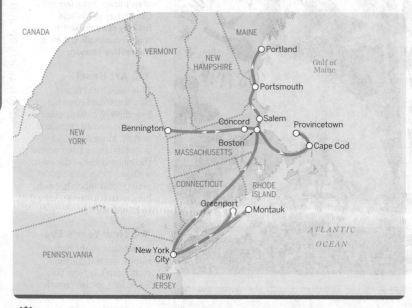

 Best of the Northeast

Get your big-city fill in the biggest city of all, then mosey into New England for small-town pleasures.

The great dynamo of art, fashion and culture, **New York City** is America at her most urbane. Spend three days blending touristy must-dos – Top of the Rock viewpoint, Upper East Side art museums, Central Park rambling – with vibrant nightlife and dining adventures, perhaps in the East Village. After big-city culture, catch your breath at the pretty beaches and enticing charms of **Greenport** and **Montauk** on Long Island. Back in NYC, catch the train to Boston, for two days visiting historic sights, dining in the North End and pub-hopping in Cambridge. Rent a car and drive to **Cape Cod**, with its idyllic dunes, forests and pretty shores. Leave time for **Provincetown**, the Cape's liveliest settlement. Then set off for a three-day jaunt taking in New England's back roads, covered bridges, picturesque towns and beautiful scenery, staying at heritage B&Bs en route. Highlights include **Salem** and **Concord** in Massachusetts; **Bennington**, Vermont; and **Portsmouth**, New Hampshire. If time allows, head onward to Maine for lobster feasts amid beautifully rugged coastlines – **Portland** is a fine place to start.

Eastern Grand Tour

4 WEEKS

This road trip loops around the East through towns large and small, as blues joints, pie shops and civil rights sights flash by.

Start in **New York City** (but hire a car cheaper in New Jersey) and hit the road for week one. Head west toward **Lancaster** to explore the idyllic back roads of Pennsylvania Dutch Country. Next is **Pittsburgh**, a surprising town of picturesque bridges and cutting-edge museums. Enter Ohio by interstate, but quickly step back in time amid the horses, buggies and byways of **Amish Country**. See the skyscrapers rising on the horizon? That's big-shouldered **Chicago**. Hang out for a few days to marvel at famous artworks and steely architecture, and chow through the city's celebrated restaurant scene.

For week two, motor south from Chicago on old Route 66, at least for a few time-warped, pie-filled miles. **Memphis** is the next destination, a mecca for Elvis fans, barbecue connoisseurs, civil rights students and blues-music buffs alike. Follow the Great River Road south from here through juke-jointed **Clarksdale**, the Civil War battlegrounds of **Vicksburg** and the antebellum mansions of **Natchez**. It's not far now to **New Orleans**, where you can hear live jazz and spoon into thick, spicy-rich gumbo.

Begin journeying back east for week three. Wheel along the Gulf Coast to the azalea-lined boulevards of **Mobile**, then inland to **Montgomery**, where museums honor civil rights pioneers like Rosa Parks, who refused to give up her seat to a white man on a city bus. Fall under the spell of live oaks in **Savannah** and pastel architecture and decadent food in **Charleston**. Take your pick of **Durham** or **Chapel Hill**, side-by-side university towns offering groovy nightlife.

Begin week four brushing up on your history in Virginia. Visit **Jamestown**, where Pocahontas helped the New World's first English settlement survive, then wander through the 18th century at nearby **Williamsburg**. A pair of big cities completes the route: **Washington, DC** is a museum free-for-all, while **Philadelphia** fires up the Liberty Bell, Ben Franklin and the mighty, meaty cheesesteak. Finally, it's back to the neon lights of NYC.

Top: Douglas Falls, Monongahela National Forest (p320)

Bottom: Faneuil Hall (p167), Boston

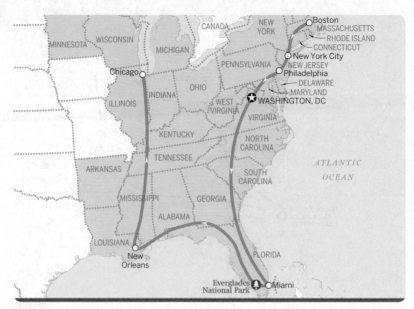

Bright Lights, Big Cities

For big, brawny, bold metropolises, the East is your place. These are the cities that never sleep.

Begin with a few days in history-rich **Boston**. Walk the Freedom Trail past Paul Revere's house. Hang out in Harvard Sq's cafes and bookstores, and chow down in North End trattorias and oyster houses. Then catch the train to **New York City**. With four days, you can indulge in iconic Manhattan and beyond. Stroll Central Park, walk the canyons of Wall St, go bohemian in Greenwich Village and catch a ferry to the Statue of Liberty. For a more local scene, join residents on the High Line, in NoLita's stylish shops and in Queens' creative microbreweries and galleries.

Next hop a train to **Philadelphia**, which is practically down the block from NYC. Philly was the birthplace of American independence, and has the Liberty Bell and Declaration of Independence artifacts to prove it. Spend a few days touring the historic sites and indulging in foodie neighborhoods like East Passyunk. Don't leave the northeast without spending a few days in **Washington, DC**, a quick trip by bus or train. Beyond the staggering number of free museums and monuments – the Air and Space Museum and Lincoln Memorial among them – the US capital has rich dining and drinking scenes in Logan Circle, Shaw and along U St. Who knows what politico might be swirling a Scotch next to you?

It's a long haul to **Miami** (flying is the easy way to go), so allocate four days to get your money's worth exploring the exotic museums and galleries, the art-deco district, Little Havana and sexy, sultry South Beach. For a change of pace, day-trip to the **Everglades** and commune with alligators. Keep the Southern thing going in jazz-loving **New Orleans**, with a soundtrack of smokin'-hot funk/brass bands and the sizzle of Cajun and Creole food. Three days of heavy eating with locals in Uptown, the Central Business District, Marigny and the Bywater should do it.

Last, but not least, **Chicago** leaps up; the *City of New Orleans* train is a scenic way to arrive. Bike to the beach, see mod art in Millennium Park and plug into the blues. Chicago rocks, like the rest of the East's big cities.

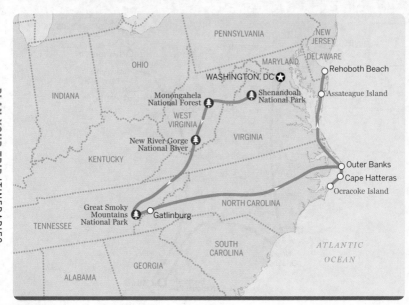

2 WEEKS **The Great Outdoors**

This trip is for those who like their nature ancient and wild. Timbered mountains, roaring rivers and sheltered islands are all on tap.

Shenandoah National Park rolls out the welcome mat: this sliver of gorgeousness straddles the Blue Ridge Mountains, so-named for their color when glimpsed in the hazy cerulean distance. Besides scenic drives, hiking is the big to-do here. Five hundred miles of paths – including 100 miles of the Appalachian Trail – wind by spring wildflowers, summer waterfalls and fiery autumn leaves. More activities await a few hours west at **Monongahela National Forest**, where you can strap on ropes for Seneca Rocks or a bicycle helmet for the Greenbrier River Trail. Adventure-sports enthusiasts will find their wet-and-wild bliss nearby at **New River Gorge National River**. Outfitters provide white-water rafting gear for the infamous class V rapids.

Next up: **Great Smoky Mountains National Park**. Though it's the USA's most popular patch of parkland, you can leave most of the crowds behind if you're willing to hike or paddle (studies have shown that 95% of tourists here never venture more than 100yds from their cars!). After a day spent in the wilderness surrounded by lush, heather-colored peaks, there's nothing quite like arriving in **Gatlinburg**, the park's kitschy base.

So goes the first week. Now it's time to fuel up for the twisty drive through the mountains and across to the coast, where the **Outer Banks** pay off big. Laid-back beach towns full of locally owned ice-cream shops and mom-and-pop motels dot the windswept barrier islands. Check out **Cape Hatteras**, with its unspoiled dunes, marshes and woodlands, or catch the ferry to remote **Ocracoke Island**, where the wild ponies run. Speaking of which: more wild horses roam **Assateague Island**, which floats to the north between Virginia and Maryland. It too offers brilliant, secluded beaches and a landscape ripe for birding, kayaking, crabbing and fishing.

Still craving surf and sand? Family-friendly, gay-friendly **Rehoboth Beach** bestows traditional gingerbread houses, kiddie amusements and a big ol' boardwalk along the oceanfront.

Plan Your Trip

Road Trips & Scenic Drives

There's no better way to experience the region than on a classic four-wheeled journey. Dawdle in diners along the Lincoln Hwy. Marvel at mansions on the Natchez Trace. Climb through the Appalachians on the Blue Ridge Pkwy. Explore Hwy 1's beaches. Or swing into bluesy joints along the Great River Road.

Blue Ridge Parkway

Snaking through the Appalachian Mountains of Virginia and North Carolina, the parkway immerses road-trippers in glorious highlands scenery, with plenty of pull-offs for vista-gaping, hiking and Southern hospitality.

Why Go

Although it skirts dozens of small towns and a few metropolitan areas, the Blue Ridge Pkwy feels far removed from modern-day America. Here, rustic log cabins with creaky rocking chairs on the front porches still dot the hillsides, while signs for folk-art shops and live-bluegrass-music joints entice travelers onto meandering side roads. Log-cabin diners dish up heaping piles of buckwheat pancakes with blackberry preserves and a side of country ham.

When you need to work off all that good Southern cooking, over 100 hiking trails can be accessed along the Blue Ridge Pkwy, from gentle nature walks to rough-and-ready tramps along the legendary Appalachian Trail. Go canoeing, kayaking or inner-tubing along rushing rivers, or dangle a fishing line over the side of a rowboat on petite lakes.

Best Experiences

Best Beaches
See dazzling coastal scenery on Florida's Hwy 1.

Best Oddball Sights
Discover goofball roadside attractions on Route 66 and the Lincoln Hwy.

Best Scenery
Watch dramatic sunsets over the Appalachian Mountains on the Blue Ridge Pkwy.

Best Music
Listen to blues at a Memphis juke joint on the Great River Road, or crazy fiddling at a Galax mountain music hall on the Blue Ridge Pkwy.

Best Food
Fork into Nashville's chicken and biscuits on the Natchez Trace, or New Orleans' famed Creole fare on the Great River Road.

Best History
Explore the Civil War super sight of Gettysburg on the Lincoln Hwy, or 450-year-old St Augustine on Florida Hwy 1.

Road Trips & Scenic Drives

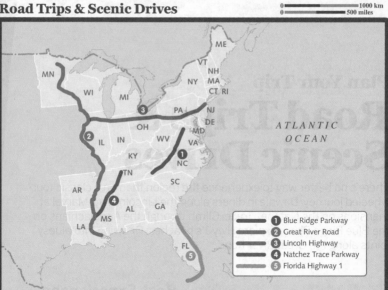

| | 0 ━━━━━ 1000 km |
| | 0 ━━━━━ 500 miles |

ATLANTIC OCEAN

1 Blue Ridge Parkway
2 Great River Road
3 Lincoln Highway
4 Natchez Trace Parkway
5 Florida Highway 1

The Route

The bucolic byway connects Virginia's Shenandoah National Park with Great Smoky Mountains National Park, straddling the North Carolina–Tennessee border. Towns along the way include Boone and Asheville in North Carolina, and Galax and Roanoke in Virginia, with Charlottesville, VA, also a short drive away. Bigger cities within range of the parkway include Washington, DC (140 miles) and Richmond, VA (95 miles).

Many road-trippers also add Skyline Drive (p311) onto their Blue Ridge route. The bendy, 105-mile Skyline connects to the parkway's northern end and ups the scenic ante by doling out mind-blowing mountain vistas on its ramble through Shenandoah National Park. One caveat: you will have to pay a $20 fee to travel the road – this is not a toll, but rather the park's admission charge.

When to Go

April through October, when visitor facilities are open (many close during winter) is best. May is best for wildflowers. Leaf-peepers pour in during October. Expect big crowds if you go during the summer or early autumn.

Resources

Blue Ridge Parkway (www.blueridgeparkway.org) Maps, activities and places to stay along the way. Also offers the free *Blue Ridge Parkway Travel Planner* to download.

Hiking the Blue Ridge Parkway (Randy Johnson; 2010) This book offers in-depth trail descriptions, topographic maps and other essential info for hikes both short and long.

Skyline Drive (www.visitskylinedrive.org) Lodging, hiking and wildlife along the picturesque addendum to the parkway.

Time & Mileage

Time At least two days, but allow five days to do it right. It's slow going on the steep, curvy roads, plus you'll want to pit-stop for hiking, eating and sightseeing.

Mileage 469 miles.

Start/End Front Royal, VA/Cherokee, NC.

Great River Road

The epic roadway edges the Mississippi River from its headwaters in northern Minnesota's pine forests all the way south to its endpoint in New Orleans. For a look at America across cultural divides – North/South, urban/rural, Baptist/bohemian – this is the road trip to make.

Why Go

The sweeping scenery inspires awe as you meander alongside America's longest river, from the rolling plains of the north down to the sun-baked cotton fields of the Mississippi Delta. Wind-hewn bluffs, dense forests, flower-filled meadows and steamy swamps are all part of the backdrop – along with smokestacks, riverboat casinos and urban sprawl: this is the good, the bad and the ugly of life on the Mississippi.

The Route

Despite the name, the Great River Road is not a single highway, but a series of linked federal, state and county roads that follow the Mississippi River as it flows through 10 different states. The one constant wherever you are is the green paddle-wheel sign that marks the way.

Small towns provide a glimpse into varying facets of American culture: there's Brainerd, MN, as seen in the Coen brothers' film *Fargo*; La Crosse, WI, where the world's largest six-pack pops its top; and Nauvoo, IL, a pilgrimage site for Mormons, complete with gleaming white temple.

The southern section of the route traces American musical history, from rock and roll in Memphis to blues in the Mississippi Delta to jazz in New Orleans. You won't go hungry either, with retro Midwestern diners, Southern barbecue joints and smoke-houses, and Cajun taverns and dance halls in Louisiana.

Major urban areas that provide easy access to the road include New Orleans, Memphis, St Louis and Minneapolis.

When to Go

May to October is best, for snow-free weather in the northern states.

Resources

Mississippi River Travel (www.experience mississippiriver.com) Great resource for history, outdoor recreation and live music in all 10 River Road states.

National Scenic Byways (www.fhwa.dot.gov/byways/byways/2279) Turn-by-turn directions.

Time & Mileage

Time Six days to drive the road from north to south; 10 days enables a more comfortable, realistic pace.

Mileage About 2000 miles.

Start/End Itasca State Park, MN/New Orleans, LA.

Lincoln Highway

America's first transcontinental roadway – begun in 1913 and paved to completion by 1925 – rambles from New York City to San Francisco. Its 1000-mile eastern portion traces a distinctive path through the nation's heartland, leaving giant coffee-pot statues, fried-chicken diners, jellybean murals and other Americana in its wake.

ADVANCE PLANNING

➡ Join an **automobile club** (p655) that provides 24-hour emergency roadside assistance and discounts on lodging and attractions.

➡ Some international automobile associations have reciprocal agreements with US clubs, so check first and bring your member card from home.

➡ International travelers might want to review the USA's **road rules** (p656) and common **road hazards** (p656).

➡ Make sure your vehicle has a spare tire, tool kit (eg jack, jumper cables, ice scraper, tire pressure gauge) and emergency equipment (eg flashers).

➡ Bring good maps, especially if you're touring off-road or away from highways. Don't rely solely on a GPS unit – it can malfunction, and in remote areas it may not even work.

➡ Always carry your **driver's license** (p655) and proof of **insurance** (p655).

Why Go

The Lincoln Hwy is authentic road-tripping, sans much of the hype and commercialization of other famous byways. While the route navigates some of the East's prominent cities (NYC and Philadelphia among them), it also steers well off the tourist path in genuine back-road style. You'll tick off seven states along the way: New York, New Jersey, Pennsylvania, West Virginia, Ohio, Indiana and Illinois.

The Route

Between New York City and Fulton, IL, the roadway cuts across the middle Atlantic and Midwestern regions. Note that the Lincoln Hwy doesn't appear on most maps, because it's no longer an official road, but rather a patchwork of federal and state highways.

The journey begins at Times Sq, where the bright lights of Broadway provide an epic send-off. From there it's on to New Jersey and Princeton, the natty Ivy League university town. Pennsylvania rolls up next, offering the Liberty Bell and Independence Hall in Philadelphia; quilts and clip-clopping horses in the Amish communities near Lancaster; the Civil War super site of Gettysburg; and river-tastic, pop-art-rich Pittsburgh. Cornfields and haunted prisons flash by in Ohio. Indiana's pit stops include more Amish areas and the town of South Bend, home to the football-crazed university of Notre Dame. In Illinois, the route swipes Chicago's suburbs, then sets a course through small farming communities pressed flat against the horizon. After that, the Lincoln Hwy heads over the Mississippi River and onward west to San Francisco.

Cities that provide easy access to the road include New York City, Philadelphia, Pittsburgh and Chicago.

When to Go

April through October is best, when the weather is snow free and attractions are open (many shut down between November and March).

Resources

Greetings from the Lincoln Highway: A Road Trip Celebration of America's First Coast-to-Coast Highway (Brian Butko; 2013) Photos, maps and stories to keep you company along the way.

Lincoln Highway Association (www.lincoln highwayassoc.org) Lots of free info online. It also sells turn-by-turn directions that are the definitive source for navigating the road.

The Lincoln Highway (Michael Wallis; 2007) Coffee-table book filled with gorgeous photos and the lowdown on route hot spots.

Time & Mileage

Time Two and a half days without stopping much, but four or five days lets you soak up the highway's essence.

Mileage About 1000 miles for the eastern portion.

Start/End NYC/Fulton, IL (for eastern portion).

ROUTE 66

For a classic American road trip, nothing beats good ol' Route 66. Nicknamed the 'Mother Road' by novelist John Steinbeck, this string of small-town main streets and country byways first connected big-shouldered Chicago with the waving palm trees of Los Angeles in 1926.

Most of the Mother Road unfurls through the western part of the country, but Illinois' 300-mile portion offers classic, time-warped moseying. Fork into thick slabs of pie in neon-lit diners; snap photos of roadside attractions like the Gemini Giant, a sky-high fiberglass spaceman; and motor on past drive-in movie theaters, mom-and-pop motels and other Americana.

Road trippers with a couple of extra weeks to spare can keep on truckin' all the way to the Pacific. The route's remaining 2100 miles wind by singular sensations such as frozen custard stands in Missouri, a totem-pole park in Oklahoma, a barbed-wire museum in Texas, the Grand Canyon in Arizona and wild and crazy Santa Monica Pier in California. See **Historic Route 66** (www.historic66.com) for more.

Top: Gemini Giant
(p539) on Route 66,
Wilmington, Illinois

Bottom: View of
autumn landscape in
North Carolina from
Blue Ridge Parkway
(p314)

Natchez Trace Parkway

With emerald mounds, jade swamps, hiking trails, opulent mansions, riverside saloons and layer upon layer of American history, the Natchez Trace Parkway is the richest drive in the South.

Why Go

Think about this as you set out: you'll be following the same path as a who's who of historic figures, including Andrew Jackson (7th president of the US and face of the $20 bill), Jefferson Davis (president of the Confederacy), James Audubon (naturalist and painter), Meriwether Lewis (famous explorer who died on the Trace in 1809), Ulysses S Grant (18th president of the US) and – wait for it – a young Elvis Presley. The drive meanders by various cultural and historic sites that let you learn more about each man.

The Route

Nashville is the easiest place to access the parkway, and for country-music fans and wannabe songwriters all over the world, a trip to the city is the ultimate pilgrimage, with boot-stomping honky-tonks, the Country Music Hall of Fame and a sweet historic district to explore. There's also good eatin' at local cafeterias, the ultimate way to indulge in everything from barbe-cue chicken and pig's feet to turnip greens and baked apples.

About 10 miles beyond Nashville, the road swings by one of the Civil War's bloodiest battlefields at Franklin, where 20,000 Confederates and 17,000 Union soldiers fought on November 30, 1864. Further along are Confederate grave sites for unknown soldiers. Several centuries-old indigenous burial mounds likewise rise up along the way. Emerald Mound, near Natchez, is one of the nation's largest, and the massive grassy pyramid still buzzes with ancient energy.

Other highlights en route include the town of Tupelo – where you can visit the humble house where Elvis grew up, learned to play the guitar and dreamed big – and tree-shaded, milky-green Cypress Swamp, filled with alligators. Natchez itself is a living antebellum museum, all sweeping spiral staircases, chandeliers and thick column houses.

When to Go

April to June and September to November are best. Summer can be hotter than hot.

Resources

Natchez Trace Parkway (www.npo.gov/natr) Park-service website that provides road construction updates, plus information on local activities and historic sites.

Natchez Trace Compact (www.scenictrace.com) State tourism bureaus of Tennessee, Alabama and

OTHER GREAT ROAD TRIPS

Mississippi band together to offer route itineraries, maps and event info.

Time & Mileage

Time Three days, though you could do it in two. Travel times aren't exactly speedy on the two-lane road.

Mileage 444 miles.

Start/End Nashville, TN/Natchez, MS.

Florida Highway 1

The coast-hugging thoroughfare features miles and miles of beaches interspersed with fascinating historical sights, from the USA's oldest city to sobering slavery exhibits to NASA rockets. Glittering Miami provides the big finale.

Why Go

For quintessential Florida sights and experiences, Hwy 1 spanning the Atlantic shoreline is it: Palm Beach's mansions, Fort Lauderdale's yachts, Miami's domino-clacking Cuban enclave of Little Havana all pop up along the way. Pristine, windswept beaches harboring endangered birds and manatees? They're here (at Canaveral National Seashore). Beaches known for hard-partying nightlife and NASCAR racing? Also here (at Daytona). Delicious seafood shacks and pastel-hued waterfront hotels are everywhere.

The Route

Begin in Florida's northeastern tip at Amelia Island, an upper-class beach-resort town since the 1890s. From there the road drifts south, past cultural parks and plantations where you can see how slaves lived. Pull over in venerable St Augustine, founded in 1565, to seek out Ponce de Leon's fountain of youth and the Pirate Museum. Lighthouses, unspoiled strands of sand and surfing hot spots flash by. Moving on you'll come to the Kennedy Space Center, where shuttles used to launch into the stratosphere. After that, art-filled West Palm Beach appears among a slew of well-heeled towns. Hwy 1 then saves the best for last: Miami. The sexy city offers eye candy galore, from mural-splashed neighborhoods to the world's largest art-deco district to

the young and glamorous locals preening around South Beach.

But let's back up a bit and cover a few basics. The road is actually called Hwy A1A (not to be confused with US 1, the larger, faster version that runs parallel). A1A is not continuous – there are a few towns where you have to detour onto other roads before picking up A1A again. Should you want more road-tripping after Miami, hop on US 1, which becomes the scenic Overseas Hwy at Key Largo and dips south to Key West – a fine way to keep the party going.

When to Go

November to April is the best time, when it's warm but not too hot.

Resources

Florida Scenic Highways (www.floridascenic highways.com) Info for specially designated parts of the highway near St Augustine and Fort Lauderdale.

Highway A1A: Florida at the Edge (Herbert L Hiller; 2007) Part travel guide, part history about the cities and towns along the way.

Time & Mileage

Time Six days to take in the sights.

Mileage 475 miles.

Start/End Amelia Island/Miami.

DOWNLOADS: BLUEGRASS SOUNDS

➡ 'Blue Moon of Kentucky' – Bill Monroe and the Blue Grass Boys

➡ 'Foggy Mountain Breakdown' – Earl Scruggs

➡ 'Orange Blossom Special' – Rouse Brothers

➡ 'Rocky Top' – Osborne Brothers

➡ 'Windy Mountain' – Lonesome Pine Fiddlers

➡ 'Flame of Love' – Jim and Jesse

➡ 'I'm a Man of Constant Sorrow' – Stanley Brothers

➡ 'Every Time You Say Goodbye' – Alison Krauss and Union Station

➡ 'Like a Hurricane' – The Dillards

Plan Your Trip

Outdoors

Smoky mountains, wave-bashed beaches, coral reefs, river-cut gorges: the eastern USA has no shortage of spectacular settings for a bit of adventure. No matter what your weakness – hiking, cycling, kayaking, rafting, surfing, diving or skiing – you'll find world-class places to commune with the great outdoors.

Best Outdoors

Best Hiking
Appalachian Trail, Shenandoah National Park (VA), Great Smoky Mountains National Park (NC and TN), Adirondack wilderness (NY)

Best Cycling
Chequamegon National Forest WI (off-road), Cape Cod Rail Trail, MA (paved); Minneapolis, MN (city riding)

Best Paddling
Boundary Waters, MN (canoeing); New River Gorge National River, VA (white-water rafting); Apostle Islands, WI (kayaking); Pictured Rocks, MI (kayaking)

Best Surfing
Cocoa Beach, FL; Long Island, NY; Coast Guard Beach, MA

Best Diving
Florida Keys, FL (coral garden); Cape Hatteras, NC (Civil War shipwrecks); Dry Tortugas, FL (sea turtles); Crystal River, FL (manatees)

Best Wildlife-Watching
Baxter State Park, ME (moose); Provincetown, MA (whales); Florida Everglades, FL (alligators, manatees, sea turtles); Wabasha, MN (eagles)

Hiking & Trekking

Almost anywhere you go, great hiking and backpacking are within easy striking distance. National parks are ideal for short and long hikes. Beyond them, you'll find troves of state-maintained footpaths. There's no limit to the terrain you can explore, from the dogwood choked **Wild Azalea Trail** (www.townofwoodworth.com/azalea-trail) in Louisiana to the multi-state **North Country National Scenic Trail** (www.nps.gov/noco), winding across rugged landscapes from New York to Minnesota.

Resources

Survive Outdoors (www.surviveoutdoors.com) Dispenses safety and first-aid tips, plus helpful photos of dangerous critters.

Wilderness Survival (Gregory Davenport; 2006) Easily the best book on surviving nearly every contingency.

American Hiking Society (www.americanhiking.org) Links to 'volunteer vacations' building trails.

Backpacker (www.backpacker.com) Premier national magazine for backpackers, from novices to experts.

Cycling

Cycling's popularity increases by the day, with cities (including New York and Chicago) adding more cycle lanes, and a growing number of greenways striping the countryside. Several abandoned rail lines across the region have been converted into paved cycling paths. They offer gentle rides through quaint villages, over bridges and alongside pastures. Massachusetts' Cape Cod Rail Trail (p192) is a popular one.

Mountain bikers should steer for Wisconsin's Chequamegon National Forest (p591), revered for its bad-ass trails and grueling **Fat Tire Festival** (www.cheqfat tire.com) in September.

Resources

Bicycling (www.bicycling.com) This magazine has information on city rides, off-road trails and much in between.

Rails-to-Trails Conservancy (www.railstotrails. org) Publishes free trail reviews at www.traillink. com.

Kayaking & Canoeing

Paddlers will find their bliss in the eastern USA. Rentals and instruction are yours for the asking. Kayaking hot spots include Wisconsin's Apostle Islands National Lakeshore (p591), for gliding through arches and sea caves on Lake Superior; Michigan's Pictured Rocks National Lakeshore (p579), to paddle by wildly colored cliffs on Lake Superior; and Maine's Penobscot Bay (p240), to poke around the briny waters and spruce-fringed islets.

Canoeing is downright legendary here, including the 12,000 miles of wet and wild routes in Minnesota's Boundary Waters (p606) and Alabama's **Bartram Canoe Trail** (lands.dcnr.alabama.gov/Bartram), with 300,000 acres of marshy delta bayous, lakes and rivers.

Resources

American Canoe Association (www.american canoe.org) Has a water trails database for canoeing and kayaking, as well as information on local paddling clubs and courses (including stand up paddleboarding).

TIPS FOR VISITING NATIONAL PARKS

➡ Park entrance fees vary, from nothing at all to $30 per vehicle.

➡ The 'America the Beautiful' annual pass ($80; store.usgs.gov/ pass), which allows admission for four adults and all children under 16 years old to all federal recreational lands for 12 calendar months, is sold at park entrances and visitor centers.

➡ Lifetime senior-citizen passes ($10) are also available for US citizens over 62.

➡ Park lodges and campgrounds book up far in advance; for summer vacations, reserve six months to one year ahead.

➡ Some parks offer first-come, first-served campgrounds; for these, try to arrive between 10am and noon, when other campers may be checking out.

➡ For overnight backpacking and some day hikes, you'll need a wilderness permit; the number of permits is often subject to quotas, so apply far in advance (up to six months before your trip, depending on park regulations).

White-Water Rafting

East of the Mississippi, West Virginia has an arsenal of famous white water. First, there's the New River Gorge National River (p320), which, despite its name, is one of the oldest rivers in the world. Slicing from North Carolina into West Virginia, it cuts a deep gorge, known as the Grand Canyon of the East, producing frothy rapids in its wake.

Then there's the Gauley (p321), arguably among the world's finest white water. Revered for its ultra steep and turbulent chutes, the venerable Appalachian river is a watery roller coaster, dropping more than 668ft and churning up 100-plus rapids in a mere 28 miles. Six more rivers, all in the same neighborhood, offer training grounds for less-experienced river rats.

THE APPALACHIAN TRAIL

Completed in 1937, the country's longest footpath is 2180 miles, crossing six national parks, traversing eight national forests and hitting 14 states from Georgia to Maine. Misty mountains, deep woods, flowery pastures and bear sightings are the rewards. Each year, roughly 2500 hardy souls attempt to hike the entire trail – only one in four makes it all the way through. But don't let that discourage you. It's estimated that two to three million people trek a portion of the Appalachian Trail annually, thanks to easy-to-access day hikes up and down its length.

Practicalities

➡ Most through-hikers start at Springer Mountain in northern Georgia and finish at Mt Katahdin in Maine's Baxter State Park (p245).

➡ They begin in March or April and finish six months later. Baxter closes for the season on October 15, so hikers must arrive before then.

➡ Hiking the route in reverse (from Maine to Georgia) is also possible, but cold weather in the north dictates you start later (in June) when the blackflies are ravenous and the trails are wet and muddy. Either way, hikers hit the weather gamut from snow to steamy humidity.

➡ Campsites, lean-tos and huts are the usual lodging options. Most hikers spend about $1000 per month for food and the occasional night in a motel or lodge, plus supplies and replacement gear.

Short Hikes & Resources

➡ If you're short on time, gorgeous and accessible areas to get a piece of the trail include Shenandoah National Park (p309) in Virginia and Harpers Ferry (p318)in West Virginia, which is also the trail headquarters (and a short Amtrak train ride from Washington, DC).

➡ The **Appalachian Trail Conservancy** (www.appalachiantrail.org) has the lowdown on all things AT: official maps and guidebooks, an online database of day hikes organized by state, terrain descriptions by state, trail updates, hiker profiles etc. It's a fantastic resource.

➡ Humorist Bill Bryson's *A Walk in the Woods* (1998) is a great recreational read about the trail. It was made into a film starring Robert Redford in 2015.

Resources

American Whitewater (www.americanwhite water.org) Works to preserve America's wild rivers; has links to local rafting clubs.

Surfing

The Atlantic states harbor some terrific and unexpected surfing spots – especially if you're after more moderate swells. The warmest waters are off Florida's Gulf Coast. Top spots to hang 10:

➡ **Cocoa Beach and Melbourne Beach, FL** Small crowds and mellow waves make it a paradise for beginners and longboarders. Just south is the Inlet, known for consistent surf and crowds to match. (p483)

➡ **Long Island, NY** More than a dozen surfing spots dot the area, from Montauk's oft-packed Ditch Plains to Nassau County's Long Beach, with its 3-mile stretch of curling waves. (p113)

➡ **Coast Guard Beach, Eastham, MA** Part of the Cape Cod National Seashore, this family-friendly beach is known for its consistent shortboard/longboard swell all summer long. (p192)

Resources

Surfer (www.surfermag.com) Has travel reports covering the eastern seaboard and just about every break in the USA.

Diving

Florida has the lion's share of great diving, with more than 1000 miles of coastline subdivided into 20 unique undersea areas. There are hundreds of sites and countless dive shops offering equipment and guided excursions. South of West Palm Beach, you'll find clear waters and fantastic year-round diving with ample reefs. In the Panhandle (p505) you can scuba in the calm and balmy waters of the Gulf of Mexico; off Pensacola (p508) and **Destin** (www. floridapanhandledivetrail.com) are fabulous wreck dives; and you can dive with manatees near Crystal River.

The Florida Keys (p477) are the crown jewel. Expect a brilliant mix of marine habitats, North America's only living coral garden and the occasional shipwreck. Key Largo is home to the John Pennekamp Coral Reef State Park (p477) and more than 200 miles of underwater idyll. The expansive reefs around Dry Tortugas National Park (p484) swarm with barracuda, sea turtles and a couple of hundred sunken ships.

Other popular places to submerge in the eastern waters include North Carolina's Cape Hatteras National Seashore (p329), where you can explore Civil War wrecks and encounter tiger sand sharks, and **Lake Ouachita** (www.lakeouachita.org), Arkansas' largest lake, known for its pristine mountain waters and 16-mile water-based trail.

Resources

Scuba Diving (www.scubadiving.com) Provides the latest on diving destinations in the US and abroad.

STEPHEN FRINK / GETTY IMAGES ©

Florida manatee

Skiing & Winter Sports

Vermont's first-rate Stowe Mountain (p220) offers sweet slopes – freeze your tail off on the lifts, but thaw out nicely après-ski in timbered bars with local brews. In Lake Placid (p124), New York, you can luge or bobsled at old Olympic facilities. Snowmobiles rev in northern Wisconsin, Michigan and Minnesota; in Minnesota, Voyageurs National Park (p607) hosts lots of wintry action on its frozen waterways.

Resources

Ski Resorts Guide (www.skiresortsguide.com) Provides lodging info, downloadable trail maps and more.

Plan Your Trip

Travel with Children

From north to south, you'll find superb attractions for all ages: bucket-and-spade fun at the beach, amusement parks, zoos, eye-popping aquariums and natural-history exhibits, hands-on science museums, camping adventures, battlefields, leisurely bike rides through the countryside and plenty of other activities likely to wow young ones.

Best Regions for Kids

New York, New Jersey & Pennsylvania

New York City offers adventure such as row boating in Central Park and kid-friendly museums. Head to the Jersey shore for boardwalk fun and to Pennsylvania for Amish Country horse-and-buggy rides.

New England

Boston's waterfront and green spaces entice with an aquarium, an 18th-century warship and pedal-powered swan boats. Plimoth Plantation, with its recreated Wampanoag and Pilgrim villages, is good family fun.

Washington, DC & the Capital Region

Washington has unrivaled allure for families with free museums, a panda-loving zoo and boundless green spaces. Virginia's Williamsburg is a slice of 18th-century America with costumed interpreters and fanciful activities.

Florida

Orlando's Walt Disney World is well worth planning a vacation around. Afterwards, hit the state's beautiful beaches.

Eastern USA for Kids

Dining with Children

The local restaurant industry seems built on family-style service: children are not just accepted at most places, but are often encouraged by special children's menus with smaller portions and lower prices. In some restaurants children under a certain age even eat for free. Restaurants usually provide high chairs and booster seats. Some restaurants may also offer children crayons and puzzles, and occasionally live performances by cartoonlike characters.

Restaurants without children's menus don't necessarily discourage kids, though higher-end restaurants might. Even at the nicer places, however, if you show up early enough (right at dinnertime opening hours, often 5pm or 6pm), you can usually eat without too much stress – and you'll likely be joined by other foodies with kids. You can ask if the kitchen will make a smaller order of a dish, or if they will split a normal-size main dish between two plates for the kids. Chinese, Mexican and Italian restaurants seem to be the best bet for finicky young eaters.

Farmers markets are growing in popularity in the region, and every sizable town has at least one a week. This is a good place to assemble a first-rate picnic, sample local specialties and support independent growers in the process. After getting your stash, head to the nearest park or waterfront.

Accommodations

Motels and hotels typically have rooms with two beds, which are ideal for families. Some also have roll-away beds or cribs that can be brought into the room for an extra charge – but keep in mind these are usually portable cribs, which not all children sleep well in. Some hotels offer 'kids stay free' programs for children up to 12 or sometimes 18 years old. Be wary of B&Bs, as many don't allow children; inquire before reserving.

Babysitting

Resort hotels may have on-call babysitting services; otherwise, ask the front-desk staff or concierge to help you make arrangements. Always ask if babysitters are licensed and insured, what they charge per hour per child, whether there's a minimum fee, and if they charge extra for transportation or meals. Most tourist bureaus list local resources for child care and recreation facilities, medical services and so on.

Driving & Flying

Every car-rental agency should be able to provide an appropriate child seat, since these are required in every state, but you need to request it when booking; expect to pay around $13 more per day.

Domestic airlines don't charge for children under two years of age. Those two years and up must have a seat, and discounts are unlikely. Rarely, some resort areas (like Disney) offer a 'kids fly free' promotion. Amtrak and other train operators run similar deals (with kids up to age 15 riding free) on various routes.

Discounts for Children

Child concessions often apply for tours, admission fees and transport, with some discounts as high as 50% off the adult rate. However, the definition of 'child' can vary from under 12 to under 16 years. Unlike in Europe, few popular sights have discount rates for families; those that do will help you save a few dollars compared to buying individual tickets. Most sights give free admission to children under two years.

EASTERN LIT FOR KIDS

➡ *Little Women* (1868) Louisa May Alcott's wonderful book about girls growing up in 19th-century Concord, Massachusetts.

➡ *Paul Revere's Ride* (1861) Henry Wadsworth Longfellow combined history, poetry and suspense in his classic.

➡ *Eloise* (1955) Kay Thompson's six-year-old Eloise lives in the Plaza Hotel in NYC, a prime place to launch into all sorts of mischief.

➡ *The Wright 3* (2006) Tween sleuths solve a mystery involving ghosts, treasure and Frank Lloyd Wright's Robie House in Chicago in Blue Balliett's book.

Children's Highlights

Outdoor Adventure

Florida Everglades, FL Kayak, canoe or join guided walks in the swamps. (p474)

New River Gorge National River, WV Go white-water rafting. (p320)

Provincetown, MA Spot humpbacks spouting on a whale-watch tour. (p193)

Mammoth Cave National Park, KY Take a jaunt through the underground chambers. (p388)

Theme Parks & Zoos

Walt Disney World, FL Immerse in the mightiest attraction of all, with four action-packed parks spread across 20,000 acres. (p502)

Bronx Zoo, NYC Hop the subway from Manhattan to one of the USA's biggest and best zoos. (p85)

Lion Country Safari, West Palm Beach, FL Drive among 900 wild creatures roaming the landscape. (p473)

Wisconsin Dells, WI Splash it up at 20-plus water parks and watch water-skiing thrill shows. (p588)

Cedar Point, OH Ride some of the planet's wildest roller coasters, then play at the mile-long beachfront and water park. (p554)

Six Flags, Washington, DC It's America's stalwart amusement-park chain, with nine coaster-rich locations in the Eastern USA, including one in Washington, DC. (p265)

Top: Frozen Niagara formation at Mammoth Cave National Park (p388), Kentucky

Bottom: Children's Museum of Indianapolis (p543), Indiana

Traveling in Time

Williamsburg, Yorktown and Jamestown, VA
Don 18th-century garb and mingle with costumed interpreters in the history-rich triangle where America began. (p301)

Fort Mackinac, MI
Plug your ears as soldiers in 19th-century costumes fire muskets and cannons. (p577)

Freedom Trail, Boston, MA
Go on a walking tour with Ben Franklin (or at least his 21st-century look-alike). (p173)

Lincoln Presidential Library & Museum, Springfield, IL
Learn about America's favorite president via holograms, a replica log cabin and other interactive features. (p540)

St Augustine, FL
Rattle along in a horse-drawn carriage through the historic streets of this 450-year-old city. (p486)

Rainy-Day Activities

National Air & Space Museum, Washington, DC
Inspire budding aviators with rockets, spacecraft, old-fashioned biplanes and ride simulators. (p251)

American Museum of Natural History, NYC
Discover the massive planetarium, immense dinosaur skeletons and 30 million other artifacts. (p75)

Port Discovery, Baltimore, MD
Roam three stories of adventure and (cleverly disguised) learning that take in an Egyptian tomb, farmers market, train, art studio and physics stations. (p286)

Museum of Science & Industry, Chicago, IL
Geek out at the biggest science center in the western hemisphere, where a fairy castle, baby chicks and mock tornadoes await. (p523)

Ben & Jerry's Ice Cream Factory, Waterbury, VT
Lick at the delicious source. (p220)

Children's Museum of Indianapolis, IN
Let 'em loose at the world's largest kids' museum, with five floors of fun, dinosaur-laden galleries. (p543)

Planning

To find family-oriented sights and activities, accommodations, restaurants and entertainment among our reviews, just look for the child-friendly icon (👪).

When to Go

➡ Peak travel season is June to August, when schools are out and the weather is warmest. Expect high prices and abundant crowds – meaning long lines at amusement and water parks, fully booked resorts and heavy traffic on the roads; book well in advance for popular destinations.

➡ High season for winter resorts (in the Catskills and White Mountains) runs from January to March.

Need to Know

➡ Many public toilets have a baby-changing table (sometimes in men's toilets, too), and gender-neutral 'family' facilities appear in airports.

➡ Medical services and facilities in America are of a high standard.

➡ Items such as baby food, formula and disposable nappies (diapers) are widely available – including organic options – in supermarkets across the country.

➡ Single parents or guardians traveling with anyone under 18 should carry proof of legal custody or a notarized letter from the non-accompanying parent(s) authorizing the trip. This isn't required, but it can help avoid potential problems entering the USA.

Resources

For more information and advice, check out Lonely Planet's *Travel with Children*. To get the kids excited, check out *Not for Parents: USA* (also by Lonely Planet), filled with cool stories about candy bars, astronauts, heroic animals and more.

Baby's Away (www.babysaway.com) Rents cribs, high chairs, car seats, strollers and even toys at locations across the country.

Family Travel Files (www.thefamilytravelfiles. com) Ready-made vacation ideas, destination profiles and travel tips.

Kids.gov (www.kids.usa.gov) Enormous, eclectic national resource; download songs and activities or even link to the CIA Kids' Page.

Travel Babees (www.travelbabees.com) Another reputable baby-gear rental outfit, with locations nationwide.

Regions at a Glance

New York City is the East's hub. More than eight million inhabitants live in this megacity, a world center for fashion, food, arts and finance. The crowd thins out in neighboring New Jersey and Pennsylvania, where beaches, mountains and literal horse-and-buggy hamlets join the landscape. New England arches north to rocky shores, clapboard fishing villages and Ivy League universities.

The Capital Region begins the march south through voluptuous valleys and a slew of historic sites. By the time you reach the true South, the pace has slowed, pecan pie tempts on the table and bluesy tunes drift from juke joints. Surreal Florida brings on mermaids, manatees, Mickey Mouse and Miami, while the sensible Great Lakes region prefers burgers and beer with its natural attractions.

New York, New Jersey & Pennsylvania

Arts
History
Outdoors

Culture Spot

Home to the Met, MoMA and Broadway – and that's just New York City. Buffalo, Philadelphia and Pittsburgh also have world-renowned cultural institutions, as well as bohemian enclaves with live-music scenes.

A Living Past

From preserved Gilded Age mansions in the Hudson Valley to Independence National Historic Park in Philadelphia and sites dedicated to formative moments in the nation's founding, the region provides an interactive education.

Wild Outdoors

The outdoors lurks just beyond the city's gaze, with hiking in the Adirondack wilderness and Catskill mountains, rafting down the Delaware River, and ocean frolics along the Jersey Shore and Hamptons.

p54

New England

Seafood
History
Outdoors

Land of Lobsters

New England is justifiably famous for its fresh seafood. Seaside eateries pepper the coast, where you can suck oysters, crack lobster claws and spoon into clam chowder while watching day-boats haul in the next meal's catch.

Legends of the Past

From the Pilgrims' landing in Plymouth and the witch hysteria in Salem to Paul Revere's revolutionary ride, New England has shaped American history.

Fall Foliage

The brilliance of fall in these parts in legendary. Changing leaves put on a fiery display all around New England, from the Litchfield Hills in Connecticut all the way up to the White Mountains in New Hampshire and Maine.

p162

Washington, DC & the Capital Region

Arts
History
Food

Museums & Music

Washington, DC has a superb collection of museums and galleries. You'll also find down-home mountain music on Virginia's Crooked Road and famous theaters and edgy art in Baltimore.

Times Past

For historical lore, Jamestown, Williamsburg and Yorktown offer windows into Colonial America, while Civil War battlefields litter the Virginia countryside. There are also fascinating presidential estates such as Mount Vernon and Monticello, plus history-rich charmers like Annapolis.

Culinary Delights

Feasts await: Maryland blue crabs, oysters and seafood platters; international restaurants in Washington, DC; and farm-to-table dining rooms in Baltimore, Charlottesville, Staunton and Rehoboth.

p246

The South

Food
Music
Charm

Biscuits & Barbecue

Slow-cooked barbecue, fried chicken and catfish, butter-smothered biscuits, corn bread, grits and spicy Cajun-Creole dishes make the South a magnificent place to fill up a plate.

Country, Jazz & Blues

Nowhere on earth has a soundtrack as influential as the South. Head to music meccas for the authentic experience: country in Nashville, blues in Memphis and big-band jazz in New Orleans – with plenty of fusions and alternative sounds all across the region.

Southern Belles

Picture-book towns such as Charleston and Savannah have long captivated visitors with their historic tree-lined streets, antebellum architecture and friendly, down-home welcome. Other charmers include Chapel Hill, Oxford, Chattanooga and Natchez.

p324

Florida

Culture
Wildlife
Beaches

Multifaceted Soul

Florida has a complicated soul: it's the home of Miami's colorful art-deco district and Little Havana, plus historical attractions in St Augustine, theme parks in Orlando and museums and island heritage in Key West.

Wildlife-Watching

Immerse yourself in aquatic life on a snorkeling or diving trip. For bigger beasts, head off on a whale-watching cruise or try to spy alligators – along with egrets, eagles, manatees and other wildlife – on an Everglades excursion.

Shades of Sand

You'll find an array of sandy shores from steamy South Beach to upscale Palm Beach, island allure on Sanibel and Captiva, and panhandle rowdiness in Pensacola.

p452

Great Lakes

Food
Music
Roadside Oddities

Heartland Cuisine

From James Beard Award–winning restaurants in Chicago and Minneapolis to fresh-from-the-dairy milkshakes, the Midwest's farms, orchards and breweries satisfy the palate.

Rock & Roll

Home to the Rock and Roll Hall of Fame, blowout fests like Lollapalooza and thrashing clubs in all the cities, the Midwest knows how to turn up the volume.

Quirky Sights

A big ball of twine, a mustard museum, a cow-doo-throwing contest: the quirks rise from the Midwest's backyards and back roads – wherever there are folks with passion, imagination and maybe a little too much time on their hands.

p510

On the Road

New York, New Jersey & Pennsylvania

Includes ➜

Best Places to Eat

➜ Upstate (p96)

➜ Smorgasburg (p101)

➜ Stonecat (p123)

➜ Reading Terminal Market (p148)

➜ Lobster House (p137)

Best Places to Stay

➜ Wythe Hotel (p92)

➜ Roxbury Motel (p119)

➜ White Pine Camp (p125)

➜ Starlux (p137)

➜ General Sutter Inn (p153)

Why Go?

Where else could you visit an Amish family's farm, camp on a mountaintop, read the Declaration of Independence and view New York, New York from the 86th floor of an art-deco landmark – all in a few days? Even though this corner of the country is the most densely populated part of the US, it's full of places where jaded city dwellers escape to seek simple lives, where artists retreat for inspiration, and pretty houses line main streets in small towns set amid stunning scenery.

Urban adventures in NYC, historic and lively Philadelphia and river-rich Pittsburgh are a must. Miles and miles of glorious beaches are within reach, from glamorous Long Island to the Jersey Shore – the latter ranges from stately to kitschy. The mountain wilderness of the Adirondacks reaches skyward just a day's drive north of New York City, a journey that perfectly encapsulates this region's heady character.

When to Go
New York City

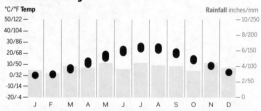

Oct–Nov Autumn in NYC brings cool temps, festivals, the marathon and gearing up for holiday season.

Feb Winter-sports buffs head to the mountains of the Adirondacks, Catskills and Poconos.

31 May–5 Sep Memorial Day through Labor Day is for beaches from Montauk to Cape May.

NEW YORK CITY

Loud and fast and pulsing with energy, New York City is symphonic, exhausting and always evolving. Maybe only a Walt Whitman poem cataloguing typical city scenes, from the humblest hole-in-the-wall to grand buildings, could begin to do the city justice. It remains one of the world centers of fashion, theater, food, music, publishing, advertising and finance.

Coming here for the first time from anywhere else is like stepping into a movie, one you've probably been unknowingly writing, one that contains all imagined possibilities. From the middle of Times Square to the most obscure corner of the Bronx, you'll find extremes. From Brooklyn's Russian enclave in Brighton Beach to the mini South America in Queens, virtually every country in the world has a bustling proxy community in the city. You can experience a little bit of everything on a visit here, as long as you take care to travel with a loose itinerary and an open mind.

History

After Henry Hudson first claimed this land in 1609 for his Dutch East India Company sponsors, he reported it to be 'as beautiful a land as one can hope to tread upon.' Soon after it was named 'Manhattan,' derived from local Munsee Native American words and meaning 'Island of Hills.'

By 1625 a colony, soon called New Amsterdam, was established, and the island was bought from the Munsee Indians by Peter Minuit. George Washington was sworn in here as the republic's first president in 1789, and when the Civil War broke out in 1861, New York City, which supplied a significant contingent of volunteers to defend the Union, became an organizing center for the movement to emancipate slaves.

Throughout the 19th century successive waves of immigrants – Irish, German, English, Scandinavian, Slavic, Italian, Greek and central European Jewish – led to a swift population increase, followed by the building of empires in industry and finance, and a golden age of skyscrapers.

After WWII New York City was the premier city in the world, but it suffered from a new phenomenon: 'white flight' to the suburbs. By the 1970s the graffiti-ridden subway system had become a symbol of New York's civic and economic decline. But NYC regained much of its swagger in the 1980s, led by colorful three-term mayor Ed Koch. The city elected its first African American mayor, David Dinkins, in 1989, but ousted him after a single term in favor of Republican Rudolph Giuliani (a 2008 primary candidate for US president). It was during Giuliani's reign that catastrophe struck on September 11, 2001, when the 110-story Twin Towers of the World Trade Center were struck

---

NEW YORK, NEW JERSEY & PENNSYLVANIA IN...

One Week

Start off with a gentle introduction in **Philadelphia**, birthplace of American independence. After a day touring the historic sites and a night sampling the great restaurants and bars, head into New Jersey for a bucolic night in **Cape May**. Stop off at another beach town like **Wildwood** or **Asbury Park** further north along the Jersey Shore, landing in **New York City** the following day. Spend the rest of your visit here, blending touristy must-dos – such as the **Top of the Rock** and **Central Park** – with vibrant nightlife and eclectic dining adventures, perhaps in the city's bustling East Village.

Two Weeks

Begin with several days in **New York City**, then a night or two somewhere in the **Hudson Valley**, before reaching the **Catskills**. After touring this bucolic region, head further north to **Lake Placid** and the **High Peaks** area of the **Adirondacks** where the outdoor-minded will have trouble leaving. Then loop back south through the **Finger Lakes** region with stops in wineries and waterfall-laden parks along the way, and a night in college-town **Ithaca**. From here you can head to **Buffalo** and **Niagara Falls** or southwest to **Pittsburgh**. Work your way back east via the **Pennsylvania Wilds**, then rest up in **Lancaster County**, where you can stay on a working Amish farm. From here it's a short jaunt to **Philadelphia**, which deserves at least a couple of nights. Follow it up with a stay at a quaint B&B in **Cape May**, then a day of boardwalk amusements in **Wildwood**.

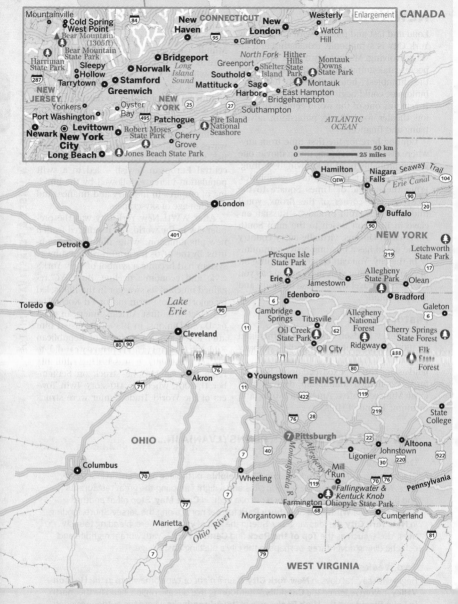

New York, New Jersey & Pennsylvania Highlights

1 Traveling round the world without ever leaving the kaleidoscope of neighborhoods and cultures that is **New York City** (p55).

2 Enjoying the kitsch and calm of the **Jersey Shore** (p133).

3 Absorbing the story of the birth of the nation in Philadelphia's **Independence National Historic Park** (p139).

4 Walking the densely forested paths of the **Catskills** (p119).

5 Exploring the wild beauty of the **Adirondacks** (p123).

6 Camping along the shores

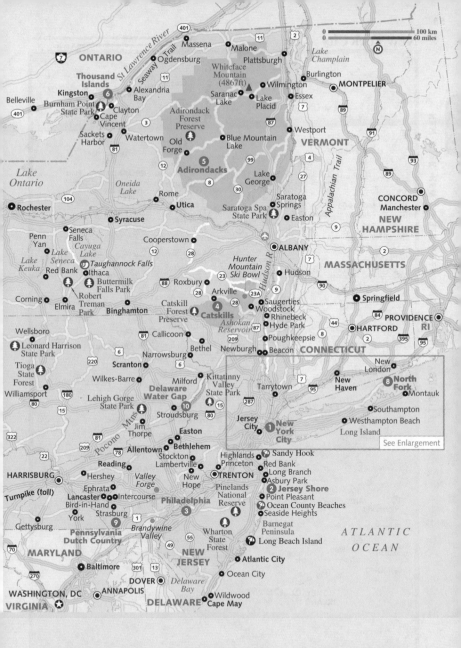

of the St Lawrence River in the **Thousand Islands** (p125).

7 Admiring great modern art and old industry in **Pittsburgh** (p155).

8 Wine tasting on Long Island's **North Fork** (p115).

9 Touring the back roads of **Pennsylvania Dutch Country** (p152).

10 Floating past bucolic scenery in the **Delaware Water Gap** (p131).

New York City

0 —————— 10 km
0 —————— 5 miles

BRONXVILLE

Cross County Pkwy

Boston Rd

ENGLEWOOD

Hudson River

Broadway

HACKENSACK

Long Island Sound

Woodlawn Cemetery

Pelham Bay Park

Hart Island

Overpeck County Park

George Washington Bridge

Cloisters

INWOOD

New York Botanical Garden

BRONXDALE

Pelham Bay Park

MetLife Stadium

FAIRVIEW

Belmont

BELMONT

Bronx Wildlife Conservation Park

City Island

KEARNY

New Jersey Turnpike

HARLEM

Yankee Stadium!

Bronx Park

THROGS NECK

GREAT NECK

See Central Park & Uptown Map (p78)

MANHATTAN

HUNTS POINT

Powells Cove

BEECHHURST

Little Neck Bay

Central Park

See Times Square, Midtown Manhattan & Chelsea Map (p70)

ASTORIA

LaGuardia Airport

COLLEGE POINT

BAYSIDE

Socrates Sculpture Park

CORONA

Citi Field

HOBOKEN

Kissena Park

See East & West Village Map (p66)

P.S.1 Contemporary Art Center

Queens Blvd

FLUSHING

Queens College

See Chinatown & Lower Manhattan Map (p62)

NEW YORK

QUEENS

Statue of Liberty

GLENDALE

BUSHWICK

JAMAICA

Brooklyn Academy of Music (BAM)

EAST NEW YORK

Upper New York Bay

Atlantic Ave

Ferry to Staten Island

Prospect Park

HOWARD BEACH

Brookville Park

BAY RIDGE

Linden Blvd

BROOKLYN

Spring Creek Park

Elders Point Marsh

John F Kennedy International Airport

Richmond County Bank Ballpark

East High Meadow

Staten Island

Fort Hamilton

Ave P

Gateway National Recreation Area

Jo Co Marsh

RICHMOND

Lower New York Bay

Bensonhurst Park

Brooklyn Marine Park

Big Channel

Key Span Park

CONEY ISLAND

Brighton Beach

Rockaway Inlet

Jacob Riis Park

Rockaway Beach

ATLANTIC OCEAN

NEW YORK

NEW JERSEY

by hijacked commercial airliners, became engulfed in balls of fire and then collapsed, killing 3000 people, the result of a now infamous terrorist attack.

The billionaire Republican Mayor Michael Bloomberg, first elected in an atmosphere of turmoil and grief, served as mayor for a controversial three terms. Considered an independent political pragmatist, he earned raves and criticism for his dual pursuit of environmental and development goals through a challenging period that has included the Global Financial Crisis and Hurricane Sandy.

Brooklyn-based Democrat Bill de Blasio became mayor in 2014, riding a wave of popular support for his proposals to address the social and economic inequalities of the city. He oversaw the creation of free pre-kindergarten education for all, greenlighted the creation of more affordable housing and tried to heal the divide between African Americans and a sometimes divisive police force.

Sights

Lower Manhattan

★Brooklyn Bridge BRIDGE

(Map p62; [S] 4/5/6 to Brooklyn Bridge-City Hall, J to Chambers St) Inspiration to artists and writers throughout the years, the Brooklyn Bridge is one of New York's best-loved monuments. Walking across it is a rite of passage for New Yorkers and visitors alike – with this in mind, walk no more than two abreast or you'll be in danger of colliding with runners and speeding cyclists.

With a span of 1596ft, it remains a compelling symbol of US achievement and a superbly graceful structure, despite the fact that its construction was plagued by budget overruns and the death of 20 workers. Among the casualties was designer John Roebling, who was knocked off a pier in 1869 while scouting a site for the western bridge tower and later died of tetanus poisoning. The bridge and the smooth pedestrian/cyclist path, beginning just east of City Hall, affords wonderful views of Lower Manhattan and Brooklyn. On the Brooklyn side, the ever-expanding Brooklyn Bridge Park is a great place to continue your stroll.

Statue of Liberty MONUMENT

(☎ 877-523-9849; www.nps.gov/stli; Liberty Island; adult/child incl Ellis Island $18/9, incl crown $21/12; 🕒 8:30am-5:30pm, check website for seasonal changes; [S] 1 to South Ferry, 4/5 to Bowling Green) In a city full of American icons, the Statue of Liberty is perhaps the most famous. Conceived as early as 1865 by French intellectual Edouard Laboulaye as a monument to the republican principles shared by France and the USA, it's still generally recognized as a symbol for the ideals of opportunity and freedom to many.

French sculptor Frédéric Auguste Bartholdi traveled to New York in 1871 to select the site, then spent more than 10 years in Paris designing and making the 151ft-tall figure of Liberty Enlightening the World. It was then shipped to New York, erected on a small island in the harbor and unveiled in 1886.

Access to the crown is limited, so reservations are required: book as far in advance as possible. Pedestal access is also limited, so reserve in advance. Keep in mind there's no elevator and the climb from the base is equal to a 22-story building. Otherwise, a visit means you can wander the grounds, take in the small museum and enjoy the view from the 16-story observation deck in the pedestal. Make the most of your visit by picking up a free audio guide when you reach the island (there's even a kid's version).

The trip to Liberty island, via ferry, is usually made in conjunction with nearby Ellis Island. Ferries leave from Battery Park and tickets include admission to both sights. Reserve in advance to cut down on long wait times.

Ellis Island LANDMARK, MUSEUM

(☎ 212-363-3200; www.nps.gov/elis; admission free, ferry incl Statue of Liberty adult/child $18/9; 🕒 8:30am-5:30pm, check website for seasonal changes; [S] 1 to South Ferry, 4/5 to Bowling Green) An icon of mythical proportions for the descendants of those who passed through here, this island and its hulking building served as New York's main immigration station from 1892 until 1954, processing an astounding 12 million arrivals – who came from far-flung corners of the globe. The process involved getting the once-over by doctors, being assigned new names if their own were deemed too difficult to spell or pronounce, and basically getting the green light to start new lives in America.

Now anybody who visits the island can get an understanding of the experience, thanks to an interactive Immigration Museum that's housed in the red-brick structure. You can peruse fascinating exhibits and watch a film that delves into the immigrant experience, explaining and how the influx changed the USA.

★National September 11 Memorial MONUMENT
(Map p62; www.911memorial.org; 180 Greenwich St; ⏲7:30am-9pm; [S] E to World Trade Center, N/R to Cortlandt St, 2/3 to Park Pl) [FREE] One of New York's most solemn spaces is the National September 11 Memorial. Titled 'Reflecting Absence', the memorial's two massive reflecting pools are as much a symbol of hope and renewal as they are a tribute to the thousands who lost their lives on September 11, 2001.

National September 11 Memorial Museum MUSEUM
(Map p62; www.911memorial.org/museum; 180 Greenwich St, near Fulton St; adult/child $24/15; ⏲9am-8pm Sun-Thu, to 9pm Fri & Sat; [S] E to World Trade Center, N/R to Cortlandt St, 2/3 to Park Pl) Just beyond the reflecting pools of the September 11 Memorial, you'll see an entrance pavilion that subtly, yet eerily, evokes a toppled tower. Inside, a gently sloping ramp leads to the subterranean exhibition galleries that recall that horrific summer day on 2001.

One World Observatory VIEWPOINT
(Map p62; ☎844-696-1776; www.oneworldobservatory.com; cnr West & Vesey Sts; adult/child $32/26; ⏲9am-8pm; [S] E to World Trade Center, N/R to Cortlandt St, 2/3 to Park Pl) Atop the highest building in the Western Hemisphere, One World Observatory, which opened in 2015, offers dazzling views from its 102-story perch. No other building in town rivals the jaw-dropping panorama of New York's urban landscape and its surrounding geography spread before you.

Aside from the sky-high spectacle, the experience also includes a video called 'Voices' about those who built the One World Trade Center; there's also a virtual time-lapse that shows the evolution of the city skyline from the 1600s to the present. Visitors are whisked up to the top in under 60 seconds in so-called 'skypods' – a surprisingly smooth ride, considering these are among the fastest elevators on the planet.

Not unexpectedly, this is a hugely popular site. Purchase tickets online: you'll need to choose the date and time of your visit.

Governors Island PARK
(www.govisland.com; ⏲10am-6pm Mon-Fri, to 7pm Sat & Sun from late May-late Sep; [S] 1 to South Ferry, then ferry from Battery Marine Terminal) [FREE] Off-limits to the public for 200 years, former military outpost Governors Island is now one of New York's most popular summer playgrounds. From late May through September, ferries make the seven-minute trip from Lower Manhattan (or Brooklyn Bridge Park's pier 6) to the 172-acre oasis. Highlights include 19th-century fortifications, open lawns, massive shade trees, a hammock grove and unsurpassed city views. There are art installations, concerts and food trucks throughout the summer. You can hire bikes when you arrive.

The **ferry** (Map p62; www.govisland.com; one-way $2; ⏲10am-4pm Mon-Fri, 10am-5:30pm Sat & Sun; [S] 1 to South Ferry) leaves every 30 to 60 minutes from the Battery Marine Terminal next to the Staten Island Ferry Whitehall Terminal in Lower Manhattan.

South Street Seaport NEIGHBORHOOD
(Map p62; www.southstreetseaport.com; [S] A/C, J/Z, 2/3, 4/5 to Fulton St) This 11-block enclave of shops, piers and sights combines the best and worst in historic preservation. It's not on the radar for most New Yorkers, but tourists are drawn to the sea air, the nautical feel, the frequent street performers and the mobbed restaurants.

The pedestrian malls, historic tall ships and riverside locale of this neighborhood create a lovely backdrop if you happen to be standing in line for discounted Broadway tickets at the downtown TKTS booth.

Bowling Green Park PARK
(Map p62; cnr State & Whitehall Sts; [S] 4/5 to Bowling Green) At Bowling Green Park, British residents relaxed with quiet games in the late 17th century. The large **Bronze Bull** here is a tourist photo stop.

National Museum of the American Indian MUSEUM
(Map p62; www.nmai.si.edu; 1 Bowling Green; ⏲10am-5pm Fri-Wed, to 8pm Thu; [S] 4/5 to Bowling Green, R to Whitehall St) [FREE] Set in Cass Gilbert's spectacular 1907 Custom House, this Smithsonian affiliate has exhibitions documenting Native American art, textiles, culture, life and beliefs.

Wall Street & the Financial District

The etymological origin of **Wall Street**, both an actual street and the metaphorical home of US commerce, is the wooden barrier built by Dutch settlers in 1653 to protect Nieuw Amsterdam from Native Americans and the British.

Battery Park & Around   NEIGHBORHOOD

The southwestern tip of Manhattan Island has been extended with landfill over the years to form **Battery Park** (Map p62; www.nycgovparks.org; Broadway at Battery Pl; ☺ sunrise-1am; Ⓢ 1 to South Ferry, 4/5 to Bowling Green), so named for the gun batteries that used to be housed at the bulkheads. **Castle Clinton** (Map p62; www.nps.gov/cacl; ☺ 8:30am-5pm; Ⓢ 1 to South Ferry, 4/5 to Bowling Green), a fortification built in 1811 to protect Manhattan from the British, was originally 900ft offshore but is now at the edge of Battery Park, with only its walls remaining.

Hudson River Park   PARK

(Map p62; www.hudsonriverpark.org; Ⓢ 1 to Franklin St, 1 to Canal St) Stretching for five miles from Battery Park to Hell's Kitchen (59th St), 550-acre Hudson River Park runs along the lower western side of Manhattan. Diversions include a bike/run/skate path that snakes along its entire length, community gardens, playgrounds, sculpture exhibitions, and renovated piers reinvented as riverfront esplanades, miniature golf courses, alfresco summertime movie theaters and concert venues.

Skyscraper Museum   MUSEUM

(Map p62; www.skyscraper.org; 39 Battery Pl; admission $5; ☺ noon-6pm Wed-Sun; Ⓢ 4/5 to Bowling Green) Housed in a ground-floor space of the Ritz-Carlton Hotel, the Skyscraper Museum features rotating exhibits plus a permanent study of high-rise history.

★ Museum of Jewish Heritage   MUSEUM

(Map p62; www.mjhnyc.org; 36 Battery Pl; adult/child $12/free, 4-8pm Wed free; ☺ 10am-5:45pm Sun-Tue & Thu, to 8pm Wed, to 5pm Fri Apr-Sep, to 3pm Fri Oct-Mar; Ⓢ 4/5 to Bowling Green) This evocative waterfront museum explores all aspects of modern Jewish identity, with often poignant personal artifacts, photographs and documentary films. Outside it stands a Holocaust memorial.

Museum of American Finance   MUSEUM

(Map p62; www.moaf.org; 48 Wall St, btwn Pearl & William Sts; adult/child $8/free; ☺ 10am-4pm Tue-Sat; Ⓢ 2/3, 4/5 to Wall St) Money makes this museum go round; its focus is on historic moments in American financial history.

Federal Reserve Bank of New York   NOTABLE BUILDING

(Map p62; ☏ 212-720-6130; www.newyorkfed.org; 33 Liberty St, at Nassau St, entry via 44 Maiden Lane; reservation required; ☺ guided tours 11:15am, noon, 12:45pm, 1:30pm, 2:15pm & 3pm Mon-Fri, museum 10am-3pm; Ⓢ A/C, J/Z, 2/3, 4/5 to Fulton St) 𝐅𝐑𝐄𝐄 The best reason to visit the Federal Reserve Bank is the chance to (briefly) ogle its high-security vault – more than 10,000 tons of gold reserves reside here, 80ft below ground. You'll only see a small part of that fortune, but signing on to a free tour (the only way down; book several months ahead) is worth the effort.

⊙ Tribeca & SoHo

The 'TRIangle BElow CAnal St,' bordered roughly by Broadway to the east and Chambers St to the south, is the more downtown of these two sister 'hoods. It has old warehouses, very expensive loft apartments and chichi restaurants.

SoHo takes its name from its geographical placement: SOuth of HOuston St. SoHo is filled with block upon block of cast-iron industrial buildings that date to the period just after the Civil War, when this was the city's leading commercial district. It had a Bohemian/artsy heyday that had ended by the 1980s, and now this super-gentrified area is a major shopping destination, home to chain stores and boutiques alike and to hordes of consumers, especially on weekends.

SoHo's cup overfloweth to the northern side of Houston St and the east side of Lafayette St, where two small areas, **NoHo** ('north of Houston') and **NoLita** ('north of Little Italy'), respectively, are known for small, independent boutiques and charming restaurants. Add them to SoHo and Tribeca for a great experience of strolling, window-shopping and cafe-hopping, and you'll have quite a packed afternoon.

⊙ Chinatown & Little Italy

Endless exotic moments await in Chinatown, one of New York City's most colorful neighborhoods. Catch the whiff of fresh fish and ripe persimmons, hear the clacking of mah-jongg tiles on makeshift tables, drool over dangling duck roasts swinging in store windows, and shop for mementos from the Far East, from rice-paper lanterns to loose oolong tea.

Little Italy, once an authentic enclave of Italian people, culture and eateries, is constantly shrinking (Chinatown keeps encroaching). Still, loyal Italian Americans, mostly from the suburbs, flock here to gather around red-and-white-checked tablecloths

Chinatown & Lower Manhattan

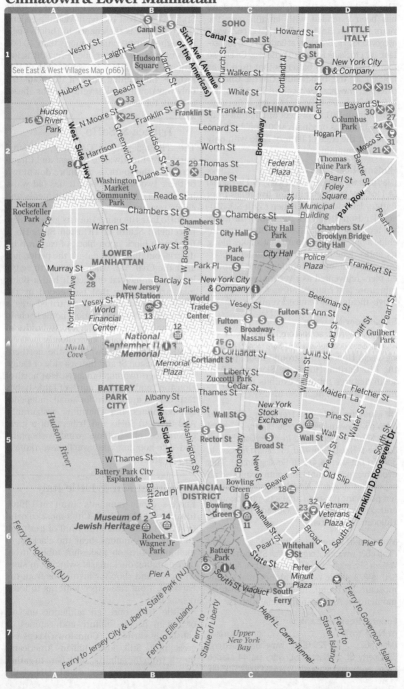

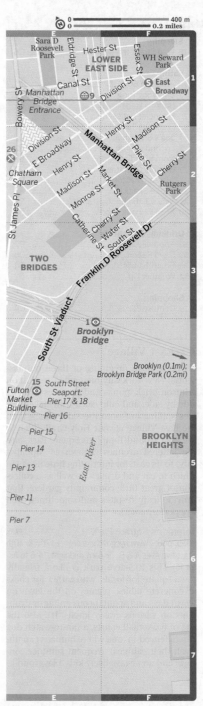

at one of a handful of longtime red-sauce restaurants along Mulberry St.

Museum of Chinese in America   MUSEUM
(Map p66; ☎212-619-4785; www.mocanyc.org; 215 Centre St, btwn Grand & Howard Sts; adult/child $10/free, Thu free; ⊙11am-6pm Tue, Wed, Fri-Sun, to 9pm Thu; ⓢN/Q/R, J/Z, 6 to Canal St) Strikingly designed and cutting-edge interactive exhibits trace the history and cultural impact of Chinese communities in the US. Also offers lectures, film series and walking tours.

St Patrick's Old Cathedral   CHURCH
(Map p66; www.oldsaintpatricks.com; 263 Mulberry St, entrance on Mott St; ⊙8am-6pm; ⓢN/R to Prince St) Though St Patrick's Cathedral is now famously located on Fifth Ave in Midtown, its first congregation was housed here, in this 1809–15 Gothic Revival church designed by Joseph-François Mangin.

◉ Lower East Side
First came the Jews, then the Latinos, followed by the hipsters and accompanying posers and frat boy bro contingents. Today, this neighborhood, once the densest in the world, is focused on being cool – offering low-lit lounges, live-music clubs and trendy bistros.

Lower East Side Tenement Museum   MUSEUM
(Map p66; ☎212-982-8420; www.tenement.org; 103 Orchard St, btwn Broome & Delancey Sts; admission $25; ⊙10am-6:30pm Fri-Wed, to 8:30pm Thu; ⓢB/D to Grand St, J/M/Z to Essex St, F to Delancey St) This museum puts the neighborhood's heartbreaking but inspiring heritage on full display in three re-creations of turn-of-the-20th-century tenements, including the late 19th-century home and garment shop of the Levine family from Poland, and two immigrant dwellings from the Great Depressions of 1873 and 1929. Visits are by tour only, with knowledgeable guides bringing the past to life. Check the website for the full range of tours that operate throughout the day. Reserve ahead (tours fill up).

New Museum of Contemporary Art   MUSEUM
(Map p66; ☎212-219-1222; www.newmuseum.org; 235 Bowery, btwn Stanton & Rivington Sts; adult/child $16/free, by donation 7-9pm Thu; ⊙11am-6pm Tue-Sun, to 9pm Thu; ⓢN/R to Prince St, F to 2nd Ave, J/Z to Bowery, 6 to Spring St) Housed in an architecturally ambitious building on Bowery, this is the city's sole museum dedicated to contemporary art – with often excellent

Chinatown & Lower Manhattan

Top Sights
1 Brooklyn Bridge E4
2 Museum of Jewish Heritage B6
3 National September 11 Memorial B4

Sights
4 Battery Park C6
5 Bowling Green Park C6
6 Castle Clinton C6
7 Federal Reserve Bank of New York C4
8 Hudson River Park A2
9 Museum at Eldridge Street Synagogue E1
10 Museum of American Finance D5
11 National Museum of the American Indian C6
12 National September 11 Memorial Museum B4
13 One World Observatory B4
14 Skyscraper Museum B6
15 South Street Seaport E4

Activities, Courses & Tours
16 Downtown Boathouse A2
17 Staten Island Ferry D7

Sleeping
18 Wall Street Inn C6

Eating
19 Amazing 66 .... D1
20 Big Wong King D1
21 Buddha Bodai D2
22 Financier Patisserie C6
23 Fraunces Tavern D6
24 Joe's Shanghai D2
25 Locanda Verde B2
26 Nom Wah Tea Parlor E2
27 Original Chinatown Ice Cream Factory D2
28 Shake Shack A3
29 Tiny's & the Bar Upstairs B2
30 Xi'an Famous Foods D2

Drinking & Nightlife
31 Apothéke D2
32 Dead Rabbit D6
33 Smith & Mills B1
34 Weather Up B2

Shopping
35 Century 21 .... C4

shows (there's no permanent collection). To save cash, stop by on Thursday evenings between 7pm and 9pm, when admission is pay what you wish.

International Center of Photography GALLERY
(ICP; Map p66; www.icp.org; 250 Bowery, btwn Houston & Prince Sts ; adult/child $14/free, Fri 5-8pm by donation; ⏰10am-6pm Tue-Thu, Sat & Sun, to 8pm Fri; [S] F to 2nd Ave, J/Z to Bowery) The city's most important showcase for major photographers, both past and present. Previous exhibitions have included work by Sebastião Salgado, Henri Cartier-Bresson and Matthew Brady. It recently moved from Midtown to this high-design space downtown.

Museum at Eldridge Street Synagogue MUSEUM
(Map p62; ☎212-219-0302; www.eldridgestreet.org; 12 Eldridge St, btwn Canal & Division Sts; adult/child $12/8, Mon free; ⏰10am-5pm Sun-Thu, 10am-3pm Fri; [S] F to East Broadway) This landmarked house of worship, built in 1887, was once the center of Jewish life before falling into squalor in the 1920s. Left to rot, it has only recently been reclaimed, and now shines with its original splendor. The on-site museum gives tours every half hour, with the last one departing at 4pm.

East Village

If you've been dreaming of those quintessential New York City moments – graffiti on crimson brick, punks and grannies walking side by side, and cute cafes with rickety tables spilling out onto the sidewalks – then the East Village is your Holy Grail. Stick to the area around Tompkins Square Park, and the lettered avenues (known as Alphabet City) to its east, for interesting little nooks in which to eat and drink – as well as a collection of great little community gardens that provide leafy respites and sometimes even live performances.

Tompkins Square Park PARK
(Map p66; www.nycgovparks.org; E 7th & 10th Sts, btwn Aves A & B; ⏰6am-midnight; [S] 6 to Astor Pl) This 10.5-acre park is like a friendly town square for locals, who gather for chess at concrete tables, picnics on the lawn on warm days and spontaneous guitar or drum jams on various grassy knolls. It's also the site of basketball courts, a fun-to-watch dog run (a fenced-in area where humans can unleash their canines), frequent summer concerts and an always-lively kids' playground.

Astor Place SQUARE
(Map p66; 8th St btwn Third & Fourth Aves; [S] N/R to 8th St-NYU, 6 to Astor Pl) This square is named after the Astor family, who built an early New York fortune on beaver pelts (check out the tiles in the wall of the Astor Place subway platform) and lived on Colonnade Row, just south of the square; four of the original nine marble-faced Greek Revival residences on Lafayette St still exist.

The large, brownstone Cooper Union, the public college founded in 1859 by glue millionaire Peter Cooper, dominates the square – you can't miss the new academic building, a wildly futuristic nine-story sculpture of glazed glass wrapped in perforated stainless steel (and LEED-certified, too) by architect Thom Mayne of Morphosis.

Russian & Turkish Baths BATHHOUSE
(Map p66; ☎ 212-674-9250; www.russianturkishbaths.com; 268 E 10th St, btwn First Ave & Ave A; per visit $35; 🕒 noon-10pm Mon-Tue & Thu-Fri, from 10am Wed, from 9am Sat, from 8am Sun; [S] L to First Ave, 6 to Astor Pl) The historic bathhouse is a great place to work out your stress in one of the four hot rooms; traditional massages are also offered. It's authentic and somewhat grungy, and you're as likely to share a sauna with a downtown couple on a date, a well-known actor looking for a time-out or an actual Russian.

West Village & Greenwich Village

Once a symbol for all things artistic, outlandish and Bohemian, this storied and popular neighborhood – the birthplace of the gay-rights movement as well as former home of Beat poets and important artists – feels worlds away from busy Broadway, and in fact almost European. Known by most visitors as 'Greenwich Village,' although that term is not used by locals (West Village encompasses Greenwich Village, which is the area immediately around Washington Square Park), it has narrow, tree-lined streets lined with eye-catching stores and lovely brownstones, as well as cafes and restaurants, making it an ideal place to wander.

Washington Square Park PARK
(Map p66; Fifth Ave at Washington Sq N; [S] A/C/E, B/D/F/M to W 4th St-Washington Sq, N/R to 8th St-NYU) This park began as a 'potter's field' – a burial ground for the penniless – and its status as a cemetery protected it from development. It is now a completely renovated and incredibly well-used park, especially on the weekend. Children use the playground, NYU students catch some rays and friends meet 'under the arch,' the renovated landmark on the park's northern edge, designed in 1889 by society architect Stanford White.

Dominating a huge swath of property in the middle of the Village, New York University, one of the largest in the country, defines the area around the park and beyond architecturally and demographically.

Christopher Street Piers/ Hudson River Park PIER, PARK
(Map p66; Christopher St & West Side Hwy; [S] 1 to Christopher St-Sheridan Sq) Like so many places in the Village, the extreme west side was once a derelict eyesore used mostly as a cruising ground. Now it's a pretty waterside hangout, bisected by the Hudson River Park's slender bike and jogging paths. It's still a place to cruise, just much less dangerous.

Sheridan Square & Around NEIGHBORHOOD
The western edge of the Village is home to **Sheridan Square** (Map p66; Christopher St & Seventh Ave; [S] 1 to Christopher St-Sheridan Sq), a small, triangular park where life-sized white statues by George Segal honor the gay community and gay pride movement that began in the nearby renovated **Stonewall Inn** sitting just across the street from the square.

A block further east, an appropriately bent street is officially named Gay St. Although gay social scenes have in many ways moved further uptown to Chelsea, **Christopher Street** is still the center of gay life in the Village.

Meatpacking District

Nestled between the far West Village and the southern border of Chelsea is the gentrified and now inappropriately named Meatpacking District. The neighborhood was once home to 250 slaughterhouses and was best known for its groups of tranny hookers, racy S&M sex clubs and, of course, its sides of beef. These days the hugely popular High Line park has only intensified an ever-increasing proliferation of trendy wine bars, eateries, nightclubs, high-end designer clothing stores, chic hotels and high-rent condos.

★ **The High Line** OUTDOORS
(Map p66; ☎ 212-500-6035; www.thehighline.org; Gansevoort St; 🕒 7am-7pm Oct-Mar, to 10pm Apr-May, to 11pm Jun-Sep; 🚌 M11 to Washington St, M11,

East & West Villages

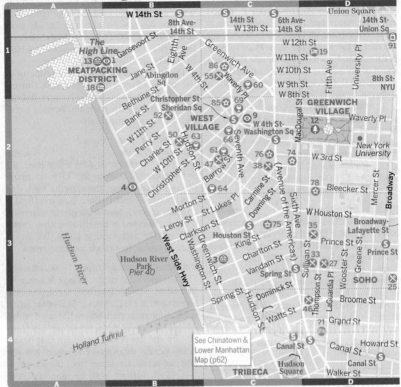

M14 to 9th Ave, M23, M34 to 10th Ave; Ⓢ L, A/C/E to 14th St-8th Ave; C/E to 23rd St-8th Ave) **FREE** With the completion of the High Line, a 30ft-high abandoned stretch of elevated railroad track transformed into a long ribbon of parkland (from Gansevoort St to W 34th St; entrances are at Gansevoort, 14th, 16th, 18th, 20th, 30th and 34th Sts with elevator access at all but 18th St), there's finally some greenery amid the asphalt jungle.

Only three stories above the streetscape, this thoughtfully and carefully designed mix of contemporary, industrial and natural elements is nevertheless a refuge and escape from the ordinary. A glass-front amphitheater with bleacher-like seating sits just above 10th Ave – bring some food and join local workers on their lunch break.

Whitney Museum of American Art MUSEUM (Map p66; 📞 212-570-3600; www.whitney.org; 99 Gansevoort St; adult/child $22/free; ⏱10:30am-6pm Mon, Wed & Sun, to 10pm Thu-Sat; Ⓢ L to 8th

Ave) After years of construction, the Whitney's new downtown location opened to much fanfare in 2015. Perched near the foot of the High Line, this architecturally stunning building – designed by Renzo Piano – makes a suitable introduction to the museum's superb collection. Inside the spacious, light-filled galleries, you'll find works by all the great American artists, including Edward Hopper, Jasper Johns, Georgia O'Keeffe and Mark Rothko.

In addition to rotating exhibits, there is a biennial on even-numbered years, an ambitious survey of contemporary art that rarely fails to generate controversy.

◎ Chelsea

This 'hood is popular for two main reasons: one, the parade of gorgeous gay men (known affectionately as 'Chelsea boys') who roam Eighth Ave, darting from gyms to

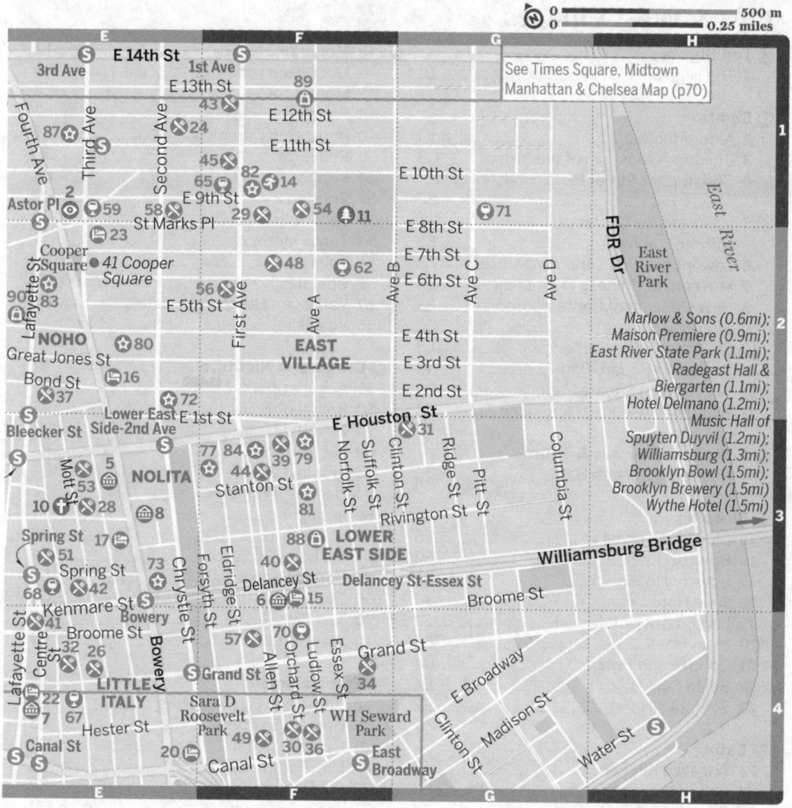

trendy happy hours; and two, as the hubs of the city's art-gallery scene, it's currently home to nearly 200 modern-art exhibition spaces, most of which are clustered west of Tenth Ave. For a handy list of specific galleries and upcoming shows, check out www.chelseagallerymap.com.

Rubin Museum of Art MUSEUM
(Map p70; ☎212-620-5000; www.rmanyc.org; 150 W 17th St at Seventh Ave; adult/child $15/free, 6-10pm Fri free; 🕐11am-5pm Mon & Thu, to 9pm Wed, to 10pm Fri, to 6pm Sat & Sun; [S]1 to 18th St) Dedicated to the art of the Himalayas and surrounding regions, this museum's impressive collection includes embroidered textiles from China, metal sculptures from Tibet, intricate Bhutanese paintings, and ritual objects and dance masks from various Tibetan regions, spanning from the 2nd to 19th centuries.

On Friday nights, museum admission is free and the cafe transforms into the K2 Lounge, where you can nibble on pan-Asian tapas, sip cocktails and enjoy a mix of DJs, films and other programs.

Chelsea Piers Complex SPORTS
(Map p70; ☎212-336-6666; www.chelseapiers.com; Hudson River at end of W 23rd St; [S]C/E to 23rd St) A waterfront sports center that caters to the athlete in everyone. It's got a four-level driving range, an indoor ice rink, a jazzy bowling alley, Hoop City for basketball, a sailing school for kids, batting cages, a huge gym, indoor rock-climbing walls – the works.

Flatiron District

The famous 1902 **Flatiron Building** (Map p70; Broadway, cnr Fifth Ave & 23rd St; [S]N/R, F/M, 6 to 23rd St) has a distinctive triangular shape to match its site. It was New York's first iron-frame high-rise, and the world's tallest building until 1909. The surrounding

East & West Villages

district is a fashionable area of boutiques, loft apartments and a burgeoning high-tech corridor, the city's answer to Silicon Valley. Peaceful **Madison Square Park**, bordered by 23rd and 26th Sts, and Fifth and Madison Aves, has an active dog run, rotating outdoor sculptures, shaded park benches and a popular burger joint.

Museum of Sex MUSEUM
(Map p70; www.museumofsex.com; 233 Fifth Ave, at 27th St; adult $17.50; ⏰10am-8pm Sun-Thu, to 9pm Fri & Sat; [S] N/R to 23rd St) Get the low-down on anything from online fetishes to homosexual necrophilia in the mallard duck at this slick, smallish ode to all things hot and sweaty.

Union Square

Like the Noah's Ark of New York, **Union Square** (Map p70; www.unionsquarenyc.org; 17th St btwn Broadway & Park Ave S; [S] L, N/Q/R, 4/5/6 to 14th St-Union Sq) rescues at least two of every kind from the curling seas of concrete. Here, amid the tapestry of stone steps and fenced-in foliage, it's not uncommon to find denizens of every ilk: suited business-folk gulping fresh air during their lunch breaks, dreadlocked loiterers tapping beats on their tabla, skateboarding punks flipping tricks on the southeastern stairs, rowdy college kids guzzling student-priced eats, and throngs of protesting masses chanting fervently for various causes.

Gramercy Park PARK
(Map p70; E 20th St btwn Park & Third Aves; [S] N/R, F/M, 6 to 23rd St) Gramercy Park, a few blocks northeast of Union Square, is named after one of New York's loveliest parks; for residents only, though, and you need a key to get in!

★**Greenmarket Farmers Market** MARKET
(Map p70; ☎212-788-7476; www.grownyc.org; 17th St btwn Broadway & Park Ave S; ⏰8am-6pm Mon, Wed, Fri & Sat) 🌿 On most days, Union Square's north end hosts the most popular of the nearly 50 greenmarkets throughout the five boroughs, where even celebrity chefs come for just-picked rarities including fiddlehead ferns, heirloom tomatoes and fresh curry leaves.

Midtown

The classic NYC fantasy – shiny skyscrapers, teeming mobs of worker bees, Fifth Ave store windows, taxi traffic – and some of the city's most popular attractions can be found here.

★**Museum of Modern Art** MUSEUM
(MoMA; Map p70; www.moma.org; 11 W 53rd St, btwn Fifth & Sixth Aves; adult/child $25/free, 4-8pm Fri free; ⏰10:30am-5:30pm Sat-Thu, to 8pm Fri, to 8pm Thu Jul-Aug; [S] E, M to 5th Ave-53rd St) Superstar of the modern art scene, MoMA's booty makes many other collections look, well, endearing. You'll find more A-listers here than at an Oscars after-party: Van Gogh, Matisse, Picasso, Warhol, Lichtenstein, Rothko, Pollock and Bourgeois. Since its founding in 1929, the museum has amassed over 150,000 artworks, documenting the emerging creative ideas and movements of the late 19th century through to those that dominate today.

For art buffs, it's Valhalla. For the uninitiated, it's a thrilling crash course in all that is beautiful and addictive about art.

Times Square LANDMARK
(Map p70; www.timessquare.com; Broadway at Seventh Ave; [S] N/Q/R, S, 1/2/3, 7 to Times Sq-42nd St) Love it or hate it, the intersection of Broadway and Seventh Ave (better known as Times Square) is New York City's hyperactive heart; a restless, hypnotic torrent of glittering lights, bombastic billboards and raw urban energy. It's not hip, fashionable or in-the-know, and it couldn't care less. It's too busy pumping out iconic, mass-marketed NYC – yellow cabs, golden arches, soaring skyscrapers and razzle-dazzle Broadway marquees.

Theater District NEIGHBORHOOD
([S] N/Q/R, S, 1/2/3, 7 to Times Sq-42nd St) The Times Square area is at least as famous as New York's official Theater District, with dozens of Broadway and off-Broadway theaters located in an area that stretches from 41st to 54th Sts, between Sixth and Ninth Aves. The Times Square branch of tourist information center New York City & Company (p111) sits smack in the middle of this famous crossroads. Broadway, the road, once ran all the way to the state capital in Albany.

Rockefeller Center NOTABLE BUILDING
(Map p70; www.rockefellercenter.com; Fifth to Sixth Aves & 48th to 51st Sts; [S] B/D/F/M to 47th-50th Sts-Rockefeller Center) During the height of the Great Depression in the 1930s, construction of the 22-acre Rockefeller Center (including the landmark art-deco skyscraper) gave jobs to 70,000 workers over nine years. It was the first project to combine retail, entertainment and office space in what is often referred to as a 'city within a city.'

In winter, the ground floor outdoor space is abuzz with ice-skaters and Christmas-tree gawkers.

NBC Studio Tours GUIDED TOUR
(Map p70; ☎212-664-3700; www.thetouratnbcstudios.com; 30 Rockefeller Plaza, at 49th St;

Times Square, Midtown Manhattan & Chelsea

W 57th St

W 55th St

Hudson River Park

Dewitt Clinton Park

Eleventh Ave

Tenth Ave

Ninth Ave

Eighth Ave

W 53rd St
55

58

W 51st St
52 65 42

Seventh Ave

57th St-7th Ave S
67

7th Ave S
64

W 49th St

Worldwide Plaza
8

50th St S
68

49th St S

W 47th St

THEATER DISTRICT

63

W 45th St
28

62

TIMES SQUARE
53

45

10

HELL'S KITCHEN
W 42nd St

37

71

42nd St-Port Authority S

42nd St-Times Sq S

19

59

Pier 83
24

Pier 81

W 40th St

74

Port Authority Bus Terminal

Broadway

495 Lincoln Tunnel

Twelfth Ave (West Side Hwy)

W 38th St

Jacob K. Javits Convention Center

W 36th St

GARMENT DISTRICT

Boltbus Bus Stop (Philadelphia & Boston)

New York City & Company 76

W 34th St

34th St-Penn Station S

W 33rd St

Megabus (Departures)

Boltbus Bus Stop (DC & Baltimore)

70

Penn Station

W 30th St

Hudson River

Eleventh Ave

W 28th St
Chelsea Park

32

Megabus (Arrivals)

28th St S

72

W 26th St

57

The High Line

Chelsea Waterside Park

23rd St S

23rd St S

36

W 23rd St

CHELSEA

51

47

27

23

Chelsea Piers

Eleventh Ave (West Side Hwy)

Tenth Ave

Ninth Ave

Eighth Ave

Seventh Ave

W 21st St

30

31

18th St S

18

W 19th St

41

W 17th St

NEW YORK
NEW JERSEY

40

W 14th St

8th Ave-14th St S

14th St S

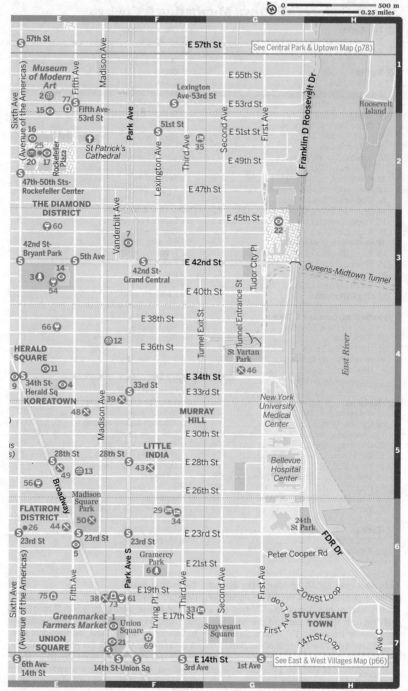

0 — 500 m
0 — 0.25 miles

57th St

E 57th St

See Central Park & Uptown Map (p78)

E 55th St

Museum of Modern Art

Lexington Ave-53rd St

E 53rd St

2
77
15

Fifth Ave-53rd St

51st St

E 51st St

16
25
20 17

Rockefeller Plaza

St Patrick's Cathedral

E 49th St

47th-50th Sts-Rockefeller Center

E 47th St

THE DIAMOND DISTRICT

E 45th St

60

22

42nd St-Bryant Park

5th Ave

E 42nd St

42nd St-Grand Central

Queens-Midtown Tunnel

3
14
54

E 40th St

66

E 38th St

12

E 36th St

St Vartan Park

HERALD SQUARE

11

E 34th St

46

9

34th St-Herald Sq

4

33rd St

E 33rd St

KOREATOWN

39

New York University Medical Center

48

MURRAY HILL

E 30th St

28th St

28th St

LITTLE INDIA

E 28th St

Bellevue Hospital Center

49

13

43

E 26th St

56

29

24th St Park

34

FLATIRON DISTRICT

44

50

E 23rd St

26

23rd St

23rd St

Peter Cooper Rd

5

Gramercy Park

E 21st St

6

E 19th St

STUYVESANT TOWN

75

38
73
61

E 17th St

33

Greenmarket Farmers Market

1

Union Square

Stuyvesant Square

UNION SQUARE

21

69

6th Ave-14th St

14th St-Union Sq

E 14th St

3rd Ave

1st Ave

See East & West Villages Map (p66)

Fifth Ave

Madison Ave

Park Ave

Lexington Ave

Third Ave

Second Ave

First Ave

(Franklin D Roosevelt Dr)

Roosevelt Island

East River

Vanderbilt Ave

Tunnel Exit St

Tunnel Entrance St

Tudor City Pl

FDR Dr

20th St Loop

First Ave Loop

14th St Loop

Ave C

Broadway

Madison Ave

Sixth Ave (Avenue of the Americas)

Park Ave S

Fifth Ave

Irving Pl

Times Square, Midtown Manhattan & Chelsea

tours adult/child $28/22, children under 6yr not admitted; S B/D/F/M to 47th-50th Sts-Rockefeller Center) NBC Studio Tours take TV fans on a walking tour through parts of the NBC Studios, home to iconic TV shows *Saturday Night Live* and *The Tonight Show Starring Jimmy Fallon*.

Competition is stiff for TV show tapings. Visit the website for details.

Top of the Rock LOOKOUT
(Map p70; www.topoftherocknyc.com; 30 Rockefeller Plaza, at 49th St, entrance on W 50th St btwn Fifth & Sixth Aves; adult/child $30/20, sunrise/sunset combo $40/22; ⊗8am-midnight, last elevator at 11pm; S B/D/F/M to 47th-50th Sts-Rockefeller Center) The 360-degree views from the tri-level observation deck 70 stories above Midtown are absolutely stunning and should not be

missed. You get an excellent view of the Empire State Building, as well as Central Park's perfect patch of green.

Radio City Music Hall   NOTABLE BUILDING

(Map p70; www.radiocity.com; 1260 Sixth Ave, at 51st St; tours adult/child $27/18; tours 10am-5pm; B/D/F/M to 47th-50th Sts-Rockefeller Center) Within the Rockefeller complex is the 6000-seat Radio City Music Hall from 1932. To get an inside look at this former movie palace and protected landmark, which has been gorgeously restored in all its art-deco grandeur, join one of the frequent guided tours that leave the lobby.

New York Public Library   BUILDING

(Stephen A Schwarzman Bldg; Map p70; 917-275-6975; www.nypl.org; Fifth Ave at 42nd St; 10am-6pm Mon & Thu-Sat, to 8pm Tue & Wed, 1-5pm Sun, guided tours 11am & 2pm Mon-Sat, 2pm Sun; B/D/F/M to 42nd St-Bryant Park, 7 to 5th Ave) FREE Flanked by two huge marble lions, the massive, superb beaux-arts library stands as testament to the value of learning and culture in the city, as well as to the wealth of the philanthropists who made its founding possible.

A magnificent 3rd-floor reading room has a painted ceiling and bountiful natural light – rows of long wooden tables are occupied by studious folk working away at laptops. This, the main branch of the entire city library system, has galleries of manuscripts on display, as well as fascinating temporary exhibits.

Bryant Park   PARK

(Map p70; www.bryantpark.org; 42nd St btwn Fifth & Sixth Aves; 7am-midnight Mon-Fri, to 11pm Sat & Sun Jun-Sep, shorter hours rest of year; B/D/F/M to 42nd St-Bryant Park, 7 to Fifth Ave) Nestled behind the grand New York Public Library building, Bryant Park is a whimsical spot for a little time-out from the Midtown madness. You'll find European coffee kiosks, alfresco chess games, summer film screenings and winter ice-skating.

Empire State Building   NOTABLE BUILDING

(Map p70; www.esbnyc.com; 350 Fifth Ave, at 34th St; 86th-fl observation deck adult/child $32/26, incl 102nd-fl observation deck $52/46; 8am-2am, last elevators up 1:15am; B/D/F/M, N/Q/R to 34th St-Herald Sq) Catapulted to Hollywood stardom both as the planned meeting spot for Cary Grant and Deborah Kerr in *An Affair to Remember,* and the vertical perch that helped to topple King Kong, the towering Empire State Building is one of the most famous members of New York's skyline. It's a limestone classic built in just 410 days, or seven million man-hours, during the depths of the Depression, at a cost of $41 million.

On the site of the original Waldorf-Astoria Hotel, the 102-story, 1472ft (to the top of the antenna) Empire State Building opened in 1931 after 10 million bricks were laid, 6400 windows installed and 328,000 sq ft of marble laid. Today you can ride the elevator to observatories on the 86th and 102nd floors, but be prepared for crowds; try to come very early or very late (and purchase your tickets ahead of time, online or pony up for $55 'express passes') for an optimal experience.

Grand Central Terminal   NOTABLE BUILDING

(Map p70; www.grandcentralterminal.com; 42nd St at Park Ave, Midtown East; 5:30am-2am; S, 4/5/6, 7 to Grand Central-42nd St) Completed in 1913, Grand Central is another of New York's stunning beaux-arts buildings, boasting 75ft-high glass-encased catwalks and a vaulted ceiling bearing a mural of the constellations streaming across it. The balconies overlooking the main concourse afford an expansive view.

There's a high-end food market and the lower level houses an excellent array of eateries.

Fifth Avenue & Around   NEIGHBORHOOD

(725 Fifth Ave, at 56th St) Immortalized in both film and song, Fifth Ave first developed its high-class reputation in the early 20th century, when it was considered desirable for its 'country' air and open spaces. A series of mansions called **Millionaire's Row** extended right up to 130th St, though most of the heirs to the millionaire mansions on Fifth Ave above 59th St sold them for demolition or converted them to the cultural institutions that now make up Museum Mile.

The avenue's Midtown stretch still boasts upmarket shops and hotels, including Trump Tower and the Plaza (corner Fifth Ave and Central Park South). While a number of the more exclusive boutiques have migrated to Madison Ave – leaving outposts of Gap and H&M in their wake – several superstars still reign over Fifth Ave above 50th St, including the famous Tiffany & Co.

Morgan Library & Museum   MUSEUM

(Map p70; www.morganlibrary.org; 29 E 36th St, at Madison Ave, Midtown East; adult/child $18/12; 10:30am-5pm Tue-Thu, to 9pm Fri, 10am-6pm Sat, 11am-6pm Sun; 6 to 33rd St) The beautifully renovated library is part of the 45-room mansion once owned by steel magnate JP Morgan. His collection features a phenomenal array of manuscripts, tapestries and books, a study filled with Italian Renaissance artwork, a marble rotunda and the three-tiered East Room main library. Temporary exhibitions delve into the lives of literary greats (Cervantes, Poe, Proust).

United Nations NOTABLE BUILDING

(UN; Map p70; ☎ 212-963-4475; http://visit.un.org; visitors' gate First Ave at 46th St, Midtown East; guided tours adult/child $20/11, children under 5yr not admitted, grounds access Sat & Sun free; ⊘ tours 9:30am-4:15pm Mon-Fri, visitor center also open 10am-4:30pm Sat & Sun; ⓢ S, 4/5/6, 7 to Grand Central-42nd St) The UN is technically on a section of international territory overlooking the East River. Take a guided 45-minute tour (English-language tours are frequent; limited tours in several other languages) of the facility and you'll get to see (when official meetings are not in session) the General Assembly, where the annual fall convocation of member nations takes place, the Security Council Chamber, the Trusteeship Council Chamber and also the Economic & Social Council Chamber.

There is a park to the south of the complex which is home to several sculptures with a peace theme.

Paley Center for Media BUILDING

(Map p70; www.paleycenter.org; 25 W 52nd St, btwn Fifth & Sixth Aves; adult/child $10/5; ⊘ noon-6pm Wed & Fri-Sun, to 8pm Thu; ⓢ E, M to 5th Ave-53rd St) TV fanatics who spent their childhood glued to the tube and proudly claim instant recall of all of Fonzi's *Happy Days* exploits can hold their heads high. This is the 'museum' for them. Search through a catalog of more than 100,000 US TV and radio programs and advertisements and a click of the mouse will play your selection on one of the library's computer screens. A comfy theater shows some great specials on broadcasting history, and there are frequent events and screenings.

Intrepid Sea, Air & Space Museum MUSEUM

(Map p70; www.intrepidmuseum.org; Pier 86, Twelfth Ave at 46th St, Midtown West; Intrepid & Growler submarine adult/child $24/19, incl Space Shuttle Pavilion $31/24; ⊘ 10am-5pm Mon-Fri, to 6pm Sat & Sun Apr-Oct, 10am-5pm Mon-Sun Nov-Mar; ⓠ M42, M50 westbound, ⓢ A/C/E to 42nd St-Port Authority Bus Terminal) The USS *Intrepid*, a hulking aircraft carrier that survived both a WWII bomb and kamikaze attacks has been transformed into a military museum with high-tech exhibits and fighter planes and helicopters for view on the outdoor flight deck. The pier area contains the guided-missile submarine *Growler*, a decommissioned Concorde and the *Enterprise* space shuttle.

Herald Square SQUARE

(Map p70; cnr Broadway, Sixth Ave & 34th St; ⓢ B/D/F/M, N/Q/R to 34th St-Herald Sq) This crowded convergence of Broadway, Sixth Ave and 34th St is best known as the home of Macy's (p110) department store, where you can still ride some of the remaining original wooden elevators to floors ranging from home furnishings to lingerie. But the busy square gets its name from a long-defunct newspaper, the *Herald,* and the small, leafy park here bustles during business hours.

Koreatown NEIGHBORHOOD

(Map p70; 31st to 36th Sts & Broadway to Fifth Ave; ⓢ B/D/F/M, N/Q/R to 34th St-Herald Sq) For kimchi and karaoke, it's hard to beat Koreatown (Little Korea). Mainly concentrated on 32nd St, with some spillover into the surrounding streets both south and north of this strip, it's a Seoul-ful jumble of Korean-owned restaurants, shops, salons and spas

Hell's Kitchen NEIGHBORHOOD

(Clinton; Map p70) For years, the far west side of Midtown was a working-class district of tenements and food warehouses known as Hell's Kitchen – supposedly its name was muttered by a cop in reaction to a riot in the neighborhood in 1881. A 1990s economic boom seriously altered the character and developers reverted to using the cleaned-up name, Clinton, a moniker originating from the 1950s; locals are split on usage.

New, primarily inexpensive ethnic restaurants have exploded along Ninth and Tenth Aves between about 37th and 55th Sts. Antique hunters should visit the **Hell's Kitchen Flea Market** (☎ 212-243-5343; 39th St btwn Ninth & Tenth Aves; ⊘ 9am-5pm Sat & Sun; ⓢ A/C/E to 42nd St), boasting 170 vendors of vintage clothing, antique jewelry, period furniture and more.

Museum of Arts & Design MUSEUM

(MAD; Map p78; www.madmuseum.org; 2 Columbus Circle, btwn Eighth Ave & Broadway; adult/child $16/free, by donation 6-9pm Thu; ⊘ 10am-6pm Tue, Wed, Sat & Sun, to 9pm Thu & Fri; ⓢ A/C, B/D, 1 to 59th St-Columbus Circle) On the southern side of the circle, exhibiting a diverse international collection of modern, folk, craft and fine-art pieces. The plush and trippy design of **Robert**, the 9th-floor restaurant, complements fantastic views of Central Park.

◉ Upper West Side

Shorthand for liberal, progressive and intellectual New York – think Woody Allen movies (although he lives on the Upper East Side) and Seinfeld – this neighborhood comprises the west side of Manhattan from Central Park to the Hudson River, and from Columbus Circle to 110th St. You'll find massive, ornate apartments, a diverse mix of stable, upwardly mobile folks (with many actors and classical musicians sprinkled throughout), and some lovely green spaces, including scenic Riverside Park.

★**Central Park**   PARK
(Map p78; www.centralparknyc.org; 59th & 110th Sts, btwn Central Park West & Fifth Ave; ⊙6am–1am;) One of the world's most renowned green spaces, Central Park checks in with 843 acres of rolling meadows, boulder-studded outcroppings, elm-lined walkways, manicured European-style gardens, a lake and a reservoir — not to mention an outdoor theater, a memorial to John Lennon, an idyllic waterside eatery (the **Loeb Boathouse**) and one very famous statue of Alice in Wonderland. The big challenge? Figuring out where to begin.

Highlights include **Sheep Meadow** (midpark from 66th to 69th Sts), where tens of thousands of people lounge and play on warm weather weekends; **Central Park Zoo** (212-439-6500; www.centralparkzoo.com; 64th St, at Fifth Ave; adult/child $12/7; ⊙10am–5:30pm Apr-Oct, to 4:30pm Nov-Mar; ; N/Q/R to 5th Ave-59th St); and the **Ramble**, a rest stop for nearly 250 migratory species of birdlife – early morning is best for sightings. A favorite tourist activity is to rent a horse-drawn carriage or hop in a **pedicab** (one hour tours from $45); the latter congregate at Central Park West and 72nd St.

★**Lincoln Center**   CULTURAL CENTER
(Map p78; 212-875-5456; lc.lincolncenter.org; Columbus Ave btwn 62nd & 66th Sts; public plazas free, tours adult/student $18/15; ; 1 to 66th St-Lincoln Center) The billion-dollar-plus redevelopment of the world's largest performing-arts center includes the dramatically redesigned **Alice Tully Hall** and other stunning venues surrounding a massive fountain; public spaces, including the roof lawn

of the North Plaza (an upscale restaurant is underneath), have been upgraded. The lavishly designed **Metropolitan Opera House** (MET), the largest opera house in the world, seats 3900 people.

Fascinating one-hour tours of the complex leave from the lobby of Avery Fisher Hall from 10:30am to 4:30pm daily; these vary from architectural to backstage tours. Free wi-fi is available on the property as well as at the **David Rubenstein Atrium** (Broadway, btwn 62nd & 63rd Sts; 1 to 66th St-Lincoln Center), a modern public space featuring a lounge area, cafe, information desk, and ticket center offering day-of discounts to Lincoln Center performances.

★**American Museum of
Natural History**   MUSEUM
(Map p78; 212-769-5100; www.amnh.org; Central Park West, at 79th St; suggested donation adult/child $22/12.50; ⊙10am–5:45pm, Rose Center to 8:45pm Fri, Butterfly Conservatory Oct-May; ; B, C to 81st St-Museum of Natural History, 1 to 79th St) Founded in 1869, this museum includes more than 30 million artifacts, interactive exhibits and loads of taxidermy. It's most famous for its three large dinosaur halls, an enormous (fake) blue whale that hangs from the ceiling above the Hall of Ocean Life and the elaborate **Rose Center for Earth & Space** – home to space-show theaters and the planetarium.

Riverside Park   OUTDOORS
(Map p78; 212-870-3070; www.riversideparknyc.org; Riverside Dr, btwn 68th & 155th Sts; ⊙6am–1am; ; 1/2/3 to any stop btwn 66th & 157th Sts) This waterside spot, running north on the Upper West Side and banked by the Hudson River from 59th to 158th Sts, is lusciously leafy. Plenty of bike paths and playgrounds make it a family favorite.

New-York Historical Society   MUSEUM
(Map p78; www.nyhistory.org; 2 W 77th St, at Central Park West; adult/child $19/6, by donation 6-8pm Fri, library free; ⊙10am–6pm Tue-Thu & Sat, to 8pm Fri, 11am–5pm Sun; B, C to 81st St-Museum of Natural History) This museum, founded in 1804, is widely credited with being the city's oldest. The quirky and wide-ranging permanent collection, including a leg brace worn by President Franklin D. Roosevelt and a 19th-century mechanical bank in which a political figure slips coins into his pocket, is now housed in a spruced-up contemporary exhibition space.

Central Park

THE LUNGS OF NEW YORK

The rectangular patch of green that occupies Manhattan's heart began life in the mid-19th century as a swampy piece of land that was carefully bulldozed into the idyllic naturescape you see today. Since officially becoming Central Park, it has brought New Yorkers of all stripes together in interesting and unexpected ways. The park has served as a place for the rich to show off their fancy carriages (1860s), for the poor to enjoy free Sunday concerts (1880s) and for activists to hold be-ins against the Vietnam War (1960s).

Since then, legions of locals – not to mention travelers from all kinds of faraway places – have poured in to stroll, picnic, sunbathe, play ball and catch free concerts and performances of works by Shakespeare.

Loeb Boathouse
Perched on the shores of the Lake, the historic Loeb Boathouse is one of the city's best settings for an idyllic meal. You can also rent rowboats and bicycles and ride on a Venetian gondola.

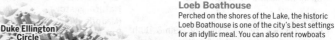

Duke Ellington Circle

Harlem Meer

The Blockhouse

North Woods

79th St Transverse

Fifth Ave

86th St Transverse

The Great Lawn

Central Park West

Conservatory Garden
The only formal garden in Central Park is perhaps the most tranquil. On the northern end, chrysanthemums bloom in late October. To the south, the park's largest crab apple tree grows by the Burnett Fountain.

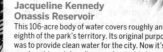

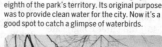

STEVEN GREAVES / GETTY IMAGES ©

Jacqueline Kennedy Onassis Reservoir
This 106-acre body of water covers roughly an eighth of the park's territory. Its original purpose was to provide clean water for the city. Now it's a good spot to catch a glimpse of waterbirds.

ANGUS OSBORN / GETTY IMAGES ©

Belvedere Castle
A so-called 'Victorian folly,' this Gothic-Romanesque castle serves no other purpose than to be a very dramatic lookout point. It was built by Central Park co-designer Calvert Vaux in 1869.

The park's varied terrain offers a wonderland of experiences. There are quiet, woodsy knolls in the north. To the south is the reservoir, crowded with joggers. There are European gardens, a zoo and various bodies of water. For maximum flamboyance, hit the Sheep Meadow on a sunny day, when all of New York shows up to lounge.

Central Park is more than just a green space. It is New York City's backyard.

FACTS & FIGURES

» **Landscape architects** Frederick Law Olmsted and Calvert Vaux

» **Year that construction began** 1858

» **Acres** 843

» **On film** Hundreds of movies have been shot on location, from Depression-era blockbusters such as *Gold Diggers* (1933) to the monster-attack flick *Cloverfield* (2008).

Conservatory Water
This pond is popular in the warmer months, when children sail their model boats across its surface. Conservatory Water was inspired by 19th-century Parisian model-boat ponds and figured prominently in EB White's classic book, *Stuart Little*.

Bethesda Fountain
This neoclassical fountain is one of New York's largest. It's capped by the *Angel of the Waters*, which is supported by four cherubim. The fountain was created by bohemian-feminist sculptor Emma Stebbins in 1868.

Metropolitan Museum of Art

Alice in Wonderland Statue

79th St Transverse

The Ramble

Fifth Ave

Delacorte Theater

The Lake

Central Park Zoo

65th St Transverse

Sheep Meadow

Strawberry Fields
A simple mosaic memorial pays tribute to musician John Lennon, who was killed across the street outside the Dakota Building. Funded by Yoko Ono, its name is inspired by the Beatles song 'Strawberry Fields Forever.'

The Mall/Literary Walk
A Parisian-style promenade – the only straight line in the park – is flanked by statues of literati on the southern end, including Robert Burns and Shakespeare. It is lined with rare North American elms.

Columbus Center

Central Park & Uptown

EDGEWATER

Hudson River

Riverside Park

Riverside Dr

West Side Hwy

Riverside Dr E

35

Broadway

W 140th St
W 137th St-City College
W 135th St
W 125th St

Amsterdam Ave
Convent Ave
St Nicholas Tce
St Nicholas Ave

City College of New York

MORNINGSIDE HEIGHTS

LaSalle St
W 122nd St
Columbia University
116th St-Columbia University

Cathedral Pkwy (110th St)

18

W 114th St
W 112th St
W 110th St (Cathedral Pkwy)
W 106th St
W 104th St
103rd St
W 102nd St
W 100th St

Duke Ellington Blvd

52

27

UPPER WEST SIDE

Morningside Dr
Morningside Ave
Morningside Park

8

116th St

10
Columbia University

W 140th St
W 135th St
St Nicholas Ave
St Nicholas Park
23
135th St
W 130th St
130th St
125th St

Frederick Douglass Blvd (Eighth Ave)
Adam Clayton Powell Jr Blvd
St Nicholas Ave

7
26

St Nicholas Ave
Cathedral Pkwy (110th St)

116th St
110th St

Central Park North (110th St)

Central Park North

Harlem Meer

The Pool
The Loch
North Meadow
Great Hill
North Woods
103rd St

Conservatory Garden

East Meadow

15

Fifth Ave

W 138th St
W 135th St
135th St
Malcolm X Blvd (Lenox Ave)
Fifth Ave

HARLEM
Martin Luther King Jr Blvd (W 125th St)
42
125th St
W 130th St
W 125th St

W 22nd St
W 20th St

118th St
116th St

Marcus Garvey Park

Madison Ave
Park Ave

Yankee Stadium (1.2mi)

Harlem River Dr

Harlem River

138th St-Grand Concourse
3rd Ave
3rd Ave-138th St

CONCOURSE VILLAGE

Major Deegan Expwy

Bruckner Blvd
E 138th St

MOTT HAVEN
Willis Ave

Bronx Kill

Cypress Ave
Brook Ave
Bruckner Blvd

Robert F Kennedy Bridge (Triborough Bridge)

Eighth Ave

Icahn Stadium

Ward's Island

Astoria Pool (0.7mi)

Robert F Kennedy Bridge (Triborough Bridge)

Franklin D Roosevelt Dr

Jefferson Park

First Ave
Second Ave
E 127th St
E 125th St
E 122nd St
E 120th St
E 118th St
E 116th St

SPANISH HARLEM
116th St (Luis Munoz Marin Blvd)

E 112th St
E 110th St
110th St

Third Ave

La Marqueta
Central Park North (110th St)

W 112th St

Lexington Ave
E 106th St
E 104th St
103rd St
E 102nd St

UPPER EAST SIDE

25

0 ⬛ 1 km
0 ⬛ 0.5 miles

ASTORIA

LONG ISLAND CITY

Rainey Park

Vernon Blvd

Roosevelt Island Bridge

East River

East River

East Channel

Main St

Roosevelt Island

The Local NYC (0.7mi);
PS 1 Contemporary
Art Center (1.2mi);
Museum of the
Moving Image (1.5mi);
Paper Factory Hotel (1.2mi);
Jackson Heights Historic
District (3.6mi)

Ed Koch
Queensboro Bridge

Mill Rock Island

Mill Rock Light Park

Carl Schurz Park

East End Ave

East River

FDR Dr

Roosevelt Island

Rockefeller University

York Ave

First Ave

Second Ave

Third Ave

Lexington Ave

Park Ave

Madison Ave

Fifth Ave

E 99th St
E 97th St
E 96th St
E 94th St
E 92nd St
E 90th St
E 88th St
E 86th St
E 84th St
E 82nd St
E 80th St
E 79th St
E 77th St
E 75th St
E 72nd St
E 70th St
E 68th St
E 65th St
E 63rd St
E 62nd St
E 59th St
E 57th St

96th St
86th St
77th St

Metropolitan Museum of Art

Conservatory Water

Frick Collection

68th St-
Hunter College

5th Ave-
59th St

Lexington Ave-
59th St

Jacqueline Kennedy Onassis Reservoir

East Dr

Great Lawn

Central Park

81st St-Museum of Natural History

Turtle Pond

The Ramble

The Lake

Strawberry Fields

Bethesda Fountain

Naumburg Bandshell

The Mall
Literary Walk

The Pond

West Dr

59th St-
Columbus Circle

West Dr

96th St
86th St
79th St
72nd St

Central Park West

Dakota Building

American Museum of Natural History

Broadway

Amsterdam Ave

West End Ave

Ninth Ave

Lincoln Center

Riverside Dr

West Side Hwy

W 97th St
W 96th St
W 94th St
W 92nd St
W 90th St
W 88th St
W 86th St
W 85th St
W 83rd St
W 81st St
W 77th St
W 75th St
W 72nd St
W 70th St
W 66th St
W 62nd St
W 60th St
W 57th St

NEW YORK
NEW JERSEY

UNION CITY

See Times Square, Midtown
Manhattan & Chelsea Map (p70)

Central Park & Uptown

◉ Upper East Side

The Upper East Side (UES) is home to New York's greatest concentration of cultural centers, including the grande dame that is the Metropolitan Museum of Art, and many refer to Fifth Ave above 57th St as Museum Mile. The real estate, at least along Fifth, Madison and Park Aves, is some of the most expensive in the world. Home to ladies who lunch as well as frat boys who drink, the neighborhood becomes decidedly less chichi the further east you go.

★ **Metropolitan Museum of Art** MUSEUM
(Map p78; ☏212-535-7710; www.metmuseum.org; 1000 Fifth Ave, at 82nd St; suggested donation adult/child $25/free; ◔10am-5.30pm Sun-Thu, to 9pm Fri & Sat; ⊕; ⓢ4/5/6 to 86th St) With more than two million objects in its collections, the Met is simply dazzling. Its great works span the world, from the chiseled

sculptures of ancient Greece to the evocative tribal carvings of Papua New Guinea. The renaissance galleries are packed with Old World masters, while the relics of ancient Egypt fire the imagination – particularly the reconstructed Temple of Dendur, complete with papyrus pond and 2000-year-old stone walls covered in hieroglyphics.

After you think you've seen enough, head to the rooftop (open early May through October) for drinks (coffee, martinis) with a sweeping view over Central Park. Note that the suggested donation (which is, truly, a *suggestion* – the rule is you simply must pay something, even if only a penny) includes same-day admission to the Cloisters (p83).

★ **Frick Collection** GALLERY
(Map p78; ☏212-288-0700; www.frick.org; 1 E 70th St, at Fifth Ave; admission $20, by donation 11am-1pm Sun, children under 10yr not admitted; ◔10am-6pm Tue-Sat, 11am-5pm Sun; ⓢ6 to 68th

St-Hunter College) This spectacular art collection sits in a mansion built by Henry Clay Frick in 1914. The 12 richly furnished rooms on the ground floor display paintings by Titian, Vermeer, El Greco, Goya and other masters. Perhaps the best asset here is that it's rarely crowded, providing a welcome break from the swarms of gawkers at larger museums, especially on weekends.

Guggenheim Museum MUSEUM

(Map p78; ☎212-423-3500; www.guggenheim.org; 1071 Fifth Ave, at 89th St; adult/child $25/free, by donation 5:45-7:45pm Sat; ⏰10am-5:45pm Sun-Wed & Fri, to 7:45pm Sat; 👪; [S] 4/5/6 to 86th St) A sculpture in its own right, architect Frank Lloyd Wright's building almost overshadows the collection of 20th-century art that it houses. Completed in 1959, the inverted ziggurat structure was derided by some critics, but it was hailed by others as an architectural icon. Stroll its sweeping spiral staircase to view masterpieces by Picasso, Pollock, Chagall, Kandinsky and others.

Neue Galerie MUSEUM

(Map p78; ☎212-628-6200; www.neuegalerie.org; 1048 Fifth Ave, cnr E 86th St; admission $20, free 6-8pm 1st Fri of every month, children under 12yr not admitted; ⏰11am-6pm Thu-Mon; [S] 4/5/6 to 86th St) This restored Carrère and Hastings mansion from 1914 is a resplendent showcase for German and Austrian art, featuring works by Gustav Klimt, Paul Klee and Egon Schiele. It also boasts the lovely, street-level eatery, Café Sabarsky.

Jewish Museum MUSEUM

(Map p78; ☎212-423-3200; www.jewishmuseum.org; 1109 Fifth Ave, at 92nd St; adult/child $15/free, Sat free, by donation 5-8pm Thu; ⏰11am-6pm Fri-Tue, to 8pm Thu; 👪; [S] 6 to 96th St) This New York City gem is tucked into a French-Gothic mansion from 1908, which houses 30,000 items of Judaica, as well as sculpture, painting and decorative arts. It hosts excellent temporary exhibits, featuring retrospectives on influential figures such as Art Spiegelman, as well as world-class shows on the likes of Chagall, Édouard Vuillard and Man Ray among other past luminaries.

Museum of the City of New York MUSEUM

(Map p78; ☎212-534-1672; www.mcny.org; 1220 Fifth Ave, btwn 103rd & 104th Sts; suggested admission adult/child $14/free; ⏰10am-6pm; [S] 6 to 103rd St) Situated in a colonial Georgian-style mansion, this local museum focuses solely on New York City's past, present and future. Don't miss the 22-minute film *Timescapes* (on the 2nd floor), which charts NYC's growth from tiny native trading post to burgeoning metropolis. Temporary exhibits cover everything from 19th-century activism to 1970s hip-hop.

👁 Morningside Heights

The Upper West Side's northern neighbor comprises the area of Broadway and west up to about 125th St. Dominating the neighborhood is Columbia University, the highly regarded Ivy League college.

Cathedral Church of St John the Divine CHURCH

(Map p78; ☎tours 212-932-7347; www.stjohndivine.org; 1047 Amsterdam Ave at W 112th St; suggested donation $10, highlights tour $6, vertical tour $15; ⏰7:30am-6pm; [S] B, C, 1 to 110th St-Cathedral Pkwy) This storied Episcopal cathedral, the largest place of worship in the United States, commands attention with its ornate Byzantine-style facade, booming vintage organ and extravagantly scaled nave – twice as wide as Westminster Abbey in London. High Mass, held at 11am Sunday, often comes with sermons by well-known intellectuals.

Columbia University UNIVERSITY

(Map p78; www.columbia.edu; Broadway at 116th St; [S] 1 to 116th St-Columbia University) Founded in 1754 as King's College, the oldest university in New York is now one of the world's premier research institutions. The principal point of interest is the main courtyard (located on College Walk at the level of 116th St), which is surrounded by various Italian Renaissance–style structures.

👁 Harlem

The heart of African American culture has been beating in Harlem since its emergence as a black enclave in the 1920s. This neighborhood north of Central Park has been the setting for extraordinary accomplishments in art, music, dance, education and letters from the likes of Frederick Douglass, Paul Robeson, James Baldwin, Alvin Ailey, Billie Holiday and many other African American luminaries. After steady decline from the 1960s to early '90s, Harlem is booming again in the form of million-dollar brownstones and condos for sale next door to neglected tenement buildings and chain stores along 125th St.

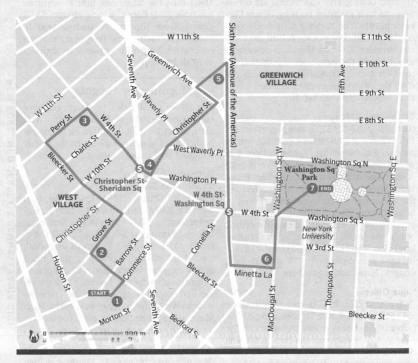

City Walk
A Village Stroll

START COMMERCE ST
END WASHINGTON SQUARE PARK
LENGTH 1 MILE; ONE HOUR

Of all the neighborhoods in New York City, Greenwich Village is the most pedestrian-friendly, with its cobbled corners that stray from the signature gridiron that unfurls across the rest of the island. Start your walkabout at the ❶ **Cherry Lane Theatre**. Established in 1924, the small theater is the city's longest continuously running off-Broadway establishment, and was the center of creative activity during the 1940s. Make a left on Bedford and you'll find ❷ **90 Bedford** on the right-hand side at the corner of Grove St. You might recognize the apartment block as the fictitious home of the cast of Friends. For another iconic TV landmark, wander up Bleecker St and make a right on Perry St, stopping at ❸ **66 Perry St**, which was used as the facade and stoop of the city's 'It Girl', Carrie Bradshaw, in Sex and the City. Make a right on W 4th St until

you reach ❹ **Christopher Park**, where two white, life-sized statues of same-sex couples stand guard. On the north side of the greenspace is the legendary Stonewall Inn, where a clutch of fed-up drag queens rioted for their civil rights in 1969, signaling the start of what would become the gay revolution. Follow Christopher St to Sixth Ave to find the ❺ **Jefferson Market Library** straddling a triangular plot of land. The 'Ruskinian Gothic' spire was once a fire lookout tower. Today the structure houses a branch of the public library; in the 1870s it was used as a courthouse. Stroll down Sixth Ave taking in the flurry of passersby, then make a left on Minetta Lane to swing by ❻ **Café Wha?**, the notorious institution where many young musicians and comedians – like Bob Dylan and Richard Pryor – got their start. End your wandering further along MacDougal St in ❼ **Washington Square Park**, the Village's unofficial town square, which plays host to loitering NYU students, buskers and a regular crowd of protestors.

For a traditional view of Harlem, visit on Sunday morning, when well-dressed locals flock to neighborhood churches. Just be respectful of the fact that these people are attending a religious service (rather than being on display for tourists). Unless you're invited by a member of a small congregation, stick to the bigger churches.

Apollo Theater HISTORIC BUILDING
(Map p78; 212-531-5300, tours 212-531-5337; www.apollotheater.org; 253 W 125th St at Frederick Douglass Blvd; admission from $20; A/C, B/D to 125th St) Not just a mythical legend but a living theater. Head here for high-profile concerts and its famous long-running amateur night, 'where stars are born and legends are made,' which takes place every Wednesday night.

Abyssinian Baptist Church CHURCH
(Map p78; www.abyssinian.org; 132 W 138th St btwn Adam Clayton Powell Jr & Malcolm X Blvds; 2/3 to 135th St) Has a superb choir and a charismatic pastor, Calvin O Butts, who welcomes tourists and prays for them. Sunday services start at 9am and 11am – the later one is *very* well attended.

Studio Museum in Harlem MUSEUM
(Map p78; 212-864-4500; www.studiomuseum.org; 144 W 125th St at Adam Clayton Powell Jr Blvd, Harlem; suggested donation $7, free Sun; noon-9pm Thu & Fri, 10am-6pm Sat, noon-6pm Sun; 2/3 to 125th St) One of the premier showcases for African American artists; look for rotating exhibits from painters, sculptors, illustrators and other installation artists.

Washington Heights

Near the northern tip of Manhattan (above 155th St), Washington Heights takes its name from the first US president, who set up a Continental Army fort here during the Revolutionary War. An isolated spot until the end of the 19th century, it attracted lots of new blood as New Yorkers sniffed out affordable rents. Still, this neighborhood manages to retain its Latino – mainly Dominican – flavor, and is an interesting mix of blocks that alternate between former downtowners and longtime residents who operate within a tight, warm community.

★**Cloisters** MUSEUM
(Map p72; 212-923-3700; www.metmuseum.org/cloisters; Fort Tryon Park, at 190th St; suggested donation adult/child $25/free; 10am-5:15pm; A to 190th St) Constructed in the 1930s using stones and fragments from several French and Spanish medieval monasteries, the romantic, castle-like creation houses medieval frescoes, tapestries, courtyards, gardens and paintings, and has commanding views of the Hudson. The walk from the subway stop to the museum through Fort Tryon Park offers fine views of the river; rock climbers head here for practice.

Brooklyn

Brooklyn is a world in and of itself; residents sometimes don't go into Manhattan for days or even weeks at a time. With 2.6 million people and growing, from well-to-do new parents seeking stately brownstones in Carroll Gardens to young band members wanting cheap rents near gigs in Bushwick, this outer borough has long surpassed Manhattan in the cool and livability factors in many people's minds. From sandy beaches and breezy boardwalks at one end to foodie destinations at the other, and with a massive range of ethnic enclaves, world-class entertainment, stately architecture and endless shopping strips in between, Brooklyn is a rival to Manhattan's attractions.

Coney Island NEIGHBORHOOD
About one hour by subway from Midtown, the wide sandy beach of Coney Island has retained its nostalgic and kitschy wood-plank boardwalk (partly destroyed and replaced after Hurricane Sandy) and famous 1927 Cyclone roller coaster, despite a sanitized makeover of the amusement park area including a handful of new adrenaline-pumping thrill rides. For better or worse, its slightly sleazy charm is a thing of the past and developers plan to transform the area into a sleek residential city complete with high-rise hotels.

Brighton Beach NEIGHBORHOOD
Walking about 1 mile east of Coney Island along the boardwalk leads to Brighton Beach ('Little Odessa'), where old-timers play chess and locals enjoy pierogies (boiled dumplings filled with meat or vegetables) and vodka shots in the sun at several boardwalk eateries. The heart of the 'hood is busy Brighton Beach Ave, with its many Russian shops, bakeries and restaurants.

Williamsburg, Greenpoint & Bushwick NEIGHBORHOOD
There is a definite Williamsburg look: skinny jeans, tattoos, a discreet body piercing, a

bushy beard for men, maybe some kind of retro head covering for a woman. Denizens of this raggedy and rowdy neighborhood across the East River on the L train seem to have the time and money to slouch in cafes and party all night in bars; a fair share of older – early 30s – transplants from Manhattan and Europe qualify as elders.

The main artery is Bedford Ave between N 10th St and Metropolitan Ave, where there are boutiques, cafes, bars and cheap eateries. But the hipster scene roams everywhere (lately Berry St is where the action is). The uber-hip even consider Williamsburg over and have long-since moved on to colonizing next door Greenpoint, a traditionally Polish neighborhood as well as the former warehouse buildings further out in Bushwick.

Brooklyn Brewery BREWERY, PUB

(☎718-486-7422; www.brooklynbrewery.com; 79 N 11th St, btwn Berry St & Wythe Ave; tours free Sat & Sun, $10 Mon-Thu; ⏲tours 5pm Mon-Thu, 1-5pm Sat, 1-4pm Sun, tasting room 6-11pm Fri, noon-8pm Sat, noon-6pm Sun; [S] L to Bedford Ave) Harking back to a time when this area of New York was a beer-brewing center, the Brooklyn Brewery not only brews and serves tasty local suds, but offers tours of its facilities. Reserve ahead for weekday (small-batch) tours.

Park Slope NEIGHBORHOOD

The Park Slope neighborhood is known for its classic brownstones, tons of great eateries and boutiques and liberal-minded stroller-pushing couples who resemble those on the Upper West Side (but have a backyard attached to their apartment).

Prospect Park OUTDOORS

(☎718-965-8951; www.prospectpark.org; Grand Army Plaza; ⏲5am-1am; [S] 2/3 to Grand Army Plaza, F to 15th St-Prospect Park) Created in 1866, Prospect Park is a showcase of resplendent greenery. A long meadow runs along the western half (where soccer, football, cricket and baseball is the order of the day). Dotted across the rest of the park you'll find hilly forests, a serene canal and a wide lake.

The **Lakeside** (www.lakesideprospectpark.com; near Ocean & Parkside Aves; ⏲11am-6pm Mon-Thu, 9am-10pm Fri & Sat, to 8pm Sun; 👪; [S] B, Q to Prospect Park) complex features two winter ice rinks (one indoor, one outdoor); in summer it becomes a roller rink and a giant wading pool with sprinklers for kiddies.

There are also free summer concerts at the Prospect Park Bandshell (near the 9th St and Prospect Park West entrance). Visit www.bricartsmedia.org for the lineup.

Brooklyn Botanic Garden GARDENS

(www.bbg.org; 1000 Washington Ave, at Crown St; adult/child $10/free, free Tue & 10am-noon Sat; ⏲8am-6pm Tue-Fri, 10am-6pm Sat & Sun; 👪; [S] 2/3 to Eastern Pkwy-Brooklyn Museum) One of Brooklyn's most picturesque attractions, this 52-acre garden is home to thousands of plants and trees, as well as a Japanese garden where river turtles swim alongside a Shinto shrine. The best time to visit is late April or early May, when the blooming cherry trees (a gift from Japan) are celebrated in Sakura Matsuri, the Cherry Blossom Festival.

Brooklyn Museum MUSEUM

(☎718-638-5000; www.brooklynmuseum.org; 200 Eastern Pkwy; suggested donation $12; ⏲11am-6pm Wed & Fri-Sun, to 10pm Thu; [S] 2/3 to Eastern Pkwy-Brooklyn Museum) This encyclopedic museum is housed in a five-story, 560,000-sq-ft beaux-arts building that houses more than 1.5 million objects, including ancient artifacts, 19th-century period rooms, and sculptures and painting from across several centuries. Admission is free on the first Saturday of every month after 5pm.

Brooklyn Heights & Downtown Brooklyn NEIGHBORHOOD

When Robert Fulton's steam ferries started regular services across the East River in the early 19th century, well-to-do Manhattanites began building stellar houses – Victorian Gothic, Romanesque, neo-Greco, Italianate and others – in Brooklyn Heights. Strolling along the tree-lined streets to gaze at them now is a lovely afternoon activity.

Follow **Montague St**, the Heights' main commercial avenue, down to the waterfront until you hit the **Brooklyn Heights Promenade**, which juts out over the Brooklyn-Queens Expwy to offer stunning views of Lower Manhattan.

★**Brooklyn Bridge Park** PARK

(☎718-222-9939; www.brooklynbridgepark.org; East River Waterfront, btwn Atlantic Ave & Adams St; ⏲6am-1am; 👪; [S] A/C to High St, 2/3 to Clark St, F to York St) [FREE] This 85-acre park is one of Brooklyn's best-loved new attractions. Wrapping around a bend on the East River, it runs for 1.3 miles from the edge of the Brooklyn Bridge in Dumbo to the west end of Atlantic Ave in Cobble Hill. It has revitalized a once barren stretch of shoreline, turning a series of abandoned piers into beautifully landscaped park land with jaw-dropping views of Manhattan.

There's lots to see and do here, with playgrounds, walkways and lawns. You'll find free open-air summertime events like film screenings (Pier 1); courts for basketball, handball and bocce, plus a skating rink (Pier 2); kayak and stand-up-paddleboard hire (Pier 4 beach). Summertime ferries to Governors Island depart from Pier 6. Pier 5 has sand volleyball courts and good food options. Empire Fulton Ferry, just past the Brooklyn Bridge, has the lovingly restored 1922 Jane's Carousel and the best views of the bridge framed against the towering skyscrapers of Lower Manhattan.

Boerum Hill, Cobble Hill & Carroll Gardens   NEIGHBORHOOD
These neighborhoods, home to a mix of families, most with Italian roots who have lived here for generations, alongside former Manhattanites looking for a real life after the city, are full of tree-lined streets with rows of attractively restored brownstones. Smith St and Court St are the two main arteries connecting to the most southerly area of the three, Carroll Gardens. The former is known as 'restaurant row', while the latter has more of the old-school groceries, bakeries and red-sauce restaurants.

Red Hook   NEIGHBORHOOD
Red Hook is a waterfront area with cobblestone streets and hulking industrial buildings. Though it's a bit of a hike from the subway line, the formerly gritty area is now home to a handful of bars and eateries, as well as a massive waterfront branch of Fairway, a beloved gourmet grocery with breathtaking views of NY harbor. A daily water taxi (www.nywatertaxi.com/tours/ikea) goes to Red Hook (near Ikea) from Lower Manhattan.

Dumbo   NEIGHBORHOOD
Dumbo's nickname is an acronym for its location: 'Down Under the Manhattan-Brooklyn Bridge Overpass', and while this north Brooklyn slice of waterfront used to be strictly for industry, it's now the domain of high-end condos, furniture shops and art galleries. The Empire-Fulton Ferry State Park hugs the waterfront and offers picture postcard Manhattan views.

◉ The Bronx

This 42-sq-mile borough to the north of Manhattan has several claims to fame: the Yankees, fondly known as the Bronx Bomb-

ers, who can be seen in all their pinstriped glory at the **Yankee Stadium** (Map p72; ☑718-293-4300, tours 646-977-8687; www.yankees.com; E 161st St at River Ave; tours $20; Ⓢ B/D, 4 to 161st St-Yankee Stadium) in spring and summer; the 'real' Little Italy, namely **Belmont** (Map p72; www.arthuravenuebronx.com), where bustling stretches of Arthur and Belmont Aves burst with Italian gourmet markets and eateries; and a super-sized attitude that's been mythologized in Hollywood movies from *The Godfather* to *Rumble in the Bronx*. But it also has some cool surprises up its sleeve: a quarter of the Bronx is parkland, including the city beach of Pelham Bay Park. Also up in these parts is the magical City Island, a little slice of New England in the Bronx.

★ New York Botanical Garden   GARDENS
(Map p72; www.nybg.org; Bronx River Pkwy & Fordham Rd; grounds only adult/child $13/3, all-garden pass $20/8, Wed & 9-10am Sat free; ☉10am-6pm Tue-Sun; ♿; Ⓡ Metro-North to Botanical Garden) There are 250 acres, with old-growth forest, a wetlands trail, nearly 3000 roses and tens of thousands of azalea plants. Springtime is fabulous.

Bronx Zoo   ZOO
(Map p72; ☑718-220-5100; www.bronxzoo.com; Bronx River Pkwy, at Fordham Rd; adult/child from $20/13, Wed free; ☉10am-5pm; 🚌BxM11, Ⓢ2 to Pelham Pkwy) Otherwise known as the Bronx Zoo, this is one of the biggest, best and most progressive zoos anywhere.

Woodlawn Cemetery   CEMETERY
(Map p72; ☑718-920-0500; www.thewoodlawncemetery.org; Webster Ave at E 233rd St; ☉8:30am-4:30pm; Ⓢ4 to Woodlawn) Famous, historic and fascinating, this 400-acre burial ground is the resting place of many notable Americans, including Miles Davis and Herman Melville.

◉ Queens

The biggest borough by size, Queens is home to over two million people. It's also the city's most ethnically diverse borough, with more than 100 nationalities speaking some 160 different languages. There are few of the tree-lined brownstone streets you find in Brooklyn, and the majority of the neighborhoods, architecturally speaking at least, do not befit this borough's royal name. However, because close to half its residents were born abroad, parts of Queens are endlessly reconstituting themselves, creating a vibrant and heady alternative universe to Manhattan. It's also home to two major airports, the Mets, a hip modern-art scene, miles of excellent beaches in the Rockaways and walking trails in the Gateway National Recreation Area (www.nps.gov/gate), a wildlife refuge in Jamaica Bay only minutes from JFK airport. The Queens Historical Society (☎718-939-0647; www.queenshistoricalsociety.org) offers tours through many areas of the massive borough.

Long Island City   NEIGHBORHOOD
(admission $15; ⊙2-9pm; ⓢG to 21st St) Neighboring Long Island City has several high-rise condominiums lining the riverfront with fantastic views of Manhattan. The area has also become a hub of art museums.

PS 1 Contemporary Art Center   ARTS CENTER
(Map p72; ☎718-784-2084; www.momaps1.org; 22-25 Jackson Ave, at 46th Ave; suggested donation $10; ⊙noon-6pm Thu-Mon) PS 1 Contemporary Art Center is dedicated solely to new, cutting-edge works. On Saturdays from late June to early September, the center's outdoor courtyard is transformed into an installation art space with DJs spinning for young crowds during the Warm Up series. Sunday sessions (May through October) feature live performances and other events.

Socrates Sculpture Park   ART
(Map p78; www.socratessculpturepark.org; Broadway, at Vernon Blvd, Long Island City; ⊙10am-dusk; ⓢN/Q to Broadway) FREE Whimsical sculp-

tures dot this 4.5-acre open-air space, right on the East River. Try to time a visit around free events – like yoga and tai chi on weekends from mid-May to late September, and movie screenings on Wednesday from early July to late August.

Astoria   NEIGHBORHOOD
Home to the largest Greek community outside of Greece, this is obviously the place to find amazing Greek bakeries, restaurants and gourmet shops, mainly along Broadway. An influx of Eastern European, Middle Eastern (Steinway Ave, known as 'Little Egypt,' is the place for falafel, kebabs and hookah pipes) and Latino immigrants have created a rich and diverse mix. Young Bohemian types have also migrated here, making the area Queens' answer to Williamsburg.

In summer, cool off at the Astoria Pool (www.nycgovparks.org/parks/astoriapark; Astoria Park, cnr 19th St & 23rd Dr; ⊙11am-7pm late Jun-early Sep; ⓢN/Q to Astoria Blvd), the city's largest and oldest.

★ Museum of the Moving Image   MUSEUM
(www.movingimage.us; 36-01 35th Ave, at 37th St, Astoria; adult/child $12/6, admission free 4-8pm Fri; ⊙10:30am-5pm Wed & Thu, to 8pm Fri, 11:30am-7pm Sat & Sun; ⓕ; ⓢM/R to Steinway St) This super-cool complex is now one of the world's top film, television and video museums. State-of-the-art galleries show off the museum's collection of 130,000-plus TV and movie artifacts.

NYC FOR CHILDREN

Contrary to popular belief, New York can be a pretty child-friendly city. Cutting-edge playgrounds have proliferated from Union Square to Battery Park and of course the city's major parks, including Central Park (p75; check out Heckscher, Adventure and Ancient playgrounds), have them in abundance. The best playgrounds in Brooklyn are at Pier 6 in Brooklyn Bridge Park (p84; there's even a small summertime water park, so bring bathing suits and towels).

For hands-on activities check out the Children's Museum of the Arts (Map p66; ☎212-274-0986; www.cmany.org; 103 Charlton St, btwn Greenwich & Hudson Sts; admission $11, by donation 4-6pm Thu; ⊙noon-6pm Mon & Fri, 10am-5pm Sat & Sun; ⓕ; ⓢ1 to Houston St, C/E to Spring St) and the Brooklyn Children's Museum (www.brooklynkids.org; 145 Brooklyn Ave, at St Marks Ave, Crown Heights; admission $9, free 3-5pm Thu; ⊙10am-5pm Tue-Sun; ⓕ; ⓢC to Kingston-Throop Aves, 3 to Kingston Ave). Kids can have close encounters with wildlife at the Central Park and Bronx zoos and the Coney Island aquarium. The boat rides to Lady Liberty, a Circle Line cruise or the cheaper ferries (Staten Island or East River ferries) offer the opportunity to chug around New York Harbor. Vintage carousels can be found in Bryant Park, Central Park and Brooklyn Bridge Park. Governors Island is a great place for a picnic, free play and biking (with big four-wheel bikes for hire).

For dining, nearly any place is fair game if you go early enough – at 5pm you'll probably be eating with other young families. Check out the weekend Arts section of the New York Times for kid-themed events and performances.

Flushing & Corona   NEIGHBORHOOD
The intersection of Main St and Roosevelt Ave, downtown Flushing, can feel like the Times Square of a city a world away from NYC. Immigrants from all over Asia, primarily Chinese and Korean, make up this neighborhood bursting at the seams with markets and restaurants filled with delicious and cheap delicacies.

Flushing Meadows Corona Park, meanwhile, is the home of Citi Field, the USTA National Tennis Center (the US Open is held here every August) and many lakes, ball fields, bike paths and grassy expanses, and was used for the 1939 and 1964 World's Fairs, of which there are quite a few faded leftovers. Kids can learn about science and technology through fun hands-on exhibits at the New York Hall of Science (☏718-699-0005; www.nysci.org; 47-01 111th St; adult/child $15/12; free 2-5pm Fri & 10-11am Sun; ☉9:30am-5pm Mon-Fri, 10am-6pm Sat & Sun; ⓈZ to 111th St). Also within this massive park is the Queens Museum (QMA; www.queensmuseum.org; suggested donation adult/child $8/free; ☉noon-6pm Wed-Sun; ⓈZ to 111th St), which faces a massive and very photogenic globe.

Jackson Heights
Historic District   NEIGHBORHOOD
(btwn Roosevelt & 34th Aves, from 70th to 90th Sts; ⓈE, F/V, R to Jackson Heights-Roosevelt Ave) A fascinating mix of Indian and South American (Roosevelt Ave) cultures, this is the place to purchase saris and 22-karat gold, dine on South Indian *masala dosas* – huge, paper-thin rice crepes folded around flavorful mixtures of masala potatoes, peas, cilantro and other earthy treats – and continue on with a plate of Colombian arepas (corn pancakes) and a bite of Argentine empanadas.

◉ Staten Island

While many New Yorkers will say that Staten Island has more in common with its neighbor, New Jersey, because of its suburban house and car cultures, there are compelling reasons to include this borough in your urban explorations. First and foremost is the Staten Island Ferry (Map p62; www.siferry.com; Whitehall Terminal at Whitehall & South Sts; ☉24hr; ⓈZ to South Ferry) FREE, which shuttles blasé commuters to work while offering breathtaking views of the Statue of Liberty and the Manhattan skyline (the world's largest Ferris wheel is to be built amid a large shopping and retail complex near the fer-

ry terminal). Not far from the ferry station on the Staten Island side is the Richmond County Bank Ballpark (p110), home to the minor-league Staten Island Yankees, as well as the hip neighborhood of St George.

🏃 Activities

Cycling
New York has hundreds of miles of designated bike lanes, making the city a surprisingly bicycle-friendly destination. For quick jaunts across town (under 30 minutes), hop on a Citi Bike (www.citibikenyc.com; 24hr/7 days $11/27), the Big Apple's bike-sharing program. Hundreds of kiosks in Manhattan and parts of Brooklyn house the bright blue bicycles and checking one out is as easy as swiping your credit card. However, unless you're an experienced urban cyclist, pedaling through the streets can be a risky activity, as bike lanes are often blocked by trucks, taxis and double-parked cars. More than 28-miles, mostly riverfront, have been integrated into the Manhattan Waterfront Greenway, a patchwork of park pathways, overpasses and a few city streets that circle the entire island of Manhattan. The mostly uninterrupted 10-mile stretch from the GW Bridge to Battery Park, including Hudson River Park, is perhaps the most spectacular. Of course Central Park and Brooklyn's Prospect Park have lovely cycling paths.

For bike rentals (other than Citi Bike), visit one of many locations of Bike and Roll (www.bikenewyorkcity.com; bikes from $10/30 per hour/half day). It has a quick-rent branch outside Central Park on 59th St and Central Park West.

Water Sports
This is an island, after all, and as such there are plenty of opportunities for boating and kayaking. The Downtown Boathouse (Map p62; www.downtownboathouse.org; Pier 26 near N Moore St; ☉9am-5:30pm Sat & Sun mid-May–mid-Oct, & 5-6:30pm Mon-Fri Jul & Aug; ⓈZ to Houston St) offers free 20-minute kayaking (including equipment) in the protected embayment of the Hudson River. Other locations include 56th St, 72nd St and Governors Island.

In Central Park, Loeb Boathouse (Map p78; ☏212-517-2233; www.thecentralparkboathouse.com; btwn 74th & 75th Sts; boating per hour $12, bike rental per hour $9-15; ☉10am-6pm Apr-Nov; ♿; ⓈB, C to 72nd St, 6 to 77th St) rents rowboats for romantic trysts, and even fills Venice-style gondolas in summer. For a sailing adventure, hop aboard the Schooner Adirondack

(Map p70; ☎212-913-9991; www.sail-nyc.com; Chelsea Piers, Pier 62 at W 22th St; tours $48-78; [S] C, E to 23rd St) at **Chelsea Piers**.

Surfers may be surprised to find a tight group of wave worshippers within city limits, at Queens' **Rockaway Beach** at 90th St, where you can hang ten after only a 75-minute ride on the A train from Midtown.

Tours

The following is a small sample of available tours.

Big Onion Walking Tours WALKING TOUR
(☎888-606-9255; www.bigonion.com; tours $20) Popular and quirky guided tours specializing in ethnic and neighborhood tours.

Circle Line BOAT TOUR
(Map p70; ☎212-563-3200; www.circleline42.com; Pier 83, W 42nd St; tickets from $29; [S] A/C/E to 42nd St-Port Authority Bus Terminal) Ferry boat tours, from semicircle to a full island cruise with guided commentary, as well as powerful speedboat trips on the *Beast*.

Municipal Art Society WALKING TOUR
(Map p78; ☎212-935-3960; www.mas.org; 111 W 57th St; tours adult/child $20/15; [S] F to 57th St) Various scheduled tours focusing on architecture and history, including daily 12.00pm tours of Grand Central Terminal.

New York City Audubon WALKING TOUR
(Map p70; ☎212-691-7483; www.nycaudubon.org; 71 W 23rd St, Ste 1523; tours free-$100; [S] F/M to 23rd St) Expert instructors and guides lead trips including birding in Central Park and the Bronx and ecology cruises of the Jamaica Bay Wildlife Refuge.

NYC Gangster Tours WALKING TOUR
(www.nycgangstertours.com; tours $25-40) Sure, it's a little schticky, but colorful and knowledgeable guides make these walking tours focusing on NYC's Italian, Chinese and Jewish mafia interesting and fun.

On Location Tours BUS TOUR
(☎212-683-2027; www.onlocationtours.com; tours $33-59) *Gossip Girl* and *How I Met Your Mother* are on the list of tours as well as long-running ones that allow you to flesh out your Carrie Bradshaw or Tony Soprano fantasies.

Festivals & Events

From cultural street fairs to foodie events, you are bound to find something that will excite you, no matter the time of year, but there's almost too much to digest in summer when outdoor celebrations proliferate.

Restaurant Week FOOD
(☎212-484-1222; www.nycgo.com; 🕒Feb & July) Dine at top restaurants with three-course dinner specials for $38 (and $25 at lunchtime).

Armory Show CULTURAL
(☎212-645-6440; www.thearmoryshow.com; Piers 92 & 94, West Side Hwy at 52nd & 54th Sts; 🕒Mar) New York's biggest contemporary art fair sweeps the city, showcasing the new work of thousands of artists from around the world.

Tribeca Film Festival FILM
(☎212-941-2400; www.tribecafilm.com; 🕒late Apr & early May) Robert De Niro co-organizes this local downtown film fest, which is quickly rising in prestige.

Fleet Week NAVAL
(☎212-245-0072; www.fleetweeknewyork.com; 🕒May) Dressed in their formal whites, an annual convocation of sailors and their naval ships and air rescue teams descend on the city.

NYC Pride GAY & LESBIAN
(☎212-807-7433; www.nycpride.org; 🕒Jun) Pride month, with a packed calendar of parties and events, culminates with a major march down Fifth Ave on the last Sunday of June.

Mermaid Parade PARADE
(www.coneyisland.com; 🕒late Jun) Something of Mardi Gras on the boardwalk, this parade turns Surf Ave on Coney Island in Brooklyn into a free-expression zone that's fun, crazy and artistic.

Village Halloween Parade PARADE
(www.halloween-nyc.com; Sixth Ave from Spring St to 16th St; 🕒7-11pm Oct 31) This fabulous parade features wildly costume-clad marchers and cheering onlookers. Anyone can join.

Sleeping

Tax adds an additional 14.75% plus $3.50 per night. A cluster of national chains, including Sheraton, Ramada and Holiday Inn, have affordably priced rooms in hotels within a few blocks of one another around 39th Ave in Long Island City, Queens, a quick N, Q or R train from midtown Manhattan directly across the East River.

Lower Manhattan & Tribeca

Wall Street Inn LUXURY HOTEL $$
(Map p62; ☎212-747-1500; www.thewallstreetinn.com; 9 S William St; r from $240; ❄📶; [S]2/3 to Wall St) Lehman Brothers once occupied this classic limestone building and, while the mood of the hotel is very early American banker, there's little risk in a stay here. Old-fashioned and warm rather than stuffy, the rooms, with luxurious marble baths, are slightly over-furnished for their size.

SoHo

Leon Hotel HOTEL $$
(Map p66; ☎212-390-8833; www.leonhotelnyc.com; 125 Canal St, btwn Bowery & Christie; r from $240; ❄📶; [S]B/D to Grand St) At the entrance to the Manhattan Bridge, this boxy space offers clean, no-frills accommodation that is a decent value for pricey NYC. Rooms are comfortable if minimally furnished, and some have quite nice views of Lower Manhattan, with One World Trade Center in plain sight. Friendly staff.

Solita SoHo HOTEL $$
(Map p66; ☎212-925-3600; www.solitasohohotel.com; 159 Grand St, at Lafayette St; r from $220; ❄📶; [S]N/Q/R, J/Z, 6 to Canal St) The Solita is a clean, functional alternative with boutique-style furnishings close to Chinatown, NoLita, Soho and the Lower East Side. Lower winter rates.

Soho Grand Hotel BOUTIQUE HOTEL $$
(Map p66; ☎212-965-3000; www.sohogrand.com; 310 W Broadway; d from $290; ❄@📶🐾; [S]6, N/Q/R, J to Canal St) The original boutique hotel of the 'hood still reigns, with its striking glass-and-cast-iron lobby stairway, and 353 rooms with cool, clean lines plus Frette linens, plasma flat-screen TVs and CO Bigelow grooming products. The lobby's Grand Lounge buzzes with action.

Lower East Side, East Village & NoLita

Bowery House HOSTEL $$
(Map p66; ☎212-837-2373; www.theboweryhouse.com; 220 Bowery btwn Prince & Spring Sts; s/d with shared bath from $90/160; ❄📶; [S]J/Z to Bowery) Across the street from the New Museum, this former 1920s-era flophouse has been resurrected as an upmarket hostel, its cubicle-sized rooms decked out with Bowery-themed film posters and custom-made mattresses (ie shorter and narrower), while communal bathrooms feature rain showers and heated floors. There's also a lounge with Chesterfield sofas and chandeliers, a bar and a roof terrace.

St Mark's Hotel HOTEL $$
(Map p66; ☎212-674-0100; www.stmarkshotel.net; 2 St Marks Pl at Third Ave; d from $140; ❄📶; [S]6 to Astor Pl) This East Village budget option draws a young, nightlife-loving crowd, who enjoy being within strolling distance of the city's best concentration of bars and cocktail lounges. Not surprisingly, the rooms are tiny, but clean and adequately equipped, with flat-screen TVs and private bathrooms in each. Wi-fi costs extra.

Blue Moon Hotel BOUTIQUE HOTEL $$
(Map p66; ☎212-533-9080; www.bluemoon-nyc.com; 100 Orchard St, btwn Broome & Delancey Sts; r incl breakfast from $250; ❄📶; [S]F to Delancey St, J/M to Essex St) You'd never guess that this quaint, welcoming brick guesthouse – full of festive colors – was once a foul tenement back in the day (the day being in 1879). Except for a few ornate touches, like wrought-iron bed frames and detailed molding, Blue Moon's clean, spare rooms are entirely modern and comfortable.

Bowery Hotel BOUTIQUE HOTEL $$$
(Map p66; ☎212-505-9100; www.theboweryhotel.com; 335 Bowery, btwn 2nd & 3rd Sts; r from $375; ❄@📶; [S]F/V to Lower East Side-Second Ave, 6 to Bleecker St) Perhaps as far as you can get from the Bowery's gritty flophouse history, this stylish hotel is all 19th-century elegance. Rooms come equipped with lots of light and sleek furnishings mixed with antiques. The baroque-style lobby bar attracts the young and chic and on-site restaurant Gemma serves upscale Italian.

Chelsea, Meatpacking District & West (Greenwich) Village

Chelsea Hostel HOSTEL $
(Map p70; ☎212-647-0010; www.chelseahostel.com; 251 W 20th St btwn Seventh & Eighth Aves; dm $40-80, s $75-100, d from $130; ❄@📶; [S]A/C/E, 1/2 to 23rd St, 1/2 to 18th St) Walkable to the Village and Midtown, Chelsea Hostel capitalizes on its convenient location with somewhat steep prices, but it's kept clean and there's access to common rooms and kitchens where other budget travelers often meet and hang.

Jane Hotel
HOTEL $

(Map p66; ☎212-924-6700; www.thejanenyc.com; 113 Jane St, btwn Washington St & West Side Hwy; r with shared/private bath from $105/250; P❉☎; S L to Eighth Ave, A/C/E to 14th St, 1/2 to Christopher St-Sheridan Sq) Originally built for sailors (obvious after one look at the cabin-sized rooms), the Jane became a temporary refuge for survivors of the *Titanic*, then a YMCA and a rock-and-roll venue. The single-bunk rooms feature flat-screen TVs and the communal showers are more than adequate.

Chelsea Lodge
HOTEL $

(Map p70; ☎212-243-4499; www.chelsealodge. com; 318 W 20th St btwn Eighth & Ninth Aves; s/d from $130/140; ❉☎; S A/C/E to 14th St, 1 to 18th St) Housed in a landmark brownstone in Chelsea, the European-style, 20-room Chelsea Lodge is a super deal. Space is tight, so you won't get more than a bed, with a TV plopped on an old wooden cabinet. There are showers and sinks in rooms, but toilets are down the hall. Six suite rooms have private bathrooms, and two come with private garden access.

Larchmont Hotel
HOTEL $

(Map p66; ☎212-989-9333; www.larchmont hotel.com; 27 W 11th St, btwn Fifth & Sixth Aves; s/d with shared bath from $110/120; ❉☎; S 4/5/6, N/Q/R to 14th St-Union Sq) Housed in a prewar building that blends in with the other fine brownstones on the block, a stay at the Larchmont is about location. The carpeted rooms are basic and in need of updating, as are the communal baths, but it's not a bad deal for the price.

Townhouse Inn of Chelsea
B&B $$

(Map p70; ☎212-414-2323; www.townhouseinnchelsea.com; 131 W 23rd St, btwn Sixth & Seventh Aves; r incl breakfast from $150; ❉☎; S F/V, 1 to 23rd St) Housed in a lone 19th-century, five-story townhouse on busy 23rd St, this 14-room B&B is a Chelsea gem. The rooms are big and welcoming, with exposed brick walls, fine linens and attractive furnishings. There's also an elegant all-Victorian library that adds to the charm. Friendly hosts have a wealth of info on the neighborhood.

🛏 Union Square, Flatiron District & Gramercy Park

Carlton Arms
HOTEL $

(Map p70; ☎212-679-0680; www.carltonarms. com; 160 E 25th St btwn Lexington & Third Aves; s/d $142/176, s/d with shared bath $96/142; S 6 to 23rd St or 28th St) Though it has a sordid past (speakeasy, drugs, prostitution), these days, the Carlton Arms feels equal parts art gallery and budget hotel. Murals cover the walls up five flights of stairs, and snake into each of the tiny guest rooms and shared bathrooms (there is a small sink in each guestroom). It draws an eclectic mix of bohemian travelers.

Hotel 17
BUDGET HOTEL $

(Map p70; ☎212-475-2845; www.hotel17ny.com; 225 E 17th St, btwn Second & Third Aves; d with shared bath from $113; ❉☎; S N/Q/R, 4/5/6 to 14th St-Union Sq, L to Third Ave) Right off Stuyvesant Sq on a leafy residential block, this no-frills, eight-floor townhouse has relatively affordable prices. Rooms are small, with traditional, basic furnishings (gray carpet, chintzy bedspreads, burgundy blinds) and lack much natural light.

The Marcel at Gramercy
BOUTIQUE HOTEL $$

(Map p70; ☎212-696-3800; www.themarcelatgramercy.com; 201 E 24th St, at Third Ave; d from $180-410; ❉@☎; S 6 to 23rd St) Minimalist with earth-tone touches, this 97-room inn is a poor-man's chic boutique and that's not a bad thing. Modernist rooms on the avenue have great views, and the sleek lounge is a great place to unwind after a day of exploring.

🛏 Midtown

Pod 51
HOTEL $

(Map p70; ☎212-355-0300; www.thepodhotel. com; 230 E 51st St, btwn Second & Third Aves, Midtown East; r from $147; ❉☎; S 6 to 51st St, E/M to Lexington Ave-53rd St) A dream come true for folks who'd like to live inside their iPod – or at least curl up and sleep with it – this affordable hot spot has a range of room types, most barely big enough for the bed. 'Pods' have bright bedding, tight workspaces, flat-screen TVs, iPod docking stations and 'rain' showerheads.

Park Savoy
HOTEL $

(Map p78; ☎212-245-5755; www.parksavoyny.com; 158 W 58th St btwn Seventh & Sixth Aves; d from $145; ❉☎; S N/Q/R to 57th St-7th Ave) The best thing about the Park Savoy is its low price and great location near Central Park. The trade-off: worn carpets, cheap bedspreads and showers with trickling water pressure, to say nothing of the unhelpful staff.

★ Yotel
HOTEL $$

(Map p70; ☎646-449-7700; www.yotel.com; 570 Tenth Ave, at 41st St, Midtown West; r from $190;

❄☂; Ⓢ A/C/E to 42nd St-Port Authority Bus Terminal, 1/2/3, N/Q/R, S, 7 to Times Sq-42nd St) Part futuristic spaceport, part Austin Powers set, this uber-cool 669-room option bases its rooms on airplane classes. Small but cleverly configured Premium cabins include automated adjustable beds, while all cabins feature floor-to-ceiling windows with killer views, slick bathrooms and iPod connectivity.

City Rooms
HOTEL **$$**

(Map p70; ☎917-475-1285; www.cityroomsnyc. com; 368 Eighth Ave btwn 28th & 29th Sts; r with shared bath from $150; ❄☂; Ⓢ C/E to 23rd St, 1 to 28th St) If you spurn luxury and don't suffer from claustrophobia, this friendly 13-room hotel is a decent option. The rooms are clean and basic, with comfortable mattresses, but extremely short on space. NYC-themed stencils add a dash of character to the otherwise white walls. Note that all rooms share bathrooms (which are also a tight fit).

414 Hotel
HOTEL **$$**

(Map p70; ☎212-399-0006; www.414hotel.com; 414 W 46th St, btwn Ninth & Tenth Aves, Midtown West; r from $285; ❄☂; Ⓢ C/E to 50th St) Set up like a guesthouse, this affordable, friendly option offers 22 tidy and tastefully decorated rooms a couple of blocks west of Times Square. Rooms facing the leafy inner courtyard, which is a perfect spot to enjoy your complimentary breakfast, are the quietest.

🛏 Upper West Side

Hostelling International New York
HOSTEL **$**

(HI; Map p78; ☎212-932-2300; www.hinewyork.org; 891 Amsterdam Ave, at 103rd St; dm $50-75; ❄☂; Ⓢ 1 to 103rd St) This red-brick mansion from the 1880s houses HI's 672 well-scrubbed bunks. It's rather 19th-century industrial, but benefits include good public areas, a backyard, a communal kitchen and a cafe.

Jazz on Amsterdam Ave
HOSTEL **$**

(Map p78; ☎646-490-7348; www.jazzhostels.com; 201 W 87th St at Amsterdam Ave; dm $50, r $130; ❄☂; Ⓢ 1 to 86th St) Only a short walk to Central Park, this hostel chain's Upper West Side branch has clean rooms, both private rooms and two- to six-bed dorms. Free wi-fi in the lobby. There are other branches in Harlem and Chelsea.

YMCA
HOSTEL **$$**

(Map p78; ☎212-912-2625; www.ymcanyc.org; 5 W 63rd St at Central Park West; d $210, s/d with shared bath from $114/160; ❄@; Ⓢ A/B/C/D to 59th St-Columbus Circle) Just steps from Central Park, this grand art-deco building has several floors – 8th to the 13th – of basic, but clean, rooms. Guests have access to an extensive but old-school gym, racquet ball courts, pool and sauna. There's also a lounge and a cafe. Other locations on the Upper East Side and Harlem.

Lucerne
HOTEL **$$**

(Map p78; ☎212-875-1000; www.thelucernehotel. com; r from $186; ❄☂🐾; Ⓢ B, C to 81st St) This unusual 1903 structure breaks away from beaux arts in favor of the baroque, with an ornately carved terracotta-colored facade. Inside is a stately 197-room hotel with nine types of guest rooms evoking a contemporary Victorian look. Think: flowered bedspreads, scrolled headboards and plush pillows with fringe.

🛏 Upper East Side

Bubba & Bean Lodges
B&B **$$**

(Map p78; ☎917-345-7914; www.bblodges.com; 1598 Lexington Ave, btwn 101st & 102nd Sts; r $130-260; ❄☂; Ⓢ 6 to 103rd St) Owners Jonathan and Clement have turned a charming Manhattan townhouse into an excellent home away from home. The five guest rooms are simply furnished, with crisp, white walls, hardwood floors and navy linens, providing the place with a modern, youthful feel. All units are equipped with private bathrooms as well as kitchenettes with cookware.

Bentley Hotel
BOUTIQUE HOTEL **$$**

(Map p78; ☎212-247-5000; www.bentleyhotelnyc. com; 500 E 62nd St, at York Ave; r from $220; ❄☂; Ⓢ N/Q/R to Lexington Ave/59th St) Featuring great East River views, the Bentley overlooks FDR Dr, as far east as you can go. Formerly an office building, the hotel has shed its utilitarian past in the form of chic boutique-hotel styling, a swanky lobby and sleek rooms.

🛏 Harlem

Harlem Flophouse
GUESTHOUSE **$**

(Map p78; ☎212-662-0678; www.harlemflophouse. com; 242 W 123rd St, btwn Adam Clayton Powell Jr & Frederick Douglass Blvds; r with shared bath $125-150; ☂; Ⓢ A/B/C/D, 2/3 to 124th St) The four attractive bedrooms have antique light fixtures, glossed-wood floors and big beds, plus classic tin ceilings and wooden shutters. Cat on the premises.

Allie's Inn B&B $$
(Map p78; ☎212-690-3813; www.alliesinn.com; 313 W 136th St btwn Frederick Douglass Blvd & Edgecombe Ave; r $175-325; ❄📶; [S]A/C, B to 135th St) This Harlem charmer has just three guest rooms, which are clean and comfortable, with oak floors, simple modern furnishings and small kitchen units. There are a growing number of appealing eating and drinking options in the neighborhood, and the subway station is just around the corner.

Brooklyn

★New York Loft Hostel HOSTEL $
(☎718-366-1351; www.nylofthostel.com; 249 Varet St, btwn Bogart & White Sts, Bushwick; dm $40-80, d $140; ❄@📶; [S]L to Morgan Ave) Live like a Williamsburg – or more accurately Bushwick – hipster in this renovated loft building. Brick walls, high ceilings, a beautiful kitchen, a back garden and a rooftop sundeck make Manhattan hostels seem like tenements.

Wythe Hotel BOUTIQUE HOTEL $$
(☎718-460-8000; wythehotel.com; 80 Wythe Ave, at N 11th St, Williamsburg; r $205-600; ❄📶) In the heart of nightlife-loving Williamsburg, the red-brick Wythe Hotel makes for a stylish getaway. The industrial-chic rooms have custom-made wallpaper (from Brooklyn's own Flavor Paper), exposed brick, polished concrete floors and original 13ft timber ceilings. There's a lovely brasserie on the ground floor and a rooftop bar with fine views of Manhattan.

Nu Hotel HOTEL $$
(☎718-852-8585; www.nuhotelbrooklyn.com; 85 Smith St; d incl breakfast $170-300; ❄@📶; [S]F, G to Bergen St) This location, only blocks from Brooklyn Heights and a nexus of attractive brownstone neighborhoods, is absolutely ideal – except for the fact that it's across the street from the Brooklyn House of Detention. It has a chic minimalist vibe and the clean all-white rooms are comfortable.

Queens

The Local NYC HOSTEL $$
(☎347-738-5251; www.thelocalny.com; 1302 44th Ave btwn 12th & 13th Sts; dm/d from $45/160; ❄📶; [S]E, M to Court Sq) This stylish hostel has clean and small, simply designed rooms, with comfy mattresses and plenty of natural light. The airy cafe-bar is a fine place to meet other travelers, with good coffees by day, and wine and beer by night. Throughout the week, there's a regular line-up of events (movie nights, live music, pub quizzes).

Paper Factory Hotel HOTEL $$
(☎718-392-7200; www.thepaperfactoryhotel.com; 37-06 36th St, Long Island City; d from $180; ❄📶; [S]M/R to 36th St) This former paper factory and warehouse has 123 rooms that evoke industrial chic. Reclaimed lumber and polished concrete feature prominently, and the artfully designed common areas are great spots to unwind.

🍴 Eating

In a city with over 20,000 restaurants, and new ones opening every single day, where are you supposed to begin? From Little Albania to Little Uzbekistan, your choice of ethnic eats is only a short subway ride away. A hotbed of buzz-worthy culinary invention and trends like artisanal doughnuts, farm-to-table pork sandwiches and *haute cuisine* reinterpretations of fried chicken, pizza and good ol' burgers and fries, NYC's restaurant scene, like the city, is constantly reinventing itself.

Lower Manhattan & Tribeca

Financier Patisserie BAKERY, SANDWICHES $
(Map p62; ☎212-344-5600; www.financierpastries.com; 62 Stone St at Mill Lane; pastries $3-4, sandwiches $8-10; 🕐7am-7pm Mon-Fri, 9am-5pm Sat & Sun; 👪; [S]2/3, 4/5 to Wall St, J/Z to Broad St) There are now three Patisserie outposts in Lower Manhattan because nobody can get enough of the buttery croissants, berry tarts or chocolate éclairs. Savory items include homemade soups, flavorful sandwiches and creamy quiches.

Shake Shack BURGERS $
(Map p62; ☎646-545-4600; www.shakeshack.com; 215 Murray St btwn West St & North End Ave; burgers $5-10; 🕐11am-11pm; [S]A/C, 1/2/3 to Chambers St) Danny Meyer's cult burger chain is fast food at its finest: cotton-soft burgers made with prime, freshly ground mince; Chicago-style hot dogs in poppy-seed potato buns; and seriously good cheesy fries. Drink local with a beer from Brooklyn brewery Sixpoint.

Fraunces Tavern AMERICAN $$
(Map p62; ☎212-968-1776; www.fraucestavern.com; 54 Pearl St; mains lunch $15-26, dinner $20-38; 🕐11am-10pm; [S]N/R to Whitehall) Can you really pass up a chance to eat where George Washington supped in 1762? Expect heaped portions of beer-battered fish and chips,

slow-roasted chicken pot pie and braised short ribs. Fraunces Tavern has great atmosphere – particularly on Sundays when there's traditional Irish music (3:30pm to 6:30pm).

★Locanda Verde   ITALIAN $$$
(Map p62; 📞212-925-3797; www.locandaverdenyc.com; 377 Greenwich St at Moore St; lunch $19-29, mains dinner $22-37; ⏱7am-11pm Mon-Fri, from 8am Sat & Sun; 🚇A/C/E to Canal St, 1 to Franklin St) Step through the velvet curtains into a scene of loosened button-downs, black dresses and slick bartenders behind a long, crowded bar. This celebrated brasserie showcases modern Italian fare like pappardelle with lamb bolognese and steamed black bass with green garlic puree. Weekend brunch features no less creative fare: try scampi and grits or lemon ricotta pancakes with blueberries.

Tiny's & the Bar Upstairs   AMERICAN $$$
(Map p62; 📞212-374-1135; www.tinysnyc.com; 135 W Broadway btwn Duane & Thomas Sts; mains lunch $16-20, dinner $22-30; ⏱8am-midnight Mon-Fri, from 9am Sat & Sun; 🚇A/C, 1/2/3 to Chambers St) Snug and adorable (book ahead!), Tiny's comes with a crackling fire in the back room and an intimate bar upstairs. Served on vintage porcelain, dishes are soulful, subtly retweaked delights; think kale salad with maple mustard and shredded Gouda, marinated shrimp with squid ink cavatelli or grilled skirt steak with pickled ramps.

✕ Chinatown, Little Italy & NoLita

Tacombi   MEXICAN $
(Map p66; www.tacombi.com; 267 Elizabeth St, btwn E Houston & Prince Sts; tacos $4-6; ⏱11am-midnight; 🚇B/D/F/M to Broadway-Lafayette St, 6 to Bleecker St) Festively strung lights, foldaway chairs and Mexican men flipping tortillas in an old VW Kombie: if you can't make it to the Yucatán shore, here's your Plan B. Casual, convivial and ever-popular, Tacombi serves up delicious tacos, tender ceviche and creamy guacamole. Wash it all down with a pitcher of sangria, a glass of horchata or a mezcal margarita.

Ruby's   CAFE $
(Map p66; 📞212-925-5755; www.rubyscafe.com; 219 Mulberry St, btwn Spring & Prince Sts; mains $10-15; ⏱9:30am-11pm; 🚇6 to Spring St, N/R to Prince St) All bases are covered at this inviting Aussie-inspired cafe. You'll find breakie-friendly avo toast (mashed avocado and fresh tomato on seven grain toast) and

pancakes with caramelized apples and pears, and lunch-pleasers like pumpkin salad, pastas and juicy burgers (best ordered with truffle fries). Flat-white coffees and bottles of Boags complete your antipodean experience.

Café Gitane   MEDITERRANEAN $
(Map p66; 📞212-334-9552; www.cafegitanenyc.com; 242 Mott St, at Prince St; mains $14-17; ⏱8:30am-midnight; 🚱; 🚇N/R to Prince St, 6 to Spring St) Clear the Gauloises smoke from your eyes and blink twice if you think you're in Paris. Label-conscious shoppers love this authentic bistro, with its dark, aromatic coffee and well-executed dishes, such as blueberry and almond *friands* (small French cake), smoked trout salad or Moroccan couscous with organic chicken.

La Esquina   MEXICAN $$
(Map p66; 📞646-613-7100; www.esquinanyc.com; 114 Kenmare St, at Petrosino Sq; tacos from $3.50, mains cafe $15-25, brasserie $18-34; ⏱noon-late; 🚇6 to Spring St) This mega-popular and quirky little spot is three places really: a stand-while-you-eat taco window (open till 2am), a casual Mexican cafe (entrance on Lafayette St) and, downstairs, a dim, slinky, cavernous brasserie requiring reservations. Standouts include grilled pulled pork tacos and mango and jicama salad, among other authentic and delicious options.

Lombardi's   PIZZA $$
(Map p66; 📞212-941-7994; www.firstpizza.com; 32 Spring St btwn Mulberry & Mott Sts; small/large pizza from $17/21; ⏱11:30am-11pm; 🚇6 to Spring St) Lombardi's was the very first pizzeria in America, opening here in 1905. It's justifiably proud of its New York style: thin crust and an even thinner layer of sauce.

Da Nico   ITALIAN $$
(Map p66; 📞212-343-1212; www.danicoristorante.com; 164 Mulberry St; mains $18-40; ⏱noon-11pm

EATING NYC: CHINATOWN

With hundreds of restaurants, from holes-in-the-wall to banquet-sized dining rooms, Chinatown is wonderful for exploring cheap eats on an empty stomach.

Xi'an Famous Foods (Map p62; 67 Bayard St; mains $6-9; S J/Z, N/Q, 6 to Canal St) Take-out counter serving delicious hand-pulled noodles and spicy cumin lamb 'burgers'; eat them in nearby Columbus Park.

Amazing 66 (Map p62; 212-334-0099; www.amazing66.com; 66 Mott St, at Canal St; mains $9-16; 11am-11pm; S 6, J, N/Q to Canal St) Terrific Cantonese lunches.

Prosperity Dumpling (Map p66; 212-343-0683; www.prosperitydumpling.com; 46 Eldridge St btwn Hester & Canal Sts; dumplings $1-3; 7:30am-10pm; S B/D to Grand St; F to East Broadway; J to Bowery) Among the best dumpling joints.

Vanessa's Dumpling House (Map p66; 212-625-8008; www.vanessasdumplinghouse.com; 118 Eldridge St, btwn Grand & Broome Sts; dumplings $1.25-5; 11am-10pm; S B/D to Grand St, J to Bowery, F to Delancey St) Great dumplings and sesame pancakes (get one with Peking duck).

Bánh Mì Saigon Bakery (Map p66; 212-941-1541; www.banhmisaigonnyc.com; 198 Grand St, btwn Mulberry & Mott Sts; sandwiches $5-6; 8am-6pm; S N/Q/R, J/Z, 6 to Canal St) Some of the best Vietnamese sandwiches in town.

Joe's Shanghai (Map p62; 212-233-8888; www.joeshanghairestaurants.com; 9 Pell St btwn Bowery & Doyers St; mains $11-18; 11am-11pm; S N/Q/R, J/Z, 6 to Canal St, B/D to Grand St) Always busy and tourist-friendly. Does good noodle and soup dishes.

Buddha Bodai (Map p62; 212-566-8388; 5 Mott St; mains $8-15; 10am-10pm; S) Serves exquisite vegetarian cuisine.

Big Wong King (Map p62; 212-964-0540; www.bigwongking.com; 67 Mott St, at Canal; mains $10-14; 8:30am-9pm; S 6, J, N/Q to Canal St) Perennial favorite. Look for the roast ducks hanging in the window.

Nom Wah Tea Parlor (Map p62; 212-962-6047; www.nowah.com; 13 Doyers St; dim sum $4-11; 10:30am-9pm; S 6, J, N/Q to Canal St) Looks like an old-school American diner, but is the oldest dim sum place in the city.

Original Chinatown Ice Cream Factory (Map p62; 212-608-4170; www.chinatownicecreamfactory.com; 65 Bayard St; ice cream $4.50-8.25; 11am-10pm; S N/Q/R, J/Z, 6 to Canal St) Refreshing scoops of green tea, ginger, durian and lychee flavored sorbets.

Sun-Thu, to midnight Fri & Sat; S J/M/Z N/Q/R/W, 6 to Canal St) If you're hell-bent on having a Little Italy dinner, Da Nico is a classic. It's family-run and traditional in feel and the extensive menu highlights both northern and southern Italian cuisine that's red-sauce predictable but delicious.

Lower East Side

Cheeky Sandwiches　SANDWICHES $
(Map p66; 646-504-8131; www.cheeky-sandwiches.com; 35 Orchard St; mains $7-9; 7am-9pm Mon-Thu, 8am-midnight Fri & Sat, 8am-9pm Sun; S F to East Broadway) This ramshackle little eatery looks like it's been airlifted in from New Orleans. The biscuit sandwiches are outstanding – try one topped with fried chicken, coleslaw and gravy. Add on chicory coffee and bread pudding and you have a great cheap meal.

Meatball Shop　ITALIAN $
(Map p66; 212-982-8895; www.themeatballshop.com; 84 Stanton St, btwn Allen & Orchard Sts; mains from $11; noon-2am Sun-Thu, to 4am Fri-Sat; S 2nd Ave; F to Delancey St; J/M/Z to Essex St) Masterfully executed meatball sandwiches have suddenly spiked in popularity, and the Meatball Shop is riding the wave of success with moist incarnations of the traditional hero. Three other branches in the city.

Doughnut Plant　DESSERT $
(Map p66; 212-505-3700; www.doughnutplant.com; 379 Grand St, at Norfolk; doughnuts $4; 6:30am-8pm; S J/M/Z to Essex St, F to Delancey St) A New York legend, Doughnut Plant whips up sweet decadence, in inventive flavors

(pistachio, tres leches, cashew and orange blossom) made from all-natural ingredients.

Clinton Street Baking Company AMERICAN $$
(Map p66; ☎ 646-602-6263; www.clintonstreetbaking.com; 4 Clinton St, btwn Stanton & Houston Sts; mains $12-20; ⏲ 8am-4pm & 6-11pm Mon-Sat, 9am-6pm Sun; [S] J/M/Z to Essex St, F to Delancey St, F to Second Ave) Mom-and-pop shop extraordinaire Clinton Street Baking Company gets the blue ribbon in so many categories – stellar blueberry pancakes, buttermilk biscuit sandwiches, fish tacos, fried chicken – that you're pretty much guaranteed a memorable meal no matter what time you stop by.

Katz's Delicatessen DELI $$
(Map p66; ☎ 212-254-2246; www.katzsdelicatessen.com; 205 E Houston St, at Ludlow St; sandwiches $13-21; ⏲ 8am-10:45pm Mon-Wed & Sun, to 2:45am Thu, open all night Fri & Sat; [S] F to 2nd Ave) One of the few remaining Jewish delicatessens in the city, Katz's attracts locals, tourists and celebrities whose photos line the walls. Massive pastrami, corned beef, brisket and tongue sandwiches are throwbacks, as is the payment system: hold on to the ticket you're handed when you walk in and pay cash only.

Fung Tu FUSION $$
(Map p66; www.fungtu.com; 22 Orchard St btwn Hester & Canal Sts; small plates $13-18, mains $24-32; ⏲ 6pm-midnight Tue-Sat, 4pm-10pm Sun; [S] F to East Broadway) Celebrated chef Jonathan Wu brilliantly blends Chinese cooking with global accents at this elegant little eatery on the edge of Chinatown. The complex sharing plates are superb (try scallion pancakes with cashew salad and smoked chicken or crepe roll stuffed with braised beef, pickled cucumbers and watercress) and pair nicely with creative cocktails like the Fung Tu Gibson.

Kuma Inn PAN-ASIAN $$
(Map p66; ☎ 212-353-8866; www.kumainn.com; 113 Ludlow St, btwn Delancey & Rivington Sts; small dishes $9-15; ⏲ 6-11pm Sun-Thu, to midnight Fri & Sat; [S] F, J/M/Z to Delancey-Essex Sts) Reservations are a must at this spot in a secretive 2nd-floor location (look for a small red door with 'Kuma Inn' painted on the concrete side). The Filipino- and Thai-inspired tapas runs the gamut, from vegetarian summer rolls (with jicama) to spicy drunken shrimp, and pan-roasted scallops with bacon and sake. Bring your own beer, wine or sake (corkage fee applies).

🍴 SoHo & NoHo

Dominique Ansel Bakery DESSERTS $
(Map p66; 189 Spring St; desserts $6-7; ⏲ 8am-7pm Mon-Sat, 9am-7pm Sun; [S] C/E to Spring St) The most famous patisserie in NYC has much more up its sleeve than just cronuts (the half-doughnut half-croissant it invented back in 2013). Buttery *kouign-amman* (a Breton cake), salted caramel éclairs and photogenic berry tarts are among the many hits. FYI: if you want a cronut before they sell out each day, arrive by 7:30am on weekdays (earlier on weekends).

Mooncake Foods ASIAN, SANDWICHES $
(Map p66; ☎ 212-219-8888; www.mooncakefoods.com; 28 Watts St , btwn Sullivan & Thompson Sts; mains from $11; ⏲ 11am-10pm; [S] 1 to Canal St) This unpretentious family-run restaurant serves some of the best sandwiches in the neighborhood. Try the smoked white-fish salad sandwich or Vietnamese pork meatball hero. Other locations in the Financial District, Chelsea and uptown in Hell's Kitchen.

Boqueria Soho TAPAS $$
(Map p66; ☎ 212-343-4255; 171 Spring St, btwn West Broadway & Thompson St; tapas $7-19; ⏲ noon-11pm; [S] C/E to Spring St) This expansive, welcoming tapas joint features delectable classics, including *pulpo a la gallega* (Galician octopus), *gambas al ajillo* (garlic marinated shrimp) and creamy tortilla (Spanish omelet). You can watch the chefs in action as you sip a pink grapefruit sangria and peer into the open kitchen.

★ Il Buco ITALIAN $$$
(Map p66; ☎ 212-533-1932; www.ilbuco.com; 47 Bond St btwn Bowery & Lafayette St; mains lunch $17-30, dinner $24-36; ⏲ noon-midnight Tue-Sat, 6pm-midnight Sun & Mon; [S] B/D/F/V to Broadway-Lafayette St; 6 to Bleecker St) This charmingly rustic nook boasts hanging copper pots, kerosene lamps and antique furniture, plus a stunning menu and wine list. Sink your teeth into seasonal and ever-changing highlights like pan-roasted black bass with celery root puree or risotto with wild nettles, melted leeks and fresh goat's cheese.

Dutch MODERN AMERICAN $$$
(Map p66; ☎ 212-677-6200; www.thedutchnyc.com; 131 Sullivan St, btwn Prince & Houston Sts; mains lunch $18-33, dinner $30-58; ⏲ 11:30am-3pm & 5:30-11pm daily, from 10am Sat & Sun; [S] C/E to Spring St, N/R to Prince St, 1 to Houston St) Oysters on ice and freshly baked homemade

pies are the notable bookends of a meal – in the middle is delectable fresh-from-the-farm comfort fare. Artisanal cocktails add to the festive cheer.

Balthazar FRENCH **$$$**

(Map p66; ☎ 212-965-1414; www.balthazarny.com; 80 Spring St, btwn Broadway & Crosby St; mains lunch $18-29, dinner $21-45; 🕒 8am-midnight; [S] 6 to Spring St; N/R to Prince St) Still the king of bistros, bustling Balthazar is never short of a discriminating mob. That's all thanks to its uplifting Paris-meets-NYC ambience and its stellar something-for-everyone menu. Highlights include the outstanding raw bar, rich onion soup, steak frites and salade Niçoise. Weekend brunch here is a very crowded (and delicious) production.

For a decadent treat to go, grab a pastry from the Balthazar bakery next door.

🍴 East Village

Every cuisine and style is represented in the East Village, though even the very best places are certainly more casual than stuffy. St Marks Place and around, from Third to Second Ave, has turned into a little Tokyo with loads of Japanese sushi and grill restaurants. Cookie-cutter Indian restaurants line Sixth St between First and Second Ave.

Tacos Morelos MEXICAN **$**

(Map p66; ☎ 347-772-5216; 438 E 9th St, btwn First Ave & Ave A; tacos from $3; 🕒 noon-midnight Sun-Thu, to 2am Fri & Sat; [S] L to 1st Ave) This famed food truck put down roots in a no-frills East Village storefront in 2013, quickly becoming one of Manhattan's favorite taco joints. Order yours with chicken, steak, roast pork, beef tongue or vegetarian. Tip: pay the $0.50 extra for the homemade tortilla.

Porchetta SANDWICHES **$**

(Map p66; ☎ 212-777-2151; www.porchetta.com; 110 E 7th St; sandwiches $10-12; 🕒 11:30am-10pm Sun-Thu, to 11pm Fri & Sat; [S] 6 to Astor Pl) This tiny white-tiled storefront serves tender boneless roasted pork that's been wrapped in a pork belly and seasoned with fennel pollen, rosemary, sage, thyme and garlic, available in sandwich or platter-with-sides versions.

Veselka UKRAINIAN **$**

(Map p66; ☎ 212-228-9682; www.veselka.com; 144 Second Ave, at 9th St; mains $10-19; 🕒 24hr; [S] L to 3rd Ave, 6 to Astor Pl) Generations of East Villagers have been coming to this bustling institution for blintzes and breakfast regardless of the hour.

Cafe Mogador MOROCCAN **$$**

(Map p66; ☎ 212-677-2226; www.cafemogador.com; 101 St Marks Pl; mains lunch $8-14, dinner $17-21; 🕒 9am-midnight; [S] 6 to Astor Pl) Family-run Mogador is a long-standing NYC classic, serving fluffy piles of couscous, char-grilled lamb and merguez sausage over basmati rice and its famous tangines – traditionally spiced, long-simmered chicken or lamb dishes served up five different ways. A garrulous young crowd packs the space, spilling out onto the small cafe tables on warm days. Brunch is also first-rate.

Luzzo's PIZZA **$$**

(Map p66; ☎ 212-473-7447; www.luzzosgroup.com; 211 First Ave, btwn 12th & 13th Sts; pizzas $18-26; 🕒 noon-11pm Sun-Thu, to midnight Fri & Sat; [S] L to 1st Ave) Fan-favorite Luzzo's occupies a thin sliver of real estate, which gets stuffed to the gills each evening as discerning diners feast on thin-crust pies, kissed with ripe tomatoes and cooked in a coal-fired oven. Cash only.

Angelica Kitchen VEGETARIAN **$$**

(Map p66; ☎ 212-228-2909; www.angelicakitchen.com; 300 E 12th St, btwn First & Second Aves; mains $17-21; 🕒 11:30am-10:30pm; 🌿; [S] L to 1st Ave) This enduring herbivore classic has a calming vibe and enough creative options to make your head spin. Some dishes get too cute names, but all do wonders with tofu, seitan, spices and soy products, and sometimes an array of raw ingredients. Cash only.

★ Momofuku Noodle Bar NOODLES **$$**

(Map p66; ☎ 212-777-7773; www.momofuku.com; 171 First Ave btwn 10th & 11th Sts; mains $17-28; 🕒 noon-11pm Sun-Thu, to 1am Fri & Sat; [S] L to 1st Ave, 6 to Astor Pl) Ramen and steamed buns are the name of the game at this infinitely creative Japanese eatery, part of the growing David Chang empire. Seating is on stools at a long bar or at communal tables. Momofuku's famous steamed chicken and pork buns are recommended.

★ Upstate SEAFOOD **$$**

(Map p66; ☎ 917-408-3395; www.upstatenyc.com; 95 First Ave, btwn 5th & 6th Sts; mains $15-30; 🕒 5-11pm; [S] F to 2nd Ave) Tiny Upstate serves outstanding seafood dishes and craft beers. The small always-changing menu features the likes of beer-steamed mussels, seafood stew, scallops over mushroom risotto, softshell crab and wondrous oyster selections. There's no freezer – seafood comes from the market each day, so you know you'll be getting only the freshest ingredients.

and the season's harvest featuring toasted quinoa and a flavorful mix of vegetables.

Chelsea, Meatpacking District & West (Greenwich) Village

Chelsea Market   MARKET $
(Map p70; www.chelseamarket.com; 75 9th Ave; ⏰7am-9pm Mon-Sat, 8am-8pm Sun; ⓢA/C/E to 14th St) This former cookie factory has been turned into an 800ft-long shopping concourse that caters to foodies with boutique bakeries, gelato shops, ethnic eats and a food court for gourmands.

★**Moustache**   MIDDLE EASTERN $
(Map p66; ✆212-229-2220; www.moustachepitza. com; 90 Bedford St btwn Grove & Barrow Sts; mains $8-17; ⏰noon-midnight; ⓢ1 to Christopher St-Sheridan Sq) Small and delightful Moustache serves up rich, flavorful sandwiches (leg of lamb, merguez sausage, falafel), thin-crust pizzas, tangy salads and hearty specialties like *ouzi* (filo stuffed with chicken, rice and spices). Start with a platter of creamy hummus or baba ghanoush, served with fluffy, piping hot pitas.

Taïm   ISRAELI $
(Map p66; ✆212-691-1287; www.taimfalafel.com; 222 Waverly Pl btwn Perry & W 11th Sts; sandwiches $7-8; ⏰11am-10pm; ⓢ1/2/3 to 14th St) This tiny joint whips up some of the best falafels in the city. There are also mixed platters, zesty salads and delicious smoothies (try the date, lime and banana). There's also a NoLita location.

Joe's Pizza   PIZZA $
(Map p66; ✆212-366-1182; www.joespizzanyc.com; 7 Carmine St btwn Sixth Ave & Bleecker St; slices from $3; ⏰10am-4am; ⓢA/C/E, B/D/F/M to W 4th St; 1 to Christopher St-Sheridan Sq or Houston St) Joe's is the Meryl Streep of pizza parlors, collecting dozens of awards and accolades over the last four decades. No-frills slices are served up indiscriminately to students, tourists and celebrities alike.

★**Foragers City Table**   MODERN AMERICAN $$
(Map p70; ✆212-243-8888; www.foragerscity grocer.com; 300 W 22nd St, cnr Eighth Ave; mains $23-36; ⏰5:30-10pm daily & 10:30am-2:30pm Sat & Sun; ✆; ⓢC/E, 1 to 23rd St) Owners of this excellent restaurant in Chelsea run a 28-acre farm in the Hudson Valley, from which much of their menu is sourced. Recent temptations include squash soup with Jerusalem artichokes and black truffles; roasted chicken with polenta; heritage pork loin;

Spotted Pig   PUB FOOD $$
(Map p66; ✆212-620-0393; www.thespottedpig. com; 314 W 11th St at Greenwich St; mains lunch $15-26, dinner $21-35; ⏰noon-2am Mon-Fri, from 11am Sat & Sun; ✆; ⓢA/C/E to 14th St; L to 8th Ave) This Michelin-starred gastro-pub is a favorite of Villagers, serving an upscale blend of hearty Italian and British dishes. Its two floors are bedecked with old-timey trinkets that give the whole place an air of relaxed elegance. It doesn't take reservations, so there is often a wait for a table. Lunch on weekdays is less crowded.

Cookshop   MODERN AMERICAN $$
(Map p70; ✆212-924-4440; www.cookshopny.com; 156 Tenth Ave btwn 19th & 20th Sts; mains $18-36; ⏰8am-11:30pm Mon-Fri, from 10am Sat & Sun; ⓢL to 8th Ave; A/C/E to 23rd St) A brilliant brunching pit stop before (or after) tackling the verdant High Line across the street, Cookshop is a lively spot for eye-opening cocktails, a perfectly baked breadbasket and a selection of inventive egg mains. Dinner is a sure-fire win as well. Ample outdoor seating on warm days.

Tía Pol   TAPAS $$
(Map p70; ✆212-675-8805; www.tiapol.com; 205 Tenth Ave btwn 22nd & 23rd Sts; small plates $4-16; ⏰noon-11pm Tue-Sun, from 5:30pm Mon; ⓢC/E to 23rd St) Wielding Spanish tapas amid closet-sized surrounds, Tía Pol is the real deal, as the hordes of locals swarming the entrance can attest. There's a great wine list and a tantalizing array of small plates: fried chickpeas, squid and ink with rice, cockles in white wine and garlic, Navarran-style trout with *serrano* ham, and fried chickpeas.

★**RedFarm**   FUSION $$$
(Map p66; ✆212-792-9700; www.redfarmnyc.com; 529 Hudson St btwn 10th & Charles Sts; mains $22-46; ⏰5pm-11pm daily & 11am-2:30pm Sat & Sun; ⓢA/C/E, B/D/F/M to W 4th St; 1 to Christopher St-Sheridan Sq) RedFarm transforms Chinese cooking into pure, delectable artistry at this small, buzzing space on Hudson St. Crispy duck and crab dumplings, sauteed black cod with black bean and Thai basil, and pastrami egg rolls are among the many creative dishes that brilliantly blend East with West. Waits can be long, so arrive early (no reservations).

Union Square, Flatiron District & Gramercy Park

Shake Shack
BURGERS $

(Map p70; 212-989-6600; www.shakeshack.com; Madison Square Park, cnr 23rd St & Madison Ave; burgers $5-10; 11am-11pm; N/R, F/M, 6 to 23rd St) Tourists line up in droves for the hamburgers and shakes at this Madison Square Park counter-window-serving institution.

★ Eataly
ITALIAN

(Map p70; www.eatalyny.com; 200 Fifth Ave, at 23rd St; 8am-11pm; F/M, N/R, 6 to 23rd St) The promised land for lovers of Italian food, this 50,000-sq-ft emporium has a countless array of tempting food counters, doling out brick-oven pizza, fresh-made pastas, pecorino-covered salads, oysters, creamy gelato, perfectly pulled espresso and much more. It's all set amid a gourmet market, with plenty of picnic ideas. The pièce de résistance is a rooftop beer garden called Birreria.

ABC Kitchen
MODERN AMERICAN $$$

(Map p70; 212-475-5829; www.abckitchennyc. com; 35 E 18th St, at Broadway; mains $16-24, dinner mains $24-40; noon-3pm & 5:30-10:30pm Mon-Fri, from 11am Sat & Sun; ; L, N/Q/R, 4/5/6 to Union Sq) Looking part gallery, part rustic farmhouse, sustainable ABC Kitchen is the culinary avatar of the chi-chi home goods department store ABC Carpet & Home. Organic gets haute in dishes like tuna sashimi with ginger and mint, or crispy pork confit with grilled ramps. For a more casual bite, try the scrumptious wholewheat pizzas.

Midtown

★ Totto Ramen
JAPANESE $

(Map p70; 212-582-0052; www.tottoramen.com; 366 W 52nd St, btwn Eighth & Ninth Aves, Midtown West; ramen $10-16; noon-midnight Mon-Fri, noon-11pm Sat, 5-11pm Sun; C/E to 50th St) Write your name and number of guests on the clipboard by the door and wait for your (cash-only) ramen revelation. Skip the chicken and go for the pork, which sings in dishes like miso ramen (with fermented soybean paste, egg, scallion, bean sprouts, onion and homemade chili paste).

El Margon
CUBAN $

(Map p70; 212-354-5013; www.margonnyc.com; 136 W 46th St, btwn Sixth & Seventh Aves, Midtown West; sandwiches $4-8, mains $10-15; 7am-5pm Mon-Fri, to 3pm Sat; B/D/F/M to 47-50th Sts-Rockefeller Center) It's still 1973 at this ever-packed Cuban lunch counter, where orange Laminex and greasy goodness never went out of style. Go for gold with the legendary cubano sandwich (a pressed panino jammed with rich roast pork, salami, cheese, pickles, mojo and mayo).

★ Danji
KOREAN $$

(Map p70; 212-586-2880; www.danjinyc.com; 346 W 52nd St, btwn Eighth & Ninth Aves, Midtown West; sharing plates $13-20; noon-2:30pm & 5pm-11pm Mon-Thu, noon-2:30pm & 5pm-midnight Fri, 5pm-midnight Sat; C/E to 50th St) Younggun chef Hooni Kim has captured tastebuds with his Michelin-starred Korean 'tapas' served in a snug and slinky contemporary space. The celebrity dish on the menu (divided into 'traditional' and 'modern' options) are the sliders, a duo of bulgogi beef and spiced pork belly served on butter-grilled buns.

Hangawi
KOREAN $$

(Map p70; 212-213-0077; www.hangawirestaurant.com; 12 E 32nd St, btwn Fifth & Madison Aves; mains lunch $11-24, dinner $19-30; noon-2:45pm & 5-10:15pm Mon-Thu, to 10:30pm Fri, 1-10:30pm Sat, 5-9:30pm Sun; B/D/T/M, N/Q/R to 34th St-Herald Sq) Sublime, flesh-free Korean is the draw at high-achieving Hangawi. Leave your shoes at the entrance and slip into a soothing, zenlike space of meditative music, soft low seating and clean, complexly flavored dishes. Show-stoppers include the leek pancakes and a seductively smooth tofu claypot in ginger sauce.

Virgil's Real Barbecue
AMERICAN BBQ $$

(Map p70; 212-921-9494; www.virgilsbbq.com; 152 W 44th St btwn Broadway & Eighth Ave; mains $14-25; 11:30am-midnight; N/R, S, W, 1/2/3, 7 to Times Sq-42nd St) Menu items cover the entire BBQ map, with Oklahoma State Fair corndogs, pulled Carolina pork and smoked Maryland ham sandwiches, and platters of sliced Texas beef brisket and Georgia chicken-fried steak.

Dhaba
INDIAN $$

(Map p70; 212-679-1284; www.dhabanyc.com; 108 Lexington Ave btwn 27th & 28th Sts; mains $12-24; noon-midnight Mon-Sat, to 10pm Sun; 6 to 28th St) Murray Hill (aka Curry Hill) has no shortage of subcontinental bites, but funky Dhaba packs one serious flavor punch. Mouthwatering standouts include the crunchy, tangy lasoni gobi (fried cauliflower with tomato and spices), and the insanely flavorful *murgh bharta* (minced chicken cooked with smoked eggplant).

There's also a good-value lunch buffet ($11 Monday to Saturday, $13 Sunday).

El Parador Cafe MEXICAN **$$**

(Map p70; ☎212-679-6812; www.elparadorcafe.com; 325 E 34th St, btwn First & Second Aves, Midtown East; mains $20-32; ⏰noon-11pm Mon-Sat, 2-10pm Sun; [S]6 to 33rd St) Well off the beaten path, this far-flung Mexican stalwart has abundant old-school charm, from the beveled candleholders and dapper Latino waiters to the satisfying south-of-the-border standbys. House classics include the mussels in red wine, cilantro and garlic, served with green chili corn bread, and the signature mole poblano (chicken stewed in a rich chili-and-chocolate-spiked sauce).

Artisanal FRENCH **$$$**

(Map p70; ☎212-725-8585; www.artisanalbistro.com; 2 Park Ave S at 32nd St; mains $24-38; ⏰10am-1am Mon-Fri, from 8:30am Sat & Sun; 🖉; [S]6 to 33rd St) For those who live, love and dream *fromage,* Artisanal is a must-eat. More than 250 varieties of cheese, from stinky to sweet, are found at this classic Parisian-style bistro. Creamy goodness aside, other favorite items include mussels, braised lamb shank and onion soup gratinée (with a three-cheese blend of course).

NoMad NEW AMERICAN **$$$**

(Map p70; ☎212-796-1500; www.thenomadhotel.com; NoMad Hotel, 1170 Broadway, at 28th St; mains $30-45; ⏰noon-2pm & 5:30-10:30pm Mon-Thu, to 11pm Fri, 11am-2pm & 5:30-11pm Sat, 11am-3pm & 5:30-10pm Sun; [S]N/R, 6 to 28th St; F/M to 23rd St) Sharing the same name as the 'It kid' hotel it inhabits, NoMad has become one of Manhattan's culinary highlights. Carved up into a series of distinctly different spaces – including a see-and-be-seen Atrium, an elegant Parlour and a snacks-only Library – the restaurant serves delicacies like roasted quail with morels, suckling pig with ramps, and foie gras marinated with rhubarb.

Grand Central Oyster Bar & Restaurant SEAFOOD **$$$**

(Map p70; ☎212-490-6650; www.oysterbarny.com; Grand Central Terminal, 42nd St at Park Ave; mains $23-38; ⏰11:30am-9:30pm Mon-Sat; [S]4/5/6 to 42nd St) This buzzing bar and restaurant within Grand Central is hugely atmostpheric, with a vaulted tiled ceiling by Catalan-born engineer Rafael Guastavino. The two dozen oyster varieties present some dizzying choices, along with clam chowder, seafood stews, pan-fried softshell crab and an overabundance of fresh fish.

🍴 Upper West Side

Jacob's Pickles AMERICAN **$$**

(Map p78; ☎212-470-5566; www.jacobspickles.com; 509 Amsterdam Ave, btwn 84th & 85th Sts; mains $15-24; ⏰10am-2am Mon-Thu, to 4am Fri, 9am-4am Sat, to 2am Sun; [S]1 to 86th St) On a restaurant-lined stretch of Amsterdam Ave, this inviting and warmly lit eatery serves upscale comfort food, like catfish tacos, wine-braised turkey leg dinner, and St Louis ribs slathered with coffee molasses barbecue sauce. The biscuits and pickles are top-notch, and you'll find two dozen or so craft beers on tap from New York, Maine and beyond.

PJ Clarke's AMERICAN **$$**

(Map p78; ☎212-957-9700; www.pjclarkes.com; 44 W 63rd St, cnr Broadway; burgers $14-19, mains $19-42; ⏰11:30am-2am; [S]1 to 66th St-Lincoln Center) Across the street from Lincoln Center, this red-checked-tablecloth spot has a buttoned-down crowd, friendly bartenders and a solid menu. If you're in a rush, belly up to the bar for a Black Angus burger and a Brooklyn Lager. A raw bar offers fresh Long Island Little Neck and Cherry Stone clams, as well as jumbo shrimp cocktails.

Barney Greengrass DELI **$$**

(Map p78; ☎212-724-4707; www.barneygreengrass.com; 541 Amsterdam Ave, at 86th St; mains $10-21; ⏰8:30am-4pm Tue-Sun; [S]1 to 86th St) Old-school Upper Westsiders and pilgrims from other neighborhoods crowd this century-old 'sturgeon king' on weekends. It serves a long list of traditional if pricey Jewish delicacies, from bagels and lox to sturgeon scrambled with eggs and onions.

Peacefood Cafe VEGAN **$$**

(Map p78; ☎212-362-2266; www.peacefoodcafe.com; 460 Amsterdam Ave, at 82nd St; mains $10-18; ⏰10am-10pm; 🖉; [S]1 to 79th St) This bright and airy vegan haven dishes up a popular fried seitan panino (served on homemade focaccia and topped with cashew, arugula, tomatoes and pesto), as well as pizzas, roasted vegetable plates and an excellent quinoa salad. There are daily raw specials, organic coffees and rich desserts. Healthy and good.

Upper East Side

JG Melon   PUB FOOD $

(Map p78; ☏ 212-744-0585; 1291 Third Ave, at 74th
St; mains $11-18; ⊙ 11:30am-4am; ⓢ 6 to 77th St)
JG's is a loud, old-school pub that has been
serving juicy burgers on tea plates since
1972. It's a local favorite for both eating and
drinking (the Bloody Marys are excellent)
and it gets crowded in the after-work hours.

Earl's Beer & Cheese   AMERICAN $

(Map p78; ☏ 212-289-1581; www.earlsny.com; 1259
Park Ave, btwn 97th & 98th Sts; grilled cheese $8;
⊙ 4pm-midnight Mon & Tue, 11am-midnight Wed-
Thu & Sun, to 2am Fri & Sat; ⓢ 6 to 96th St) Chef
Corey Cova's comfort-food outpost channels
a hipster hunting vibe. The NY state cheddar
grilled cheese is a paradigm shifter, served
with pork belly, fried egg and kimchi. Other popular dishes: mac 'n' cheese, a braised
pork shoulder taco, and a Sriracha tomato
soup. Earl's also has an excellent craft beer
selection.

Candle Cafe   VEGAN $$

(Map p78; ☏ 212-472-0970; www.candlecafe.com;
1307 Third Ave, btwn 74th & 75th Sts; mains $15-22;
⊙ 11:30am-10:30pm Mon-Sat, to 9:30pm Sun; ☑;
ⓢ 6 to 77th St) The moneyed yoga set piles
into this attractive vegan cafe serving a long
list of sandwiches, salads, comfort food and
market-driven specials. The specialty here is
the house-made seitan.

Jones Wood Foundry   BRITISH $$

(Map p78; ☏ 212-249-2700; www.joneswoodfound-
ry.com; 401 E 76th St, btwn First & York Aves; mains
lunch $12-24, dinner $19-26; ⊙ 11am-11pm; ☎;
ⓢ 6 to 77th St) Inside a narrow brick building that once housed an ironworks, the
Jones Wood Foundry is a British-inspired
gastropub serving first-rate beer-battered
fish and chips, bangers and mash, lamb and
rosemary pie and other hearty temptations.
On warm days, grab a table on the enclosed
courtyard patio.

Tanoshi   SUSHI $$$

(Map p78; ☏ 646-727-9056; www.tanoshisushinyc.
com; 1372 York Ave, btwn 73rd & 74th Sts; chef's sushi
selection around $80; ⊙ 6-10:30pm Mon-Sat; ⓢ 6 to
77th St) The setting may be humble, but the
flavors are simply magnificent at this small,
wildly popular sushi spot: think Hokkaido
scallops, Atlantic shad, seared salmon belly
or mouthwatering uni (sea urchin). Only
sushi is on offer and only *omakase* – the
chef's selection of whatever is particularly

outstanding that day. It's BYO beer, sake or
what-not. Reserve well in advance.

Harlem

★**Red Rooster**   MODERN AMERICAN $$

(Map p78; ☏ 212-792-9001; www.redrooster
harlem.com; 310 Malcolm X Blvd btwn 125th & 126th
Sts, Harlem; mains $18-30; ⊙ 11:30am-10:30pm
Mon-Fri, 10am-11pm Sat & Sun; ⓢ 2/3 to 125th St)
Transatlantic super-chef Marcus Samuels-
son laces upscale comfort food with a world
of flavors at his effortlessly cool, swinging
brasserie. Try blackened catfish with curried
peas and pickled mango, meatballs with lin-
gonberries and buttermilk mashed potatoes,
or mac 'n' cheese with lobster.

Amy Ruth's Restaurant   SOUTHERN $$

(Map p78; ☏ 212-280-8779; www.amyruthsharlem.
com; 113 W 116th St near Malcolm X Blvd; mains
$12-24; ⊙ 11am-11pm Mon, 8:30am-11pm Tue-Thu,
8:30am-5am Fri, 7:30am-5am Sat, 7:30am-11pm
Sun; ⓢ B, C, 2/3 to 116th St) This perennially
crowded restaurant is *the* place to go for
classic soul food, serving up fried catfish,
mac 'n' cheese and fluffy biscuits. But it's
the waffles that are most famous – dished
up 14 different ways, including with shrimp.
Our favorite is the 'Rev Al Sharpton': waffles
topped with succulent fried chicken.

Dinosaur Bar-B-Que   STEAK $$

(Map p78; ☏ 212-694-1777; www.dinosaurbarbque.
com; 700 W 125th St at Twelfth Ave; mains $13-25;
⊙ 11:30am-11pm Mon-Thu, to midnight Fri & Sat,
noon-10pm Sun; ☎; ⓢ 1 to 125th St) Get messy
with dry-rubbed, slow-pit-smoked ribs, slabs
of juicy steak, and succulent burgers. The
very few vegetarian options include a fantastic version of Creole-spiced deviled eggs.
There's live music weekend nights (from
10:30pm).

Brooklyn

Of course it's impossible to begin to do justice to Brooklyn's eating options – it's as
much a foodie's paradise as Manhattan. Virtually every ethnic cuisine has a significant
presence somewhere in this borough. As far
as neighborhoods close to Manhattan go:
Williamsburg is chockablock with eateries,
as are Fifth and Seventh Aves in Park Slope.
Smith St is 'Restaurant Row' in the Carroll
Gardens and Cobble Hill neighborhoods.
Atlantic Ave, near Court St, has a number
of excellent Middle Eastern restaurants and
groceries.

Mile End DELI $
(☎ 718-852-7510; www.mileendbrooklyn.com; 97A Hoyt St, Boerum Hill; sandwiches $9-15; 🕙 8am-10pm Mon-Fri, from 10am Sat & Sun; [S] A/C/G to Hoyt Schermerhorn Sts) Mile End is small, like its portions, but big on flavors. Try a smoked beef brisket on rye with mustard – the bread is sticky soft and the meat will melt in your mouth.

Tom's Restaurant DINER $
(☎ 718-636-9738; 782 Washington Ave, at Sterling Pl, Prospect Heights; mains $8-12; 🕙 7am-4pm Mon-Sat, from 8am Sun; [S] 2/3 to Eastern Pkwy-Brooklyn Museum) Inspiration for the eponymously named Suzanne Vega song, this old-school soda fountain diner's specialty is its variety of pancakes (eg pumpkin walnut). Coffee and cookies are served to those waiting in the line that invariably snakes out the door on weekend mornings.

Chuko JAPANESE $
(☎ 718-576-6701; www.barchuko.com; 552 Vanderbilt Ave, cnr Dean St, Prospect Heights; ramen $13; 🕙 noon-3pm & 5:30-10pm Sun-Thu, to 11pm Fri & Sat; 🌿; [S] B/Q to 7th Ave, 2/3 to Bergen St) This cozy wood-lined ramen shop brings a top-notch noodle game to Prospect Heights. Steaming bowls of al dente ramen are paired with silky broths, including an excellent roasted pork and a full-bodied vegetarian. Don't overlook the appetizers, particularly the fragrant salt-and-pepper chicken wings.

★ **Pok Pok** THAI $$
(☎ 718-923-9322; www.pokpokny.com; 117 Columbia St, cnr Kane St; sharing plates $12-18; 🕙 5:30-10:30pm Mon-Fri, from 10am Sat & Sun; [S] F to Bergen St) Andy Ricker's NYC outpost is a smashing success, wowing diners with a rich and complex menu inspired by Northern Thailand street food. Fiery fish-sauce-slathered chicken wings, spicy green papaya salad with salted black crab, smoky grilled eggplant salad and sweet pork belly with ginger, turmeric and tamarind are among the many unique dishes.

The setting is fun and ramshackle, with a small backyard festooned with fairy lights. Waits can be long; thankfully there's a great little bar (**Whiskey Soda Lounge**) across the street, which serves imaginative concoctions (tamarind whiskey sours, Vietnamese coffee spiked with brandy) as well as bar nibbles from Pok Pok's menu.

SMORGASBURG!

On weekends, it's well worth planning a day around Brooklyn's **Smorgasburg** (www.smorgasburg.com; 🕙 11am-6pm Sat & Sun Apr-Nov). At this sprawling food market you can nibble your way around the globe with over 100 food vendors on hand. Among the countless temptations you'll find chocolate salted caramel doughnuts (**Dough**), pork and crackling sandwiches (**Porchetta**), Japanese-inspired tacos (**Takumi**), sweet potato masala (**Dosa Royale**), Mexican street food (**Cemita's**), cold brew coffee (**Grady's**), strawberry rhubarb popsicles (**People's Pops**) and much more.

On Saturdays you'll find it at **East River State Park** (www.nysparks.com/parks/155; Kent Ave, btwn 8th & 9th Sts; 🕙 9am-dusk; 👪; [S] L to Bedford Ave) and Sundays at Pier 5 in **Brooklyn Bridge Park** (p84). Check the website for more details.

Battersby MODERN AMERICAN $$
(☎ 718-852-8321; www.battersbybrooklyn.com; 255 Smith St, btwn Douglass & Degraw Sts; mains $17-32, tasting menu $75-95; 🕙 5:30-11pm Mon-Sat, to 10pm Sun; [S] F, G to Bergen St) A top choice in Brooklyn, Battersby serves magnificent seasonal dishes. The small menu changes regularly, but be on the lookout for veal sweetbreads, pappardelle with duck ragu, chatham cod with braised fennel and delightfully tender lamb. The space is Brooklyn-style quaint (plank floors, brick walls, tin ceiling), but tiny and cramped.

To get in without a long wait, plan ahead: arrive at opening time or make a reservation – accepted only for folks partaking of the tasting menu.

Juliana's PIZZA $$
(☎ 718-596-6700; www.julianaspizza.com; 19 Old Fulton St, btwn Water & Front Sts; pizza $16-32; 🕙 11:30am-11pm; [S] A/C to High St) Legendary pizza maestro Patsy Grimaldi has returned to Brooklyn, with delicious thin-crust perfection in both classic and creative combos (like the No 5, with smoked salmon, goat's cheese and capers). It's in Dumbo and the Brooklyn waterfront.

Marlow & Sons
MODERN AMERICAN **$$**

(☏718-384-1441; www.marlowandsons.com; 81 Broadway, btwn Berry St & Wythe Ave; mains lunch $14-18, dinner $24-28; ⊘8am-midnight; Ⓢ J/M/Z to Marcy Ave, L to Bedford Ave) The dimly lit, wood-lined space feels like an old farmhouse cafe, which hosts a buzzing nighttime scene as diners and drinkers crowd in for oysters, tip-top cocktails and a changing menu of locavore specialties (smoked pork loin, crunchy crust pizzas, carmelized turnips, fluffy Spanish-style tortillas). Brunch is also a big draw, though prepare for lines.

Roberta's
PIZZA **$$**

(☏718-417-1118; www.robertaspizza.com; 261 Moore St, near Bogart St, Bushwick; pizzas $14-18; ⊘11am-midnight; ☍; Ⓢ L to Morgan Ave) This hipster-saturated warehouse restaurant in Bushwick consistently produces some of the best pizza in New York. Service can be lackadaisical and the waits long, but the brick-oven pies are the right combination of chewy and fresh.

Water Table
MODERN AMERICAN **$$$**

(☏917-499-5727; www.thewatertablenyc.com; Skyport Marina, 23rd St & FDR Drive, Greenpoint; prix fixe $75; ⊘7:30-10pm Thu-Sat, 6-8pm Sun; Ⓢ1 Scoring high on novelty, the Water Table is set inside a rustically converted WWII navy patrol boat. The three-course dinner (smoked scallop lobster bisque, kale salad, New England dry rub chicken, and seafood stew were recent selections) would seem a bit pricey if not for the memorable experience of sailing past soaring skyscrapers and the Statue of Liberty by night. Reserve a spot online.

🍷 Drinking & Nightlife

Watering holes come in many forms in this city: sleek lounges, pumping clubs, cozy pubs and booze-soaked dives – no smoke, though, thanks to city law. The majority are open to 4am, though closing (and opening) times do vary; most nightclubs are open from 10pm. Here's a highly selective sampling.

Lower Manhattan

★ Dead Rabbit
COCKTAIL BAR

(Map p62; ☏646-422-7906; www.deadrabbitnyc. com; 30 Water St; ⊘11am-4am; Ⓢ R to Whitehall St, 1 to South Ferry) Far from dead, this rabbit has won a warren full of awards for its magnificent cocktails. During the day, hit the sawdust-sprinkled taproom for specialty beers, historic punches and pop-inns (lightly hopped ale spiked with different flavors). Come evening, scurry upstairs to the cozy Parlour for 72 meticulously researched cocktails.

Smith & Mills
COCKTAIL BAR

(Map p62; ☏212-226-2515; www.smithandmills. com; 71 N Moore St btwn Hudson & Greenwich Sts; ⊘11am-2am Sun-Wed, to 3am Thu-Sat; Ⓢ1 to Franklin St) Petite Smith & Mills ticks all the cool boxes: unmarked exterior, kooky industrial interior and expertly crafted cocktails. Space is limited so head in early if you fancy kicking back on a plush banquette. A seasonal menu spans light snacks to a particularly notable burger.

Weather Up
COCKTAIL BAR

(Map p62; ☏212-766-3202; www.weatherupnyc. com; 159 Duane St btwn Hudson St & W Broadway; ⊘5pm-midnight Mon-Wed, to 2am Thu-Sun; Ⓢ1/2/3 to Chambers St) Softly lit subway tiles, amiable barkeeps and seductive cocktails set the stage for a fine night out. Try a Whizz Bang (Scotch whiskey, dry vermouth, housemade grenadine, orange bitters and absinthe) while munching fine snacks, including oysters slapped with gin-martini granita.

🍸 Chinatown, SoHo & NoLita

Mulberry Project
COCKTAIL BAR

(Map p66; ☏646-448-4536; www.mulberryproject. com; 149 Mulberry St, btwn Hester & Grand Sts; ⊘5pm-2am Sun-Thu, to 4am Fri & Sat; Ⓢ N/Q/R, J/Z, 6 to Canal St) Lurking behind an unmarked door is this intimate, cavernous cocktail den, with its festive, 'garden-party' backyard one of the best spots to imbibe in the 'hood.

Apothéke
COCKTAIL BAR

(Map p62; ☏212-406-0400; www.apothekenyc. com; 9 Doyers St; ⊘6:30pm-2am Mon-Sat, 8pm-2am Sun; Ⓢ J to Chambers St, 4/5/6 to Brooklyn Bridge-City Hall) It takes a little effort to track down this former opium den turned apothecary bar on Doyers St. Inside, skilled barkeeps work like careful chemists, using local and organic produce from greenmarkets or the rooftop herb garden to produce intense, flavorful 'prescriptions.' Toast to your health with the invigorating Harvest of Mexico (roasted corn, Herba Sainte, mezcal, agave, lime and habanero-infused bitters).

Spring Lounge
DIVE BAR

(Map p66; ☏212-965-1774; www.thespringlounge. com; 48 Spring St, at Mulberry St; ⊘8am-4am Mon-Sat, from noon Sun; Ⓢ6 to Spring St, N/R to Prince St) This neon-red rebel has never let anything get in the way of a good time. These days, this pretension-free drinking den is best known for its kooky stuffed sharks, early-start regulars and come-one-come-all late-night revelry. Fueling the fun are cheap drinks and free grub (hot dogs on Wednesdays from 5pm, bagels on Sundays from noon, while they last).

East Village & the Lower East Side

Ten Bells TAPAS BAR

(Map p66; ☎ 212-228-4450; www.tenbellsnyc.com; 247 Broome St, btwn Ludlow & Orchard Sts; 🕐 5pm-2am Mon-Fri, from 3pm Sat & Sun; [S] F to Delancey St, J/M/Z to Essex St) This charmingly tucked-away tapas bar has a grotto-like design, with flickering candles, dark tin ceilings, brick walls and a U-shaped bar that's an ideal setting for conversation with a new friend. The chalkboard menu features excellent wines by the glass, which go nicely with *boquerones* (marinated anchovies) and other Iberian hits. The entrance is unsigned.

Wayland BAR

(Map p66; ☎ 212-777-7022; www.thewaylandnyc.com; 700 E 9th St, cnr Ave C; 🕐 5pm-4am; [S] L to 1st Ave) Whitewashed walls, weathered floorboards and salvaged lamps give this urban outpost a Mississippi flair, which goes just right with the live music (bluegrass, jazz, folk) from Sunday through Wednesday. Decent drink specials and $1 oysters from 5pm to 7pm on weekdays.

Angel's Share BAR

(Map p66; ☎ 212-777-5415; 2nd fl, 8 Stuyvesant St, near Third Ave & E 9th St; 🕐 6pm-1:30am Sun-Thu, until 2:30am Fri & Sat; [S] 6 to Astor Pl) Show up early and snag a seat at this hidden gem, behind a Japanese restaurant on the same floor. It's quiet and elegant with creative cocktails, but you can't stay if you don't have a table or a seat at the bar, and they tend to go fast.

Immigrant WINE & BEER

(Map p66; ☎ 646-308-1724; www.theimmigrantnyc.com; 341 E 9th St, btwn First & Second Aves; 🕐 5pm-1am Sun-Wed, to 2am Thu-Sat; [S] L to 1st Ave, 4/6 to Astor Pl) Wholly unpretentious, these twin boxcar-sized bars could easily become your neighborhood local if you decide to stick around town. Enter the right side for the wine bar. The left entrance takes you into the taproom, where the focus is on unique microbrews. Both have a similar design – chandeliers, exposed brick, vintage charm.

West Village & Chelsea

Bell Book & Candle BAR

(Map p66; ☎ 212-414-2355; www.bbandcnyc.com; 141 W 10th St btwn Waverley & Greenwich Ave; 🕐 5:30pm-2am Sun-Wed, to 4am Thu-Sat; [S] A/B/C, B/D/F/M to W 4th St; 1 to Christopher St-Sheridan Sq) Step down into this candelit gastropub for strong, inventive libations and hearty pub grub. A twenty-something crowd gathers around the small, packed bar (for $1 oysters and happy-hour drink specials early in the night), though there's a lot more seating hidden in the back, with big booths ideal for larger groups.

Employees Only BAR

(Map p66; ☎ 212-242-3021; www.employeesonlynyc.com; 510 Hudson St near Christopher St; 🕐 6pm-4am; [S] 1 to Christopher St-Sheridan Sq) Duck behind the neon 'Psychic' sign to find this hidden hangout. The bar gets busier as the night wears on. Bartenders are ace mixologists, fizzing up crazy, addictive libations like the Ginger Smash and the Mata Hari. Great for late-night drinking, and eating, courtesy of the on-site restaurant that serves till 3:30am.

Buvette WINE BAR

(Map p66; ☎ 212-255-3590; www.ilovebuvette.com; 42 Grove St btwn Bedford & Bleecker Sts; 🕐 9am-2am; [S] 1 to Christopher St-Sheridan Sq; A/C/E, B/D/F/M to W 4th St) The rustic-chic decor here (think delicate tin tiles and a swooshing marble countertop) make it the perfect place for a glass of wine – no matter the time of day. For the full experience at this self-proclaimed *gastrotèque,* grab a seat at one of the surrounding tables, and nibble on small plates while enjoying the Old-World wines (mostly from France and Italy).

Frying Pan BAR

(Map p70; ☎ 212-989-6363; www.fryingpan.com; Pier 66 at W 26th St; 🕐 noon-midnight May-Oct; [S] C/E to 23rd St) The lightship *Frying Pan* and the two-tiered dockside bar where it's parked are fine go-to spots for a sundowner. On warm days, the rustic open-air space brings in the crowds, who come to laze on deck chairs, eat burgers off the sizzling grill, drink ice-cold beers and admire the waterside views.

🍸 Union Square, Flatiron District & Gramercy Park

Old Town Bar & Restaurant
BAR

(Map p70; 212-529-6732; www.oldtownbar. com; 45 E 18th St, btwn Broadway & Park Ave S; 11:30am-1:30am Mon-Sat, 1pm-midnight Sun; L, N/Q/R, 4/5/6 to 14th St-Union Sq) It still looks like 1892 in here, with the original tile floors and tin ceilings – the Old Town is an 'old world' drinking-man's classic (and woman's: Madonna lit up at the bar here, when lighting up was still legal, in her 'Bad Girl' video). There are cocktails around, but most come for beers and a burger (from $12).

Flatiron Room
COCKTAIL BAR

(Map p70; 212-725-3860; www.theflatironroom. com; 37 W 26th St btwn Sixth Ave & Broadway; 5pm-2am Mon-Sat, to midnight Sun; N/R to 28th St) This beautifully designed drinking den has vintage wallpaper, a glittering chandelier, hand-painted coffer ceilings and artfully lit cabinets filled with rare whiskeys. The fine cocktails pair nicely with high-end sharing plates (sweet potato tacos, wild mushroom flatbread, roasted bone marrow). There's also live music (jazz, bluegrass) most nights. Reservations essential.

🍸 Midtown

★ Rum House
COCKTAIL BAR

(Map p70; 646-490-6924; www.therum-housenyc.com; 228 W 47th St, btwn Broadway & Eighth Ave, Midtown West; 1pm-4am; N/Q/R to 49th St) Inside this beautifully polished drinking parlor, you'll find well-crafted drinks, red leather banquettes and a classy old-timey vibe. There's live music daily – sometimes just a lone pianist, other times a jaunty jazz trio or sentimental torch singer.

Campbell Apartment
COCKTAIL BAR

(Map p70; 212-953-0409; www.hospitality holdings.com; Grand Central Terminal, 15 Vanderbilt Ave, at 43rd St; noon-midnight Sun-Thu, to 2am Fri & Sat; S, 4/5/6, 7 to Grand Central-42nd St) This sublime, deliciously buttoned-up gem in Grand Central was once the office of a '20s railroad magnate fond of Euro eccentricities: think Florentine-style carpets, decorative wooden ceiling beams and a soaring lead-glass window. Suitably tucked away from the hordes, reach it from the lift beside the Oyster Bar or the stairs to the West Balcony.

Russian Vodka Room
BAR

(Map p70; 212-307-5835; www.russianvodka-room.com; 265 W 52nd St, btwn Eighth Ave & Broadway; 4pm-2am Mon-Thu, to 4am Fri & Sat; C/E to 50th St) Actual Russians aren't uncommon at this swanky and welcoming bar. The lighting is dark and the corner booths intimate, but more importantly the dozens of infused vodkas, from cranberry to horseradish, are fun to experiment with.

Lantern's Keep
COCKTAIL BAR

(Map p70; 212-453-4287; www.thelanternskeep. com; Iroquois Hotel, 49 W 44th St, btwn Fifth & Sixth Aves; 5pm-midnight Mon-Fri, 6pm-1am Sat; B/D/F/M to 42nd St-Bryant Park) Cross the lobby of the Iroquois Hotel and slip into this dark, intimate cocktail salon. Its specialty is pre-Prohibition libations, shaken and stirred by passionate, personable mixologists. Reservations recommended.

Top of the Strand
COCKTAIL BAR

(Map p70; www.topofthestrand.com; Strand Hotel, 33 W 37th St, btwn Fifth & Sixth Aves; 5pm-midnight Mon & Sun, to 1am Tue-Sat; B/D/F/M to 34th St) For that 'Oh my God, I'm in New York' feeling, head to the Strand Hotel's rooftop bar, order a martini and admire the jaw-dropping view of the Empire State Building.

Rudy's Bar & Grill
DIVE BAR

(Map p70; 646-707-0890; www.rudysbarnyc. com; 627 Ninth Ave, at 44th St, Midtown West; 8am-4am Mon-Sat, noon-4am Sun; A/C/E to 42nd St-Port Authority Bus Terminal) The big pantless pig in a red jacket out front marks Hell's Kitchen's best divey mingler, with cheap pitchers of Rudy's two beers, half-circle booths covered in red duct tape, and free hot dogs. A mix of folks come to flirt or watch muted Knicks games as classic rock plays.

Bryant Park Grill
BAR, RESTAURANT

(Map p70; 212-840-6500; www.arkrestaurants. com/bryant_park.html; 25 W 40th St btwn Fifth & Sixth Aves; 11:30am-11pm; B/D/F/M to 42nd St-Bryant Park, 7 to Fifth Ave) When the weather is warm, head to this lovely restaurant and bar situated at the eastern end of Bryant Park. The patio bar is a perfect spot for a twilight cocktail or three.

Jimmy's Corner
DIVE BAR

(Map p70; 212-221-9510; 140 W 44th St, btwn Sixth & Seventh Aves, Midtown West; 10am-4am; N/Q/R, 1/2/3, 7 to 42nd St-Times Sq; B/D/F/M to

42nd St-Bryant Park) This skinny, welcoming, completely unpretentious dive off Times Square is owned by an old boxing trainer – as if you wouldn't guess by all the framed photos of boxing greats. The jukebox covers Stax to Miles Davis.

Upper West Side

79th Street Boat Basin
BAR
(Map p78; 212-496-5542; www.boatbasincafe.com; W 79th St, in Riverside Park; noon-11pm Apr-Oct; 1 to 79th St) A covered, open-sided party spot under the ancient arches of a park overpass, this is an Upper West Side favorite once spring hits. Order a pitcher, some snacks and enjoy the sunset view over the Hudson River.

Manhattan Cricket Club
COCKTAIL LOUNGE
(Map p78; 646-823-9252; www.mccnewyork.com; 226 W 79th St, btwn Amsterdam Ave & Broadway; 6pm-2am Tue-Sat; 1 to 79th St) Above an Australian bistro, this elegant drinking lounge is modeled on the classy Anglo-Aussie cricket clubs of the early 1900s. Sepia-toned photos of batsmen adorn the gold brocaded walls, while mahogany bookshelves and Chesterfield sofas create a fine setting for quaffing well-made but pricey cocktails.

Dead Poet
BAR
(Map p78; 212-595-5670; www.thedeadpoet.com; 450 Amsterdam Ave, btwn 81st & 82nd Sts; noon-4am; 1 to 79th St) This skinny, mahogany-paneled pub has been a neighborhood favorite for over a decade, with a mix of locals and students nursing pints of Guinness and cocktails named after dead poets.

Barcibo Enoteca
WINE BAR
(Map p78; 212-595-2805; www.barciboenoteca.com; 2020 Broadway, cnr 69th St; 4:30pm-11:30am Tue-Fri, from 3:30pm Sat-Mon; 1/2/3 to 72nd St) Just north of Lincoln Center, this casual chic marble-table spot is ideal for sipping, with a long list of vintages from all over Italy, including 40 different varieties sold by the glass.

Upper East Side

Auction House
BAR
(Map p78; 212-427-4458; 300 E 89th St; 7:30pm-4am; 4/5/6 to 86th St) Dark maroon doors lead into a candlelit hangout that's perfect for a relaxing drink. Victorian-style couches and overstuffed chairs are strewn about the wood-floored rooms, while oil paintings of nudes adorn the exposed brick walls.

Penrose
BAR
(Map p78; 212-203-2751; www.penrosebar.com; 1590 Second Ave, btwn 82nd & 83rd Sts; 3pm-4am Mon-Thu, noon-4am Fri, 10:30am-4am Sat & Sun; 4/5/6 to 86th St) The Penrose brings a dose of style to the Upper East Side, with craft beers, vintage mirrors, floral wallpaper and friendly bartenders setting the stage for fine evening among friends.

Brooklyn

★Maison Premiere
COCKTAIL BAR
(347-335-0446; www.maisonpremiere.com; 298 Bedford Ave, btwn 1st & Grand Sts, Williamsburg; 4pm-2am Mon-Fri, from 11am Sat & Sun; L to Bedford Ave) This old-timey place features a chemistry-lab-style bar full of syrups and essences and suspendered bartenders to mix them all up. The epic cocktail list includes more than 20 absinthe drinks and a raw bar provides a long list of snacks on the half shell.

Radegast Hall & Biergarten
BEER HALL
(718-963-3973; www.radegasthall.com; 113 N 3rd St, at Berry St, Williamsburg; noon-2am; L to Bedford Ave) This lively Austro-Hungarian beer hall in Williamsburg offers up a huge selection of Bavarian brews as well as a kitchen full of munchable meats.

Spuyten Duyvil
BAR
(718-963-4140; www.spuytenduyvilnyc.com; 359 Metropolitan Ave, btwn Havemayer & Roebling, Williamsburg; 5pm-late Mon-Fri, from noon Sat & Sun; L to Lorimer St, G to Metropolitan Ave) Red ceilings, vintage maps on the walls and tattered furniture recede into the background when perusing the staggering beer selection of this hallowed brew parlor. A leafy patio opens in good weather.

Hotel Delmano
COCKTAIL BAR
(718-387-1945; www.hoteldelmano.com; 82 Berry St, at N 9th St; 5pm-late Mon-Fri, frm 2pm Sat & Sun; L to Bedford Ave) This low-lit cocktail bar aims for the speakeasy vibe, with old mirrors, unpolished floorboards and vintage chandeliers.

Pine Box Rock Shop
BAR
(718-366-6311; www.pineboxrockshop.com; 12 Grattan St, btwn Morgan Ave & Bogart St, Bushwick; 4pm-4am Mon-Fri, from 2pm Sat & Sun; L to Morgan Ave) The cavernous Pine Box is

GAY & LESBIAN NYC

Few cities make being queer so utterly fabulous. New York's vibrant gay scene is spread across Hell's Kitchen, Chelsea and the West Village, with an ever-expanding choice of gay and gay-friendly eateries, bars, clubs and shops. For nightlife, here are a few highlights:

Eastern Bloc (Map p66; ☎212-777-2555; www.easternblocnyc.com; 505 E 6th St, btwn Aves A & B, East Village; ⏰7pm-4am; [S] F to 2nd Ave) Though the theme may be 'Iron Curtain,' the drapery is most definitely velvet and taffeta at this East Village gay bar. Spring forth into the crowded sea of boys – some flirting with the topless barkeeps, others pretending not to stare at the retro '70s porno playing on the TVs.

Industry (Map p70; ☎646-476-2747; www.industry-bar.com; 355 W 52nd St, btwn Eighth & Ninth Aves, Midtown West; ⏰4pm-4am; [S] C/E, 1 to 50th St) One of the hottest gay bars in Hell's Kitchen, this slick 4000-sq-ft watering hole has handsome lounge areas, a pool table, and a stage for top-notch drag divas.

Therapy (Map p70; ☎212-397-1700; www.therapy-nyc.com; 348 W 52nd St, btwn Eighth & Ninth Aves, Midtown West; ⏰5pm-2am Sun-Thu, to 4am Fri & Sat; [S] C/E, 1 to 50th St) This long-running multilevel space still draws throngs to Hell's Kitchen with its nightly shows (from music to boylesque).

Flaming Saddles (Map p70; ☎212-713-0481; www.flamingsaddles.com; 793 Ninth Ave, btwn 52nd & 53rd Sts, Midtown West; ⏰3pm-4am Mon-Fri, noon-4am Sat & Sun; [S] C/E to 50th St) *Coyote Ugly* meets *Calamity Jane* at this Hell's Kitchen hangout, complete with studly bar-dancing barmen, aspiring urban cowboys and a rough 'n' ready vibe.

Marie's Crisis (Map p66; ☎212-243-9323; www.manhattan-monster.com; 59 Grove St, btwn Seventh Ave & Bleecker St, West Village; ⏰4pm-4am; [S] 1 to Christopher St-Sheridan Sq) One-time hooker hangout turned showtune piano bar. It's old-school fun, no matter how jaded you were when you went in.

Stonewall Inn (Map p66; ☎212-488-2705; www.thestonewallinnnyc.com; 53 Christopher St, West Village; ⏰2pm-4am; [S] 1 to Christopher St-Sheridan Sq) Site of the Stonewall riots in 1969, this historic bar draws varied crowds nightly for parties that cater to everyone under the rainbow flag.

Henrietta Hudson (Map p66; ☎212-924-3347; www.henriettahudson.com; 438 Hudson St, West Village; ⏰ 5pm-2am Mon & Tue, 4pm-4am Wed-Fri, 2pm-4am Sat & Sun; [S] 1 to Houston St) All sorts of cute young dykes, many from neighboring New Jersey and Long Island, storm this sleek 'bar & girl'. Varying theme nights bring in spirited DJs, who spin a mix of hip-hop, house and Latin beats.

a former Bushwick casket factory that has 16 drafts to choose from, as well as spicy, pint-sized Bloody Marys. Run by a friendly musician couple, the walls are filled with local artwork and a performance space in the back hosts regular gigs.

61 Local BAR
(☎718-875-1150; www.61local.com; 61 Bergen St, btwn Smith St & Boerum Pl, Cobble Hill; ⏰7am-late Mon-Fri, from 9am Sat & Sun; 📶; [S] F, G to Bergen) A roomy brick-and-wood hall in Cobble Hill manages to be both chic and warm, with large communal tables, a mellow vibe and a good selection of craft beers. There's a simple menu of charcuterie and other snacks.

Sunny's BAR
(☎718-625-8211; www.sunnysredhook.com; 253 Conover St, btwn Beard & Reed Sts, Red Hook; ⏰6pm-late Tue-Fri, from 2pm Sat, 4-11pm Sun; 🚌 B61 to Coffey & Conover Sts, [S] F, G to Carroll St) Way out in Red Hook, this super-inviting longshoreman bar – the sign says 'bar' – is straight out of *On the Waterfront*. Every Saturday at 10pm it hosts a foot-stomping bluegrass jam.

☆ Entertainment

Those with unlimited fuel and appetites can gorge themselves on a seemingly infinite number of entertainments – from Broadway shows to performance art in someone's Brooklyn living room, and everything in between. *New York* magazine and the weekend editions of the *New York Times* are great guides for what's on once you arrive.

Live Music

Joe's Pub LIVE MUSIC
(Map p66; ☎ 212-539-8778; www.joespub.com; Public Theater, 425 Lafayette St, btwn Astor Pl & 4th St; [S] R/W to 8th St-NYU, 6 to Astor Pl) Part cabaret theater, part rock and new-indie venue, this small and lovely supper club hosts a wonderful variety of styles, voices and talent.

Rockwood Music Hall LIVE MUSIC
(Map p66; ☎ 212-477-4155; www.rockwoodmusichall.com; 196 Allen St, btwn Houston & Stanton Sts; [S] F/V to Lower East Side-Second Ave) This bread-box-sized concert space features a rapid-fire flow of bands and singer/songwriters on three different stages. Many shows are free.

Pianos LIVE MUSIC
(Map p66; ☎ 212-505-3733; www.pianosnyc.com; 158 Ludlow St, at Stanton St; cover $8-10; ⏲ noon-4am; [S] F to 2nd Ave) A Lower East Side stalwart, two-story Pianos stages a mix of genres and styles, leaning more toward pop, punk and new wave, but throwing in some hip-hop and indie for good measure.

Bowery Ballroom LIVE MUSIC
(Map p66; ☎ 212-533-2111; www.boweryballroom.com; 6 Delancey St, at Bowery St; [S] J/Z to Bowery) This terrific, medium-sized venue has the perfect sound and feel for more blown-up indie-rock acts (Interpol, Belle & Sebastian, Morrissey).

Le Poisson Rouge LIVE MUSIC
(Map p66; ☎ 212-505-3474; www.lepoissonrouge.com; 158 Bleecker St; [S] A/C/E, B/D/F/M to W 4th St-Washington Sq) This Bleecker St basement club is one of the premier venues for experimental contemporary, from classical to indie rock to electro-acoustic.

Mercury Lounge LIVE MUSIC
(Map p66; ☎ 212-260-4700; www.mercuryloungenyc.com; 217 E Houston St btwn Essex & Ludlow Sts; cover charge $10-15; ⏲ 4pm-4am; [S] F/V to Lower East Side-2nd Ave) The Mercury dependably pulls in a new or comeback band that draws the downtown crowds.

Beacon Theatre LIVE MUSIC
(Map p78; www.beacontheatre.com; 2124 Broadway, btwn 74th & 75th Sts; [S] 1/2/3 to 72nd St) This Upper West Side venue hosts big acts in an environment that's more intimate than a big concert arena.

Radio City Music Hall CONCERT VENUE
(Map p70; ☎ 212-247-4777; www.radiocity.com; Sixth Ave, at W 50th St; [S] B/D, F, M to 47-50th Sts) The architecturally grand concert hall in Midtown hosts the likes of Tony Bennett, Kelly Clarkson and the famous Christmas spectacular.

Irving Plaza LIVE MUSIC
(Map p70; www.irvingplaza.com; 17 Irving Pl at 15th St; [S] L, N/Q/R/W, 4/5/6 to 14th St-Union Sq) A great 1000-seat setting for quirky mainstream acts.

Webster Hall CLUB
(Map p66; ☎ 212-353-1600; www.websterhall.com; 125 E 11th St, near Third Ave; ⏲ 10pm-4am Thu-Sat; [S] L, N/Q/R/W, 4/5/6 to 14th St-Union Sq) The granddaddy of dancehalls.

★ **Brooklyn Bowl** LIVE MUSIC
(☎ 718-963-3369; www.brooklynbowl.com; 61 Wythe Ave, btwn 11th & 12th Sts; ⏲ 6pm-2am Mon-Thu, to 4am Fri, noon-4am Sat, noon-2am Sun; [S] L to Bedford Ave, G to Nassau Ave) This 23,000-sq-ft venue inside the former Hecla Iron Works Company combines bowling, microbrews, food and groovy live music.

Bell House LIVE MUSIC
(www.thebellhouseny.com; 149 7th St, Gowanus; ⏲ 5pm-4am; 📶; [S] F, G, R to 4th Ave-9th St) A converted warehouse in the industrial neighborhood of Gowanus, the Bell House features live performances, indie rockers, DJ nights, comedy shows and burlesque parties.

Jalopy LIVE MUSIC
(www.jalopy.biz; 315 Columbia St, at Woodhull St, Red Hook; [S] F, G to Carroll St) This fringe Carroll Gardens/Red Hook banjo shop and bar features bluegrass, country and ukulele shows, including a feel-good Roots 'n' Ruckus show on Wednesday nights.

Music Hall of Williamsburg LIVE MUSIC
(www.musichallofwilliamsburg.com; 66 N 6th St, btwn Wythe & Kent Aves, Williamsburg; show $15-35; [S] L to Bedford Ave) This popular Williamsburg music venue is *the* place to see indie bands in Brooklyn. (For many groups traveling through New York, this is their one and only spot.)

Theater

In general, 'Broadway' productions are staged in the lavish, early 20th-century theaters surrounding Times Square.

Choose from current shows by checking print publications, or a website such as **Theater Mania** (☎ 212-352-3101;

www.theatermania.com). You can purchase tickets through Telecharge ($\boxed{\mathcal{J}}$ 212-239-6200; www.telecharge.com) and Ticketmaster ($\boxed{\mathcal{J}}$ 800-448-7849, 800-745-3000; www.ticketmaster.com) for standard ticket sales, or TKTS ticket booths (www.tdf.org/tkts; cnr Front & John Sts; ⊘11am-6pm Mon-Sat, to 4pm Sun; $\boxed{S}$ A/C to Broadway-Nassau; 2/3, 4/5, J/Z to Fulton St) for same-day tickets to a selection of Broadway and off-Broadway musicals at up to 50% off regular prices.

Some distinguished theaters:

★ **Public Theater**　　　THEATER

(Map p66; $\boxed{\mathcal{J}}$ 212-539-8500; www.publictheater.org; 425 Lafayette St, btwn Astor Pl & E 4th St; $\boxed{S}$ R/N to 8th St, 6 to Astor Pl) Excellent downtown venue that stages works by some of the best contemporary and classic playwrights.

★ **St Ann's Warehouse**　　　THEATER

($\boxed{\mathcal{J}}$ 718-254-8779; www.stannswarehouse.org; 45 Water St, Dumbo; $\boxed{S}$ A/C to High St) This avant-garde performance company hosts innovative theater and dance happenings that attract the Brooklyn literati.

PS 122　　　THEATER

(Map p66; $\boxed{\mathcal{J}}$ 212-477-5288; www.ps122.org; 150 First Ave at E 9th St) Catch dance shows, film screenings and various festivals for up-and-coming talents.

Playwrights Horizons　　　THEATER

(Map p70; $\boxed{\mathcal{J}}$ 212-279-4200; www.playwrightshorizons.org; 416 W 42nd St, btwn Ninth & Tenth Aves, Midtown West; $\boxed{S}$ A/C/E to 42nd St-Port Authority Bus Terminal) An excellent place to catch what could be the next big thing.

New York Theater Workshop　　　THEATER

(Map p66; $\boxed{\mathcal{J}}$ 212-460-5475; www.nytw.org; 79 E 4th St, btwn Second & Third Aves; $\boxed{S}$ F to 2nd Ave) A treasure to those seeking cutting-edge, contemporary plays with purpose.

Comedy

Comedy Cellar　　　COMEDY

(Map p66; $\boxed{\mathcal{J}}$ 212-254-3480; www.comedycellar.com; 117 MacDougal St btwn W 3rd & Minetta Ln; cover $12-24; $\boxed{S}$ A/C/E, B/D/F/M to W 4th St-Washington Sq) This long-established basement club in Greenwich Village is one of New York's best comedy venues.

Caroline's on Broadway　　　COMEDY

(Map p70; $\boxed{\mathcal{J}}$ 212-757-4100; www.carolines.com; 1626 Broadway, at 50th St; $\boxed{S}$ N/Q/R to 49th St, 1 to 50th St) A top spot to catch US comedy big guns and sitcom stars.

★ **Upright Citizens Brigade Theatre**　　　COMEDY

(Map p70; $\boxed{\mathcal{J}}$ 212-366-9176; www.ucbtheatre.com; 307 W 26th St btwn Eighth & Ninth Aves; cover $5-10; $\boxed{S}$ C/E to 23rd St) Improv venue featuring well-known, emerging and probably-won't-emerge comedians in a small basement theater nightly.

Cinemas

★ **Film Forum**　　　CINEMA

(Map p66; $\boxed{\mathcal{J}}$ 212-727-8110; www.filmforum.com; 209 W Houston St btwn Varick St & Sixth Ave; $\boxed{S}$ 1 to Houston St) The long and narrow theaters can't dent cineastes' love for this institution showing revivals, classics and documentaries.

JAZZ

From bebop to free improvisation, in classic art-deco clubs and at intimate jam sessions, New York remains one of the great capitals of jazz.

Smalls (Map p66; $\boxed{\mathcal{J}}$ 212-252-5091; www.smallsjazzclub.com; 183 W 4th St; 7:30pm-12:30am cover $20, after $10; ⊘4pm-4am; $\boxed{S}$ 1 to Christopher St-Sheridan Sq) is a subterranean jazz dungeon that rivals the world-famous **Village Vanguard** (Map p66; $\boxed{\mathcal{J}}$ 212-255-4037; www.villagevanguard.com; 178 Seventh Ave at 11th St; cover around $30; ⊘7:30pm-12:30am; $\boxed{S}$ 1/2/3 to 14th St) in terms of sheer talent. Of course, the latter has hosted every major star of the past 50 years; there's a one-drink minimum and a serious no-talking policy.

Heading uptown, **Dizzy's Club Coca-Cola: Jazz at the Lincoln Center** (Map p78; $\boxed{\mathcal{J}}$ tickets to Dizzy's Club Coca-Cola 212-258-9595, tickets to Rose Theater & Allen Room 212-721-6500; www.jazz.org; Time Warner Center, Broadway at 60th St; $\boxed{S}$ A/C, B/D, 1 to 59th St-Columbus Circle), one of Lincoln Center's three jazz venues, has stunning views overlooking Central Park and nightly shows featuring top lineups. Further north on the Upper West Side, check out the **Smoke Jazz & Supper Club-Lounge** (Map p78; $\boxed{\mathcal{J}}$ 212-864-6662; www.smokejazz.com; 2751 Broadway, btwn W 105th & 106th Sts; ⊘5:30pm-3am Mon-Sat, 11am-3am Sun; $\boxed{S}$ 1 to 103rd St), which gets crowded on weekends.

IFC Center CINEMA
(Map p66; ☎212-924-7771; www.ifccenter.com; 323 Sixth Ave at 3rd St; tickets $14; [S]A/C/E, B/D/F/M to W 4th St-Washington Sq) This three-screen art-house cinema shows new indies, cult classics and foreign films.

Landmark Sunshine Cinema CINEMA
(Map p66; ☎212-260-7289; www.landmarktheatres.com; 143 E Houston St, btwn Forsyth & Eldridge Sts; [S]F/V to Lower East Side-Second Ave) Housed in a former Yiddish theater; shows first-run indies.

Anthology Film Archives CINEMA
(Map p66; ☎212-505-5181; www.anthologyfilmarchives.org; 32 Second Ave, at 2nd St; [S]F to 2nd Ave) Film studies majors head to this school-house-like building for independent and avant-garde cinema.

Performing Arts

★Carnegie Hall LIVE MUSIC
(Map p70; ☎212-247-7800; www.carnegiehall.org; W 57th St at Seventh Ave, Midtown West; 🕐tours 11:30am, 12:30pm, 2pm & 3pm Mon-Fri, 11:30am & 12:30pm Sat, 12:30pm Sun Oct-May; [S]N/Q/R to 57th St-7th Ave) Since 1891, the historic Carnegie Hall has hosted performances by the likes of Tchaikovsky, Mahler and Prokofiev, as well as Stevie Wonder, Sting and João Gilberto. It's mostly closed in July and August.

★Brooklyn Academy of Music PERFORMING ARTS
(BAM; Map p72; www.bam.org; 30 Lafayette Ave, at Ashland Pl, Fort Greene; 📶; [S]D, N/R to Pacific St, B, Q, 2/3, 4/5 to Atlantic Ave) Sort of a Brooklyn version of the Lincoln Center – in its all-inclusiveness rather than its vibe, which is much edgier – the spectacular academy also hosts everything from modern dance to opera, cutting-edge theater and music concerts.

Symphony Space LIVE MUSIC
(Map p78; ☎212-864-5400; www.symphonyspace.org; 2537 Broadway, btwn 94th & 95th Sts; [S]1/2/3 to 96th St) A multigenre space with several facilities in one. This Upper West Side gem is home to many performance series as well as theater, cabaret, comedy, dance and world-music concerts throughout the week.

Shopping

Home to myriad fashion boutiques, flea markets, booksellers, record stores, antique shops and gourmet grocers – New York City is quite simply one of the best shopping destinations on the planet.

Downtown

Downtown's coolest offerings are in NoLita (just east of SoHo), the East Village and the Lower East Side. SoHo has more expensive and equally fashionable stores, while Broadway from Union Sq to Canal St is lined with big retailers like H&M and Urban Outfitters, as well as dozens of jeans and shoe stores.

ABC Carpet & Home HOMEWARES, GIFTS
(Map p70; ☎212-473-3000; www.abchome.com; 888 Broadway, at 19th St; 🕐10am-7pm Mon-Wed, Fri & Sat, to 8pm Thu, noon-6pm Sun; [S]L, N/Q/R, 4/5/6 to 14th St-Union Sq) A mecca for home designers, this beautifully curated, six-level store heaves with housewares, designer jewelry and global gifts.

★Strand Book Store BOOKS
(Map p66; ☎212-473-1452; www.strandbooks.com; 828 Broadway at 12th St; 🕐9:30am-10:30pm Mon-Sat, from 11am Sun; [S]L, N/Q/R, 4/5/6 to 14th St-Union Sq) The city's preeminent bibliophile warehouse, selling new and used books.

★Century 21 FASHION
(Map p62; www.c21stores.com; 22 Cortlandt St btwn Church St & Broadway; 🕐7:45am-9pm Mon-Fri, 10am-9pm Sat, 11am-8pm Sun; [S]A/C, J/Z, 2/3, 4/5 to Fulton St, N/R to Cortlandt St) A four-level department store loved by New Yorkers of every income. It's shorthand for designer bargains.

Other Music MUSIC
(Map p66; ☎212-477-8150; www.othermusic.com; 15 E 4th St, btwn Lafayette St & Broadway; 🕐11am-9pm Mon-Fri, noon-8pm Sat, noon-7pm Sun; [S]6 to Bleecker St) This indie-run CD store feeds its loyal fan base with a clued-in selection of offbeat lounge, psychedelic, electronica, indie rock etc, available new and used. There's also vinyl.

Obscura Antiques ANTIQUES
(Map p66; ☎212-505-9251; 207 Ave A, btwn 12th & 13th Sts; 🕐noon-8pm Mon-Sat, to 7pm Sun; [S]L to 1st Ave) Browsing here is like stepping into a small cabinet of curiosities with taxidermy, tiny (dental?) instruments, old poison bottles, glass eyes, cane toad purses, anatomical drawings and other great gift ideas for that special someone (your mother-in-law?).

Idlewild Books BOOKS
(Map p70; ☎212-414-8888; www.idlewildbooks.com; 12 W 19th St, btwn Fifth & Sixth Aves; 🕐noon-7.30pm Mon-Thu, to 6pm Fri & Sat, to 5pm Sun; [S]L, N/Q/R, 4/5/6 to 14th St-Union Sq) This wondrous

WATCHING SPORTS IN NYC

The uber-successful **New York Yankees** (☑718-293-6000, tickets 877-469-9849; www.yankees.com; tickets $20-300) play at **Yankee Stadium** (Map p72; ☑718-293-4300, tickets 212-926-5337; E 161st St at River Ave, the Bronx; tours $20; Ⓢ B/D, 4 to 161st St-Yankee Stadium), while the more historically beleaguered **New York Mets** (☑718-507-8499; www.mets.com; tickets $19-130) play at **Citi Field** (Map p72; 126th St, at Roosevelt Ave, Flushing, Queens; Ⓢ7 to Mets-Willets Pt). For less-grand settings but no-less-pleasant outings, check out the minor-league **Staten Island Yankees** (☑718-720-9265; www.siyanks.com; tickets $12) at **Richmond County Bank Ballpark** (75 Richmond Tce, Staten Island ⛴ Staten Island Ferry) or the **Brooklyn Cyclones** (☑718-372-5596; www.brooklyncyclones.com; tickets from $15, $10 on Wed) at **MCU Park** (Map p72; 1904 Surf Ave & W 17th St, Coney Island; Ⓢ D/F, N/Q to Coney Island-Stillwell Ave).

For basketball, you can get courtside with the NBA's **New York Knicks** (www.nyknicks.com; tickets from $109) at **Madison Square Garden** (Map p70; www.thegarden.com; Seventh Ave btwn 31st & 33rd Sts, Midtown West; Ⓢ1/2/3 to 34th St-Penn Station), called the 'mecca of basketball,' and the **Brooklyn Nets** (www.nba.com/nets; tickets from $15), who play at the **Barclays Center** (www.barclayscenter.com; cnr Flatbush & Atlantic Aves, Prospect Heights; Ⓢ B/D, N/Q/R, 2/3, 4/5 to Atlantic Ave) near downtown Brooklyn. Also playing at Madison Square Garden, the women's WNBA league team **New York Liberty** (☑212-564-9622, tickets 212-465-6073; www.nyliberty.com; tickets $10-85) provides a more laid-back time.

New York City's NFL (pro-football) teams, the **Giants** (☑201-935-8222; www.giants.com) and **Jets** (☑800-469-5387; www.newyorkjets.com), share **MetLife Stadium** (Map p72; www.metlifestadium.com; 1 MetLife Stadium Dr; ⛟351 from Port Authority, 🚆NJ Transit from Penn Station to Meadowlands) in East Rutherford, NJ.

---

travel bookshop stocks fiction, travelogues, history, cookbooks, foreign-language titles and other stimulating fare.

Economy Candy CANDY
(Map p66; ☑212-254-1531; www.economycandy.com; 108 Rivington St at Essex St; ⊘9am-6pm Tue-Fri, 10am-6pm Sat-Mon; Ⓢ F, J/M/Z to Delancey St-Essex St) Bringing sweetness to the 'hood since 1937, this candy shop is stocked with floor-to-ceiling goods in package and bulk.

🏠 Midtown & Uptown

Midtown's Fifth Ave and the Upper East Side's Madison Ave have the famous high-end fashion and clothing by international designers.

Uniqlo FASHION
(Map p70; www.uniqlo.com; 666 Fifth Ave, at 53rd St; ⊘10am-9pm Mon-Sat, 11am-8pm Sun; Ⓢ E, M to Fifth Ave-53rd St) Uniqlo is Japan's answer to H&M and this is its showstopping 89,000-sq-ft flagship megastore. The forte here is affordable, fashionable, quality basics, from tees and undergarments, to Japanese denim, cashmere sweaters and high-tech parkas.

Macy's DEPARTMENT STORE
(Map p70; www.macys.com; 151 W 34th St, at Broadway; ⊘9am-9.30pm Mon-Fri, 10am-9:30pm

Sat, 11am-9.30pm Sun; Ⓢ R/T/F/M N/Q/R to 34th St-Herald Sq) The grande dame of Midtown department stores sells everything from jeans to kitchen appliances.

Bloomingdale's DEPARTMENT STORE
(Map p78; www.bloomingdales.com; 1000 Third Ave, at E 59th St, Midtown East; ⊘10am-8:30pm Mon-Sat, 11am-7pm Sun; 🚻; Ⓢ4/5/6 to 59th St, N/Q/R to Lexington Ave-59th St) Uptown, the sprawling, overwhelming Bloomingdale's is akin to the Metropolitan Museum of Art for shoppers.

ℹ️ Information

INTERNET ACCESS

Free wi-fi hot spots include Bryant Park, Battery Park, Tompkins Square Park, Union Square Park, Lincoln Center and many cafes in the city.

New York Public Library (Map p84; ☑212-930-0800; www.nypl.org; E 42nd St, at Fifth Ave; Ⓢ B, D, F or M to 42nd St-Bryant Park) Free wi-fi and internet terminals.

MEDIA

WFUV-90.7FM The area's best alternative-music radio station.

WNYC 820AM or 93.9FM National Public Radio's local affiliate.

Daily News (www.nydailynews.com) A daily tabloid, leaning toward the sensational.

New York (www.newyorkmagazine.com) Weekly featuring NYC-centric news and listings for the arts and culture-oriented reader.

New York Post (www.nypost.com) Famous for spicy headlines, celebrity scandal-laden Page Six and good sports coverage.

New York Times (www.nytimes.com) The 'Gray Lady' is the newspaper of record for readers throughout the US.

NY1 (www.ny1.com) This is the city's all-day news station on Time Warner Cable's Channel 1.

Village Voice (www.villagevoice.com) The weekly tabloid is still a good resource for events, clubs and music listings.

MEDICAL SERVICES

New York County Medical Society (☑ 212-684-4670; www.nycms.org) Makes doctor referrals by phone, based on type of problem and language spoken.

Tisch Hospital (New York University Langone Medical Center; ☑ 212-263-7300; 550 First Ave; ☑ 24hr) Medical care downtown.

Travel MD (☑ 212-737-1212; www.travelmd.com) A 24-hour house-call service for travelers and residents.

TOURIST INFORMATION

New York City & Company (Map p70; ☑ 212-484-1222; www.nycgo.com; 151 W 34th St btwn Seventh Ave & Broadway, at 53rd St; ☑ 9am-7pm Mon-Fri, 10am-7pm Sat, 11am-7pm Sun; ☑ 1/2/3, A/C/E to 34th St-Herald Sq) The official information service of the Convention & Visitors Bureau, it has helpful multilingual staff. Other branches include Chinatown (Map p62; cnr Canal, Walker & Baxter Sts; ☑ 10am-6pm; ☑ 6/J/N/Q to Canal St) and Lower Manhattan (Map p62; City Hall Park at Broadway; ☑ 9am-6pm Mon-Fri, 10am-5pm Sat & Sun; ☑ 4/5/A/C to Fulton St).

ⓘ Getting There & Away

AIR

Three major airports serve New York City. The biggest is **John F Kennedy International Airport** (JFK; ☑ 718-244-4444; www.panynj.gov), in the borough of Queens, which is also home to **La Guardia Airport** (LGA; www.panynj.gov/aviation/lgaframe). **Newark Liberty International Airport** (EWR; ☑ 973-961-6000; www.panynj.gov), across the Hudson River in Newark, NJ, is another option.

BUS

The massive and confusing **Port Authority Bus Terminal** (Map p70; ☑ 212-564-8484; www.panynj.gov; 41st St at Eighth Ave; ☑ A, C, E, N, Q, R, 1, 2, 3, & 7) is the gateway for buses into and out of Manhattan.

A number of comfortable and reliably safe bus companies depart from curbside locations, including **BoltBus** (☑ 877-265-8287; www.boltbus.com) and **Megabus** (☑ 877-462-6342; us.megabus.com), linking NYC to Philadelphia ($9-15, two hours), Boston ($17-36, 4¼ hours) and Washington, DC ($16-36, 4½ hours); there's free wi-fi on board.

CAR & MOTORCYCLE

Note that renting a car in the city is expensive, starting at about $80 a day including tax for a compact car.

FERRY

Seastreak (www.seastreak.com) goes to Sandy Hook (return $45) in New Jersey from Pier 11 near Wall St and from E 35th St. There's also a weekend, summer-only ferry to Martha's Vineyard (one-way/round-trip $165/240, five hours) in Massachusetts from E 35th St.

TRAIN

Penn Station (33rd St, btwn Seventh & Eighth Aves; ☑ 1/2/3/A/C/E to 34th St-Penn Station) is the departure point for all **Amtrak** (☑ 800-872-7245; www.amtrak.com) trains, including service to Boston (3¾ hours) and Washington, DC (3 hours). Also arriving into Penn Station (NYC), as well as points in Brooklyn and Queens, is the **Long Island Rail Road** (LIRR; ☑ 718-217-5477; www.mta.info/lirr; furthest zone one-way off-peak/peak $27/34), which serves several hundred-thousand commuters each day. New Jersey Transit (p131) also operates trains from Penn Station (NYC), with services to the suburbs and the Jersey Shore. Another option for getting into New Jersey, but strictly to points north of the city such as Hoboken and Newark, is the **New Jersey PATH** (☑ 800-234-7284; www.panynj.gov/path), which runs trains on a separate-fare system ($2.75) along the length of Sixth Ave, with stops at 34th, 23rd, 14th, 9th and Christopher Sts and the World Trade Center station.

The only train line that departs from Grand Central Terminal, Park Ave at 42nd St, is the **Metro-North Railroad** (☑ 511; www.mta.info/mnr), which serves the northern city suburbs, Connecticut and locations throughout the Hudson Valley.

ⓘ Getting Around

TO/FROM THE AIRPORT

Taxis from JFK to Midtown cost a $52 flat rate (plus toll and tip). You'll have to pay the metered fare from LaGuardia (around $30) and Newark Airport (around $55, not including toll and tip).

A cheaper but slow option to/from JFK is the AirTrain ($5 one way), which connects to subway lines into the city ($2.75; coming from the city, take the Far Rockaway–bound A train). A faster route to Penn Station is to take the AirTrain to Jamaica

Station ($5 one way) and hopping aboard the LIRR ($10, one way) train, which only makes a few stops before arriving at Penn Station in the city.

To/from Newark, the AirTrain links all terminals to a New Jersey Transit train station, which connects to Penn Station in NYC ($13 one way combined NJ Transit/AirTrain ticket).

For LaGuardia, you can take the M60 bus, which goes to/from Manhattan across 125th St in Harlem and makes stops along Broadway on the Upper West Side.

All three airports are also served by express buses ($16) and shuttle vans (from $20); such companies include the **NYC Airporter** (www.nycairporter.com), which leaves every 30 or so minutes for Grand Central Terminal, Port Authority Terminal and Penn Station; and **Super Shuttle Manhattan** (www.supershuttle.com), which picks you (and others) up anywhere, on demand, with a reservation.

BICYCLE

NYC has a bike-sharing program, called Citi Bike (p87).

CAR & MOTORCYCLE

Traffic and parking are always problematic and anxiety-provoking. If you do drive, be aware of local laws: you can't make a right on red (like you can in the rest of the state), and every other street is one way.

FERRY

The **East River Ferry** (www.eastriverferry.com) service (one way $4, every 20 minutes) connects spots in Brooklyn (Greenpoint, North and South Williamsburg and Dumbo) and Queens (Long Island City) with Manhattan (Pier 11 at Wall St and E 35th St). And **New York Water Taxi** (☑ 212-742-1969; www.nywatertaxi.com; hop-on-hop-off service 1-day $31) has a fleet of zippy yellow boats that run along several different routes, including a hop-on, hop-off weekend service around Manhattan and Brooklyn.

ℹ️ METROCARDS

All buses and subways use the yellow-and-blue MetroCard, which you can purchase or add value to at an easy-to-use automated machine at any station. You can use cash or an ATM or credit card. Just select 'Get new card' and follow the prompts. The card itself costs $1. You then select one of two types of Metro-Card. The 'pay-per-ride' is $2.75 per ride, though the MTA tacks on an 11% bonus on MetroCards over $5.50. Tip: if you're not from the US, when the machine asks for your zipcode, enter 99999.

PUBLIC TRANSPORTATION

The New York subway system, run by the **Metropolitan Transport Authority** (MTA; ☑ 718-330-1234; www.mta.info), is iconic, cheap ($2.75 per ride, regardless of the distance traveled), round-the-clock and often the fastest and most reliable way to get around the city. It's also safer and (a bit) cleaner than it used to be.

TAXI

Current taxi fares are $2.50 for the initial charge (first one-fifth mile), 50¢ each additional one-fifth mile, as well as per 60 seconds of being stopped in traffic, $1 peak surcharge (weekdays 4pm to 8pm), and 50¢ night surcharge (8pm to 6am daily). Tips are expected to be 10% to 15%; minivan cabs can hold five passengers. You can only hail a cab that has a lit light on its roof.

NEW YORK STATE

Upstate New York – anywhere outside the city, essentially – and downstate share virtually nothing but a governor and dysfunctional legislature in the capital, Albany. This incongruity produces political gridlock, but it's a blessing for those who cherish a hike up a mountaintop as much as a bar crawl around the Lower East Side. Upstate is defined largely by its inland waterways. The Hudson River heads straight north from NYC, like an escape route. From Albany, the 524-mile Erie Canal cuts due west to Lake Erie, by the world-famous Niagara Falls and Buffalo, a lively city despite its epic winters. And the St Lawrence River forms the border with Canada in the under-the-radar Thousand Islands area. Another patch of water is the Finger Lakes region, and the college town of Ithaca, known for its wines. Add in the rugged backcountry of the Adirondack mountains and the lush farms of the Catskills, plus miles and miles of sandy beaches along Long Island, and it's easy to understand why people leave the city, never to return.

ℹ️ Information

511 NY (☑ in NY 511, elsewhere 800-465-1169; www.511ny.org) Statewide traffic and transit info, with weather advisories and more.

I Love NY (☑ 800-225-5697; www.iloveny.com) Comprehensive state tourism bureau.

New York State Office of Parks, Recreation and Historic Preservation (☑ 518-474-0456; www.nysparks.com) Camping, lodging and general info on all state parks. Reservations can be made up to nine months in advance.

NEW YORK FACTS

Nicknames Empire State, Excelsior State, Knickerbocker State

Population 19.8 million

Area 54,5226 sq miles, including water

Capital city Albany (population 98,400)

Other cities New York City (population 8.4 million)

Sales tax 4%, plus additional municipal taxes (total usually around 8%)

Birthplace of Poet Walt Whitman (1819–92), President Theodore Roosevelt (1858–1919), President Franklin D Roosevelt (1882–1945), first lady Eleanor Roosevelt (1884–1962), painter Edward Hopper (1882–1967), movie star Humphrey Bogart (1899–1957), comic Lucille Ball (1911–89), filmmaker Woody Allen (b 1935), actor Tom Cruise (b 1962), athlete Michael Jordan (b 1963), pop star Jennifer Lopez (b 1969)

Home of Six Nations of the Iroquois Confederacy, first US cattle ranch (1747, in Montauk, Long Island), US women's suffrage movement (1848), Erie Canal (1825)

Politics Democratic governor Andrew Cuomo, NYC overwhelmingly Democratic, upstate more conservative

Famous for Niagara Falls (half of it), the Hamptons, wineries, Hudson River

Unusual river Genesee River is one of the few rivers in the world that flows south–north, from south-central New York into Lake Ontario at Rochester

Driving distances NYC to Albany 150 miles, NYC to Buffalo 375 miles

Long Island

Technically, the 118 miles of Long Island includes the boroughs of Brooklyn and Queens on the west edge, but in the popular imagination, 'Long Island' begins only where the city ends, in a mass of traffic-clogged expressways and suburbs that every teenager aspires to leave. (Levittown, the first planned 1950s subdivision, is in central Nassau County.) But there's plenty more out on 'Lawn-guy-land' (per the local accent). Push past the central belt of 'burbs to windswept dunes, glitzy summer resorts, fresh farms and wineries, and whaling and fishing ports established in the 17th century. Then you'll see why loyalists prefer the nickname 'Strong Island.'

❶ Getting There & Around

Thanks to the Long Island Rail Road (p111), which runs three lines from NYC's Penn Station to the furthest east ends of the island, it's possible to visit without a car. Additionally, the **Hampton Jitney** (☑212-362-8400; www.hamptonjitney. com; one way $30) and **Hampton Luxury Liner** (☑631-537-5800; www.hamptonluxuryliner. com; one way $45) buses connect Manhattan to various Hamptons' villages and Montauk; the former also picks up in Brooklyn, and runs to the North Fork. With a car, however, it is easier to visit several spots on the island in one go. I-495, aka the Long Island Expwy (LIE), runs down the middle of the island – but avoid rush hour, when it's commuter hell.

North Shore

Relatively close to NYC, the so-called 'Gold Coast' is where the Vanderbilts, Chryslers and Guggenheims, not to mention Gatsby, summered in the roaring '20s. Now it's mostly suburban, but a few remnants of the age survive, along with some pretty wild spots. Near the town of Port Washington, **Sands Point Preserve** (☑516-571-7901; www.sandspointpreserve.org; 127 Middle Neck Rd, Sands Point; parking $10, Falaise tours $10; ☉8am-5pm, to 7pm Jul-Aug, Falaise tours hourly noon-3pm Thu-Sun mid-May–Nov), formerly the Guggenheim estate, covers forest and a beautiful bayfront beach; the visitor center is in Castle Gould, built in the 19th century by railroad heir Howard Gould. Visitors can also tour the 1923 mansion Falaise, one of the few intact and furnished mansions from that era. Further east, beyond the town of Oyster Bay, **Sagamore Hill** (☑516-922-4788; www.nps.gov/sahi; 12 Sagamore Hill Rd, Oyster Bay; museum & grounds free, house tours adult/child $10/free; ☉9am-5pm Wed-Sun) is where president

Theodore Roosevelt and his wife raised six children. A nature trail from behind the museum ends at a picturesque beach. The 23-room Victorian home was rehabilitated in 2015; it's accessible by guided tour, but can get very crowded in summer.

South Shore

Easily accessible by public transit, these beaches can get crowded, but they're a fun day out. The train runs directly to **Long Beach**, just over the border from NYC, and its main town strip is busy with ice-cream shops, bars and eateries. Just east, **Jones Beach State Park** (☑ 516-785-1600; www.nysparks.com; 1 Ocean Pkwy; parking $10, lounge chairs $10, pools adult/child $3/1, mini-golf $5; ⊙ 10am-7pm, though hours vary by area) is a 6-mile microcosm of beach culture, with surfers, old-timers, local teens and gay men each claiming patches of sand. Access is by train to Freeport, then a bus; in July and August, LIRR sells a combo ticket (round-trip $20.50).

The next barrier island east is **Fire Island National Seashore** (☑ 631-687-4750; www.nps.gov/fiis; dune camping permit $20) FREE. Except for the west end, where a bridge crosses the bay to **Robert Moses State Park**, the island is accessible only by **ferry** (☑ 631-665-3600; www.fireislandferries.com; 99 Maple Ave, Bay Shore; one-way adult/child $10/5) and is free of cars – regulars haul their belongings on little wagons instead. The island is edged with a dozen or so tiny hamlets, mostly residential. Party center Ocean Beach Village and quieter Ocean Bay Park (take ferries from the Bayshore LIRR stop) have a few hotels; Cherry Grove and the Pines (ferries from Sayville) are gay enclaves, also with hotels. Lodging is not cheap; **Seashore Condo Motel** (☑ 631-583-5860; www.seashorecondomotel.com; Bayview Ave, Ocean Bay Park; r from $219; ☎) is a typical no-frills option. At the east end (ferry from Patchogue), there is camping with services at **Watch Hill** (☑ 631-567-6664; www.watchhillfi.com; tent sites $25; ⊙ early May-late Oct) and backcountry camping in the dunes beyond. Bring plenty of cash to the island.

The Hamptons

This string of villages is a summer escape for Manhattan's wealthiest, who zip to mansions by helicopter. Mere mortals take the Hampton Jitney and chip in on rowdy rental houses. Behind the glitz is a long cultural history, as noted artists and writers have lived here.

The area is small, connected by often traffic-clogged Montauk Hwy. **Southampton**, to the west, has many of the nightclubs, as well as good museums. Its sweeping beaches are gorgeous; in summer nonresidents can park only at Coopers Beach (per day $40) and Road D (free). **Bridgehampton** has its share of boutiques and fine restaurants; it's where you turn north to **Sag Harbor**, a one-time whaling town with pretty, narrow old streets. **East Hampton** is where the highest-profile celebrities party – and sometimes act, in plays at **Guild Hall** (☑ 631-324-0806; www.guildhall.org; 158 Main St; ⊙ museum 11am-5pm Jul-Aug, Fri-Mon only Sep-Jun) FREE.

⊙ Sights

Parrish Art Museum MUSEUM
(☑ 631-283-2118; www.parrishart.org; 279 Montauk Hwy, Water Mill; adult/child $10/free, Wed free; ⊙ 10am-5pm Wed-Mon, to 8pm Fri) In a sleek long barn designed by Herzog & de Meuron, this institution spotlights local artists such as Jackson Pollock, Willem de Kooning and Chuck Close.

For more Pollock, make reservations to see his nearby paint-drizzled **studio and home** (☑ 631-324-4929; 830 Springs-Fireplace Rd, East Hampton; adult/child $10/5; ⊙ tours hourly 11am-4pm Thu-Sat May-Oct).

Shinnecock Nation Cultural Center & Museum MUSEUM
(☑ 631-287-4923; www.shinnecockmuseum.com; 100 Montauk Hwy, Southampton; adult/child $15/8.50; ⊙ 11am-5pm Thu-Sun; ♿) The 1300-member Shinnecock tribe runs this museum and living-history village, one of the few reminders of Native American life on Long Island.

Southampton Historical Museum MUSEUM
(☑ 631-283-2494; www.southamptonhistorical museum.org; 17 Meeting House Ln, Southampton; adult/child $4/free; ⊙ 11am-4pm Wed-Sun Mar-Dec) Before the Hamptons was the Hamptons, there was this clutch of nicely maintained old buildings, including a whaling captain's mansion.

🛏 Sleeping & Eating

Bridge Inn MOTEL $$
(☑ 631-537-2900; www.hamptonsbridgeinn.com; 2668 Montauk Hwy, Bridgehampton; r from $209; ❄🛜🏊) Get your foot in the Hamptons door at this clean and sleek motel, tucked behind hedges like all the neighboring mansions.

Provisions CAFE $
(cnr Bay & Division Sts, Sag Harbor; sandwiches $9-16; ⊙8am-6pm; ✐) Find gourmet sustenance at this natural foods market with take-out sandwiches.

Candy Kitchen DINER $
(2391 Montauk Hwy, Bridgehampton; mains $5-12; ⊙7am-7:30pm; ✦) An antidote to glitz, this corner diner has been serving good soups, ice cream and other staples since 1925.

Nick & Toni's MEDITERRANEAN $$$
(☑631-324-3550; 136 North Main St, East Hampton; pizzas $17, mains $24-42; ⊙6-10pm Wed-Mon, to 11pm Fri & Sat, also 11:30am-2:30pm Sun) A good bet for celebrity sightings, this institution serves Italian food with ingredients from nearby farms.

Montauk

Toward the east-pointing tip of Long Island's South Fork, you'll find the mellow town of Montauk, aka 'The End,' and the famous surfing beach **Ditch Plains**. With the surfers have come affluent hipsters and boho-chic hotels like Surf Lodge and Ruschmeyer's. But the area is still far less of a scene than the Hamptons, with proudly blue-collar residents and casual seafood restaurants.

The road divides after **Napeague State Park**, with Montauk Hwy going direct; Old Montauk Hwy bears right to hug the water. The roads converge at the edge of central Montauk and Fort Pond, a small lake. Two miles east is a large inlet called Lake Montauk, with marinas strung along its shore. Another 3 miles is **Montauk Point State Park**, with the wind-whipped **Montauk Point Lighthouse** (☑631-668-2544; www.montauklighthouse.com; 2000 Montauk Hwy; adult/child $10/4; ⊙10:30am-5:30pm in summer, reduced hours rest of year), active since 1796.

🛏 Sleeping

Hither Hills State Park CAMPGROUND $
(☑631-668-2554; www.nysparks.com; 164 Old Montauk Hwy; tent & RV sites weekday/weekend $56/64, reservation fee $9) These wooded dunes have 168 sites for tents and RVs; online reservations are a must.

Ocean Resort Inn HOTEL $$
(☑631-668-2300; www.oceanresortinn.com; 95 S Emerson Ave; r/ste from $135/185; ❄🤖) All rooms at this small, L-shaped hotel open onto a large porch or balcony. It's walking distance to the beach and the main town.

Sunrise Guesthouse GUESTHOUSE $$
(☑631-668-7286; www.sunrisebnb.com; 681 Old Montauk Hwy; r $130, ste $195; ❄🤖) A good old-school option a few miles west of town, just across the road from the beach.

🍴 Eating & Drinking

Lobster Roll SEAFOOD $$
(1980 Montauk Hwy, Amagansett; mains $14-28; ⊙11:30am-10pm summer) 'Lunch' is the sign to look for on the roadside west of Montauk, marking the clam-and-lobster shack that's been in operation since 1965.

Cyril's Fish House SEAFOOD $$
(2167 Montauk Hwy, Amagansett; mains $15-22; ⊙11am-7pm summer) As much an outdoor party as a seafood shack, this place puts the islands in Long Island with its signature Bailey's banana coladas (aka BBCs).

★**Westlake Fish House** SEAFOOD $$
(☑631-668-3474; 352 W Lake Dr; mains $21-36; ⊙noon-9pm Thu-Sun, to 10pm Fri & Sat; ✦) In the marina of the same name, this is a great place for seafood, all caught the same day.

Montauket BAR
(88 Firestone Rd; ⊙from noon Thu-Sun) Experts agree: this is the best place to watch the sun go down on Long Island.

North Fork & Shelter Island

The North Fork of Long Island is known for its farmland and vineyards – bucolic, though weekends can draw rowdy limo-loads on winery crawls. Still, Rte 25, the main road through the towns of **Jamesport**, **Cutchogue** and **Southold**, is pretty and edged with farm stands.

The largest town on the North Fork is **Greenport**, a laid-back place with working fishing boats, a history in whaling and an old carousel in its Harbor Front Park. It's compact and easily walkable from the LIRR station. If you're driving, you can carry on to **Orient**, with its sandy point, and **Orient Beach State Park** (☑631-323-2440; 40000 Main Rd, Orient; per car $8; ⊙from 8am year-round, swimming only Jul-Aug), a slip of a peninsula with clean beaches and a calm bay for kayaking.

Like a little pearl in Long Island's claw, **Shelter Island** rests between the North and South Forks. **North Ferry** (☑631-749-0139; www.northferry.com; on foot $2, with bicycle $3, with car one-way/same-day return $11/16; ⊙every 10-20min 6am-midnight) connects to Greenport; **South Ferry** (☑631-749-1200;

www.southferry.com; on foot $1, with bicycle $4, vehicle & driver one-way/same-day round-trip $14/17; ⊙ every 15min 6am-1:30am Jul-Aug, to midnight Sep-Jun) runs to North Haven, near Sag Harbor. The island is a smaller, lower-key version of the Hamptons, with a touch of maritime New England. Parking is limited; long Crescent Beach, for instance, has spots only by permit. If you don't mind a few hills, it's a nice place to visit by bike. On the southern part of the island, 2000-acre Mashomack Nature Preserve (☑631-749-1001; www.nature.org; Rte 114; ⊙9am-5pm Mar-Sep, to 4pm Oct-Feb) is great for kayaking.

🛏 Sleeping & Eating

Greenporter Hotel   BOUTIQUE HOTEL $$
(☑631-477-0066; www.greenporterhotel.com; 326 Front St, Greenport; r from $199; ❋ 🤶 ❄) An older motel redone with white walls and Ikea furniture, this place is good value for the area. Its on-site restaurant, Cuvée, is very good.

North Fork Table & Inn   INN $$$
(☑631-765-0177; www.nofoti.com; 57225 Main Rd, Southold; r from $250) A favorite foodies' escape, this four-room inn has an excellent farm-to-table restaurant (three-course prix-fixe $75), run by alums of the esteemed Manhattan restaurant Gramercy Tavern.

Four & Twenty Blackbirds   DESSERTS $
(☑347-940-6717; 1010 Village Ln, Orient; pie slice $5; ⊙8am-6pm Wed-Mon mid-May–Sep) An outpost of the Brooklyn pie experts, with delectable fruit and chocolate varieties.

Love Lane Kitchen   MODERN AMERICAN $$
(☑631-298-8989; 240 Love Ln, Mattituck; mains lunch $12-15, dinner $16-30; ⊙8am-9:30pm Thu-Mon, 7am-4pm Tue & Wed) At this popular place on a cute street, local meat and vegetables drive the global-diner menu: burgers, of course, plus spicy chickpeas and duck tagine.

Claudio's   SEAFOOD $$$
(☑631-477-0627; 111 Main St, Greenport; mains $25-36; ⊙11:30am-9pm Sun-Thu, to 10pm Fri & Sat) A Greenport legend, owned by the Portuguese Claudio family since 1870. For a casual meal, hit Claudio's Clam Bar, on the nearby pier.

Hudson Valley

Just north of New York City, the vistas of the Hudson River inspired the 19th-century Hudson River School of landscape painting

as well as scores of wealthy families, who built grand estates here. Today it's dotted with farms and parks, and populated by longtime nature-lovers and more recent city escapees. The towns closer to NYC are more populated and suburban but easy to reach by Metro-North train; the further north you go, the more rural (and sometimes desolate) the towns can be.

❶ Getting There & Away

Metro-North Railroad (p111) runs as far north as Poughkeepsie out of NYC's Grand Central; another line runs through New Jersey and gives access to Harriman. Amtrak (www.amtrak.com) also stops in Rhinecliff (for Rhinebeck), Poughkeepsie and Hudson. For New Paltz, you'll need the bus: Short Line (☑212-736-4700; www.shortlinebus.com), which also does a day trip to Storm King.

Lower Hudson Valley

Several magnificent homes can be found near Tarrytown and Sleepy Hollow, east of the Hudson. For arts, beeline north to formerly industrial Beacon, revived as an outpost of the avant-garde. For a taste of the outdoors, the village of Cold Spring offers good hiking on Bull Hill and other trails not far from the train station. If you have a car, cross to the Hudson's west bank to explore Harriman State Park (☑845-947-2444; www.nysparks.com; Seven Lakes Dr, Ramapo; parking per car $8) and adjacent Bear Mountain State Park (☑845-786-2701; www.nysparks.com; Palisades Pkwy, Bear Mountain; parking per car $8 summer; ⊙8am-dusk), with views down to Manhattan from its 1303ft peak.

◎ Sights

Sunnyside   HISTORIC BUILDING
(☑914-591-8763, Mon-Fri 914-631-8200; www.hudsonvalley.org; 3 W Sunnyside Ln, Sleepy Hollow; adult/child $12/6; ⊙tours 10:30am-3:30pm Wed-Sun May-Oct; 🚼) Washington Irving, famous for tales such as *The Legend of Sleepy Hollow*, built this imaginative home. Tour guides in 19th-century costume tell good stories.

Kykuit   HISTORIC SITE
(☑914-366-6900; www.hudsonvalley.org; 381 N Broadway, Sleepy Hollow; tours adult/child $25/23; ⊙tour hours vary May-early Nov, closed Tue) This onetime Rockefeller summer home has a remarkable collection of modern art.

West Point HISTORIC SITE
(US Military Academy Visitors Center; ☑ 845-938-2638; www.usma.edu; 2107 N South Post Rd, West Point; 1hr tours adult/child $14/11; ⊙ 9am-4:45pm) A bus tours the scenic grounds of this US Army academy, which has been training officers since 1802. The museum (free) is a must for military buffs.

Storm King Art Center GALLERY
(☑ 845-534-3115; www.stormking.org; 1 Museum Rd, New Windsor; adult/child $15/8; ⊙ 10am-5:30pm Wed-Sun Apr-Oct, to 4:30pm Nov) ✐ This 500-acre sculpture park, established in 1960, has works by Mark di Suvero, Andy Goldsworthy and others, all carefully placed in nooks formed by the land's natural breaks and curves.

★ **Dia Beacon** GALLERY
(Beacon; ☑ 845-440-0100; www.diaart.org; 3 Beekman St, Beacon; adult/child $12/free; ⊙ 11am-6pm Thu-Mon Apr-Oct, 11am-4pm Fri-Mon Nov-Mar) This former factory houses monumental contemporary sculpture by the likes of Richard Serra and Dan Flavin, plus ever-changing, always surprising installations.

✗ **Eating**

The Hop MODERN AMERICAN $$
(☑ 845-440-8676; 554 Main St, Beacon; sandwiches $15, mains $24-36; ⊙ noon-10pm Wed-Mon, to midnight Fri & Sat) Craft beer and cider is this casual spot's raison d'être, and it goes perfectly with local cheeses and hearty creations like the Huff-n-Puff, a pork burger with ham and bacon.

Blue Hill at Stone Barns MODERN AMERICAN $$$
(☑ 914-366-9600; www.bluehillfarm.com; 630 Bedford Rd, Pocantico Hills; prix fixe $218; ⊙ cafe & farm 10am-4:30pm Wed-Sun, restaurant 5-10pm Wed-Sat, from 1pm Sun) ✐ Go maximum locavore at chef Dan Barber's farm (it also supplies his Manhattan restaurant). By day, visitors are welcome to tour the fields and pastures, and there's a very basic cafe.

New Paltz

On the west bank of the Hudson is New Paltz, a conclave of hippies old and young. You'll find a campus of the State University of New York here, as well as historic **Huguenot St**, a strip of early 18th-century stone houses. It's also the gateway to Shawangunk Ridge (aka 'The Gunks'), for hiking and some of the best rock climbing in the eastern US, particularly in the **Mohonk Preserve** (☑ 845-255-0919; www.mohonkpreserve.org; 3197 Rte 55, Gardiner;

day pass hikers/climbers & cyclists $12/17; ⊙ 9am-5pm) and nearby **Minnewaska State Park Preserve** (☑ 845-255-0752; www.nysparks.com; 5281 Rte 44-55, Kerhonkson; per vehicle $10). For climbing instruction and equipment, contact **Alpine Endeavors** (☑ 877-486-5769; www.alpineendeavors.com; Rosendale).

To stay in style in the area, visit the landmark Victorian-era castle that is the **Mohonk Mountain House** (☑ 845-255-1000; www.mohonk.com; 1000 Mountain Rest Rd; d all-inclusive from $558; ✲ ☎ ☒ ☼); its all-inclusive rates cover a huge range of activities. Day guests are welcome for hiking for the price of a meal (reserve ahead) or an entrance fee ($26/21 per adult/child per day, less on weekdays). At the other end of the spectrum is the excellent **New Paltz Hostel** (☑ 845-255-6676; www.newpaltzhostel.com; 145 Main St; dm $30, r from $70).

Poughkeepsie & Hyde Park

The largest town in the Hudson Valley, **Poughkeepsie** (puh-*kip*-see) is home to Vassar, a college that was women-only until 1969, as well as an IBM office – once the 'Main Plant' where notable early computers were built. Most visitors head north to pastoral **Hyde Park** for Roosevelt lore or to visit the 'other CIA' – the Culinary Institute of America, the country's most prestigious cooking school. It also has an old **drive-in movie theater** (☑ 845-229-4738; www.hydeparkdrivein.com; 4114 Albany Post Rd, Hyde Park; adult/child $9/6; ⊙ mid-Apr–mid-Sep) and

---

🛈 APPALACHIAN TRAIL ACCESS

The Appalachian Trail covers a total of 390 miles in New York, New Jersey and Pennsylvania. One of the most accessible stretches is through **Harriman and Bear Mountain State Parks**, on nicely varied but not too strenuous terrain. The trail passes close to Metro-North's Harriman Station (though no other services there). In New Jersey, the trail runs along the east side of the **Delaware Water Gap**, and the town of the same name, actually in Pennsylvania, is very hiker-friendly. The majority of the route (230 miles) is in Pennsylvania, where it reaches the Appalachian Mountains for which it's named. The trail runs north of Pennsylvania Dutch Country, and about 20 miles west of **Gettysburg**.

Roller Magic (✆845-229-6666; www.hydepark-rollermagic.com; 4178 Albany Post Rd, Hyde Park; admission $7, skate rental $2; ⊙7:30-10:30pm Fri, also 1-4:30pm Sat & Sun) skating rink, home of the local roller derby team.

◉ Sights

Walkway Over the Hudson
PARK

(✆845-454-9649; www.walkway.org; 61 Parker Ave, Poughkeepsie; ⊙7am-sunset) Once a railroad bridge crossing the Hudson, this is now the world's longest pedestrian bridge – 1.28 miles – and a state park.

Franklin D Roosevelt Home
HISTORIC BUILDING

(✆845-486-7770; www.nps.gov/hofr; 4097 Albany Post Rd, Hyde Park; adult/child $18/free, museum only $9/free; ⊙9am-5pm) FDR served three terms as president and instituted lasting progressive programs; he also made the decision to drop the A-bomb on Japan to end WWII. A tour of his home, relatively modest considering his family wealth, is interesting, but it can be unpleasantly crowded in summer.

In this case, better to focus on the excellent museum, built around FDR's own library, where he recorded his groundbreaking radio program of 'fireside chats.' You can also visit Val-Kill (✆845-229-9422; www.nps.gov/elro; 54 Valkill Park Rd, Hyde Park; adult/child $10/free; ⊙9am-5pm daily May-Oct, Thu-Mon Nov-Apr), Eleanor Roosevelt's cottage hideaway.

Vanderbilt Mansion
HISTORIC SITE

(✆877-444-6777; www.nps.gov/vama; 119 Vanderbilt Park Rd, Hyde Park; grounds free, tours adult/child $10/free; ⊙9am-5pm) The railroad-wealthy Vanderbilt family's summer 'cottage' is a beaux arts spectacle, with most of the original furnishings.

🛏 Sleeping & Eating

★Roosevelt Inn
MOTEL $

(✆845-229-2443; www.rooseveltinnofhydepark.com; 4360 Albany Post Rd, Hyde Park; r $85-115; ⊙closed Jan & Feb) A fantastically clean roadside motel; its pine-paneled 'rustic' rooms are a bargain.

Journey Inn
INN $$

(✆845-229-8972; www.journeyinn.com; 1 Sherwood Pl, Hyde Park; r $160-215) Across the road from the Vanderbilt Mansion, this country home has tastefully designed theme rooms (Kyoto, Tuscany, Roosevelt) and better-than-average breakfast.

Bocuse
MODERN FRENCH $$$

(✆845-451-1012; www.ciarestaurantgroup.com; 1946 Campus Dr, Hyde Park; mains $26-31; ⊙11:30am-1pm & 6-8:30pm Tue-Sat) One of several excellent student-run restaurants at the Culinary Institute of America, this place does traditional truffles and modern tableside tricks like liquid-nitrogen ice cream. Lunch is good value. For a snack, head for Apple Pie Cafe (✆845-905-4500; sandwiches $10-15; ⊙7:30am-5pm Mon-Fri).

Rhinebeck & Hudson

Midway up the east side of the Hudson, Rhinebeck has a charming main street. The surrounding land is farms and wineries, as well as the holistic Omega Institute (✆877-944-2002; www.eomega.org; 150 Lake Dr), for every kind of healing and yoga, and super-liberal Bard College. As a result, Rhinebeck cafes tend to host interesting conversations. The northernmost town in the river valley, Hudson is still a bit ragged but has been partially remade by a small community of ex-NYC artists and writers. Warren St is lined with antiques shops, design stores, galleries and cafes.

◉ Sights

Old Rhinebeck Aerodrome
MUSEUM

(✆845-752-3200; www.oldrhinebeck.org; 9 Norton Rd, Red Hook; adult/child Mon-Fri $10/3, airshows adult/child $20/5, flights $75; ⊙10am-5pm May-Oct, airshows from 2pm Sat & Sun) This museum has a collection of vintage planes that date back as far as 1909. On weekends you can watch an airshow or take a ride in an old biplane.

★Olana
HISTORIC SITE

(✆518-828-0135; www.olana.org; 5720 Rte 9G, Hudson; tours adult/child $12/free, grounds per vehicle $5; ⊙grounds 8am-sunset daily, tours 10am-4pm Tue-Sun May-Oct, self-guided tour only 2-5pm Sat) In pure aesthetic terms, this is finest of the Hudson Valley mansions, as landscape painter Frederic Church designed every detail, inspired by his travels in the Middle East and his appreciation of the river view.

🛏 Sleeping & Eating

Wm Farmer and Sons
GUESTHOUSE $$

(✆518-828-1635; www.wmfarmerandsons.com; 20 S Front St, Hudson; r from $149; ✵🕿) This rustic-chic former boarding house, steps from the train station and a short walk to Warren St, has rough-hewn furniture and claw-foot tubs. Its restaurant gets high marks.

Helsinki
MODERN AMERICAN **$$**

(☑ 518-828-4800; www.helsinkihudson.com; 405 Columbia St, Hudson; mains $13-25; ⊙ 5-10pm Thu-Tue) This restored carriage house is a sort of clubhouse for the valley's working artists. A music venue showcases rock, jazz and even global touring acts, while the restaurant does locally sourced cuisine like garlicky kale salads.

Catskills

This mountainous region west of the Hudson Valley hosts a mix of cultures, both manmade and natural. The romantic image of mossy gorges and rounded peaks, as popularized by Hudson Valley School painters, encouraged a preservation movement; in 1894 the state constitution was amended so that thousands of acres are 'forever kept as wild forest lands.'

In the 20th century, the Catskills became synonymous with so-called 'borscht belt' hotels, summer escapes for middle-class NYC Jews. Those hotels have all closed, but Jewish communities still thrive in many towns – as does a back-to-the-land, hippie ethos on numerous small farms. In the past decade, more sophisticated places have opened, catering to nostalgic NYC hipsters in search of weekends away. In the fall, this is the closest place to NYC with really dramatic colors in the trees.

❶ Getting There & Around

Having a car is near essential; be sure you have a paper map, as the 'forever wild' ethos of the forest preserve means mobile-phone service is often nonexistent.

There is some bus service: the most useful is **Trailways** (☑ 800-858-8555; www.trailwaysny.com), from NYC through Kingston to Woodstock ($28, three hours) and Phoenicia ($32.25, 3½ hours).

Route 28 & Around

Starting off I-87, this road cuts through the heart of the Catskills and past some of the best places to eat and sleep in the area. Before the road narrows, it passes glittering **Ashokan Reservoir**, one source for NYC's drinking water. In denser forest is **Phoenicia**, a one-street town that's a pleasant place for a meal and a splash in the creek.

In **Arkville**, you can turn north on Rte 30 through **Roxbury**. Then head back east on Rte 23, which passes through colorfully painted **Tannersville**, an only-in-the-Catskills collision of skiers from nearby Hunter Mountain and Orthodox Jewish vacationers. A few miles east is the mile-long trail to New York's tallest waterfalls, **Kaaterskill Falls**; the trail starts near a horseshoe curve in Rte 23A.

🏃 Activities

Town Tinker Tube Rental WATER SPORTS
(☑ 845-688-5553; www.towntinker.com; 10 Bridge St, Phoenicia; tubes per day $15, package incl transportation $25; ▣) Visit this outfitter for everything you need to ride an inner tube down wet and wild (and cold!) Esopus Creek.

Belleayre Beach SWIMMING
(☑ 845-254-5202; 33 Friendship Manor Rd, Pine Hill; per person/car $3/10; ⊙ 10am-6pm mid-Jun–Labor Day, to 7pm Sat & Sun) At the base of Belleayre ski area, this lake is a popular and refreshing swimming spot.

🛌 Sleeping

Phoenicia Lodge MOTEL **$**
(☑ 845-688-7772; www.phoenicialodge.com; 5987 Rte 28, Phoenicia; r from $90, cottage from $110; ❋ 🛜 ❋) This classic roadside motel has cozy, wood-paneled rooms and a touch of mid-century modern decor. Groups can opt for a cottage or suite.

★ Roxbury Motel BOUTIQUE HOTEL **$$**
(☑ 607-326-7200; www.theroxburymotel.com; 2258 County Rd 41, Roxbury; r $158-550; ❋ 🛜) Every room is a work of art: sleep in a glam version of a Flintstones cave, Oz' Emerald City or even a dreamy cream pie. (A couple of more subdued rooms are available for $100.) Breakfast is continental but generous, and there's a full spa.

🍴 Eating

★ Phoenicia Diner AMERICAN **$**
(5681 Rte 28, Phoenicia; mains $9-12; ⊙ 7am-5pm Thu-Mon; ☑) Farm-fresh and fabulous, this roadside place is a must for all-day breakfast and nourishing versions of club sandwiches and burgers.

Last Chance Cheese AMERICAN **$$**
(☑ 518-589-6424; 6009 Main St, Tannersville; mains $9-20; ⊙ 11am-midnight Fri & Sat, to 9pm Sun, to 4pm Mon) This four-decade-old institution is part roadhouse with live bands, part candy store and part restaurant, serving hearty meals.

THE OTHER WOODSTOCK

Bethel Woods Center for the Arts
(☑ 866-781-2922; www.bethelwoodscenter.org; 200 Hurd Rd; museum adult/child $15/6; ☉ museum 10am-7pm daily May-Sep, 10am-5pm Thu-Sun Oct-Apr) The site of the Woodstock Music & Art Fair, on Max Yasgur's farm outside Bethel, is 70 miles from the town of Woodstock. It's now home to an amphitheater with great summer concerts and an evocative museum dedicated to the hippie movement and the 1960s.

Peekamoose   MODERN AMERICAN **$$$**
(☑ 845-254-6500; 8373 Rte 28, Big Indian; mains $20-36; ☉ 4-10pm Thu-Mon) The finest restaurant in the Catskills, this renovated farmhouse has been promoting local products for more than a decade. The main dining room can feel a bit austere; some regulars prefer the cozier bar.

Woodstock & Saugerties

A minor technicality: the 1969 music *festival* was actually held in Bethel, an hour away. Nonetheless, the *town* of Woodstock still cultivates the free spirit of that era, with rainbow tie-dye style and local grassroots everything, from radio to movies to a farmers market (Wednesdays in summer; fittingly billed as a 'farm festival'). Just 7 miles east, Saugerties is not nearly as quaint and feels by comparison like the big city, but the lighthouse on the point in the Hudson is well worth a visit.

For a very rural drive, head to **West Saugerties** (FYI, rock aficionados: site of Big Pink, the house made famous by Bob Dylan and the Band) and take Platte Clove Rd (Cty Rd 16) northwest. The seven winding miles are some of the most scenic in the Catskills. The road eventually emerges around Tannersville.

◉ Sights

Opus 40   SCULPTURE PARK
(☑ 845-246-3400; www.opus40.org; 50 Fite Rd, Saugerties; adult/child $10/3; ☉ 11am-5:30pm Thu-Sun May-Sep) Beginning in 1938, artist Harvey Fite worked for nearly four decades to coax an abandoned quarry into an immense work of land art, all sinuous walls, canyons and pools.

Saugerties Lighthouse   LIGHTHOUSE
(☑ 845-247-0656; www.saugertieslighthouse.com; 168 Lighthouse Dr, Saugerties; tours suggested donation adult/child $5/3; ☉ sunrise-sunset, tours noon-3pm Sun summer) **FREE** A half-mile nature trail leads to this 1869 landmark on the point where Esopus Creek joins the Hudson. You can also stay the night in the lighthouse's two-room B&B ($225), but you must book at least six months ahead.

⊨ Sleeping & Eating

White Dove Rockotel   INN **$$**
(☑ 845-306-5419; www.thewhitedoverockotel.com; 148 Tinker St, Woodstock; r $135-169, ste $255-325; ☎) A couple of Phish fans run this purple-painted Victorian. The four party-ready rooms are decorated with psychedelic concert posters, record players and vintage vinyl.

Cucina   ITALIAN **$$**
(☑ 845-679-9800; 109 Mill Hill Rd, Woodstock; mains $16-26; ☉ 5am-late, from 11am Sat & Sun) Sophisticated seasonal Italian fare, including thin-crust pizzas, in a farmhouse with a large communal table.

Finger Lakes

Stretching across west-central New York, the rolling hills are cut through with 11 long narrow lakes – the eponymous fingers. The Finger Lakes region is an outdoor paradise, as well as the state's premier wine-growing region, with more than 80 vineyards.

❶ Getting There & Around

Ithaca is the region's major hub: **Short Line** (www.coachusa.com; 710 W State St) has eight daily departures from NYC ($53.50, five hours). **Ithaca Tompkins Regional Airport** (ITH; ☑ 607-257-0456; www.flyithaca.com; 1 Culligan Dr) has direct flights to Detroit, Newark and Philadelphia. For renting a car in the area, however, you may find cheaper in Rochester or Syracuse.

Ithaca & Cayuga Lake

An idyllic home for college students and first-wave hippies, Ithaca, on the southern tip of Cayuga Lake, is the largest town around the Finger Lakes. With art-house cinemas, good eats and great hiking ('Ithaca is gorges' goes the slogan, for all the surrounding canyons and waterfalls), it's both a destination in itself and a convenient halfway point between NYC and Niagara Falls.

The center of Ithaca is a pedestrian street called the Commons. On a steep hill above is Ivy League Cornell University, founded in 1865, with a small business strip at the campus's front gates, called Collegetown. The drive from Ithaca up scenic Rte 89 to Seneca Falls, at the north end of Cayuga Lake, takes about an hour.

For maps and other info, head to the **Visit Ithaca Information Center** (✆607-272-1313; www.visitithaca.com; 904 E Shore Dr).

⊙ Sights & Activities

Exploring Ithaca's gorges can start in town, at **Cascadilla Gorge**, where the trail starts a few blocks from the Commons and climbs to campus. Or head north to **Taughannock Falls State Park** (✆607-387-6739; www.nysparks.com; 1740 Taughannock Blvd, Trumansburg; per car $7), where you can rent a canoe on the lake, or **Buttermilk Falls State Park** (✆607-273-5761; www.nysparks.com; 112 E Buttermilk Falls Rd; per car $7) and **Robert H Treman State Park** (✆607-273-3440; www.nysparks.com; 105 Enfield Falls Rd; per car $7), both south of town. All have stunning waterfalls, camping space and swimming holes, open in high summer; the one at Robert H Treman is especially large and popular. Birders shouldn't miss **Sapsucker Woods** (✆800-843-2473; www.birds.cornell.edu; 159 Sapsucker Woods Rd; ⊙visitor center 8am-5pm Mon-Thu, to 4pm Fri, 9:30am-4pm Sat, 11am-4pm Sun Apr-Dec only) FREE, managed by Cornell's world-renowned ornithology department.

Herbert F Johnson Museum of Art MUSEUM
(✆607-255-6464; www.museum.cornell.edu; 114 Central Ave; ⊙10am-5pm Tue- Sun) FREE Inside the brutal IM Pei building is an eclectic collection, pleasantly crowded on the walls and ranging from medieval wood carvings to modern masters. There's a nice view from the veranda, and just down the hill behind is Fall Creek, with a scenic bridge across it.

Sciencenter MUSEUM
(✆607-272-0600; www.sciencenter.org; 601 1st St; adult/child $8/6; ⊙10am-5pm Tue-Sat, from noon Sun; ☺) The local children's museum, where the definition of science includes both compost and mini-golf.

Women's Rights National Historical Park MUSEUM
(✆315-568-0024; www.nps.gov/wori; 136 Fall St, Seneca Falls; ⊙9am-5pm Wed-Sun) FREE In the quiet, post-industrial town of Seneca Falls is the chapel where Elizabeth Cady Stanton and friends declared in 1848 that 'all men and women are created equal,' the first step toward suffrage. The adjacent museum tells the story, including the complicated relationship with abolition.

LOCAL KNOWLEDGE

FINGER LAKES WINERIES

With its cool climate and short growing season, the Finger Lakes region is similar to Germany's Rhine valley, and is similarly strong in off-dry whites such as Riesling. More than 80 wineries make it easy to spend a day sipping. It pays to pack a picnic lunch; food options at wineries are limited. A few to try:

Cayuga & Seneca Lakes

Lucas Vineyards (www.lucasvineyards.com; 3862 Cty Rd 150, Interlaken; ⊙10:30am-6pm Jun-Aug, to 5:30pm Mon-Sat Sep-May) One of the pioneer wineries in the region.

Sheldrake Point Winery (www.sheldrakepoint.com; 7448 Cty Rd 153, Ovid; ⊙10am-5:30pm Apr-Oct, 11am-5pm Fri-Mon Nov-Mar) Lake views and award-winning Chardonnays.

Hazlitt 1852 Vineyards (5712 Rte 414, Hector; ⊙11am-5pm) Long-established, with a solid Pinot Noir.

Keuka Lake

Keuka Spring Vineyards (www.keukaspringwinery.com; 243 E Lake Rd, Penn Yan; ⊙10am-5pm Apr-Nov, Sat & Sun only Dec-Mar) Just south of Penn Yan, a local favorite in a pastoral setting.

Dr Konstantin Frank (www.drfrankwines.com; 9749 Middle Rd, Hammondsport; ⊙9am-5pm Mon-Sat, from noon Sun) Don't miss the rkatsiteli, an acidic and floral white.

Keuka Lake Vineyards (www.klvineyards.com; 8882 Cty Rd 76, Hammondsport; ⊙10am-5pm May-Nov, Fri-Sun only Dec-Apr) Try the vignoles.

WORTH A TRIP

CORNING

An hour's drive southwest of Ithaca is the town of Corning, put on the map by Corning Glass Works, a company most Americans associate with sturdy Corningware plates but which now excels in industrial materials of all kinds. Here, the massive **Corning Museum of Glass** (☏ 800-732-6845; www.cmog.org; 1 Museum Way; adult/child $18/free; ⊙ 9am-5pm, to 8pm Memorial Day-Labor Day; ♿) presents the substance as both art and science, illustrated through live glass-blowing demonstrations and workshops to make your own glass crafts. Just over the river, in the former city hall, is the **Rockwell Museum of Western Art** (☏ 607-937-5386; www.rockwellmuseum.org; 111 Cedar St; adult/child $10/free; ⊙ 9am-5pm, to 8pm summer; ♿), a varied collection from beautiful pottery to contemporary Native American work. It's a manageable size, and a combination ticket with the glass museum ($25) makes it an easy add-on.

Corning is a pretty town, still energetic thanks to the corporate headquarters here. Stroll Market St, around the corner from the Rockwell Museum, for coffee, snacks and a bit of shopping.

🛏 Sleeping

Perhaps due to Cornell's prestigious hotel school, local lodging is generally excellent, but, with one exception, not cheap. Budget travelers might also consider Keuka Lake.

Hillside Inn   HOTEL $
(☏ 607-272-9507; www.hillsideinnithaca.com; 518 Stewart Ave; r from $69; ❄ 🐾) A bit ramshackle, with rooms in odd corners, but homey. Plus, very close to campus (though a steep walk up from the Commons).

Frog's Way B&B   GUESTHOUSE $
(☏ 607-592-8402; www.frogsway-bnb.com; 211 Rachel Carson Way; r $100; 🐾) 🌿 Get the full green Ithaca experience at this house in Eco-Village, a planned community just west of town. Two rooms share a bathroom; breakfast is organic and local, of course.

★ William Henry Miller Inn   B&B $$
(☏ 607-256-4553; www.millerinn.com; 303 N Aurora St; r from $195; ❄ 🐾) Gracious and grand, and only a few steps from the Commons, this is a historic home with luxurious rooms – three have Jacuzzis – and a gourmet breakfast.

Buttonwood Grove Winery   CABIN $$
(☏ 607-869-9760; www.buttonwoodgrove.com; 5986 Rte 89, Romulus; r $140; ⊙ Apr-Nov; 🐾) The winery rents out four comfortably furnished log cabins, all with lake views. Slightly rustic and remote – you can see the stars at night.

Inn on Columbia   INN $$
(☏ 607-272-0204; www.columbiabb.com; 228 Columbia St; r from $195; ❄ 🐾) Several homes clustered in a quiet residential area, with a refreshing modern style.

🍴 Eating & Drinking

Restaurants with outdoor seats line North Aurora St south of Seneca St, around the corner from the Commons. Ithaca's **Farmers Market** (☏ 607-273-7109; www.ithacamarket.com; 545 3rd St; ⊙ Apr-Dec) is the region's standout; check the website for hours. Ithaca excels in natural elixirs – local mini-chain Gimme! Coffee for standard caffeine, **Mate Factor** (143 E State St; mains $9; ⊙ 9am-9pm Mon-Thu, to 3pm Fri, from noon Sun) for the South American upper and even **Sacred Root Kava Lounge** (☏ 607-272-5282; 139 W State St; ⊙ 4pm-midnight Mon-Sat) to chill in the Polynesian style.

Ithaca Bakery   DELI $
(☏ 607-273-7110; 400 N Meadow St; sandwiches $9; ⊙ 6am-8pm) An epic selection of pastries, smoothies, sandwiches and prepared food, serving Ithacans of every stripe. Ideal for picnic goods.

Glenwood Pines   BURGERS $
(☏ 607-273-3709; 1213 Taughannock Blvd; burgers $6; ⊙ 11am-10pm) If you work up an appetite hiking at Taughannock Falls, stop by this roadside restaurant for good burgers.

★ Moosewood Restaurant   VEGETARIAN $$
(☏ 607-273-9610; www.moosewoodcooks.com; 215 N Cayuga St; mains $8-18; ⊙ 11:30am-9pm; 🍴) Established in 1973, this near-legendary restaurant is run by a collective. It has a slightly upscale feel, with a full bar and global menu.

Felicia's Atomic Lounge & Cupcakery   COCKTAIL BAR
(☏ 607-273-2219; 508 W State St; ⊙ noon-midnight Tue-Thu, to 1am Fri, 10:30am-1am Sat, to

11pm Sun) Felicia's does a super-creative and locally sourced brunch on weekends, then serves up cocktails, snacks and live bands at night.

Seneca & Keuka Lakes

Pretty **Geneva**, at the northern tip of Seneca Lake, is a lively little town, thanks to the student population at Hobart & William Smith Colleges. South Main St is lined with impressive turn-of-the-century homes, and the restored 1894 **Smith Opera House** (☑315-781-5483; www.thesmith.org; 82 Seneca St) is a vibrant center for performing arts.

To the west, Y-shaped Keuka Lake is edged by two small state parks that keep it relatively pristine; it's a favorite for trout fishing. The nicest town for visitors is sweet little **Hammondsport**, on the southwest end. An old canal on the north end has a rustic bike trail to Seneca Lake.

🛏 Sleeping

Keuka Lakeside Inn   MOTEL **$$**
(☑607-569-2600; www.keukalakesideinn.com; 24 Water St, Hammondsport; r $120; 🌸🛜) What this place lacks in historic charm (it's a simple motel block), it more than makes up for in location, right on the edge of the water. The 17 rooms have all been redone since 2010, with a crisp style.

Belhurst Castle   INN **$$**
(☑315-781-0201; www.belhurst.com; 4069 West Lake Rd, Geneva; r $160-295; 🌸🛜) This 1880s lakefront folly is worth a stop just to see its ornate interior (its casual Stonecutter's restaurant has live music on weekends) and the gorgeous view. The best rooms in the main mansion have stained glass, heavy antique furniture and fireplaces. It's a popular wedding locale, so book ahead.

🍴 Eating & Drinking

★**Stonecat**   AMERICAN **$$$**
(☑607-546-5000; 5315 Rte 414, Hector; mains $23-31; ⊘noon-3pm & 5-9pm Wed-Sat, from 10:30am Sun May-Oct) This foodie haven on the southeast side of Seneca Lake is mostly casual but serious where it counts: smart service, impeccable local ingredients, and excellent wine and cocktails. Sunday brunch, with mellow live music and dishes like duck-confit eggs benedict, is popular, as is Wednesday for the snacky bar menu.

Microclimate   WINE BAR
(☑315-787-0077; 38 Linden St, Geneva; ⊘5-10pm Sun & Mon, 4:30pm-midnight Wed & Thu, to 1am Fri & Sat) This cool little wine bar serves tasting flights that compare locally produced varietals with their international counterparts.

The Adirondacks

The Adirondack Mountains may not compare in drama and height with mountains in the western US, but they make up for it in size, covering 9375 sq miles, from the center of the state up to the Canada border. And with 46 peaks over 4000ft high, this area is some of the most wild-feeling terrain in the east. Like the Catskills to the south, much of the Adirondacks' dense forest is protected by the state constitution, and it's a great place to see the color show of autumn leaves. Hiking, canoeing and backcountry camping are the most popular activities, and there's good fishing, along with power-boating on the bigger lakes.

ℹ Getting There & Around

Both **Greyhound** (☑800-231-2222; www.greyhound.com) and **Trailways** (☑800-858-8555; www.trailwaysny.com) serve various towns in the Adirondacks, though a car is essential for exploring widely. **Amtrak** (www.amtrak.com) runs a day to Ticonderoga ($68, five hours) and Westport ($68, six hours), on Lake Champlain, with a bus connection to Lake Placid ($93, seven hours); once there, you can take the town shuttle to activities.

Lake George

The gateway to the Adirondacks is a tourist town with arcades and paddle-wheel boat rides on the crystalline, 32-mile-long lake. Small motels and mini-resorts line Rte 9 all the way to the village of **Bolton Landing**; a nice older one on the lakefront in town is **Lake Crest Inn** (☑518-668-3374; www.lakecrestinn.com; 376 Canada St; r from $119; 🌸🛜🐾); its clean rooms have, shall we say, vintage style. For perfectly fried seafood and massive lobster rolls, visit **Saltwater Cowboy** (☑518-685-3116; 164 Canada St; mains $11-28; ⊘11am-9pm).

A major draw in the area: the wonderfully secluded state-maintained **campgrounds** (☑800-456-2267; www.dec.ny.gov/outdoor; tent sites $28) on the lake's numerous islands. You'll need to reserve ahead and rent your own power boat or canoe. If canoeing, focus on sites in the southern end of the Narrows

DON'T MISS

LOCAL MUSEUMS

Adirondack Museum (📞518-352-7311; www.adkmuseum.org; 9097 Rte 30, Blue Mountain Lake; adult/child $18/6; ⏲10am-5pm late May–mid-Oct; 🖐) Set on 30 acres, this museum has creative exhibits on the mountains' human-centered stories, from mining and logging industries to quirky hermits and Victorian tourists. You can easily spend half a day here.

Wild Center (📞518-359-7800; www.wildcenter.org; 45 Museum Dr, Tupper Lake; adult/child $20/13; ⏲10am-6pm late May-early Sep, to 5pm Sep–mid-Oct, to 5pm Fri-Sun May; 🖐) Dedicated to local ecosystems, this hands-on museum has everything from rare frogs to live river otters. Outdoors is a trail to the river and, new in 2015, the Wild Walk, connected platforms and bridges in the treetops, with amazing views. Ticket prices are lower off-season; if you've also visited the Adirondack Museum, show your receipt for $2 discount.

Great Camp Sagamore (Sagamore Institute; 📞315-354-5311; www.greatcampsagamore. org; Sagamore Rd, Raquette Lake; tours adult/child $16/8; ⏲hours vary late May–mid-Oct) 'Great camps,' big compounds of log cabins built by wealthy families, were a popular way of vacationing in the Adirondacks. Many have been turned into kids' summer camps, but this one, a former Vanderbilt vacation estate on the west side of the Adirondacks, is open for tours, workshops and overnight stays on occasional history-oriented weekends.

area, a one- or two-hour paddle from Bolton Landing, and go on a weekday, when powerboat traffic is much lighter.

Lake Placid

The tiny resort town of Lake Placid is synonymous with snow sports – it hosted the Winter Olympics in 1932 and 1980. Elite athletes still train here; the rest of us can ride real bobsleds, speed-skate and more. Mirror Lake (the main lake in town) freezes thick enough for ice-skating, tobogganing and dogsledding. The town is also pleasant in summer, as the unofficial center of the High Peaks region of the Adirondacks. There are good hiking trails around, for instance on Rte 73 toward **Keene** – look for the pullout in Cascade Pass for a 2.2-mile hike to Cascade Peak.

⊙ Sights & Activities

Olympic Center   STADIUM
(Olympic Museum; 📞box office 518-523-3330, museum 518-302-5426; www.whiteface.com; 2634 Main St; museum adult/child $7/5, skating shows adult/child $10/8; ⏲10am-5pm, skating shows 4:30pm Fri, 7:30pm Sat; 🖐) This hockey stadium hosted the 1980 'Miracle on Ice', when the upstart US team trumped the unstoppable Soviets. This and more Olympic triumphs are covered in the museum. Year-round, there are usually figure-skating shows on Fridays and Saturdays.

Whiteface Mountain Toll Road   MOUNTAIN
(Veterans Memorial Hwy; www.whiteface.com; Cty Rd 18; car with driver $11, passenger $8; ⏲8:45am-5:30pm Jul–mid-Oct, Sat & Sun only May-Jun) Whiteface is the only peak in the Adirondacks accessible by car, with a neat castle-style lookout and cafe at the top. It can be socked in with clouds, making for an unnerving drive up, but when the fog clears, the 360-degree view is awe-inspiring.

Olympic Sports

One major draw at Lake Placid is the opportunity to play like an Olympian (or just watch athletes train). Most activities are managed by **Whiteface Mountain** (📞518-946-222; www.whiteface.com; 5021 Rte 86, Wilmington; full-day lift ticket adult/child $89/57) ski area (where the Olympic ski races were held) but located in other spots around the area. Among other activities, you can do a half-mile on the **bobsled** track ($90) or a modified **biathlon** (cross-country skiing and shooting; $55). A private group organizes **speed-skating** rental and tutorials ($20) at the Olympic Center. Many sports are modified for summer – bobsledding on wheels, for instance. For the very energetic, Whiteface's Olympic Sites Passport ticket ($35) can be a good deal, covering admission at sites (such as the tower at the **ski-jump** complex) and offering discounts on some activities.

🛏 Sleeping & Eating

⭐ Adirondack Loj LODGE $
(☑ 518-523-3441; www.adk.org; 1002 Adirondack Loj Rd; dm/r $60/169) The Adirondack Mountain Club runs this rustic retreat on the shore of Heart Lake. Lean-tos and cabins are also available, and trails take off in all directions.

Hotel North Woods HISTORIC HOTEL $$
(☑ 518-523-1818; www.hotelnorthwoods.com; 2520 Main St; r from $140; ✳🐾) Lake Placid's oldest hotel got a total rehab in 2015. Its stylish modern-rustic rooms have either lake views or balconies facing the forest.

ADK Corner Store SANDWICHES $
(☑ 518-523-1689; 188 Newman Rd; sandwiches from $4; ⊙ 5:30am-9pm) This general store caters to the early-start hiker with great breakfast sandwiches.

⭐ Chair 6 MODERN AMERICAN $$$
(☑ 518-523-3630; 5993 Sentinel Rd; breakfasts $12, dinner mains $26-34, five-course menu $60; ⊙ 8am-9pm Wed-Mon) So much flavor in such a tiny house: try venison dumplings for dinner, or sweet potato pancakes for breakfast.

Saranac Lake

A short drive from Lake Placid, this town is not so tourist-oriented, and gives a better idea of regular Adirondacks life. **St Regis Canoe Outfitters** (☑ 518-891-1838; www.canoeoutfitters.com; 73 Dorsey St) can provide gear, maps and tips for exploring the gemlike lakes to the north; you can even do a combo canoe-train trip with the **Adirondack Scenic Railroad** (☑ 800-819-2291; www.adirondack-rr.com; 42 Depot St; round-trip to Lake Placid adult/child $19/11). The town built up in the early 20th century as a retreat for tuberculosis patients, and it still has a sturdy, if slightly scruffy, main street. Check on the grand old **Hotel Saranac** (www.hotelsaranac.com; 100 Main St) – it was being renovated in 2015. If you prefer the wilderness, book at the excellent **White Pine Camp** (☑ 518-327-3030; www.whitepinecamp.com; 432 White Pine Rd, Paul Smiths; r from $165, cabins from $315), 14 miles north on Osgood Pond, one of the best places to stay in the Adirondacks.

Lake Champlain

This 125-mile lake divides New York from Vermont. The road along its eastern shore is exceptionally scenic – you may want to drive this way when going to or coming from Lake George.

◉ Sights & Activities

Fort Ticonderoga FORT
(☑ 518-585-2821; www.fortticonderoga.org; 100 Fort Ti Rd; adult/child $19.50/8; ⊙ 9:30am-5pm mid-May–mid-Oct) In a major victory in the American Revolution, the Green Mountain Boys took this fort from the British in 1775. With costumed guides, reenactments, a museum and hiking trails, it's possible to spend a full day here.

Crown Point State Historic Site FORT
(☑ 518-597-4666; www.nysparks.com; 21 Grandview Dr, Crown Point; museum adult/child $4/free; ⊙ grounds 9am-6pm, museum 9:30am-5pm Thu-Mon May–mid-Oct) The remains of two major 18th-century forts occupy a dramatic promontory where Lake Champlain narrows.

Ausable Chasm OUTDOORS
(☑ 518-834-7454; www.ausablechasm.com; 2144 Rte 9, Ausable; adult/child hiking $18/10, rafting $12/10; ⊙ 9am-4pm, to 5pm summer, to 3pm Dec-Mar; 🐾) This 2-mile-long fissure can be explored on foot or by raft – good to do with kids, for managed adventure. Incongruously, across the parking lot, there's also a free museum about the Underground Railroad.

🛏 Sleeping & Eating

Essex Inn INN $$$
(☑ 518-963-4400; www.essexinnessex.com; 2297 Main St, Essex; r from $250; ✳🐾) A 200-year-old charmer, with rooms decorated with period furnishings, plus a wide veranda and back garden. Its restaurant, Room 12, serves excellent fresh food.

Wind-Chill Factory ICE CREAM $
(☑ 518-585-3044; 794 Rte 9N, Ticonderoga; burgers from $5, ice cream from $3; ⊙ 11am-8pm in season) This humble ice-cream stand has fresh flavors, and its burgers use locally raised beef.

Thousand Islands

To downstate New Yorkers, this region is the mythical source of a salad dressing made of ketchup, mayonnaise and relish. In fact, it's a scenic wonderland along the St Lawrence River, with more than 1800 islands of all sizes. The area was a Gilded Age playground; now it's more populist. Pros: beautiful sunsets, good-value lodging and the exotic sound of Canadian radio. Cons: very large mosquitoes; bring ample repellent.

Where the river meets Lake Ontario is the French-heritage village of **Cape Vincent**, marked by the 1854 **Tibbetts Point Lighthouse**. Fifteen miles east along the Seaway Trail (Rte 12), **Clayton** has a pretty old main strip and a few good eating options. Further east, **Alexandria Bay** (Alex Bay) is the center of tourism in the area. Clayton is the most attractive place to spend the night, but if you're traveling with kids, Alex Bay is preferable, as there's entertainment such as mini-golf and a **drive-in movie theater** (☑315-482-3874; www.baydrivein.com; Rte 26; adult/child $6/2; ☉Fri-Sun; ⓜ). Both towns have boat-tour operators with similar offerings – **Clayton Island Tours** (☑315-686-4820; www.claytonislandtours.com; 39621 Chateau Ln, Clayton; 2hr tour adult/child $22/12) and **Uncle Sam Boat Tours** (☑315-482-2611; www.usboattours.com; 45 James St, Alexandria Bay; 2hr tours adult/child $22/11), respectively.

❶ Getting There & Around

JetBlue (☑1-800-538-2583; www.jetblue.com) has flights from NYC to Hancock International Airport (SYR) in Syracuse, where you can rent a car.

◉ Sights & Activities

★ Boldt Castle　　　　　　　　CASTLE
(☑800-847-5263; www.boldtcastle.com; Heart Island; adult/child $8.50/6; ☉10am-6:30pm mid-May–mid-Oct) This Gothic gem was (partly) built by George C Boldt, a Prussian immigrant who rose to the uppermost class by managing Manhattan's Waldorf-Astoria hotel in the late 19th century. Midway through construction, Boldt's wife died suddenly, and the project was abandoned. One floor has been finished the way Boldt intended; the rest is a ghostly monument.

Access to the castle is by boat (additional fee) from Clayton or Alexandria Bay.

Singer Castle　　　　　　　　CASTLE
(☑877-327-5475; www.singercastle.com; Dark Island; adult/child $14.25/6.25; ☉10am-4pm mid-May–mid-Oct) This castle, full of secret passages and hidden doors, is less visited – a plus in summer, when Boldt Castle can be very busy. Romantics should check the option of staying overnight in the main bedroom ($700!). Uncle Sam runs boats from Alex Bay; **Schermerhorn Harbor**

(☑315-324-5966; www.schermerhornharbor.com; 71 Schermerhorn Landing, Hammond) also visits.

Antique Boat Museum　　　　　MUSEUM
(☑315-686-4104; www.abm.org; 750 Mary St, Clayton; adult/child $14/free; ☉9am-5pm mid-May–mid-Oct; ⓜ) This museum lets you row old skiffs as you learn about them. You can also tour George Boldt's glam 1903 houseboat; reserve a tour time in advance.

Wellesley Island State Park　　OUTDOORS
(☑315-482-2722; www.nysparks.com; 44927 Cross Island Rd, Fineview; beach $7; ☉year-round; swimming 11am-7pm Jul-Aug) **FREE** This is essentially a 2600-acre floating village attached to the mainland by the Thousand Islands International Bridge (toll $2.75). The park is full of wildlife and has a nature center and a beautiful swimming beach. Camping options here are excellent, with riverfront tent sites, cabins and family cottages.

🛏 Sleeping & Eating

★ Wooden Boat Inn　　　　　　MOTEL $
(☑315-686-5004; www.woodenboatinn.com; 606 Alexandria St, Clayton; r from $89, boat $175; ❀🛜) The six motel rooms are great value, but anyone with a nautical bent should book the boat trawler moored on the riverfront.

HI Tibbetts Point Lighthouse　　HOSTEL $
(☑315-654-3450; www.hihostels.com; 33439 Cty Rte 6, Cape Vincent; dm $30, r from $65; ☉Jul-mid-Sep) The lighthouse keepers' house is now this well-kept hostel. Book ahead – there are only 18 beds.

Otter Creek Inn　　　　　　　MOTEL $
(☑315-482-5248; www.ottercreekinnabay.com; 2 Crossmon St Extension, Alexandria Bay; r from $95; ❀🛜) This motel sits next to a quiet bay, away from the sometimes rowdy town center (easy walking distance, though).

Lyric Coffee House　　　　　　CAFE $$
(☑315-686-4700; 246 James St, Clayton; mains $7-20; ☉8am-5pm, to 8pm Fri & Sat summer, Sat-Mon only winter; 🛜) A nice break from the burgers-and-BBQ menus in these parts, this cafe has great cakes, sandwiches and daily specials such as duck terrine; there's live music some Fridays and Saturdays.

Western New York

Much activity in this region revolves around Buffalo, New York State's (very distant) second-largest city, with about 250,000 people.

The area first developed thanks to the hydroelectric power of Niagara Falls and the Erie Canal, which linked the Great Lakes to the Atlantic Ocean. The falls are now better known as a tourist destination, with 12 million visitors annually.

Buffalo

The winters are long and cold, and abandoned industrial buildings dot the skyline, but Buffalo stays warm with a vibrant creative community and strong local pride. Settled by the French in 1758, the city is believed to derive its name from *beau fleuve* (beautiful river). With power from nearby Niagara Falls, it boomed in the early 1900s; Pierce-Arrow cars were made here, and it was the first American city to have electric streetlights. Its strong bones include art-deco masterpieces and a gracious park system laid out by Frederick Law Olmsted, of NYC's Central Park fame. It's about an eight-hour trip from NYC through the Finger Lakes region and only half an hour south of Niagara Falls.

◎ Sights

Architecture buffs will enjoy a stroll around downtown, marked by the towering art-deco **City Hall** (☑716-852-3300; www.preservation-buffaloniagara.org; 65 Niagara Sq; ⊙tours noon Mon-Fri) **FREE** and the **Theatre District**, a string of beautiful late 19th-century buildings along Main St. For more detail, join a tour with **Explore Buffalo** (☑716-245-3032; www.explorebuffalo.org; 1 Symphony Circle). **Elmwood Ave** is a lively thoroughfare, leading north to the State Univeristy of New York's Buffalo campus and Olmsted's **Delaware Park**.

This is a hard-core sports town: the **Buffalo Bills** (www.buffalobills.com) play pro football in a stadium in the suburb of Orchard Park; the **Buffalo Sabres** (www.sabres.com) rule ice hockey at HarborCenter downtown; and the minor-league baseball team, **Buffalo Bisons** (www.bisons.com), play in a trendy-traditional downtown ballpark.

★**Martin House**   ARCHITECTURE
(☑716-856-3858; www.darwinmartinhouse.org; 125 Jewett Pkwy; tours basic/extended $17/35; ⊙tours hourly 10am-3pm, closed Tue & some Thu) An early work of Frank Lloyd Wright's, in his horizontal Prairie style, the 15,000-sq-ft Martin House has been meticulously restored and even rebuilt. A guided tour reveals the exacting details; the very worthwhile longer tour visits three neighboring buildings. Buy tickets online; Wright fans may want the combo ticket to Graycliff, a vacation home outside Buffalo.

Albright-Knox Art Gallery   MUSEUM
(☑716-882-8700; www.albrightknox.org; 1285 Elmwood Ave; adult/child $12/5; ⊙10am-5pm, closed Mon) Renowned for its collection of Ruscha, Rauschenberg and other abstract expressionists, this sizable museum occupies a neoclassical building from Buffalo's 1901 Pan-American Exposition. Its temporary exhibits are particularly creative and compelling.

Burchfield Penney Art Center   MUSEUM
(☑716-878-6011; www.burchfieldpenney.org; 1300 Elmwood Ave; adult/child $10/free; ⊙10am-5pm Tue, Wed, Fri & Sat, to 9pm Thu, 1-5pm Sun) Dedicated to artists of Western New York, past and present, this museum shows great range. Namesake Charles Burchfield's paintings and prints reflect the local landscape.

Theodore Roosevelt Inaugural National Historic Site   MUSEUM
(☑716-884-0095; www.nps.gov/thri; 641 Delaware Ave; adult/child $10/5; ⊙tours hourly 9:30am-3:30pm Mon-Fri, from 12:30pm Sat & Sun) Guided tours of the Ansley-Wilcox house tell the dramatic tale of Teddy's emergency swearing-in here in 1901, after President William McKinley was assassinated while attending Buffalo's Pan-American Exposition.

Canalside   PARK
(☑716-574-1537; www.canalsidebuffalo.com; 44 Prime St) Buffalo's once derelict waterfront now offers summer parkland and winter ice skating. The area includes the **Buffalo & Erie County Naval & Military Park** (☑716-847-1773; www.buffalonavalpark.org; 1 Naval Park Cove; adult/child $10/6; ⊙10am-5pm Apr-Oct, Sat & Sun Nov), with two WWII-era ships and a submarine, and **BFLO Harbor Kayak** (☑716-288-5309; www.bfloharborkayak.com; 1 Naval Park Cove; tours from $25; ⊙Memorial Day-Labor Day).

⊨ Sleeping

★**Hostel Buffalo Niagara**   HOSTEL $
(☑716-852-5222; www.hostelbuffalo.com; 667 Main St; dm/r $25/65; ✸@🛜) Conveniently located in Buffalo's downtown Theatre District, this hostel occupies three floors of a former school, with a basement rec room, plenty of kitchen and lounge space, and spotless if insitutional bathrooms. Services include laundry facilities, bikes, and lots of info on local music, food and arts happenings.

Hotel @ The Lafayette
BOUTIQUE HOTEL **$$**
(☑716-853-1505; www.thehotellafayette.com; 391 Washington St; r $169, ste from $199; P❂❋🐾) This seven-story early 1900s building has been restored with stylish furnishings in its rooms. The location is handy, with a very good brewpub, Pan-American Grill, set in some of the fantastically ornate public spaces. Also recommended: the same owners' **Lofts on Pearl** (☑716-856-0098; www.loftsonpearl.com; 92 Pearl St; ste from $169), a few blocks away.

Mansion on Delaware Avenue
HOTEL **$$$**
(☑716-886-3300; www.mansionondelaware.com; 414 Delaware Ave; r/ste from $195/390; P❋@🐾) For truly special accommodations and flawless service, head to this hotel in a grand and regal home c 1862. Room 200 has a fireplace and floor-to-ceiling windows. Amenities include daily self-serve drinks in the lounge, and car service around central Buffalo.

🍴 Eating

The neighborhood of Allentown is a strong destination for dining (and nightlife), and food trucks rally around Larkin Sq, east of downtown. Also keep an eye out for branches of Mighty Taco, Buffalo's answer to Taco Bell, as famed for its weird ads as its satisfying burritos, as well as extra-savory Ted's Hot Dogs, in the northeast suburb of Williamsville and other spots around western New York.

⭐ Anchor Bar
AMERICAN **$**
(☑716-886-8920; 1047 Main St; 10/20 wings $13/20; ⊙11am-11pm) Admirably, the place that invented that ultimate bar snack, Buffalo wings (here, of course, they're just called 'wings'), is not a massive tourist trap, but a functioning neighborhood hangout, with a broad menu beyond the spicy, deep-fried chicken. There's live music, often jazz, Thursday, Friday and Saturday nights.

Sweetness 7
CAFÉ **$**
(301 Parkside Ave; crepes $10; ⊙8am-6pm; 🐾) A comfy, somewhat hippie-feeling cafe with sweet and savory crepes, good coffee and fresh baked goods. It can get packed, but Delaware Park is just across the road. There's another branch on Buffalo's **west side** (220 Grant St; ⊙7am-6pm, from 8am Sat & Sun; 🐾).

Cantina Loco
MEXICAN **$**
(☑716-551-0160; 191 Allen St; mains $7; ⊙4-10pm Mon-Thu, to 11pm Fri & Sat, 4-8pm Sun) Hip and always packed, this Allentown restaurant with a backyard patio serves up tacos, burritos and quesadillas. Some come with a twist like the Koreatown (short ribs and kimchi). The desserts are excellent and super-efficient bartenders know their mescals.

Parkside Candy
SWEETS **$**
(3208 Main St; ⊙11am-6pm Mon-Thu, to 9pm Fri & Sat, noon-8pm Sun) A landmark sweet shop, with decor as beautiful as the lollipops and bonbons. Sponge candy (aka honeycomb toffee) is a Buffalo favorite.

Ulrich's 1868 Tavern
GERMAN **$$**
(☑716-989-1868; 674 Ellicott St; mains $15; ⊙11am-9pm Mon & Tue, to 10pm Wed & Thu, to 11pm Fri, 3-10pm Sat) Buffalo's oldest bar has been partially modernized and now draws a slightly younger clientele. Traditional German schnitzel is on the menu alongside western New York pub food such as beef on weck, a roast-beef sandwich on a caraway-flecked roll.

Betty's
AMERICAN **$$**
(☑716-362-0633; 370 Virginia St; mains $9-22; ⊙8am-9pm Tue-Thu, to 10pm Fri, 9am-10pm Sat, 9am-2pm Sun; 🐾) On a quiet Allentown corner, bohemian Betty's does flavorful, fresh interpretations of American comfort food like meatloaf. Brunch is deservedly popular.

🍺 Drinking & Entertainment

With a young populace and most bars open till 4am, Buffalo can keep you out late. The bars along Chippewa St (aka the Chip Strip) cater primarily to a mainstream college crowd, while nearby Allentown has a more eclectic scene. For events listings, pick up the excellent free weeklies *Artvoice* (www.artvoice.com) and *The Public* (www.dailypublic.com).

Founding Fathers
BAR
(☑716-855-8944; 75 Edward St; ⊙11:30am-2am Mon-Fri, 4pm-4am Sat, 4-10pm Sun) Any questions about American history? Ask the knowledgeable owner of this laid-back neighborhood bar with a presidential theme. You'll also find free popcorn and nachos and good sandwiches ($9).

Allen Street Hardware Cafe
BAR
(☑716-882-8843; 245 Allen St; ⊙5pm-4am, music from 9pm) One of the more sophisticated options in Allentown, with a good restaurant (mains $14 to $25) and eclectic local music.

Nietzsche's
LIVE MUSIC
(☑716-886-8539; www.nietzsches.com; 248 Allen St; ⊙1pm-2am Mon & Tue, from noon Sun & Wed, to 4am Thu & Fri, 3pm-4am Sat) One of the original Allentown dives, with live music every night.

ℹ Information

Visit Buffalo Niagara (☑ 800-283-3256; www.visitbuffaloniagara.com; 403 Main St; ⊙ 9am-5pm Mon-Fri) The helpful tourism board has a great website, good walking-tour pamphlets and a small gift shop.

ℹ Getting There & Around

Buffalo Niagara International Airport (BUF; ☑ 716-630-6000; www.buffaloairport.com; 4200 Genesee St), about 10 miles east of downtown, is a regional hub. JetBlue Airways offers affordable round-trip fares from New York City. **NFTA** (☑ 716-855-7300; www.nfta.com), the local transit service, runs express bus 204 to the **Buffalo Metropolitan Transportation Center** (☑ 716-855-7300; www.nfta.com; 181 Ellicott St) downtown. (Greyhound buses also pull in here.) NFTA local bus 40 goes to the American side of Niagara Falls ($2, one hour); express bus 60 also goes to the area, but requires a transfer. From Amtrak's downtown **Exchange Street Station** (☑ 716-856-2075; www.amtrak.com; 75 Exchange St), you can catch trains to NYC ($63, eight hours), Niagara Falls ($14, one hour), Albany ($50, six hours) and Toronto ($45, four hours). It's desolate late at night; you may prefer to use the **Buffalo-Depew Station** (www.amtrak.com; 55 Dick Rd), 8 miles east.

Niagara Falls

It's a tale of two cities: Niagara Falls, New York (USA), and Niagara Falls, Ontario (Canada). Both overlook a natural wonder – 150,000 gallons of water per second, plunging more than 1000ft – and both provide a load of tourist kitsch surrounding it. The Canadian side, with its somewhat better views and much larger town, is where almost everyone visits. The view from the New York side is still impressive, though the town is much quieter, even a bit derelict. It's easy to walk across the Rainbow Bridge between the two – be sure to bring your passport.

👁 Sights & Activities

The area around the falls is New York's first state park, pleasantly landscaped by Frederick Law Olmsted in the 1880s. (Unfortunately, this came at the expense of the town of Niagara Falls, as many central blocks were razed in the process.) From the walking paths, you can see the **American Falls** and their western portion, the **Bridal Veil Falls**. Walk out on the deck of the **Prospect Point Observation Tower** (☑ 716-278-1796; admission $1, free from 5pm and off-season; ⊙ 9:30am-7pm) for a better view, or midway across the windy Rainbow Bridge, where you can also see the Horseshoe Falls on the Canadian side.

Upstream from the main falls, cross the small bridge to **Goat Island**, which forms the barrier between the American Falls and Horseshoe Falls. From Terrapin Point, on the southwest corner, there's a fine view of Horseshoe Falls. Additional pedestrian bridges lead further to the **Three Sisters Islands** in the upper rapids.

Cave of the Winds   VIEWPOINT
(☑ 716-278-1730; Goat Island Rd; adult/child $14/11; ⊙ 9am-7:30pm mid-May–Oct) On the north corner of Goat Island, don a rain poncho (provided) and take an elevator down to walkways just 25ft from the crashing water at the base of Bridal Veil Falls. (Despite the name, the platforms run in front of the falls, not into a cave.)

Wax Museum at Niagara   MUSEUM
(☑ 716-285-1271; Prospect & Old Falls Sts; adult/child $7/5; ⊙ 10am-9pm) Not the most state-of-the-art museum, but huge, entertaining and packed with interesting stories: massacres, stunt-jumpers and that time the water stopped flowing. Pose for a photo in an actual barrel someone rode over the falls.

★ **Maid of the Mist**   BOAT TRIP
(☑ 716-284-8897;   www.maidofthemist.com; 1 Prospect Pt; adult/child $17/9.90; ⊙ 9am-7pm summer; check website for other times) The traditional way to see Niagara Falls is on this boat cruise, which has ferried soaking visitors into the rapids right below the falls since 1846. It typically runs from mid-May through October, with departures from the bank below Prospect Point.

🛏 Sleeping & Eating

Many national hotel chains are represented, but the quality is poor compared with the Canadian side. The majority of restaurants near the falls are Indian, catering to the high number of Indian tourists, and their buffets are decent value.

Giacomo   BOUTIQUE HOTEL **$$$**
(☑ 716-299-0200; www.thegiacomo.com; 220 1st St; r from $250; P ❄ 🛜) A rare bit of style on either the US or Canadian sides, the luxe Giacomo occupies part of a gorgeous art-deco office tower, with spacious, ornately decorated rooms. Even if you're not staying here, have a drink in the 19th-floor lounge (from 5pm) for spectacular views and music on Thursday and Friday.

ⓘ BORDER CROSSING: CANADIAN NIAGARA FALLS

The Canadian side of the falls is naturally blessed with superior views. **Horseshoe Falls**, on the west half of the river, are wider than Bridal Veil Falls on the eastern, American side, and they're especially photogenic from Queen Victoria Park. The **Journey Behind the Falls** (☑ 905-354-1551; 6650 Niagara Pkwy; adult/child Apr-Dec $16.75/10.95, Jan-Mar $11.25/7.30; ⊙ 9am-10pm) gives access to a spray-soaked viewing area (similar to Cave of the Winds).

The Canadian town is also livelier, in an over-the-top touristy way. Chain hotels and restaurants dominate, but there is a HI hostel, and some older motels have the classic honeymooners' heart-shaped tubs. For more local info, visit the **Niagara Falls Tourism office** (☑ 905-356-6061; www.niagarafallstourism.com; 5400 Robinson St; ⊙ 9am-5pm), near the base of the Skylon Tower observation deck.

Crossing the Rainbow Bridge and returning costs US$3.25/1 per car/pedestrian. Walking takes about 10 minutes; car traffic can grind to a standstill in summer. US citizens and overseas visitors must show a passport or an enhanced driver's license at immigration at either end. Driving a rental car from the US over the border should not be a problem, but check with your rental company.

Zaika   INDIAN $

(421 3rd St; buffet $14; ⊙ 11:30am-9pm Sun-Thu, to 10pm Fri & Sat; ☑⚫) Zaika is a cut above the Indian joints immediately adjacent to the falls. À la carte items are available when it's not too crowded, but the buffet is fresh and varied.

Buzzy's   PIZZA $

(7617 Niagara Falls Blvd; mains $7-15; ⊙ 11am-11pm Sun-Thu, to midnight Fri & Sat) Enjoy excellent NYC-style pizza and other bar food at this long-established place a good drive east of the falls.

ⓘ Information

Niagara Tourism (☑ 716-282-8992; www. niagara-usa.com; 10 Rainbow Blvd; ⊙ 9am-7pm Jun-Sep, to 5pm Oct-May) At the bridge crossing to Goat Island, this office is stocked with very good maps and information for all of western New York. The combo pass it sells is not great value, though, as the museum and aquarium it gives admission to are quite small.

ⓘ Getting There & Around

NFTA (p129) bus 40 connects downtown Buffalo and Niagara Falls ($2, one hour); the stop in Niagara Falls is at 1st St and Rainbow Blvd. Express bus 60 goes to a terminal east of the town center; you'll have to transfer to bus 55 to reach the river. The **Amtrak train station** (☑ 716-285-4224; 2701 Willard Ave) is about 2 miles northeast of downtown; the station on the Canadian side is more central, but coming from NYC, you have to wait for Canadian customs. From Niagara Falls, daily trains go to Buffalo ($14, 35 minutes), Toronto ($34, three hours) and NYC ($63, nine hours). **Greyhound** (www.greyhound.com; 240 1st St) buses stop at the Quality Inn.

Parking costs $8 to $10 a day on either side of the falls. Most midrange hotels offer complimentary parking to guests, while upscale hotels on the Canadian side tend to charge $15 to $20 a day. To avoid traffic mayhem in summer, you can park along Niagara Falls Blvd and ride the NFTA bus 55 west to the river. At the falls, the Niagara Scenic Trolley runs a loop around the American side.

NEW JERSEY

Everything you've seen on TV, from the Mc-Mansions of *Real Housewives of New Jersey* to the thick accents of *The Sopranos,* is at least partially true. But Jersey (natives lose the 'New') is at least as well defined by its high-tech and banking headquarters, and a quarter of it is lush farmland (hence the 'Garden State' nickname). And on the 127 miles of beautiful beaches, you'll find, yes, the guidos and guidettes of *Jersey Shore,* but also many other oceanfront towns, each with a distinct character.

ⓘ Information

Edible Jersey (www.ediblejersey.com) Where to enjoy the bounty of the Garden State; also a free print quarterly.

New Jersey Monthly (www.njmonthly.com) Monthly glossy for residents and visitors.

NJ.com (www.nj.com) Statewide news from all the major dailies including the *Newark Star-Leger* and Hudson County's *Jersey Journal.*

ⓘ Getting There & Around

Though many New Jersey folks do love their cars, there are other transportation options.

PATH Train (www.panynj.gov/path) Connects lower Manhattan to Hoboken, Jersey City and Newark.

NJ Transit (☑ 973-275-5555; www.njtransit.com) Operates buses and trains around the state, including bus service to NYC's Port Authority and downtown Philadelphia, and trains to Penn Station, NYC.

New York Waterway (☑ 800-533-3779; www.nywaterway.com) Its ferries run up the Hudson River and from the NJ Transit train station in Hoboken to the World Financial Center in Lower Manhattan.

Northern New Jersey

Stay east and you'll experience the Jersey (sub)urban jungle. Go west to find its opposite: the peaceful, refreshing landscape of the Delaware Water Gap.

Hoboken & Jersey City

A sort of TV-land version of a cityscape, Hoboken is a cute little urban pocket just across the Hudson River from NYC. On weekends the bars come alive, and loads of restaurants line commercial Washington St. Gritty *On the Waterfront* was filmed here, but today the riverside is leafy and revitalized – and has dazzling views of Manhattan.

High-rise condominiums and financial towers have transformed the Jersey City waterfront from a primarily blue-collar zone into an upwardly mobile address. The 1200-acre **Liberty State Park** (☑ 201-915-3440; www.libertystatepark.org; Morris Pesin Dr; ☺ 6am-10pm) hosts outdoor concerts with the Manhattan skyline as a backdrop; the expansive **Liberty Science Center** (☑ 201-200-1000; www.lsc.org; 222 Jersey City Blvd; adult/child $19.75/15.75, extra for IMAX & special exhibits; ☺ 9am-4pm Mon-Fri, to 5:30pm Sat & Sun; ⊞) is at one end. Ellis Island and the Statue of Liberty are not far; **ferries** (☑ 877-523-9849; www.statuecruises.com; adult/child from $18/9; ☺ from 9am mid-Feb–Labor Day) leave from here. Movie buffs can head inland to the **Landmark Loew's Jersey Theatre** (☑ 201-798-6055; www.loewsjersey.org; 54 Journal Sq; ☺ 10am-6pm Mon-Fri, plus movie screenings), a classic cinema, half-restored, with a working pipe organ.

Delaware Water Gap

The beautiful spot where the Delaware River makes a tight S-curve through the ridge of the Kittatinny Mountains, was, in the pre-air-conditioning days, a popular resort destination. In 1965 the **Delaware Water Gap National Recreation Area** (☑ 570-426-2452; www.nps.gov/dewa) was established, covering land in both New Jersey and Pennsylvania, and it's still an unspoiled recreational spot – just 70 miles east of New York City. The 30-mile road on the Pennsylvania side has several worthwhile stops including the small but pretty **Raymondskill Falls**, the **Pocono Environmental Education Center** (☑ 570-828-2319; www.peec.org; 538 Emery Rd, Dingmans Ferry; ☺ 9am-5pm; ⊞) ⌷ and the developed but stunning **Bushkill Falls** (☑ 570-588-6682; www.visitbushkillfalls.com; Bushkill Falls Rd, off Rte 209; adult/child $13.50/8; ☺ opens 9am, closing times vary, closed Dec-Mar).

On the New Jersey side, bump along unpaved Old Mine Rd, one of the oldest continually operating commercial roads in the US, to trailheads for day hikes such as the one to the top of 1574ft Mt Tammany in **Worthington State Forest** (☑ 908-841-9575; www.njparksandforests.org; Old Mine Rd; ☺ sunrise-sunset).

For river fun, contact **Adventure Sports** (☑ 570-223-0505; www.adventuresport.com; Rte 209, Marshalls Creek; canoe/kayak $43/47 per day; ☺ 9am-6pm Mon-Fri, from 8am Sat & Sun May-Oct) for everything you need for a day or, better, multiday trip on the water. Camping along the way, at sites accessible only by canoe or kayak, is a great way to see the area.

Northeast of here, **High Point State Park** (☑ 973-875-4800; www.njparksandforests.org; 1480 Rte 23, Sussex; per vehicle $10; ☺ 8am-8pm Apr-Oct, to 4:30pm Nov-Mar) has a monument that, at 1803ft above sea level, affords wonderful views of surrounding lakes, hills and farmland.

For food and lodging, visit charming **Milford**, PA, on the north end of the gap; it has several good restaurants, as well as **Grey Towers** (☑ 570-296-9630; www.greytowers.org; 122 Old Owego Turnpike; tours adult/child $8/free; ☺ grounds dawn-dusk), the gorgeous chateau-style home of Gifford Pinchot, former governor of Pennsylvania and founder of the US Forest Service. On the south end, the somewhat groovier town of Delaware Water Gap, PA, has the **Deer Head Inn** (☑ 570-424-2000; www.deerheadinn.com; 5 Main St, Delaware Water Gap; r from $90; ⊞ ⌷), with Victorian rooms and great live jazz on weekends.

Princeton & the Delaware River

Settled by an English Quaker missionary, the tiny town of Princeton is filled with lovely architecture and several noteworthy sites, number one of which is its Ivy League **Princeton University** (✆609-258-3000; www.princeton.edu), which was built in the mid-1700s and soon became one of the largest structures in the early colonies. You can rove around on your own or join a free student-led tour. The town is more upper-crust than collegiate, with preppie boutiques edging central **Palmer Sq**.

About 20 miles west, on the banks of the Delaware River, is **Lambertville** and its sister town across the water, **New Hope**, PA. New Hope has a faintly hippie-meets-goth sensibility (Doc Martens sold here!) while Lambertville is preppier. Together they're good for an afternoon stop if you're road-tripping. Browse the stalls at **Golden Nugget Antique & Flea Market** (✆609-397-0811; www.gnmarket. com; 1850 River Rd, Lambertville; ⊙6am-4pm Wed, Sat & Sun), and stroll along the peaceful towpaths that edge the river. A few miles south is where George Washington crossed the Delaware in Trenton in 1776 (as depicted in Emanuel Leutze's iconic painting).

As for **Trenton**, the state capital just south along the river, it's small and fairly scruffy. Its

motto – 'Trenton makes, the world takes' – strikes another downbeat note, considering the riverside city no longer manufactures anything. But travelers with an affection for urban underdogs may appreciate its several historic sites, museum and farmers market.

◉ Sights & Activities

★**Princeton University**

Art Museum MUSEUM
(✆609-258-3788; www.princetonartmuseum.org; McCormick Hall; ⊙10am-5pm Tue-Sat, to 10pm Thu, 1-5pm Sun) FREE This wide-ranging collection is particularly strong on antiquities, Asian art and photography.

Bucks County River Country BOATING
(✆215-297-5000; www.rivercountry.net; 2 Walters Lane, Point Pleasant; tube $22-26, canoe $70; ⊙rental 9am-3pm, return by 5pm) North of Lambertville, on the Pennsylvania side, this outfitter rents rafts, tubes and canoes for floating down the serene Delaware River, plus transportation back to base.

🛏 Sleeping & Eating

Accommodations are expensive and hard to find during reunions and graduation, from Memorial Day to the end of the month.

Inn at Glencairn B&B $$
(✆609-497-1737; www.innatglencairn.com; 3301 Lawrenceville Rd; r from $199; 🛜) The best

value in the Princeton area: five serene rooms in a renovated Georgian manor, 10 minutes' drive from campus.

Nassau Inn
INN $$$

(☎609-921-7500; www.nassauinn.com; 10 Palmer Sq; r from $259; ✷ ⊛ ✷) Pricey, due to its prime location, and the history-soaked rooms can feel a little frumpy (some may prefer the new wing). Visit the classic bar even if you don't stay the night.

Olives
BAKERY, DELI $

(22 Witherspoon St; sandwiches $7; ⊙7am-8pm Mon-Fri, from 8am Sat, 9am-6pm Sun) Reasonably priced, Greek-inspired food, mainly for takeout.

Swan
AMERICAN $

(☎609-397-1960; 43 S Main St, Lambertville; burgers $11; ⊙5-10pm Mon-Fri, from 1pm Sat, 1-9pm Sun) This late 19th-century building – once the village hotel – is a scenic place for a burger. The same owners also have the bar, **Boat House** (8 Coryell St, Lambertville; ⊙4:30-11pm), on the towpath, which oozes even more historic atmosphere.

Mistral
MEDITERRANEAN $$$

(☎609-688-8808; 66 Witherspoon St; sharing plates $17-28; ⊙5-9pm Mon-Wed, 11:30am-9pm Thu & Sun, 11.30am-10pm Fri & Sat) Princeton's most creative restaurant, largely Mediterranean, with an occasional dash of Asian. The BYOB policy offsets the menu prices.

Jersey Shore

Perhaps the most famous and revered feature of New Jersey is its sparkling shore – and heading 'down the shore' (in local parlance, never 'to the beach') is an essential summer ritual. Stretching from Sandy Hook to Cape May, the coastline is dotted with resort towns both tacky and tony. In 2012 much of the shore was devastated by Hurricane Sandy – the roller coaster at Seaside Heights was even knocked into the ocean. Repairs are ongoing, but the area has largely returned to its vibrant state. It's mobbed on summer weekends (traffic is especially bad on the bridges to the barrier islands), and finding good-value accommodation is nearly as difficult as locating un-tattooed skin; campgrounds can be low-cost alternatives. But by early fall, you could find yourself blissfully alone on the sand.

Sandy Hook

The northernmost tip of the Jersey Shore is the **Sandy Hook Gateway National Recreation Area** (☎718-354-4606; www.nps.gov/gate; parking $15 summer) **FREE**, a 7-mile barrier island at the entrance to New York Harbor. From your beach blanket, you can see the NYC skyline. The wide beaches, including New Jersey's only legal nude beach (Gunnison), are edged by a system of bike trails, while the bay side is great for fishing or bird-watching. The **Sandy Hook Lighthouse** (☎732-872-5970; ⊙visitor center 9am-5pm, tours 1-4:30pm) **FREE** is the oldest in the country. Bug spray is recommended as biting flies can be a nuisance at dusk.

A fast ferry service, **Seastreak** (☎800-262-8743; www.seastreak.com; 2 First Ave, Atlantic Highlands; one way/return $26/45, bicycle $5), runs between Sandy Hook (and the Highlands) and Pier 11 in Lower Manhattan.

Asbury Park & Ocean Grove

During decades of economic stagnation, the town of Asbury Park had nothing more to its name than the fact that state troubadour Bruce Springsteen got his start at the **Stone Pony** (☎732-502-0600; www.stoneponyonline.com; 913 Ocean Ave) nightclub here in the mid-1970s. But since 2000, blocks of previously abandoned Victorian homes have seen such a revival that Asbury is sometimes called the Brooklyn of New Jersey. The downtown, several blocks of Cookman and Bangs Aves, has antiques shops, hip restaurants (from vegan to French bistro) and bars, and an art-house cinema. On the boardwalk, pinball fans shouldn't miss the **Silver Ball Museum** (☎732-774-4994; www.silverballmuseum.com; 1000 Ocean Ave; per hour/half-day $10/15; ⊙11am-9pm Mon-Thu, to 1am Fri & Sat, 10am-10pm Sun; ⊛), dozens of mint-condition games, all ready to play.

Immediately south of Asbury Park, Ocean Grove is a kind of time and culture warp. 'God's square mile at the Jersey Shore,' as it's still known, was founded by Methodists in the 19th century as a revival camp, and it's still a 'dry' town – no liquor sold here – and the beach is closed Sunday mornings. Its Victorian architecture is so covered in gingerbread trim you want to eat it. At the center, around a 6500-seat wooden auditorium with a huge pipe organ, the former revival camp is now **Tent City** – a historic site with more than a hundred quaint canvas tents used as summer homes. Among the many beautiful B&Bs, **Quaker Inn** (☎732-775-7525; www.quakerinn.com;

ⓘ BEACH FEES

Many communities on the Jersey Shore charge $5 or so for access, issuing a badge (also called a tag) for the day. From Long Beach Island north to near Sandy Hook, all beaches have a fee; the southern shore is mostly but not entirely free.

39 Main St, Ocean Grove; r $90-200; ⚘) is a good deal, and don't miss **Nagle's Fountain** (☎ 732-776-9797; 43 Main Ave; ice cream $3; ⊘ 8:30am-9pm Wed-Mon; ⚘) for an ice-cream sundae.

Barnegat Peninsula

Locals call this 22-mile stretch 'the barrier island,' though it is technically a peninsula, connected to the mainland on the north end at **Point Pleasant Beach**. Surfers should seek out **Inlet Beach** in Manasquan, immediately north (not on the peninsula), for the shore's most reliable year-round waves.

South of **Mantoloking** and **Lavallette**, midway down the island, a bridge from the mainland (at Toms River) deposits the hordes in **Seaside Heights**, notorious location of the MTV reality show *Jersey Shore*. As campy as the show was, it did capture the deliciously tacky essence of a certain shore culture. It's still a sticky pleasure to lick a Kohr's orange-vanilla twist cone and stroll through the boardwalk's raucous, deeply tanned, scantily clad crowds. You can refuel at an above-average number of bars. Also look out for the 1932 wooden carousel, still undergoing post-Sandy restoration in 2015.

For a bit of quiet, escape south to residential **Seaside Park** and the wilderness of Island Beach State Park beyond.

◎ Sights & Activities

Island Beach State Park   PARK
(☎ 732-793-0506; www.njparksandforests.org; Seaside Park; summer weekday/weekend $12/20; ⊘ dawn-dusk) Of the 10 miles of relatively untouched beach, one is open for swimming; the rest makes a nice bike ride. On the bay side, the lush tidal marshes are good for kayaking.

Jenkinson's   AMUSEMENT PARK
(☎ 732-295-4334; www.jenkinsons.com; 300 Ocean Ave, Point Pleasant Beach; aquarium adult/child $11/7; ⊘ rides noon-11pm, aquarium 10am-10pm Ju-Aug, hours vary off-season; ⚘) The focus is on kids at this boardwalk in Point Pleasant Beach: small-scale rides, mini-golf, an aquarium and plenty of candy.

Casino Pier   AMUSEMENT PARK
(☎ 732-793-6488; www.casinopiernj.com; 800 Ocean Terrace, Seaside Heights; rides from $5, water park adult/child $35/29; ⊘ noon-late Jun-Aug, hours vary rest of year; ⚘) The amusement pier at the north end of the Seaside boardwalk has a few kiddie rides and more extreme thrills for the 48in-and-taller set, plus a chairlift that runs above the boardwalk. Nearby is Breakwater Beach, a water park with tall slides.

🛏 Sleeping & Eating

Staying in Seaside Heights proper is too noisy to recommend in summer, but can be a good deal off-season.

Surf & Stream Campground   CAMPGROUND $
(☎ 732-349-8919; www.surfnstream.com; 1801 Ridgeway Rd, Toms River; campsites from $45; ☎) A well-tended alternative to the crash-pad motels in Seaside Heights.

Luna-Mar Motel   MOTEL $
(☎ 732-793-7955; www.lunamarmotel.com; 1201 N Ocean Ave, Seaside Park; r from $129; ❄ ☎ ⊗) Directly across the road from the beach, this tidy motel has tile floors (no sandy carpets). Rates include beach badges.

★**Klee's**   PUB FOOD $
(www.kleesbarandgrill.com; 101 Blvd, Seaside Heights; pizza from $8, mains $9-20; ⊘ 10:30am-11pm Mon-Thu, to midnight Fri & Sat) Don't ask why an Irish bar has the best thin-crust pizza on the shore – just enjoy. The rest of the menu is solid, if standard, and comes in mammoth portions.

Music Man   ICE CREAM $
(www.njmusicman.com; 2305 Grand Central Ave, Lavallette; ice cream $3-8; ⊘ 11am-midnight, shows from 5:30pm; ⚘) Have a little razzle-dazzle with your ice-cream sundae – the waitstaff belt out Broadway show tunes all night. Cash only.

Long Beach Island

Accessible only by a bridge (Rte 72) across Manahawkin Bay, Long Beach Island is an 18-mile-long barrier island at the dead center of the Jersey Shore. LBI, as it's known, is a string of townships, all with beautiful beaches and strong surf culture (Ron Jon started here). South of the bridge, **Long Beach** and

Beach Haven are where the action is, and quieter, more affluent Surf City, Harvey Cedars and Barnegat Light are to the north.

The landmark Barnegat Lighthouse (☑ 609-494-2016; www.njparksandforests.org; off Long Beach Blvd; lighthouse adult/child summer $3/1; ☺ park 8am-6pm, lighthouse 10am-4:30pm), in the small state park at the northern tip of the island, offers panoramic views at the top. On the southern end, the Jolly Roger (☑ 609-492-6931; www.jollyrogerlbi.com; 5416 S Long Beach Blvd, Beach Haven; r $150-180; ☺ Apr-Oct; ✹ 🛜) is an excellent little motel. Tucked down a residential street is Hudson House (☑ 609-492-9616; 19-E 13th St, Beach Haven; ☺ 5pm-1am summer), a friendly dive bar with pinball, shuffleboard and lots of lore. And there are seven – count 'em, *seven* – mini-golf courses on the island.

Atlantic City

Atlantic City (AC) may be the largest city on the shore, but that currently doesn't mean much, as the vision of Vegas on the East Coast has foundered, and casinos gone bankrupt. But the hotels can be a bargain and the lovely beach is free and often empty because most visitors are indoors playing the slots. And in contrast with many homogenous beach enclaves, the population here is more diverse.

As for the Prohibition-era glamour depicted in the HBO series *Boardwalk Empire,* there's little trace – though you can still ride along the boardwalk on a nifty wicker rolling chair. As you do, consider that the first boardwalk was built here, and if Baltic Ave rings a bell, it's because the game Monopoly uses AC's street names. A later contribution: the Miss America pageant, though it's now held in Vegas; the Miss'd America drag pageant fills the gap.

⊙ Sights

Atlantic City Historical Museum MUSEUM
(☑ 609-347-5839; www.atlanticcityexperience.org; Garden Pier, S New Jersey Ave at the boardwalk; ☺ 10am-5pm Sat-Wed) FREE Small but informative – you'll learn all about AC's quirkiest details, such as the high-diving horses that once leapt off a 40ft tower at Steel Pier.

Lucy the Elephant MONUMENT
(☑ 609-823-6473; www.lucytheelephant.org; 9200 Atlantic Ave, Margate; adult/child $8/4; ☺ 10am-8pm Mon-Sat, 10am-5pm Sun, check for winter hours) This six-story wooden pachyderm was constructed in 1881 as a land developer's weird scheme to attract customers. It's in Margate (just south of AC), and you can now climb up inside on a guided tour (on the half-hour).

🛏 Sleeping & Eating

The casinos often have very low midweek room rates. A handful of motor inns and cheap motels are on Pacific Ave, a block inland from the boardwalk.

Chelsea BOUTIQUE HOTEL $
(☑ 800-548-3030; www.thechelsea-ac.com; 111 S Chelsea Ave; r from $99; 🅿 ✹ @ 🛜 ✈) This stylish place looks a little better in the photos than in real life (maintenance can be patchy). But it's reasonably priced, either in the quieter Luxe section or slightly groovier (and cheaper) style in the Annex.

Kelsey & Kim's Café BARBECUE $
(☑ 609-350-6800; 201 Melrose Ave; mains $9-12; ☺ 7am-10pm) In the pretty residential Uptown area, this friendly cafe does excellent Southern comfort food, from morning grits and waffles to fried whiting and barbecue brisket. BYOB makes it a deal.

White House Subs SANDWICHES $
(☑ 609-345-8599; 2301 Arctic Ave; sandwiches $7-16; ☺ 10am-8pm Mon-Thu, to 9pm Fri-Sun; 🚗) Legendary, giant and delicious sub sandwiches. A half is plenty for two.

Knife and Fork Inn AMERICAN $$$
(☑ 609-344-1133; www.knifeandforkinn.com; 3600 Atlantic Ave; mains $26-45; ☺ 4-10pm, from 11:30am Fri) This vestige of Prohibition style was restored in 2005. Happy hour, 4pm to 6:30pm, is a good way to see the interior murals and mahogany trim.

ⓘ Information

Atlantic City Weekly (www.acweekly.com) The free paper has listings for events, clubs and food.
DO AC (www.atlanticcitynj.com) The local tourism organization has a main branch on the Boardwalk (☑ 609-348-7100; Boardwalk at Mississippi Ave; ☺ 9:30am-5:30pm) and another on the AC Expwy (☑ 609-449-7130; Atlantic City Expwy; ☺ 9am-5pm).

ⓘ Getting There & Around

Small **Atlantic City International Airport** (ACY; ☑ 609-645-7895; www.acairport.com) is a 20-minute drive from the town center. If you happen to be coming from Florida (where most of the flights come from), it's a great option for South Jersey or Philadelphia.

PINE BARRENS

New Jersey is America's most densely populated state, but you'd never know it in the million or so acres of state parks and wildlife refuges that make up **Pinelands National Reserve** (☑609-894-7300; www.nj.gov/pinelands). That's the official name, but to Jersey natives, the area will always be the Pine Barrens, an apt adjective for the flat, sandy-soil forest and eerie cedar bogs. And never mind its rare conifers and orchids – this is foremost the home of the sinister 'Jersey Devil.' Ask any local you meet about it – or read John McPhee's 1968 classic, *The Pine Barrens*.

The 50-mile **Batona Trail** cuts through east–west, rewarding hikers with wild blueberries in midsummer. The route passes the **Apple Pie Hill Fire Tower**, giving a view over a veritable sea of forest. (You can drive to the tower too; turn on paved Ringler Rd, rather than sand roads suggested by some GPS.)

Batsto Village (☑609-561-0024; www.batstovillage.org; 31 Batsto Rd, Hammonton; mansion tours $3; ⊙9am-4pm, mansion Fri-Sun only; 🚻) This 18th-century village is an open-air museum about the bog-iron industry, as well as a nature center. Guided tours of the central Batsto Mansion are available on weekends.

Whitesbog Village (☑609-893-4646; www.whitesbog.org; 120-34 Whitesbog Rd, Browns Mills; ⊙dawn-dusk; 🚻) Visit one of New Jersey's first cranberry bogs, and the place where the highbush blueberry was cultivated. Nature trails wind through the property. Check the website for organized tours & events.

Micks Pine Barrens Canoe Rental (☑609-726-1380; www.mickscanoerental.com; 3107 Rte 563; per day kayak/canoe $45/55; ⊙9am-5pm Mon-Fri, from 8:30am Sat & Sun) This outfitter has maps and other details for water trips in the area.

Atsion Campground (☑609-268-0444; www.njparksandforests.org; 744 Hwy 206, Shamong; campsites $25; ⊙Apr-Oct) Try to reserve a lakeside spot.

Panico's at the Red Barn (☑609-567-3412; 31 Myrtle St, Hammonton; pie slice $5, mains $9-12; ⊙8am-5pm) This rather grandmotherly place serves fruit pies and omelets with farm-fresh vegetables.

The only train service is NJ Transit (p131) from Philadelphia (one way $10, 1½ hours), arriving at the **train station** (☑973-491-9400; 1 Atlantic City Expwy) next to the convention center. AC's **bus station** (☑609-345-5403; 1901 Atlantic Ave) receives NJ Transit and Greyhound service from NYC ($25 to $36, 2½ hours) and Philadelphia (1½ hours). A casino will often refund much of the fare (in chips, coins or coupons) if you get a bus, such as Greyhound's Lucky Streak service, directly to its door. When leaving AC, buses first stop at various casinos and only stop at the bus station if not already full.

Ocean City, Strathmere & Sea Isle

South of Atlantic City are several smaller beach communities. Ocean City is an old-fashioned family spot, maintaining its wholesome reputation with a no-alcohol policy. It has child-centric arcades, a small waterpark, mini-golf courses and themed playlands along its lively boardwalk. Motels are plentiful, relatively cheap and old-fashioned, as are the myriad crab shacks and seafood joints. On the next barrier island down, Sea Isle City and Strathmere are both low-key – the closest you'll get to 'secret' shore spots. Strathmere's beach is free, and **DiGenni's Centennial Guest House** (☑609-263-6945; centennialguesthouse@gmail.com; 127 39th St, Sea Isle City; r from $75; 🚻) in Sea Isle is a homey treat, with shared bathrooms, outdoor showers and ceiling fans.

Wildwoods

The three towns of **North Wildwood**, **Wildwood** and **Wildwood Crest** are a virtual outdoor museum of 1950s motel architecture and neon signs. The vintage style has been self-consciously preserved – visit the **Doo Wop Experience** (☑609-523-1958; www.doowopusa.org; 4500 Ocean Ave, Wildwood; ⊙4-9pm Tue & Thu, to 8pm Wed & Fri, 9am-9pm Sat & Sun Jun-Aug, trolley tours 8pm Tue & Thu Jun-Aug) FREE for the whole story, loads of old neon and even a trolley tour around the best landmarks.

The community has a relaxed atmosphere, somewhere between wild party and clean-cut fun. The beach is the widest in New

Jersey, and there's no admission fee. Along the 2-mile boardwalk, several massive piers have roller coasters and rides best suited to aspiring astronauts. A miniature rubber-tired **tram** (one way $3; ⊘11am-1am) runs the length of the boardwalk, intermittently chirping 'Watch the tram car, *please.*'

With some 250 small motels – no corporate chains here – in the area, and rooms from $50 to $250, you're spoiled for choice. A typical option is the **Starlux** (✐609-522-7412; www.thestarlux.com; 305 E Rio Grande Ave, Wildwood; r from $157, trailers $240; ⏏), decked out with lava lamps and boomerang-print bedspreads; it even rents two chrome Airstream trailers. For breakfast, **Key West Cafe** (✐609-522-5006; 4701 Pacific Ave, Wildwood; mains $8-10; ⊘7am-2pm) does the best pancakes and eggs.

Cape May

Established in 1620, Cape May is a town with deep history and some 600 gorgeous Victorian buildings. Its sweeping beaches are a draw in summer, but its year-round population of more than 4000 makes it a lively off-season destination, unlike most of the rest of the Jersey Shore. Whales can be spotted off the coast May to December, and migratory birds are plentiful in spring and fall. And thanks to the location on New Jersey's southern tip (it's Exit 0 from the turnpike), you can watch the sun both rise and set over the water.

◉ Sights & Activities

Cape May Lighthouse   LIGHTHOUSE
(✐609-884-5404; 215 Lighthouse Ave; adult/child $8/3; ⊘9am-8pm summer, hours vary rest of year) In the lush wetlands of Cape May Point State Park, this 1869 lighthouse gives a fine view. It's also open full-moon nights April through September. At the base are exhibits on wildlife in the area.

Cape May Bird Observatory   BIRD-WATCHING
(✐609-884-2736; www.birdcapemay.org; 701 East Lake Dr; ⊘9am-4:30pm Apr-Oct, closed Tue Nov-Mar) **FREE** Cape May is one of the country's top birding spots, with more than 400 species during migration season. The mile-long loop trail here is a good introduction.

Aqua Trails   KAYAKING
(✐609-884-5600; www.aquatrails.com; 1600 Delaware Ave; per hour single/double $25/35, tours single/double from $45/75) Based at Cape May's

nature center, this outfitter rents gear and leads tours through the wetlands at sundown and during the full moon.

🛏 Sleeping & Eating

★**Congress Hall**   HOTEL $$$
(✐609-884-8421; www.caperesorts.com; 200 Congress Pl; r from $259; ❄ 🐾 ⌨) Opened in 1816, the enormous Congress Hall is a local landmark, now suitably modernized without wringing out all the history. The same company manages several other excellent hotels in the area.

★**Lobster House**   SEAFOOD $$
(✐609-884-8296; 906 Schellengers Landing Rd; mains $14-30; ⊘11:30am-3pm & 4:30-10pm Apr-Dec, to 9pm rest of year) This clubby-feeling classic on the wharf serves local oysters and scallops. No reservations means very long waits – go early or late.

Mad Batter   AMERICAN $$
(19 Jackson St; breakfast $8-11, dinner mains $32; ⊘8am-9pm summer, hours vary rest of year) Tucked in a white Victorian, this restaurant is locally beloved for brunch – including fluffy oat pancakes and rich clam chowder. (Dinner is fine, but pricier.)

❶ Getting There & Away

NJ Transit (p131) buses serve Cape May, direct from NYC ($45, three hours) and connecting from Philadelphia. For onward car travel, the **Cape May-Lewes Ferry** (✐800-643-3779; www.cmlf.com; 1200 Lincoln Blvd; car/passenger $45/10; ⊘hourly in summer 7am-7pm, check website rest of year) crosses the bay in 1½ hours to Lewes, DE, near Rehoboth Beach.

PENNSYLVANIA

More than 300 miles across, stretching from the East Coast to the edge of the Midwest, Pennsylvania contains multitudes. Philadelphia, once the heart of the British colonial empire, is very much a part of the east, a link on the Boston–Washington metro corridor. Outside the city, though, the terrain turns pastoral, emphasized by the Pennsylvania Dutch – that is, Mennonite, Amish and others – who tend their farms by hand, as if it were still the 18th century. West of here, the Appalachian mountains begin, as do the so-called Pennsylvania Wilds, a barely inhabited patch of deep forest. In the far west edge of the state, Pittsburgh, the state's only other large city and once a staggeringly wealthy steel manufacturing center, is fascinating in its combination of rust-belt decay and new energy.

Philadelphia

With giant NYC less than 100 miles north and Washington, DC, due south, Philadelphia often gets knocked down the must-visit list. In many ways, though, the City of Brotherly Love can be as rewarding as its bigger neighbors. It has its own distinct traditions, and outsize food, music and art scenes – unfettered by crushing real-estate prices. Because the city's oldest buildings are so well preserved, America's early history and its role in building democracy is sometimes more accessible here than in the capital. Moreover, it's a beautiful place that is easy and rewarding to explore, its streets dotted with gracious squares and linked with cobbled alleys.

For a time in its early years, Philadelphia was the second-largest city in the British empire, after London, then, along with Boston, the Empire's undoing. From the start of the Revolutionary War until 1790 (when Washington, DC, was founded), it was the new nation's capital. Eventually, NYC rose as a cultural, commercial and industrial center, and Philly slipped into a decline, enhanced by the loss of industrial jobs. Some areas of the city are still blighted, but its core, from the manicured campuses of the University of Pennsylvania to the redbrick buildings of Old City, is solid.

⊙ Sights & Activities

Most visitors will spend time in central Philadelphia, an area between the Delaware and Schuylkill (*skoo*-kill) Rivers. It's easy to navigate and distances are walkable, or a short bus ride at most. If you head west of the Schuylkill, you hit the area known as University City, with several campuses; for this trip, the nifty underground trolley comes in handy.

⊙ Old City

The area along the Delaware River bounded by Walnut, Vine and 6th Sts has been dubbed 'America's most historic square mile,' thanks to its role in the American Revolution and the earliest years of American democracy. A large, L-shaped chunk of the neighborhood is designated **Independence National Historic Park**, with many of the buildings managed by the National Park Service.

Front St used to mark the edge of the river port (now a freeway separates it from the wharves at **Penn's Landing**), and the blocks adjacent are lined with centuries-old homes and warehouses, now converted to lofts, galleries and shops. The mix of modern use and history makes this a fascinating place to stroll, even at the height of the summer tourist crush.

Liberty Bell Center HISTORIC SITE
(Map p144; www.nps.gov/inde; 526 Market St; ⊙9am-5pm, to 7pm late May-early Sep) **FREE**
A glass-walled building protects this icon of Philadelphia history from the elements. You can peek from outside, or join the line to file past, reading about the 2080lb object's history along the way. The queue starts on the building's north end, where the foundations of George Washington's house are marked.

The gist of the story: the bell was made in 1751 to commemorate the 50th anniversary of Pennsylvania's constitution. Mounted in Independence Hall, it tolled on the first public reading of the Declaration of Independence. The crack developed in the 19th century, and it was retired in 1846.

★ **Independence Hall** HISTORIC BUILDING
(Map p144; ☑877-444-6777; www.nps.gov/inde; 520 Chestnut St; ⊙9am-5pm, to 7pm late May-early Sep) **FREE** The 'birthplace of American government,' a modest Quaker building, is where delegates from the 13 colonies met to approve the Declaration of Independence on July 4, 1776. Entrance is at the corner of Chestnut and 5th Sts. Even without a ticket, you can pass through to see **Congress Hall** (☑215-965-2305; cnr S 6th & Chestnut Sts; ⊙9am-5pm, tours every 20-30min) **FREE**, where the congress met when Philly was the nation's capital.

★ **Benjamin Franklin Museum** MUSEUM
(Map p144; www.nps.gov/inde; Market St, btwn 3rd & 4th Sts; adult/child $5/2; ⊙9am-5pm, to 7pm late May-early Sep) In the courtyard south of Market St, underground, is a museum dedicated to Benjamin Franklin's storied life as a printer (he started the nation's first newspaper), inventor (bifocals! lightning rods!) and statesman who signed the Declaration of Independence.

In the same courtyard, don't miss the newspaper office where Franklin worked – park rangers demonstrate the printing press.

National Constitution Center   MUSEUM

(Map p144; 215-409-6600; www.constitution-center.org; 525 Arch St; adult/child $14.50/8; ⊙9:30am-5pm Mon-Fri, to 6pm Sat, noon-5pm Sun;) This whiz-bang museum makes the US Constitution jump off the page, starting with a dramatic theater-in-the-round presentation. This exits into a dizzying array of interactive exhibits, from voting booths to trivia games. You can also see an original version of the Bill of Rights. Go early, both for lighter crowds and a fresher brain – this place is hard to skim through.

Elfreth's Alley   HISTORIC SITE

(Map p144; 215-627-8680; www.elfrethsalley.org; off 2nd St, btwn Arch & Race Sts; tours $5; ⊙museum noon-5pm Fri-Sun) This tiny, cobblestone lane has been occupied since the 1720s. One home is a museum that leads a tour inside and down the alley. The 32 well-preserved brick row houses are inhabited by regular Philadelphians, so be considerate in the narrow space.

National Museum of American Jewish History   MUSEUM

(Map p144; 215-923-3811; www.nmajh.org; 101 S Independence Mall E; adult/child $12/free; ⊙10am-5pm Tue-Fri, to 5:30pm Sat & Sun) With lots of multimedia displays, this museum is a solid introduction to the role of Jewish culture in the US in everything from entertainment to the civil rights movement.

United States Mint   HISTORIC BUILDING

(Map p144; 215-408-0112; www.usmint.gov; 151 N Independence Mall E; ⊙9am-4:30pm Mon-Fri, incl Sat summer) FREE Take the 45-minute self-guided tour to see coins being made, and to admire the Tiffany mosaics inside this stately building.

Dream Garden   HISTORIC BUILDING

(Map p144; 215-238-6450; 601 Walnut St; ⊙8am-6pm Mon-Fri, 10am-1pm Sat) FREE In the east lobby of the Curtis Center is a masterpiece of American craft: a luminous wall-size Tiffany mosaic of more than 100,000 pieces of glass, depicting a lush landscape by Maxfield Parrish.

Independence Seaport Museum   MUSEUM

(Map p140; 215-413-8655; www.phillyseaport.org; 211 S Columbus Blvd; adult/child $15/10; ⊙10am-5pm, to 7pm Thu-Sat summer; ; 21, 25, 76) Worth the trek to Penn's Landing, this well-done museum honors Philadelphia's shipyards, which operated until 1995. You

---

ⓘ VISITING INDEPENDENCE NATIONAL HISTORIC PARK

This national park includes old buildings, museums, landmarks such as the Liberty Bell, and even a restaurant, **City Tavern** (Map p144; 215-413-1443; www.citytavern.com; 138 S 2nd St; mains $22-30; ⊙11:30am-9pm), with waiters in 18th-century costume. With some exceptions, most sites are open 9am to 5pm every day and entrance is free. Independence Hall requires a timed ticket; reserve online (fee $1.50) or go in the morning to the Independence Visitor Center (p151) for same-day tickets (and good maps).

In peak summer, the central park of Independence Mall and surrounding major sights can be an epic tourist scene. You can still find quiet in lesser-known park buildings. Just pick a dot on the map and head for it – there are cool historical details in every corner.

---

can walk through an 1892 steel warship and a WWII submarine.

⊙ Society Hill

Architecture from the 18th and 19th centuries defines this lovely residential neighborhood, bounded by Front, Walnut, Lombard and 8th Sts. Come here just to ramble past brick row homes and down some of the city's prettiest alleys. (The anachronistic Society Hill Towers, designed by IM Pei, overshadow a bit on the north side.) Two 18th-century mansions are open for tours: **Physick House** (Map p144; 215-925-7866; www.philalandmarks.org; 321 S 4th St; admission $8; ⊙noon-4pm Thu-Sat, 1-4pm Sun, by appt Jan & Feb), home of an influential surgeon, and **Powel House** (Map p144; 215-627-0364; www.philalandmarks.org; 244 S 3rd St; adult/child $5/free; ⊙noon-4pm Thu-Sat, 1-4pm Sun, by appt Jan & Feb), the original interior of which is installed in the Philadelphia Museum of Art. At the south edge is Headhouse Shambles, a market hall built in the early 1800s and now the site of the city's largest **farmers market** (Map p140; www.thefoodtrust.org; 2nd St, south of Lombard St; ⊙10am-2pm Sun May-Oct).

⊙ Chinatown & Around

The fourth-largest Chinatown in the USA, Philly's version has existed since the 1860s, thanks to Chinese immigrants who built

Philadelphia

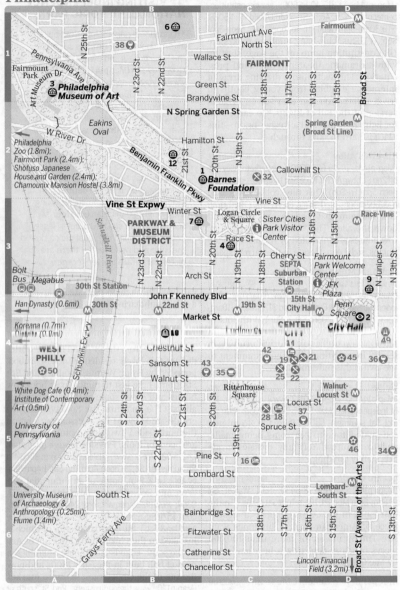

America's transcontinental railroads. Now many residents come from Malaysia, Thailand and Vietnam in addition to every province in China. The multicolored, four-story

Chinese Friendship Gate (Map p140; N 10th St, btwn Cherry & Arch Sts) is the neighborhood's most conspicuous landmark.

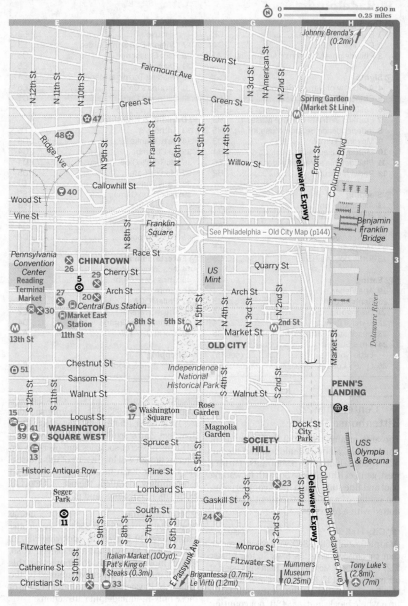

African American Museum in Philadelphia MUSEUM

(Map p144; 215-574-0380; www.aampmuseum.org; 701 Arch St; adult/child $14/10; 10am-5pm Thu-Sat, from noon Sun;) The ground floor has exhibits on notable African American Philadelphians – a bit kid-oriented, but these stories aren't commonly told elsewhere in the city.

Philadelphia

◉ Center City & Rittenhouse Square

The area around City Hall is the engine of Philadelphia, all office buildings and big hotels, concert halls and restaurants. Further west, genteel Rittenhouse Sq, with its wading pool and fine statues, is a quiet counterpoint, the center of an elegant residential district dotted with a few cafés.

★ City Hall   BUILDING
(Map p140; ☏ 215-686-2840; www.phlvisitorcenter.com; cnr Broad & Market Sts; tower $6, tour & tower $12; ⊕ 9am-5pm Mon-Fri, also 11am-4pm one Sat per month, tour at 12:30pm, tower closes at 4:15pm Mon-Fri) Completed in 1901, City Hall takes up a whole block, and, at 548ft, not counting the 27-ton bronze statue of William Penn, it's the world's tallest structure without a steel frame. The view from the observation deck near the top of the tower takes in most of the city (reserve tickets ahead). The daily interior tour is a treat too. In winter, there's ice skating on the west-side plaza.

Masonic Temple   HISTORIC BUILDING
(Map p140; ☏ 215-988-1917; www.pagrandlodge.org; 1 N Broad St; adult/child $13/5; ⊕ tours 10am, 11pm, 1pm, 2pm & 3pm Tue-Fri, 10am, 11am & noon Sat) Fans of secret societies and over-the-top interior design will love a tour of this church-like building. Each meeting room sports an astonishingly detailed theme – Moorish, Egyptian, Renaissance and more.

Mütter Museum   MUSEUM
(Map p140; ☏ 215-560-8564; www.muttermuseum.org; 19 S 22nd St; adult/child $15/10; ⊕ 10am-5pm) Know what a bezoar is? If so, you're morbid enough to appreciate this trove of medical oddities. Maintained by the College of Physicians, this is definitely one of those only-in-Philadelphia attractions.

◉ Fairmount

Starting at JFK Plaza (where the iconic red-and-blue *Love* statue, by sculptor Robert Indiana, stands), the Benjamin Franklin Pkwy is lined with museums and other civic landmarks. It runs northwest, ending at the Philadelphia Museum of Art and Fairmount Park.

★ Philadelphia Museum of Art   MUSEUM

(Map p140; ☑ 215-763-8100; www.philamuseum. org; 2600 Benjamin Franklin Pkwy; adult/child $20/free; ◷10am-5pm Tue, Thu, Sat & Sun, to 8:45pm Wed & Fri) To many, this building is simply the steps Sylvester Stallone ran up in the 1976 flick *Rocky*. But well beyond that, this is one of the nation's finest treasure troves, featuring excellent collections of Asian art, Renaissance masterpieces, post-impressionist works and modern pieces by Picasso, Duchamp and Matisse. Especially neat are the complete rooms: a medieval cloister, a Chinese temple, an Austrian country house.

There's so much to see that a ticket gives admission for two days, here and at the separate Perelman Building, two nearby historic homes and the **Rodin Museum** (Map p140; www.rodinmuseum.org; 2151 Benjamin Franklin Pkwy; admission suggested $10; ◷10am-5pm Wed-Mon). Wednesday and Friday nights are pay-what-you-wish (but note the Perelman is closed).

★ Barnes Foundation   MUSEUM

(Map p140; ☑ 215-278-7200; www.barnesfoundation.org; 2025 Benjamin Franklin Pkwy; adult/child $25/10; ◷10am-5pm Wed-Mon) In the first half of the 20th century, collector and educator Albert C Barnes amassed a remarkable trove of artwork by Cézanne, Degas, Matisse, Renoir, Van Gogh and other European stars. Alongside, he set beautiful pieces of folk art from Africa and the Americas – an artistic desegregation that was shocking at the time. Today's Barnes Foundation is a modern shell, inside which is a faithful reproduction of Barnes' original mansion (still in the Philadelphia suburbs).

The art is hung according to his vision, a careful juxtaposition of colors, themes and materials. In one room, all the portraits appear to be staring at a central point. Even more remarkable: you've likely never seen any of these works before, because Barnes' will limits reproduction and lending.

Franklin Institute Science Museum   MUSEUM

(Map p140; ☑ 215-448-1200; www.fi.edu; 222 N 20th St; adult/child $19.95/15.95; ◷9:30am-5pm; ▪; ▣33, 38, 48) Blockbuster science displays, such as under-the-skin Bodies series, plus a planetarium and a Ben Franklin memorial and show.

Academy of Natural Sciences   MUSEUM

(Map p140; ☑ 215-299-1000; www.ansp.org; 1900 Benjamin Franklin Pkwy; adult/child $15.95/13.95; ◷10am-4:30pm Mon-Fri, to 5pm Sat & Sun; ▪; ▣32, 33, 38) Kid-pleasing exhibits such as a butterfly room and a terrific dinosaur exhibition where you can dig for fossils and bones.

Eastern State Penitentiary   MUSEUM

(Map p140; ☑ 215-236-3300; www.easternstate. org; 2027 Fairmount Ave; adult/child $14/10; ◷10am-5pm) The modern prison didn't just happen – it was invented, and Eastern State Penitentiary was the first one, opened in 1829 and finally closed in 1971. An excellent audioguide leads you through the eerie, echoing halls. There's also broader information on America's current prison system, and fascinating art installations throughout.

From mid-September through Halloween, the prison hosts a truly terrifying haunted house.

Fairmount Park   OUTDOORS

(www.phila.gov/parksandrecreation) **FREE** The snaking Schuylkill River bisects this 9200-acre green space, the largest city park in the US. On the east bank, admire the Victorian-era rowing clubs at Boathouse Row; there's a fine view from in front of the art museum. On either side of the river are playing fields and lawns, public art, historic houses and a very large **zoo** (☑ 215-243-1100; www. philadelphiazoo.org; 3400 W Girard Ave; adult/child $20/18; ◷9:30am-5pm Mar-Oct, to 4pm Nov-Feb; ▪; ▣38, trolley15). In cherry-blossom season especially, don't miss the 16th-century-style **Shofuso Japanese House and Garden** (☑ 215-878-5097; www.shofuso.com; Horticultural Dr; adult/child $7/5; ◷10am-4pm Wed-Fri, 11am-5pm Sat & Sun Apr-Oct).

◉ South Philadelphia

South St, dotted with slightly grungy, youth-oriented bars and music venues, marks the approximate border of South Philadelphia, generally held up as the stronghold of old-style, working-class Philly culture, of the Italian, Irish and German variety. In practice, it's a lot more mixed than that, with distinct enclaves of Mexicans, Vietnamese, African Americans and even that other burgeoning 'ethnic' group, Hipster Coffee Shop Owners.

Philadelphia – Old City

Philadelphia's Magic Gardens GARDENS
(Map p140; ☎ 215-733-0390; www.phillymagic-gardens.org; 1020 South St; adult/child $7/3; ⊙ 11am-6pm Sun-Thu, to 8pm Fri & Sat Apr-Oct, to 5pm Nov-Mar; ☝) The ongoing life's work of Isaiah Zagar, this is a folk-art wonderland of mirror mosaics, bottle walls and quirky sculpture. Zagar has done work around the city – visit here first, and you'll know what to look for.

Italian Market MARKET
(☎ 215-278-2903; www.italianmarketphilly.org; S 9th St, btwn Fitzwater & Wharton Sts; ⊙ 9am-5pm Tue-Sat, to 2pm Sun) A vibrant part of South Philadelphia, this long commercial strip is lined with produce stalls, while the stores are butchers, fishmongers and delis. The northern end is still predominantly Italian; south of Washington St skews Mexican, so you can pick up tortillas and tortellini in the same trip.

Mummers Museum MUSEUM
(☎ 215-336-3050; www.mummersmuseum.com; 1100 S 2nd St; admission by donation; ⊙ 9:30am-4pm Wed-Sat; ☐ 4,57) The Mummers Parade, a dazzling display of homegrown costumes, is a local New Year's ritual with roots in South

Philadelphia – Old City

◉ Top Sights
1	Benjamin Franklin Museum	C3
2	Independence Hall	B4

◉ Sights
3	African American Museum in Philadelphia	A2
4	Congress Hall	A4
5	Dream Garden	A4
6	Elfreth's Alley	D2
7	Liberty Bell Center	A3
8	National Constitution Center	B2
9	National Museum of American Jewish History	B3
10	Physick House	B5
11	Powel House	C5
12	United States Mint	B2

🛏 Sleeping
13	Apple Hostels	C3
14	Penn's View Hotel	D3

✕ Eating
15	Amada	C3
16	City Tavern	C4
17	Franklin Fountain	C3
18	Han Dynasty	C3
19	Wedge + Fig	C1
20	Zahav	C4

🍷 Drinking & Nightlife
21	Olde Bar	D4

🛍 Shopping
22	Shane Confectionery	D3

NEW YORK, NEW JERSEY & PENNSYLVANIA PHILADELPHIA

Philly and, before that, Germany and Switzerland. Learn to tell your Fancy Brigades from your String Bands at this museum – and even try on a costume or two.

◉ University City

This neighborhood, separated from downtown Philly by the Schuylkill River, feels like one big college town. That's because it's home to both Drexel University and the Ivy League University of Pennsylvania ('U Penn'), founded in 1740. The leafy, bustling campus makes for a pleasant afternoon stroll; you might also visit two museums.

University Museum of Archaeology & Anthropology MUSEUM
(☏ 215-898-4000; www.penn.museum; 3260 South St; adult/child $15/10; ☺ 10am-5pm Tue & Thu-Sun, to 8pm Wed; 🚍 21, 30, 40, Ⓜ 36th St Station) Penn's magical museum contains archaeological treasures from ancient Egypt, Mesopotamia, the Mayan world and more.

Institute of Contemporary Art GALLERY
(☏ 215-898-7108; www.icaphila.org; 118 S 36th St; ☺ 11am-8pm Wed, to 6pm Thu & Fri, to 5pm Sat & Sun) FREE Worth a stop if you're in the area; usually two exhibits up at a time, from retrospectives to themed group shows.

🚶 Tours

Mural Tours TROLLEY TOUR
(☏ 215-925-3633; www.muralarts.org/tours; tours free-$30) FREE Guided trolley, train and walking tours of the city's numerous outdoor murals. A free self-guided tour and map is available online.

Taste of Philly Food Tour TOUR
(☏ 800-838-3006; www.tasteofphillyfoodtour.com; adult/child $17/10; ☺ 10am Wed & Sat) Snack and learn Philly food lore at the Reading Terminal Market, with a local writer. Reservations required.

🎉 Festivals & Events

Mummers Parade CARNIVAL
(www.mummers.com; ☺ Jan 1) Uniquely Philly: the closest parallel may be New Orleans' Mardi Gras krewes, with their elaborate costumes, music and deep lore – but in the bracing cold of winter. It often stretches more than a mile through the city center.

Fringe Festival PERFORMING ARTS
(www.fringearts.com; ☺ Sep) Philly's performance fest has been running since 1996. Also on: Feastival, featuring local chefs.

🛏 Sleeping

Because central Philadelphia is so compact, your hotel, no matter the neighborhood, will never be too far from your day's activities. Busy, businessy Center City is where most hotels are located, while B&Bs provide quieter alternatives in the residential blocks around Rittenhouse Sq. There is no shortage of rooms, especially with the national chains (the Loews, Sofitel and Westin can all be recommended). For parking, plan on paying $20 to $45 per day for space in a hotel lot; on-street parking is difficult in the center.

★ Apple Hostels HOSTEL $
(Map p144; ☏ 215-922-0222; www.applehostels.com; 32 Bank St; dm $38, r from $80; ❄ @ 🛜) This gem of a hostel is hidden down an Old

City alley. The apple-green color scheme is a bit intense, but the HI-affiliated place is strong on details: power outlets in lockers, USB ports and reading lights at every bed, free coffee and earplugs. The huge kitchen is spotless; so are the laundry machines.

There are male, female and coed dorms, plus two private rooms. The friendly staff run nightly activities such as walking tours, pasta nights and a bar crawl.

Chamounix Mansion Hostel HOSTEL $

(☑ 215-878-3676; www.philahostel.org; 3250 Chamounix Dr, West Fairmount Park; dm $25; ⊙ closed mid-Dec–mid-Jan; P @ ; 🖳 38) In a lovely wooded area on the north side of the city, this HI hostel is best for guests with a car. In its public areas, set with 19th-century furnishings, the place looks more like a B&B than a hostel; the dorms themselves are basic but clean.

★ Alexander Inn BOUTIQUE HOTEL $$

(Map p140; ☑ 215-923-3535; www.alexanderinn.com; cnr 12th & Spruce Sts; s/d from $119/129; ✳ @ 🛜) Online photos undersell this place. The impeccably kept rooms have a subdued, slightly vintage style; some have old-fashioned half-size tubs. The continental breakfast is a bit generic – but you're in a good area for something more interesting

Morris House Hotel BOUTIQUE HOTEL $$

(Map p140; ☑ 215-922-2446; www.morrishouse-hotel.com; 225 S 8th St; r from $179; ✳ 🛜) In a landmark building near Washington Sq, Morris House conjures colonial elegance without too much formality or frilliness. Beyond the 15 rooms, its finest asset is the courtyard garden (with a locally loved dinner restaurant), a true respite from the city. In winter, cozy up by the fireplace.

Hotel Palomar DESIGN HOTEL $$

(Map p140; ☑ 215-563-5006; www.hotelpalomar-philadelphia.com; 117 S 17th St; r from $229; P ✳ 🛜) One of Philadelphia's two hotels in the excellent Kimpton chain (the other is the more central Monaco), the Palomar is preferable for its lower rates and its quieter location, a few blocks from Rittenhouse Sq. The rooms have a dark but not serious elegance (leopard-spot bathrobes).

Independent BOUTIQUE HOTEL $$

(Map p140; ☑ 215-772-1440; www.theindependenthotel.com; 1234 Locust St; r from $145; ✳ 🛜) A good Center City option housed in a handsome brick Georgian-Revival building with a four-story atrium. The 24 wood-floored rooms are uncluttered and sunny, and the complimentary off-site gym pass and wine and cheese every evening sweeten the deal.

Penn's View Hotel HISTORIC HOTEL $$

(Map p144; ☑ 215-922-7600; www.pennsviewhotel.com; cnr Front & Market Sts; r from $149; ✳ 🛜) Penn's View shows its age – mostly in a good way. The rooms, some with fireplace or balcony, have a quaint style, with oriental rugs.

PENNSYLVANIA FACTS

Nicknames Keystone State, Quaker State

Population 12.8 million

Area 46,055 sq miles

Capital city Harrisburg (population 49,500)

Other cities Philadelphia (population 1.55 million), Pittsburgh (population 306,000), Erie (population 101,000)

Sales tax 6%

Birthplace of Writer Louisa May Alcott (1832–88), dancer Martha Graham (1894–1991), anthropologist Margaret Mead (1901–78), artist Andy Warhol (1928–87), movie star Grace Kelly (1929–82)

Home of US Constitution, the Liberty Bell, first daily newspaper (1784), first auto service station (1913), first computer (1946)

Politics 'Swing state,' Democrat governor, majority Republican state house and senate

Famous for Soft pretzels, Amish people, Philadelphia cheesesteak, Pittsburgh steel mills

Wildlife Home of the largest herd of wild elk east of the Mississippi

Driving distances Philadelphia to NYC 95 miles, Philadelphia to Pittsburgh 306 miles

Maintenance is an occasional issue, and while river views are nice, the nearby freeway is noisy if windows are open. Still, it's great value for its location on the edge of Old City.

La Reserve
B&B $$

(Map p140; ☑ 215-735-1137; www.lareservebandb.com; 1804 Pine St; r $155, without bathroom $120; ❄ 🛜) This 1850s row house sits on a quiet street south of Rittenhouse Sq. The 12 rooms have well-worn charm, with faded oriental rugs, plush drapes, high ceilings and (it seems) the fragile furniture of a minor 19th-century French aristocrat. Some may find the style fussy, but the price is right.

Rittenhouse 1715
BOUTIQUE HOTEL $$$

(Map p140; ☑ 215-546-6500; www.rittenhouse1715.com; 1715 Rittenhouse Square St; r from $289; ❄ 🛜) Around the corner from Rittenhouse Sq, this 1911 mansion is a top-notch choice for those who prefer their luxury small and local. The place oozes old-world sophistication, the 23 rooms are more than comfortable, and the staff is friendly and efficient. But this is a B&B in its bones; some may prefer the amenities of a larger hotel.

🍴 Eating

Philly is a great food town, full of variety and mostly reasonably priced – though you can splash out if you want to. The liveliest new restaurant areas are East Passyunk in the south and Northern Liberties and Fishtown north of Old City, along the river. Stephen Starr and Jose Garces are two rival restaurateurs who together account for some two dozen on-trend operations – you'll almost certainly wind up in one of their places during your visit. Wherever you go, it's a good idea to make reservations; most restaurants are on OpenTable (OpenTable.com). For cheap eats, including the legendary Philly cheesesteak, South St is a go-to spot. Finally, don't miss local gelato chain Capogiro, with branches all over the city.

🍴 Old City

⭐ Franklin Fountain
ICE CREAM $

(Map p144; ☑ 215-627-1899; 116 Market St; sundaes $10; ◷ 11am-midnight Sun-Thu, to 1am Fri & Sat; 🖑) A fantastic yet kitsch-free throwback, from the phosphates and vintage ice-cream flavors (try the teaberry) right down to the ancient telephone and the carton cups (cash only). Also check out the owners'

equally old-school **Shane Confectionery** (Map p144; ☑ 215-922-1048; 110 Market St; ◷ 11am-10pm, to 11pm Fri & Sat) down the block, with historic hot chocolate in the back.

Wedge + Fig
SANDWICHES $

(Map p144; 160 N 3rd St; sandwiches $10; ◷ 11am-8pm Tue-Sat, 10:30am-3:30pm Sun) Grilled-cheese fans will be bowled over by the options at this 'cheese bistro,' which also has big fresh salads and heartier mains. Two bonuses: BYOB policy and a cute garden.

⭐ Zahav
MIDDLE EASTERN $$

(Map p144; ☑ 215-625-8800; 237 St James Pl, off Dock St; mains $14; ◷ 5-10pm Sun-Thu, to 11pm Fri & Sat) Sophisticated 'modern Israeli' cuisine, drawing primarily from North African, Persian and Levantine kitchens. Pick your own meze and grills, or go for the $54 Mesibah (Party Time) set menu. In a slightly incongruous building on Society Hill Towers grounds.

Han Dynasty
CHINESE $$

(Map p144; ☑ 215-922-1888; 123 Chestnut St; mains $13-21; ◷ 11:30am-10pm Sun-Tue & Thu, to midnight Wed, to 10:30pm Fri & Sat) Part of a local mini-empire of sizzling Szechuan goodness. This location has the bonus of a glam dining room in an old bank building. There's another branch in **University City** (☑ 215-222-3711; 3711 Market St; ◷ 11:30am-10pm Sun-Tue & Thu, to midnight Wed, to 10:30pm Fri & Sat).

Amada
SPANISH $$

(Map p144; ☑ 215-625-2450; 217 Chestnut St; tapas $6-20; ◷ 11:30am-2:30pm & 5-10pm Mon-Fri, from 10:30am Sat & Sun) See why Jose Garces was an Iron Chef – his traditional Spanish tapas are fresh and garlicky, and the atmosphere is bustling and loud at the long communal tables.

✕ Chinatown

Banh Mi Cali
VIETNAMESE $

(Map p140; 900 Arch St; sandwiches $5; ⊘9:30am-7:30pm) For cheap, fast eats after Old City sightseeing, nothing beats one of these 'Vietnamese hoagies,' as locals call *banh mi*.

Nan Zhou Hand Drawn Noodle House
CHINESE $

(Map p140; 1022 Race St; mains $6-10; ⊘11am-10pm, to 10:30pm Fri & Sat) Delicious and inexpensive meat soups (skip the skimpy seafood options) with perfectly chewy noodles, plus standard stir-fries and less common treats like pig ears. Cash only.

Rangoon
BURMESE $

(Map p140; 112 N 9th St; mains $9-17; ⊘11:30am-9pm Sun-Thu, to 10pm Fri & Sat) This Burmese spot offers a huge array of tantalizing specialties from spicy red-bean shrimp and curried chicken with egg noodles to coconut tofu.

Original Dim Sum Garden
CHINESE $

(Map p140; 59 N 11th St; mains $6; ⊘11am-10:30pm Sun-Fri, to 11pm Sat) Not the most salubrious looking hole in the wall near the bus station, but some of the tastiest buns and soup dumplings in the city.

✕ Center City & Around

★ Reading Terminal Market
MARKET $

(Map p140; ☑215-922-2317; www.readingterminal-market.org; 51 N 12th St; ⊘8am-6pm Mon-Sat, 9am-5pm Sun) Among the many highlights at this massive, multiethnic food market: Beiler's doughnuts, Miller's Twist buttery pretzels, Tommy Dinic's roast pork and Amish meals at Dutch Eating Place. On weekends, due to crowds, think twice about visiting with small children or large groups (at least with the latter, you can fan out to join different lines).

Luke's Lobster
SEAFOOD $

(Map p140; 130 S 17th St; sandwiches $8-15; ⊘11am-9pm Sun-Thu, to 10pm Fri & Sat) Part of an East Coast mini-chain serving authentic tastes of Maine, from sustainably sourced seafood. Wash down your buttered-bun lobster roll with a wild-blueberry soda.

Federal Donuts
FAST FOOD $

(Map p140; ☑215-665-1101; 1632 Sansom St; doughnuts $1.50, chicken $9; ⊘7am-7pm) All fried, all day: in the morning, the menu is cake doughnuts and quality coffee. After 11am comes the super-crispy Korean-style fried chicken. There's a branch in University City (3428 Sansom St; ⊘7am-7pm), next to White Dog Cafe.

Abe Fisher
JEWISH $$

(Map p140; ☑215-867-0088; 1623 Sansom St; small plates $10-14, 4-course prix fixe $39; ⊘5-10pm Sun-Thu, to 11pm Fri & Sat) 'Foods of the Jewish diaspora,' taken to a higher, slightly whimsical level. Seltzer flows freely; beets abound. Next door, under the same ownership, is equally hot snack bar Dizengoff (1625 Sansom St; hummus from $9; ⊘10:30am-7pm; ☑), for hummus straight out of Tel Aviv.

CLASSIC PHILLY FLAVOR

Philadelphians argue over the nuances of cheesesteaks – hot sandwiches of thin-sliced, griddle-cooked beef on a chewy roll – like biblical scholars parsing Deuteronomy. What a visitor most needs to know is how to order. Say first the kind of cheese – **prov** (provolone), **American** (melty yellow) or **whiz** (molten orange Cheez Whiz!) then **wit** (with) or **widdout** (without), referring to fried onions: 'Prov wit,' for instance, or 'whiz widdout.'

Pat's King of Steaks (1237 E Passyunk Ave; sandwiches $8; ⊘24hr) Pat's invented the cheesesteak, way back in 1930.

Jim's Steaks (Map p140; 400 South St; sandwiches $8; ⊘10am-1am Mon-Thu, to 3am Fri & Sat, from 11am Sun) 'Pizza steak' – topped with tomato sauce – is an option, as are cold hoagies. More comfortable than most, with indoor seats and beer.

Tony Luke's (39 E Oregon Ave; sandwiches $7; ⊘6am-midnight Mon-Thu, to 2am Fri & Sat, 11am-8pm Sun) Famous for its roast pork sandwich with broccoli rabe and provolone. A veggie-only version is great too.

Little Nonna's
ITALIAN $$

(Map p140; 215-546-2100; 1234 Locust St; mains $20-24; 11:45am-2:45pm & 5-10pm Mon-Sat, 5-10pm Sun) 'Sunday gravy,' that delectable tomato-meat sauce that's a staple of Italian-American tables, is served every night at this homey BYOB.

Parc Brasserie
FRENCH $$$

(Map p140; 215-545-2262; 227 S 18th St; mains from $23; 7:30am-11pm Sun-Thu, to midnight Fri & Sat) Soak up the elegant Rittenhouse vibe at this enormous, polished bistro right on the park. Dinner is a little steep, but brunch and lunch are good value, and prime people-watching time.

South Philadelphia

The area around the corner of Washington and 11th Sts is chockablock with Vietnamese restaurants, not to mention the Italian Market (p144). There are classic cheesesteak places here too – in sharp contrast with the everything-artisanal restaurant scene further south on E Passyunk Ave.

Sabrina's Cafe
BREAKFAST $

(Map p140; 910 Christian St; breakfast $10-14; 8am-5pm;) Sabrina's made its name with brunch: stuffed French toast, gooey pork sandwiches – in short, what you need to ease into the day, in a pretty atmosphere. There's also a branch in **Fairmount** (Map p140; 1804 Callowhill St; 8am-10pm Tue-Sat, to 4pm Sun & Mon), near the art museum.

★ Le Virtù
ITALIAN $$$

(215-271-5626; 1927 E Passyunk Ave; mains $24-28; 5-10pm Mon-Sat, 4-9:30pm Sun) The owner of this restaurant is dedicated, obsessively so, to the cuisine of Abruzzo, the region east of Rome, where he long studied with home cooks. He also runs more casual **Brigantessa** (267-318-7341; 1520 E Passyunk Ave; pizzas $16, mains $26; 5pm-midnight) up the street, with a slightly broader menu that includes pizzas. Tuesday is BYOB.

University City

Koreana
KOREAN $

(3801 Chestnut St; mains $9; 11am-10pm) Satisfying students and others interested in good, inexpensive Korean fare; enter from the parking lot in the back of the shopping plaza.

★ White Dog Cafe
ORGANIC $$

(215-386-9224; 3420 Sansom St; dinner mains $18-29; 11:30am-9:30pm Mon-Fri, 10am-10pm Sat, 10am-9pm Sun) If the atmosphere and food here seems more refined than your average farm-to-table restaurant, it's because it has been serving since 1983. Come here for your spring ramps and morels, peak summer tomatoes and plenty more.

Distrito
MEXICAN $$

(215-222-1657; 3945 Chestnut St; mains $9-30; 11:30am-10pm;) Vibrant pink and lime decor is a fitting backdrop for modern Mexican-ish street snacks. Kids will be delighted to sit in the old VW Bug.

Drinking & Nightlife

As one might expect in a city with strong working-class pride, dive bars are well represented, but so are chic cocktail lounges, wine bars and gastropubs intensely focused on local brews. In fact, Old City boasts the highest concentration of liquor licenses in the US after New Orleans, most on S 2nd and S 3rd Sts. Another party strip is on South St, particularly the east end. The whole craft-beer-and-indie-rock scene can be found in Northern Liberties and Fishtown. Impromptu parties happen the first Friday night of the month in Old City, particularly along N 3rd St, when galleries and shops are open late and serving wine. For gay and lesbian bars, look no further than 'The Gayborhood,' roughly bounded by Chestnut, Pine, Juniper and 11th Sts; it's so established that the street signs are trimmed with rainbows.

Cafes

La Colombe
COFFEE

(Map p140; 130 S 19th St; 7am-7pm Mon-Fri, from 8am Sat & Sun) Many cafes now carry the beans from these excellent local coffee roasters (since 1994), but this is the original, in a pleasant spot near Rittenhouse Sq.

Anthony's
CAFE

(Map p140; 903 S 9th St; gelato $3.50; 7am-7pm, to 8pm Sat, to 5pm Sun) Classic Italian Market spot for espresso, cannoli and panini.

Bars

★ Monk's Cafe
BAR

(Map p140; www.monkscafe.com; 264 S 16th St; 11:30am-2am, kitchen to 1am) Hop fans crowd this mellow, wood-paneled place for Belgian and American craft beers on tap. There's also a reasonably priced menu, with typical mussels-and-fries as well as a daily vegan special.

★ Trestle Inn
BAR

(Map p140; ☑267-239-0290; 339 N 11th St; ⏰5pm-2am Wed-Sat) On a dark corner in the so-called 'Eraserhood' (the semi-industrial zone where director David Lynch found inspiration for his film *Eraserhead*), this classed-up old dive has craft cocktails and go-go dancers.

Olde Bar
COCKTAIL BAR

(Map p144; ☑215-253-3777; 125 Walnut St; cocktails $10-15; ⏰5pm-midnight, from 4pm Sat, bar 11am-2am) This Jose Garces remake of a classic Philly oyster house (formerly Bookbinders) kept the stately, nostalgic vibe while improving the cocktails as well as the solid regional dishes ($15 to $20), such as snapper soup and pepper pot.

Tria Cafe
WINE BAR

(Map p140; 1137 Spruce St; glass wine $9-12; ⏰noon-late) An elegant but informal wine bar with an excellent menu of small plates and sandwiches (snacks $4 to $10). There's also one near Rittenhouse Sq (Map p140; 123 S 18th St; ⏰noon-late), and a new-in-2015 taproom (Map p140; 2005 Walnut St; ⏰noon-late) that applies the same thoughtfulness to beer.

Dirty Franks
BAR

(Map p140; 347 S 13th St; ⏰11am-2am) The regulars at this place call it an 'institution' with some irony. Like many Philly dives, it offers the 'citywide special,' a shot of Jim Beam and a can of PBR for $3.

Fiume
BAR

(229 S 45th St; ⏰6pm-2am) To find this unmarked dive in University City, enter next to Abyssinia restaurant). Live rock and bluegrass and good craft beers.

McGillin's Olde Ale House
IRISH PUB

(Map p140; www.mcgillins.com; 1310 Drury St; ⏰11am-2am) Philadelphia's oldest continually operating tavern (since 1860) – it remained open as a speakeasy in the Prohibition years – is a chummy Irish-style pub, with karaoke on Wednesdays and Sundays.

Tavern on Camac
GAY & LESBIAN

(Map p140; www.tavernoncamac.com; 243 S Camac St; ⏰piano bar 4pm-2am, club 9pm-2am Tue-Sun) One of the longest-established gay bars in Philly, with a piano bar and restaurant downstairs. Upstairs is a small club, called

Ascend; Wednesday is ladies' night, Friday and Saturday have DJs.

Paris Wine Bar
WINE BAR

(Map p140; 2301 Fairmount Ave; glass wine $8-11; ⏰5pm-midnight Thu-Sat) Handy for a post-museum glass of wine, this French-ish place (with an English-ish pub adjacent) serves PA vintages on tap and light meals ($11 to $15) and has occasional live jazz.

☆ Entertainment

Philadelphia's culture scene hums, both with home-grown talent and great touring acts. For classical music and ballet, ticket prices are low compared with NYC; likewise, you could see a great rock show for $10. And totally free are the daily classical and pop concerts on the lavish 1909 Wanamaker Organ (Map p140; www.wanamakerorgan.com; 1300 Market St; ⏰concerts noon Mon-Sat, also 5:30pm Mon, Tue, Thu & Sat, 7pm Wed) FREE, inside Macy's.

In sports, the Philadelphia Eagles (www.philadelphiaeagles.com) are legendary, not entirely for the team's (unreliable) performance but for the fervid fans, who party pre-game outside Lincoln Financial Field (www.lincolnfinancielfield.com; 1 Lincoln Financial Field Way) in South Philly (pro baseball and basketball stadiums are in the same area). The season runs August through January.

Johnny Brenda's
LIVE MUSIC

(☑215-739-9684; www.johnnybrendas.com; 1201 N Frankford Ave; tickets $10-15; ⏰kitchen 11am-1am, showtimes vary; Ⓜ Girard) The hub of Fishtown/Northern Liberties' indie-rock scene, this is a great small venue with a balcony, plus a solid restaurant and bar with equally indie-minded beers.

Kimmel Center
PERFORMING ARTS

(Map p140; ☑215-790-5800; www.kimmelcenter.org; 300 S Broad St) The city's most active and prestigious arts institution, this modern concert hall hosts the Philadelphia Orchestra, the Pennyslvania Ballet and more. It also manages the gorgeous old baroque Academy of Music (Map p140; 240 S Broad St) – it's a real treat to see a show here.

PhilaMOCA
PERFORMING ARTS

(Philadelphia Mausoleum of Contemporary Art; Map p140; ☑267-519-9651; www.philamoca.org; 531 N 12th St) A former tombstone store, then producer Diplo's studios, this eclectic space now hosts movies, live shows, art, comedy and more.

Union Transfer

CONCERT VENUE

(Map p140; ☎ 215-232-2100; www.utphilly.com; 1026 Spring Garden St; tickets $15-40) Opened in 2011, this music hall is one of the best spaces for bigger-name bands, with eclectic booking and good bar service.

Chris' Jazz Club

JAZZ

(Map p140; ☎ 215-568-3131; www.chrisjazzcafe. com; 1421 Sansom St; cover $10-20) Showcasing local talent along with national greats, this intimate space features a 4pm piano happy hour Tuesday through Friday and good bands Monday through Saturday nights.

World Cafe Live

LIVE MUSIC

(Map p140; ☎ 215-222-1400; www.worldcafelive. com; 3025 Walnut St; cover $10-40; ⊙ from 11am Mon-Fri, from 5pm Sat & Sun) Home to U Penn's radio station, WXPN, this former factory has upstairs and downstairs performance spaces for jazz, folk and global acts, plus good food.

ℹ Information

Hospital of the University of Pennsylvania (☎ 800-789-7366; www.pennmedicine.org; 800 Spruce St; ⊙ 24hr) Philadelphia's largest medical facility.

Independence Visitor Center (Map p144; ☎ 800-537-7676; www.phlvisitorcenter.com; 599 Market St; ⊙ 8:30am-6pm Sep-May, 8:30am-7pm Jun-Aug) Run by the city and the National Park Service, the center covers the national park and all of the sights in Philadelphia.

Philadelphia Magazine (www.phillymag.com) Monthly glossy, with excellent food writing by Jason Sheehan.

Philadelphia Visitor Center (www.phlvisitor center.com) The city tourism service has convenient branches at Logan Sq (Map p140; ☎ 267-514-4761; www.phlvisitorcenter.com; 200 N 18th St; ⊙ 11am-4pm May-Sep) and JFK Plaza (Map p140; ☎ 215-683-0246; 1599 JFK Blvd; ⊙ 10am-5pm Mon-Sat).

Philadelphia Weekly (www.philadelphiaweekly. com) Free alternative rag available at street boxes around town.

ℹ Getting There & Away

AIR

Philadelphia International Airport (PHL; ☎ 215-937-6937; www.phl.org; 8000 Essington Ave; 🚉 Airport Line), 7 miles southwest of Center City, is a hub for American Airlines, and served by direct international flights.

BUS

Greyhound (☎ 215-931-4075; www.greyhound. com), **Peter Pan Bus Lines** (www.peterpanbus.

com) and **NJ Transit** (☎ 973-275-5555; www. njtransit.com) all depart from the **central bus station** (Map p140; 1001 Filbert St) downtown, near the convention center; Greyhound goes nationwide, Peter Pan focuses on the northeast and NJ Transit gets you to New Jersey. The former two offer cheaper online fares; Greyhound to Washington, DC, for example, can be $14.50 (3½ hours).

From near 30th St Station, **Megabus** (Map p140; www.us.megabus.com; JFK Blvd & N 30th St) serves major cities in the northeast, and Toronto. For NYC and Boston, Greyhound subsidiary **Bolt Bus** (Map p140; ☎ 877-265-8287; www.boltbus.com; JFK Blvd & N 30th St) has the roomiest buses; fares to NYC (2½ hours) can be as low as $7 when booked online.

CAR & MOTORCYCLE

From the north and south, I-95 (Delaware Expwy) follows the east edge of the city along the Delaware River, with several exits for Center City. In the north of the city, I-276 (Pennsylvania Turnpike) runs east over the river to connect with the New Jersey Turnpike.

TRAIN

Just west of downtown across the Schuylkill, beautiful neoclassical **30th St Station** (www. amtrak.com; 30th & Market Sts) is a major hub. From here, Amtrak provides service on its Northeast Corridor line to New York City ($54 to $196, one to 1½ hours) and Boston ($96 to $386, five to 5¾ hours), and Washington, DC ($53 to $242, two hours), as well as to Lancaster (from $16, one hour) and Pittsburgh (from $55, 7½ hours).

A slower but cheaper way to get to NYC is on regional **Septa** (☎ 215-580-7800; www.septa. org) to Trenton ($9, 50 minutes), then NJ Transit to NYC's Penn Station ($15.50, 1½ hours).

ℹ Getting Around

Septa (☎ 215-580-7800; www.septa.org) operates Philadelphia's transit system, including the Airport Line train ($8.75, 25 minutes, every 30 minutes), which stops in University City and Center City. A taxi to the center costs a flat fare of $28.50.

Downtown, it's barely 2 miles between the Delaware and the Schuylkill, so you can walk most places. To rest your feet or travel further afield, choose from a web of Septa buses, two subway lines and a trolley (fare $2.25). Purchase multiple tokens (phasing out in 2016) or the stored-value Key card (phasing in) for discounted fares. Market St is the main artery – hop on buses here to cross the center, or go underground to take the trolley to University City. In high tourist seasons, the purple **Phlash** (www.ridephillyphlash.com; ride/day pass $2/5; ⊙ 10am-6pm daily May-Aug & Dec, Fri-Sun only Sep-Nov) bus makes a loop around major tourist sites; pay on board with exact change.

Philly's bike-share system is **Indego** (☑844-446-3346; www.rideindego.com). Walk-up rates are $4 for 30 minutes; a 30-day membership is a steal at $15, but you must order the key ahead of time.

Cabs, especially around City Center, are easy to hail. The flag drop or fare upon entry is $2.70, then $2.30 per mile or portion thereof. All licensed taxis have GPS and most accept credit cards.

Pennsylvania Dutch Country

Lancaster County and the broader area roughly between Reading and the Susquehanna River is the center of the so-called Pennyslvania Dutch community (now often corrected to Pennsylvania German). These are myriad religious orders and cultures, of Germanic roots and established here since the 18th century. Amish, Mennonites and German Baptist (Brethren) are the best known. One common cultural thread: all are devoted to various degrees of low-tech, plain living.

Somewhat paradoxically, this simple life, with its picturesque horse-drawn buggies and ox teams tilling fields, attracts busloads of visitors and is spawning an astoundingly kitschy tourist industry that can be off-putting. But if you get onto the back roads, you can appreciate the quiet these religious orders have preserved. And some of that kitsch is undeniably fun.

The city of **Lancaster**, population 60,000, has a nice old downtown and some good restaurants that use the fruits of the surrounding farmland; its First Friday party on Prince St draws a good local crowd. The main PA Dutch tourist zone is east of here: along Rte 30 and Old Philadelphia Pike (Rte 340), between **Ronks**, **Bird-in-Hand**, **Intercourse** and **Paradise**. The stretch is essentially farmland interrupted by strip malls and attractions such as kiddie theme park Dutch Wonderland, and souvenir shop Dutch Haven, shaped like a windmill (which does nevertheless make a killer shoo-fly pie and some serious birch beer).

South of Lancaster, **Strasburg** and **Christiana** are pleasant tiny towns, as are, to the north, **Ephrata** and **Lititz**. Lititz is home to Wilbur Chocolates, what locals prefer to giant Hershey's (based north of here),

and America's first pretzel factory, Sturgis. Ephrata is the headquarters of Ten Thousand Villages, a massive Mennonite-run fairtrade imports store with branches all over.

◉ Sights

★**Strasburg Railroad**   TRAIN
(☑866-725-9666; www.strasburgrailroad.com; 301 Gap Rd, Ronks; coach class adult/child $14/8; ⊘multiple trips daily, times vary by season; ☋) It's only a 45-minute ride to Paradise and back, but this steam train is a treat, with grand old carriages (wood-stove-heated in winter) running on a line laid down in 1832. Package tickets are available for the **Railroad Museum of Pennsylvania** (☑717-687-8628; www.rrmuseumpa.org; 300 Gap Rd, Ronks; adult/child $10/8; ⊘9am-5pm Mon-Sat, from noon Sun, closed Sun & Mon winter; ☋) across the road, which has scores of mechanical marvels to admire.

For a fully rail-themed trip, book a night in a train car motel room at the **Red Caboose** (☑717-687-5000; www.redcaboosemotel.com; 312 Paradise Ln, Ronks; s/d from $95/129; ☀☋☋), or just visit its **restaurant** (☑717-687-7759; breakfasts $8, dinners $14; ⊘7:30am-3pm Tue & Wed, to 8pm Thu-Sat, to 4pm Sun).

Landis Valley Museum   MUSEUM
(☑717-569-0401; www.landisvalleymuseum.org; 2451 Kissel Hill Rd, Lancaster; adult/child $12/8; ⊘9am-5pm, from noon Sun, closed Mon & Tue Jan-Feb) Based on an 18th-century village, this open-air museum is the best way to get an overview of the early PA Dutch culture and Mennonites in particular. Costumed staff are on hand to demonstrate tinsmithing, for instance, and there's a beautiful crafts exhibit.

Ephrata Cloister   MUSEUM
(☑717-733-6600; www.ephratacloister.org; 632 W Main St, Ephrata; adult/child $10/6; ⊘9am-5pm, from noon Sun, closed Mon & Tue Jan-Feb, tours hourly 10am-3pm) One of the area's myriad breakaway religious sects established this community in 1732; despite celibacy vows and infighting, it lasted until 1934. Now it has an almost ghost-town feel. You can walk around alone, but ideally join a tour, to see inside all the buildings.

Lancaster Mennonite Historical Society   MUSEUM
(☑717-393-9745; www.lmhs.org; 2215 Millstream Rd, Lancaster; museum $5; ⊘8:30am-4:30pm Tue-Sat) The small museum here displays beautiful glass and woodwork along with the story

WORTH A TRIP

GETTYSBURG

This town 145 miles west of Philadelphia, now quite tranquil and pretty, is synonymous with one of the bloodiest battles of the Civil War. Over three days in July 1863, some 8000 people were killed. Later that year, President Abraham Lincoln delivered his Gettysburg Address ('Four score and seven years ago...'), reinforcing the war's mission of equality.

Gettysburg National Military Park (☎717-334-1124; www.nps.gov/gett; 1195 Baltimore Pike; museum adult/child $12.50/8.50, ranger tours per vehicle $65, bus tours adult/child $30/18; ☺museum 8am-6pm Apr-Oct, to 5pm Nov-Mar, grounds 6am-10pm Apr-Oct, to 7pm Nov-Mar) covers 8 sq miles of land marked with monuments and trails. The museum at the visitor center is a must-see, for the awe-inspiring cyclorama – a life-size, 360-degree painting – of Pickett's Charge, the especially disastrous battle on the last day. Originally made in 1884, the painting was restored and reinstalled in 2008, with a dramatic light show and narration. Out in the park, you can explore on your own, or on a bus tour or – most recommended – on a two-hour ranger-led tour in your own car.

Gettysburg itself is a pretty town, worth spending the night in, but plan ahead in summer, especially in July, when the town is mobbed with battle reenactors. For accommodations, try **Brickhouse Inn** (☎717-338-9337; www.brickhouseinn.com; 452 Baltimore St; r from $149; [P]❄️🛜), two adjacent old buildings with a lovely back garden; the owners take breakfast so seriously there's even a pie course. **Dobbin House** (☎717-334-2100; 89 Steinwehr Ave; sandwiches $10, mains $25; ☺tavern 11:30am-9pm, main restaurant from 5pm), built in 1776, is an inn and restaurant. The food is average, but the setting, all candlelit and creaky, is great. The tavern in the basement has a cheaper bar menu, with burgers and soups.

of how Mennonites established themselves in this area. There's a well-stocked shop and bookstore, too.

◌̆ Tours

Aaron & Jessica's Buggy Rides　　TOUR
(☎717-768-8828; www.amishbuggyrides.com; 3121 Old Philadelphia Pike, Bird-in-Hand; adult/child tours from $10/6; ☺9am-5pm Mon-Sat; 👶) Hop in one of those black horse-drawn buggies, for a 30-minute cruise through the country or an hour-long farm tour. Drivers are Amish, Mennonite or Brethren and open to questions.

🛏 Sleeping

★Quiet Haven　　MOTEL $
(☎717-397-6231; www.quiethavenmotel.com; 2556 Siegrist Rd, Ronks; r from $76) If your vision of a PA Dutch getaway is sitting in a rocking chair and gazing out over farmland, book in at this family-owned motel, surrounded by green fields. Most of the 15 rooms still have a hint of 1960s flair.

A Farm Stay　　ACCOMMODATION SERVICE $
(www.afarmstay.com; r from $80; 👶) This website is a network of 20 or so lodging options on area farmland – some more typical B&Bs and others full working farms where guests are welcome to pet goats and milk cows.

★General Sutter Inn　　INN $$
(☎717-626-2115; www.generalsutterinn.com; 14 East Main St, Lititz; s/d/ste from $70/110/185; ❄️🛜) At this 18th-century inn, 10 rooms are furnished with tasteful antiques, and on the incongruous top floor, six suites have a loose rock-and-roll theme. Downstairs is the popular Bulls Head Pub, for Scotch eggs and cask ales.

Fulton Steamboat Inn　　HOTEL $$
(☎717-299-9999; www.fultonsteamboatinn.com; 1 Hartman Bridge Rd, Lancaster; r from $140; ❄️🛜🏊) Even if you know the inventor of the steamboat was born in this area, this nautical-themed hotel is a bit gimmicky. But the brass fixtures and flowery wallpaper are all well kept, the rooms are comfortable, and there's even an indoor pool.

Cork Factory　　BOUTIQUE HOTEL $$
(☎717-735-2075; www.corkfactoryhotel.com; 480 New Holland Ave, Lancaster; r from $159; ❄️🛜) An abandoned brick behemoth now houses this stylish hotel. It's a short drive from downtown.

✗ Eating

Local aficionados agree, the best PA Dutch cooking is done for church suppers. Keep an eye out for special events.

★ **Katie's Kitchen** AMERICAN $
(200 Hartman Bridge Rd, Ronks; mains $8; ⊘7:30am-7:30pm) This typical PA Dutch diner serves locals and tourists alike with dishes such as creamed chipped beef and 'egg-in-the-nest.' Food is freshly cooked, and fortunately available in half-portions.

★ **Tomato Pie Cafe** SANDWICHES $
(☑717-627-1762; 23 N Broad St, Lititz; mains $8; ⊘7am-9pm Mon-Sat; 🛜🗲) The creative, fresh food and the complex coffee drinks wouldn't be out of place in a city, but the atmosphere is pure friendly small town.

Central Market MARKET $
(☑717-735-6890; www.centralmarketlancaster. com; 23 N Market St, Lancaster; snacks from $2; ⊘6am-4pm Tue & Fri, to 2pm Sat) The produce and food stalls at this indoor market represent a great cross-section of Lancaster. You can pick up fresh PA Dutch sausages or horseradish, as well as Thai noodles and Lebanese salads.

Bird-in-Hand Farmers Market MARKET $
(☑717-393-9674; 2710 Old Philadelphia Pike; pretzels $2, lunches $8; ⊘8:30am-5:30pm Fri & Sat, also Wed Apr-Nov, Thu Jul-Oct) A one-stop shop of Dutch Country highlights, both genuine and tourist-friendly. Load up on tasty home-made jams, pastries, pretzels, beef jerky and more. Two lunch counters serve meals.

Dienner's BUFFET $
(2855 Lincoln Hwy, Ronks; dinner $11-15; ⊘7am-6pm Mon-Thu, to 8pm Fri & Sat) Pace yourself at this all-you-can-eat PA Dutch extravaganza: one of the three buffet lines is dedicated to sweets. The food tends toward bland, but everyone will find something to like; daily specials like chicken pot pie are generally good.

★ **Lancaster Brewing Co** PUB FOOD $$
(302 N Plum St; mains $16-24; ⊘11:30am-10pm; 🍴) This brewery, established in 1995, is a local favorite. The restaurant serves hearty but delicious food – lamb chops with tzatziki, say, and housemade sausage. But you can't beat specials like $5 all-you-can-eat wings.

Maison EUROPEAN $$$
(☑717-293-5060; 230 N Prince St, Lancaster; mains $26-30; ⊘5-11pm Wed-Sat; 🗲) A husband-and-wife team run this homey but meticulous place downtown, giving local farm products a rustic Italian-French treatment: pork braised in milk, fried squash blossoms, hand-made gnocchi, depending on the season.

ℹ Information

Discover Lancaster Visitors Center (☑800-723-8824; www.padutchcountry.com; 501 Greenfield Rd; ⊘10am-4pm, to 5pm summer) Just off Rte 30, with info on all of Pennsylvania, good area maps and free coffee, which goes with cinnamon rolls sold in the parking lot.

ℹ Getting There & Around

A car is the most practical way; get a good map (mobile service is poor) and take smaller roads. If you have time, you could go Amish-style: Amtrak serves the **Lancaster train station** (☑800-872-7245; www.amtrak.com; 53 McGovern Ave, Lancaster) with frequent trains from Philadelphia ($16, 1¼ hours), but only once-daily service to Pittsburgh ($51, 6¼ hours). Lancaster's bus system, **RRTA** (Red Rose Transit Authority; ☑717-393-3315; www.redrosetransit.com; 225 North Queen St, Lancaster; fare from $1.70, transfer from $.05), covers the greater county. Bike rental is a possibility, though the terrain is hilly and road shoulders thin or nonexistent; **Intercourse Bike Works** (☑717-929-0327; www.intercourse-bikeworks.com; 3614 Old Philadelphia Pike, Intercourse; ⊘10am-5pm Mon-Sat) rents bikes and leads tours many summer Saturdays.

Pennsylvania Wilds

North-central Pennsylvania, called 'the Wilds,' is largely deep forest, with an occasional regal building or grand mansion, remnants of a time when lumber, coal and oil brought wealth to this now little-visited patch of the state. Several museums (in Titusville, Bradford and Galeton) tell the boom and bust story. Since the bust, this swath of 12 counties has reverted to its wild state; much of the area is national forest or state park land.

Scenic **Rte 6** cuts through east–west, with the tiny college town of **Mansfield** as an eastern gateway. Just west of here, **Pine Creek Gorge** cuts south; its deeper end (1450ft) is down near Waterville, but it's more accessible, with good views and trails along the rim and down into the canyon, on the north end at **Colton Point State Park** (☑570-724-3061; www.visitpaparks.com; 4797 Rte 660, Wellsboro) FREE. Follow signs outside the pretty, gas-lamp-lit town of **Wellsboro**.

Further west, stop at **Kinzua Bridge Skywalk** (☑814-965-2646; www.visitanf.com; 1721 Lindholm Rd, Mt Jewett; ⊘dawn-dusk) FREE, a

300ft-high train viaduct, partially destroyed in 2003 by a tornado and now an observation point with an unnerving glass floor and views of the ruined steel piers in the valley below.

Deeper in the Wilds is Cherry Springs State Park (☑814-435-5010; www. visitpaparks. com; 4639 Cherry Springs Rd, Coudersport; campsites from $17). Due its position on a mountaintop, it is one of the best places for stargazing east of the Mississippi, and people book the campsites well ahead in July and August, when the Milky Way is almost directly overhead.

🛏 Sleeping & Eating

Mansfield Inn   MOTEL **$**
(☑570-662-2136; www.mansfieldinn.com; 26 S Main St, Mansfield; r from $60; ❖❀☎) There may be more charming B&Bs deeper in the PA Wilds, but this well-maintained motel is hard to beat for straight-ahead value.

Lodge at Glendorn   LODGE **$$$**
(☑800-843-8568; www.glendorn.com; 1000 Glendorn Dr, Bradford; r from $550) Legacy of the Wilds' former industrial wealth, this 1200-acre estate was developed by an early 20th-century oil baron. Its 'big house' and log cabins (all with wood-burning fireplaces) are now the state's finest resort. The restaurant is excellent, and the nightly fee includes activities from skeet shooting to curling.

Yorkholo Brewing   AMERICAN **$**
(☑570-662-0241; 19 N Main St, Mansfield; mains $11-14; ⊘4-10pm Mon & Tue, 11am-10pm Wed-Sat, to 9pm Sun; ☑) A welcome alternative to standard diner food in this area, this brick-walled brewpub has fresh salads, creative pizzas and some excellent Belgian-style beers.

Pittsburgh

For decades in the second half of the 20th century, Pittsburgh looked like it would be another notch in America's rust belt, a desolate city where the once-churning steel mills and blast furnaces had all shuttered. But thanks to latent wealth and some creative thinking, it has earned a reputation for being one of the more livable small cities in the country. It has a distinct topography, a mass of green hills (the climate is very rainy) rising straight up from the Monongahela and Allegheny Rivers, which converge here and join the Ohio, all connected by picturesque

bridges – Istanbul in western Pennysylvania, if you squint hard enough. It's a far more cultured city than a population of 300,000 would suggest, with top-notch museums and universities, abundant greenery and several bustling neighborhoods with lively restaurant and bar scenes.

Carnegie is the biggest name in Pittsburgh – Scottish-born Andrew modernized steel production, and his legacy is still synonymous with the city and its many cultural and educational institutions. Second-biggest: Heinz, of ketchup fame, a company established here in 1869.

◉ Sights & Activities

Points of interest in Pittsburgh are scattered in every neighborhood, and because of the hills, it's a bit difficult to walk between them. You could drive, but the bus goes everywhere and gives you a chance to enjoy the views.

◉ Downtown & the Strip District

The so-called Golden Triangle where the Monongahela and Allegheny converge is Pittsburgh's center of finance, business and high culture. Every Friday from May to October, there's a farmers market in Market Sq, a slick modern piazza surrounded by restaurants. Just south is PPG Place, a clutch of dazzling 1980s glass office towers, with **ice skating** (www.ppgplace.com; adult/child $8/7, skate rental $3; ⊘mid-Nov–Feb) in winter. Northeast of downtown, along the Allegheny, are the warehouses of the **Strip District**, a longtime hub for wholesalers and now a lively stretch of ethnic food stores and cafes; it's even livelier on Saturdays, when street vendors add to the mix.

Fort Pitt Museum   MUSEUM
(☑412-281-9284; www.heinzhistorycenter.org; 601 Commonwealth Pl; adult/child $6/3; ⊘10am-5pm) This museum tells the story of the French and Indian War of the mid-18th century, which brought Pittsburgh into being. The surrounding waterfront, a state park, is lovely on a summer day.

Heinz History Center   MUSEUM
(☑412-454-6000; www.heinzhistorycenter.org; 1212 Smallman St; adult/child incl Sports Museum $15/6; ⊘10am-5pm) Local history and lore is shared with verve and color – there's even an exhibit dedicated to children's TV host and native son Fred Rogers. It also contains

the **Western Pennsylvania Sports Museum**, focusing on Pittsburgh's many beloved champs.

North Side

This part of town across the Allegheny River is mobbed when the Steelers (football, at **Heinz Field**) or Pirates (baseball, at **PNC Park**) are playing; bridges from downtown close to cars at this time. But this is also where the city's best art museums are, and the pretty **Mexican War Streets** neighborhood (streets are named for battles) is a pleasant place to stroll among the restored row houses – look for colorful **Randyland** on Arch St.

★ **Andy Warhol Museum**　　　　MUSEUM
(☏ 412-237-8300; www.warhol.org; 117 Sandusky St; adult/child $20/10, 5-10pm Fri $10/5; ⊙ 10am-5pm Tue-Sun, to 10pm Fri) This six-story museum celebrates Pittsburgh's coolest native son, who moved to NYC, got a nose job and made himself famous with pop art. The exhibits start with Warhol's earliest drawings and commercial illustrations and include a simulated Velvet Underground happening, a DIY 'screen test,' and pieces of Warhol's extensive knickknack collection.

★ **Mattress Factory**　　　　ARTS CENTER
(☏ 412-231-3169; www.mattress.org; 500 Sampsonia Way; adult $20; ⊙ 10am-5pm Tue-Sat, 1-5pm Sun, café 11:30am-3pm Tue-Sat) Since 1977, this art space has hosted the absolute avant-garde. It now occupies several neighborhood buildings, and always has something surprising on. Note the good café here too, as there's a shortage of food in the area.

National Aviary　　　　ZOO
(☏ 412-323-7235; www.aviary.org; 700 Arch St; adult/child $14/12; ⊙ 10am-5pm; ⊕) Often overlooked due to its proximity to the excellent science center and children's museum, this is nonetheless a fantastic opportunity to see all kinds of birds up close and very personal, in big open habitats.

Carnegie Science Center　　　　MUSEUM
(☏ 412-237-3400; www.carnegiesciencecenter.org; 1 Allegheny Ave; adult/child $19/12, IMAX & special exhibits extra; ⊙ 10am-5pm, to 7pm Sat; ⊕) A cut above the average science museum, with exhibits on everything from outer space to candy, this is a favorite with Pittsburgh parents.

South Side & Mt Washington

Across the Monongahela River is the South Side, which rises steeply to a ridge called Mt Washington. The neighborhood called the **South Side Slopes** is a fascinating community of houses on the incline, accessible via steep, winding roads and hundreds of stairs. Most visitors come for the dozens of bars in the flatland along E Carson St.

★ **Monongahela & Duquesne Inclines**　　　　TRAM
(www.duquesneincline.org; one-way adult/child $2.50/1.25; ⊙ 5:30am-12:45am Mon-Sat, from 7am Sun) These two funiculars, built in the late 19th century, are Pittsburgh icons, zipping up the steep slope of Mt Washington every five to 10 minutes. They provide commuters a quick connection and they give visitors great city views, especially at night. You can make a loop, going up one, walking along aptly named Grandview Ave (about 1 mile, or take bus 40) and coming down the other.

If you ride just one, make it the Duquesne (du-*kane*). At the top, you can pay 50¢ to see the gears and cables at work. Outside the station, **Altius** (☏ 412-904-4442; 1230 Grandview Ave; mains $28-44, bar snacks $8-18; ⊙ 5-10pm Mon-Thu, to 11pm Fri & Sat, to 9pm Sun) restaurant is a good place to enjoy the view over a drink.

Oakland & Around

The University of Pittsburgh and Carnegie Mellon University are here, and the surrounding streets are packed with cheap eateries, cafes, shops and student homes.

Carnegie Museums　　　　MUSEUM
(☏ 412-622-3131; www.carnegiemuseums.org; 4400 Forbes Ave; adult/child both museums $20/12; ⊙ 10am-5pm Tue-Sat, from noon Sun; ⊕) Founded in 1895, these neighboring institutions are both tremendous troves of knowledge. The **Carnegie Museum of Art** has European treasures and an excellent architectural collection, while the **Carnegie Museum of Natural History** features a complete *Tyrannosaurus rex* skeleton and beautiful old dioramas.

Cathedral of Learning　　　　TOWER
(☏ 412-624-6001; 4200 Fifth Ave; audio tour adult/child weekends only $4/2; ⊙ 9am-4pm Mon-Sat, from 11am Sun) FREE Soaring 42 stories, this Gothic tower at the center of University of Pittsburgh is a city landmark. Visit to see

DON'T MISS

FALLINGWATER

A Frank Lloyd Wright masterpiece, **Fallingwater** (☎724-329-8501; www.fallingwater.org; 1491 Mill Run Rd, Mill Run; adult/child $25/18, grounds only $8; ☺tours Thu-Tue mid-Mar–Nov, weekends only Dec, closed Jan & Feb) is south of Pittsburgh, and a visit here makes a good day out in the pretty area known as the Laurel Highlands. Completed in 1939 as a weekend retreat for the Kaufmanns, owners of a Pittsburgh department store, Fallingwater melds elegantly with the natural setting, including the stream that runs through. It is furnished largely as the Kaufmanns left it. Access is by guided tour only; reservations are recommended. The attractive forested grounds open at 8:30am, and there's a good cafe (it closes before the last tour ends).

A 20-minute drive away – crossing the pretty Youghiogheny River, where you can go rafting – is a smaller Wright home, **Kentuck Knob** (☎724-329-1901; www.kentuckknob.com; 723 Kentuck Rd, Chalk Hill; adult/child $22/16; ☺tours daily Mar-Nov, weekends in Dec, closed Jan & Feb), which he designed when he was in his 80s. Nowhere near as extravagant, as it adheres more closely to his austere Usonian principles, it is nonetheless interesting for its use of hexagons – and it is seldom crowded. Tours last about an hour and include a jaunt through the current owners' sculpture garden.

You can even spend a night nearby at **Polymath Park** (☎877-833-7829; www.frank lloydwrightovernight.net; 187 Evergreen Ln, Acme; house from $199 ; ✿ ☎), a kind of mini-resort with one Wright home and three others designed by his apprentices. Don't expect loads of Wright flair – these are all Usonia-style homes, and the furniture is not Wright's designs. Still, it's a pretty area and a rare opportunity for architecture buffs. The homes are open for tours, and there's a restaurant here too – though you could also stop for an exceptionally good fish sandwich en route at **Johnny L's Sandwich Works** (1240 S Main St, Greensburg; sandwiches $7; ☺11am-11pm Mon-Sat).

the delightful Nationality Rooms, themed classrooms ranging from Russian to Syrian to African.

Frick Art & Historical Center MUSEUM
(☎412-371-0600; www.thefrickpittsburgh.org; 7227 Reynolds St; tours adult/child $12/6; ☺10am-5pm Tue-Sun; ☐P1, 71C) FREE Henry Clay Frick, of Manhattan's Frick Museum fame, built his steel fortune in Pittsburgh. This Frick shows a small art collection (beautiful medieval icons), plus his cars. For more art and general splendor, join a tour of Clayton, the family mansion. The cafe here is excellent; reserve.

Phipps Conservatory GARDENS
(☎412-622-6914; www.phipps.conservatory.org; 1 Schenley Park; adult/child $15/11; ☺9:30am-5pm, to 10pm Fri; ☎) ✐ An impressive steel-and-glass greenhouse with beautifully designed and curated gardens, at the northwest corner of Schenley Park.

◉ Squirrel Hill & Shadyside

These long-established wealthier neighborhoods have an almost village-like atmosphere, each with a central business street lined with boutiques and cafés. **Squirrel Hill** is home to Pittsburgh's large Jewish community, the city's best kosher eateries, butchers and Judaica shops. In **Shadyside**, Walnut St is the bustling main strip. The leafy campus of **Chatham University**, located between the two neighborhoods, is a nice place to stroll.

◉ Lawrenceville, Bloomfield & East Liberty

Formerly gritty Lawrenceville, along the Allegheny northeast of the Strip District, has become one of the city's coolest neighborhoods. Butler St from around 34th St all the way up to 54th St is a spotty strip of shops, galleries, studios, bars and eateries on every hipster's radar. East of Allegheny Cemetery (a trove of history itself) are the slightly gentrifying Garfield and Bloomfield neighborhoods, still both strong Polish and Italian enclaves. Due east is the intensely overhauled East Liberty area, now home to a Google office.

Center for PostNatural History MUSEUM
(☎412-223-7698; www.postnatural.org; 4913 Penn Ave; admission by donation; ☺6-8pm 1st Fri of month, noon-4pm Sun & by appointment) FREE 'Postnatural history,' according to the artist founder of this quirky museum, is the field

of plants and animals manipulated by humankind. Learn all about spider-silk-making goats, selective breeding and more.

👉 Tours

Rivers of Steel   TOUR
(☑ 412-464-4020; www.riversofsteel.com; 623 E 8th Ave, Homestead; tours adult/child $20/12.50; ☺ museum 10am-4pm Mon-Fri, Carrie Furnace tours 10am & 11am Sat May-Oct, also 10am Fri Jun-Aug) This organization leads tours of Carrie Blast Furnace, a huge and derelict structure on the riverfront. At the group's offices in Homestead, there's a neat free museum about the area's industrial labor history. Great info online too.

Alan Irvine Storyteller Tours   TOUR
(☑ 412-508-2077; www.alanirvine.com; tours $15) This historian brings the city's past to life in a journey through several neighborhoods.

'Burgh Bits & Bites   TOUR
(☑ 412-901-7150; www.burghfoodtour.com; tours $39) These food tours through various neighborhoods are a fun way to discover the city's unique ethnic eats.

Pittsburgh History & Landmarks Foundation   TOUR
(☑ 412-471-5808; www.phlf.org; 100 W Station Sq Dr; some tours free, others from $5) This group runs a free walking tour from Market Sq on Fridays at noon, among other excursions.

🛏 Sleeping

Many hotels cater to business travelers, so rates are significantly lower on weekends. Pittsburgh has no real hostel, although there seem to be eternal plans for one. An Ace Hotel was set to open in East Liberty in 2016.

★ Priory   INN $$
(☑ 412-231-3338; www.thepriory.com; 614 Pressley St; s/d/ste from $105/170/235; P ❋ ☎) The monks had it good when this was still a Catholic monastery: spacious rooms, high ceilings, a fireplace in the parlor. Breakfast, with its pastries and cold cuts, is reminiscent of a European hostel. It's on the North Side, in the historic-but-scruffy Deutschtown area.

Friendship Suites   APARTMENT $$
(☑ 412-392-1935; www.friendshipsuites.com; 301 Stratford Ave; r/ste/apt $129/145/175; ❋ ☎) In several neighboring buildings, these fully furnished small apartments on the edge of East Liberty are not bursting with style, but they're good value and close to transportation.

Morning Glory Inn   B&B $$
(☑ 412-721-9174; www.gloryinn.com; 2119 Sarah St; r/ste from $155/190; P ❋ ☎) An Italianate-style Victorian brick town house, the Morning Glory is in the heart of the lively South Side. The overall decor (white wicker, floral patterns) might strike some as too frilly, but there's a charming backyard patio and delicious breakfasts.

Parador Inn   B&B $$
(☑ 412-231-4800; www.theparadorinn.com; 939 Western Ave; r $160; P ❋ ☎) A Victorian mansion renovated with a Caribbean color sensibility, this North Side inn delights the eyes in each of the nine rooms.

Mansions on Fifth   B&B $$
(☑ 412-381-5105; www.mansionsonfifth.com; 5105 Fifth Ave; r from $225; P ❋ ☎) These two early 20th-century homes are convenient to the University of Pittsburgh and the Carnegie Museums. Rooms are spacious and plush, but it's the stained glass, intricate tile and other details that set it apart.

Monaco   DESIGN HOTEL $$$
(☑ 412-471-1170; www.monaco-pittsburgh.com; 620 William Penn Pl; r from $279; P ❋ ☎) The cool Kimpton chain opened this place in 2015, done up in eye-popping colors. Enthusiastic staff and a good restaurant make it the best value downtown.

Omni William Penn Hotel   HOTEL $$$
(☑ 412-281-7100; www.omnihotels.com; 530 William Penn Pl; r from $299; P ❋ ☎) Pittsburgh's stateliest old hotel, built by Henry Frick, has great public spaces, but the rooms feel a bit stuck in the '90s. Worth booking if you can find it at a discount.

🍴 Eating

E Carson St on the South Side has the highest concentration of restaurants, but the Strip District comes a close second. As in many categories, Lawrenceville has the most up-and-coming activity. Catering to a large Catholic population, many Pittsburgh restaurants serve fish on Fridays, and fried-fish sandwiches are especially popular.

☜ Downtown & the Strip District

Grazing is easy in the Strip, with all kind of food vendors and one-of-a-kind markets such as mega-grocery Wholey, Greek Stamoolis Brothers and the epic cheese counter at Pennsylvania Macaroni (though note many businesses are closed Sunday).

Original Oyster House SEAFOOD $
(20 Market Sq; mains $9; ⊙10am-10pm Mon-Sat, 11am-7pm Sun) Operating in one form or another since 1870, this place often has a line out the door for its fish sandwiches. It is not quite the best in the area, but the bar side is a historical gem. Cash only.

Enrico Biscotti Cafe ITALIAN $
(2022 Penn Ave; mains $10; ⊙11am-3pm Mon-Fri, from 7am Sat) Bread, pizza and torta rustica round out the menu alongside the biscotti. Charismatic owner Larry Laguttata offers a bread-baking class ($85) every Sunday.

Prantl's BAKERY $
(438 Market St; cake slice $3; ⊙7am-6pm Mon-Fri, 9am-4pm Sat, 10am-3pm Sun) Don't leave Pittsburgh without tasting burnt almond torte, Prantl's signature. Also in **Shadyside** (5525 Walnut St; ⊙7:30am-6pm Tue-Sat, 9am-4pm Sun & Mon).

Primanti Bros FAST FOOD $
(☑412-263-2142; www.primantibros.com; 46 18th St; sandwiches $6; ⊙24hr) The sandwiches Pittsburghers miss when they move away: hot, greasy and always stuffed with french fries and coleslaw. Other outlets are in **Oakland** (3803 Forbes Ave; ⊙10am-midnight, to 3am Thu-Sat), **Market Sq downtown** (2 S Market Sq; ⊙10am-midniight, to 2am Fri & Sat) and **South Side** (1832 E Carson St; ⊙11am-2am, from 10am Sat & Sun).

Pamela's DINER $
(60 21st St; mains $6-9; ⊙7am-3pm Mon-Sat, from 8am Sun) Unpretentious Pamela's has a few branches around the city, all with a classic chrome diner look and its signature lacy-thin pancakes. Cash only.

★Bar Marco ITALIAN $$
(☑412-471-1900; 2216 Penn Ave; mains $18-26, tasting menu $75; ⊙5-11pm Wed-Sun, to 10pm Mon, also 10am-3pm Sat & Sun; ☝) One of the city's more sophisticated kitchens, with an excellent brunch too. Snack in the bar or reserve in the Wine Room, for the chef's great-value tasting menu. Refreshing no-tipping policy.

☜ North Side

Wilson's Bar-B-Q BARBECUE $
(700 N Taylor Ave; mains $8.50; ⊙noon-8pm Mon-Sat) Your clothes will smell like a campfire after a plastic-plate meal in this zero-frills place, but the ribs can't be beat.

☜ South Side

Zenith VEGAN $
(☑412-481-4833; 86 S 26th St; mains $7-10; ⊙11:30am-8:30pm Thu-Sat, 11am-2:30pm Sun; ☝) A meal here is like eating in an antique shop, as everything, including the Formica tables, is for sale. The buffet Sunday brunch ($11.50) draws a great community of regulars.

Dish Osteria Bar ITALIAN $$
(☑412-390-2012; www.dishosteria.com; 128 S 17th St; mains $20-26; ⊙5pm-2am Mon-Sat, kitchen till midnight) An intimate locals' fave, with sometimes extravagant Mediterranean dishes such as fettuccine with lamb ragù.

☜ Oakland

★Conflict Kitchen FAST FOOD $
(☑412-802-8417; 221 Schenley Dr; mains $8-12; ⊙11am-6pm) This takeout stand near the Cathedral of Learning reinvents itself periodically, cooking food from another country the US has issues with. It has so far been Afghani, Palestinian and Cuban, among other cuisines.

Original Hot Dog Shop FAST FOOD $
(☑412-621-7388; 3901 Forbes Ave; sandwiches $4-7; ⊙10am-1:30am Tue-Sat, to 9pm Sun & Mon) Affectionately nicknamed 'The Dirty O,' this neon-lit shop is a late-night favorite. With good chili dogs and mountains of twice-fried fries, inebriation isn't necessary – just very common.

☜ Lawrenceville & East Liberty

★Smoke BBQ Taqueria MEXICAN $
(☑412-224-2070; 4115 Butler St; tacos $6; ⊙11am-11pm; ☝) Two Austin, TX, natives combine barbecue skills with Mexican flour-tortilla tech for super-savory food and even good veg options. BYOB; there's a great beer store adjacent.

Coca Cafe
CAFE **$**

(3811 Butler St; mains $10-14, dinner small plates $10-15; ☺8am-3pm Mon-Wed, to 5pm Thu, to 9pm Fri, 9am-9pm Sat, to 2pm Sun; 🖉) Creative and fresh breakfasts (eggplant benedict, say) are a big draw here, but this two-room cafe is pleasant any time. Good coffee, too.

Franktuary
FAST FOOD **$**

(3810 Butler St; hot dogs from $3.50; ☺11:30am-11:30pm Tue-Thu, to 1am Fri & Sat, to 3pm Sun) Giving dignity to the simple frankfurter, with quality meat and toppings ('vestments,' per the menu) such as blue cheese to kimchi. Good salads and a full cocktail list make it a meal.

Cure
MODERN AMERICAN **$$$**

(🖉412-252-2595; 5336 Butler St; mains $28-34; ☺5-10pm) This gold-lit temple to the pig is so devoted it even serves garlic-and-caper-studded lard with the bread. Its 'charcroute' plate presents all its lovely housemade preserved meats.

🍷 Drinking & Nightlife

E Carson St on the South Side is the biggest party strip in town, while Lawrenceville has many of the cooler bars. Most gay bars are in a short stretch of Liberty Ave downtown. Drinks are a steal but bring cash. Also, many places still allow smoking.

★ Allegheny Wine Mixer
WINE BAR

(5326 Butler St; ☺5pm-midnight Tue-Thu, to 1am Fri-Sun) All the perks of a high-end wine bar – great list, smart staff, tasty nibbles – in the comfort of a neighborhood dive.

Gooski's
BAR

(3117 Brereton St; beers $3; ☺11am-2am) Pierogi, punk rock and a near-legendary bartender have made this a consistently great dive bar in Polish Hill for decades.

Park House
BAR

(403 E Ohio St; ☺5pm-2am Mon-Sat) A friendly bar in Deutschtown on the North Side, with free peanuts, popcorn and music. A menu of hummus and falafel balances out the beer. Wednesday is bluegrass night.

Bloomfield Bridge Tavern
BAR

(🖉412-682-8611; 4412 Liberty Ave; ☺5pm-2am Tue-Sat) 'The Polish Party Place' is a pub with an '80s-rec-room look, excellent pierogi and sauerkraut, and indie-rock bands on the weekends.

Kelly's
COCKTAIL BAR

(6012 Penn Circle S; drinks from $6; ☺11:30am-2am Mon-Sat) This old bar has weathered the East Liberty neighborhood's shift to upwardly mobile style with class, developing great Prohibition-era cocktails while keeping the crackly vinyl booths.

Brillobox Bar
BAR

(www.brillobox.net; 4104 Penn Ave; ☺5pm-2am Tue-Sun) Live music and DJs (upstairs, with a cover), veg-friendly food and 'starving artist Sunday' $7 dinner make this a popular spot just up the hill from the Lawrenceville strip.

Nied's Hotel
BAR

(5438 Butler St; beers $2; ☺7am-midnight or later, closed Sun) An anchor in Upper Lawrenceville since 1941, this great community restaurant-bar serves one of the city's better fish sandwiches ($2), and its house band is a crowd-pleaser. In summer, bands play in the 'amphitheater' (empty lot) next door.

Wigle Whiskey Garden at the Barrelhouse
BAR

(🖉412-224-2827; www.wiglewhiskey.com; 1055 Spring Garden Ave; ☺5-9pm Wed-Fri, from 3pm Sat, 11am-4pm Sun) This craft whiskey maker's barreling facility on the North Side hosts bands and bingo in a pretty outdoor space. Its **distillery** (2401 Smallman St; ☺10am-6pm Tue-Sat, to 4pm Sun), in the Strip District, is open for tours and tastings too.

☆ Entertainment

★ Elks Lodge
LIVE MUSIC

(🖉412-321-1834; 400 Cedar Ave; cover $5; ☺bluegrass 8pm Wed, big band 7pm 1st & 3rd Thu) Find out why Pittsburgh is known as the Paris of Appalachia at the Elks' Banjo Night, when the stage is packed with players and the audience sings along to all the bluegrass classics. Also hosts big-band night twice a month, with dance classes first. On the North Side in Deutschtown.

Pittsburgh Cultural Trust
PERFORMING ARTS

(🖉412-471-6070; www.pgharts.org; 803 Liberty Ave) An umbrella group for all the arts in downtown's Cultural District, from Pittsburgh Opera to global-minded Pittsburgh Dance Council to creative theater from Bricolage. Check the website for an events calendar and tickets.

Rex Theater   LIVE MUSIC
(☑ 412-381-6811; www.rextheatre.com; 1602 E Carson St) A favorite South Side venue, a converted movie theater, for touring jazz, rock and indie bands.

MCG Jazz   LIVE MUSIC
(☑ 412-322-0800; www.mcgjazz.org; 1815 Metropolitan St; ☺ Oct-Apr) Part of a community arts-and-crafts school on the North Side, this 350-seat venue hosts top jazz musicians.

Row House Cinema   CINEMA
(☑ 412-904-3225; www.rowhousecinema.com; 4115 Butler St; ticket $9) This art-house and repertory cinema in Lawrenceville has theme weeks and gives a discount for wearing a costume.

ⓘ Information

Greater Pittsburgh Convention & Visitors Bureau Main Branch (☑ 412-281-7711; www.visitpittsburgh.com; 120 Fifth Ave, Suite 2800; ☺ 10am-6pm Mon-Fri, to 4pm Sat, to 3pm Sun) Publishes the *Official Visitors Guide* and provides maps and tourist advice.
Pittsburgh City Paper (www.pghcitypaper.com) Independent local alt-weekly with good arts listings.
Pittsburgh Post-Gazette (www.post-gazette.com) A major daily.
Pop City (www.popcitymedia.com) Weekly e-magazine with a focus on arts and community.
University of Pittsburgh Medical Center (☑ 412-647-2345; www.upmc.com; 200 Lothrop St; ☺ 24hr) Pittsburgh's top hospital.

ⓘ Getting There & Away

AIR
Pittsburgh International Airport (☑ 412-472-3525; www.pitairport.com; 1000 Airport Blvd), 18 miles west of downtown, has direct connections to Europe, Canada and major US cities via a slew of airlines.

BUS
The **Greyhound bus station** (Grant Street Transportation Center; ☑ 412-392-6514; www.greyhound.com; 55 11th St) has frequent buses to Philadelphia (from $33, six to seven hours), New York (from $31, 8½ to 11 hours) and Chicago ($68, 11 to 14 hours).

CAR & MOTORCYCLE
Pittsburgh is accessible via I-76 or I-79 from the west and from the east on I-70. It's about a six-hour drive from NYC and about three hours from Buffalo.

TRAIN
Pittsburgh has a magnificent old train station – and **Amtrak** (☑ 800-872-7245; www.amtrak.com; 1100 Liberty Ave) drops you off in a dismal modern building behind it. Service runs to Philadelphia (from $55, 7½ hours) and NYC (from $73, 9½ hours). One also runs to Chicago ($107, 10 hours) and Washington, DC ($50, eight hours).

ⓘ Getting Around

PortAuthority (www.portauthority.org) provides public transportation around Pittsburgh, including the 28X Airport Flyer ($3.75, 40 minutes, every 30 minutes 5:30am to midnight) from the airport to downtown and Oakland. Taxis cost about $40 (not including tip) to downtown. Various shuttles also make downtown runs for $25 or so per person one way.

Driving in Pittsburgh can be frustrating – roads end with no warning or deposit you suddenly on bridges. Parking is scarce downtown. Where possible, use the extensive bus network, which includes a fast express busway (routes beginning with P). There is also a limited light-rail system, the T, useful for the South Side. Rides on the T downtown are free; other in-city fares are $2.50, and $1 for a transfer.

New England

Best Places to Eat

➡ Row 34 (p178)

➡ Chatham Fish Pier Market (p191)

➡ Fore Street (p238)

➡ Nudel (p201)

➡ Art Cliff Diner (p197)

Best Places to Stay

➡ Verb Hotel (p177)

➡ Carpe Diem (p194)

➡ Inn at Shelburne Farms (p223)

➡ The Attwater (p207)

Why Go?

The history of New England is the history of America. It's the Pilgrims who came ashore at Plymouth Rock and the minutemen who fought for American independence. It's hundreds of years of progressive thinkers who dared to dream and dared to do. Nowadays, New England is still at the cutting edge of culture, with top-notch art museums and music festivals.

For outdoor adventure, the region undulates with the rolling hills and rocky peaks of the ancient Appalachian Mountains. Plus, nearly 5000 miles of coastline make for unlimited opportunities for fishing, swimming, surfing and sailing. Those are surefire ways to work up an appetite. Fortunately, New England is a bounty of epicurean delights: pancakes drenched in maple syrup; just-picked fruit and sharp cheddar cheese; and – most importantly – sublimely fresh seafood that is the hallmark of this region.

When to Go

Boston

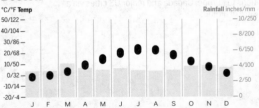

May–Jun	Jul–Aug	Sep–Oct
Uncrowded sights and lightly trodden trails. Whale-watching begins.	Top tourist season with summer festivals and warmer ocean water.	New England's blazing foliage peaks from mid-September to mid-October.

History

When the first European settlers arrived, New England was inhabited by native Algonquians who lived in small tribes, raising corn and beans, hunting game and harvesting the rich coastal waters.

In 1602 English captain Bartholomew Gosnold landed at Cape Cod and sailed north to Maine; but it wasn't until 1614 that Captain John Smith, who charted the region's coastline for King James I, christened the land 'New England.' With the arrival of the Pilgrims at Plymouth in 1620, European settlement began in earnest. Over the next century the colonies expanded, often at the expense of the indigenous people.

Although subjects of the British Crown, New Englanders governed themselves with their own legislative councils and they came to view their affairs as separate from those of England. In the 1770s King George III imposed a series of taxes to pay for England's involvement in costly wars. The colonists, unrepresented in the British parliament, protested under the slogan 'no taxation without representation.' Attempts to squash the protests eventually led to battles at Lexington and Concord, setting off the War for Independence. The historic result was the birth of the USA in 1776.

Following independence, New England became an economic powerhouse, its harbors booming centers for shipbuilding, fishing and trade. New England's famed Yankee Clippers plied ports from China to South America. A thriving whaling industry brought unprecedented wealth to Nantucket and New Bedford. The USA's first water-powered cotton-spinning mill was established in Rhode Island in 1793.

No boom lasts forever. By the early 20th century many of the mills had moved south. Today education, finance, biotechnology and tourism are linchpins of the regional economy.

Local Culture

New Englanders tend to be reserved by nature, with the Yankee brusqueness standing in marked contrast to the casual outgoing nature of some other American regions. This taciturn quality shouldn't be confused with unfriendliness, as it's simply a more formal regional style.

Particularly in rural areas, folks take pride in their ingenuity and self-sufficient character. These New Englanders remain fiercely independent, from the fishing boat crews who brave Atlantic storms to the small Vermont farmers who fight to keep operating independently within America's agribusiness economy. Fortunately for the farmers and fishers, buy-local and go-organic movements have grown by leaps and bounds throughout New England. From bistros in Boston to small towns in the far north the menus are greening.

One place you won't find that ol' Yankee reserve is at the ball field. New Englanders are fanatical about sports. Attending a Red Sox game is as close as you'll come to a modern-day gladiators-at-the-coliseum scene – wild cheers and nasty jeers galore.

Generally regarded as a liberal enclave, New England is at the forefront on progressive political issues from gay rights to health-care reform. Indeed the universal health-insurance program in Massachusetts became the model for President Obama's national plan.

NEW ENGLAND IN...

One Week

Start in **Boston**, following the **Freedom Trail**, dining at a cozy **North End bistro** and exploring the city's highlights. Spend a day ogling the mansions in **Newport**. Then hit the beaches on **Cape Cod** or hop a ferry to **Nantucket** or **Martha's Vineyard**. End the week with a jaunt north to New Hampshire's **White Mountains** or the **Maine coast**.

Two Weeks

On your second week, take a leisurely drive through the **Litchfield Hills** and the **Berkshires.** Bookend the week with visits to the lively burgs of **Providence** and **Burlington**. Alternatively, plan an extended stay on the Maine coast, with time to explore **Bar Harbor** and kayak along the shores of **Acadia National Park**. Wrap it up in Maine's vast wilderness, where you can work up a sweat on a hike up the northernmost peak of the **Appalachian Trail** or take an adrenaline-pumping ride down the **Kennebec River**.

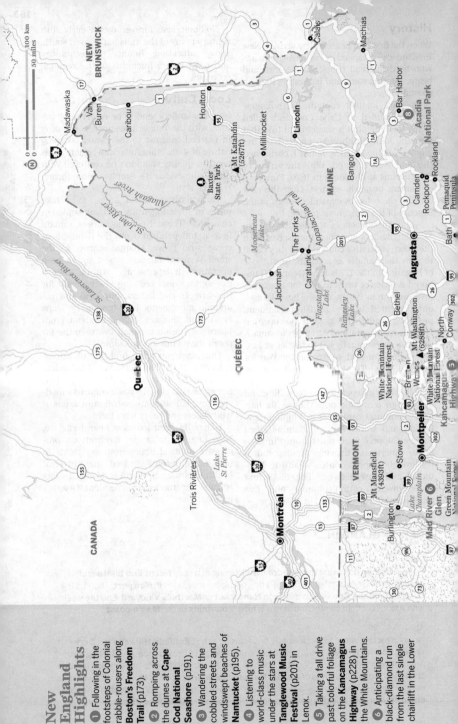

New England Highlights

1 Following in the footsteps of Colonial rabble-rousers along **Boston's Freedom Trail** (p173).

2 Romping across the dunes at **Cape Cod National Seashore** (p191).

3 Wandering the cobbled streets and windswept beaches of **Nantucket** (p195).

4 Listening to world-class music under the stars at **Tanglewood Music Festival** (p201) in Lenox.

5 Taking a fall drive past colorful foliage on the **Kancamagus Highway** (p228) in the White Mountains.

6 Anticipating a black-diamond run from the last single chairlift in the Lower

100 km
50 miles

48 at Mad River Glen (p219).

❼ Catching your breath as raptors swoop past at VINS Nature Center (p218).

❽ Enjoying lofty views from a ladder trail at Acadia National Park (p241).

❾ Cracking open a steamed lobster at the Lobster Dock (p240) in Boothbay Harbor.

MASSACHUSETTS

From the woodsy hills of the Berkshires to the sandy beaches of Cape Cod, Massachusetts is filled with opportunities to explore the great outdoors. From Plymouth Rock to the Revolutionary War, the Commonwealth is rich with history. And from Boston's universities and museums to the Berkshires' summer theaters and Tanglewood, its cultural offerings are world class. Your challenge lies in the deciding: which Massachusetts will you discover?

ⓘ Information

Massachusetts Department of Conservation and Recreation (☏ 617-626-1250; www.mass.gov/eea) Offers camping in 29 state parks.

Massachusetts Office of Travel & Tourism (☏ 617-973-8500; www.massvacation.com) Information about events and activities throughout the state, including an excellent guide to green tourism and resources especially for gay and lesbian travelers.

Boston

For all intents and purposes, Boston is the oldest city in America. And you can hardly walk a step over its cobblestone streets without running into some historic site. But Boston has not been relegated to the past. The city's art and music scenes continue to charm and challenge contemporary audiences; cutting-edge urban planning projects are reshaping the city; and scores of universities guarantee an infusion of cultural energy year after year.

History

When the Massachusetts Bay Colony was established by England in 1630, Boston became its capital. It's a city of firsts: Boston Latin School, the first public school in the USA, was founded in 1635, followed a year later by Harvard, the nation's first university. The first newspaper in the colonies was printed here in 1704, America's first labor union organized here in 1795 and the country's first subway system opened in Boston in 1897.

Not only were the first battles of the American Revolution fought nearby, but Boston was also home to the first African American regiment to fight in the US Civil War. Waves of immigrants, especially Irish in the mid-18th century and Italians in the early 20th century, have infused the city with European influences.

Today Boston remains at the forefront of higher learning and its universities have spawned world-renowned industries in biotechnology, medicine and finance.

◉ Sights

Boston's small size means that it's easy to walk and difficult to drive. Most of Boston's main attractions are found in or near the city center. Begin at Boston Common, where you'll find the tourist office and the start of the Freedom Trail

◉ Boston Common, Beacon Hill & Downtown

Rising above Boston Common is Beacon Hill, one of the city's most historic and affluent neighborhoods. To the east is Downtown Boston, with a curious mix of Colonial sights and modern office buildings.

★**Boston Common** PARK
(Map p174; btwn Tremont, Charles, Beacon & Park Sts; ⊙6am-midnight; P ⚐; T Park St) The Boston Common has served many purposes over the years, including as a campground for British troops during the Revolutionary War and as green grass for cattle grazing until 1830. The Common today serves picnickers, sunbathers and people-watchers. In winter, the **Frog Pond** (Map p174; www.bostonfrogpond.com; Boston Common; admission adult/child $5/free, rental $10/5; ⊙10am-4pm Mon, to 9pm Tue-Sun mid-Nov–mid-Mar; ⚐; T Park St) attracts ice-skaters, while summer draws theater lovers for **Shakespeare on the Common** (Map p174; www.commshakes.org; Boston Common; ⊙8pm Tue-Sat, 7pm Sun Jul & Aug; T Park St). This is also the starting point for the Freedom Trail.

Massachusetts State House   NOTABLE BUILDING

(Map p174; www.sec.state.ma.us; cnr Beacon & Bowdoin Sts; ⊘9am-5pm, tours 10am-3:30pm Mon-Fri; ⊤Park St) FREE High atop Beacon Hill, Massachusetts' leaders and legislators attempt to turn their ideas into concrete policies and practices within the State House. John Hancock provided the land (previously part of his cow pasture); Charles Bulfinch designed the commanding state capitol; but it was Oliver Wendell Holmes who called it 'the hub of the solar system' (thus earning Boston the nickname 'the Hub'). Free 40-minute tours cover the history, artwork, architecture and political personalities of the State House.

Granary Burying Ground   CEMETERY

(Map p174; Tremont St; ⊘9am-5pm; ⊤Park St) Dating to 1660, this atmospheric spot is crammed with historic headstones, many with evocative (and creepy) carvings. This is the final resting place of all your favorite revolutionary heroes including Paul Revere, Samuel Adams, John Hancock and James Otis. Benjamin Franklin is buried in Philadelphia, but the Franklin family plot contains his parents.

Old South Meeting House   HISTORIC BUILDING

(Map p174; www.osmh.org; 310 Washington St; adult/child $6/1; ⊘9:30am-5pm Apr-Oct, 10am-4pm Nov-Mar; ⊤Downtown Crossing or State) 'No tax on tea!' That was the decision on December 16, 1773, when 5000 angry colonists gathered here to protest British taxes, leading to the Boston Tea Party. Visit the graceful meeting house to check out an exhibit about the history of the building and listen to an audio of the historic pre–Tea Party meeting.

Old State House   HISTORIC BUILDING

(Map p174; www.revolutionaryboston.org; 206 Washington St; adult/child $10/free; ⊘9am-6pm Jun-Aug, to 5pm Sep-May; ⊤State) Dating to 1713, the Old State House is Boston's oldest surviving public building, where the Massachusetts Assembly used to debate the issues of the day before the revolution. The building is best known for its balcony, where the Declaration of Independence was first read to Bostonians in 1776. Inside, the Old State House contains a small museum of revolutionary memorabilia, with videos and multimedia presentations about the Boston Massacre, which took place out front.

Faneuil Hall   HISTORIC BUILDING

(Map p174; www.nps.gov/bost; Congress St; ⊘9am-5pm; ⊤Haymarket or Government Center) FREE 'Those who cannot bear free speech had best go home,' said Wendell Phillips. 'Faneuil Hall is no place for slavish hearts.' Indeed, this public meeting place was the site of so much rabble-rousing that it earned the nickname the 'Cradle of Liberty'. After the revolution, Faneuil Hall was a forum for meetings about abolition, women's suffrage and war. The historic hall is normally open to the public, who can hear about the building's history from National Park Service (NPS) rangers.

★New England Aquarium   AQUARIUM

(Map p174; www.neaq.org; Central Wharf; adult/child $25/18; ⊘9am-5pm Mon-Fri, to 6pm Sat & Sun, 1hr later Jul & Aug; ℗⊛; ⊤Aquarium) ✐ Teeming with sea creatures of all sizes, shapes and colors, this giant fishbowl is the centerpiece of downtown Boston's waterfront. The main attraction is the newly renovated three-story Giant Ocean Tank, which swirls with thousands of creatures great and small, including turtles, sharks and eels. Countless side exhibits explore the lives and habitats of other underwater oddities, as well as penguins and marine mammals.

NEW ENGLAND BOSTON

MASSACHUSETTS FACTS

Nickname Bay State

Population 6.7 million

Area 7840 sq miles

Capital city Boston (population 646,000)

Other cities Worcester (population 182,500), Springfield (population 153,700)

Sales tax 6.25%

Birthplace of Inventor Benjamin Franklin (1706–90), John F Kennedy (1917–63), authors Jack Kerouac (1922–69) and Henry David Thoreau (1817–62)

Home of Harvard University, Boston Marathon, Plymouth Rock

Politics Democratic

Famous for Boston Tea Party, first state to legalize gay marriage

Driving distances Boston to Provincetown 115 miles, Boston to Northampton 104 miles, Boston to Acadia National Park 280 miles

State Sweets Boston Cream Pie, Dunkin' Donuts, Fig Newtons

Boston

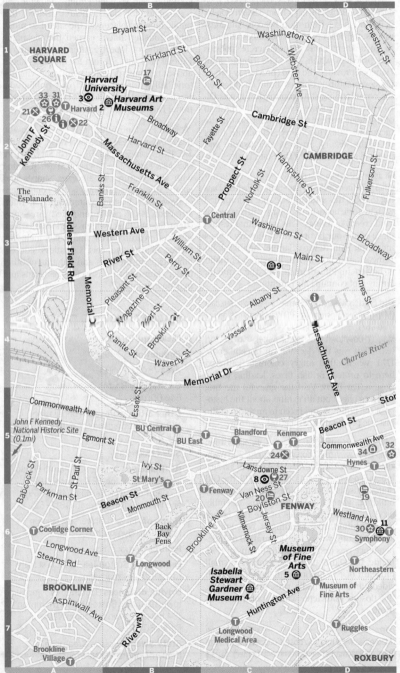

NEW ENGLAND

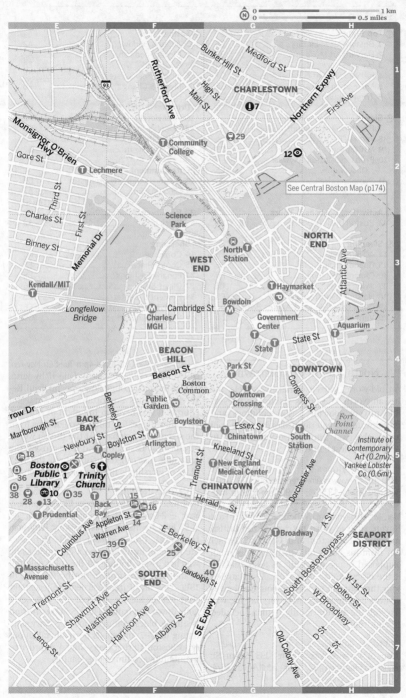

0 1 km
0 0.5 miles

NEW ENGLAND

CHARLESTOWN

Medford St
Bunker Hill St
High St
Main St
Rutherford Ave
Northern Expwy
First Ave

7

29

Community College

12

Monsignor O'Brien Hwy

Gore St
Third St
Charles St
First St
Binney St
Memorial Dr

Lechmere

Science Park

See Central Boston Map (p174)

Kendall/MIT

Longfellow Bridge

WEST END
North Station

NORTH END

Atlantic Ave

Haymarket

Bowdoin

Cambridge St
Charles/MGH

Government Center

Aquarium

State St
State

BEACON HILL
Beacon St

Park St

DOWNTOWN

Congress St

Boston Common

Downtown Crossing

Public Garden

Boylston

BACK BAY

Berkeley St
Boylston St

Marlborough St
Newbury St
Copley
Arlington

Essex St
Chinatown

South Station

Kneeland St

New England Medical Center

Fort Point Channel

Institute of Contemporary Art (0.2mi); Yankee Lobster Co (0.6mi)

row Dr

18

23

Boston Public Library
1

6 Trinity Church

36
38
28 **13**
10 **35**
Prudential

15
16
Back Bay
14

Tremont St

CHINATOWN

Herald St

Columbus Ave
Appleton St
Warren Ave

E Berkeley St

Broadway

A St

SEAPORT DISTRICT

South Boston Bypass

W 1st St
Bolton St
W Broadway

39
37

25

40
Randolph St

SE Expwy

Massachusetts Avenue

SOUTH END

Tremont St
Shawmut Ave
Washington Street
Harrison Ave
Albany St

Lenox St

D St
E St

Old Colony Ave

Boston

◉ North End & Charlestown

An old-world warren of narrow streets, the Italian North End offers visitors an irresistible mix of colorful period buildings and mouthwatering eateries. Colonial sights spill across the river into Charlestown, home to America's oldest battleship.

Paul Revere House   HISTORIC SITE

(Map p174; www.paulreverehouse.org; 19 North Sq; adult/child $3.50/1; ⊙9:30am-5:15pm mid-Apr–Oct, to 4:15pm Nov–mid-Apr, closed Mon Jan–Mar; ⊛; ⊤Haymarket) When silversmith Paul Revere rode to warn patriots of the British march to Lexington and Concord, he set out from his home on North Sq. This small clapboard house was built in 1680, making it the oldest house in Boston. A self-guided tour through the house and courtyard gives visitors a glimpse of what everyday life was like for the Revere family (which included 16 children!).

Old North Church   CHURCH

(Map p174; www.oldnorth.com; 193 Salem St; requested donation $3, tour adult/child $6/4; ⊙9am-5pm Mar–Oct, 10am-4pm Tue–Sun Nov–Feb; ⊤Haymarket or North Station) 'One if by land, Two if by sea...' Longfellow's poem, 'Paul Revere's Ride,' has immortalized this graceful church. It was here, on the night of April 18, 1775, that the sexton hung two lanterns from the steeple, as a signal that the British would advance on Lexington and Concord via the sea route. Also called Christ Church, this 1723 place of worship is Boston's oldest church.

USS Constitution   HISTORIC SITE

(Map p168; www.oldironsides.com; Charlestown Navy Yard; ⊙2-6pm Tue-Fri, 10am-6pm Sat & Sun; ⊛; ⊟93 from Haymarket, ⊠Inner Harbor Ferry from Long Wharf, ⊤North Station) FREE 'Her sides are made of iron!' So cried a crewman as he watched a shot bounce off the thick oak hull of the USS *Constitution* during the War of 1812. This bit of irony earned the legendary ship her nickname. Indeed, she has never gone down in a battle. The USS *Constitution* is still the oldest commissioned US Navy ship, dating to 1797, and she is normally taken out onto Boston Harbor every July 4 in order to maintain her commissioned status.

Bunker Hill Monument MONUMENT
(Map p168; www.nps.gov/bost; Monument Sq; ⊙9am-5:30pm Jul & Aug, to 4:15pm Sep-Jun; ﹩; 🚌93 from Haymarket, ⊤Community College) FREE
This 220ft granite obelisk monument commemorates the turning-point battle that was fought on the surrounding hillside on June 17, 1775. Ultimately, the Redcoats prevailed, but the victory was bittersweet, as they lost more than one-third of their deployed forces, while the colonists suffered relatively few casualties. Climb the 294 steps to the top of the monument to enjoy the panorama of the city, the harbor and the North Shore.

⊙ **Seaport District**

Following the HarborWalk, it's a pleasant stroll into the up-and-coming Seaport District.

★**Boston Tea Party Ships & Museum** MUSEUM
(Map p174; www.bostonteapartyship.com; Congress St Bridge; adult/child $25/15; ⊙10am-5pm, last tour 4pm; ﹩; ⊤South Station) 'Boston Harbor a teapot tonight!' To protest unfair taxes, a gang of rebellious colonists dumped 342 chests of tea into the water. The 1773 protest – the Boston Tea Party – set into motion the events leading to the Revolutionary War. Nowadays, replica Tea Party Ships are moored at the reconstructed Griffin's Wharf, alongside an excellent experiential museum dedicated to the revolution's most catalytic event.

Institute of Contemporary Art MUSEUM
(ICA; www.icaboston.org; 100 Northern Ave; adult/child $15/free; ⊙10am-5pm Tue, Wed, Sat & Sun, to 9pm Thu & Fri; ﹩; 🚌SL1 or SL2, ⊤South Station) Boston is fast becoming a focal point for con-temporary art in the 21st century, with the Institute of Contemporary Arts leading the way. The building is a work of art in itself: a glass structure cantilevered over a waterside plaza. The vast light-filled interior allows for multimedia presentations, educational programs and studio space. More importantly, it allows for the development of the ICA's permanent collection.

⊙ **Chinatown, Theater District & South End**

Compact Chinatown offers enticing Asian eateries, while the overlapping Theater District is clustered with performing-arts venues. To the west, the sprawling South End boasts one of America's largest concentrations of Victorian row houses, a burgeoning art community and a terrific restaurant scene.

⊙ **Back Bay**

Extending west from Boston Common this well-groomed neighborhood boasts graceful brownstone residences, grand edifices and tony shopping on Newbury St.

★**Public Garden** GARDENS
(Map p174; www.friendsofthepublicgarden.org; Arlington St; ⊙6am-midnight; ﹩; ⊤Arlington) Adjoining Boston Common, the Public Garden is a 24-acre botanical oasis of Victorian flower beds, verdant grass and weeping willow trees shading a tranquil lagoon. The old-fashioned pedal-powered **Swan Boats** (Map p174; www.swanboats.com; Public Garden; adult/child $3/1.50; ⊙10am-5pm Jun-Aug, to 4pm mid-Apr–May, noon-4pm Sep; ⊤Arlington) have been delighting children for generations. The most endearing

BOSTON IN...

Two Days

Spend one day reliving revolutionary history by following the **Freedom Trail**. Take time to lounge on the **Boston Common**, peek in the **Old State House** and imbibe a little history at the **Union Oyster House**. Afterwards, stroll into the **North End** for an Italian dinner. On your second day, rent a bike and ride along the Charles River. Go as far as **Harvard Sq** to cruise the campus and browse the bookstores.

Four Days

On your third day, peruse the impressive American collection at the **Museum of Fine Arts**. In the evening, catch a performance of the world-famous **Boston Symphony Orchestra** or watch the Red Sox play at **Fenway Park**.

Spend your last day discovering Back Bay. Window-shop and gallery-hop on **Newbury St**, go to the top of the **Prudential Center** and browse the **Boston Public Library**.

WORTH A TRIP

JFK SITES

John F Kennedy Library & Museum (www.jfklibrary.org; Columbia Point; adult/child $14/10; ☺9am-5pm; ⓣ JFK/UMass) The legacy of JFK is ubiquitous in Boston, but the official memorial to the 35th president is the presidential library and museum – a striking modern marble building designed by IM Pei. The architectural centerpiece is the glass pavilion, with soaring 115ft ceilings and floor-to-ceiling windows overlooking Boston Harbor. The museum is a fitting tribute to JFK's life and legacy. The effective use of video recreates history for visitors who may or may not remember the early 1960s.

John F Kennedy National Historic Site (www.nps.gov/jofi; 83 Beals St; ☺9:30am-5pm Wed-Sun May-Oct; ⓣ Coolidge Corner) Four of the nine Kennedy children were born and raised in this modest house, including Jack, who was born in the master bedroom in 1917. Matriarch Rose Kennedy oversaw the restoration of the house in the late 1960s; today her narrative sheds light on the Kennedys' family life. Guided tours allow visitors to see furnishings, photographs and mementos that have been preserved from the time the family lived here.

statue in the Public Garden is *Make Way for Ducklings,* depicting Mrs Mallard and her eight ducklings, the main characters in the beloved book by Robert McCloskey.

★**Boston Public Library** LIBRARY
(Map p168; www.bpl.org; 700 Boylston St; ☺9am-9pm Mon-Thu, to 5pm Fri & Sat year-round, also 1-5pm Sun Oct-May; ⓣ Copley) Dating from 1852, the esteemed Boston Public Library lends credence to Boston's reputation as the 'Athens of America.' The old McKim building is notable for its magnificent facade and exquisite interior art. Pick up a free brochure and take a self-guided tour; alternatively, free guided tours depart from the entrance hall (times vary).

★**Trinity Church** CHURCH
(Map p168; www.trinitychurchboston.org; 206 Clarendon St; adult/child $7/free; ☺9am-4:30pm Mon, Fri & Sat, to 5:30pm Tue-Thu, 1-5pm Sun; ⓣ Copley) A masterpiece of American architecture, Trinity Church is the country's ultimate example of Richardsonian Romanesque. The granite exterior, with a massive portico and side cloister, uses sandstone in colorful patterns. The interior is an awe-striking array of vibrant murals and stained glass, most by artist John LaFarge, who cooperated closely with architect Henry Hobson Richardson to create an integrated composition of shapes, colors and textures. Free architectural tours are offered following Sunday service at 11:15am.

Prudential Center Skywalk Observatory LOOKOUT
(Map p168; www.skywalkboston.com; 800 Boylston St; adult/child $16/11; ☺10am-10pm Mar-Oct, to 8pm Nov-Feb; Ⓟⓗ; ⓣ Prudential) Technically called the Shops at Prudential Center, this landmark Boston building is not much more than a fancy shopping mall. But it does provide a bird's-eye view of Boston from its 50th-floor skywalk. Completely enclosed by glass, the skywalk offers spectacular 360-degree views of Boston and Cambridge, accompanied by an entertaining audio tour (with a special version catering to kids). Alternatively, enjoy the same view from **Top of the Hub** (Map p168; ☏617-536-1775; www.topofthehub.net; 800 Boylston St; ☺11:30am-1am; ☎; ⓣ Prudential) for the price of a drink.

◉ Fenway & Kenmore Square

Kenmore Sq is best for baseball and beer, while the southern part of the Fenway is dedicated to higher-minded cultural pursuits.

★**Museum of Fine Arts** MUSEUM
(MFA; Map p168; www.mfa.org; 465 Huntington Ave; adult/child $25/10; ☺10am-5pm Sat-Tue, to 10pm Wed-Fri; ⓗ; ⓣ Museum or Ruggles) Since 1876, the Museum of Fine Arts has been Boston's premier venue for showcasing art by local, national and international artists. Nowadays, the museum's holdings encompass all eras, from the ancient world to contemporary times, and all areas of the globe, making it truly encyclopedic in scope. Most recently, the museum has added gorgeous new wings dedicated to the Art of the Americas and to contemporary art, contributing to Boston's emergence as an art center in the 21st century.

★ **Isabella Stewart Gardner Museum**   MUSEUM
(Map p168; www.gardnermuseum.org; 280 The Fenway; adult/child $15/free; ⊙11am-5pm Mon, Wed & Fri-Sun, to 9pm Thu; 🚻; T Museum) The magnificent Venetian-style palazzo that houses this museum was home to 'Mrs Jack' Gardner herself until her death in 1924. A monument to one woman's taste for acquiring exquisite art, the Gardner is filled with almost 2000 priceless objects, primarily European, including outstanding tapestries and Italian Renaissance and 17th-century Dutch paintings. The four-story greenhouse courtyard is a masterpiece and a tranquil oasis that alone is worth the price of admission.

◉ **Cambridge**

On the north side of the Charles River lies politically progressive Cambridge, home to academic heavyweights Harvard University and Massachusetts Institute of Technology (MIT). Harvard Square overflows with cafes, bookstores and street performers.

★ **Harvard University**   UNIVERSITY
(Map p168; www.harvard.edu; Massachusetts Ave; tours free; ⊙tours hourly 10am-3pm Mon-Sat; T Harvard) Founded in 1636 to educate men for the ministry, Harvard is America's oldest college. The original Ivy League school has eight graduates who went on to be US presidents, not to mention dozens of Nobel laureates and Pulitzer Prize winners. It educates 6500 undergraduates and about 12,000 graduates yearly in 10 professional schools. The geographic heart of Harvard University – where red-brick buildings and leaf-covered paths exude academia – is Harvard Yard.

★ **Harvard Art Museums**   MUSEUM
(Map p168; www.harvardartmuseums.org; 32 Quincy St; adult/child $15/free; ⊙10am-5pm; T Harvard) Architect extraordinaire Renzo Piano has overseen a renovation and expansion of Harvard's art museums, allowing the university's massive 250,000-piece collection to come together under one very stylish roof. Harvard's art spans the globe, with separate collections devoted to Asian and Islamic cultures (formerly the Arthur M Sackler Museum), Northern European and Germanic cultures (formerly the Busch-Reisinger Museum) and other Western art, especially European modernism (formerly the Fogg).

🖝 **Tours**

★ **Urban AdvenTours**   BICYCLE TOUR
(Map p174; ✆617-379-3590; www.urbanadventours.com; 103 Atlantic Ave; tours $55; 🚲; T Aquarium)
🖋 Founded by avid cyclists who believe the best views of Boston are from a bicycle. The City View Ride provides a great overview of how to get around by bike, but there are other specialty tours such as Bikes at Night and the Emerald Necklace tour.

Boston by Foot   WALKING TOUR
(www.bostonbyfoot.com; adult/child $15/10; 🚶) This fantastic nonprofit offers 90-minute walking tours, with neighborhood-specific walks and specialty theme tours such as Literary Landmarks, the Dark Side of Boston and Boston for Little Feet – a kid-friendly version of the Freedom Trail.

NPS Freedom Trail Tour   WALKING TOUR
(Map p174; www.nps.gov/bost; Faneuil Hall; ⊙10am & 2pm Apr-Oct; T State) **FREE** Show up at least 30 minutes early to snag a spot on one of the free, ranger-led Freedom Trail tours provided by the NPS. Tours depart from the visitor center in Faneuil Hall, and follow a portion of the Freedom Trail (not including Charlestown), for a total of 90 minutes. Each tour is limited to 30 people.

Boston Duck Tours   BOAT TOUR
(Map p168; ✆617-267-3825; www.bostonducktours.com; adult/child $36/25; 🚲; T Aquarium, Science Park or Prudential) These ridiculously popular tours use WWII amphibious vehicles that cruise the downtown streets before splashing into the Charles River. The 80-minute tours depart from the Museum

DON'T MISS

BOSTON GOES GREEN

The gateway to the newly revitalized waterfront is the **Rose Kennedy Greenway** (Map p174; www.rosekennedygreenway.org; 🚲; T Aquarium or Haymarket). Where once was a hulking overhead highway, now winds a 27-acre strip of landscaped gardens and fountain-lined greens, with an artist market for Saturday shoppers, and food trucks for weekday lunchers. Cool off in the whimsical Rings Fountain, walk the calming labyrinth, or take a ride on the custom-designed Greenway carousel.

Central Boston

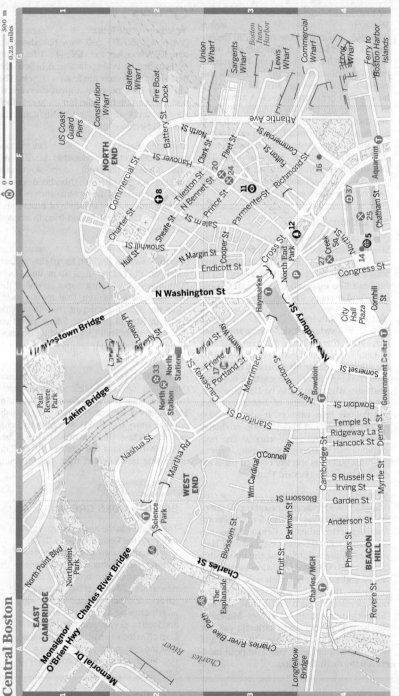

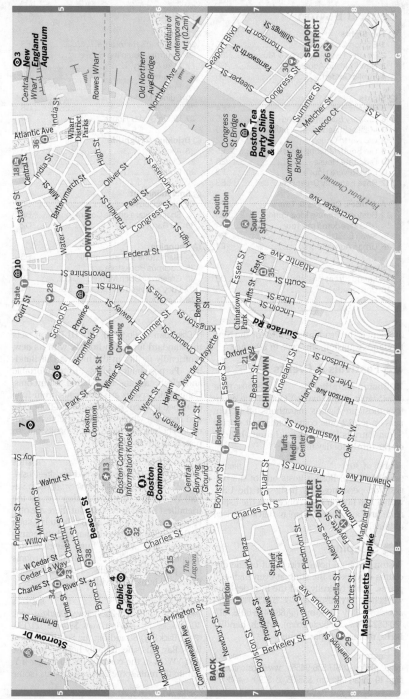

NEW ENGLAND

Central Boston

Top Sights
1 Boston Common C6
2 Boston Tea Party Ships & Museum F7
3 New England Aquarium G5
4 Public Garden B6

Sights
5 Faneuil Hall E4
6 Granary Burying Ground D5
7 Massachusetts State House C5
8 Old North Church F2
9 Old South Meeting House E5
10 Old State House E5
11 Paul Revere House F3
12 Rose Kennedy Greenway E3

Activities, Courses & Tours
13 Boston Common Frog Pond C5
14 NPS Freedom Trail Tour E4
15 Swan Boats B6
16 Urban AdvenTours F4

Sleeping
17 Friend Street Hostel D3
18 Harborside Inn F5
19 HI-Boston C7

Eating
20 Giacomo's Ristorante F3
21 Gourmet Dumpling House D7
22 Mike & Patty's B8
23 Paramount B5
24 Pomodoro F3
25 Quincy Market E4
26 Row 34 G8
27 Union Oyster House E4

Drinking & Nightlife
28 Alley Bar E5
29 Club Café A8
30 Drink G7

Entertainment
31 Opera House C6
32 Shakespeare on the Common B6
33 TD Garden D2

Shopping
34 Blackstone's of Beacon Hill B5
35 Calamus Bookstore E7
36 Greenway Open Market F5
37 Lucy's League F4
38 Ruby Door B5

of Science, the Prudential Center or the New England Aquarium. Reserve in advance.

Festivals & Events

★Boston Marathon SPORTING EVENT
(www.baa.org; 3rd Mon Apr) One of the country's most prestigious marathons takes runners on a 26.2-mile course ending at Copley Sq on Patriots Day, a Massachusetts holiday on the third Monday in April.

Fourth of July HOLIDAY
(www.july4th.org) Boston hosts one of the biggest Independence Day bashes in the USA, with a free Boston Pops concert on the Esplanade and a fireworks display that's televised nationally.

Sleeping

Boston has high hotel prices, but online discounts can lessen the sting at even high-end places. You'll typically find the best deals on weekends. Try also **Bed & Breakfast Associates Bay Colony** (888-486-6018, 617-720-0522; www.bnbboston.com), which handles B&Bs, rooms and apartments.

HI-Boston HOSTEL $
(Map p174; 617-536-9455; www.bostonhostel.org; 19 Stuart St; dm $55-65, d $199; ; T Chinatown or Boylston) HI-Boston sets the standard for urban hostels, with its new, ecofriendly facility in the historic Dill Building. Purpose-built rooms are comfortable and clean, as are the shared bathrooms. Community spaces are numerous, from fully equipped kitchen to trendy ground-floor cafe, and there's a whole calendar of activities on offer. The place is large, but it books out, so reserve in advance.

Friend Street Hostel HOSTEL $
(Map p174; 617-248-8971; www.friendstreethostel.com; 234 Friend St; dm $45-50; ; T North Station) We believe them when they say it's the friendliest hostel in Boston. But there are other reasons to love this affable hostelry, such as the spick-and-span kitchen and the comfy common area with the huge flatscreen TV. Sleeping six to 10 people each, dorm rooms have painted brick walls, wide-plank wood floors and bunk beds with thin mattresses.

40 Berkeley HOSTEL $$
(Map p168; 617-375-2524; www.40berkeley.com; 40 Berkeley St; s/d/tr/q from $95/103/121/130; ; T Back Bay) Straddling the South End and Back Bay, this safe, friendly hostelry was the first YWCA in the country. It's no longer a Y, but it still rents some 200 basic rooms (some

overlooking the lovely garden) to guests on a nightly and long-term basis. Bathrooms are shared, as are other useful facilities including the telephone, library, TV room and laundry.

★**Newbury Guest House** GUESTHOUSE **$$**
(Map p168; ☏617-437-7666, 617-437-7668; www.newburyguesthouse.com; 261 Newbury St; d from $209; P❉🛜; ⊤Hynes or Copley) Dating to 1882, these three interconnected brick and brownstone buildings offer a prime location in the heart of Newbury St. A recent renovation has preserved the charming features such as ceiling medallions and in-room fireplaces, but now the rooms feature clean lines, luxurious linens and modern amenities. Each morning, a complimentary continental breakfast is laid out next to the marble fireplace in the salon.

★**Oasis Guest House
& Adams B&B** GUESTHOUSE **$$**
(Map p168; ☏617-230-0105, 617-267-2262; www.oasisguesthouse.com; 22 Edgerly Rd; s/d without bathroom $109/149, r with bathroom from $189; P❉🛜; ⊤Hynes or Symphony) These homey side-by-side (jointly managed) guesthouses offer a peaceful, pleasant oasis in the midst of Boston's chaotic city streets. Thirty-odd guest rooms occupy four attractive brick, bow-front town houses on this tree-lined lane. The modest, light-filled rooms are tastefully and traditionally decorated, most with queen beds, floral quilts and nondescript prints.

Irving House GUESTHOUSE **$$**
(Map p168; ☏617-547-4600; www.irvinghouse.com; 24 Irving St; s/d without bathroom $135/165, r with bathroom from $185; P❉🍴🛜; ⊤Harvard) 🌿 Call it a big inn or a homey hotel, this property welcomes the world-weariest of travelers. The 44 rooms range in size, but every bed is covered with a quilt and big windows let in plenty of light. There is a bistro-style atmosphere in the brick-lined basement, where you can browse the books on hand, plan your travels or munch on free continental breakfast.

Chandler Inn HOTEL **$$**
(Map p168; ☏617-482-3450; www.chandlerinn.com; 26 Chandler St; r from $179; ❉🛜; ⊤Back Bay) Small but sleek rooms show off a designer's touch, giving them a sophisticated, urban glow. Travelers appreciate the plasma TVs and iPod docks, all of which come at relatively affordable prices. As a bonus, congenial staff provide super service. Across the street, the inn rents out 11 newly renovated, modern apartments of various sizes, under the

BOSTON STRONG

On Patriot's Day 2013, the nation (and the world) turned their eyes to Boston when two bombs exploded near the finish line of the Boston Marathon, killing three and injuring hundreds. Several days later, an MIT police officer was shot dead and the entire city was locked down, as Boston became a battleground for the War on Terror. The tragedy was devastating, but Boston can claim countless heroes, especially the many victims who have inspired others with their courage and fortitude throughout their recoveries.

moniker **Chandler Studios** (Map p168; www.chandlerstudiosboston.com; 54 Berkeley St; ste from $269; ❉🛜; ⊤Back Bay).

★**Verb Hotel** BOUTIQUE HOTEL **$$$**
(Map p168; ☏855-695-6678; www.theverbhotel.com; 1271 Boylston St; r from $250; P❉🛜🏊🐕; ⊤Kenmore) The Verb Hotel took a down-and-out HoJo property and turned it into Boston's most radical, retro, rock and roll hotel. The style is mid-century modern; the theme is music. Memorabilia is on display throughout the joint, with a jukebox cranking out tunes in the lobby. Classy, clean-lined rooms face the swimming pool or Fenway Park. A+ for service and style.

★**Harborside Inn** BOUTIQUE HOTEL **$$$**
(Map p174; ☏617-723-7500; www.harborsideinn-boston.com; 185 State St; r from $269; P❉🏠🛜; ⊤Aquarium) Steps from Faneuil Hall and the waterfront, this boutique hotel inhabits a respectfully renovated 19th-century mercantile warehouse. The 116 rooms are on the small side, but comfortable and appropriately nautically themed. Note that Atrium Rooms face the atrium (ahem) and Cabin Rooms have no windows at all. Add $20 for a city view (worth it).

🍴 Eating

New England cuisine is known for summertime clambakes and Thanksgiving turkey. But the Boston dining scene changes it up with wide-ranging international influences and contemporary interpretations. Indulge in affordable Asian fare in Chinatown and Italian feasts in the North End; or head to the South End for the city's trendiest foodie scene.

SEAFOOD SPECIALTIES

Lobster The mighty crustacean, steamed, and usually served in its shell

Lobster roll The succulent meat of the tail and claws, mixed with a touch of mayo and served on a grilled hotdog bun

Clam chowder Or, as Bostonians say, *chow-dah*, combines chopped clams, potatoes and clam juice in a milk base

Oysters Usually served raw on the half-shell, with lemon and cocktail sauce

Steamers Soft-shelled clams, steamed and served in a bucket of briny broth

Beacon Hill & Downtown

Quincy Market
FOOD COURT $

(Map p174; www.faneuilhallmarketplace.com; Congress St; ⊙10am-9pm Mon-Sat, noon-6pm Sun; 🛜🦪♿; ⓣHaymarket) Behind Faneuil Hall, this food court offers a variety of places under one roof: the place is packed with about 20 restaurants and 40 food stalls. Choose from chowder, bagels, Indian, Greek, baked goods and ice cream, and take a seat at one of the tables in the central rotunda.

★Paramount
CAFETERIA $$

(Map p174; www.paramountboston.com; 44 Charles St; mains breakfast & lunch $6-12, dinner $15-23; ⊙7am-10pm Mon-Thu, to 11pm Fri, 8am-11pm Sat, to 10pm Sun; 🦪♿; ⓣCharles/MGH) This old-fashioned cafeteria is a neighborhood favorite. A-plus diner fare includes pancakes, home fries, burgers and sandwiches, and big, hearty salads. Banana and caramel French toast is an obvious go-to for the brunch crowd. Don't sit down until you get your food! At dinner, add table service and candlelight, and the place goes upscale without losing its down-home charm.

Union Oyster House
SEAFOOD $$$

(Map p174; www.unionoysterhouse.com; 41 Union St; mains lunch $15-20, dinner $22-32; ⊙11am-9:30pm; ⓣHaymarket) The oldest restaurant in Boston, ye olde Union Oyster House has been serving seafood in this historic red-brick building since 1826. Countless history-makers have propped themselves up at this bar, including Daniel Webster and John F Kennedy. (Apparently JFK used to order the lobster bisque.) Overpriced but atmospheric.

North End

★Pomodoro
ITALIAN $$

(Map p174; 📋617-367-4348; 351 Hanover St; mains brunch $12, dinner $23-24; ⊙5-11pm Mon-Fri, noon-11pm Sat & Sun; ⓣHaymarket) Pomodoro has a new (only slightly larger) location, but it's still one of the North End's most romantic settings for delectable Italian. The food is simple but perfectly prepared: fresh pasta, spicy tomato sauce, grilled fish and meats, and wine by the glass. If you're lucky, you might be on the receiving end of a complimentary tiramisu for dessert. Cash only.

Giacomo's Ristorante
ITALIAN $$

(Map p174; www.giacomosblog-boston.blogspot.com; 355 Hanover St; mains $14-19; ⊙4:30-10:30pm Mon-Sat, 4-9:30pm Sun; 🦪; ⓣHaymarket) Customers line up before the doors open so they can guarantee themselves a spot in the first round of seating at this North End favorite. Enthusiastic and entertaining waiters plus cramped quarters ensure that you get to know your neighbors. The cuisine is no-frills southern Italian fare, served in unbelievable portions. Cash only.

Seaport District

Yankee Lobster Co
SEAFOOD $

(www.yankeelobstercompany.com; 300 Northern Ave; mains $11-20; ⊙10am-9pm Mon-Sat, 11am-6pm Sun; 🚌SL1 or SL2, ⓣSouth Station) The Zanti family has been fishing for three generations, so they definitely know their stuff. A relatively recent addition is this retail fish market, scattered with a few tables in case you want to dine in. And you do. Order something simple like clam chowder or a lobster roll, accompany it with a cold beer, and you will not be disappointed.

★Row 34
SEAFOOD $$

(Map p174; 📋617-553-5900; www.row34.com; 383 Congress St; oysters $2-3, mains lunch $13-18, dinner $21-28; ⊙11:30am-10pm Mon-Fri, 5-10pm Sat & Sun; ⓣSouth Station) In the heart of the new Seaport District, this is a 'workingman's oyster bar' (by working man, they mean yuppie). Set in a sharp, post-industrial space, the place offers a dozen types of raw oysters and clams, alongside an amazing selection of craft beers. There's also a full menu of cooked seafood, ranging from the traditional to the trendy.

City Walk
Freedom Trail

START BOSTON COMMON
FINISH BUNKER HILL MONUMENT
LENGTH 2.5 MILES; THREE HOURS

Trace America's earliest history along the Freedom Trail, which covers Boston's key revolutionary sites. The well-trodden route is marked by a double row of red bricks, starting at the **1 Boston Common** (p166), America's oldest public park. Follow the trail north to the gold-domed **2 State House** (p167), designed by Charles Bulfinch, America's first homegrown architect. Rounding Park St takes you past the Colonial-era **3 Park Street Church**; the **4 Granary Burying Ground** (p167), where victims of the Boston Massacre lie buried; and **5 King's Chapel**, topped with one of Paul Revere's bells. Continue down School St, past the site of **6 Boston's first public school** and the **7 Old Corner Bookstore**, a haunt of 19th-century literati.

Nearby, the **8 Old South Meeting House** (p167) tells the backstory of the Boston Tea Party. There are more Revolutionary exhibits at the **9 Old State House** (p167). Outside, a ring of cobblestones at the intersection marks the **10 Boston Massacre Site**, the first violent conflict of the American Revolution. Next up is **11 Faneuil Hall** (p167), a public market since Colonial times.

Cross the Greenway to Hanover St, the main artery of the North End. Treat yourself to lunch before continuing to North Sq, where you can tour the **12 Paul Revere House** (p170), the Revolutionary hero's former home. Follow the trail to the **13 Old North Church** (p170), where a lookout in the steeple signaled to Revere that the British were coming, setting off his famous midnight gallop.

Walk northwest on Hull St, where you'll find more Colonial graves at **14 Copp's Hill Burying Ground**. Then cross the Charlestown Bridge to reach the **15 USS Constitution** (p170), the world's oldest commissioned warship. To the north lies **16 Bunker Hill Monument** (p171), the site of the first battle fought in the American Revolution.

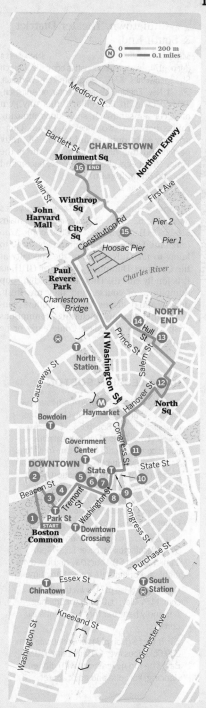

✗ Chinatown, Theater District & South End

Mike & Patty's
SANDWICHES $

(Map p174; www.mikeandpattys.com; 12 Church St; sandwiches $7-9; ⊗7:30am-2pm Wed-Sun; 🖉; ⊤New England Medical Center or Arlington) Tucked away in Bay Village, this tiny gem of a corner sandwich shop does amazing things between two slices of bread. There are only eight options and they're all pretty perfect, but the hands-down favorite is the Fancy (fried egg, cheddar cheese, bacon and avocado on multigrain).

★Gourmet Dumpling House
CHINESE, TAIWANESE $

(Map p174; 52 Beach St; dumplings $2-8, mains $10-15; ⊗11am-1am; 🖉; ⊤Chinatown) *Xiao long bao*. That's all the Chinese you need to know to take advantage of the specialty at the Gourmet Dumpling House (or GDH, as it is fondly called). They are Shanghai soup dumplings, of course, and they are fresh, doughy and delicious. The menu offers plenty of other options, including scrumptious crispy scallion pancakes. Come early or be prepared to wait.

GAY & LESBIAN BOSTON

Out and active gay communities are visible all around Boston and Cambridge, especially in the South End. **Calamus Bookstore** (Map p174; www.calamus-books.com; 92 South St; ⊗9am-7pm Mon-Sat, noon-6pm Sun; ⊤South Station) is an excellent source of information about community events and organizations. Pick up a copy of the free weekly *Bay Windows* (www.baywindows.com). Other GLBT venues:

Midway Café (www.midwaycafe.com; 3496 Washington St; cover $5; ⊗4pm-2am; ⊤Green St) Thursday night is dyke night, but queers are cool at any time.

Alley Bar (Map p174; www.thealleybar.com; 14 Pi Alley; ⊤Downtown Crossing) A friendly bear bar that welcomes all comers.

Club Café (Map p174; www.clubcafe.com; 209 Columbus Ave; ⊗11am-2am; ⊤Back Bay) The fun never stops with dinner, dancing, karaoke and gay cabaret.

Myers & Chang
ASIAN $$

(Map p168; 🖉617-542-5200; www.myersandchang. com; 1145 Washington St; small plates $10-18; ⊗11:30am-10pm Sun-Thu, to 11pm Fri & Sat; 🖉; 🖫SL4 or SL5, ⊤New England Medical Center) This super-hip Asian spot blends Thai, Chinese and Vietnamese cuisines, which means delicious dumplings, spicy stir-fries and oodles of noodles. The kitchen staff does amazing things with a wok, and the menu of small plates allows you to sample a wide selection of dishes. The vibe is casual but cool, international and original.

✗ Back Bay & Fenway

★Courtyard
MODERN AMERICAN $$

(Map p168; www.thecateredaffair.com; 700 Boylston St; mains $17-22; ⊗11:30am-4pm Mon-Fri; 🖉; ⊤Copley) The perfect destination for an elegant luncheon with artfully prepared food is – believe it or not – the Boston Public Library. Overlooking the beautiful Italianate courtyard, this grown-up restaurant serves seasonal, innovative and exotic dishes (along with a few standards). After 2pm, the Courtyard serves a delightful afternoon tea ($32), with a selection of sandwiches, scones and sweets.

★Island Creek Oyster Bar
SEAFOOD $$$

(Map p168; 🖉617-532-5300; www.islandcreekoys-terbar.com; 500 Commonwealth Ave; oysters $2.50-4, mains lunch $18-21, dinner $25-35; ⊗4pm-1am; ⊤Kenmore) Island Creek has united 'farmer, chef and diner in one space' – and what a space it is. ICOB serves up the region's finest oysters, along with other local seafood, in an ethereal new-age setting. The specialty – lobster roe noodles topped with braised short ribs and grilled lobster – lives up to the hype.

✗ Cambridge

★Clover Food Lab
VEGETARIAN $

(Map p168; www.cloverfoodlab.com; 7 Holyoke St; mains $6-7; ⊗7am-midnight Mon-Sat, to 7pm Sun; 🛜🖉♿; ⊤Harvard) 🖉 Clover is on the cutting edge. It's all high-tech with its 'live' menu updates and electronic ordering system. But it's really about the food – local, seasonal, vegetarian food – that is cheap, delicious and fast. How fast? Check the menu. Interesting tidbit: Clover started as a food truck (and still has a few trucks making the rounds).

★Alden & Harlow
MODERN AMERICAN $

(Map p168; 🖉617-864-2100; www.aldenharlow. com; 40 Brattle St; small plates $9-17; ⊗5pm-1am

Sun-Wed, to 2am Thu-Sat; 🖊; T Harvard) This spanking-new place in a cozy subterranean space is offering a brand-new take on American cooking. The small plates are made for sharing, so everyone in your party gets to sample. And you will want to sample, because these local ingredients are prepared in ways you've never seen before. By the way, it's no secret that the 'Secret Burger' is amazing.

🍷 Drinking & Nightlife

⭐ Bleacher Bar   SPORTS BAR
(Map p168; www.bleacherbarboston.com; 82a Lansdowne St; ⊘11am-1am Sun-Wed, to 2am Thu-Sat; T Kenmore) Tucked under the bleachers at Fenway Park, this classy bar offers a view onto center field. It's not the best place to watch the game, as the place gets packed, but it's a fun way to experience America's oldest ballpark, even when the Sox are not playing. Gentlemen: enjoy the view from the loo!

If you want a seat in front of the window, get your name on the waiting list an hour or two before game time; once seated, diners have 45 minutes in the hot seat.

⭐ Drink   COCKTAIL BAR
(Map p174; www.drinkfortpoint.com; 348 Congress St; ⊘4pm-1am; 🚌 SL1 or SL2, T South Station) There is no cocktail menu at Drink. Instead you have a little chat with the bartender, and he or she will whip something up according to your specifications. The bar takes seriously the art of drink mixology – and you will too, after you sample one of its concoctions. The subterranean space creates a dark, sexy atmosphere, which makes for a great date destination.

Beat Hotel   BAR
(Map p168; www.beathotel.com; 13 Brattle St; ⊘4pm-midnight Mon-Wed, to 2am Thu & Fri, 10am-2am Sat, to midnight Sun; T Harvard) A great addition to Harvard Sq, this vast, underground bistro packs in good-looking patrons for international food, classy cocktails and live jazz and blues. It's inspired by the Beat Generation writers – and named for a rundown Parisian motel where they hung out – but there's nothing down-and-out about this hot spot.

Warren Tavern   PUB
(Map p168; www.warrentavern.com; 2 Pleasant St; ⊘11am-1am Mon-Fri, 10am-1am Sat & Sun; T Community College) One of the oldest pubs in Boston, the Warren Tavern has been pouring pints for its customers since George Washington and Paul Revere drank here. It is named for General Joseph Warren, a fallen hero of

---

ℹ CHEAP SEATS

BosTix kiosks (www.bostix.org; ⊘10am-6pm Tue-Sat, 11am-4pm Sun) Offers discounted tickets to theater productions citywide (up to 25% off for advance purchases online). Discounts up to 50% are available for same-day purchase: check the website to see what's available. Purchases must be made in person, in cash, at outlets on Copley Sq or at Quincy Market.

---

the Battle of Bunker Hill (shortly after which – in 1780 – this pub was opened). Also recommended as a lunch stop.

☆ Entertainment

For up-to-the-minute listings, grab a copy of the free *Boston Phoenix*.

Live Music

⭐ Club Passim   LIVE MUSIC
(Map p168; ☑ 617-492-7679; www.clubpassim.org; 47 Palmer St; tickets $15-30; T Harvard) Folk music in Boston seems to be endangered outside of Irish bars, but the legendary Club Passim does such a great job booking top-notch acts that it practically fills in the vacuum by itself. The colorful, intimate room is hidden off a side street in Harvard Sq, just as it has been since 1969.

⭐ Red Room @ Café 939   LIVE MUSIC
(Map p168; www.cafe939.com; 939 Boylston St; ⊘8-11pm Wed-Sun; T Hynes) Run by Berklee students, the Red Room @ 939 has emerged as one of Boston's least predictable and most enjoyable music venues. The place has an excellent sound system and a baby grand piano; most importantly, it books interesting, eclectic up-and-coming musicians. Check out wicked local Wednesdays to sample the local sound. Buy tickets in advance at the Berklee Performance Center.

Sinclair   LIVE MUSIC
(Map p168; www.sinclaircambridge.com; 52 Church St; tickets $15-18; ⊘5pm-1am Mon, 11am-1am Tue-Sun; T Harvard) This is a great small venue to hear live music. The acoustics are excellent and the mezzanine level allows you to escape the crowds on the floor. The club attracts a good range of local and regional bands and DJs.

Classical Music & Theater

★ **Boston Symphony Orchestra**   CLASSICAL MUSIC

(BSO; Map p168; ☑617-266-1200; www.bso.org; 301 Massachusetts Ave; tickets $30-115; ⊤ Symphony) Flawless acoustics match the ambitious programs of the world-renowned Boston Symphony Orchestra. From September to April, the BSO performs in the beauteous **Symphony Hall** (Map p168; www.bso.org; 301 Massachusetts Ave; ⊙ tours 4pm Wed & 2pm Sat, reservation required), featuring an ornamental high-relief ceiling and attracting a fancy-dress crowd. In summer months, the BSO retreats to Tanglewood in Western Massachusetts.

Opera House   LIVE PERFORMANCE

(Map p174; www.bostonoperahouse.com; 539 Washington St; ⊤ Downtown Crossing) This lavish theater has been restored to its 1928 glory, complete with mural-painted ceiling, gilded molding and plush velvet curtains. The glitzy venue regularly hosts productions from the Broadway Across America series, and is also the main performance space for the Boston Ballet.

Sports

★ **Fenway Park**   BASEBALL

(Map p168; www.redsox.com; 4 Yawkey Way; bleachers $12-40, grandstand $29-78, box $50-75; ⊤ Kenmore) From April to September you can watch the Red Sox play at **Fenway Park** (Map p168; www.redsox.com; 4 Yawkey Way; tours adult/child $18/12; ⊙ 10am-5pm; ⬛; ⊤ Kenmore), the nation's oldest and most storied ballpark.

Unfortunately, it is also the most expensive – not that this stops the Fenway faithful from scooping up the tickets. There are sometimes game-day tickets on sale starting 90 minutes before the opening pitch.

TD Garden   BASKETBALL, ICE HOCKEY

(Map p174; ☑information 617-523-3030, tickets 617-931-2000; www.tdgarden.com; 150 Causeway St; ⊤ North Station) The TD Garden is home to the Bruins, who play hockey here from September to June, and the Celtics, who play basketball from October to April. It's the city's largest venue, so big-name musicians perform here, too.

🛍 Shopping

Newbury St in the Back Bay and Charles St on Beacon Hill are Boston's best shopping destinations for the biggest selection of shops, both traditional and trendy. Harvard Sq is famous for bookstores and the South End is the city's up-and-coming art district. **Copley Place** (Map p168; www.simon.com; 100 Huntington Ave; ⊙ 10am-8pm Mon-Sat, noon-6pm Sun; ⊤ Back Bay) and the **Prudential Center** (Map p168; www.prudentialcenter.com; 800 Boylston St; ⊙ 10am-9pm Mon-Sat, 11am-8pm Sun; 🛜; ⊤ Prudential), both in Back Bay, are big indoor malls.

★ **Ruby Door**   JEWELRY

(Map p174; www.therubydoor.com; 15 Charles St; ⊙ 11am-6pm Mon-Sat; ⊤ Charles/MGH) What will you find behind the ruby door? Gorgeous, hand-crafted jewelry, much of it featuring intriguing gemstones and unique vintage

---

BOSTON FOR CHILDREN

Boston is one giant history museum, the setting for many educational and lively field trips. Cobblestone streets and costume-clad tour guides can bring to life events from American history. Hands-on experimentation and interactive exhibits fuse education and entertainment.

Changing stations are ubiquitous in public restrooms and many restaurants offer children's menus and high chairs. You'll have no trouble taking your kid's stroller on the T.

A good place to start your family's exploration is the **Public Garden** (p171), where Swan Boats ply the lagoon and tiny tots climb on the bronze ducklings. Across the street at the **Boston Common** (p166), kids can cool their toes in the Frog Pond, ride the carousel and romp at the playground. At the **New England Aquarium** (p167), kids of all ages will enjoy face-to-face encounters with underwater creatures.

Great tours for kids:

Boston for Little Feet (p173) The only Freedom Trail walking tour designed especially for children aged six to 12.

Urban AdvenTours (p173) Rents kids' bikes and helmets, as well as bike trailers for toddlers.

Boston Duck Tours (p173) Quirky quackiness is always a hit.

elements. Designer and owner Tracy Chareas reworks antique and vintage jewels into thoroughly modern pieces of art. There is also plenty of more affordable jewelry for bauble lovers. Great for browsing, with no pressure to buy.

Blackstone's of Beacon Hill GIFTS, ACCESSORIES
(Map p174; www.blackstonesbeaconhill.com; 46 Charles St; ⊙10am-6:30pm Mon-Sat, 11am-5pm Sun; ⊤Charles/MGH) Here's a guarantee: you will find the perfect gift for that certain someone at Blackstone's. This little place is crammed with classy, clever and otherwise unusual items. Highlights include the custom-designed stationery, locally made handicrafts and quirky Boston-themed souvenirs like clocks and coasters. Otherwise, you can't go wrong with a solar-powered rotating globe – everyone needs one!

Lucy's League CLOTHING
(Map p174; www.rosterstores.com/lucysleague; North Market, Faneuil Hall; ⊙10am-9pm Mon-Sat, to 6pm Sun; ⊤Government Center) We're not advocating those pink Red Sox caps, but sometimes a girl wants to look good while she's supporting the team. At Lucy's League, fashionable sports fans will find shirts, jackets and other gear sporting the local teams' logos in super-cute styles designed to flatter the female figure.

Converse SHOES, CLOTHING
(Map p168; www.converse.com; 348 Newbury St; ⊙10am-7pm Mon-Fri, to 8pm Sat, 11am-6pm Sun; ⊤Hynes) Converse started making shoes right up the road in Malden, Massachusetts way back in 1908. Chuck Taylor joined the 'team' in the 1920s and the rest is history. This retail store (one of three in the country) carries sneakers, denim and other gear. The iconic shoes come in all colors and patterns; make them uniquely your own in the in-store customization area.

Sault New England CLOTHING, GIFTS
(Map p168; www.saultne.com; 577 Tremont St; ⊙11am-7pm Tue-Sun; ⊤Back Bay) Blending prepster and hipster, rustic and chic, this little basement boutique packs in a lot of intriguing stuff. The eclectic mix of merchandise runs the gamut from new and vintage clothing to coffee-table books and homemade terrariums. A New England theme runs through the store, with nods to the Kennedys, *Jaws* and LL Bean.

DON'T MISS

OPEN MARKETS

Part flea market and part artists' market, this weekly outdoor event is a fabulous opportunity for strolling, shopping and people-watching. More than 100 vendors set up shop under white tents. It's never the same two weeks in a row, but there's always plenty of arts and crafts, as well as edgier art, vintage clothing, jewelry, local farm produce and homemade sweets. In summer months, catch it on Saturday on the **Rose Kennedy Greenway** (Map p174; www.newenglandopenmarkets.com; Rose Kennedy Greenway; ⊙11am-5pm Sat May-Oct; 🖨; ⊤Aquarium) and Sunday in the **South End** (Map p168; www.newenglandopenmarkets.com; Thayer St; ⊙10am-4pm Sun May-Oct; 🚊SL4 or SL5, ⊤New England Medical Center).

Olives & Grace GIFTS
(Map p168; www.olivesandgrace.com; 623 Tremont St; ⊙10am-7pm; ⊤Back Bay) This little shoebox of a store offers an eclectic array of gift items – many from New England – all of them made with love and thoughtfulness by artisans. The most enticing items are the foodstuffs, including chocolate bars, hot sauces, raw honey, saltwater taffy and, um, beef jerky.

Lunarik Fashions ACCESSORIES
(Map p168; 279 Newbury St; ⊙11am-7pm Mon-Fri, 10am-8pm Sat, noon-6pm Sun; ⊤Hynes) Like a modern woman's handbag, Lunarik is packed with useful stuff, much of it by local designers. Look for whimsical collage-covered pieces by Jenn Sherr, beautiful hand-crafted jewelry by Dasken Designs, and the best-selling richly colored leather handbags by Saya Cullinan. Who wouldn't want to pack their stuff into that!

ℹ Information

INTERNET ACCESS
Aside from hotels, wireless access is common at cafes, on buses and even in public spaces like Faneuil Hall and the Greenway. Many cafes charge a fee, though they may offer the first hour free of charge.
Boston Public Library (www.bpl.org; 700 Boylston St; ⊙9am-9pm Mon-Thu, to 5pm Fri & Sat year-round, 1-5pm Sun Oct-May; 🖨; ⊤Copley) Internet access free for 15-minute intervals.

GETTING TO NYC

The cheapest travel between Boston and NYC is by bus, including **Lucky Star Bus** (www.luckystarbus.com; South Station; one way $20; 🛜) and **Megabus** (www.megabus.com; South Station; one-way $10-30; 🛜), both departing from South Station. **Go Bus** (www.gobuses. com; Alewife Brook Pkwy; one way $18-34; 🛜; T Alewife) departs from Alewife station in Cambridge.

Or get a visitor courtesy card at the circulation desk and sign up for one hour of free terminal time. Arrive first thing in the morning to avoid long waits.

Wired Puppy (www.wiredpuppy.com; 250 Newbury St; ⊙ 6:30am-7:30pm; 🛜; T Hynes) Free wireless access and free computer use in case you don't have your own. This is also a comfortable, cozy place to just come and drink coffee.

MEDIA

Boston Globe (www.boston.com) One of two major daily newspapers, the *Globe* publishes an extensive Calendar section every Thursday and the daily Sidekick, both of which include entertainment options.

Improper Bostonian (www.improper.com) A sassy biweekly distributed free from sidewalk dispenser boxes.

TOURIST INFORMATION

Cambridge Visitor Information Kiosk (Map p168; www.cambridge-usa.org; Harvard Sq; ⊙ 9am-5pm Mon-Fri, 1-5pm Sat & Sun; T Harvard) Detailed information on current Cambridge happenings and self-guided walking tours.

Boston Common Information Kiosk (GBCVB Visitors Center; Map p174; www.bostonusa.com; Boston Common; ⊙ 8:30am-5pm; T Park St) Starting point for the Freedom Trail and many other walking tours.

USEFUL WEBSITES

My Secret Boston (www.mysecretboston.com) Not-that-secret restaurants, nightlife, cultural and family events.

Universal Hub (www.universalhub.com) Round-up of local news, with rich local commentary.

City of Boston (www.cityofboston.gov) Official website of Boston city government with links to visitor services.

Getting There & Away

Getting in and out of Boston is easy. The train and bus stations are conveniently side by side, and the airport is a short subway ride away.

AIR

Logan International Airport (📞 800-235-6426; www.massport.com/logan), just across Boston Harbor from the city center, is served by major US and foreign airlines and has full services.

BUS

South Station is the terminal for an extensive network of long-distance buses operated by Greyhound and regional bus companies.

TRAIN

MBTA Commuter Rail (📞 800-392-6100, 617-222-3200; www.mbta.com) trains connect Boston's North Station with Concord and Salem and Boston's South Station with Plymouth and Providence.

The **Amtrak** (📞 800-872-7245; www.amtrak. com; South Station) terminal is at South Station; trains to New York cost $75 to $125 for the Northeast Regional (4¼ hours) or $130 to $170 on the speedier *Acela Express* (3½ hours).

Getting Around

TO/FROM THE AIRPORT

Logan International Airport is just a few miles from downtown Boston: take the blue-line subway or the silver-line bus.

CAR

Driving in Boston is not for the faint of heart. It's easier to get around the city on public transportation.

SUBWAY

The **MBTA** (📞 617-222-3200; www.mbta.com; per ride $2.10-2.65; ⊙ 5:30am-12:30am Sun-Thu, to 2am Fri & Sat) operates the USA's oldest subway (known as the 'T'), built in 1897. Five color-coded lines – red, blue, green and orange – radiate from the downtown stations of Park St, Downtown Crossing and Government Center. 'Inbound' trains are headed for one of these stations, 'outbound' trains away from them. Note that the silver line is actually a 'bus rapid transit service' that is useful for Logan airport and some other destinations.

TAXI

Taxis are plentiful; expect to pay between $15 and $25 between two points within the city limits. Flag taxis on the street or find them at major hotels. For airport transfers, call **Cabbie's Cab** (📞 617-547-2222; www.cabbiescab.com; airport $35).

Around Boston

Boston may be the state capital, but it's not the only town in Massachusetts with traveler appeal. Up and down the coast, destinations with rich histories, vibrant cultural scenes and unique events merit a venture outside the city. Easily accessible from Boston by car or train, these are ideal day-trip destinations.

Lexington & Concord

Students of history and lovers of liberty can trace the events of the fateful day that started a revolution – April 19, 1775. Follow in the footsteps of British soldiers and colonial minutemen, who tromped out to Lexington to face off on the town green, then continued on to Concord for the battle at the Old North Bridge.

A century later, Concord harbored a vibrant literary community, including the likes of Nathaniel Hawthorne, Ralph Waldo Emerson, Henry David Thoreau and Louisa May Alcott, whose homes are now open for visitors. The **Concord Chamber of Commerce** (www.concordchamberofcommerce.org; 58 Main St; ⊘10am-4pm Mar-Oct) has full details on the sites, as well as walking tours of Concord.

★ **Old North Bridge**   HISTORIC SITE
(www.nps.gov/mima; Monument St; ⊘dawn-dusk) A half-mile north of Memorial Sq in Concord center, the wooden span of Old North Bridge is the site of the 'shot heard around the world' (as Emerson wrote in his poem 'Concord Hymn'). This is where enraged minutemen fired on British troops, forcing them to retreat to Boston. Daniel Chester French's first statue,

Minute Man, presides over the park from the opposite side of the bridge.

Battle Green   HISTORIC SITE
(Massachusetts Ave) The historic Battle Green is where the skirmish between patriots and British troops jump-started the War for Independence. The **Lexington Minuteman Statue** (crafted by Henry Hudson Kitson in 1900) stands guard at the southeast end of Battle Green, honoring the bravery of the 77 minutemen who met the British here in 1775, and the eight who died.

Minute Man National Historic Park   PARK
(www.nps.gov/mima; 250 North Great Rd, Lincoln; ⊘9am-5pm Apr-Oct; [⊞]) **FREE** Two miles west of Lexington center, the route that British troops followed to Concord has been designated the Minute Man National Historic Park. The visitors center at the eastern end of the park shows an informative multimedia presentation depicting Paul Revere's ride and the ensuing battles.

Walden Pond   STATE PARK
(www.mass.gov/dcr/parks/walden; 915 Walden St; parking $5; ⊘dawn-dusk) **FREE** Thoreau took the naturalist beliefs of Transcendentalism out of the realm of theory and into practice when he left the comforts of town and built a rustic cabin at Walden Pond. Now a state park, the glacial pond is surrounded by acres of forest preserved by the nonprofit Walden Woods project. The site of Thoreau's cabin is on the northeast side, marked by a cairn and signs.

❶ Getting There & Away

MBTA buses 62 and 76 run from Alewife T-station (Cambridge) to Lexington center, though they don't run on Sunday. For Concord, take the **MBTA**

NEW ENGLAND AROUND BOSTON

GRAB A BIKE

Note that the Hubway pricing is designed so a bike ride can substitute for a cab ride (eg to make a one-way trip or run an errand). For leisurely riding or long trips, go for a longer-term rental.

Hubway (www.thehubway.com; 24/72hr membership $6/12, 30/60/90 minutes free/$2/4; ⊘24hr) Boston's bike-share program is the Hubway. There are 140 Hubway stations around Boston, Cambridge, Brookline and Somerville, stocked with 1300 bikes that are available for short-term loan. Purchase a temporary membership at any bicycle kiosk, then pay by the half-hour for the use of the bikes (free under 30 minutes). Return the bike to any station in the vicinity of your destination.

Urban AdvenTours (www.urbanadventours.com; 103 Atlantic Ave; per day $35; ⊘9am-6pm Mon-Sat; [T] Aquarium) Bikes available for rental include road bikes and mountain bikes, in addition to the standard hybrids. For an extra fee these guys will bring your bike to your doorstep in a BioBus powered by vegetable oil.

commuter rail (☑ 617-222-3200, 800-392-6100; www.mbta.com; Concord Depot, 90 Thoreau St) from North Station to Concord Depot ($8.50, 40 minutes, 12 daily).

Salem

A lot of history is packed into this gritty city. The town's very name conjures up images of diabolical witchcraft and women being burned at the stake. The famous Salem witch trials of 1692 are engrained in the national memory, and the town embraces its role as 'Witch City', with witchy museums, spooky tours and Halloween madness.

These incidents obscure Salem's true claim to fame: its glory days as a center for clipper-ship trade with the Far East. The **NPS Regional Visitor Center** (www.nps.gov/sama; 2 New Liberty St; ⊕9am-5pm) has complete information about the National Historic Site and environs.

★ Salem Maritime National Historic Site

HISTORIC SITE

(www.nps.gov/sama; 193 Derby St; ⊕9am-5pm) **FREE** This National Historic Site comprises the Custom House, the wharves and the other buildings that are remnants of the shipping industry that once arrived here. Of the 50 wharves that once lined Salem Harbor, only three remain, the longest of which is **Derby Wharf**. Visitors can stroll out to the end and peek inside the 1871 lighthouse or climb aboard the tall ship *Friendship*.

★ Peabody Essex Museum

ART MUSEUM

(www.pem.org; 161 Essex St; adult/child $18/free; ⊕10am-5pm Tue-Sun; ☝) All of the art, artifacts and curiosities that Salem merchants brought back from the Far East were the foundation for this museum. Founded in 1799, it is the country's oldest museum in continuous operation. The building itself is impressive, with a light-filled atrium, and is a wonderful setting for the vast collections, which focus on New England decorative arts and maritime history. Predictably, PEM is also strong in Asian art, especially the collection from pre-industrial Japan.

❶ Getting There & Away

The **MBTA commuter rail** (www.mbta.com) runs from Boston's North Station to Salem depot ($7, 30 minutes). **Boston Harbor Cruises** (Salem Ferry; www.bostonharborcruises.com; 10 Blaney St; round-trip adult/child $27/22; ⊕May-Oct) operates the ferry from Long Wharf to Salem (1 way adult/child $25/20, 50 minutes).

Plymouth

Plymouth calls itself 'America's Home Town.' It was here that the Pilgrims first settled in the winter of 1620, seeking a place where they could practice their religion without interference from government. An innocuous, weathered ball of granite – the famous **Plymouth Rock** – marks the spot where where they supposedly first stepped ashore in this foreign land, and many museums and historic houses in the surrounding streets recall their struggles, sacrifices and triumphs.

★ Mayflower II

HISTORIC SITE

(www.plimoth.org; State Pier, Water St; adult/child $12/8; ⊕9am-5pm Apr-Nov; ☝) If Plymouth Rock tells us little about the Pilgrims, *Mayflower II* speaks volumes. It is a replica of the small ship in which they made the fateful voyage. Actors in period costume are often on board, recounting harrowing tales from the journey.

WITCH CITY

The city of Salem embraces its witchy past with a healthy dose of whimsy. But the history offers a valuable lesson about what can happen when fear and frenzy are allowed to trump common sense and compassion.

By the time the witch hysteria of 1692 had finally died down, a total of 156 people had been accused, 55 people had pleaded guilty and implicated others to save their own lives, and 14 women and five men had been hanged. Stop by at the **Witch Trials Memorial** (Charter St), a simple but dramatic monument that honors the innocent victims.

The most authentic of more than a score of witchy museums, the **Witch House** (Jonathan Corwin House; www.witchhouse.info; 310 Essex St; adult/child $8.25/4.25, tour extra $2; ⊕10am-5pm Mar-Nov) was once the home of Jonathan Corwin, a local magistrate who investigated witchcraft claims.

For an informative, accurate overview of Salem's sordid past, sign up with **Hocus Pocus Tours** (www.hocuspocustours.com; adult/child $16/8), which is neither hokey nor pokey.

★ **Plimoth Plantation** MUSEUM
(www.plimoth.org; 137 Warren Ave; adult/child $26/15; ⊗9am-5pm Apr-Nov; 🖶) Three miles south of Plymouth center, Plimoth Plantation authentically recreates the Pilgrims' settlement, in its primary exhibit entitled **1627 English Village**. Everything in the village – costumes, implements, vocabulary, artistry, recipes and crops – has been painstakingly researched and remade. Costumed interpreters, acting in character, explain the details of daily life and answer your questions as you watch them work and play.

ℹ Getting There & Away

Plymouth & Brockton (P&B; www.p-b.com) buses travel hourly from Boston South Station (adult/child $15/8, one hour). Alternatively, take the **MBTA commuter rail** (📞617-222-3200, 800-392-6100; www.mbta.com) ($10.50, 90 minutes), also from South Station.

Cape Cod

Fringed with 400 miles of sparkling shoreline, the Cape offers a beach for every mood. Besides sun, surf and sand, there are lighthouses to climb, oysters to eat, art to admire, and trails to hike or bike. Find all the info you need at the **Cape Cod Chamber of Commerce** (📞508-362-3225; www.capecodchamber.org; MA 132 at US 6, Hyannis; ⊗9am-5pm Mon-Sat, 10am-2pm Sun).

Sandwich

Cape Cod's oldest town (founded in 1637) makes a perfect first impression as you cross over the canal from the mainland. In the village center, white-steepled churches, period homes and a working grist mill surround a picturesque swan pond. Before you leave town, take a stroll across the **Sandwich boardwalk**, which extends 1350 scenic feet across an expansive marsh to Town Neck Beach.

◉ Sights

Heritage Museums & Gardens MUSEUM
(www.heritagemuseumsandgardens.org; 67 Grove St; adult/child $18/8; ⊗10am-5pm; 🖶) Fun for kids and adults alike, this 76-acre site sports a superb vintage automobile collection in a Shaker-style round barn, a working 1912 carousel, folk art collections and an outdoor play area for kids. The grounds also contain one

LOBSTER ICE CREAM

Lobster mania takes a new twist at **Ben & Bill's Chocolate Emporium** (📞508-548-7878; 209 Main St; cones $5; ⊗9am-11pm) where the crustacean has crawled onto the ice-cream menu. Forget plain vanilla. Step up to the counter and order a scoop of lobster ice cream. Now there's one you won't find with the old 31 flavors folks.

of the country's finest rhododendron gardens, which is ablaze with color in early June.

If museums and gardens sound sedate, think again. The on-site **Adventure Center** (www.heritageadventurepark.org; 67 Grove St; adult/child $43/38; ⊗9am-6pm daily Jun-Oct, 9am-6pm Sat & Sun only May & Nov) has five 'aerial trails' that offer a whole new perspective on the forest and gardens.

Sandwich Glass Museum MUSEUM
(www.sandwichglassmuseum.org; 129 Main St; adult/child $9/2; ⊗9:30am-5pm Apr-Dec, to 4pm Wed-Sun Feb-Mar) Artfully displayed here is the town's 19th-century glass-making heritage. Glass-blowing demonstrations are given hourly throughout the day.

Cape Cod Canal CANAL
(www.capecodcanal.us; 🖶🐾) **FREE** The Cape Cod Canal was dug in 1914 to save ships the treacherous 135-mile sail around the tip of the Cape. The 7-mile canal is bordered on both sides by paved bike paths, also ideal for ideal for walking, in-line skating and fishing. In Sandwich, get more info at the **Cape Cod Canal Visitors Center** (www.capecodcanal.us; 60 Ed Moffitt Dr; ⊗10am-5pm May-Oct) **FREE**, near the marina.

🛏 Sleeping & Eating

Shawme-Crowell State Forest CAMPGROUND $
(📞508-888-0351; www.reserveamerica.com; MA 130; tent sites $17; 🐾) You'll find 285 shady campsites in this 760-acre woodland near MA 6A.

Belfry Inn & Bistro B&B $$$
(📞508-888-8550; www.belfryinn.com; 8 Jarves St; r incl breakfast $179-299; 🌬🐾) Ever fall asleep in church? Then you'll love the rooms, some with stained-glass windows, in this creatively restored former church. If you're uneasy about the angel Gabriel watching over you in bed, Belfry has two other nearby inns with

SCENIC DRIVE: CAPE COD BAY

The best way to explore the Cape is on the **Old King's Highway (MA 6A)**, which snakes along Cape Cod Bay from Sandwich to Orleans. The longest continuous stretch of historic district in the USA, it's lined with gracious period homes, antique shops and art galleries, all of which make for good browsing en route.

conventional rooms. There's also a lovely high-ceiling, stained-glass restaurant.

Seafood Sam's   SEAFOOD **$$**
(☑ 508-888-4629; www.seafoodsams.com; 6 Coast Guard Rd; mains $8-20; ⊙11am-9pm; 🖼️) Sam's is a good family choice for fish and chips, fried clams and lobster rolls. Dine at outdoor picnic tables overlooking Cape Cod Canal and watch the fishing boats sail by.

Falmouth

Crowd-pleasing beaches, a terrific bike trail and the quaint seaside village of Woods Hole are the highlights of the Cape's second-largest town.

🎯 Sights & Activities

Old Silver Beach   BEACH
(off MA 28A; 🖼️) Deeply indented Falmouth has 70 miles of coastline, none of it finer than this long, sandy stretch of beach. A rock jetty, sandbars and tidal pools provide fun diversions for kids. Parking costs $20.

★ Shining Sea Bikeway   CYCLING
A bright star among the Cape's stellar bike trails, this 10.7-mile beaut runs along the entire west coast of Falmouth, offering unspoiled views of salt ponds, marsh and seascapes. Bike rentals are available at the north end of the trail.

🛏️ Sleeping

Falmouth Heights Motor Lodge   MOTEL **$$**
(☑ 508-548-3623; www.falmouthheightsresort. com; 146 Falmouth Heights Rd; r incl breakfast $129-259; ❄️🐾🛜🏊) Don't be fooled by the name. This tidy operation is no drive-up motor lodge – it's not even on the highway. All 28 rooms are a cut above the competition. The beach and Vineyard ferry are minutes away.

Tides Motel of Falmouth   MOTEL **$$**
(☑ 508-548-3126; www.tidesmotelcapecod.com; 267 Clinton Ave; r $180) It's all about the water. This place is smack on its own private beach, and you could spit into the ocean from your deck. Frankly, the same rooms elsewhere would be a yawn. But you came to the Cape for the water, right?

🍴 Eating

Maison Villatte   CAFE **$**
(☑ 774-255-1855; 267 Main St; snacks $3-10; ⊙7am-7pm Wed-Sat, to 5pm Sun) A pair of French bakers crowned in toques work the ovens, creating crusty artisan breads, flaky croissants and sinful pastries at this bakery-cafe. Hearty sandwiches and robust coffee make it an ideal lunch spot.

Pickle Jar Kitchen   MODERN AMERICAN **$**
(☑ 508-540-6760; www.picklejarkitchen.com; 170 Main St; mains $7-14; ⊙7am-3pm Wed-Mon; 🖼️) Hearty, healthy comfort food, prepared with seasonal ingredients and lots of love. Look for satisfying hash for breakfast, delicious sammies for lunch, and lots of fresh fruit and veggies all around. And of course, don't miss the housemade pickles.

Clam Shack   SEAFOOD **$**
(☑ 508-540-7758; 227 Clinton Ave; mains $6-15; ⊙11:30am-7:30pm) A classic of the genre, right on Falmouth Harbor. It's tiny, with picnic tables on the back deck and lots of fried seafood.

Hyannis

Ferries, buses and planes all converge on the Cape's commercial hub. Hyannis is a launching point for boats to Nantucket and Martha's Vineyard. It was also the summer home of the Kennedys – and the site where Teddy passed away in 2009.

🎯 Sights

Hyannis is blessed with a couple of wide, warm-water beaches that are ideal for swimming. **Kalmus Beach** (Ocean St, Hyannis) is popular for windsurfing, while **Craigville Beach** (Craigville Beach Rd, Centerville) is where the college set goes; parking at either costs $15 to $20.

Cape Cod, Martha's Vineyard & Nantucket

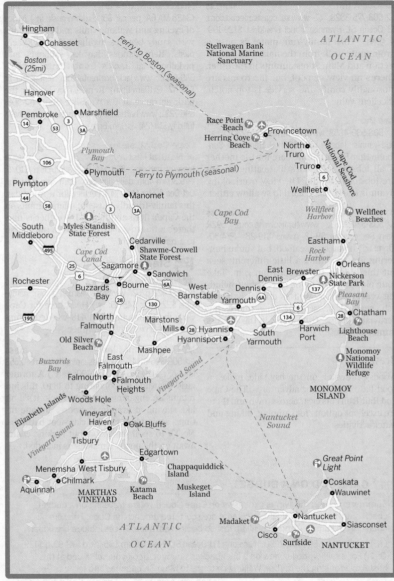

John F Kennedy Hyannis Museum MUSEUM (www.jfkhyannismuseum.org; 397 Main St, Hyannis; adult/child $10/5; ⊙ 9am-5pm Mon-Sat, noon-5pm Sun) Celebrates America's 35th president with photographs, videos and mementos.

For more Kennedy nostalgia, pick up a map of the **Hyannis Kennedy Legacy Trail** (www.kennedylegacytrail.org) FREE. The museum also holds the **Cape Cod Baseball League Hall of Fame.**

🛏 Sleeping & Eating

SeaCoast Inn
MOTEL **$$**

(☑ 508-775-3828; www.seacoastcapecod.com; 33 Ocean St, Hyannis; r incl breakfast $129-199; ❄@🛜) This family-run motel is just a two-minute walk from the harbor in one direction and Main St restaurants in the other. There's no view or pool, but the rooms are thoroughly comfy and service is top-notch. Excellent value.

Raw Bar
SEAFOOD **$$**

(☑ 508-539-4858; www.therawbar.com; 230 Ocean St, Hyannis; lobster rolls $26; ⊙11am-8pm Sun-Thu, to 11pm Fri-Sat) Come here for the mother of all lobster rolls – it's like eating an entire lobster in a bun. The view overlooking Hyannis Harbor isn't hard to swallow either.

Tumi
SEAFOOD **$$**

(☑ 508-534-9289; www.tumiceviche.com; 592R Main St; ceviche $9-12, mains $19-28; ⊙4:30-10pm; ☑) If you love seafood, but you're hankering for something a little different, seek out this hidden Italian-Peruvian gem. Take your pick from 10 kinds of ceviche (including vegetarian), as well as other raw shellfish, seafood pasta and some interesting Peruvian options. Hint: the R in the address stands for 'rear'.

Brewster

Woodsy Brewster, on the bay side, makes a good base for outdoor adventures. The Cape Cod Rail Trail cuts clear across town and there are excellent options for camping, hiking and water activities.

⦿ Sights & Activities

Nickerson State Park
PARK

(3488 MA 6A; per car $5; ⊙dawn-dusk; ☑) Miles of cycling and walking trails and eight ponds with sandy beaches highlight this 2000-acre oasis. Rent canoes, kayaks, sailboats and pedalboats at **Jack's Boat Rental** (☑508-349-9808; www.jacksboatrental.com; rentals per hr $32-47; ⊙10am-6pm). Rent a bicycle near the park entrance at **Barb's Bike Shop** (☑508-896-7231; www.barbsbikeshop.com; bicycles per half/full day $18/24; ⊙9am-6pm).

Cape Cod Museum of Natural History
MUSEUM

(www.ccmnh.org; 869 MA 6A; adult/child $10/5; ⊙9:30am-4pm daily Jun-Sep, 11am-3pm Wed-Sun Oct-Dec & Mar-May; ☑) Perfect for a rainy day, this family-friendly museum offers exhibits on the Cape's flora and fauna. If weather is fine, there's a **boardwalk trail** across a salt marsh to a remote beach.

🛏 Sleeping

⭐ Nickerson State Park
CAMPGROUND **$**

(☑877-422-6762; www.reserveamerica.com; campsites $22; yurts $45-55; ☑) Head here for Cape Cod's best camping with 418 wooded campsites. Reserve early in summer.

⭐ Old Sea Pines Inn
B&B **$$**

(☑508-896-6114; www.oldseapinesinn.com; 2553 MA 6A; r $120-165, ste $155-190; @🛜) A former girls' boarding school dating to 1840, this inn retains an engaging yesteryear look. It's a bit like staying at grandma's house: antique fittings, sepia photographs, claw-foot bathtubs. No TV to spoil the mood, but rocking chairs await on the porch. Breakfast is included.

ⓘ CAPE COD ON A BUDGET

Summertime, and the livin' is expensive on Cape Cod. If you're traveling on a budget, check out these excellent HI hostels that are scattered around the Cape. They are all open only in summer, and they fill up fast so book in advance. Prices include breakfast.

HI-Hyannis (☑508-775-7990; hiusa.org; 111 Ocean St, Hyannis; dm $35-39, d $79-99, q $129; @🛜) For a million-dollar view on a backpacker's budget, book yourself a bed at this hostel overlooking the harbor. Walking distance to Main St, beaches and ferries.

Hostelling International Eastham (☑508-255-2785; hiusa.org; 75 Goody Hallett Dr; dm $33-36; 🛜) This hostel is close to the beach and the bike trail, but surrounded by quiet woods. Basic cabins serve as dormitories, sleeping five to eight people each.

Hostelling International Truro (☑508-349-3889; hiusa.org; N Pamet Rd; dm incl breakfast $45; @) Budget digs don't get more atmospheric than this former coast-guard station perched amid undulating dunes and a short stroll to the beach. It's so remote that wild turkeys are the only traffic along the road.

✖ Eating

★ Brewster Fish House SEAFOOD $$
(☑ 508-896-7867; www.brewsterfish.com; 2208 MA 6A; lunch mains $12-18, dinner $25-32; ⊙11:30am-3pm & 5-9:30pm) Once a retail fish market, this tiny, unassuming bistro has earned fiercely loyal patrons, thanks to artful presentations of classic seafood dishes. Just 11 tables, and no reservations.

Cobie's SEAFOOD $$
(☑ 508-896-7021; www.cobies.com; 3260 MA 6A; mains $9-23; ⊙11am-9pm; 🚸) Conveniently located near Nickerson State Park, this roadside clam shack dishes out fried seafood that you can crunch and munch at outdoor picnic tables.

Chatham

Main St Chatham is lined with upscale inns and shops – a hallmark of this genteel town; but there's something for everyone here. At **Chatham Fish Pier** (Shore Rd), fishers unload their catch and seals bask on nearby shoals. A mile south on Shore Rd, **Chatham Light** (⊙20min tours 1-3:30pm Wed May-Oct) FREE overlooks picturesque **Lighthouse Beach**, an endless expanse of sea and sandbars.

The two uninhabited islands off the elbow comprise the 7600-acre **Monomoy National Wildlife Refuge** (www.fws.gov/northeast/monomoy) 🌿. Take a boat tour with the **Beachcomber** (☑ 508-945-5265; www.sealwatch.com; Crowell Rd; North Beach water taxi adult/child $20/10; seal-watching trips adult/child $29/25; ⊙10am-5pm) or **Monomoy Island Excursions** (☑ 508-430-7772; www.monomoysealcruise.com; 702 MA 28, Harwich Port; 1½hr tours adult/child $36/30) to get a good look at hundreds of gray seals, harbor seals and shorebirds.

🛏 Sleeping

Chatham Highlander MOTEL $$
(☑ 508-945-9038; www.chathamhighlander.com; 946 Main St; r $119-209; ❄🛜🏊) The rooms here, about 1 mile from the town center, are straightforward but large and clean. Unlike some stodgier resorts in town that cater to an older set, this motel welcomes families; kids will love the pair of heated pools.

Hawthorne Motel MOTEL $$$
(www.thehawthorne.com; 196 Shore Rd; d $225-330; ⊙May-Oct; ❄🛜🏊) Here's your chance to wake up to a fabulous sunrise over the sandbars. It's pricey for a motel, but the rooms are tasteful, service is charming and the view is

ℹ SNACK ATTACK

On your way into Hyannis, stop at the **Cape Cod Potato Chip Factory** (☑ 508-775-3358; www.capecodchips.com; 100 Breeds Hill Rd, Hyannis; ⊙9am-5pm Mon-Fri) FREE for a free tour and a free sample. From MA 132 (just west of the airport), take Independence Rd a half-mile north to the factory.

unbeatable. If you can drag yourself away from the private beach, it's a short walk into town.

✖ Eating

Chatham Cookware Café CAFE $
(☑ 508-954-1250; www.chathamcookware.com; 524 Main St; sandwiches $8; ⊙6:30am-4pm) No, it's not a place to buy pots and pans, but rather *the* downtown spot for a coffee fix, homemade muffins and sandwiches.

★ Chatham Fish Pier Market SEAFOOD $$
(☑ 508-945-3474; www.chathamfishpiermarket.com; 45 Barcliff Ave; mains $12-25; ⊙10am-6pm Wed-Sun) If you like it fresh and local to the core, this salt-sprayed fish shack, with its own sushi chef and day boats, is for you. The chowder's incredible, the fish so fresh it was swimming earlier in the day. It's all takeout, but there are shady picnic tables and a harbor full of sights.

Cape Cod National Seashore

Cape Cod National Seashore PARK
(www.nps.gov/caco; beach pass pedestrian/car $3/20) Cape Cod National Seashore extends some 40 miles around the curve of the Outer Cape and encompasses most of the shoreline from Eastham to Provincetown. It's a treasure trove of unspoiled beaches, dunes, salt marshes and forests. Thanks to President John F Kennedy, this vast area was set aside for preservation in the 1960s, just before a building boom hit the rest of his native Cape Cod.

The **Salt Pond Visitor Center** (☑ 508-255-3421; 50 Doane Rd, cnr US 6 & Nauset Rd, Eastham; ⊙9am-5pm) FREE is the place to start. Here you will find exhibits and films about the area's ecology, as well as information on the park's numerous cycling and hiking trails, some of which begin right at the center.

NEW ENGLAND CAPE COD

Coast Guard Beach
BEACH

Just down the beach from the Salt Pond Visitor Center, Coast Guard Beach is a stunner that attracts everyone from surfers to beachcombers. The view of untouched Nauset Marsh from the dunes above the beach is nothing short of spectacular.

Nauset Light
LIGHTHOUSE

(www.nausetlight.org; ☉1-4pm or 4:30-7:30pm Sun May-Oct, 4:30-7:30pm Wed Jul & Aug) Photogenic Nauset Light has been shining over Cape Cod since 1877. It stands proudly over Nauset Light Beach, which stretches north from Coast Guard Beach.

Wellfleet

Wellfleet is one of Cape Cod's unsung gems, offering some unspoiled beaches, dozens of art galleries, and plenty of opportunities to slurp those glorious oysters.

👁 Sights

Wellfleet Beaches
BEACHES

Ocean-side Wellfleet is part of the Cape Cod National Seashore, so the pristine beaches backed by undulating dunes. **Marconi Beach** has a monument to Guglielmo Marconi, who sent the first wireless transmission across the Atlantic from this site. The adjacent **White Crest Beach** and **Cahoon Hollow Beach** offer high-octane surfing. Rent your gear at **SickDay Surf Shop** (☎508-214-4158; www.sickdaysurf.com; 361 Main St; surfboards per day $30; ☉9:30am-5pm Mon-Fri).

Wellfleet Bay Wildlife Sanctuary
NATURE RESERVE

(www.massaudubon.org; West Rd, off US 6; adult/child $5/3; ☉8:30am-dusk; 🚹) 🅿 Birders flock to Mass Audubon's 1100-acre sanctuary, where trails cross tidal creeks, salt marshes and beaches.

🎉 Festivals & Events

Wellfleet OysterFest
FOOD

(www.wellfleetoysterfest.org; ☉mid-Oct) The town becomes a food fair for a weekend, with a beer garden, an oyster-shucking contest and, of course, belly-busters of the blessed bivalves.

🛏 Sleeping & Eating

Even'Tide Motel
MOTEL $$

(☎508-349-3410; www.eventidemotel.com; 650 US 6; r $89-187, cottages per week $1400-2800; ☉May-Oct; ❄ ⛱) This 31-room motel, set back from the highway in a grove of pine trees, also has nine cottages. It's a simple, friendly place with a large indoor pool, picnic facilities and a small playground.

PB Boulangerie & Bistro
BAKERY $

(☎508-349-1600; www.pbboulangeriebistro.com; 15 Lecount Hollow Rd; pastries from $3; ☉7am-7pm Tue-Sun) When you walk through the door and scan the glass cases full of flaky fruit tarts and chocolate croissants, you'll think you've died and gone to Paris. Cape Cod's only Michelin-starred chef is behind this gem.

Mac's Seafood Market
SEAFOOD $$

(☎508-349-9611; www.macsseafood.com; 265 Commercial St, Wellfleet Town Pier; mains $7-20; ☉11am-3pm Mon-Thu, to 8pm Fri-Sun; 🅿 🚹) Head here for market-fresh seafood at bargain prices. Fried fish standards are paired with snappy-fresh oysters harvested from nearby flats. Order at a window and chow down at picnic tables overlooking Wellfleet Harbor. **Mac's Shack** (☎508-349-6333; 91 Commercial St; mains $15-30; ☉4:30-9:45pm) is a proper full-service restaurant up the street.

⭐ Entertainment

★ Beachcomber
LIVE MUSIC

(☎508-349-6055; www.thebeachcomber.com; 1120 Cahoon Hollow Rd; ☉5pm-1am Jun-Aug) It's a bar. It's a restaurant. It's a dance club. It's the coolest summertime hangout on the entire Cape,

---

DON'T MISS

CAPE COD RAIL TRAIL

One of the finest cycling trails in New England, the **Cape Cod Rail Trail** follows a former railroad track for 22 glorious miles past cranberry bogs, through quaint villages, and along sandy ponds ideal for a dip. The path begins in Dennis on MA 134 and continues all the way to Wellfleet. If you have time to do only part of the trail, begin at Nickerson State Park in Brewster and head for the Cape Cod National Seashore in Eastham. Bicycle rentals are available at the trailhead in Dennis, at Nickerson State Park and opposite the National Seashore's **Salt Pond Visitor Center** (p191).

set in a former lifesaving station right on Cahoon Hollow Beach. You can watch the surf action till the sun goes down, and after dark some really hot bands take the stage.

Wellfleet Drive-In CINEMA
(☎508-349-7176; www.wellfleetcinemas.com; US 6; adult/child $9/6; 🅿) Park your car at this 1950s-era drive-in, where everything except the feature flick is true to the era. Grab a bite to eat at the old-fashioned snack bar, hook the mono speaker over the car window and settle in for a double feature.

Provincetown

Provincetown is as far as you can go on the Cape, and more than just geographically. Fringe writers and artists began making a summer haven in Provincetown a century ago. Today this sandy outpost has morphed into the hottest gay and lesbian destination in the Northeast. Flamboyant street scenes, brilliant art galleries and unbridled nightlife paint the town center. Away from Commercial St, Provincetown's untamed coastline and vast beaches beg exploring. Sail off on a whalewatch, cruise the night away, get lost in the dunes – but whatever you do, don't miss this unique corner of New England.

◉ Sights & Activities

Provincetown is a perfect gateway to the Cape Cod National Seashore (p191). On the wild tip of the Cape, **Race Point Beach** is a breathtaking stretch of sand with crashing surf and undulating dunes as far as the eye can see. The west-facing **Herring Cove Beach** is popular for swimming and sunset-watching. Eight exhilarating miles of **paved bike trails** crisscross the forest and dunes, providing access to both beaches. Get more information or sign up for a tour at **Province Lands Visitor Center** (www.nps.gov/caco; Race Point Rd; car/bike/pedestrian $15/3/3; ⊙9am-5pm; 🅿) 🌊.

★**Provincetown Art Association & Museum** MUSEUM
(PAAM; www.paam.org; 460 Commercial St; adult/child $10/free; ⊙11am-8pm Mon-Thu, to 10pm Fri, to 5pm Sat & Sun) Founded in 1914 to celebrate the town's thriving art community, this vibrant museum showcases the works of artists who have found their inspiration in Provincetown. Chief among them is Edward Hopper, who had a home and gallery in the Truro dunes.

DON'T MISS

FIRST PORT OF CALL

Erected in 1860 as a church, **Provincetown Public Library** (www.provincetownlibrary.org; 356 Commercial St; ⊙10am-5pm Mon & Fri, to 8pm Tue-Thu, 1-5pm Sat & Sun; 🅿) was turned into a museum a century later, complete with a half-size replica of Provincetown's race-winning schooner *Rose Dorothea*. When the museum went bust, the town converted the building to a library. One catch: the boat was too big to remove. So it's still there, with bookshelves built around it. Pop upstairs and take a look.

Pilgrim Monument & Provincetown Museum MUSEUM
(www.pilgrim-monument.org; High Pole Rd; adult/child $12/4; ⊙9am-5pm Apr-Nov, to 7pm Jul & Aug) Climb to the top of the USA's tallest all-granite structure (253ft) for a sweeping view of town and coast. At the base of the c 1910 tower an evocative museum depicts the landing of the *Mayflower* Pilgrims and other Provincetown history.

Whydah Pirate Museum MUSEUM
(www.whydah.com; MacMillan Wharf; adult/child $10/8; ⊙10am-5pm May-Oct) See the salvaged booty from a pirate ship that sank off Cape Cod in 1717.

East End Gallery District GALLERIES
(Commercial St) With the many artists who have worked here, it's no surprise that Provincetown hosts some of the finest art galleries in the region. Most of them are packed into the East End of Commercial St: begin at PAAM and start walking southwest for the town's finest browsing.

★**Dolphin Fleet Whale Watch** WHALE-WATCHING
(☎800-826-9300; www.whalewatch.com; MacMillan Wharf; adult/child $46/31; ⊙Apr-Oct; 🅿) 🌊 Provincetown is the perfect launch point for whale-watching, since it's the closest port to Stellwagen Bank National Marine Sanctuary, a summer feeding ground for humpback whales. Dolphin offers as many as 12 whale-watch tours daily. Humpback whales have a flair for acrobatic breaching and come surprisingly close to the boats, offering great photo ops.

GAY & LESBIAN PROVINCETOWN

Provincetown is awash with gay clubs, drag shows and cabarets. And don't be shy if you're straight – everyone's welcome.

A-House (Atlantic House; www.ahouse.com; 4 Masonic Pl; ⊙ pub noon-1am, club 10pm-1am) P-town's gay scene got its start here and it's still one of the leading bars in town. Includes an intimate 1st-floor pub with fireplace, as well as a dance club and cabaret through a separate entrance.

Boatslip Resort (www.boatsliplresort.com; 161 Commercial St; ⊙ 4-7pm) Hosts wildly popular afternoon tea dances.

Crown & Anchor (www.onlyatthecrown.com; 247 Commercial St; ⊙ hours vary) The queen of the gay scene, this multiwing complex has a nightclub, a video bar, a leather bar and a steamy cabaret that takes it to the limit.

Pied Bar (www.piedbar.com; 193 Commercial St; ⊙ noon-1am May-Oct) This woman-owned waterfront lounge is a popular dance spot for all genders. The main event is the 'After Tea T-Dance,' so folks head here after the Boatslip. Also hosts 'Women's Week' in October.

🎉 Festivals & Events

Provincetown Carnival　　　　CARNIVAL
(www.ptown.org/carnival; ⊙ 3rd week of August) Mardi Gras, drag queens, flowery floats – this is the ultimate gay party event in this gay party town, attracting tens of thousands of revelers.

🛏 Sleeping

Provincetown offers nearly 100 guesthouses, without a single chain hotel to mar the view. In summer it's wise to book ahead, doubly so on weekends. If you do arrive without a booking, the chamber of commerce keeps tabs on available rooms.

Dunes' Edge Campground　　CAMPGROUND $
(☑ 508-487-9815; www.dunesedge.com; 386 US 6; tent/RV sites $49/61; ⊙ mid-May–mid-Oct) Camp amid the dunes at this family-friendly campground.

Moffett House　　　　　　GUESTHOUSE $$
(☑ 508-487-6615; www.moffetthouse.com; 296a Commercial St; d without bathroom $75-164, d with bathroom $115-185; ▣ 🕾 🎴) Set back in a quiet alleyway, this guesthouse has a bonus: free bicycles. Rooms are basic – feels sort of like crashing with a friend – but you get kitchen privileges and lots of ops to meet fellow travelers.

Captain's House　　　　　　　B&B $$
(☑ 508-487-9353; www.captainshouseptown.com; 350A Commercial St; r without bathroom $100-175, r with bathroom $210; ▣ ▣ 🕾) Occupying an actual former sea captain's house, this

small B&B is a charming affordable option in the heart of P-town. Rooms are small, but cozy and comfortable. Your hosts Peter and Mauricio are equally charming. Breakfast features Mauricio's delicious homemade granola.

★ Carpe Diem　　　　BOUTIQUE HOTEL $$$
(☑ 508-487-4242; www.carpediemguesthouse.com; 12 Johnson St; r incl breakfast $279-469; ▣ ▣ 🕾) Sophisticated yet relaxed, this boutique inn blends a soothing mix of smiling Buddhas, orchid sprays and artistic decor. Each guest room is inspired by a different gay literary genius; the room themed on poet Raj Rao, for example, has sumptuous embroidered fabrics and hand-carved Indian furniture. The on-site spa includes a Finnish sauna, hot tub and massage therapy.

Revere Guesthouse　　　　　B&B $$$
(☑ 508-487-2292; www.reverehouse.com; 14 Court St; r incl breakfast $169-359; ▣ 🕾) Tasteful rooms, fresh-baked breakfast goodies and welcoming little touches will make you feel right at home here. The setting is peaceful, yet just minutes from all the action.

🍴 Eating

Cafe Heaven　　　　　　　　CAFE $
(☑ 508-487-9639; 199 Commercial St; mains $7-12; ⊙ 8am-10pm; 🎴) Light and airy but small and crowded, this art-filled storefront is an easy-on-the-wallet eating place. The menu ranges from sinful croissant French toast to healthy salads. Don't be deterred by the wait – the tables turn over quickly.

★ Mews Restaurant & Cafe
MODERN AMERICAN **$$$**
(☑508-487-1500; www.mews.com; 429 Commercial St; mains bistro $13-22, restaurant $27-31; ☺5:30-10pm) Want affordable gourmet? Skip the excellent but pricey restaurant and go upstairs to the bar for a fab view, great martinis and scrumptious bistro fare.

Lobster Pot
SEAFOOD **$$$**
(☑508-487-0842; www.ptownlobsterpot.com; 321 Commercial St; mains $22-37; ☺11:30am-9pm) True to its name, this bustling fish house is *the* place for lobster. Service can be s-l-o-w. Best way to beat the crowd is to come mid-afternoon.

▼ Drinking

Aqua Bar
BAR
(207 Commercial St; ☺10am-1am) Imagine a food court where the options include a raw bar, sushi, gelato and other international delights. Add a fully stocked bar with generous tenders pouring the drinks. Now put the whole place in a gorgeous seaside setting, overlooking a little beach and beautiful harbor. Now, imagine this whole scene at sunset. That's no fantasy, that's Aqua Bar.

Ross' Grill
BAR
(www.rossgrille.com; 237 Commercial St; ☺11:30am-10pm) For an romantic place to have a drink with a water view, head to the bar at this smart bistro. The food also gets rave reviews.

Harbor Lounge
COCKTAIL BAR
(www.theharborlounge.com; 359 Commercial St; ☺noon-10pm) The Harbor Lounge takes full advantage of its seaside setting, with floor-to-ceiling windows and a boardwalk stretching out into the bay. Candlelit tables and black leather sofas constitute the decor – nothing else is needed. The cocktails are surprisingly affordable, with many martini concoctions to sample.

❶ Information

Provincetown Business Guild (www.ptown.org) Oriented to the gay community.

Provincetown Chamber of Commerce (www.ptownchamber.com; 307 Commercial St; ☺9am-6pm) The town's helpful tourist office is at MacMillan Wharf, where the ferries dock.

Provincetown on the Web (www.provincetown.com) Online guide with the entertainment scoop.

Wired Puppy (www.wiredpuppy.com; 379 Commercial St; ☺6:30am-10pm; 🛜) Free online computers for the price of an espresso.

❶ Getting There & Away

Plymouth & Brockton buses (www.p-b.com) connect Provincetown to Boston ($31, 3½ hours) and other towns on the Cape. From mid-May to mid-October, **Bay State Cruise Company** (☑877-783-3779; www.boston-ptown.com; 200 Seaport Blvd, Boston; ☺mid-May–mid-Oct) runs a ferry (round-trip $88, 1½ hours) between Boston's World Trade Center Pier and MacMillan Wharf. From late June to early September, the **Plymouth-to-Provincetown Express Ferry** (www.p-townferry.com; State Pier, 77 Water St) plies that route twice a day (round-trip $45, 1½ hours).

Nantucket
Nantucket is New England at her most rose-covered, cobblestoned, picture-postcard perfect. the island's only population center, Nantucket Town, was once home port to the world's largest whaling fleet. Now a national Historic Landmark, the town boasts leafy streets lined with gracious period homes and public buildings. Walk up cobbled Main St, where the grandest whaling-era mansions are lined up in a row. Get your questions answered at the Visitors Services kiosk (☑508-228-0925; www.nantucket-ma.gov; 25 Federal St; ☺9am-5pm), near the ferry dock.

◉ Sights & Activities

★ Nantucket Whaling Museum
MUSEUM
(13 Broad St; adult/child $20/5; ☺10am-5pm mid-May–Oct, 11am-4pm Nov–mid-May) Occupies a former spermaceti (whale-oil) candle factory. The evocative exhibits relive Nantucket's 19th-century heyday as the whaling center of the world. A 46ft-long sperm-whale skeleton, a rigged whaleboat and assorted whaling implements recount the history.

Beaches
Right in town, Children's Beach has calm water and a playground. For wilder, less frequented strands, pedal a bike or hop on a bus to Surfside Beach, 2 miles to the south. The best place to catch the sunset is Madaket Beach, 5.5 miles west of town.

Cycling
Cycling around Nantucket is an unbeatable way to explore the island. Dedicated bike paths connect the town with the main beaches and the villages of Madaket and 'Sconset – no place is more than 8 miles away. Rent bikes near Steamboat Wharf.

NANTUCKET BREW

Enjoy a hoppy pint of Whale's Tale Pale at **Cisco Brewers** (☎508-325-5929; www.ciscobrewers.com; 5 Bartlett Farm Rd; tours $20; ☺10am-7pm Mon-Sat & noon-6pm Sun, tours 1pm & 4pm daily), the friendliest brewery you'll likely ever see. In addition to brewery tours, there are a few bars where you can hear spirited live music played on the mountain banjo in the late afternoons. Bonus: in season, Cisco operates a free shuttle bus from the Visitor Services kiosk.

🛌 Sleeping

HI Nantucket　　　　　　　　HOSTEL **$**
(Star of the Sea; ☎508-228-0433; hiusa.org; 31 Western Ave; dm $42-45; ☺mid-May–mid-Sep; ❷) Occupying an 1873 lifesaving station, this atmospheric hostel has a million-dollar spot near Surfside Beach. Prices include breakfast.

Barnacle Inn　　　　　　　　B&B **$$**
(☎508-228-0332; www.thebarnacleinn.com; 11 Fair St; r without/with bathroom from $115/125; ❄🕾) This is what old Nantucket is all about: folksy owners and simple, quaint accommodations that hearken to earlier times. Rooms in this turn-of-the-19th-century inn offer excellent value. Breakfast included.

✗ Eating

Downyflake　　　　　　　DINER, BAKERY **$**
(☎508-228-4533; www.thedownyflake.com; 18 Sparks Ave; mains $5-10; ☺6am-2pm Mon-Sat, to 1pm Sun) First and foremost, the doughnuts are tried-and-true, old-fashioned goodness, in three varieties only (plain, sugar and chocolate). That should be enough. But there's also a full-service diner, with delicious blueberry pancakes for breakfast and burgers, reubens and tuna melts for lunch.

Black-Eyed Susan's　　　　　　CAFE **$$**
(☎508-325-0308; www.black-eyedsusans.com; 10 India St; breakfast mains $8-12, dinner $24-26; ☺7am-1pm daily, 6-10pm Mon-Sat; ✐) No reservations, no credit cards and no alcohol (unless you bring it yourself). Yet islanders line up out the door to get one of a dozen tables at this understated gem. This is New American at its finest: you've eaten these ingredients, but never before in these creative, decidedly delicious combinations.

Club Car　　　　AMERICAN, SEAFOOD **$$**
(☎508-228-1101; www.theclubcar.com; 1 Main St; mains $12-30; ☺11:30am-1am) This converted railroad car is a vestige of the actual railroad that sank in the sands of Nantucket. The lively place dishes up sing-along piano music and consistently good food, including an excellent lobster roll.

ℹ Getting There & Around

AIR

Cape Air (www.flycapeair.com) flies from Boston, Hyannis and Martha's Vineyard to Nantucket Memorial Airport (ACK).

BOAT

The **Steamship Authority** (☎508-477-8600; www.steamshipauthority.com) runs ferries throughout the day between Hyannis and Nantucket. The fast ferry (round-trip adult/child $69/35) takes an hour; the slow ferry (round-trip adult/child $37/19) takes 2¼ hours. Also from Hyannis, **Hy-Line Cruises** (☎508-778-2600, 888-492-8082; www.hylinecruises.com; Ocean St Dock) has a high-speed ferry (adult/child $77/51, one hour, five or six daily) and a slow ferry ($45/free, two hours, two daily).

BUS

Getting around Nantucket is a snap. The **NRTA Wave** (www.nrtawave.com; rides $1-2, day pass $7; ☺late May-Sep) operates buses around town and to 'Sconset, Madaket and the beaches. Buses have bike racks, so cyclists can bus one way and pedal back.

Martha's Vineyard

Bathed in scenic beauty, Martha's Vineyard attracts wide-eyed day-trippers, celebrity second-home owners, and urbanites seeking a restful getaway. The Vineyard remains untouched by the kind of rampant commercialism found on the mainland. Instead you'll find cozy inns, chef-driven restaurants and a bounty of green farms and grand beaches.

Vineyard Haven is the island's commercial center. Most ferries arrive in Oak Bluffs, which is the center of all summer fun on the Vineyard. Edgartown has a rich maritime history and more of a patrician air.

◉ Sights & Activities

Campgrounds & Tabernacle　　　HISTORIC SITE
(Oak Bluffs) Oak Bluffs started out in the mid-19th century as a summer retreat for a revivalist church, whose members enjoyed a

day at the beach as much as a gospel service. They built some 300 cottages, each adorned with whimsical gingerbread trim. These brightly painted cottages – known today as the Campgrounds – surround Trinity Park and its open-air Tabernacle (1879), a venue for festival and concerts.

For a peek inside one, visit the **Cottage Museum** (www.mvcma.org; 1 Trinity Park; adult/child $2/50¢; ⊙10am-4pm Mon-Sat & 1-4pm Sun May-Sep), which contains exhibits on CMA history.

Flying Horses Carousel HISTORIC SITE

(www.mvpreservation.org; 15 Lake Ave, Oak Bluffs; rides $2.50; ⊙10am-10pm; ▣) Take a nostalgic ride on the USA's oldest merry-go-round, which has been captivating kids of all ages since 1876. The antique horses have manes of real horse hair and, if you stare into their glass eyes, you'll see neat little silver animals inside.

Katama Beach BEACH

(Katama Rd; ▣) The Vineyard's best beach lies 4 miles south of Edgartown center. Also called South Beach, Katama stretches for three magnificent miles. Rugged surf will please surfers on the ocean side, while some swimmers may prefer the protected salt ponds on the inland side.

Cycling

A scenic bike trail runs along the coast connecting Oak Bluffs, Vineyard Haven and Edgartown – it's largely flat so makes a good pedal for families. Rent bicycles at **Anderson's Bike Rental** (☑508-693-9346; www.andersonsbikerentals.com; 1 Circuit Ave Extension; bicycles per day adult/child $20/15; ⊙9am-6pm) near the ferry terminal.

🛏 Sleeping

HI Martha's Vineyard HOSTEL $

(☑508-693-2665; http://hiusa.org; 525 Edgartown–West Tisbury Rd; dm $35-39, d/q $99/135; ⊙mid-May–mid-Oct; @🔊) Reserve early for a bed at this popular purpose-built hostel in the center of the island. It has everything you'd expect of a top-notch hostel: a solid kitchen, bike delivery and no curfew. The hostel is 1 mile east of the village of West Tisbury; take bus 3 from Vineyard Haven.

Nashua House INN $$

(☑508-693-0043; www.nashuahouse.com; 30 Kennebec Ave, Oak Bluffs; r without/with bathroom from $99/129; ❄🔊) Despite the (mostly) shared bathrooms, these accommodations are spotlessly clean, cozily comfortable and quite lovely. There's no breakfast, but there are coffee and snacks all day. Staff is eager to please.

Down the road, the **Madison Inn** (☑508-693-2760; www.madisoninnmv.com; 18 Kennebec Ave; r incl breakfast from $169; ❄🔊) is the slightly more upscale sister property.

Narragansett House B&B $$

(☑508-693-3627; www.narragansetthouse.com; 46 Narragansett Ave, Oak Bluffs; d $150-235; ❄🔊) On a quiet residential street, this B&B occupies two nearby Victorian gingerbread-trimmed houses, just a stroll from the town center. The wide porch and blooming gardens are both delightful places to enjoy your complimentary breakfast.

Edgartown Inn GUESTHOUSE $$$

(☑508-627-4794; www.edgartowninn.com; 56 N Water St, Edgartown; r $200-325; ❄🔊) This stately inn was built in 1798 as a sea captain's home, but later was converted into an inn, welcoming such distinguished guests as Nathaniel Hawthorne and Daniel Webster. Nowadays, it is a lovely, relatively affordable inn with period furnishings and old-fashioned charm.

✕ Eating

★ Art Cliff Diner CAFE $

(☑508-693-1224; 39 Beach Rd, Vineyard Haven; mains $8-16; ⊙7am-2pm Thu-Tue) 🖉 The place for breakfast and lunch. Chef-owner Gina Stanley adds flair to everything she touches, from the almond-encrusted French toast to the fresh-fish tacos. The food is thoroughly modern, but the diner itself is charmingly retro.

MV Bakery BAKERY $

(☑508-693-3688; www.mvbakery.com; 5 Post Office Sq, Oak Bluffs; baked goods $1-3; ⊙7am-5pm) Inexpensive coffee, apple fritters and cannoli are served all day, but the best time to swing by is from 9pm to midnight, when folks line up at the back door to buy hot doughnuts straight from the baker.

Among the Flowers Café CAFE $$

(☑508-627-3233; www.amongtheflowersmv.com; 17 Mayhew Lane, Edgartown; mains $8-20; ⊙8am-10pm; ▣) This is a sweet spot, hidden among the flowers on a garden patio off the main drag. It's a darling setting for delicious food, even if it is served on paper plates. In-the-know folks line up at breakfast time for decadent cinnamon rolls, waffles and omelets. But you won't be disappointed at lunch, especially if you order the lobster roll.

Slice of Life

CAFE $$

(📞 508-693-3838; www.sliceoflifemv.com; 50 Circuit Ave, Oak Bluffs; mains $8-24; ⊙8am-9pm; 🖋) The look is casual; the fare is gourmet. At breakfast, there's kick-ass coffee, portobello omelets and fab potato pancakes. At dinner the roasted cod with sun-dried tomatoes is a savory favorite. And the desserts – decadent crème brûlée and luscious lemon tarts – are as good as you'll find anywhere.

🍷 Drinking & Nightlife

Offshore Ale Co

BREWPUB

(www.offshoreale.com; 30 Kennebec Ave, Oak Bluffs; ⊙11:30am-10pm) This popular microbrewery offers about a half-dozen different ales, including the award-winning Beach Road Nut Brown Ale. Seasonal favorites feature the bounty of the island, such as blueberries or sugar pumpkins.

Lampost

NIGHTCLUB

(www.lampostmv.com; 6 Circuit Ave, Oak Bluffs; ⊙4pm-1am) Head to this combo bar and nightclub for the island's hottest dance scene. Downstairs, you'll find some 100 brands of beer on offer at the Dive Bar (www.divebarmv. com; 6 Circuit Ave; ⊙noon-1:30am Jun-Sep).

☆ Entertainment

★ Flatbread Company

LIVE MUSIC

(www.flatbreadcompany.com; 17 Airport Rd; ⊙4pm-late May-Sep) Formerly the home of Carly Simon's legendary Hot Tin Roof, Flatbread continues the tradition, staging the best bands on the island. And it makes damn good organic pizzas too. It's adjacent to Martha's Vineyard Airport.

❶ Getting There & Around

BOAT

Frequent ferries operated by the Steamship Authority (p196) link Woods Hole to both Vineyard Haven and Oak Bluffs (round-trip $17, 45 minutes). If you're bringing a car, book well in advance.

From Falmouth Harbor, the passenger-only ferry **Island Queen** (📞 508-548-4800; www.island-queen.com; 75 Falmouth Heights Rd) sails to Oak Bluffs several times daily in summer (round-trip $20, 40 minutes).

From Hyannis, **Hy-Line Cruises** (📞 508-778-2600; www.hylinecruises.com; Ocean St Dock) operates a slow ferry ($45, 1½ hours, daily) and a high-speed ferry ($72, 55 minutes, several daily) to Oak Bluffs.

BUS

Martha's Vineyard Regional Transit Authority (www.vineyardtransit.com; per ride $2.50, day pass $7) operates a bus network around the island. Bus 13 travels frequently between the three main towns, while other buses go to more out-of-the-way destinations.

Central Massachusetts

Poking around this central swath of Massachusetts between big-city Boston and the fashionable Berkshires, provides a taste of the less-touristed stretch of the state. But it's no sleeper, thanks largely to a score of colleges that infuse a youthful spirit to the region.

The **Central Massachusetts Convention & Visitors Bureau** (📞 508-755-7400; www.centralmass.org; 91 Prescott St, Worcester; ⊙9am-5pm Mon-Fri) and the **Greater Springfield Convention & Visitors Bureau** (📞 413-787-1548;

OFF THE BEATEN TRACK

UP-ISLAND

Known as **Up-Island**, the rural western half of Martha's Vineyard is a patchwork of rolling hills, small farms and open fields frequented by wild turkeys and deer. Feast your eyes and your belly at the picturesque fishing village of **Menemsha**, where you'll find seafood shacks where the boats unload their catch at the back door. Watch oysters being shucked and lobsters steamed while you dine al fresco on a harborside bench.

The coastal **Aquinnah Cliffs**, also known as the **Gay Head Cliffs**, are a National Natural Landmark. These 150ft-high cliffs glow with an amazing array of colors in the late-afternoon light. You can hang out at **Aquinnah Public Beach** (parking $15), just below the multihued cliffs, or walk a mile north along the shore to an area that's popular with nude sunbathers.

Much of this area is protected in one form or another. **Cedar Tree Neck Sanctuary** (www.sheriffsmeadow.org; Indian Hill Rd, off State Rd; ⊙8:30am-5:30pm) 𝐅𝐑𝐄𝐄 has an inviting 2.5-mile hike across native bogs and forest to a coastal bluff with views of Cape Cod. **Felix Neck Wildlife Sanctuary** (www.massaudubon.org; Edgartown–Vineyard Haven Rd; adult/child $4/3; ⊙dawn-dusk; ♿) is a birder's paradise with 4 miles of trails skirting marshes and ponds.

www.valleyvisitor.com; 1441 Main St, Springfield; ⊕8:30am-5pm Mon-Fri) provide regional visitor information.

Springfield

Workaday Springfield gave birth to two American cultural icons, both of which are memorialized here.

★**Naismith Memorial Basketball Hall of Fame**   MUSEUM
(www.hoophall.com; 1000 W Columbus Ave; adult/child $22/15; ⊕10am-5pm; P⛑) Basketball devotees will be thrilled to shoot baskets, feel the center-court excitement and learn about the sport's history and great players.

Dr Seuss National Memorial Sculpture Garden   PARK
(www.catinthehat.org; 21 Edwards St; ⊕dawn-dusk; ⛑) **FREE** Life-size bronze sculptures of the Cat in the Hat and other wonky characters look beseechingly at passers-by. Oh me, oh my. Welcome to the world of Theodor Seuss Geisel, Springfield's favorite native son.

Northampton

The region's best dining, hottest nightlife and most interesting street scenes all await in this uber-hip burg known for its liberal politics and outspoken lesbian community. Easy to explore on foot, the eclectic town center is chockablock with cafes, funky shops and art galleries. **Greater Northampton Chamber of Commerce** (☑413-584-1900; www.explorenorthampton.com; 99 Pleasant St; ⊕9am-5pm Mon-Fri year-round, 10am-2pm Sat & Sun May-Oct) is information central.

⊙ Sights

Smith College   COLLEGE CAMPUS
(www.smith.edu; Elm St; P) Founded 'for the education of the intelligent gentlewoman' in 1875, Smith College is one of the largest women's colleges in the country, with 2600 students. The verdant 125-acre campus holds an eclectic architectural mix of nearly 100 buildings as well as a pretty pond.

Smith College Museum of Art   MUSEUM
(www.smith.edu/artmuseum; Elm St at Bedford Tce; adult/child $5/2; ⊕10am-4pm Tue-Sat, noon-4pm Sun; P) This impressive campus museum boasts a 25,000-piece collection which is particularly strong in 17th-century Dutch and 19th- and 20th-century European and North American paintings, including works by

DON'T MISS

WORCESTER DINERS

The state's second-largest city nurtured a great American icon: the diner. Here, in this rustbelt city, you'll find a dozen of them tucked behind warehouses, underneath old train trestles, or steps from dicey bars. **Miss Worcester Diner** (☑508-753-5600; 300 Southbridge St; mains $6-10; ⊕5am-2pm Mon-Fri, 6am-2pm Sat & Sun) is a classic of the genre. Built in 1948, it was a showroom diner of the Worcester Lunch Car Company, which produced 650 diners at its factory right across the street. Harleys parked on the sidewalk and Red Sox paraphernalia on the walls set the tone. Enticing selections such as banana-bread French toast compete with the usual greasy-spoon menu of chili dogs and biscuits with gravy. It's one tasty slice of Americana.

Degas, Winslow Homer, Picasso and James Abbott McNeill Whistler.

🛏 Sleeping

Autumn Inn   MOTEL $$
(☑413-584-7660; www.hampshirehospitality.com; 259 Elm St/MA 9; r incl breakfast $119-179; P@🛜🏊) Despite the motel layout, this two-story place near Smith campus has an agreeable ambience and large, comfy rooms.

Hotel Northampton   HISTORIC HOTEL $$
(☑413-584-3100; www.hotelnorthampton.com; 36 King St; r $185-275; P🛜) Northampton's finest sleep since 1927, the 100-room hotel in the town center features period decor and well-appointed rooms.

🍴 Eating

Haymarket Café   CAFE $
(☑413-586-9969; www.haymarketcafe.com; 185 Main St; items $5-10; ⊕7am-10pm; 🛜) Northampton's coolest (and perhaps longest-standing) hangout for bohemians and caffeine addicts, the Haymarket serves up heady espresso, fresh juices and an extensive vegetarian menu.

Paul & Elizabeth's   SEAFOOD $$
(☑413-584-4832; www.paulandelizabeths.com; 150 Main St; mains $13-17; ⊕11:30am-9:15pm; 🛜) 🌿 This airy, plant-adorned restaurant, known locally as P&E's, sits on the top floor

of Thornes Marketplace and is the town's premier natural-foods restaurant. It serves delectable vegetarian and seafood, often with an Asian bend.

Bela VEGETARIAN $$
(☑413-586-8011; www.belaveg.com; 68 Masonic St; mains $9-13; ⊙noon-8:30pm Tue-Sat; ☑🖼) 🌱 This cozy vegetarian restaurant puts such an emphasis on fresh ingredients that the chalkboard menu changes daily depending on what local farmers are harvesting. Cash only.

Drinking & Entertainment

For a smallish town, Northampton sees a great line-up of indie bands, folk artists and jazz musicians, who play at the restored **Calvin Theatre** (☑413-586-8686; www.iheg.com; 19 King St) or other smaller venues around town.

Northampton Brewery BREWPUB
(www.northamptonbrewery.com; 11 Brewster Ct; ⊙11:30am-1am; 🛜🖼) 🌱 The oldest operating brewpub in New England enjoys a loyal summertime following thanks to its generously sized outdoor deck and delicious libations.

Diva's LESBIAN
(www.divasofnoho.com; 492 Pleasant St; ⊙10pm-2am Tue-Sat) The city's main gay-centric club hosts dance nights, drag shows, Latin nights and other high-energy weekly events. Located about a mile south of the main intersection on Rte 5.

Amherst

This college town, a short drive from Northampton, is built around the mega **University of Massachusetts** (UMass; www.umass.edu) and two small colleges, the liberal **Hampshire College** (www.hampshire.edu) and the prestigious **Amherst College** (www.amherst.edu). Contact the admissions offices for campus tours and event information. Amherst is also something of a literary center, thanks to two noteworthy museums.

Emily Dickinson Museum MUSEUM
(www.emilydickinsonmuseum.org; 280 Main St; adult/child $10/5; ⊙11am-4pm Wed-Mon Mar-Dec) The lifelong home of poet Emily Dickinson (1830–86), also known as the 'belle of Amherst.' Her verses on love, nature and immortality have made her one of the most important poets in the US. Tours depart every half-hour.

Eric Carle Museum of Picture Book Art MUSEUM
(www.carlemuseum.org; 125 W Bay Rd; adult/child $9/6; ⊙10am-4pm Tue-Fri, to 5pm Sat, noon-5pm Sun; 🖼) Co-founded by the author and illustrator of *The Very Hungry Caterpillar,* this superb museum celebrates book illustrations from around the world. All visitors (grown-ups included) are encouraged to express their own artistic sentiments in the **hands-on art studio**.

The Berkshires

Tranquil towns and a wealth of cultural attractions are nestled in these cool green hills. For more than a century the Berkshires have been a favored retreat for wealthy Bostonians and New Yorkers. And we're not just talking Rockefellers – the entire Boston symphony summers here as well. The **Berkshire Visitors Bureau** (☑413-743-4500; www.berkshires.org; 66 Allen St, Pittsfield; ⊙10am-5pm) provides information on the whole region.

Great Barrington

Woolworths, diners and hardware stores have given way to art galleries, urbane boutiques and locavore restaurants on Main St, Great Barrington. The picturesque Housatonic River flows through the center of town, with the **River Walk** (www.gbriverwalk.org) offering a perfect perch from which to admire it. Access the walking path from Main St (behind Rite-Aid) or from Bridge St. At the intersection of Main and Railroad Sts, you'll find an artful mix of galleries and eateries.

Gypsy Joynt CAFE $$
(☑413-644-8811; www.gypsyjoyntcafe.net; 293 Main St; mains $10-15; ⊙11am-midnight Wed-Sat, to 9pm Sun, to 4pm Mon; 🛜🌱) This is a family affair, with three generations pitching in to serve innovative pizzas, beefy sandwiches and bountiful salads. Most everything is organic and locally sourced. The Gypsy Joynt also throws in great coffee, live music and a super boho atmosphere.

Baba Louie's PIZZA $$
(☑413-528-8100; www.babalouiespizza.com; 286 Main St; pizzas $12-18; ⊙11:30am-9:30pm; 🛜🌱) Baba's is known for its wood-fired pizza with organic sourdough crust, and guys with dreadlocks. There's a pizza for every taste, including vegan and gluten-free options.

Barrington Brewery BREWPUB
(www.barringtonbrewery.net; 420 Stockbridge Rd; mains $8-20; 11:30am-9:30pm;) Solar-powered microbrews – you know you're in Great Barrington! Outdoor seating is divine on a balmy summer night. Located 2 miles north of the town center on the road to Stockbridge.

Stockbridge

This timeless New England town, with not even a single traffic light, looks like something straight out of a Norman Rockwell painting. No coincidence! Rockwell (1894–1978), the most popular illustrator in US history, lived on Main St and used the town and its residents as subjects. See his slice-of-life artwork up close, as well has his studio, at the evocative **Norman Rockwell Museum** (413-298-4100; www.nrm.org; 9 Glendale Rd/MA 183; adult/child $18/6; 10am-5pm).

Lenox

The refined village of Lenox is the cultural heart of the Berkshires, thanks to the open-air **Tanglewood Music Festival** (888-266-1200; www.tanglewood.org; 297 West St/MA 183, Lenox; late Jun-early Sep). One of the country's premier music series, Tanglewood hosts the Boston Symphony Orchestra and guest artists like James Taylor and Yo-Yo Ma. Buy a lawn ticket, spread a blanket, uncork a bottle of wine and enjoy the quintessential Berkshires experience. Other excellent summertime cultural fare includes **Shakespeare & Company** (413-637-1199; www.shakespeare.org; 70 Kemble St; late Jun-early Sep) and the renowned **Jacob's Pillow Dance Festival** (413-243-0745; www.jacobspillow.org; 358 George Carter Rd, Becket; mid-Jun–Aug).

Sleeping

Cornell in Lenox B&B $$
(413-637-4800; www.cornellbb.com; 203 Main St; r incl breakfast from $149; @) With three historic houses on 4 acres, Cornell offers a variety of comfortable room layouts and friendly, accommodating service.

Birchwood Inn INN $$$
(413-637-2600; www.birchwood-inn.com; 7 Hubbard St; r incl breakfast $249-379;) The oldest house in Lenox (1767), the Birchwood Inn offers gorgeous period rooms, scrumptious breakfast and warm hospitality.

HANCOCK SHAKER VILLAGE

Just west of the town of Pittsfield, **Hancock Shaker Village** (www.hancockshakervillage.org; US 20; adult/youth/child $20/8/free; 10am-5pm mid-Apr–Oct;) is a fascinating museum illustrating the lives of the Shakers, the religious sect that founded the village in 1783. The Shakers believed in communal ownership, the sanctity of work and celibacy, the latter of which proved to be their demise. Their handiwork – graceful in its simplicity – includes wooden furnishings and 20 buildings, the most famous of which is the round stone barn.

Eating

Haven Cafe & Bakery CAFE $
(413-637-8948; www.havencafebakery.com; 8 Franklin St; mains $8-15; 7:30am-3pm;) It looks like a cafe, but the sophisticated food evokes a more upscale experience. Try inventive egg dishes for breakfast or fancy salads and sandwiches for lunch – all highlighting local organic ingredients.

Nudel AMERICAN $$$
(413-551-7183; www.nudelrestaurant.com; 37 Church St; mains $22-26; 5:30-9:30pm Tue-Sun) A driving force in the area's sustainable-food movement, just about everything on Nudel's menu is seasonally inspired and locally sourced. Incredible flavors. Nudel doesn't take reservations, so arrive early to avoid a long wait.

Williamstown

Cradled by the Berkshire's rolling hills, Williamstown is a picture-perfect New England college town revolving around the leafy campus of **Williams College** (www.williams.edu). It's a mini cultural capital, with two stellar art museums holding down opposite ends of the town. In summer months, the **Williamstown Theatre Festival** (413-597-3400; www.wtfestival.org;) mounts a mix of classics and contemporary works by up-and-coming playwrights, attracting plenty of well-known thespians to the stage.

NEW ENGLAND THE BERKSHIRES

WORTH A TRIP

SCENIC DRIVE

For the finest fall foliage drive in Massachusetts, head west on MA 2 from Greenfield to Williamstown on the 63-mile route known as the **Mohawk Trail** (www.mohawktrail.com). The lively Deerfield River slides alongside, with roaring, bucking stretches of white water that turn leaf-peeping into an adrenaline sport for kayakers.

◉ Sights

★ Clark Art Institute   MUSEUM

(www.clarkart.edu; 225 South St, Williamstown; adult/child $20/free; ☉ 10am-5pm Tue-Sun) Set on a gorgeous 140-acre campus, the Sterling & Francine Clark Art Institute is a gem among small art museums. The collections are particularly strong in the Impressionists, but the highlight is the rich collection of paintings by Winslow Homer, George Innes and John Singer Sargent.

Williams College Museum of Art   MUSEUM

(www.wcma.org; 15 Lawrence Hall Dr, Williamstown; ☉ 10am-5pm, closed Wed Sep-May) FREE Gracing the center of town, this is the sister museum of the Clark Art Institute. Around half of its 13,000 pieces comprise the American Collection, with substantial works by notables such as Edward Hopper (*Morning in a City*), Winslow Homer and Grant Wood, to name a few.

⌂ Sleeping

River Bend Farm B&B   B&B $$

(☏ 413-458-3121; www.riverbendfarmbb.com; 643 Simonds Rd/US 7, Williamstown; r incl breakfast $120; ☉ Apr-Oct; ✳ ☎) Step back to the 18th century in this Georgian Colonial B&B, furnished with real-deal antiques and boasting five fireplaces. Four doubles share two bathrooms. Located one mile north of town. Credit cards are not accepted.

Maple Terrace Motel   MOTEL $$

(☏ 413-458-9677; www.mapleterrace.com; 555 Main St, Williamstown; d incl breakfast $128-188; ☎ ⊠) The Maple Terrace is a simple, yet cozy 15-room place on the eastern outskirts of town. The Swedish innkeepers have snazzed up the grounds with gardens that make you want to linger.

✕ Eating & Drinking

Pappa Charlie's Deli   DELI $

(☏ 413-458-5969; 28 Spring St; mains $5-9; ☉ 7:30am-8pm) The stars themselves created the lunch sandwiches that bear their names. (Order a Politician and get anything you want on it.)

★ Mezze Bistro & Bar   FUSION $$

(☏ 413-458-0123; www.mezzerestaurant.com; 777 Cold Spring Rd/US 7, Williamstown; mains $16-28; ☉ 5-9pm) Situated on 3 acres, Mezze's farm-to-table approach begins with an edible garden right on site. Much of the rest of the seasonal menu, from small-batch microbrews to organic meats, is locally sourced as well.

Hops & Vines   BEER GARDEN

(www.hopsandvinesma.com; ☉ noon-10pm Tue-Sat, to 8pm Sun; ☎) This two-sided bar and restaurant offers an experience for every mood. The quirky, casual ambiance and excellent beer selection make 'Hops' the hands-down favorite, but some occasions call for a classy dining room like 'Vines'.

North Adams

Gritty North Adams is a former manufacturing center that was long dominated by the vast campus of the Sprague Electric Company. When Sprague closed in the 1980s, the site was converted into the USA's largest contemporary museum. North Adams is also a jumping-off point for Mt Greylock, the highest mountain in Massachusetts.

◉ Sights

MASS MoCA   MUSEUM

(www.massmoca.org; 87 Marshall St, North Adams; adult/child $18/8; ☉ 10am-6pm Jul & Aug, 11am-5pm Wed-Mon Sep-Jun; ⊞) The museum encompasses 222,000 sq ft and over 25 buildings, including art construction areas, performance centers and 19 galleries. One gallery is the size of a football field, giving installation artists the opportunity to take things into a whole new dimension. Bring your walking shoes!

Mt Greylock State Reservation   PARK

(☏ 413-499-4262; www.mass.gov/dcr; parking $5-6; ☉ visitor center 9am-5pm) FREE At 3491ft, the state's highest peak may seem modest, but the summit rewards you with a panorama stretching across three mountain ranges and five states. The reservation has 45 miles of hiking trails, including several routes to the top. Alternatively, you can drive up the auto road (open May to October). There's also a rustic, seasonal summit lodge.

🛏 Sleeping & Eating

Porches BOUTIQUE HOTEL **$$**
(☑ 413-664-0400; www.porches.com; 231 River St, North Adams; r incl breakfast $135-225; ✸ 🎧 ✉ 🐾) Across the street from MASS MoCA, the artsy rooms here offer soothing color palettes, tasteful furnishings and – appropriately – private porches.

Public Eat & Drink PUB FOOD **$$**
(☑ 413-664-4444; www.publiceatanddrink.com; 34 Holden St, North Adams; mains $10-22; ⊘4-10pm Mon-Wed, 11:30am-10pm Thu-Sun; ☑) Come to this cozy North Adams pub for an excellent selection of craft beers and gourmet pub fare, such as brie burgers, flatbread pizzas and bistro steak.

RHODE ISLAND

America's smallest state makes up for its lack of land with 400 miles of craggy coastline, deeply indented bays and enticing beaches. The state capital, Providence, is home to stellar artistic and academic institutions, cutting-edge galleries and top-notch dining, all with a dash of urban grit. Down the coast, Newport shines with opulent mansions, pretty yachts and world-class music festivals. Don't forget that this is the Ocean State, so there's no shortage of beaches, boats and other ways to appreciate the deep blue.

History

Ever since it was founded in 1636 by Roger Williams, a religious outcast from Boston, Providence has enjoyed an independent frame of mind. Williams' guiding principle, the one that got him ostracized from Massachusetts, was that all people should have freedom of conscience. He put his liberal beliefs into practice when settling Providence, purchasing the land from the local Narragansett Native Americans and remaining on friendly terms with them – a bold experiment in tolerance and peaceful coexistence.

As Providence and Newport grew and merged into a single colony, competition and conflict with area tribes sparked several wars, leading to the decimation of the Wampanoag, Pequot, Narragansett, and Nipmuck peoples.

Rhode Island was also a prolific slave trader and its merchants would control much of that trade in the years after the Revolutionary War.

The city of Pawtucket was an early player in the American industrial revolution, with the 1790 establishment of the water-powered Slater Mill. Industrialism impacted the character of Providence and surrounds, particularly along the Blackstone River, creating urban density. As with many small East-Coast cities, these urban areas went into a precipitous decline in the 1940s and '50s as manufacturing industries (textiles and costume jewelry) faltered. In the 1960s, preservation efforts salvaged the historic architectural framework of Providence and Newport. The former has emerged as a lively place with a dynamic economy and the latter, equally lively, survives as a museum city.

ⓘ Information

Providence Journal (www.providencejournal.com) The state's largest daily newspaper.
Rhode Island Parks (www.riparks.com) Offers camping in five state parks.
Rhode Island Tourism Division (☑ 800-556-2484; www.visitrhodeisland.com) Distributes visitor information on the whole state.

RHODE ISLAND FACTS

Nicknames Ocean State, Little Rhody

Population 1.05 million

Area 1034 sq miles

Capital city Providence (population 178,400)

Other city Newport (population 24,000)

Sales tax 7%

Birthplace of Broadway composer George M Cohan (1878–1942) and toy icon Mr Potato Head (b 1952)

Home of The first US tennis championships

Politics Majority vote Democrat

Famous for Being the smallest state

Official state bird A chicken? Why not? The Rhode Island Red revolutionized the poultry industry

Driving distances Providence to Newport 37 miles, Providence to Boston 50 miles

Providence

Rhode Island's capital city, Providence offers some fine urban strolling, whether in the crisp autumn afternoons or balmy summer mornings. Wander through Brown University's leafy campus on 18th-century College Hill; follow the Riverwalk into Downcity for eating, drinking and browsing. Get your questions answered at the **Providence Visitor Information Center** (☏ 401-751-1177; www.goprovidence.com; Rhode Island Convention Center, 1 Sabin St; ◷ 9am-5pm Mon-Sat).

◉ Sights

Exit 22 off I-95 deposits you Downcity, while the university area is on the East Side of the Providence River.

★ **Brown University**   ACADEMIC INSTITUTION
(www.brown.edu) Covering much of College Hill, the campus of Brown University exudes Ivy League charm. The centerpiece is **University Hall**, a 1770 brick edifice that was used as a barracks during the Revolutionary War. To explore the campus, start at the wrought-iron gates at the top of College St and make your way across the green toward Thayer St.

College Hill   NEIGHBORHOOD
East of the Providence River, College Hill contains over 100 Colonial, Federal and Revival houses dating from the 18th century. Stroll down **Benefit Street** for a sampling. Don't miss the Greek Revival **Providence Athenaeum** (www.providenceathenaeum.org; 251 Benefit St; ◷ 9am-7pm Mon-Thu, to 5pm Fri & Sat, 1-5pm Sun) **FREE**, designed by William Strickland and completed in 1838. Inside, plaster busts of Greek gods and philosophers preside over the collection.

RISD Museum of Art   MUSEUM
(www.risdmuseum.org; 224 Benefit St; adult/child $12/3; ◷ 10am-5pm Tue-Sun, to 9pm Thu; ⊞) Wonderfully eclectic, the Rhode Island School of Design's art museum showcases everything from ancient Greek art to 20th-century American paintings and decorative arts. Free admission on Sundays.

State House   HISTORIC BUILDING
(www.sos.ri.gov; 82 Smith St; ◷ 8:30am-4:30pm Mon-Fri, hourly tours 9am-2pm) **FREE** The focal point of Providence, the State House was designed by McKim, Mead and White.

DON'T MISS

BONFIRES AFTER DARK

Occasionally and throughout the summer, much of central Providence takes on a carnival atmosphere, as 100 flaming braziers illuminate the water at the convergence of the Providence, Moshassuck and Woonasquatucket rivers. Pedestrians can witness the spectacle of **WaterFire** (www.waterfire.org) from the bridges and riverside, while also enjoying live music, outdoor theater and ballroom dancing. WaterFire occurs about a dozen times a year from May to October and begins at sunset.

It is crowned with one of the world's largest self-supporting marble domes. Go inside to see a replica of the Liberty Bell, as well as Gilbert Stuart's famous portrait of George Washington (which you might also see on the $1 bill in your wallet).

Roger Williams Park   PARK
(1000 Elmwood Ave) **FREE** The parkland was donated in 1871 by a descendent of Roger Williams himself. Today this 430-acre expanse of greenery includes lakes and ponds, forest copses and broad lawns, picnic grounds and a planetarium, not to mention the excellent **zoo** (www.rwpzoo.org; adult/child $15/10; ◷ 10am-4pm Oct-Mar, to 5pm Apr-Sep; P ⊞). The park is about 4 miles south of downtown Providence; take exit 17 off I-95.

🛏 Sleeping

Old Court B&B   HISTORIC INN $$
(☏ 401-751-2002; www.oldcourt.com; 144 Benefit St; r weekday $135-185, weekend $165-215) Well positioned among the historic buildings of College Hill, this three-story, 1863 Italianate home has stacks of charm. Enjoy eccentric wallpaper, good jam at breakfast and occasional winter discounts.

Christopher Dodge House   B&B $$
(☏ 401-351-6111; www.providence-hotel.com; 11 W Park St; r incl breakfast $149-189; P) This 1858 Federal-style house is furnished with early American reproduction furniture and marble fireplaces. Austere on the outside, it has elegant proportions, large, shuttered windows and wooden floors on the inside.

Providence Biltmore
HISTORIC HOTEL $$$

(☑ 401-421-0700; www.providencebiltmore.com; 11 Dorrance St; r Mon-Fri/Sat & Sun from $169/229; P 🛜) The granddaddy of Providence's hotels, the Biltmore dates to the 1920s. The lobby, both intimate and regal, nicely combines dark wood, twisting staircases and chandeliers, while well-appointed rooms stretch many stories above the old city. Lovely views from the upper floors.

✖ Eating

Both the Rhode Island School of Design and Johnson & Wales University have top-notch culinary programs that annually turn out creative new chefs. The large student population on the East Side ensures that there are plenty of affordable places along Thayer St in College Hill. For Italian eats, head to Federal Hill, just west of Downcity.

East Side Pocket
MEDITERRANEAN $

(☑ 401-453-1100; www.eastsidepocket.com; 278 Thayer St; mains $4-7; ⊙ 10am-1am Mon-Sat, to 10pm Sun; ☑) Fabulous falafels and wraps at student-friendly prices.

Haven Brothers Diner
DINER $

(Washington St; meals $5-10; ⊙ 5pm-3am) Legend has it that the Haven Brothers started as a horse-drawn lunch wagon in 1893. Climb up a rickety ladder to get basic diner fare alongside everyone from prominent politicians to college kids pulling an all-nighter, to drunks.

Aspire
MODERN AMERICAN $$

(☑ 401-521-3333; www.aspirerestaurant.com; 311 Westminster St; mains $10-20; ⊙ 6:30am-9pm Mon-Thu, to 11pm Fri-Sat, to 3pm Sun; ☑) Aspire has a swanky, chandelier-lit interior, but the reason to come here is the delightful patio seating, known as A-Garden. It's a perfect place to sample the seasonal small-plate menu. The place seems to be understaffed; but if you have to wait for your food, this is a fine setting to do it in.

★ birch
MODERN AMERICAN $$$

(☑ 401-272-3105; www.birchrestaurant.com; 200 Washington St; 4-course dinner $49, beverage pairings $35; ⊙ 5-10pm Thu-Mon) Eighteen chairs surround a U-shaped bar at this innovative kitchen. The intimate size and style of the place means attention to detail is exacting in both the decor and the food, which focuses on small-batch and hyper-seasonal produce. Reservations are essential.

🍷 Drinking & Nightlife

Trinity Brewhouse
MICROBREWERY

(www.trinitybrewhouse.com; 186 Fountain St; ⊙ 11:30am-1am Sun-Thu, to 2am Fri-Sat) This microbrewery in the Downcity entertainment district brews terrific British-style beers.

AS220
CLUB

(www.as220.org; 115 Empire St; ⊙ food noon-10pm, bar 5pm-1am) A longstanding outlet for all forms of Rhode Island art, AS220 (say 'A-S-two-twenty') books experimental bands, hosts readings and provides gallery space for a very active artistic community.

The Salon
BAR, CLUB

(www.thesalonpvd.com; 57 Eddy St; ⊙ 5pm-1am Tue-Thu, to 2am Fri-Sat) The Salon mixes ping-pong tables and pinball machines with '80s pop and pickleback shots (whiskey with a pickle juice chaser). Downstairs, you'll find live music, DJs and dance parties.

❶ Getting There & Away

TF Green Airport (PVD; www.pvdairport.com; I-95, exit 13, Warwick), 20 minutes south of downtown Providence, is served by major US airlines and car-rental companies.

Peter Pan Bus Lines (www.peterpanbus.com) connects Providence with Boston ($8, one hour) and New York ($30, 3¾ hours). **Amtrak** (www.amtrak.com; 100 Gaspee St) trains also link cities in the Northeast with Providence.

Rhode Island Public Transit Authority (RIPTA; www.ripta.com; one way $2, day pass $6) bus 60 links Providence with Newport.

Newport

Established by religious moderates fleeing persecution from Massachusetts Puritans, this 'new port' flourished to become the fourth richest city in the newly independent colony. Downtown, the Colonial-era architecture is beautifully preserved.

In later years, bolstered by the boom in shipping, wealthy industrialists made Newport their summer vacation spot and built opulent country 'cottages' down lantern-lined Bellevue Ave. Modelled on Italianate palazzos, French chateaux and Elizabethan manor houses, and decorated with priceless furnishings and artwork, they remain the town's premier attraction, alongside a series of topnotch summer music festivals. Get the scoop at the **Newport Visitor Center** (☑ 401-845-9123; www.discovernewport.com; 23 America's Cup Ave; ⊙ 9am-5pm).

◉ Sights

Several of the city's grandest mansions are managed by the **Preservation Society of Newport County** (📞 401-847-1000; www.newportmansions.org; 424 Bellevue Ave; 5-site ticket adult/child $33/11). Each mansion takes about 90 minutes to tour. Or gawk at them from the 3.5-mile **Cliff Walk**, which hugs the coast behind the mansions. Start the walk at Ruggles Ave near the Breakers.

★ Breakers MANSION

(www.newportmansions.org; 44 Ochre Point Ave; adult/child $21/7; ⊙ 9am-5pm Apr-mid-Oct, hours vary mid-Oct–Mar; 🅿) If you have time for only one Newport mansion, make it this extravagant 70-room, 1895 Italian Renaissance megapalace built for Cornelius Vanderbilt II, patriarch of America's then-richest family.

★ The Elms MANSION

(www.newportmansions.org; 367 Bellevue Ave; adult/child $16/7, servant life tour adult/child $15/5; ⊙ 9am-5pm Apr–mid-Oct, hours vary mid-Oct–Mar; 🅿🚻) Built in 1901, the Elms is a replica of Château d'Asnières, built near Paris in 1750. Here you can take a 'behind-the-scenes' tour which will have you snaking through the servants' quarters and up onto the roof.

★ Rough Point MANSION

(www.newportrestoration.com; 680 Bellevue Ave; adult/child $25/free; ⊙ 10am-2pm Thu-Sat mid-Apr-mid-May, 10am-3:45pm Tue-Sun mid-May–mid-Nov; 🅿) Once called the 'richest little girl in the world,' Doris Duke (1912–93) was just 13 years old when she inherited this English manor estate from her father. Duke had a passion for travel and art collecting; Rough Point houses many of her holdings, from Ming dynasty ceramics to Renoir paintings.

★ Fort Adams State Park PARK

(www.fortadams.org; Harrison Ave; fort tours adult guided/self-guided $12/6, child $6/3; ⊙ sunrise-sunset) Fort Adams is America's largest coastal fortification and is the centerpiece of this gorgeous state park, which juts out into Narragansett Bay. It's the venue for the Newport Jazz and Folk Festivals.

Rosecliff MANSION

(548 Bellevue Ave; adult/child $16/7; ⊙ 9am-4pm Apr–mid-Oct, hours vary mid-Oct–Mar; 🅿) A 1902 masterpiece of architect Stanford White, Rosecliff resembles the Grand Trianon at Versailles. Its immense ballroom had a starring role in Robert Redford's *The Great Gatsby*.

International Tennis Hall of Fame MUSEUM

(www.tennisfame.com; 194 Bellevue Ave; adult/child $15/free; ⊙ 10am-5pm) The historic Newport Casino building (1880) served as a summer club for Newport's wealthiest residents. Now it houses this newly revamped museum, with plenty of interactive and high-tech exhibits about the game.

Touro Synagogue National Historic Site SYNAGOGUE

(www.tourosynagogue.org; 85 Touro St; adult/child $12/free; ⊙ noon-1.30pm Sun-Fri May-Jun, 10am-4pm Sun-Fri Jul & Aug, to 1:30pm Sun-Fri Sep-Oct, noon-1.30pm Sun Nov-Apr) Tour the oldest synagogue (c 1763) in the USA, an architectural gem that treads the line between austere and lavish.

🏃 Activities

★ America's Cup Charters YACHT TOURS

(📞 401-846-9886; www.americacupcharters.com; 49 America's Cup Ave, Newport Harbor Hotel Marina; sunset tour adult/child $75/40; ⊙ May-Sep; 🚻) Take the ultimate waterborne tour aboard a 12m America's Cup racing yacht. Ticketed two-hour sunset sails and private charters are available daily in season and offer a thrilling experience.

★ Sail Newport SAILING

(📞 401-846-1983; www.sailnewport.org; 60 Fort Adams Dr; 6hr instruction $150-179, sailboat rental per 3hr $73-138; ⊙ 9am-7pm; 🚻) As you'd expect in the hometown of the prestigious America's Cup, the sailing in breezy Newport is phenomenal.

🎊 Festivals & Events

Newport Folk Festival MUSIC

(www.newportfolk.org; Fort Adams State Park; 1-/3-day pass $49/120, parking $18; ⊙ late Jul) Big-name stars and up-and-coming groups perform at Fort Adams State Park. Bring sunscreen.

Newport Jazz Festival MUSIC

(www.newportjazzfest.org; Fort Adams State Park; tickets $40-85, 3-day $155; ⊙ early Aug) The roster reads like a who's who of jazz, with the likes of Dave Brubeck and Wynton Marsalis.

Newport Music Festival MUSIC

(www.newportmusic.org; tickets $30-45; ⊙ mid-Jul) This internationally regarded festival offers classical music concerts in many of the great mansions.

📥 Sleeping

★**Newport International Hostel**　　HOSTEL $
(William Gyles Guesthouse; ☎401-369-0243; www.
newporthostel.com; 16 Howard St; dm $35-65;
☺Apr-Dec; 🛜) Welcome to Rhode Island's only
hostel, run by an informal and knowledgeable
host. The tiny guesthouse offers spare, clean
digs in a dormitory room, as well as a simple
breakfast and laundry facilities. Private rooms
are also available.

Sea Whale Motel　　MOTEL $$
(☎888-257-4096; www.seawhale.com; 150 Aquid-
neck Ave, Middletown; d $109-229; 🅿🛜) This
owner-occupied motel is a lovely place to
stay with rooms facing Easton's Pond and
flowers hung about the place. Rooms have
little pizzazz, but they are comfortable and
neat with fridges and microwaves. The motel
is about 2 miles from town and 400 yards
from the beach.

★**The Attwater**　　BOUTIQUE HOTEL $$$
(☎401-846-7444; www.theattwater.com; 22 Liberty
St; r from $259; 🅿❈🛜) This newish hotel has
the bold attire of a midsummer beach party
with turquoise, lime green and coral prints,
ikat headboards and snazzily patterned geometric rugs. Picture windows and porches
capture the summer light and rooms come
furnished with thoughtful luxuries such as
iPads, Apple TV and beach bags.

🍴 Eating

★**Rosemary & Thyme Cafe**　　BAKERY, CAFE $
(☎401-619-3338; www.rosemaryandthymecafe.
com; 382 Spring St; baked goods $2-5, sandwiches
& pizza $6-8; ☺7:30am-3pm Tue-Sat, to 11:30am
Sun; 🍴) With a German baker in the kitchen
it's hardly surprising that the counter here is
piled high with buttery croissants, apple and
cherry tarts and plump muffins. At lunch
time there are gourmet salads and sandwiches, including an award-winning grilled
cheese.

Salvation Café　　CAFE $$
(☎401-847-2620; www.salvationcafe.com; 140
Broadway; mains $12-25; ☺5pm-midnight daily, plus
11am-3pm Sun) A funky, eclectic decor and bril-
liant food are in store at this bohemian cafe.
The multi-ethnic menu ranges far and wide,
from pad Thai to Moroccan spiced lamb, but
seldom misses the mark.

The Mooring　　SEAFOOD $$$
(☎401-846-2260; www.mooringrestaurant.com;
Sayer's Wharf; sandwiches $12-16, mains $19-38;

☺11:30am-10pm) A harborfront setting and a
menu brimming with fresh seafood make this
an unbeatable combination for seaside dining. Tip: if it's packed, take the side entrance
to the bar, grab a stool and order the meaty
clam chowder and a 'bag of doughnuts' (tangy
lobster fritters).

🍷 Drinking & Entertainment

Coffee Grinders　　COFFEEHOUSE
(www.coffeegrindernewport.com; 33 Bannister's
Wharf; ☺8am-5pm, longer hours in summer) Enjoy
espresso and a pastry on some benches at this
small shingled shack at the end of Bannister's
Wharf. You'll be surrounded by water, with
great views over yacht activity and crustaceans being unloaded at the Aquidneck Lobster Company.

Newport Blues Café　　CLUB
(www.newportblues.com; 286 Thames St; ☺7pm-
1am Tue-Sat, shows 10pm) This popular rhythm-
and-blues bar and restaurant draws top acts
to an old brownstone. It's an intimate space
with many enjoying quahogs, house-smoked
ribs or pork loins at tables adjoining the
small stage.

ℹ️ Getting There & Away

Peter Pan (www.peterpanbus.com) has several
daily buses to Boston ($22, two hours), while **RIP-
TA** (www.ripta.com) operates frequent buses (one
way $2, day pass $6) from the visitor center to the
mansions and beaches, and as far as Providence.

Rhode Island Beaches

If you're wondering why it's called the Ocean
State, drive down Rte 1A to check out the
South County Beaches (☎800-548-4662;
www.southcountyri.com). Surfers, head to the
mile-long **Narragansett Town Beach** in Narragansett. The nearby **Scarborough State
Beach** is among Rhode Island's finest, with
a wide sandy shore, a classic pavilion and inviting boardwalks. At the state's southwestern
tip, **Watch Hill** is a wonderful place to turn
back the clock, with its Flying Horse Carousel
and Victorian mansions.

CONNECTICUT

Sandwiched between sexy New York City
and quainter quarters in northern New England, Connecticut often gets short shrift from
travelers. But the Constitution State has long

BLOCK ISLAND

Separated from the rest of Rhode Island by 12 miles of open ocean, this unspoiled island offers simple pleasures: rolling farms, uncrowded beaches and miles of quiet hiking and cycling trails.

Ferries dock at **Old Harbor**, the main town, which has changed little since its ginger-bread houses were built in the late 19th century. A lovely beach stretches several miles to the north. About 2 miles away, the **Clay Head Nature Trail** (off Corn Neck Rd) follows high clay bluffs above the beach, offering good bird-watching along the way.

A mere 7 miles long, Block Island is perfect for exploration by bicycle; rent them near the ferry dock. The **Block Island Chamber of Commerce** (☑ 800-383-2474; www. blockislandchamber.com), at the ferry dock, can help with accommodations, but be aware the island's inns typically book out in summer and many require minimum stays.

The **Block Island Ferry** (☑ 401-783-4613; www.blockislandferry.com) offers several options for getting to the island. From Point Judith in Narragansett, there is a high-speed ferry (round-trip adult/child $36/20, 30 minutes) and a traditional ferry (adult/child $28/14, one hour). The latter is the only car ferry, for which reservations are essential. There is an additional fast ferry from Newport (adult/child $50/26, one hour).

been luring artists, celebrities and moneyed Manhattanites, who appreciate the rural landscape sprinkled with small vineyards and genteel Colonial towns.

History

The name 'Connecticut' comes from the Mohegan name for the great river that bisects the state. A number of Native American tribes (including the Mohegan, as well as the Pequot and others) were here when the first European explorers, primarily Dutch, appeared in the early 17th century. The first English settlement was at Old Saybrook in 1635, followed a year later by the Connecticut Colony, built by Massachusetts Puritans under Thomas Hooker. A third colony was founded in 1638 in New Haven. After the Pequot War (1637), the Native Americans were no longer a check to colonial expansion in New England, and Connecticut's English population grew. In 1686 Connecticut was brought into the Dominion of New England.

The American Revolution swept through Connecticut, leaving scars with major battles at Stonington (1775), Danbury (1777), New Haven (1779) and Groton (1781). Connecticut became the fifth state in 1788. It embarked on a period of prosperity, propelled by its whaling, shipbuilding, farming and manufacturing industries (from firearms to bicycles to household tools), which lasted well into the 19th century.

The 20th century brought world wars and the depression but, thanks in no small part to Connecticut's munitions industries, the state was able to fight back. Everything from planes to submarines was made in the state, and when the defense industry began to decline in the 1990s, the growth of other businesses (such as insurance) helped pick up the slack.

ℹ Information

There are welcome centers at the Hartford airport and on I-95 and I-84 when entering the state by car.

Connecticut Tourism Division (www.ctvisit.com) Distributes visitor information for the entire state.

Hartford Courant (www.courant.com) The state's largest newspaper.

Hartford

Connecticut's capital city, Hartford has been lovingly dubbed the 'filing cabinet of America.' But this underappreciated city – one of the oldest in New England – harbors a rich cultural heritage. Besides being the former 'insurance capital' of America, it is also a former publishing center, which means that Hartford was home to some of the country's most celebrated writers. The **Greater Hartford Welcome Center** (☑ 860-244-0253; www. letsgoarts.org/welcomecenter; 100 Pearl St; ⊙ 9am-5pm Mon-Fri) distributes tourist information.

Options for sleeping in Hartford are limited to national chain hotels.

⊙ Sights

★ Mark Twain House & Museum MUSEUM
(www.marktwainhouse.org; 351 Farmington Ave; adult/child $19/11; ⊙9:30am-5:30pm, closed Tue in Mar) It was at this former home of Samuel Langhorne Clemens, aka Mark Twain, that the legendary author penned many of his greatest works, including *The Adventures of Huckleberry Finn* and *Tom Sawyer*. The house itself, a Victorian Gothic with fanciful turrets and gables, reflects Twain's quirky character.

★ Wadsworth Atheneum MUSEUM
(www.thewadsworth.org; 600 Main St; adult/child $10/5; ⊙11am-5pm Wed-Fri, 10am-5pm Sat & Sun) The nation's oldest public-art museum, the Wadsworth Atheneum houses nearly 50,000 pieces. On display are paintings by members of the Hudson River School, European Old Masters, 19th-century Impressionist works, sculptures by Connecticut artist Alexander Calder; and a small yet outstanding array of surrealist works.

Harriet Beecher Stowe House MUSEUM
(www.harrietbeecherstowe.org; 77 Forest St; adult/child $10/7; ⊙9:30am-5pm Tue-Sat, noon-5pm Sun) Next door to the Twain house is the house of the woman who wrote the anti-slavery book *Uncle Tom's Cabin*. It rallied so many Americans against slavery that Abraham Lincoln once credited Stowe with starting the US Civil War.

Old State House HISTORIC BUILDING
(www.ctoldstatehouse.org; 800 Main St; adult/child $6/3; ⊙10am-5pm Tue-Sat Jul–mid-Oct, Mon-Fri mid-Oct–Jul; ⊞) Connecticut's original capitol building, designed by Charles Bulfinch, was the site of the trial of the *Amistad* prisoners. Gilbert Stuart's famous 1801 portrait of George Washington hangs in the senate chamber. Dedicated museum space houses interactive exhibits aimed at kids, as well as a **Museum of Curiosities** that features a two-headed calf, a narwhal's horn and a variety of mechanical devices.

✕ Eating & Drinking

Salute ITALIAN $$
(☎860-899-1350; www.salutect.com; 100 Trumbull St; lunch mains $9-13, dinner $12-20; ⊙11:30am-11pm Mon-Thu, to midnight Fri-Sat, 3-10pm Sun; ✐) Charming service is the hallmark of this urban gem, which offers a contemporary take on Italian flavors. Regulars rave about the cheesy garlic bread, but other offerings are a tad more sophisticated. The pleasant patio overlooks Bushnell Park.

Bin 228 WINE BAR $$
(☎860-244-9463; www.bin228winebar.com; 228 Pearl St; paninis & small plates $8-15; ⊙11:30am-10pm Mon-Thu, to midnight Fri, 4pm-midnight Sat) This wine bar serves Italian fare – paninis, cheese platters, salads – alongside its expansive all-Italian wine list. On weekends, the kitchen stays open until midnight (later for drinks).

City Steam Brewery Café BREWPUB
(citysteam.biz; 942 Main St; ⊙11:30am-1am Mon-Sat, 4-10pm Sun) This big and boisterous place has housemade beers on tap. The Naughty Nurse Pale Ale is a bestseller, but the seasonals are also worth a try. The brewery's basement is home to the **Brew Ha Ha Comedy Club** (tickets $10-15; ⊙Fri & Sat), where you can yuk it up with visiting comedians from New York and Boston.

❶ Getting There & Away

Central **Union Station** (www.amtrak.com; 1 Union Pl) links Hartford to cities throughout the Northeast, including New Haven (from $14, one hour) and New York City ($42 to $60, three hours).

Litchfield Hills

The rolling hills in the northwestern corner of Connecticut are sprinkled with lakes and carpeted with forests. Historic Litchfield is the hub of the region, but lesser-known villages such as Bethlehem, Kent, Lakeville and Norfolk are just as photogenic. The **Western Connecticut Convention & Visitors Bureau** (☑ 800-663-1273; www.litchfieldhills.com) has information on the region.

Litchfield

Founded in 1719, Litchfield prospered from the commerce brought by stagecoaches en route between Hartford and Albany, and its many handsome period buildings are a testimony to that era. A row of shops, restaurants and historic buildings overlooks the picturesque green. Stroll along North and South Sts to see the finest homes, including the 1773 **Tapping Reeve House & Law School** (www.litchfieldhistoricalsociety.org, 82 South St, adult/child $5/free; ⊙ 11am-5pm Tue-Sat, 1-5pm Sun mid-Apr–Nov), the country's first law school.

Connecticut's largest wildlife preserve, the **White Memorial Conservation Center** (www.whitememorialcc.org; US 202; park free, museum adult/child $6/3; ⊙ park dawn-dusk, museum 9am-5pm Mon-Sat & noon-5pm Sun), 2 miles west of town, has 35 miles of walking trails and good bird-watching.

Lake Waramaug

The most beautiful of the dozens of lakes and ponds in the Litchfield Hills is Lake Waramaug. As you make your way around North Shore Rd, stop at **Hopkins Vineyard** (☑ 860-868-7954; www.hopkinsvineyard.com; 25 Hopkins Rd; ⊙ 10am-5pm Mon-Sat & 11am-5pm Sun Mar-Dec, 10am-5pm Fri-Sun only Jan-Mar) for wine tastings. The view from the bar is worth the trip, particularly when the foliage changes in the fall. Across the street, the 19th-century **Hopkins Inn** (☑ 860-868-7295; www.thehopkinsinn.com; 22 Hopkins Rd, Warren; r without/with bathroom from $125/135, apt $150; P ❄ 🐾) has lake-view accommodation and a recommended restaurant.

Connecticut Coast

Connecticut has a surprisingly delightful and diverse strip of coastline. At the eastern end of the state, Mystic houses a magnificent recreated 19th-century whaling town, spread across 17 acres. Well-preserved historic towns grace the banks of the mighty Connecticut River. The western end of the state's coastline is largely a bedroom community connected by commuter rail to New York City; but the artsier (and more academic) elements are on display in New Haven.

Mystic

From simple beginnings in the 17th century, the village of Mystic grew to become a prosperous whaling center and one of the great shipbuilding ports of the East Coast. In the mid-19th century, Mystic's shipyards launched clipper ships, gunboats and naval transport vessels, many from the George Greenman & Co Shipyard, now the site of the state's largest tourist attraction. The charming town center – complete with sailboats bobbing and drawbridge clanging – makes Mystic a popular summertime destination. The **Greater Mystic Chamber of Commerce** (☑ 860 572 9578; www.mysticchamber.org; 12 Roosevelt Ave; ⊙ 9am-4:30pm), next to the train station, has visitor information.

◉ Sights & Activities

There's no shortage of outfits in Mystic ready to whisk you away on a watery adventure. Sail away on the schooner **Argia** (☑ 860-536-0416; www.argiamystic.com; 15 Holmes St; adult/child $44/35) or take a historic harbor tour on the **Mystic Express** (1 Holmes St; adult/child $20/10; ⊙ 11am Sat-Sun May-Jun, daily Jun-Oct). There are also cruises and boat rentals at the Seaport Museum.

★ **Mystic Seaport Museum**   MUSEUM
(www.mysticseaport.org; 75 Greenmanville Ave/CT 27; adult/child $25/16; ⊙ 9am-5pm mid-Feb–Oct, to 4pm Nov-Dec; P 🐾) America's maritime history springs to life as costumed interpreters ply their trades at this sprawling re-created 19th-century seaport village. You can explore several historic sailing vessels, including the *Charles W Morgan* (built in 1841), the last surviving wooden whaling ship in the world.

Mystic Aquarium &
Institute for Exploration   AQUARIUM

(www.mysticaquarium.org; 55 Coogan Blvd; adult/child $35/25; ⊙9am-4pm Mar-Nov, to 5pm Apr-Aug, from 10am Dec-Feb; ⊕) This state-of-the-art aquarium boasts more than 6000 species of sea creatures, as well as an outdoor viewing area for watching seals and sea lions below the waterline and a penguin pavilion. The aquarium's most famous (and controversial) residents are the three beluga whales, who reside in the Arctic Coast exhibit.

🛏 Sleeping

⭐**Steamboat Inn**   INN $$$

(☑860-536-8300; www.steamboatinnmystic.com; 73 Steamboat Wharf; d incl breakfast $160-280; ℗❄🛜) Located right in the heart of downtown Mystic, the 11 rooms of this historic inn have wraparound water views and luxurious amenities, including two-person whirlpool tubs. Antiques lend the interior a romantic atmosphere. Bonus: complimentary bikes.

✕ Eating & Drinking

⭐**Captain Daniel Packer Inne**   AMERICAN $$

(☑860-536-3555; www.danielpacker.com; 32 Water St; mains $14-24; ⊙11am-10pm) This 1754 historic house has a low-beam ceiling, creaky floorboards and a casual (and loud) pub downstairs. Upstairs, the dining room has river views and an imaginative American menu.

Engine Room   BURGERS $$

(860-415-8117; 14 Holmes St; mains $12-20; ⊙noon-10pm Thu-Mon, 4-10pm Tue-Wed; 🖉⊕) Promising beer, bourbon and burgers, this place delivers, with dozens of enticing beers on tap and perfectly cooked, damn tasty burgers coming off the grill. (We didn't try the bourbon.) Evocatively set in the old Lathrup Marine Engine building, it's an excellent place to eat and drink, even for vegetarians.

Oyster Club   SEAFOOD $$$

(☑860-415-9266; www.oysterclubct.com; 13 Water St; oysters $2, lunch mains $12-18, dinner $18-34; ⊙4-9pm Mon-Thu, noon-10pm Fri-Sun) A little off the main drag, this is the place locals come for oysters served grilled or raw. The deck out back, also known as the Treehouse, is the best perch in town.

Lower Connecticut River Valley

Several lovely Colonial-era towns grace the banks of the Connecticut River, offering up their rural charm at an unhurried pace.

WORTH A TRIP

GILLETTE CASTLE

Looming on the hilltop above East Haddam is **Gillette Castle** (☑860-526-2336; www.ct.gov/dep/gillettecastle; 67 River Rd; adult/child $6/2; ⊙castle 10am-4:30pm late May–mid-Oct, grounds 8am-dusk year-round; ℗), a turreted mansion built in 1919. The eccentric actor William Gillette made his fortune in the role of Sherlock Holmes. His fascinating home is modeled on the medieval castles of Germany. The surrounding 125 acres are a designated state park with loads of walking trails and picnic areas.

In summer, you can cross the Connecticut River on the **Chester-Hadlyme Ferry** (car/pedestrian $5/2; ⊙7am-6:45pm Mon-Fri, 10:30am-5pm Sat & Sun Apr-Nov). It's a short, five-minute river crossing on the *Selden III*, the second-oldest ferry in America (since 1769). The ferry affords great views of the river and the castle, and deposits passengers at the foot of the castle in East Haddam.

The **River Valley Tourism District** (☑860-787-9640; www.visitctriver.com) provides information on the region.

OLD LYME

Set near the mouth of the Connecticut River, Old Lyme is the picturesque setting for the Lyme Art Colony, which cultivated the American Impressionist movement in the early 20th century. It all started when art patron Florence Griswold opened her estate to visiting artists, many of whom offered paintings in lieu of rent. Her Georgian mansion, now the **Florence Griswold Museum** (www.flogris.org; 96 Lyme St; adult/child $10/free; ⊙10am-5pm Tue-Sat, 1-5pm Sun; ℗) contains a fine selection of both Impressionist and Barbizon paintings.

ESSEX

The main town along the lower Connecticut River is tree-lined Essex, established in 1635. The well-preserved Federal-period houses along Main St are legacies of rum and tobacco fortunes made in the 19th century. The landmark **Griswold Inn** (☑860-767-1776; www.griswoldinn.com; 36 Main St; r incl breakfast $115-205, ste $190-324; ℗🛜) has been Essex's physical and social centerpiece since 1776.

Connecticut River Museum
MUSEUM

(www.ctrivermuseum.org; 67 Main St; adult/child $9/6; ⊙10am-5pm Tue-Sun; P ⚓) Next to the steamboat dock, the Connecticut River Museum meticulously recounts the history of the region. Exhibits include a reproduction of the world's first submarine, *Turtle,* a hand-propelled vessel built by a Yale student in 1776.

The museum runs summer **schooner cruises** (adult/child $30/18; ⊙1:30pm & 3:30pm daily, Jun-Oct) and weekend **eagle-watch tours** (per person $40, h 11am & 1pm Fri-Sun, Jan-Mar).

Essex Steam Train & Riverboat Ride
STEAM TRAIN

(☏ 860-767-0103; www.essexsteamtrain.com; 1 Railroad Ave; adult/child $19/10, with cruise $29/19; ⚓) The old-fashioned way to see the river valley is to hop aboard this antique steam locomotive that runs six scenic miles to the town of Deep River. There you can connect with a cruise on a Mississippi-style riverboat, before returning by train. There's also an excursion to Gillette Castle.

New Haven

Head straight to New Haven Green, graced by old Colonial churches and the ivy-covered walls of Yale University. The oldest planned city in America (1638), New Haven is laid out in orderly blocks spreading out from the Green, making it a cinch to get around. Opposite the green, **INFO New Haven** (☏ 203-773-9494; www.infonewhaven.com; 1000 Chapel St; ⊙10am-9pm Mon-Sat, noon-5pm Sun) is the city's helpful tourist office.

⊙ Sights

★ **Yale University**
UNIVERSITY

(www.yale.edu) Each year, thousands of high-school students make pilgrimages to Yale, nursing dreams of attending the country's third-oldest university, which boasts such notable alums as Noah Webster, Eli Whitney, Samuel Morse, and Presidents William H Taft, George HW Bush, Bill Clinton and George W Bush. You don't need to share the students' ambitions in order to take a stroll around the campus, just pick up a map at the **Visitors Center** (☏ 203-432-2300; www.yale.edu/visitor; 149 Elm St; walking tours free; ⊙9am-4:30pm Mon-Fri, 11am-4pm Sat & Sun, walking tours 10:30am & 2pm Mon-Fri, 1:30pm Sat) or join a free, one-hour guided tour.

★ **Yale University Art Gallery**
MUSEUM

(artgallery.yale.edu; 1111 Chapel St; ⊙10am-5pm Tue-Fri, to 8pm Thu, 11am-5pm Sat & Sun) **FREE** America's oldest university art museum boasts American masterworks by Edward Hopper and Jackson Pollock, as well as a superb European collection that includes Vincent van Gogh's *The Night Café.*

Peabody Museum of Natural History
MUSEUM

(www.peabody.yale.edu; 170 Whitney Ave; adult/child $9/5; ⊙10am-5pm Mon-Sat, noon-5pm Sun; P ⚓) Wannabe paleontologists will be thrilled by the dinosaurs here. There are also excellent anthropology exhibits, including a replica of an Egyptian tomb.

Yale Center for British Art
MUSEUM

(www.ycba.yale.edu; 1080 Chapel St; ⊙10am-5pm Tue-Sat, noon-5pm Sun) **FREE** The most comprehensive British art collection outside the UK. Closed for conservation at the time of research, the museum is expected to reopen in 2016.

🛏 Sleeping

Hotel Duncan
HISTORIC HOTEL $

(☏ 203-787-1273; www.hotelduncan.net; 1151 Chapel St; s/d $65/85; ❄ ☎) Though the shine has rubbed off this New Haven gem it's the enduring features that still make it worth a stay, like the handsome lobby and the hand-operated elevator.

Study at Yale
HOTEL $$$

(☏ 203-503-3900; www.studyatyale.com; 1157 Chapel St; r $199-259; P ☎) The Study at Yale manages to evoke a mid-century modern sense of sophistication without being over-the-top or intimidating. Ultra-contemporary touches include in-room iPod docking stations and cardio machines with built-in televisions.

✖ Eating

★ **Frank Pepe**
PIZZA $

(☏ 203-865-5762; www.pepespizzeria.com; 157 Wooster St; pizza $10-20; ⊙11:30am-10pm; ☑ ⚓) Pepe's serves delectable, crispy, thin-crust pizza, fired in a coal oven, just as it has since 1925. Go for 'Frank Pepe's original tomato pie' or try a New Haven specialty white-clam pizza. No credit cards.

Booktrader Cafe CAFE $

(☑ 203-787-8147; www.booktraderatyale.com; 1140 Chapel St; sandwiches $7-10; ⊙7:30am-9pm Mon-Fri, 9am-9pm Sat, to 7pm Sun; 🛜🍴) This light-filled, book-filled atrium is a delightful place to devour scrumptious sandwiches and spell-binding literature. In nice weather, there's a shady patio.

Caseus Fromagerie Bistro CHEESE SHOP $$

(☑ 203-624-3373; www.caseusnewhaven.com; 93 Whitney Ave; mains $12-25; ⊙11:30am-2:30pm Mon-Sat & 5:30-9pm Wed-Sat; 🍴) With a bou-tique cheese counter piled with locally sourced labels and a concept menu devoted to *le grand fromage*, Caseus has hit upon a winning combination. After all, what's not to like about a perfectly executed mac 'n' cheese or the dangerously delicious poutine (pommes frites, cheese curds and velouté).

☆ Entertainment

New Haven has a first-rate theater scene. The free weekly *New Haven Advocate* (www.ctnow.com) has current entertainment listings.

Toad's Place MUSIC

(☑ 203-624-8623; www.toadsplace.com; 300 York St) Toad's is one of New England's premier music halls, having earned its rep hosting the likes of the Rolling Stones, U2 and Bob Dylan.

Shubert Theater THEATER

(☑ 203-562-5666; www.shubert.com; 247 College St) Dubbed 'Birthplace of the Nation's Great-est Hits,' since 1914 the Shubert has been host-ing ballet and Broadway musicals on their trial runs before heading off to New York City.

Yale Repertory Theatre THEATER

(☑ 203-432-1234; www.yalerep.org; 1120 Chapel St) Performing classics and new works in a con-verted church.

ℹ Getting There & Away

By train from New York City skip Amtrak and take **Metro North** (www.mta.info; one way $10-16), which has near-hourly services and the lowest fares. Heading north, you can take Amtrak to Hartford ($14, one hour) or Boston (from $54, 2½ hours). **Greyhound Bus Lines** (www.greyhound.com) also connects New Haven to scores of cities including Hartford ($15, one hour) and Boston ($23 to $27, four hours).

VERMONT

Vermont, we like your crunchy soul. Green, upbeat and a little bit quirky, it's a pretty place that embraces its natural beauty with a respectful *joie de vivre*. And the eating is darn good too, from the artisanal cheeses to Ben & Jerry's ice cream to the buckets of maple syrup. Fortunately, there are plenty of ways to work it off: hike the trails of the Green Mountains, paddle a kayak on Lake Champlain or hit the snowy slopes.

Vermont gives true meaning to the word rural. Its capital would barely rate as a small town in other states and even its largest city, Burlington, has just 42,200 contented souls. The countryside is a blanket of rolling green, with 80% of the state forested and most of the rest given over to some of the prettiest farms you'll ever see. The Green Mountain State is also home to more than 100 covered bridges. So take your time, meander down quiet side roads, stop in those picturesque villages, and sample a taste of the good life.

History

Frenchman Samuel de Champlain explored Vermont in 1609, becoming the first European to visit these lands long inhabited by the na-tive Abenaki.

Vermont played a key role in the Amer-ican Revolution in 1775 when Ethan Allen led a local militia, the Green Mountain Boys, to Fort Ticonderoga, capturing it from the British. In 1777 Vermont declared independ-ence as the Vermont Republic, adopting the first New World constitution to abolish slav-ery and establish a public school system. In 1791, Vermont was admitted to the USA as the 14th state.

The state's independent streak is as long and deep as a vein of Vermont marble. Long a land of dairy farmers, Vermont is still largely agricultural and has the lowest population of any New England state.

ℹ Information

Vermont Dept of Tourism (www.vermont vacation.com) Online information by region, season and other user-friendly categories.

Vermont Public Radio (VPR; www.vpr.net) Ver-mont's excellent statewide public radio station. The radio frequency varies across the state, but the following selection covers most areas: Burl-ington (northwestern Vermont – 107.9); Brattle-boro (southeastern Vermont – 88.9); Manchester

VERMONT FACTS

Nickname Green Mountain State

Population 626,500

Area 9217 sq miles

Capital city Montpelier (population 7755)

Other city Burlington (population 42,200)

Sales tax 6%

Birthplace of Mormon leader Brigham Young (1801–77), President Calvin Coolidge (1872–1933)

Home of More than 100 covered bridges

Politics Independent streak, leaning Democrat

Famous for Ben & Jerry's ice cream

Sudsiest state Most microbreweries per capita in the USA

Driving distances Burlington to Brattleboro 151 miles, Burlington to Boston 216 miles

(southwestern Vermont – 106.9), and St Johnsbury (northeastern Vermont – 88.5).

Vermont State Parks (☏888-409-7579; www.vtstateparks.com) Complete camping and parks information.

Southern Vermont

The southern swath of Vermont holds the state's oldest towns and plenty of scenic back roads.

Brattleboro

Ever wonder where the 1960s counter-culture went? It's alive and well in this riverside burg overflowing with artsy types and more tie-dye per capita than any other place in New England.

⊙ Sights

Paralleling the Connecticut River, Main St is lined with period buildings, including the handsome art-deco **Latchis Building**. The surrounding area boasts several **covered bridges**; pick up a map at the Bennington Chamber of Commerce.

Brattleboro Museum & Art Center   MUSEUM
(www.brattleboromuseum.org; 10 Vernon St; adult/student/child under 18yr $8/4/free; ⊙11am-5pm Wed-Mon) Located in a 1915 railway station, this museum hosts rotating exhibitions of contemporary art, including multimedia works by local artists.

⌷ Sleeping

If all you're after is a cheap sleep, there are plenty of motels on Putney Rd north of town; take Exit 3 off I-91.

Latchis Hotel   HOTEL $$
(☏802-254-6300, 800-798-6301; www.latchis.com; 50 Main St; r incl breakfast $115-170, ste $185; ☏) The decor is retro and your view from an interior room may be a red-brick wall, but this art-deco hotel has charm. And you can't beat the prime downtown location and the attached historic theater.

Forty Putney Road B&B   B&B $$$
(☏800-941-2413, 802-254-6268; www.fortyputneyroad.com; 192 Putney Rd; r incl breakfast $159-329; @☏) In a sweet riverside location just north of town, this 1930 B&B has a cheery pub, pool table, hot tub, a glorious backyard, four rooms and a separate self contained cottage. Easy access to river trails from the property.

✗ Eating

Brattleboro Food Co-op   DELI $
(☏802-257-0236; www.brattleborofoodcoop.com; 2 Main St; sandwiches $7-9; ⊙7am-9pm Mon-Sat, 9am-9pm Sun) ✐ At this thriving downtown community market, load up your basket with wholefood groceries, organic produce, and local cheeses, or visit the juice bar and deli for healthy takeaway treats.

Whetstone Station   PUB FOOD $$
(☏802-490-2354; www.whetstonestation.com; 36 Bridge St; mains $10-22; ⊙11:30am-10pm Sun-Thu, to 11pm Fri & Sat) At sunset, dine on the deck overlooking the Connecticut River for one of the finest views in town. This busy brewery and eatery has 20 or so craft beers on tap – with house and guest brewery selections – plus a wide range of craft bottles and cans. For a light but filling meal, try the grilled sirloin tips with a dipping sauce. Fantastic! Welcoming service, too.

TJ Buckley's   AMERICAN $$$
(☏802-257-4922; www.tjbuckleys.com; 132 Elliot St; mains $40; ⊙5:30-9pm Thu-Sun) ✐ Chef-owner Michael Fuller founded this

exceptional, upscale 18-seat eatery in an authentic 1927 diner over 30 years ago. The oral menu of four nightly changing items is sourced largely from local organic farms. Reserve ahead.

❶ Information

Brattleboro Chamber of Commerce (✆877-254-4565, 802-254-4565; www.brattle borochamber.org; 180 Main St; ⊙9am-5pm Mon-Fri) Stop by for a free historical society walking-tour map.

Bennington

Southern Vermont is rural, and cozy Bennington, with about 15,000 inhabitants, ranks as the region's largest town. An interesting mix of cafes and shops downtown line Main St, while the adjacent Old Bennington historic district boasts Colonial homes, the early 19th-century **Old First Church**, where poet Robert Frost is buried, and a trio of covered bridges. A hilltop granite obelisk commemorating the 1777 Battle of Bennington towers above it all.

◉ Sights

Bennington Battle Monument   HISTORIC SITE
(www.benningtonbattlemonument.com; 15 Monument Circle; adult/child 6-14yr $5/1; ⊙9am-5pm mid-Apr–Oct) This striking structure, which rises more than 300ft, offers an unbeatable 360-degree view of the surrounding countryside. An elevator whisks you painlessly to the top.

Bennington Museum   MUSEUM
(✆802-447-1571; www.benningtonmuseum. org; 75 Main St; adult/child under 18yr $10/free; ⊙10am-5pm daily, closed Jan, closed Wed Nov-Jun) Between downtown and Old Bennington, this museum's houses an outstanding early Americana collection which includes Bennington pottery and the Bennington Flag, one of the oldest surviving American Revolutionary flags, and works by American folk artist 'Grandma Moses.'

🛏 Sleeping & Eating

Greenwood Lodge
& Campsites   HOSTEL, CAMPGROUND $
(✆802-442-2547; www.campvermont.com/greenwood; VT 9, Prospect Mountain; 2-person tent/RV site $29/35, dm $30-36, private room 1/2 people $72/75; ⊙mid-May–late Oct; 🛜) Nestled in the Green Mountains 8 miles east of town, this 120-acre space with three ponds holds one of Vermont's best-sited hostels and campgrounds.

Henry House   B&B $$
(✆802-442-7045; www.thehenryhouseinn.com; 1338 Murphy Rd, North Bennington; r incl breakfast $100-155; 🛜) Sit on the rocking chair and watch the traffic trickle across a covered bridge at this Colonial home on 25 peaceful acres, built in 1769 by American Revolution hero William Henry.

Blue Benn Diner   DINER $
(✆802-442-5140; 314 North St; mains $7-16; ⊙6am-4:45pm Mon-Fri, 7am-3:45pm Sat & Sun; 🍴) This classic 1950s-era diner serves breakfast all day and a healthy mix of American and international fare. Enhancing the retro experience are little tabletop jukeboxes where you can play Willie Nelson's 'Moonlight in Vermont' till your neighbors scream for mercy. Cash only.

Pangaea   INTERNATIONAL $$$
(✆802-442-7171; www.vermontfinedining.com; 1 Prospect St, North Bennington; lounge mains from $10-23, restaurant mains $30; ⊙lounge from 5pm daily, restaurant 5-9pm Tue-Sat) Offering fine

---

WORTH A TRIP

SCENIC DRIVE: COVERED BRIDGES OF BENNINGTON

North of Bennington, a 30-minute detour takes you across three picture-perfect covered bridges spanning the Wallomsac River. To get started, turn west onto VT 67A just north of Bennington's tourist office and continue 3.5 miles, bearing left on Murphy Rd at the 117ft-long **Burt Henry Covered Bridge** (1840). Exhale, slow down: you're back in horse-and-buggy days. After curving to the left, Murphy Rd next loops through the **Paper Mill Bridge**, which takes its name from the 1790 mill whose gear works are still visible along the river below. Next turn right onto VT 67A, go half a mile and turn right onto Silk Rd where you'll soon cross the **Silk Road Bridge** (c 1840). Continue southeast for two more miles, bearing left at two T-intersections, to reach the **Bennington Battle Monument**.

Vermont & New Hampshire

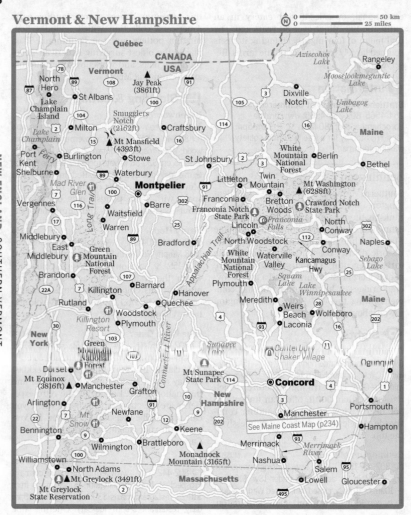

dining for every budget, this top-end North Bennington restaurant sits side-by-side with a more casual, intimate lounge. Opt for gourmet burgers served on the riverside terrace out back, or head to the tastefully decorated dining room next door for international specialties like *filet mignon* on risotto and topped with pancetta and taleggio.

ℹ Information

Bennington Area Chamber of Commerce
(☎ 802-447-331; www.bennington.com; 100 Veterans Memorial Dr; ⊙10am-5pm Mon-Fri) One mile north of downtown. The chamber also

runs the Bennington Welcome Center (100 Route 279, 7am to 9pm), near the Rte 279 and US 7 interchange, which is open daily.

Manchester

Sitting in the shadow of Mt Equinox, Manchester's been a fashionable summer retreat since the 19th century. The mountain scenery, the agreeable climate and the Batten Kill River – Vermont's best trout stream – continue to draw vacationers today.

Manchester Center, at the town's north end, sports cafes and upscale outlet stores. Further south lies dignified Manchester Village, lined with marble sidewalks, stately homes and the posh Equinox hotel.

◉ Sights & Activities

The **Appalachian Trail**, which overlaps the **Long Trail** in southern Vermont, passes just east of Manchester. For trail maps and details on shorter day hikes, stop by the **Green Mountain National Forest office** (☑ 802-362-2307; www.fs.usda.gov/greenmountain; 2538 Depot St, Manchester Center; ◷ 8am-4:30pm Mon-Fri).

★ **Hildene**   HISTORIC SITE
(☑ 802-362-1788, 800-578-1788; www.hildene.org; 1005 Hildene Rd/VT 7A; adult/child $16/5, guided tours $5/2; ◷ 9:30am-4:30pm) This stately 24-room Georgian Revival mansion was home to members of Abraham Lincoln's family from the 1800s until 1975, when it was converted into a museum. The collection of family heirlooms includes the hat Lincoln probably wore while delivering the Gettysburg Address – one of the three surviving Lincoln top hats. The gorgeous grounds offer 12 miles of walking and cross-country ski trails.

American Museum of Fly Fishing & Orvis   MUSEUM
(www.amff.com; 4070 Main St; adult/child 5-14yr $5/3; ◷ 10am-4pm Tue-Sun Jun-Oct, Tue-Sat Nov-May) In this small museum, check out fly-fishing gear once owned by America's manliest men, including Ernest Hemingway, Babe Ruth, Zane Grey and former president George Bush. Another exhibit traces the history of trout fishing and fly fishing.

BattenKill Canoe   BOATING
(☑ 802-362-2800; www.battenkill.com; 6328 VT 7A, Arlington; canoe/kayak rental $73/45; ◷ 9:30am-5:30pm May-Oct) These outfitters 6 miles south of Manchester rent paddling equipment and organize trips on the lovely Battenkill River.

Skyline Drive   SCENIC DRIVE
(☑ 802-362-1114; www.equinixmountain.com; car & driver $15, extra passenger $5; ◷ 9am-5pm late May-Oct, cars admitted until 4pm) For spectacular views, drive to the summit of **Mt Equinox** (3816ft) via Skyline Drive, a private 5-mile toll road off VT 7A.

⊨ Sleeping & Eating

Aspen Motel   MOTEL $
(☑ 802-362-2450; www.theaspenatmanchester. com; 5669 Main St/VT 7A; r $85-150; ❊ ☎ ❄)

Rhododendrons and bright flowers set a pretty stage at this family-run motel set back serenely from the road. The 24-room motel is within walking distance of Manchester Center.

Inn at Manchester   INN $$
(☑ 802-362-1793, 800-273-1793; www.innatmanchester.com; 3967 Main St/VT 7A; r/ste incl breakfast from $165/255; ❊ @ ☎ ❄) The hospitality is what you notice first at this delightful inn and carriage house in the heart of downtown. Relax in comfy rooms with quilts and country furnishings or step out your door for the big front porch, afternoon teas, an expansive backyard and a wee pub. The new Celebration Barn works well for weddings and meetings.

Spiral Press Café   CAFE $
(☑ 802-362-9944; cnr VT 11 & VT 7A; mains $8-10; ◷ 7:30am-7pm Mon-Sat, 8:30-7pm Sun; ☎) Attached to the fabulous Northshire Bookstore, Manchester Center's favorite cafe draws locals and tourists alike with good coffee, tasty cookies, flaky croissants and delicious sandwiches.

Ye Olde Tavern   AMERICAN $$$
(☑ 802-362-0611; www.yeoldetavern.net; 5183 Main St; mains $18-35; ◷ 5-9pm) At this gracious roadside 1790s inn, hearthside dining at candlelit tables enhances the wide-ranging menu of 'Yankee favorites' such as traditional pot roast (cooked in the tavern's own ale) or local venison (a Friday evening special).

❶ Information

Manchester and the Mountains Regional Chamber of Commerce (☑ 802-362-6313; www. visitmanchestervt.com; 39 Bonnet St, Manchester Center; ◷ 9am-5pm Mon-Fri, 10am-3pm Sat, 11am-3pm Sun; ☎) Spiffy office has free wi-fi.

Central Vermont

Nestled in the Green Mountains, central Vermont is classic small-town, big-countryside New England. Its picturesque villages and venerable ski resorts have been luring travelers for generations.

Woodstock & Quechee

The archetypal Vermont town, Woodstock has streets lined with graceful Federal- and Georgian-style houses. The Ottauquechee River, spanned by a covered bridge, meanders right through the heart of town. Quechee (*kwee-chee*), 7 miles to the northeast, is famous for

WORTH A TRIP

MONTSHIRE MUSEUM OF SCIENCE

Play a musical fence. Study leaf cutter ants in action. Wander a riverside trail. And view current images from the Hubble telescope. Yep, the hands-on exhibits at the family-friendly **Montshire** (☎802-649-2200; www.montshire.org; 1 Montshire Rd; adult/child 2-12yr $14/11; ⏰10am-5pm; 🚼) are pretty darn cool and tend to be more thoughtful and engaging than those at other children's museums. Here, the focus is on the science, with exhibits tackling questions in ecology, technology and the physical and natural sciences. Adults will learn something too.

The museum sits on a scenic 110-acre perch beside the Connecticut River, 20 miles east of Woodstock. The Montshire is also easy to reach if you're in downtown Hanover, NH – just drive across the river.

its dramatic gorge, dubbed 'Vermont's Little Grand Canyon.'

◉ Sights

★ Quechee Gorge CANYON
(⏰visitor center 9am-5pm) FREE Quechee Gorge, an impressive 170ft-deep, 3000ft-long chasm cut by the Ottauquechee River, can be viewed from above or explored via nearby walking trails. The adjacent **visitor center** (5966 Woodstock Rd; ⏰ 9am-5pm) has trail maps and local information

★ VINS Nature Center RAPTOR CENTER
(☎802-359-5000; www.vinsweb.org; 6565 Woodstock Rd; adult/child 4-17yr $13.50/11.50; ⏰10am-5pm mid-Apr–Oct, to 4pm Nov–mid-Apr; 🚼) 🏞 You may feel like ducking during the live raptor show when several magnificent raptors show off their mad flight skills. Visit this nature center, a mile west of Quechee Gorge, for a close-up look at bald eagles, snow owls, and red-tailed hawks. More than 40 raptors are rehabilitated here.

Marsh-Billings-Rockefeller National Historical Park PARK
(☎802-457-3368; www.nps.gov/mabi; 53 Elm St, Woodstock; mansion tours adult/child under 16yr $8/free, trails free; ⏰visitor center 10am-5pm late May-Oct, tours 10am-4pm) Encompassing the historic home and estate of early American conservationist George Perkins Marsh, Vermont's only national park offers mansion tours on the hour, plus 20 miles of trails and carriage roads for walkers, cross-country skiers and snowshoers. Advance reservations are recommended for tours. Specialty tours may be substituted for the mansion tour on certain days, so call ahead to confirm which tour is being offered.

Billings Farm & Museum FARM
(☎802-457-2355; www.billingsfarm.org; 69 Old River Rd, Woodstock; adult/child 5-15yr/child 3-4yr $14/8/4; ⏰10am-5pm daily May-Oct, to 4pm Sat & Sun Nov-Feb; 🚼) 🏞 A mile north of the village green, this historic farm delights children with its pretty Jersey cows and hands-on demonstrations of traditional farm life. Family-friendly seasonal events include wagon and sleigh rides, a pumpkin and apple festival and old-fashioned Halloween, Thanksgiving and Christmas celebrations.

🛏 Sleeping

Quechee State Park CAMPGROUND $
(☎802-295-2990; www.vtstateparks.com/htm/quechee.htm; 5800 Woodstock Rd/US 4, Quechee; tent & RV sites/lean-tos from $20/25; ⏰mid-May–mid-Oct) Perched on the edge of Quechee Gorge, this 611-acre spot has 45 pine-shaded campsites and seven lean-tos.

Ardmore Inn B&B $$
(☎802-457-3887; www.ardmoreinn.com; 23 Pleasant St, Woodstock; r incl breakfast $219-259; ❄🛜) Congenial owners and lavish breakfasts enhance the considerable appeal of this stately, centrally located 1867 Victorian–Greek Revival inn with five antique-laden rooms.

Shire Riverview Motel MOTEL $$
(☎802-457-2211; www.shiremotel.com; 46 Pleasant St/US 4, Woodstock; r $149-209; ❄🛜) Spring the extra few dollars for a river view at this 42-room motel, which features a wraparound porch overlooking the Ottauquechee River. Expect classic, not-too-fancy decor and a few country prints.

Eating

Mon Vert Cafe
CAFE **$**

(☑ 802-457-7143; www.monvertcafe.com; 67 Central St; breakfast $6-13, lunch $9-11; ⊙ 7:30am-5pm Mon-Thu, to 6pm Fri & Sat) Pop into this bright and airy cafe for croissants, scones, and egg sandwiches in the morning or settle in on the patio for salads and paninis at lunch. Enjoy the maple latte anytime. Ingredients are sourced locally, and farms and food purveyors are listed on the wall.

Melaza Caribbean Bistro
PUERTO RICAN **$$**

(☑ 802-457-7110; www.melazabistro.com; 71 Central St; small plates $5-12, mains $16-25; ⊙ 5:30-8:30 Sun, Wed & Thu, to 9pm Fri & Sat) Service was a little too casual on our visit, but all was forgiven after the first bite of the perfectly seasoned rice and chicken *sofrito*, served with avocados and brava sauce. Unwind here after day of exploring, with a glass of wine and an enticing mix of Puerto Rican and tropically inspired tapas and entrees.

★ Simon Pearce
Restaurant
NEW AMERICAN **$$$**

(☑ 802-295-1470; www.simonpearce.com; 1760 Main St, Quechee; lunch $13-19, dinner $22-38; ⊙ 11:30am-2:45pm & 5:30-9pm Mon-Sat, 10:30am-2:45 & 5:30-9pm Sun) Reserve ahead for a window table suspended over the river in this converted brick mill, where fresh-from-the-farm local ingredients are used to inventive effect. The restaurant's beautiful stemware is blown by hand in the Simon Pearce Glass workshops next door. The Vermont cheddar soup is always a good choice.

ℹ Information

Woodstock Area Chamber of Commerce Welcome Center (☑ 802-432-1100; www.woodstockvt.com; Mechanic St, Woodstock; ⊙ 9am-5pm) On a riverside backstreet, two blocks from the village green.

Killington

A half-hour's drive west of Woodstock, **Killington Resort** (☑ 802-422-6200; www.killington.com; adult/senior/child 7-18yr lift ticket weekend $92/78/71, midweek $84/71/65) is New England's answer to Vail, boasting more than 200 runs on seven mountains, a vertical drop of 3150ft and 29 lifts. Thanks to the world's most extensive snowmaking system, Killington has one of the East's longest ski seasons.

Come summer, mountain bikers and hikers claim the slopes.

Killington is jam-packed with accommodations, from cozy ski lodges to chain hotels. Most are along Killington Rd, the 6-mile road that heads up the mountain from US 4. The **Killington Chamber of Commerce** (☑ 802-773-4181; www.killingtonchamber.com; 2319 US 4, Killington; ⊙ 10am-5pm Mon-Fri, to 2pm Sat) has all the nitty-gritty.

Mad River Valley

The Mad River Valley, centered around the towns of Warren and Waitsfield, boasts two significant ski areas: **Sugarbush** (☑ 802-583-6300, 800-537-8427; www.sugarbush.com; 1840 Sugarbush Access Rd, Warren; adult lift ticket weekend/midweek $91/84; discount if purchased online) and **Mad River Glen** (☑ 802-496-3551; www.madriverglen.com; VT 17; adult lift ticket weekend/midweek $75/60), in the mountains west of VT 100. Opportunities abound for cycling, canoeing, horseback riding, kayaking, gliding and other activities. Stop at the **Mad River Valley Chamber of Commerce** (☑ 802-496-3409, 800-828-4748; www.madrivervalley.com; 4061 Main St, Waitsfield; ⊙ 9am-5pm Mon-Fri) for a mountain of information.

Northern Vermont

Boasting some of New England's lushest and prettiest landscapes, northern Vermont cradles the fetching state capital of Montpelier, the ski mecca of Stowe, the vibrant college town of Burlington and the state's highest mountains.

Montpelier

America's smallest capital, Montpelier is a thoroughly likable town of period buildings backed by verdant hills and crowned by the gold-domed 19th-century **State House** (www.vtstatehouse.org; 115 State St; ⊙ tours 10am-3:30pm Mon-Fri, 11am-2:30pm Sat Jul-Oct) **FREE**. Tours of the capitol building run on the hour and the half hour. Right across the street, the **Capitol Region Visitors Center** (☑ 802-828-5981; 134 State St; ⊙ 6am-5pm Mon-Fri, 9am-5pm Sat & Sun) has tourist information.

Bookstores, boutiques and restaurants throng the town's twin thoroughfares, State and Main Sts. Forget about junk food – Montpelier prides itself on being the only state capital in the USA without a McDonald's!

The bakery-cafe La Brioche (www.neci.edu/labrioche; 89 Main St; pastries $1-5, sandwiches $5-8; ⊙7am-6pm Mon-Fri, to 3pm Sat), run by students from Montpelier's New England Culinary Institute, gets an A-plus for its innovative sandwiches and flaky French pastries.

Stowe & Around

With Vermont's highest peak, Mt Mansfield (4393ft), as its backdrop, Stowe ranks as Vermont's classiest ski destination. It packs all the alpine thrills you could ask for – both cross-country and downhill skiing, with gentle runs for novices and challenging drops for pros. Cycling, hiking and kayaking take center stage in the summer. Lodgings and eateries are thick along VT 108 (Mountain Rd), which continues northwest from Stowe village to the ski resorts.

◉ Sights & Activities

In warm weather, don't miss the drive through dramatic Smugglers Notch, northwest of Stowe on VT 108 (closed by heavy snows in winter). This narrow pass slices through mountains with 1000ft cliffs on either side. Roadside trails lead into the surrounding high country.

★ Ben & Jerry's Ice Cream Factory   FACTORY
(☏802-882-1240; www.benjerrys.com; 1281 VT 100, Waterbury; adult/child under 13yr $4/free; ⊙9am-9pm Jul–mid-Aug, to 7pm mid-Aug–Oct, 10am-6pm Nov-Jun; ⓐ) A far cry from the abandoned Burlington gas station where ice cream pioneers Ben Cohen and Jerry Greenfield first set up shop in 1978, this legendary factory, just north of I-89 in Waterbury, draws crowds for tours that include a campy moo-vie and a taste tease of the latest flavor.

Behind the factory, a mock cemetery holds 'graves' of Holy Cannoli and other long-forgotten flavors.

Long Trail   HIKING
Vermont's 300-mile Long Trail, which passes west of Stowe, follows the crest of the Green Mountains and runs the entire length of Vermont, with rustic cabins, lean-tos and campsites along the way. Its caretaker, the Green Mountain Club (☏802-244-7037; www.greenmountainclub.org; 4711 Waterbury-Stowe Rd/VT 100) ✐, has full details on the Long Trail and shorter day hikes around Stowe.

★ Stowe Recreation Path   OUTDOORS
(www.stowerec.org/paths; ⓐⓑ) ✐ This flat to gently rolling 5.3-mile path offers a fabulous four-season escape for all ages, as it rambles through woods, meadows and outdoor sculpture gardens along the West Branch of the Little River, with sweeping views of Mt Mansfield in the distance. Bike, walk, skate, ski and/or swim in one of the swimming holes along the way. If you're traveling with your dog, veer onto the 1.8-mile Quiet Path extension, open only to joggers and walkers, and their dogs.

Stowe Mountain Resort   SKIING
(☏888-253-4849, 802-253-3000; www.stowe.com; 5781 Mountain Rd) This venerable resort encompasses two major mountains, Mt Mansfield (vertical drop 2360ft) and Spruce Peak (1550ft). It offers 48 beautiful trails: 16% beginner, 55% intermediate and 29% for hardcore backcountry skiers.

Umiak Outdoor Outfitters   OUTDOORS
(☏802-253-2317; www.umiak.com; 849 S Main St; ⊙9am-6pm) Rents kayaks, snowshoes and telemark skis, offers boating lessons and leads river and moonlight snowshoe tours.

AJ's Ski & Sports   EQUIPMENT RENTAL
(☏802 253 4593, 000 226 6257; www.stowesports.com; 350 Mountain Rd; ⊙9am-6pm) Rents bikes, ski and snowboard equipment in the village center.

🛏 Sleeping

Smugglers Notch State Park   CAMPGROUND $
(☏888-409-7579, 802-253-4014; www.vtstateparks.com/htm/smugglers.htm; 6443 Mountain Rd; tent & RV sites/lean-tos from $20/$27; ⊙mid-May–mid-Oct) This 35-acre park, 8 miles northwest of Stowe, is perched on the mountainside, with 20 tent and trailer sites and 14 lean-tos.

Stowe Motel & Snowdrift   MOTEL, APARTMENT $$
(☏802-253-7629, 800-829-7629; www.stowemotel.com; 2043 Mountain Rd; r $108-188, ste $192-208, apt $172-240; ⓐ🖧🏊) Active guests will do just fine at this motel, set on 16 acres and home to a tennis court, hot tubs, lawn games and free bicycles or snowshoes for use on the adjacent Stowe Recreation Path. Units range from simple to deluxe.

Trapp Family Lodge   LODGE $$$
(☏802-253-8511, 800-826-7000; www.trappfamily.com; 700 Trapp Hill Rd; r from $295; ⓐ🖧🏊ⓟ) The setting is appropriately breathtaking, and you'd surely be forgiven if you broke into

song. Surrounded by wide-open fields and mountain vistas, this Austrian-style chalet, built by Maria von Trapp of *Sound of Music* fame, boasts Stowe's best setting. Traditional lodge rooms are complemented by guesthouses scattered across the 2700-acre property. A network of trails offers stupendous hiking, snowshoeing and cross-country skiing. Pet fee is $50 per night.

✖ Eating

Harvest Market MARKET $
(☏ 802-253-3800; www.harvestatstowe.com; 1031 Mountain Rd; ⊗ 7am-5:30pm) Before heading for the hills, stop here for coffee, pastries, Vermont cheeses, sandwiches, gourmet deli items, wines and local microbrews.

Pie-casso PIZZA $$
(☏ 802-253-4411; www.piecasso.com; 1899 Mountain Rd; sandwiches $9-13, pizza $11-22; ⊗ 11am-10pm Sun-Thu, to 11pm Fri & Sat) Organic arugula chicken salad and portobello panini supplement the menu of excellent hand-tossed pizzas. There's a bar and live music, too.

Gracie's Restaurant BURGERS $$
(☏ 802-253-8741; www.gracies.com; 18 Edson Hill Rd; mains $12-44; ⊗ 5pm until close) Halfway between the village and the mountain, this animated, dog-themed eatery serves big burgers, hand-cut steaks, Waldorf salad and garlic-laden shrimp scampi.

★ Hen of the Wood AMERICAN $$$
(☏ 802-244-7300; www.henofthewood.com; 92 Stowe St, Waterbury; mains $22-29; ⊗ 5-9pm Tue-Sat) 🍴 Arguably the finest dining in northern Vermont, this chef-driven restaurant in Waterbury gets rave reviews for its innovative farm-to-table cuisine. The setting in a historic grist mill rivals the extraordinary food, which features densely flavored dishes, like ham-wrapped rabbit loin and sheep's-milk gnocchi.

❶ Information

Stowe Area Association (☏ 802-253-7321; www.gostowe.com; 51 Main St; ⊗ 9am-5pm Mon-Sat, to 8pm Jun-Oct & Jan-Mar) In the heart of the village.

Burlington

This hip college town on the shores of scenic Lake Champlain is one of those places that makes you think, wouldn't it be great to live here? The cafe and club scene is on par with a much bigger city, while the slow, friendly pace is pure small town. And where else can

SCENIC DRIVE: VERMONT'S GREEN MOUNTAIN BYWAY

Following Vermont's Green Mountain spine through the state's rural heart, the **VT 100** rambles past rolling pastures speckled with cows, tiny villages with country stores and white-steepled churches, and verdant mountains crisscrossed with hiking trails and ski slopes. It's the quintessential side trip for those who want to slow down and experience Vermont's bucolic essence. The road runs north to south all the way from Massachusetts to Canada. Even if your time is limited, don't miss the scenic 45-mile stretch between Waterbury and Stockbridge, an easy detour off I-89. For details about attractions along the way, visit www.vermont-byways.us.

you walk to the end of Main St and paddle off in a kayak?

◎ Sights

Burlington's shops, cafes and pubs are concentrated around Church St Marketplace, a bustling brick-lined pedestrian mall midway between the University of Vermont and Lake Champlain.

★ Shelburne Museum MUSEUM
(☏ 802-985-3346; www.shelburnemuseum.org; 6300 Shelburne Rd/US 7, Shelburne; adult/youth 13-17yr/child 5-12yr $24/14/12; ⊗ 10am-5pm mid-May–Oct; ♿) Wear your walking shoes for this extraordinary 45-acre museum, which showcases a Smithsonian-caliber collection of Americana – 150,000 objects in all. The mix of folk art, decorative arts and more is housed in 39 historic buildings, most of them relocated here from other parts of New England to ensure their preservation. Located 9 miles south of Burlington.

Shelburne Farms FARM
(☏ 802-985-8686; www.shelburnefarms.org; 1611 Harbor Rd, Shelburne; adult/child 3-17yr $8/5; ⊗ 9am-5:30pm mid-May–mid-Oct, 10am-5pm mid-Oct–mid-May; ♿) 🍴 This 1400-acre estate, designed by landscape architect Frederick Law Olmsted (who also designed New York's Central Park), was both a country house for the aristocratic Webb family and a working farm, with stunning lakefront perspectives. Still a working farm, the property

today welcomes visitors. Guests can milk a cow in the farmyard (11am, 2pm), sample the farm's superb cheddar cheese, tour the magnificent barns and walk the network of trails. Enjoy afternoon tea while a guest at the award-winning inn, or stop by for farm-sourced produce and local meats at its restaurant.

Echo Lake Aquarium & Science Center
SCIENCE CENTER

(☑ 802-864-1848; www.echovermont.org; 1 College St; adult/child 3-17yr $13.50/10.50; ⊙10am-5pm; ⊕) Examining the colorful past, present and future of Lake Champlain, this lakeside museum features a multitude of small aquariums and rotating science exhibits with plenty of hands-on, kid-friendly activities. Don't miss the Into the Lake exhibit which spotlights Champ, a local 'sea monster' allegedly dwelling in the lake.

Magic Hat Brewery
BREWERY

(☑ 802-658-2739; www.magichat.net; 5 Bartlett Bay Rd, South Burlington; ⊙10am-7pm Mon-Sat Jun–mid-Oct, to 6pm Mon-Thu, to 7pm Fri & Sat mid-Oct-May, noon-5pm Sun year-round) Drink in the history of one of Vermont's most dynamic microbreweries on the fun, free, self-guided tour. Afterwards, sample a few of the eight brews on tap in the on-site Growler Bar. Recent samples included the Peppercorn Pilsner, made with pink peppercorns, and the Electric Peel, a grapefruit IPA.

🏃 Activities

Ready for outdoor adventures? Head to the waterfront, where options include boating on Lake Champlain and cycling, in-line skating and walking on the 7.5-mile shorefront Burlington Bike Path. Jump-off points and equipment rentals for all these activities are

BURLINGTON'S SECRET GARDEN

Hidden away less than 2 miles from Burlington's city center is one of Vermont's most idyllic green spaces. Tucked among the lazy curves of the Winooski River, the Intervale Center (www.intervale.org; 180 Intervale Rd) FREE encompasses a dozen organic farms and a delightful trail network, open to the public 365 days a year for hiking, biking, skiing, berry picking and more; check the website for details.

within a block of each other near the waterfront end of Main St.

Local Motion
BICYCLE RENTAL

(☑ 802-652-2453; www.localmotion.org; 1 Steele St; bicycles per day $32; ⊙9am-6pm July & Aug, 10am-6pm May & Jun, Sept & Oct; ⊕) 🌿 Rents quality bikes beside the Burlington Bike Path between Main St and King St.

Whistling Man Schooner Company
SAILING

(☑ 802-598-6504; www.whistlingman.com; Boathouse, 1 College St, at Lake Champlain; 2hr cruises adult/child under 13yr $40/25; ⊙3 trips daily, late May–early Oct) Explore Lake Champlain on the *Friend Ship*, a 17-passenger, 43-foot sailboat.

🛏 Sleeping

Burlington's budget and midrange motels are on the outskirts of town, clustered along Shelburne Rd (US 7) in South Burlington, Williston Rd (US 2) east of I-89 exit 14, and US 7 north of Burlington in Colchester (I-89 exit 16).

North Beach Campground
CAMPGROUND $

(☑ 802-862-0942; www.enjoyburlington.com; 60 Institute Rd; tent/RV site $36/41; ⊙May–mid-Oct; 🛜) Two miles north of downtown, this wonderful spot on Lake Champlain offers 137 campsites on 45 wooded acres, with picnic tables, fire rings, hot showers, a playground, beach and bike path.

Burlington Hostel
HOSTEL $

(☑ 802-540-3043; www.theburlingtonhostel.com; 53 Main St; dm incl breakfast $40; ❄@🛜) Just minutes from Church St and Lake Champlain, Burlington's hostel offers both mixed and single sex dorms, with eight beds per room.

Lang House
B&B $$

(☑ 802-652-2500; www.langhouse.com; 360 Main St; r incl breakfast $199-259; ❄@🛜) The Lang House may be Burlington's most elegant B&B, but you can still kick back and relax like the proletariat - this is Burlington, after all. This tastefully restored 19th-century Victorian home and carriage house occupies a centrally located spot not far from downtown. Reserve ahead for one of the 3rd-floor rooms with lake views.

Hilton Garden Inn Burlington Downtown
HOTEL $$

(☑ 802-951-0099; www.hiltongardeninn3.hilton.com; 101 Main St; r from $229; 🅿❄@🛜🏊) Hip *and* historic? Yep, and the combination works seamlessly at this Hilton Garden, which opened in 2015. Housed in a former armory, the hotel is within walking distance of Church St Marketplace and Lake Champlain. The airy pavilion lobby pops with bright colors and crisp decor. Rooms are a bit less exuberant but come with Serta beds, mini-fridges, and microwaves. Note that weekends book up far in advance. Parking is $16 per night and valet only.

★ Inn at Shelburne Farms   INN $$$

(☎ 802-985-8498; www.shelburnefarms.org/stay-dine; 1611 Harbor Rd, Shelburne; r with private/shared bath from $210/165, cottage from $320, guesthouse from $450; ☺ May-Oct; ☎) At this historic 1400-acre estate (p221) on the shore of Lake Champlain, 7 miles south of Burlington, guests stay in a gracious, welcoming country manor house, or in four independent, kitchen-equipped cottages and guest houses scattered across the property. The attached farm-to-table restaurant is superb. And those lake sunsets? Ahhhh.

✗ Eating

On Saturday mornings, City Hall Park hosts Burlington's thriving **farmers market** (www.burlingtonfarmersmarket.org) in downtown.

Penny Cluse Cafe   CAFE $

(☎ 802-651-8834; www.pennycluse.com; 169 Cherry St; mains $6-12.25; ☺ 6:45am-3pm Mon-Fri, 8am-3pm Sat & Sun) ✐ Did somebody say bucket-o-spuds? Oh yes, they did. And that's just the first thing listed on the enticing menu at Penny Cluse, one of Burlington's most popular downtown eateries. The kitchen also whips up pancakes, biscuits and gravy, omelets and tofu scrambles along with sandwiches, fish tacos, salads and excellent *chile relleno*. Expect long lines on weekends. One quibble? Weak coffee on our visit. Sad face.

City Market   MARKET $

(☎ 802-861-9700; www.citymarket.coop; 82 S Winooski Ave; sandwiches $8-10; ☺ 7am-11pm) ✐ If there's a natural-foods heaven, it must look something like this downtown co-op: chock-full of local produce and products (with more than 1000 Vermont-based producers represented) and a huge takeout deli.

Stone Soup   VEGETARIAN $

(☎ 802-862-7616; www.stonesoupvt.com; 211 College St; buffet per lb $10.75, sandwiches under $10; ☺ 7am-9pm Mon-Fri, 9am-9pm Sat; ☎✐) Squeeze in at lunchtime for the small but excellent vegetarian- and vegan-friendly buffet at this longtime local favorite. Also good: homemade soups, sandwiches on home-baked bread, a salad bar and pastries.

★ Pizzeria Verita   PIZZA $$

(☎ 802-489-5644; www.pizzeriaverita.com; 156 Paul St; pizza $8-18; ☺ 5-10pm Sun-Thu, to 11pm Fri & Sat) You can't walk two steps in Burlington without somebody recommending new-on-the-scene Pizzeria Verita. And their recommendation is spot-on. It's heaven on a thin crust. Step into this modernly rustic trattoria (you know what we mean – wine casks for bar tables, etc) for the *quatro formaggi,* the *funghi rustico* or the Ring of Fire with hot cherry peppers.

At the bar, sip interesting seasonal cocktails and Vermont craft beers.

Daily Planet   INTERNATIONAL $$

(☎ 802-862-9647; www.dailyplanet15.com; 15 Center St; mains $11-24; ☺ 4-9pm Sun-Thu, to 9:30pm Fri & Sat; ☎✐) This stylish downtown haunt serves everything from confit duck poutine to burgers with tasty trimmings to pan-roasted lamb lollipops to caramelized sea scallops. The bar stays open until 2am nightly.

Leunig's Bistro   FRENCH $$$

(☎ 802-863-3759; www.leunigsbistro.com; 115 Church St; lunch $12-22, dinner $18-34; ☺ 11am-10pm Mon-Thu, to 11pm Fri, 9am-11pm Sat, to 10pm Sun) With sidewalk seating and an elegant, tin-ceilinged dining room, this convivial Parisian-style brasserie is a longstanding Burlington staple. It's as much fun for the people-watching (windows face busy Church St Marketplace) as for the excellent wine list and food.

🍷 Drinking & Nightlife

The free weekly *Seven Days* (www.7dvt.com) has event and entertainment listings.

Radio Bean   BAR

(www.radiobean.com; 8 N Winooski Ave; ☺ 8am-2am Mon-Sat, 10am-2am Sun; ☎) This funky cafe-bar features its own low-power FM radio station, a trendy attached eatery serving international street food, and live performances nightly that include jazz, acoustic music and poetry readings.

Vermont Pub & Brewery   MICROBREWERY

(www.vermontbrewery.com; 144 College St; mains $5-18; ☺ 11:30am-1am Sun-Wed, to 2am Thu-Sat) Specialty and seasonal brews, including weekly limited releases, are made on the premises, accompanied by British-style pub fare.

Splash at the Boathouse
BAR

(☑ 802-658-2244; www.splashattheboathouse. com; 0 College St; ⊙ 10am-2am mid-May–Sep) Perched atop Burlington's floating boathouse, this restaurant-bar with stellar views over Lake Champlain is perfect for kicking back with an evening cocktail or microbrew at sunset.

☆ Entertainment

Nectar's
LIVE MUSIC

(www.liveatnectars.com; 188 Main St; ⊙ 7pm-2am Sun-Tue, 5pm-2am Wed-Sat) Nectar's celebrated its 40th birthday in 2015, and the joint still rocks out with a mix of theme nights and live acts. Indie darlings Phish got their start here.

 Shopping

You'll find boutiques and smart craft shops along Church St Marketplace. Don't miss the **Frog Hollow Craft Center** (www.froghollow.org; 85 Church St; ⊙ 10am-6pm Mon-Wed, to 8pm Thu-Sat, 11am-7pm Sun mid-Apr–Nov, reduced hours rest of the year) FREE, a collective featuring some of the finest work in Burlington.

ⓘ Information

University of Vermont Medical Center (☑ 802-847-0000, www.uvmhealth.org; 111 Colchester Ave; ⊙ 24hr) Vermont's largest hospital. Has a 24hr level 1 trauma center.

Lake Champlain Regional Chamber of Commerce (☑ 802-863-3489, 877-686-5253; www.vermont.org; 60 Main St; ⊙ 8am-5pm Mon-Fri) Downtown tourist office.

ⓘ Getting There & Away

Greyhound (☑ 800-231-2222, 802-864-6811; www.greyhound.com; 1200 Airport Dr) offers bus service between Burlington International Airport and Boston and Montreal. **Megabus** (☑ 877-462-6342; www.megabus.com; 116 University Pl) runs from the University of Vermont campus in Burlington to Amherst, MA and New York City. **Amtrak's Vermonter train** (☑ 800-872-7245; www.amtrak. com/vermonter-train) runs south daily to Brattleboro, New York City and Washington, DC. **Lake Champlain Ferries** (☑ 802-864-9804; www. ferries.com; King St Dock; adult/child 6-12yr/car $8/3.10/30) runs ferries mid-June through September across the lake to Port Kent, NY (one hour 20 minutes).

NEW HAMPSHIRE

New Hampshire needs to work on its marketing: The Granite State? Live Free or Die? Do they want anyone to visit? In truth, this state has the scale of things just right for residents and travelers: the towns are small and personable, the mountains majestic and rugged. The heart of New Hampshire is unquestionably the granite peaks of the White Mountain National Forest. Outdoor enthusiasts of all stripes flock to New England's highest range (6288ft at Mt Washington) for cold-weather skiing, summer hiking and brilliant fall foliage scenery. And don't be fooled by that politically conservative label that people stick on the state. The aforementioned state mantra, 'Live Free or Die,' indeed rings from every automobile license plate, but residents here pride themselves on their independent spirit more than right-wing politics.

History

Named in 1629 after the English county of Hampshire, New Hampshire was one of the first American colonies to declare its independence from England in 1776. During the 19th-century industrialization boom, the state's leading city, Manchester, became such a powerhouse that its textile mills were the world's largest.

New Hampshire played a high-profile role in 1944 when president Franklin D Roosevelt gathered leaders from 44 Allied nations to remote Bretton Woods for a conference to rebuild global capitalism. It was at the Bretton Woods Conference that the World Bank and the International Monetary Fund emerged.

In 1963 New Hampshire, long famed for its anti-tax sentiments, found another way to raise revenue – by becoming the first state in the USA to have a legal lottery.

ⓘ Information

Welcome centers are situated at major state border crossings.

New Hampshire Division of Parks & Recreation (☑ 603-271-3556; www.nhstateparks.org) Offers information on hiking, biking, camping and other outdoor activities.

New Hampshire Division of Travel & Tourism Development (☑ 603-271-2665; www.visitnh. gov) Order a visitor's guide and check out the adventure itineraries.

Portsmouth

America's third-oldest city (1623), Portsmouth wears its history on its sleeve. Its roots are in shipbuilding, but New Hampshire's sole coastal city also has a hip, youthful energy. The old maritime warehouses along the harbor now house cafes and boutiques. Elegant period homes built by shipbuilding tycoons have been converted into B&Bs.

◉ Sights & Activities

Strawbery Banke Museum MUSEUM
(☑603-433-1100; www.strawberybanke.org; cnr Hancock & Marcy Sts; adult/child 5-17yr $20/10; ☺10am-5pm May-Oct) Spread across a 10-acre site, the Strawbery Banke Museum is an eclectic blend of period homes that date back to the 1690s. Costumed guides recount tales that took place among the 40 buildings (10 furnished). Strawbery Banke includes **Pitt Tavern** (1766), a hotbed of American revolutionary sentiment, **Goodwin Mansion** (a grand 19th-century house from Portsmouth's most prosperous time) and **Abbott's Little Corner Store** (1943). The admission ticket is good for two consecutive days.

USS Albacore MUSEUM
(☑603-436-3680; http://ussalbacore.org; 600 Market St; adult/child 7-13yr $7/3; ☺9:30am-5pm Jun–mid-Oct, to 4pm Thu-Mon mid-Oct–May) Audio recollections add context as you squeeze through the narrow compartments packed inside the USS *Albacore* – which was home to 55 officers and crew in its heyday. Like a fish out of water, this 205ft-long submarine is now a beached museum on a grassy lawn. Launched from Portsmouth Naval Shipyard in 1953, the *Albacore* was once the world's fastest submarine.

Isles of Shoals Steamship Co CRUISE
(☑603-431-5500; www.islesofshoals.com; 315 Market St; adult/child 4-12yr $28/18; 🚢) From mid-June through September the company runs an excellent tour of the harbor and the historic Isles of Shoals aboard a replica 1900s ferry. Also offers sunset, country music, reggae and dinner cruises.

🛏 Sleeping

Ale House Inn INN **$$**
(☑603-431-7760; www.alehouseinn.com; 121 Bow St; r $209-359; 🅿🛜) Thank you for the two Smuttynose beers, Ale House Inn. We like it here already. Portsmouth's snazziest

boutique, this brick warehouse for the Portsmouth Brewing Company fuses contemporary design with comfort. Rooms are modern with clean lines of white and flatscreen TVs, plush tan sofas fill the suites. Deluxe rooms feature an in-room iPad. Rates include use of vintage cruising bikes.

Port Inn MOTEL **$$**
(☑603-436-4378; www.choicehotels.com; 505 Rte 1 Bypass; r/ste incl breakfast $127/178; ❄@🛜🐾🐕) Wrapped neatly around a small courtyard, this welcoming motel is conveniently located off I-95, about a mile and a half southwest of downtown. In the rooms, monochromatic pillows and throws add a dash of color to classic furnishings. Pets are $20 per night.

🍴 Eating & Drinking

Head to the intersection of Market and Congress Sts, where restaurants and cafes are thick on the ground.

Friendly Toast
DINER $

(☑ 603-430-2154; www.thefriendlytoast.com; 113 Congress St; breakfast $8-14, lunch $11-19; ⊙ 7am-9pm Sun-Thu, to 10pm Thu, 2am Fri & Sat; ☜ 🐾) Fun, whimsical furnishings set the scene for filling sandwiches, omelets, Tex-Mex and vegetarian fare at this retro diner. The breakfast menu is huge and is served around the clock – good thing since weekend morning waits can be long.

Surf
SEAFOOD $$

(☑ 603-334-9855; www.surfseafood.com; 99 Bow St; lunch $9-18, dinner $12-38; ⊙ 4-9pm Sun-Thu, to 10pm Fri & Sat) We're not sure if the view of the Pisquataqua River complements the food or the food complements the view, especially at sunset at this airy restaurant. Either way, both are a satisfying way to close out the day. The seafood offerings have some global flair, with shrimp and avocado quesadillas, haddock crepes, and shrimp vindaloo with curry sauce.

Black Trumpet Bistro
INTERNATIONAL $$$

(☑ 603-431-0887; www.blacktrumpetbistro.com; 29 Ceres St; mains $19-31; ⊙ 5:30-9pm) With brick walls and sophisticated ambience, this bistro serves unique combinations (anything from pork sirloin with collard greens to quail with sausage stuffing). The full menu is also available at its wine bar upstairs, which whips up equally inventive cocktails.

Thirsty Moose Taphouse
PUB

(www.thirstymoosetaphouse.com; 21 Congress St; bar snacks $5-13, mains $10-14; ⊙ 11am-1pm) From Abita to Widmer Bros, with Clown Shoes in between, this convivial spot pours more than 100 beers on tap, leaning heavily on New England brews (and a staff that can walk you through most – it's impressive). A fine spot to kick back and relax. Bites include *poutine* (fries drenched in cheese and gravy), sandwiches and burgers.

ℹ️ Information

Greater Portsmouth Chamber of Commerce
(☑ 603-436-3988; www.portsmouthchamber. org; 500 Market St; ⊙ 8:30am-5pm Mon-Thu, to 7pm Fri, 10am-5pm Sat & Sun Jun–mid-Oct, 8:30am-5pm Mon-Fri mid-Oct–May) Also operates an information kiosk in the city center at Market Sq.

Monadnock State Park & Around

The climb to the 3165ft summit of Mt Monadnock (www.nhstateparks.org; 116 Poole Rd, Jaffrey, NH 124; adult/child 6-11yr $4/2) is rocky and steep, but the view from the boulder-capped summit is oh-so-worth-the-burn. Mt Monadnock, in the southwestern corner of the state, is the most hiked summit in New England. 'Mountain That Stands Alone' in Algonquian, Monadnock is relatively isolated from other peaks, which means hikers who make the 5-mile round-trip to the summit are rewarded with unspoiled views of three states. Best bet for first-timers? Hike up on the White Dot Trail and return via the White Cross Trail.

The best post-hike reward? Everyone knows it's a heaping scoop of ice cream from Kimball Farm (www.kimballfarm.com; 158 Turnpike Rd; small scoop $5; ⊙ ice cream 10am-10pm) just up the road. Choose from more than 50 flavors, including chocolate raspberry, maple walnut, and coffee Oreo. For a drink or an overnight stay near the Monadnock Inn (☑ 603-532-7800; www.monadnockinn.com; 379 Main St; r $110-190), where the tavern is cozy and your room may include a wine birdcage.

Lake Winnipesaukee

A popular summer retreat for families looking for a break from the city, New Hampshire's largest lake stretches 28 miles in length, contains 274 islands and offers abundant opportunities for swimming, boating and fishing.

Weirs Beach

This lakeside town dishes up a curious slice of honky-tonk Americana with its celebrated video arcades, mini-golf courses and go-cart tracks. The Lakes Region Chamber of Commerce (☑ 603-524-5531; www.lakesregion chamber.org; 383 S Main St, Laconia; ⊙ 9am-3pm Mon-Fri, 10am-5pm Sat) supplies information about the area.

Mount Washington Cruises (☑ 603-366-5531; www.cruisenh.com; 211 Lakeside Ave; cruises $30-47) operates scenic lake cruises, the pricier ones with champagne brunch and live music, from Weirs Beach aboard the old-fashioned MS *Mount Washington*.

Winnipesaukee Scenic Railroad (☑603-745-2135; www.hoborr.com; 211 Lakeside Ave, Weirs Beach; adult/child 3-11yr 1hr $12/14, 2hr $14/18) offers train rides along the shore of Lake Winnipesaukee.

Wolfeboro

On the opposite side of Lake Winnipesaukee, and a world away from the ticky-tacky commercialism of Weirs Beach, sits genteel Wolfeboro. Anointing itself 'the oldest summer resort in America,' the town is awash with graceful period buildings, including several that are open to the public. The **Wolfeboro Chamber of Commerce** (☑603-569-2200; www.wolfeborochamber.com; 32 Central Ave; ⊙10am-3pm Mon-Fri, to noon Sat), in the old train station, has the scoop on everything from boat rentals to lakeside beaches.

Wolfeboro is home to the **Great Waters Music Festival** (☑603-569-7710; www.greatwaters.org; ⊙Jun-Aug), featuring folk, jazz and blues artists at different venues throughout town.

Off NH 28, about 4 miles north of town, is lakeside **Wolfeboro Campground** (☑603-569-9881; www.wolfeborocampground.com; 61 Haines Hill Rd; tent & RV sites $32; ⊙mid-May–mid-Oct) with 50 wooded campsites.

For breakfast, lunch or coffee with a Lake Winnipesaukee view, stop by the **Downtown Grille Cafe** (www.downtowngrillecafe.com; 33 S Main St; breakfast $3.25-7, lunch $8-12; ⊙7am-3pm), which serves a tasty array of omelets, sandwiches, wraps and burgers. The cozy bar at **Wolfe's Tavern** (www.wolfestavern.com; Wolfeboro Inn, 90 N Main St; bar menu appetizers $5-12, sandiwches $11-13; ⊙8am-10pm) offers numerous regional beers and a bar menu with pork belly tacos, calamari and sandwiches. Ice cream from **Bailey's Bubble** (☑603-569-3612; www.baileysbubble.com; 5 Railroad Ave; small scoop $2.75; ⊙11am-10pm May-mid-Oct, shorter hours spring and fall) is always a good idea.

White Mountains

What the Rockies are to Colorado the White Mountains are to New Hampshire. New England's loftiest mountain range is a magnet for adventurers, with boundless opportunities for everything from hiking and kayaking to skiing. Those who prefer to take it in from the comfort of a car seat won't be disappointed either, as scenic drives wind over rugged mountains ripping with waterfalls, sheer rock faces and sharply cut gorges.

You'll find information on the White Mountains at ranger stations throughout the **White Mountain National Forest** (www.fs.usda.gov/whitemountain) and chambers of commerce in the towns along the way.

Mount Washington Valley

Stretching north from the eastern terminus of the Kancamagus Hwy, Mt Washington Valley includes the towns of Conway, North Conway, Intervale, Glen, Jackson and Bartlett. Every conceivable outdoor activity is available. The area's hub and biggest town, North Conway, is also a center for outlet shopping, including some earthy stores like LL Bean.

◉ Sights & Activities

★**Conway Scenic Railroad** TRAIN (☑603-356-5251; www.conwayscenic.com; 38 Norcross Circle; Notch Train adult/child 4-12yr/child 1-3yr from $55/39/11, Valley Train from $16.50/11.50; ⊙mid-Jun–Oct; ▦) The **Notch Train**, built in 1874 and restored in 1974, offers New England's most scenic journey. The spectacular five- to 5½-hour trip passes through Crawford Notch. Accompanying live commentary recounts the railroad's history and folklore. Reservations required.

Alternatively, the same company operates the antique steam **Valley Train**, which makes a shorter journey south through the Mt Washington Valley, stopping in Conway and Bartlett. Look for seasonal excursions like the Pumpkin Patch Express in October and the Polar Bear Express in November and December.

★**Mount Washington Observatory Weather Discovery Center** MUSEUM (☑603-356-2137; www.mountwashington.org; 2779 White Mountain Hwy; adult/child 7-17yr $2/1; ⊙10am-5pm) If you don't have time to drive to the summit of Mt Washington but you think wild weather is cool, take an hour to explore this small but fascinating weather museum instead. Shoot an air cannon, interrupt a mini-tornado and learn why temperatures are so extremely cold atop Mount Washington. What happens when you push the red button inside the mock observatory shack? All we'll say is, hold on tight.

WORTH A TRIP

SCENIC DRIVE: WHITE MOUNTAIN NATIONAL FOREST

One of New England's finest, the 35-mile **Kancamagus Hwy (NH 112)** is a beauty of a road cutting through the **White Mountain National Forest** (p227) between Conway and Lincoln. Laced with excellent hiking trails, scenic lookouts and swimmable streams, this is as natural as it gets. There's absolutely no development along the entire highway, which reaches its highest point at **Kancamagus Pass** (2868ft).

Pick up brochures and hiking maps at the **Saco Ranger District Office** (603-447-5448; 33 Kancamagus Hwy; 8am-4:30pm) at the eastern end of the highway near Conway. On the western end, stop by the National Forest desk at the **White Mountains Visitor Center** in North Woodstock.

Coming from Conway, 6.5 miles west of the Saco ranger station, you'll see **Lower Falls** on the north side of the road – stop here for the view and a swim. No trip along this highway is complete without taking the 20-minute hike to the breathtaking cascade of **Sabbaday Falls**; the trail begins at Mile 15 on the south side of the road. The best place to spot moose is along the shores of **Lily Pond**; stop at the roadside overview at Mile 18. At the Lincoln Woods ranger station, which is near the Mile 29 marker, cross the suspension footbridge over the river and hike 3 miles to **Franconia Falls**, the finest swimming hole in the entire national forest, complete with a natural rock slide. Parking anywhere along the highway costs $3 per day (honor system) or $5 per week; just fill out an envelope at any of the parking areas.

The White Mountain National Forest is ideal for campers, and you'll find several campgrounds run by the forest service accessible from the Kancamagus Hwy. Most are on a first-come, first-served basis; pick up a list at the Saco ranger station.

Echo Lake State Park   PARK

(www.nhstateparks.org; River Rd; adult/child 6-11yr $4/2) Two miles west of North Conway via River Rd, this placid mountain lake lies at the foot of **White Horse Ledge**, a sheer rock wall. A scenic trail circles the lake, which has a small beach. There is also a mile-long auto road and hiking trail leading to the 700ft-high **Cathedral Ledge**, with panoramic White Mountains views. Both Cathedral Ledge and White Horse Ledge are excellent for rock climbing. This is also a fine spot for swimming and picknicing.

Saco Bound   CANOEING

(603-447-2177; www.sacobound.com; 2561 E Main/US 302, Conway; rentals per day $26-45; late Apr–mid-Oct) Saco Bound Inc organizes canoe trips with shuttle service ($12 TO $15 per canoe/kayak), including the introductory trip to Weston's Bridge. Also runs overnight camping trips. Inner tubes (adult/child under 12 $20/10) available for rent, too.

🛏 Sleeping

North Conway in particular is thick with sleeping options from resort hotels to cozy inns.

White Mountains Hostel   HOSTEL $

(603-447-1001; www.whitemountainshostel.com; 36 Washington St, Conway; dm/r $20/20-30;) Set in an early-1900s farmhouse, this cheery place in Conway is now under new ownership. The environmentally conscientious hostel has dorm bedrooms with bunk beds and five private rooms, and a communal lounge and kitchen. Excellent hiking, bicycling and kayaking opportunities are all found nearby. Our only gripe is the location, which is 5 miles south of the action in North Conway.

Not a party hostel, but a great choice if you want to explore the outdoors.

Saco River Camping Area   CAMPGROUND $

(603-356-3360; www.sacorivercampingarea.com; 1550 White Mountain Hwy/NH 16; tent/RV sites from $33/43, huts $47; May–mid-Oct;) A riverside campground, away from the highway, with 140 wooded and open sites as well as rustic huts (literally walls and a roof; no electricity or kitchen). Canoe and kayak rental available.

Cranmore Inn   B&B $$

(603-356-5502; www.cranmoreinn.com; 80 Kearsarge St; r incl breakfast $149-369;) Under new ownership and recently renovated, the Cranmore has lost the country frills. Rooms now sport a fresh, more contemporary style. In addition to standard rooms, there are several two-room suites and one apartment with a kitchen. The inn has been operating as a country inn since 1863. There's a year-round hot tub on-site, perfect for post-hike sore muscles.

Hampton Inn North Conway
HOTEL $$$

(☑ 603-356-7736;   www.hamptoninn3.hilton.com;
1788 White Mountain Hwy; r from $279; ✴ @ 🛜 ≋)
Traveling with high-energy kids? Let them
loose in the 5000-sq-ft indoor water park,
with two slides, at this super welcoming loca-
tion of the national chain.

✖ Eating

Peach's
CAFE $

(☑ 603-356-5860;   www.peachesnorthconway.com;
2506 White Mountain Hwy; breakfast $6-10, lunch
$8-9; ⊙ 7am-2:30pm) Away from the in-town
bustle, this perennially popular little house
is an excellent option for soups, sandwiches
and breakfast. Who can resist fruit-smothered
waffles and pancakes and fresh-brewed cof-
fee, served in somebody's cozy living room?

Moat Mountain Smoke House
& Brewing Co
PUB FOOD $$

(☑ 603-356-6381; www.moatmountain.com; 3378
White Mountain Hwy; mains $10-23; ⊙ 11:30am-
midnight) With its great food, on-point service
and tasty homemade beers, Moat Mountain
wins best all around for New Hampshire
brewpubs. Come here for a wide array of
American fare, with a nod to the South: BBQ
sandwiches, beefy chili, juicy burgers, wood-
grilled pizzas and a delicious curried crab
and corn bisque. Wash it down with one of
the numerous brews made on-site.

The friendly bar is also a popular local
hangout.

ℹ Information

Mt Washington Valley Chamber of Commerce
(☑ 603-356-5701; www.mtwashingtonvalley.org;
2617 White Mountain Hwy; ⊙ 9am-5pm) Tourist
information just south of the town center. Hours
are notoriously unreliable.

North Woodstock & Lincoln

The twin towns of Lincoln and North Woodstock break up the drive between the Kancamagus Hwy and Franconia Notch State Park,
so they are a handy place to stop for a bite or
a bed. The towns straddle the Pemigewasset
River at the intersection of NH 112 and US 3.
Ratchet up the adrenaline by zipping 2000ft
down a hillside while strapped to just a cable
with the treetop zip line at **Alpine Adventure**
(☑ 603-745-9911; www.alpinezipline.com; 41 Main St,
Lincoln; zips from $64; ⊙ 11am-4pm).

🛏 Sleeping & Eating

Woodstock Inn
INN $$

(☑ 603-745-3951; www.woodstockinnnh.com; US 3;
r incl breakfast with shared/private bath from
$147/178; ✴ 🛜) Anchoring downtown North
Woodstock, this Victorian country inn fea-
tures 34 individually appointed rooms across
five separate buildings (three in a cluster, two
across the street), each with modern ameni-
ties but old-fashioned style. For dinner, you
have your choice of the on-site upscale restau-
rant and microbrewery (Woodstock Station &
Microbrewery).

Woodstock Inn Station
& Brewery
PUB FOOD $$

(☑ 603-745-3951; www.woodstockinnnh.com;
mains $12-24; ⊙ 11:30am-10pm) On warm days,
the sunny front patio is a nice place to eat,
drink and watch the world go by. Formerly a railroad station, this eatery tries to be
everything to everyone, with more than
150 items on the menu. Pasta, sandwiches
and burgers are the most interesting. The
beer-sodden rear tavern is one of the most
happening places in this neck of the woods.

ℹ Information

Lincoln/Woodstock Chamber of Commerce
(☑ 603-745-6621; www.lincolnwoodstock.com;
126 Main St/NH 112, Lincoln; ⊙ 9am-5pm Mon-
Fri) Offers area information.

White Mountains Visitor Center (☑ 603-745-
8720, National Forest 603-745-3816; www.visit
whitemountains.com; 200 Kancamagus Hwy;
⊙ visitor info 8:30am-5pm, National Forest desk
9am-3pm daily mid-May–Oct, Fri, Sat & Sun only
Nov–mid-May) A life-size stuffed moose (not
real) sets a mood for adventure while brochures
and trail maps provide the details. You can also
buy a White Mountain National Forest Pass
here ($3/5 per day/week), which is required for
extended stops at national forest trailheads.

Franconia Notch State Park

Franconia Notch is the most celebrated mountain pass in New England, a narrow gorge
shaped over the eons by a rushing stream slicing through the craggy granite. I-93, in places
feeling more like a country road than a highway, runs straight through the state park. The
Franconia Notch State Park visitor center
(☑ 603-745-8391; www.nhstateparks.org; I-93, exit
34A; ⊙ 9am-5pm mid-May–Oct), 4 miles north
of North Woodstock, can give you details on
hikes in the park, which range from short nature walks to day-long treks.

Take a walk or a bike ride on the 8.8-mile **bike path** that tracks the Pemigewasset River and links Flume Gorge and Cannon Mountain. Bike rentals available at the tramway (half/full day $25/40).

◉ Sights & Activities

Cannon Mountain Aerial Tramway CABLE CAR (☑ 603-823-8800; www.cannonmt.com; I-93, exit 34B; round-trip adult/child 6-12yr $17/14; ⊙ 9am-5pm late May–mid-Oct; ⊕) This tramway shoots up the side of Cannon Mountain, offering a breathtaking view of Franconia Notch. In 1938 the first passenger aerial tramway in North America was installed on this slope. It was replaced in 1980 by the current, larger cable car, capable of carrying 80 passengers up to the summit in five minutes – a 2022ft, 1-mile ride. Or, visitors can hike up the mountain and take the tramway down.

Flume Gorge HIKING (www.nhstateparks.org; adult/child 6-12yr $16/13; ⊙ 9am-5pm May-Oct) To see this natural wonder, take the 2-mile self-guided nature walk that includes the 800ft boardwalk through the Flume, a natural cleft (12ft to 20ft wide) in the granite bedrock. The granite walls tower 70ft to 90ft above you with moss and plants growing from precarious niches and crevices Signs explain how nature formed this natural phenomenon. A nearby covered bridge is thought to be one of the oldest in the state, perhaps erected as early as the 1820s.

Echo Lake BEACH (☑ 603-823-8800; I-93, exit 34C; adult/child 6-11yr $4/2; ⊙ 10am-5pm mid-Jun–Aug) Despite its proximity to the highway, this little lake at the foot of Cannon Mountain is a pleasant place to pass an afternoon swimming, kayaking or canoeing (rentals $20 per hour) in the crystal-clear waters. And many people do. The small beach gets packed, especially on weekends.

⌊ Sleeping

Lafayette Place Campground CAMPGROUND $ (☑ 877-647-2757; www.reserveamerica.com; campsites $25; ⊙ mid-May–early Oct) This popular campground has 97 wooded tent sites that are in heavy demand in summer. Reservations are accepted for 89 of the sites. For the others, arrive early in the day and hope for the best. Many of the state park's hiking trails start here.

Bretton Woods & Crawford Notch

Before 1944, Bretton Woods was known primarily as a low-key retreat for wealthy visitors who patronized the majestic Mt Washington Hotel. After President Roosevelt chose the hotel for the historic conference that established a new post-WWII economic order, the town's name took on worldwide recognition. The countryside, with Mt Washington looming above it, is as magnificent today as it was back then. The **Twin Mountain-Bretton Woods Chamber of Commerce** (☑ 800-245-8946; www.twinmountain.org; cnr US 302 & US 3; ⊙ 9am-5pm Jul & Aug, 9am-5pm Fri-Sun foliage season, closed rest of yr) information booth details about the area.

The state's largest ski area, **Bretton Woods** (☑ 603-278-3320; www.brettonwoods. com; US 302; Sat, Sun & holidays lift ticket adult/child 13-17/child 6-12 & seniors $85/65/49, Mon-Fri $75/58/43) offers downhill and cross-country skiing, and a zipline in warmer months (May-Sep).

US 302 heads south from Bretton Woods to Crawford Notch (1773ft) through stunning mountain scenery ripe with towering cascades. **Crawford Notch State Park** (☑ 603-271-3556, www.nhstateparks.org; 1464 US Route 302, adult/child 6-11yr $4/2) maintains an extensive system of hiking trails, including short hikes around a pond and to a waterfall, and a longer trek up Mt Washington.

⌊ Sleeping

AMC Highland Center LODGE $$ (☑ information 603-278-4453, reservations 603-466-2727; www.outdoors.org/lodging/whitemountains/highland; NH 302, Bretton Woods; dm incl breakfast & dinner adult/child $106/55, s/d incl breakfast & dinner $153/89) This cozy Appalachian Mountain Club (AMC) lodge is set amid the splendor of Crawford Notch, an ideal base for hiking the many trails criss-crossing the Presidential Range. The grounds are beautiful, rooms are basic but comfortable, meals are hearty and guests are outdoor enthusiasts. Discounts are available for AMC members. The information center, open to the public, has loads of information about regional hiking.

★ **Omni Mt Washington Hotel & Resort** HOTEL $$$ (☑ 603-278-1000; www.omnihotels.com; 310 Mt Washington Hotel Rd, Bretton Woods; r from $339, ste $869; ☀ @ 🛜 ☰) Open since 1902, this grand hotel maintains a sense of fun – note the moose's head overlooking the lobby and the framed images of local wildflowers in many of the guest rooms. It also offers 27 holes of golf, red-clay tennis courts, an equestrian center and a spa. A sunset cocktail on the back porch, with the mountains before you, is perfection. There's a $27.25 daily resort fee.

Mount Washington

From Pinkham Notch (2032ft), on NH 16 about 11 miles north of North Conway, a system of hiking trails provides access to the natural beauties of the **Presidential Range**, including lofty Mt Washington (6288ft), the highest mountain east of the Mississippi and north of the Smoky Mountains.

Hikers need to be prepared: Mt Washington's weather is notoriously severe and can turn on a dime. Dress warmly – not only does the mountain register New England's coldest temperatures (in summer, the average at the summit is 45°F/7°C) but unrelenting winds make it feel colder than the thermometer reading. In fact, Mt Washington holds the record for the USA's strongest wind gust – 231mph!

The **Pinkham Notch Visitor Center** (☑ 603-278-4453; www.outdoors.org; NH 16; ☺ 6:30am-10pm May-Oct, to 9pm Nov-Apr), run by the Appalachian Mountain Club (AMC), is the area's informational nexus for like-minded adventurers and a good place to buy hiking necessities, including topographic trail maps and the handy *AMC White Mountain Guide*.

One of the most popular trails up Mt Washington begins at the Visitor Center and runs 4.2 strenuous miles to the summit, taking four to five hours to reach the top and a bit less on the way down.

If your quads aren't up for a workout, the **Mt Washington Auto Road** (☑ 603-466-3988; www.mountwashingtonautoroad.com; 1 Mt Washington Auto Rd, off NH 16; car & driver $28, extra adult/child 5-12yr $8/6; ☺ 7:30-6pm early Jun-Aug, shorter hr mid-May–early Jun, Sep-mid-Oct), 2.5 miles north of Pinkham Notch Camp, offers easier summit access, weather permitting.

While purists walk, and the out-of-shape drive, the quaintest way to reach the summit is to take the **Mt Washington Cog Railway** (☑ 603-278-5404; www.thecog.com; 3168 Bass Station Rd; adult/child 4-12yr $68/39; ☺ May-Oct). Since 1869, coal-fired steam-powered locomotives have followed a 3.5-mile track up a steep mountainside trestle for a jaw-dropping excursion.

OFF THE BEATEN TRACK

AMC WHITE MOUNTAIN HUTS

The Appalachian Mountain Club manages eight overnight huts along the Appalachian Trail in the Presidential Range. In summer and early fall a small 'croo' at each hut welcomes hikers, prepares meals and shares information about conservation and natural sciences. The hut system here has been in operation for more than 125 years. If you're a hiker but not sure about backpacking, an overnight hut trip is a great way to test the waters. Just pack overnight clothes, toiletries, trail snacks, water, and a headlamp. The croo will take care of the rest. It ain't fancy – hikers sleep in bunks in co-ed dorms with rustic bathrooms – but the views and the community? Awesome. Reservations are key. (www.outdoors.org/lodging/huts).

Dolly Copp Campground (☑ 603-466-2713, reservations 877-444-6777; www.fs.usda.gov; NH 16; tent & RV sites $22; ☺ mid-May–mid-Oct), a USFS campground 6 miles north of the AMC's Pinkham Notch facilities, has 176 simple campsites.

Hanover

The archetypal New England college town, Hanover has a town green that is bordered on all four sides by the handsome brick edifices of Dartmouth College. Virtually the whole town is given over to this Ivy League school; chartered in 1769, Dartmouth is the nation's ninth-oldest college.

Main St, rolling down from the green, is surrounded by perky pubs, shops and cafes that cater to the collegian crowd. The Appalachian Trail runs along Main St right through downtown.

◎ Sights

Dartmouth College   COLLEGE
(☑ 603-646-1110; www.dartmouth.edu) Hanover is all about Dartmouth College, so hit the campus. Join a free student-guided **campus walking tour** (☑ 603-646-2875; https://admissions.dartmouth.edu; 6016 McNutt Hall), or grab a map at the admissions office across from the green in McNutt Hall. Maps are also available online. Don't miss the **Baker-Berry Library**, splashed with the grand *Epic of American*

Civilization, painted by the outspoken Mexican muralist José Clemente Orozco (1883–1949), who taught at Dartmouth in the 1930s.

Hood Museum of Art — MUSEUM

(☑ 603-646-2808; http://hoodmuseum.dartmouth.edu/; E Wheelock St; ⊙10am-5pm Tue, Thu-Sat, to 9pm Wed, noon-5pm Sun) FREE Shortly after the university's founding in 1769 Dartmouth began to acquire artifacts of artistic or historical interest. Since then the collection has expanded to include nearly 65,000 items, which are housed at the Hood Museum of Art. The collection is particularly strong in American pieces, including Native American art. One of the highlights is a set of Assyrian reliefs from the Palace of Ashurnasirpal that date to the 9th century BC. Special exhibits often feature contemporary artists.

🛏 Sleeping & Eating

Storrs Pond Recreation Area — CAMPGROUND $

(☑ 603-643-2134; www.storrspond.com; 59 Oak Hill DR/NH 10; tent/RV sites $32/40; ⊙ Jun–early Oct; 🛜) As well as woodsy sites next to a 15-acre pond, this private campground has tennis courts and two sandy beaches for swimming. 18 RV sites available and 12 tent sites. From I-89 exit 13, take NH 10 north and look for signs.

Hanover Inn — INN $$$

(☑ 603-643-4300, 800-443-7024; www.hanoverinn.com; 2 E Wheelock St, cnr W Wheelock & S Main Sts; r from $249; 🖨🛜🐾) A 2800lb handmade granite table now anchors the lobby at the recently revamped Hanover Inn, the city's loveliest guesthouse. Owned by Dartmouth College, the inn has nicely appointed rooms with custom art work, collegiate-style throws, and elegant wood furnishings. It has a farm-to-table restaurant on site. Pets are $50 per night.

Lou's — DINER $

(☑ 603-643-3321; www.lousrestaurant.net; 30 S Main St; breakfast $8-12, lunch $9-12; ⊙6am-3pm Mon-Fri, 7am-3pm Sat & Sun) A Dartmouth institution since 1947, this is Hanover's oldest establishment, always packed with students meeting for a coffee or perusing their books. From the retro tables or the Formica-topped counter, order typical diner food like eggs, sandwiches and burgers. The bakery items – I'm talking about you ginger molasses cookie – are also highly recommended.

Canoe Club Bistro — CAFE $$

(☑ 603-643-9660; www.canoeclub.us; 27 S Main St; lunch $12-24, dinner $10-23; ⊙11:30am-11:30pm) 🍴 This smart cafe does a fine job with grilled food – not just burgers and steaks, but also a range of farm-to-table fare with global accents including a crispy pork schnitzel and malay curry shrimp. There's also live entertainment nightly, anything from acoustic to jazz to a Monday night magic show.

Drinking & Entertainment

Murphy's on the Green — PUB

(☑ 603-643-4075; wwwmurphysonthegreen.com; 11 S Main St; mains $12-24; ⊙ 4pm-12:30am Mon-Thu, 11-12:30am Fri-Sun) This classic collegiate tavern is where students and faculty meet over pints (it carries over 10 beers on tap, including local microbrews like Long Trail Ale) and satisfying pub fare (mains $12 to $24). Stained-glass windows, church-pew seating and book-lined shelves enhance the cozy atmosphere.

Hopkins Center for the Arts — PERFORMING ARTS

(☑ 603-646-2422; www.hop.dartmouth.edu; 4 E Wheelock St) A long way from the big-city lights of New York and Boston, Dartmouth hosts its own entertainment at this outstanding performing-arts venue. The season brings everything from movies to live performances by international companies.

🛈 Information

Hanover Area Chamber of Commerce

(☑ 603-643-3115; www.hanoverchamber.org; 53 S Main St, Suite 208; ⊙9am-4pm Mon-Fri) For tourist information. It's inside the Nugget Building and also maintains an **information booth** (⊙9:30am-3pm Mon-Wed, to 6pm Thu & Fri, 10am-3pm Sat & Sun) on the village green, staffed daily from late June to early September.

MAINE

Maine is New England's frontier – a land so vast it could swallow the region's five other states with scarcely a gulp. The sea looms large with mile after mile of sandy beaches, craggy sea cliffs and quiet harbors. While time-honored fishing villages and seaside lobster joints are the fame of Maine, inland travel also offers ample reward. Maine's rugged interior is given over to rushing rivers, dense forests and lofty mountains just aching to be explored.

As a traveler in the Pine Tree State, your choices are as spectacularly varied as the landscape. You can opt to sail serenely along the coast on a graceful schooner or rip through white-water rapids on a river raft, spend the night in an old sea captain's home-turned-B&B, or camp among the moose on a backwoods lake.

History

It's estimated that 20,000 Native Americans from tribes known collectively as Wabanaki ('People of the Dawn') inhabited Maine when the first Europeans arrived. The French and English vied to establish colonies in Maine during the 1600s but, deterred by the harsh winters, these settlements failed.

In 1652 Massachusetts annexed the territory of Maine to provide a front line of defense against potential attacks during the French and Indian Wars. And indeed Maine at times did become a battlefield between English colonists in New England and French forces in Canada. In the early 19th century, in an attempt to settle sparsely populated Maine, 100-acre homesteads were offered free to settlers willing to farm the land. In 1820 Maine broke from Massachusetts and entered the Union as a state.

In 1851 Maine became the first state to ban the sale of alcoholic beverages, the start of a temperance movement that eventually took hold throughout the United States. It wasn't until 1934 that Prohibition was finally lifted.

ℹ Information

If you're entering the state on I-95 heading north, stop at the well-stocked visitor information center on the highway.

Maine Bureau of Parks and Land (☑ 800-332-1501; www.campwithme.com) Offers camping in 12 state parks.

Maine Office of Tourism (☑ 888-624-6345; www.visitmaine.com; 59 State House Station, Augusta) These folks maintain information centers on the principal routes into the state – Calais, Fryeburg, Hampden, Houlton, Kittery and Yarmouth. Each facility is open 9am to 5:30pm, with extended hours in summer. Many offer wi-fi.

Southern Maine Coast

Maine's most touristed quarter, this seaside region lures visitors with its sandy beaches, resort towns and outlet shopping. The best place to stop for the latter is the southernmost town of Kittery, which is chockablock with outlet stores.

MAINE FACTS

Nickname Pine Tree State

Population 1.3 million

Area 35,387 sq miles

Capital city Augusta (population 18,700)

Other cities Portland (population 66,300)

Sales tax 5.5%

Birthplace of Poet Henry Wadsworth Longfellow (1807–82)

Home of Horror novelist Stephen King

Politics Split between Democrats and Republicans

Famous for Lobster, moose, blueberries, LL Bean

State drink Maine gave the world Moxie, America's first (1884) and spunkiest soft drink

Driving distances Portland to Acadia National Park 160 miles, Portland to Boston 150 miles

Ogunquit

Aptly named, Ogunquit means 'Beautiful Place by the Sea' in the native Abenaki tongue, and its 3-mile beach has long been a magnet for summer visitors. Ogunquit Beach, a sandy barrier beach, separates the Ogunquit River from the Atlantic Ocean, offering beachgoers the appealing option to swim in cool ocean surf or in the warmer, calmer cove.

As a New England beach destination, Ogunquit is second only to Provincetown for the number of gay travelers who vacation here. Most of the town lies along Main St (US 1), lined with restaurants, shops and motels. For waterfront dining and boating activities head to Perkins Cove at the south end of town.

◉ Sights & Activities

A highlight is walking the scenic 1.5-mile Marginal Way, the coastal footpath that skirts the 'margin' of the sea from Shore Rd, near the center of town, to Perkins Cove. A sublime stretch of family-friendly coastline, Ogunquit Beach, also called Main Beach by locals, begins right in the town center at

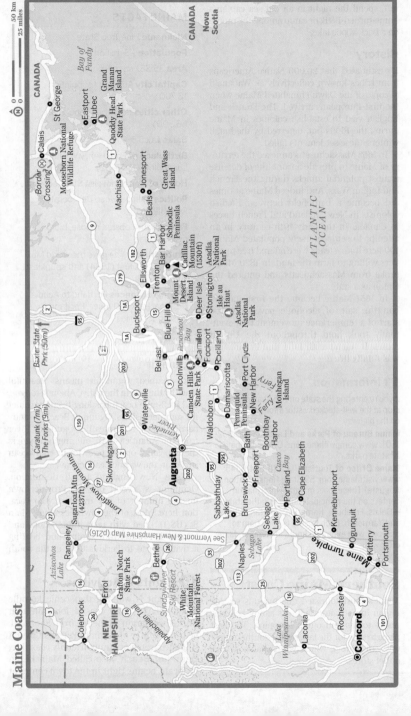

Maine Coast

CANADA
Nova Scotia

Bay of
Fundy

CANADA

Grand
Manan
Island

Eastport
Lubec
Quoddy Head
State Park

St George

Border
Crossing
Calais

Moosehorn National
Wildlife Refuge

Jonesport

Great Wass
Island

Beals

Machias

Schoodic
Peninsula

Bar Harbor

Cadillac
Mountain
(1530ft)

Acadia
National
Park

ATLANTIC
OCEAN

Ellsworth

Trenton

Mount
Desert
Island

Deer Isle

Stonington

Isle au
Haut

Acadia
National
Park

Bucksport

Blue Hill

Penobscot
Bay

Baxter State
Prk (50mi)

Belfast

Camden
Rockport
Rockland

Lincolnville

Camden Hills
State Park

Port Clyde

New Harbor

Monhegan
Island

Waterville

Damariscotta

Waldoboro

Pemaquid
Peninsula

Ferry

Ferry

Skowhegan

Caratunk (7mi);
The Forks (9mi)

Kennebec River

Augusta

Bath

Boothbay
Harbor

Sugarloaf Mtn.
(4237ft)

Longfellow Mountains

Sabbathday
Lake

Brunswick

Freeport

Casco
Bay

Portland

Cape Elizabeth

Rangeley

Aziscohos
Lake

Errol

Colebrook

Bethel

Grafton Notch
State Park

Sunday River
Ski Resort

Appalachian Trail

White
Mountain
National Forest

NEW
HAMPSHIRE

See Vermont & New Hampshire Map (p216)

Naples

Sebago
Lake

Sebago
Lake

Kennebunkport

Ogunquit

Kittery

Portsmouth

Maine Turnpike

Rochester

Laconia

Lake
Winnipesaukee

Concord

50 km
25 miles

the end of Beach St. Want to escape town? Park at **Footbridge Beach** just north at the end of Ocean St.

Finestkind Scenic Cruises   CRUISES
(☎207-646-5227; www.finestkindcruises.com; Perkins Cove; adult/child 4-11yr from $18/9) Offers many popular trips, including a 50-minute lobstering trip, a sunset cocktail cruise and a two-hour cruise aboard the twin-sailed *Cricket*.

🛏 Sleeping

Pinederosa Camping   CAMPGROUND $
(☎207-646-2492; www.pinederosa.com; 128 North Village Rd, Wells; campsites from $35; ☺mid-Jun–early Sep; 🐾🐕) This wholesome, wooded campground has 85 well-tended sites, some of which overlook the Ogunquit River. Amenities include a lovely in-ground heated pool and camp store. Ogunquit Beach is about 3 miles away.

Gazebo Inn   B&B $$
(☎207-646-3733; www.gazeboinnogt.com; 572 Main St; r/ste incl breakfast $239-269/299-599; 🛜🐾) This stately 1847 farmhouse features 14 rooms that feel more like a private boutique hotel. Rustic-chic touches include heated wood floors, stone fireplaces in the bathrooms, and a media room with beamed ceilings and a wall-size TV.

Ogunquit Beach Inn   B&B $$
(☎207-646-1112; www.ogunquitbeachinn.com; 67 School St; r incl breakfast $179-209; @🛜) In a tidy little Craftsman-style bungalow, this gay-and-lesbian-friendly B&B has colorful, homey rooms and chatty owners who know all about the best new bistros and bars in town. The central location makes walking to dinner a breeze.

🍴 Eating

You'll find Ogunquit's restaurants on the south side of town at Perkins Cove and in the town center along Main St.

Bread & Roses   BAKERY $
(www.breadandrosesbakery.com; 246 Main St; snacks $3-10; ☺7am-9pm Sun-Thu, to 11pm Sat & Sun Jun-Aug, shorter hours rest of the year; 🧒) 🌿 Get your coffee and blueberry-scone fix at this teeny slip of a bakery, in the heart of downtown Ogunquit. The cafe fare, like veggie burritos and organic egg-salad sandwiches, is good for a quick lunch. No seating.

★Lobster Shack   SEAFOOD $$
(www.lobster-shack.com; 110 Perkins Cove Rd; mains $5-29; ☺11am-8pm) If it's available, the homemade chowder and lobster roll special ($19) is the way to go. Lobster Shack is a great choice if you're craving good seafood and aren't particular about the view. This reliable joint serves lobster in all its various incarnations.

Barnacle Billy's   SEAFOOD $$$
(☎207-646-5575; www.barnbilly.com; 183 Shore Rd; mains $3-21; ☺11am-9pm Apr-Oct) This big, noisy barn of a restaurant overlooking Perkins Cove is a longtime favorite for casual seafood – steamers, crab rolls, clam chowder and, of course, whole lobsters.

☆ Entertainment

Ogunquit Playhouse   THEATER
(☎207-646-5511; www.ogunquitplayhouse.org; 10 Main St; 🎭) First opened in 1933, presents both showy Broadway musicals and children's theater each summer.

ℹ Information

Ogunquit Chamber of Commerce (☎207-646-2939; www.ogunquit.org; 36 Main St; ☺9am-5pm Mon-Sat, 11am-4pm Sun) Located on US 1, near the Ogunquit Playhouse and just south of the town's center.

Kennebunkport

On the Kennebunk River, Kennebunkport fills with tourists in summer who come to stroll the streets, admire the century-old mansions and get their fill of sea views. Be sure to take a drive along **Ocean Ave**, which runs along the east side of the Kennebunk River and then follows a scenic stretch of the Atlantic that holds some of Kennebunkport's finest estates, including the summer home of former president George Bush Snr. To view the Bush compound, drive almost 2 miles from US 9 downtown then look for a small pullover and marker.

Three public beaches extend along the west side of the Kennebunk River and are known collectively as **Kennebunk Beach**. The center of town spreads out from Dock Sq, which is along ME 9 (Western Ave) at the east side of the Kennebunk River bridge.

🛌 Sleeping

Franciscan Guest House   GUESTHOUSE **$$**
(☑207-967-4865; www.franciscanguesthouse.com;
26 Beach Ave; r/ste $119-209/200-259; ❋ 🛜 ❋)
You can almost smell the blackboard chalk
inside this high school–turned-guesthouse,
on the peaceful grounds of the St Anthony
Monastery. Guest rooms, once classrooms,
are basic and unstylish – acoustic tile, faux-
wood paneling, motel beds. If you don't
mind getting your own sheets out of the
supply closet (there's no daily maid service),
staying here's a great value and a unique
experience.

Kennebunkport Inn   INN **$$$**
(☑207-967-2621; www.kennebunkportinn.com; 1
Dock Sq; r from $199; ❋ @ 🛜) Crisp blues and
whites evoke a breezy, nautical mood at this
finger-popping inn on Dock Square, Get
comfortable in the stylish rooms, beside the
sundeck firepit or at the in-house bar and restaurant. Complimentary bikes are available
for your riding pleasure. Ocean Ave – and its
scenic estates – are short ride away.

🍴 Eating

Clam Shack   SEAFOOD **$$**
(☑207-967-3321; www.theclamshack.net; 2 Western
Ave; mains $4 30; ⊘11am to close May mid Oct)
Standing in line at this teeny gray hut, perched
on stilts above the river, is a time-honored
Kennebunkport summer tradition. Order a
box of succulent fried whole-belly clams or a
one-pound lobster roll, which is served with
your choice of mayo or melted butter. Out-
door seating only. In June, you might catch
former first lady Barbara Bush here celebrat-
ing her birthday. Cash only.

Closing time is based on the crowd, any-
time between 6 and 9:30pm.

★ Bandaloop   BISTRO **$$**
(☑207-967-4994; www.bandaloop.biz; 2 Ocean
Ave; small plates $8-12, mains $18-31; ⊘5-9:30pm;
🍴) 🌱 The Casco Bay garlic mussels? Hands
down the tastiest bowl of mussels we've ever
had. We recommend washing them down
with a Peak's organic ale. And the rest of the
menu? Local, organic and deliciously innovative, running the gamut from a rosemary
grilled sirloin to Vermont cheddar mac-and-
cheese to a massaged kale salad with hemp
seeds, beets and pecans.

Portland

The 18th-century poet Henry Wadsworth
Longfellow referred to his childhood city as
the 'jewel by the sea,' and, thanks to a hefty
revitalization effort, Portland once again
sparkles. Its lively waterfront, burgeoning
gallery scene and manageable size add up
to great exploring. Foodies, rev up your taste
buds: cutting-edge cafes and chef-driven restaurants have turned Portland into the hottest dining scene north of Boston.

Portland sits on a hilly peninsula surrounded on three sides by water: Back Cove,
Casco Bay and the Fore River. It's easy to
find your way around. Commercial St (US
1A) runs along the waterfront through the
Old Port, while the parallel Congress St is
the main thoroughfare through downtown.

◉ Sights

Old Port   NEIGHBORHOOD
Handsome 19th-century brick buildings line
the streets of the Old Port, with Portland's
most enticing shops, pubs and restaurants
located within this five-square-block district.
By night, flickering gas lanterns add to the atmosphere. What to do here? Eat some wicked
fresh seafood, down a local microbrew, buy
a nautical-themed t-shirt from an up-and-
coming designer, peruse the many tiny local
art galleries. Don't forget to wander the au-
thentically stinky wharfs, ducking into a fishmongers to order some lobsters.

Portland Museum of Art   MUSEUM
(☑207-775-6148; www.portlandmuseum.org; 7 Congress Sq; adult/child $12/6, 5-9pm Fri free; ⊘10am-
5pm Sat-Thu, to 9pm Fri, closed Mon mid-Oct–May)
Founded in 1882, this well-respected museum
houses an outstanding collection of American artists. Maine artists, including Winslow
Homer, Edward Hopper, Louise Nevelson and
Andrew Wyeth, are well represented. You'll
also find a few works by European masters,
including Degas, Picasso and Renoir. The majority of works are found in the postmodern
Charles Shipman Payson building, designed
by the firm of famed architect IM Pei.

Fort Williams Park   LIGHTHOUSE
(⊙sunrise-sunset) 🌱 **FREE** Four miles southeast of Portland on Cape Elizabeth, 90-acre
Fort Williams Park is worth visiting simply
for the panoramas and picnic possibilities.
Stroll around the ruins of the fort, a late-19th-
century artillery base, checking out the WWII
bunkers and gun emplacements (a German

U-boat was spotted in Casco Bay in 1942) that still dot the rolling lawns. Strange as it may seem, the fort actively guarded the entrance to Casco Bay until 1964.

Adjacent to the fort stands the **Portland Head Light**, the oldest of Maine's 52 functioning lighthouses. It was commissioned by George Washington in 1791 and staffed until 1989, when machines took over. The keeper's house has been passed into service as the **Museum at Portland Head Light** (☏ 207-799-2661; www.portlandheadlight.com; 1000 Shore Rd; lighthouse museum adult/child 6-18yr $2/1; ⊙ 10am-4pm Jun-Oct), which traces the maritime and military history of the region.

Longfellow House　　　　HISTORIC BUILDING
(☏ 207-879-0427; www.mainehistory.org; 489 Congress St; guided tour adult/child 7-17yr $15/3; ⊙ 10am-5pm Mon-Sat, noon-5pm Sun May-Oct, closed Sun & Mon Nov-Apr) Visitors have been checking out dusty artifacts in the home of revered American poet Henry Wadsworth Longfellow for more than 110 years. A thought that can creep you out if you think about it too much while squinting at the framed needlepoint displays – just like the thousands who have squinted before you. Most now dead. But whatever. Longfellow grew up in this Federal-style house, built in 1788 by his Revolutionary War hero grandfather. The house has been impeccably restored to look like it did in the 1800s, complete with original furniture and artifacts. Tours last one hour.

🏃 Activities

For a whole different angle on Portland and Casco Bay, hop one of the boats offering narrated scenic cruises out of Portland Harbor.

Casco Bay Lines　　　　CRUISE
(☏ 207-774-7871; www.cascobaylines.com; 56 Commercial St; adult $13-24, child $7-11) This outfit cruises the Casco Bay islands delivering mail, freight and visitors looking to bike or explore. It also offers cruises to Bailey Island (adult/child 5-9yr $26/12).

Maine Island Kayak Company　　　KAYAKING
(☏ 207-766-2373; www.maineislandkayak.com; 70 Luther St, Peak Island; tour $65; ⊙ May-Nov) On Peak Island, a 15-minute cruise from downtown on the Casco Bay Lines, this well-run outfitter offers fun day and overnight trips exploring the islands of Casco Bay.

Maine Brew Bus　　　　TOUR
(☏ 207-200-9111; www.themainebrewbus.com; tour $50-75; ⊙ tour times vary) Hop aboard the green bus for tours and tastings at some of Portland's most beloved breweries and brewpubs, from Allagash to Sebago. Lunch at a brewpub is included on the Casco Fiasco tour.

Portland Schooner Company　　　CRUISE
(☏ 207-766-2500; www.portlandschooner.com; 56 Commercial St; adult/child under 13yr $42/21; ⊙ May-Oct) Offers tours aboard an elegant, early-20th-century schooner. In addition to two-hour sails, you can book overnight tours ($250 per person, including dinner and breakfast).

🛏 Sleeping

Portland has a healthy selection of midrange and upscale B&Bs, though very little at the budget end. The most idyllic accommodations are in the old town houses and grand Victorians in the West End.

Inn at St John　　　　INN $$
(☏ 207-773-6481; www.innatstjohn.com; 939 Congress St; r incl breakfast $125-275; P ⊛) On the western fringe of downtown, this turn-of-the-century hotel has a stuck-in-time feel, from the old-fashioned pigeonhole mailboxes behind the lobby desk to the narrow, sweetly floral rooms. Ask for a room away from noisy Congress St. The value rooms come with a private hall bath or shared hall bath. Book early for big weekends.

Morrill Mansion　　　　B&B $$
(☏ 207-774-6900; www.morrillmansion.com; 249 Vaughan St; r incl breakfast $169-239; ⊛) Charles Morrill, the original owner of this 19th-century West End town house, made his fortune by founding B&M baked beans, still a staple of Maine pantries. His home has been transformed into a handsome B&B, with eight guest rooms furnished in a trim, classic style. Think hardwood floors, lots of tasteful khaki and taupe shades.

Some rooms are a bit cramped; if you need lots of space, try the two-room Morrill Suite.

Portland Harbor Hotel　　　HOTEL $$$
(☏ 207-775-9090; www.portlandharborhotel.com; 468 Fore St; r from $339; P ⊛ ⊛) This independent hotel has a classically coiffed lobby, where guests relax on upholstered leather chairs surrounding the glowing fireplace. The rooms carry on the classicism, with sunny gold walls and pert blue toile bedspreads. The windows face Casco Bay, the interior garden or the street; garden rooms are quieter. Parking is $18 (valet only). Pets are $25 per night.

✖ Eating

Two Fat Cats Bakery BAKERY $
(☑207-347-5144; www.twofatcatsbakery.com; 47 India St; treats $3-7; ☺8am-6pm Mon-Fri, to 5pm Sat, to 4pm Sun, closed Mon Jan & Feb) Tiny bakery serving pastries, pies, melt-in-your-mouth chocolate-chip cookies and fabulous Whoopie Pies.

DuckFat SANDWICHES $
(☑207-774-8080; www.duckfat.com; 43 Middle St; small fries $5, sandwiches $10-14; ☺11am-10pm) DuckFat has the best fries we've tasted in our many decades of fry-eating. No lie. Fried in – yes – duck fat, they're shatteringly crisp, with melt-in-your-mouth fluffy centers. Dipping sauces, like truffle ketchup, are good, but unnecessary. Panini are also excellent. But again, it's about the fries. Decor is 'hipster fast-food joint,' with a blackboard menu and a handful of bistro tables.

★ Green Elephant VEGETARIAN $$
(☑207-347-3111; www.greenelephantmaine.com; 608 Congress St; mains $10-15; ☺11:30am-2:30pm, 5-9:30pm Mon-Sat, to 9pm Sun; ☑) They'll spice it as hot as you like it at this Zen-chic, Thai-inspired cafe, which serves brilliant vegetarian fare in an airy and spare nook downtown. Start with the crispy spinach wontons, then move on to one of the exotic soy creations like garlic and ginger tofu or a flavorful curry like the panang coconut curry with vegetables.

Susan's Fish & Chips SEAFOOD $$
(☑207-878-3240; www.susansfishnchips.com; 1135 Forest Ave/US 302; mains $9-22; ☺11am-8pm) Pop in for chowder and fish and chips at this no-fuss but welcoming eatery on US 302, where the tartar sauce comes in mason jars. Located in a former garage.

J's Oyster SEAFOOD $$
(☑207-772-4828; www.jsoyster.com; 5 Portland Pier; sandwiches $5-18, mains $25-31; ☺11:30am-11pm) Maybe not the friendliest place on the planet, but this well-loved dive has the cheapest raw oysters in town. Eat 'em on the deck overlooking the pier. The oyster-averse have plenty of sandwiches and seafood mains to choose from.

★ Fore Street NEW AMERICAN $$$
(☑207-775-2717; www.forestreet.biz; 288 Fore St; small plates $13-22, mains $28-40; ☺5:30-10pm Sun-Thu, to 10:30 Fri & Sat) Roasting is a high art at Fore Street, one of Maine's most lauded restaurants. Chickens turn on spits in the open kitchen as chefs slide iron kettles of mussels into the wood-burning oven. Local, seasonal eating is taken very seriously, and the menu changes daily to offer what's freshest. The large, noisy dining room nods towards its warehouse past with exposed brick and pine paneling.

Offerings may include a fresh pea salad, periwinkles (a local shellfish) in herbed cream, and roast bluefish with pancetta. The chilled and smoked seafood platter, offered daily, is a palate pleaser. Reservations needed, but you may be able to snag a bar seat between 5:30 and 6pm.

♟ Drinking & Entertainment

Gritty McDuff's Brew Pub BREWPUB
(www.grittys.com; 396 Fore St; ☺11am-1am) Gritty is an apt description for this party-happy Old Port pub. You'll find a generally raucous crowd drinking excellent beers – Gritty brews its own award-winning ales downstairs.

Port City Music Hall CONCERT HALL
(☑207-956-6000; www.portcitymusichall.com; 504 Congress St) This three-story performance space hosts big-name and smaller-name bands.

🛍 Shopping

For boutiques, galleries and craft shops, head downtown to Exchange and Fore Sts in Old Port.

Portland Farmers Market FARMERS MARKET
(http://portlandmainefarmersmarket.org; ☺7am-noon Sat, to 1pm Mon & Wed May-Nov) Vendors hawk everything from Maine blueberries to homemade pickles on Saturdays in summer and fall in Deering Oaks Park downtown (Park Ave at Forest Ave). On Monday and Wednesday the market is in Monument Sq on Congress St. Saturdays only in winter at 200 Anderson St.

Harbor Fish Market FISHMONGER
(☑207-775-0251; www.harborfish.com; 9 Custom House Wharf; ☺8:30am-5:30pm Mon-Sat, 9am-noon Sun) On Custom House Wharf, this iconic fishmonger packs lobsters and seafood for roadtrips, island trips, flights, and ships to anywhere in the US.

Maine Potters Market POTTERY
(www.mainepottersmarket.com; 376 Fore St; ☺10am-9pm daily) A cooperatively owned gallery featuring the work of a dozen or so different Maine ceramists.

ⓘ Information

Greater Portland Convention & Visitors Bureau (www.visitportland.com; Ocean Gateway Bldg, 14 Ocean Gateway Pier; ⊙9am-5pm Mon-Fri, to 4pm Sat & Sun Jun-Oct, hours vary rest of year) Stop by for brochures and maps.

ⓘ Getting There & Around

Portland International Jetport (PWM; ☑20 7-874-8877; www.portlandjetport.org) has non-stop flights to cities in the eastern US.

Greyhound (www.greyhound.com; 950 Congress St) buses and **Amtrak** (☑800-872-7245; www.amtrak.com; 100 Thompson's Point Rd) trains connect Portland and Boston; both take about 2½ hours and charge $14 to $34 one way.

The local bus **Metro** (www.gpmetrobus.com; fares $1.50), which runs throughout the city, has its main terminus at Monument Sq, the intersection of Elm and Congress Sts.

Central Maine Coast

Midcoast Maine is where the mountains meet the sea. You'll find craggy peninsulas jutting deep into the Atlantic, alluring seaside villages and endless opportunities for hiking, sailing and kayaking.

Freeport & Around

The fame and fortune of Freeport, 16 miles northeast of Portland, began a century ago when Leon Leonwood Bean opened a shop to sell equipment to hunters and fishers heading north into the Maine wilderness. Bean's good value earned him loyal customers, and over the years the LL Bean Store has expanded.

⊙ Sights

LL Bean Flagship Store OUTDOOR EQUIPMENT (www.llbean.com; 95 Main St; ⊙24hr) A 10ft-tall model of the Bean Boot marks the entrance to the LL Bean store, which has expanded to add sportswear to its outdoor gear. Although a hundred other stores have joined the pack in Freeport, the wildly popular LL Bean is still the epicenter of town and one of the most popular tourist attractions in Maine. It's part store, part outdoor-themed amusement park, with an archery range, an indoor trout pond and a coffee shop.

DeLorme Mapping Company BUILDING (☑207-846-7100; www.delorme.com; 2 DeLorme Dr; ⊙9:30am-6pm Mon-Sat, to 5pm Sun) Don't miss a visit to this office, with its giant 5300-sq-ft rotating globe, Eartha, in nearby Yarmouth at

WHOOPIE!

Looking like steroid-pumped Oreos, these marshmallow-cream-filled chocolate snack cakes are a staple of bakeries and seafood-shack dessert menus across the state. Popular both in Maine and in Pennsylvania's Amish country, whoopie pies are said to be so named because Amish farmers would shout 'whoopie!' when they discovered one in their lunch pail. Don't leave the state without trying at least one. For our money, Portland's **Two Fat Cats Bakery** has the best.

exit 17 off I-95. Maker of the essential *Maine Atlas and Gazetteer,* DeLorme also creates maps and software for every destination in the United States. You'll find regional hiking guides and trail maps here, too.

✖ Eating & Drinking

★**Harraseeket Lunch & Lobster Co** SEAFOOD $$ (☑207-865-4888; www.harraseeketlunchand lobster.com; 36 Main St, South Freeport; mains $5-29; ⊙11am-7:45pm, to 8:45pm Jul & Aug; 🚸) Head down to the marina to feast on lobster at this iconic red-painted seafood shack. If it's nice out, grab a picnic table – or just do like the locals and sit on the roof of your car. Come early to beat the crowds. Finish with a slice of blueberry pie. BYOB. Cash or check only.

Gritty McDuff's Brew Pub PUB FOOD $$ (www.grittys.com; 187 Lower Main St; mains $10-14) Kids getting cranky, and momma needs a beer? Let the young ones run wild on the back lawn while you sip an IPA and savor a cheeseburger on the deck. This offshoot of the popular Gritty's in Portland is 2 miles south of LL Bean.

Bath

Bath has been renowned for shipbuilding since Colonial times and that remains the raison d'être for the town today. **Bath Iron Works**, one of the largest shipyards in the USA, builds steel frigates and other ships for the US Navy. The substantial **Maine Maritime Museum** (☑207-443-1316; www.maine-maritimemuseum.org; 243 Washington St; adult/child under 17yr $15/10; ⊙9:30am-5pm), south of the ironworks on the Kennebec River,

PEMAQUID PENINSULA

Adorning the southernmost tip of the Pemaquid Peninsula, **Pemaquid Point** is one of the most wildly beautiful places in Maine, with its tortured igneous rock formations pounded by treacherous seas. Perched atop the rocks in the 7-acre **Lighthouse Park** (☎207-677-2494; www.bristolparks.org; Pemaquid Point; adult/child under 12yr $2/free; ☺sunrise-sunset daily, facilities early May-Oct, lighthouse 10:30am-5pm) is the 11,000 candle power Pemaquid Light, built in 1827. A climb to the top will reward you with a fine coastal view. A star of the 61 surviving lighthouses along the Maine coast, you may well be carrying an image of Pemaquid Light in your pocket without knowing it – it's the beauty featured on the back of the Maine state quarter. The keeper's house now serves as the **Fishermen's Museum** (☺9am-5pm early-May–Oct) displaying period photos, old fishing gear and lighthouse paraphernalia. Admission is included in the park fee. Pemaquid Peninsula is 15 miles south of US 1 via ME 130.

showcases the town's centuries-old maritime history, which included construction of the six-mast schooner *Wyoming*, the largest wooden vessel ever built in the USA.

Boothbay Harbor

On a fjord-like harbor, this picturesque fishing village with narrow, winding streets is thick with tourists in the summer. Other than eating lobster, the main activity here is hopping on boats. **Balmy Days Cruises** (☎207-633-2284; www.balmydaycruises.com; Pier 8; harbor tour adult/child 3--11yr $18/9 (Mar-Nov), day-trip cruise to Monhegan adult/child 3-11yr $39/19 (Jun-early Oct), sailing tour adult/child under 12yr $26/18 (mid-Jun-mid-Sep)) runs one-hour harbor tour cruises, day trips to Monhegan Island and 1.5 hour sailing trips around the scenic islands near Boothbay. The **Boothbay Harbor Region Chamber of Commerce** (☎207-633-2353; www.boothbayharbor.com; 192 Townsend Ave; ☺8am-5pm Mon-Fri, 10am-4pm Sat & Sun Jun-mid-Oct, closed wknds mid-Oct-May) provides visitor information.

Sleeping & Eating

Topside Inn   B&B $$
(☎207-633-5404; www.topsideinn.com; 60 McKown St; r incl breakfast $199-360; ☎) Under new ownership, this grand gray mansion atop McKown Hill has Boothbay's best harbor views. Rooms are elegantly turned out in crisp nautical prints and beachy shades of sage, sea grass and khaki. Main-house rooms have more historic charm, but rooms in the two adjacent modern guesthouses are sunny and lovely, too. Enjoy the sunset from an Adirondack chair on the inn's sloping, manicured lawn.

Lobster Dock   SEAFOOD $$
(www.thelobsterdock.com; 49 Atlantic Ave; mains $6-25; ☺11:30am-8:30pm) Of all the lobster joints in Boothbay Harbor, this sprawling wooden waterfront shack is one of the best. It's also a little different. You don't order at the counter but a server stops by your table. Take your pick of traditional fried seafood platters, sandwiches and steamers, plus a couple of seafood pastas, but whole butter-dripping lobster is definitely the main event.

Rockland, Camden & Around

The pretty towns of Rockland, Rockport and Camden hug the coast. Rockland is a thriving commercial port with an inviting downtown lined with eateries and independently owned shops. With rolling hills as a backdrop and a harbor full of sailboats, Camden is a gem. Both towns are home to Maine's famed fleet of windjammers, which attract nautical-minded souls. Rockport sits prettily between the two towns.

Lobster fanatics (and who isn't!) won't want to miss the **Maine Lobster Festival** (www.mainelobsterfestival.com; ☺early Aug), New England's ultimate homage to the crusty crustacean, held in Rockland.

The **Camden-Rockport-Lincolnville Chamber of Commerce** (☎207-236-4404; www.camdenme.org; 2 Public Landing; ☺9am-5pm), near the harbor, provides visitor information on the region.

Sights & Activities

★**Rockland Breakwater Lighthouse**   LIGHTHOUSE
(www.rocklandharborlights.org) Stroll down the 4300ft granite breakwater (nearly one mile long) to gape at the sweet white light sitting atop the brick-and white house with a

sweeping view of town. The breakwater took 18 years to build.

Camden Hills State Park — PARK

(☑ 207-236-3109; wwwmmaine.gov; 280 Belfast Rd/US 1; adult/child 3-11yr $4.50/1; ☺ 9am-sunset) A favorite hike in this densely forest park is the 45-minute (half mile) climb up Mt Battie, which offers exquisite views of Penobscot Bay. Simple trail maps are available at the park entrance, just over 1.5 miles northeast of Camden center on US 1. The picnic area has short trails down to the shore. Feeling lazy? You can also drive to the summit.

Maine Media Workshops — ART CLASSES

(www.mainemedia.edu; 70 Camden St, Rockport) One of the world's leading instructional centers in photography, film and digital media, this institute offers more than 450 beginner- through professional-level workshops throughout the year. Intensive one-week workshops are taught by leaders in their fields. Changing exhibitions of student and faculty work are displayed in a gallery (18 Central St) in Rockport.

🛏 Sleeping & Eating

Island View Inn — MOTEL $$

(☑ 207-596-0040; www.islandviewinnmaine.com; 908 Commercial St, Rockport; r/ste $119/189-259; ✳🐾🛜🏊) Each room comes with a pair of binoculars at this inviting motel, where scanning Penobscot Bay for wildlife from your balcony is a nice way to start the day. Rooms are bright, crisp and spacious with modern but comfy decor. On Route 1 between Rockland and Rockport. A fantastic low-price option.

Boynton-McKay Food Co — BREAKFAST; COFFEE $

(☑ 207-236-2465; www.boynton-mckay.com; mains $6.25-10; ☺ 7am-3pm Tue-Sat, 8am-3pm Sun) Watch the world go by while you sip coffee and dig into a skillet breakfast of eggs, chorizo and Monterey Jack cheese. In a former apothecary shop in downtown Camden, this snug but sunny cafe and coffee shop fills quickly, so get here early. Fresh lunch fare includes salads and sandwiches.

Clan MacLaren — SANDWICHES $

(☑ 207-593-7778; www.clanmaclaren.net; 395 Main St, Rockland; mains $7-10; ☺ 10am-4:30pm Mon-Sat) Fresh, simple and oh-so-tasty subs and paninis are the draw at Clan MacClaren, a welcoming lunch spot in downtown Rockland. Per the website, the owners descend from the Scottish MacLaren clan. Ordering the Erin MacLaren (a not-so-Scottish combo of salami and provolone) will get your brogue rolling.

Cappy's — SEAFOOD $$

(☑ 207-236-2254; www.cappyschowder.com; 1 Main St, Camden; mains $10-26; ☺ 11am-11pm; 🛜) Renovated in 2015, this friendly longtime favorite is popular with locals and tourists alike. Known best for its bar and its convivial atmosphere, it does serve an excellent bowl of chowder and other casual New England fare.

Acadia National Park

The only national park in New England, Acadia (www.nps.gov/acad) encompasses an unspoiled wilderness of undulating coastal mountains, towering sea cliffs, surf-pounded beaches and quiet ponds. The dramatic landscape offers a plethora of activities for both leisurely hikers and adrenaline junkies.

The park, which celebrates its centennial in 2016 (www.acadiacentennial2016.org), was established on land that John D Rockefeller donated to the national parks system to save from encroaching lumber interests. Today you can hike and bike along the same carriage roads that Rockefeller once rode his horse and buggy on. The park covers over 62 sq miles, including most of mountainous Mt Desert Island and tracts of land on the Schoodic Peninsula and Isle au Haut, and holds a wide diversity of wildlife including moose, puffins and bald eagles.

👁 Sights & Activities

👁 Park Loop Road

Unfurling for 27 gorgeous miles, Park Loop Rd, is the main sightseeing jaunt through the park (mid-April to November). If you're up for a frigid swim or just want to stroll Acadia's longest beach, stop at Sand Beach. About a mile beyond Sand Beach you'll come to Thunder Hole, where wild Atlantic waves crash into a deep, narrow chasm with such force that it creates a thundering boom, loudest during incoming tides. Look to the south to see Otter Cliffs, a favorite rock-climbing spot that rises vertically from the sea. At Jordan Pond choose from a 1-mile nature trail loop around the south side of the pond or a 3.2-mile trail that skirts the entire pond perimeter. After you've worked up an appetite, reward yourself with a relaxing afternoon tea on the lawn of Jordan Pond House (p242).

Near the end of Park Loop Rd a side road leads up to Cadillac Mountain.

Cadillac Mountain

The majestic centerpiece of Acadia National Park is Cadillac Mountain (1530ft), the highest coastal peak in the eastern US, reached by a 3.5-mile spur road off Park Loop Rd. Four trails lead to the summit from four directions should you prefer hiking boots to rubber tires. The panoramic 360-degree view of ocean, islands and mountains is a winner any time of the day, but it's truly magical at dawn when hardy souls flock to the top to watch the sun rise over Frenchman Bay.

Other Activities

Some 125 miles of hiking trails crisscross Acadia National Park, from easy half-mile nature walks and level rambles to mountain treks up steep and rocky terrain. A standout is the 3-mile round-trip Ocean Trail, which runs between Sand Beach and Otter Cliffs and takes in the most interesting coastal scenery in the park. Look for a trail summary on the park website. The helpful *A Walk in the Park: Acadia's Hiking Guide* by Tom St. Germain ($11) is for sale in the Hull Visitor Center.

The park's 45 miles of carriage roads are the prime attraction for cycling. You can rent quality mountain bikes, replaced new at the start of each season, at Acadia Bike (207-288-9605; www.acadiabike.com; 48 Cottage St; per day $23; 8am-6pm Jul & Aug, 9am-6pm May & Jun, Sep & Oct).

Rock climbing on the park's sea cliffs and mountains is breathtaking. Gear up with Acadia Mountain Guides (207-288-8186; www.acadiamountainguides.com; 228 Main St, Bar Harbor; half-day outing $75-140; May-Oct); rates include a guide, instruction and equipment.

Scores of ranger-led programs, including nature walks, birding talks and kids' field trips, are available in the park. Check out the stars fom the sand during the Stars over Sand Beach program. Check the schedule online or at the Hulls Cove Visitor Center.

Sleeping & Eating

The park has two campgrounds, both wooded and with running water, showers and barbecue pits. A third is set to open in the fall of 2015.

There are scores of restaurants, inns and hotels in Bar Harbor, just a mile beyond the park.

Acadia National Park Campgrounds CAMPGROUND $
(877-444-6777; www.nps.gov/acad; campsites $22-30) Four miles south of Southwest Harbor, Seawall has both by-reservation and walk-up sites. Five miles south of Bar Harbor on ME 3, year-round Blackwoods fills quickly in summer, when reservations are strangely recommended. Both sites have restrooms and pay showers. Both are also densely wooded but only a few minutes' walk to the ocean. A third campground with 92 campsites, Schoodic Woods, was scheduled to open in September 2015 on the Schoodic Peninsula.

Jordan Pond House AMERICAN $$
(207-276-3316; www.thejordanpondhouse.com; afternoon tea $10.50, mains $9-24; 11am-8pm mid-May–Oct) Afternoon tea at this lodge-like teahouse has been an Acadia tradition since the late 1800s. Steaming pots of Earl Grey come with hot popovers (hollow rolls made with egg batter) and strawberry jam. Eat outside on the broad lawn overlooking the lake. The park's only restaurant, Jordan Pond also does fancy but often mediocre lunches and dinners.

Information

Granite mountains and coastal vistas greet you upon entering Acadia National Park. The park is open year-round, though Park Loop Rd and most facilities are closed in winter. An admission fee is charged from May 1 to October 31. The fee, which is valid for seven consecutive days, is $25 per vehicle, $20 per motorcycle and $12 on bike or foot between mid-June and early October (no fee rest of the year).

Start your exploration at Hulls Cove Visitor Center (207-288-3338; ME 3; 7-day park admission per vehicle $25, motorcycle $20, walkers & cyclists $12; 8:30am-4:30pm mid-Apr–Jun, Sep & Oct, 8am-6pm Jul & Aug), from where the 27-mile Park Loop Rd circumnavigates the eastern portion of the park.

Getting There & Around

The convenient Island Explorer (www.explore acadia.com; late Jun-early Oct) runs eight shuttle bus routes throughout Acadia National Park and to adjacent Bar Harbor, linking trailheads, campgrounds and accommodations.

Bar Harbor

Set on the doorstep of Acadia National Park, this alluring coastal town once rivaled Newport, RI as a trendy summer destination for

HOIST THE SAILS

Feel the wind in your hair and history at your side aboard the gracious, multimasted sailing ships known as windjammers. The sailing ships, both historic and replicas, gather in the harbors at Camden and neighboring Rockland to take passengers out on day trips and overnight sails.

Day sails cruise for two hours in Penobscot Bay from June to October for around $40 and you can usually book your place on the day. On the Camden waterfront, look for the 86ft wooden tall ship **Appledore** (☑ 207-236-8353; www.appledore2.com) and the two-masted schooner **Olad** (☑ 207-236-2323; www.maineschooners.com).

Other schooners make two- to six-day cruises, offer memorable wildlife viewing (seals, whales and puffins) and typically include stops at Acadia National Park, small coastal towns and offshore islands for a lobster picnic.

You can get full details on several glorious options in one fell swoop through the **Maine Windjammer Association** (☑ 800-807-9463; www.sailmainecoast.com), which represents eight traditional tall ships, several of which have been designated National Historic Landmarks. Among them is the granddaddy of the schooner trade, the *Lewis R French*, America's oldest (1871) windjammer. Rates range from $400 for a two-day cruise to $1100 for a six-day voyage and are a bargain when you consider they include meals and accommodations. Reservations for the overnight sails are a must. Prices are highest in midsummer.

wealthy Americans. Today, many of the old mansions have been turned into inviting inns and the town has become a magnet for outdoor enthusiasts. The **Bar Harbor Chamber of Commerce** (☑ 207-288-5103; www. barharborinfo.com; 1201 Bar Harbor Rd/ME 3, Trenton; ☺ 9am-5pm Mon-Fri May-Aug, hours vary fall, closed Nov-Apr) has a convenient welcome center just before the bridge onto Mt Desert Island.

🏃 Activities

Bar Harbor Whale Watch Co　　　CRUISE
(☑ 207-288-2386;　　　　www.barharborwhales.com; 1 West St; adult $29-63, child 6-14 yr $18-35, child under 6yr free-$9; ☺ mid-May–Oct) Operates four-hour whale-watching and puffin-watching cruises, among other options.

Downeast Windjammer Cruises　　　CRUISE
(☑ 207-288-4585; www.downeastwindjammer.com; 19 Cottage St; adult/child 6-11yr/2-5yr $38/30/5) Offers two-hour cruises on the majestic 151ft, four-masted schooner *Margaret Todd*.

Acadian Nature Cruises　　　CRUISE
(☑ 207-801-2300; www.acadiannaturecruises.com; 119 Eden St; adult/child 6-14yr/under 6yr $30/18/5; ☺ mid-May–Oct) See whales, porpoises, bald eagles, seals and more on these narrated two-hour nature cruises.

🛏 Sleeping

There's no shortage of sleeping options in Bar Harbor in summer, ranging from period B&Bs to the usual chain hotels. Note that many inns and B&B's close from late fall to early spring.

Holland Inn　　　B&B $$
(☑ 207-288-4804; www.hollandinn.com; 35 Holland Ave; r incl breakfast $145-185; ☺ late Apr-Oct; ❋ 🖵) In a quiet residential neighborhood within walking distance of downtown, this restored 1895 house with two adjacent buildings has 13 inviting, unfrilly rooms. Ambience is low-key – you'll feel like you're staying in a friend's private home – and the breakfasts are gourmet. Innkeeper Evin Carson will tell you everything you need to know for a great time in Bar Harbor.

Bar Harbor Grand Hotel　　　HOTEL $$
(☑ 207-288-5226; 207-288-5226; 269 Main St; r incl breakfast $239; ☺ Apr-early Nov; ❋ 🖵) A replica of Bar Harbor's 19th-century Rodick House Hotel, this four-story property offers a lofty view of the town. Decor is classic, if a bit uninspired, but the staff is accommodating and the hotel is open a bit longer in the season than other local properties.

🍴 Eating

Cafe This Way　　　AMERICAN $$
(☑ 207-288-4483; www.cafethisway.com; 14½ Mount Desert St; mains breakfast $6-17, dinner $18-28; ☺ 7-11:30am Mon-Sat, 8am-1pm Sun, 5:30-9pm nightly May-Oct; 🖍) In a sprawling white cottage, this quirky eatery is *the* place for breakfast, with plump Maine blueberry pancakes and eggs Benedict with smoked salmon. It also serves

eclectic, sophisticated dinners, like roasted duck with blueberries, Moroccan-style squash and tuna tempura. Sit in the garden.

2 Cats CAFE $$
(☑207-288-2808; www.2catsbarharbor.com; 130 Cottage St; mains $7-20; ☺7am-1pm; 🖋) On weekends crowds line up for smoked-trout omelets and homemade muffins at this sunny, arty little cafe. Lunch offerings include slightly heartier fare, such as burritos and seafood dishes.

Mâche Bistro FRENCH $$$
(☑207-288-0447; www.machebistro.com; 321 Main Street; mains $18-29; ☺5:30 until close Mon-Sat early May-Oct) Almost certainly Bar Harbor's best midrange restaurant, Mâche serves contemporary French-inflected fare in a stylishly renovated cottage. The changing menu highlights the local riches – think pumpkin-seed-dusted scallops, lobster-and-brie flatbread, and wild blueberry trifle. Specialty cocktails add to the appeal. Reservations are crucial.

Downeast Maine

The 900-plus miles of coastline running northeast from Bar Harbor are sparsely populated, slower-paced and foggier than southern and western Maine. Highlights include the **Schoodic Peninsula**, whose tip is a noncontiguous part of Acadia National Park; the lobster fishing villages of **Jonesport** and **Beals**; and **Great Wass Island**, a nature preserve with walking paths and good bird-watching, including the chance to see puffins.

Machias, with a branch of the University of Maine, is the center of commerce along this stretch of coast. **Lubec** is about as far east as you can go and still be in the USA; folks like to watch the sun rise at nearby **Quoddy Head State Park** so they can say they were the first in the country to catch the sun's rays.

Interior Maine

Sparsely populated northern and western Maine is rugged outdoor country. River rafting, hiking trails up Maine's highest mountain and the ski town of Bethel make the region a magnet for adventurers.

Sabbathday Lake

The nation's only active Shaker community is at Sabbathday Lake, 25 miles north of Portland. Founded in the early 18th century, a handful of devotees keep the Shaker tradition of simple living, hard work and fine artistry alive. You can tour several of their buildings on a visit to the **Shaker Museum** (☑207-926-4597; www.maineshakers.com; adult/child 6-12yr $10/2; ☺10am-4:30pm Mon-Sat late May–mid-Oct). To get there, take exit 63 off the Maine Turnpike and continue north for 8 miles on ME 26.

Bethel

The rural community of Bethel, nestled in the rolling Maine woods 12 miles east of New Hampshire on ME 26, offers an engaging combination of mountain scenery, outdoor escapades and good-value accommodations. **Bethel Area Chamber of Commerce** (☑207-824-2282; www.bethelmaine.com; 8 Station Pl; ☺9am-5pm Jun–mid-Oct, closed Sat & Sun mid-Oct–May) provides information for visitors.

🏃 Activities

Bethel Outdoor Adventure KAYAKING
(☑207-824-4224; www.betheloutdooradventure.com; 121 Mayville Rd/US 2; per day kayak/canoe $46/67; ☺8am-6pm mid-May-mid-Oct) This downtown outfitter rents canoes, kayaks and bicycles, and it arranges lessons, guided trips and shuttles to and from the Androscoggin River.

Grafton Notch State Park HIKING
(☑207-824-2912; www.maine.gov; ME 26; adult/child 5-11yr $3/1; ☺9am-sunset May 15-Oct 15) If you're ready for a hike, head to this park north of Bethel for pretty mountain scenery, waterfalls and lots of trails of varying lengths. Walking in for the trails is okay in the off-season.

Sunday River Ski Resort SKIING
(☑800-543-2754; www.sundayriver.com; ME 26; full-day lift ticket adult/child 13-18yr/6-12yr & seniors $89/69/57; 🏂) Six miles north of Bethel along ME 5/26, Sunday River has eight mountain peaks and 135 trails, with 15 lifts. It's regarded as one of the region's best family ski destinations. They've also got summer activities, including chairlift rides, ziplines, hiking trails, disc golf and a mountain-bike park. Two huge lodges have more than 400 rooms.

🛏 Sleeping

Chapman Inn   B&B $
(📞 207-824-2657; www.chapmaninn.com; 2 Church St; dm/rm/ste incl breakfast $35/$89-129/139; ❊ 🛜) This roomy downtown guesthouse has character in spades. The nine private rooms are done up in florals and antiques, with slightly sloping floors attesting to the home's age. In winter, skiers bunk down in the snug dorm, complete with a wood-paneled game room presided over by a massive mounted moose head. Breakfast is a lavish spread of homemade pastries and made-to-order omelets.

Sudbury Inn & Suds Pub   INN $$
(📞 207-824-2174; www.sudburyinn.com; 151 Main St; r/ste incl breakfast $119-139/189-199; ⊙ pub from 11:30am daily, restaurant 5:30-9pm Thu-Sat; ❊) The choice place to stay in downtown Bethel, this historic inn has 17 rooms, a pub with 29 beers on tap, pizza and live weekend entertainment. It also has an excellent dinner restaurant serving Maine-centric fare (mains $20 to $34).

Caratunk & The Forks

For white-water rafting at its best, head to the **Kennebec River**, below the Harris Dam, where the water shoots through a dramatic 12-mile gorge. With rapid names like Whitewasher and Magic Falls, you know you're in for an adrenaline rush.

The adjoining villages of Caratunk and The Forks, on US 201 south of Jackman, are at the center of the Kennebec River rafting operations. The options range from rolling rapids and heart-stopping drops to calmer waters where children as young as seven can join in. Rates range from $99 to $120 per person for a day-long outing. Multiday packages, with camping or cabin accommodations, can also be arranged.

Reliable operators include **Crab Apple Whitewater** (📞 800-553-7238; www.crabapplewhitewater.com) and **Three Rivers Whitewater** (📞 877-846-7238; www.threeriverswhitewater.com).

Baxter State Park

Set in the remote forests of northern Maine, **Baxter State Park** (📞 207-723-5140; www.baxterstateparkauthority.com; per car $14) centers on Mt Katahdin (5267ft), Maine's tallest mountain and the northern terminus of the 2175-mile **Appalachian Trail** (www.nps.gov/appa). This vast 209,500-acre park is maintained in a wilderness state – no electricity and no running water (bring your own or plan on purifying stream water) – and there's a good chance you'll see moose, deer and black bear. Baxter has extensive hiking trails, several leading to the top of Mt Katahdin, which can be hiked round-trip in a day as long as you're in good shape and get an early start.

At **Millinocket**, south of Baxter State Park, there are motels, campgrounds, restaurants and outfitters that specialize in white-water rafting and kayaking on the Penobscot River. Get information from the **Katahdin Area Chamber of Commerce** (📞 207-723-4443; www.katahdinmaine.com; 1029 Central St, Millinocket; ⊙ 9am-2pm Mon-Fri).

Washington, DC & the Capital Region

Best Places to Eat

➡ Rose's Luxury (p268)

➡ Woodberry Kitchen (p282)

➡ Mama J's (p300)

➡ Blue Pete's (p306)

➡ Oakhart Social (p307)

Best Places to Stay

➡ Hotel Lombardy (p266)

➡ The Georges (p313)

➡ Peaks of Otter (p314)

➡ HI Richmond (p299)

➡ Colonial Williamsburg Historic Lodging (p302)

Why Go?

No matter your politics, it's hard not to fall for the nation's capital. Iconic monuments, vast (and free) museums and venerable restaurants serving global cuisines are just the beginning of the great DC experience. There's much to discover: cobblestoned neighborhoods, sprawling markets, heady multicultural nightspots and verdant parks – not to mention the corridors of power, where visionaries and demagogues alike still roam.

Beyond the Beltway, the diverse landscapes of Maryland, Virginia, West Virginia and Delaware offer potent enticement to travel beyond the marble city. Craggy mountains, rushing rivers, vast nature reserves (including islands where wild horses run), sparkling beaches, historic villages and the magnificent Chesapeake Bay form the backdrop to memorable adventures: sailing, hiking, rafting, camping or just sitting on a pretty stretch of shoreline, planning the next seafood feast. It's a place where traditions run deep, from the nation's birthplace to Virginia's still-thriving bluegrass scene.

When to Go
Washington DC

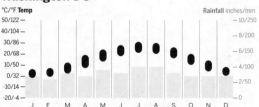

May–Apr Cherry blossoms bring crowds to the city during DC's most popular festival.

Jun–Aug Beaches and resorts heave; prices are high and accommodations scarce.

Sep–Oct Fewer crowds and lower prices, but with pleasant temperatures and fiery fall scenery.

History

Native Americans populated this region long before European settlers arrived. Many of the area's geographic landmarks are still known by their Native American names, such as Chesapeake, Shenandoah, Appalachian and Potomac. In 1607 a group of 108 English colonists established the first permanent European settlement in the New World: Jamestown. During the early years, colonists battled harsh winters, starvation, disease and, occasionally, hostile Native Americans.

Jamestown survived, and the Royal Colony of Virginia came into being in 1624. Ten years later, fleeing the English Civil War, Lord Baltimore established the Catholic colony of Maryland at St Mary's City, where a Spanish Jewish doctor treated a town council that included a black Portuguese sailor and Margaret Brent, the first woman to vote in North American politics. Delaware was settled as a Dutch whaling colony in 1631, practically wiped out by Native Americans, and later resettled by the British. Celts displaced from Britain filtered into the Appalachians, where their fiercely independent culture persists today. Border disputes between Maryland, Delaware and Pennsylvania led to the creation of the Mason–Dixon line, which eventually separated the industrial North from the agrarian, slave-holding South.

The fighting part of the Revolutionary War finished here with the British surrender at Yorktown in 1781. To diffuse regional tension, central, swampy Washington, District of Columbia (DC), was made the new nation's capital. But divisions of class, race and economy were strong, and this area in particular split along its seams during the Civil War (1861–65): Virginia seceded from the Union, while its impoverished western farmers, long resentful of genteel plantation owners, seceded from Virginia. Maryland stayed in the Union, but its white slave-owners rioted against Northern troops, while thousands of black Marylanders joined the Union Army.

Local Culture

The North–South tension long defined this area, but the region has also swung between the cultures of Virginia aristocrats, miners, waterfolk, immigrants and the ever-changing rulers of Washington, DC. Since the Civil War, local economies have made the shift from agriculture and manufacturing to high technology and the servicing and staffing of the federal government.

Many African Americans settled this border region, either as slaves or escapees running for Northern freedom. Today African Americans still form the visible underclass of its major cities, but in the rough arena of the disadvantaged they compete with Latino immigrants, mainly from Central America.

At the other end of the spectrum, ivory towers – in the form of world-class universities and research centers such as the National Institute of Health – attract intelligentsia from around the world. The local high schools are often packed with the children of scientists and consultants who staff some of the world's most prestigious think tanks.

All of this has spawned a culture that is, in turns, as sophisticated as a journalists' book club, as linked to the land as bluegrass festivals in Virginia and as hooked into the main vein of African American culture as Tupac Shakur, go-go, Baltimore Club and DC Hardcore. And, of course, there's always politics, a subject continually simmering under the surface here.

WASHINGTON, DC

The USA's capital teems with iconic monuments, vast museums and the corridors of power where visionaries and demagogues roam. But it's more than that. It's also home to tree-lined neighborhoods and groovy markets, with ethnically diverse restaurants, large numbers of immigrants and a dynamism percolating just beneath the surface. There's always a buzz here – no surprise, as DC gathers more overachieving and talented types than any city of this size deserves.

Plan on jam-packed days sightseeing in the countless museums (most of them free). At night, join the locals sipping DC-made brews and chowing in cozy restaurants in buzzy quarters such as U St and Logan Circle.

History

Following the Revolutionary War, a balance was struck between Northern and Southern politicians, who wanted to plant a federal city somewhere between their power bases. Potential capitals such as Boston, Philadelphia and Baltimore were rejected by Southern plantation owners, as too urban-industrial so it was decided a new city would be carved at midway point of the 13 colonies, along the banks of the Potomac River. Maryland and Virginia donated the land.

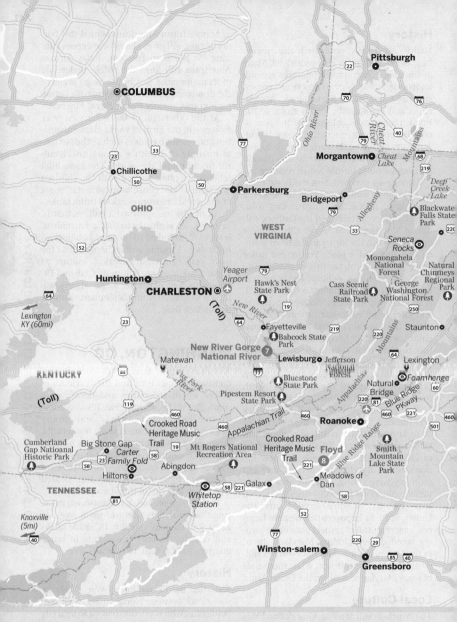

Washington, DC & the Capital Region Highlights

1 Visiting Washington's **Smithsonian Institution museums** (p259), then watching the sun set over **Lincoln Memorial** (p250).

2 Tracing America's roots at the living-history museum of **Colonial Williamsburg** (p302).

3 Exploring the region's nautical past with a pub crawl through Baltimore's cobblestoned port-town neighborhood of **Fell's Point** (p280).

4 Taking a Sunday drive along **Skyline Drive** (p311), followed by hiking and camping

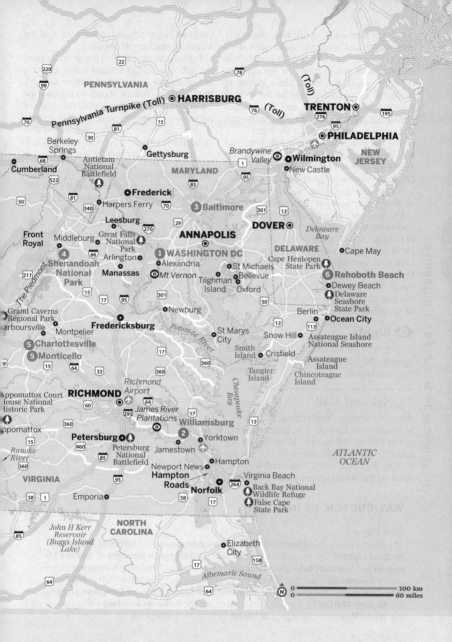

PENNSYLVANIA

220
99
22
78
HARRISBURG ⊙
76 (Toll)
TRENTON ⊙
195
Pennsylvania Turnpike (Toll)
81
15
276 (Toll)
95
70
30
Berkeley Springs
PHILADELPHIA ⊙
NEW JERSEY
68
Cumberland
Antietam National Battlefield
Gettysburg
Brandywine Valley
Wilmington
New Castle
522
81
340
MARYLAND
83
95
50
Frederick
Harpers Ferry
70
Baltimore ❸
301
13
DOVER ⊙
Delaware Bay
Leesburg
29
Front Royal
Middleburg
270
ANNAPOLIS
DELAWARE
Cape May
211
❹
Great Falls National Park
WASHINGTON DC ❶
Cape Henlopen State Park
Rehoboth Beach ❻
66
Arlington
Alexandria
St Michaels
Dewey Beach
Shenandoah National Park
Manassas
Mt Vernon
Bellevue
Delaware Seashore State Park
15
17
95
301
Tilghman Island
Oxford
Berlin
13
Ocean City
Grand Caverns Regional Park
Newburg
50
113
Charboursville
Fredericksburg
St Marys City
Snow Hill
Assateague Island National Seashore
❺ Charlottesville
Montpelier
17
Smith Island
Crisfield
❺ Monticello
360
Assateague Island Chincoteague Island
9
64
33
360
Tangier Island
95
Richmond Airport
Chesapeake Bay
Appomattox Court House National Historic Park
RICHMOND
60
64
James River Plantations
295
17
Williamsburg
13
appomattox
360
❷
Yorktown
ATLANTIC OCEAN
15
Petersburg
Jamestown
460
85
Petersburg National Battlefield
Ranoke River
360
Newport News
Hampton
VIRGINIA
95
Hampton Roads
Virginia Beach
Back Bay National Wildlife Refuge
58
1
Emporia
Norfolk
264
58
False Cape State Park
17
NORTH CAROLINA
John H Kerr Reservoir (Buggs Island Lake)
85
Elizabeth City
158
64
17
Albemarle Sound
64
0 —————— 100 km
Ⓝ 0 —————— 60 miles

under the stars in **Shenandoah National Park** (p309).
❺ Marveling at Thomas Jefferson's masterpieces of **Monticello** (p309) and the

University of Virginia (p307) in historic Charlottesville.
❻ Strolling the boardwalk in the family- and gay-friendly resort of **Rehoboth Beach** (p291).

❼ Tackling the rapids of **New River Gorge National River** (p320) in Fayetteville.
❽ Feeling the beat of the clog dancers at a jamboree in **Floyd** (p316).

DC was torched by the British during the War of 1812, and ceded the south-bank slave port of Alexandria to Virginia in 1846 (when abolition talk was buzzing in the capital). Over the years, DC evolved along diverging tracks: as a marbled temple to the federal government on one hand, and as an urban ghetto for northbound African Americans and overseas immigrants on the other.

The city finally got its own mayor in 1973 (Walter Washington, among the first African American mayors of a major American city); Congress governed it prior to that. Today, DC residents are taxed just as other American citizens are, yet lack a voting seat in Congress.

DC has undergone extensive gentrification since the late 1990s. With the election of Barack Obama in 2008, the city gained a bit of cool cachet – New Yorkers are coming here now, instead of the other way around. Unfortunately, they've jacked up the cost of living. DC's costs are among the highest in the nation, and as the city's economy keeps on booming, it's likely to stay that way.

⊙ Sights

Be prepared for big crowds from late March through July, and for sticky-hot days June through August.

⊙ National Mall

When you imagine Washington, DC, you likely imagine this 1.9-mile-long lawn: anchored at one end by the Lincoln Memorial; at the other by Capitol Hill; intersected by the Reflecting Pool and WWII Memorial; and centered on the Washington Monument. This is the heart of the city, and in some ways, of the American experiment itself.

Perhaps no other symbol has so well housed the national ideal of massed voices affecting radical change – from Martin Luther King Jr's 1963 'I Have a Dream' speech to marches for marriage equality in the 2000s. Hundreds of rallies occur here every year: the Mall, framed by great monuments and museums, and shot through with tourists, dog walkers and idealists, acts as a loudspeaker for any cause.

★ Lincoln Memorial   MONUMENT

(www.nps.gov/linc; 2 Lincoln Memorial Circle NW; ⊙24hr; ☐ Circulator, Ⓜ Foggy Bottom-GWU) FREE Anchoring the Mall's west end is the hallowed shrine to Abraham Lincoln, who gazes peacefully across the reflecting pool beneath his neoclassical Doric-columned abode. To the left of Lincoln you can read the words of the Gettysburg Address, and the hall below highlights other great Lincoln-isms; on the steps, Martin Luther King Jr delivered his famed 'I Have a Dream' speech.

★ Vietnam Veterans Memorial   MONUMENT

(www.nps.gov/vive; 5 Henry Bacon Dr NW; ⊙24hr; ☐ Circulator, Ⓜ Foggy Bottom-GWU) FREE The opposite of DC's white, gleaming marble is this black, low-lying 'V,' an expression of the psychic scar wrought by the Vietnam War. The monument follows a descent deeper into the earth, with the names of the 58,272 dead soldiers – listed in the order in which they died – chiseled into the dark wall. It's a subtle, but profound monument – and all the more surprising as it was designed by 21-year-old undergraduate student Maya Lin in 1981.

WASHINGTON, DC IN...

Two Days

Start at the much-loved **National Air and Space Museum** and **National Museum of Natural History**. Continue down the Mall to the **Washington Monument**, **Lincoln Memorial** and **Vietnam Veterans Memorial**. Have dinner at **Founding Farmers** or somewhere **Downtown**. Next day, start at the **Capitol** and tour the statue-cluttered halls. Then walk across the street to the **Supreme Court** and **Library of Congress**. Hungry? Try **Eastern Market** for a snack. Later, check out the **National Archives** and saunter by the **White House**. At night go to **U Street** for jazz, rock and clubs.

Four Days

On day three, go to **Georgetown** for a stroll along the Potomac, followed by window-shopping and lunch at **Martin's Tavern**. Afterward, visit the lovely gardens of **Dumbarton Oaks**. In the evening, catch a show at the **Kennedy Center**. On day four, start at **Dupont Circle** and gape at the enormous mansions along **Embassy Row**. Swing into the **Phillips Collection**, **National Gallery of Art**, **Newseum** or any other top museums you might have missed. For dinner, browse 14th St in **Logan Circle**.

★ **Washington Monument** MONUMENT
(www.nps.gov/wamo; 2 15th St NW; ☉9am-5pm, to 10pm Jun-Aug; 🚌Circulator, Ⓜ Smithsonian) FREE Just peaking at 555ft (and 5in), the Washington Monument is the tallest building in the district. It took two phases of construction to complete; note the different hues of the stone. A 70-second elevator ride whisks you to the observation deck for the city's best views. Same-day tickets for a timed entrance are available at the kiosk (15th St, btwn Madison Dr NW & Jefferson Dr SW; ☉from 8:30am) by the monument. Arrive early.

★ **National Air & Space Museum** MUSEUM
(📞202-633-1000; www.airandspace.si.edu; cnr 6th St & Independence Ave SW; ☉10am-5:30pm, to 7:30pm mid-Mar–early Sep; 🚻; 🚌Circulator, Ⓜ L'Enfant Plaza) FREE The Air and Space Museum is one of the most popular Smithsonian museums. Everyone flocks to see the Wright brothers' flyer, Chuck Yeager's Bell X-1, Charles Lindbergh's *Spirit of St Louis,* Amelia Earhart's natty red plane and the Apollo Lunar Module. An IMAX theater, planetarium and flight simulators are all here ($7 to $9 each). More avionic pieces reside in Virginia at the Steven F Udvar-Hazy Center, an annex to hold this museum's leftovers.

★ **United States Holocaust Memorial Museum** MUSEUM
(📞202-488-0400; www.ushmm.org; 100 Raoul Wallenberg Pl SW; ☉10am-5:20pm, to 6:20pm Mon-Fri Apr & May; Ⓜ Smithsonian) FREE For a deep understanding of the Holocaust – its victims, perpetrators and bystanders – this harrowing museum is a must-see. The main exhibit gives visitors the identity card of a single Holocaust victim, whose story is revealed as you take a winding route into a hellish past marked by ghettos, rail cars and death camps. It also shows the flip side of human nature, documenting the risks many citizens took to help the persecuted.

National Gallery of Art MUSEUM
(📞202-737-4215; www.nga.gov; Constitution Ave NW, btwn 3rd & 7th Sts; ☉10am-5pm Mon-Sat, 11am-6pm Sun; 🚌Circulator, Ⓜ Archives) FREE The staggering collection spans the Middle Ages to the present. The neoclassical west building showcases European art through the early 1900s; highlights include a da Vinci painting and a slew of impressionist and postimpressionist works. The IM Pei-designed east building displays modern art,

WASHINGTON, DC FACTS

Nickname DC, the District, Chocolate City

Population 659,000

Area 68.3 sq miles

Capital city Exactly!

Sales tax 5.75%

Birthplace of Duke Ellington (1899–1974), Marvin Gaye (1939–84), Dave Chappelle (b 1973)

Home of The Redskins, cherry blossoms, all three branches of American government

Politics Overwhelmingly Democrat

Famous for National symbols, partying interns, struggle for Congressional recognition

Unofficial motto and license-plate slogan Taxation Without Representation

Driving distances Washington, DC, to Baltimore: 40 miles; Washington, DC, to Virginia Beach: 210 miles

with works by Picasso, Matisse, Pollock and a massive Calder mobile over the entrance lobby. Alas, it's closed (except for the lobby) until 2016 for renovations. A trippy underground walkway connects the two wings.

National Sculpture Garden GARDENS
(cnr Constitution Ave NW & 7th St NW; ☉10am-7pm Mon-Thu & Sat, 10am-9:30pm Fri, 11am-7pm Sun; 🚌Circulator, Ⓜ Archives) FREE The National Gallery of Art's 6-acre garden is studded with whimsical sculptures such as Roy Lichtenstein's *House,* a giant Claes Oldenburg typewriter eraser and Louise Bourgeois' leggy *Spider*. They are scattered around a fountain – a great place to dip your feet in summer. From November to March the fountain becomes a festive ice rink (adult/child $8/7, skate rental $3).

In summer, the garden hosts free evening jazz concerts on Fridays from 5pm to 8:30pm.

National Museum of Natural History MUSEUM
(www.mnh.si.edu; cnr 10th St & Constitution Ave NW; ☉10am-5:30pm, to 7:30pm Jun-Aug; 🚻; 🚌Circulator, Ⓜ Smithsonian) FREE Smithsonian museums don't get more popular than this

Washington, DC

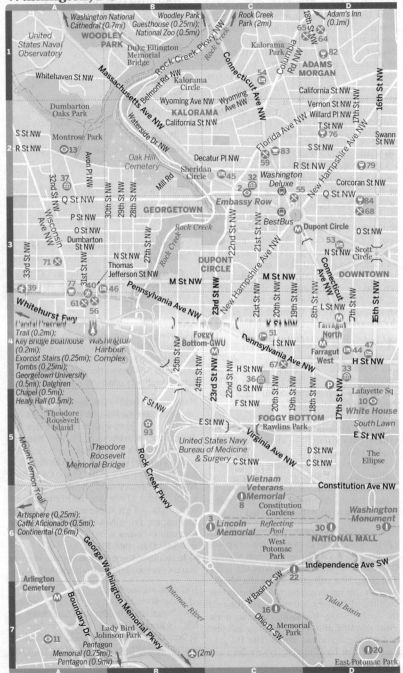

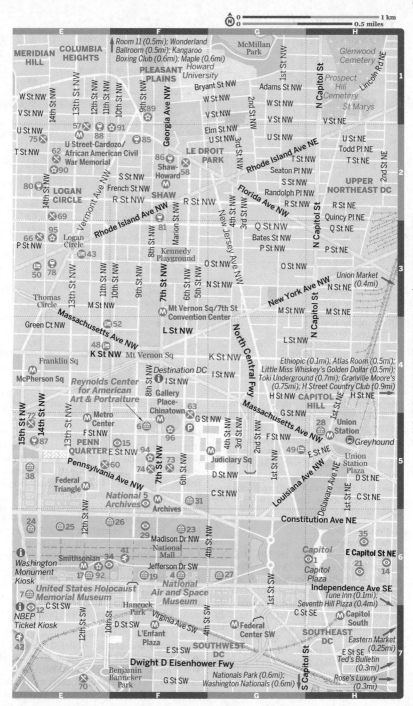

WASHINGTON, DC & THE CAPITAL REGION

MERIDIAN HILL
COLUMBIA HEIGHTS
PLEASANT PLAINS
Howard University
McMillan Park
Glenwood Cemetery

Room 11 (0.5mi); Wonderland Ballroom (0.5mi); Kangaroo Boxing Club (0.6mi); Maple (0.6mi)

Prospect Hill Cemetery
St Marys

W St NW
V St NW
U St NW
T St NW

Bryant St NW
W St NW
V St NW
Elm St NW
U St NW

Adams St NW
W St NW
V St NW
U St NW

U St NE
Todd Pl NE
T St NE
V St NE

LE DROIT PARK

U Street–Cardozo/ African Civil War Memorial

Rhode Island Ave NE

UPPER NORTHEAST DC

Shaw-Howard
SHAW
S St NW
French St NW
R St NW

Seaton Pl NW
Randolph Pl NW
R St NW
R St NE
Quincy Pl NE
Q St NE

LOGAN CIRCLE
Logan Circle
P St NW

Rhode Island Ave NW
R St NW
Florida Ave NW

Q St NW
Bates St NW
P St NW
O St NW

P St NE

Thomas Circle
M St NW

Kennedy Playground
N St NW

Union Market (0.4mi)
N St NE
M St NE

New York Ave NW

Massachusetts Ave NW
Green Ct NW

Mt Vernon Sq/7th St Convention Center
L St NW

M St NE
L St NW

Franklin Sq
K St NW
Mt Vernon Sq
K St NW

Ethiopic (0.1mi); Atlas Room (0.5mi); Little Miss Whiskey's Golden Dollar (0.5mi); Toki Underground (0.7mi); Granville Moore's (0.75mi); H Street Country Club (0.9mi)

McPherson Sq
Destination DC
I St NW
I St NW

H St NW
CAPITOL HILL
H St NE

Reynolds Center for American Art & Portraiture
Gallery Place-Chinatown
G St NW

Massachusetts Ave NW
G St NW
G St NE

Metro Center
F St NW
PENN QUARTER
E St NW

Union Station
Greyhound

Pennsylvania Ave NW

F St NW
E St NE
Union Station Plaza
D St NE

Federal Triangle
Judiciary Sq
Louisiana Ave NW
D St NE
C St NE

National Archives
Archives
C St NW

Constitution Ave NE

Madison Dr NW
National Mall

Capitol
E Capitol St NE

Smithsonian
Jefferson Dr SW

Capitol Plaza
Independence Ave SE

Washington Monument Kiosk
National Air and Space Museum

Tune Inn (0.1mi); Seventh Hill Pizza (0.4mi)

United States Holocaust Memorial Museum
C St SW

C St SE
Capitol South

NBEP Ticket Kiosk
Hancock Park
D St SW
Virginia Ave SW
L'Enfant Plaza

Federal Center SW
SOUTHEAST DC

Eastern Market (0.25mi)
Ted's Bulletin (0.3mi)

Dwight D Eisenhower Fwy
E St SW
SOUTHWEST DC
G St SW

E St SE
Rose's Luxury (0.3mi)

Benjamin Banneker Park
Nationals Park (0.6mi); Washington Nationals (0.6mi)

Washington, DC

one, so crowds are pretty much guaranteed. Wave to Henry, the elephant who guards the rotunda, then zip to the 2nd floor's Hope Diamond. The 45.52-carat bauble has cursed its owners, including Marie Antoinette, or so the story goes. The beloved dinosaur hall is under renovation until 2019, but the giant squid (1st floor, Ocean Hall) and tarantula feedings (2nd floor, Insect Zoo) fill in the thrills at this kid-packed venue.

National Museum of American History   MUSEUM

(www.americanhistory.si.edu; cnr 14th St & Constitution Ave NW; ⊙10am-5:30pm, to 7:30pm Jun-Aug; ⌖; ⌕Circulator, ⓜSmithsonian) **FREE** The museum collects all kinds of artifacts of the American experience. The centerpiece is the flag that flew over Fort McHenry in Baltimore during the War of 1812 – the same flag that inspired Francis Scott Key to pen *The Star-Spangled Banner*. Other highlights include Julia Child's kitchen (1st floor, Food exhibition), Dorothy's ruby slippers and a

piece of Plymouth Rock (both on the 2nd floor, American Stories exhibition).

National Museum of African American History and Culture   MUSEUM

(www.nmaahc.si.edu; 1400 Constitution Ave NW; ⊙10am-5:30pm; ⌕Circulator, ⓜSmithsonian, Federal Triangle) **FREE** This most recent addition to the Smithsonian fold covers the diverse African American experience and how it helped shape the nation. The collection includes everything from Harriet Tubman's hymnal to Emmett Till's casket to Louis Armstrong's trumpet. The institution is constructing a brand-spankin' new building for the museum, to open in 2016. In the meantime, find exhibits from the collection on show at the next-door National Museum of American History (on the 2nd floor).

National WWII Memorial   MONUMENT

(www.nps.gov/wwii; 17th St; ⊙24hr; ⌕Circulator, ⓜSmithsonian) **FREE** Dedicated in 2004, the WWII memorial honors the 400,000 Americans who died in the conflict, along with the 16 million US soldiers who served between

1941 and 1945. The plaza's dual arches symbolize victory in the Atlantic and Pacific theaters. The 56 surrounding pillars represent each US state and territory. Stirring quotes speckle the monument. You'll often see groups of veterans paying their respects.

Hirshhorn Museum MUSEUM
(www.hirshhorn.si.edu; cnr 7th St & Independence Ave SW; ⊙10am-5:30pm; 🚼; 🚌Circulator, Ⓜ L'Enfant Plaza) FREE The Smithsonian's cylindrical modern art museum stockpiles sculptures and canvases from modernism's early days to pop art to contemporary art. Special exhibits ring the 2nd floor. Rotating pieces from the permanent collection circle the 3rd floor, where there's also a swell sitting area with couches, floor-to-ceiling windows and a balcony offering Mall views.

Smithsonian Castle NOTABLE BUILDING
(📞202-633-1000; www.si.edu; 1000 Jefferson Dr SW; ⊙8:30am-5:30pm; 🚌Circulator, Ⓜ Smithsonian) James Renwick designed this turreted red-sandstone fairytale in 1855. Today, the castle houses the **Smithsonian Visitors Center**, which makes a good first stop on the Mall. Inside you'll find history exhibits, multilingual touch-screen displays, a staffed information desk, free maps, a cafe – and the tomb of James Smithson, the institution's founder. His crypt lies inside a little room by the main entrance off the Mall.

Freer-Sackler Museums of Asian Art MUSEUM
(www.asia.si.edu; cnr Independence Ave & 12th St SW; ⊙10am-5:30pm; 🚌Circulator, Ⓜ Smithsonian) FREE This is a lovely spot in which to while away a Washington afternoon. Japanese silk scrolls, smiling Buddhas, rare Islamic manuscripts and Chinese jades spread through cool, quiet galleries. The Freer and Sackler are actually separate venues, connected by an underground tunnel. The Sackler focuses more on changing exhibits, while the Freer, rather incongruously, also houses works by American painter James Whistler. Don't miss the blue-and-gold, ceramics-crammed Peacock Room.

National Mall

Folks often call the Mall 'America's Front Yard,' and that's a pretty good analogy. It is indeed a lawn, unfurling scrubby green grass from the Capitol west to the Lincoln Memorial. It's also America's great public space, where citizens come to protest their government, go for scenic runs and connect with the nation's most cherished ideals writ large in stone, landscaping, monuments and memorials.

You can sample quite a bit in a day, though it'll be a full one that requires roughly 4 miles of walking. Start at the **Vietnam Veterans Memorial ❶**, then head counterclockwise around the Mall, swooping in on the **Lincoln Memorial ❷**, **Martin Luther King Jr Memorial ❸** and **Washington Monument ❹**. You can also pause for the cause of the Korean War and WWII, among other monuments that dot the Mall's western portion.

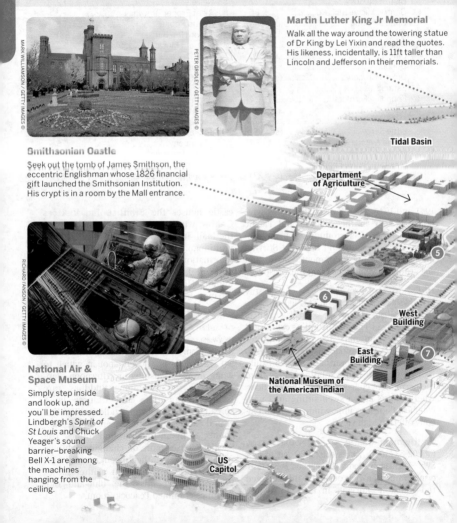

Martin Luther King Jr Memorial

Walk all the way around the towering statue of Dr King by Lei Yixin and read the quotes. His likeness, incidentally, is 11ft taller than Lincoln and Jefferson in their memorials.

MARK WILLIAMSON / GETTY IMAGES ©

PETER GRIDLEY / GETTY IMAGES ©

Smithsonian Castle

Seek out the tomb of James Smithson, the eccentric Englishman whose 1826 financial gift launched the Smithsonian Institution. His crypt is in a room by the Mall entrance.

Tidal Basin

Department of Agriculture

RICHARD I'ANSON / GETTY IMAGES ©

National Air & Space Museum

Simply step inside and look up, and you'll be impressed. Lindbergh's *Spirit of St Louis* and Chuck Yeager's sound barrier–breaking Bell X-1 are among the machines hanging from the ceiling.

West Building

East Building

National Museum of the American Indian

US Capitol

Then it's onward to the museums, all fabulous and all free. Begin at the **Smithsonian Castle ❺** to get your bearings – and to say thanks to the guy making all this awesomeness possible – and commence browsing through the **National Air & Space Museum ❻**, **National Gallery of Art & National Sculpture Garden ❼** and **National Museum of Natural History ❽**.

TOP TIPS

Start early, especially in summer. You'll avoid the crowds, but more importantly you'll avoid the blazing heat. Try to finish with the monuments and be in the air-conditioned museums by 10:30am. Also, consider bringing snacks, since the only food available is from scattered cart vendors and museum cafes.

Lincoln Memorial

Commune with Abe in his chair, then head down the steps to the marker where Martin Luther King Jr gave his 'Dream' speech. The view of the Reflecting Pool and Washington Monument is one of DC's best.

STEVEN GREAVES /GETTY IMAGES ©

Korean War Veterans Memorial

National WWII Memorial

National Museum of African American History & Culture

National Museum of American History

National Sculpture Garden

Vietnam Veterans Memorial

Check the symbol that's beside each name. A diamond indicates 'killed, body recovered.' A plus sign indicates 'missing and unaccounted for.' There are approximately 1200 of the latter.

Washington Monument

As you approach the obelisk, look a third of the way up. See how it's slightly lighter in color at the bottom? Builders had to use different marble after the first source dried up.

National Museum of Natural History

Wave to Henry, the elephant who guards the rotunda, then zip to the 2nd floor's Hope Diamond. The 45.52-carat bauble has cursed its owners, including Marie Antoinette, or so the story goes.

National Gallery of Art & National Sculpture Garden

Beeline to Gallery 6 (West Building) and ogle the Western Hemisphere's only Leonardo da Vinci painting. Outdoors, amble amid whimsical sculptures by Miró, Calder and Lichtenstein. Also check out IM Pei's design of the East Building.

EDDIE BRADY / GETTY IMAGES ©

ℹ EATING ON THE MALL

Stock up on snacks before visiting the Mall, since there are few good dining options. One exception: the unique **Mitsitam Native Foods Cafe** (www.mitsitamcafe.com; cnr 4th St & Independence Ave SW, National Museum of the American Indian; mains $10-18; ⊙11am-5pm; 🚌Circulator, Ⓜ L'Enfant Plaza) in the American Indian Museum.

Like all Smithsonian institutions, the venues host free lectures, concerts and film screenings, though the ones here typically have an Asian bent; the website has the schedule. Alas, the Freer is closed for structural renovations from January 1, 2016 until summer of 2017. The Sackler will stay open throughhout the period.

National Museum of the American Indian — MUSEUM

(www.nmai.si.edu; cnr 4th St & Independence Ave SW; ⊙10am-5:30pm; 🚻; 🚌Circulator, Ⓜ L'Enfant Plaza) FREE Ensconced in honey-colored, undulating limestone, this museum makes a striking architectural impression. Inside it offers cultural artifacts, costumes, video and audio recordings related to the indigenous people of the Americas. Exhibits are largely organized and presented by individual tribes, which provides an intimate, if sometimes disjointed, overall narrative. The 'Our Universes' gallery (on Level 4) about Native American beliefs and creation stories is intriguing.

Bureau of Engraving & Printing — LANDMARK

(www.moneyfactory.gov; cnr 14th & C Sts SW; ⊙9-10:45am, 12:30-3:45pm & 5-6pm Mon-Fri Mar-Aug, reduced hours Sep-Feb; Ⓜ Smithsonian) FREE Cha-ching! The nation's paper currency is designed and printed here. Guides lead 40-minute tours during which you peer down onto the work floor where millions of dollars roll off the presses and get cut (by guillotine!). In peak season (March to August), timed entry tickets are required. Get in line early at the **ticket kiosk** (Raoul Wallenberg Pl, aka 15th St). It opens at 8am.

◉ Tidal Basin

It's magnificent to stroll around this constructed inlet and watch the monument lights wink across the Potomac River. The blooms here are loveliest during the Cherry Blossom Festival, the city's annual spring rejuvenation, when the basin bursts into a pink-and-white floral collage. The original trees, a gift from the city of Tokyo, were planted in 1912.

Martin Luther King Jr Memorial — MONUMENT

(www.nps.gov/mlkm; 1850 W Basin Dr SW; ⊙24hr; 🚌Circulator, Ⓜ Smithsonian) FREE Opened in 2011, this is the Mall's first memorial dedicated to a nonpresident, as well as to an African American. Sculptor Lei Yixin carved the piece. Besides Dr King's image, known as the *Stone of Hope*, there are two blocks behind him that represent the Mountain of Despair. A wall inscribed with King's stirring quotes flanks the statues. It sits in a lovely spot on the banks of the Tidal Basin.

Franklin Delano Roosevelt Memorial — MONUMENT

(www.nps.gov/frde; 400 W Basin Dr SW; ⊙24hr; 🚌Circulator, Ⓜ Smithsonian) FREE The 7.5-acre memorial pays tribute to the US's longest-serving president and the era in which he governed. Visitors are taken through four red-granite 'rooms' that narrate FDR's time in office, from the Depression to the New Deal to WWII. The story is told through statuary and inscriptions, punctuated with fountains and peaceful alcoves. It's especially pretty at night, when the marble shimmers in the glossy stillness of the Tidal Basin.

Jefferson Memorial — MONUMENT

(www.nps.gov/thje; 900 Ohio Dr SW; ⊙24hr; 🚌Circulator, Ⓜ Smithsonian) FREE Set on the south bank of the Tidal Basin amid the cherry trees, this memorial honors the third US president, political philosopher, drafter of the Declaration of Independence and founder of the University of Virginia. Designed by John Russell Pope to resemble Jefferson's library at the university, the rounded monument was initially derided by critics as 'the Jefferson Muffin.' Inside is a 19ft bronze likeness, and excerpts from Jefferson's writings are etched into the walls.

◉ Capitol Hill

The Capitol, appropriately, sits atop Capitol Hill (we'd say it's more of a stump, but hey), across a plaza from the dignified Supreme Court and Library of Congress. Congressional office buildings surround the plaza. A pleasant brownstone residential district stretches from E Capitol St to Lincoln Park.

SMITHSONIAN INSTITUTION MUSEUMS

It's not a single place, as commonly thought: rather, the Smithsonian Institution (www.si.edu) consists of 19 museums, the National Zoo and nine research facilities. Most are in DC, but others are further flung in the US and abroad. Together they comprise the world's largest museum and research complex – and it's all free to visitors. You could spend weeks wandering endless corridors taking in the great treasures, artifacts and ephemera from America and beyond; massive dinosaur skeletons, lunar modules and artworks from every corner of the globe are all part of the largesse. For perspective, consider this: of the approximately 140 million objects in the Smithsonian's collection, only 1% are on display at any given time. Thanks go to the curious Englishman James Smithson (1765–1829): he never visited the USA but in his will bequeathed the fledgling nation $508,318 to found an 'establishment for the increase and diffusion of knowledge.'

Most Smithsonian museums are open daily (except Christmas Day). Some have extended hours in summer. Be prepared for lines and bag checks.

★ **Capitol**   LANDMARK

(www.visitthecapitol.gov; First St NE & E Capitol St; ⊙8:30am-4:30pm Mon-Sat; Ⓜ Capitol South) **FREE** Since 1800, this is where the legislative branch of American government – ie Congress – has met to write the country's laws. The lower House of Representatives (435 members) and upper Senate (100) meet respectively in the south and north wings of the building. Enter via the underground visitor center below the East Plaza. Guided tours of the building are free, but you need a ticket. Get one at the information desk, or reserve online in advance (there's no fee).

Library of Congress   LIBRARY

(www.loc.gov; 1st St SE; ⊙8:30am-4:30pm Mon-Sat; Ⓜ Capitol South) **FREE** The world's largest library – 29 million books and counting – awes in both scope and design. The centerpiece is the 1897 Jefferson Building. Gawk at the Great Hall, done up in stained glass, marble and mosaics of mythical characters, the Gutenberg Bible (c 1455), Thomas Jefferson's round library and the reading-room viewing area. Free tours of the building take place between 10:30am and 3:30pm on the half-hour.

Supreme Court   LANDMARK

(☑ 202-479-3030; www.supremecourt.gov; 1 1st St NE; ⊙9am-4:30pm Mon-Fri; Ⓜ Capitol South) **FREE** The highest court in the USA sits in a pseudo-Greek temple that you enter through 13,000lb bronze doors. Arrive early to watch arguments (periodic Monday through Wednesday, October to April). You can visit the permanent exhibits and the building's five-story marble-and-bronze spiral staircase year-round. On days when court is not in session you can also hear lectures (every hour on the half-hour) in the courtroom.

Folger Shakespeare Library   LIBRARY

(www.folger.edu; 201 E Capitol St SE; ⊙10am-5pm Mon-Sat, noon-5pm Sun; Ⓜ Capitol South) **FREE** Bard-o-philes will be all of a passion here, as the library holds the largest collection of old Billy's works in the world. Stroll through the Great Hall to see Elizabethan artifacts, paintings, etchings and manuscripts. The highlight is a rare First Folio that you can leaf through digitally. The evocative theater on site stages Shakespearean plays.

National Postal Museum   MUSEUM

(www.postalmuseum.si.edu; 2 Massachusetts Ave NE; ⊙10am-5:30pm; ♿; Ⓜ Union Station) **FREE** The Smithsonian-run Postal Museum is way cooler than you might think. Level 1 has exhibits on postal history from the Pony Express to modern times, where you'll see antique mail planes and touching old letters from soldiers and pioneers. Level 2 holds the world's largest stamp collection. Join the stamp geeks pulling out drawers and snapping photos of the world's rarest stamps (the Ben Franklin Z Grill!), or start your own collection by choosing from thousands of free international stamps (Guyana, Congo, Cambodia...).

◉ White House Area & Foggy Bottom

An expansive park called the Ellipse borders the Mall; on the east side is the power-broker block of Pennsylvania Ave. Foggy Bottom was named for the mists that belched out of a local gasworks; now home to the State Department and George Washington University, it's an upscale (if not terribly lively) neighborhood crawling with students and professionals.

★ **White House**   LANDMARK
(☑ tours   202-456-7041;   www.whitehouse.gov;
☉ tours 7:30-11:30am Tue-Thu, to 1:30pm Fri & Sat;
Ⓜ Federal Triangle, McPherson Sq, Metro Center)
FREE The White House has survived both
fire (the Brits torched it in 1814) and insults
(Jefferson groused that it was 'big enough
for two emperors, one Pope and the grand
Lama'). Tours must be arranged in advance.
Americans must apply via one of their state's
members of Congress, and non-Americans
must apply through either the US consulate
in their home country or their country's consulate in DC. Applications are taken from 21
days to six months in advance; three months
ahead is the recommended sweet spot.

White House Visitor Center   MUSEUM
(www.nps.gov/whho; 1450 Pennsylvania Ave NW;
☉ 7:30am-4pm; Ⓜ Federal Triangle) **FREE** Getting inside the White House can be tough,
so here is your backup plan. Browse artifacts
such as Roosevelt's desk for his fireside chats
and Lincoln's cabinet chair. Multimedia exhibits give a 360-degree view into the White
House's rooms. It's not the same as seeing the
real deal first-hand, but the center does do its
job very well, giving good history sprinkled
with great anecdotes on presidential spouses,
kids, pets and dinner preferences.

STEVEN F UDVAR-HAZY CENTER

The National Air and Space Museum on
the Mall is so awesome they made an
attic for it: the **Steven F Udvar-Hazy
Center** (www.airandspace.si.edu/visit/ud-
var-hazy-center; 14390 Air & Space Museum
Pkwy; ☉ 10am-5:30pm, to 6:30pm late
May-early Sep; ♿; Ⓜ Wiehle-Reston East for
bus 983) **FREE**, in Chantilly, VA. It's three
times the size of the DC museum and
sprawls through two massive hangars
near Dulles Airport. Highlights include
the SR-71 Blackbird (the fastest jet in
the world), the space shuttle *Discovery*
(which was retired in 2011) and the
Enola Gay (the B-29 that dropped the
atomic bomb on Hiroshima).

  Though the museum is free, parking
costs $15. To get here on public trans-
portation, take the metro silver line to
Wiehle-Reston East station. Then transfer to the Fairfax Connector bus 983
and take it one stop to the museum.

Textile Museum   MUSEUM
(www.museum.gwu.edu; 701 21st St NW; admission
$8; ☉ 11:30am-6:30pm Mon & Wed-Fri, 10am-5pm
Sat, 1-5pm Sun, closed Tue; Ⓜ Foggy Bottom-GWU)
This gem is the country's only textile museum. Galleries hold exquisite fabrics and carpets. Exhibits revolve around a theme, say
Asian textiles depicting dragons or Kuba
cloth from the Democratic Republic of Congo, and rotate a few times a year. Bonus: the
museum shares space with George Washington University's Washingtonia trove of
historic maps, drawings and ephemera.

Renwick Gallery   MUSEUM
(www.americanart.si.edu/renwick; 1661 Pennsylvania
Ave NW; ☉ 10am-5:30pm; ♿; Ⓜ Farragut West)
FREE Part of the Smithsonian empire, the
Renwick Gallery is set in a stately 1859 mansion and exhibits a superb collection of American crafts and decorative-art pieces. Closed
until early 2016 for infrastructure upgrades.

◉ **Downtown**

This neighborhood bustles day and night,
and several major sights are located here.
It's also DC's shiny theater district and convention hub.

★ **National Archives**   LANDMARK
(☑ 866-272-6272;   www.archives.gov/museum;
700 Pennsylvania Ave NW; ☉ 10am-5:30pm Sep-
mid-Mar, to 7pm mid-Mar-Aug; Ⓜ Archives) **FREE**
It's hard not to feel a little in awe of the big
three documents in the National Archives:
the Declaration of Independence, the Constitution and the Bill of Rights, plus one of
four copies of the Magna Carta. Taken together, it becomes clear just how radical the
American experiment was for its time. The
Public Vaults, a bare scratching of archival
bric-a-brac, make a flashy rejoinder to the
main exhibit.

★ **Reynolds Center for American
Art & Portraiture**   MUSEUM
(☑ 202-633-1000; www.americanart.si.edu; cnr 8th
& F Sts NW; ☉ 11:30am-7pm; Ⓜ Gallery Pl) **FREE** If
you only visit one art museum in DC, make
it the Reynolds Center, which combines the
National Portrait Gallery and the American
Art Museum. There is, simply put, no better
collection of American art in the world than
at these two Smithsonian museums. Famed
works by Edward Hopper, Georgia O'Keeffe, Andy Warhol, Winslow Homer and loads
more celebrated artists fill the galleries.

Ford's Theatre

HISTORIC SITE

(📞 202-426-6924; www.fords.org; 511 10th St NW; ⊙ 9am-4:30pm; Ⓜ Metro Center) FREE On April 14, 1865, John Wilkes Booth assassinated Abraham Lincoln in his box seat here. Timed-entry tickets let you see the flag-draped site. They also provide entry to the basement museum (displaying Booth's .44-caliber pistol, his muddy boot etc) and to Petersen House (across the street), where Lincoln died. Arrive early because tickets do run out. Reserve online ($6.25 fee) to ensure admittance.

Newseum

MUSEUM

(www.newseum.org; 555 Pennsylvania Ave NW; adult/child $23/14; ⊙ 9am-5pm; 👪; Ⓜ Archives, Judiciary Sq) This six-story, highly interactive news museum is worth the admission price. You can delve into the major events of recent years (the fall of the Berlin Wall, September 11, Hurricane Katrina), and spend hours watching moving film footage and perusing Pulitzer Prize–winning photographs. The concourse level displays FBI artifacts from news stories, such as the Unabomber's cabin and John Dillinger's death mask.

⊙ U Street, Shaw & Logan Circle

These neighborhoods have changed in recent years than almost anywhere else in DC. The U Street Corridor, DC's richest nightlife zone, has quite a history: it was once the 'Black Broadway,' where Duke Ellington and Ella Fitzgerald hit their notes in the early 1900s, and later the smoldering epicenter of the 1968 race riots. The area's history is acknowledged by the African American Civil War Memorial at the U Street metro station. After a troubled descent, it's had a vibrant rebirth in recent years; a stroll around this neighborhood is a must.

U Street becomes part of the larger Shaw district, which is DC's current 'it' neighborhood. But it's not annoyingly trendy – the breweries, bars and cafes that seem to pop up weekly are true local places. Logan Circle, next door, is also booming: walk down 14th St NW and hot-chef wine bars, gastropubs, tapas places and oyster bars flash by. The side streets hold stately old manors that give the area its class.

⊙ Dupont Circle

A well-heeled splice of the gay community and the DC diplomatic scene, this is city life at its best. Great restaurants, bars, bookstores and cafes, captivating architecture and the electric energy of a lived-in, happening neighborhood make Dupont worth a linger. Most of the area's historic mansions have been converted into embassies.

★ Embassy Row

ARCHITECTURE

(www.embassy.org; Massachusetts Ave NW btwn Observatory & Dupont Circles NW; Ⓜ Dupont Circle) How quickly can you leave the country? It takes about five minutes; just stroll north along Massachusetts Ave from Dupont Circle (the actual traffic circle) and you pass more than 40 embassies housed in mansions that range from elegant to imposing to discreet. Technically they're on foreign soil, as embassy grounds are the embassy nation's territory.

Phillips Collection

MUSEUM

(www.phillipscollection.org; 1600 21st St NW; Sat & Sun $10, Tue-Fri free, ticketed exhibitions per day $12; ⊙ 10am-5pm Tue, Wed, Fri & Sat, to 8:30pm Thu, 11am-6pm Sun, chamber-music series 4pm Sun Oct-May; Ⓜ Dupont Circle) The first modern-art museum in the country (opened in 1921) houses a small but exquisite collection of European and American works. Renoir's *Luncheon of the Boating Party* is a highlight, along with pieces by Gauguin, Van Gogh, Matisse, Picasso and many other greats. The intimate rooms, set in a restored mansion, put you unusually close to the artworks. The permanent collection is free on weekdays.

⊙ Georgetown

Thousands of the bright and beautiful, from Georgetown students to ivory-tower academics and diplomats, call this leafy, aristocratic neighborhood home. At night, chockablock M St becomes congested with traffic, a weird mix of high-school cruising and high-street boutique.

Dumbarton Oaks

GARDENS, MUSEUM

(www.doaks.org; 1703 32nd St NW; museum free, gardens adult/child $8/5; ⊙ museum 11:30am-5:30pm Tue-Sun, gardens 2-6pm) The mansion's 10 acres of enchanting formal gardens are straight out of a storybook. In springtime, the blooms – including heaps of cherry blossoms – are stunning. The mansion itself is worth a walk-through to see exquisite Byzantine and pre-Columbian art (including El Greco's *The Visitation*) and the fascinating library of rare books.

Georgetown Waterfront Park   PARK

(Water St NW, btwn 30th St & Key Bridge; 🚻) The park is a favorite with couples on first dates, families on an evening stroll and power players showing off their big yachts. Benches dot the way, where you can sit and watch the rowing teams out on the Potomac River. Alfresco restaurants cluster near the harbor at 31st St NW. They ring a terraced plaza filled with fountains (which become an ice rink in winter). The docks are also here for sightseeing boats that ply the Potomac to Alexandria, VA.

Georgetown University   UNIVERSITY

(www.georgetown.edu; cnr 37th & O Sts NW) Georgetown is one of the nation's top universities, with a student body that's equally hardworking and hard-partying. Founded in 1789, it was America's first Roman Catholic university. Notable Hoya (derived from the Latin *hoya saxa*, 'what rocks') alumni include Bill Clinton, as well many international royals and heads of state. Near the campus' east gate, medieval-looking **Healy Hall** impresses with its tall, Hogwarts-esque clock tower. Pretty **Dalghren Chapel** and its quiet courtyard hide behind it.

Exorcist Stairs   FILM LOCATION

(3600 Prospect St NW) The steep set of stairs dropping down to M St is a popular track for joggers, but more famously it's the spot where demonically possessed Father Karras tumbles to his death in 1973 horror classic *The Exorcist*. Come on foggy nights, when the stone steps really are creepy as hell.

Tudor Place   MUSEUM

(www.tudorplace.org; 1644 31st St NW; 1hr house tour adult/child $10/3, self-guided garden tour $3; ☉10am-4pm Tue-Sat, from noon Sun, closed Jan) This 1816 neoclassical mansion was owned by Thomas Peter and Martha Custis Peter, the granddaughter of Martha Washington. Today the mansion functions as a small museum, and features furnishings and artwork from Mt Vernon, which give a nice insight into American decorative arts. The grand, 5-acre gardens bloom with roses, lilies, poplar trees and exotic palms.

◉ Upper Northwest DC

The far reaches of northwest DC are primarily made up of leafy residential neighborhoods.

National Zoo   ZOO

(www.nationalzoo.si.edu; 3001 Connecticut Ave NW; ☉10am-6pm Apr-Oct, to 4:30pm Nov-Mar, grounds 6am-8pm daily, to 6pm Nov-Mar; Ⓜ Cleveland Park, Woodley Park-Zoo/Adams Morgan) **FREE** Home to over 2000 individual animals (400 different species) in natural habitats, the National Zoo is famed for its giant pandas Mei Xiang and Tian Tian, along with their cub Bao Bao (born to Mei Xiang in 2013). Other highlights include the African lion pride, Asian elephants, and dangling orangutans swinging 50ft overhead from steel cables and interconnected towers (aka the 'O Line').

Washington National Cathedral   CHURCH

(☎ 202-537-6200; www.nationalcathedral.org; 3101 Wisconsin Ave NW; adult/child $10/$6, admission free Sun; ☉10am-5:30pm Mon-Fri, to 8pm some days May-Sep, 10am-4:30pm Sat, 8am-4pm Sun; Ⓜ Tenleytown-AU to southbound bus 31, 32, 36, 37) This Gothic cathedral, as dramatic as its European counterparts, blends both the spiritual and the profane in its architectural treasures. The stained-glass windows are stunning (check out the 'Space Window' with an imbedded lunar rock); you'll need binoculars to spy the Darth Vader gargoyle on the exterior. Specialized tours delve deeper into the esoteric; call or go online for the schedule. There's also an excellent cafe here.

◉ Anacostia

The drive from Georgetown eastbound to Anacostia takes about 30 minutes – and the patience to endure a world of income disparity. The neighborhood's poverty in contrast to the Mall, sitting mere miles away, forms one of DC's (and America's) great contradictory panoramas. Some high-end condos have sprung up around Nationals Park, the baseball stadium for the Washington Nationals.

Yards Park   PARK

(www.yardspark.org; 355 Water St SE; ☉7am-2hr past sunset; Ⓜ Navy Yard) The riverside green space is just down the road from the Nationals' stadium. There are shaded tables by the water, a wooden boardwalk, fountains and a funky modernist bridge that looks like a giant, open-faced plastic straw. Look left

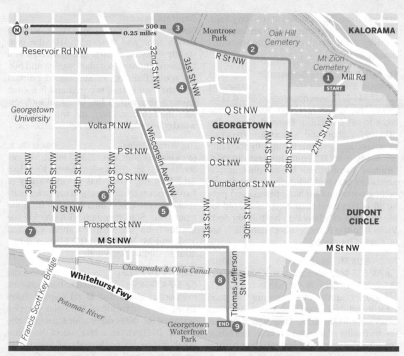

Reservoir Rd NW · Montrose Park · Oak Hill Cemetery · KALORAMA · 32nd St NW · 31st St NW · R St NW · Mt Zion Cemetery · Mill Rd · START · Georgetown University · Volta Pl NW · Wisconsin Ave NW · Q St NW · GEORGETOWN · P St NW · 29th St NW · 28th St NW · 27th St NW · 36th St NW · 35th St NW · 34th St NW · 33rd St NW · P St NW · O St NW · O St NW · Dumbarton St NW · N St NW · 31st St NW · 30th St NW · DUPONT CIRCLE · Prospect St NW · M St NW · M St NW · Francis Scott Key Bridge · Whitehurst Fwy · Chesapeake & Ohio Canal · Thomas Jefferson St NW · Potomac River · Georgetown Waterfront Park · END

🏃 City Walk
Genteel Georgetown

START MT ZION CEMETERY
END GEORGETOWN WATERFRONT PARK
LENGTH 3 MILES; THREE HOURS

Georgetown, in all its leafy, filigreed-manor glory, is a prime neighborhood for ambling.

African American **❶ Mt Zion Cemetery**, near the intersection of 27th and Q Sts, dates from the early 1800s. The nearby Mt Zion church (1334 29th St) was a stop on the Underground Railroad; escaping slaves hid in a vault in the cemetery.

The entrance to **❷ Oak Hill Cemetery** is a few blocks away at 30th and R Sts NW. Stroll the obelisk-studded grounds and look for graves of prominent Washingtonians such as Edwin Stanton (Lincoln's war secretary). Up the road, **❸ Dumbarton Oaks** offers exquisite Byzantine art and sprawling, fountain-dotted gardens: the blooms in springtime are stunning.

George Washington's step-granddaughter Martha Custis Peter owned **❹ Tudor Place**, the neoclassical mansion at 1644 31st St.

It features some of George's furnishings from Mount Vernon and pretty, landscaped grounds.

Head over to Wisconsin Ave NW and stop in at **❺ Martin's Tavern**, where John F Kennedy proposed to Jackie Bouvier. Walk along N St and you'll pass several Federal-style townhouses in the 3300 block. The Kennedys lived at **❻ 3307 N St** from 1958 to 1961, before they left for the White House.

At the corner of 36th St and Prospect Ave, stare down the **❼ Exorcist Stairs**, where demonically possessed Regan of *The Exorcist* sent victims to their screaming deaths. Joggers use the stairs by day; at night the steps are legitimately creepy as hell.

Go down to M St NW, popping in to whatever boutiques and high-end chain stores your wallet permits. At Jefferson St turn right and sniff your way to **❽ Baked & Wired** to replenish with a monster cupcake and cappuccino. From there you can stroll down to **❾ Georgetown Waterfront Park** to watch boats along the Potomac River.

and you'll see ships docked at the Navy Yard. Several new restaurants and an excellent brewery at the park's edge ensure you won't hunger or thirst.

Frederick Douglass National Historic Site
HISTORIC SITE

(☏877-444-6777; www.nps.gov/frdo; 1411 W St SE; ☉9am-5pm Apr-Oct, to 4:30pm Nov-Mar; ⓂAnacostia to bus B2) FREE Escaped slave, abolitionist, author and statesman Frederick Douglass occupied this beautifully sited hilltop house from 1878 until his death in 1895. Original furnishings, books, photographs and other personal belongings paint a compelling portrait of both the private and public life of this great man. Keep an eye out for his wire-rim eyeglasses on his roll-top desk. Visits into the home – aka Cedar Hill – are by guided tour only.

Anacostia Museum
MUSEUM

(☏202-633-4820; www.anacostia.si.edu; 1901 Fort Pl SE; ☉10am-5pm; ⓂAnacostia to bus W2, W3) FREE This Smithsonian museum has good rotating exhibitions on the African American experience in the USA. They typically focus on art (quilts of a certain region; landscape paintings by an overlooked artist) or history (the first black baseball teams in the area; a slave family's story). The museum also serves as a community hall for the surrounding neighborhood of Anacostia. Call ahead, as it often closes between installations.

🏃 Activities

Hiking & Cycling

C&O Canal Towpath
WALKING, CYCLING

(www.nps.gov/choh; 1057 Thomas Jefferson St NW) The shaded hiking-cycling path – part of a larger national historic park – runs alongside a waterway constructed in the mid-1800s to transport goods all the way to West Virginia. Step on at Jefferson St for a lovely green escape from the crowd.

In its entirety, the gravel path runs for 185 miles from Georgetown to Cumberland, MD. Lots of cyclists do the 14-mile ride from Georgetown to Great Falls, MD. The tree-lined route goes over atmospheric wooden bridges and past waterwheels and old lock houses. It's mostly flat, punctuated by occasional small hills. The park's website and **Bike Washington** (www.bikewashington.org/canal) have trail maps.

Capital Crescent Trail
CYCLING

(www.cctrail.org; Water St) Stretching between Georgetown and Bethesda, MD, the constantly evolving Capital Crescent Trail is a fabulous (and very popular) jogging and biking route. Built on an abandoned railroad bed, the 11-mile trail is paved and is a great leisurely day trip. It has beautiful lookouts over the Potomac River, and winds through woodsy areas and upscale neighborhoods.

Big Wheel Bikes
BICYCLE RENTAL

(www.bigwheelbikes.com; 1034 33rd St NW; per 3hr/day $21/35; ☉11am-7pm Tue-Fri, 10am-6pm Sat & Sun) Big Wheel has a wide variety of two-wheelers to rent, and you can practically spin onto the C&O Canal Towpath from the front door. Staff members also provide the lowdown on the nearby Capital Crescent Trail and Mt Vernon Trail. There's a three-hour minimum for rentals.

Capital Bikeshare
BICYCLE RENTAL

(☏877-430-2453; www.capitalbikeshare.com; membership 24hr/3 days $7/15) Capital Bikeshare has a network of 2500-plus bicycles scattered at 300-odd stations around the region. To check out a bike, select the membership (one day or three days), insert your credit card, and off you go. The first 30 minutes are free, after that, rates rise fast ($2/6/14 per extra 30/60/90 minutes). Call or go online for complete details.

Boating

Tidal Basin Boathouse
BOATING

(www.tidalbasinpaddleboats.com; 1501 Maine Ave SW; 2-/4-person boat rental $14/22; ☉10am-6pm mid-Mar–Aug, Wed-Sun only Sep–mid-Oct, closed mid-Oct–mid-Mar; 🚌Circulator, ⓂSmithsonian) It rents paddleboats to take out on the Tidal Basin. Make sure you bring a camera. There are great views, of the Jefferson Memorial in particular, from the water.

Key Bridge Boathouse
KAYAKING

(www.boatingindc.com; 3500 Water St NW; ☉hours vary Mar-Oct) Located beneath the Key Bridge, the boathouse rents canoes, kayaks and stand-up paddleboards (prices start at $15 per hour). It also offers guided, 90-minute kayak trips ($45 per person) in summer that glide past the Lincoln Memorial as the sun sets. If you have a bike, the boathouse is a mere few steps from the Capital Crescent Trail.

Tours

DC by Foot WALKING TOUR
(www.dcbyfoot.com) Guides for this pay-what-you-want walking tour offer engaging stories and historical details on different jaunts covering the National Mall, Lincoln's assassination, Georgetown's ghosts, U Street's food and many more. Most takers pay around $10 per person.

Bike & Roll BICYCLE TOUR
(www.bikeandrolldc.com; adult/child from $40/30; ⊙mid-Mar–Nov) Offers day and evening bike tours around the Mall and Capitol Hill. The 'Monuments at Night' tour is especially atmospheric. The company also arranges combo boat-bike trips to Mt Vernon.

DC Brew Tours BUS TOUR
(☑202-759-8687; www.dcbrewtours.com; tours $85; ⊙noon & 5pm Thu & Fri, 11am & 5pm Sat & Sun) DC Brew Tours offers five-hour jaunts by van that take in four breweries. Routes vary, but could include DC Brau, Right Proper Brewing, Chocolate City, 3 Stars and Atlas Brew Works, among others. Tastings of 15-plus beers and a beer-focused meal are part of the package. Departure is from downtown at 710 12th St NW, by the Metro Center station.

Festivals & Events

National Cherry Blossom Festival CULTURAL
(www.nationalcherryblossomfestival.org; ⊙late Mar–early Apr) DC at her prettiest.

Smithsonian Folklife Festival CULTURAL
(www.festival.si.edu; ⊙Jun & Jul) This fun family event, held over two weekends in June and July, features distinctive regional folk art, crafts, food and music.

Independence Day CULTURAL
(⊙Jul 4) Not surprisingly, a big deal here, celebrated on July 4 with a parade, an open-air concert and fireworks over the Mall.

WASHINGTON, DC FOR CHILDREN

The top destination for families is undoubtedly the (free!) **National Zoo** (p262). Other museums around the city will also entertain and educate children of all ages. Institutions with especially good programming include:

National Air and Space Museum (p251)

National Museum of Natural History (p251)

Newseum (p261)

National Gallery of Art (p251)

Some other family hot spots:

Carousel (tickets $3.50; ⊙10am-6pm; ☑Circulator, Ⓜ Smithsonian) Take a spin on the old-fashioned merry-go-round on the Mall, then romp around the wide-open lawn.

Discovery Theater (www.discoverytheater.org; 1100 Jefferson Dr SW; tickets $6-12; ☑; ☑Circulator, Ⓜ Smithsonian) The Smithsonian's kids' theater focuses on cultural plays and storytelling.

Yards Park (p262) Play and splash in this enticing green space.

Six Flags America (☑301-249-1500; www.sixflags.com/america; 13710 Central Ave, Upper Marlboro, MD; adult/child $60/40; ⊙May-Oct, hours vary) The park offers a full array of roller coasters and tamer kiddie rides. It's located about 15 miles east of downtown DC in Maryland.

Good resources for parents:

DC Cool Kids features activity guides, insider tips from local youngsters on things to do, and museum info.

Smithsonian Kids has educational games and projects, plus the lowdown on pint-sized activities at the museums.

Our Kids has loads of listings for kid-centric shows and events, family-friendly restaurants and activity ideas.

🛏 Sleeping

Lodging is expensive in DC. The high-season apex is mid-March through April (cherry-blossom season). Crowds and rates also peak in May, June, September and October. Hotel tax adds 14.5% to rates. If you have a car, figure on $35 to $55 per day for in-and-out privileges.

Airbnb can also be a good option in the city. For B&Bs and private apartments city-wide, contact **Bed & Breakfast DC** (www.bedandbreakfastdc.com).

🏠 Capitol Hill

Hotel George　　　BOUTIQUE HOTEL **$$**
(☑ 202-347-4200; www.hotelgeorge.com; 15 E St NW; r from $300; P ➗ ✳ @ 🛜 🐾; Ⓜ Union Station) DC's first chic boutique hotel is still one of its best. Chrome-and-glass furniture and modern art frame the bold interior. Rooms exude a cool, creamy-white Zen. The pop-art presidential accents (paintings of American currency, artfully rearranged and diced up) are a little overdone, but that's a minor complaint about what is otherwise the hippest lodging on the Hill.

🏠 Downtown & White House Area

Hostelling International – Washington DC　　　HOSTEL **$**
(☑ 202-737-2333; www.hiwashingtondc.org; 1009 11th St NW; dm $33-55, r $110-150; ➗ ✳ @ 🛜; Ⓜ Metro Center) Top of the budget picks, this large, friendly hostel attracts a laid-back international crowd and has loads of amenities: lounge rooms, a pool table, a 60in TV for movie nights, free tours, free continental breakfast and free wi-fi.

★ Hotel Lombardy　　　BOUTIQUE HOTEL **$$**
(☑ 202-828-2600; www.hotellombardy.com; 2019 Pennsylvania Ave NW; r $180-330; P ➗ ✳ @ 🛜; Ⓜ Foggy Bottom-GWU) Done up in Venetian decor (shuttered doors, warm gold walls), and beloved by World Bank and State Department types, this European boutique hotel has multilingual staff and an international vibe – you hear French and Spanish as often as English in its halls. The attitude carries into rooms decorated with original artwork and Chinese and European antiques.

Morrison-Clark Inn　　　HISTORIC HOTEL **$$**
(☑ 202-898-1200; www.morrisonclark.com; 1015 L St NW; r $150-250; P ➗ ✳ @ 🛜; Ⓜ Mt Vernon Sq) Listed on the Register of Historic Places and helmed by a doting staff, the elegant Morrison-Clark comprises two 1864 Victorian residences filled with fine antiques, chandeliers, richly hued drapes and other features evocative of the pre–Civil War South. Some rooms are on the small side, but more options are coming: the inn is expanding into a church next door.

Club Quarters　　　HOTEL **$$**
(☑ 202-463-6400; www.clubquarters.com/washington-dc; 839 17th St NW; r $125-205; P ➗ ✳ @ 🛜; Ⓜ Farragut West) Club Quarters is a no-muss, no-fuss kind of place often used by business travelers on the go. Room are small and without views, they lack charm or quirk, but the bed is restful, the desk workable, the wi-fi fast enough and the coffee maker well stocked. Oh, and the prices are reasonable in an area where they're usually sky-high.

★ Hay-Adams Hotel　　　HERITAGE HOTEL **$$$**
(☑ 202-638-6600; www.hayadams.com; 800 16th St NW; r from $350; P ✳ @ 🛜 🐾; Ⓜ McPherson Sq) One of the city's great heritage hotels, the Hay is a beautiful old building where 'nothing is overlooked but the White House.' The property has a palazzo-style lobby and probably the best rooms of the old-school, luxury genre in the city, all puffy mattresses like clouds shaded by four-poster canopies and gold-braid tassels.

🏠 U Street, Shaw & Logan Circle

Hotel Helix　　　BOUTIQUE HOTEL **$$**
(☑ 202-462-9001; www.hotelhelix.com; 1430 Rhode Island Ave NW; r $200-300; P ➗ ✳ @ 🛜 🐾; Ⓜ McPherson Sq) Modish and highlighter bright, the Helix is playfully hip – the perfect hotel for the bouncy international set that makes up the surrounding neighborhood. Little touches suggest a youthful energy (Pez dispensers in the minibar) balanced with worldly cool (like the pop-punk decor). All rooms have comfy, crisp-sheet beds and 37in flat-screen TVs.

Chester Arthur House　　　B&B **$$**
(☑ 877-893-3233; www.chesterarthurhouse.com; 23 Logan Circle NW; r $175-215; ➗ ✳ 🛜; Ⓜ U St) Snooze in one of four rooms in this beautiful Logan Circle row house, located a stumble from the restaurant boom along P and 14th Sts. The 1883 abode is stuffed with crystal chandeliers, antique oil paintings and a

mahogany-paneled staircase, plus ephemera from the hosts' global expeditions.

Adams Morgan

Adam's Inn   B&B $
(202-745-3600; www.adamsinn.com; 1746 Lanier Pl NW; r $109-179, without bathroom $79-100; P⊖✳@⟆; M Woodley Park) Tucked on a shady residential street, the 26-room inn is known for its personalized service, fluffy linens and handy location just a few blocks from 18th St's global smorgasbord. Inviting, homey rooms sprawl through two adjacent townhouses and a carriage house. The common areas have a nice garden patio, and there's a general sense of sherry-scented chintz.

Taft Bridge Inn   B&B $$
(202-387-2007; www.taftbridgeinn.com; 2007 Wyoming Ave NW; r $179-205, without bathroom $100-140; P⊖✳⟆; M Dupont Circle) Named for the bridge that leaps over Rock Creek Park just north, this beautiful 19th-century Georgian mansion is an easy walk to 18th St or Dupont Circle. The inn has a paneled drawing room, classy antiques, six fireplaces and a garden. Some of the 12 rooms have a Colonial Americana theme, accentuated by Amish quilts; others are more tweedy, exuding a Euro-renaissance vibe.

Dupont Circle

★ Tabard Inn   BOUTIQUE HOTEL $$
(202-785-1277; www.tabardinn.com; 1739 N St NW; r $195-250, without bathroom $135-155; ⊖✳@⟆; M Dupont Circle) Named for the inn in *The Canterbury Tales,* the Tabard spreads through a trio of Victorian-era row houses. The 40 rooms are hard to generalize: all come with vintage quirks such as iron bed frames and wing-backed chairs, though little accents distinguish – a Matisse-like painted headboard here, Amish-looking quilts there. There are no TVs, and wi-fi can be dodgy, but the of-yore atmospherics prevail.

Continental breakfast is included. Downstairs the parlor, beautiful restaurant and bar have low ceilings and old furniture, highly conducive to curling up with a vintage port and the Sunday *Post.*

Embassy Circle Guest House   B&B $$
(202-232-7744; www.dcinns.com; 2224 R St NW; r $180-300; ⊖✳⟆; M Dupont Circle) Embassies surround this 1902 French country–style home, which sits a few blocks from Dupont's nightlife hubbub. The 11 big-windowed rooms are decked out with Persian carpets and original art on the walls; they don't have TVs or radios, though they do each have wi-fi. Staff feeds you well throughout the day, with a hot organic breakfast, afternoon cookies, and an evening wine and beer soiree.

Embassy Circle's sister property – the **Woodley Park Guest House** (202-667-0218; www.dcinns.com; 2647 Woodley Rd NW; r $180-250, without bathroom $135-165; P✳⟆; M Woodley Park-Zoo, Adams Morgan) in farther-flung northwest DC – is a hot spot.

Georgetown

Graham Georgetown   BOUTIQUE HOTEL $$
(202-337-0900; www.thegrahamgeorgetown. com; 1075 Thomas Jefferson St NW; r $270-350; P⊖✳@⟆; M Foggy Bottom-GWU to DC Circulator) Set smack in the heart of Georgetown, the Graham occupies the intersection between stately tradition and modernist hip. Rooms have tasteful floral prints and duochrome furnishings with geometric accents. Even the most basic rooms have linens by Liddell Ireland and L'Occitane bath amenities, which means you'll be as fresh, clean and beautiful as the surrounding Georgetown glitterati.

✕ Eating

Washington's dining scene is booming. The number of restaurants has doubled over the past decade, with small, independent spots helmed by local chefs leading the way. There's also a delicious glut of global cuisines (Salvadoran, Ethiopian, Vietnamese, French) and traditional Southern fare (fried chicken, grits, biscuits and sweet iced tea).

✕ Capitol Hill

This hood has two particularly rich veins for eating and drinking. You'll find 8th St SE (near Eastern Market) – also known as Barracks Row – packed with venues. So is H St NE, an edgy corridor a mile east of Union Station; catch bus X2 or a taxi (about $8). The District's long-awaited streetcars might be rolling there soon, as well.

Toki Underground   ASIAN $
(202-388-3086; www.tokiunderground.com; 1234 H St NE; mains $10-12; ⟆11:30am-2:30pm & 5-10pm Mon-Thu, to midnight Fri & Sat; ⟆X2 from Union Station) Spicy ramen noodles and dumplings sum up wee Toki's menu. Steaming pots

obscure the busy chefs, while diners slurp and sigh contentedly. The eatery doesn't take reservations and there's typically a wait. Take the opportunity to explore surrounding bars; Toki will text when your table is ready. The restaurant isn't signposted; look for the Pug bar, and Toki is above it.

Maine Avenue Fish Market
SEAFOOD $

(1100 Maine Ave SW; mains $7-13; ☺8am-9pm; Ⓜ L'Enfant Plaza) The pungent, open-air Maine Avenue Fish Market is a local landmark. No-nonsense vendors sell fish, crabs, oysters and other seafood so fresh it's almost still flopping. They'll kill, strip, shell, gut, fry or broil your desire, which you can take to the waterfront benches and eat blissfully (mind the seagulls!).

Atlas Room
AMERICAN $$

(☏202-388-4020; www.theatlasroom.com; 1015 H St NE; mains $21-25; ☺5:30-9:30pm Tue-Thu, 5:30-10pm Fri & Sat, 5-9pm Sun; ☐X2 from Union Station) Set in a snug, candle-shimmering room, Atlas is a neighborhood favorite on edgy H St. The bistro takes cues from classical French and Italian gastronomy but blends them in approachable American ways using seasonal ingredients. In summer you might enjoy crab fritters, while in winter a braised daube of beef will melt your tongue (in a good way!).

Ted's Bulletin
AMERICAN $$

(☏202-544-8337; www.tedsbulletincapitolhill.com; 505 8th St SE; mains $10-19; ☺7am-10pm Sun-Thu, to 11pm Fri & Sat; ♿; Ⓜ Eastern Market) Plop into a booth in the art-deco-meets-diner ambience, and loosen the belt. Beer biscuits and sausage gravy for breakfast, meatloaf with ketchup glaze for dinner and other hipster spins on comfort foods hit the table. You've got to admire a place that lets you substitute pop tarts for toast. Breakfast is available all day.

Ethiopic
ETHIOPIAN $$

(☏202-675-2066; www.ethiopicrestaurant.com; 401 H St NE; mains $12-18; ☺5-10pm Tue-Thu, from noon Fri-Sun; ☝; Ⓜ Union Station) In a city with no shortage of Ethiopian joints, Ethiopic stands above the rest. Top marks go to the various *wats* (stews) and the signature *tibs* (sauteed meat and veg), derived from tender lamb that has sat in a bath of herbs and hot spices. Vegans get lots of love here.

★ Rose's Luxury
MODERN AMERICAN $$$

(☏202-580-8889; www.rosesluxury.com; 717 8th St SE; small plates $12-14, family-style plates $28-33; ☺5:30-10pm Mon-Thu, to 11pm Fri &

Sat; Ⓜ Eastern Market) Rose's is DC's most buzzed-about eatery – and that was before *Bon Appetit* named it the nation's best new restaurant in 2014. Crowds fork into worldly Southern comfort food as twinkling lights glow overhead and candles flicker around the industrial, half-finished room. Rose's doesn't take reservations, but ordering your meal at the upstairs bar can save time (and the cocktails are delicious).

✕ Downtown & White House Area

★ Red Apron Butchery
DELI $

(☏202-524-5244; www.redapronbutchery.com; 709 D St NW; mains $5-10; ☺7:30am-8pm Mon-Fri, 9am-8pm Sat, 9am-5pm Sun; Ⓜ Archives) Red Apron makes a helluva breakfast sandwich. Plop into one of the comfy booths and wrap your lips around the ricotta, honey and pine-nut 'aristocrat' or the egg and chorizo 'buenos dias.' They're all heaped onto tigelle rolls, a sort of Italian flatbread. But you have to order before 10:30am (2:30pm on weekends).

Daikaya
JAPANESE $

(☏202-589-1600; www.daikaya.com; 705 6th St NW; mains $13-14; ☺11:30am-10pm Sun & Mon, to 11pm Tue-Thu, to midnight Fri & Sat; Ⓜ Gallery Pl) Daikaya offers two options. Downstairs it's a casual ramen-noodle shop, where locals swarm in and slurp with friends in the slick wooden booths. Upstairs it's a sake-pouring Japanese izakaya (tavern), with rice-bowl lunches and fishy small plates for dinner. Note the upstairs closes between lunch and dinner (ie between 2pm and 5pm).

★ Founding Farmers
MODERN AMERICAN $$

(☏202-822-8783; www.wearefoundingfarmers. com; 1924 Pennsylvania Ave NW; mains $14-26; ☺11am-10pm Mon, 11am-11pm Tue-Thu, 11am-midnight Fri, 9am-midnight Sat, 9am-10pm Sun; ☝; Ⓜ Foggy Bottom-GWU, Farragut West) ✿ A frosty decor of pickled goods in jars adorns this buzzy dining space. The look is a combination of rustic-cool and modern art that reflects the nature of the food: locally sourced, New American fare. Buttermilk fried chicken and waffles and zesty pork and lentil stew are a few of the favorites. The restaurant is located in the IMF building.

Rasika
INDIAN $$

(☏202-637-1222; www.rasikarestaurant.com; 633 D St NW; mains $14-28; ☺11:30am-2:30pm Mon-Fri, 5:30-10:30pm Mon-Thu, 5-11pm Fri & Sat;

DON'T MISS

MARKET FARE

A couple of groovy markets offer good eats:

Union Market (www.unionmarketdc.com; 1309 5th St NE; ⊙ 11am-8pm Tue-Sun; Ⓜ NoMa) The cool crowd hobnobs here as foodie entrepreneurs sell their banana-ginger chocolates, herbed goat cheeses and smoked meats; pop-up restaurants use the space to try out concepts for everything from Taiwanese ramen to Indian dosas. Craft beers and coffee drinks help wash it all down. Tables dot the sunlit warehouse, and many locals make an afternoon of it, nibbling and reading. The market is about a half-mile walk from the NoMa Metro station in Northeast DC.

Eastern Market (www.easternmarket-dc.org; 225 7th St SE; ⊙ 7am-7pm Tue-Fri, to 6pm Sat, 9am-5pm Sun; Ⓜ Eastern Market) One of the icons of Capitol Hill, Eastern Market sprawls with delectable chow and good cheer. The covered arcade holds a bakery, dairy, butcher, blue-crab-and-shrimp company, and vendors of fresh produce. It's not that large...until the weekend, when artisans and farmers join the fun and the market spills out onto the street.

🖉; Ⓜ Archives) Rasika is as cutting edge as Indian food gets. The room resembles a Jaipur palace decorated by a flock of modernist art-gallery curators. Narangi duck is juicy, almost unctuous, and pleasantly nutty thanks to the addition of cashews; the deceptively simple *dal* (lentils) has the right kiss of sharp fenugreek. Vegans and vegetarians will feel a lot of love here.

Old Ebbitt Grill
AMERICAN $$

(☎ 202-347-4800; www.ebbitt.com; 675 15th St NW; mains $12-22; ⊙ 7:30am-1am Mon-Fri, from 8:30am Sat & Sun; Ⓜ Metro Center) The Grill has occupied its prime, by the White House, real estate since 1846. Political players (and lots of tourists) pack into the brass and wood interior, the sound of their conversation rumbling across a dining room where thick burgers, crab cakes and fish-and-chip type fare are rotated out almost as quickly as the clientele. Pop in for a drink and oysters during happy hour.

★ Central
Michel Richard
MODERN AMERICAN $$$

(☎ 202-626-0015; www.centralmichelrichard. com; 1001 Pennsylvania Ave NW; mains $19-34; ⊙ 11:30am-2:30pm Mon-Fri, 5-10:30pm Mon-Thu, 5-11pm Fri & Sat; Ⓜ Federal Triangle) Michel Richard is known for his high-end eating establishments in the District, but Central stands out as a special experience. It's aimed at hitting a comfort-food sweet spot. You're dining in a four-star bistro where the food is old-school favorites with a twist: lobster burgers, a sinfully complex meatloaf and fried chicken that redefines what fried chicken can be.

✕ U Street, Shaw & Logan Circle

★ Ben's Chili Bowl
AMERICAN $

(www.benschilibowl.com; 1213 U St; mains $5-10; ⊙ 6am-2am Mon-Thu, 6am-4am Fri, 7am-4am Sat, 11am-midnight Sun; Ⓜ U St) Ben's is a DC institution. The main stock in trade is half-smokes, DC's meatier, smokier version of the hot dog, usually slathered in mustard, onions and the namesake chili. For nearly 60 years presidents, rock stars and Supreme Court justices have come in to indulge in the humble diner; but, despite the hype, Ben's remains a true neighborhood establishment. Cash only.

★ Compass Rose
INTERNATIONAL $$

(☎ 202-506-4765; www.compassrosedc.com; 1346 T St NW; small plates $10-15; ⊙ 5pm-2am Sun-Thu, to 3am Fri & Sat; Ⓜ U St) Compass Rose feels like a secret garden, set in a discreet townhouse a whisker from 14th St's buzz. The exposed brick walls, rustic wood decor and sky-blue ceiling give it a casually romantic air. The menu is a mash-up of global comfort foods, so dinner might entail, say, a Chilean *lomito* (pork sandwich), Lebanese *kefta* (ground lamb and spices) and Georgian *khachapuri* (buttery, cheese-filled bread).

Estadio
SPANISH $$

(☎ 202-319-1404; www.estadio-dc.com; 1520 14th St NW; tapas $5-15; ⊙ 11:30am-2pm Fri-Sun; 5-10pm Mon-Thu, to 11pm Fri & Sat, to 9pm Sun; Ⓜ U St) Estadio buzzes with a low-lit, date-night vibe. The tapas menu (which is the focus) is as deep as an ocean trench. There are three variations of *Iberico* ham and a delicious foie gras, scrambled egg and truffle open-faced sandwich. Wash it down with some traditional *calimocho* (red wine and Coke). No reservations after 6pm, which usually means a wait at the bar.

Bistro Bohem
EASTERN EUROPEAN **$$**
(☑ 202-735-5895; www.bistrobohem.com; 600 Florida Ave NW; mains $12-21; ☺ 5-11pm Mon-Thu, 5pm-2am Fri, 10am-2am Sat, 10am-11pm Sun; ☏; Ⓜ Shaw-Howard U) Cozy Bistro Bohem is a community favorite for its rib-sticking Czech schnitzels, goulash and pilsners, served with a side of local art on the walls and occasional live jazz. By day the action shifts to adjoining Kafe Bohem, which opens at 7am (8am weekends) for espresso, pastries and flat sandwiches. The warm, bohemian environs make you swear you're in Prague.

Tico
LATIN AMERICAN **$$**
(☑ 202-319-1400; www.ticodc.com; 1926 14th St NW; small plates $9-14; ☺ 4pm-midnight Sun-Thu, from 10am Fri & Sat; ☑; Ⓜ U St) Loud, fun and clattering, Tico draws a young and artsy crowd for its nouveau tacos, small plates and 140 tequilas. Top honors go to the scallop ceviche with crispy rice, the Manchego cheese fritters and hibiscus margaritas. Vegetarians get some love from the edamame tacos, roasted cauliflower and other dishes. The bright hued, mural splashed eatery is mega popular, so make reservations.

★ Le Diplomate
FRENCH **$$$**
(☑ 202-332-3333; www.lediplomatedc.com; 1601 14th St NW; mains $22-31; ☺ 5-10pm Mon & Tue, 5-11pm Wed & Thu, 5pm-midnight Fri, 9:30am-midnight Sat, 9:30am-10pm Sun; Ⓜ U St) This charming French bistro is a relative newcomer, but it has skyrocketed to one of the hottest tables in town. DC celebrities galore cozy up in the leather banquettes and at the sidewalk tables. They come for an authentic slice of Paris, from the *coq au vin* (wine-braised chicken) and aromatic baguettes to the vintage curios and nudie photos decorating the bathrooms. Make reservations.

✗ Adams Morgan

The area around 18th St and Columbia Rd NW is loaded with ethnic eateries and funky diners.

Diner
AMERICAN **$**
(www.dinerdc.com; 2453 18th St NW; mains $9-17; ☺ 24hr; ☏; Ⓜ Woodley Park-Zoo/Adams Morgan) The Diner serves hearty comfort food, any time of the day or night. It's ideal for wee-hour breakfast scarf-downs, weekend bloody-Mary brunches (if you don't mind crowds) or any time you want unfussy, well-prepared American fare. Omelets, fat pancakes, mac 'n' cheese, grilled Portobello sandwiches and burgers hit the tables with aplomb. It's a good spot for kids, too.

★ Donburi
JAPANESE **$**
(☑ 202-629-1047; www.facebook.com/donburidc; 2438 18th St NW; mains $9-12; ☺ 11am-10pm; Ⓜ Woodley Park-Zoo/Adams Morgan) Hole-in-the-wall Donburi has 15 seats at a wooden counter where you get a front-row view of the slicing, dicing chefs. *Donburi* means 'bowl' in Japanese, and that's what arrives steaming hot and filled with, say, panko-coated shrimp atop rice and blended with the house's sweet-and-savory sauce. It's a simple, authentic meal. There's often a line, but it moves quickly. No reservations.

It's located in the same building as the DC Arts Center.

✗ Dupont Circle

★ Afterwords Cafe
AMERICAN **$$**
(☑ 202-387-3825; www.kramers.com; 1517 Connecticut Ave; mains $15-21; ☺ 7:30am-1am Sun-Thu, 24hr Fri & Sat; Ⓜ Dupont Circle) Attached to Kramerbooks, this buzzing spot is not your average bookstore cafe. The packed indoor tables, wee bar and outdoor patio overflow with good cheer. The menu features tasty bistro fare and an ample beer selection, making it a prime spot for happy hour, for brunch and at all hours on weekends (open 24 hours, baby!).

Duke's Grocery
CAFE **$$**
(☑ 202-733-5623; www.dukesgrocery.com; 1513 17th St NW; mains $11-16; ☺ 5:30-10pm Mon, 8am-10pm Tue & Wed, to 1am Thu & Fri, 11am-1am Sat, to 10pm Sun; ☏; Ⓜ Dupont Circle) 'The taste of East London in East Dupont' is the Duke's tagline, and that means black pudding and baked beans in the morning, spiced-lentil rotis in the afternoon and Brick Lane salt-beef sandwiches late night. Couples on low-maintenance dates and groups of chit-chatty friends angle for tables by the bay windows to people-watch. The genial vibe invites all-day lingering.

Bistrot du Coin
FRENCH **$$**
(☑ 202-234-6969; www.bistrotducoin.com; 1738 Connecticut Ave NW; mains $14-24; ☺ 11:30am-11pm Sun-Wed, to 1am Thu-Sat; Ⓜ Dupont Circle) The lively and much-loved Bistrot du Coin

TOP CAFES

Baked & Wired (202-333-2500; www.bakedandwired.com; 1052 Thomas Jefferson St NW; baked goods $3-6; 7am-8pm Mon-Thu, to 9pm Fri, 8am-9pm Sat, 9am-8pm Sun;) This cheery little Georgetown cafe whips up beautifully made coffees and delectable desserts; it's a fine spot to join students in both real and virtual chatter (free wi-fi, of course).

Ching Ching Cha (1063 Wisconsin Ave NW; teas $6-12; 11am-9pm) An airy, Zen-like teahouse that feels a world away from the shopping mayhem of Georgetown's M Street. Stop in for a pot of rare tea (more than 70 varieties), or try the steamed dumplings, sweets and other little snacks.

Filter (www.filtercoffeehouse.com; 1726 20th St NW; 7am-7pm Mon-Fri, 8am-7pm Sat & Sun; ; Dupont Circle) On a quiet street in Dupont, Filter is a jewel-box-sized cafe with a tiny front patio, a hipsterish, laptop-toting crowd and, most importantly, great coffee. Those who seek caffeinated perfection can get a decent flat white here.

is a neighborhood favorite for roll-up-your-sleeves, working-class French fare. The kitchen sends out consistently good onion soup, classic *steak-frites* (grilled steak and French fries), cassoulet, open-face sandwiches and nine varieties of its famous *moules* (mussels). Regional wines from around the motherland accompany the food by the glass, carafe and bottle.

★**Little Serow** THAI $$$
(www.littleserow.com; 1511 17th St NW; fixed menu per person $45; 5:30-10pm Tue-Thu, to 10:30pm Fri & Sat; Dupont Circle) Little Serow has no phone, no reservations and no sign on the door. It only seats groups of four or fewer (larger parties will be separated) but, despite all this, people line up around the block. And what for? Superlative northern Thai cuisine. The single-option menu – which consists of six or so hot-spiced courses – changes by the week.

Komi FUSION $$$
(202-332-9200; www.komirestaurant.com; 1509 17th St NW; set menu $135; 5-9:30pm Tue-Thu, to 10pm Fri & Sat; Dupont Circle) There is an admirable simplicity to Komi's changing menu, which is rooted in Greece and influenced by everything – primarily genius. Suckling pig for two; scallops and truffles; roasted baby goat. Komi's fairytale of a dining space doesn't take groups larger than four, and you need to reserve way in advance – like, now.

Georgetown

★**Chez Billy Sud** FRENCH $$
(202-965-2606; www.chezbillysud.com; 1039 31st St NW; mains $17-29; 11:30am-2pm Tue-Fri, 11am-2pm Sat & Sun, 5-10pm Tue-Thu & Sun, 5-11pm Fri & Sat;) An endearing little bistro tucked

away on a residential block, Billy's mint-green walls, gilt mirrors and wee marble bar exude laid-back elegance. Mustachioed servers bring baskets of warm bread to the white-linen–clothed tables, along with crackling pork and pistachio sausage, golden trout, tuna nicoise salad and plump cream puffs.

Martin's Tavern AMERICAN $$
(202-333-7370; www.martins-tavern.com; 1264 Wisconsin Ave NW; mains $17-32; 11am-1:30am Mon-Thu, 11am-2:30am Fri, 9am-2:30am Sat, 8am-1:30am Sun) John F Kennedy proposed to Jackie in booth three at Georgetown's oldest saloon, and if you're thinking of popping the question there today, the attentive waitstaff keep the champagne chilled for that very reason. With an old-English country scene, including the requisite fox-and-hound hunting prints on the wall, this DC institution serves unfussy classics such thick burgers, crab cakes and icy-cold beers.

Upper Northwest DC

★**Comet Ping Pong** PIZZA $
(www.cometpingpong.com; 5037 Connecticut Ave NW; pizzas $12-15; 5-10pm Mon-Thu, 11:30am-11pm Fri & Sat, to 10pm Sun; ; Van Ness-UDC) Proving that DC is more than a city of suits and corporate offices, Comet Ping Pong offers a fun and festive counterpoint to the marble city, with its ping-pong tables, industrial chic interior and delicious thin-crust pizzas cooked up in a wood-burning oven.

★**Macon** FUSION $$
(202-248-7807; www.maconbistro.com; 5520 Connecticut Ave NW; mains $22-28; 5-10pm Tue-Thu, to 11pm Fri & Sat, 10am-2pm & 5-10pm Sun; Friendship Heights then bus E2) Macon,

LOCAL KNOWLEDGE

EAT STREETS

14th St NW (Logan Circle) DC's most happening road: an explosion of hot-chef bites and bars.

18th St NW (Adams Morgan) Korean, West African, Japanese and Latin mash-up, plus late-night snacks.

11th St NW (Columbia Heights) Ever-growing scene of hipster cafes and edgy gastropubs.

8th St SE (Capitol Hill) Known as Barracks Row, it's the locals' favorite for welcoming comfort-food-type spots.

H St NE (Capitol Hill) Hip strip of pie cafes, noodle shops and foodie pubs.

9th St NW (Shaw) Aka 'Little Ethiopia', it has all the wats and injera you can handle.

Georgia, meets Mâcon, France, in this wild mash-up of delectable southern cooking with creative European accents. The space is always buzzing, as a local, well-dressed crowd comes to feast on fried catfish with smoked aïoli, seared chicken breast with almondine sauce, and piping hot biscuits served with pepper jelly. Creative cocktails, refreshing microbrews and an appealing all-French wine list round out the menu.

Columbia Heights

Hipsters and Latino immigrants share the sidewalks in this unassuming neighborhood, set a short distance from U St.

Maple ITALIAN **$$**
(☎202-588-7442; www.dc-maple.com; 3418 11th St NW; mains $14-22; ⏰5:30pm-midnight Mon-Thu, 5pm-1am Fri & Sat, 11am-11pm Sun; Ⓜ Columbia Heights) At snug Maple, ladies in thrifty dresses and black tights fork into rich pasta dishes next to guys clad in T-shirts and tattoo sleeves on a reclaimed wood bar. House-made limoncello, Italian craft beers and unusual wine varietals also move across the lengthy slab (the wood type, incidentally, is what gives the venue its name).

Kangaroo Boxing Club AMERICAN **$$**
(KBC; ☎202-505-4522; www.kangaroodc.com; 3410 11th St NW; mains $13-18; ⏰5-11pm Mon-Thu, 5pm-1:30am Fri, 10am-1:30am Sat, 10am-10pm Sun; Ⓜ Columbia Heights) The gastropub concept –

but a hip, laid-back, Brooklyn-esque gastropub – is all the rage among DC's hip young things and the restaurateurs who cater to them. Enter the KBC: it has a quirky theme (vintage boxing), a delicious menu (burgers, barbecue, sweet spoon bread and loaded mac 'n' cheese and the like) and a deep beer menu.

Drinking & Nightlife

See the free alternative weekly *Washington City Paper* (www.washingtoncitypaper.com) for comprehensive listings. DC is a big happy-hour town – practically all bars have some sort of drink special for a few hours between 4pm and 7pm.

Capitol Hill

Little Miss Whiskey's Golden Dollar BAR
(www.littlemisswhiskeys.com; 1104 H St NE; ⏰5pm-2am; 🚇X2 from Union Station) If Alice had returned from Wonderland so traumatized by her near-beheading that she needed a stiff drink, we imagine she'd pop down to Little Miss Whiskey's. She'd love the whimsical-meets-dark-nightmares decor. And she'd probably have fun with the club kids partying on the upstairs dance floor on weekends. She'd also adore the weirdly fantastic back patio.

★**Bluejacket Brewery** BREWERY
(☎202-524-4862; www.bluejacketdc.com; 300 Tingey St SE; ⏰11am-1am Sun-Thu, to 2am Fri & Sat; Ⓜ Navy Yard) Beer lovers' heads will explode in Bluejacket. Pull up a stool at the mod-industrial bar, gaze at the silvery tanks bubbling up the ambitious brews, then make the hard decision about which of the 25 tap beers you want to try. A dry-hopped kolsch? Sweet-spiced stout? A cask-aged farmhouse ale? Four-ounce tasting pours help with decision-making.

H Street Country Club BAR
(www.thehstreetcountryclub.com; 1335 H St NE; ⏰5pm-1am Mon-Thu, 4pm-3am Fri, 11am-3am Sat, 11am-1am Sun; 🚇X2 from Union Station) The Country Club is two levels of great. The bottom floor is packed with pool tables, skeeball and shuffleboard, while the top contains its own mini-golf course ($7 to play) made up to resemble a tour of the city on a small scale. You putt-putt past a trio of Lego lobbyists, through Beltway traffic snarls and past a King Kong–clad Washington Monument.

Granville Moore's
PUB

(www.granvillemoores.com; 1238 H St NE; ◷5pm-midnight Mon-Thu, 5pm-3am Fri, 11am-3am Sat, 11am-midnight Sun; ☐X2 from Union Station) Besides being one of DC's best places to grab frites and a steak sandwich, Granville Moore's has an extensive Belgian beer menu that should satisfy any fan of low-country boozing. With raw, wooden fixtures and walls that look as if they were made from daub and mud, the interior resembles a medieval barracks. The fireside setting is ideal on a winter's eve.

Tune Inn
BAR

(331 Pennsylvania Ave SE; mains $7-14; ◷8am-2am Sun-Fri, to 3am Sat; Ⓜ Capitol South, Eastern Market) Dive bar Tune Inn has been around for decades and is where the neighborhood's older residents come to knock back Budweisers. The mounted deer heads and antler chandelier set the mood, as greasy-spoon grub and all-day breakfasts get scarfed in the vinyl-backed booths.

🍷 U Street, Shaw & Logan Circle

★ Right Proper Brewing Co
BREWERY

(www.rightproperbrewery.com; 624 T St NW; ◷5-11pm Tue-Thu, to midnight Fri & Sat, to 10pm Sun; Ⓜ Shaw-Howard U) As if the artwork – a chalked mural of the National Zoo's giant pandas with laser eyes destroying downtown DC – wasn't enough, Right Proper Brewing Co makes sublime ales in a building where Duke Ellington used to play pool. It's the Shaw district's neighborhood clubhouse, a big, sunny space filled with folks gabbing at reclaimed wood tables.

Churchkey
BAR

(www.churchkeydc.com; 1337 14th St NW; ◷4pm-1am Mon-Thu, 4pm-2am Fri, noon-2am Sat, noon-1am Sun; Ⓜ McPherson Sq) Coppery, mod-industrial Churchkey glows with hipness. Fifty beers flow from the taps, including five brainwalloping, cask-aged ales. If none of those please you, another 500 types of brew are available by the bottle (including gluten-free suds). Churchkey is the upstairs counterpart to Birch & Barley, a popular nouveau comfort-food restaurant, and you can order much of its menu at the bar.

Cork Wine Bar
WINE BAR

(www.corkdc.com; 1720 14th St NW; ◷5pm-midnight Tue & Wed, 5pm-1am Thu-Sat, 11am-3pm & 5-10pm Sun; Ⓜ U St) This dark 'n' cozy wine bar manages to come off as foodie magnet

and friendly neighborhood hangout all at once, which is a feat. Around 50 smart wines are available by the glass and 160 types by the bottle. Accompanying nibbles include cheese and charcuterie platters, as well as small plates such as chicken livers on marmalade-dolloped rosemary bruschetta.

Dacha Beer Garden
BEER GARDEN

(www.dachadc.com; 1600 7th St NW; ◷4-10:30pm Mon-Thu, 4pm-midnight Fri, noon-midnight Sat, noon-10:30pm Sun; Ⓜ Shaw-Howard U) Happiness reigns in Dacha's freewheeling beer garden. Kids and dogs bound around the picnic tables, while adults hoist glass boots filled with German brews. When the weather gets nippy, staff bring heaters and blankets and stoke the fire pit. And it all takes place under the sultry gaze of Elizabeth Taylor (or a mural of her, which sprawls across the back wall).

U Street Music Hall
CLUB

(www.ustreetmusichall.com; 1115 U St NW; ◷hours vary; Ⓜ U St) **FREE** This is the spot to get your groove on sans the VIP/bottle-service crowd. Two local DJs own and operate the basement club. It looks like a no-frills rock bar, but it has a pro sound system, cork-cushioned dance floor and other accoutrements of a serious dance club. Alternative bands also thrash a couple of nights per week to keep it fresh.

🍷 Dupont Circle & Adams Morgan

★ Dan's Cafe
BAR

(2315 18th St NW; ◷7pm-2am Tue-Thu, to 3am Fri & Sat; Ⓜ Woodley Park-Zoo/Adams Morgan) This is one of DC's great dive bars. The interior looks sort of like an evil Elks Club, all unironically old-school 'art,' cheap paneling and dim lights barely illuminating the unapologetic slumminess. It's famed for its

BEER TOWN

Washington is serious about beer, and even brews much its own delicious stuff. That trend started in 2009, when DC Brau became the District's first brewery to launch in more than 50 years (several more beer makers followed). As you drink around town, keep an eye out for local concoctions from Chocolate City, 3 Stars, Atlas Brew Works, Hellbender and Lost Rhino (from northern Virginia).

WASHINGTON, DC & THE CAPITAL REGION DRINKING & NIGHTLIFE

GAY & LESBIAN WASHINGTON, DC

The community concentrates in Dupont Circle, but U St, Shaw, Capitol Hill and Logan Circle also have lots of gay-friendly businesses. The free weeklies *Washington Blade* and *Metro Weekly* have the nightlife lowdown.

Cobalt (www.cobaltdc.com; 1639 R St NW; ☺5pm-2am; Ⓜ Dupont Circle) Featuring lots of hair product and faux-tanned gym bodies, Cobalt tends to gather a better-dressed late-20s-to-30-something crowd who come for fun (and loud!) dance parties throughout the week.

Nellie's (www.nelliessportsbar.com; 900 U St NW; ☺5pm-1am Mon-Thu, from 3pm Fri, from 11am St & Sun; Ⓜ Shaw-Howard U) The vibe here is low-key; Nellie's is a good place to hunker down among a friendly crowd for tasty bar bites, event nights (including karaoke Tuesdays) and early-evening drink specials.

JR's (www.jrsbar-dc.com; 1519 17th St NW; ☺4pm-2am Mon-Thu, 4pm-3am Fri, 1pm-3am Sat, 1pm-2am Sun; Ⓜ Dupont Circle) This popular gay hangout is a great spot for happy hour and is packed more often than not. Embarrassing show-tunes karaoke is great fun on Monday nights.

whopping, mix-it-yourself drinks, where you get a ketchup-type squirt bottle of booze, a can of soda and bucket of ice for barely $20. Cash only.

Bar Charley　BAR
(www.barcharley.com; 1825 18th St NW; ☺5pm-12:30am Mon-Thu, 4pm-1:30am Fri, 10am-1:30am Sat, 10am-12:30am Sun; Ⓜ Dupont Circle) Bar Charley draws a mixed crowd from the neighborhood – young, old, gay and straight. They come for groovy cocktails sloshing in vintage glassware and ceramic tiki mugs, served at very reasonable prices by DC standards. Try the gin and gingery Suffering Bastard. The beer list isn't huge, but it is thoughtfully chosen with some wild ales. Around 60 wines are available, too.

Tabard Inn Bar　BAR
(www.tabardinn.com; 1739 N St NW; ☺11:30am-1:30am Mon-Fri, from 10:30am Sat & Sun; Ⓜ Dupont Circle) The Tabard Inn Bar is in a hotel, but plenty of locals come to swirl an Old Fashioned or gin and tonic in the wood-beamed, lodge-like lounge. On warm nights, maneuver for an outdoor table on the ivy-clad patio.

🍷 Georgetown & White House Area

Tombs　PUB
(www.tombs.com; 1226 36th St NW; ☺11:30am-1:30am Mon-Thu, to 2:30am Fri & Sat, 9:30am-1:30am Sun) Every college of a certain pedigree has 'that' bar – the one where faculty and students alike sip pints under athletic regalia of the old school. The Tombs is

Georgetown's contribution to the genre. If it looks familiar, think back to the '80s: the subterranean pub was one of the settings for the film *St Elmo's Fire*.

Round Robin　BAR
(1401 Pennsylvania Ave NW, Willard InterContinental Hotel; ☺noon-1am Mon-Sat, to midnight Sun; Ⓜ Metro Center) Dispensing drinks since 1850, the bar at the Willard Hotel is one of DC's most storied watering holes. The small, circular space is done up in Gilded Age accents, all dark wood and velvet-green walls, and while it's touristy, you'll still see officials here likely determining your latest tax hike over a mint julep or single-malt Scotch.

🍷 Columbia Heights

★ Room 11　CAFE
(www.room11dc.com; 3234 11th St NW; ☺8am-1am Sun-Thu, to 2am Fri & Sat; Ⓜ Columbia Heights) Room 11 isn't much bigger than an ambitious living room, and as such it can get pretty jammed. On the plus side, everyone is friendly, the intimacy is warmly inviting on chilly winter nights and there's a spacious outdoor area for when it gets too hot inside. The low-key crowd sips excellent wines hand-selected by the management and whiz-bang cocktails.

Wonderland Ballroom　BAR
(www.thewonderlandballroom.com; 1101 Kenyon St NW; ☺5pm-2am Mon-Thu, 4pm-3am Fri, 11am-3pm Sat, 10am-2am Sun; 🐾; Ⓜ Columbia Heights) Wonderland embodies the edgy, eccentric Columbia Heights vibe to perfection. The interior is decked out in vintage signs and found objects to the point it could be a

folk-art museum, the outdoor patio is a good spot for meeting strangers, and the upstairs dance floor is a good place to take said strangers for a bit of bump and grind.

☆ Entertainment

Live Music

Black Cat   LIVE MUSIC
(www.blackcatdc.com; 1811 14th St NW; MU St) A pillar of DC's rock and indie scene since the 1990s, the battered Black Cat has hosted all the greats of years past (White Stripes, the Strokes, Arcade Fire and others). If you don't want to pony up for $20-a-ticket bands on the upstairs main stage (or the smaller Backstage below), head to the Red Room for jukebox, pool and strong cocktails.

9:30 Club   LIVE MUSIC
(www.930.com; 815 V St NW; admission from $10; MU St) This place, which can pack 1200 people into a surprisingly compact venue, is the granddaddy of the live music scene in DC. Pretty much every big name that comes through town ends up on this stage, and a concert here is the first-gig memory of many a DC-area teenager. Headliners usually take the stage between 10:30pm and 11:30pm.

Bohemian Caverns   JAZZ
(www.bohemiancaverns.com; 2001 11th St NW; admission $7-22; ⊙7pm-midnight Mon-Thu, 7:30pm-2am Fri & Sat, 6pm-midnight Sun; MU St) Back in the day, Bohemian Caverns hosted the likes of Miles Davis, John Coltrane and Duke Ellington. Today you'll find a mix of youthful renegades and soulful legends. Monday night's swingin' house band draws an all-ages crowd.

Performing Arts

Kennedy Center   PERFORMING ARTS
(☑202-467-4600; www.kennedy-center.org; 2700 F St NW; MFoggy Bottom-GWU) Sprawled on 17 acres along the Potomac River, the magnificent Kennedy Center hosts a staggering array of performances – more than 2000 each year among its multiple venues, including the Concert Hall (home to the National Symphony) and Opera House (home to the National Opera). A free shuttle bus runs to and from the Metro station every 15 minutes from 9:45am (noon on Sunday) to midnight.

Shakespeare Theatre Company   THEATER
(☑202-547-1122; www.shakespearetheatre.org; 450 7th St NW; MArchives) The nation's foremost Shakespeare company presents masterful works by the bard, as well as plays by George Bernard Shaw, Oscar Wilde, Ibsen, Eugene O'Neill and other greats. The season spans about a half-dozen productions annually, plus a free summer Shakespeare series on-site for two weeks in late August.

Studio Theatre   THEATER
(www.studiotheatre.org; 1501 14th St NW; MDupont Circle) The contemporary four-theater complex has been staging Pulitzer Prize–winning and premiere plays for more than 35 years. It cultivates a lot of local actors.

Sports

★ Washington Nationals   BASEBALL
(www.nationals.com; 1500 S Capitol St SE; 🐦; MNavy Yard) The major-league Nats play baseball at **Nationals Park** (www.nationals.com; 1500 S Capitol St SE; MNavy Yard) beside the Anacostia River. Don't miss the mid-fourth-inning 'Racing Presidents' – an odd foot race between giant-headed caricatures of George Washington, Abraham Lincoln, Thomas Jefferson, Teddy Roosevelt and William Taft. The stadium itself is spiffy, and hip eateries and mod Yards Park have cropped up around it as the area gentrifies.

Washington Redskins   FOOTBALL
(☑301-276-6800; www.redskins.com; 1600 Fedex Way, Landover, MD; MMorgan Blvd) Washington's NFL team, the Redskins, plays September through January at FedEx Field. The team has experienced a lot of controversy recently, and not only because of its woeful play. Many groups have criticized the Redskins' name and logo as insulting to Native Americans. The US Patent and Trademark Office agreed, and revoked the team's trademark.

Washington Capitals   HOCKEY
(http://capitals.nhl.com; 601 F St NW; MGallery Pl) Washington's rough-and-tumble pro hockey team skates at the Verizon Center from October to April. Tickets start from around $40.

ⓘ KENNEDY CENTER FREEBIES

Don't have the dough for a big-ticket show? No worries. Each evening the Kennedy Center's **Millennium Stage** (www.kennedy-center.org/millennium; Kennedy Center; MFoggy Bottom-GWU) puts on a first-rate music or dance performance at 6pm in the Grand Foyer. The cost is absolutely nada. Check the website to see who's playing.

Washington Wizards BASKETBALL
(www.nba.com/wizards; 601 F St NW; M Gallery Pl)
Washington's winning pro basketball team
plays at the Verizon Center from October
through April. The lowest-price tickets are
around $30 for the nosebleed section, and
the cost goes way up from there.

ℹ Orientation

Remember: lettered streets go east–west, and
numbered streets, north–south. On top of that
the city is divided into four quadrants with identical addresses in different divisions – F and 14th
NW puts you near the White House, while F and
14th NE puts you near Rosedale Playground.

ℹ Information

Cultural Tourism DC (www.culturaltourismdc.
org) Offers a large range of DIY neighborhood
walking tours.

Destination DC (☑ 202-789-7000; www.
washington.org) DC's official tourism site, with
the mother lode of online information.

George Washington University Hospital
(☑ 202-715-4000; 900 23rd St NW; M Foggy
Bottom-GWU)

Washington City Paper (www.washington
citypaper.com) Free edgy weekly with entertainment and dining listings.

Washington Post (www.washingtonpost.com)
Respected daily city (and national) paper. Its
tabloid-format daily *Express* is free.

ℹ Getting There & Away

AIR

Ronald Reagan Washington National Airport
(DCA; www.metwashairports.com) DC's smaller
airport, located 4.5 miles south of DC in Arlington, VA.

Dulles International Airport (IAD; www.
metwashairports.com) Found 26 miles west of
DC, in Virginia. It's the larger airport, and handles most international flights.

**Baltimore/Washington International Thur-
good Marshall Airport** (BWI; ☑ 410-859-7111;
www.bwiairport.com) Set 30 miles northeast,
in Maryland. It's a Southwest Airlines hub, and
often has cheaper flights.

BUS

Cheap bus services to and from Washington
abound. Most charge around $25 for a one-way
trip to NYC, which takes four to five hours. Tickets usually need to be bought online.

BoltBus (☑ 877-265-8287; www.boltbus.com;
50 Massachusetts Ave NE; 🛜) The best of the
budget options for NYC trips; it uses Union
Station as its terminal.

BestBus (☑ 202-332-2691; www.bestbus.com;
20th St & Massachusetts Ave NW; 🛜) Several
trips to/from NYC daily. The main bus stop
is by Dupont Circle; there's another at Union
Station.

Greyhound (☑ 202-589-5141; www.greyhound.
com; 50 Massachusetts Ave NE) Provides
nationwide service. The terminal is at Union
Station.

Megabus (☑ 877-462-6342; http://us.
megabus.com; 50 Massachusetts Ave NE; 🛜)
Offers the most trips to NYC (more than 20 per
day), as well as other east-coast cities; arrives
at/departs from Union Station.

Washington Deluxe (☑ 866-287-6932; www.
washny.com; 1610 Connecticut St NW; 🛜)
Good express service to/from NYC. It has stops
at both Dupont Circle and Union Station.

TRAIN

The magnificent beaux-arts Union Station is the
city's rail hub. Trains depart at least once per hour
for major east coast cities, including New York
City (3½ hours) and Boston (six to eight hours).

Amtrak (☑ 800-872-7245; www.amtrak.com)
Trains depart for nationwide destinations, includ-
ing New York City (3½ hours), Chicago (18 hours),
Miami (24 hours) and Richmond, VA (three hours).

MARC (Maryland Rail Commuter; www.mta.
maryland.gov) This regional rail service for the
Washington, DC–Baltimore metro area runs
trains frequently to Baltimore and other Maryland towns; also goes to Harpers Ferry, WV.

ℹ Getting Around

TO/FROM THE AIRPORT

Ronald Reagan Washington National Airport
Has its own Metro station. Trains (around
$2.50) depart every 10 minutes or so between
5am and midnight (to 3am Friday and Saturday) and reach downtown in 20 minutes. Taxis
cost $13 to $22 and take 10 to 30 minutes.

**Baltimore/Washington International Thur-
good Marshall Airport** Both local MARC trains
and Amtrak travel from the airport to DC's
Union Station. Trains leave once or twice per
hour, but there's no service after 9:30pm (and
limited service on weekends). It takes 30 to 40
minutes; fares start at $6. Or consider the B30
bus, which runs to the Greenbelt Metro station
(75 minutes, $10.50 for total bus/Metro fare).

Washington Dulles International Airport The
Metro Silver Line is slated to reach Dulles in
2018. In the meantime, options include taxis
(30 to 60 minutes, $62 to $73), the Metrobus
5A and the Washington Flyer.

Metrobus 5A (www.wmata.com) Runs every 30
to 40 minutes from Dulles to the Rosslyn Metro
station (Blue, Orange and Silver Lines) and on
to central DC (L'Enfant Plaza) between 5:50am
(6:30am weekends) and 11:35pm. Total time to

the center is about an hour; total bus/Metro fare is about $9.

Washington Flyer (☑ 888-927-4359; www. washfly.com) The company's Silver Line Express bus runs every 15 to 20 minutes from Dulles airport (main terminal, arrivals level door 4) to the Wiehle-Reston East Metro station between 6am and 10:40pm (from 7:45am weekends). Total time to DC's center is 60 to 75 minutes, total bus-Metro cost around $11.

PUBLIC TRANSPORTATION

The system is a mix of Metro trains (subway) and buses, but the Metro is the main way to go. Buy a rechargeable SmarTrip card at any station. It costs $10, with $8 of that stored for fares. You can add value as needed. Without a SmarTrip card, each ride is subject to a $1 surcharge for using a disposable fare card. Use the card to enter *and* exit station turnstiles. The card is also usable on buses. Another option: buy an unlimited-ride day pass for $14.50.

Metrorail (☑ 202-637-7000; www.wmata.com) The Metro will get you to most sights, hotels and business districts, and to the Maryland and Virginia suburbs. Trains start running at 5am Monday through Friday (from 7am on weekends); the last service is around midnight Sunday through Thursday and 3am on Friday and Saturday. Machines inside stations sell computerized fare cards; fares are based on distance traveled.

DC Circulator (www.dccirculator.com; fare $1) Red Circulator buses run along handy local routes, including Union Station to/from the Mall (looping by all major museums and memorials), Union Station to/from Georgetown (via K St), Dupont Circle to/from Georgetown (via M St), and the White House area to/from Adams Morgan (via 14th St). Buses operate from roughly 7am to 9pm weekdays (to midnight or so on weekends).

Metrobus (www.wmata.com; fare $1.75) Operates clean, efficient buses throughout the city and suburbs, typically from early morning until late evening.

TAXI

Taxis are relatively easy to find (less so at night), but costly. **DC Yellow Cab** (☑ 202-544-1212) is reliable. The rideshare company Uber is used more in the District.

MARYLAND

Maryland is often described as 'America in Miniature,' and for good reason: this small state possesses all of the best bits of the country, from the Appalachian Mountains in the west to sandy white beaches in the east. A blend of Northern streetwise and Southern down-home gives this most osmotic of border states an appealing identity crisis. Its main city, Baltimore, is a sharp, demanding port town; the Eastern Shore jumbles art-and-antique-minded city refugees and working fisher-folk; while the DC suburbs are packed with government and office workers seeking green space, and the poor seeking lower rents. Yet it all somehow works – scrumptious blue crabs, Natty Boh beer and lovely Chesapeake country being the glue that binds all. This is also an extremely diverse and progressive state, and was one of the first in the country to legalize gay marriage.

History

George Calvert established Maryland as a refuge for persecuted English Catholics in 1634 when he purchased St Mary's City from the local Piscataway tribespeople, with whom he initially tried to coexist. Puritan refugees drove both Piscataway and Catholics from control and shifted power to Annapolis; their harassment of Catholics produced the Tolerance Act, a flawed but progressive law that allowed freedom of any (Christian) worship in Maryland – a North American first.

That commitment to diversity has always characterized this state, despite a mixed record on slavery. Although state loyalties were split during the Civil War, a Confederate invasion was halted here in 1862 at Antietam. Following the war, Maryland harnessed its black, white and immigrant work force, splitting the economy between Baltimore's industry and shipping, and the later need for services in Washington, DC. Today, the answer to 'What makes a Marylander?' is 'all of the above': the state mixes rich, poor, the foreign-born, urban sophisticates and rural villages like few other states do.

Baltimore

Once among the most important port towns in America, Baltimore – or 'Bawlmer' to locals – is a city of contradictions. On one hand it remains something of an ugly duckling – a defiant, working-class, gritty city still tied to its nautical past. But in recent years Baltimore has begun to grow into a swan – or, more accurately, gotten better at showing the world the swan that was always there, in the form of world-class museums, trendy shops, ethnic restaurants, boutique hotels, culture and sports. 'B'more' (another nickname) does this all with a twinkle in the eye and a wisecrack on the lips; this quirky city spawned Billie Holiday and John Waters. Yet it remains intrinsically tied to the water, from the Disney-fied Inner Harbor and cobblestoned streets of portside Fell's Point to the shores of Fort McHenry, birthplace of America's national anthem, 'The Star-Spangled Banner.' There's an intense, sincere friendliness to this burg, which is why Baltimore lives up to its final, most accurate nickname: 'Charm City.'

⊙ Sights & Activities

⊙ Harborplace & Inner Harbor

This is where most tourists start and, unfortunately, end their Baltimore sightseeing. The Inner Harbor is a big, gleaming waterfront-renewal project of shiny glass, air-conditioned malls and flashy bars that manages to capture the maritime heart

MARYLAND FACTS

Nickname The Old Line State, the Free State

Population 5.8 million

Area 12,407 sq miles

Capital city Annapolis (population 39,000)

Other cities Baltimore (621,000), Frederick (66,000), Hagerstown (40,000), Salisbury (30,500)

Sales tax 6%

Birthplace of Abolitionist Frederick Douglass (1818–95), baseball great Babe Ruth (1895–1948), actor David Hasselhoff (b 1952), author Tom Clancy (b 1947), swimmer Michael Phelps (b 1985)

Home of 'The Star-Spangled Banner,' Baltimore Orioles, TV crime shows *The Wire* and *Homicide: Life on the Street*

Politics Staunch Democrats

Famous for Blue crabs, lacrosse, Chesapeake Bay

State sport Jousting

Driving distances Baltimore to Annapolis 29 miles; Baltimore to Ocean City 147 miles

of this city, albeit in a safe-for-the-family kinda way. But it's also just the tip of Baltimore's iceberg.

National Aquarium   AQUARIUM
(☑ 410-576-3833; www.aqua.org; 501 E Pratt St, Piers 3 & 4; adult/child $35/22; ⊙ 9am-5pm Sun-Thu, to 8pm Fri, to 6pm Sat) ✎ Standing seven stories high and capped by a glass pyramid, this is widely considered to be the best aquarium in America, with 17,000 creatures (over 750 species), a rooftop rainforest, a central ray pool and a multistory shark tank. There's also a reconstruction of the Umbrawarra Gorge in Australia's Northern Territory, complete with 35ft waterfall, rocky cliffs and free-roaming birds and lizards.

The largest exhibit contains eight bottlenose dolphins kept in captivity, though at press time the aquarium was exploring the possibility of retiring them to an oceanside sanctuary (freeing them in the wild is not an option, since they lack survival skills). Kids will love the 4-D Immersion Theater (admission costs an additional $5). There are loads of unique, behind-the-scenes tours, as well as dolphin and shark sleepovers. Go on weekdays (right at opening time) to beat the crowds.

Baltimore Maritime Museum   MUSEUM
(☑ 410-539-1797; www.historicships.org; 301 E Pratt St, Piers 3 & 5; adult 1/2/4 ships $11/14/18, child $5/6/7; ⊙ 10am-4:30pm) Ship-lovers can take a tour through four historic ships: a Coast Guard cutter that saw action in Pearl Harbor, a 1930 lightship, a submarine active in WWII and the **USS Constellation** – one of the last sail-powered warships built (in 1797) by the US Navy. Admission to the 1856 Seven Foot Knoll Lighthouse, on Pier 5, is free.

⊙ Downtown & Little Italy

You can easily walk from downtown Baltimore to Little Italy, but follow the delineated path: there's a rough housing project along the way.

**National Great Blacks
in Wax Museum**   MUSEUM
(☑ 410-563-3404; www.greatblacksinwax.org; 1601 E North Ave; adult/child $13/11; ⊙ 9am-6pm Mon-Sat, noon-6pm Sun Feb & Jul-Aug, closed Mon rest of year) This excellent African American history museum has exhibits on Frederick Douglass, Jackie Robinson, Martin Luther King Jr and Barack Obama, as well as lesser-known figures, such as explorer Matthew Henson. The

museum also covers slavery, the Jim Crow era and African leaders – all told in surreal fashion through Madame Tussaud–style wax figures.

Star-Spangled Banner Flag House & 1812 Museum   MUSEUM
(☑410-837-1793; www.flaghouse.org; 844 E Pratt St; adult/child $8/6; ☉10am-4pm Tue-Sat; ♿) This historic home, built in 1793, is where Mary Pickersgill sewed the gigantic flag that inspired America's national anthem. Costumed interpreters and 19th-century artifacts transport visitors back in time to dark days during the War of 1812; there's also a hands-on discovery gallery for kids.

Jewish Museum of Maryland   MUSEUM
(☑410-732-6400; www.jewishmuseummd.org; 15 Lloyd St; adult/student/child $8/4/3; ☉10am-5pm Sun-Thu) Maryland has traditionally been home to one of the largest, most active Jewish communities in the country, and this is a fine place to explore their experience in America. It also houses two wonderfully preserved historical synagogues. Call or go online for the scheduled times of synagogue tours.

Edgar Allan Poe House & Museum   MUSEUM
(☑410-396-7932; www.poeinbaltimore.org; 203 N Amity St; adult/student/child $5/4/free; ☉11am-4pm Sat & Sun late May-Dec) Home to Baltimore's most famous adopted son from 1832 to 1835, it was here that the macabre poet and writer first found fame after winning a $50 short-story contest. After moving around, Poe later returned to Baltimore in 1849, where he died under mysterious circumstances. His grave can be found in nearby Westminster Cemetery.

◉ Mt Vernon

★ Walters Art Museum   MUSEUM
(☑410-547-9000; www.thewalters.org; 600 N Charles St; ☉10am-5pm Wed-Sun, to 9pm Thu) FREE Don't pass up this excellent, eclectic gallery: it spans more than 55 centuries, from ancient to contemporary, with excellent displays of Asian treasures, rare and ornate manuscripts and books, and a comprehensive French paintings collection.

Washington Monument   MONUMENT
(mvpconservancy.org; 699 Washington Pl; suggested donation $5; ☉4-9pm Thu, noon-5pm Fri-Sun) For the best views of Baltimore, climb the 228 steps of the 178ft-tall Doric column dedicated to America's Founding Father, George Washington. It was designed by Robert Mills, who also created DC's Washington Monument, and is looking better than ever after a $6 million restoration project. The ground floor contains a museum about Washington's life. To climb the monument, call or email ahead.

Maryland Historical Society   MUSEUM
(www.mdhs.org; 201 W Monument St; adult/child $9/6; ☉10am-5pm Wed-Sat, noon-5pm Sun) With more than 350,000 objects and seven million books and documents, this is one of the largest collections of Americana in the world. Highlights include one of three surviving Revolutionary War officer's uniforms, photographs from the 1930s Civil Rights movement in Baltimore and Francis Scott Key's original manuscript of 'the Star-Spangled Banner.' There are often excellent temporary exhibits that explore the role of Baltimore residents in historic events.

◉ Federal Hill & Around

On a bluff overlooking the harbor, **Federal Hill Park** lends its name to the comfortable neighborhood that's set around Cross St Market and comes alive after sundown.

★ American Visionary Art Museum   MUSEUM
(AVAM; ☑410-244-1900; www.avam.org; 800 Key Hwy; adult/child $16/10; ☉10am-6pm Tue-Sun) Housing a jaw-dropping collection of self-taught (or 'outsider' art), AVAM is a celebration of unbridled creativity utterly free of arts-scene pretension. You'll find broken-mirror collages, homemade robots and flying apparatuses, elaborately sculptural works made of needlepoint, and gigantic model ships painstakingly created from matchsticks.

Fort McHenry National Monument & Historic Shrine   HISTORIC SITE
(☑410-962-4290; 2400 E Fort Ave; adult/child $7/free; ☉9am-5pm) On September 13 and 14, 1814, this star-shaped fort successfully repelled a British Navy attack during the Battle of Baltimore. After a long night of bombs bursting in the air, prisoner Francis Scott Key saw, 'by dawn's early light,' the tattered flag still waving, inspiring him to pen 'The Star-Spangled Banner,' which was set to the tune of a popular drinking song.

SCENIC DRIVE: MARITIME MARYLAND

Maryland and Chesapeake Bay have always been inextricable, but there are some places where the old-fashioned way of life on the bay seems to have changed little over the passing centuries.

About 150 miles south of Baltimore, at the edge of the Eastern Shore, is **Crisfield**, the top working water town in Maryland. Get visiting details at the **J Millard Tawes Historical Museum** (☑410-968-2501; www.crisfieldheritagefoundation.org/museum; 3 Ninth St; adult/child $3/1; ⊙10am-4pm Mon-Sat), which doubles as a visitor center. Any seafood you eat will be first-rate, but for a true Shore experience, **Watermens Inn** (☑410-968-2119; 901 W Main St; mains $12-25; ⊙11am-8pm Thu & Sun, to 9pm Fri & Sat, closed Mon-Wed) is legendary; in an unpretentious setting you can feast on local catch from an ever-changing menu. You can find local waterfolk at their favorite hangout – **Gordon's Confectionery** (831 W Main St) – having 4am coffee before shipping off to check and set traps.

From here you can leave your car and take a boat to **Smith Island** (www.visitsmithisland.com), the only offshore settlement in the state. Settled by fisherfolk from the English West Country some 400 years ago, the island's tiny population still speak with what linguists reckon is the closest thing to a 17th-century Cornish accent.

We'll be frank: this is more of a dying fishing town than charming tourist attraction, although there are B&Bs and restaurants (check the website for details). But it's also a last link to the state's past, so if you approach Smith Island as such, you may appreciate the limited amenities on offer. These notably include paddling through miles of some of the most pristine marshland on the eastern seaboard. Ferries will take you back to the mainland (and the present day) at 3:45pm.

Fell's Point & Canton

Once the center of Baltimore's shipbuilding industry, the historic cobblestoned neighborhood of Fell's Point is now a gentrified mix of 18th-century homes and restaurants, bars and shops. The neighborhood has been the setting for several films and TV series, most notably *Homicide: Life on the Street*. Further east, the slightly more sophisticated streets of Canton fan out, with its grassy square surrounded by great restaurants and bars.

North Baltimore

The 'Hon' expression of affection – an oft-imitated, never-quite-duplicated 'Bawl-merese' peculiarity – originated in **Hampden**, an area straddling the line between working class and hipster-creative class. Spend a lazy afternoon browsing kitsch, antiques and vintage clothing along the **Avenue** (aka W 36th St). To get to Hampden, take the I-83 N, merge onto Falls Rd (northbound) and take a right onto the Avenue. The prestigious **Johns Hopkins University** (3400 N Charles St) is nearby.

★ **Evergreen Museum** MUSEUM
(☑410-516-0341; http://museums.jhu.edu; 4545 N Charles St; adult/child $8/5; ⊙11am-4pm Tue-Fri, noon-4pm Sat & Sun) Well worth the drive, this grand 19th-century mansion provides a fascinating glimpse into upper-class Baltimore life of the 1800s. The house is packed with fine art and masterpieces of the decorative arts – including paintings by Modigliani, glass by Louis Comfort Tiffany and exquisite Asian porcelain – not to mention the astounding rare-book collection, numbering some 32,000 volumes.

More impressive than the collection, however, is the compelling story of the Garrett family, who were world travellers (John W was an active diplomat for some years) and astute philanthropists, as well as lovers of the arts, if not always successful performers in their own right – though that didn't stop Alice from taking to the stage (her own, which you'll see in the intimate theater below the house).

☞ Tours

Baltimore Ghost Tours WALKING TOUR
(☑410-357-1186; www.baltimoreghosttours.com; adult/child $15/10; ⊙7pm Fri & Sat Mar-Nov) Offers several walking tours exploring the spooky and bizarre side of Baltimore. The popular Fell's Point ghost walk departs from Max's on Broadway (731 S Broadway). Book online to save $2 per ticket.

✷ Festivals & Events

Honfest
CULTURAL

(www.honfest.net; ⊘ Jun) Put on your best 'Bawlmerese' accent and head to Hampden for this celebration of kitsch, beehive hair-dos, rhinestone glasses and other Baltimore eccentricities.

Artscape
CULTURAL

(www.artscape.org; ⊘ mid-July) America's largest free arts festival features art displays, live music, theater and dance performances.

🛏 Sleeping

Stylish and affordable B&Bs are mostly found in the downtown burbs of Canton, Fell's Point and Federal Hill.

HI-Baltimore Hostel
HOSTEL $

(✆ 410-576-8880; www.hiusa.org/baltimore; 17 W Mulberry St, Mt Vernon; dm $31; ✸@⊛) Located in a beautifully restored 1857 mansion, the HI-Baltimore has four-, eight- and 12-bed dorms. Helpful management, nice location and a filigreed classical chic look make this one of the region's best hostels. Breakfast included.

★ Inn at 2920
B&B $$

(✆ 410-342-4450; www.theinnat2920.com; 2920 Elliott St, Canton; r $185-272; ✸@⊛) ❀ Housed in a former bordello, this boutique B&B offers five individual rooms; high-thread-count sheets; sleek, avant-garde decor; and the nightlife-charged neighborhood of Canton right outside your door. The Jacuzzi bathtubs and green sensibility of the owners add a nice touch.

Hotel Brexton
HOTEL $$

(✆ 443-478-2100; www.brextonhotel.com; 868 Park Ave, Mt Vernon; r $130-240; P✸⊛✸) This red-brick 19th-century landmark building has recently been reborn as an appealing, if not overly lavish, hotel. Rooms offer a mix of wood floors or carpeting, comfy mattresses, mirrored armoires and framed art prints on the walls. Curious historical footnote: Wallis Simpson, the woman for whom Britain's King Edward VIII abdicated the throne, lived in this building as a young girl.

It's in a good location, just a short walk to the heart of Mt Vernon.

✗ Eating

Baltimore is an ethnically rich town that sits on top of the greatest seafood repository in the world, not to mention the fault line between the down-home South and cutting-edge innovation of the Northeast.

Dooby's Coffee
CAFE $

(www.doobyscoffee.com; 802 N Charles St, Mt Vernon; mains lunch $8-11, dinner $13-18; ⊘ 7am-11pm Mon-Fri, 8am-midnight Sat, 8am-5pm Sun; ⊛) A short stroll from the Washington Monument, this hip but unpretentious place is equal parts sunny cafe and creative eating and drinking spot. Come in the morning for tasty pastries and egg-and-Gruyère sandwiches, or at lunchtime for Korean-style rice bowls and toasted sandwiches. At night, there are bourbon-braised sticky ribs, steaming bowls of mushroom-and-leek ramen and other Asian infusions.

Papermoon Diner
DINER $

(www.papermoondiner24.com; 227 W 29th St, Harwood; mains $9-17; ⊘ 7am-midnight Sun-Thu, to 2am Fri & Sat) This brightly colored, quintessential Baltimore diner is decorated with thousands of old toys, creepy mannequins and other quirky knickknacks. The real draw here is the anytime breakfast – fluffy buttermilk pancakes, crispy bacon and crab-and-artichoke-heart omelets. Wash it down with a caramel-and-sea-salt milkshake.

Artifact
CAFE $

(www.artifactcoffee.com; 1500 Union Ave, Woodberry; mains $7-13; ⊘ 7am-5pm Mon-Tue, to 7pm Wed-Fri, 8am-7pm Sat & Sun; ⊛✷) Artifact serves the city's best coffee, along with tasty light meals such as egg muffins, spinach salad, vegetarian *banh mi* and pastrami sandwiches. It's inside a former mill space, handsomely repurposed from its industrial past. It's a two-minute stroll from the Woodberry light-rail station.

Vaccaro's Pastry
ITALIAN $

(www.vaccarospastry.com; 222 Albemarle St, Little Italy; desserts around $7; ⊘ 9am-10pm Sun-Thu, to midnight Fri & Sat) Vaccaro's serves some of the best desserts and coffee in town. The cannolis are legendary.

Lexington Market
FAST FOOD $

(www.lexingtonmarket.com; 400 W Lexington St, Mt Vernon; ⊘ 8:30am-6pm Mon-Sat) Around since 1782, Mt Vernon's Lexington Market is one of Baltimore's true old-school food markets. It's a bit shabby on the outside, but the food is great. Don't miss the crab cakes at Faidley's (✆ 410-727-4898; www.faidleyscrabcakes.com; mains $10-20; ⊘ 9:30am-5pm Mon-Sat) seafood stall, because my goodness, they are amazing.

★ **Thames St Oyster House**   SEAFOOD **$$**
(☑ 443-449-7726; www.thamesstreetoysterhouse.
com; 1728 Thames St, Fell's Point; mains $14-29;
⊙ 11:30am-2:30pm Wed-Sun, 5-10pm daily) An
icon of Fell's Point, this vintage dining and
drinking hall serves some of Baltimore's
best seafood. Dine in the polished upstairs
dining room with views of the waterfront,
take a seat in the backyard, or plunk down
at the bar in front (which stays open till
midnight) and watch the drink-makers and
oyster-shuckers in action.

Birroteca   PIZZA **$$**
(☑ 443-708-1935; www.bmorebirroteca.com; 1520
Clipper Rd, Roosevelt Park; pizzas $17-19; ⊙ 5-11pm
Mon-Fri, noon-midnight Sat, to 10pm Sun) Amid
stone walls and indie rock, Birroteca fires
up delicious thin-crust pizzas in imagina-
tive combos (like duck confit with fig-onion
jam). There's craft beer, good wines, fancy
cocktails and impressively bearded bartenders. It's about a half-mile from either Hampden's 36th St or the Woodberry light-rail
station.

Helmand   AFGHAN **$$**
(☑ 410-752-0311; 806 N Charles St, Mt Vernon;
mains $14-17; ⊙ 5-10pm Sun-Thu, to 11pm Fri & Sat)
The Helmand is a longtime favorite for its
kaddo borawni (pumpkin in yogurt garlic
sauce), vegetable platters and flavorful beef-
and-lamb meatballs followed by cardamom
ice cream. If you've never tried Afghan cui-
sine, this is a great place to do so.

LP Steamers   SEAFOOD **$$**
(☑ 410-576-9294; 1100 E Fort Ave, South Baltimore;
mains $10-28; ⊙ 11:30am-9:30pm) LP is the best
in Baltimore's seafood stakes: working class,
teasing smiles and the freshest crabs on the
southside.

★ **Woodberry Kitchen**   AMERICAN **$$$**
(☑ 410-464-8000; www.woodberrykitchen.com;
2010 Clipper Park Rd, Woodberry; mains $24-39;
⊙ dinner 5-10pm Mon-Thu, to 11pm Fri & Sat, to 9pm
Sun, brunch 10am-2pm Sat & Sun) The Wood-
berry takes everything the Chesapeake re-
gion has to offer, plops it into an industrial
barn and creates culinary magic. The entire
menu is like a playful romp through the best
of local produce, seafood and meats, from
Maryland rockfish with Carolina Gold grits
to Shenandoah Valley lamb with collard
greens, and hearty vegetable dishes plucked
from nearby farms. Reserve ahead.

Food Market   MODERN AMERICAN **$$$**
(☑ 410-366-0606; www.thefoodmarketbaltimore.
com; 1017 W 36th St, Hampden; mains $20-34;
⊙ 5-11pm daily plus 9am-3pm Fri-Sun) On Hampden's lively restaurant- and shop-lined main
drag, the Food Market was an instant success when it opened back in 2012. Award-
winning local chef Chad Gauss elevates
American comfort fare to high art in dishes
like bread-and-butter-crusted sea bass with
black-truffle vinaigrette, and crab cakes with
lobster mac 'n' cheese.

🍷 **Drinking & Nightlife**

On weekends, Fell's Point and Canton turn
into temples of alcoholic excess that would
make a Roman emperor blush. Mt Vernon
and North Baltimore are a little more civilized, but any one of Baltimore's neighborhoods houses a cozy local pub. Closing time
is generally 2am.

Brewer's Art   PUB
(☑ 410-547-6925; 1106 N Charles St, Mt Vernon;
⊙ 4pm-2am) In a vintage early-20th-century
mansion, Brewer's Art serves well-crafted
Belgian-style microbrews to a laid-back Mt
Vernon crowd. There's tasty pub fare (mac
'n' cheese, portobello wraps) in the bar, and
upscale American cuisine in the elegant
back dining room. Head to the subterranean
drinking den downstairs for a more raucous
crowd. During happy hour (4pm to 7pm)
drafts are just $3.75.

Club Charles   BAR
(☑ 410-727-8815; 1724 N Charles St, Mt Vernon;
⊙ 6pm-2am) Hipsters adorned in the usual
skinny jeans and vintage T-shirt uniform, as
well as characters from other walks of life,
flock to this 1940s art-deco cocktail lounge
to enjoy good tunes and cheap drinks.

Ale Mary's   BAR
(☑ 410-276-2044; 1939 Fleet St, Fell's Point;
⊙ 4pm-2am Mon-Fri, from 10am Sat & Sun) Its
name and decor pay homage to Maryland's
Catholic roots, with crosses and rosaries
scattered about. It draws a buzzing neighborhood crowd that comes for strong drinks and
good, greasy bar food (tater tots, cheesesteak
subs) as well as mussels and Sunday brunch.

Little Havana   BAR
(☑ 410-837-9903; 1325 Key Hwy, Federal Hill;
⊙ 4pm-2am Mon-Thu, from 11:30am Fri-Sun) A
good after-work spot and a great place to
sip mojitos on the waterfront deck, this
converted brick warehouse is a major draw

BALTIMORE FOR CHILDREN

Most attractions are centered on the Inner Harbor, including the **National Aquarium** (p278), perfect for pint-sized visitors. Kids can run wild o'er the ramparts of historic **Fort McHenry National Monument & Historic Shrine** (p279), too.

Maryland Science Center (☑410-685-2370; www.mdsci.org; 601 Light St; adult/child $19/16; ☺10am-5pm Mon-Fri, to 6pm Sat, 11am-5pm Sun, longer hours in summer) is an awesome center featuring a three-story atrium, tons of interactive exhibits on dinosaurs, outer space and the human body, and the requisite IMAX theater ($4 extra).

Two blocks north is the converted fish market of **Port Discovery** (☑410-727-8120; www.portdiscovery.org; 35 Market Pl; admission $15; ☺10am-5pm Mon-Sat, noon-5pm Sun, reduced hours in winter), which has a playhouse, a laboratory, a TV studio and even a pharaoh's tomb. Wear your kids out here.

At **Maryland Zoo in Baltimore** (www.marylandzoo.org; Druid Hill Park; adult/child $18/13; ☺10am-4pm daily Mar-Dec, 10am-4pm Fri-Mon Jan & Feb), lily-pad hopping, adventures with Billy the Bog Turtle and grooming live animals are all in a day's play here.

---

on warm, sunny days (especially around weekend brunch time).

☆ Entertainment

Baltimoreans *love* sports. The town plays hard and parties even harder, with tailgating parties in parking lots and games showing on numerous televisions.

Baltimore Orioles   BASEBALL
(☑888-848-2473; www.orioles.com) The Orioles play at **Oriole Park at Camden Yards** (333 W Camden St, Downtown), arguably the best ballpark in America. Daily tours (adult/child $9/6) of the stadium are offered during the regular season (April to October).

Baltimore Ravens   FOOTBALL
(☑410-261-7283; www.baltimoreravens.com) The Ravens play at **M&T Bank Stadium** (1101 Russell St, Downtown) from September to January.

ℹ Information

Baltimore Area Visitor Center (☑877-225-8466; www.baltimore.org; 401 Light St, Inner Harbor; ☺9am-6pm May-Sep, 10am-5pm Oct-Apr) Located on the Inner Harbor. Sells the **Harbor Pass** (adult/child $50/40), which gives admission to five major area attractions.
Baltimore Sun (www.baltimoresun.com) Daily city newspaper.
City Paper (www.citypaper.com) Free alt-weekly.
Enoch Pratt Free Library (400 Cathedral St, Mt Vernon; ☺10am-7pm Mon-Wed, to 5pm Thu-Sat, 1-5pm Sun; ☎) There's free wi-fi and some public access computers (also free).
University of Maryland Medical Center (☑410-328-9400; 22 S Greene St, University of Maryland-Baltimore) Has a 24-hour emergency room.

ℹ Getting There & Away

The Baltimore/Washington International Thurgood Marshall Airport (p276) is 10 miles south of downtown via I-295.

Departing from a terminal 2 miles southwest of Inner Harbor, **Greyhound** (www.greyhound.com) and **Peter Pan Bus Lines** (☑410-752-7682; 2110 Haines St, Carroll-Camden) have numerous buses from Washington, DC ($10 to $14, roughly every 45 minutes, one hour), and from New York ($14 to $50, 12 to 15 per day, 4½ hours). The **BoltBus** (☑877-265-8287; www.boltbus.com; 1610 St Paul St, Carroll-Camden; ☎) has six to nine buses a day to/from NYC ($15 to $33); it departs from a streetside location outside of Baltimore's Penn Station.

Penn Station (1500 N Charles St, Charles North) is in north Baltimore. MARC operates weekday commuter trains to/from Washington, DC ($7, 71 minutes). **Amtrak** (☑800-872-7245; www.amtrak.com) trains serve the East Coast and beyond.

ℹ Getting Around

Light-Rail (☑866-743-3682; mta.maryland.gov/light-rail; one way/day pass $1.60/3.50; ☺6am-midnight Mon-Sat, 7am-11pm Sun) runs from BWI airport to Lexington Market and Penn Station. Train frequency is every five to 10 minutes. MARC trains run hourly on weekdays (and six to nine times daily on weekends) between Penn Station and BWI airport for $4. Check **Maryland Transit Administration** (MTA; www.mtamaryland.com) for all local transportation schedules and fares.

Supershuttle (☑800-258-3826; www.supershuttle.com; ☺5:30am-12:30am) provides a BWI-van service to the Inner Harbor for $16.

Baltimore Water Taxi (☑410-563-3900; www.baltimorewatertaxi.com; Inner Harbor; daily pass adult/child $12/6; ☺10am-11pm Mon-Sat, to 9pm Sun) docks at all harborside attractions and neighborhoods.

Annapolis

Annapolis is as charming as state capitals get. The Colonial architecture, cobblestones, flickering lamps and brick row houses are worthy of Dickens, but the effect isn't artificial: this city has preserved, rather than created, its heritage.

Perched on Chesapeake Bay, Annapolis revolves around the city's rich maritime traditions. It's home to the US Naval Academy, whose 'middies' (midshipmen students) stroll through town in their starched white uniforms. Sailing is not just a hobby here, but a way of life, and the city docks are crammed with vessels of all shapes and sizes.

◉ Sights & Activities

Annapolis has more 18th-century buildings than any other city in America, including the homes of all four Marylanders who signed the Declaration of Independence.

Think of the State House as a wheel hub from which most attractions fan out, leading to the City Dock and historic waterfront.

US Naval Academy   UNIVERSITY
(visitor center 410-293-8687; www.usnabsd. com./for visitors; Randall St btwn Prince George and King George Sts) The undergraduate college of the US Navy is one of the most selective universities in America. The **Armel-Leftwich visitor center** (410-293-8687; tourinfo@usna. edu; Gate 1, City Dock entrance; tours adult/child $10.50/8.50; ⊗9am-5pm) is the place to book tours and immerse yourself in all things Academy-related. Come for the formation weekdays at 12:05pm sharp, when the 4000 midshipmen and -women conduct a 20-minute military marching display in the yard. Photo ID is required for entry. If you've got a thing for American naval history, revel in the **Naval Academy Museum** (410-293-2108; www.usna.edu/museum; 118 Maryland Ave; ⊗9am-5pm Mon-Sat, 11am-5pm Sun) FREE.

Maryland State House   HISTORIC BUILDING
(410-946-5400; 91 State Circle; ⊗9am-5pm) FREE The country's oldest state capitol in continuous legislative use, the grand 1772 State House also served as national capital from 1733 to 1734. The Maryland Senate is in action here from January to April. The upside-down giant acorn atop the dome stands for wisdom.

Banneker-Douglass Museum   MUSEUM
(http://bdmuseum.maryland.gov; 84 Franklin St; ⊗10am-4pm Tue-Sat) FREE A short stroll from the State House, this small but worthwhile museum highlights great achievements of Marylanders of African American ancestry. There are permanent exhibits on the likes of US Supreme Court justice Thurgood Marshall, explorer Matthew Henson and public intellectual Frederick Douglass, as well as temporary exhibitions that often run the gamut from historical forays into the Civil Rights era to today's crop of great African American artists, musicians and writers.

Hammond Harwood House   MUSEUM
(410-263-4683; www.hammondharwoodhouse. org; 19 Maryland Ave; adult/child $10/5; ⊗noon-5pm Tue-Sun Apr-Dec) Of the many historical homes in town, the 1774 HHH is the one to visit. It has a superb collection of decorative arts, including furniture, paintings and ephemera dating to the 18th century, and is one of the finest existing British Colonial homes in America. Knowledgeable guides help bring the past to life on 50-minute house tours (held at the top of the hour).

William Paca House & Garden   HISTORIC BUILDING
(410-990-4543; www.annapolis.org; 186 Prince George St; adult/child $10/6; ⊗10am-5pm Mon-Sat, noon-5pm Sun) Take a tour (offered hourly on the half-hour) through this Georgian mansion for an insight into 18th-century life for the upper class in Maryland. Don't miss the blooming garden in spring.

Kunta Kinte–Alex Haley Memorial   MONUMENT
At the City Dock, the Kunta Kinte–Alex Haley Memorial marks the spot where Kunta Kinte – ancestor of *Roots* author Alex Haley – was brought in chains from Africa.

☞ Tours

Four Centuries Walking Tour   WALKING TOUR
(www.annapolistours.com; adult/child $18/10) A costumed docent will lead you on this great introduction to all things Annapolis. The 10:30am tour leaves from the visitor center and the 1:30pm tour leaves from the information booth at the City Dock; there's a slight variation in sights visited by each, but both cover the country's largest concentration of 18th-century buildings, influential African Americans and colonial spirits who don't want to leave.

The associated one-hour **Pirates of the Chesapeake Cruise** (☎410-263-0002; www.chesapeakepirates.com; admission $20; ☺mid-Apr–Sep; ⚓) is good 'yar'-worthy fun, especially for the kids.

Woodwind   CRUISE
(☎410-263-7837; www.schoonerwoodwind.com; 80 Compromise St; sunset cruise adult/child $44/27; ☺mid-Apr–Oct) This beautiful 74ft schooner offers two-hour day and sunset cruises. Or splurge for the *Woodwind* 'boat & breakfast' package (rooms $305, including breakfast), one of the more unique lodging options in town.

🛌 Sleeping

ScotLaur Inn   GUESTHOUSE $$
(☎410-268-5665; www.scotlaurinn.com; 165 Main St; r $95-140; 🅿 🕸 🛜) The folks from Chick & Ruth's Delly offer 10 rooms, each with wrought-iron beds, floral wallpaper and private bath. The quarters are small but have a familial atmosphere (the guesthouse is named after the owners' children Scott and Lauren, whose photos adorn the hallways).

O'Callaghan Hotel   HOTEL $$
(☎410-263-7700; www.ocallaghanhotels-us.com; 174 West St; r $99-180; 🕸 🛜) This Irish chain offers attractively furnished rooms that are nicely equipped, with big windows, a writing desk, brass fixtures and comfy mattresses. It's on West St, just a short stroll to a good selection of bars and restaurants, and about a 12-minute walk to the old quarter.

Historic Inns of Annapolis   HOTEL $$
(☎410-263-2641; www.historicinnsofannapolis.com; 58 State Circle; r $140-200; 🕸 🛜) The Historic Inns comprise three different boutique guesthouses, each set in a heritage building in the heart of old Annapolis: the Maryland Inn, the Governor Calvert House and the Robert Johnson House. Common areas are packed with period details, and the best rooms boast antiques, a fireplace and attractive views (while the cheapest are small and cramped and could use a good cleaning).

🍴 Eating & Drinking

With the Chesapeake at its doorstep, Annapolis has superb seafood.

49 West   CAFE $
(☎410-626-9796; 49 West St; mains $7-15; ☺7:30am-midnight; 🛜) This comfy, art-filled coffeehouse is a good spot for coffee and light bites during the day (sandwiches, soups, salads) and heartier bistro fare by night, along with wines and cocktails. There's live music some nights.

Chick & Ruth's Delly   DINER $
(☎410-269-6737; www.chickandruths.com; 165 Main St; mains $7-14; ☺6:30am-11:30pm; ⚓) A cornerstone of Annapolis, the Delly is bursting with affable quirkiness and a big menu, heavy on sandwiches and breakfast fare. Patriots can relive grade-school days reciting the Pledge of Allegiance, weekdays at 8:30am (and 9:30am on weekends).

★ Vin 909   AMERICAN $$
(☎410-990-1846; 909 Bay Ridge Ave; small plates $13-16; ☺5:30-10pm Tue-Sun & noon-3pm Wed-Fri) Perched on a little wooded hill and boasting intimate but enjoyably casual ambience, Vin is the best thing happening in Annapolis for food. Farm-sourced goodness features in the form of duck confit, BBQ sliders and homemade pizzas with toppings that include wild

> **WASHINGTON, DC & THE CAPITAL REGION** ANNAPOLIS

MARYLAND BLUE CRABS

Eating at a crab shack, where the dress code stops at shorts and flip-flops, is the quintessential Chesapeake Bay experience. Folks in these parts take their crabs seriously, and can spend hours debating the intricacies of how to crack a crab, the proper way to prepare crabs and where to find the best ones. There is one thing Marylanders can agree on: they must be blue crabs (scientific name: *Callinectes sapidus*, 'beautiful swimmers'). Sadly, blue crab numbers have suffered with the continuing pollution of the Chesapeake Bay, and many crabs you eat here are imported from elsewhere.

Steamed crabs are prepared very simply, using beer and Old Bay seasoning. One of the best crab shacks in the state is near Annapolis at **Jimmy Cantler's Riverside Inn** (www.cantlers.com; 458 Forest Beach Rd, Annapolis; mains $17-32; ☺11am-11pm Sun-Thu, to midnight Fri & Sat), located 4 miles northeast of the Maryland State House, across the Severn River Bridge; here, eating a steamed crab has been elevated to an art form – a hands-on, messy endeavor, normally accompanied by corn on the cob and ice-cold beer. Another fine spot is across the bay at the Crab Claw (p286).

mushrooms, foie gras and Spanish chorizo. There's a great wine selection, including over three-dozen wines by the glass.

No reservations are accepted, so go early to beat the often lengthy waits.

Boatyard Bar & Grill SEAFOOD $$
(☑ 410-216-6206; www.boatyardbarandgrill.com; 400 4th St; mains $14-27; ⊙ 8am-midnight; 🖝) This bright, nautically themed restaurant is an inviting spot for crab cakes, fish and chips, fish tacos and other seafood. Happy hour (3pm to 7pm) draws in the crowds with 99¢ oysters and $3 drafts. It's a short drive (or 10-minute walk) from the City Dock, across the Spa Creek Bridge.

Rams Head Tavern PUB FOOD $$$
(☑ 410-268-4545; www.ramsheadtavern.com; 33 West St; mains $12-32; ⊙ 11am-2am Mon-Sat, from 10am Sun) Serves pub fare and refreshing microbrews in an attractive exposed-brick and oak-paneled setting. Well-known bands perform next door at the Rams Head On Stage (tickets $22 to $80).

❶ Information

There's a **visitor center** (☑ 410-280-0445; www.visitannapolis.org; 26 West St; ⊙ 9am-5pm) and a seasonal information booth at City Dock.

❶ Getting There & Away

Greyhound (www.greyhound.com) runs buses to Washington, DC (once daily). **Dillon's Bus** (www.dillonbus.com; tickets $4.25) has 26 weekday-only commuter buses between Annapolis and Washington, DC, connecting with various DC Metro lines.

Eastern Shore

Just across the Chesapeake Bay Bridge, nondescript suburbs give way to unbroken miles of bird-dotted wetlands, serene waterscapes, endless cornfields, sandy beaches and friendly little villages. The Eastern Shore retains its charm despite the growing influx of city-dwelling yuppies and day-trippers. This area revolves around the water: working waterfront communities still survive off Chesapeake Bay and its tributaries, and boating, fishing, crabbing and hunting are integral to local life.

St Michaels & Tilghman Island

The prettiest little village on the Eastern Shore, St Michaels lives up to its motto as the 'Heart and Soul of Chesapeake Bay.' It's a mix of old Victorian homes, quaint B&Bs, boutique shops and working docks, where escape artists from Washington mix with salty-dog watermen. During the War of 1812, inhabitants rigged up lanterns in a nearby forest and blacked out the town. British naval gunners shelled the trees, allowing St Michaels to escape destruction. The building now known as the Cannonball House (Mulberry St) was the only structure to have been hit.

At the end of the road over the Hwy 33 drawbridge, tiny Tilghman Island still runs a working waterfront, where local captains take visitors out on graceful sailing vessels.

◉ Sights & Activities

Chesapeake Bay
Maritime Museum MUSEUM
(☑ 410-745-2916; www.cbmm.org; 213 N Talbot St, St Michaels; adult/child $13/6; ⊙ 9am-5pm May-Oct, 10am-4pm Nov-Apr; 🖝) At the lighthouse, the Chesapeake Bay Maritime Museum delves into the deep ties between shore folk and America's largest estuary.

Lady Patty Classic Yacht Charters SAILING
(☑ 410-886-1127; www.ladypatty.com; 6176 Tilghman Island Rd, Tilghman Island; cruise adult/child from $27/42; ⊙ May-Oct) Lady Patty Yacht Charters runs memorable two hour sails on the Chesapeake.

🛏 Sleeping & Eating

Parsonage Inn INN $$
(☑ 410-745-8383; www.parsonage-inn.com; 210 N Talbot St; r $160-225; 🅿🐾) Laura Ashley's most lurid fantasies probably resemble the rooms in the red-brick Parsonage Inn, which is run by a very hospitable innkeeper (and her canine companion). Off-season prices drop as low as $90 per night.

Crab Claw SEAFOOD $$
(☑ 410-745-2900; www.thecrabclaw.com; 304 Burns St, St Michaels; mains $16-30; ⊙ 11am-9pm mid-Mar–Oct) Next door to the Chesapeake Bay Maritime Museum, the Crab Claw serves up tasty Maryland blue crabs to splendid views over the harbor. Avoid the seafood sampler, unless you're a fan of deep-fried seafood.

Oxford

Oxford is a small village with a history dating back to the 1600s and a fine spread of leafy streets and waterfront homes. Although you can drive there via US 333, it's well worth taking the old-fashioned **ferry** ([⏎]410-745-9023; www.oxfordbellevueferry.com; Bellevue Rd near Bellevue Park; one way car/additional passenger/pedestrian $12/1/3; ☺9am-sunset mid-Apr–mid-Nov) from Bellevue. Try to go around sunset for memorable views.

Once in Oxford, don't miss the chance to dine at the celebrated **Robert Morris Inn** ([⏎]410-226-5111; www.robertmorrisinn.com; 314 N Morris St; mains $17-29; ☺7:30-10am, noon-2:30pm & 5:30-9:30pm), near the ferry dock. Award-winning crab cakes, grilled local rockfish and medallions of spring lamb are nicely matched with wines and best followed by pavlova with berries and other desserts. You can also overnight in one of the inn's heritage-style rooms (from $145).

Berlin & Snow Hill

Imagine a typical small-town-America Main St, cute that vision up by a few points, and you've come close to these Eastern Shore villages. Most buildings here are handsomely preserved, and antique shops litter the area.

In **Berlin**, the **Globe Theater** ([⏎]410-641-0784; www.globetheater.com; 12 Broad St; mains $10-26; ☺11am-10pm; ☎) is a lovingly restored main stage that serves as a restaurant, bar, art gallery and theater for nightly live music; the kitchen serves eclectic American fare with global accents.

There are B&Bs galore, but we prefer the **Atlantic Hotel** ([⏎]410-641-3589; www.atlantichotel.com; 2 N Main St; r $125-275; [P][✳][☎]), a Gilded Era lodger that gives guests the time-warp experience with all the modern amenities.

A few miles from Berlin, **Snow Hill** has a splendid location along the idyllic Pocomoke River. Get on the water with the **Pocomoke River Canoe Company** ([⏎]410-632-3971; www.pocomokerivercanoe.com; 2 River St; canoe hire per hr/day $15/50). They'll even take you upriver so you can have a leisurely paddle downstream. Nearby **Furnace Town** ([⏎]410-632-2032; www.furnacetown.com; Old Furnace Rd; adult/child $7/4; ☺10am-5pm Mon-Sat Apr-Oct, from noon Sun; [P][♿]), off Rte 12, is a living-history museum that marks the old location of a 19th-century iron-smelting town. In Snow Hill itself, while away an odd, rewarding half-hour in the **Julia A Purnell Museum** ([⏎]410-632-0515; 208 W Market St; adult/child $2/; ☺10am-4pm Tue-Sat, from 1pm Sun Apr-Oct), a tiny structure that feels like an attic for the entire Eastern Shore.

Staying in town? Check out Snow Hill's **River House Inn** ([⏎]410-632-2722; www.river-houseinn.com; 201 E Market St; r $160-210, cottage $275-350; [P][✳][☎][≋]), with a lush backyard that overlooks a scenic bend of the river. The **Blue Dog Cafe** ([⏎]410-251-7193; www.bluedogsnowhill.com; 300 N Washington St; mains $10-21) serves up tasty crab cakes, burgers and Cajun-style shrimp. There's live music some nights – from old-fashioned brass bands to fiddle players and singing waitstaff.

Ocean City

'The OC' is where you'll experience the American seaside resort at its tackiest. Here you can take a spin on nausea-inducing thrill rides, buy a T-shirt with obscene slogans and drink to excess at cheesy theme bars. The center of action is the 2.5-mile-long boardwalk, which stretches from the inlet to 27th St. The beach is attractive, but you'll have to contend with horny teenagers, heavy traffic and noisy crowds; the beaches north of the boardwalk are much quieter.

🛏 Sleeping

The **visitor center** ([⏎]800-626-2326; www.ococean.com; Coastal Hwy at 40th St; ☺9am-5pm), in the convention center on Coastal Hwy, can help you find lodgings.

King Charles Hotel　　　　　GUESTHOUSE $$
([⏎]410-289-6141; www.kingcharleshotel.com; cnr N Baltimore Ave & 12th St; r $115-190; [P][✳][☎]) This place could be a quaint summer cottage, except it happens to be a short stroll to the heart of the boardwalk action. It has aging but clean rooms with small porches attached, and it's quiet.

🍴 Eating & Drinking

Surf 'n' turf and all-you-can-eat deals are the order of the day.

Liquid Assets　　　　MODERN AMERICAN $$
([⏎]410-524-7037; cnr 94th St & Coastal Hwy; mains $13-34; ☺11:30am-11pm) Like a diamond in the rough, this bistro and wine shop is hidden in a strip mall in north OC. The menu is a refreshing mix of innovative seafood, grilled meats and regional classics.

Seacrets　　　　　　　　　　　　BAR
(www.seacrets.com; cnr W 49th St & the Bay; ☺8am-2am) A Jamaican-themed, rum-soaked bar straight out of MTV's *Spring Break*. You can drift around in an inner tube while sipping a drink and people-watching at OC's most famous meat market.

WORTH A TRIP

ASSATEAGUE ISLAND

Just 8 miles south but a world away from Ocean City is Assateague Island seashore, a perfectly barren landscape of sand dunes and beautiful secluded beaches. This undeveloped barrier island is populated by the only herd of wild horses on the East Coast, made famous in the book *Misty of Chincoteague*.

The island is divided into three sections. In Maryland there's **Assateague State Park** (☑410-641-2918; Rte 611; admission/campsites $6/28; ☺ campground late Apr–Oct) and federally administered **Assateague Island National Seashore** (☑410-641-1441; www.nps.gov/asis; Rte 611; admission pedestrian/vehicle/campsite per week $3/15/25; ☺ visitor center 9am-5pm). **Chincoteague National Wildlife Refuge** (www.fws.gov/refuge/chincoteague; 8231 Beach Road, Chincoteague Island; daily/weekly pass $8/15 ; ☺ 5am-10pm May-Sep, 6am-6pm Nov-Feb, to 8pm Mar, Apr & Oct; P ♿) ✐ is in Virginia.

As well as swimming and sunbathing, recreational activities include birding, kayaking, canoeing, crabbing and fishing. There are no services on the Maryland side of the island, so you must bring all your own food and drink. Don't forget insect repellent: the mosquitoes and biting horseflies can be ferocious!

❶ Getting There & Around

Greyhound (☑410-289-9307; www.greyhound.com; 12848 Ocean Gateway) buses run daily to and from Washington, DC (four hours), and Baltimore (3½ hours).

Ocean City Coastal Highway Bus (day pass $3) runs up and down the length of the beach, from 6am to 3am. There's also a tram ($3) that runs along the boardwalk

Western Maryland

The western spine of Maryland is mountain country. The Appalachian peaks soar to 3000ft above sea level, and the surrounding valleys are packed with rugged scenery and Civil War battlefields. This is Maryland's playground, where hiking, skiing, rock climbing and white-water rafting draw the outdoors-loving crowd.

Frederick

Halfway between the battlefields of Gettysburg, PA and Antietam is Frederick; its handsome 50-square-block historic district resembles an almost perfect cliche of a mid-sized city.

◉ Sights

National Museum of Civil War Medicine   MUSEUM
(www.civilwarmed.org; 48 E Patrick St; adult/student/child $9.50/7/free; ☺ 10am-5pm Mon-Sat, from 11am Sun) This museum provides a fascinating, and sometimes gruesome, look at the health conditions soldiers and doctors faced during the war, as well as important medical advances that resulted from the conflict.

🛏 Sleeping & Eating

Hollerstown Hill B&B   B&B $$
(☑301-228-3630; www.hollerstownhill.com; 4 Clarke Pl, ; $145-175, P ♿ 🐾) The elegant friendly Hollerstown has four pattern-heavy rooms, two resident terriers and an elegant billiards room. This lovely Victorian sits right in the middle of the historic downtown area of Frederick, so you're within easy walking distance of all the goodness. No children under 16.

Brewer's Alley   GASTROPUB $$
(☑301-631-0089; 124 N Market St; mains $10-26; ☺ noon-11:30pm; 🔊) This bouncy brewpub is one of our favorite places in Frederick for several reasons. First, the beer: house-brewed, plenty of variety, delicious. Second, the burgers: enormous, half-pound monstrosities of staggeringly yummy proportions. Third, the rest of the menu: excellent Chesapeake seafood (including a wood-fired pizza topped with crab) and Frederick county farm produce and meats.

❶ Getting There & Away

Frederick is accessible via **Greyhound** (☑301-663-3311; www.greyhound.com) and **MARC** (☑301-682-9716) trains, located across from the visitor center at 100 S East St.

Antietam National Battlefield

The site of the bloodiest day in American history is now, ironically, supremely peaceful, quiet and haunting – uncluttered save for plaques and statues. On September 17, 1862, General Robert E Lee's first invasion of the North was stalled here in a tactical stalemate that left more than 23,000 dead, wounded or missing – more casualties than America had suffered in all her previous wars combined. Poignantly, many of the battlefield graves are inscribed with German and Irish names, a roll call of immigrants who died fighting for their new homeland. The **visitor center** (☑ 301-432-5124; State Rd 65; 3-day pass per person/family $4/6; ☉ 9am-5pm) shows a short film (playing on the hour and half-hour) about the events that transpired here. It also sells books and materials, including self-guided driving and walking tours of the battlefield.

Cumberland

At the Potomac River, the frontier outpost of Fort Cumberland (not to be confused with the Cumberland Gap between Virginia and Kentucky) was the pioneer gateway across the Alleghenies to Pittsburgh and the Ohio River. Today Cumberland has expanded into the outdoor recreation trade to guide visitors to the region's rivers, forests and mountains. Sights are a short stroll from the pedestrian-friendly streets of downtown Cumberland.

◉ Sights & Activities

C&O Canal National
Historic Park   NATIONAL PARK
(www.nps.gov/choh; FREE) A marvel of engineering, the C&O Canal was designed to stretch alongside the Potomac River from Chesapeake Bay to the Ohio River. Construction on the canal began in 1828 but halted here in 1850 by the Appalachian Mountains. The park's protected 185-mile corridor includes a 12ft-wide towpath, hiking and bicycling trail, which goes all the way from here to Georgetown in DC. The **Cumberland Visitor Center** (☑ 301-722-8226; 13 Canal St; ☉ 9am-5pm; P) has displays chronicling the importance of river trade in eastern seaboard history.

Allegany Museum   MUSEUM
(www.alleganymuseum.org; 3 Pershing St; ☉ 10am-4pm Tue-Sat, from 1pm Sun) FREE Set in the old courthouse, this is an intriguing place to

delve into Cumberland's past, with exhibits by local folk artist and woodcarver Claude Yoder; a model of the old shanty town that sprang up along the canal; 1920s firefighting gear; beautifully garbed mechanized puppets and other curiosities.

Western Maryland Scenic Railroad   TOUR
(☑ 800-872-4650; www.wmsr.com; 13 Canal St; adult/child $35/18; ☉ 11:30am Fri-Sun May-Dec) Outside the Cumberland visitor center, near the start of the C&O Canal, passengers can catch steam-locomotive rides, traversing forests and steep ravines to Frostburg, a 3½-hour round-trip.

Cumberland Trail Connection   CYCLING
(☑ 301-777-8724; www.ctcbikes.com; 14 Howard St, Canal Pl; half-day/day/week from $20/30/120; ☉ 8am-7pm) Conveniently located near the start of the C&O Canal, this outfit rents out bicycles (cruisers, touring bikes and mountain bikes), and also arranges shuttle service anywhere from Pittsburgh to DC.

⌕ Sleeping & Eating

Inn on Decatur   GUESTHOUSE $$
(☑ 301-722-4887; www.theinnondecatur.net; 108 Decatur St; d $125-136; ✲ ☎) Offers comfy guestrooms just a short stroll to pedestrianized Baltimore St in downtown Cumberland. The friendly owners have a wealth of knowledge on the area, and also lead bike tours (rentals available).

Queen City Creamery & Deli   DINER $
(☑ 240-979-4125; 108 Harrison St; mains $6-9; ☉ 7am-9pm) This retro soda fountain is like a 1940s time warp, with creamy shakes and homemade frozen custard, thick sandwiches and belly-filling breakfasts.

DELAWARE

Wee Delaware, the nation's second-smallest state (96 miles long and less than 35 miles across at its widest point) is overshadowed by its neighbors – and often overlooked by visitors to the Capital Region. And that's too bad, because Delaware has a lot more on offer than just tax-free shopping and chicken farms.

Long white sandy beaches, cute Colonial villages, a cozy countryside and small-town charm characterize the state that happily calls itself the 'Small Wonder.'

WORTH A TRIP

DEEP CREEK LAKE

In the extreme west of the panhandle, Maryland's largest freshwater lake is an all-seasons playground. The crimson and copper glow of the Alleghenies attracts thousands during the annual **Autumn Glory Festival** (www.visit-deepcreek.com; ⊙ early Oct), rivaling New England's leaf-turning backdrops.

History

In Colonial days Delaware was the subject of an aggressive land feud between Dutch, Swedish and British settlers. The former two imported classically northern European middle-class concepts, the latter a plantation-based aristocracy – which is partly why Delaware remains a typically mid-Atlantic cultural hybrid today.

The little state's big moment came on December 7, 1787, when Delaware became the first colony to ratify the US Constitution, thus becoming the first state in the Union. It remained in that union throughout the Civil War, despite supporting slavery. During this period, as throughout much of the state's history, the economy drew on its chemical industry. DuPont, the world's second-largest chemical company, was founded here in 1802 as a gunpowder factory by French immigrant Eleuthère Irénée du Pont. Low taxes drew other firms (particularly credit card companies) in the 20th century, boosting the state's prosperity.

Delaware Beaches

Delaware's 28 miles of sandy Atlantic beaches are the best reason to linger. Most businesses and services are open year-round. Off-season (outside of June to August), bargains abound.

Lewes

In 1631 the Dutch gave this whaling settlement the pretty name of Zwaanendael, or Valley of the Swans, before promptly getting massacred by local Nanticokes. The name was changed to Lewes (*loo*-iss) when William Penn gained control of the area. Today it's an attractive seaside gem with a mix of English and Dutch architecture.

The **visitor center** (www.leweschamber.com; 120 Kings Hwy; ⊙ 10am-4pm Mon-Fri, 9am-3pm Sat, 10am-2pm Sun) provides useful insight into attractions and outings in the surrounding area.

◉ Sights & Activities

Zwaanendael Museum   MUSEUM
(102 Kings Hwy; ⊙ 10am-4:30pm Tue-Sat, 1:30-4:30pm Sun) **FREE** This small, appealing museum is a good place to learn about the Dutch roots of Lewes.

Quest Fitness Kayak   KAYAKING
(✆ 302-745-2925; www.questfitnesskayak.com; 514 E Savannah Rd; kayak hire per 2/8hr $25/50) For aquatic action, Quest Fitness Kayak operates a kayak rental stand next to the Beacon Motel. It also runs scenic paddle tours around the Cape (adult/child $65/35).

⬛ Sleeping & Eating

Hotel Rodney   HOTEL $$
(✆ 302-645-6466; www.hotelrodneydelaware.com; 142 2nd St; r $150-260; ❐ ❄ ❡ ⛨) This charming boutique hotel features exquisite bedding and antique furniture, and also has some modern touches.

Wharf   SEAFOOD $$
(✆ 302-645-7846; 7 Anglers Rd; mains $13-29; ⊙ 11:30am-1am; ❐ ♿) Across the drawbridge, the Wharf has a relaxing waterfront location and serves a big selection of seafood and pub grub. Live music on weekends.

ⓘ Getting There & Away

Cape May–Lewes Ferry (✆ 800-643-3779; www.capemaylewesferry.com; 43 Cape Henlopen Dr; per motorcycle/car $37/45, per adult/child $10/5) Runs daily 90-minute ferries across Delaware Bay to New Jersey from the terminal, 1 mile from downtown Lewes. For foot passengers, a seasonal shuttle bus ($4) operates between the ferry terminal and Lewes. Reservations recommended.

Cape Henlopen State Park

One mile east of Lewes, more than 4000 acres of dune bluffs, pine forests and wetlands are preserved at this lovely **state park** (✆ 302-645-8983; www.destateparks.com/park/cape-henlopen/; 15099 Cape Henlopen Dr; admission per car out-of-state/in-state $10/5; ⊙ 8am-sunset) that's popular with bird-watchers, beachgoers and campers. You can see clear to Cape May from the observation tower. **North**

Shores beach draws many gay and lesbian couples.

Rehoboth Beach & Dewey Beach

As the closest stretch of sand to Washington, DC (121 miles), **Rehoboth Beach** is often dubbed 'the Nation's Summer Capital.' It is both a family-friendly and gay-friendly destination. To escape the chaos of busy Rehoboth Ave (and the heavily built-up outskirts), wander into the side streets downtown. There you'll find a mix of gingerbread houses, posh restaurants and kiddie amusements, plus a wide beach fronted by a mile-long boardwalk.

Less than 2 miles south on Hwy 1 is the tiny hamlet of **Dewey Beach**. Unapologetically known as 'Do Me' Beach for its (heterosexual) hook-up scene and hedonistic nightlife, Dewey is a major party beach. Another 3 miles past Dewey is **Delaware Seashore State Park** (☑302-227-2800; www.destateparks.com/park/delaware-seashore/; 39415 Inlet Rd; per vehicle $10; ☉8am-sunset), a windswept slice of preserved dunes and salty breezes possessed of a wild, lonely beauty.

🛏 Sleeping

As elsewhere on the coast, prices skyrocket in high season (June to August). Cheaper lodging options are located on Rte 1.

Crosswinds Motel MOTEL $$
(☑302-227-7997; www.crosswindsmotel.com; 312 Rehoboth Ave; r $110-220; P❄☎) In the heart of Rehoboth Ave, this simple but nicely designed motel is great value for money, with welcome amenities (minirefridgerator, coffeemaker, flat-screen TV). Walk to the beach in 12 minutes.

🍴 Eating & Drinking

Cheap eats are available on the boardwalk. For classier dining, browse the inviting restaurants sprinkled along Wilmington Ave.

Henlopen City Oyster House SEAFOOD $$$
(50 Wilmington Ave; mains $14-34; ☉from 3pm) Seafood lovers won't want to miss this spot, where an enticing raw bar and mouthwatering seafood dishes draw crowds (arrive early; no reservations). Good microbrews, cocktails and wine selection.

★ Dogfish Head MICROBREWERY
(www.dogfish.com; 320 Rehoboth Ave; mains $9-25; ☉noon-late) This iconic brewery serves up tasty pizzas, burgers, crab cakes and

other pub fare, which go perfectly with the award-winning IPAs.

❶ Getting There & Around

BestBus (www.bestbus.com) Offers bus service from Rehoboth to DC ($40, 2½ hours) and NYC ($46, 4½ hours). Runs summertime only (late May through early September).

Jolly Trolley (one way/round-trip $3/5; ☉8am-2am Jun-Aug) Connects Rehoboth and Dewey Beaches, and makes frequent stops along the way.

Northern & Central Delaware

The grit of Wilmington is balanced by the rolling hills and palatial residences of the Brandywine Valley, particularly the soaring estate of Winterthur. Dover is cute, friendly and gets a little lively after hours.

Wilmington

A unique cultural milieu (African Americans, Jews and Caribbeans) and an energetic arts scene make this town worth a visit. The **visitor center** (☑800-489-6664; www.visitwilmingtonde.com; 100 W 10th St; ☉9am-4:30pm Mon-Fri) is downtown.

DELAWARE FACTS
....

Nickname The First State, Small Wonder

Population 917,000

Area 1982 sq miles

Capital city Dover (population 36,000)

Sales tax None

Birthplace of Rock musician George Thorogood (b 1952), actress Valerie Bertinelli (b 1960), actor Ryan Phillippe (b 1974)

Home of Vice President Joe Biden, the Du Pont family, DuPont chemicals, credit card companies, lots of chickens

Politics Democrat

Famous for Tax-free shopping, attractive beaches

State bird Delaware Blue Hen chicken

Driving distances Wilmington to Dover 52 miles; Dover to Rehoboth Beach 43 miles

---

DON'T MISS

CYCLING THE JUNCTION & BREAKWATER TRAIL

For a scenic ride between Rehoboth and Lewes, rent a bicycle and hit the 6-mile **Junction & Breakwater Trail**. Named after the former rail line that operated here in the 1800s, this smooth, graded greenway travels through wooded and open terrain, over coastal marshes and past farmland. Pick up a map from the Rehoboth visitor center or from **Atlantic Cycles** (✷ 302-226-2543; www.atlanticcycles.net; 18 Wilmington Ave; half-/full day from $16/24), also in Rehoboth, which offers inexpensive rentals. In Lewes, try **Ocean Cycles** (✷ 302-537-1522; www.oceancycles.com; 526 E Savannah Rd) at the Beacon Motel.

◉ Sights & Activities

Delaware Art Museum   MUSEUM
(✷ 302-571-9590; www.delart.org; 2301 Kentmere Pkwy; adult/child $12/6, Sun free; ◷ 10am-4pm Wed-Sun) The Delaware Art Museum exhibits work of the local Brandywine School, including Edward Hopper, John Sloan and three generations of Wyeths.

Wilmington Riverfront   WATERFRONT
The Wilmington Riverfront consists of several blocks of redeveloped waterfront shops, restaurants and cafes; the most striking building is the **Delaware Center for the Contemporary Arts** (✷ 302-656-6466; www.thedcca.org; 200 S Madison St; ◷ 10am-5pm Tue & Thu-Sat, noon-5pm Wed & Sun) FREE, which consistently displays innovative exhibitions.

⌑ Sleeping & Eating

Inn at Wilmington   HOTEL $$
(✷ 855-532-2216; www.innatwilmington.com; 300 Rocky Run Pkwy; r from $120; P✷✷) This is a charming, good-value option 5 miles north of downtown.

Iron Hill Brewery   BREWERY $$
(✷ 302-472-2739; www.ironhillbrewery.com; 620 Justison St; mains $11-27; ◷ 11:30am-11pm) The spacious and airy multilevel Iron Hill Brewery is set in a converted brick warehouse on the riverfront. Satisfying microbrews go nicely with hearty pub grub.

ℹ Getting There & Away

Wilmington is accessible by Greyhound bus from the **Wilmington Transportation Center** (100 S French St). **Amtrak** (www.amtrak.com; 100 S French St) trains connect with DC (1½ hours), Baltimore (45 minutes) and New York (1¾ hours).

Brandywine Valley

After making their fortune, the French-descended Du Ponts turned the Brandywine Valley into a sort of American Loire Valley. It remains a nesting ground for the wealthy and ostentatious to this day.

◉ Sights & Activities

Winterthur   HISTORIC SITE
(✷ 302-888-4600; www.winterthur.org; 5105 Kennett Pike, Rte 52; adult/child $20/5; ◷ 10am-5pm Tue-Sun) Six miles northwest of Wilmington is the 175-room estate of industrialist Henry Francis du Pont and his collection of antiques and American arts, one of the world's largest.

Brandywine Creek State Park   PARK
(✷ 302-577-3534; www.destateparks.com/park/brandywine-creek/; 41 Adams Dam Rd; per vehicle $8; ◷ 8am-sunset) Brandywine Creek State Park is the gem of the area. This green space would be impressive anywhere, but is doubly so considering how close it is to prodigious urban development. Nature trails and shallow streams wend through the park.

Wilderness Canoe Trips   CANOEING
(✷ 302-654-2227; www.wildernesscanoetrips.com; 2111 Concord Pike; kayak/canoe trip from $47/57, per tube $19) Call this outfit for for information on paddling or tubing down Brandywine Creek.

New Castle

As cute as a colonial kitten, New Castle is a web of cobblestoned streets and beautifully preserved 18th-century buildings lying near a riverfront (that said, however, the surrounding area is unfortunately a bit of an urban wasteland). Sights include the **Old Court House** (✷ 302-323-4453; 211 Delaware St, New Castle; ◷ 10am-3:30pm Wed-Sat, 1:30-4:30pm Sun) FREE, the arsenal on the Green, churches and cemeteries dating back to the 17th century.

The five-room **Terry House B&B** (✷ 302-322-2505; www.terryhouse.com; 130 Delaware St, New Castle; r $90-110; P✷) is idyllically set in the historic district.

A few doors down, **Jessop's Tavern** (☑302-322-6111; 114 Delaware St, New Castle; mains $14-24; ☺11:30am-10pm Mon-Sat, to 9pm Sun) serves up Dutch pot roast, 'Pilgrim's Feast' (oven-roasted turkey with all the fixings) and Belgian beers in a Colonial atmosphere.

Dover

Dover's city center is quite attractive; the row-house–lined streets are peppered with restaurants and shops, while broadleaf trees spread their branches over pretty little lanes.

◉ Sights & Activities

First State Heritage Park
Welcome Center & Galleries   MUSEUM
(☑302-739-9194; www.destateparks.com/park/first-state-heritage/; 121 Martin Luther King Blvd N; ☺9am-4:30pm Mon-Sat, 1:30-4:30pm Sun) FREE Delve into the history of Delaware at the First State Heritage Park, which serves as a welcome center for the city of Dover, the state of Delaware and the adjacent state house. This so-called park without boundaries includes some two dozen historic sites within a few blocks of one another. Start out at the Welcome Center & Galleries, which has exhibitions exploring Delaware's history. You can also pick up more info here on other key sites nearby.

Old State House   MUSEUM
(☑302-744-5055; http://history.delaware.gov/museums/; 25 The Green; ☺9am-4:30pm Mon-Sat, from 1:30pm Sun) FREE Built in 1791 and since restored, the Old State House contains art galleries and in-depth exhibits on the First State's history and politics.

🛏 Sleeping & Eating

State Street Inn   B&B $$
(☑302-734-2294; www.statestreetinn.com; 228 N State St; r $125-135; ✳) Although it's a bit over the top in its cuteness and flower-patterned wallpapers and sheets, the State Street remains a solid accommodation choice, with friendly, knowledgeable service and an unbeatable central location.

Golden Fleece   PUB FOOD $
(☑302-674-1776; 132 W Lockerman St; mains $4-10; ☺4pm-midnight) The best bar in Dover also serves up some good food. First priority is maintaining the atmosphere of an old English pub, which meshes well with the sur-rounding red-brick Dover historical center. Has an outdoor patio for summer nights.

Bombay Hook National Wildlife Refuge

Bombay Hook National
Wildlife Refuge   PARK
(☑302-653-9345; www.fws.gov/refuge/Bombay_Hook; 2591 Whitehall Neck Rd, Smyrna; per vehicle/pedestrian $4/2; ☺sunrise-sunset) Hundreds of thousands of waterfowl use this protected wetland as a stopping point along their migration routes. A 12-mile wildlife driving trail, running through 16,251 acres of saltwater marsh, cordgrass and tidal mud flats, manages to encapsulate all of the soft beauty of the DelMarVa peninsula in one perfectly preserved ecosystem. There are also short walking trails and observation towers.

VIRGINIA

Beautiful Virginia is a state steeped in history. It's the birthplace of America, where English settlers established the first permanent colony in the New World in 1607. From then on, the Commonwealth of Virginia has played a lead role in nearly every major American drama, from the Revolutionary and Civil Wars to the Civil Rights movement and the attacks of September 11, 2001.

Virginia's natural beauty is as diverse as its history and people. Chesapeake Bay and the wide sandy beaches kiss the Atlantic Ocean. Pine forests, marshes and rolling green hills form the soft curves of the central Piedmont region, while the rugged Appalachian Mountains and stunning Shenandoah Valley line its back.

History

Humans have occupied Virginia for at least 5000 years. Several thousand Native Americans were already here in May 1607, when Captain James Smith and his crew sailed up Chesapeake Bay and founded Jamestown, the first permanent English colony in the New World. Named for Queen Elizabeth I – aka the 'Virgin Queen' – the territory originally occupied most of America's eastern seaboard. By 1610 most of the colonists had died from starvation in their quest for gold, until colonist John Rolfe (husband of Pocahontas) discovered Virginia's real riches: tobacco.

A feudal aristocracy grew out of tobacco farming, and many gentry scions became Founding Fathers, including native son George Washington. In the 19th century the slave-based plantation system grew both in size and incompatibility with the industrializing North; Virginia seceded in 1861 and became the epicenter of the Civil War. Following its defeat the state walked a tense cultural tightrope, accruing a layered identity that included older aristocrats, a rural and urban working class, waves of immigrants and, today, the burgeoning tech-heavy suburbs of DC. The state revels in its history, yet still wants to pioneer the American experiment; thus, while Virginia only reluctantly desegregated in the 1960s, today it houses one of the most ethnically diverse populations of the New South.

Northern Virginia

Hidden within its suburban sprawl, Northern Virginia (NoVa) mixes small-town charm with metropolitan chic. Colonial villages and battlefields bump up against skyscrapers, shopping malls and world-class arts venues.

Arlington

Green-conscious and well trimmed, Arlington sits just across the Potomac River from DC. It has a couple of crucial capital sites, along with tempting dining and nightlife options. Most are easy-peasy to reach via the Metro.

Sights

Arlington National Cemetery HISTORIC SITE
([☎] 877-907-8585; www.arlingtoncemetery.mil; ⊙ 8am-7pm Apr-Sep, to 5pm Oct-Mar; Ⓜ Arlington Cemetery) FREE The county's best-known attraction is the somber final resting place for more than 400,000 military personnel and their dependents, with veterans of every US war from the Revolution to Iraq. The cemetery is spread over 612 hilly acres. Departing from the visitor center, bus tours are a handy way to visit the cemetery's memorials.

Highlights include the Tomb of the Unknowns, with its elaborate Changing of the Guard ceremony, and the gravesite of John F and Jacqueline Kennedy, marked by an eternal flame.

Pentagon BUILDING
([☎] 703-697-1776; pentagontours.osd.mil; Arlington, VA; ⊙ memorial 24hr, tours by appointment; Ⓜ Pentagon) South of Arlington Cemetery is the Pentagon, the largest office building in the world. Outside you may visit the **Pentagon Memorial** (www.pentagonmemorial.org; Ⓜ Pentagon) FREE; 184 illuminated benches honor each person killed in the September 11, 2001, terrorist attack on the Pentagon. To get inside the building, you'll have to book a free guided tour on the website. Make reservations 14 to 90 days in advance.

Artisphere ARTS CENTER
([☎] 703-875-1100; www.artisphere.com; 1101 Wilson Blvd; ⊙ 4-11pm Wed-Fri, noon-11pm Sat, noon-5pm Sun; [⁂]; Ⓜ Rosslyn) For something completely different from memorials and museums, check out the excellent exhibits at this sleek, modern arts complex, which opened in 2011. Its several theaters host live performances (many free), including world music, film and experimental theater. There's also a cafe, restaurant and bar.

✖ Eating & Drinking

In addition to hotels, there are dozens of chic restaurants and bars located along Clarendon and Wilson Blvds, clustered near the Rosslyn and Clarendon Metro stations.

★ **Myanmar** BURMESE $
([☎] 703-289-0013; 7810 Lee Hwy, Falls Church; mains $10-14; ⊙ noon-10pm; Ⓜ Dunn Loring Merrifield, then bus 2A) Myanmar's decor is bare bones; the service is slow; the portions are small; and the food is delicious. This is home-cooked Burmese: curries prepared with lots of garlic, turmeric and oil, chili fish, mango salads and chicken swimming in rich gravies.

Caffé Aficionado CAFE $
(1919 N Lynn St; sandwiches around $8; ⊙ 7am-6pm Mon-Fri, 8am-3pm Sat; Ⓜ Rosslyn) This friendly cafe whips up excellent lattes, pastries, waffles and thick baguette-style sandwiches. The space is tiny though, so you may have to get it to go (and enjoy it at the Freedom Park or on the Mt Vernon Trail).

Eden Center VIETNAMESE $$
(www.edencenter.com; 6571 Wilson Blvd, Falls Church; mains $9-15; ⊙ 9am-11pm; [⁂]; Ⓜ East Falls Church then bus 26A) One of Washington's most fascinating ethnic enclaves isn't technically in Washington. Instead, drive west past Arlington to Falls Church, VA and the Eden Center, which is, basically, a bit of Saigon that got lost in America. And we mean 'Saigon' – this is a shopping center/strip mall entirely occupied and operated by South Vietnamese refugees and their descendants.

Continental LOUNGE
(www.continentalpoollounge.com; 1911 N Fort Myer
Dr; ☺11:30am-2am Mon-Fri, 6pm-2am Sat & Sun;
M Rosslyn) A stone's throw from many Rosslyn
hotels, this buzzing pool lounge evokes a trippy, tropical vibe with its murals of palm trees,
oversized tiki heads and color-saturated bar
stools. All of which sets the stage for an alternative night of shooting pool, playing ping-
pong or trying your hand at shuffleboard.

☆ Entertainment

★ **Iota** LIVE MUSIC
(www.iotaclubandcafe.com; 2832 Wilson Blvd;
tickets $10-15; ☺4pm-2am Mon-Thu, from 10am
Fri-Sun; ☎; M Clarendon) With shows almost
every night of the week, Iota is the best venue for live music in Clarendon's music strip.
Bands span genres: folk, reggae, traditional
Irish and Southern rock are all distinct possibilities. Tickets are available at the door
only (no advance sales) and this place packs
'em in (the seating is first come, first served).

Alexandria

The charming Colonial village of Alexandria
is just 5 miles – and 250 years – away from
Washington. Once a salty port town, today
it is a posh collection of red-brick Colonial
homes, cobblestone streets, flickering gas
lamps and a waterfront promenade. King St,
the main thoroughfare, is packed with boutiques, outdoor cafes and neighborhood bars
and restaurants.

◉ Sights

★ **Carlyle House** HISTORIC BUILDING
(☏703-549-2997; www.nvrpa.org/park/carlyle_
house_historic_park; 121 N Fairfax St; admission $5;
☺10am-4pm Tue-Sat, noon-4pm Sun; M King St
then trolley) If you have time for just one historic house tour in Alexandria, make it this
one. It dates from 1753 when merchant and
city founder John Carlyle built the most lavish mansion in town (which in those days was
little more than log cabins and muddy lanes).
The Georgian Palladian-style house is packed
with paintings, historic relics and period furnishings that help bring the past to life.

Freedom House Museum MUSEUM
(☏708-836-2858; www.nvul.org/freedomhouse;
1315 Duke St; ☺10am-4pm Mon-Thu, to 3pm Fri;
M King St then trolley) FREE For a look at one
of the darkest eras of American history, pay
a visit to this small museum on Duke St. In

VIRGINIA FACTS

Nickname Old Dominion

Population 8.4 million

Area 42,774 sq miles

Capital city Richmond (population 205,000)

Other cities Virginia Beach (450,000),
Norfolk (247,000), Chesapeake
(231,000), Richmond (215,000), Newport News (183,000)

Sales tax 5.3 to 6%

Birthplace of George Washington
(1732–99) and seven other US presidents, Confederate General Robert E
Lee (1807–70), tennis ace Arthur Ashe
(1943–93), author Tom Wolfe (b 1931),
actor Sandra Bullock (b 1964)

Home of The Pentagon, the CIA, more
technology workers than any other state

Politics Republican

Famous for American history, tobacco,
apples, Shenandoah National Park

State beverage milk

Driving distances Arlington to Shenandoah 113 miles; Richmond to Virginia
Beach 108 miles

the 1830s, this nondescript brick building
housed the headquarters of the largest domestic slave-trading company in the country. Among the shackles, iron bars and low
ceilings in the basement, multimedia exhibits give a glimpse of what life was like for the
enslaved people held here.

**George Washington Masonic
National Memorial** MONUMENT, LOOKOUT
(www.gwmemorial.org; 101 Callahan Dr at King St;
admission $7, incl guided tour $10; ☺9am-5pm;
M King St) Alexandria's most prominent
landmark features a fine view from its 333ft
tower, where you can see the Capitol, Mt
Vernon and the Potomac River. It is modeled
after Egypt's Lighthouse of Alexandria, and
honors the first president (who was initiated
into the shadowy Masons in Fredericksburg
in 1752 and later became Worshipful Master
of Alexandria Lodge No 22).

Torpedo Factory Art Center ARTS CENTER
(www.torpedofactory.org; 105 N Union St; ☺10am-
6pm, to 9pm Thu; M King St then trolley) FREE

What do you do with a former munitions dump and arms factory? How about turn it into one of the best art spaces in the region? Three floors of artist studios and free creativity are on offer in Old Town Alexandria, as well as the opportunity to buy paintings, sculptures, glassworks, textiles and jewelry direct from creators. The Torpedo Factory anchors Alexandria's revamped waterfront with a marina, parks, walkways, residences and restaurants.

✖ Eating & Drinking

Eamonn's Dublin Chipper   PUB FOOD $
(www.eamonnsdublinchipper.com; 728 King St; mains $7-10; ⊙11:30am-11pm, to 1am Fri & Sat; MKing St then trolley) You'll find no better execution of the fish and chips genre than at this upscale temple to classic pub fare. How authentic is it? It imports Batchelors baked beans from Ireland, and also serves deep-fried Mars Bars, Milky Way and Snickers. Like many resto-pubs in this part of Old Town, Eamonn's is a good place for a drink on weekend nights.

Brabo Tasting Room   BELGIAN $$
(703-894-5252; www.braborestaurant.com; 1600 King St; mains $16-20; ⊙7:30-10:30am & 11:30am-11pm; MKing St then trolley) The inviting and sunlit Brabo Tasting Room serves its signature mussels, tasty wood-fired tarts and gourmet sandwiches, with a good beer and wine selection. In the morning, stop by for brioche French toast and Bloody Marys. Brabo restaurant, next door, is the high-end counterpart serving seasonal fare.

Restaurant Eve   AMERICAN $$$
(703-706-0450; www.restauranteve.com; 110 S Pitt St; mains $36-45, 6-course tasting menu $135; ⊙11:30am-2:30pm Mon-Fri, 5:30-10:30pm Mon-Sat; ; MKing St then trolley) One of Alexandria's best (and priciest) dining rooms, Eve blends great American ingredients, precise French technique and first-rate service. Splurge here on the tasting menus, which are simply on another level of gastronomic experience.

PX   BAR
(www.barpx; 728 King St, entrance on S Columbus St; ⊙6pm-midnight Wed-Thu, to 1:30am Fri & Sat; MKing St then trolley) This elegant, low-lit drinking den is a magical spot to linger over a cocktail or two. Jauntily attired bartenders shake up beautifully hued elixirs to a well-dressed crowd, perfectly in keeping with the speakeasy theme. True to form, there's no sign, just a blue light and a red door to mark the entrance. It's best to reserve ahead.

As expected, cocktails are in the $14 to $18 range, so sip sloooowly.

☆ Entertainment

Basin Street Lounge   JAZZ
(703-549-1141; www.219restaurant.com; 219 King St; admission Fri & Sat $5; ⊙shows 9pm Tue-Sat; MKing St then trolley) Tortoise-shell glasses and black turtlenecks ought to be the uniform of choice at this low-key jazz venue and cigar bar, located above the 219 Restaurant. The extensive whiskey selection, amber lighting and long wooden bar make a fine backdrop to bluesy jazz performances.

❶ Information

The **visitor center** (703-838-5005; www.visitalexandriava.com; 221 King St; ⊙10am-5pm) issues parking permits and discount tickets to historic sites.

❶ Getting There & Away

To get to Alexandria from downtown DC, take the Metro to the King St station. A free trolley makes the 1-mile journey between the Metro station and the waterfront (every 15 minutes, from 10am to 10:15pm Sunday to Wednesday, and until midnight Thursday to Saturday).

Mount Vernon

One of the most visited historic shrines in the nation, **Mt Vernon** (703-780-2000, 800-429-1520; www.mountvernon.org; 3200 Mount Vernon Memorial Hwy; adult/child $17/9; ⊙8am-5pm Apr-Aug, 9am-4pm Nov-Feb, to 5pm Mar, Sep & Oct, gristmill & distillery 10am-5pm Apr-Oct) was the beloved home of George and Martha Washington, who lived here from the time of their marriage in 1759 until George's death in 1799. Now owned and operated by the Mt Vernon Ladies Association, the estate offers glimpses of 18th-century farm life and the first president's life as a country planter. Mt Vernon does not gloss over the Founding Father's slave ownership: visitors can tour the slave quarters and burial ground. Other sights include Washington's **distillery and gristmill** (5513 Mount Vernon Memorial Hwy; ⊙10am-5pm Apr-Oct), 3 miles south of the estate.

Mt Vernon is 16 miles south of DC off the Mt Vernon Memorial Hwy. By public transportation, take the Metro to Huntington, then switch to Fairfax Connector bus

101. Grayline (☑202-289-1999; www.grayline.
com; adult/child incl Mt Vernon admission $90/30)
and OnBoard Tours (☑301-839-5261; www.
onboardtours.com; adult/child incl Mt Vernon admission from $80/70) run bus tours from DC,
stopping at Arlington and Mt Vernon.

Several companies offer seasonal boat
trips from DC and Alexandria; the cheapest
is Potomac Riverboat Company (☑703-
684-0580; www.potomacriverboatco.com; adult/
child incl Mt Vernon admission $42/22). A healthy
alternative is to take a lovely bike ride along
the Potomac River from DC (18 miles from
Roosevelt Island). You can even bike one way
from the Alexandria waterfront and return
by boat with Bike and Roll DC (☑202-842-
2453; www.bikeandrolldc.com; adult/child $63/40).

Manassas

On July 21, 1861, Union and Confederate
soldiers clashed in the first major land
battle of the Civil War. Expecting a quick
victory, DC residents flocked here to picnic and watch the First Battle of Bull Run
(known in the South as First Manassas).
The surprise Southern victory erased any
hopes of a quick end to the war. Union
and Confederate soldiers again met on the
same ground for the larger Second Battle of
Manassas in August 1862; again the South
was victorious. Today, Manassas National
Battlefield Park is a curving green hills-
cape, sectioned into fuzzy fields of tall grass
and wildflowers by split-rail wood fences.
Start your tour at the Henry Hill Visitor
Center (☑703-361-1339; www.nps.gov/mana;
adult/child $3/free; ⊙8:30am-5pm) to watch
the orientation film and pick up park and
trail maps.

Daily Amtrak (www.amtrak.com; one way $16-
28) and Virginia Railway Express (VRE; www.
vre.org; one way $9.10; ⊙Mon-Fri) trains make
the 50-minute journey between DC's Union
Station and the historic Old Town Manassas Railroad Station (9451 West St); from
there it's a 6-mile taxi ride to the park. There
are several restaurants and bars around the
Manassas train station, but the rest of the
city is a mess of strip malls and suburban
sprawl.

Fredericksburg

Fredericksburg is a pretty town with a historical district that's almost a cliché of small-
town Americana. George Washington grew

up here, and the Civil War exploded in the
streets and surrounding fields. Today, the
main street is a pleasant amble of bookstores, gastropubs and cafes.

◎ Sights

Fredericksburg & Spotsylvania
National Military Park   HISTORIC SITE
(www.nps.gov/frsp) FREE More than 13,000
Americans were killed during the Civil War
in four battles fought in a 17-mile radius covered by this park, today maintained by the
NPS (National Park Service). Don't miss the
burial site of Stonewall Jackson's amputated
arm near the Fredericksburg Battlefield
visitor center (☑540-373-6122; www.nps.gov/
frsp; 1013 Lafayette Blvd; film $2; ⊙9am-5pm)
FREE.

James Monroe Museum
& Memorial Library   HISTORIC SITE
(☑540-654-1043; http://jamesmonroemuseum.
umw.edu; 908 Charles St; adult/child $6/2;
⊙10am-5pm Mon-Sat, from 1pm Sun) The museum's namesake was the nation's fifth president. US history nerds will delight in the
small curious collection of Monroe memorabilia, including the desk on which he wrote
the famous Monroe Doctrine.

Mary Washington House HISTORIC BUILDING
(☑540-373-5630; 1200 Charles St; adult/child
$5/2; ⊙11am-5pm Mon-Sat, noon-4pm Sun) At
the 18th-century home of George Washington's mother, knowledgeable tour guides
in period costume shed light on Mary and
what life was like in her time. The lovely garden is an excellent recreation from the era.

🛏 Sleeping & Eating

You'll find dozens of restaurants and cafes
along historic Caroline and William Sts.

Richard Johnston Inn   B&B $$
(☑540-899-7606; www.therichardjohnstoninn.
com; 711 Caroline St; r $125-250; P ❄ 🛜) In an
18th-century brick mansion, this cozy B&B
scores points for location, comfort and
friendliness.

Foode   AMERICAN $$
(☑540-479-1370; www.foodeonline.com; 1006C/D
Caroline St; mains lunch $9-11, dinner $15-25;
⊙11am–3pm & 4:30pm–8pm Tue-Sat, 10am-2pm
Sun; 🍴) 🍃 Foode serves up tasty farm-to-
table fare in a rustic but artsy setting.

ℹ Getting There & Away

Virginia Railway Express ($11.55, 1½ hours) and **Amtrak** ($26 to $50, 1¼ hours) trains depart from the **Fredericksburg train station** (200 Lafayette Blvd) with service to DC.

Greyhound has buses to/from DC ($15 to $24, five per day, 1½ hours) and Richmond ($15 to $27, three per day, one hour). The **Greyhound station** (☏ 540-373-2103; 1400 Jefferson Davis Hwy) is roughly 1.5 miles west of the historic district.

Richmond

Richmond has been the capital of the Commonwealth of Virginia since 1780. It's an old-fashioned Southern city that's grounded in tradition on one hand, but full of income disparities and social tensions on the other. Yet it's an undeniably handsome town, with red-brick row houses, a rushing river and leafy parks.

Its history is ubiquitous and, sometimes, uncomfortable; this was where patriot Patrick Henry gave his famous 'Give me Liberty, or give me Death!' speech, and where the slave-holding Southern Confederate States placed their capital. Today the 'River City' is a surprisingly dynamic place, with a buzzing food-and-drink scene, fascinating neighborhoods and a wide range of attractions.

◉ Sights

American Civil War Center at Historic Tredegar   MUSEUM
(www.tredegar.org; 500 Tredegar St; adult/child $8/4; ☻ 9am-5pm) Located in an 1861 gun foundry, this fascinating site explores the causes and course of the Civil War from the perspectives of Union, Confederate and African American experiences. Next door is a free site run by the National Park Service that delves into Richmond's role during the war. This is one of 13 protected area sites that make up **Richmond National Battlefield Park** (www.nps.gov/rich).

Canal Walk   WATERFRONT
(www.rvariverfront.com; btwn 5th and 17th Sts) The 1.25-mile waterfront Canal Walk between the James River and the Kanawha (ka-*naw*) and Haxall Canals is a lovely way of seeing a dozen highlights of Richmond history in one go. There's also a pedestrian bridge across to Belle Isle, a scruffy but intriguing island in the James.

Belle Isle   PARK
(www.jamesriverpark.org) A long pedestrian bridge leads from Tredegar St (just past the national park site) out to this car-free island. Once a quarry, power plant and POW camp during the Civil War (though never all at once), today this is one of Richmond's finest city parks. The big flat rocks are lovely for sunbathing, and hiking and biking trails abound – but don't swim in the James River. It's polluted and the currents are treacherous.

White House of the Confederacy   HISTORIC SITE
(www.moc.org; cnr 12th & Clay Sts; adult/child $10/6; ☻ 10am-5pm) While this was once a shrine to the Southern 'Lost Cause,' the Confederate White House is recommended for its quirky insights (did you know the second-most powerful man in the Confederacy may have been a gay Jew?).

Virginia State Capitol   BUILDING
(www.virginiacapitol.gov; cnr 9th & Grace Sts, Capitol Sq; ☻ 8am-5pm Mon-Sat, 1-5pm Sun) FREE Designed by Thomas Jefferson, the capitol building was completed in 1788 and houses the oldest legislative body in the Western Hemisphere – the Virginia General Assembly, established in 1619. Free tours available.

Virginia Historical Society   MUSEUM
(www.vahistorical.org; 428 North Blvd; adult/student $6/4; ☻ 10am-5pm Mon-Sat, from 1pm Sun) The VHS is looking grander than ever following a multi-million-dollar renovation. Changing and permanent exhibits trace the history of the Commonwealth from prehistoric to present times.

St John's Episcopal Church   CHURCH
(www.historicstjohnschurch.org; 2401 E Broad St; tours adult/child $7/5; ☻ 10am-4pm Mon-Sat, from 1pm Sun) It was here that firebrand Patrick Henry uttered his famous battle cry – 'Give me Liberty, or give me Death!' – during the rebellious 1775 Second Virginia Convention. His speech is re-enacted from 1pm to 3pm on Sundays in summer.

Virginia Museum of Fine Arts   MUSEUM
(VMFA; ☏ 804-340-1400; www.vmfa.museum; 200 North Blvd; ☻ 10am-5pm Sun-Wed, to 9pm Thu & Fri) FREE Has a remarkable collection of European works, sacred Himalayan art and one of the largest Fabergé egg collections on display outside Russia. Also hosts excellent temporary exhibitions (admission ranges from free to $20).

VINEYARDS OF VIRGINIA

Home to some 230 vineyards, Virginia has a rising presence in the wine world. Good places to begin the foray lie just outside of DC in Loudon County. For maps, wine routes and loads of other viticultural info, visit www.virginiawine.org.

King Family Vineyards (☑434-823-7800; www.kingfamilyvineyards.com; 6550 Roseland Farm, Crozet; tastings $8; ☉10am-5:30pm) Consistently ranks as one of Virginia's best wineries. Bring a picnic (the winery also sells gourmet goodies) and enjoy the expansive scenery. At 1pm on summer Sundays (late May to mid-October), you can also catch a free polo match. It's 18 miles east of Charlottesville.

Jefferson Vineyards (☑434-977-3042; www.jeffersonvineyards.com; 1353 Thomas Jefferson Pkwy, Charlottesville; tastings $10; ☉10am-6pm) Near Charlottesville, this winery harvests from its namesake's original 1774 vineyard site. It also hosts twice-monthly free outdoor concerts in summer.

Bluemont Vineyard (☑540-554-8439; www.bluemontvineyard.com; 18755 Foggy Bottom Rd, Bluemont; tastings $5; ☉11am-6pm Wed-Mon) Bluemont produces ruby-red Nortons and crisp Viogniers, though it's equally famous for its spectacular location – at a 950ft elevation with sweeping views over the countryside.

Chrysalis Vineyards (☑540-687-8222; www.chrysaliswine.com; 23876 Champe Ford Rd, Middleburg; tastings $7-10; ☉10am-6pm) Proudly using the native Norton grape (which dates back to 1820), Chrysalis produces highly drinkable reds and whites – including a refreshing Viognier. The pretty estate hosts a bluegrass fest in October.

Tarara Vineyard (☑703-771-7100; www.tarara.com; 13648 Tarara Lane, Leesburg; tastings $10; ☉11am-5pm) On a bluff overlooking the Potomac, this 475-acre estate provides guided tours showing the grape's journey from vine to glass. The winery has a 6000-sq-ft cave/cellar, and visitors can pick fruit in the orchard or hike the 6 miles of trails through rolling countryside. Tarara also hosts summertime Saturday-evening concerts and three major wine festivals.

Poe Museum　　　　MUSEUM
(☑804-648-5523; www.poemuseum.org; 1914-16 E Main St; adult/student $6/5; ☉10am-5pm Tue-Sat, from 11am Sun) Contains the world's largest collection of manuscripts and memorabilia of poet Edgar Allan Poe, who lived and worked in Richmond.

Hollywood Cemetery　　　　CEMETERY
(☑804-649-0711; www.hollywoodcemetery.org; entrance cnr Albemarle & Cherry Sts; ☉8am-5pm, to 6pm summer) FREE This tranquil cemetery, perched above the James River rapids, contains the gravesites of two US presidents (James Monroe and John Tyler), the only Confederate president (Jefferson Davis) and 18,000 Confederate soldiers. Free walking tours are given at 10am Monday through Saturday and 2pm on Sunday.

Monument Avenue Statues　　　　STATUE
(btwn N Lombardy St & Roseneath Rd) Monument Ave, a tree-lined boulevard in northeast Richmond, holds statues of such revered Southern heroes as JEB Stuart, Robert E Lee, Matthew Fontaine Maury, Jefferson Davis, Stonewall Jackson and – in a nod to diversity – African American tennis champion Arthur Ashe.

🛏 Sleeping

★**HI Richmond**　　　　HOSTEL $
(www.hiusa.org; 7 N 2nd St; dm around $30; ❄🤚) Inside a historic 1924 building, this new, eco-friendly hostel has a great central location and bright rooms (both dorms and private rooms), with high ceilings and loads of original details. There's a kitchen for guests, inviting common areas, and it's also completely accessible for travelers with disabilities.

Linden Row Inn　　　　BOUTIQUE HOTEL $$
(☑804-783-7000; www.lindenrowinn.com; 100 E Franklin St; r $100-190; P❄@🤚) This antebellum gem has 70 attractive rooms (with period Victorian furnishings) spread among neighboring Greek Revival town houses in an excellent downtown location. Friendly southern hospitality and thoughtful extras (free passes to the YMCA, free around-town shuttle service) sweeten the deal.

Museum District B&B
B&B **$$**

(☏ 804-359-2332; www.museumdistrictbb.com; 2811 Grove Ave; r from $150; P✳❀) In a fine location near the dining and drinking of Carytown, this stately 1920s brick B&B has earned many admirers for its warm welcome. Rooms are comfortably set and guests can enjoy the wide front porch, cozy parlor with fireplace, and excellent cooked breakfasts – plus wine and cheese in the evenings.

Jefferson Hotel
LUXURY HOTEL **$$$**

(☏ 804-649-4750; www.jeffersonhotel.com; 101 W Franklin St; r $365; P✳❀▣) The Jefferson is Richmond's grandest hotel and one of the finest in America. The vision of tobacco tycoon and Confederate major Lewis Ginter, the beaux-arts-style hotel was completed in 1895. According to rumor, the magnificent grand staircase in the lobby served as the model for the famed stairs in *Gone with the Wind*.

Even if you don't stay here, it's worth having a peek inside. If you have time, try the hotel's afternoon tea, served beneath Tiffany stained glass in the Palm Court lobby (from 3pm Friday to Sunday), or have a drink at the grand Lemaire Bar.

✕ Eating

You'll find dozens of restaurants along the cobbled streets of Shockoe Slip and Shockoe Bottom. Further west in Carytown (W Cary St between S Blvd and N Thompson St) are even more dining options.

★ Mama J's
AMERICAN **$**

(415 N 1st St; mains $7-10; ⊙ 11am-9pm Sun-Thu, to 10pm Fri & Sat) Set in the historic African American neighborhood of Jackson Ward, Mama J's serves up delicious fried chicken and legendary fried catfish, along with collard greens, mac 'n' cheese, candied yams and other fixings. The service is friendly and the lines are long – go early to beat the crowds.

17th Street Farmers Market
MARKET **$**

(cnr 17th & E Main Sts; ⊙ 8:30am-4pm Sat & Sun) For cheap eats and fresh produce, check out this bustling market, which runs from late April through early October. On Sundays, the market sells antiques.

Sub Rosa
BAKERY **$**

(620 N 25th St; pastries $3-5; ⊙ 7am-6pm Tue-Fri, 8:30am-5pm Sat & Sun) In the historic Church Hill neighborhood, Sub Rosa is a wood-fired bakery serving some of the best baked goods in the south.

Kuba Kuba
CUBAN **$**

(1601 Park Ave; mains $7-17; ⊙ 9am-9:30pm Mon-Sat to 8pm Sun) In the Fan district, this tiny hole in the wall feels like a bodega straight out of Old Havana, with mouth-watering roast pork dishes, Spanish-style omelets and panini at rock-bottom prices.

Sidewalk Cafe
AMERICAN **$**

(2101 W Main St; mains $9-18; ⊙ 11:30am-2am Mon-Fri, from 9am Sat & Sun) A much-loved local haunt, Sidewalk Cafe feels like a dive bar (year-round Christmas lights, wood-paneled walls, kitschy artwork), but the food is first rate. There's outdoor seating on the sidewalk, daily specials (eg Taco Tuesdays) and legendary weekend brunches.

The Daily
MODERN AMERICAN **$$**

(☏ 804-342-8990; 2934 W Cary St; mains $10-25; ⊙ 7am-10pm Sun-Thu, to midnight Fri & Sat; ✐) ❏ In the heart of Carytown, the Daily is a great dining and drinking choice no matter the time of day. Stop by for lump crab omelets at breakfast, blackened mahimahi BLT at lunch and seared scallops by night. Extensive vegan options, first-rate cocktails and a buzzing, artfully designed space (complete with dramatically lit trees) seal the deal.

Millie's Diner
MODERN AMERICAN **$$**

(☏ 804-643-5512; 2603 E Main St; lunch $9-12, dinner $22-26; ⊙ 11am-2:30pm & 5:30-10:30pm Tue-Fri, 9am-3pm & 5:30-10:30pm Sat & Sun) Lunch, dinner or weekend brunch – Richmond icon Millie's does it all, and does it well. It's a small but handsomely designed space, with creative seasonal fare. The Devil's Mess – an open-faced omelet with spicy sausage, curry, veg, cheese and avocado – is legendary.

Boathouse at Rocketts Landing
SEAFOOD **$$$**

(☏ 804-622-2628; 4708 E Old Main St; mains $14-32; ⊙ 5pm-midnight Mon-Thu, from 3pm Fri, from noon Sat & Sun) The Boathouse serves good seafood plates (crispy calamari, Chapel Creek oysters, sesame-seared tuna) and pub fare in a fabulous setting overlooking the James River. The breezy deck is also a fine spot for a sundowner. It's located about 1 mile south of Shockoe Bottom.

♟ Drinking & Entertainment

Legend Brewing Company
MICROBREWERY

(☏ 804-232-3446; www.legendbrewing.com; 321 W 7th St; ⊙ 11:30am-11pm Mon-Sat, to 10pm Sun) On the south side of the James River, this place has excellent microbrews, tasty pub grub and fine views of the city from its popular outdoor deck. There's live bluegrass on Sundays (6:30pm), rock and other music on Fridays (8pm), and free brewery tours on Saturdays (1pm).

From downtown, it's a short hop across the bike- and pedestrian-friendly Manchester (S 9th St) Bridge.

Saison   COCKTAIL BAR
(23 W Marshall St; ☺5pm-2am) This classy drinking den attracts serious cocktail lovers, who clink glasses over creative libations, craft beer and farm-to-table fare. It's in Jackson Ward, near downtown.

Capital Ale House   BAR
(623 E Main St; ☺11am-1:30am) Popular with political wonks from the nearby state capitol, this downtown pub has a superb beer selection (more than 50 on tap and 250 bottled) and decent pub grub.

Cary Street Cafe   LIVE MUSIC
(☑804-353-7445; www.carystreetcafe.com; 2631 W Cary St; ☺8am-2am Mon-Fri, from 11am Sat & Sun) Live music (plus the odd karaoke crooner) emanates from this excellent bar just about every night of the week. This spot is proudly pro-hippie, but doesn't just bust hippie tunes; the gigs juke from reggae and folk to alt-country and gypsy rock.

Byrd Theater   CINEMA
(☑804-353-9911; www.byrdtheatre.com; 2908 W Cary St; tickets from $2) You can't beat the price at this classic 1928 cinema, which shows second-run films. Wurlitzer-organ concerts precede the Saturday-night shows.

ℹ️ Information

Johnston-Willis Hospital (☑804-330-2000; 1401 Johnston-Willis Dr)
Post Office (700 E Main St; ☺7:30am-5pm Mon-Fri)
Richmond-Times Dispatch (www.richmond.com) Daily newspaper.
Richmond Visitor Center (☑804-783-7450; www.visitrichmondva.com; 405 N 3rd St; ☺9am-5pm)
Style Weekly (www.styleweekly.com) Alternative weekly with listings of events, restaurants, nightlife and the arts.

ℹ️ Getting There & Around

The cab fare from **Richmond International Airport** (RIC; ☑804-226-3000; www.flyrichmond.com), 10 miles east of town, costs about $30.

Amtrak (☑800-872-7245; www.amtrak.com) trains stop at the **main station** (7519 Staples Mill Rd), 7 miles north of town (accessible to downtown via bus 27). More-convenient but less-frequent trains stop downtown at the **Main St Station** (1500 E Main St).

A new **Bikeshare** program is slated to launch by 2016.
Greater Richmond Transit Company (GRTC; ☑804-358-4782; www.ridegrtc.com; fares from $2) Runs local buses. Takes exact change only.
Greyhound/Trailways Bus Station (☑804-254-5910; www.greyhound.com; 2910 North Blvd)

Petersburg

About 25 miles south of Richmond, the little town of Petersburg played a big role in the Civil War as a major railway junction, transporting Confederate troops and supplies. Union troops laid a 10-month siege of Petersburg in 1864–65, the longest on American soil. The **Siege Museum** (☑804-733-2404; 15 W Bank St; adult/child $5/4, incl Old Blandford Church $11/9; ☺10am-5pm) relates the plight of civilians during the siege. Several miles east of town, **Petersburg National Battlefield** (nps.gov/pete; per vehicle/pedestrian $5/3; ☺9am-5pm) is where Union soldiers planted explosives underneath a Confederate breastwork, leading to the Battle of the Crater (novelized and cinematized in *Cold Mountain*). West of downtown in Pamplin Historical Park, the excellent **National Museum of the Civil War Soldier** (☑804-861-2408; www.pamplinpark.org; 6125 Boydton Plank Rd; adult/child $13/8; ☺9am-5pm) illustrates the hardships faced by soldiers on both sides of the conflict.

Historic Triangle

This is America's birthplace. Nowhere else in the country has such a small area played such a pivotal role in the nation's history. The nation's roots were planted in Jamestown, the first permanent English settlement in the New World; the flames of the American Revolution were fanned at the Colonial capital of Williamsburg; and America finally won its independence from Britain at Yorktown.

You'll need at least two days to do the Triangle any justice. A daily free shuttle travels between the Williamsburg visitor center, Yorktown and Jamestown.

Williamsburg

If you visit only one historical town in Virginia, make it Williamsburg – home to Colonial Williamsburg, one of the largest, most comprehensive living-history museums in the world. If any place is going to get kids into history, this is it, but it's plenty of fun for adults, too.

The actual town of Williamsburg, Virginia's capital from 1699 to 1780, is a stately place. The prestigious campus of the College of William & Mary adds a decent dash of youth culture, with coffee shops, cheap pubs and fashion boutiques.

◉ Sights

Colonial Williamsburg   HISTORIC SITE
(www.colonialwilliamsburg.org; adult/child 1-day $41/21, multi-day $51/26; ⊙9am-5pm) The restored capital of England's largest colony in the New World is a must-see attraction for visitors of all ages. This is not some phony, fenced-in theme park: Colonial Williamsburg is a living, breathing, working history museum with a painstakingly researched environment that brilliantly captures America of the 1700s.

➡ The Site

The 301-acre historic area contains 88 original 18th-century buildings and several hundred faithful reproductions. Costumed townsfolk and 'interpreters' in period dress go about their colonial jobs as blacksmiths, apothecaries, printers, barmaids, soldiers and patriots, breaking character only long enough to pose for a snapshot.

Costumed patriots including Patrick Henry and Thomas Jefferson still deliver impassioned speeches for freedom, but the park doesn't gloss over America's less glorious moments. Today's re-enactors debate and question slavery, women's suffrage, the rights of indigenous Americans and whether or not it is even moral to engage in revolution.

➡ Entrance

Walking around the historic district and patronizing the shops and taverns is free, but entry to building tours and most exhibits is restricted to ticketholders. Expect crowds, lines and petulant children, especially in summer.

To park and to purchase tickets, follow signs to the **visitor center** (☎757-220-7645; 101 Visitor Center Dr; ⊙8:45am-5pm), found north of the historic district between Hwy 132 and Colonial Pkwy; kids can also hire period costumes here for $25 per day. Start off with a 30-minute film about Williamsburg, and ask about the day's programs and events.

Parking is free; shuttle buses run frequently to and from the historic district, or you can walk along the tree-lined footpath. You can also buy tickets at the **Merchants Square information booth** (W Duke of Gloucester St; ⊙9am-5pm).

College of William & Mary   HISTORIC BUILDING
(www.wm.edu; 200 Stadium Dr) Chartered in 1693, the College of William & Mary is the second-oldest college in the country and retains the oldest academic building in continued use in the USA, the **Sir Christopher Wren Building**. The school's alumni include Thomas Jefferson, James Monroe and comedian Jon Stewart.

🛏 Sleeping

The visitor center can help find and book accommodations at no cost. If you stay in Colonial Williamsburg, guesthouses can provide discount admission tickets (adult/child $30/15).

Governor's Inn   HOTEL $
(☎757-220-7940; www.colonialwilliamsburg.com; 506 N Henry St; r $70-93; P🌐🐾🏊) Williamsburg's official 'economy' choice is a big box by any other name, but rooms are clean, and guests can use the pool and facilities of the Woodlands Hotel. It's in a great location near the visitor center, three blocks from the historic district.

**Williamsburg Woodlands
Hotel & Suites**   HOTEL $$
(☎757-220-7960; www.colonialwilliamsburg.com; 105 Visitor Center Dr; r from $165; P🌐🐾🏊) This good-value option has comfy, carpeted rooms (some of which go a bit heavy on the patterned wallpaper) near the main visitor center in Colonial Williamsburg. The splash park, games (mini-golf, volleyball court) and complimentary breakfast make it a hit with families.

**★ Colonial Williamsburg
Historic Lodging**   GUESTHOUSE $$$
(☎888-965-7254, 757-220-7978; www.colonialwilliamsburg.com; 136 E Francis St; r $220) For true 18th-century immersion, guests can stay in one of 26 original Colonial houses inside the historic district. Accommodations range in

size and style, though the best have period furnishings, canopy beds and wood-burning fireplaces.

✖ Eating

You'll find many restaurants, cafes and pubs in Merchants Sq, adjacent to Colonial Williamsburg.

Cheese Shop
DELI $

(410 W Duke of Gloucester St, Merchants Sq; mains $6-8; ⊙ 10am-8pm Mon-Sat, 11am-6pm Sun) This gourmet deli showcases some flavorful sandwiches and antipasti, plus baguettes, pastries, wine, beer and wonderful cheeses.

Aromas
CAFE $

(www.aromasworld.com; 431 Prince George St; mains $6-15; ⊙ 7am-10pm Mon-Sat, 8am-8pm Sun; 🛜) One block north of Merchants Sq, Aromas is an inviting coffeehouse serving a wide range of fare, plus wine and beer. It has outdoor seating and live music (jazz on Tuesdays; wide-ranging sounds on weekends).

King's Arms Tavern
MODERN AMERICAN $$$

(☑888-965-7254; 416 E Duke of Gloucester St; lunch mains $14-16, dinner $32-37; ⊙ 11:30am-2:30pm & 5-9pm) Of the four restaurants within Colonial Williamsburg, this is the most elegant, serving early-American cuisine, such as game pie – venison, rabbit and duck braised in port-wine sauce.

❶ Getting There & Around

Williamsburg Transportation Center (☑757-229-8750; cnr Boundary & Lafayette Sts)
Amtrak (www.amtrak.com) trains run from here twice a day to Washington, DC ($44, four hours), and Richmond ($21, one hour).

Jamestown

On May 14, 1607, a group of 104 English men and boys settled on this swampy island, bearing a charter from the Virginia Company of London to search for gold and other riches. Instead, they found starvation and disease. By January of 1608, only about 40 colonists were still alive, and these had resorted to cannibalism to survive. The colony survived the 'Starving Time' with the leadership of Captain James Smith and help from Powhatan, a local Native American leader. In 1619 the elected House of Burgesses convened, forming the first democratic government in the Americas.

◉ Sights & Activities

Historic Jamestowne
HISTORIC SITE

(☑757-856-1250; www.historicjamestowne.org; 1368 Colonial Pkwy; adult/child $14/free; ⊙ 8:30am-4:30pm) Run by the NPS, this is the original Jamestown site. Start your visit at the on-site museum and check out the statues of John Smith and Pocahontas. The original Jamestown ruins were rediscovered in 1994; visitors can watch the ongoing archaeological work at the site.

Jamestown Settlement
HISTORIC SITE

(☑757-253-4838; www.historyisfun.org; 2110 Jamestown Rd; adult/child $17/8, incl Yorktown Victory Center $21/11; ⊙ 9am-5pm; P ♿) Popular with kids, the state-run Jamestown Settlement reconstructs the 1607 James Fort; a Native American village; and full-scale replicas of the first ships that brought the settlers to Jamestown, along with living-history fun. Multimedia exhibits and costumed interpreters bring the 17th century to life.

Yorktown

On October 19, 1781, British General Cornwallis surrendered to George Washington here, effectively ending the American Revolution. Overpowered by massive American guns on land and cut off from the sea by the French, the British were in a hopeless position. Although Washington anticipated a much longer siege, the devastating barrage quickly overwhelmed Cornwallis, who surrendered within days.

Yorktown itself is a pleasant waterfront village overlooking the York River, with a nice range of shops, restaurants and pubs.

◉ Sights & Activities

Yorktown Battlefield
HISTORIC SITE

(☑757-898-3400; www.nps.gov/york; 1000 Colonial Pkwy; incl Historic Jamestowne adult/child $7/free; ⊙ 9am-5pm; P ♿) 🌿 Yorktown Battlefield, run by the NPS, is the site of the last major battle of the American Revolution. Start your tour at the visitor center and check out the orientation film and the display of Washington's original tent. The 7-mile Battlefield Rd Tour takes you past the major highlights. Don't miss a walk through the last British defensive sites, Redoubts 9 and 10.

Yorktown Victory Center
MUSEUM

(☑757-887-1776; www.historyisfun.org; 200 Water St; adult/child $10/6; ⊙ 9am-5pm; P ♿) 🌿 The state-run Yorktown Victory Center is an interactive, living-history museum that focuses on reconstruction, re-enactment and the Revolution's impact on the people who lived through it. At the re-created encampment, costumed Continental soldiers fire cannons and discuss food preparation and field medicine of the day.

✖ Eating

Carrot Tree   CAFE $
(☑ 757-988-1999; 323 Water St; mains $7-9; ☺ 11am-4pm; ✦) On the waterfront, Carrot Tree is a good, affordable spot serving wraps, salads and veggie burgers.

James River Plantations

The grand homes of Virginia's slave-holding aristocracy were a clear sign of the era's class divisions. A string of them line scenic Hwy 5 on the north side of the river, though only a few are open to the public.

⊙ Sights & Activities

Sherwood Forest   HISTORIC SITE
(☑ 804-829-5377; www.sherwoodforest.org; 14501 John Tyler Memorial Hwy, Charles City; self-guided tours adult/child $10/free; ☺ grounds 9am-5pm) The longest frame house in the country, this was the home of 10th US president John Tyler. Full tours are available by advance appointment only ($35 per person), though the grounds are open to self-guided tours.

Berkeley Plantation   HISTORIC SITE
(☑ 804-829-6018; www.berkeleyplantation.com; 12602 Harrison Landing Rd, Charles City; adult/child $11/7.50; ☺ 9:30am-4:30pm) Berkeley was the site of the first official Thanksgiving in 1619. It was the birthplace and home of Benjamin Harrison V, a signatory to of the Declaration of Independence, and his son William Henry Harrison, the 9th US president.

Shirley Plantation   HISTORIC SITE
(☑ 800-829-5121; www.shirleyplantation.com; 501 Shirley Plantation Rd, Charles City; adult/child $11/7.50; ☺ 9:30am-4:30pm) Shirley, situated picturesquely on the river, is Virginia's oldest plantation (1613) and is perhaps the best example of how a British-model plantation actually appeared, with its tidy row of brick service and trade houses – tool barn, ice house, laundry, etc – leading up to the big house.

Hampton Roads

The Hampton Roads (named not for asphalt, but the confluence of the James, Nansemond and Elizabeth Rivers and Chesapeake Bay) have always been prime real estate. The Powhatan Confederacy fished these waters and hunted the fingerlike protrusions of the Virginia coast for thousands of years before John Smith arrived in 1607. Today Hampton Roads is known for congestion and a cultural mishmash of history, the military and the arts.

Norfolk

As home to the world's largest naval base, it's not surprising that Norfolk has had a reputation as a rowdy port town filled with drunken sailors. In recent years the city has worked hard to clean up its image through development, gentrification and focusing on its burgeoning arts scene.

⊙ Sights

Naval Station Norfolk   MILITARY SITE
(☑ 757-444-7955; www.cnic.navy.mil/norfolksta; 9079 Hampton Blvd; adult/child $10/5) The world's largest navy base, and one of the two jet airfields in the country, this is a must-see. The 45-minute bus tours are conducted by naval personnel and must be booked in advance (hours vary). Photo ID is required for adults.

Nauticus   MUSEUM
(☑ 757-664-1000; www.nauticus.org; 1 Waterside Dr; adult/child $16/11.50; ☺ 10am-5pm Tue-Sat, noon-5pm Sun) This massive, interactive, maritime-themed museum has exhibits on undersea exploration, the aquatic life of the Chesapeake Bay and US Naval lore. The highlight for visitors is clambering around the decks and inner corridors of the USS Wisconsin. Built in 1943, it was the largest (887ft long) and last battleship built by the US Navy.

Chrysler Museum of Art   MUSEUM
(☑ 757-664-6200; www.chrysler.org; 245 W Olney Rd; ☺ 10am-5pm Tue-Sat, noon-5pm Sun) FREE A glorious setting for an eclectic collection of artifacts from ancient Egypt to the present day, including works by Monet, Matisse, Renoir, Warhol and a world-class collection of Tiffany blown glass.

🛏 Sleeping

For waterfront digs, there are tons of budget to midrange options lining Ocean View Ave (which actually borders the bay).

Tazewell Hotel　　　　　　　　　HOTEL $
(☑757-623-6200; www.thetazewell.com; 245 Granby St; r from $89; ✳🛜) Set in a heritage 1906 building, the Tazewell has a great location in the heart of the Granby St dining and drinking district. The carpeted rooms have aging wooden furnishings, and the place could use an update, but it's still a good value. There's a low-lit wine bar and Italian restaurant on the 1st floor.

Page House Inn　　　　　　　　　B&B $$
(☑757-625-5033; www.pagehouseinn.com; 323 Fairfax Ave; r $160-245; P✳🛜) Opposite the Chrysler Museum of Art, this luxurious B&B is a cornerstone of Norfolk elegance.

🍴 Eating

Two of the best dining strips are downtown's Granby St and Ghent's Colley Ave.

Cure　　　　　　　　　　　　　　CAFE $
(www.curenorfolk.com; 503 Botetourt St; mains $6-9; ⊙8am-10pm Mon-Sat, 9am-8pm Sun; 🛜) The Cure is a picture-perfect neighborhood cafe on the edge of the historic district, with tasty and creative sandwiches, great coffee (from Counter Culture), and microbrews and charcuterie later in the day.

Field Guide　　　　　　MODERN AMERICAN $
(429 Granby St; mains $8-10; ⊙11am-10pm Tue-Thu, to 1am Fri & Sat) On restaurant-lined Granby St, Field Guide is a standout for its market-fresh fare: zingy salads, flavor-rich rice bowls and decadent sandwiches, plus fun cocktails (try a margarita slushie). It's a casual but hip affair, with communal tables and a sliding garage door that opens wide on sunny days.

Press 626 Cafe & Wine Bar　　　MODERN AMERICAN $$
(☑757-282-6234; 626 W Olney Rd; mains lunch $8-13, dinner $16-26; ⊙11am-11pm Mon-Fri, from 5pm Sat, 10:30am-2:30pm Sun; ☑) Embracing the Slow Food movement, the very charming Press 626 has a wide-ranging menu, with pressed gourmet sandwiches (at lunch), seared scallops, bouillabaisse and a great wine selection.

🍷 Drinking & Entertainment

Elliot's Fair Grounds　　　　　　CAFE
(806 Baldwin Ave; ⊙7am-10pm Mon-Sat, from 8am Sun; 🛜) This tiny, funky coffeehouse attracts everyone from students to sailors. Aside from good caffeinated drinks, Elliot's serves sandwiches and desserts.

Taphouse Grill at Ghent　　　　　PUB
(931 W 21st St; ⊙11am-2am) Good microbrews are served and good local bands jam at this warm little pub.

ℹ Getting There & Around

The region is served by **Norfolk International Airport** (NIA; ☑757-857-3351), 7 miles northeast of downtown Norfolk. **Greyhound** (☑757-625-7500; www.greyhound.com; 701 Monticello Ave) runs buses to Virginia Beach ($16, 35 minutes), Richmond ($32, 2¾ hours) and Washington, DC ($50, 6½ hours).

Hampton Roads Transit (☑757-222-6100; www.gohrt.com) serves the entire Hampton Roads region. Buses ($1.75) run from downtown throughout the city and to Newport News and Virginia Beach.

Newport News

The city of Newport News comes off as a giant example of suburban sprawl, but there are several attractions here, notably the amazing **Mariners' Museum** (☑757-596-2222; www.marinersmuseum.org; 100 Museum Dr; adult/child $14/9; ⊙9am-5pm Mon-Sat, from 11am Sun), one of the biggest, most comprehensive maritime museums in the world. The on-site **USS Monitor Center** houses the dredged carcass of the Civil War–era *Monitor,* one of the world's first ironclad warships, as well as a life-size replica of the real deal.

The **Virginia Living Museum** (☑757-595-1900; www.thevlm.org; 524 J Clyde Morris Blvd; adult/child $17/13; ⊙9am-5pm, from noon Sun; P🖐) 🖋 is a fine introduction to Virginia's terrestrial and aquatic life, set in naturalistic ecosystems. The complex comprises open-air animal enclosures, an aviary, gardens and a planetarium.

Virginia Beach

With 35 miles of sandy beaches, a 3-mile concrete oceanfront boardwalk and nearby outdoor activities, it's no surprise that Virginia Beach is a prime tourist destination. The city has worked hard to shed its reputation as a rowdy 'Redneck Riviera,' and hey, the beach *is* wider and cleaner now and there are fewer louts. Beach aside, you'll find some lovely parks and nature sites beyond the crowded high-rises lining the shore. Expect thick crowds and heavy traffic if visiting in the summer.

◉ Sights

Virginia Aquarium
& Marine Science Center　　　AQUARIUM
(☑757-385-3474; www.virginiaaquarium.com; 717 General Booth Blvd; adult/child $22/15; ☺9am-5pm) If you want to see an aquarium done right, come here. In various habitats, you can see a great array of aquatic life, including sea turtles, river otters and Komodo dragons.

First Landing State Park　　　NATURE RESERVE
(2500 Shore Dr; admission per vehicle $6-7) This 2888-acre woodland has 20 miles of **hiking trails**, plus opportunities for camping, cycling, fishing, kayaking and swimming.

Virginia Museum of
Contemporary Art　　　MUSEUM
(www.virginiamoca.org; 2200 Parks Ave; adult/child $7.70/5.50; ☺10am-9pm Tue, to 5pm Wed-Fri, to 4pm Sat & Sun) Has excellent rotating exhibitions housed in a fresh, ultramodern building.

Back Bay National
Wildlife Refuge　　　NATURE RESERVE
(www.fws.gov/backbay; per vehicle/pedestrian Apr-Oct $5/2, Nov-Mar free; ☺sunrise-sunset) This 9250-acre wildlife and migratory-bird marshland habitat is most stunning during the December migration season.

Great Dismal Swamp
National Wildlife Refuge　　　NATURE RESERVE
(☑757-986-3705; www.fws.gov/refuge/great_dismal_swamp; 3100 Desert Rd, Suffolk; ☺sunrise-sunset; ▣) ✎ FREE Some 30 miles southwest of Virginia Beach, this 112,000-acre refuge, which straddles the North Carolina border, is rich in flora and fauna, including black bears, bobcats and more than 200 bird species.

◻ Sleeping

Angie's Guest Cottage
& Hostel　　　GUESTHOUSE $
(☑757-491-1830; www.angiescottage.com; 302 24th St; dm $32, d $70-110; ▣❄) Located just one block from the beach, Angie's offers dormitories and private rooms with kitchenettes. It's a good value for the area.

First Landing State Park　　　CAMPGROUND $
(☑800-933-7275; http://dcr.virginia.gov; Cape Henry; campsites $28, cabins from $75; ▣) ✎ You couldn't ask for a prettier campground than the one at this bayfront state park, though the cabins have no water view.

✗ Eating

★ **Blue Pete's**　　　SEAFOOD $$
(☑757-426-2278; www.bluepetespungo.com; 1400 N Muddy Creek Rd; mains $10-25; ☺5-10pm Wed-Fri, noon-10pm Sat & Sun) Perched over a peaceful creek near Back Bay, Blue Pete's has an enchanting woodland setting and a wide-ranging menu: crab cakes, brisket sandwiches, pastas and coconut-breaded shrimp.

Mahi Mah's　　　SEAFOOD $$$
(☑757-437-8030; www.mahimahs.com; 615 Atlantic Ave; mains $10-36; ☺7am-midnight Sun-Thu, to 2am Fri & Sat; ▣) This oceanfront local is the go-to for scrumptious seafood. From happy hour (when oysters are 50¢) onwards, it's a buzzing spot for a drink.

❶ Information

The I-264 runs straight to the **visitor center** (☑800-822-3224; www.visitvirginiabeach.com; 2100 Parks Ave; ☺9am-5pm) and the beach.

❶ Getting There & Around

Greyhound (☑757-422-2998; www.greyhound.com; 971 Virginia Beach Blvd) has five buses a day to Richmond ($15.50, 3½ hours), which also stop in Norfolk and Newport News; transfer in Richmond for services to Washington, DC; Wilmington; NYC and beyond. Buses depart from Circle D Food Mart, 1 mile west of the boardwalk.

Hampton Roads Transit runs the Virginia Beach Wave trolley (tickets $2), which plies Atlantic Ave in summer.

The Piedmont

Central Virginia's rolling central hills and plateaus separate the coastal lowlands from the mountainous frontier. The fertile valley gives way to dozens of wineries, country villages and grand colonial estates.

Charlottesville

Set in the shadow of the Blue Ridge Mountains, Charlottesville is regularly ranked as one of the country's best places to live. This culturally rich town of 45,000 is home to the University of Virginia (UVA), which attracts Southern aristocracy and artsy lefties in equal proportion. With the UVA grounds and pedestrian downtown area overflowing with students, couples, professors and the occasional celebrity under a blanket of blue skies, 'C-ville' is practically perfect.

Charlottesville Visitor Center (☑877-386-1103; www.visitcharlottesville.org; 610 E Main St; ◷9am-5pm) is a helpful office in the heart of downtown.

◉ Sights

University of Virginia UNIVERSITY
(☑434-924-0311; www.uvaguides.org; 400 Ray C Hunt Dr, Charlottesville) Thomas Jefferson founded the University of Virginia, whose classically designed buildings and grounds embody the spirit of communal living and learning that Jefferson envisioned. Free, student-led guided tours of the campus depart daily from the Harrison Institute at 10am, 11am and 2pm during the school year. The Jefferson-designed **Rotunda** (☑434-924-7969; rotunda.virginia.edu; 1826 University Ave), a scale replica of Rome's Pantheon, re-opens in 2016 following restoration. UVA's **Fralin Art Museum** (☑434-924-3592; 155 Rugby Rd; ◷noon-5pm Tue-Sun) FREE has an eclectic, interesting collection of American, European and Asian arts.

⌂ Sleeping

There's a good selection of budget and mid-range chain motels lining Emmet St/US 29 north of town. If you're after a reservation service, try **Guesthouses** (☑434-979-7264; www.va-guesthouses.com; r from $150), which provides cottages and B&B rooms in private homes. Two-night minimum stays are commonly required on weekends.

Fairhaven GUESTHOUSE $
(☑434-933-2471; www.fairhavencville.com; 413 Fairway Ave; r $65-75; P✲☎) This friendly and welcoming guesthouse is a great deal if you don't mind sharing facilities (there's just one bathroom for the three rooms). Each room has wood floors, with comfy beds and a cheerful color scheme, and guests can use the kitchen, living room or backyard. It's about a 1-mile walk to the pedestrian mall.

English Inn HOTEL $$
(☑434-971-9900; www.englishinncharlottesville.com; 2000 Morton Dr; r $120-160; P✲☎☲) British hospitality and furnishings and a Tudor facade accent this unique hotel. It's

1.5 miles north of UVA. Cheaper rates on weekdays.

South Street Inn B&B $$
(☑434-979-0200; www.southstreetinn.com; 200 South St; r $150-190, ste $230-275; P✲☎) In the heart of downtown Charlottesville, this elegant 1856 building has gone through previous incarnations as a girls' finishing school, a boarding house and a brothel. Now it houses heritage-style rooms – a total of two dozen, which gives this place more depth and diversity than your average B&B. Includes breakfast.

✕ Eating & Drinking

The Downtown Mall, a pedestrian zone lined with dozens of shops and restaurants, is great for people-watching and outdoor dining on warm days. Follow Main St west for another good selection of restaurants. The Belmont area (about a half-mile southeast of the Downtown Mall) has a handful of local eating and drinking options. At night the bars along University Ave attract students and 20-somethings.

Feast! AMERICAN $
(416 W Main St; mains $8-10; ◷10am-7pm Mon-Fri, 9am-6pm Sat) Inside the Main St Market, Feast! is a fine spot to load up on picnic fare, with wines, cheeses, fruits and other temptations, plus fresh sandwiches (made to order from 11am to 3pm), soups and salads.

Citizen Burger AMERICAN $
(212 E Main St; mains $12-15; ◷noon-midnight Sun-Thu, to 2am Fri & Sat) On the pedestrian mall, Citizen Burger serves up delicious burgers and microbrews in a buzzing brick-lined dining room. The ethos is local and sustainable (organically raised, grass-fed cows, Virginia-made cheeses and beers). Don't miss the truffle fries.

Blue Moon Diner AMERICAN $
(www.bluemoondiner.net; 512 W Main St; mains $8-12; ◷8am-10pm Mon-Fri, 9am-3pm Sat & Sun) Serving breakfast all day, the Blue Moon is a festive retro-style diner that also has Virginia beers on tap and live music (Wednesday through Friday nights). Pancakes come decorated with unusual portraits.

★Oakhart Social MODERN AMERICAN $$
(☑434-995-5449; 511 W Main St; small plates $7-15; ◷5pm-2am Tue-Sun) The stylish new kid on the block serves creative, seasonally inspired small plates (grilled octopus with garbanzo

puree, sweet and crispy pork-belly salad) as well as wood-fired pizzas, in a handsomely laid-back setting. The front patio is a festive spot to sit and sip a refreshing 'Corpse Reviver #2,' and other well-made cocktails.

Whiskey Jar   SOUTHERN $$
(☑434-202-1549; 227 West Main St; mains lunch $10-15, dinner $12-32; ⊙11am-midnight Mon-Thu, to 2am Fri & Sat, 10am-2:30pm Sun; ☑) The Whiskey Jar does neo–Southern comfort food in a rustic setting of wooden furniture, where waitstaff wear plaid and drinks are served out of Mason jars. There's great barbecue and a huge (125 varieties!) whiskey selection.

The Local   MODERN AMERICAN $$
(☑434-984-9749; 824 Hinton Ave; mains $13-25; ⊙5:30-10pm Sun-Thu, to 11pm Fri & Sat) The Local has earned many fans for its locavore-loving menu (try roast squash with goat cheese or roast duck with blood-orange gastrique) and the elegant, warmly lit interior (exposed brick trimmed with colorful oil paintings). It offers sidewalk and rooftop dining in warmer months, plus great cocktails.

ⓘ Getting There & Around

Amtrak (www.amtrak.com; 810 W Main St) Two daily trains to Washington, DC (from $33, three hours).

Charlottesville Albemarle Airport (CHO; ☑434-973-8342; www.gocho.com) Ten miles north of downtown; offers regional flights.

Greyhound/Trailways Terminal (☑434-295-5131; 310 W Main St) Runs three daily buses to both Richmond (from $21, 1¼ hours) and Washington, DC (from $28, three hours).

Trolley (⊙6:40am-11:30pm Mon-Sat, 8am-5pm Sun) A free trolley connects W Main St with UVA.

Barboursville & Around
BARBOURSVILLE
Take Hwy 20 north of Charlottesville for a scenic drive amid rolling hills, past forested strands and picturesque farms. About a half-hour from Charlottesville (18 miles), you'll reach the tiny settlement of Barboursville, home to one of the oldest and best vineyards in the region. Spread across 900 acres, the **Barboursville Vineyards** (☑540-832-3824; www.bbv.wine.com; 17655 Winery Rd; tastings $7; ⊙tasting room 10am-5pm Mon-Sat, from 11am Sun) has earned high praise for its fine Cabernet Francs, and you can plan an afternoon of wine-tasting (a great value, considering

the many wines you can sample), strolling the grounds, having a picnic (a shop sells goodies to go with the wine), or indulging in a decadent meal at the **Palladio** (☑540-832-7848; Barboursville Winery; 2-/4-course lunch $41/55, four-course dinner $80; ⊙noon-2:30pm Wed-Sun & 6:30-9:30pm Fri & Sat) restaurant. On the grounds, you'll find the ruins of the estate of James Barbour, the former governor of Virginia and friend of Thomas Jefferson, who designed the building. You can overnight at the Vineyard's lavish **1804 Inn** (Barboursville Winery; r $240-450; P✳🛜).

MONTPELIER
Thomas Jefferson gets all the attention in these parts, but it's well worth branching out and visiting James Madison's **Montpelier** (www.montpelier.org; 11350 Constitution Hwy; adult/child $18/7; ⊙9am-5pm Apr-Oct, 10am-4pm Nov-Mar), a spectacular estate 25 miles northeast of Charlottesville (off Hwy 20). Madison was a brilliant but shy man who devoted himself to his books; he's almost singlehandedly responsible for developing and writing the US Constitution. **Guided tours** shed a light on the life and times of James as well as his gifted and charismatic wife Dolley, plus other residents of the estate; carefully reconstructed cabins show what life was like for Madison's slaves. There's an archaeology lab, where on-site archaeologists can explain recent findings. **Hiking trails** lead through the forests beyond the estate; the ambitious can even walk 4 miles to the **Market at Grelen** (www.themarketatgrelen.com; 15091 Yager Rd, Somerset; sandwiches $7; ⊙cafe 11:30am-2pm Tue-Sun, shop 10am-4pm Tue-Sat), a charming lunch spot and garden center, where you can pick your own berries on the rolling 600-acre grounds.

Appomattox Court House & Around
At the McLean House in the town of Appomattox Court House, General Robert E Lee surrendered the Army of Northern Virginia to General Ulysses S Grant, in effect ending the Civil War. Instead of coming straight here, follow **Lee's retreat** (☑800-673-8732; www.varetreat.com) on a winding, 25-stop tour that starts in **Petersburg** at Southside Railroad Station (River St and Cockade Alley) and cuts through some of the most attractive countryside in Virginia. Best take a detailed road map, as the trail is not always clearly marked.

MONTICELLO & AROUND

Monticello ([phone]434-984-9800; www.monticello.org; 931 Thomas Jefferson Pkwy; adult/child $25/8; [hours]9am-6pm Mar-Oct, 10am-5pm Nov-Feb) is an architectural masterpiece designed and inhabited by Thomas Jefferson, Founding Father and third US president. 'I am as happy nowhere else and in no other society, and all my wishes end, where I hope my days will end, at Monticello,' wrote Jefferson, who spent 40 years building his dream home, finally completed in 1809. Today it is the only home in America designated a UN World Heritage site. Built in Roman neoclassical style, the house was the centerpiece of a 5000-acre plantation tended by 150 slaves. Monticello today does not gloss over the complicated past of the man who declared that 'all men are created equal' in the Declaration of Independence, while owning slaves and likely fathering children with slave Sally Hemings. Jefferson and his family are buried in a small wooded plot near the home.

Visits to the house are conducted by guided tours only; you can take self-guided tours of the plantation grounds, gardens and cemetery. A high-tech exhibition center delves deeper into Jefferson's world – including exhibits on architecture, enlightenment through education, and the complicated idea of liberty. Frequent shuttles run from the visitor center to the hilltop house, or you can take the wooded footpath.

It's well worth planning a trip around the nearby 1784 **Michie Tavern** ([phone]434-977-1234; www.michietavern.com; 683 Thomas Jefferson Pkwy; buffet adult/child $18/11; [hours]11:15am-3:30pm), which spreads a filling Southern-style lunch buffet. Another excellent attraction is James Monroe's estate **Ash Lawn-Highland** ([phone]434-293-8000; www.ashlawnhighland.org; 2050 James Monroe Pkwy; adult/child $14/8; [hours]9am-6pm Apr-Oct, 11am-5pm Nov-Mar), 2.5 miles east of Monticello.

Monticello is about 4.5 miles northwest of downtown Charlottesville.

You'll finish at the 1700-acre **Appomattox Court House National Historic Park** ([phone]434-352-8987; www.nps.gov/apco; admission Jun-Aug $4, Sep-May $3; [hours]8:30am-5pm). The park comprises over two dozen restored buildings. A number of buildings are open to visitors, and set with original and period furnishings from 1865. Highlights include the parlor of the **McLean House**, where Lee and Grant met; the **Clover Hill Tavern**, used by Union soldiers to print 30,000 parole passes for Confederate soldiers; and the dry-goods-filled **Meeks General Store**.

The town of **Appomatox** (3 miles southwest of the national park) is small but charming, with a main street dotted with antique shops (a gold mine for hunters of Civil War memorabilia). Stop in **Baine's Books and Coffee** (www.bainesbooks.com; 205 Main St; snacks $3-6; [hours]8:30am-8pm Mon-Sat, 9am-5pm Sun) for sandwiches, quiche and scones (plus live bluegrass several nights a week). If you need a place to stay, nearby **Longacre** ([phone]800-758-7730; www.longacreva.com; 1670 Church St; r from $90; [P][*]) looks as if it got lost somewhere in the English countryside and decided to set up shop in Virginia. Its elegant rooms are set with antiques, and lush grounds surround the sprawling Tudor house.

Shenandoah Valley

Local lore says Shenandoah was named for a Native American word meaning 'Daughter of the Stars.' True or not, there's no question this is God's country, one of the most beautiful places in America. The 200-mile-long valley and its Blue Ridge Mountains are packed with picturesque small towns, wineries, preserved battlefields and caverns. This was once the western border of Colonial America, settled by Scotch–Irish frontiersmen who were Highland Clearance refugees. Outdoor activities – hiking, camping, fishing, horseback riding and canoeing – abound.

Shenandoah National Park

One of the most spectacular national parks in the country, Shenandoah ([phone]540-999-3500; www.nps.gov/shen; 1-week pass per car $20) is like a new smile from nature: in spring and summer the wildflowers explode; in fall the leaves burn bright red and orange; and in winter a cold, starkly beautiful hibernation period sets in. White-tailed deer are a common sight and, if you're lucky, you might spot a black bear, bobcat or wild turkey. The park lies just 75 miles west of Washington, DC.

⚡ Activities

There are two visitor centers in the park, **Dickey Ridge** (☎540-635-3566; Skyline Dr, Mile 4.6; ⊙9am-5pm Apr-Nov) in the north and **Harry F Byrd** (☎540-999-3283; Skyline Dr, Mile 50; ⊙9am-5pm Apr-Nov) in the south. Both have maps and backcountry permits, as well as information on horseback riding, hang gliding, cycling (only on public roads) and other outdoors activities. Shenandoah has more than 500 miles of hiking trails, including 101 miles of the Appalachian Trail.

Old Rag Mountain   HIKING
This is a tough, 8-mile circuit trail that culminates in a rocky scramble that's suitable only for the physically fit. Your reward is the summit of Old Rag Mountain and, along the way, some of the best views in Virginia.

Big Meadows   HIKING
A very popular area, with four easy-to-medium-difficulty hikes. The **Lewis Falls** and **Rose River** trails run by the park's most spectacular waterfalls; the former accesses the Appalachian Trail.

Bearfence Mountain   HIKING
A short trail leads to a spectacular 360-degree viewpoint. The circuit hike is only 1.2 miles, but it involves a strenuous scramble over rocks.

Riprap Trail   HIKING
Three trails of varying difficulty. **Blackrock Trail** is an easy 1-mile loop that yields fantastic views. You can either hike the moderate 3.4-mile Riprap Trail to **Chimney Rock**, or detour and make a fairly strenuous 9.8-mile circuit that connects with the Appalachian Trail.

🛏 Sleeping & Eating

Camping is at four **NPS campgrounds** (☎877-444-6777; www.recreation.gov): **Mathews Arm** (Mile 22.1; campsite $15; ⊙May-Oct), **Big Meadows** (Mile 51.3; campsite $20; ⊙late Mar-Nov), **Lewis Mountain** (Mile 57.5; campsite $15, no reservations; ⊙mid-Apr–Oct) and **Loft Mountain** (Mile 79.5; campsite $15; ⊙mid-May–Oct). Camping elsewhere requires a backcountry permit, available for free from any visitor center.

For not-so-rough lodging, stay at **Skyland Resort** (☎540-999-2212; Skyline Dr, Mile 41.7; r $115-210, cabins $97-235; ⊙Apr-Oct; P☀🛜🐾), **Big Meadows Lodge** (☎540-999-2221; Skyline Dr, Mile 51.2; r $94-210; ⊙mid-May–Oct; 🛜)

or **Lewis Mountain Cabins** (☎540-999-2255; Skyline Dr, Mile 57.6; cabins $117; ⊙Apr-Oct; P🐾); booking is available online at www.goshenandoah.com.

Skyland and Big Meadows both have restaurants and taverns with occasional live music. Big Meadows offers the most services, including gas, laundry and camp store. It's best to bring your own food into the park if you're going camping or on extended hikes.

ℹ Getting There & Around

Amtrak (www.amtrak.com) trains run to Staunton, in the Shenandoah Valley, once a day from Washington, DC (from $34, four hours). You'll really need your own wheels to explore the length and breadth of the park, which can be easily accessed from several exits off I-81.

Front Royal & Around

The northernmost tip of Skyline Dr looks like a drab strip of gas stations, but a friendly main street and some cool caverns nearby. Stop at the **visitor center** (☎800-338-2576; 414 E Main St; ⊙9am-5pm) before heading 'up' the valley. Kids may enjoy mini-train rides ($5) and the mirror maze ($6).

🅞 Sights & Activities

Skyline Caverns   CAVE
(☎800-296-4545; www.skylinecaverns.com; entrance to Skyline Dr, Front Royal; adult/child $20/10; ⊙9am-5pm) Front Royal's claim to fame is Skyline Caverns, which boasts rare white-spiked anthodites – mineral formations that look like sea urchins.

Museum of the Shenandoah Valley MUSEUM
(☎888-556-5799, 540-662-1473; www.themsv.org; 901 Amherst St, Winchester; adult/student/child $10/8/free, admission Wed free; ⊙10am-4pm Tue-Sun) Located in the town of Winchester, some 25 miles north of Front Royal, the Museum of the Shenandoah Valley comprises an 18th-century house museum filled with period furnishings, a 6-acre garden and a multimedia museum that delves into the valley's history.

Luray Caverns   CAVE
(☎540-743-6551; www.luraycaverns.com; Rte 211, Luray; adult/child $26/14; ⊙9am-7pm daily Jun-Aug, to 6pm Sep-Nov, Apr & May, to 4pm Mon-Fri Dec-Mar) If you can only fit one cavern into your itinerary, head 25 miles south from Front Royal to the world-class Luray Caverns

and hear the 'Stalacpipe Organ' – hyped as the largest musical instrument on Earth.

🛏 Sleeping & Eating

Woodward House on Manor Grade   B&B **$$**
(☏ 540-635-7010, 800-635-7011; www.acountry-home.com; 413 S Royal Ave/US 320, Front Royal; r $110-155, cottage $225; 🅿 🏶) Offers seven cheerful rooms and a separate cottage (with wood-burning fireplaces). Sip your coffee on the deck and don't let the busy street below distract from the Blue Ridge Mountain vista.

Element   FUSION **$$**
(☏ 540-636-9293; www.jsgourmet.com; 206 S Royal Ave, Front Royal; mains lunch $8-14, dinner $14-22; ☺ 11am-3pm & 5-10pm Tue-Sat; 🍴) 🍷 Element is a foodie favorite for quality bistro fare. The small dinner menu features changing specials such as roasted quail with Mexican corn salad and sweet potatoes; at lunch, come for gourmet sandwiches, soups and salads.

Apartment 2G   FUSION **$$$**
(☏ 540-636-9293; www.jsgourmet.com; 206 S Royal Ave, Front Royal; 5-course meal $50; ☺ from 6:30pm Sat) 🍷 The best restaurant in Front Royal is open just once a week. Owned and operated by a husband-and-wife team – two chefs from the acclaimed Inn at Little Washington – the Apartment's culinary philosophy is simple: uncompromisingly fresh ingredients fashioned into ever-changing five-course fixed menus.

Staunton & Around

This small-town beauty has much going for it, including a historic and walkable town center, a great foodie scene, several microbreweries, some intriguing museums and a first-rate theater. Add to this an abundance of outdoor activities nearby and you may find yourself looking into local real estate when you get here.

⊙ Sights

The pedestrian-friendly, handsome center boasts more than 200 buildings designed by noted Victorian architect TJ Collins. There's an artsy yet unpretentious bohemian vibe thanks to the presence of Mary Baldwin, a small, women's liberal arts college.

Blackfriars Playhouse   THEATER
(☏ 540-851-1733; www.americanshakespeare-center.com; 10 S Market St; tickets $24-37) Don't leave Staunton without catching a show at

SCENIC DRIVE: SKYLINE DRIVE
....

A 105-mile-long road running down the spine of the Blue Ridge Mountains, Shenandoah National Park's **Skyline Drive** redefines the definition of 'Scenic Route.' You're constantly treated to an impressive view, but keep in mind the road is bendy, slow-going (35mph limit) and is congested in peak season. It's best to start this drive just south of Front Royal, VA; from here you'll snake over Virginia wine and hill country. Numbered mileposts mark the way; there are lots of pull-offs. Our favorite is around Mile 51.2, where you can take a moderately difficult 3.6-mile-loop hike to **Lewis Spring Falls**.

the Blackfriars Playhouse, where the American Shakespeare Center company performs in the world's only re-creation of Shakespeare's original indoor theater.

Woodrow Wilson
Presidential Library   HISTORIC SITE
(www.woodrowwilson.org; 20 N Coalter St; adult/student/child $14/7/5; ☺ 9am-5pm Mon-Sat, from noon Sun) History buffs should check out the Woodrow Wilson Presidential Library across town. Stop by and tour the hilltop Greek Revival house where Wilson grew up, which has been faithfully restored to its original 1856 appearance.

Frontier Culture Museum   MUSEUM
(☏ 540-332-7850; www.frontiermuseum.org; 1290 Richmond Rd; adult/student/child $10/9/6; ☺ 9am-5pm mid-Mar–Nov, 10am-4pm Dec–mid-Mar) The excellent Frontier Culture Museum has authentic historic buildings from Germany, Ireland and England, plus re-created West African dwellings and a separate area of American frontier dwellings on the site's 100-plus acres. Costumed interpreters (aided by bleating livestock) do an excellent job showing what life was like for the disparate ancestors of today's Virginians. It's 2 miles southeast of the center.

🛏 Sleeping

Frederick House   B&B **$$**
(☏ 540-885-4220; www.frederickhouse.com; 28 N New St; r $120-185; 🅿 ❄ 🏶) Stay right downtown in the thoroughly mauve and immensely welcoming Frederick House, which

consists of five historical residences with 25 varied rooms and suites – all with private bathrooms and some with antique furnishings and decks.

Anne Hathaway's Cottage   B&B $$
(☏540-885-8885; www.anne-hathaways-cottage.com; 950 W Beverley St; r $130-160; P❄☎) Head out of town to Anne Hathaway's Cottage, named for Shakespeare's wife, who would have thoroughly enjoyed a night in one of the three rooms in this ridiculously romantic Tudor-style, thatched-roof cottage.

✖ Eating & Drinking

West Beverley St is sprinkled with restaurants and cafes.

Split Banana   ICE CREAM $
(7 W Beverley St; ice cream $2.60-5.20; ⊙noon-11pm; ⭐) This locals' favorite ice cream parlor has delicious flavors, served up in a charmingly old-fashioned setting.

Byers Street Bistro   MODERN AMERICAN $$
(☏540-887-6100;   www.byersstreetbistro.com; 18 Byers St; mains lunch $9-14, dinner $16-26; ⊙11am-midnight) By the train station, Byers Street Bistro cooks up high-end pub grub (applewood bacon and carmelized onion pizzas, mahimahi tacos, Angus burgers, slow-roasted babyback ribs) that's best enjoyed at the outdoor tables on warm days. Come on Friday and Saturday nights for live bands (bluegrass, blues and folk).

Zynodoa   SOUTHERN $$$
(☏540-885-7775; 115 E Beverley St; mains $22-29; ⊙5-9:30pm Sun-Tue, to 10:30pm Wed-Sat; ✐) ✐ Classy Zynodoa puts together some fine dishes in the vein of Virginia artisan cheeses, Shenandoah-sourced roasted chicken and

SCENIC DRIVE: VIRGINIA'S HORSE COUNTRY

About 40 miles west of Washington, DC, suburban sprawl gives way to endless green farms, vineyards, quaint villages and palatial estates and ponies. This is 'Horse Country,' where wealthy Washingtonians pursue their equestrian pastimes.

The following route is the most scenic drive to Shenandoah National Park. From DC, take Rte 50 West to **Middleburg**, a too-cute-for-words town of B&Bs, taverns, wine shops and boutiques. The **National Sporting Library** (☏540-687-6542; www.nsl.org; 102 The Plains Rd, Middlesburg; museum admission $10, library free; ⊙10am-5pm Wed-Sat, from 1pm Sun) is a museum and research center devoted to horse and field sports such as foxhunting, dressage, steeplechase and polo. About 20 miles northeast of Middleburg is **Leesburg**, another town with colonial charm and historic sites. Stop in **Morven Park** (☏703-777-2414; www.morvenpark.org; 17263 Southern Planter Lane, Leesburg; grounds admission free, mansion tours adult/child $10/5; ⊙grounds dawn-dusk daily, tours hourly noon-4pm Mon, Fri & Sat, 1-4pm Sun) for a tour of a staggering Virginia home on 1000 acres. For more Greek Revival grandeur, visit **Oatlands Plantation** (☏703-777-3174; www.oatlands.org; 20850 Oatlands Plantation Lane, Leesburg; adult/child $12/8, grounds only $8; ⊙10am-5pm Mon-Sat, 1-5pm Sun Apr-Dec), outside of town.

The area has a wealth of appealing dining options. Stop in the **Shoes Cup & Cork** (☏703-771-7463; www.shoescupandcork.com; 17 N King St, Leesburg; mains lunch $8-16, dinner $15-25; ⊙7am-5pm Mon-Wed, to 9pm Thu & Fri, 9am-9pm Sat & Sun) in Leesburg for creative American fare or **Chimole** (☏703-777-7011; 10 S King St, Leesburg; tapas $8-18; ⊙5-9pm Sun & Wed, to 11pm Thu-Sat) for wine and Latin American tapas. In Middleburg, the **Red Fox Inn & Tavern** (☏540-687-6301; www.redfox.com; 2 E Washington St, Middlesburg; mains lunch $11-18, dinner $26-42; ⊙8am-10am, 11:30am-2:30pm & 5-8:30pm Mon-Sat, 10am-2:30pm & 5-7:30pm Sun) has first-rate American cooking served in a beautifully preserved 1728 dining room.

Located 6 miles west of Middleburg, the **Welbourne B&B** (☏540-687-3201; www.welbourneinn.com; 22314 Welbourne Farm Lane, Middleburg; r $143; ❄☎❄❄) has five heritage rooms set in a historic landmark house (c 1770) surrounded by 520 acres. The **Leesburg Colonial Inn** (☏703-777-5000; www.theleesburgcolonialinn.com; 19 S King St; d $70-150) has a great central location and unbeatable prices.

Further down the road at the foothills of the Blue Ridge Mountains is **Sperryville.** Its many galleries and shops are a must-stop for antique-lovers. Continue 9 miles west to reach the Thornton Gap entrance of Skyline Dr in Shenandoah National Park.

and rainbow trout from Casta Line (raised nearby). Local farms and wineries are the backbone of Zynodoa's larder (and, by extension, your table).

Redbeard Brewery MICROBREWERY
(www.redbeardbrews.com; 102 S Lewis St; ⊙ 4-11pm Thu & Fri, 1-11pm Sat & Sun) A small-batch brewery that serves up tasty IPAs, saison, ambers and other seasonal selections. There's often a barbecue food truck parked out back on weekends. Occasional live music, too.

Lexington & Around

This is the place to see Southern gentry at their stately best, as cadets from the Virginia Military Institute jog past the prestigious academics of Washington & Lee University. The **visitor center** (☎540-463-3777; 106 E Washington St; ⊙9am-5pm) has handy maps with self-guided walking tours.

◉ Sights & Activities

Founded in 1749, colonnaded **Washington & Lee University** is one of the top small colleges in America. The **Lee Chapel & Museum** (☎540-458-8768; http://leechapel.wlu.edu; ⊙9am-4pm Mon-Sat, 1pm-4pm Sun Nov-Mar, to 5pm Apr-Oct) inters Robert E Lee, while his horse Traveller is buried outside. One of the four Confederate banners surrounding Lee's tomb is set in an original flagpole, a branch a rebel soldier turned into a makeshift standard.

Virginia Military Institute UNIVERSITY
(VMI; www.vmi.edu; Letcher Ave) You'll either be impressed or put off by the extreme discipline of the cadets at Virginia Military Institute, the only university to have sent its entire graduating class into combat (plaques to student war dead are touching and ubiquitous). The **VMI Museum** (☎540-464-7334; ⊙9am-5pm) FREE houses the stuffed carcass of Stonewall Jackson's horse, a homemade American flag made by an alumnus prisoner of war in Vietnam, and a tribute to VMI students killed in the War on Terror.

Contact the museum for a free guided tour of the campus, offered at noon. A full-dress parade takes place most Fridays at 4:30pm during the school year. The school's **George C Marshall Museum** (☎540-463-2083; www.marshallfoundation.org/museum/; adult/student $5/2; ⊙11am-4pm Tue-Sat) honors the creator of the Marshall Plan for post-WWII European reconstruction.

Stonewall Jackson House HISTORIC BUILDING
(www.stonewalljackson.org; 8 E Washington St; adult/child $8/6; ⊙9am-5pm Mon-Sat, from 1pm Sun) One of the most revered generals of the south, Thomas Jonathon 'Stonewall' Jackson lived in this handsome brick two-story house from 1851 to 1861, while he taught at nearby VMI. The house is remarkably preserved, with guided tours providing fascinating insight into Jackson's life and times. His body (all but his left arm, anyway) is buried in the cemetery a few blocks away.

Natural Bridge & Foamhenge LANDMARK
Yes, it's a kitschy tourist trap, and yes, vocal creationists who insist it was made by the hand of God are dominating the site, but the 215ft-high **Natural Bridge** (www.naturalbridge-va.com; bridge adult/child $20/12, bridge & caverns $28/18; ⊙9am-dusk), 15 miles from Lexington, is still pretty cool. It was surveyed by a 16-year-old George Washington, who supposedly carved his initials into the wall, and was once owned by Thomas Jefferson. You can also take a tour of some exceptionally deep caverns here.

Just up the road, check out **Foamhenge** (www.thefoamhenge.com; Hwy 11) FREE, a marvelous full-sized replica of Stonehenge made entirely of Styrofoam. There are fine views – and even an on-site wizard. It's 1 mile north of Natural Bridge.

⌫ Sleeping

★**The Georges** BOUTIQUE HOTEL $$
(☎540-463-2500; thegeorges.com; 11 N Main St; r from $165; P❈🐾) Set in two historic buildings on opposite sides of Main St, the Georges has beautifully set rooms, each custom-designed with high-end furnishings. The great location, friendly service and on-site eateries (with locally focused cuisine) add to the appeal.

Applewood Inn & Llama Trekking INN $$
(☎800-463-1902; www.applewoodbb.com; 242 Tarn Beck Lane; r $164-172; P❈) The charming, eco-minded Applewood Inn & Llama Trekking offers accommdations and a slew of outdoorsy activities (including, yes, llama trekking) on a farm in a bucolic valley just a 10-minute drive away from downtown Lexington.

✗ Eating & Drinking

Pure Eats AMERICAN $
(107 N Main St; mains $7-9; ⊙8am-2:30pm & 5-8pm Tue-Thu, 8am-8pm Fri-Sun) In a former gas station, Pure Eats whips up delicious

doughnuts and egg-and-cheese biscuits in the morning, and burgers and milkshakes later in the day.

Blue Sky Bakery SANDWICHES $
(125 W Nelson St; mains $7-10; ⊙10:30am-4pm Mon-Fri) This local favorite has tasty focaccia sandwiches, hearty soups and fresh salads.

Red Hen SOUTHERN $$$
(☑540-464-4401; 11 E Washington St; mains $24-30; ⊙5-9:30pm Tue-Sat; ☑) ✐ Reserve well ahead for a memorable meal at Red Hen, which features a creative menu showcasing the fine local produce.

Haywood's COCKTAIL BAR
(11 N Main St; ⊙5-10pm Wed-Sun) For a kitschy good time, stop by this small, cozy piano bar, where you can sometimes catch a lounge singer lighting up the crowd alongside a piano-playing colleague.

☆ Entertainment

Hull's Drive-in CINEMA
(☑540-463-2621; www.hullsdrivein.com; 2367 N Lee Hwy/US 11; adult/child $7/3; ⊙7pm Fri-Sun May-Oct) For old-fashioned amusement, catch a movie at this drive-in movie theater, set 5.5 miles north of Lexington.

Blue Ridge Highlands & Southwest Virginia

The southwestern tip of Virginia is the most rugged part of the state. Turn onto the Blue Ridge Pkwy or any side road and you'll immediately plunge into dark strands of dogwood and fir, fast streams and white waterfalls. You're bound to see Confederate flags in the small towns, but there's a proud hospitality behind the fierce veneer of independence.

Blue Ridge Parkway

Where Skyline Dr ends, the **Blue Ridge Parkway** (www.blueridgeparkway.org) picks up. The road is just as pretty and runs from the southern Appalachian ridge in Shenandoah National Park (at Mile 0) to North Carolina's Great Smoky Mountains National Park (at Mile 469). Wildflowers bloom in spring, and fall colors are spectacular, but watch out for foggy days; the lack of guardrails can make for hairy driving. There are a dozen visitor centers scattered over the Pkwy, and any of them make a good kick-off point to start your trip.

◉ Sights & Activities

There are all kinds of sights running along the parkway.

Mabry Mill HISTORIC SITE
(Mile 176) One of the most-photographed buildings in the state, the mill nestles in such a fuzzy green vale you'll think you've entered the opening chapter of a Tolkien novel.

Humpback Rocks HIKING
(Mile 5.8) Tour 19th-century farm buildings or take the steep trail to Humpback Rocks, offering spectacular 360-degree views.

Sherando Lake Recreation Area SWIMMING
(☑540-291-2188; off Mile 16) In George Washington National Forest, you'll find two pretty lakes (one for swimming, one for fishing), with hiking trails and campsites. To get there, take Rte 664 W.

Peaks of Otter HIKING
(Mile 86) There are trails to the tops of these mountains: Sharp Top, Flat Top and Harkening Hill. Shuttles run to the top of Sharp Top, or you can try a fairly challenging hike (3 miles return) to the summit.

🛏 Sleeping

There are nine local **campgrounds** (☑877-444-6777; www.recreation.gov; campsites $19; ⊙May-Oct), four in Virginia. Sites are generally open from April to November.

★ Peaks of Otter LODGE $$
(☑540-586-1081; www.peaksofotter.com; 85554 Blue Ridge Pkwy, Mile 86; r $97-145; ※ ⍨) A pretty, split-rail-surrounded lodge on a small lake that's nestled between two of its namesake mountains. It has a restaurant and wi-fi, but no public phones and no cellphone reception.

Roanoke & Around

Illuminated by the giant star atop Mill Mountain, Roanoke is the largest city in the valley and is the self-proclaimed 'Capital of the Blue Ridge.'

There are good eating and drinking options downtown (near Market and Campbell Sts), and appealing options 3 miles west along Grandin Rd.

◉ Sights & Activities

Mill Mountain Park PARK
Mill Mountain Park has walking trails, a discovery center, a zoo and grand views of Roanoke. You can drive up (via Walnut Ave SE)

or hike up (take the Monument Trail just off Sylvan Ave SE or the Star Trail near Riverland Rd SE)

Taubman Museum of Art   MUSEUM
(www.taubmanmuseum.org; 110 Salem Ave SE; ☺10am-5pm Tue-Sat, to 9pm Thu & 1st Fri of month; **P**) **FREE** The striking Taubman Museum of Art is set in a sculptural steel-and-glass edifice that's reminiscent of the Guggenheim Bilbao. Inside, you'll find a superb collection of artworks spanning 3500 years; it's particularly strong in 19th- and 20th-century American works.

National D-Day Memorial   MONUMENT
(☑540-587-3619; www.dday.org; US 460 & Hwy 122; adult/child $10/6; ☺10am-5pm) About 30 miles east of Roanoke, the tiny town of Bedford suffered the most casualties per capita in the US during WWII, and hence was chosen to host the moving National D-Day Memorial. Among its towering arch and flower garden is a cast of bronze figures re-enacting the storming of the beach, complete with bursts of water symbolizing the hail of bullets the soldiers faced.

🛏 **Sleeping & Eating**

Rose Hill   B&B $$
(☑540-400-7785; www.bandbrosehill.com; 521 Washington Ave; r $100-125) Rose Hill is a charming and welcoming three-room B&B in Roanoke's historic district.

Texas Tavern   DINER $
(114 Church Ave SW; burgers $1.30-2.45; ☺24hr) The legendary Texas Tavern is a boxcar-sized diner serving juicy burgers.

Local Roots   MODERN AMERICAN $$
(☑540-206-2610; www.localrootsrestaurant.com; 1314 Grandin Rd; mains lunch $11-13, dinner $21-33; ☺11:30am-2pm & 5-10pm Tue-Sun) Local Roots serves up catfish and chips, black bass, bison steak and other delectable fare.

Lucky's   MODERN AMERICAN $$
(☑540-982-1249; www.eatatlucky.com; 18 Kirk Ave SW; mains $17-25; ☺5-9pm Mon-Wed, to 10pm Thu-Sat) Lucky's has excellent cocktails (try 'The Cube') and a seasonally inspired menu of small plates (hickory-smoked porchetta, roasted oysters) and heartier mains (buttermilk fried chicken, morel and asparagus gnocchi).

Mt Rogers National Recreation Area

This seriously beautiful district is well worth a visit from outdoor enthusiasts. Hike, fish or cross-country ski among ancient hardwood trees and the state's tallest peak. The **park headquarters** (☑276-783-5196, 800-628-7202; www.fs.usda.gov/gwj; 3714 Hwy 16, Marion) offers maps and recreation directories. The NPS operates five campgrounds in the area; contact park headquarters for details.

Abingdon

One of the most photogenic towns in Virginia, Abingdon retains fine Federal and Victorian architecture in its historic district, and hosts the bluegrass **Virginia Highlands Festival** over the first half of August. The **visitor center** (☑800-435-3440; www.visitabingdonvirginia.com; 335 Cummings St; ☺9am-5pm) has exhibits on local history.

◉ **Sights & Activities**

Barter Theatre   THEATER
(☑276-628-3991; www.bartertheatre.com; 133 W Main St; performances from $25) Founded during the Depression, Barter Theatre earned its name from audiences trading food for performances. Actors Gregory Peck and Ernest Borgnine cut their teeth on Barter's stage.

Heartwood   ARTS CENTER
(☑276-492-2400; www.myswva.org/heartwood; One Heartwood Circle; ☺9am-5pm Mon-Wed & Fri-Sat, to 9pm Thu, 10am-3pm Sun) Heartwood is a showcase of regional crafts, cuisine (sandwiches, salads, Virginia wines) and traditional music. Don't miss Thursday nights, when bluegrass bands and barbecue draw a festive local crowd. It's about 3 miles east of town (off Hwy 11).

Virginia Creeper Trail   TRAIL
(www.vacreepertrail.org) Named for the railroad that once ran this route, the Virginia Creeper Trail travels 33 miles between Whitetop Station (near the North Carolina border) and downtown Abingdon. Several outfitters rent bicycles, organize outings and run shuttles, including **Virginia Creeper Trail Bike Shop** (☑276-676-2552; www.vacreepertrailbikeshop.com; 201 Pecan St; per 2hr/day $10/20; ☺9am-6pm Sun-Fri, from 8am Sat), near the trailhead.

🛏 Sleeping

Alpine Motel MOTEL **$**
(☏276-628-3178; www.alpinemotelabingdon.com; 882 E Main St; s/d from $59/69; P❄🔊) The Alpine Motel is a simple but good-value option, with carpeted rooms, old TVs, and chirping birds across the way; it's located about 2 miles west of downtown.

Martha Washington Inn HOTEL **$$$**
(☏276-628-3161; www.marthawashingtoninn.com; 150 W Main St; r from $225; P❄@🔊❄) Opposite the Barter, this is the region's premier historic hotel, a Victorian sprawl of historical classiness and wrought-iron style.

🍴 Eating & Drinking

128 Pecan MODERN AMERICAN **$$**
(☏276-698-3159; 128 Pecan St; mains $9-22; ⏱11am-9pm Tue-Sat; 🔊) This local favorite serves up excellent sandwiches, tacos and heartier meat or seafood dishes, with seating on a front veranda. It's a short stroll to the Virginia Creeper Trail.

The Tavern MODERN AMERICAN **$$$**
(☏276-628-1118; 222 E Main St; mains $28-42; ⏱5-9pm Mon-Sat) Inside the oldest building in town (built in 1779) you'll find tasty crab cakes, French onion soup and oysters served in a cozy setting, with low ceilings and brick floors.

Wolf Hills Brewery MICROBREWERY
(350 Park St; ⏱5-8pm Mon-Fri, from 1pm Sat, 1-5pm Sun) For satisfying microbrews and the occasional live music session, head to Wolf Hills Brewery.

The Crooked Road

When Scotch–Irish fiddle-and-reel married African American banjo-and-percussion, American mountain or 'old-time' music was born, spawning such genres as country and bluegrass. The latter genre still dominates the Blue Ridge, and Virginia's Heritage Music Trail, the 250-mile-long Crooked Road (www.myswva.org/tcr), takes you through nine sites associated with that history, along with some eye-stretching mountain scenery. It's well worth taking a detour and joining the music-loving fans of all ages who kick up their heels (many arrive with tap shoes) at these festive jamborees. During a live show you'll witness elders connecting to deep cultural roots and a new generation of musicians keeping that heritage alive and evolving.

FLOYD

Tiny, cute-as-a-postcard Floyd is nothing more than an intersection between Hwy 8 and 221, but life explodes on Friday nights at the **Floyd Country Store** (☏540-745-4563; www.floydcountrystore.com; 206 S Locust St; ⏱11am-5pm Tue-Thu, to 11pm Fri, to 5pm Sat, noon-5pm Sun). Every Friday starting at 6:30pm, $5 gets you four bluegrass bands in four hours and the chance to watch happy crowds jam along to regional heritage. No smokin', no drinkin', but there's plenty of dancin' (of the jig-and-tap style) and good cheer. On weekends, there's lots of live music happening nearby.

🛏 Sleeping

Oak Haven Lodge INN **$**
(☏540-745-5716; www.oakhavenlodge.com; 323 Webb's Mill Rd, Route 8; r $75-90; P❄🔊) Just a mile north of Floyd, this good-value place has spacious rooms (some with Jacuzzi tubs) that open onto a shared balcony with rocking chairs.

Hotel Floyd HOTEL **$$**
(☏540-745-6080; www.hotelfloyd.com; 120 Wilson St; r $119-169; P❄🔊❄) 🌿 Built with eco-friendly materials and furnishings, Hotel Floyd is a model of sustainability. Works by local artisans adorn its attractive rooms.

🍴 Eating & Drinking

Harvest Moon MARKET **$**
(227 N Locust St; ⏱9am-6:30pm Mon-Sat, noon-6pm Sun) A great place to stock up on picnic fare.

Oddfella's FUSION **$$**
(☏540-745-3463; 110 N Locust St; lunch mains $8-10, dinner $13-26; ⏱11am-2:30pm Tue-Sat, 4-10pm Thu-Sat, 10am-3pm Sun; P🌿) 🌿 When you're all jigged out, head for Oddfella's, a comfy spot for Tex-Mex fare (plus tapas) – and tasty microbrews.

Dogtown Roadhouse PIZZA **$$**
(302 S Locust St; mains $10-18; ⏱5-10pm Thu, to midnight Fri, noon-midnight Sat, noon-10pm Sun) The lively Dogtown Roadhouse is the go-to for pizzas (fired up in a wood-burning oven) and microbrews, with live rock on Friday and Saturday nights.

GALAX

Galax claims to be the world capital of mountain music, although it feels like anywhere-else-ville outside of the immediate downtown area, which is on the National Register of Historic Places. The main attraction is the **Rex Theater** (☑ 276-236-0329; www.rextheatergalax.com; 113 E Grayson St), a musty, red-curtained belle of yore. Frequent bluegrass acts cross its stage, but the easiest one to catch is the Friday-night live WBRF 98.1 show (admission $5), which pulls in crowds from across the mountains.

Tom Barr of **Barr's Fiddle Shop** (☑ 276-236-2411; www.barrsfiddleshop.com; 105 S Main St; ⊙ 9am-5pm Mon-Sat) is the Stradivarius of the mountains, a master craftsman sought out by fiddle and mandolin aficionados from across the world. The **Old Fiddler's Convention** (www.oldfiddlersconvention.com), held over five days in August in Galax is one of the premier mountain-music festivals in the world.

Doctor's Inn (☑ 276-238-9998; www.the-doctorsinnvirginia.com; 406 W Stuart Dr; r $140-150; ☏ ✳ ☎) is a welcoming guesthouse with antique-filled chambers and excellent breakfasts.

Creek Bottom Brews (☑ 276-236-2337; 307 Meadow St; mains $7-16; ⊙ 11am-9pm Tue-Sat, 1-6pm Sun) has a changing lineup of craft brews, which go nicely with the brick-oven pizza and smoked chicken wings fired up on site.

WEST VIRGINIA

Wild and wonderful West Virginia is often overlooked by both American and foreign travelers. It doesn't help that the state can't seem to shake its negative stereotypes. That's too bad, because West Virginia is one of the prettiest states in the Union. With its line of unbroken green mountains, raging white-water rivers and snowcapped ski resorts, this is an outdoor-lovers' paradise.

Created by secessionists from secession, the people here still think of themselves as hardscrabble sons of miners, and that perception isn't entirely off. But the Mountain State is also gentrifying and, occasionally, that's a good thing: the arts are flourishing in the valleys, where some towns offer a welcome break from the state's constantly evolving outdoor activities.

History

Virginia was once the biggest state in America, divided between the plantation aristocracy of the Tidewater and the mountains of what is now West Virginia. The latter were settled by tough farmers who staked out inde-

CARTER FAMILY FOLD

In a tiny hamlet of southwest Virginia, formerly known as Maces Spring (today part of Hiltons), you'll find one of the hallowed birthplaces of mountain music. The **Carter Family Fold** (☑ 276-386-6054; www.carterfamilyfold. org; 3449 AP Carter Hwy, Hiltons; $10/1 adult/child; ⊙ 7:30pm Sat) continues the musical legacy begun by the talented Carter family back in 1927. Every Saturday night, the 900-person arena hosts first-rate bluegrass and gospel bands; there's also a museum with family memorabilia and the original mid-1800s log cabin where AP Carter was born. With no nearby lodging, your best bet is to stay in Abingdon (30 miles east); Kingsport, TN (12 miles southwest); or Bristol, TN (25 miles southeast).

pendent freeholds across the Appalachians. Always resentful of their Eastern brethren and their reliance on cheap (ie slave) labor, the mountaineers of West Virginia declared their independence from Virginia when the latter tried to break off from America during the Civil War.

Yet the scrappy, independent-at-all-costs stereotype was challenged in the late 19th and early 20th centuries, when miners here formed cooperative unions and fought employers in some of the bloodiest battles in American labor history. That mix of chip-on-the-shoulder resentment toward authority and look-out-for-your-neighbor community values continues to characterize West Virginia today.

ℹ Information

West Virginia Division of Tourism (☑ 800-225-5982; www.wvtourism.com) operates welcome centers at interstate borders and in **Harpers Ferry** (☑ 866-435-5698; www.wveasterngateway.com; 37 Washington Ct). Check the Division of Tourism's website for info on the state's myriad adventure-tourism opportunities.

Eastern Panhandle

The most accessible part of the state has always been a mountain getaway for DC types.

Harpers Ferry

History lives on in this attractive town, set with steep cobblestoned streets, framed by the Shenandoah Mountains and the confluence of the rushing Potomac and Shenandoah Rivers. The lower town functions as an open-air museum, with more than a dozen buildings that you can wander through to get a taste of 19th-century small-town life. Exhibits narrate the town's role at the forefront of westward expansion, American industry and, most famously, the slavery debate – in 1859 old John Brown tried to spark a slave uprising here and was hanged for his efforts; the incident rubbed friction between North and South into the fires of Civil War.

Pick up a pass to visit the historic buildings at the **Harpers Ferry National Historic Park Visitor Center** (☑ 304-535-6029; www.nps.gov/hafe; 171 Shoreline Dr; per person/vehicle $5/10; ☺ 9am-5pm; ♠) ⟋ off Hwy 340. You can also park and take a free shuttle from here. Parking is extremely limited in Harpers Ferry proper.

Sights

You can freely enter over a dozen buildings that are part of the Harpers Ferry National Historic Park. Start your exploring at the information center on Shenandoah St, near the riverfront. From there, you can pick up a map and stroll into nearby buildings, all of which offer a unique perspective on life in the past.

Black Voices   MUSEUM

(High St; ☺ 9am-5pm) **FREE** This worthwhile, interactive exhibit has narrated stories of hardships and hard-won victories by African Americans from the times of enslavement through the Civil Rights era. Across the street is the Storer College exhibit, which gives an overview of the groundbreaking educational center and Niagara movement that formed in its wake.

John Brown Museum   MUSEUM

(Shenandoah St; ☺ 9am-5pm) **FREE** Across from Arsenal Sq, this three-room gallery gives a fine overview (through videos and period relics) of the events surrounding John Brown's famous raid.

Master Armorer's House   HISTORIC SITE

(☑ 304-535-6029; www.nps.gov/hafe; Shenandoah St; ☺ 9am-5pm) **FREE** One of the free sites in the historic district, this 1858 house explains how rifle technology developed here went on to revolutionize the firearms industry.

Storer College Campus   HISTORIC SITE

(www.nps.gov/hafe; Fillmore St) Founded immediately after the Civil War, Storer College grew from a one-room schoolhouse for freed slaves to a respected college open to all races and creeds. It closed in 1955. You can freely wander the historic campus, reachable by taking the path to upper town, past St Peter's church, Jefferson Rock and Harper Cemetery.

John Brown Wax Museum   MUSEUM

(☑ 304-535-6342; www.johnbrownwaxmuseum. com; 168 High St; adult/child $7/5; ☺ 9am-4:30pm Apr-May & Sep-Nov, 10am-5:30pm Jun-Aug, 9am-4:30pm Sat & Sun only Mar & Dec, closed Jan-Feb) Not to be confused with the National Park–run museum, this private wax museum is a kitschy (and rather overpriced) attraction that pays tribute to the man who led an ill-conceived slave rebellion here. The exhibits are laughably old-school; nothing says historical accuracy like scratchy vocals, jerky animatronics and dusty old dioramas.

Activities

There are great hikes in the area, from three-hour scrambles to the scenic overlook from the Maryland Heights Trail, past Civil War fortifications on the Loudoun Heights Trail or along the Appalachian Trail. You can also cycle or walk along the C&O Canal towpath.

Appalachian Trail Conservancy   HIKING

(☑ 304-535-6331; www.appalachiantrail.org; cnr Washington & Jackson Sts; ☺ 9am-5pm) The 2160-mile Appalachian Trail is headquartered here at this tremendous resource for hikers.

River Riders   ADVENTURE SPORTS

(☑ 800-326-7238; www.riverriders.com; 408 Alstadts Hill Rd) The go-to place for rafting, canoeing, tubing, kayaking and multiday cycling trips, plus cycle rental. There's even a new 1200ft zip line that opened in 2014.

O Be Joyfull   WALKING TOUR

(☑ 732-801-0381; www.obejoyfull.com; 175 High St; day/night tours $22/14) Offers eye-opening historical daytime walking tours (lasting three to four hours) around Harpers Ferry, as well as a spooky 90-minute evening tour.

🛏 Sleeping

Teahorse Hostel
HOSTEL $

(📞304-535-6848; www.teahorsehostel.com; 1312 Washington St; dm/ste $33/150; 🅿️❄️@🛜) Popular with cyclists on the C&O Canal towpath and hikers on the Appalachian Trail, Teahorse is a welcoming place with comfy rooms and common areas (including an outdoor patio). It's located 1 mile (uphill) from the historic lower town of Harpers Ferry.

HI-Harpers Ferry Hostel
HOSTEL $

(📞301-834-7652; www.hiusa.org; 19123 Sandy Hook Rd, Knoxville, MD; dm/d $25/61; ☺May–mid-Nov; 🅿️❄️@🛜) Located 2 miles from downtown on the Maryland side of the Potomac River, this friendly hostel has plenty of amenities, including a kitchen, laundry and lounge area with games and books.

Jackson Rose
B&B $$

(📞304-535-1528; www.thejacksonrose.com; 1167 W Washington St; r Mon-Fri/Sat & Sun $135/150; ❄️🛜) This marvelous 18th-century brick residence with stately gardens has three attractive guest rooms, including a room where Stonewall Jackson lodged briefly during the Civil War. Antique furnishings and vintage curios are sprinkled about the house, and the cooked breakfast is excellent. It's a 600m walk downhill to the historic district. No children under 12.

Town's Inn
INN $$

(📞304-932-0677; www.thetownsinn.com; 179 High St; r $120-140; ❄️) Spread between two neighboring pre–Civil War residences, the Town's Inn has rooms ranging from small and minimalist to charming heritage-style quarters. It's set in the middle of the historic district and has an indoor-outdoor restaurant as well.

🍴 Eating

Potomac Grille
AMERICAN $

(186 High St; mains $10-16; ☺noon-9pm) Serves good pub food (fish and chips, crab cakes, huge burgers) and local brews in an old-fashioned tavern atmosphere in the historic district. The outdoor patio has fine views over the train station and Maryland Heights.

Beans in the Belfry
AMERICAN $

(📞301-834-7178; 122 W Potomac St, Brunswick, MD; sandwiches around $7; ☺9am-9pm Mon-Sat, 8am-7pm Sun; 🛜♿) Across the river in Brunswick, MD (roughly 10 miles east), you'll find this converted red-brick church sheltering

---

WEST VIRGINIA FACTS

Nickname Mountain State

Population 1.85 million

Area 24,230 sq miles

Capital city Charleston (population 52,000)

Other cities Huntington (49,000), Parkersburg (31,500), Morgantown (29,500), Wheeling (28,500)

Sales tax 6%

Birthplace of Olympic gymnast Mary Lou Retton (b 1968), writer Pearl S Buck (1892–1973), pioneer aviator Chuck Yeager (b 1923), actor Don Knotts (1924–2006)

Home of the National Radio Astronomy Observatory, much of the American coal industry

Politics Republican

Famous for Mountains, John Denver's 'Take Me Home, Country Roads,' the Hatfield–McCoy feud

State slogan 'Wild and Wonderful'

Driving distances Harpers Ferry to Fayetteville 280 miles; Fayetteville to Morgantown 148 miles

---

mismatched couches and kitsch-laden walls, featuring light fare (chili, sandwiches, quiche) and a tiny stage where live folk, blues and bluegrass bands strike up several nights a week. Sunday jazz brunch ($18) is a hit.

Canal House
AMERICAN $$

(1226 Washington St; mains $11-24; ☺noon-8pm Mon, to 9pm Fri & Sat, to 6pm Sun; ♿) Roughly 1 mile west (and uphill) from the historic district, Canal House is a perennial favorite for delicious sandwiches, locally sourced seasonal fare and friendly service in a flower-trimmed stone house. Outdoor seating. You can bring your own beer or wine.

ℹ️ Getting There & Around

Amtrak (www.amtrak.com; one way $13-16) trains run to Washington's Union Station (once daily, 71 minutes). **MARC trains** (http://mta.maryland.gov; one way $11) run three times daily during the week (Monday to Friday).

Berkeley Springs

America's first spa town (George Washington relaxed here) is an odd jumble of spiritualism, artistic expression and pampering spa centers. Farmers in pickups sporting Confederate flags and acupuncturists in tie-dye smocks regard each other with bemusement on the roads of Bath (still the official name).

◉ Sights & Activities

The Berkeley Springs State Park's **Roman Baths** (☑ 304-258-2711; www.berkeleyspringssp.com; 2 S Washington St; 30min bath $22, 1hr massage $85-95; ⊙ 9am-4:30pm mon-Fri, 10am-3pm Sat) are uninspiring soaks in dimly lit, individual tile-lined rooms, but it's the cheapest spa deal in town, and you can also book a massage there. (Fill your water bottle with some of the magic stuff at the fountain outside the door.) In the summer, kids will enjoy the spring-fed (but chlorinated) outdoor **swimming pool** (adult/child $3/2; ⊙ 10am-6pm) in the middle of the green.

✖ Eating & Drinking

Cacapon State Park   CABIN $
(☑ 304-258-1022; 818 Cacapon Lodge Dr; lodge/cabins from $69/91) Cacapon State Park has simple lodge accommodations plus modern and rustic cabins (some with fireplaces) in a peaceful wooded setting, 9 miles south of Berkeley Springs (off US 522). The park has hiking, lake swimming, horseback riding and a golf course.

Country Inn of Berkeley Springs   HOTEL $$
(☑ 304-258-1200; www.thecountryinnwv.com; 110 S Washington St; d from $120; P✳☎) The Country Inn, right next to the park, offers luxurious treatment plus lodging package deals. There's a good restaurant on hand.

Tari's   FUSION $$
(☑ 304-258-1196; 33 N Washington St; lunch $9-12, dinner $19-29; ⊙ 11am-9pm; ☑) ✐ Tari's is a very Berkeley Springs sort of spot, with fresh local food and good vegetarian options served in a laid-back atmosphere with all the right hints of good karma abounding. The Caribbean-spiced mahimahi tacos are a delicious way to satisfy one's lunch cravings.

Monongahela National Forest

Almost the entire eastern half of West Virginia is marked as green parkland on the map, and all that goodness falls under the auspices of this stunning national forest. Within its 1400 sq miles are wild rivers, caves and the highest peak in the state, **Spruce Knob**. More than 850 miles of trails include the 124-mile **Allegheny Trail**, for hiking and backpacking, and the 75-mile rails-to-trails **Greenbrier River Trail**, popular with cyclists.

Elkins, at the forest's western boundary, is a good base of operations. The **National Forest Service Headquarters** (☑ 304-636-1800; www.fs.usda.gov/mnf/; 200 Sycamore St; campsites $5-37, primitive camping free) distributes recreation directories for hiking, cycling and camping. After the hike, enjoy wood-fired pizzas, almond-crusted trout and wine at **Vintage** (304-636-0808; 25 Randolph Ave, Elkins; mains $12-29; ⊙ 11am-10pm).

In the southern end of the forest, **Cranberry Mountain Nature Center** (☑ 304-653-4826; cnr Hwys 150 & 39/55; ⊙ 9am-4:30pm Thu-Mon mid-Apr-Oct) FREE has scientific information on the forest and the surrounding 750-acre bog ecosystem, the largest of its kind in the state.

The surreal landscapes at **Seneca Rocks**, 35 miles southeast of Elkins, attract rock climbers up the 900ft-tall sandstone strata. **Seneca Shadows Campground** (☑ 877-444-6777; www.recreation.gov; campsites $15-40; ⊙ Apr-Oct) lies 1 mile east.

Southern West Virginia

This part of the state has carved out a viable stake as adventure-sports capital of the eastern seaboard.

New River Gorge National River

The New River is actually one of the oldest in the world, and the primeval forest gorge it runs through is one of the most breathtaking in the Appalachians. The NPS protects a stretch of the New River that falls 750ft over 50 miles, with a compact set of rapids up to Class V concentrated at the northernmost end.

Canyon Rim visitor center (☎304-574-2115; www.nps.gov/neri; 162 Visitor Center Rd Lansing, WV, GPS 38.07003 N, 81.07583 W; ◷9am-5pm; ✿) ✎, just north of the impressive gorge bridge, is only one of five NPS visitor centers along the river. It has information on scenic drives (including a memorable outing to the abandoned mining town of **Nuttallburg**), river outfitters, gorge climbing, hiking and mountain biking, as well as white-water rafting to the north on the **Gauley River**. Rim and gorge trails offer beautiful views. There are several free basic camping areas.

For a hair-raising stroll over the gorge, sign up for a tour with **Bridgewalk** (☎304-574-1300; www.bridgewalk.com; per person $69; ◷10am-3pm), which takes visitors out across the catwalk below the bridge.

Hawks Nest State Park offers views from its rim-top **lodge** (☎304-658-5212; www.hawksnestsp.com; 49 Hawks Nest Park Rd; r $91-98, ste $111-134; ✾☎). It has short hiking trails and an aerial tram (open May to October) to the river, where you can sign up for a jet-boat ride.

Babcock State Park (☎304-438-3004; www.babcocksp.com; 486 Babcock Rd; cabins $76-121, campsites $21-24) has hiking, canoeing, horseback riding, camping and cabin accommodations. The park's highlight is its very photogenic **Glade Creek Grist Mill**.

The reputable **Adventures on the Gorge** (☎855-379-8738; www.adventuresonthegorge.com; 219 Chestnutburg Rd, Lansing; cabin from $150) offers a wide range of activities, including white-water rafting ($94 to $144 per person), zip-lining, rappelling and more. It has camping, a range of cabins and several popular restaurants.

Fayetteville & Around

Pint-sized Fayetteville acts as jumping-off point for New River thrill-seekers and is an artsy mountain enclave besides. On the third Saturday in October, hundreds of BASE jumpers parachute from the 876ft-high New River Gorge Bridge during the massive **Bridge Day Festival**.

ROADSIDE MYSTERIES

See gravity and the known limits of tackiness defied at the **Mystery Hole** (☎304-658-9101; www.mysteryhole.com; 16724 Midland Trail, Ansted; adult/child $7/6; ◷10:30am-6pm), one of the great attractions of roadside America. Everything inside this madhouse *tilts at an angle!* It's located 1 mile west of Hawks Nest State Park. Call ahead to check open days.

Among the many state-licenced rafting outfitters in the area, **Cantrell Ultimate Rafting** (☎304-877-8235; www.cantrellultimaterafting.com; 49 Cantrell Dr; half-/full-day rafting from $89/109) stands out for its white-water rafting trips. **Hard Rock** (☎304-574-0735; www.hardrockclimbing.com; 131 South Court St; half-/full day from $80/150) offers trips and training courses for rock climbers. Mountain biking is superb in the area, on the graded loops of the **Arrowhead Trails**. Hire wheels at **New River Bikes** (☎304-574-2453; www.newriverbikes.com; 221 N Court St; bike hire per day $35, tours $59-110; ◷10am-6pm Mon-Sat).

The **Beckley Exhibition Coal Mine** (☎304-256-1747; www.beckley.org/exhibition_coal_mine; adult/child $20/12; ◷10am-6pm Apr-Oct) in nearby Beckley is a museum for the region's coal heritage. Visitors can descend 1500ft to a former coal mine. Bring a jacket, as it's cold underground!

River Rock Retreat Hostel (☎304-574-0394; www.riverrockretreatandhostel.com; Lansing-Edmond Rd; dm $26; ℗✾), located less than 1 mile north of the New River Gorge Bridge, has basic, clean rooms and plenty of common space. Owner Joy Marr is a wealth of local information.

Start the day with breakfast and coffee under stained-glass windows at **Cathedral Café** (☎304-574-0202; 134 S Court St; mains $6-10; ◷7:30am-4pm Sun-Thu, to 9pm Fri & Sat; ☎✎) ✎. The **Secret Sandwich Society** (103 Keller Ave; mains $9-12; ◷11am-10pm Wed-Mon) has delicious burgers, hearty salads and a changing lineup of local microbrews.

Eastern & Southern USA Cuisine

Look at the photos of these dishes and tell us your mouth didn't just water. Eating is serious business in the region, and locals' time-honed, fiercely guarded recipes for barbecue sauce, fried chicken, apple pie and more are yours to seek out and yield to.

1. New York hot dog
The garlicky, all-beef frank is griddled to a crackling snap and dressed with spicy brown mustard, sauerkraut and onions.

2. Chicago deep-dish pizza
A hulking mass of crust rises three inches above the plate and cradles a molten pile of cheese and chunky tomato sauce.

3. Gumbo
The spicy soup/stew teems with oysters, shrimp and crab (or smoked meats if you're inland).

4. Pie
The South prefers pecan, Florida likes key lime, the Midwest bakes sugar cream and the Northeast enjoys fruit between its crusts.

5. Southern-style barbecue
The variations are mind-blowing, but expect some version of slow-cooked, wood-smoked pork, with sauces sweet or vinegary.

6. Wisconsin cheese
The chunks go way beyond cheddar, from cave-aged Gouda to cocoa-rubbed goat's-milk cheese and stinky Limburger.

7. Seafood
The region's bounty makes a heckuva chowder (rich, creamy soup), including oysters, clams and Maine's mighty lobsters.

8. Kentucky bourbon
The silky, caramel-colored whiskey gets its unique taste from corn and barrel aging. Drink it straight or with water.

9. Microbrews
It's a golden age for hopheads: you'll find small-batch brewers pouring delicious suds regionwide.

10. Corn bread
Mix cornmeal and buttermilk, bake in a cast-iron skillet, and voila: the bread of the South, best consumed butter-smothered.

11. Southern-fried chicken
All chefs have a secret recipe for the batter, but the constant is that the bird will pop out of the pan crisp outside and moist inside.

12. Cajun food
The bayou country's rustic fare marries native spices like sassafras and chili peppers to provincial French cooking. Try the jambalaya.

DAVID MURRAY AND JULES SELMES / GETTY IMAGES ©

RITA MAAS / GETTY IMAGES ©

BRIAN HAGIWARA / GETTY IMAGES ©

JEFF GREENBERG / ALAMY ©

DANA HOFF / GETTY IMAGES ©

RICHARD LEVINE / ALAMY ©

BROOKLYN BREWERY

JOHN PEACOCK / GETTY IMAGES ©

EKASH / GETTY IMAGES ©

The South

Best Places to Eat

➜ The Optimist (p395)
➜ Decca (p383)
➜ Cúrate (p343)
➜ Boucherie (p441)
➜ Octopus Bar (p396)

Best Places to Stay

➜ Crash Pad (p377)
➜ La Belle Esplanade (p437)
➜ 21c Museum Hotel (p382)
➜ Lodge on Little St Simons (p407)
➜ Capital Hotel (p422)

Why Go?

Beneath its hospitable exterior, the South has a feisty streak. It's a unique combination of 'Hey y'all' and 'Don't tell me what to do.' This dissonance makes the region a bit of a conundrum to outsiders, as well as a compelling place to visit. Well, that and the lyrical dialect, complicated political history and exuberant food. Nurtured by deep roots yet shaped by hardship, the South has a rich legacy in politics and culture. Icons like Martin Luther King Jr, Rosa Parks and Bill Clinton, and novelists like William Faulkner, Eudora Welty and Flannery O'Connor are all Southern born. So are barbecue and grits, bourbon and Coca-Cola, and bluegrass and the blues.

The cities are some of the country's most fascinating, from antebellum beauties like New Orleans and Savannah to New South powerhouses like Atlanta and Nashville. Natural treasures include golden beaches and forested mountain ranges. Tying it all together? That Southern hospitality.

When to Go
New Orleans

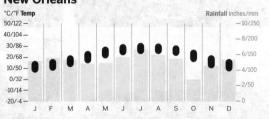

Nov–Feb Winter is generally mild here, and Christmas is a capital-E Event.

Apr–Jun Spring is lush and warm, abloom with fragrant jasmine, gardenia and tuberose.

Jul–Sep Summer is steamy, often unpleasantly so, and locals hit the beaches.

NORTH CAROLINA

The conservative Old South and the liberal New South are jostling for political dominance in the fast-growing Tar Heel State, home to hipsters, hog farmers, hi-tech wunderkinds and an increasing number of craft brewers. For the most part, though, from the ancient mountains in the west to the sandy barrier islands of the Atlantic, the various cultures and communities here coexist.

Agriculture is an important economic force, and there are 52,200 farms across the state. North Carolina leads the nation in tobacco production and is the second-largest producer of pigs. But new technologies also drive the economy, and more than 190 businesses operate in Research Triangle Park alone. Other important industries include finance, nanotechnology and Christmas trees. Craft brewers have contributed nearly $800 million to the economy.

Though the bulk of North Carolinians live in the business-oriented urban centers of the central Piedmont region, most travelers stick to the scenic routes along the coast and through the Appalachian Mountains.

So come on down, grab a platter of barbecue and watch the Duke Blue Devils battle the Carolina Tar Heels on the basketball court. College hoops rival Jesus for Carolinians' souls.

History

Native Americans have inhabited North Carolina for more than 10,000 years. Major tribes included the Cherokee in the mountains, the Catawba in the Piedmont and the Waccamaw in the Coastal Plain.

North Carolina was the second territory to be colonized by the British, named in memory of King Charles I (Carolus in Latin), but the first colony to vote for independence from the Crown. Several important Revolutionary War battles were fought here.

The state was a sleepy agricultural backwater through the 19th century, earning it the nickname the 'Rip Van Winkle State.' Divided on slavery (most residents were too poor to own slaves), North Carolina was the last state to secede during the Civil War, but went on to provide more Confederate soldiers than any other state.

North Carolina was a civil rights hotbed in the mid-20th century, with highly publicized lunch-counter sit-ins in Greensboro and the formation of the influential Student Nonviolent Coordinating Committee (SNCC) in Raleigh. The latter part of the century brought finance to Charlotte, and technology and medicine to the Raleigh-Durham area, driving a huge population boom and widening cultural diversity.

ℹ Information

North Carolina Division of Tourism (☎919-733-8372; www.visitnc.com; 301 N Wilmington St, Raleigh; ⊗8am-5pm Mon-Fri) Sends out good maps and information, including its annual *Official Travel Guide*.

North Carolina State Parks (www.ncparks.gov) Offers info on North Carolina's 41 state parks and recreation areas, many of which have camping (campsite fees range from $10 to $45).

North Carolina Coast

The coastline of North Carolina stretches just over 300 miles. Remarkably, it remains underdeveloped and the beach is often visible from coastal roads. Yes, the wall of cottages stretching south from Corolla to Kitty Hawk can seem endless, but for the most part the state's shores remain free of flashy, highly commercialized resort areas. Instead you'll find rugged, windswept barrier islands, Colonial villages once frequented by pirates and laid-back beach towns full of locally owned ice-cream shops and mom-and-pop motels. Even the most touristy beaches have a small-town vibe.

For solitude, head to the isolated Outer Banks (OBX), where fishermen still make their living hauling in shrimp and the older locals speak in an archaic British-tinged brogue. The Hwy 158 bypass from Kitty Hawk to Nags Head gets congested in summer, but the beaches themselves still feel uncrowded. Further south, Wilmington is known as a center of film and TV production, and its surrounding beaches are popular with local spring breakers and tourists.

Outer Banks

These fragile ribbons of sand trace the coastline for 100 miles, cut off from the mainland by various sounds and waterways. From north to south, the barrier islands of Bodie (pronounced 'Body'), Roanoke, Hatteras and Ocracoke, essentially large sandbars, are linked by bridges and ferries. The far-northern communities of **Corolla** (pronounced kur-*all*-ah, not like the car), **Duck** and **Southern Shores** are former duck-hunting

The South Highlights

1 Donning a costume and joining the crowds during Mardi Gras in **New Orleans** (p429).

2 Hiking and camping in the magnificent **Great Smoky Mountains National Park** (p344).

3 Stomping your boots in honky-tonks along Lower Broadway in **Nashville** (p366).

4 Driving windswept Hwy 12 the length of North Carolina's **Outer Banks** (p325) and riding the ferry to Ocracoke Island.

5 Touring the grand antebellum homes and

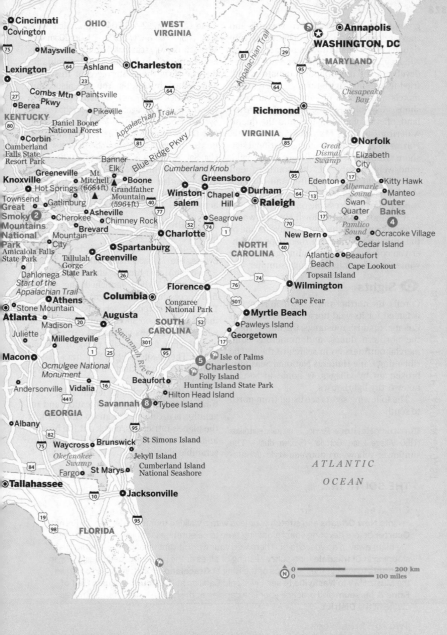

dining on Lowcountry fare in **Charleston** (p346).

6 Learning the story of segregation and the Civil Rights movement at the **Birmingham Civil Rights Institute** (p409).

7 Exploring Arkansas' **Ozark Mountains** (p425), where folk music reigns.

8 Falling for the hauntings, murderous tales and Southern hospitality in Georgia's living romance novel, the architecturally pristine **Savannah** (p402).

grounds for the northeastern wealthy, and they are quiet and upscale. The nearly contiguous Bodie Island towns of **Kitty Hawk**, **Kill Devil Hills** and **Nags Head** are heavily developed and more populist in nature, with fried-fish joints, drive-through beer shops, motels and dozens of sandals 'n' sunblock shops. **Roanoke Island**, west of Bodie Island, offers Colonial history and the quaint waterfront town of **Manteo**. Further south, **Hatteras Island** is a protected national seashore with a few teeny villages and a wild, windswept beauty. At the southern end of OBX, wild ponies run free and old salts shuck oysters and weave hammocks on **Ocracoke Island**, accessible only by ferry.

A meandering drive down Hwy 12, which connects much of the Outer Banks, is one of the truly great American road trips, whether you come during the stunningly desolate winter months or in the sunny summer.

◉ Sights

Corolla, the northernmost town on Hwy 158, is famed for its wild horses. Descendants of Colonial Spanish mustangs, the horses roam the northern dunes, and numerous commercial outfitters go in search of them. The ribboning Cape Hatteras National Seashore, broken up by villages, is home to several noteworthy lighthouses.

The following sights are listed from north to south.

Currituck Heritage Park   HISTORIC BUILDINGS
(1160 Village Lane, Corolla; ◷dawn-dusk) The sunflower-yellow, art-nouveau-style **Whale-**head Club (☑252-453-9040; www.visitcurrituck.com; adult/child 6-12yr $5/3; ◷tours 10am-4pm Mon-Sat, may vary seasonally), built in the 1920s as a hunting 'cottage' for a Philadelphia industrialist, is the centerpiece of this manicured park in Corolla. You can also climb the redbrick **Currituck Beach Lighthouse** (www.currituckbeachlight.com; adult/child under 8yr $7/free; ◷9am-5pm late Mar-Nov). The modern **Outer Banks Center for Wildlife Education** (www.ncwildlife.org/obx; ◷9am-4:30pm Mon-Sat; ▣) **FREE** is home to an 8000-gallon aquarium, a life-size marsh diorama and an interesting film about area history. The center also offers numerous kids' classes and activities.

**Wright Brothers
National Memorial**   PARK, MUSEUM
(☑252-473-2111; www.nps.gov/wrbr; US 158 Bypass, Mile 7.5; adult/child under 16yr $4/free; ◷9am-5pm) Self-taught engineers Wilbur and Orville Wright launched the world's first successful airplane flight on December 17, 1903 (it lasted 12 seconds). A boulder marks the take-off spot. Climb a nearby hill, where the brothers conducted earlier glider experiments, for fantastic views of sea and sound. The on-site **Wright Brothers Visitor Center** has a reproduction of the 1903 flyer and exhibits.

The 30-minute 'Flight Room Talk,' a lecture about the brothers' dedication and ingenuity, is excellent. For an up-close look at the plane's intricacies, check out the bronze-and-steel replica behind the hill; it's okay to scramble aboard.

THE SOUTH IN...

One Week

Fly into **New Orleans** and stretch your legs with a walking tour in the legendary **French Quarter** before devoting your remaining time to celebrating jazz history and partying the night away in a zydeco joint. Then wind your way upward through the languid Delta, stopping in **Clarksdale** for a sultry evening of blues at the juke joints before alighting in **Memphis** to walk in the footsteps of the King at **Graceland**. From here, head on down the Music Hwy to **Nashville** to see Elvis' gold Cadillac at the **Country Music Hall of Fame & Museum** and practice your line dancing at the honky-tonks (country-music clubs) of the **District**.

Two to Three Weeks

From Nashville, head east to hike amid the craggy peaks and waterfalls of **Great Smoky Mountains National Park** before a revitalizing overnight in the arty mountain town of **Asheville** and a tour of the scandalously opulent **Biltmore Estate**, America's largest private home. Plow straight through to the coast to loll on the sandy barrier islands of the isolated **Outer Banks**, then head down the coast to finish up in **Charleston**, with decadent food and postcard-pretty architecture.

Fort Raleigh National Historic Site   HISTORIC BUILDING

In the late 1580s, three decades before the Pilgrims landed at Plymouth Rock, a group of 116 British colonists disappeared without a trace from their Roanoke Island settlement. Were they killed off by drought? Did they run away with a Native American tribe? The fate of the 'Lost Colony' remains one of America's greatest mysteries. Explore their story in the **visitor center** (www.nps.gov/fora; 1401 National Park Dr, Manteo; ☉grounds dawn-dusk, visitor center 9am-5pm) **FREE**. One of the site's star attractions is the beloved musical the **Lost Colony Outdoor Drama** (www.thelostcolony.org; 1409 National Park Dr; adult/child 6-12yr $30/10; ☉7:30pm Mon-Sat late May-late Aug).

The play, from Pulitzer Prize–winning North Carolina playwright Paul Green, dramatizes the fate of the colonists and will celebrate its 80th anniversary in 2017. It plays at the Waterside Theater throughout summer.

Other attractions include exhibits, artifacts, maps and a free film to fuel the imagination, hosted at the visitor center. The 16th-century-style **Elizabethan Gardens** (www.elizabethangardens.org; 1411 National Park Dr; adult/child 6-17yr $9/6; ☉9am-7pm Jun-Aug, shorter hours Sep-May) include a Shakespearian herb garden and rows of beautifully manicured flower beds. A commanding statue of Queen Elizabeth I stands guard at the entrance.

Cape Hatteras National Seashore   ISLANDS

(www.nps.gov/caha) Extending some 70 miles from south of Nags Head to the south end of Ocracoke Island, this fragile necklace of islands remains blissfully free from overdevelopment. Natural attractions include local and migratory water birds, marshes, woodlands, dunes and miles of empty beaches.

Bodie Island Lighthouse   LIGHTHOUSE

(☏255-473-2111; Bodie Island Lighthouse Rd, Bodie Island; museum free, tours adult/child under 11yr $8/4; ☉visitor center 9am-5pm, tours 9am-4:30pm late Apr-early Oct; ♿) Built in 1872, this photogenic lighthouse opened its doors to visitors in 2013. The 156ft-high structure still has its original Fresnel lens – a rarity. It's just over 200 steps to the top. The lighthouse keeper's former home is now the visitor center.

Pea Island National Wildlife Refuge   PRESERVE

(☏252-987-2394; www.fws.gov/refuge/peaisland; Hwy 12; ☉visitor center 9am-4pm, trails dawn-dusk) At the northern end of Hatteras Island, this 5834-acre preserve is a bird-watcher's heaven, with two nature trails (both are fully accessible to people with disabilities) and 13 miles of unspoiled beach. Viewer scopes inside the visitor center overlook an adjacent pond. Check the online calendar for details about guided bird walks, turtle talks and canoe tours.

Cape Hatteras Lighthouse   LIGHTHOUSE

(www.nps.gov/caha; climbing tours adult/child under 12yr $8/4; ☉visitor center 9am-5pm Sep-May, to 6pm Jun-Aug, lighthouse 9am-5:30pm Jun-Aug, until 4:30pm spring & fall) At 208ft, this striking black-and-white-striped edifice is the tallest brick lighthouse in the US and is one of North Carolina's most iconic images. Climb the 248 steps then check out the interesting exhibits about local history in the Museum of the Sea, located in the lighthouse keeper's former home.

NORTH CAROLINA FACTS

Nickname Tar Heel State

Population 9.9 million

Area 48,711 sq miles

Capital city Raleigh (population 431,000)

Other cities Charlotte (population 792,000)

Sales tax 4.75% plus municipality taxes, plus an additional hotel-occupancy tax of up to 8%

Birthplace of President James K Polk (1795–1849), jazzman John Coltrane (1926–67), Nascar driver Richard Petty (b 1937), singer-songwriter Tori Amos (b 1963)

Home of America's first state university, the Biltmore Estate, Krispy Kreme doughnuts

Politics Conservative in rural areas, increasingly liberal in urban ones

Famous for The Andy Griffith Show, first airplane flight, college basketball

Pet name Natives are called 'tar heels,' a nickname of uncertain origin but said to be related to their pine-tar production and their legendary stubbornness

Driving distances Asheville to Raleigh 247 miles, Raleigh to Wilmington 131 miles

Graveyard of the Atlantic Museum MUSEUM

(☑ 252-986-2995; www.graveyardoftheatlantic.
com; 59200 Museum Dr; ⊙10am-4pm) FREE
Exhibits about shipwrecks, piracy and salvaged cargo are highlights at this maritime
museum at the end of the road. There have
been more than 2000 shipwrecks off the
coast of the Outer Banks. According to one
exhibit, in 2006 a container washed ashore
near Frisco, releasing thousands of Doritos
bags. One local told us that residents were
enjoying Doritos casseroles for months!
Donations appreciated.

🏃 Activities

The same strong wind that helped the
Wright brothers launch their biplane today propels windsurfers, sailors and hang
gliders. Other popular activities include
kayaking, fishing, cycling, horse tours,
stand-up paddleboarding and scuba diving.
The coastal waters kick up between August
and October, creating perfect conditions for
bodysurfing.

Kitty Hawk Kites ADVENTURE SPORTS

(☑ 252-449-2210; www.kittyhawk.com; 3925 S
Croatan Hwy, Mile 12.5; electric bike rental per day
$30, kayaks $39-49, stand-up paddleboards $60)
In business more than 30 years, Kitty Hawk
Kites has several locations along the OBX
coast. They offer beginners' kiteboarding
lessons (five hours, $400) in Kitty Hawk and
Rodanthe and hang-gliding lessons at Jockey's Ridge State Park (from $109). Also rents
kayaks, sailboats, stand-up paddleboards,
bikes and inline skates and offers a variety
of tours and courses.

Corolla Outback Adventures DRIVING TOUR

(☑ 252-453-4484; www.corollaoutback.com; 1150
Ocean Trail, Corolla; 2hr tour adult/child under 13yr
$50/25) Tour operator Jay Bender, whose
family started Corolla's first guide service,
knows his local history and his local horses.
Tours bounce you down the beach and
through the dunes to see the wild mustangs
that roam the northern Outer Banks.

🛏 Sleeping

Crowds swarm the Outer Banks in summer, so
reserve in advance. The area has few massive
chain hotels, but hundreds of small motels,
rental cottages and B&Bs; the visitor centers
offer referrals. Also check www.outer-banks.
com. For cottage rentals, try www.sunreal-
tync.com or www.southernshores.com.

Campgrounds CAMPGROUND $

(☑ 252-473-2111; www.nps.gov/caha; tent sites
$20-23; ⊙ late spring-early fall) The National
Park Service runs four campgrounds on the
islands which feature cold-water showers
and flush toilets. They are located at Oregon
Inlet (near Bodie Island Lighthouse), Cape
Point and Frisco (near Cape Hatteras Lighthouse) and Ocracoke (☑ 800-365-2267; www.
recreation.gov). Sites at Oregon Inlet, Frisco
and Ocracoke can be reserved; Cape Point
is first-come, first-served. You'll enjoy close
proximity to the coast at these campsites,
but you won't find many trees for shade.

Breakwater Inn MOTEL $$

(☑ 252-986-2565; www.breakwaterhatteras.com;
57896 Hwy 12; r/ste $159/189, motel $104/134;
🅿❄🛜🐾) The end of the road doesn't look
so bad at this three-story inn. Rooms come
with kitchenettes and private decks that have
views of the sound. On a budget? Try one of
the older 'Fisherman's Quarters' rooms, with
microwave and refrigerator. The inn is near
the Hatteras–Ocracoke ferry landing.

Shutters on the Banks HOTEL $$

(☑ 252-441-5581; www.shuttersonthebanks.com;
405 S Virginia Dare Trail; r $159-284, ste $229-725;
🅿❄🛜🐾) Centrally located in Kill Devil
Hills, this welcoming beachfront hotel exudes a snappy, colorful style. The inviting
rooms come with plantation windows and
colorful bedspreads as well as a flat-screen
TV, refrigerator and microwave. Some
rooms come with a full kitchen.

Sanderling Resort & Spa RESORT $$$

(☑ 252-261-4111; www.sanderling-resort.com; 1461
Duck Rd; r $399-539; 🅿❄🛜🐾) Two dozen re-
vamped rooms opened their doors in 2015,
giving this posh place a stylish kick in the
pants. Or should we say the Lululemons? Because yes, the resort does offer sunrise yoga
on the beach. Decor is impeccably tasteful,
and the attached balconies are an inviting
place to enjoy the ocean sounds and breezes.

The property includes several restaurants
and bars, and a spa offering luxe massage.
Daily resort fee is $25 from mid-May to Oc-
tober, $15 from November to mid-May.

🍴 Eating & Drinking

The main tourist strip on Bodie Island has
the most restaurants and nightlife options.
Many places are only open Memorial Day
(last Monday in May) through early fall, or
have reduced hours in the off-season.

OCRACOKE ISLAND

Crowded in summer and desolate in winter, Ocracoke Village (www.ocracokevillage.com) is a funky little community that moves at a slower pace. The village is at the southern end of 14-mile-long Ocracoke Island and is accessed from Hatteras via the free Hatteras–Ocracoke ferry (p332). The ferry lands at the northeastern end of the island. With the exception of the village, the National Park Service owns the island.

The older residents still speak in the 17th-century British dialect known as 'Hoi Toide' (their pronunciation of 'high tide') and refer to non-islanders as 'dingbatters.' Edward Teach, aka Blackbeard the pirate, used to hide out in the area and was killed here in 1718. You can camp by the beach where wild ponies run, have a fish sandwich in a local pub, bike around the village's narrow streets or visit the 1823 Ocracoke Lighthouse, the oldest one still operating in North Carolina.

The island makes a terrific day trip from Hatteras Island, or you can stay the night. There are a handful of B&Bs, a park service campground near the beach and rental cottages.

Locals and tourists converge at Ocracoke Coffee (www.ocracokecoffee.com; 226 Back Rd; 7am-6pm Mon-Sat, to 1pm Sun), home of the Grasshopper latte (chocolate mint and toffee), and friendly Howard's Pub (1175 Irvin Garrish Hwy; mains $9-25; 11am-10pm early Mar-late Nov, may stay open later Fri & Sat), a big old wooden pub that's been an island tradition for beer and fried seafood since the 1850s.

Want to get on the water? Take a kayaking tour with Ride the Wind (252-928-6311; www.surfocracoke.com; 486 Irvin Garrish Hwy; 2-2½ hr tours adult $39-45; child under 13yr $18; 9am-9pm Mon-Sat, to 8pm Sun). The sunset tours are easy on the arms, and the guides (we hear) are easy on the eyes.

THE SOUTH NORTH CAROLINA COAST

John's Drive-In SEAFOOD, ICE CREAM $
(www.johnsdrivein.com; 3716 N Virginia Dare Trail; mains $2-16; 11am-5pm Thu-Tue) A Kitty Hawk institution for perfectly fried baskets of mahi-mahi, to be eaten at outdoor picnic tables and washed down with one of hundreds of possible milkshake combinations. Some folks just come for the soft-serve.

⭐ **Blue Moon Beach Grill** SEAFOOD, SANDWICHES $$
(252-261-2583; www.bluemoonbeachgrill.com; 4104 S Virginia Dare Trail, Mile 13; mains $10-29) Would it be wrong to write an ode to a side of french fries? Because Lord almighty, the lightly spiced fries at this casual hot spot are the stuff of sonnets and monologues. And we haven't even mentioned the BLT with seared mahi-mahi, Applewood bacon, local Currituck tomatoes and a jalapeño rémoulade for slathering. Other choices include seafood sandwiches, burgers and voodoo pasta.

The strip mall view won't inspire poetry, but the friendly staff, come-as-you-are atmosphere and upbeat play list – Elvis' 'Jailhouse Rock' – will invigorate your spirit for sure.

Trio WINE BAR
(www.obxtrio.com; 3708 N Croatan Hwy, Mile 4.5; cheese plates $7-21, tapas $7-11, panini $9-10; 11am-11pm Mon-Sat, noon-11pm Sun) This sim-ple but stylish wine bar is a welcome – and welcoming – addition to OBX. Select from two-dozen wines in the self-service tasting bar then complement your choice with housemade hummus, a cheese plate or one of seven different panini. The retail store sells a wide selection of craft beer, wine and artisanal cheese.

ℹ Orientation

Hwy 12, also called Virginia Dare Trail or 'the coast road,' runs close to the Atlantic for the length of the Outer Banks. US 158/Croatan Hwy, usually called 'the Bypass,' begins just north of Kitty Hawk and merges with US 64 as it crosses onto Roanoke Island. Locations are usually given in terms of 'mile posts' (Mile or MP), beginning with Mile 0 at the foot of the Wright Memorial Bridge at Kitty Hawk.

ℹ Information

The best sources of information are at the main visitor centers. Many smaller centers are open seasonally. Also useful is www.outerbanks.org. The entire Manteo waterfront has free wi-fi.

Aycock Brown Visitor Center (252-261-4644; www.outerbanks.org; US 158, Mile 1, Kitty Hawk; 9am-5:30pm Mar-Oct, to 5pm Nov-Feb) On the bypass in Kitty Hawk; has maps and information.

Hatteras Island Visitor Center (📞252-473-2111; www.nps.gov/caha; ⊙9am-6pm Jun-Aug, to 5pm Sep-May) Beside Cape Hatteras Lighthouse.

Ocracoke Island Visitor Center (📞252-928-4531; www.nps.gov/caha; ⊙9am-5pm) Near the southern ferry dock.

Outer Banks Welcome Center on Roanoke Island (📞252-473-2138; www.outerbanks.org; 1 Visitors Center Circle, Manteo; ⊙9am-5:30pm Mar-Oct, to 5pm Nov-Feb) Just east of Virginia Dare Memorial Bridge on the US 64 Bypass.

🛈 Getting There & Around

No public transportation exists to or on the Outer Banks. However, the **North Carolina Ferry System** (📞800-293-3779; www.ncdot.gov/ferry) operates several routes, including the free one-hour Hatteras–Ocracoke car ferry, which runs at least hourly from 5am to midnight from Hatteras in high season; reservations aren't accepted. North Carolina ferries also run between Ocracoke and Cedar Island (one-way car/motorcycle $15/10, 2¼ hours) and Ocracoke and Swan Quarter on the mainland ($15/10, 2¾ hours) every three hours or so; reservations are recommended in summer for these two routes.

Crystal Coast

The southern Outer Banks are collectively called the 'Crystal Coast,' at least for tourist offices' promotional purposes. Less rugged than the northern beaches, they include several historic coastal towns, sparsely populated islands, and vacation-friendly beaches.

An industrial and commercial stretch of US 70 goes through **Morehead City**, with plenty of chain hotels and restaurants. The **Bogue Banks**, across the sound from Morehead City via the Atlantic Beach Causeway, have several well-trafficked beach communities – try Atlantic Beach if you like the smell of coconut suntan oil and doughnuts.

Just north, postcard-pretty **Beaufort** (bowfort), the third-oldest town in the state, has a charming boardwalk and lots of B&Bs. Blackbeard himself is said to have lived in the Hammock House off Front St. You can't go inside, but some claim you can still hear the screams of the pirate's murdered wife at night.

⊙ Sights

North Carolina Maritime Museum MUSEUM
(http://ncmaritimemuseums.com/beaufort; 315 Front St, Beaufort; ⊙9am-5pm Mon-Fri, 10am-5pm

Sat, 1-5pm Sun) FREE The pirate Blackbeard was a frequent visitor to the Beaufort area in the early 1700s. In 1996 the wreckage of his flagship, the *Queen Anne's Revenge*, was discovered at the bottom of Beaufort Inlet. You'll see plates, bottles and other artifacts from the ship in this small but engaging museum, which also spotlights the seafood industry as well as maritime rescue operations.

North Carolina Aquarium AQUARIUM
(www.ncaquariums.com; 1 Roosevelt Blvd, Pine Knoll Shores; adult/child 3-12yr $11/9; ⊙9am-5pm; 🚼) Aquatic life from the North Carolina mountains to the sea is covered in this small but engaging aquarium. The fast-moving river otters are mesmerizing, and there's a cool exhibit re-creating the local shipwreck of a U-352 German submarine.

Fort Macon State Park FORT
(www.ncparks.gov; 2303 E Fort Macon Rd, Atlantic Beach; ⊙8am-9pm Jun-Aug, shorter hours Sep-May) FREE This sturdy, five-sided fort, with 26 vaulted rooms, was completed in 1834. Exhibits in rooms near the entrance spotlight the fort's construction as well as the daily lives of soldiers stationed there. The fort, built from brick and stone, changed hands twice during the Civil War.

🛏 Sleeping & Eating

Hampton Inn Morehead City HOTEL $$$
(📞252-240-2300; www.hamptoninn3.hilton.com; 4035 Arendell St, Morehead City; r from $209; 🅿❄@🛜🏊) Yep, it's part of a national chain, but the helpful staff and the views of Bogue Sound make this Hampton Inn a nice choice, plus it's convenient to US 70 for those driving the coast. Rates drop significantly on weeknights in summer.

El's Drive-In SEAFOOD $
(3706 Arendell St, Morehead City; mains $2-14; ⊙10:30am-10pm Sun-Thu, to 10:30pm Fri & Sat) The food is brought to you by carhop at this legendary seafood spot, open since 1959. Our recommendation? The fried shrimp burger with ketchup and slaw plus a side of fries. Cash only.

Front Street Grill at Stillwater RESTAURANT $$
(www.frontstreetgrillatstillwater.com; 300 Front St, Beaufort; brunch & lunch $11-17, dinner $17-30; ⊙11:30am-9pm Tue-Thu & Sun, to 10pm Fri & Sat) The view reigns supreme at this inviting seafood spot overlooking Taylor's Creek. Nibble chili-lime shrimp tacos at lunch or seared

backfin crabcakes at dinnertime. Enjoy people-watching at the small Rhum Bar.

Wilmington

Wilmington is pretty darn fun, and it's worth carving out a day or two for a visit if you're driving the coast. This seaside charmer may not have the name recognition of Charleston and Savannah, but eastern North Carolina's largest city has historic neighborhoods, azalea-choked gardens and cute cafes aplenty. All that plus reasonable hotel prices. At night the historic riverfront downtown becomes the playground for local college students, craft beer enthusiasts, tourists and the occasional Hollywood type – there are so many movie studios here the town has earned the nickname 'Wilmywood'.

⦿ Sights

Wilmington sits at the mouth of the Cape Fear River, about 8 miles from the beach. The historic riverfront is perhaps the city's most important sight, abounding with boutiques and boardwalks. Nearby Wrightsville Beach bustles with fried-fish joints, shops selling sunglasses and summer crowds.

A free trolley (www.wavetransit.com) runs through the historic district from morning through evening.

Cape Fear Serpentarium   ZOO
(☏ 910-762-1669; www.capefearserpentarium.com; 20 Orange St; admission $9; ⊘ 11am-5pm Mon-Fri, to 6pm Sat & Sun) Herpetologist Dean Ripa's museum is a fun and informative place to spend an hour or two – if you don't mind standing in a building slithering with venomous snakes, giant constrictors and big-teethed crocodiles. They're all behind glass but... ssssssss. Just hope there's not an earthquake. One sign explains the effects of a bite from a bushmaster: 'It is better to just lie down under a tree and rest, for you will soon be dead.' Enjoy! Cash only.

The Serpentarium may close on Monday and Tuesday in the off-season. Live feedings are held at 3pm on Saturday and Sunday, but call ahead to confirm.

Battleship North Carolina   HISTORIC SITE
(www.battleshipnc.com; 1 Battleship Rd; adult/child 6-11yr $14/6; ⊘ 8am-5pm Sep-May, to 8pm Jun-Aug) Self-guided tours take you through the decks of this 45,000-ton megaship, which earned 15 battle stars in the Pacific theater in WWII before it was decommissioned in

1947. Sights include the bake shop and galley, the print shop, the engine room, the powder magazine and the communications center. Note that there are several steep stairways leading to lower decks. Take the Cape Fear Bridge from downtown to get here.

Airlie Gardens   GARDENS
(www.airliegardens.org; 300 Airlie Rd; adult/child 4-12yr $9/3; ⊘ 9am-5pm, closed Mon in winter) In spring, wander past thousands of bright azaleas at this 67-acre wonderland, also home to bewitching formal flower beds, seasonal gardens, pine trees, lakes and trails. The Airlie Oak dates to 1545.

🛏 Sleeping & Eating

There are numerous budget hotels on Market St, just north of downtown. Restaurants directly on the waterfront can be crowded and mediocre; head a block or two inland for the best eats and nightlife.

★ CW Worth House   B&B $$
(☏ 910-762-8562; www.worthhouse.com; 412 S 3rd St; r $154-194; ❋ @ 🛜) One of our favorite B&Bs in North Carolina, this turreted 1893 home is dotted with antiques and Victorian touches, but still manages to feel kick-back and cozy. Breakfasts are top-notch. The B&B is within a few blocks of downtown.

Best Western Plus Coastline Inn   HOTEL $$
(☏ 910-763-2800; www.bestwestern.com; 503 Nutt St; r/ste $209/239; ❋ @ 🛜 🐾) We're not sure what we like best: the gorgeous views of the Cape Fear River, the wooden boardwalk or the short walk to downtown fun. Standard rooms aren't huge, but they do pop with a bit of modern style. Every room has a river view. Pet fee is $20 per day.

Fork & Cork   BURGERS, SANDWICHES $
(www.theforkncork.com; 122 Market St; ⊘ 11am-11pm Mon-Thu, 11am-midnight Sat, noon-10pm Sun) The kitchen's not afraid of kicky flavors at new-on-the-scene Fork & Cork, a former food truck that has cleaned up nice – just look at those exposed brick walls. Juicy burgers like the Hot Mess – with bacon, jalapeños, grilled onions, and blue and cheddar cheese – draw raves, as do the poutine, duck wings and the day's mac 'n' cheese.

Flaming Amy's Burrito Barn   MEXICAN $
(☏ 910-799-2919; www.flamingamys.com; 4002 Oleander Dr; mains $5-9; ⊘ 11am-10pm) The burritos are big and tasty at Flaming Amy's, a scrappy barn filled with kitschy decor from

Elvis to Route 66. Burritos include the Philly Phatboy, the Thai Mee Up and the jalapeño-and-pepper-loaded Flaming Amy itself. Everyone in town is here or on the way.

 Drinking & Nightlife

Flytrap Brewing MICROBREWERY
(www.flytrapbrewing.com; 319 Walnut St; ⊙3-10pm Mon-Thu, noon-midnight Fri & Sat, noon-10pm Sun) Half-a-dozen new microbreweries have opened in Wilmington in the last few years, and the one consistently recommended is Flytrap. Located in a bright space in the Brooklyn Arts District just a short walk from Front St, the brewery specializes in American and Belgian-style ales. Look for food-truck fare and live music on weekend nights.

The brewery is named for the Venus flytrap, the carnivorous plant whose only native habitat is within 60 miles of Wilmington.

 Entertainment

Dead Crow Comedy Room COMEDY
(☑910-399-1492; www.deadcrowcomedy.com; 265 N Front St; tickets $13-16) Dark, cramped, underground and in the heart of downtown, just like a comedy club should be. Before heading out, stop in for improv, open mike nights and touring comedians. Bar service and full menu available.

ℹ Information

Visitor Center (☑877-406-2356, 910-341-4030; www.wilmingtonandbeaches.com; 505 Nutt St; ⊙8:30am-5pm Mon-Fri, 9am-4pm Sat, 1-4pm Sun) The visitor center, in an 1800s freight warehouse, has a walking-tour map of downtown.

The Triangle

The cities of Raleigh, Durham and Chapel Hill form a rough triangle in the central Piedmont region. Three top research universities – Duke, University of North Carolina and North Carolina State – are located here, as is the 7000-acre computer and biotech-office campus known as Research Triangle Park. Swarming with egghead computer programmers, bearded peace activists and hip young families, each town has its own unique personality, despite being only a few miles apart. In March, everyone – we mean *everyone* – goes crazy for college basketball.

ℹ Getting There & Around

Raleigh-Durham International Airport (RDU; ☑919-840-2123; www.rdu.com), a significant hub, is a 25-minute (15 mile) drive northwest of downtown Raleigh.

In 2014 **Greyhound** (☑919-834-8275; 2210 Capital Blvd) moved from downtown Raleigh to a location 3 miles northeast and not easy to reach for pedestrians and connections. For a better downtown stop, try Durham (515 W Pettigrew St), near the Amtrak station in the Durham Station Transportation Center. The **Triangle Transit Authority** (☑919-549-9999; www.triangle-transit.org; adult $2.25) operates buses linking Raleigh, Durham and Chapel Hill to each other and the airport. Rte 100 runs from downtown Raleigh to the airport, and the Regional Transit Center near Research Triangle Park where there are connections to Durham and Chapel Hill.

Raleigh

Founded in 1792 specifically to serve as the state capital, Raleigh remains a rather staid government town with major sprawl issues. Still, the handsome downtown has some neat (and free!) museums and galleries, and the food and music scene is on the upswing. The handsome 1840 **state capitol** is a fine example of Greek Revival architecture.

 Sights

⭐**North Carolina Museum of Art** MUSEUM
(www.ncartmuseum.org; 2110 Blue Ridge Rd; ⊙10am-5pm Tue-Thu, Sat & Sun, 10am-9pm Fri, park dawn-dusk) **FREE** The light-filled glass-and-anodized-steel West Building won praise from architecture critics nationwide when it opened in 2010. The fine and wide-ranging collection, with everything from ancient Greek sculptures to commanding American landscape paintings to elaborate African masks, is worthy as well. Short on time? Then stretch your legs on the winding outdoor sculpture trail. It's a few miles west of downtown.

North Carolina Museum of Natural Sciences MUSEUM
(www.naturalsciences.org; 11 W Jones St; ⊙9am-5pm Mon-Sat, noon-5pm Sun, to 9pm 1st Fri of month) **FREE** Whale skeletons hang from the ceiling. Butterflies flutter past your shoulder. Emerald tree boas make you shiver. And swarms of unleashed elementary school children rampage all over the place if you arrive after 10am on a school day. Be warned. The glossy new **Nature Research Center**, fronted by a three-story multimedia globe, spotlights

scientists and their projects. Visitors can watch them at work. Skywalks lead to the main museum building, which also holds habitat dioramas and well-done taxidermy.

Don't miss the exhibit about the Acrocanthosaurus dinosaur, a three-ton carnivore known as the Terror of the South. Its toothy skull is the stuff of nightmares.

North Carolina Museum of History MUSEUM
(www.ncmuseumofhistory.org; 5 E Edenton St; ☺9am-5pm Mon-Sat, noon-5pm Sun) FREE This engaging museum is low on tech but high on straightforward information. Artifacts in the *Story of North Carolina* exhibit include a 3000-year-old canoe; the state's oldest house, dating from 1742; a restored slave cabin; and a 1960s sit-in lunch counter. The special exhibits typically shine too.

🛏 Sleeping & Eating

Downtown is pretty quiet at nights and on weekends, except for the City Market area at E Martin and S Person Sts. Just to the northwest, the Glenwood South neighborhood hops with cafes, bars and clubs. Raleigh claims to have the most live music in the state. Check www.themostnc.for upcoming shows.

You'll find plenty of moderately priced chain hotels around exit 10 off I-440 and off I-40 near the airport.

Umstead Hotel & Spa HOTEL $$$
(☑919-447-4000; www.theumstead.com; 100 Woodland Pond Dr; r $329-389, s $409-599; P ❄ @ ⚲ ⚐) In a wooded suburban office park, the Umstead caters to visiting biotech CEOs with simple, sumptuous rooms and a Zen-like spa. A 3-acre lake sits behind the property complete with a quarter-mile walking trail. The pet fee is $200 per stay, and the hotel has a new fenced playground for Fido, DogWoods.

Raleigh Times PUB FOOD $
(www.raleightimesbar.com; 14 E Hargett St; mains $8-14; ☺11am-2am) Chase plates of BBQ nachos and PBR-battered fish and chips with pints of North Carolina craft brews at this popular downtown pub.

Beasley's Chicken + Honey SOUTHERN $
(www.ac-restaurants.com; 237 Wilmington St; mains $7-13; ☺11:30am-10pm Mon-Wed, 11:30am-midnight Thu & Fri, 11am-midnight Sat, 11am-10pm Sun) You'll need to loosen your belt after a meal at this crispy venture from James Beard Award winner and local restaurant maven Ashley Christensen. Inside this airy downtown eatery, fried chicken is the star – on a biscuit, with waffles, in a pot pie. The sides are decadent too.

If you've ever wanted to try collard greens, the creamed ones here are a good place to start.

Cowfish Sushi Burger Bar BURGERS, SUSHI $$
(☑919-784-0400; www.thecowfish.com; 4208 Six Forks Rd; burgers $11-16, sushi $12-29) The name doesn't lie at this busy eatery in North Hills. Popular with families as well as stylish after-work crowds, this burger-and-sushi joint serves great food in a fun atmosphere. And yes, the sushi and burger menus do overlap – on the 'burgushi' menu – but it all seems to work. Portions are generous too. The amusing pop art on the walls is worth a closer look.

ⓘ Information

Raleigh Visitor Information Center (☑919-834-5900; www.visitraleigh.com; 500 Fayetteville St; ☺8:30am-5pm Mon-Fri, 9am-5pm Sat) Hands out maps and other info. Office is closed on Sundays, but the city visitor guide and map are available on the counter.

Durham & Chapel Hill

Ten miles apart, these two university towns are twinned by their rival basketball teams and left-leaning attitudes. Chapel Hill is a pretty Southern college town whose culture revolves around the nearly 30,000 students at the prestigious University of North Carolina, founded in 1789 as the nation's first state university. A funky, forward-thinking place, Chapel Hill is renowned for its indie rock scene and loud 'n' proud hippie culture. Down the road, Durham is a once-gritty tobacco-and-railroad town whose fortunes collapsed in the 1960s and have only recently begun to revive. Though still fundamentally a working-class Southern city, the presence of top-ranking Duke University has long drawn progressive types to the area and Durham is now making its name as a hot spot for gourmands, artists and gays and lesbians.

The hip former mill town of **Carrboro** is just west of downtown Chapel Hill. Here, the big lawn at **Weaver Street Market** (www.weaverstreetmarket.com) grocery co-op serves as an informal town square, with live music and free wi-fi.

In Durham, activity revolves around the renovated brick tobacco warehouses of the handsome downtown: check out Brightleaf

Sq and the American Tobacco Campus for shopping and outdoor dining.

⊙ Sights

★ Duke Lemur Center   ZOO
(☑ 919-489-3364; www.lemur.duke.edu; 3705 Erwin Rd, Durham; adult/child $10/7; 🏵) The secret is out: the Lemur Center is the coolest attraction in Durham. Located about 2 miles from the main campus, this research and conservation center is home to the largest collection of endangered prosimian primates outside their native Madagascar. Only a robot could fail to melt at the sight of these big-eyed fuzzy-wuzzies. Visits are by guided tour only. To guarantee a tour spot, make your reservation well ahead of your visit. Call at least three weeks in advance for weekdays, and one to two months ahead for weekends.

Duke University   UNIVERSITY, GALLERY
(www.duke.edu; Campus Dr) Endowed by the Duke family's cigarette fortune, the university has a Georgian-style East Campus and a neo-Gothic West Campus notable for the towering 1930s **Duke Chapel** (https://chapel. duke.edu; 401 Chapel Dr). This breathtaking place, with its 210ft tower and colorful, Bible-themed glass windows, is impressive. The **Nasher Museum of Art** (http://nasher. duke.edu; 2001 Campus Dr; adult/child under 16yr $5/free; ⊙10am-5pm Tue, Wed, Fri & Sat, to 9pm Thu, noon-5pm Sun) is also worth a gander, as is the heavenly 55-acre **Sarah P Duke Gardens** (www.gardens.duke.edu; 420 Anderson St; ⊙8am to dusk) FREE. Metered parking on campus is $2 per hour.

University of North Carolina   UNIVERSITY
(www.unc.edu) America's oldest public university has a classic quad lined with flowering pear trees and gracious antebellum buildings. Don't miss the Old Well, said to give good luck to students who drink from it. Pick up a map of the school at the **visitor center** (☑ 919-962-1630; 250 E Franklin St; ⊙9am-5pm Mon-Fri) inside the Morehead Planetarium and Science Center or the Chapel Hill Visitor Center (p337).

Durham Bulls Athletic Park   STADIUM
(www.dbulls.com; 409 Blackwell St, Durham; tickets $7-10; 🏵) Have a quintessentially American afternoon of beer and baseball watching the minor-league Durham Bulls (of 1988 Kevin Costner film *Bull Durham* fame), who play from April to early September.

🛏 Sleeping

There are plenty of cheap chain motels off I-85 in north Durham.

Duke Tower   HOTEL $
(☑ 866-385-3869, 919-687-4444; www.duketower .com; 807 W Trinity Ave, Durham; ste $88-103; 🅿 ❄ 🛜 🏊 🐾) For less than most local hotel rooms you can enjoy a condo with hardwood floors, full kitchen and a Tempur-Pedic mattress. The decor is nothing fancy, but a central pool, picnic tables and grills add a community feel. Located in Durham's historic downtown tobacco-mill district. Pet fee is $5 per night.

★ Carolina Inn   HOTEL $$$
(☑ 919-933-2001; www.carolinainn.com; 211 Pittsboro St, Chapel Hill; r from $259; 🅿 ❄ 🛜) Even if you're not a Tar Heel, this lovely on-campus inn will win you over with its hospitality and historic touches. The charm starts in the snappy lobby then continues through the hallways, lined with photos of alums and championship teams. Classic decor – inspired by Southern antiques – feels fresh in the bright rooms, where silhouettes of famous graduates join the party.

Spring through fall, stop by on Friday afternoon for Fridays on the Front Porch, with food trucks and live music.

🍴 Eating

The region abounds with top-notch restaurants. Downtown Durham has scads of great eateries, coffee shops and bars in close proximity. Most of Chapel Hill's better restaurants are found along Franklin St.

Neal's Deli   BREAKFAST, DELI $
(www.nealsdeli.com; 100 E Main St, Carrboro; breakfast $3-6, lunch $5-10; ⊙7:30am-4pmTue-Fri, 8am-4pm Sat & Sun) Before starting your day, dig into a delicious buttermilk breakfast biscuit at this tiny deli in downtown Carrboro. The egg, cheese and bacon is some kind of good. For lunch, Neal's serves sandwiches and subs, from chicken salad to pastrami to a three-cheese pimiento with a splash of bourbon. A good coffee shop, Open Eye Cafe, is next door.

Toast   SANDWICHES $
(www.toast-fivepoints.com; 345 W Main St, Durham; sandwiches $8; ⊙11am-3pm Mon, to 8pm Tue-Sat) Families, couples, solos and the downtown lunch crowd – everybody loves this tiny Italian sandwich shop, one of the eateries at the

forefront of downtown Durham's revitalization. Order your panini (hot and grilled), tramezzini (cold) or crostini (bundle of joy) at the counter then grab a table by the window – if you can – for people-watching.

Guglhupf Bakery & Cafe
BAKERY, CAFE **$$**
(www.guglhupf.com; 2706 Durham-Chapel Hill Blvd, Durham; breakfast $7-9, lunch $8-10, dinner $15-23; ⊗ bakery 7am-6pm Tue-Fri, to 5pm Sat, 8:30am-2pm Sun, cafe till 10pm Tue-Sun) We like Guglhupf for lunch, when skirt steak sandwiches with blue cheese, housemade bratwurst on sub rolls and grilled pear salads bring an upbeat crowd to the sunny patio at this superior German-style bakery and cafe. Add a German pilsner and a chocolate mousse tart – with salted caramel – and call it a day. Check website for full opening hours.

★ Lantern
ASIAN **$$$**
(☑ 919-969-8846; www.lanternrestaurant.com; 423 W Franklin St, Chapel Hill; mains $23-32; ⊗ 5:30-10pm Mon-Sat) If you only have time for one dinner in the Triangle, dine here. This modern Asian spot, sourced with North Carolina ingredients, has earned a slew of accolades and chef Andrea Reusing is a James Beard Award winner. The current menu includes NC crabcakes with Japanese mustard, tea-smoked chicken and coconut-braised pork shank. For dessert? Warm brown buttercake with strawberries and peppercorn ice cream.

For special occasions, the stylish front rooms are just right, but for a more casual, convivial atmosphere try the bar and lounge in back.

⬤ Drinking & Nightlife

Chapel Hill has an excellent music scene. For entertainment listings, pick up the free weekly *Independent* (www.indyweek.com). A good cluster of brew providers – both coffee and beer – are within walking distance along Geer St and Rigbee Ave.

★ Cocoa Cinnamon
COFFEE
(www.cocoacinnamon.com; 420 W Geer St, Durham; ⊗ 7:30am-10pm Mon-Thu, 7:30am-midnight Fri & Sat, 9am-9pm Sun; ⊛) If someone tells you that you *must* order a hot chocolate at Cocoa Cinnamon, ask them to be more specific. This talk-of-the town coffee shop offers several cocoas, and newbies may be paralyzed by the plethora of chocolatey awesomeness. Come to this one-time service station to enjoy cocoa, teas, single-source coffee, and the energetic vibe.

The wi-fi is strong and the Mac count high. Indoor and outdoor seating.

Fullsteam Brewery
BREWERY
(www.fullsteam.ag; 726 Rigsbee Ave, Durham; ⊗ 4pm-midnight Mon-Thu, 2pm-2am Fri, noon-2am Sat, noon-midnight Sun) Calling itself a 'plow-to-pint' brewery, Fullsteam has gained national attention for pushing the boundaries of beer with wild, super-Southern concoctions like the Summer Basil Farmhouse Ale and the Carver Sweet Potato Lager. Mixed-age crowds.

Top of the Hill
PUB
(www.thetopofthehill.com; 100 E Franklin St, Chapel Hill; ⊗ 11am-2am) The 3rd-story patio of this downtown restaurant and microbrewery, nicknamed TOPO, is *the* place for the Chapel Hill preppy set to see and be seen after football games. Now serving organic spirits from its own distillery.

☆ Entertainment

Cat's Cradle
MUSIC
(☑ 919-967-9053; www.catscradle.com; 300 E Main St, Carrboro) Everyone from Nirvana to Arcade Fire has played the Cradle, hosting the cream of the indie-music world for three decades. Most shows are all-ages.

ℹ Information

Chapel Hill Visitor Center (☑ 919-245-4320; www.visitchapelhill.org; 501 W Franklin St, Chapel Hill; ⊗ 8:30am-5pm Mon-Fri, 10am-2pm Sat) Lots of helpful information including a UNC campus map.
Durham Visitor Center (☑ 919-687-0288; www.durham-nc.com; 101 E Morgan St, Durham; ⊗ 8:30am-5pm Mon-Fri, 10am-2pm Sat) Has information and maps.

Charlotte

The largest city in North Carolina and the biggest US banking center after New York, Charlotte has the sprawling, sometimes faceless look of many New South suburban megalopolises. But though the Queen City, as it's known, is primarily a business town, it's got a few good museums, stately old neighborhoods and lots of fine food.

Busy Tryon St cuts through skyscraper-filled 'uptown' Charlotte, home to banks, hotels, museums and restaurants. The renovated textile mills of the NoDa neighborhood (named for its location on N Davidson St) and the funky mix of boutiques and restaurants

LOCAL KNOWLEDGE

THE BARBECUE TRAIL

North Carolina pulled-pork BBQ is practically a religion in these parts, and the rivalry between Eastern Style (with a thin vinegar sauce) and Western Style (with a sweeter, tomato-based sauce) occasionally comes to blows. The North Carolina Barbecue Society has an interactive **Barbecue Trail Map** (www.ncbbqsociety.com), directing pilgrims to the best spots. So try both styles, then take sides (hint: Eastern style is better. Just kidding! Sort of).

in the Plaza-Midwood area, just northeast of uptown, have a hipper vibe. Uptown's new **Romare Bearden Park** (300 S Church St) is a pretty place to watch the sunset.

For more information about the city's greenways and new bike-share program visit https://charlotte.bcycle.com.

Sights & Activities

Billy Graham Library RELIGIOUS SITE
(www.billygrahamlibrary.org; 4330 Westmont Dr; 9:30am-5pm Mon-Sat) FREE This multimedia 'library' is a tribute to the life of superstar evangelist and 'pastor to the presidents' Billy Graham, a Charlotte native. The 90-minute tour, 'The Journey of Faith', starts with a gospel-preaching animatronic cow then spotlights key moments in Graham's life, including his transformative 1949 tent revival in Los Angeles (where he first inspired *Unbroken* hero, Louis Zamperini). The tour is engaging and informative, especially if you're curious about Graham's journey and the roots of modern evangelicalism.

Levine Museum of the New South MUSEUM
(www.museumofthenewsouth.org; 200 E 7th St; adult/child 6-18yr $8/5; 10am-5pm Mon-Sat, noon-5pm Sun) Interested in the South's complicated post–Civil War history? Then set aside an hour or two for the comprehensive *From Cotton Fields to Skyscrapers* exhibit at this slick museum, which spotlights the cotton industry, Jim Crow laws, sit-ins, women's advancement and recent immigration trends.

NASCAR Hall of Fame MUSEUM
(www.nascarhall.com; 400 E Martin Luther King Blvd; adult/child 5-12yr $20/13; 10am-6pm) The race car simulator at this rip-roaring museum hurtles you onto the track and into an eight-car race that feels surprisingly real. Elsewhere, learn the history of this American-born sport (which traces back to moonshine running), check out six generations of race cars and test your pit crew skills. NASCAR, if you're wondering, is short for National Association for Stock Car Auto Racing.

One quibble? Exhibits are geared toward visitors who have some knowledge of cars and racing, so casual fans be warned!

★US National Whitewater Center ADVENTURE SPORTS
(www.usnwc.org; 5000 Whitewater Center Pkwy; all-sport day pass adult/child under 10yr $54/44, individual activities $20-25, 3hr canopy tours $89; dawn-dusk) A beyond-awesome hybrid of nature center and waterpark, this 400-acre facility is home to the largest artificial white-water river in the world, whose rapids serve as training grounds for Olympic canoe and kayak teams. Paddle it yourself as part of a guided rafting trip, or try one of the center's other adventurous activities: multiple ropes courses, an outdoor rock-climbing wall, paddleboarding, zip lines and miles of wooded hiking and mountain-biking trails. Parking is $5.

Sip a craft brew and watch the kayaks in action from the Pump House Biergarten.

Sleeping & Eating

Because so many uptown hotels cater to the business traveler, rates are often lower on weekends. Cheaper chains cluster off I-85 and I-77.

Uptown eating and drinking options draw the preppy young banker set; you'll see more tattoos at the laid-back bars and bistros of NoDa. Numerous breweries have opened across the city in the last few years. Several of the best line N Davidson St. See www.charlottesgotalot.com/breweries for a full list.

Dunhill Hotel BOUTIQUE HOTEL $$
(704-332-4141; www.dunhillhotel.com; 237 N Tryon St; r from $219; P ❄ @) The staff shines at this heart-of-uptown hotel, and the property has been welcoming guests since 1929. Classic decor gives a nod to the 1920s, but large flat-screen TVs and Keurig coffeemakers keep the rooms firmly in the 21st century. Parking is $18 per night.

Hyatt Place Charlotte Downtown HOTEL $$
(704-227-0500; www.charlottedowntown.place.hyatt.com; 222 S Caldwell St, GPS: 459 E 3rd St;

r from $229; P ✳ 🛜) The breakfast spread is impressive at this mod hotel perched on the edge of uptown. Rooms are spare and contemporary, and big windows offer sweeping views of the city. Get tipsy in style at Fahrenheit, the sultry rooftop bar. The hotel lobby is on the 10th floor.

Valet parking is $20 per night, but a cheaper, machine-pay city lot is behind the hotel.

Price's Chicken Coop   SOUTHERN $

(www.priceschickencoop.com; 1614 Camden Rd; mains $2-12; ⊙10am-6pm Tue-Sat) A Charlotte institution, scruffy Price's regularly makes 'Best Fried Chicken in America' lists. Line up to order your 'dark quarter' or 'white half' from the army of white-jacketed cooks, then take your bounty outside – there's no seating. Latta Park is a few blocks east on E Park Ave if you want to spread out. Cash only but an ATM on-site.

Amelie's French Bakery & Cafe   CAFE $

(www.ameliesfrenchbakery.com; 2424 N Davidson St; pastries $2-6, sandwiches $6; ⊙24hr; 🛜) Stop by for fancy coffees, cheesy sandwiches on croissants and baguettes, and a decadent line-up of cookies, tarts, petits fours and slices of cake. It's an inviting place to plan your day or spend some time online. And it's open all the time.

★ Soul Gastrolounge

Tapas   SUSHI, SANDWICHES $$

(☑704-348-1848; www.soulgastrolounge.com; 1500 Central Ave; small plates $8-20, sushi $5-24, sandwiches $6-15; ⊙5pm-2am Mon-Sat, 11am-3pm & 5pm-2am Sun) In Plaza Midtown, this sultry but welcoming speakeasy serves a globally inspired selection of small plates. Choices are wide-ranging, from skewers to sushi rolls to Cuban and Vietnamese sandwiches, but the kitchen takes care to infuse each little snowflake with unique, satisfying flavors. The dancing tuna rolls with jalapeños and two spicy mayos is highly recommended if you like heat.

❶ Information

Check out the alt-weekly *Creative Loafing* (www. clclt.com) for entertainment listings.

Main Library (www.cmlibrary.org; 310 N Tryon ST; ⊙10am-8pm Mon-Thu, until 5pm Fri & Sat; 🛜♿) The public library has internet terminals and wi-fi.

Visitor Center (☑704-331-2700; www. charlottesgotalot.com; 330 S Tryon St; ⊙9am-5pm Mon-Sat) The downtown visitor center publishes maps and a visitors' guide.

❶ Getting There & Around

Charlotte Douglas International Airport (CLT; ☑704-359-4027; www.charmeck.org/depart ments/airport; 5501 Josh Birmingham Pkwy) is a US Airways hub with direct flights from Europe and the UK. Both the **Greyhound station** (601 W Trade St) and **Amtrak** (1914 N Tryon St) are handy to uptown. **Charlotte Area Transit** (www. charmeck.org; one-way fare $2.20) runs local bus and light-rail services. The Charlotte Transit Center in uptown is on Brevard St between 4th and Trade St.

North Carolina Mountains

The Cherokee came to these ancient mountains to hunt, followed by 18th-century Scots-Irish immigrants looking for a better life. Lofty towns like Blowing Rock drew the sickly, who came for the fresh air. Today, scenic drives, leafy trails and roaring rivers draw outdoor adventurers.

The Appalachians in the western part of the state include the Great Smoky, Blue Ridge, Pisgah and Black Mountain subranges. Carpeted in blue-green hemlock, pine and oak trees, these cool hills are home to cougars, deer, black bears, wild turkeys and great horned owls. Hiking, camping, climbing and rafting adventures abound,

BIKE-SHARING IN THE CAROLINAS

If you like exploring cities by bicycle, consider buying a 24-hour pass under the B-cycle bike-share programs in Charlotte, NC ($8; https://charlotte. bcycle.com) and Greenville, SC ($5; https://greenville.bcycle.com). In Charlotte, 24 bike stations dot uptown and nearby greenways, with 200 bikes available. In Greenville, there are 10 stations, many along popular Main St and near the Swamp Rabbit Trail, with 35 bikes in service. Note that these are bike *sharing* programs, not rentals. To encourage turnover, the 24-hour pass includes rides taken in 30 to 60 minute increments within the 24-hour time period. You must check the bikes in and out to avoid additional fees. Pay by credit card at the station kiosk.

and there's another jaw-dropping photo opportunity around every bend.

High Country

The northwestern corner of the state is known as 'High Country.' Its main towns are Boone, Blowing Rock and Banner Elk, all short drives from the Blue Ridge Pkwy. Boone is a lively college town, home to Appalachian State University (ASU). Blowing Rock and Banner Elk are quaint tourist centers near the winter ski areas.

⊙ Sights & Activities

Hwy 321 from Blowing Rock to Boone is studded with gem-panning mines and other tourist traps. In Boone, check out the shops on King St and keep an eye out for the bronze statue of local bluegrass legend Doc Watson. He's strumming his guitar on the corner of King and Depot Sts.

Grandfather Mountain HIKING
(☑ 828-733-4337; www.grandfather.com; Blue Ridge Pkwy, Mile 305; adult/child 4-12yr $20/9; ⊙ 8am-7pm Jun-Aug, closes earlier Sep-May) Hold up. Is the Mile High Suspension Bridge really swinging 1 mile above the ground? Not exactly, so don't fret if you don't love heights. The park's star attraction is 1-mile *above sea level*, but the chasm beneath? It's 80ft deep. Nothing to sneeze at, but the distance is a bit less horrifying. Lose the crowds on one of 11 hiking trails; the most difficult include steep hands-and-knees scrambles. A small museum and wildlife reserve spotlights local plants and animals.

In 2008 the family that owns the mountain sold the backcountry to the state park system, which opened the adjacent **Grandfather Mountain State Park** (www.ncparks.gov) the following year.

River and Earth Adventures OUTDOORS
(☑ 828-963-5491; www.raftcavehike.com; 1655 Hwy 105; half-/full-day rafting from $60/100; ⊛) Offers everything from family-friendly caving trips to rafting Class V rapids at Watauga Gorge. Eco-conscious guides even pack organic lunches. Canoe ($60), kayak ($35 to $60) and tube ($20) rentals.

⏣ Sleeping & Eating

Chain motels abound in Boone. You'll find private campgrounds and B&Bs scattered throughout the hills.

Mast Farm Inn B&B $$
(☑ 828-963-5857; www.themastfarminn.com; 2543 Broadstone Rd, Valle Crucis; r/cottages from $189/319; ℗ ❋ ☎) In the beautiful hamlet of Valle Crucis, this restored farmhouse defines rustic chic with worn hardwood floors, clawfoot tubs and handmade toffees on your bedside table. Eight cabins and cottages also available. The upscale mountain cuisine at the inn's restaurant, Simplicity, is worth a trip in itself. The Over Yonder, focusing on simpler Appalachian fare, opened in 2014.

Six Pence Pub PUB FOOD $$
(www.sixpencepub.com; 1121 Main St, Blowing Rock; mains $6-14; ⊙ restaurant 11:30am-10:30pm Sun-Thu, to midnight Fri & Sat, bar to 2am) The bartenders keep a sharp but friendly eye on things at this lively British pub, where the shepherd's pie comes neat, not messy.

Hob Nob Farm Cafe CAFE $$
(www.hobnobfarmcafe.com; 506 West King St, Boone; breakfast & lunch $3-11, dinner $9-14; ⊙ 10am-10pm Wed-Sun; ⊛) Gobble up avocado-tempeh melts, Thai curry bowls and sloppy burgers made from local beef at a wildly painted cottage near ASU. Brunch is served until 5pm.

ⓘ Information

Visitor Center (☑ 828-264-1299; www.highcountryhost.com; 1700 Blowing Rock Rd, Boone; ⊙ 9am-5pm Mon-Sat, to 3pm Sun) The High Country visitor center has info on accommodations and outdoors outfitters.

Asheville

With its homegrown microbreweries, decadent chocolate shops and stylish New Southern eateries, Asheville is one of the trendiest small cities in the East. Glossy magazines swoon for the place. But don't be put off by all the flash. At heart, Asheville is still an overgrown mountain town, and it holds tight to its traditional roots. Just look around. There's a busker fiddling a high lonesome tune on Biltmore Ave. Over there, hikers chow down after climbing Mt Pisgah. Cars swoop on and off the Blue Ridge Pkwy, which swings around the city. A huge artist population and a visible contingent of hard-core hippies also keep things real.

⊙ Sights & Activities

Downtown is compact and easy to negotiate on foot. The art-deco buildings remain

SCENIC DRIVE: BLUE RIDGE PARKWAY

You won't find one stoplight on the entire Blue Ridge Pkwy, which traverses the southern Appalachians from Virginia's Shenandoah National Park at Mile 0 to North Carolina's Great Smoky Mountains National Park at Mile 469.

Commissioned by President Franklin D Roosevelt as a Depression-era public-works project, it's one of America's classic drives. North Carolina's piece of the parkway twists and turns for 262 miles of killer mountain vistas.

The **National Park Service** (NPS; www.nps.gov/blri; ☉ May-Oct) runs campgrounds and visitor centers. Note that restrooms and gas stations are few and far between. For more details about stops, visit www.blueridgeparkway.org.

Parkway highlights and campgrounds include the following, from the Virginia border south:

Cumberland Knob (Mile 217.5) NPS visitor center; easy walk to the knob.

Doughton Park (Mile 241.1) Trails and camping.

Blowing Rock (Mile 291.8) Small town named for a craggy, commercialized cliff that offers great views, occasional updrafts and a Native American love story.

Moses H Cone Memorial Park (Mile 294.1) A lovely old estate with carriage trails and a craft shop.

Julian Price Memorial Park (Mile 296.9) Camping.

Grandfather Mountain (Mile 305.1) Hugely popular for its mile-high pedestrian 'swinging bridge.' Also has a nature center and a small wildlife reserve.

Linville Falls (Mile 316.4) Short hiking trails to the falls; campsites.

Little Switzerland (Mile 334) Old-style mountain resort.

Mt Mitchell State Park (Mile 355.5) Highest peak east of the Mississippi (6684ft); hiking and camping.

Craggy Gardens (Mile 364) Hiking trails explode with rhododendron blossoms in summer.

Folk Art Center (Mile 382) High-end Appalachian crafts for sale.

Blue Ridge Pkwy Visitor Center (Mile 384) Inspiring film, interactive map, trail information.

Mt Pisgah (Mile 408.8) Hiking, camping, restaurant, inn.

Graveyard Fields (Mile 418) Short hiking trails to waterfalls.

much as they were in 1930. The shopping's fantastic, with everything from hippie-dippy candle shops to vintage shops to trendy boutiques and high-end local art. Start your shopping on Lexington Ave. West Asheville is an up-and-coming area, still gritty but very cool. On Friday nights, look for the drum circle on Pack Square in the heart of downtown.

★ **Biltmore Estate**   HOUSE, GARDENS
(☎ 800-411-3812; www.biltmore.com; 1 Approach Rd; adult/child 10-16yr $60/30; ☉ house 9am-4:30pm) The country's largest privately owned home, and Asheville's number-one tourist attraction, the Biltmore was built in 1895 for shipping and railroad heir George Washington Vanderbilt II. He modeled it after the grand chateaux he'd seen on his various European jaunts. Viewing the estate and its 250 acres of gorgeously manicured grounds and gardens takes several hours.

Tours of the house are self-guided. To get the most out of your visit, pay an extra $10 for the informative audio tour. Also available is a behind-the-scenes guided tour ($17) covering the servants, guest rooms and parties. In summer, children visiting with an adult are free.

Beyond the house, there are numerous cafes, a gift shop the size of a small supermarket, a hoity-toity hotel and an award-winning winery with free tastings. In Antler Village, the new Biltmore Legacy exhibit *The Vanderbilts at Home and Abroad* provides a more personal look at the family.

Chimney Rock Park
PARK

(www.chimneyrockpark.com; Hwy 64/74A; adult/child 5-15yr $15/7; ☉8:30am-5:30pm mid-Mar–Oct, hours vary Nov-mid-Mar) Views of the Broad River and Lake Lure are superb from atop the namesake chimney – a 315ft granite monolith. An elevator takes visitors up to the chimney, but the real draw is the exciting hike around the cliffs to a 404ft waterfall. The park, once privately owned, is now part of the state park system; access to the rock is still managed commercially. The park is a 20-mile drive southeast of Asheville.

Thomas Wolfe Memorial
HOUSE

(www.wolfememorial.com; 52 N Market St; museum free, house tours adult/child 7-17yr $5/2; ☉9am-5pm Tue-Sat) This downtown memorial, with a small museum and a separate house tour, honors *Look Homeward Angel* author Thomas Wolfe. The author grew up in Asheville, which was the inspiration for the novel's setting.

Tours

Brews Cruise
MICROBREWERIES

(☑828-545-5181; www.ashevillebrewscruise.com; per person $57) Tour several of Asheville's microbreweries, with samples.

Lazoom Comedy Tour
COMEDY

(☑828-225-6932; www.lazoomtours.com; per person $21-29) For a hysterically historical tour of the city, hop on the purple bus – and bring your own booze.

🛏 Sleeping

The **Asheville Bed & Breakfast Association** (☑877-262-6867; www.ashevillebba.com) handles bookings for numerous area B&Bs, from gingerbread cottages to alpine cabins.

Sweet Peas
HOSTEL $

(☑828-285-8488; www.sweetpeashostel.com; 23 Rankin Ave; dm/pod/r $28/35/60; P❄@☎) This spick-and-span hostel gleams with IKEA-like style, with shipshape steel bunk beds and blond-wood sleeping 'pods.' The loftlike space is very open and can be noisy (a downstairs pub adds to the ruckus) – what you lose in privacy and quiet, you gain in style, cleanliness, sociability and an unbeatable downtown location.

Campfire Lodgings
CAMPGROUND $$

(☑828-658-8012; www.campfirelodgings.com; 116 Appalachian Village Rd; tent sites $35-38, RV sites $45-65, yurts $115-135, cabins $160; P❄☎) All yurts should have flat-screen TVs, don't you think? Sleep like the world's most stylish Mongolian nomad in one of these furnished multiroom tents, on the side of a wooded hill. Cabins and tent sites are also available. Wi-fi access at RV sites, which have stunning valley views.

Omni Grove Park Inn
RESORT $$$

(☑828-252-2711; www.omnihotels.com; 290 Macon Ave; r from $349; P❄@☎❄❄) This titanic arts-and-crafts-style stone lodge has a hale-and-hearty look that sets a tone for adventure. But no worries modern mavens, the well-appointed rooms sport 21st-century amenities. The spa is an underground grotto with stone pools and an indoor waterfall. Feeling sporty? The property offers a golf course and tennis courts, and the Nantahala Outdoor Center (p345) has a 'basecamp' here.

The hotel turned 100 in 2013. The resort fee is $25 per day. The pet fee is $150 per stay.

Aloft Asheville
HOTEL $$$

(☑828-232-2838; www.aloftasheville.com; 51 Biltmore Ave; r from $320; P❄@☎❄❄) With a giant chalkboard in the lobby, a groovy young staff and an outdoor clothing store on the 1st floor, this place looks like the seventh circle of hipster. The only thing missing is a wool-cap-wearing bearded guy drinking a hoppy microbrew– oh, wait, over there. We jest. Once settled, you'll find the staff knowledgeable, the rooms spacious and the vibe convivial.

The hotel is close to several downtown hot spots, including Wicked Weed Brewery and the Orange Peel.

🍴 Eating

Asheville is a great foodie town – many visitors come here just to eat!

⭐ White Duck Taco Shop
MEXICAN $

(www.whiteducktacoshop.com; 12 Biltmore Ave; tacos under $7; ☉11:30am-9pm) The chalkboard menu at this downtown taco shop will give you fits – every taco sounds like a must-have flavor bomb: spicy buffalo chicken with blue cheese sauce, crispy pork belly, mole-roasted duck. Even better? These soft tacos are hefty. The chips and salsa appetizer comes with three salsas, and it works well for a group. The margaritas are mighty fine too.

In the River Arts District? Stop by the original location at 1 Roberts St.

12 Bones BARBECUE $
(www.12bones.com; 5 Riverside Dr; dishes $6-21; ⊙11am-4pm Mon-Fri) How good is the BBQ? Well, President Obama and wife Michelle stopped by a few years ago for a meal. The slow-cooked meats are smoky tender, and the sides, from the jalapeño cheese grits to the buttery green beans, will have you kissing your mama and blessing the day you were born. Order at the counter and grab a picnic table.

**French Broad
Chocolate Lounge** BAKERY, DESSERTS $
(www.frenchbroadchocolates.com; 10 S Pack Sq; desserts under $7; ⊙11am-11pm Sun-Thu, to midnight Fri & Sat) This beloved downtown chocolate shop may have moved to larger, glossier digs beside Pack Square Park, but she hasn't lost her chocolate heart. Small-batch organic chocolates, chunky chocolate brownies, chocolate-dipped ginger cookies, a sippable 'liquid truffle'...hey, where'd you go?

★**Cúrate** SPANISH, TAPAS $$
(☑828-239-2946; www.curatetapasbar.com; 11 Biltmore Ave; small plates $4-20) This convivial place celebrates the simple charms and sensual flavors of traditional Spanish tapas, with a few Southern twists here and there: tender lamb skewers with Moorish spices; spicy chorizo wrapped in potato chips; sautéed shrimp with sliced garlic. This is a place to savor the flavors, order another glass of garnacha and converse with your dinner companions, not your phone.

Reservations are a must, especially on weekends, but you can probably snag a bar seat fairly quickly after 9pm. And calling it Karate is only funny once.

🍷 **Drinking & Nightlife**

Downtown Asheville has a range of bars and cafes, from frat-boy beer halls to hippie holes-in-the-wall to spare new microbreweries. West Asheville has a more laid-back townie vibe. Stop by the visitor center or ask your hotel for a copy of the free *Field Guide to Breweries*, which provides key details and maps for the breweries (currently 27), taprooms and beer pubs on the **Asheville Ale Trail** (www.ashevillealetrail.com).

Wicked Weed MICROBREWERY
(www.wickedweedbrewing.com; 91 Biltmore Ave; ⊙11:30-11pm Mon & Tue, to midnight Wed & Thu, to 1am Fri & Sat, noon-11pm Sun) Henry VIII called hops 'a wicked and pernicious weed' that ruined the taste of beer. His subjects kept quaffing it anyway – just like the hordes at this restaurant and microbrewery, which overflows with hoppy brews and lively crowds. In a former gas station with a wide front patio, it's a big and breezy spot to chill.

The downstairs taproom can get elbow-to-elbow on weekend nights.

Hi-Wire Brewing Co MICROBREWERY
(www.hiwirebrewing.com; 197 Hilliard Ave; ⊙4-11pm Mon-Thu, 2pm-2am Fri, noon-2am Sat, 1-10pm Sun) Beers are named for old-school circus acts at this swift-growing downtown brewery. The brews are easy drinking, and the taproom is a chilled place to hang with friends on a Saturday afternoon.

Thirsty Monk BEER HALL
(www.monkpub.com; 92 Patton Ave; ⊙4pm-midnight Mon-Thu, noon-2am Fri & Sat, noon-10pm Sun) Try a variety of North Carolina craft beers and plenty of Belgian ales at this scruffy but lovable beer bar.

☆ **Entertainment**

Orange Peel LIVE MUSIC
(www.theorangepeel.net; 101 Biltmore Ave; tickets $10-35) For live music, try this warehouse-sized place showcasing big-name indie and punk.

ℹ **Information**

Pack Memorial Library (67 Haywood Ave; ⊙10am-8pm Mon-Thu, to 6pm Fri, to 5pm Sat; 🛜) Free wi-fi, and computers with free internet.
Visitor Center (☑828-258-6129; www.exploreasheville.com; 36 Montford Ave; ⊙8:30am-5:30pm Mon-Fri, 9am-5pm Sat & Sun) The shiny visitor center is at I-240 exit 4C. You can buy Biltmore admission tickets here, with a reduced rate for the audio tour. Downtown, there is a satellite visitor center, with restrooms, beside Pack Square Park.

ℹ **Getting There & Around**

Asheville Transit (www.ashevilletransit.com; tickets $1) has 17 local bus routes that run from about 5:30am to 10:30pm Monday through Saturday, with reduced hours Sunday. There are free bike racks on the front of buses. **Greyhound** (2 Tunnel Rd) is about 1 mile northeast of downtown.

Twenty minutes south of town, **Asheville Regional Airport** (AVL; ☑828-684-2226; www.flyavl.com) has a handful of nonstop flights, including to/from Atlanta, Charlotte, Chicago and New York.

Great Smoky Mountains National Park

This moody and magical place sprawls across 521,000 acres in both North Carolina and Tennessee. It is one of the world's most diverse areas; landscapes range from deep, dim spruce forest to sunny meadows carpeted with daisies and Queen Anne's lace to wide, coffee-brown rivers. There's ample hiking and camping, and opportunities for horseback riding, bike rental and fly-fishing. Unfortunately, with more than 10 million annual visitors – which is the highest of any national park in the US – the place can get annoyingly crowded. The North Carolina side has less traffic than the Tennessee side, however, so even at the height of summer tourist season you'll still have room to roam.

Newfound Gap Rd/Hwy 441 is the only thoroughfare that crosses Great Smoky Mountains National Park, winding through the mountains from Gatlinburg, TN, to the town of Cherokee and the busy Oconaluftee Visitor Center (☑ 828-497-1904; www.nps.gov/grsm; 1194 Newfound Gap Rd, North Cherokee, NC; ☉ 8am-7:30pm Jun-Aug, hours vary Sep-May), in the southeast. Pick up your backcountry camping permits here. The Oconaluftee River Trail, one of only two in the park that allows leashed pets and bicycles, leaves from the visitor center and follows the river for 1.5 miles.

SMOKY MOUNTAINS DAY HIKES

These are a few of our favorite short hikes on, or bordering, the North Carolina side of the park.

Charlie's Bunion Follow the Appalachian Trail 4 miles from the Newfound Gap overlook to a rocky outcrop for sweeping mountain-and-valley views.

Big Creek Trail Hike an easy 2 miles to Mouse Creek Falls or go another 3 miles to a backcountry campground; the trailhead is near I-40 on the park's northeastern edge.

Boogerman Trail Moderate 7-mile loop passing old farmsteads; accessible via Cove Creek Rd.

Chasteen Creek Falls From Smokemont campground, this 4-mile round-trip passes a small waterfall.

The on-site **Mountain Farm Museum** (☑ 865-436-1200; www.nps.gov/grsm; ☉ dusk-dawn) FREE is a restored 19th-century farmstead, complete with barn, blacksmith shop and smokehouse (with real pig heads!), assembled from original buildings from different parts of the park. Just north is the 1886 **Mingus Mill** (☉ 9am-5pm daily mid-Mar–mid-Nov, plus Thanksgiving weekend) FREE, a turbine-powered mill that still grinds wheat and corn much as it always has. A few miles away the **Smokemont Campground** (www.nps.gov/grsm; tent & RV sites $20) is the only North Carolina campground open year-round.

To the east, remote **Cataloochee Valley** has several historic buildings to wander through and is a prime location for elk and black bears.

Around Great Smoky Mountains National Park

The state's westernmost tip is blanketed in parkland and sprinkled with tiny mountain towns. The area has a rich but sad Native American history – many of the original Cherokee inhabitants were forced off their lands during the 1830s and marched to Oklahoma on the Trail of Tears. Descendants of those who escaped are known as the Eastern Band of the Cherokee and many still live on the 56,000-acre Qualla Boundary territory at the edge of Great Smoky Mountains National Park.

The town of **Cherokee** anchors the Qualla Boundary with ersatz Native American souvenir shops, fast-food joints and **Harrah's Cherokee Casino** (www.caesars.com/harrahs-cherokee; 777 Casino Dr; ☉ 24hr), which has an impressive water and video display, the Rotunda, in the lobby. The best sight is the modern and engaging **Museum of the Cherokee Indian** (☑ 828-497-3481; www.cherokeemuseum.org; 589 Tsali Blvd/Hwy 441, at Drama Rd; adult/child 6-12yr $11/7; ☉ 9am-5pm daily, to 7pm Mon-Sat Jun-Aug), with an informative exhibit about the Trail of Tears.

South of Cherokee, the contiguous Pisgah and Nantahala National Forests have more than a million acres of dense hardwood trees, windswept mountain balds and some of the country's best white water. Both contain portions of the Appalachian Trail. **Pisgah National Forest** highlights include the bubbling baths in the village of **Hot Springs** (www.hotspringsnc.org), the natural waterslide at **Sliding Rock**, and the 3.2-mile round-trip hike to the summit of 5721ft **Mt Pisgah**, which has a view of Cold Mountain (of book and movie fame). **Nantahala National Forest** has several recreational lakes and dozens of roaring waterfalls.

Just north of Nantahala is quaint **Bryson City**, an ideal jumping-off point for outdoor adventures. It's home to the huge and highly recommended **Nantahala Outdoor Center** (NOC; ☑ 828-366-7502, 888-905-7238; www.noc. com; 13077 Hwy 19/74; kayak/canoe rental per day $30/50, guided trips $30-189), which specializes in wet and wild rafting trips down the Nantahala River. The 500-acre site also offers zip-lining and mountain biking. It even has its own lodge, a hostel, a year-round restaurant and one seasonal BBQ and beer joint (May through September). The Appalachian Trail rolls across the property, too.

From the Bryson City depot, the **Great Smoky Mountains Railroad** (☑ 800-872-4681; www.gsmr.com; 226 Everett St; Nantahala Gorge trip adult/child 2-12yr from $55/31) runs scenic train excursions through the dramatic river valley.

For lodging and dining try the lofty **Fryemont Inn** (☑ 828-488-2159; www.fryemontinn. com; 245 Fryemont St; lodge/ste/cabins from $110/180/245; nonguests breakfast $5-9, dinner $21-31; ⊙ restaurant 8am-10am & 6-8pm Sun-Tue, 6-9pm Fri & Sat mid-Apr–late Nov; ℗ ✷), a family-owned lodge and restaurant. The bark-covered inn has a front-porch view of the Smokies and downtown Bryson City.

SOUTH CAROLINA

Moss-draped oaks. Stately mansions. Wide beaches. Rolling mountains. And an ornery streak as old as the state itself. Ah yes, South Carolina, where the accents are thicker and the traditions more dear. From its Revolutionary War patriots to its 1860s secessionist government to its current crop of outspoken legislators, the Palmetto State has never shied away from a fight.

From the silvery sands of the Atlantic Coast, the state climbs westward from the Coastal Plain across the Piedmont and up into the Blue Ridge Mountains. Most travelers stick to the coast, with its splendid antebellum cities and palm-tree-studded beaches. But the interior has a wealth of sleepy old towns, wild and undeveloped state parks and spooky black-water swamps. Along the sea islands you hear the sweet songs of the Gullah, a culture and language created by former slaves who held onto many West African traditions through the ravages of time.

From well-bred, gardenia-scented Charleston to bright, tacky Myrtle Beach, South Carolina is always a fascinating destination.

History

More than 28 separate tribes of Native Americans have lived in what is now South Carolina, many of them Cherokee who were later forcibly removed during the Trail of Tears era.

The English founded the Carolina colony in 1670, with settlers pouring in from the royal outpost of Barbados, giving the port city known as Charles Towne a Caribbean flavor. West African slaves were brought over to turn the thick coastal swamps into rice paddies and by the mid-1700s the area was deeply divided between the slave-owning aristocrats of the Lowcountry and the poor Scots-Irish and German farmers of the rural backcountry.

South Carolina was the first state to secede from the Union, and the first battle of the Civil War occurred at Fort Sumter in Charleston Harbor. The end of the war left much of the state in ruins.

South Carolina traded in cotton and textiles for most of the 20th century. It remains a relatively poor agricultural state, though with a thriving coastal tourism business.

In recent years the Palmetto State has garnered headlines because of its politicians, from Nikki Haley, the state's first woman governor, to Congressman Joe Wilson, who yelled 'You lie!' during a speech by President Obama to Congress. Congressman Mark Sanford, while serving as governor, famously claimed that he was hiking the Appalachian Trail when he was in fact visiting his Argentinian girlfriend.

In 2015, following the shooting of nine members of a historically black church for what appeared to be racially motivated reasons, the state legislature voted to remove the Confederate flag from the grounds of the state capitol, where it had flown since 1962.

ℹ Information

South Carolina Department of Parks, Recreation & Tourism (☑ 803-734-1700; www. discoversouthcarolina.com; 1205 Pendleton St, Columbia; ☎) Sends out the state's official vacation guide. The state's nine highway

SOUTH CAROLINA FACTS

Nickname Palmetto State

Population 4.8 million

Area 30,109 sq miles

Capital city Columbia (population 133,300)

Other cities Charleston (population 127,900)

Sales tax 6%, plus up to 8.5% extra tax on accommodations

Birthplace of Jazzman Dizzy Gillespie (1917–93), political activist Jesse Jackson (b 1941), boxer Joe Frazier (b 1944), *Wheel of Fortune* hostess Vanna White (b 1957)

Home of The first US public library (1698), museum (1773) and steam railroad (1833)

Politics Leans Republican

Famous for Firing the first shot of the Civil War, from Charleston's Fort Sumter

State dance The shag

Driving distances Columbia to Charleston 115 miles, Charleston to Myrtle Beach 97 miles

welcome centers offer free wi-fi. Ask inside for password.

South Carolina State Parks (☑ camping reservations 866-345-7275, 803-734-0156; www.southcarolinaparks.com) The helpful website lists activities and hiking trails, and allows online reservations for campsites ($6 to $40 per night).

Charleston

This lovely city will embrace you with the warmth and hospitality of an old and dear friend – who died in the 18th century. We jest, but the cannons, cemeteries and carriage rides do conjure an earlier era. And that historic romanticism, along with the food and Southern graciousness, is what makes Charleston one of the most popular tourist destinations in the South, drawing more than 4.8 million visitors every year.

How best to enjoy its charms? Charleston is a city for savoring – stroll past the historic buildings, admire the antebellum architecture, stop to smell the blooming jasmine and enjoy long dinners on the verandah. It's also a place for romance; everywhere you turn another blushing bride is standing on the steps of yet another charming church.

In the high season the scent of gardenia and honeysuckle mixes with the tang of horses from the aforementioned carriage tours that clip-clop down the cobblestones. In winter the weather is milder and the crowds thinner, making Charleston a great bet for off-season travel.

History

Well before the Revolutionary War, Charles Towne (named for Charles II) was one of the busiest ports on the eastern seaboard, the center of a prosperous rice-growing and trading colony. With influences from the West Indies and Africa, France and other European countries, it became a cosmopolitan city, often compared to New Orleans.

A tragic but important component of the city's history? Slavery. Charleston was a key port and trade center for the slave industry, and bustling slave auction houses clustered near the Cooper River. The first shots of the Civil War rang out at Fort Sumter, in Charleston's harbor. After the war, as the labor-intensive rice plantations became uneconomical without slave labor, the city's importance declined.

A mass shooting in the historically black Emanuel African Methodist Episcopal (AME) Church in 2015 reopened questions about the city's racially fraught past and its effects on the present.

⊙ Sights

◉ Historic District

The quarter south of Beaufain and Hasell Sts has the bulk of the antebellum mansions, shops, bars and cafes. At the southernmost tip of the peninsula are the antebellum mansions of the Battery. A loose path, the **Gateway Walk**, winds through several church grounds and graveyards between **St John's Lutheran Church** (5 Clifford St) and **St Philip's Church** (146 Church St).

Old Exchange & Provost Dungeon HISTORIC BUILDING
(www.oldexchange.org; 122 E Bay St; adult/child 7-12yr $10/5; ☉9am-5pm; ⊕) Kids love the creepy dungeon, used as a prison for pirates and for American patriots held by the British during the Revolutionary War. The

cramped space sits beneath a stately Georgian Palladian customs house completed in 1771. Costumed guides lead the dungeon tours. Exhibits about the city are displayed on the upper floors.

Combination ticket with the Old Slave Mart Museum is adult/child $15/8.

Old Slave Mart Museum   MUSEUM
(www.nps.gov/nr/travel/charleston/osm.htm; 6 Chalmers St; adult/child 5-17yr $7/5; ☺9am-5pm Mon-Sat) Ryan's Mart was an open-air market that auctioned African men, women and children in the mid-1800s. It's now a museum about South Carolina's shameful past. Text-heavy exhibits illuminate the slave experience; the few artifacts, such as leg shackles, are especially chilling. For first-hand stories, listen to the oral recollections of former slave Elijah Green and others.

Combination ticket with the Old Exchange is adult/child $15/8.

Gibbes Museum of Art   GALLERY
(www.gibbesmuseum.org; 135 Meeting St; adult/child $9/7; ☺10am-5pm Tue-Sat, 1-5pm Sun) Houses a decent collection of American and Southern works. The contemporary collection includes works by local artists, with Lowcountry life as a highlight. The museum was closed for renovations in 2015 but is scheduled to reopen in the spring of 2016.

Battery & White Point Gardens   GARDENS
The Battery is the southern tip of the Charleston Peninsula, buffered by a seawall. Stroll past cannons and statues of military heroes in the gardens then walk the promenade and look for Fort Sumter.

Kahal Kadosh Beth Elohim   SYNAGOGUE
(www.kkbe.org; 90 Hasell St; ☺tours 10am-noon & 1:30-3:30pm Mon-Thu, 10am-noon & 1-3pm Fri, 1-3:30pm Sun) The oldest continuously used synagogue in the country. There are free docent-led tours; check website for times.

Rainbow Row   AREA
With its candy-colored houses, this stretch of lower E Bay St is one of the most photographed areas of town. The houses are around the corner from White Point Garden.

Historic Homes
About half a dozen majestic historic homes are open to visitors. Discounted combination tickets may tempt you to see more, but one or two will be enough for most people. Guided tours run every half-hour and start before the closing times noted in our reviews.

Aiken-Rhett House   HISTORIC BUILDING
(www.historiccharleston.org; 48 Elizabeth St; adult/child 6-16yr $12/5; ☺10am-5pm Mon-Sat, 2-5pm Sun) The only surviving urban plantation, this house gives a fascinating glimpse into antebellum life. The role of slaves is also presented, and you can wander into their dorm-style quarters behind the main house. The Historic Charleston Foundation manages the house with a goal of preserving and conserving, but not restoring, the property, meaning there have been few alterations.

Joseph Manigault House   HISTORIC BUILDING
(www.charlestonmuseum.org; 350 Meeting St; adult/child 13-17yr/child 3-12yr $12/10/5; ☺9am-5pm Mon-Sat, noon-5pm Sun) The three-story Federal-style house was once the showpiece of a French Huguenot rice planter. Don't miss the tiny neoclassical temple in the garden.

Nathaniel Russell House   HISTORIC BUILDING
(www.historiccharleston.org; 51 Meeting St; adult/child 6-16yr $12/5; ☺10am-5pm Mon-Sat, 2-5pm Sun) A spectacular, self-supporting spiral staircase is the highlight at this 1808 Federal-style house, built by a Rhode Islander, known in Charleston as 'the king of the Yankees.' The small but lush English garden is also notable as is the square-circle-rectangle footprint of the home.

◉ **Marion Square**

Formerly home to the state weapons arsenal, this 10-acre park is Charleston's living room, with various monuments and an excellent Saturday farmers market.

Charleston Museum   MUSEUM
(www.charlestonmuseum.org; 360 Meeting St; adult/child 13-17yr/child 3-12yr $12/10/5; ☺9am-5pm Mon-Sat, noon-5pm Sun) Founded in 1773, this claims to be the country's oldest museum. It's helpful and informative if you're looking for historic background before strolling through the historic district. Exhibits spotlight various periods of Charleston's long and storied history.

Artifacts include a whale skeleton, slave tags and the 'secession table' used for the signing of the state's secession documents. And don't miss Charleston's polar bear.

◉ **Aquarium Wharf**

Aquarium Wharf surrounds pretty Liberty Sq and is a great place to stroll and watch the tugboats guiding ships into the fourth-largest

THE SOUTH CHARLESTON

GULLAH CULTURE

African slaves were transported from the region known as the Rice Coast (Sierra Leone, Senegal, Gambia and Angola) to a landscape of remote islands that was shockingly similar – swampy coastlines, tropical vegetation and hot, humid summers.

These new African Americans were able to retain many of their homeland traditions, even after the fall of slavery and well into the 20th century. The resulting Gullah (also known as Geechee) culture has its own language, an English-based Creole with many African words and sentence structures, and many traditions, including fantastic story-telling, art, music and crafts. The Gullah culture is celebrated annually with the energetic **Gullah Festival** (www.theoriginalgullahfestival.org; ⊙ late May) in Beaufort.

container port in the US. The wharf is one of two embarkation points for tours to Fort Sumter; the other is at Patriot's Point.

Fort Sumter HISTORIC SITE
The first shots of the Civil War rang out at Fort Sumter, on a pentagon-shaped island in the harbor. A Confederate stronghold, the fort was shelled to bits by Union forces from 1863 to 1865. A few original guns and fortifications give a feel for the momentous history. The only way to get here is by **boat tour** (☑ boat tour 843-722-2628, park 843-883-3123; www.nps.gov/fosu; adult/child 4-11yr $19/12), which depart from 340 Concord St at 9.30am, noon and 2.30pm in summer (less frequently in winter) and from Patriot's Point in Mt Pleasant, across the river, at 10:45am, 1:30pm and 4pm from mid-March to late August (less frequently the rest of the year).

⊙ Tours

Listing all of Charleston's walking, horse-drawn carriage, bus and boat tours could take up this entire book. Ask at the visitor center for the gamut.

Culinary Tours of Charleston CULINARY
(☑ 843-722-8687; www.culinarytoursofcharleston.com; 2½hr tour $50) You'll likely sample grits, pralines and BBQ on the Savor the Flavors of Charleston walking tour of restaurants and markets.

Adventure Harbor Tours BOAT
(☑ 843-442-9455; www.adventureharbortours.com; adult/child 3-12yr $55/30) Runs fun trips to uninhabited Morris Island – great for shelling.

Charleston Footprints WALKING
(☑ 843-478-4718; www.charlestonfootprints.com; 2hr tour $20) A highly rated walking tour of historical Charleston sights.

⭐ Festivals & Events

Lowcountry Oyster Festival FOOD
(www.charlestonrestaurantassociation.com/low-country-oyster-festival; ⊙ Jan) Oyster-lovers in Mt Pleasant feast on 80,000lb of the salty bivalves in January.

Spoleto USA PERFORMING ARTS
(www.spoletousa.org; ⊙ May) This 17-day performing-arts festival is Charleston's biggest event, with operas, dramas and concerts staged across the city.

MOJA Arts Festival PERFORMING ARTS
(www.mojafestival.com; ⊙ Sep) Spirited poetry readings and gospel concerts mark this two-week celebration of African American and Caribbean culture.

🛏 Sleeping

Staying in the historic downtown is the most attractive option, but it's also the most expensive, especially on weekends and in high season. The rates below are for high season (spring and early summer). The chain hotels on the highways and near the airport offer significantly lower rates. Hotel parking in central downtown is usually between $12 and $20 a night; accommodations on the fringes of downtown often have free parking.

The city is bursting with charming B&Bs serving Southern breakfasts and Southern hospitality. They fill up fast, so try using an agency such as **Historic Charleston B&B** (☑ 843-722-6606; www.historiccharlestonbedandbreakfast.com; 57 Broad St; ⊙ 9am-5pm Mon-Fri).

James Island County Park CAMPGROUND $
(☑ 843-795-4386; www.ccprc.com; 871 Riverland Dr; tent sites from $25, 8-person cottages $169; 🛜) A great budget option, this 643-acre park southwest of downtown has meadows, a marsh and a dog park. Rent bikes and kayaks or play the disc golf course. The park

offers shuttle services to downtown and Folly Beach ($10). Reservations are highly recommended. There are 124 campsites and 10 marsh-adjacent rental cottages. Cottages require a one-week rental June to August.

1837 Bed & Breakfast
B&B $$

(☎ 877-723-1837, 843-723-7166; www.1837bb.com; 126 Wentworth St; r $135-189; P ✳ ☎) Close to the College of Charleston, this B&B may bring to mind the home of your eccentric, antique-loving aunt. The 1837 has nine charmingly overdecorated rooms, including three in the old brick carriage house.

Indigo Inn
BOUTIQUE HOTEL $$

(☎ 843-577-5900; www.indigoinn.com; 1 Maiden Lane; r $249; P ✳ ☎ ☒) Our favorite part? The tasty ham biscuits at breakfast. Other perks include a prime location in the middle of the historic district and an oasis-like private courtyard, where guests can enjoy free wine and cheese by the fountain. Decor gives a nod to the 18th century, and the beds are quite comfy. Pets are $40 per night.

Town & Country Inn & Suites
HOTEL $$

(☎ 843-571-1000; www.thetownandcountryinn. com; 2008 Savannah Hwy; r/ste from $169/189; P ✳ @ ☎ ☒) About six miles from downtown, Town & Country offers modern and stylish rooms at a reasonable price. The inn is a good launch pad if you want to get a jump on traffic for a morning visit to the Ashley River plantations.

★ Ansonborough Inn
HOTEL $$$

(☎ 800-522-2073; www.ansonboroughinn.com; 21 Hasell St; r from $299; P ✳ @ ☎) Droll neo-Victorian touches like the Persian-carpeted glass elevator, the closet-sized British pub and the formal portraits of dogs add a sense of fun to this intimate historic district hotel, which also manages to feel like an antique sailing ship. Huge guest rooms mix old and new, with worn leather couches, high ceilings and flat-screen TVs.

Complimentary wine and cheese social, with great pimiento cheese, runs from 5pm to 6pm.

Vendue Inn
INN $$$

(☎ 843-577-7970; www.vendueinn.com; 19 Vendue Range; r/ste $265/435; P ✳ ☎) Fresh off a $4.8 million revamp and expansion, this boutique inn exudes a smart modern style that is also very inviting. Reimagined as an art hotel, it displays artwork property-wide, and the inn itself unfurls like a masterpiece of

architecture and design. Simplicity and comfort blend seamlessly in rooms in the main building, while eye-catching art adds oomph to classically styled rooms across the street.

The popular Rooftop Bar is worth a stop even if you're not staying here. Parking is $16 per night.

✗ Eating

Charleston is one of America's finest eating cities, and there are enough fabulous restaurants here for a town three times its size. The 'classic' Charleston establishments stick to fancy seafood with a French flair, while many of the trendy up-and-comers are reinventing Southern cuisine with a focus on the area's copious local bounty, from oysters to heirloom rice to heritage pork. On Saturday, stop by the terrific **farmers market** (Marion Sq; ☉ 8am-1pm Sat Apr-Oct).

Sugar Bakeshop
BAKERY $

(www.sugarbake.com; 59 1/2 Cannon St; pastries under $4; ☉ 10am-6pm Mon-Fri, 11am-5pm Sat) The staff is as sweet as the cupcakes at Sugar, a teensy space north of downtown. If available, try the Lady Baltimore cupcake, a retro Southern specialty with dried fruit and white frosting.

Artisan Meat Share
SANDWICHES $

(www.artisanmeatsharecharleston.com; 33 Spring St; sandwiches $7-12; ☉ 11am-7pm Mon-Fri, 10am-7pm Sat & Sun) Meat, man, meat. Stuffed in a biscuit. Piled high on potato bread. Or lurching across your charcuterie board – damn that's fresh. Order at the counter, find a seat if you can, then give a nod to artisan hipsters, bless their hearts. You know the drill: fresh, local, delicious and the condiments are housemade. The pea and peanut salad is superb.

Gaulart & Maliclet
FRENCH $

(www.fastandfrenchcharleston.com; 98 Broad St; breakfast under $7, lunch $5-9, dinner $5-18; ☉ 8am-4pm Mon, to 10pm Tue-Thu, to 10:30pm Fri & Sat) Oooh la la. Locals crowd around the shared tables at this tiny spot, known as 'Fast & French,' to nibble on Gallic cheeses and sausages or nightly specials ($16) that include bread, soup, a main dish and wine.

Fleet Landing
SEAFOOD $$

(☎ 843-722-8100; www.fleetlanding.net; 186 Concord St; lunch $9-23, dinner $10-26; ☉ 11am-4pm daily, 5-10pm Sun-Thu, to 11pm Fri & Sat) Come here for the perfect Charleston lunch: a river view, a cup of she-crab soup with a splash of sherry, and a big bowl of shrimp and grits. Housed in an old naval building on a pier, Fleet Landing is a convenient and scenic spot to enjoy fresh fish, a fried seafood platter or a burger after a morning of downtown exploring.

Smothered in tasso ham gravy, the shrimp and grits here look dirty, not high-falutin', and they're our favorite version in the city.

Poe's Tavern
PUB FOOD $$
(www.poestavern.com; 2210 Middle St, Sullivan's Island; mains $9-13; ⊘11am-2am) On a sunny day the front porch of Poe's on Sullivan's Island is the place to be. The tavern's namesake, master of the macabre Edgar Allan Poe, was once stationed at nearby Fort Moultrie. The burgers are superb, and the Amontillado comes with guacamole, jalapeño jack, pico de gallo and chipotle sour cream. Quoth the raven: 'Gimme more.'

Xiao Bao Biscuit
ASIAN $$
(www.xiaobaobiscuit.com; 224 Rutledge Ave, cnr of Spring St; lunch $10, dinner small plates $8-10, mains $12-17; ⊘11:30am-2pm & 5:30-10pm Mon-Sat) Exposed brick walls, concrete floor and housed in a former gas station – this casual but stylish eatery hits the hipster high marks. But the food? Now we're talking. The short but palate-kicking menu spotlights simple pan-Asian fare enhanced by local ingredients and spicy flavors. For something different and memorable, try the *okonomiyaki* – a cabbage pancake – with egg and bacon.

Hominy Grill
NEW SOUTHERN $$
(www.hominygrill.com; 207 Rutledge Ave; breakfast $8-16, lunch & dinner mains $9-19; ⊘7:30am-9pm Mon-Fri, 9am-9pm Sat, to 3pm Sun; 🖉) Slightly off the beaten path, this neighborhood cafe serves modern, vegetarian-friendly Lowcountry cuisine in an old barbershop. The shaded patio is tops for brunch.

★FIG
NEW SOUTHERN $$$
(☑843-805-5900; www.eatatfig.com; 232 Meeting St; mains $29-31; ⊘5:30-10:30pm Mon-Thu, to 11pm Fri & Sat) FIG has been a long-time foodie favorite, and it's easy to see why. Welcoming staff, efficient but unrushed service, and top-notch nouvelle Southern fare from James Beard Award winner Mike Lata. The six nightly dishes embrace what's fresh and local from the sea and local farms and mills. FIG stands for Food is Good. And the gourmands agree.

Reservations highly recommended, but rogue solos might be able to snag a seat quickly at the communal table or bar.

Drinking & Nightlife

Balmy Charleston evenings are perfect for lifting a cool cocktail or dancing to live blues. Check out the weekly *Charleston City Paper* and the 'Preview' section of Friday's *Post & Courier*.

Husk Bar
BAR
(www.huskrestaurant.com; 76 Queen St; ⊘from 4pm) Adjacent to Husk restaurant, this intimate brick-and-worn-wood spot recalls a speakeasy, with historic cocktails such as the Monkey Gland (gin, OJ, raspberry syrup).

Rooftop at Vendue Inn
BAR
(www.vendueinn.com; 23 Vendue Range; ⊘11:30am-10pm Sun-Thu, to midnight Fri & Sat) This rooftop bar has the best views of downtown, and the crowds to prove it. Enjoy crafts, cocktails and live music on Sundays (6pm to 9pm).

Closed for Business
PUB
(www.closed4business.com; 453 King St; ⊘11am-2am Mon-Sat, 10am-2pm Sun) A wide beer selection and raucous neighborhood pub vibe.

🔒 Shopping

The historic district is clogged with overpriced souvenir shops and junk markets. Head instead to King St: hit lower King for antiques, middle King for cool boutiques, and upper King for trendy design and gift shops. The main stretch of Broad St is known as 'Gallery Row' for its many art galleries.

Shops of Historic Charleston Foundation
GIFTS
(www.historiccharleston.org; 108 Meeting St; ⊘9am-6pm Mon-Sat, noon-5pm Sun) This place showcases jewelry, home furnishings and furniture inspired by the city's historic homes.

Charleston Crafts Cooperative
CRAFTS
(www.charlestoncrafts.org; 161 Church St; ⊘10am-6pm) A pricey, well-edited selection of contemporary South Carolina–made crafts such as sweetgrass baskets, hand-dyed silks and wood carvings.

Blue Bicycle Books   BOOKS
(www.bluebicyclebooks.com; 420 King St; ⊙10am-7:30pm Mon-Sat, 1-6pm Sun) Excellent new-and-used bookshop with a great selection of Southern history and culture.

ℹ Information

The City of Charleston maintains free public internet (wi-fi) access throughout the downtown area.

Charleston City Paper (www.charlestoncity-paper.com) Published each Wednesday, this alt-weekly has good entertainment and restaurant listings.

Police Station (☑ non-emergencies 843-577-7434; 180 Lockwood Blvd) The police station is just northwest of downtown.

Post & Courier (www.postandcourier.com) Charleston's daily newspaper.

Post Office (www.usps.com; 83 Broad St; ⊙11:30am-3:30pm) At the corner of Broad St and Meeting St.

University Hospital (Medical University of South Carolina; ☑ 843-792-1414; www.musc health.org; 171 Ashley Ave; ⊙24hr) Emergency room.

Visitor Center (☑843-853-8000; www. charlestoncvb.com; 375 Meeting St; ⊙8:30am-5pm Apr-Oct, to 5pm Nov-Mar) Find help with accommodations and tours or watch a half-hour video on Charleston history in this spacious renovated warehouse.

ℹ Getting There & Around

Charleston International Airport (CHS; ☑843-767-7000; www.chs-airport.com; 5500 International Blvd) is 12 miles outside of town in North Charleston, with nonstop flights to 18 destinations.

The **Greyhound station** (3610 Dorchester Rd) and the **Amtrak train station** (4565 Gaynor Ave) are both in North Charleston.

CARTA (www.ridecarta.com; one-way fare $1.75) runs city-wide buses; the free DASH street-cars do three loop routes from the visitor center.

Mt Pleasant

Across the Cooper River from Charleston is the residential and vacation community of Mt Pleasant, originally a summer retreat for early Charlestonians, along with the slim barrier resort islands of Isle of Palms and Sullivan's Island. Though increasingly glutted with traffic and strip malls, the area still has some charm, especially in the historic downtown, called the Old Village. Some good seafood restaurants overlook the water at Shem

---

MEXICAN HAT DANCE

Yes, that's a giant sombrero rising above I-95 on the North Carolina–South Carolina state line. *Bienvenidos* to **South of the Border** (www.thesouthoftheborder. com; 3346 Hwy 301 N Hamer), a Mexican-flavored monument to American kitsch. Begun in the 1950s as a fireworks stand – pyrotechnics are illegal in North Carolina – it's morphed into a combo rest stop, souvenir mall, motel and (mostly defunct) amusement park, promoted on hundreds of billboards by a wildly stereotypical Mexican cartoon character named Pedro. The place has been looking tired, but it's still worth a quick stop for a photo and some taffy.

Creek, where it's fun to dine creekside at sunset and watch the incoming fishing-boat crews unload their catch. This is also a good place to rent kayaks to tour the estuary.

◉ Sights

Patriot's Point Naval & Maritime Museum   MUSEUM
(☑866-831-1720; www.patriotspoint.org; 40 Patriots Point Rd; adult/child 6-11yr $20/12; ⊙9am-6:30pm) Patriot's Point Naval & Maritime Museum is home to the USS *Yorktown*, a giant aircraft carrier used extensively in WWII. You can tour the ship's flight deck, bridge and ready rooms and get a glimpse of what life was like for its sailors. Also on-site is a submarine, a naval destroyer, the Medal of Honor Museum and a re-created 'fire base' from Vietnam. You can also catch the Fort Sumter boat tour (p348). Parking is $5.

Boone Hall Plantation   HISTORIC BUILDING
(☑843-884-4371; www.boonehallplantation.com; 1235 Long Point Rd; adult/child 6-12yr $20/10; ⊙8:30am-6:30pm Mon-Sat, noon-5pm Sun early Mar-Aug, shorter hours Sep-Jan, closed Feb) Just 11 miles from downtown Charleston on Hwy 17N, Boone Hall Plantation is famous for its magical Avenue of Oaks, planted by Thomas Boone in 1743. Boone Hall is still a working plantation, though strawberries, tomatoes and Christmas trees long ago replaced cotton as the primary crop. The main house, built in 1936, is the fourth house on the site. The most compelling buildings are the Slave Street cabins, built between 1790 and 1810 and now lined with exhibits.

Ashley River Plantations

Three spectacular plantations line the Ashley River about a 20-minute drive from downtown Charleston. You'll be hard-pressed for time to visit all three in one outing, but you could squeeze in two (allow at least a couple of hours for each). Ashley River Rd is also known as SC 61, which can be reached from downtown Charleston via Hwy 17.

◉ Sights

★ **Middleton Place** HISTORIC BUILDING, GARDENS
(☏843-556-6020; www.middletonplace.org; 4300 Ashley River Rd; gardens adult/child 6-13yr $28/10, house museum tour adult & child extra $15; ⊙9am-5pm) Designed in 1741, this plantation's vast gardens are the oldest in the US. One hundred slaves spent a decade terracing the land and digging the precise geometric canals for the owner, wealthy South Carolina politician Henry Middleton. The bewitching grounds are a mix of classic formal French gardens and romantic woodland, bounded by flooded rice paddies and rare-breed farm animals. Union soldiers burned the main house in 1865; a 1755 guest wing, now housing the house museum, still stands.

The on-site inn is a series of ecofriendly modernist glass boxes overlooking the Ashley River. Enjoy a traditional Lowcountry plantation lunch of she-crab soup and hoppin' john at the highly regarded cafe.

Magnolia Plantation HOUSE, GARDENS
(www.magnoliaplantation.com; 3550 Ashley River Rd; adult/child 6-10yr $15/10, tours $8; ⊙8am-5:30pm Mar-Oct, to 4:30pm Nov-Feb) Up for a spooky stroll? Then follow the boardwalk through the trees and bog on the Swamp Garden tour – it's a unique experience. The 500-acre plantation, which has been owned by the Drayton family since 1676, is a veritable theme park. Enjoy a tram tour, a petting zoo and a guided house tour. At the reconstructed slave cabins, the Slavery to Freedom Tour traces the African American experience at the plantation.

Drayton Hall HOUSE
(☏843-769-2600; www.draytonhall.org; 3380 Ashley River Rd; adult/child $18/8; ⊙9am-5pm Mon-Sat, 11am-5pm Sun, last tour 3:30pm) This 1738 Palladian brick mansion was the only plantation house on the Ashley River to survive the Revolutionary and Civil Wars and the great earthquake of 1886. Guided tours explore the unfurnished house, which has been preserved, but not restored. Walking trails wander along the river and a marsh.

Lowcountry

From just north of Charleston, the southern half of the South Carolina coast is a tangle of islands cut off from the mainland by inlets and tidal marshes. Here, descendants of West African slaves known as the Gullah maintain small communities in the face of resort and golf-course development. The landscape ranges from tidy stretches of shimmery, oyster-gray sand to wild, moss-shrouded maritime forests.

Charleston County Sea Islands

Several islands are within an hour's drive of Charleston. About 8 miles south of Charleston, **Folly Beach** is good for a day of sun and sand. **Folly Beach County Park** (☏843-588-2426; www.ccprc.com; 1100 W Ashley Ave, Folly Beach; parking per vehicle $7-10, walk-in/bicycle free; ⊙9am-7pm May-Aug, 10am-6pm Mar, Apr, Sep & Oct, 10am-5pm Nov-Feb), on the west side, has public changing areas and beach-chair rentals. The other end of the island is popular with surfers.

Upscale rental homes, golf courses and the swanky **Sanctuary Resort** mark **Kiawah Island**, just southeast of Charleston, while nearby **Edisto Island** (*ed*-is-tow) is a homespun family vacation spot without a single traffic light. At its southern tip, **Edisto Beach State Park** (☏843-869-2156; www.southcarolinaparks.com; adult/child 6-15yr $5/3; tent/RV sites from $20/26, cabins from $110) has a gorgeous, uncrowded beach and oak-shaded hiking trails and campgrounds.

🛏 Sleeping

The Sanctuary at Kiawah Island Golf Resort RESORT $$$
(☏843-768-2121; www.kiawahresort.com; 1 Sanctuary Beach Dr; r/ste from $570/1675, villa from $275, house from $8,100 per week; ❈@🛜❄) Ready to swank it up? Consider an idyll at the Sanctuary, sitting prettily by the sea 21 miles south of downtown Charleston. Hotel rooms glow with freshly classic decor – think soft greens, four-poster beds, Italian linens, custom-made mattresses and marble showers. Villas and houses also available. Amenities include two tennis complexes, 90 holes of golf, a spa and Kamp Kiawah for the kids.

Beaufort & Hilton Head

The southernmost stretch of South Carolina's coast is popular with a mostly upscale set of golfers and B&B aficionados, but the area's got quirky charms aplenty for everyone.

On Port Royal Island, the darling colonial town of **Beaufort** (byoo-furt) is often used as a set for Hollywood films about the South. The streets of the historic district are lined with antebellum homes and magnolias dripping with Spanish moss. The riverfront downtown has gobs of linger-worthy cafes and galleries.

South of Beaufort, some 20,000 young men and women go through boot camp each year at the **Marine Corps Recruit Depot** on Parris Island, made notorious by Stanley Kubrick's *Full Metal Jacket*. The facility has been 'welcoming' recruits for 100 years. Come for Friday graduations to see newly minted marines parade proudly for family and friends. You may be asked to show ID and car registration before driving onto the base.

East of Beaufort, the Sea Island Pkwy/Hwy 21 connects a series of marshy, rural islands, including **St Helena Island**, considered the heart of Gullah country and the site of a coastal state park.

Across Port Royal Sound, tiny **Hilton Head Island** is South Carolina's largest barrier island and one of America's top golf spots. There are dozens of courses, many enclosed in posh private residential communities called 'plantations.' The overall set-up is a bit unwelcoming. Summer traffic and miles of stoplights also make it hard to appreciate the beauty of the island, but there are some lush nature preserves and wide, white beaches hard enough for bike riding. Stop by the **visitor center** (☎800-523-3373; www.hiltonheadisland.org; 1 Chamber of Commerce Dr; ⊙8:30am-5:30pm Mon-Fri), on the island, for information and brochures.

◉ Sights

Parris Island Museum　　MUSEUM
(☎843-228-2951; www.mcrdpi.marines.mil; 111 Panama St; ⊙10am-4:30pm) FREE This fascinating museum with antique uniforms and weaponry, and covers marine corps history. There are also a few rooms dedicated to local history. Don't miss the introductory movie.

BOWEN'S ISLAND RESTAURANT

Down a long dirt road through Lowcountry marshland near Folly Beach, this unpainted wooden **shack** (1870 Bowen's Island Rd; ⊙5-10pm Tue-Sat) is one of the South's most venerable seafood dives – grab an oyster knife and start shucking! Cool beer and friendly locals give the place its soul.

Penn Center　　MUSEUM
(☎843-838-2474; www.penncenter.com/museum; 16 Penn Center Circle W; adult/child 6-16yr $5/3; ⊙9am-4pm Mon-Sat) Once the home of one of the nation's first schools for freed slaves, the Penn Center on St Helena Island has a small museum that covers Gullah culture and traces the history of Penn School.

Hunting Island State Park　　PARK
(☎843-838-2011; www.southcarolinaparks.com; 2555 Sea Island Pkwy; adult/child 6-15yr $5/3; ⊙visitor center 9am-5pm Mon-Fri, 11am-5pm Sat & Sun) Lush and inviting, Hunting Island State Park impresses visitors with acres of spooky maritime forest, tidal lagoons and empty, bone-white beach. The Vietnam War scenes from *Forrest Gump* were filmed in the marsh, a nature-lover's dream. Campgrounds fill up quickly in summer. Climb the **lighthouse** ($2) for sweeping coastal views.

⛺ Sleeping & Eating

Hunting Island State Park Campground　　CAMPGROUND $
(☎reservations 866-345-7275, office 843-838-2011; www.southcarolinaparks.com; 2555 Sea Island Pkwy; tent sites $18.50-29, RV sites $23-32, cabin $23-201; ⊙6am-6pm, to 9pm early Mar-early Nov) At South Carolina's most visited park, you can camp under pine trees or palm trees. Several campsites are just steps from the beach. All sites are available by walk-up or reservation, but reservations are advisable in summer.

City Loft Hotel　　HOTEL $$
(☎843-379-5638; www.citylofthotel.com; 301 Carteret St, Beaufort; r/ste $209/229; ❋🛜) The chic City Loft Hotel adds a refreshing dash of modern style to a town heavy on historic homes and stately oak trees. Enjoy flat-screen

MUST-EAT SOUTHERN FOODS

Barbecue – region-wide, especially in North Carolina and Tennessee

Fried chicken – region-wide

Cornbread – region-wide

Shrimp and grits – South Carolina and Georgia coasts

Lowcountry boil/Frogmore stew – crabs, shrimp, oysters and other local seafood boiled in a pot with corn and potatoes; South Carolina and Georgia coasts

Boudin – Cajun pork and rice sausage; Southern Louisiana

Gumbo/jambalaya/étouffée – rice and seafood or meat stew or a mixture; Southern Louisiana

Po'boy – sandwich, traditionally with fried seafood or meat; Southern Louisiana

Collards – a leafy green, often cooked with ham; region-wide

Pecan pie, coconut cake, red velvet cake, sweet-potato pie – region-wide

Bourbon – Kentucky

TVs in the bedroom and bathroom, artisan-tile showers and Memory Foam–topped beds. Other perks include a gym, complimentary bicycle use and an on-site coffee shop.

Sgt White's SOUTHERN, BARBECUE $
(1908 Boundary St, Beaufort; meat & three platter $9; ⊙ 11am-3pm Mon-Fri) A retired Marine ser-geant serves up classic meat and three plat-ters. At the counter, order your juicy BBQ ribs or meat dish, then choose three sides, which can include collards, okra stew and cornbread.

North Coast

Stretching from the North Carolina border south to the city of Georgetown, the coastal region known as the Grand Strand bustles with some 60 miles of fast-food joints, beach resorts and three-story souvenir shops. What was once a laid-back summer destin-ation for working-class people from across the Southeast has become some of the most overdeveloped real estate in the country. Whether you're ensconced in a behemoth resort or sleeping in a tent at a state park, all you need to enjoy your stay is a pair of flip-flops, a margarita and some quarters for the pinball machine.

Myrtle Beach

The towering Sky Wheel spins fantastically beside the coast in downtown Myrtle Beach, anchoring a 60-mile swath of sun-bleached

excess. Love it or hate it, Myrtle Beach means summer vacation, American-style.

Bikers take advantage of the lack of hel-met laws to let their graying ponytails fly in the wind, bikini-clad teenagers play video games and eat hot dogs in smoky arcades, and whole families roast like chickens on the white sand.

North Myrtle Beach, actually a separate town, is slightly lower-key, with a thriving culture based on the 'shag' (no, not that kind of shag) – a jitterbug-like dance invented here in the 1940s.

It ain't for nature-lovers, but with enor-mous outlet malls and innumerable mini-golf courses, water parks, daiquiri bars and T-shirt shops, it's a rowdy good time.

⊙ Sights & Activities

The beach itself is pleasant enough – wide, hot and crowded with umbrellas. Beach-front Ocean Blvd has the bulk of the ham-burger stands and seedy gift shops. Hwy 17 is choked with over-the-top mini-golf cours-es. Several amusement park and shopping mall hybrids teem with people at all hours.

Brookgreen Gardens GARDENS
(www.brookgreen.org; adult/child 4-12yr $15/7; ⊙ 9:30am-5pm, to 8pm Apr) These magical gar-dens, 16 miles south of town on Hwy 17S, are home to the largest collection of American sculpture in the country, set amid more than 9000 acres of rice plantation turned sub-tropical garden paradise. Seasonal blooms are listed on the website.

SkyWheel
AMUSEMENT PARK

(www.myrtlebeachskywheel.com; 1110 N Ocean Blvd; adult/child 3-11yr $13/9; ⊘11am-midnight) The 187ft high SkyWheel overlooks the 1.2-mile coastal boardwalk. One ticket includes three revolutions in an enclosed gondola. At night the wheel is bewitching, with more than a million dazzling colored lights.

Broadway at the Beach
MALL

(www.broadwayatthebeach.com; 1325 Celebrity Circle; ⊘10am-11pm May-Jun, shorter hours rest of year) With shops, restaurants, nightclubs, rides, an aquarium and a giant-screen digital movie theater, this is Myrtle Beach's nerve center.

Family Kingdom
AMUSEMENT PARK

(www.family-kingdom.com; combo pass $38; ⊛) An old-fashioned amusement-and-water-park combo overlooking the ocean. Hours vary seasonally. Closed in winter.

🛏 Sleeping

Hundreds of hotels, ranging from retro family-run motor inns to vast resort complexes, have prices that vary widely by season; a room might cost $30 in January and more than $150 in July. The following are high-season rates.

Myrtle Beach State Park
CAMPGROUND $

(☑843-238-5325; www.southcarolinaparks.com; 4401 S Kings Hwy; rustic tents May-Jun $30, tent/RV sites from $38/42, cabins from $149; P🐾🛜🏊) Sleep beneath the pines or rent a cabin, all just steps from the shore. The park is 3 miles south of central Myrtle Beach.

Best Western Plus
Grand Stand Inn & Suites
HOTEL $$

(☑843-448-1461; www.myrtlebeachbestwestern.com; 1804 S Ocean Blvd; r/ste from $157/177; ✳@🛜🏊) Yes, it's part of a large national chain, but rates are reasonable, the beach is steps away and the complimentary breakfast is filling. The hotel sprawls across two buildings, one of them oceanfront and one just across Ocean Blvd. Rooms sport a bit of modern style. The boardwalk is 1 mile north.

Hampton Inn Broadway at
the Beach
HOTEL $$$

(☑843-916-0600; www.hamptoninn3.hilton.com; 1140 Celebrity Circle; r/ste from $249/389; ✳@🛜🏊) The bright rooms overlooking the lake and Broadway at the Beach are a great choice at this hotel, which feels less hectic than properties along Ocean Blvd. If you're traveling with pre-teens, you may feel more comfortable letting them roam the adjacent shops and attractions rather than the boardwalk.

✗ Eating

The hundreds of restaurants are mostly high-volume and middlebrow – think buffets longer than bowling alleys and 24-hour doughnut shops. Ironically, good seafood is hard to come by; locals go to the nearby fishing village of **Murrells Inlet**.

Prosser's BBQ
SOUTHERN $$

(www.prossersbbq.com; 3750 Business Hwy 17, Murrells Inlet; buffet breakfast/lunch/dinner $6.50/9/12-14; ⊘6:30-10:30am Mon-Sat, 11am-2pm Mon-Sat, 11am-2:30pm Sun, 4-8:30pm Tue-Sat; ⊛) The gut-busting lunch buffet is down-home delicious. It includes fried fish and chicken, sweet potato soufflé, mac 'n' cheese, green beans and vinegary pulled pork. Your best bet on Murrells Inlet's 'restaurant row.' Worth the drive.

Aspen Grille
SOUTHERN $$$

(☑843-449-9191; www.aspen-grille.com; 5101 N Kings Hwy; mains $20-55) Impress your palate, escape the madness and shake off the fried seafood baskets that bind you at Aspen Grille. Sophisticated yet inviting, it seems worlds away from the roar of the Kings Hwy. Chef Curry Martin serves fresh and locally sourced fare with style and Southern sensibilities. Think shrimp and cheese grits with pan gravy and andouille sausage.

If triggerfish is the catch of the day, don't miss it. Live music and half off wines on Wednesday nights.

☆ Entertainment

★ Fat Harold's Beach Club
DANCE

(www.fatharolds.com; 212 Main St; ⊘from 4pm Mon & Tue, from 11am Wed-Sun) Folks groove to doo-wop and old-time rock and roll at this North Myrtle institution, which calls itself 'Home of the Shag.' The dance, that is. Free shag lessons are offered at 7pm every Tuesday.

ⓘ Information

Visitor Center (☑843-626-7444; www.visitmyrtlebeach.com; 1200 N Oak St; ⊘8:30am-5pm Mon-Fri, 9am-5pm Sat, 10am-2pm Sun May-Aug, 9am-2pm Sat and closed Sun Sep-May) Has maps and brochures.

EXPLORING THE SWAMP AT CONGAREE NATIONAL PARK

Inky-black water, dyed with tannic acid leached from decaying plant matter. Bone-white cypress stumps like the femurs of long-dead giants. Spanish moss as dry and gray as witches' hair. There's nothing like hiking or canoeing through one of South Carolina's unearthly swamps to make you feel like a character in a Southern Gothic novel.

Near Columbia, the 22,000-acre **Congaree National Park** (☑803-776-4396; www. nps.gov/cong; 100 National Park Rd, Hopkins; ⊘visitor center 9am-5pm Tue-Sat), America's largest contiguous, old-growth floodplain forest, has camping and free ranger-led canoe trips (reserve in advance). Casual day-trippers can wander the 2.4-mile elevated board-walk. Look carefully at the Blue Sky mural in the visitor center – the scene seems to change as you move.

Between Charleston and Myrtle Beach, **Francis Marion National Forest** has 259,000 acres of black-water creeks, camping, and hiking trails, including the 42-mile Palmetto Trail, which runs along old logging routes. Charleston-based Nature Adventures Outfitters leads kayak and canoe trips.

❶ Getting There & Around

The traffic coming and going on Hwy 17 Business/Kings Hwy can be infuriating. To avoid 'the Strand' altogether, stay on the Hwy 17 bypass, or take Hwy 31/Carolina Bays Pkwy, which parallels Hwy 17 between Hwy 501 and Hwy 9.

Myrtle Beach International Airport (MYR; ☑843-448-1589; www.flymyrtlebeach.com; 1100 Jetport Rd) is located within the city limits, as is the **Greyhound** (☑843-448-2472; 511 7th Ave N) station.

Greenville & the Upcountry

Cherokee once roamed the state's mountain foothills, which they called 'The Great Blue Hills of God.' The region today is known as the Upcountry. Geographically, it's the spot where the Blue Ridge Mountains drop dramatically to meet the Piedmont.

The region is anchored by Greenville, home to one of the most photogenic downtowns in the South. The Reedy River twists through the city center, and its dramatic falls tumble beneath Main St at **Falls Park** (www.fallspark.com). Pedal along the river on the **Swamp Rabbit Trail** on one of the new bike-share bikes (https://greenville.bcycle.com). Dowtown Main St rolls past a lively array of indie shops, good restaurants and craft-beer pubs. Whimsical quotes, called 'Thoughts on a Walk' dot the sidewalk. Kids will get a kick out of **Mice on Main**, a find-the-bronze-mouse scavenger hunt inspired by the book *Goodnight Moon*.

The region's marquee natural attraction is Table Rock Mountain, a 3124ft-high mountain with a striking granite face. The 7.2-mile round-trip hike to its summit at **Table Rock State Park** (☑864-878-9813; www.south carolinaparks.com; 158 Ellison Lane, Pickens; adult/child 6-15yr $5/3 Jun-Nov, adult/child under 16yr $2/free Dec-May; ⊘7am-7pm Sun-Thu, to 9pm Fri & Sat, extended hours mid-May–early Nov) is a popular local challenge. For overnight stays, camping is available (campsites $16 to $21) as are cabins built by the Civilian Conservation Corps ($52 to $181).

🛏 Sleeping & Eating

Drury Inn & Suites   HOTEL **$$**
(☑864-288-4401; www.druryhotels.com; 10 Carolina Point Pkwy; r/ste from $107/166; 🅿❋@🛜) It's not downtown and it's part of a cookie-cutter chain, but the price includes a nightly happy hour with a hearty array of appetizers as well as a filling breakfast. The hotel is on I-85, 7 miles from downtown.

Lazy Goat   MEDITERRANEAN **$$**
(☑864-679-5299; www.thelazygoat.com; 170 River Pl; lunch $5-15, dinner small plates $5-10, dinner mains $12-25; ⊘11:30am-9pm Mon-Wed, to 10pm Thu-Sat) Nibble pimiento cheese and ciabatta bread and sip wine beside the river at this stylish spot, known for its Mediterranean small plates.

TENNESSEE

Most states have one official state song. Tennessee has seven. And that's not just a random fact – Tennessee has music deep within its soul. Here, the folk music of the Scots-Irish in the eastern mountains combined with the bluesy rhythms of the African Americans in the western Delta to give birth to the modern country music that makes Nashville famous.

These three geographic regions, represented by the three stars on the Tennessee flag, have their own unique beauty: the heather-colored peaks of the Great Smoky Mountains; the lush green valleys of the central plateau around Nashville; and the hot, sultry lowlands near Memphis.

In Tennessee you can hike shady mountain trails in the morning, and by evening whoop it up in a Nashville honky-tonk or walk the streets of Memphis with Elvis' ghost.

ℹ Information

Department of Environment & Conservation (✉ 888-867-2757; www.state.tn.us/environment/parks) Check out the well-organized website for camping, hiking and fishing info for Tennessee's more than 50 state parks.

Department of Tourist Development (✉ 615-741-2159; www.tnvacation.com; 312 8th Ave N, Nashville) Has welcome centers at the state borders.

Memphis

Memphis doesn't just attract tourists. It draws pilgrims. Music-lovers lose themselves to the throb of blues guitar on Beale St. Barbecue connoisseurs descend to stuff themselves silly on smoky pulled pork and dry-rubbed ribs. Elvis fanatics fly in to worship at the altar of the King at Graceland. You could spend days hopping from one museum or historic site to another, stopping only for barbecue, and leave happy.

But once you get away from the lights and the tourist buses, Memphis is a different place entirely. Named after the capital of ancient Egypt, it has a certain baroque ruined quality that's both sad and beguiling. Though poverty is rampant – Victorian mansions sit beside tumbledown shotgun shacks (a narrow style of house popular in the South) and college campuses lie in the shadow of eerie abandoned factories – whiffs of a renaissance are in the air. Neighborhoods once downtrodden, abandoned and/or otherwise reclaimed by kudzu – South Main, Binghampton, Crosstown and others – are being reinvented with kitschy boutiques, hipster lofts and daring restaurants, all dripping with Memphis' wild river-town spirit.

◉ Sights

◔ Downtown

The pedestrian-only stretch of Beale St is a 24-hour carnival zone, where you'll find deep-fried funnel cakes, to-go beer counters, and music, music, music. Although locals don't hang out here much, visitors tend to get a kick out of it. Look out for the Memphis Music Hall of Fame and the Blues Hall of Fame, both of which opened in 2015.

★**National Civil Rights Museum**   MUSEUM
(Map p360; www.civilrightsmuseum.org; 450 Mulberry St; adult $15, student & senior $14, child $12; ⊙9am-5pm Mon & Wed-Sat, 1-5pm Sun Sep-May, to 6pm Jun-Aug) Housed across the street from the Lorraine Motel, where the Rev Dr Martin Luther King Jr was fatally shot on April 4, 1968, is the gut-wrenching National Civil Rights Museum. Five blocks south of Beale St, this museum's extensive exhibits and detailed timeline chronicle the struggle for African American freedom and equality.

TENNESSEE FACTS

Nickname Volunteer State

Population 6.54 million

Area 42,146 sq miles

Capital city Nashville (population 634,000)

Other cities Memphis (population 653,000)

Sales tax 7%, plus local taxes of up to about 15%

Birthplace of Frontiersman Davy Crockett (1786–1836), soul diva Aretha Franklin (b 1942), singer Dolly Parton (b 1946)

Home of Graceland, Grand Ole Opry, Jack Daniel's distillery

Politics Pretty darn conservative, with liberal hot spots in urban areas

Famous for 'Tennessee Waltz,' country music, Tennessee walking horses, soul music

Odd law In Tennessee, it's illegal to fire a gun at any wild game, other than whales, from a moving vehicle

Driving distances Memphis to Nashville 213 miles, Nashville to Great Smoky Mountains National Park 223 miles

Both Dr King's cultural contribution and his assassination serve as prisms for looking at the Civil Rights movement, its precursors and its continuing impact on American life.

The turquoise exterior of the 1950s motel and two preserved interior rooms remain much as they were at the time of King's death.

Memphis Rock 'n' Soul Museum MUSEUM
(Map p360; www.memphisrocknsoul.org; 191 Beale St; adult/child \$12/9; ⊙10am-7pm) The Smithsonian's museum, next to FedEx Forum, examines how African American and white music mingled in the Mississippi Delta to create the modern rock and soul sound.

Gibson Beale Street Showcase FACTORY TOUR
(Map p360; www2.gibson.com; 145 Lt George W Lee Ave; admission \$10, no children under 5yr; ⊙hourly tours 11am-4pm Mon-Sat, noon-4pm Sun) Take the fascinating 45-minute tours, which vary throughout the day by worker presence and noise level, of this enormous place to see

master craftspeople transform solid blocks of wood into Les Pauls.

WC Handy House Museum MUSEUM
(Map p360; www.wchandymemphis.org; 352 Beale St; adult/child \$6/4; ⊙11am-4pm Tue-Sat winter, to 5pm summer) On the corner of 4th St, this shotgun shack once belonged to the composer called the 'father of the blues.' He was the first to transpose the 12 bars and later wrote 'Beale Street Blues' in 1916.

Peabody Ducks MARCHING DUCKS
(Map p360; www.peabodymemphis.com; 149 Union Ave; ⊙11am & 5pm; ⊕) FREE A tradition dating to the 1930s begins every day at 11am sharp when five ducks file from the Peabody Hotel's gilded elevator, waddle across the red-carpeted lobby, and decamp in the marble lobby fountain for a day of happy splashing. The ducks make the reverse march at 5pm, when they retire to their penthouse accompanied by their red-coated Duckmaster.

Get here early to secure your spot among the heavy crowds (the mezzanine has the best views).

North of Downtown

Mud Island   PARK
(Map p360; www.mudisland.com; 125 N Front St; ⏱10am-5pm Tue-Sun mid-Apr-Oct; 🖈) **FREE** A small peninsula jutting into the Mississippi, Mud Island is downtown Memphis' best-loved green space. Hop the monorail ($4, or free with Mississippi River Museum admission) or walk across the bridge to the park, where you can jog and rent bikes.

Slave Haven Underground Railroad Museum/Burkle Estate   MUSEUM
(www.slavehavenundergroundrailroadmuseum.org; 826 N 2nd St; adult/child $10/8; ⏱10am-4pm Mon-Sat, to 5pm Jun-Aug) This unimposing clapboard house is thought to have been a way station for runaway slaves on the Underground Railroad, complete with trapdoors, cellar entry and cubby-holes.

East of Downtown

★Sun Studio   STUDIO TOUR
(📞800-441-6249; www.sunstudio.com; 706 Union Ave; adult/child $12/free; ⏱10am-6:15pm) This dusty storefront is ground zero for American rock and roll music. Starting in the early 1950s, Sun's Sam Phillips recorded blues artists such as Howlin' Wolf, BB King and Ike Turner, followed by the rockabilly dynasty of Jerry Lee Lewis, Johnny Cash, Roy Orbison and, of course, the King himself (who started here in 1953).

Packed 40-minute guided tours (no children under five allowed; hourly from 10:30am to 5:30pm) through the tiny studio offer a chance to hear original tapes of historic recording sessions. Guides are full of anecdotes; you can pose for photos on the 'X' where Elvis once stood, or buy a CD of the 'Million Dollar Quartet,' Sun's spontaneous 1956 jam session between Elvis, Johnny Cash, Carl Perkins and Jerry Lee Lewis. From here, hop on the studio's free shuttle (hourly, starting at 11:15am), which does a loop between Sun Studio, Beale St and Graceland.

Children's Museum of Memphis   MUSEUM
(www.cmom.com; 2525 Central Ave; admission $12; ⏱9am-5pm, to 6pm summer; 🖈) Gives the kids a chance to let loose and play in, on and with exhibits such as an airplane cockpit or tornado generator.

Overton Park

Stately homes surround this 342-acre rolling green oasis – home to the Memphis Zoo – off Poplar Ave in the middle of this often gritty city. If Beale St is Memphis' heart, then Overton Park is its lungs.

Brooks Museum of Art   GALLERY
(www.brooksmuseum.org; 1934 Poplar Ave; adult/child $7/3; ⏱10am-4pm Wed & Fri, to 8pm Thu, to 5pm Sat, from 11am Sun) At this well-regarded art museum on the park's western fringe, the excellent permanent collection encompasses everything from Renaissance sculpture to Impressionists to abstract expressionists.

Levitt Shell   ARCHITECTURE, CONCERT VENUE
(www.levittshell.org; 1928 Poplar Ave) A historic band shell and the site of Elvis' first concert in 1954. Today the mod-looking white shell hosts free concerts all summer.

South of Downtown

★Graceland   HISTORIC BUILDING
(📞901-332-3322; www.graceland.com; Elvis Presley Blvd/US 51; tours house only adult/child $36/16, expanded tours from $40/19; ⏱9am-5pm Mon-Sat, to 4pm Sun, shorter hours & closed Tue Dec; 🅿) If you only make one stop in Memphis, it should be here: the sublimely kitschy, gloriously bizarre home of the King of Rock and Roll. Though born in Mississippi, Elvis Presley was a true son of Memphis, raised in the Lauderdale Courts public housing projects, inspired by blues clubs on Beale St, and discovered at Sun Studio. In the spring of 1957, the already-famous 22-year-old spent $100,000 on a Colonial-style mansion, named Graceland by its previous owners.

The King himself had the place, ahem, redecorated in 1974. With a 15ft couch, fake waterfall, yellow vinyl walls and green shag-carpet ceiling – it's a virtual textbook of ostentatious '70s style. You'll begin your tour at the visitor plaza on the other side of Elvis Presley Blvd. Book ahead in the busy season (June to August and important Elvis dates) to ensure a prompt tour time. The basic self-guided mansion tour comes with an engaging multimedia iPad narration. Pay just $4 extra to see the car museum, and $9 extra to tack on the two custom planes (check out the blue-and-gold private bathroom on the *Lisa Marie*, a Convair 880 Jet).

Priscilla Presley (who divorced Elvis in 1973) opened Graceland to tours in 1982,

THE SOUTH MEMPHIS

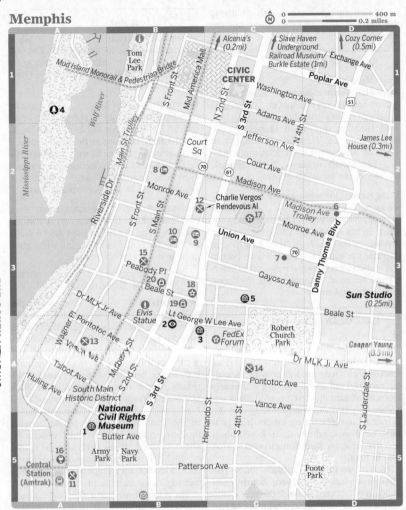

THE SOUTH MEMPHIS

and now millions come to pay homage to the King who died here (in the upstairs bathroom) from heart failure in 1977. Throngs of fans still weep at his grave, next to the swimming pool out back. Graceland is 9 miles south of downtown on US 51, also called 'Elvis Presley Blvd.' A free shuttle runs from Sun Studio (p359). Parking costs $10.

★ Stax Museum of
American Soul Music   MUSEUM
(☎901-942-7685; www.staxmuseum.com; 926 E McLemore Ave; adult/child $13/10; ☉10am-

5pm Tue-Sat, 1-5pm Sun) Wanna get funky? Head directly to Soulsville USA, where this 17,000-sq-ft museum sits on the site of the old Stax recording studio. This venerable spot was soul music's epicenter in the 1960s, when Otis Redding, Booker T and the MGs and Wilson Pickett recorded here.

Dive into soul music history with photos, displays of '60s and '70s stage clothing, and above all, Isaac Hayes' 1972 Superfly Cadillac outfitted with shag-fur and 24-carat-gold exterior trim.

Memphis

Full Gospel Tabernacle Church   CHURCH
(787 Hale Rd; ☉ services 11am) On Sunday, put on your smell goods and head to services in South Memphis, where soul music legend turned reverend Al Green presides over a powerful choir. Visitors are welcome; it's a fascinating cultural experience.

☞ Tours

American Dream Safari   CULTURAL
(Map p360; ☑ 901-428-3602; www.american-dreamsafari.com; 343 Madison Ave; walking tours per person $15, driving tours per vehicle from $200) Southern culture junkie Tad Pierson shows you the quirky, personal side of Memphis – juke joints, gospel churches, decaying buildings – on foot or in his pink Cadillac (if you can get ahold of him, that is).

Blues City Tours   BUS TOUR
(Map p360; ☑ 901-522-9229; www.bluescitytours.com; adult/child from $24/19) A variety of themed bus tours, including an Elvis tour and a Memphis Music Tour.

✦ Festivals & Events

Trolley Night   ART
(www.gosouthmain.com/trolley-night.html; S Main St; ☉ 6-9pm last Fri of month) FREE On Trolley Night galleries on South Main stay open late and pour wine for the people.

Beale Street Music Festival   MUSIC
(www.memphisinmay.org; Tom Lee Park; 3-day passes $95; ☉ 1st weekend in May) You've heard of Coachella, New Orleans Jazz Fest and Bonnaroo, but Memphis' Beale Street Music Festival gets very little attention, consider-ing it offers one of the country's best lineups of old-school blues masters, up-and-coming rockers and gloriously past their prime pop and hip-hop artists.

⌂ Sleeping

Chain motels lie off I-40, exit 279, across the river in West Memphis, AR. Look out for the new Guest House at Graceland, a 450-room luxury hotel steps from Graceland due to open in 2016.

⌂ Downtown

Talbot Heirs   GUESTHOUSE $$
(Map p360; ☑ 901-527-9772; www.talbothouse.com; 99 S 2nd St; ste $130-195; ❋ @ ☎) Incon-spicuously located on the 2nd floor of a busy downtown street, this cheerful guesthouse is one of Memphis' best kept and most unique secrets. Spacious suites are more like hip studio apartments than hotel rooms, with Asian rugs, funky local artwork and kitchens stocked with (included!) snacks.

Big stars like Harvey Keitel, Matt Damon and John Grisham have nested here as well as Bobby Whitlock of Derek and the Dom-inos fame, who signed a piano.

Peabody Hotel   HOTEL $$
(Map p360; ☑ 901-529-4000; www.peabodymem-phis.com; 149 Union Ave; r from $219; ❋ ☎ ⊠) Memphis' most storied hotel has been ca-tering to a who's who of Southern gentry since the 1860s. The current incarnation, a 13-story Italian Renaissance Revival–style building, dates to the 1920s and remains a social center, with a spa, shops, restaurants,

an atmospheric lobby bar and 464 guest rooms in soothing turquoise tones.

Madison Hotel　　　　BOUTIQUE HOTEL **$$$**
(Map p360; ☑ 901-333-1200; www.madisonhotel memphis.com; 79 Madison Ave; r from $259; P ✳ @ 🛜 ☲) If you're looking for a sleek treat, check into these swanky, music-themed boutique sleeps. The rooftop Sky Terrace ($10 for nonguests) is one of the best places in town to watch a sunset, and stylish rooms have nice touches like hardwood entryways, high ceilings and Italian linens.

★ **James Lee House**　　　　B&B **$$$**
(☑ 901-359-6750; www.jamesleehouse.com; 690 Adams Ave; r $245-450; P ✳ @ 🛜) This exquisite Victorian mansion sat abandoned for 56 years in the city's historic Victorian Village on the edge of downtown; $2 million later and the owner's keen eye for detail and design, and it's one of Memphis' most refined sleeps.

Dating in parts to 1848 and 1872, a glorious renovation preserved crown moldings, mirrors, cornices, 14 fireplaces and some hardwood flooring. The five spacious suites are impeccably furnished, and there's a peaceful garden with original fountain.

East of Downtown

Pilgrim House Hostel　　　　HOSTEL **$**
(☑ 901-273-8341; www.pilgrimhouse.org; 1000 S Cooper St; dm/r $25/55; P ✳ @ 🛜) Yes, it's in a church. No, no one will try to convert you. Dorms and private rooms are clean and spare. An international crowd plays cards and chats (no alcohol) in open common areas flush with secondhand furniture, and all guests must do a brief daily chore.

South of Downtown

Graceland RV Park & Campground　　　　CAMPGROUND **$**
(☑ 901-396-7125; www.graceland.com/visit/ graceland_campground.aspx; 3691 Elvis Presley Blvd; tent sites/cabins from $25/47; P 🛜 ☲) Keep Lisa Marie in business when you camp out or sleep in the no-frills log cabins (with shared bathrooms) next to Graceland.

Heartbreak Hotel　　　　HOTEL **$$**
(☑ 901-332-1000; www.graceland.com/visit/heart breakhotel.aspx; 3677 Elvis Presley Blvd; d from $115; P ✳ @ 🛜 ☲) At the end of Lonely St (seriously) across from Graceland, this basic hotel is tarted up with all things Elvis. Ramp up the already-palpable kitsch with one of

the themed suites, such as the red-velvet Burnin' Love room. Good value.

Days Inn Graceland　　　　MOTEL **$$**
(☑ 901-346-5500; www.daysinn.com; 3839 Elvis Presley Blvd; r from $100; P ✳ 🛜 ☲) With a guitar-shaped pool, gold records and Elvis memorabilia in the lobby and neon Cadillacs on the roof, the Days Inn manages to out-Elvis the neighboring Heartbreak Hotel. Guest rooms themselves are clean but nothing special.

✗ Eating

Locals come to blows over which of the city's chopped-pork sandwiches or dry-rubbed ribs are the best. Barbecue joints are scattered across the city; the ugliest exteriors often yield the tastiest goods. Hip young locals head to the South Main Arts District, Midtown's Cooper-Young or Overton Square neighborhoods, all fashionable evening enclaves.

Downtown

Gus's World Famous Fried Chicken　　　　FRIED CHICKEN **$**
(Map p360; 310 S Front St; plates $5.65-9.95; ◷11am-9pm Sun-Thu, to 10pm Fri & Sat) Fried chicken connoisseurs across the globe twitch in their sleep at night, dreaming about the gossamer-light fried chicken at this downtown concrete bunker with the fun, neon-lit interior and vintage jukebox. On busy nights, waits can top an hour.

LUNCHBOXeats　　　　SOUTHERN **$**
(Map p360; www.lunchboxeats.com; 288 S 4th St; sandwiches $8-11; ◷10:30am-3pm; 🛜) Classic soul food gets a seriously tasty makeover at this creative sandwich shop, resulting in such ridiculousness as chicken and waffle sandwiches (Belgian waffles serve as the slices of 'bread'); crawfish étouffée sloppy Joes; a pork butt, onion and mac 'n' cheese club sandwich and more, served on traditional school lunch trays.

Alcenia's　　　　SOUTHERN **$**
(www.alcenias.com; 317 N Main St; mains $9.55-11; ◷11am-5pm Tue-Fri, 9am-3pm Sat) The only thing sweeter than Alcenia's famous 'Ghetto-Aid' (a diabetes-inducing fruit drink) is owner Betty-Joyce 'BJ' Chester-Tamayo – don't be surprised to receive a kiss on the top of the head as soon as you sit down.

The lunch menu at this funky little gold-and purple-painted cafe rotates daily – look for killer fried chicken and catfish, melt-in-the-mouth spiced cabbage and an exquisite eggy custard pie.

Arcade
DINER $

(Map p360; www.arcaderestaurant.com; 540 S Main St; mains $7-10; ⊙ 7am-3pm Sun-Wed, to 11pm Thu-Sat) Step inside this ultra-retro diner, Memphis' oldest, and wander to the Elvis booth, strategically located near the rear exit. The King used to sit here and eat griddle-fried peanut butter and banana sandwiches and would bolt out the door if fan-instigated pandemonium ensued. Crowds still pack in for sublime sweet-potato pancakes – as fluffy, buttery and addictive as advertised.

The rest of the dishes are standard greasy-spoon fare (don't tell Elvis).

Charlie Vergos' Rendezvous
BARBECUE $$

(Map p360; ☑ 901-523-2746; www.hogsfly.com; 52 S 2nd St; mains $8-20; ⊙ 4:30-10:30pm Tue-Thu, 11am-11pm Fri, from 11:30am Sat) Tucked in its own namesake alleyway off Monroe Ave, this subterranean institution sells an astonishing 5 tons of its exquisite dry-rubbed ribs weekly. The ribs don't come with any sauce, but the pork shoulder does, so try a combo and you'll have plenty of sauce to enjoy. The beef brisket is also tremendous. Expect a wait.

Majestic Grille
EUROPEAN $$$

(Map p360; ☑ 901-522-8555; www.majesticgrille. com; 145 S Main St; mains $16-47; ⊙ 11am-10pm Mon-Thu, to 11pm Fri & Sat, to 9pm Sun; 🕾) Set in an old silent-movie theater near Beale St, with pre-talkie black and whites strobing in the handsome dark-wood dining room, the Majestic serves classic continental fare, from roasted half chicken, to seared tuna and grilled pork tenderloin, and four varieties of hand-cut filet mignon.

✕ East of Downtown

★ Payne's Bar-B-Q
BARBECUE $

(1762 Lamar Ave; sandwiches $4.50-8.50, plates $7.50-10.50; ⊙ 11am-5:30pm Tue-Sat) We'd say this converted gas station has the best chopped-pork sandwich in town, but we don't want to have to fight anyone.

Bar DKDC
GASTROPUB $

(www.bardkdc.com; 964 S Cooper St; dishes $5-14; ⊙ 5pm-3am Tue-Sat) Cheap and flavorful global street food is the calling at this ever-evolving Cooper-Young staple. South American *arepas*, Vietnamese *banh-mi* sandwiches, Caribbean jerked fish, Greek *souvlaki* – you get the idea. The space

JACK DANIEL'S DISTILLERY

The irony of the recently revamped **Jack Daniel's Distillery** (www.jackdaniels. com; 182 Lynchburg Hwy; ⊙ 9am-4:30pm) FREE being in a 'dry county' is lost on no one – local liquor laws dictate that no hard stuff can be sold within county lines, but they do give out small samples on their free hour-long tours. For $10 you can take a two-hour Distillery Tour (book in advance), where you'll get a more generous sample and a scenic tour of the countryside. This is the oldest registered distillery in the US; the folks at Jack Daniel's have been dripping whiskey through layers of charcoal then aging it in oak barrels since 1866. It's located off Hwy 55 in tiny Lynchburg.

sports an eclectic decor, chalkboard wine list and friendly bartenders.

Cozy Corner
BARBECUE $

(www.cozycornerbbq.com; 745 N Pkwy; mains $4.95-12.75; ⊙ 11am-6pm Tue-Sat) Slouch in a torn vinyl booth and devour an entire barbecued Cornish game hen ($11.75), the house specialty at this pug-ugly cult favorite. Ribs and wings are spectacular too, and the fluffy, silken sweet-potato pie is an A-plus specimen of the classic Southern dessert. (Note: during renovations Cozy Corner will be serving across the street at 726 N Pkwy.)

Brother Juniper's
BREAKFAST $

(www.brotherjunipers.com; dishes $3.50-13; ⊙ 6:30am-1pm Tue-Fri, 7am-12:30pm Sat, 8am-1pm Sun) This humble breakfast spot started as a chain out of San Francisco's Haight-Ashbury district to feed the homeless; today, the Memphis location is the last man standing and it's pretty much unanimously voted the best breakfast in town. Think huge portions of omelets, pancakes, breakfast burritos, waffles, biscuits and home fries. A must.

Hog & Hominy
SOUTHERN, ITALIAN $$

(☑ 901-207-7396; www.hogandhominy.com; 707 W Brookhaven Circle; pizza $14-17; ⊙ 11am-2pm & 5-10pm Tue-Thu, to late Fri-Sat, 10:30am-10pm Sun; 🕾) The chef-driven, Southern-rooted Italian at this Brookhaven Circle hot spot has grabbed the nation's attention, winning best-new-this and best-new-that from everyone from *GQ* to *Food & Wine* magazines. Small plates (often with adventurous ingredients like frog legs, pig ears and beef hearts) and perfect brick-oven pizza are the mainstays; along with seasonal cocktails, craft beers and bocce.

Soul Fish Cafe
SEAFOOD $$

(www.soulfishcafe.com; 862 S Cooper St; mains $9.50-16; 11am-10pm Mon-Sat, to 9pm Sun) A cute cinderblock cafe in the Cooper-Young neighborhood, known for delectable po'boys, fried fish plates and some rather indulgent cakes.

★ Restaurant Iris
NEW SOUTHERN $$$

(901-590-2828; www.restaurantiris.com; 2146 Monroe Ave; mains $27-39; 5-10pm Mon-Sat) Chef Kelly English crafts special, avant-garde Southern fusion dishes that delight foodies, hence the James Beard noms. He's got a fried-oyster-stuffed steak, a sublime shrimp and grits, and some scrumptious Brussels sprouts dressed up with smoky bacon and sherry, all served in a refined residential home. Next door he has opened Second Line, a more affordable New Orleans bistro.

Sweet Grass
SOUTHERN $$$

(901-278-0278; www.sweetgrassmemphis.com; 937 S Cooper St; mains $23-32; 5:30pm-late Tue-Sun, 11am-2pm Sun) Contemporary Low-country cuisine (the seafood-heavy cooking of the South Carolina and Georgia coasts) wins raves at this casual Midtown restaurant, split between a more rambunctious bar side and a more refined bistro side (different menus). The shrimp and grits is one of the best you'll try.

🍷 Drinking & Nightlife

The East Memphis neighborhoods of Cooper-Young and Overton Square offer the best concentration of hip bars and restaurants. Both are about 4 miles east of downtown. Last call is 3am.

★ Wiseacre Brewing Co
MICROBREWERY

(www.wiseacrebrew.com; 2783 Broad Ave; beers $5, tours $10; 4-9pm Wed-Fri, 1-9pm Sat) Our favorite Memphis taproom is in the warehouse district of Binghampton, 5 miles east of downtown. Sample year-round and seasonal craft brews on the outside deck, which features a wraparound porch hugging two enormous, near 100-year-old cement wheat silos.

Earnestine & Hazel's
BAR

(Map p360; www.earnestineandhazelsjukejoint. com; 531 S Main St; 5pm-3am Sun-Fri, from 11am Sat) One of the great dive bars in Memphis has a 2nd floor full of rusty bedsprings and claw-foot tubs, remnants of its brothel past. Its Soul Burger is the stuff of legend. Things heat up after midnight.

Hammer & Ale
BEER HALL

(www.hammerandale.com; 921 S Cooper; beers $5; 2-9pm Tue-Thu, 11am-10pm Fri-Sat, noon-3pm Sun;) Hopheads descend on this barn-like Cooper-Young craft beer bar decked out in light cypress woods throughout. Memphis breweries Wiseacre, High Cotton, Memphis Made and Ghost River are represented among the 24 taps of mostly Southern microbrews. Cash *not* accepted!

☆ Entertainment

Beale St is the obvious spot for live blues, rock and jazz. There's no cover at most clubs, or it's only a few bucks, and the bars are open all day, while neighborhood clubs tend to start filling up around 10pm. Check the *Memphis Flyer* (www.memphisflyer.com) online calendar for listings.

Wild Bill's
BLUES

(1580 Vollintine Ave; cover Fri Sat $10; Wed Thu noon-9pm, noon-3am Fri-Sat) Don't even think of showing up at this gritty hole-in-the-wall before midnight. Order a 40oz beer and a basket of wings then sit back to watch some of the greatest blues acts in Memphis from 11pm Friday and Saturday only. Expect some stares from the locals; it's worth it for the kick-ass, ultra-authentic jams.

Lafayette's Music Room
LIVE MUSIC

(901-207-5097; www.lafayettes.com/memphis; 2119 Madison Ave; cover Fri-Sat $5; 11am-10pm Mon-Wed, to midnight Tue & Sun, to 2am Fri-Sat) This newly reopened historic Overton Square music venue once hosted Kiss and Billy Joel in its '70s heyday. The lights were out for 38 years, but it's now one of the most intimate music venues in town.

Hi-Tone Cafe
LIVE MUSIC

(www.hitonememphis.com; 412-414 N Cleveland St; cover $5-20) In new digs in Crosstown, this unassuming little dive is one of the city's best places to hear live local bands and touring indie acts.

Young Avenue Deli
LIVE MUSIC

(www.youngavenuedeli.com; 2119 Young Ave; ⏰11am-3pm Mon-Sat, from 11:30am Sun) This Midtown favorite has food, pool, occasional live music and a laid-back young crowd.

Rum Boogie
BLUES

(Map p360; www.rumboogie.com; 182 Beale St) Huge, popular and loud, this Cajun-themed Beale St club hops every night to the tunes of a tight house blues band.

🔒 Shopping

Beale St abounds with cheesy souvenir shops, while Cooper-Young is the place for boutiques and bookshops. The streets around South Main have been branded an arts district.

City & State
FOOD & DRINK, ACCESSORIES

(www.cityandstate.us; 2625 Broad Ave; coffee $2.50-4.75; ⏰7am-6pm Mon-Sat, 8am-2pm Sun; 📶) This fabulous new artisan-centric store and coffeehouse in Binghampton stocks exquisitely curated everyday coolness (handcrafted soaps, boutique camping items, waxed canvas lunch bags, ceramic pour-over coffee mugs) and is the only place in Memphis for a barista-level coffee experience.

A Schwab's
GIFTS

(Map p360; www.a-schwab.com; 163 Beale St; ⏰noon-7pm Mon-Wed, to 7pm Thu, to 10pm Fri & Sat, 11am-6pm Sun) It has everything from denim shirts to flasks to rubber duckies to fine hats to overalls. But the real attractions are the antiques upstairs. Think vintage scales and irons, hat stretchers and a cast-iron anchor of a cash register.

Lanksy Brothers
CLOTHING

(Map p360; ☑901-425-3960; www.lanskybros. com; 126 Beale St; ⏰9am-6pm Sun-Wed, to 9pm Thu-Sat) The 'Clothier to the King,' this mid-century men's shop once outfitted Elvis with his two-tone shirts. Today it has a retro line of menswear (including blue suede shoes!) plus gifts and women's clothes. It has relocated in its original location on Beale St (in addition to its store in the Peabody Hotel).

❶ Information

Commercial Appeal (www.commercialappeal. com) Daily newspaper with local entertainment listings.

Main Post Office (Map p360; www.usps.com; 555 S 3rd St; ⏰9:30am-6pm Mon-Fri) Downtown postal services.

Memphis Flyer (www.memphisflyer.com) Free weekly distributed on Wednesday; has entertainment listings.

Memphis Visitor's Center (☑888-633-9099; www.memphistravel.com; 3205 Elvis Presley Blvd; ⏰9am-6pm Apr-Sep, to 5pm Oct-Mar, to 4pm Sun Nov-Feb) City information center near exit for Graceland.

Police Station (☑901-636-4099; www.memphispolice.org; 545 S Main St) Terribly hard to find. It's above Amtrak's Central Station.

Regional Medical Center at Memphis (☑901-545-7100; www.the-med.org; 877 Jefferson Ave) Has the only level-one trauma center in the region.

Tennessee State Visitor Center (☑901-543-6757; www.tnvacation.com; 119 N Riverside Dr; ⏰7am-11pm) Brochures for the whole state.

❶ Getting There & Around

Memphis International Airport (MEM; ☑901-922-8000; www.memphisairport.org; 2491 Winchester Rd) is 12 miles southeast of downtown via I-55; taxis to Downtown cost about $30.

Memphis Area Transit Authority (MATA; www.matatransit.com; 444 N Main St; fares $1.75) operates local buses; buses 2 and 20 go to the airport.

MATA's vintage trolleys ($1, every 12 minutes) ply Main St and Front St downtown. **Greyhound** (☑901-395-8770; www.greyhound.com; 3033 Airways Blvd) is located at the MATA's Airways Transit Center near Memphis International Airport. Amtrak's **Central Station** (www.amtrak. com; 545 S Main St) is right downtown.

Shiloh National Military Park

'No soldier who took part in the two day Battle at Shiloh ever spoiled for a fight again,' said one veteran of the bloody 1862 clash, which took place among these lovely fields and forests. Ulysses S Grant, then a major general, led the Army of Tennessee. After a vicious Confederate assault on the first day that took Grant by surprise, his creative maneuver on the second day held Pittsburg Landing, and turned the Confederates back. During the fight over 3500 soldiers died and nearly 24,000 were wounded. A relative unknown at the beginning of the war, Grant went on to lead the Union to victory and eventually became the 18th president of the United States.

Vast **Shiloh National Military Park** (☑731-689-5696; www.nps.gov/shil; 1055 Pittsburg Landing Rd; ⏰park dawn-dusk, visitor center 8am-5pm) FREE is located just north of the Mississippi border near the town of Crump, TN, and can only be seen by car. Sights include the Shiloh National Cemetery, and an overlook of the Cumberland River where Union reinforcement troops arrived by ship. The visitor center offers maps, shows a video about the battle, and sells an audio driving tour.

Nashville

Imagine you're an aspiring country singer arriving in downtown Nashville after days of hitchhiking, with nothing but your battered guitar on your back. Gaze up at the neon lights of Lower Broadway, take a deep breath of smoky, beer-perfumed air, feel the boot-stompin' rumble from deep inside the crowded honky-tonks, and say to yourself: 'I've made it.'

For country-music fans and wannabe songwriters all over the world, a trip to Nashville is the ultimate pilgrimage. Since the 1920s the city has been attracting musicians who have taken the country genre from the 'hillbilly music' of the early 20th century to the slick 'Nashville sound' of the 1960s to the punk-tinged alt-country of the 1990s.

Its many musical attractions range from the Country Music Hall of Fame to the revered Grand Ole Opry to Jack White's niche of a record label. It also has a lively university community, some excellent down-home grub and some seriously kitschy souvenirs.

◉ Sights

◉ Downtown

The historic **2nd Ave N** business area was the center of the cotton trade in the 1870s and 1880s, when most of the Victorian warehouses were built; note the cast-iron and masonry facades. Today it's the heart of the **District**, with shops, restaurants, underground saloons and nightclubs. It's a bit like the French Quarter meets Hollywood Boulevard drenched in bourbon and country twang. South of Lower Broadway is the **SoBro** district, revitalized by the opening of the $635-million **Music City Center** (www.nashvillemusiccitycenter.com; Broadway St, btwn 5th & 8th Aves) convention center, restaurants, bars and hotels. Two blocks west of 2nd Ave N, **Printers Alley** is a narrow cobblestoned lane known for its nightlife since the 1940s. Along the Cumberland River, **Riverfront Park** is a landscaped promenade that's

being redeveloped; **West Riverfront Park**, an 11-acre civic park will include over 1 mile of multi-use greenway trails, Nashville's first downtown dog park, ornamental gardens, a 1.5-acre event lawn called The Green and an amphitheater.

★ **Country Music Hall of Fame & Museum**   MUSEUM
(www.countrymusichalloffame.com; 222 5th Ave S; adult/child $25/15, with audio tour $27/18, with Studio B 1hr tour $40/30; ⊙9am-5pm) Following a $100 million expansion in 2014, this monumental museum, reflecting the near-biblical importance of country music to Nashville's soul, is a must-see, whether you're a country music fan or not. Gaze at Carl Perkins' blue suede shoes, Elvis' gold Cadillac (actually white) and gold piano (actually gold), and Hank Williams' western-cut suit with musical note appliqués.

Highlights of the ambitious 210,000-sq-ft expansion include the 800-seat CMA Theater, the Taylor Swift Education Center and the relocation of the legendary letterpress operation of Hatch Show Print (p374). Written exhibits trace country's roots, computer touch screens access recordings and photos from the enormous archives, and the fact-and music-filled audio tour is narrated by contemporary stars.

Ryman Auditorium   HISTORIC BUILDING
(www.ryman.com; 116 5th Ave N; adult/child self-guided tours $15/10, backstage tours $20/15; ⊙9am-4pm) The so-called 'Mother Church of Country Music' has hosted a laundry list of performers, from Martha Graham to Elvis, and Katherine Hepburn to Bob Dylan. The soaring brick tabernacle (1892) was built by wealthy riverboat captain Thomas Ryman to house religious revivals, and watching a show from one of its 2000 seats can still be described as a spiritual experience.

The *Grand Ole Opry* (p374) took place here for 31 years until it moved out to the Opryland complex in Music Valley in 1974. Today, the *Opry* returns to the Ryman during winter. In 2015 a $14 million visitor experience renovation installed a new event space, cafe and bars.

Johnny Cash Museum & Store   MUSEUM
(www.johnnycashmuseum.com; 119 3rd Ave; adult/child $16/12; ⊙8am-7pm) The new museum dedicated to 'The Man in Black' is smallish but houses the most comprehensive collection of Johnny Cash artifacts and memorabilia in the world, officially endorsed by the Cash family.

Tennessee State Museum   MUSEUM
(www.tnmuseum.org; 5th Ave, btwn Union & Deaderick Sts; ⊙10am-5pm Tue-Sat, 1-5pm Sun; ⚑) **FREE** For history buffs, this engaging but not-flashy museum on the ground floor of a massive office tower provides a worthy look at the state's past, with Native American handicrafts, a life-size log cabin and quirky historical artifacts such as President Andrew Jackson's inaugural hat.

Frist Center for the Visual Arts   GALLERY
(www.fristcenter.org; 919 Broadway; adult/child $12/free; ⊙10am-5:30pm Mon-Wed & Sat, to 9pm Thu & Fri, 1-5pm Sun) A top-notch post office turned art museum and complex hosting traveling exhibitions of everything from American folk art to Picasso.

Tennessee State Capitol   HISTORIC BUILDING
(www.capitol.tn.gov; Charlotte Ave; ⊙tours 9am-4pm Mon-Fri) **FREE** This 1845–59 Greek Revival building was built from local limestone and marble by slaves and prison inmates working alongside European artisans. Around back, steep stairs lead down to the **Tennessee Bicentennial Mall**, whose outdoor walls are covered with historical facts about Tennessee's history, and the wonderful daily **Farmers Market**.

Free tours leave from the Information Desk on the 1st floor of the Capitol every hour on the hour.

◉ West End

Along West End Ave, starting at 21st Ave, sits prestigious **Vanderbilt University**, founded in 1883 by railway magnate Cornelius Vanderbilt. The 330-acre campus buzzes with some 12,000 students, and student culture influences much of Midtown's vibe.

Parthenon   PARK, GALLERY
(www.parthenon.org; 2600 West End Ave; adult/child $6/4; ⊙9am-4:30pm Tue-Sat, 12:30-4:30pm Sun) Yes, that is indeed a reproduction Athenian Parthenon sitting in **Centennial Park**. Originally built in 1897 for Tennessee's Centennial Exposition and rebuilt in 1930 due to popular demand, the full-scale plaster copy of the 438 BC original now houses an art museum with a collection of American paintings and a 42ft statue of the Greek goddess Athena.

Music Row   AREA
(Music Sq West & Music Sq East) Just west of downtown, sections of 16th and 17th Aves, called Music Sq West and Music Sq East, are home to the production companies, record labels, agents, managers and promoters who run Nashville's country-music industry, including the famed RCA Studio B.

Historic RCA Studio B   LANDMARK
(www.countrymusichalloffame.org; 1611 Roy Acuff Pl; tours adult/child $40/30) One of Music Row's most historic studios, this is where Elvis, the Everly Brothers and Dolly Parton all recorded numerous hits. It's marked by the Heartbreak Hotel guitar sculpture emblazoned with a pelvis-jutting image of the King. You can tour the studio via the Country Music Hall of Fame's Studio B Tour, included with their Platinum Package.

◉ Music Valley

This suburban tourist zone is about 10 miles northeast of downtown at Hwy 155/Briley Pkwy, exits 11 and 12B, and reachable by bus.

Grand Ole Opry House   MUSEUM
(☑615-871-6779; www.opry.com; 2802 Opryland Dr; tours adult/child $22/17; ⊙tours 9am-4pm) This unassuming modern brick building seats 4400 for the Grand Ole Opry (p374) on Tuesday, Friday and Saturday from March to November and Wednesday from June to August. Guided backstage tours are offered every 15 minutes daily from October to March.

Willie Nelson Museum   MUSEUM
(www.willienelsongeneralstore.com; 2613 McGavock Pike; admission $8; ⊙8:30am-9pm) 'Outlaw Country' star Willie Nelson sold all his worldly goods to pay off $16.7 million in tax debt in the early 1990s. You can see them at this quirky museum not far from the Grand Ole Opry.

☞ Tours
★NashTrash   BUS TOUR
(☑615-226-7300; www.nashtrash.com; 722 Harrison St; tours $32-35) The big-haired 'Jugg Sisters' lead a campy frolic through the risqué side of Nashville history while guests sip BYO booze on the big pink bus. Buy in advance: tours can sell out *months* in advance. Meet the bus at the south end of the Nashville Farmers Market.

Tommy's Tours   BUS TOUR
(☑615-335-2863; www.tommystours.com; 2120 Lebanon Pike; tours $35) Wisecracking local Tommy Garmon leads highly entertaining three-hour tours of country-music sights.

Nashville

Rolf and Daughters (0.6mi)

Monell's (0.5mi)

Silo (0.5mi)

Jackson St

7th Ave N

6th Ave N

5th Ave N

10

Bicentennial Mall

Herman St

10th Ave N

41

James Robertson Pkwy

12

Music City Central

Harrison St

8

Charlotte Ave

Deaderick St

9

Gay St

Legislative Plaza

70

Union St

12

Jo Johnson Ave

6th Ave N

40

7th Ave N

16th Ave N

Charlotte Ave

10th Ave N

8th Ave N

13th Ave N

12th Ave N

11th Ave N

US Courthouse

Patterson St

Broadway

2

9th Ave S

McGavock St

State St

Church St

16

Music City Hostel (0.1mi)

16th Ave N

Demonbreun St

17th Ave N

Hayes St

MIDTOWN

10th Ave S

18th Ave N

McGavock

12th Ave S

11th Ave S

14

West End Ave

Demonbreun St

18

Broadway

22

27

Parthenon (1.3mi)

20

Pine St

11

19th Ave S

Division St

33

Gleaves St

THE GULCH

Division St

Music Circle N

Music Square W

23

Music Circle S

MUSIC ROW

Hawkins St

12th Ave S

24

3

Chet Atkins Pl

6

18th Ave S

Hawkins St

South St

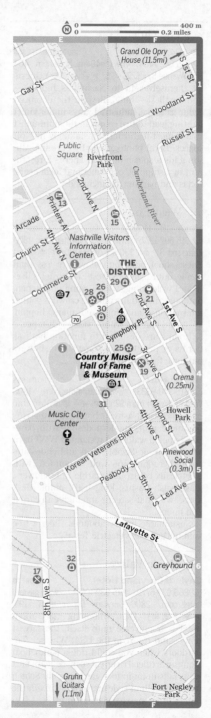

Nashville

◎ Top Sights

◎ Sights

✪ Activities, Courses & Tours

🛏 Sleeping

✪ Eating

☕ Drinking & Nightlife

✪ Entertainment

🛍 Shopping

🎊 Festivals & Events

CMA Music Festival   MUSIC
(www.cmafest.com; ⊙ Jun) Draws tens of thousands of country-music fans to town.

Tennessee State Fair   FAIR
(www.tnstatefair.org; ⊙ Sep) Nine days of racing pigs, mule-pulls and cake bake-offs.

🛏 Sleeping

Bargain-bin chain motels cluster on all sides of downtown, along I-40 and I-65. Music Valley has a glut of family-friendly midrange chains.

🛏 Downtown

★ Nashville Downtown Hostel HOSTEL $
(☎615-497-1208; www.nashvillehostel.com; 177 1st Ave N; dm $35-40, r $128-140; ℗) Well located and up-to-the-minute in style and function. The common space in the basement, with its rather regal exposed stone walls and beamed rafters, is your all-hours mingle den. Dorm rooms are on the 3rd and 4th floors, and have lovely wood floors, exposed timber columns, silver-beamed ceilings and four, six or eight bunks to a room.

Hotel Indigo BOUTIQUE HOTEL $$
(☎615-891-6000; www.hotelindigo.com; 301 Union St; r from $199; ℗🐾❄@🛜) Part of a boutique international chain, the Indigo has a fun, pop-art look, with 160 rooms (30 of which are brand new). Avoid the original (but tacky) Terrazo floor rooms in favor of those spacious King Rooms, with brand-new hardwood floors, high ceilings, flat-screens, leather headboards and office chairs.

Union Station Hotel HOTEL $$$
(☎615-726-1001; www.unionstationhotelnashville.com; 1001 Broadway; r from $259; ℗❄🛜) This soaring Romanesque gray stone castle was Nashville's train station back in the days when rail travel was a grand affair; today it's downtown's most iconic hotel. The vaulted lobby is dressed in peach and gold with inlaid marble floors and a stained-glass ceiling.

Rooms are tastefully modern, with flat-screen TVs and deep soaking tubs, and are set for an upcoming renovation.

Hermitage Hotel HOTEL $$$
(☎888-888-9414, 615-244-3121; www.thehermitagehotel.com; 231 6th Ave N; r from $399; ℗❄🛜) Nashville's first million-dollar hotel was a hit with the socialites when it opened in 1910. The beaux-arts lobby feels like a czar's palace, every surface covered in rich tapestries and ornate carvings. The original art-deco men's room, dating to the 1930s, is worth a pop-in, as is the Capitol Grille restaurant, which sources from its own farm.

Rooms are upscale, with plush, four-poster beds, marble baths with soaking tubs, and mahogany furniture (ask for those ending in -08-14 for Capitol views).

🛏 The Gulch

★ 404 BOUTIQUE HOTEL $$$
(☎615-242-7404; www.the404nashville.com; 404 12th Avenue S; r $275-425; ℗🐾❄@🛜) Guests let themselves in to Nashville's hippest – and smallest – hotel. Beyond the ebonized cedar frontage, industrial grays under violet lighting lead to five rooms in the minimalist space, most featuring painstakingly hip loft spaces. Local photography by Caroline Allison adds a splash of color. There's a restaurant in a shipping container and local beers, sodas and parking are included.

🛏 West End

Music City Hostel HOSTEL $
(☎615-692-1277; www.musiccityhostel.com; 1809 Patterson St; dm $30-35, d $85-100; ℗❄@🛜) These squat brick bungalows are less than scenic, but Nashville's West End hostel is lively and welcoming, with a common kitchen, outdoor grill and fire pit. The crowd is young, international and fun, and many hoppin' West End bars are within walking distance.

Rooms are designed to function both as dorms or privates and some share showers but have their own toilet.

Hutton Hotel HOTEL $$$
(☎615-340-9333; www.huttonhotel.com; 1808 West End Ave; r from $259; ℗🐾❄@🛜) ✒ One of our favorite Nashville boutique hotels riffs on mid-century-modern design with bamboo-paneled walls and reclaimed WWI barn wood flooring. Sizable rust- and chocolate-colored rooms are well appointed with electrically controlled marble rain showers, glass wash basins, king beds, ample desk space, wide flat-screens and high-end carpet and linens.

Sustainable luxury abounds. Take a free spin in the hotel's electric Tesla!

🛏 Music Valley

Gaylord Opryland Hotel RESORT $$
(☎866-972-6779, 615-889-1000; www.gaylordhotels.com; 2800 Opryland Dr; r from $199; ℗❄@🛜🏊) This whopping 2882-room hotel is a universe unto itself, the largest non-casino resort in the USA. Why set foot outdoors when you could ride a paddleboat along an artificial river, eat sushi beneath faux waterfalls in an indoor garden or sip Scotch in an antebellum-style mansion, all *inside* the hotel's three massive glass atriums.

THE SOUTH NASHVILLE

✕ Eating

The classic Nashville meal is the 'meat-and-three' – a heaping portion of meat, served with your choice of three home-style sides. Gentrifying Germantown offers a handful of cafes and restaurants, including two standouts. Five Points in East Nashville is the epicenter of Nashville's hipster scene and is covered with cafes, restaurants and shops, with most of the action in the area of Woodlawn St between 10th and 11th.

✕ Downtown & Germantown

Arnold's   SOUTHERN $
(www.arnoldscountrykitchen.com; 605 8th Ave S; meals $9-10; ☻10:30am-2:45pm Mon-Fri) Grab a tray and line up with college students, garbage collectors and country-music stars at Arnold's, king of the meat-and-three. Slabs of drippy roast beef are the house specialty, along with fried green tomatoes, cornbread two ways, and big gooey wedges of chocolate meringue pie.

★ Rolf and Daughters   MODERN EUROPEAN $$
(☑615-866-9897; www.rolfanddaughters.com; 700 Taylor St; mains $17-26; ☻5:30-10pm; ☎) The epicenter of Germantown's foodie revival is this stunning kitchen run by Belgian chef Philip Krajeck, whose earthy pastas, rustic sauces and seasonal-changing 'modern peasant food' will stand your taste buds on end as if to say, 'What was *that?*'

Standouts of the European-inspired, locally sourced fare – it's a feeding frenzy here as the menu fluctuates with the arrival of the season's first crops – include *garganelli verde* (green from fresh spinach) and a devastatingly good pastured chicken with preserved lemon and garlic confit. Reservations? Certainly. But there's a communal table and bar for walk-ins as well.

Silo   NEW SOUTHERN $$
(☑615-750-2912; www.silotn.com; 1222 4th Ave N; mains $17-26; ☻5-11pm Tue-Sun, bar from 4pm) This Southern-influenced farm-to-table bistro in Germantown is easy on the eyes: Amish-crafted carpentry and pendant lighting by artist John Beck. The food follows suit. Though the menu changes faster than your Twitter feed, dishes like braised rabbit in housemade pasta and pan-seared Gulf corvina pop with savory and rich deliciousness.

Monell's   SOUTHERN $$
(☑615-248-4747; www.monellstn.com; 1235 6th Ave N; all you can eat $13-18; ☻10:30am-2pm Mon, 8:30am-4pm & 5-8:30pm Tue-Fri, 8:30am-8:30pm Sat, 8:30am-4pm Sun) In an old brick house just north of the District, Monell's is beloved for down-home Southern food served family style. This is not just a meal, it's an experience, as platter after platter of skillet-fried chicken, pulled pork, corn pudding, baked apples, mac and cheese and mashed potatoes keep coming...and coming. Clear your afternoon schedule!

★ Etch   MODERN AMERICAN $$$
(☑615-522-0685; www.etchrestaurant.com; 303 Demonbreun St; dinner mains $21-38; ☻11am-2pm & 5-10pm Mon-Thu, 11am-2pm & 5-10:30pm Fri, 5-10:30pm Sat; ☎) Well-known Nashville chef Deb Paquette's Etch serves some of Nashville's most inventive cuisine – comfort food whose flavors and textures have been manipulated into tantalizing combinations that surpass expectations in every bite. Octopus and shrimp bruschetta, roasted cauliflower with truffled pea pesto, cocoa-chili-spiced venison, grilled filet with sourdough baked potato bread pudding – all masterpieces. Reservations essential.

✕ The Gulch

★ Biscuit Love   BREAKFAST $
(www.biscuitlovebrunch.com; 316 11th Ave; biscuits $10-14; ☻7am-3pm; ☎) Championing everything that is wrong about American breakfast, Biscuit Love started life as a food truck in 2012. Its gluttonous gourmet takes on the Southern biscuit and gravy experience took off, allowing it to graduate to this supremely cool brick-and-mortar location in the Gulch.

Look no further than the menu's first item, the East Nasty – a perfectly fluffy buttermilk biscuit smothered by an insanely good piece of fried chicken thigh, aged chedder and perfect sausage gravy. If that's wrong, we don't wanna be right!

✕ West End & Midtown

★ Hattie B's   SOUTHERN $
(www.hattieb.com; 112 19th Ave S; quarter/half plates from $8.50/12; ☻11am-10pm Mon-Thu, to midnight Fri-Sat, to 4pm Sun) Hattie's may be the hipsterized, social-media savvy yin to Prince's Hot Chicken's off-the-grid yang, but if this isn't Nashville's best cayenne-rubbed 'hot' fried chicken, our name is mud. Perfectly moist, high-quality bird comes devilishly fried to levels that top out at 'Shut

WORTH A TRIP

PLANTATIONS NEAR NASHVILLE

Hermitage (☑ 615-889-2941; www.thehermitage.com; 4580 Rachel's Lane; adult/child $20/14, with multimedia player $28/18; ⊙ 8:30am-5pm mid-Mar–mid-Oct 15, 9am-4:30pm mid-Oct–mid-Mar) The former home of seventh president Andrew Jackson lies 15 miles east of downtown Nashville. The 1150-acre plantation is a peek into what life was like for a Mid-South gentleman farmer in the 19th century. Tour the Federal-style brick mansion, now a furnished house museum with costumed interpreters, and see Jackson's original 1804 log cabin and the old slave quarters (Jackson was a lifelong supporter of slavery, at times owning up to 100 slaves; a special exhibit tells their stories).

Belle Meade Plantation (☑ 615-356-0501; www.bellemeadeplantation.com; 5025 Harding Pike; adult/student 13-18yr/child under 13yr $18/12/10; ⊙ 9am-5pm) The Harding-Jackson family began raising thoroughbreds here (6 miles west of Nashville) in the early 1800s. Several Kentucky Derby winners have been descendants of Belle Meade's studly sire, Bonnie Scotland, who died in 1880. Yes, Bonnie can be a boy's name! The 1853 mansion is open to visitors, as are various interesting outbuildings, including a model slave cabin, and wine tasting is available on-site, too.

the Cluck Up!' hot and they mean business ('Damn Hot' was our limit). Get in line.

Fido   CAFE $
(www.fidocafe.com; 1812 21st S; mains $5-11; ⊙ 7am-11pm; 🛜) A Hillsboro institution, known for excellent coffees and breakfasts, as well as an affordable menu of salads and sandwiches. It's generally packed, yet spacious enough to accommodate the rather appealing crowd.

Pancake Pantry   BREAKFAST $
(www.pancakepantry.com; 1796 21st Ave S; mains $6.50-10; ⊙ 6am-3pm Mon-Fri, to 4pm Sat-Sun) For 50-plus years, crowds have been lining up around the block for tall stacks of pancakes done up every which way at this iconic breakfast joint. Honestly, the pancakes underwhelmed us – until we doused them in that cinnamon cream syrup. Paradise found!

✕ East Nashville

⭐ **The Pharmacy**   BURGERS, BEER GARDEN $
(www.thepharmacynashville.com; 731 Mcferrin Ave; burgers $8-11; ⊙ 11am-10pm Sun-Thu, to 11pm Fri-Sat; 🛜) Prepare to go to war for a table at this burger bar, constantly voted Nashville's best, be it at the welcoming communal table, bar or spectacular backyard beer garden. Tattooed staff sling burgers, sausages and old-school sides (tater tots!) washed back with specialty beers and hand-mixed old fashioned sodas.

Pied Piper Creamery   ICE CREAM $
(www.thepiedpipercreamery.com; 114 S 11th St; scoops $3.75; ⊙ noon-9pm Sun-Thu, to 10pm Fri

& Sat) Thicker, smoother and more packed with goodness than any other ice-cream shop in town. How to choose: Toffee Loaded Coffee? Chocolate with Cinnamon and Cayenne Pepper? Trailer Trash, with Oreo, Reese's Pieces, Snickers, Butterfinger, Twix *and* Nestlé's Crunch? It's in Five Points.

I Dream of Weenie   HOT DOGS $
(www.facebook.com/IDreamofWeenie; 113 S 11th St; hot dogs $3-5; ⊙ 11am-4pm Mon-Thu, to 6pm Fri, 10:30am-6pm Sat, to 4pm Sun) Quick and easy, this VW bus turned hot-dog stand in Five Points slings beef, turkey or vegetarian tubular products drowned in indulgent toppings (hint: pimiento cheese with chili!).

✕ Greater Nashville

Prince's Hot Chicken   FRIED CHICKEN $
(123 Ewing Dr; quarter/half/whole chicken $6/11/22; ⊙ 11:30-10pm Tue-Thu, to 4am Fri-Sat; 🅿) Tiny, faded, family-owned Prince's serves Nashville's most legendary 'hot chicken.' It's set in a gritty, northside strip mall and attracts everyone from hipsters to frat boys to entire immigrant families to local heads to hillbillies.

Fried up mild (total lie), medium (what a joke), hot (verging on insanity), Xhot (extreme masochism) and XXXHot (suicide), its chicken will burn a hole in your stomach, and take root in your soul. Cash only.

King Market Cafe   LAOTIAN, THAI $
(www.kingmarkettn.com; 300 Church St, Antioch Pike; dishes $6.50-11.50; ⊙ 9am-7:30pm) An authentic Southeast Asian cafe set inside

an Asian grocer in the Antioch Pike area –
an east Nashville suburb where this city
suddenly seems much less homogeneous.
It does noodle dishes, soups, curries and
stir-fries, a Thai-style country pork sausage,
deep-fried mackerel, and adventurous eats
like fried pork intestine. Worth a trip.

🍷 Drinking & Nightlife

Nashville has the nightlife of a city three
times its size, and you'll be hard-pressed to
find a place that doesn't have live music. College students, bachelor-party-goers, Danish
backpackers and conventioneers all rock out
downtown, where neon-lit Broadway looks
like a country-fried Las Vegas. Bars and
venues in neighborhoods such as East Nashville, Hillsboro Village, Germantown, the
Gulch, 12 South and SoBro tend to attract
more locals, with many places clustered
near Vanderbilt University.

★ Butchertown Hall   BEER HALL
(www.butchertownhall.com; 1416 Fourth Ave N; beer
$5-8; ⊙ 11am-late Mon-Fri, from 10am Sat-Sun; 🛜)
This hipster hangout in Germantown plays
to the neighborhood's historical roots – it's
the first beer hall in the neighborhood since
1909. The 2200-sq-ft space is gorgeous:
vaulted ceilings, oversized subway tiles and
stacked stone and chopped wood strategi-
cally used as earthy-accented space divid-
ers. There are 31 taps specializing in local
and rarer German options as well as cask-
conditioned English ales.

The Latin-leaning, smoke-and-brimstone-
heavy German-Southern comfort food is not
to be missed, either.

Patterson House   COCKTAIL BAR
(www.thepattersonnashville.com; 1711 Division
St; cocktails $12-14; ⊙ 5pm-3am; 🛜) Without
a doubt Nashville's best spot for artisanal
cocktails, so much so there is often a wait
(yes, for a drink at a bar!). There is no service without a seat, either at the 30-stool bar
or in the surrounding banquets. Meticulous
Prohibition-era mixology is sipped amid vintage chandeliers and checks are delivered
inside novels.

Acme Feed & Seed   BAR, LIVE MUSIC
(www.theacmenashville.com; 101 Broadway;
⊙ 11am-late Mon-Fri, from 10am Sat-Sun; 🛜)
This ambitious, four-floor takeover of an
old 1875 farm supply warehouse has finally
given Nashvillians a reason to go downtown
even when family is *not* visiting. The 1st

floor is devoted to lightning-fast pub grub,
craft beers and live music that's defiantly
un-country most nights (Southern rock,
indie, roots etc).

Head up a level for a casual cocktail lounge
complete with rescued furniture, vintage
pinball, walls made from old printing plates
and a cornucopia of music memorabilia. And
then there's the open-air rooftop, with unrivaled views over the Cumberland River and
straight down the belly of Broadway.

Pinewood Social   LOUNGE
(☑ 615-751-8111; www.pinewoodsocial.com; 33 Peabody St; ⊙ 7am-1am Mon-Fri, 9am-1am Sat-Sun) This
all-in-one off-downtown hipster retreat aims
to relieve you of your money from sunrise to
sundown. Inside a stylish former trolley barn,
there's a Crema coffeehouse, restaurant, bar
and six vintage reclaimed wooden bowling
lanes ($40 per hour). Outside is an artificial
lawn and pool and bocce ball.

Hops + Craft   BAR
(www.hopscrafts.com; 319 12th Ave S; beer $4.75-
6.60; ⊙ 2-11pm Mon-Thu, noon-midnight Fri, from
11am Sat, noon-11pm Sun; 🛜) You won't be rav-
ing about the ambiance on any postcards
home, but this small (and devoted!) bar
in the Gulch is Nashville's best for diving
head-first into the local craft beer scene.
Knowledgeable and friendly bartenders offer tastings on any number of their 36 draft
offerings.

No 308   COCKTAIL BAR
(www.bar308.com; 407 Gallatan Ave; cocktails $11-
14; ⊙ 5pm-3am) Cool kids gather at this unassuming East Nashville cocktail bar to knock
back adult shots inspired by Beat novelists
chosen from worn leather-bound menus.
Pick your poison amid low coffee tables, taxidermy, black banquets and a long bar featuring lacquered pages of classic literature.

★ Barista Parlor   COFFEE
(www.baristaparlor.com; 519 Gallatin Ave; coffee $5-
6; ⊙ 7am-8pm Mon-Fri, 8am-8pm Sat-Sun) Unre-
pentantly hipster coffee joint housed inside
a huge former transmission shop in East
Nashville. Some of America's best beans are
put through methods all but fiendish coffee
nerds will need defined (V60, Kone, Chemex
etc). The lone turntable preserving vinyl is a
mere afterthought. Prepare to wait – the art
shall not be compromised.

The espresso comes courtesy of the
famed, rare (and hand-built!) $18,000 Slayer
machine.

Crema

COFFEE

(www.crema-coffee.com; 15 Hermitage Ave; coffee $2.75-5; ⊙7am-7pm Mon-Fri, 8am-6pm Sat, 9am-4pm Sun; 🛜) This hard-core, downtown-adjacent coffeehouse serves the best brew within relative walking distance of Broadway.

Soulshine

PUB

(www.soulshinepizza.com; 1907 Division St; ⊙11am-10pm Sun-Wed, to midnight Thu-Sat) A two-story, concrete-floor, brickhouse pub and pizzeria in Midtown that attracts more jam-band-appreciating, middle-of-the-road types. Bands rock the wide rooftop patio most nights.

☆ Entertainment

Nashville's opportunities for hearing live music are unparalleled. As well as the big venues, many talented country, folk, bluegrass, Southern-rock and blues performers play smoky honky-tonks, college bars, coffee shops and organic cafes for tips. Cover charges are rare.

★ Station Inn

LIVE MUSIC

(☑615-255-3307; www.stationinn.com; 402 12th Ave S; ⊙open mike 7pm, live bands 9pm) Sit at one of the small cocktail tables, squeezed together on the worn-wood floor in this beer-only dive, illuminated with stage lights and neon signs, and behold the lightning fingers of bluegrass savants. We are talking stand-up bass, banjo, mandolin, fiddle and a modicum of yodeling.

Famed duo Doyle and Debbie, a cult-hit parody of a washed-up country-music duo, perform most Tuesdays ($20; reservations essential on ☑615-999-9244).

Bluebird Cafe

CLUB

(☑615-383-1461; www.bluebirdcafe.com; 4104 Hillsboro Rd; cover free-$20; ⊙shows 6:30pm & 9:30pm) It's in a strip mall in suburban South Nashville, but don't let that fool you: some of the best original singer-songwriters in country music have graced this tiny stage. Steve Earle, Emmylou Harris and the Cowboy Junkies have all played the Bluebird, which is the setting for the popular television series, *Nashville*. Try your luck at Monday open-mike nights.

It's first-come, first-served seating, and it's best to show up at least an hour before the show begins. No talking during the show or you'll get bounced.

Tootsie's Orchid Lounge

HONKY-TONK

(☑615-726-7937; www.tootsies.net; 422 Broadway; ⊙10am-late) FREE The most venerated of the downtown honky-tonks, Tootsie's is a blessed dive oozing boot-stomping, hillbilly, beer-soaked grace. In the 1960s club owner and den mother 'Tootsie' Bess nurtured Willie Nelson, Kris Kristofferson and Waylon Jennings on the come up. A new rooftop and stage, added in 2014, is one of Broadway's best parties-with-views.

Grand Ole Opry

MUSICAL THEATER

(☑615-871-6779; www.opry.com; 2802 Opryland Dr; tickets $40-70) Though you'll find a variety of country shows throughout the week, the performance to see is the *Grand Ole Opry*, a lavish tribute to classic Nashville country music, every Tuesday, Friday and Saturday night. Shows return to the Ryman from November to June.

Robert's Western World

HONKY-TONK

(www.robertswesternworld.com; 416 Broadway; ⊙11am-2am) FREE Buy a pair of boots, a beer or a burger at Robert's, a longtime favorite on the strip. Music starts at 11am and goes all night; Brazilbilly, the house band, rocks it after 10pm on weekends. All ages are welcome before 6pm, afterward it's strictly 21 and up.

Ryman Auditorium

CONCERT VENUE

(☑615-889-3060; www.ryman.com; 116 5th Ave N) The Ryman's excellent acoustics, historic charm and large seating capacity have kept it the premier venue in town, with big names frequently passing through. The *Opry* returns for winter runs.

Nashville Symphony

SYMPHONY

(☑615-687-6400; www.nashvillesymphony.org; 1 Symphony Pl) Hosts maestros, the local symphony and major pop stars from Randy Travis to Smokey Robinson, in the shiny new, yet beautifully antiquated, Schermerhorn Symphony Hall.

🔒 Shopping

Lower Broadway has tons of record shops, boot stores and souvenir stalls. The 12th Ave South neighborhood is the spot for ultra-trendy boutiques and vintage stores.

★ Hatch Show Print

ART, SOUVENIRS

(www.hatchshowprint.com; 224 5th Ave S; tours $15; ⊙9am-5pm Mon-Wed, to 8pm Thu-Sat) One of the oldest letterpress print shops in the US, Hatch has been using old-school, hand-cut blocks to print its bright, iconic posters since Vaudeville. The company has produced graphic ads and posters for almost every country star since and have now graduated to newly expanded digs inside the revamped Country Music Hall of Fame (p366).

There are three daily tours (12:30pm, 2pm and 3:30pm); an expanded retail space; and a gallery, where you can purchase re-strikes made from original wood plates dating from the 1870s to 1960s and one-of-a-kind monoprints reinterpreted from original woodblocks by Nashville legend Jim Sherraden.

★ **Third Man Records**   MUSIC
(www.thirdmanrecords.com; 623 7th Ave S; ⊙10am-6pm Mon-Sat, 1-4pm Sun) In a still-industrial slice of downtown you'll find Jack White's boutique record label, shop and novelty lounge, complete with its own lathe and live venue. It sells only Third Man recordings on vinyl and CD, collectible T-shirts, stickers, headphones and Pro-Ject record players. You'll also find White's entire catalog of recordings; and you can record yourself on vinyl ($15).

Live shows go off in the studio's **Blue Room** once a month. They're typically open to the public (about $10), but are only announced a couple weeks in advance. Attendees receive an exclusive colored vinyl Black and Blue of the performance.

Two Old Hippies   CLOTHING, LIVE MUSIC
(www.twooldhippies.com; 401 12th Ave S; ⊙10am-8pm Mon-Thu, to 9pm Fri-Sat, 11am-6pm Sun) Only in Nashville would an upscale retro-inspired clothing shop have a bandstand with regular live shows of high quality. And, yes, just like the threads, countrified hippie rock is the rule. The shop itself has special jewelry, fitted tees, excellent belts, made in Tennessee denim, a bounty of stage-worthy shirts and jackets and some incredible acoustic guitars.

There's live music four nights a week at 6pm and an open mike for kids on Sundays at 1pm.

Imogene + Willie   CLOTHING
(www.imogeneandwillie.com; 2601 12th Ave S; ⊙10am-6pm Mon-Fri, 11am-6pm Sat, 1-5pm Sun) This independent purveyor of style in the hip neighborhood of 12 South does built-to-last, custom-tailored denim ($250) that ships to you within a week or two.

Ernest Tubb   MUSIC
(www.etrecordshop.com; 417 Broadway; ⊙10am-10pm Sun-Thu, to midnight Fri-Sat) Marked by a

---

WORTH A TRIP

FRANKLIN

About 20 miles south of Nashville off I-65, the historic town of **Franklin** (www.historicfranklin.com) has a charming downtown and beautiful B&Bs. It was also the site of one of the Civil War's bloodiest battlefields. On November 30, 1864, some 37,000 men (20,000 Confederates and 17,000 Union soldiers) fought over a 2-mile stretch of Franklin's outskirts. Nashville's sprawl has turned much of that battlefield into suburbs, but the **Carter House** (☑615-791-1861; www.boft.org; 1140 Columbia Ave, Franklin; adult/senior/child $15/12/8; ⊙9am-5pm Mon-Sat, 11-5pm Sun; 🚻🏛) property preserves up to a 20-acre chunk of the Battle of Franklin. The house is one of the most bullet-ridden Civil War properties left in the USA (more than 1000 holes are estimated across its various buildings).

---

giant neon guitar sign, this is the best place to shop for country and bluegrass records.

Boot Country   BOOTS
(www.twofreeboots.com; 304 Broadway; ⊙10am-10:30pm Mon-Thu, to 11pm Fri & Sat, 11am-7:30pm Sun) If you're into leather, or worn rawhide, or anything close, they do all manner of boots here. Buy one pair, get two free. No joke!

Gruhn Guitars   MUSIC
(www.gruhn.com; 2120 8th Ave S; ⊙9:30am-6pm Mon-Sat) This renowned vintage instrument store has expert staff, and at any minute some unassuming virtuoso may just walk in, grab a guitar, mandolin or banjo off the wall and jam.

Pangaea   GIFTS
(www.pangaeanashville.com; 1721 21st Ave S; ⊙10am-6pm Mon-Thu, to 9pm Fri & Sat, noon-5pm Sun) There are no groovier shops in town. What with the beaded belts and silly scarves, funky hats and summery dresses, retro Portuguese soaps, Lionel Richie koozies, Day of the Dead figurines and literary-inspired jewelry.

❶ Information

Downtown Nashville and Centennial Park have free wi-fi, as do many hotels, restaurants and coffee shops.

Main Police Station ([☑]615-862-7611; 601 Korean Veterans Blvd) Nashville's Central Precinct.

Nashville Scene (www.nashvillescene.com) Free alternative weekly with entertainment listings.

Nashville Visitors Information Center ([☑]800-657-6910, 615-259-4747; www.visit musiccity.com; 501 Broadway, Bridgestone Arena; ⊘8am-5:30pm Mon-Sat, 10am-5pm Sun) Pick up free city maps here at the glass tower. A second, smaller center (150 4th Ave N; ⊘8am-5pm Mon-Fri) is run out of the corporate offices in the Regions Bank Building lobby.

Out & About Nashville (www.outandabout-nashville.com) A monthly covering the local gay and lesbian scene.

Post Office (www.usps.com; 601 Broadway; ⊘6am-6pm Mon-Fri, to 12:30pm Sat) The most convenient downtown post office.

Tennessean (www.tennessean.com) Nashville's daily newspaper.

Vanderbilt University Medical Center ([☑]615-322-5000; www.mc.vanderbilt.edu; 1211 Medical Center Dr) Widely regarded as Tennessee's best hospital.

❶ Getting There & Around

Nashville International Airport (BNS; [☑]615-275-1075, www.nashintl.com; One Terminal Dr), 8 miles east of town, is not a major air hub. **Metropolitan Transit Authority** (MTA; www.nash-villemta.org; fares $1.70-2.25) bus 18 links the airport and downtown; **Jarmon Transportation** (www.jarmontransportation.com; fares $15) runs airport shuttles to major downtown and West End hotels. Taxis charge a flat rate of $25 to downtown or Opryland.

SCENIC DRIVE: NASHVILLE'S COUNTRY TRACKS

About 25 miles southwest of Nashville off Hwy 100, drivers pick up the Natchez Trace Parkway, which leads 444 miles southwest to Natchez, MS. This northern section is one of its most attractive stretches, with broad-leafed trees leaning together to form an arch over the winding road. Near the parkway entrance, stop at the landmark Loveless Cafe (www.lovelesscafe.com; 8400 Hwy 100 , Nashville; breakfast $7.25-14.25; ⊘7am-9pm), a 1950s roadhouse famous for its biscuits with homemade preserves, country ham and ample portions of Southern fried chicken.

Greyhound ([☑]615-255-3556; www.grey-hound.com; 709 5th Ave S) is downtown. The MTA operates city bus services, based downtown at **Music City Central** (400 Charlotte Ave), including the free Music City Circuit, whose three routes hit the majority of Nashville attractions. Express buses go to Music Valley.

Nashville B-Cycle ([☑]615-625-2153; www.nashville.bcycle.com), the city's public bike-share scheme, offers more than 30 stations throughout the city center. Your first hour is free; after that your credit card will be charged $1.50 per half-hour. Daily, weekly and monthly plans are also available.

Eastern Tennessee

Dolly Parton, Eastern Tennessee's most famous native, loves her home region so much she has made a successful career out of singing about girls who leave the honeysuckle-scented embrace of the Smoky Mountains for the false glitter of the city. They're always sorry. Largely a rural region of small towns, rolling hills and river valleys, the eastern third of the state has friendly folks, hearty country food and pastoral charm. The lush, heather-tinted Great Smoky Mountains are great for hiking, camping and rafting, while the region's two main urban areas, Knoxville and Chattanooga, are easygoing riverside cities with lively student populations.

Chattanooga

Named 'the dirtiest city in America' in the 1960s, today the city is recognized as being one of the country's greenest, with miles of well-used waterfront trails, electric buses and pedestrian bridges crossing the Tennessee River. With world-class rock-climbing, hiking, biking and water-sports opportunities, it's one of the South's best cities for outdoorsy types. And it's gorgeous now, too; just check out those views from the Bluff View Art District!

The city was once a major railway hub throughout the 19th and 20th centuries, hence the 'Chattanooga Choo-Choo,' which was originally a reference to the Cincinnati Southern Railway's passenger service from Cincinnati to Chattanooga and later the title of a 1941 Glen Miller tune. The eminently walkable downtown is an increasingly gentrified maze of historic stone and brick buildings and some tasty gourmet kitchens. There's a lot to love about the 'Noog.

👁 Sights & Activities

Coolidge Park is a good place to start a riverfront stroll. There's a carousel, well-used playing fields and a 50ft climbing wall attached to one of the columns supporting the **Walnut Street Bridge**. Abutting that park, the city has installed gabions to restore the wetlands and attract more bird life. Check them out by strolling to the edge of the cool, floating decks that jut over the marsh. The much larger **Tennessee River Park** is an 8-mile, multi-use greenway that runs from downtown through Amincola Marsh and along South Chickamauga Creek. Plans are to expand its reach to a full 22 miles. **Chattanooga Nightfall** is a free concert series every Friday from May 1 to September 4 at Miller Plaza.

Hunter Museum of American Art   GALLERY
(www.huntermuseum.org; 10 Bluff View; adult/child $10/5; ⊙10am-5pm Mon, Tue, Fri & Sat, to 8pm Thu, noon-5pm Wed & Sun) Set high on the river bluffs, this striking melted-steel and glass edifice is easily the most singular architectural achievement in Tennessee. Oh, and its 19th- and 20th-century art collection is fantastic. Permanent exhibits are free the first Sunday of the month (special exhibits cost $5).

Lookout Mountain   OUTDOORS
(www.lookoutmountain.com; 827 East Brow Rd; adult/child $49/30; ⊙varies; 🚠) Some of Chattanooga's oldest and best-loved attractions are 6 miles outside the city. Admission price includes: the **Incline Railway**, which chugs up a steep incline to the top of the mountain; the world's longest underground waterfall, **Ruby Falls**; and **Rock City**, a garden with a dramatic clifftop overlook.

Outdoor Chattanooga   OUTDOORS
(📞423-643-6888; www.outdoorchattanooga.com; 200 River St) A city-run agency promoting active recreation; the website is a good resource for outdoor information, including river and trail suggestions, though walk-in visitors may be disappointed by the lack of spur-of-the-moment guidance.

🛏 Sleeping & Eating

⭐ Crash Pad   HOSTEL $
(📞423-648-8393; www.crashpadchattanooga.com; 29 Johnson St; dm/d/tr $30/79/99; 🅿❄@🛜) 🗲 The South's best hostel, run by climbers, is a sustainable den of coolness in Southside, the 'Noog's hippest downtown

neighborhood. Coed dorms overachieve: built-in lights, power outlets, fans and privacy curtains for each bed. Privates feature exposed concrete and bedside tables built into the bedframes. Access throughout is via hi-tech fobs; linens, padlocks and breakfast supplies are all included.

Up to 95% of the materials were reclaimed from the previous building and there's solar power to boot. It's the first LEED platinum-certified hostel *in the world*. Book ahead – it fills with outdoor enthusiasts of all ilk on the weekends.

Stone Fort Inn   BOUTIQUE HOTEL $$
(📞423-267-7866; www.stonefortinn.com; 120 E 10th St; r $165-214; 🅿❄🛜) Ceilings are high, craft furnishings are vintage and service is mostly phenomenal at this 16-room historic downtown boutique hotel. Each room is unique but all are awash in exposed brick and we're partial to the ones with private terraces and outdoor Jacuzzi tubs. Its Appalachian-style, farm-to-table restaurant is one of city's best.

Chattanooga Choo-Choo   HOTEL $$
(📞423-308-2440; www.choochoo.com; 1400 Market St; r/railcars from $155/189; 🅿❄@🛜🏊) Fresh off a centennial birthday and the wraps of an $8 million expansion at time of research, the city's grand old railway terminal is a bustling hotel, complete with 48 authentic Victorian railcar rooms, a retro Gilded Age bar and a stunning grand portico in the lobby. Standard rooms and suites, in separate buildings, are spacious but ordinary.

★ **Public House** NEW SOUTHERN **$$**
(☑ 423-266-3366; www.publichousechattanooga.
com; 1110 Market St; mains $8.50-32; ☺ 11am-
2:30pm & 5-9pm Mon-Thu, to 10pm Fri, noon-3pm &
5-10pm Sat) A rather chic pub and restaurant
in the refurbished warehouse district; the in-
house bar, Social, is a dark welcoming brick
house, the dining room is draped, bright
and homey, and both rooms serve a tasty
upscale menu (there's a divine pimiento
cheese and bacon burger).

St John's Meeting Place AMERICAN **$$$**
(☑ 423-266-4571; www.stjohnsmeetingplace.com;
1274 Market St; mains $14-33; ☺ 5-9:30pm Mon-
Thu, to 10pm Fri & Sat) The culinary anchor
of Chattanooga's Southside is widely considered the city's best night out. It's Johnny
Cash black (black granite floor, black-glass
chandeliers, black banquets) lending an
unorthodox but mod elegance for a foodie
habitat. The farm-to-table cuisine features
bacon-wrapped quail, lamb tenderloin, pork
belly/shoulder fried rice, local trout and so
on. Live jazz Thursdays from 6pm to 9pm.

ⓘ Information

Visitor Center (☑ 800-322-3344; www.chatta-
noogafun.com; 215 Broad St; ☺ 10am-5pm) Easy
to miss, located in an outdoor public breezeway.

ⓘ Getting There & Around

Chattanooga's modest **airport** (CHA; ☑ 423-
855-2202; www.chattairport.com; 1001 Airport
Rd) is just east of the city. The **Greyhound
station** (☑ 423-892-1277; www.greyhound.com;
960 Airport Rd) is just down the road. For access
to most downtown sites, ride the free electric
shuttle buses that ply the center and the North
Shore. The visitor center has a route map.

Roadies should fill out an online application
and take part in **Bike Chattanooga** (www.bike-
chattanooga.com), the city-sponsored bicycle-
sharing program. Bikes are lined and locked up
at 31 stations throughout the city. Rides under
60 minutes are free.

Knoxville

Once known as the 'underwear capital of
the world' for its numerous textile mills,
Knoxville is home to the University of Tennessee. Downtown's **Market Square** is full
of ornate 19th-century buildings and lovely
outdoor cafes shaded by pear trees, while
Old Town and **Hundred Block** are arty,
renovated warehouse districts centered on
Gay St, where the best nightlife blooms.

◉ Sights & Activities

Sunsphere LANDMARK
(☑ 865-251-6860; World's Fair Park, 810 Clinch Ave;
☺ 9am-10pm Apr-Oct, 11am-6pm Nov-Mar) The
city's visual centerpiece is the Sunsphere, a
golden orb (disco ball!) atop a tower that's
the main remnant of the 1982 World Fair.
You can take the elevator up to the 4th-floor
viewing deck to see the skyline, an updated
exhibit on the city or, one more floor up, a
cocktail at Icon Ultra Lounge.

Women's Basketball Hall of Fame MUSEUM
(www.wbhof.com; 700 Hall of Fame Dr; adult/child
$10/6; ☺ 10am-5pm Mon-Sat summer, 11am-5pm
Tue-Fri, 10am-5pm Sat winter; ⓓ) You can't miss
the massive orange basketball that marks
the Women's Basketball Hall of Fame, a nifty
look at the sport from the time when women
were forced to play in full-length dresses.

🛏 Sleeping & Eating

★ **Oliver Hotel** BOUTIQUE HOTEL **$$**
(☑ 865-521-0050; www.theoliverhotel.com; 700
Hall of Fame Dr; r $150-250; ℗ ✳ @ 🛜) Hipster
receptionists man Knoxville's only boutique
hotel, with 28 modern rooms with marble
sink tops and rain-shower heads in the
baths, plush linens and hand-crafted coffee
tables. It has a suave, upmarket vibe and the
Peter Kern Library bar draws craft cocktail
enthusiasts.

★ **Oli Bea** BREAKFAST **$**
(www.olibea.net; mains $6-12; ☺ 7am-1pm Mon-Sat;
🛜) It's worth sleeping in Knoxville just to
wake up to the Mexicanized Southern break-
fast fare at this morning stop in the Old City.
You'll find gussied up standards (country
ham, sage sausage, organic chicken or duck
eggs) but it's really about gourmet South
of the Border fare: pork confit *carnitas*
tostadas, *chilaquiles*, breakfast burritos –
all full-stop fabulous!

Knox Mason NEW SOUTHERN **$$**
(www.knoxmason.com; 131 S Gay St; mains $16-24;
☺ 4-11pm Tue-Thu, to midnight Fri-Sat, 10am-2pm
Sun) In the historic 100 Block of Gay St, this
is the go-to for seasonally focused, locally
sourced creative New Southern fare.

ⓘ Information

Visitor Center (☑ 800-727-8045; www.visit-
knoxville.com; 301 S Gay St; ☺ 8:30am-5pm
Mon-Sat, 9am-5pm Sun) Besides tourism info,
the visitor center also welcomes bands across
the Americana genre for WDVX's Blue Plate

Special, a free concert series at noon Monday to Saturday.

Great Smoky Mountains National Park

The Cherokee called this territory Shaconage (shah-*cone*-ah-jey), meaning roughly 'land of the blue smoke', for the heather-colored mist that hangs over the ancient peaks. The Southern Appalachians are the world's oldest mountain range, with mile upon mile of cool, humid deciduous forest.

The 815-sq-mile **park** (www.nps.gov/grsm) **FREE** is the country's most visited (double that of the Grand Canyon!) and, while the main arteries and attractions can get crowded, 95% of visitors never venture further than 100yd from their cars, so it's easy to leave the teeming masses behind. There are sections of the park in Tennessee and North Carolina.

Unlike most national parks, Great Smoky charges no admission fee. Stop by a visitor center to pick up a park map and the free *Smokies Guide*. The remains of the 19th-century settlement at **Cades Cove** are some of the park's most popular sights, as evidenced by the teeth-grinding summer traffic jams on the loop road.

Mt LeConte offers terrific hiking, as well as the only non-camping accommodations, **LeConte Lodge** (☑ 865-429-5704; www.leconte lodge.com; cabins per person adult/child 4-12yr $136/85). Though the only way to get to the lodge's rustic, electricity-free cabins is via five uphill hiking trails varying in length from 5.5 miles (Alum Cave Trail) to 8 miles (Boulevard), it's so popular you need to reserve up to a year in advance. You can drive right up to the dizzying heights of **Clingmans Dome**, the third-highest peak east of the Mississippi, with a futuristic observation tower (though it's clouded over more often than not).

With nine operating campgrounds offering about 900 campsites, you'd think finding a place to pitch would be easy. Not so in the busy summer season, so plan ahead. You can make **reservations** (☑ 800-365-2267; www.recreation.gov; camping site per night $17-23) for some sites; others are first-come, first-served. Cades Cove and Smokemont campgrounds are open year-round; others are open March to October.

Backcountry camping (☑ reservations 865-436-1231; www.nps.gov/grsm/planyourvisit/backcountry-camping.htm; per night $4) is an excellent option, which is only chargeable up to five nights (beyond that, it's free). A permit is required; you can make reservations and get permits at the ranger stations or visitor centers.

ℹ Information

The park's four interior visitor centers are **Sugarlands Visitor Center** (☑ 865-436-1291; www.nps.gov/grsm; 107 Park Headquarters Rd; ☺ 8am-7:30pm, hours vary Sep-May), at the park's northern entrance near Gatlinburg; **Cades Cove Visitor Center** (Cades Cove Loop Rd; ☺ 9am-7pm Apr-Aug, earlier Sep-Mar), halfway up Cades Cove Loop Rd, 24 miles off Hwy 441 from the Gatlinburg entrance; the Oconaluftee Visitor Center (p344), at the park's southern entrance near Cherokee in North Carolina; and the new **Clingmans' Dome Visitor Center** (Clingmans Dome Rd; ☺ 10am-6pm Apr-Oct, 9:30am-5pm Nov).

Gatlinburg

Wildly kitschy Gatlinburg hunkers at the entrance of the Great Smoky Mountains National Park, waiting to stun hikers with the scent of fudge, cotton candy and pancakes, and various oddity museums and campy attractions.

⊙ Sights & Activities

★**Ole Smoky Moonshine Holler** DISTILLERY (www.olesmokymoonshine.com; 903 Parkway; ☺ 10am-11pm) At first glance, this stone-and-wood moonshine distillery, Tennessee's first licensed moonshine maker, appears to have a Disney flair, but it's the real deal. Gathering around the hysterical bartenders, drinking the free hooch and taking in all of their colorful commentary, is Gatlinburg's best time.

Ober Gatlinburg Aerial Tramway SKI AREA (www.obergatlinburg.com; 1001 Parkway; adult/child $12.50/9.50; ☺ 9:30am-5:40pm Sun-Fri, to 6:30pm Sat) Ride the scenic 2-mile aerial tramway to the Bavarian-themed Ober Gatlinburg Ski Resort.

🛏 Sleeping & Eating

Bearskin Lodge LODGE $$ (☑ 877-795-7546; www.thebearskinlodge.com; 840 River Rd; r from $110; P ❋ 🛜 🏊) This shingled riverside lodge is blessed with timber accents and a bit more panache than other Gatlinburg comers. All of the spacious rooms have flat-screen TVs and some come

DOLLYWOOD

A self-created ode to the patron saint of East Tennessee, the big-haired, bigger-bosomed country singer Dolly Parton, **Dollywood** (☑ 865-428-9488; www.dollywood.com; 2700 Dollywood Parks Blvd; adult/child $59/47; ⊙ Apr-Dec) features Appalachian-themed rides and attractions, a water park, the new DreamMore Resort and more. Find it looming above **Pigeon Forge** (www.mypigeonforge.com), a secondhand Vegas-like mess drunk on American kitsch 9 miles north of Gatlinburg.

with gas fireplaces and private balconies jutting over the river.

Three Jimmys   AMERICAN $
(www.threejimmys.com; 1359 East Pkwy; mains $10-25; ⊙ 11am-10pm; ☎) Escape the tourist hordes on the main drag and grab a bite at this locals' favorite with friendly waitresses ('Here's your menu, baby...') and a long list of everything: BBQ, turkey Reubens, burgers, champagne chicken, steaks, a great spinach salad and so on.

KENTUCKY

With an economy based on bourbon, horse racing and tobacco, you might think Kentucky would rival Las Vegas as Sin Central. Well, yes and no. For every whiskey-soaked Louisville bar there's a dry county where you can't get anything stronger than ginger ale. For every racetrack there's a church. Kentucky is made of such strange juxtapositions. A geographic and cultural crossroads, the state combines the friendliness of the South, the rural frontier history of the West, the industry of the North and the aristocratic charm of the East. Every corner is easy on the eye, but there are few sights more heartbreakingly beautiful than the rolling limestone hills of horse country, where thoroughbred breeding is a multimillion-dollar industry. In spring the pastures bloom with tiny azure buds, earning it the moniker 'Bluegrass State.'

① Information

The boundary between Eastern and Central time goes through the middle of Kentucky.

Kentucky State Parks (☑ 800-255-7275; www.parks.ky.gov) Offers info on hiking, caving, fishing, camping and more in Kentucky's 52 state parks. So-called 'Resort Parks' have lodges. 'Recreation Parks' are for roughin' it.

Kentucky Travel (☑ 800-225-8747, 502-564-4930; www.kentuckytourism.com) Sends out a detailed booklet on the state's attractions.

Louisville

Best known as the home of the Kentucky Derby, Louisville (or Luhvul, as the locals say) is handsome, underrated and undeniably cool. A major Ohio River shipping center during the days of westward expansion, Kentucky's largest city is on the come up, with hip bars, superb farm-to-table restaurants, and an engaging, young and increasingly progressive population. It's a fun place to spend a few days, checking out the museums, wandering the old neighborhoods and sipping some bourbon.

◉ Sights & Activities

The Victorian-era Old Louisville neighborhood, just south of downtown, is well worth a stroll. Don't miss **St James Court**, just off Magnolia Ave, with its utterly charming gas-lamp-lit park. There are several wonderful **historic homes** (☑ 502-899-5079; www.historichomes.org) in the area open for tours, including Thomas Edison's old shotgun cottage.

★ **Churchill Downs**   RACETRACK
(www.churchilldowns.com; 700 Central Ave) On the first Saturday in May, a who's who of upper-crust America puts on their seersucker suits and most flamboyant hats and descends for the 'greatest two minutes in sports': the Kentucky Derby, the longest-running consecutive sporting event in North America.

After the race, the crowd sings 'My Old Kentucky Home' and watches as the winning horse is covered in a blanket of roses. Then they party. Actually, they've been partying for a while. The **Kentucky Derby Festival** (www.kdf.org), which includes a balloon race, a marathon, and the largest fireworks display in North America, starts two weeks before the big event. Most seats at the derby are by invitation only or have been reserved years in advance. On Derby Day, $60 gets you into the infield, which is a debaucherous rave with no seats, as well as the classier Paddock Area, where you can see the horses getting ready for each race. It's crowded and it was previously hard to see races, but the newly installed 4K video board (the world's largest) has alleviated that minor detail. If you are a connoisseur of the thoroughbreds, warm-ups and other races take place from April to June and again in September and November, where it's possible to snag $3 seats.

Kentucky Derby Museum   MUSEUM
(www.derbymuseum.org; Gate 1, Central Ave; adult/senior/child $14/13/6; ⊙8am-5pm Mon-Sat, 11am-5pm Sun mid-Mar–mid-Nov, from 9am Mon-Sat, 11am-5pm Sun Dec–mid-Mar) On the racetrack grounds, the museum has exhibits on derby history, including a peek into the life of jockeys and a roundup of the most illustrious horses. Highlights include a 360-degree HD film about the race, the 30-minute walking tour of the grandstands (which includes some engaging yarns) and mint juleps in the museum cafe.

The 90-minute 'Inside the Gates Tour' ($11) leads you through the jockey's quarters and posh VIP seating areas known as Millionaire's Row.

Muhammad Ali Center   MUSEUM
(www.alicenter.org; 144 N 6th St; adult/senior/child $9/8/4; ⊙9:30am-5pm Tue-Sat, noon-5pm Sun) ✐ A love offering to the city from its most famous native, and an absolute must-see. For a black man from the South during his era, to rejoice in his own greatness and beauty was revolutionary and inspiring to behold – and this museum captures it all.

Louisville Slugger
Museum & Factory   MUSEUM
(www.sluggermuseum.org; 800 W Main St; adult/senior/child $12/11/7; ⊙9am-5pm Mon-Sat, 11am-5pm Sun; 🖼) Look for the 120ft baseball bat leaning against the museum. Hillerich & Bradsby Co have been making the famous Louisville Slugger here since 1884. Admission includes a plant tour and a hall of baseball memorabilia, including Babe Ruth's bat, and a free mini slugger.

Frazier History Museum   MUSEUM
(www.fraziermuseum.org; 829 W Main St; adult/student/child $12/10/8; ⊙9am-5pm Mon-Sat, noon-5pm Sun) Surprisingly ambitious for a

midsized city, this state-of-the-art museum covers 1000 years of history with grisly battle dioramas and costumed interpreters demonstrating swordplay and staging mock debates.

Kentucky Science Center   MUSEUM
(☑502-561-6100; www.kysciencecenter.org; 727 W Main St; adult/child $13/11; ⊙9:30am-5:30pm Sun-Thu, to 9pm Fri & Sat; 🖼) Set in a historic building on Main St there are three floors of exhibits that illuminate biology, physiology, physics, computing and more for families (kids love it). For an extra $8 to $10 you can catch a film in the IMAX theater.

Big Four Bridge   WALKING, CYCLING
(East River Rd) Built between 1888 and 1895, the Big Four Bridge, which spans the Ohio River and reaches the Indiana shores, has been closed to vehicular traffic since 1969 but was reopened in 2013 as a pedestrian and cycling path; excellent city and river views throughout.

KENTUCKY FACTS

Nickname Bluegrass State

Population 4.4 million

Area 39,728 sq miles

Capital city Frankfort (population 25,500)

Other cities Louisville (population 750,000), Lexington (population 310,000)

Sales tax 6%

Birthplace of 16th US president Abraham Lincoln (1809–65), 'gonzo' journalist Hunter S Thompson (1937–2005), boxer Muhammad Ali (b 1942), actresses Ashley Judd (b 1968) and Jennifer Lawrence (b 1990)

Home of Kentucky Derby, Louisville Slugger, bourbon

Politics From generally to extremely conservative in rural areas

Famous for Horses, bluegrass music, basketball, bourbon, caves

Ongoing internal conflict North vs South allegiance during the Civil War

Driving distances Louisville to Lexington 77 miles, Lexington to Mammoth Cave National Park 135 miles

THE SOUTH LOUISVILLE

🛏 Sleeping

Chain hotels cluster near the airport off I-264.

Rocking Horse B&B
B&B $$

(☎ 502-583-0408; www.rockinghorse-bb.com; 1022 S 3rd St; r from $125; ▣✳@🛜) On a stretch of 3rd St once known as Millionaire's Row, this 1888 Richardsonian Romanesque mansion is chock-full of astounding historic detail. The six guest rooms are decorated with Victorian antiques and splendid original stained glass. Guests can eat their two-course breakfast in the English country garden or sip complimentary port in the parlor. The cheapest room sacrifices space and a bathtub for a street-facing balcony.

⭐ 21c Museum Hotel
HOTEL $$$

(☎ 502-217-6300; www.21chotel.com; 700 W Main St; r from $239; ▣✳🛜) This contemporary art museum–hotel features edgy design details: video screens project your distorted image and falling language on the wall as you wait for the elevator; water-blurred, see-through glass urinal walls line the men's rooms. Rooms, though not as interesting as the five contemporary art galleries/common areas, have iPod docks and mint julep kits.

Brown Hotel
HOTEL $$$

(☎ 502-583-1234; www.brownhotel.com; 335 West Broadway; r $179-399; ▣😊✳🛜) Opera stars, queens and prime ministers have trod the marble floors of this storied downtown hotel, now restored to all its 1920s glamor with 294 comfy rooms and an impressive lobby bourbon bar under original English Renaissance gilded ceilings.

THE HAUNTED HOSPITAL

Towering over Louisville like a mad king's castle, the abandoned **Waverly Hills Sanatorium** once housed victims of an early 20th-century tuberculosis epidemic. When patients died, workers dumped their bodies down a chute into the basement. No wonder the place is said to be one of America's most haunted buildings. Search for spooks with a nighttime ghost-hunting **tour** (☎ 502-933-2142; www.therealwaverlyhills. com; 4400 Paralee Lane; 2hr tours/2hr ghost hunt/overnight $22.50/50/100; ⊙ Fri & Sat Mar-Aug); the genuinely fearless can even spend the night! Many claim it's the scariest place they've ever been.

In 1926, Louisville's signature dish, the Hot Brown (open-faced turkey sandwich with turkey, bacon, pimientos, and Mornay sauce) was invented here and is still served in all three in-house restaurants.

🍴 Eating

The number of incredible kitchens multiplies every year, especially in the engaging **NuLu** ('New Louisville') area, where there are numerous galleries and boutiques to explore. The **Highlands** area around Bardstown and Baxter Rds is another popular nightlife and dining spot.

Gralehaus
MODERN AMERICAN $

(www.gralehaus.com; 1001 Baxter Ave; mains $6-13; ⊙ 8am-4pm Sun-Tue, to 10pm Wed-Sat; 🛜) There's breakfast all day at this small eatery housed in a historic early 20th-century home and you should indeed indulge in their chef-centric takes on traditional Southern comforts at all hours (think locally sourced biscuits and duck gravy, lamb and grits). Serious signature coffee drinks excel as well.

Upstairs, three rustic-chic rooms feature craft-beer-stocked mini-bars, hardwood ceilings and edgy furnishings.

The Post
DELI $

(www.thepostlouisville.com, 1045 Goss Ave; mains $3-13; ⊙ 11am-2am Wed-Mon; 🛜) In gentrifying Germantown, New York–style pizza by the slice, sub sandwiches and great spaces (sunny patio out the front, comfy bar in the back) evoke a pricier atmosphere and cooler vibe than your bill suggests.

⭐ Mayan Cafe
MEXICAN $$

(☎ 502-566-0651; www.themayancafe.com; 813 E Market St; mains $14-23; ⊙ 11am-2:30pm & 5-10pm Mon-Thu, to 10:30pm Fri-Sat; 🛜) 🍃 Check your visions of piñatas and mariachis at the door – Chef Bruce Ucán's subtle farm-to-table Mexican mainstay is a journey about flavor, not patriotic pomp and circumstance. Impossibly fresh, sustainably produced seasonal menus draw heavily from the Yucatán Peninsula and dishes nail that just-right wallop between taste and texture.

Garage Bar
GASTROPUB $$

(www.garageonmarket.com; 700 E Market St; dishes $5-17; 🛜) The best thing to do on a warm afternoon in Louisville is to make your way to this uber-hip converted NuLu service station (accented by two kissing Camaros) and order a round of basil gimlets and the ham platter (a tasting of four regionally cured hams, served with fresh bread and preserves; $21).

Then move onto the menu which ranges from the best brick-oven pizza in town to divine rolled oysters.

★ Decca
MODERN AMERICAN $$$

(☎ 502-749-8128; www.deccarestaurant.com; 812 E Market St; mains $24-31; ⏱ 5:30-10pm Mon-Thu, to 11pm Fri & Sat; 🛜) A beautiful space with a cork-and-wood floor, fountain-strewn patio and gorgeous Laguiole cutlery opened by a chef from San Francisco (albeit a Southerner by birth). Kentuckians were skeptical, but Annie Pettry wooed and won. The emphasis of the delectable, seasonally changing menu is wood-fired roasts.

But they aren't afraid to give veggies the treatment, too – the wood-grilled broccoli with almonds and anchovy is an absolute knockout.

Proof
NEW SOUTHERN $$$

(☎ 502-217-6360; www.proofonmain.com; 702 W Main St; mains $11-34; ⏱ 7-10am, 11am-2pm & 5:30-10pm Mon-Thu, to 11pm Fri, 7am-3pm & 5:30-11pm Sat, to 1pm Sun; 🛜) Arguably Louisville's best restaurant. The cocktails ($8 to $15) are incredible, the wine and bourbon 'library' (they're known to pour from exclusive and rare barrels of Woodford Reserve and Van Winkle) is long and satisfying, and startling dishes range from country ham falafel to a deliciously messy bison burger or a high-minded take on 'hot' fried chicken.

🍷 Drinking & Nightlife

The free *Weekly Leo* (www.leoweekly.com) lists local gigs.

Holy Grale
PUB

(www.holygralelouisville.com; 1034 Bardstown Rd; ⏱ 4pm-late; 🛜) One of Bardstown's best bars is housed in an old church, with a menu of funked-up pub grub (blistered shishito peppers, red curry mussels) and a buzzworthy beer list dependent on rarer German, Danish, Belgian and Japanese brews on tap. The most intense beers (up to 13% alcohol) can be found in the choir loft. Hallelujah!

Crescent Hill Craft House
BAR

(www.crafthousebrews.com; 2636 Frankfort Ave; beers $5-6.50; ⏱ 4pm-midnight Mon-Thu, to 2am Fri, noon-2am Sat-Sun; 🛜) The new darling of the artsy-upscale Crescent Hill neighborhood, 6 miles east of downtown, this bar-restaurant devotes its taps to 40 great-value microbrews, all of which are from Kentuck-

iana and projected on a side wall complete with alcohol content and IBU units.

Knock them back behind the hoity-toity (and at times progressively vegetarian) bar food like poutine with short ribs, pork belly BLTs or smoked eggplant barley burgers.

Ei8ht Up
BAR

(www.8uplouisville.com; 350 West Chestnut St; cocktails $8-14; ⏱ 4pm-midnight Sun-Thu, to 2am Fri-Sat; 🛜) Louisville's newest and hottest drinking den, on the rooftop of a Hilton Garden Inn (don't hold that against it). It's all about the open-air terrace, a come-one, come-all cornucopia of all leanings and persuasions, and its expansive good-time bar surrounded by a variety of cozy, fire-lit lounge areas.

Please & Thank You
CAFE

(www.pleaseandthankyoulouisville.com; 800 E Market St; drinks $2-4.75; ⏱ 7am-6pm Mon-Fri, 8am-6pm Sat, 8am-4pm Sun; 🛜) The kind of indie cafe that makes a neighborhood. It does creamy espresso and home-baked bread pudding, creative scones and coffee cakes, zucchini bread and gooey chocolate-chip cookies. Oh, and it also sells vinyl records, which only adds to its anti-Starbucks mystique.

Shopping

★ Joe Ley Antiques
ANTIQUES

(www.joeley.com; 615 E Market St; ⏱ 10am-5pm Tue-Sat) Go down the rabbit hole into this massive, three-story brick-and-stained glass antique emporium crammed with collectibles from eight decades. Think homely dolls, freaky furniture and chunky jewelry – and everything else *including* the kitchen sink.

Butchertown Market
BOUTIQUES

(www.thebutchertownmarket.com; 1201 Story Ave; ⏱ 10am-6pm Mon-Fri, to 5pm Sat) This converted slaughterhouse complex that's been turned into a grab bag of quirky, cute and artsy boutiques is a zoo of desirables. Whether it's funky jewelry, kooky gifts, exquisite Cellar Door chocolates, craftsman metal fixtures, bath and body products or baby clothes, someone is selling it here.

Taste
WINE

(☎ 502-409-4646; www.tastefinewinesandbourbons.com; 634 E Market St; tastings $3-5.50; ⏱ 11am-8pm Tue-Wed, to late Thu & Fri, 10:30am-late Sat) A high-end wine shop that sells small-batch wines and bourbons, and offers sips of either (or both) to help you decide (or perhaps it muddles the whole process).

Come, sip, buy. The 10-option wine list turns over every Tuesday.

ⓘ Information

Visitor Center (☑ 502-379-6109; www.goto louisville.com; 301 S 4th St; ⊙ 10am-6pm Mon-Sat, noon-5pm Sun) Stuffed with brochures and helpful staff.

ⓘ Getting There & Around

Louisville's International Airport (SDF; ☑ 502-367-4636; www.flylouisville.com; 600 Terminal Drive) is 5 miles south of town on I-65. Get there by cab for a flat rate of $20 or local bus 2. The **Greyhound station** (☑ 502-561-2805; www.greyhound.com; 720 W Muhammad Ali Blvd) is just west of downtown. **TARC** (www.ridetarc.org; 1000 W Broadway; fares $1.75) runs local buses from the Union Station depot, including its free ZeroBus, an electric bus fleet that circles Main, Market and 4th Sts, taking in most of the city's attractions and coolest restaurants. Buses do not require exact change, but there is no mechanism for giving change back.

Bluegrass Country

Drive through northeast Kentucky's Bluegrass Country on a sunny day and glimpse horses grazing in the brilliant green hills dotted with ponds, poplar trees and handsome estate houses. These once-wild woodlands and meadows have been a center of horse breeding for almost 250 years. The region's natural limestone deposits – you'll see limestone bluffs rise majestic from out of nowhere – are said to produce especially nutritious grass. The area's principal city, Lexington, is called the 'Horse Capital of the World.'

Lexington

Even the prison looks like a country club in Lexington, home of million-dollar houses and multimillion-dollar horses. Once the wealthiest and most cultured city west of the Allegheny Mountains, it was called 'the Athens of the West.' It's home to the University of Kentucky and is the heart of the thoroughbred industry. The small downtown has some pretty Victorian neighborhoods, but most of the attractions are in the countryside.

◉ Sights & Activities

It's well worth taking a drive into the countryside, where postcard-perfect horse farms dot the landscape like a farmland fairy-tale

across pastureland peppered with picket fences and whinnying thoroughbreds.

Kentucky Horse Park MUSEUM, PARK (www.kyhorsepark.com; 4089 Iron Works Pkwy; adult/child $16/8, horseback riding $25; ⊙ 9am-5pm daily mid-Mar–Oct, Wed-Sun Nov–mid-Mar; ⊞) An educational theme park and equestrian sports center sits on 1200 acres just north of Lexington. Horses representing 50 different breeds live in the park and participate in special live shows.

Also included, the **International Museum of the Horse**, with its neat dioramas of the horse through history, from the tiny prehistoric 'eohippus' to Pony Express mail carriers, and the **American Saddlebred Museum**, devoted to America's favorite native horse. Guided 35-minute horseback rides are offered seasonally and closer-look farm tours can be arranged.

Thoroughbred Center FARM (☑ 859-293-1853; www.thethoroughbredcenter. com; 3380 Paris Pike; adult/child $15/8; ⊙ tours 9am Mon-Sat Apr-Oct) Most farms are closed to the public, but you can see working racehorses up close here, with tours of the stables, practice tracks and paddocks.

Ashland HISTORIC BUILDING (www.henryclay.org; 120 Sycamore Rd; adult/child $10/5; ⊙ 10am-4pm Tue-Sat, 1-4pm Sun Mar-Dec) Just 1.5 miles east of downtown, part historic home of one of Kentucky's favorite sons, part public park, this was the Italianate estate of famed statesman and great compromisor Henry Clay (1777–1852).

A gorgeous property set in the midst of a tony historic neighborhood, it's well worth the admission to enter the home, but you can walk the property for free, peer into the carriage house where his coach is on display, and you can see the, ahem, privy (outhouse), too.

Mary Todd-Lincoln House HISTORIC BUILDING (www.mtlhouse.org; 578 W Main St; adult/child $10/5; ⊙ 10am-4pm Mon-Sat mid-Mar–mid-Nov) This modest 1806 house has articles from the first lady's childhood and her years as Abe's wife, including original White House pieces. Tours hourly on the hour; last at 3pm.

🛏 Sleeping

Look for the Lexington opening of trendy 21C Museum Hotel downtown at the corner of Main and Upper in the historic First National Bank Building by mid-2016.

Kentucky Horse Park CAMPGROUND $
(☎ 859-259-4257; www.kyhorsepark.com; 4089 Iron Works Pkwy; sites $20, powered sites $26-35; 🛜 ❄) There are 260 paved sites, plus showers, laundry, grocery, playgrounds and more. Primitive camping is also available.

★ **Lyndon House** B&B $$
(☎ 859-420-2683; www.lyndonhouse.com; 507 N Broadway; r from $179; P ❄ @) A detail-oriented ordained-minister-turned-foodie is your host at this discerning and spacious downtown B&B in a historic mansion dating to 1885. Anton takes hospitality seriously, as he does breakfast. The seven rooms feature period furnishings and all the mod-cons; and you're steps from a long list of restaurants and breweries.

✕ Eating & Drinking

Lexington's vibiest concentration of cutting-edge bars and restaurants is along and around revitalized Jefferson Ave between W 6th and Main, which includes several craft breweries.

★ **County Club** BARBECUE $
(www.countyclubrestaurant.com; 555 Jefferson St; mains $8-12; ⊙ 5-10pm Tue-Thu, from 11am Fri-Sun; 🛜) This smoked-meat sanctuary occupies the former storage garage of a Sunbeam bread factory. Though the service is best described as hipster aloof, the wares – a burger, brisket on rye, Sriracha-lime smoked chicken wings, flank steak etc – are moist, tender and perfectly smoked. Douse it all in four housemade sauces (vinegar, sweet, smoked habenero and mustard – oh, that mustard!). The rotating list of daily specials and draft beers help you forget the metallic vibe.

Stella's Kentucky Deli DELI $
(www.stellaskentuckydeli.com; 143 Jefferson St; sandwiches $3.50-9; ⊙ 10:30am-4pm Mon-Tue, to 9pm Wed-Thu, 9am-1pm Fri-Sat, 9am-9pm Sun; 🛜) This don't-miss deli has 30 years under its apron, but the latest owners refocused a few years back, upping the cool quotient and concentrating on invaluable provisions from local farmers. Great sandwiches, soups and salads, along with seasonal brews, are served in a colorful historic home with reclaimed tin roof and sociable bar.

Doodles CAFE $
(www.doodlesrestaurant.com; 262 N Limestone; mains $4-10; ⊙ 8am-2pm Tue-Sun; 🛜) 🥪 Breakfast fiends should head to this former gas station to fill up on scrumptious comfort

WORTH A TRIP

BLUEGRASS BONANZA!

Kentuckian Bill Monroe is considered the founding father of bluegrass music; his band, the Blue Grass Boys, gave the genre its name. Bluegrass has its roots in the old-time mountain music, mixed with the fast tempo of African songs and spiced with lashings of jazz. Any banjo picker or fiddle fan will appreciate the historic exhibits at the **International Bluegrass Music Museum** (www.bluegrassmuseum.org; 107 Daviess St; adult/student $5/2; ⊙ 10am-5pm Tue-Sat, 1-4pm Sun) in Owensboro, where you can stumble into a jam session on the first Thursday of the month. If you miss it, head to the city's free **Friday After 5** (www.fridayafter5.com) concert series throughout summer, which also features bluegrass at 7pm. The pretty Ohio River town, about 100 miles west of Louisville, also hosts the **ROMP Bluegrass Festival** (www.rompfest.com; tickets $15-50; ⊙ late Jun).

food led by shrimp and grits (with green onion rémoulade and country ham), oatmeal brûleé and local egg casseroles; all organic and local where possible.

Natural Provisions FRENCH $$
(264 Walton Ave; mains $15-25; ⊙ 11am-3pm & 4-10pm; 🛜) This industrial-chic culinary complex in a former bottling factory houses a French brasserie, a boulangerie/coffee shop and gourmet beer hall/market; together, they bear the weight of Lexington's new cradle of cool. It oozes hipness from its colorful button-tufted banquets to its long, stylish bar with deer-antler beer taps. *Voilà*! Meet Lexington, Version 2.0.

Coles 735 Main MODERN AMERICAN $$$
(☎ 859-266-9000; www.coles735main.com; 735 E Main St; mains $19-33; ⊙ 5-10pm Mon-Thu, to 11pm Fri-Sat; 🛜) Original fox-and-hound murals line the walls of this long-standing restaurant location (eight have tried and failed over the course of decades) but Coles 735 Main has spruced up what looks like little more than a chiropractic office, thrown in a Provençal color scheme, a charming front patio and, most importantly, nailed the food and drink.

You'll find it packed as early as 7pm on a Monday – Lexingtonians have embraced the change, flocking here for bourbon cocktails and top-end local takes on both classic (killer grit fries with pecorino cheese) and more adventurous dishes.

Country Boy Brewing MICROBREWERY
(www.countryboybrewing.com; 436 Chair Ave) True to its name, Country Boy – all trucker hats, taxidermy and camo – delivers the best beer in the most authentically Kentuckian climate. Up to 16 taps are devoted to their own experimental concoctions, brewed with a rural Mikkeller-like approach (spruce-needle ales, crab-apple saisons, jalapeño smoked porters) and another eight for guests. There's no food, but a different food truck pulls round each night.

THE BOURBON TRAIL

Silky, caramel-colored bourbon whiskey was likely first distilled in Bourbon County, north of Lexington, around 1789. Today 90% of all bourbon that comes out of the US is produced in Kentucky, thanks to its pure, limestone-filtered water. Bourbon must contain at least 51% corn, and be stored in charred oak barrels for a minimum of two years. While connoisseurs drink it straight or with water, you must try a mint julep, the archetypal Southern drink made with bourbon, simple syrup and crushed mint.

The **Oscar Getz Museum of Whiskey History** (www.whiskeymuseum.com; 114 N 5th St; ⊙10am-4pm Tue-Sat, noon-4pm Sun), in Bardstown, tells the bourbon story with old moonshine stills and other artifacts.

Most of Kentucky's distilleries, which are centered on Bardstown and Frankfort, offer tours. Check out Kentucky's official **Bourbon Trail website** (www.kybourbontrail.com). Note that it doesn't include every distillery.

To get around the dilemma of drinking and driving, sit back with your whiskey snifter on a tour with **Mint Julep Tours** (☑502-583-1433; www.mintjuleptours.com; 140 N Fourth St, Suite 326; tours from $99).

Distilleries near Bardstown:

Heaven Hill (www.bourbonheritagecenter.com; 1311 Gilkey Run Rd; tours $10-40; ⊙10am-5pm Mon-Fri, noon-4pm Sun, closed Sun-Mon Jan-Feb) Distillery tours are offered, but you may also opt to explore the interactive Bourbon Heritage Center.

Jim Beam (☑502-543-9877; www.americanstillhouse.com; 149 Happy Hollow Rd; tours per person $10; ⊙9am-5:30pm Mon-Sat, noon-4:30pm Sun) Watch a film about the Beam family and sample small-batch bourbons at the country's largest bourbon distillery. Beam makes Knob Creek (good), Knob Creek Single Barrel (better), Basil Hayden's (velvety) and the fabulous Booker's (high-proof enlightenment).

Maker's Mark (☑270-865-2099; www.makersmark.com; 3350 Burks Spring Rd; tours $9; ⊙9:30am-3:30pm Mon-Sat, 11:30-3:30pm Sun, closed Sun Jan-Feb) This restored Victorian distillery is like a bourbon theme park, with an old gristmill and a gift shop where you can seal your own bottle in molten red wax.

Willet (☑502-348-0899; www.kentuckybourbonwhiskey.com; Loretto Rd; tours $7-12; ⊙9am-5:30pm Mon-Fri, 10am-5:30pm Sat, noon-4:30 Sun Mar-Dec) A craftsman, family-owned distillery making small-batch bourbon in its own patented style. It's a gorgeous 120-acre property and one of our favorites. Tours run throughout the day.

Distilleries near Frankfort/Lawrenceburg:

Buffalo Trace (☑800-654-8471; www.buffalotracedistillery.com; 1001 Wilkinson Blvd; ⊙9am-5:30pm Mon-Sat, noon-5:30pm Sun Apr-Oct) **FREE** The nation's oldest continuously operating distillery has highly regarded tours and free tastings.

Four Roses (☑502-839-3436; www.fourrosesbourbon.com; 1224 Bonds Mills Rd; tours $5; ⊙9am-4pm Mon-Sat, noon-4pm Sun, closed summer) One of the most scenic distilleries, in a riverside Spanish Mission–style building. Free tastings.

Woodford Reserve (☑859-879-1812; www.woodfordreserve.com; 7855 McCracken Pike; tours $10-30; ⊙10am-3pm Mon-Sat, 1-3pm Sun Mar-Dec) The historic site along a creek is restored to its 1800s glory; the distillery still uses old-fashioned copper pots. By far the most scenic of the lot.

☆ Entertainment

Keeneland Association RACETRACK
(☑ 859-254-3412; www.keeneland.com; 4201 Versailles Rd; general admission $5; ☺ races Apr & Oct) Second only to Churchill Downs in terms of quality of competition, races run in April and October, when you can also glimpse champions train from sunrise to 10am. Frequent horse auctions lure sheiks, sultans, hedgefund princes and those who love (or serve) them.

Red Mile RACETRACK
(www.theredmile.com; 1200 Red Mile Rd; admission $2; ☺ races Aug–first week of Oct) Head here to see live harness racing in the covered grandstand or in the plush comfort of the clubhouse, where drivers on sulkies race champion standardbred pacers and trotters on the most historic mile-long harness track in the world. Live races are in the fall, but you can watch and wager on simulcast racing year-round.

ℹ Information

Visitor Center (☑ 859-233-7299; www.visitlex. com; 401 W Main St; ☺ 9am-5pm Mon-Fri, from 10am Sat, noon-5pm Sun) Pick up maps and area information from the visitor center, located downtown in an upscale restaurant complex known as the Square.

ℹ Getting There & Around

Blue Grass Airport (LEX; ☑ 859-425-3100; www.bluegrassairport.com; 4000 Terminal Dr) is west of town, with about a dozen domestic nonstops. **Greyhound** (☑ 859-299-0428; www. greyhound.com; 477 W New Circle Rd) is two miles from downtown. **Lex-Tran** (www.lextran. com) runs local buses ($1; bus 6 goes to the Greyhound station, bus 21 goes to the airport and Keeneland weekdays from 6:30am to 8:50am and 1:30pm to 6:10pm only) as well as the free Colt trolley, a diesel/electric hybrid trolleybus that operates on two downtown routes, taking in most major points of interest and nightlife.

Central Kentucky

The Bluegrass Pkwy runs from I-65 in the west to Rte 60 in the east, passing through some of the most luscious pastureland in Kentucky.

About 40 miles south of Louisville is **Bardstown**, the 'Bourbon Capital of the World'. The historic downtown comes alive for the **Kentucky Bourbon Festival** (www. kybourbonfestival.com; Bardstown; ☺ Sep). Have a meal, some bourbon and a good night's sleep in the dim limestone environs of **Old Talbott Tavern** (☑ 502-348-3494; www. talbotts.com; 107 W Stephen Foster Ave; r from $69; mains $10-23; P ❄), which has been welcoming the likes of Abraham Lincoln and Daniel Boone since the late 1700s.

Follow Hwy 31 southwest to **Hodgenville** and the **Abraham Lincoln Birthplace** (www. nps.gov/abli; 2995 Lincoln Farm Road, Hodgenville; ☺ 8am-4:45pm, to 6:45pm summer) **FREE**, a faux-Greek temple constructed around an old log cabin. Ten minutes away is Honest Abe's boyhood home at Knob Creek, with access to hiking trails.

About 25 miles (30 minutes) southwest of Lexington is **Shaker Village at Pleasant Hill** (www.shakervillageky.org; 3501 Lexington Rd; adult/child $10/5; riverboat rides $10/5; ☺ 10am-5pm), home to a community of the Shaker religious sect until the early 1900s. Tour impeccably restored buildings, set amid buttercup meadows and winding stone paths. There's a charming **inn** (☑ 859-734-5611; www. shakervillageky.org; 3501 Lexington Rd; r $110-300; P ⧖) and restaurant, a paddle-boat ride beneath the limestone bluffs along the Kentucky River, and a gift shop.

Daniel Boone National Forest

More than 700,000 acres of rugged ravines and gravity-defying sandstone arches cover much of the Appalachian foothills of eastern Kentucky. The main **ranger station** (☑ 859-745-3100; www.fs.fed.us/r8/boone; 1700 Bypass Rd) is in Winchester.

An hour southeast of Lexington is the **Red River Gorge**, whose cliffs and natural arches make for some of the best rock climbing in the country. **Red River Outdoors** (☑ 859-230-3567; www.redriveroutdoors.com; 415 Natural Bridge Rd; full-day guided climb for two from $100, cabins from $110) offers guided climbing trips, cabins on the ridge line and yoga. **Red River Climbing** (www.redriverclimbing.com) offers detailed route information on their website. Climbers and hikers (only) can also pay $2 to camp out behind **Miguel's Pizza** (www. miguelspizza.com; 1890 Natural Bridge Rd; pizza from $10; ☺ 7am-8:45pm Mon-Thu, to 9:45pm Fri & Sat; ⧖) in the hamlet of Slade, which also runs a climbing shop. Bordering Red River Gorge is the **Natural Bridge State Resort Park** (☑ 606-663-2214; www.parks.ky.gov; 2135 Natural Bridge Rd; r $109-154, cottages $149-239; P ⧖ ✦), notable for its sandstone arch, it's a family-friendly park, with camping, rooms and cottages at its Hemlock Lodge and 20 miles of short hiking trails. If you don't want to leg it, you can ride the sky lift over the arch ($13 return).

Mammoth Cave National Park

With the longest cave system on earth, **Mammoth Cave National Park** (www.nps.gov/maca; 1 Mammoth Cave Pkwy, exit 53, off I-65; tours adult $5-55, child $3.50-20; ☺8am-6pm, to 6:30pm summer) has some 400 miles of surveyed passageways. Mammoth is at least three times longer than any other known cave, with vast interior cathedrals, bottomless pits and strange, undulating rock formations. The caves have been used for prehistoric mineral-gathering, as a source of saltpeter for gunpowder and as a tuberculosis hospital. Guided tours have been offered since 1816. The area became a national park in 1941 and now attracts 600,000 visitors each year.

The only way to see the caves is on the excellent **ranger-guided tours** (☎800-967-2283) and it's wise to book ahead, especially in summer. Tours range from subterranean strolls to strenuous, day-long spelunking adventures (adults only). The Historic tour is particularly interesting.

In addition to the caves, the park contains 85 miles of trails – all for hiking, 60 miles designated for horseback riding and 25 miles for mountain biking. There are also three campgrounds with restrooms, though only a few sites have electricity or water hookups ($12 to $50), and 13 free backcountry campsites. Get your backcountry permit at the park visitor center.

GEORGIA

The largest state east of the Mississippi River is a labyrinth of geographic and cultural extremes: right-leaning Republican politics rub against liberal idealism; small, conservative towns merge with sprawling, progressive, financially flush cities; northern mountains rise to the clouds and produce roaring rivers, while coastal marshlands teem with fiddler crabs and swaying cordgrass. Georgia's southern beaches and islands are a treat. And so are its restaurant kitchens.

🛈 Information

Your own car is the most convenient way to move around Georgia. I-75 bisects the state running north–south; I-20 runs east–west.

Discover Georgia (☎800-847-4842; www.exploregeorgia.org) For statewide tourism information.
Georgia Department of Natural Resources (☎800-864-7275; www.gastateparks.org) For information on camping and activities in state parks.

Atlanta

With 5.5 million residents in the metro and outlying areas, the so-called capital of the South continues to experience explosive growth thanks to southbound Yankees and international immigrants alike. It's also booming as a tourist destination. Beyond the big-ticket downtown attractions you'll find a constellation of superlative restaurants, a palpable Hollywood influence (Atlanta has become a highly popular production center) and iconic African American history.

Without natural boundaries to control development, Atlanta keeps growing. Yet for all this suburbanization, Atlanta is a pretty city covered with trees and elegant homes. Distinct neighborhoods are like friendly small towns stitched together. The economy is robust, the population is young and creative, and racial tensions are minimal in 'the city too busy to hate.'

⊙ Sights & Activities

⊚ Downtown

Downtown Atlanta is undergoing yet another transformation, continuing the recent trend of developers and politicians focusing on making the urban core more vibrant and livable. Two new world-class museums and a new Atlanta Falcons football stadium (and subsequent demolition of the 23-year-old Georgia Dome) by the 2017 NFL season have once again given the capital of the South a new face.

World of Coca-Cola   MUSEUM
(www.woccatlanta.com; 121 Baker St; adult/senior/child $16/14/12; ☺10am-5pm Sun-Thu, 9am-5pm Fri-Sat) This self-congratulatory museum might prove entertaining to fizzy beverage and rash commercialization fans. The climactic moment comes when guests sample Coke products from around the world – a taste-bud-twisting good time! But there are also Andy Warhol pieces on view, a 4D film, company history and promotional materials aplenty.

Center for Civil and Human Rights MUSEUM
(www.civilandhumanrights.org; 100 Ivan Allen Jr
Blvd; adult/senior/child $15/13/10; ⊘10am-5pm
Mon-Sat, noon-5pm Sun) This striking 2014 addition to Atlanta's Centennial Park is a sobering $68 million memorial to the American
Civil Rights and Global Human Rights Movements. Beautifully designed and thoughtfully
executed, the indisputable highlight centers
around an absolutely harrowing interactive
mock Woolworth's lunch-counter sit-in sim-
ulation that will leave you speechless and
drive some to tears.

College Football Hall of Fame MUSEUM
(www.cfbhall.com; 250 Marietta St; adult/senior/
child $20/18/17; ⊘10am-5pm Sun-Fri, 9am-6pm
Sat; ⊞) It is impossible to overstate the importance of college football to American
culture. This new museum, relocated from
Indiana in 2014 and revamped into this
three-story, 94,256-sq-ft gridiron sanctuary, is
a supremely cool and suitable shrine.

Pledge your allegiance to your team of
choice upon entry and your interactive experience is customized as you make your
way past famous trophies like the coveted
Heisman and hands-on experiences like Fight
Song Karaoke or attempting to kick a 20-yard
field goal. Needless to say, kids go nuts here.

CNN Center TV STUDIO
(☑404-827-2300; www.cnn.com/tour/atlanta; 1
CNN Center; tours adult/senior/child $16/15/13;
⊘9am-5pm) The 55-minute behind-the-
scenes tour through the headquarters of the
international, 24-hour news giant is a good
time for fans. Although visitors don't get
very close to Wolf Blitzer (or his cronies), the
9am and noon timeslots offer the best bets
for seeing anchors live on-air.

⊙ Midtown

Midtown is like a hipper version of downtown, with plenty of great bars, restaurants
and cultural venues.

★**High Museum of Art** GALLERY
(www.high.org; 1280 Peachtree St NE; adult/child
$19.50/12; ⊘10am-5pm Tue-Thu & Sat, to 9pm Fri,
noon-5pm Sun) Atlanta's modern High Museum was the first to exhibit art lent from
Paris' Louvre, and is a destination as much
for its architecture as its world-class exhibits. The striking whitewashed multilevel
building houses a permanent collection of
eye-catching late 19th-century furniture,

GEORGIA FACTS

Nickname Peach State

Population 10 million

Area 59,425 sq miles

Capital city Atlanta (population
5.5 million)

Other cities Savannah (population
142,772)

Sales tax 7%, plus 6% extra on hotel
accommodations

Birthplace of Baseball legend Ty Cobb
(1886–1961), president Jimmy Carter
(b 1924), civil rights leader Martin
Luther King Jr (1929–68), singer Ray
Charles (1930–2004)

Home of Coca-Cola, the world's busiest
airport, Gone with the Wind

Politics Socially conservative as a
whole; Atlanta has been known to swing
both ways

Famous for Peaches

Odd law Donkeys may not be kept in
bathtubs. Seriously, don't do it.

Driving distances Atlanta to St Marys
343 miles, Atlanta to Dahlonega
75 miles

early American modern canvases from the
likes of George Morris and Albert Gallatin,
and postwar work from Mark Rothko.

Atlanta Botanical Garden GARDENS
(☑404-876-5859; www.atlantabotanicalgarden.
org; 1345 Piedmont Ave NE; adult/child $19/13;
⊘9am-7pm Tue, to 5pm Wed-Sun) In the northwest corner of Piedmont Park, the stunning
30-acre botanical garden has a Japanese garden, winding paths and the amazing Fuqua
Orchid Center.

**Margaret Mitchell House
& Museum** LANDMARK
(☑404-249-7015; www.margaretmitchellhouse.
com; 990 Peachtree St, at 10th St; adult/student/
child $13/10/8.50; ⊘10am-5pm Mon-Sat, noon-
5:30pm Sun) A shrine to the author of Gone
With the Wind. Mitchell wrote her epic in
a small apartment in the basement of this
historic house, though nothing inside it actually belonged to her.

Atlanta

0   0.5 miles
0   1 km

Westside Provisions District (0.75mi)

Center for Puppetry Arts (0.3mi);
(14mi)

High Museum of Art (0.1mi);
Hotel Artmore (0.2mi);
Woodruff Arts Center (0.2mi);
Amtrak Station (1mi)

Atlanta Botanical Garden (0.4mi)

Piedmont Park

Ponce de Leon Pl

Virginia Ave

Monroe Dr

Eastside Beltline Trail

Ave

Greenwood

Seal Pl

Charles Allen Dr

Decatur (4mi)

Glen Iris Dr

City Hall East

Highland Inn (0.7mi)

Monroe Dr

Ponce de Leon Ave

North Ave

Linden Ave

Boulevard Pl

Durant Pl

Glendale

Argonne Ave

Penn Ave

Myrtle St

Piedmont Ave

3rd St

5th St

6th St

8th St

9th St

10th St

12th St

11th St

Old 10th St

Crescent Ave

Peachtree Pl

Peachtree St NE

Peachtree St NE

8th St

7th St

Juniper St NE

6th St

5th St

4th St

3rd St

Biltmore Pl

Cypress St

W Peachtree St

Spring St

Spring St NW

Williams St

Techwood Dr

Fowler St

8th St

6th St

4th St

5th St

10th St

5th St

Georgia Institute of Technology

Bobby Dodd Stadium

Bobby Dodd Way

Techwood Dr

North Ave

Downtown Connector

Tech Pkwy NW

Octane (0.6mi);
The Optimist (0.6mi);
Terminal West (0.9mi)

MIDTOWN

N4 Midtown

N3 North Ave

13

28

16

27

26

20

2

10

25

24

8

29

30

19

75

85

401

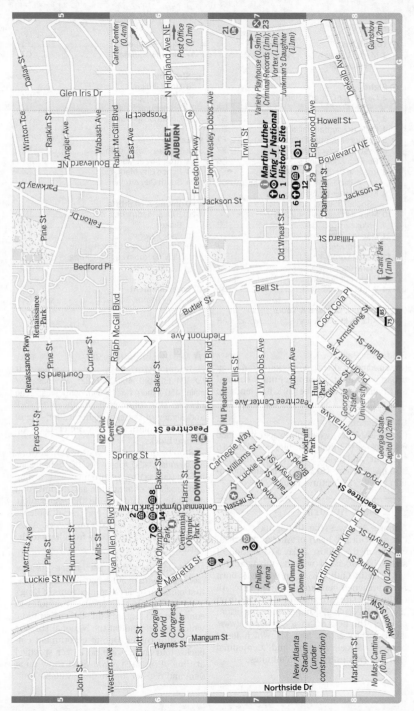

THE SOUTH

Atlanta

Piedmont Park PARK

(www.piedmontpark.org) A glorious, rambling urban park and the setting of many cultural and music festivals. The park has fantastic bike paths, and a Saturday **Green Market**.

Skate Escape CYCLING

(☑404-892-1292; www.skateescape.com; 1086 Piedmont Ave NE) Rents out bicycles (from $6 per hour) and in-line skates ($6 per hour). It also has tandems ($12 per hour) and mountain bikes ($25 for three hours).

⊙ Sweet Auburn

Auburn Ave was the thumping commercial and cultural heart of African American culture in the 1900s. Today a collection of sights is associated with its most famous son, Martin Luther King Jr, who was born here, preached here and is buried here. All of the King sites are a few blocks' walk from the MARTA (p399) King Memorial station; or catch the new **Atlanta Streetcar** (www.theatlantastreetcar.com; fares $1), which loops between Sweet Auburn and Centennial Olympic Park every 10 to 15 minutes.

★**Martin Luther King Jr National Historic Site** HISTORIC SITE

(☑404-331-5190, 404-331-6922; www.nps.gov/malu; 450 Auburn Ave; ⊙9am-5pm) FREE The historic site commemorates the life, work and legacy of the civil rights leader, one of the great Americans. The center takes up several blocks.

Stop by the excellent **visitor center** (www.nps.gov/malu; 450 Auburn Ave NE; ⊙9am-5pm, to 6pm summer) to get oriented with a map and brochure of area sites, and exhibits that elucidate the context – ie the segregation, systematic oppression and racial violence that inspired and fueled King's work. A 1.5-mile landscaped trail leads from here to the Carter Center.

Martin Luther King Jr Birthplace LANDMARK

(www.nps.gov/malu; 501 Auburn Ave) FREE Free, first-come, first-served guided tours of King's childhood home take about 30 minutes to complete and require same-day registration, which can be made at the National Historic Site visitor center. Due to government cutbacks, tour times were no longer specified at time of research – you must show up at 9am and register for the next available tour.

**King Center for
Non-Violent Social Change** MUSEUM
(www.thekingcenter.org; 449 Auburn Ave NE;
⊙9am-5pm, to 6pm summer) Across from
the National Historic Site visitor center,
this place has more information on King's
life and work and a few of his personal effects, including his Nobel Peace Prize. His
gravesite is surrounded by a long reflecting
pool and can be viewed any time.

First Ebenezer Baptist Church CHURCH
(www.historicebenezer.org; 407 Auburn Ave NE;
⊙tours 9am-5pm, to 6pm Summer) `FREE` Martin
Luther King Jr, his father and grandfather
were all pastors here, and King Jr's mother
was the choir director. Sadly she was murdered here by a deranged gunman while she
sat at the organ in 1974. A multimillion-dollar
restoration, completed in 2011, brought the
church back to the 1960–68 period when
King Jr served as co-pastor with his father.

Sunday services are now held at a new
Ebenezer across the street.

⊙ Virginia-Highland

Families enjoy the historic homes and quiet, leafy streets off North Highland Ave. The
main focal point of the area is the triangular
Virginia-Highland intersection turned commercial district, chockablock with restaurants, cafes and boutiques – corporate and
indie.

Carter Center LIBRARY, MUSEUM
(☑404-865-7100; www.jimmycarterlibrary.org;
441 Freedom Pkwy; adult/senior/child $8/6/free;
⊙9am-4:45pm Mon-Sat, noon-4:45pm Sun) Located on a hilltop overlooking downtown, it
features exhibits highlighting Jimmy Carter's 1977–81 presidency, including a replica
of the Oval Office and his Nobel Prize. Don't
miss the tranquil Japanese garden and new
butterfly garden out back. The 1.5-mile-long,
landscaped, **Freedom Park Trail** leads from
here to the Martin Luther King Jr National
Historic Site through **Freedom Park**.

🎇 Festivals & Events

Atlanta Jazz Festival MUSIC
(www.atlantafestivals.com; Piedmont Park; ⊙May)
The month-long event culminates in live
concerts in Piedmont Park on Memorial Day
weekend.

Atlanta Pride Festival GAY & LESBIAN
(www.atlantapride.org; ⊙Oct) Atlanta's annual
GLBT festival.

ATLANTA BELTLINE

The **Atlanta BeltLine** (www.beltline.org)
🏃 is an enormous sustainable redevelopment project that is repurposing an
existing 22-mile rail corridor encircling
the city into 33 miles of connected
multiuse trails. It is the most comprehensive transportation and economic
development effort ever undertaken in
Atlanta and among the largest, most
wide-ranging urban redevelopment
programs currently underway in the
United States. At the time of research,
four trails totaling 6.8 miles were complete. Of most interest to tourists is the
2.2-mile Eastside Trail, connecting the
hip urban neighborhood of Inman Park
with Piedmont Park in Midtown.

National Black Arts Festival CULTURAL
(☑404-730-7315; www.nbaf.org; ⊙Jul) Artists
from across the country converge to celebrate African American music, theater, literature and film.

🛏 Sleeping

Rates at downtown hotels tend to fluctu-
ate wildly depending on whether there is a
large convention in town. The least expensive option is to stay in one of the many
chain hotels along the MARTA line outside
downtown and take the train into the city
for sightseeing.

★**Urban Oasis B&B** B&B $$
(☑770-714-8618; www.urbanoasisbandb.com;
130A Krog St NE; r $125-195; P❄🐾) Hidden
from view inside a gated and repurposed
1950s cotton sorting warehouse, this won-
derful retro-modern loft B&B is urban dwell-
ing at its best. Enter into a huge and funky
common area stealing hordes of natural
light through massive windows and make
your way to one of three rooms, all discern-
ingly appointed with Haywood Wakefield
mid-Century Modern furnishings. It's on the
doorstep of famed Atlanta chef Kevin Rath-
bun's culinary empire, the Krog Street Mar-
ket, Edgewood, Inman Park MARTA *and* the
Beltline. Two-night minimum.

Hotel Artmore BOUTIQUE HOTEL $$
(☑404-876-6100; www.artmorehotel.com; 1302 W
Peachtree St; r $139-399; P❄@🐾) This funky
art-deco gem wins all sorts of accolades:

excellent service, a wonderful courtyard with fire pit and a superb location across the street from Arts Center MARTA station. The 1924 Spanish-Mediterranean architectural landmark has been completely revamped into an artistic boutique hotel that's become an urban sanctuary for those who appreciate their trendiness with a dollop of discretion.

Social Goat B&B B&B $$
(☏404-626-4830; www.thesocialgoatbandb.com; 548 Robinson Ave SE; r $155-245; P✳🖉) Skirting Grant Park, this wonderfully restored 1900 Queen Anne Victorian mansion has six rooms decorated in country French style and is loaded down with period antiques. More importantly, however, you'll share the real estate with goats, turkeys, chickens and cats!

Hotel Indigo BOUTIQUE HOTEL $$
(☏404-874-9200; www.hotelindigo.com; 683 Peachtree St; r $109-179; P✳@🖉) A boutique-style chain hotel, the music-themed Indigo offers a whimsical personality and local in-room touches like custom-stitched domes on the bedspreads that echo the iconic Islamic-style domes of the Fox Theatre across the street. The outstanding Midtown location is within walking distance of bars, restaurants and MARTA.

A second location at **230 Peachtree St** (☏888-233-9450; www.hotelindigo.com; 230 Peachtree St NE; P✳@🖉) near Centennial Park will open by 2016.

Highland Inn INN $$
(☏404-874-5756; www.thehighlandinn.com; 644 N Highland Ave; s/d from $73/103; P✳🖉) This European-style 65-room independent inn, built in 1927, has appealed to touring musicians over the years. Rooms aren't huge, but it's as affordably comfortable as in Atlanta city proper – to say nothing of its great location in the Virginia-Highland area. It's one of the few with single rooms.

★Stonehurst Place B&B $$$
(☏404-881-0722; www.stonehurstplace.com; 923 Piedmont Ave NE; r $199-429; P✳@🖉) Built in 1896 by the Hinman family, this elegant B&B has all the modern amenities one could ask for, is fully updated with ecofriendly water treatment and heating systems, and has original Warhol illustrations on the wall. Well located, it's an exceptional choice if you have the budget.

🍴 Eating

After New Orleans, Atlanta is the best city in the South to eat and the food culture here is nothing short of obsessive. The **Westside Provisions District** (www.westsidepd.com; 100-1210 Howell Mill Rd; P), **Krog Street Market** (www.krogstreetmarket.com; 99 Krog St) and **Ponce City Market** (675 Ponce De Leon Ave NE) are all newish and hip mixed-use residential and restaurant complexes sprinkled among Atlanta's continually transitioning urban neighborhoods.

Downtown & Midtown

Empire State South NEW SOUTHERN $$
(www.empirestatesouth.com; 999 Peachtree St; mains $5-36; ⏲7am-10pm Mon-Wed, to 11pm Thu-Sat, 10:30am-2pm Sun; 🖉) This rustic-hip Midtown bistro serves imaginative New Southern fare and does not disappoint, be it at breakfast (they make their own bagels, the attention to coffee detail approaches Pacific Northwest levels and they mix fried chicken, bacon *and* pimiento cheese!) or throughout the remains of the day.

No Mas! Cantina MEXICAN $$
(☏404-574-5678; www.nomascantina.com; 180 Walker St SW; mains $7-20; ⏲11am-10pm Sun-Thu, 11am-11pm Fri & Sat; 🖉🍴) Though the design overkill feels a bit like dining inside a hungover piñata, locals are sold on the festive Mexican at this downtown Castleberry Hill cantina. Despite its quiet location, it's walking distance from the New Atlanta Stadium, Phillips Arena, CNN Center and Centennial Park.

South City Kitchen SOUTHERN $$$
(☏404-873-7358; www.southcitykitchen.com; 1144 Crescent Ave; mains $18-36; ⏲11am-3:30pm & 5-10pm Sun-Thu, to 10:30pm Fri & Sat) An upscale Southern kitchen featuring tasty updated staples like buttermilk fried chicken served with sautéed collards and mash, and a Georgia trout, pan-fried with roasted heirloom carrots. Start with fried green tomatoes, a Southern specialty *before* the movie.

Westside

West Egg Cafe DINER $
(www.westeggcafe.com; 1100 Howell Mill Rd; mains $6.25-8; ⏲7am-3pm Mon & Tue, to 9pm Wed-Fri, 8am-9pm Sat, to 6pm Sun; P🖉🍴) Belly up to the marble breakfast counter or grab a table and dive into black bean cakes and eggs,

WALKER STALKERS: WELCOME TO WOODBURY!

The post-apocalyptic world of flesh-eating zombies on AMC's *The Walking Dead* has had much of the world paralyzed in front of their TVs and devices since its inaugural season in 2010, and the whole end-of-days showdown takes place right here in the Peach State. The city of Atlanta and the historic small town of Senoia and its surrounds, about an hour's drive south of Atlanta, are the setting for the fanatically popular show. **Atlanta Movie Tours** (☑855-255-3456; www.atlantamovietours.com; 327 Nelson St SW) offers two good-time Zombie tours to filming locations, one in Atlanta proper and another around Senoia (our favorite), narrated by extras from the show who are chomping at the bits to reveal all sorts of insidery tidbits about cast members and filming. Additionally, because its an active film set from May to November, the show's actors can often be seen around Senoia grabbing a morning coffee at **Senoia Coffee & Cafe** (www.senoiacoffeeandcafe. com; 1 Main St; mains $2.75-19; ⏰7:30am-3pm Mon-Thu, to 9pm Fri, to 6pm Sat) or partying at Zac Brown's restaurant, **Southern Ground Social Club** (www.southerngroundsocialclub. com; 18 Main St; ⏰11am-midnight Tue-Thu, to 2am Fri-Sat) – Norman Reedus drove himself right past our tour van on the way to the studio. The entire town, on the National Register of Historic Places, has been transformed into zombie central. Be sure to pop into the **Woodbury Shoppe** (www.woodburyshoppe.com; 48 Main St; ⏰11am-5pm Mon-Sat, 1-5pm Sun), the official *Walking Dead* souvenir shop, which includes a *Walking Dead*–themed cafe downstairs and a small museum.

turkey sausage Benedict, pimento cheese and bacon omelet, or a fried green tomato BLT. It's all reimagined versions of old-school classics, served in a stylish and spare dining room.

Star Provisions SELF-CATERING $
(www.starprovisions.com; 1198 Howell Mill Rd; ⏰10am-midnight Mon-Sat; 🛜) DIY gourmands will feel at home among the cheese shops and butcher cases, bakeries, organic cafe and kitchen hardware depots attached to the city's finest dining establishment, **Bacchanalia** (☑404-365-0410; www.starprovisions. com/bacchanalia; 1198 Howell Mill Rd; prix-fixe per person $85; ⏰from 6pm). Excellent picnic accoutrements.

★**Cooks & Soldiers** BASQUE $$
(☑404-996-2623; www.cooksandsoldiers.com; 691 14th St; dishes $8-32; ⏰5-10pm Sun-Wed, to 11pm Thu, to 2am Fri-Sat; 🛜) A game-changing Westside newcomer, this Basque-inspired hot spot specializes in small plate *pintxos* (Basque tapas) and wood-fired *asadas* (grills) designed to share. Both the food and cocktails are outstanding. Highlights: blood orange gin and tonic, a black-truffled White American grilled cheese, a dehydrated tomato tartar and a perfectly charred Berkshire pork tenderloin with hazelnut romesco.

★**The Optimist** SEAFOOD $$$
(☑404-477-6260; www.theoptimistrestaurant. com; 914 Howell Mill Rd; mains $21-33; ⏰11:30am-2:30pm & 5-10pm Mon-Thu, to 11pm Fri-Sat; 🛜) 🍃

Guidebook space could never do this Westside sustainable-seafood mecca justice. In a word: astonishing! Start with the Spanish charred octopus, braised for four hours in red wine; move on to a duck-fat-poached swordfish or whole fish in garlicky ginger sauce and a side of corn-milk hushpuppies; finish with a scoop of housemade salted-caramel ice cream.

This is one of the South's most buzzed about hot spots, not a word of it heresy. If you cannot get a reservation, plop yourself down at the massive fresh-oyster bar. Alternatively, just practice your putting skills on their three-hole green and smell that miraculous food – a better option than actually eating at lesser establishments.

⚡ Virginia-Highland & Around

Little Five Points is Atlanta's bohemian home and has a fun vibe on weekends. Inman Park is a transitional neighborhood, set just east of downtown.

Sevananda SELF-CATERING $
(www.sevananda.coop; 467 Moreland Ave NE, Little Five Points; ⏰8am-10pm) Voted Atlanta's best health-food store and a gold mine for self-caterers.

★**Fox Brothers** BARBECUE $$
(www.foxbrosbbq.com; 1238 DeKalb Ave NE; dishes $10-27; ⏰11am-10pm Sun-Thu, to 11pm Fri & Sat; 🛜) At this longtime Atlanta classic, set in Inman

MARTIN LUTHER KING JR: A CIVIL RIGHTS GIANT

Martin Luther King Jr, the quintessential figure of the American Civil Rights movement and arguably America's greatest leader, was born in 1929, the son of an Atlanta preacher and choir leader. His lineage was significant not only because he followed his father to the pulpit of Ebenezer Baptist Church, but also because his political speeches rang out with a preacher's inflections.

In 1955 King led the year-long 'bus boycott' in Montgomery, AL, which resulted in the US Supreme Court removing laws that enforced segregated buses. From this successful beginning King emerged as an inspiring moral voice.

His nonviolent approach to racial equality and peace, which he borrowed from Gandhi and used as a potent weapon against hate, segregation and racially motivated violence – a Southern epidemic at the time – makes his death all the more tragic. He was assassinated on a Memphis hotel balcony in 1968, four years after receiving the Nobel Peace Prize and five years after giving his legendary 'I Have a Dream' speech in Washington, DC.

King remains one of the most recognized and respected figures of the 20th century. Over 10 years he led a movement that essentially ended a system of statutory discrimination in existence since the country's founding.

Park, ribs are scorched and smoked perfectly with a hint of charcoaled crust on the outside and tender on the inside. It's also known for its exceptional Texas-style brisket and Brunswick-stew-smothered tator tots. Always packed.

Vortex　　　　　　　　　　BURGERS $$
(www.thevortexbarandgrill.com; 438 Moreland Ave NE; burgers $8.25-16.25; ⊙11am-midnight Sun-Thu, to 2am Fri & Sat) An NC-17 joint cluttered with Americana memorabilia, where alterna-hipsters mingle alongside Texas tourists and Morehouse College steppers at the Godfather of Atlanta burger joints, which veer from impressive to outlandish but are always some of the most heralded and heart-stopping in Atlanta. The 20ft-tall skull facade is a Little Five Points landmark of pre–Olympic Games outrageousness.

★**Octopus Bar**　　　　　　ASIAN FUSION $$
(www.octopusbaratl.com; 560 Gresham Ave SE, East Atlanta; dishes $9-15; ⊙10:30pm-2:30am Mon-Sat) Do they keep odd hours? Is seating difficult to come by? Does it take so long to get your fusion grub because the chefs are too busy fielding industry complaints from a room full of sous chefs and servers? The answer, of course, is yes, to all of the above.

So leave your hang-ups at the hotel – this is punk-rock dining – and get to know what's good at this indoor-outdoor patio dive nuanced with graffed-up walls and ethereal electronica. No reservations, so line up early.

✗ East Atlanta

★**Gunshow**　　　　　　NEW SOUTHERN $$$
(☑404-380-1886; www.gunshowatl.com; 924 Garrett St SE; dishes $12-20; ⊙6-9pm Tue-Sat; 🕾) Celebrity chef Kevin Gillespie's latest light-bulb moment is an unorthodox evening out. Guests do not order at the three nightly seatings, but rather choose between 12 or so smallish dishes, dreamed up by five chefs in the open kitchen, who then hawk their blood, sweat and culinary tears dim-sum-style tableside.

It can be agonizing, turning your nose up at a smoked ham hock confit because you're holding out for the Saigon-style Kobe beef tartar, but it's a dining experience like no other and Atlanta's hottest table. Reservations open 30 days out.

✗ Decatur

Independent Decatur, 6 miles east of downtown, is a countercultural enclave and a bona-fide foodie destination. Like most traditional Southern towns, the gazebo-crowned **Courthouse Square** is the center of the action, with a number of restaurants, cafes and shops surrounding it.

Victory　　　　　　　　　　SANDWICHES $
(www.vicsandwich.com; 340 Church St; sandwiches $4-5; ⊙11am-2am; 🕾) This spare, converted Decatur brick house is a wonderful bargain gourmet sandwich counter where baguettes are stuffed with white anchovies and lemon

mayo, or chicken and ghost pepper jack, among other intriguing options.

★ Leon's Full Service FUSION $$
(☏ 404-687-0500; www.leonsfullservice.com; 131 E Ponce de Leon Ave; mains $12-24; ⊘ 5pm-1am Mon, 11:30am-1am Tue-Thu & Sun, to 2am Fri & Sat; 🛜) Leon's can come across as a bit pretentious, but the gorgeous concrete bar and open floor-plan spilling out of a former service station and onto a groovy heated deck with floating beams remains cooler than thou and fully packed at all times.

Everything, from the beer, wine and cocktails (spirits are all craft, small-batch creations) to the menu, show love and attention to detail. No reservations.

Cakes & Ale MODERN AMERICAN $$$
(☏ 404-377-7994; www.cakesandalerestaurant.com; 155 Sycamore St; mains $9-32; ⊘ 11:30am-2:30pm & 6-10pm Tue-Thu, 11:30am-2:30pm & 5:30-10:30pm Fri-Sat) A Chez Panisse alum and pastry mastermind run this hip eatery. The bakery next door has life-affirming hot chocolate along with a case of delectable pastries, while the restaurant features spare but stunning selections that could mean perfectly grilled *framani soppresata* sandwiches with chard, preserved-lemon ricotta and Dijon (a lunch standout), and pork guinea hen or lamb at dinner.

 Drinking & Nightlife

Edgewood, very near Sweet Auburn, is the latest edgy neighborhood to be flipped into the *en vogue* nightlife destination.

Brick Store Pub BAR
(www.brickstorepub.com; 125 E Court Sq; draft beers $5-12) Beer hounds geek out on Atlanta's best craft beer selection at this pub in Decatur, with some 30 meticulously chosen drafts (including those in the more intimate Belgian beer bar upstairs). It serves nearly 300 beers by the bottle from a 15,000-bottle vault and draws a fun, young crowd every night.

Argosy GASTROPUB
(www.argosy-east.com; 470 Flat Shoals Ave SE; ⊘ 5pm-2:30am Mon-Fri, from 11am Sat-Sun; 🛜) This East Atlanta gastropub nails it with an extensive list of rare craft beers, perfect bar food (the Don-a-Tello pizza is insanely good) and a space that shocks and awes. The multi-angled bar snakes its way through the largely masculine space, a gorgeous specimen at which to socialize, and living-room-style lounge areas pepper the remaining real estate.

Kimball House COCKTAIL BAR
(www.kimball-house.com; 303 E Howard Ave; cocktails $8-12; ⊘ 5pm-1am Sun-Thu, to 2am Fri-Sat) Housed in an atmospheric restored train depot slightly off the grid in Decatur, Kimball House harbors a vaguely saloonlike feel and specializes in craft cocktails, absinthe service and a long list of flown-in-fresh oysters.

Sister Louisa's Church of the Living Room and Ping Pong Emporium BAR
(www.sisterlouisaschurch.com; 466 Edgewood Ave; ⊘ 5pm-3am Mon-Fri, 1pm-3am Sat, to midnight Sun; 🛜) This cradle of Edgewood's bar revival fosters a church theme, but it's nothing like Westminster Abbey. Sacrilegious art peppers every patch of free wall space, the kind of offensive stuff that starts wars in some parts. Praise the resistance to fancy craft cocktails and join the congregation, chuckling at the artistry or staring at mesmerizing table-tennis matches.

THE SOUTH ATLANTA

GAY & LESBIAN ATLANTA

Atlanta – or 'Hotlanta' as some might call it – is one of the few places in Georgia with a noticeable and active gay and lesbian population. Midtown is the center of gay life; the epicenter is around Piedmont Park and the intersection of 10th St and Piedmont Ave, where you can check out **Blake's** (www.blakesontheparkatlanta.com; 227 10th St NE), Atlanta's classic gay bar, or the appropriately named hot spot of the moment, **10th & Piedmont** (www.communitashospitality.com/10th-and-piedmont; 991 Piedmont Ave NE; ⊘ 11:30am-4pm & 5-10pm Mon-Thu, 11:30am-4pm & 5-11pm Fri, 10am-4pm & 5-11pm Sat, 10am-4pm & 5-10pm Sun), good for both food and late-night shenanigans. The town of Decatur, east of downtown Atlanta, has a significant lesbian community. For news and information, grab a copy of *David Atlanta* (www.davidatlanta.com); also check out www.gayatlanta.com.

Atlanta Pride Festival (p393) is a massive annual celebration of the city's gay and lesbian community. Held in October in and around Piedmont Park.

Park Tavern   BAR
(www.parktavern.com; 500 10th Street NE;
⊕4:30pm-midnight Mon-Fri, from 11:30am Sat
& Sun; 🛜) The outdoor patio of this staple
microbrewery-restaurant on the edge of
Piedmont Park is one of the most beautiful
spots in Atlanta to sit back and drink away a
weekend afternoon.

Octane   CAFE
(www.octanecoffee.com; 1009-B Marietta St; coffee
$2.50-5; ⊕7am-11pm Mon-Thu, 7am-midnight Fri,
8am-11pm Sat-Sun; 🛜) 🍴 This industrial-hip
coffeehouse near Georgia Tech's campus, the
original of three locations in the city, brews
the joe of choice for severe caffeine junkies,
following a 'direct trade' philosophy. It remains Atlanta's most serious coffeehouse.

☆ Entertainment

Atlanta has big-city nightlife with lots of
live music and cultural events. For listings,
check out **Atlanta Coalition of Performing Arts** (www.atlantaperforms.com). The **Atlanta Music Guide** (www.atlantamusicguide.
com) maintains a live-music schedule, plus a
directory of local venues and links to online
ticketing.

Theater

Woodruff Arts Center   ARTS
(www.woodruffcenter.org; 1280 Peachtree St NE,
at 15th St) An arts campus hosting the High
Museum, the Atlanta Symphony Orchestra
and the Alliance Theatre.

Fox Theatre   THEATER
(📞855-285-8499; www.foxtheatre.org; 660
Peachtree St NE; ⊕box office 10am-6pm Mon-Fri,
to 3pm Sat) A spectacular 1929 movie palace
with fanciful Moorish and Egyptian designs.
It hosts Broadway shows and concerts in an
auditorium holding more than 4500 people.
Tours are also available.

Live Music & Nightclubs

Cover charges at the following vary nightly.
Check the respective websites for music cal-
endars and ticket prices.

Terminal West   LIVE MUSIC
(887 W Marietta St) Voted Atlanta's best
live-music venue, it's inside a beautifully revamped 100-year-old iron and steel foundry
on the Westside.

Eddie's Attic   LIVE MUSIC
(📞404-377-4976; www.eddiesattic.com; 515b N Mc-
Donough St) In East Atlanta, this is one of the
city's best venues for live folk and acoustic
music, renowned for breaking local artists;
nonsmoking atmosphere seven nights a week.

Variety Playhouse   LIVE MUSIC
(www.variety-playhouse.com; 1099 Euclid Ave NE) A
smartly booked and well-run concert venue
featuring a variety of touring artists. It's the
anchor that keeps Little Five Points relevant.

🛍 Shopping

Junkman's Daughter   VINTAGE
(www.thejunkmansdaughter.com; 464 Moreland Ave
NE; ⊕11am-7pm Mon-Fri, from noon Sun) A defiant
and fiercely independent cradle of counter-
culture since 1982, this 10,000-sq-ft alternative superstore stocks racks of vintage, ornery
bumper stickers, kitschy toys and tchotchkes,
Star Wars lunch boxes, incense, wigs, offensive coffee mugs and a whole lot more. It put
Little Five Points on the map.

Criminal Records   MUSIC
(www.criminalatl.com; 1154 Euclid Ave; ⊕11am-9pm
Mon-Sat, noon-7pm Sun) A throwback record
store with used and new pop, soul, jazz and
metal, on CD or vinyl. It has a fun music-
related book section, and some decent comic
books.

ℹ Information

EMERGENCY & MEDICAL SERVICES

Atlanta Medical Center (www.atlantamed-
center.com; 303 Pkwy Dr NE) A tertiary care
hospital considered Atlanta's best since 1901.

Atlanta Police Department (📞404-614-6544;
www.atlantapd.org) Atlanta's police department.

MEDIA

Atlanta (www.atlantamagazine.com) A monthly
general-interest magazine covering local
issues, arts and dining.

Atlanta Daily World (www.atlantadailyworld.
com) The nation's oldest continuously running
African American newspaper (since 1928).

Atlanta Journal-Constitution (www.ajc.com)
Atlanta's major daily newspaper, with a good
travel section on Sunday.

Creative Loafing (www.clatl.com) For hip tips
on music, arts and theater, this free alternative
weekly comes out every Wednesday.

POST

Post Office (📞800-275-8777; www.usps.com;
190 Marietta St NW, CNN Center; ⊕11am-4pm
Mon-Fri) Little Five Points (455 Moreland Ave
NE; ⊕9am-11am & noon-5pm Mon-Fri); North
Highland (1190 N Highland Ave NE; ⊕8:30am-
6pm Mon-Fri, to noon Sat); Phoenix Station

ATLANTA FOR CHILDREN

Atlanta has plenty of activities to keep children entertained, delighted and educated.

Center for Puppetry Arts (⌨ tickets 404-873-3391; www.puppet.org; 1404 Spring St NW; museum $8.25, performances $16.50-20.59; ⊙ 9am-3pm Tue-Fri, 10am-5pm Sat, noon-5pm Sun; ⛨) A wonderland for visitors of all ages and hands-down one of Atlanta's most unique attractions, the museum houses a treasury of puppets, some of which you get to operate yourself. A major addition is the Worlds of Puppetry Museum, housing the most comprehensive collection of Jim Henson puppets and artifacts in the world.

Imagine It! Children's Museum of Atlanta (www.childrensmuseumatlanta.org; 275 Centennial Olympic Park Dr NW; admission $12.75; ⊙ 10am-4pm Mon-Fri, to 5pm Sat & Sun; ⛨) A hands-on museum geared towards kids aged eight and under. Adults aren't allowed in without a youngster in tow.

Georgia Aquarium (www.georgiaaquarium.com; 225 Baker St; adult/child $39/33; ⊙ 10am-5pm Sun-Fri, 9am-6pm Sat; ℗ ⛨) Whale sharks, beluga whales and more than 100,000 other animals representing 500 species swimming about in 8 million gallons of fresh and marine water make this the world's second-largest aquarium. It would be remiss not to note that holding whales and dolphins in captivity has fallen out of favor since the release of the 2013 documentary *Blackfish*.

Skyview Atlanta (www.skyviewatlanta.com; 168 Luckie St NW; adult/senior/child $13.50/12.15/8.50; ⊙ noon-10pm Sun-Thu, to 11pm Fri, 10am-11pm Sat; ⛨) Soar 200ft above the Atlanta skyline in this 20-story, 42-gondola Ferris wheel installed in 2013.

(41 Marietta St NW; ⊙ 9am-5pm Mon-Fri) Postal services around town.

USEFUL WEBSITES

Scout Mob (www.scoutmob.com) Tips on what's new and hot in Atlanta.

Atlanta Travel Guide (www.atlanta.net) Official site of the Atlanta Convention & Visitors Bureau with excellent links to shops, restaurants, hotels and upcoming events. Its website also lets you buy a CityPass, a tremendous money saver that bundles admission to five of the city's attractions for a discounted price (see www.citypass.com/atlanta for more).

❶ Getting There & Away

Atlanta's huge **Hartsfield-Jackson International Airport** (ATL; Atlanta; www.atlanta-airport. com), 12 miles north of downtown, is a major regional hub and an international gateway. The **Greyhound terminal** (www.greyhound.com; 232 Forsyth St) is next to the MARTA Garnett station. The **Amtrak station** (www.amtrak.com; 1688 Peachtree St NW, at Deering Rd) is just north of downtown.

❶ Getting Around

The **Metropolitan Atlanta Rapid Transit Authority** (MARTA; ⌨ 404-848-5000; www. itsmarta.com; fares $2.50) rail line travels to/from the airport to downtown, along with less useful commuter routes. Each customer must purchase a Breeze card ($1; www.breezecard.

com), which can be loaded and reloaded as necessary. The shuttle and car-rental agencies have desks in the airport situated at baggage claim.

North Georgia

The southern end of the great Appalachian Range extends some 40 miles into Georgia's far north, providing superb mountain scenery, some decent wines, and frothing rivers. Fall colors emerge late here, peaking in October. A few days are warranted to see sites like the 1200ft-deep **Tallulah Gorge** (⌨ 706-754-7981; www.gastateparks.org/tallulahgorge; entry per vehicle $5), and the mountain scenery and hiking trails at **Vogel State Park** (⌨ 706-745-2628; www.gastateparks.org/vogel; entry per vehicle $5) and **Unicoi State Park** (⌨ 706-878-4726; www.gastateparks.org/unicoi; entry per vehicle $5).

Dahlonega

In 1828 Dahlonega was the site of the first gold rush in the USA. The boom these days is in tourism, as it's an easy day excursion from Atlanta and is a fantastic mountain destination. Not only is it a hotbed of outdoor activities, but downtown Dahlonega around Courthouse Square is a delightful melange of tasting rooms, gourmet emporiums, great food, countrified shops and foothill charm.

◉ Sights & Activities

Amicalola Falls State Park   HIKING
(☑706-265-4703; www.gastateparks.org/ami
calolafalls; 280 Amicalola Falls State Park Rd,
Dawsonville; entry per vehicle $5; ☉7am-10pm)
Amicalola Falls State Park, 18 miles west of
Dahlonega on Hwy 52, features the 729ft
Amicalola Falls, the tallest cascading waterfall in the Southeast. The park offers spectacular scenery, a lodge, and excellent hiking
and mountain-biking trails.

★Frogtown Cellars   WINERY
(☑706-865-0687; www.frogtownwine.com; 700
Ridge Point Dr; tastings $15; ☉noon-5pm Mon-Fri,
to 6pm Sat, 12:30-5pm Sun) Frogtown Cellars is
a beautiful winery and has a killer deck on
which to sip libations and nibble cheese. It
bills itself as the most awarded North American winery *not* in California.

🛏 Sleeping & Eating

★Hiker Hostel   HOSTEL $
(☑770-312-7342; www.hikerhostel.com; 7693 Hwy
19N; dm/r/cabin $18/42/55; P✳@☎) On Hwy
19N, 7 miles or so from town, this hostel is
owned by an avid pair of cycling and outdoors enthusiasts. It caters to those looking
to explore the Appalachian Trail. The hostel
is a converted log cabin; each bunk room
has its own bath and it is wonderfully neat
and clean.

Two stylish new shipping-container cabins are built from reclaimed materials from
throughout Georgia.

Spirits Tavern   BURGERS $
(www.spirits-tavern.com; 19 E Main St; burgers $12;
☉11am-11pm Sun-Thu, to 1am Fri, to midnight Sat;
☎) Dahlonega's only full bar dishes up surprisingly creative burgers, in Angus beef or
free-range, hormone-free turkey versions,
including crunchy mac 'n' cheese, Greek,
Asian and Cajun versions.

Crimson Moon Café   CAFE $
(www.thecrimsonmoon.com; 24 N Park St; mains
$6.50-18; ☉11am-4pm Mon & Tue, to 9pm Wed &
Thu, 10am-midnight Fri, 8:30am-midnight Sat, to
9pm Sun; ☎) An organic coffeehouse offering
great Southern comfort food and an intimate live-music venue.

Back Porch Oyster Bar   SEAFOOD $$
(☑706-864-8623; www.backporchoysterbar.net;
19 N Chestatee St; mains $9-31; ☉11:30am-9pm
Mon-Thu, to 10pm Fri-Sat, to 8pm Sun; ☎) Oysters,
ahi and clams are among the bounty flown

in fresh daily to be shucked, seared and
steamed at this neighborhood fish house,
with a front porch overlooking the square
that's perfect for taking it all down.

ℹ Information

Visitor Center (☑706-864-3513; www.dahlon-
ega.org; 13 S Park St; ☉9am-5:30pm Mon-Fri,
10am-5pm Sat) The visitor center has plenty
of information on area sites and activities,
including hiking, canoeing, kayaking, rafting and
mountain biking.

Athens

A beery, artsy and laid-back college town
roughly 70 miles east of Atlanta, Athens has
an extremely popular football team (the Uni-
versity of Georgia Bulldogs), a world-famous
music scene (which has launched artists in-
cluding the B-52s, R.E.M. and Widespread
Panic) and a burgeoning restaurant culture.
The university drives the culture of Athens
and ensures an ever-replenishing supply of
young bar-hoppers and concert-goers, some
of whom stick around long after graduation
and become 'townies.' The pleasant, walk-
able downtown offers a plethora of funky
choices for eating, drinking and shopping.

◉ Sights

★Georgia Museum of Art   MUSEUM
(www.georgiamuseum.org; 90 Carlton St; ☉10am-
5pm Tue-Wed, Fri & Sat, to 9pm Thu, 1-5pm Sun)
FREE A smart, modern gallery open to the
public where brainy, arty types set up in
the wired lobby for personal study while art
hounds gawk at modern sculpture in the
courtyard garden and the tremendous collec-
tion from American realists of the 1930s.

**State Botanical Garden
of Georgia**   GARDENS
(www.botgarden.uga.edu; 2450 S Milledge Ave;
☉8am-6pm Oct-Mar, to 8pm Apr-Sep) Truly gor-
geous, with winding outdoor paths and a
socio-historical edge, Athens' gardens rival
those in Atlanta. Signs provide smart con-
text for its amazing collection of plants,
which runs the gamut from rare and threat-
ened species to nearly 5 miles of top-notch
woodland walking trails.

🛏 Sleeping & Eating

Athens does not have a great selection of
lodging. There are standard chains just out
of town on W Broad St.

★**Graduate Athens**   INN **$$**
(📞706-549-7020; www.graduateathens.com; 295 E Dougherty St; r $99-169, ste $159-229; P ❄ @ 🛜 🖼) This newly revamped 122-room boutique hotel, the inaugural address of a new college-campus chain, is drowning in sexified retro hipness, from potted plants inside old-school Dewey Decimal card catalog filing cabinets in the lobby to the sweet Crosley turntables and classic video games in the suites.

Local accents, such as chalkboard-art of the chemical formula for sweet tea, fortify local allure. Also on-site is a great coffeehouse, bar and grill and live-music venue, all inside an old Confederate iron foundry.

Hotel Indigo   BOUTIQUE HOTEL **$$**
(📞706-546-0430; www.indigoathens.com; 500 College Ave; r weekend/weekday from $169/139; P ❄ @ 🛜 🖼) 🍽 Rooms are spacious, loftlike pods of cool at this eco-chic boutique hotel. Part of the Indigo chain, it's a Leadership in Energy and Environmental Design gold-certified sustainable standout. Green elements include regenerative elevators and priority parking for hybrid vehicles; 30% of the building was constructed from recycled content.

White Tiger   BARBECUE **$**
(www.whitetigergourmet.com; 217 Hiawassee Ave; mains $6.50-10.50; ⏱11am-3pm Tue-Wed, 11am-3pm & 6-8pm Thu-Sat, 10am-2pm Sun) The 100-year-old structure doesn't invite confidence, but this off-the-beaten path local favorite does killer wood-smoked pulled pork sandwiches, burgers and even BBQ-smoked tofu for the vegetarians. Chef Ken Manring honed his skills in much higher-brow kitchens before settling in Athens.

Ike & Jane   CAFE **$**
(www.ikeandjane.com; 1307 Prince Ave; mains $3.50-8; ⏱6:30am-5pm Mon-Fri, 8am-2pm Sat-Sun) This sunny little shingle in Normal Town serves decadent doughnuts bedazzled with crazy creative ingredients like red velvet, Cap'n Crunch cereal and peanut butter, banana and bacon. If that's all a bit much for you, the pimento cheese biscuit or roasted jalapeño and egg sandwich are both divine.

Ted's Most Best   ITALIAN **$**
(www.tedsmostbest.com; 254 W Washington St; mains $7.50-9) This atmospheric budget eatery occupies a former Michelin tire shop (oh, the irony) and is a great spot for cheap eats. Pizzas and panini are what drives it,

but the outdoor patio and sandbox/bocce court (when the little ones haven't commandeered it) is the real star of the show.

National   NEW SOUTHERN **$$**
(📞706-549-3450; www.thenationalrestaurant.com; 232 W Hancock Ave; mains $12-29; ⏱11:30am-10pm Mon-Thu, to late Fri-Sat, 5-10pm Sun; 🛜) An effortlessly cool bistro on the downtown outskirts, favored for its daily-changing, eclectic menu that jumps from roasted chicken breast with za'atar to lamb sandwiches with fennel-caper mayo. The bar is one where you may want to sit and sip a while. Outstanding vegetarian choices.

★**Five & Ten**   AMERICAN **$$$**
(📞706-546-7300; www.fiveandten.com; 1653 S Lumpkin St; mains $24-36; ⏱5:30-10pm Sun-Thu, to 11pm Fri & Sat, 10:30am-2:30pm Sun) 🍽 Driven by sustainable ingredients, Five & Ten ranks among the South's best restaurants. Its menu is earthy and slightly gamey: sweetbreads, black-eyed-pea hummus and Frogmore stew (stewed corn, sausage and potato). In an about-face, Tuesday is *tonkotsu*-style ramen night. Reservations mandatory.

🍷 **Drinking & Entertainment**

Nearly 100 bars and restaurants dot Athens' compact downtown area, so it's not hard to find a good time. Pick up a free copy of **Flagpole** (www.flagpole.com) to find out what's on.

Trapeze Pub   BEER HALL
(www.trappezepub.com; 269 N Hull St; beers $4.50-8; ⏱11am-2am Mon-Sat, to midnight Sun; 🛜) Downtown's best craft beer bar installed itself well before the suds revolution. You'll find 33 taps, including loyal fav Creature Comforts, and another 100 or so at any given time in bottles. Soak it all up with Belgian-style fries, the best in town.

World Famous   COCKTAIL BAR
(www.facebook.com/theworldfamousathens; 351 N Hull; cocktails $4-9; ⏱11am-2m Mon-Sat, 11:30-midnight Sun; 🛜) This trendy newcomer serves commendable craft cocktails in Mason jars amid retro French farmhouse decor. Also hosts intimate comedy and live-music events.

The Old Pal   BAR
(www.theoldpal.com; 1320 Prince Ave; cocktails $7-9; ⏱4pm-2am Mon-Sat; 🛜) Dark and taxidermied, the Old Pal is Normal Town's thinking man's bar, devoted to seasonal craft cocktails and a thoughtfully curated bourbon list. It's

a beautiful space that has been showered with local preservation awards.

Normal Bar   BAR
(www.facebook.com/normal.bar.7; 1365 Prince Ave; ⏰4pm-2am Mon-Thu, from 3pm Fri & Sat) This lovable dark storefront bar, a bit out of the way in Normal Town, is very unstudentlike but still very much Athens. The beer goes from PBR cheap to local craftsman IPA-sophisticati. There's a terrific wine list and the crowd is young, cute and doesn't care either way. It's the quintessential neighborhood bar.

Hendershots   COFFEE
(www.hendershotscoffee.com; 237 Prince Ave; coffee $2.15-5.35; ⏰6:30am-11pm Mon-Thu, to midnight Fri, 7:30am-midnight Sat, 7am-10pm Sun; 🛜) This is not Athens' best coffee, but it is its coolest coffeehouse, which pulls triple duty as a great bar and live-music venue. Pick your poison.

40 Watt Club   LIVE MUSIC
(📞706-549-7871; www.40watt.com; 285 W Washington St; admission $5-25) Athens' most storied joint has lounges, a tiki bar and $2.50 PBRs, and has welcomed indie rock to its stage since R.E.M., the B-52s and Widespread Panic owned this town. It's still where the big hitters play when they visit and has recently embraced comedy as well.

ⓘ Information
Athens Welcome Center (📞706-353-1820; www.athenswelcomecenter.com; 280 E Dougherty St; ⏰10am-5pm Mon-Sat, noon-5pm Sun) The Athens Welcome Center, in a historic antebellum house at the corner of Thomas St, provides maps and information on local tours.

South Georgia
Once the unbounded urban sprawl of Atlanta meets the rear-view mirror, a more rustic and definitively genteel Georgia emerges, with swampy Savannah holding court as the state's irresistible Southern belle. But there's more to the region than antebellum architecture and Spanish moss: Georgia's wild and preserved barrier-island-riddled coast is an often overlooked stunner.

Savannah
Like a proper Southern belle with an electric-blue streak in her hair, this grand historic town revolves around formal antebellum architecture and the revelry of local students from Savannah College of Art and Design (SCAD). It sits alongside the Savannah River, about 18 miles from the coast, amid Lowcountry swamps and mammoth live oak trees dripping with Spanish moss. With its colonial mansions and beautiful squares, Savannah preserves its past with pride and grace. However, unlike its sister city of Charleston, SC, which retains its reputation as a dignified and refined cultural center, Savannah is a little gritty, lived-in, and real.

⊙ Sights & Activities
The Central Park of Savannah is a sprawling rectangular green space called **Forsyth Park**. The park's beautiful fountain is a quintessential photo op. Savannah's **riverfront** is mostly populated with forgettable shops and cafes, but it's worth a short stroll. As is **Jones Street**, among Savannah's prettiest thanks to the mossy oaks that hold hands from either side.

A $20 multivenue ticket gets you into the Jepson Center for the Arts, Telfair Academy and the Owens-Thomas House.

★ Wormsloe Plantation
Historic Site   HISTORIC SITE
(www.gastateparks.org/Wormsloe; 7601 Skidaway Rd; adult/senior/child 6-17yr/child 1-5yr $10/9/4.50/2; ⏰9am-5pm Tue-Sun) A short drive from downtown, on the beautiful **Isle of Hope**, this is one of the most photographed sites in town. The real draw is the dreamy entrance through a corridor of mossy, ancient oaks that runs for 1.5 miles, known as the **Avenue of the Oaks**.

But there are other draws, including an existing antebellum mansion still lived in by the descendants of the original owner, Noble Jones, some old colonial ruins, and a touristy site where you can see folks demonstrate blacksmithing and other bygone trades. There are two flat, wooded walking trails here, too.

Owens-Thomas House   HISTORIC BUILDING
(www.telfair.org; 124 Abercorn St; adult/senior/child $20/18/free; ⏰noon-4pm Sun-Mon, 10am-4:30pm Tue-Sat) Completed in 1819 by British architect William Jay, this gorgeous villa exemplifies English Regency-style architecture, which is known for its symmetry.

The guided tour is fussy, but it delivers interesting trivia about the spooky 'haint blue' ceiling paint in the slaves' quarters (made from crushed indigo, buttermilk and crushed oyster shells) and the number of years by which this mansion preceded the White House in getting running water (nearly 20).

Mercer-Williams House   HISTORIC BUILDING
(www.mercerhouse.com; 429 Bull St; adult/student $12.50/8; ⊙10:30am-4:10pm Mon-Sat, noon-4pm Sun) Although Jim Williams, the Savannah art dealer portrayed by Kevin Spacey in the film version of *Midnight in the Garden of Good and Evil,* died back in 1990, his infamous mansion didn't become a museum until 2004. You're not allowed to see the upstairs, where Williams' family still lives, but the downstairs is an interior decorator's fantasy.

Telfair Academy of Arts & Sciences MUSEUM
(www.telfair.org; 121 Barnard St; adult/child $12/5; ⊙noon-5pm Sun-Mon, 10am-5pm Tue-Sat) Considered Savannah's top art museum, the historic Telfair family mansion is filled with 19th-century American art, silver from that era, and a smattering of European pieces.

SCAD Museum of Art   ART MUSEUM
(www.scadmoa.org; 601 Turner Blvd; adult/child under 14yr $10/free; ⊙10am-5pm Tue-Wed, to 8pm Thu, to 5pm Fri, noon-5pm Sun) Brand new and architecturally striking, this brick, steel, concrete and glass longhouse delivers your modern art fix. With groovy, creative sitting areas inside and out, and fun rotating exhibitions.

Jepson Center for the Arts   GALLERY
(JCA; www.telfair.org; 207 W York St; adult/child $12/5; ⊙noon-5pm Sun-Mon, 10am-5pm Tue-Sat; 📷) Looking pretty darn space-age by Savannah's standards, the JCA focuses on 20th- and 21st-century art.

Savannah Bike Tours   BICYCLE TOUR
(✆912-704-4043; www.savannahbiketours.com; 41 Habersham St; tours $25) This outfit offers two-hour bike tours on its fleet of cruisers.

🛏 Sleeping

Luckily for travelers, it's become stylish for Savannah hotels and B&Bs to serve hors d'oeuvres and wine to guests in the evening. Cheap sleeps are difficult to find and all accommodations should be booked in advance.

Savannah Pensione   GUESTHOUSE $
(✆912-236-7744; www.savannahpensione.com; 304 E Hall St; s/d/tr without bath from $48/57/77, d/tr from $71/82; P❄@) It was run as a hos-

tel for some 15 years but the owner of this basic neighborhood crash-pad got tired of backpackers traipsing up and down the historic steps of the 1884 Italianate mansion. Fair enough. Now a bare-bones and vibeless pensione, it still offers the cheapest historic quarter rooms, though its potential is criminally unrealized.

Dorm beds can be had for $26, but only for groups of three or more who know each other.

Thunderbird Inn   MOTEL $$
(✆912-232-2661; www.thethunderbirdinn.com; 611 W Oglethorpe Ave; r $109; P❄🛜) A 'tad Palm Springs, a touch Vegas' best describes this vintage-chic 1964 motel that wins its own popularity contest – a 'Hippest hotel in Savannah' proclamation greets guests in the '60s-soundtracked lobby. In a land of stuffy B&Bs, this groovy place is an oasis, made all the better by local Savannah College of Art and Design student art.

Krispy Kreme doughnuts for breakfast!

Azalea Inn   INN $$
(✆912-236-2707; www.azaleainn.com; 217 E Huntingdon St; r/villa from $199/299; P❄🛜🏊) A humble stunner on a quiet street, we love this sweet canary-yellow historic inn near Forsyth Park. The 10 house rooms aren't huge, but are well done with varnished darkwood floors, crown moldings, four-poster beds and a small dipping pool out back. Three new villas offer more modern luxury for long-term stays.

Kehoe House   B&B $$$
(✆912-232-1020; www.kehoehouse.com; 123 Habersham St; r from $239; ❄🛜) This romantic, upscale Renaissance Revival B&B dates to 1892 and twins are said to have died in a chimney here, making it one of America's most haunted hotels. If you're skittish, steer clear of rooms 201 and 203! Ghosts aside, it's a beautifully appointed worthwhile splurge on picturesque Columbia Sq.

Mansion on Forsyth Park   HOTEL $$$
(✆912-238-5158; www.mansiononforsythpark.com; 700 Drayton St; r weekend/weekday $299/199; P❄@🛜🏊) A choice location and chic design highlight the luxe accommodations on offer at the 18,000-sq-ft Mansion – the sexy bathrooms alone are practically worth the money. The best part of the hotel-spa is the amazing local and international art that crowds its walls and hallways – more than 400 pieces in all.

Savannah

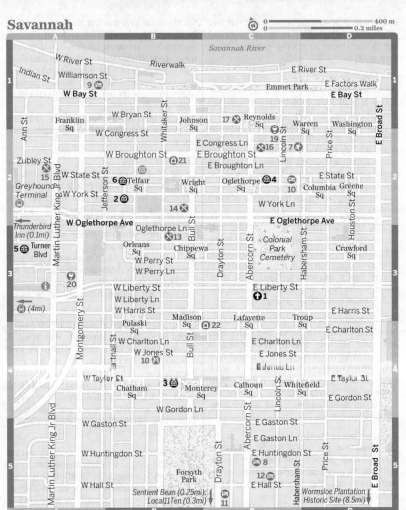

Savannah River

Bohemian Hotel
BOUTIQUE HOTEL **$$$**

(☎912-721-3800; www.bohemianhotelsavannah. com; 102 West Bay St; r weekend/weekday $359/269; P✳@☎) Enjoy sleek, dark, Gothic hallways, a riverside perch and small touches like driftwood-and-oyster chandeliers. Rooms are stunning, though too low-lit for some. Personalized service makes it feel far more intimate than its 75 rooms indicate.

✕ Eating

Angel's BBQ
BARBECUE **$**

(www.angels-bbq.com; 21 W Oglethorpe Lane; sandwiches/plates $6.50/9; ⊙11:30am until sold out

Wed-Sat) Utterly low-brow and hidden down an uneventful lane, Angel's pulled-pork sandwiches and sea-salted fries will leave you humbled and thoroughly satisfied – and that's before you tear through the impressive list of housemade sauces.

Leopold's Ice Cream
ICE CREAM **$**

(www.leopoldsicecream.com; 212 E Broughton St; scoops $2.75-4.75; ⊙11am-11pm Sun-Thu, to midnight Fri-Sat; ☎) This classic American ice-cream parlor feels like the Last Man Standing, having been scooping up its creamy Greek recipes since 1919. Tutti Frutti was invented here, but we dig coffee, pistachio, honey

Savannah

almond and cream, and caramel swirl. Hurry up and wait.

⭐ **Collins Quarter** CAFE $$
(www.thecollinsquarter.com; 151 Bull St; mains $9-17; ◷6:30am-11pm; 🛜) If you have ever talked coffee with an Australian, you know they are particularly fussy about their java. This wildly popular newcomer is Australian-owned and turns Australian-roasted Brooklyn coffee into their beloved flat whites and long blacks. Beyond Savannah's best coffee, it serves excellent fusion fare, including a drool-inducing brisket burger. There's booze, too!

Wilkes' House SOUTHERN $$
(www.mrswilkes.com; 107 W Jones St; lunch adult/child $20/10; ◷11am-2pm Mon-Fri, closed Jan) The line outside can begin as early as 8am at this first-come, first-served, Southern comfort food institution. Once the lunch bell rings and you are seated family-style, the kitchen unloads on you: fried chicken, beef stew, meatloaf, cheese potatoes, collard greens, black-eyed peas, mac 'n' cheese, rutabaga, candied yams, squash casserole, creamed corn *and* biscuits.

It's like Thanksgiving and the Last Supper rolled into one massive feast, chased with sweet tea.

Olde Pink House NEW SOUTHERN $$$
(☏912-232-4286; 23 Abercorn St; mains $15-37; ◷11am-10:30pm, closed lunch Sun-Mon) Classic Southern food done upscale; our favorite appetizer is Southern sushi – shrimp and grits rolled in a coconut-crusted nori roll. Dine in the slender digs upstairs, or go underground to the fabulous tavern where the piano player rumbles and the room is cozy, funky and perfect. The building is a 1771 landmark and this is Savannah's most consistently great restaurant.

The Grey NEW SOUTHERN $$$
(☏912-662-5999; www.thegreyrestaurant.com; 109 Martin Luther King Jr Blvd; mains $25-44; 🛜) A wonderfully retro makeover of the 1960s Greyhound Bus Terminal gives us Savannah's latest culinary darling, where chef Mashama Bailey's 'Port City Southern' cuisine is a delightful immigrant-infused take on local grub. Bearded hipsters work the best seats in the house, around the U-shaped centerpiece bar, where scrumptious pork-belly country pasta and a gargantuan pork shank are standouts. Reservations essential.

Local11Ten MODERN AMERICAN $$$
(☏912-790-9000; www.local11ten.com; 1110 Bull St; mains $16-35; ◷6-10pm Mon-Sat) Upscale, sustainable, local, fresh: these elements help create an elegant, well-run restaurant that's easily one of Savannah's best. Start with a deconstructed rabbit ravioli, then move on to the fabulous seared sea scallops in mint beurre blanc or the harissa-marinated bison hanger steak and a salted caramel pot de crème for a happy ending. Wait. Scratch that. The menu already changed.

🍷 **Drinking & Nightlife**

River St, with its plastic cup open container laws, is the bar-hopping, spring-break-like nightlife corridor.

THE SOUTH SOUTH GEORGIA

Rocks on the Roof
BAR

(www.bohemianhotelsavannah.com/dining/lounge; 102 West Bay St; ⏱11am-midnight Sun-Wed, to 1am Thu-Sat; 🛜) The expansive, viewriffic rooftop bar at the Bohemian Hotel is breezy, fun and best when the weather is fine and the fire pit is glowing.

Distillery Ale House
BAR

(www.distilleryalehouse.com; 416 W Liberty St; ⏱11am-late Mon-Sat, from noon Sun) Formerly the Kentucky Distilling Co, opened in 1904 and closed at Prohibition, this is oddly *not* Savannah's local throat-burning swill house, but rather its go-to craft beer bar. Also popular with tourists and families for bar food.

Abe's on Lincoln
BAR

(17 Lincoln St) Ditch the tourists – drink with the locals in dark, dank, all-wood environs.

Sentient Bean
CAFE

(www.sentientbean.com; 13 E Park Ave; coffee $1.50-4.75; ⏱7am-10pm; 🛜) 🌿 Everything you want from an indie coffeehouse: terrific brew, gourmet breakfasts, spacious boho interior and hipster clientele and baristas, all awash in sustainability. It's Savannah's favorite and just across from Forsyth Park.

🛍 Chopping

West Broughton St is Savannah's preeminent shopping district – with both corporate and indie entities shoulder to shoulder, and all of it punctuated with a distinctly SCAD flavor.

Savannah Bee Company
FOOD

(www.savannahbee.com; 104 W Broughton St; ⏱10am-8pm Mon-Sat, 11am-5pm Sun) This internationally renowned honey dreamland is one of Savannah's must-stops. Expect artisanal honey of infinite variety and limitless free tastings.

ShopSCAD
ARTS & CRAFTS

(www.shopscadonline.com; 340 Bull St; ⏱9am-5:30pm Mon-Fri, to 6pm Sat, noon-5pm Sun) All the wares at this funky, kitschy boutique were designed by students, faculty and alumni of Savannah's prestigious art college.

❶ Information

Candler Hospital (www.sjchs.org; 5353 Reynolds St; ⏱24hr) Medical services.

Post Office (www.usps.com; 118 Barnard St; ⏱8am-5pm Mon-Fri) Historic district postal services.

Savannah Chatham Metropolitan Police (☎912-651-6675; www.scmpd.org; cnr E Oglethorpe Ave & Habersham St) Police headquarters.

Savannah Visitor Center (☎912-944-0455; www.savannahvisit.com; 301 Martin Luther King Jr Blvd; ⏱8:30am-5pm Mon-Fri, 9am-5pm Sat & Sun) Excellent resources and services are available in this center, based in a restored 1860s train station. Many privately operated city tours start here. There is also a small interactive tourist-info kiosk in the new visitor center at Forsyth Park.

❶ Getting There & Around

The **Savannah/Hilton Head International Airport** (SAV; ☎912-966-3743; www.savannahairport.com; 400 Airways Ave) is about 5 miles west of downtown off I-16. Taxis from the airport to the historic district cost a standard $28. **Greyhound** (www.greyhound.com; 610 W Oglethorpe Ave) has connections to Atlanta (about five hours), Charleston, SC (about two hours) and Jacksonville, FL (2½ hours). The **Amtrak station** (www.amtrak.com; 2611 Seaboard Coastline Dr) is just a few miles west of the historic district.

Savannah is very foot-friendly. **Chatham Area Transit** (CAT; www.catchacat.org; per ride $1.50) operates local buses that run on bio-diesel, including a free shuttle (the Dot) that makes its way around the historic district and stops within a couple of blocks of nearly every major site.

CAT Bike (www.catbike.boyolo.oom; ⏱por 30min $2) Convenient bike-hire scheme, run by Chatham Area Transit, with stations around town. It's free for the first hour.

Brunswick & the Golden Isles

Georgia has a coast? Oh yes, a righteously beautiful one, blessed with a string of picturesque islands ranging from rustic to kitschy to indulgent. With its large shrimp-boat fleet and downtown historic district shaded beneath lush live oaks, Brunswick dates from 1733 and has charms you might miss when sailing by on I-95 or the Golden Isle Pkwy (US Hwy 17). During WWII Brunswick shipyards constructed 99 Liberty transport ships for the navy. Today a 23ft scale model at **Mary Ross Waterfront Park** (Bay St) stands as a memorial to those ships and their builders.

🛏 Sleeping

Hostel in the Forest
HOSTEL $

(☎912-264-9738; www.foresthostel.com; 3901 Hwy 82; per person $25; 🐾) The only budget base in the area is this set of bare-bones octagonal

CUMBERLAND ISLAND

An unspoiled paradise, a backpacker's fantasy, a site for day trips or extended stays – it's clear why the family of 19th-century industrialist and philanthropist Andrew Carnegie used Cumberland as a retreat long ago. Most of this southernmost barrier island is now occupied by the **Cumberland Island National Seashore** (www.nps.gov/cuis; admission $4). Almost half of its 36,415 acres consists of marsh, mudflats and tidal creeks. On the ocean side are 16 miles of wide, sandy beach that you might have all to yourself. The island's interior is characterized by maritime forest. Ruins from the Carnegie estate **Dungeness** are astounding, as are the wild turkeys, tiny fiddler crabs and beautiful butterflies. Feral horses roam the island and are a common sight.

The only public access to the island is via boat to/from the quirky, lazy town of **St Marys** (www.stmaryswelcome.com). Convenient and pleasant **ferries** (☑877-860-6787; www.nps.gov/cuis; round-trip adult/senior/child $25/23/15) leave from the mainland at the St Marys dock at 9am and 11:45am and return at 10:15am and 4:45pm (with an extra 2:45pm departure in spring and summer). Reservations are staunchly recommended well before you arrive, and visitors are required to check in at the **visitors center** (☑912-882-4336; www.nps.gov/cuis; ⊗8am-4pm) at the dock at least 30 minutes prior to departure. December through February, the ferry does not operate on Tuesday or Wednesday.

On Cumberland Island, the only private accommodations (two-night minimum stay) are at the **Greyfield Inn** (☑904-261-6408; www.greyfieldinn.com; r incl meals $425-635), a mansion built in 1900. Camping is available at **Sea Camp Beach** (☑912-882-4335; www.nps.gov/cuis; tent sites per person $4), set among magnificent live oaks.

Note: there are no stores or waste bins on the island. Eat before arriving or bring lunch, and take your trash with you.

cedar huts and tree houses (sans air or heat) on an ecofriendly, sustainable campus. You must pay a member fee of $10 to stay and it's all very hippy-dippy with dinner included. It's tucked in the woods 10 miles outside Brunswick; phone reservations only.

St Simons Island

Famous for its golf courses, resorts and majestic live oaks, St Simons Island is the largest and most developed of the Golden Isles. It lies 75 miles south of Savannah and just 5 miles from Brunswick. The southern half of the island is a thickly settled residential and resort area.

Little St Simons is an all-natural jewel, accessible by boat only to guests at the exclusive **Lodge on Little St Simons** (☑888-733-5774; www.littlessi.com; 1000 Hampton Pt; all-inclusive d from $450) or to their **day trippers** (☑888-733-5774; www.littlestsimonsisland.com; Hampton Point Dr; per person $95; ⊗trips 10:30am).

◉ Sights & Activities

Sea Island   ISLAND
(www.seaisland.com) Sea Island offers tracts of coastal wilderness amid a tidewater estuary, but access is limited to guests of its three luxury hotels unless you make dining reservations at the Cloister's Georgian Room.

Massengale Park   PARK, BEACH
(1350 Ocean Blvd) East Beach, the island's best, is accessible from Massengale Park.

🍴 Sleeping & Eating

St Simons Inn by the Lighthouse   INN $$
(☑912-638-1101; www.saintsimonsinn.com; 609 Beachview Dr; r weekend/weekday from $159/139; P❄🖥🏊) Cute and comfortable good-value inn, accented with white wooden shutters. It's well located next to the downtown drag and a short pedal from East Beach. Continental breakfast included.

Southern Soul BBQ   BARBECUE $
(www.southernsoulbbq.com; 2020 Demere Rd; mains $5-17; ⊗11am-10pm) Succulent slow oak-smoked pulled pork, burnt-tipped brisket and daily specials like jerk chicken burritos. There are a number of wonderful house-made sauces and a great patio from which to take it all in. Packed always.

Halyards   SEAFOOD $$$
(☑912-638-9100; www.halyardsrestaurant.com; 55 Cinema Lane; mains $14-42; ⊗5-9pm Mon-Wed, to 10pm Thu-Sat; 🐾) 🌿 Chef Dave Snyder's classy sustainable seafooder consistently

hogs best-of-everything awards on St Simons, and for good reason. Go for the Chef's Highlights (our mahi-mahi over boursin grits, haricot verts and orange-vanilla butter was perfect).

Jekyll Island

An exclusive refuge for millionaires in the late 19th and early 20th centuries, Jekyll is a 4000-year-old barrier island with 10 miles of beaches. Today it's an unusual clash of wilderness, historically preserved buildings, modern hotels and a massive campground. It's an easily navigable place – you can get around by car, horse or bicycle, but there's a $6 parking fee per 24 hours.

⊙ Sights & Activities

Georgia Sea Turtle Center   WILDLIFE
(☑ 912-635-4444; www.georgiaseaturtlecenter. org; 214 Stable Rd; adult/child $7/5; ⊙ 9am-5pm, closed Mon Nov-Mar; ⓐ) An endearing attraction is the Georgia Sea Turtle Center, a conservation center and turtle hospital where patients are on view for the public. Behind the Scenes tours ($22; 3pm) and Turtle Walks ($14; 8:30pm and 9:30pm; June 1 to July 31) are also available

⊨ Sleeping & Eating

Villas by the Sea   CONDOS $
(☑ 912-635-2521; www.villasbythesearesort.com; 1175 N Beachview Dr; r/condo from $99/129; P ❉ 🛜 ≋) A nice choice on the north coast close to the best beaches. Rooms are spacious and the one-, two- and three-bedroom condos, set in a complex of lodge buildings sprinkled over a garden, are not fancy but plenty comfy.

★ **Jekyll Island Club Hotel**   HISTORIC HOTEL $$
(☑ 912-635-2600; www.jekyllclub.com; 371 Riverview Dr; d/ste from $189/299, resort fee $15; P ❉ @ 🛜 ≋) A posh and storied historic hotel and the backbone of the island, featuring a rambling array of rooms spread out over five historic structures. Plans are in the works for 41 new beachfront suites.

Latitude 31 Restaurant & Rah Bar SEAFOOD $
(www.latitude31jekyllisland.com; 370 Riverview Dr; mains $6-36; ⊙ 11am-3pm & 5-10pm) This casual outdoor seafooder on the Jekyll Island wharf is a great spot for a sunset drink and fresh seafood.

ALABAMA

History suffuses Alabama, a description which could be true of many states. But there are few places where the perception of said history is so emotionally fraught. The Mississippian Native American culture built great mound cities here, and Mobile is dotted with Franco-Caribbean architecture. But for many, the word Alabama is synonymous with the American Civil Rights movement.

Perhaps such a struggle, and all of the nobility and desperation it entailed, was bound for a state like this, with its Gothic plantations, hardscrabble farmland and fiercely local sense of place. From the smallest hunting town to river-bound cities, Alabama is a place all its own, and its character is hard to forget. Some visitors have a hard time looking beyond the state's past, but the troubling elements of that narrative are tied up in a passion that constantly manifests in Alabama's arts, food and culture.

ⓘ Information

Alabama Bureau of Tourism & Travel (www. alabama.travel) Sends out a vacation guide and has a website with extensive tourism options.

Alabama State Parks (1-800-252-7275; www. alapark.com) There are 23 parks statewide with camping facilities ranging from primitive ($16) to 15-person cabins ($200). Advance reservations are suggested for weekends and holidays.

Birmingham

Birmingham is a treasure of unexpected cool. This hilly, shady town, founded as an iron mine, is still a center for manufacturing – Mercedes-Benz USA is based out of nearby Tuscaloosa. In addition, universities and colleges pepper the town, and all of this comes together to create a city with an unreservedly excellent dining and drinking scene. The past also lurks in Birmingham, once named 'Bombingham,' and the history of the Civil Rights movement is very much at your fingers.

⊙ Sights & Activities

Art-deco buildings abound in trendy **Five Points South**, where you'll find shops, restaurants and nightspots. Once industrial **Avondale** is where the hipsters are congregating. Equally noteworthy is the upscale **Homewood** community's quaint commercial drag on 18th St S, close to the Vulcan which looms illuminated above the city and is visible from nearly all angles, day and night.

★ Birmingham
Civil Rights Institute   MUSEUM
(☎ 866-328-9696; www.bcri.org; 520 16th St N; adult/senior/child $12/5/3, Sun free; ◎10am-5pm Tue-Sat, 1-5pm Sun) A maze of moving audio, video and photography exhibits tell the story of racial segregation in America, and the Civil Rights movement, with a focus on activities in and around Birmingham. There's an extensive exhibit on the 16th Street Baptist Church (located across the street), which was bombed in 1963; it's the beginning of the city's Civil Rights Memorial Trail.

Birmingham Museum of Art   GALLERY
(www.artsbma.org; 2000 Rev Abraham Woods Jr Blvd; ◎10am-5pm Tue-Sat, noon-5pm Sun) FREE This very fine museum collects works from Asia, Africa, Europe and the Americas. Don't miss the work of Rodin, Botero and Dalí in the sculpture garden.

Birmingham
Civil Rights Memorial Trail   WALKING TOUR
(www.bcri.org; 520 16th St N) Seven blocks long, this is a poignant walk perfect for the whole family. Installed in 2013 for the 50th anniversary of the Civil Rights campaign, the walk depicts 22 moving scenes with plaques, statues and photography, some of it quite conceptual and moving – to whit, a gauntlet of snapping, sculpted dog statues pedestrians must traverse. The experience peels back yet another layer of the sweat and blood behind a campaign that changed America.

Vulcan Park   PARK
(☎ 205-933-1409; www.visitvulcan.com; 1701 Valley View Dr; observation tower & museum adult/child $6/4, 6-10pm $4; ◎7am-10pm, observation tower 10am-10pm Mon-Sat, from noon Sun, museum 10am-6pm Mon-Sat, from noon Sun; 🚼🐾) Imagine Christ the Redeemer in Rio, but made of iron and depicting a beefcake Roman god of metalworking. Vulcan is visible from all over the city – this is actually the world's largest cast-iron statue – and the park he resides in offers fantastic views, along with an **observation tower**. A small on-site museum explores Birmingham history.

🛏 Sleeping

By the time you read this, the grand old **Redmont Hotel** (www.redmontbirmingham.com; 2101 5th Ave N; ✳@🛜), closed for renovation at the time of writing, will have reopened.

Hotel Highland   HOTEL $$
(☎ 205-933-9555; www.thehotelhighland.com; 1023 20th St S; r from $129; P✳@🛜) Nuzzled right up next to the lively Five Points district, this colorful, slightly trippy but modern hotel is very comfortable and a good deal. The rooms are thankfully a bit less bright and funky than the lobby.

🍴 Eating

For such a small Southern city, student-oriented Birmingham has a wide variety of eateries and cafes, and plenty of free live music on weekends.

Saw's BBQ   BARBECUE $
(☎ 205-879-1937; www.sawsbbq.com; 1008 Oxmoor Road; mains $9-16; ◎11am-8pm Mon-Sat; 🚼) Saw's has exploded onto the Birmingham barbecue scene with a vengeance, offering some of the most mouthwatering smoked meat in the city, served in a family-friendly atmosphere. Stuffed potatoes make a nice addition to your meal, and the

---

ALABAMA FACTS

Nickname The Heart of Dixie

Population 4.8 million

Area 52,419 sq miles

Capital city Montgomery (population 201,300)

Other cities Birmingham (population 212,113)

Sales tax 4%, but up to 11% with local taxes

Birthplace of Author Helen Keller (1880–1968), civil rights activist Rosa Parks (1913–2005), musician Hank Williams (1923–53)

Home of The University of Alabama Crimson Tide

Politics Republican stronghold – Alabama hasn't voted Democratic since 1976

Famous for Rosa Parks, the Civil Rights movement, and football

Bitter rivalry University of Alabama vs Auburn University

Driving distances Montgomery to Birmingham 91 miles, Mobile to Dauphin Island 38 miles, Mobile to Tuscaloosa 196 miles

smoked chicken with a tangy local white sauce is divine – although with that said, bring on the ribs!

Eagle's Restaurant
AMERICAN $

(☑ 205-320-0099; www.eaglesrestaurant.com; 2610 16th St N; mains $5.50-15; ☺ 10:30am-4pm Sun-Fri) Tucked away on a lonely strip is Eagle's, home of Birmingham's best soul food. Decidedly popular with the local African American population, Eagle's operates on a meat-and-two/three model: order a main, be it steak and gravy, neckbones and potatoes or chicken wings, then pick from a buffet tray of side options. It's delicious, cheap and local as anything.

Chez Fonfon
FRENCH $$

(☑ 205-939-3221; www.fonfonbham.com; 2007 11th St S; mains $14.50-24; ☺ 11am-10pm Tue-Thu, to 10:30pm Fri, 4:30-10:30pm Sat) The name of this place merits a slight snicker, but save your smiles for the food, because it's very good French bistro fare. Hanger steak comes with a fresh green salsa and crispy, warm frites, while trout sizzles next to some golden potatoes. Despite a 'no dress code' rule, folks tend to look nice, and reservations are recommended.

 Drinking & Entertainment

There's a silly amount of good bars in Birmingham, many concentrated in Avondale and Five Points.

The Collins Bar
BAR

(☑ 205-323-7995; 2125 2nd Ave N; ☺ 4pm-midnight Tue-Thu, to 2am Fri & Sat, 6pm-midnight Sun) Birmingham's beautiful people pack into this cool space after work and on weekends, sipping handmade cocktails under giant paper planes and a Birmingham-centric Periodic Table of the Elements. There's no drink menu – tell the bartender what flavors you like and they'll mix something special for you.

Marty's
BAR

(1813 10th Ct S; ☺ 4pm-6am) Take note: Marty's is technically a drinking club; the first time you visit, you pay a $2 membership fee. That club status allows Marty's to stay open late, attracting an unapologetically geeky crowd to a friendly bar packed with comic book art, *Star Wars* memorabilia, role-playing game references and the occasional live-music gig.

Garage Café
BAR

(☑ 205-322-3220; www.garagecafe.us; 2304 10th Terrace S; ☺ 3pm-midnight Sun-Mon, 11am-2am Tue-Sat) A crowd of hipsters and older drinking pros knock back their brew while tapping their toes to live music in a courtyard full of junk, antiques, ceramic statues and quite literally, the kitchen sink.

41 Street Pub & Aircraft Sales
BAR

(☑ 205-202-4187; 130 41st St S; ☺ 4:30pm-midnight Mon-Thu, 4:30pm-2am Fri, 1pm-2am Sat, 1pm-noon Sun) A slick wooden bar fronts a large open space offset with some shuffleboard tables. Behind the bar, strong drinks (the Moscow Mule is a winner) are served to an attractive, hipster crowd in shiny copper mugs.

❶ Getting There & Around

The **Birmingham International Airport** (BHM; www.flybirmingham.com) is about 5 miles northeast of downtown.

Greyhound (☑ 205-253-7190; www.greyhound.com; 618 19th St N), north of downtown, serves cities including Huntsville, Montgomery, Atlanta, GA, Jackson, MS, and New Orleans, LA (10 hours). **Amtrak** (☑ 205-324-3033; www.amtrak.com; 1819 Morris Ave), downtown, has trains daily to New York and New Orleans.

Birmingham Transit Authority (www.bjcta.org; adult $1.25) runs local buses.

Moundville

One of the largest and best preserved sites of the pre-Columbian Mississippian civilization sits outside of modern Moundville, about 17 miles south of Tuscaloosa. Here, on the dark forested banks of the Black Warrior River, you will find the grassy remains of the Mississippian mound city and an excellent museum, all managed by **Moundville Archaeological Park** (☑ 205-348-9826; www.moundville.ua.edu; 634 Mound Park; adult/senior/children $8/7/6; ☺ museum 9am-5pm, park 9am-dusk).

Within the complex you will find 26 mounds of varying sizes, arranged in a manner that suggests a highly stratified social structure. The museum is filled with pre-Columbian art, including pottery and disks inscribed with underwater panthers, feathered serpents and skulls. The highest mound at the site is topped by a small replica hut (closed to the public at the time of research).

ROLL TIDE!

Roll Tide! It's the call you'll hear pretty much everywhere in the town of Tuscaloosa, 60 miles southwest of Birmingham, but especially on Saturday afternoons in the fall. During football season, students and alumni gather in the **University of Alabama** (www. ua.edu) quad, hours before kickoff, for a pregame party like none other. White tents, wired with satellite TV, fill the expansive lawn. Barbecue is smoked and devoured, cornhole (drunken bean-bag toss) is played. At game time all migrate to **Bryant-Denny Stadium** (☑205-348-3600; www.rolltide.com; 920 Paul W Bryant Dr), a 102,000-capacity football stadium that looks out onto the rolling hills and is always packed with rabid fans, and with good reason. The Alabama Crimson Tide have won 19 national championships, including the last two, and three of the last four. Get a full dose of Crimson Tide football history at the **Paul W Bryant Museum** (☑205-348-4668; www.bryantmuseum.com; 300 Paul W Bryant Dr; adult/senior & child $2/1; ⊗9am-4pm), named for the greatest coach of them all. Or so the legend goes...

Montgomery

In 1955 Rosa Parks refused to give up her seat to a white man on a city bus, launching a bus boycott and galvanizing the Civil Rights movement nationwide. The city has commemorated that incident with a museum, which along with a few other civil rights sights, is the main reason to visit. Alabama's capital, Montgomery is an otherwise charming but sleepy city.

⊙ Sights

Montgomery's pleasant **Riverwalk** is accessed via a tunnel from downtown and is an extended plaza along a bend in the river with a natural amphitheater and a riverboat dock.

Rosa Parks Museum   MUSEUM
(☑334-241-8615; www.troy.edu/rosaparks; 251 Montgomery St; adult/child 4-12yr $7.50/5.50; ⊗9am-5pm Mon-Fri, 9am-3pm Sat;) This museum, set in front of the bus stop where Rosa Parks took her stand, features a video re-creation of that pivotal moment that launched the 1955 boycott. The experience is very managed – you're given a small opportunity to explore on your own, but otherwise the museum feels something like an interactive movie. For the price of an additional full admission ticket, you can visit the children's wing, a kids-oriented time-travel exhibit to the Jim Crow South.

Civil Rights Memorial Center   MEMORIAL
(www.splcenter.org/civil-rights-memorial; 400 Washington Ave; adult/child $2/free; ⊗9am-4:30pm Mon-Fri, 10am-4pm Sat) With its circular design crafted by Maya Lin, this haunting memorial focuses on 40 martyrs of the Civil Rights movement. Some cases remain unsolved. Martin Luther King Jr was the most famous, but there were many 'faceless' deaths along the way, both white and African American. The memorial is part of the Southern Poverty Law Center, a legal foundation committed to racial equality and equal opportunity for justice under the law.

Scott & Zelda Fitzgerald Museum   MUSEUM
(☑334-264-4222; www.fitzgeraldmuseum.net; 919 Felder Ave; adult/child donation $5/2; ⊗10am-3pm Tue-Sat, noon-5pm Sun) ◢ The writers' home from 1931 to 1932 now houses first editions, translations and original artwork by Zelda from her sad last days when she was committed to a mental health facility. Unlike many 'homes of famous people,' there's a ramshackle charm to this museum – while the space is curated, you also feel as if you've stumbled into the Fitzgerald's attic, exemplified by loving handwritten letters from Zelda to Scott.

⊨ Sleeping & Eating

Montgomery isn't known for its restaurants and accommodations, and can be done on a day trip, but there are a couple of finds. **The Alley**, a dining and entertainment district, has helped perk up a dormant downtown.

Renaissance Hotel   HOTEL $$
(☑334-481-5000; www.marriott.com; 201 Tallapoosa St; r from $150;) Yes, it's corporate and kind of faceless, but it is also well located and easily Montgomery's nicest address.

Central
STEAK $$$

(☑334-517-1121; www.central129coosa.com; 129 Coosa St; mains $18-39; ⊙11am-2pm Mon-Fri, 5:30pm-late Mon-Sat; ☑) The gourmand's choice, this stunner has an airy interior with a reclaimed-wood bar. The booths are sumptuous and these guys were doing farm to table before it was 'A Thing'; The menu specializes in wood-fired fish, chicken, steaks and chops sourced from the region. Dishes like a pesto walnut pasta are nice for vegetarians.

❶ Information

Montgomery Area Visitor Center (☑334-261-1100; www.visitingmontgomery.com; 300 Water St; ⊙8:30am-5pm Mon-Sat) Has tourist information and a helpful website.

❶ Getting There & Around

Montgomery Regional Airport (MGM; ☑334-281-5040; www.montgomeryairport.org; 4445 Selma Hwy) is about 15 miles from downtown and is served by daily flights from Atlanta, GA, Charlotte, NC, and Dallas, TX. **Greyhound** (☑334-286-0658; www.greyhound.com; 950 W South Blvd) also serves the city. The **Montgomery Area Transit System** (www.montgomerytransit.com; tickets $2) operates city bus lines.

Selma

On Bloody Sunday, March 7, 1965, the media captured state troopers and deputies beating and gassing African Americans and white sympathizers near the **Edmund Pettus Bridge** (Broad St & Walter Ave). The crowd was marching to the state capital (Montgomery) to demonstrate against the murder of a local black activist by police during a demonstration for voting rights.

When the scene was broadcast on every network later that night, it marked one of the first times anyone outside the South had witnessed the horrifying images of the struggle, of booted policemen using night sticks and attack dogs on peaceful marchers while whites waving Confederate flags jeered from the sidelines. Shock and outrage was widespread, and support for the movement grew. Martin Luther King arrived swiftly in Selma and after another aborted attempt due to the threat of violence, helped lead what became 8000 people on a four-day, 54-mile march to Montgomery, culminating with a classic King speech on the capitol steps. Soon after, President Johnson signed the Voting Rights Act of 1965.

Selma's story is told at the **National Voting Rights Museum** (☑334-418-0800; www.nvrmi.com; 1012 Water Ave; adult/senior & student $6.50/4.50; ⊙10am-4pm Mon-Thu, by appt only Fri-Sun), near the Edmund Pettus Bridge, and at two interpretive sites run by the National Park Service: the **Selma Interpretive Center** (☑334-872-0509; www.nps.gov/semo; 2 Broad St; ⊙9am-4:30pm Mon-Sat) and the **Lowndes County Interpretive Center** (☑334-877-1983; www.nps.gov/semo; 7002 US Hwy 80; ⊙9am-4:30pm) halfway between Selma and Montgomery. Both centers contain small, solid exhibitions that delve into the history of Jim Crow and the Civil Rights movement.

Selma is a quiet, poor town located in the heart of the Alabama 'Black Belt,' so named

THE SOUTH SELMA

THE CARNIVOROUS BOG

The pitcher plant is the vegetarian's revenge: a carnivorous plant topped with a lovely, fluting champagne rim of petals. Insects are drawn into the plant's interior cavity, which is lined with a slippery surface; the bugs fall into a pocket of liquid at the flower's base and are digested into nutrients.

Blankets of white-topped pitcher plants can be found at the **Splinter Hill Bog** (www.nature.org; off Co Rd 47, Bay Minette, GPS N 31°02.638', W -87°68.500'; ⊙dawn-dusk), a 2100-acre plot of land owned and protected by the nonprofit Nature Conservancy. Walk into the pitcher plant bogs (almost immediately visible once you depart the parking area) and you may notice that the clouds of midges, mosquitoes and flies so common in Southern woodlands and wetlands are mysteriously absent. That's because many of these insects are busily being digested by a graceful field of wildflowers.

Besides pitcher plants, this is an area of startling diversity; in some spots scientists have found over 60 different species of plants in a square yard, which constitutes some of the highest concentrations of biodiversity in North America. For more information, check out *America's Amazon*, a documentary on this region, which forms part of the Mobile-Tensaw Delta.

for both its dark, high-quality soil and a large population of African Americans. A point of interest is the Mishkan Israel (503 Broad St), an enormous redbrick synagogue that once housed a thriving local Jewish community. Many of the members of said community have left the South, but occasionally, a service is held.

If you're hungry, swing into Lannie's (☑334-874-4478; 2115 Minter Ave; mains $5-11; ☺9am-9pm Mon-Sat), which cranks out some of the finest barbecue around.

Mobile

Wedged between Mississippi and Florida, the only real Alabama coastal city is Mobile (mo-*beel*), a busy industrial seaport with a smattering of green space, shady boulevards and four historic districts. It's ablaze with azaleas in early spring, and festivities are held throughout February for Mardi Gras (www.mobilemardigras.com), which has been celebrated here for nearly 200 years (it actually predates Mardi Gras in New Orleans).

◉ Sights

USS Alabama   BATTLESHIP
(www.ussalabama.com; 2703 Battleship Pkwy; adult/child $15/6; ☺8am-6pm Apr-Sep, to 5pm Oct-Mar) USS *Alabama* is a 690ft behemoth famous for escaping nine major WWII battles unscathed. It's a worthwhile self-guided tour for its awesome size and might. While there, you can also tour a submarine and get up close and personal with military aircraft. Parking's $2.

🛏 Sleeping & Eating

Battle House   HOTEL $$
(☑251-338-2000; www.marriott.com; 26 N Royal St; r from $139; P❋@☎❄) By far the best address in Mobile. Stay in the original historic wing with its ornate domed marble lobby, though the striking new tower is on the waterfront. Rooms are spacious, luxurious, four-star chic.

Callaghan's Irish Social Club   PUB FOOD $
(☑251-433-9374; www.callaghansirishsocialclub. com; 916 Charleston St; burgers $7-9; ☺11am-11pm Mon-Thu, to midnight Fri & Sat, 10am-11pm Sun) This ramshackle pub is located in a 1920s-era building that used to house a meat market. It serves a mean burger and a cold beer, and often feature live-music acts.

🍷 Drinking & Nightlife

OK Bicycle Shop   BAR
(☑251-432-2453; 661 Dauphin St; ☺11am-3am) This sweet bar carries a bicycle theme throughout; there's a fantastic outdoor space for humid Mobile nights.

MISSISSIPPI

The state named for the most vital waterway in North America encompasses, appropriately enough, a long river of identities. Mississippi features palatial mansions and rural poverty; haunted cotton flats and lush hill country; honey-dipped sand on the coast and serene farmland in the north. Oft mythologized and misunderstood, this is the womb of some of the rawest history – and music – in the country.

❶ Getting There & Away

There are three routes most folks take when traveling through Mississippi. I-55 and US-61 both run north–south from the state's northern to southern borders. US-61 goes through the delta, and I-55 flows in and out of Jackson. The gorgeous Natchez Trace Pkwy runs diagonally across the state from Tupelo to Natchez.

❶ Information

Mississippi Division of Tourism Development (☑866-733-6477, 601-359-3297; www.visit mississippi.org) Has a directory of visitor bureaus and thematic travel itineraries. Most are well thought-out and run quite deep.

Mississippi Wildlife, Fisheries, & Parks (☑800-467-2757; www.mississippistateparks.reserve america.com) Camping costs from $13 (tent only) to $35 (beachfront camping), depending on the facilities; some parks have cabins for rent.

Oxford

Oxford both confirms and explodes preconceptions you may have of Mississippi's most famous college town. Frat boys in Ford pickup trucks and debutante sorority sisters? Sure. But they're alongside doctoral candidates debating critical theory, and a lively arts scene. Local culture revolves around the Square, where you'll find bars, restaurants and decent shopping, and the regal University of Mississippi (www.olemiss.edu), aka Ole Miss. All around are quiet residential streets,

414

SOUTH OXFORD

sprinkled with antebellum homes and shaded by majestic oaks.

Sights & Activities

The gorgeous, 0.6-mile-long and rather painless **Bailee's Woods Trail** connects two of the town's most popular sights: Rowan Oak and the University of Mississippi Museum. **The Grove**, the shady heart of Ole Miss (the university), is generally peaceful, except on football Saturdays, when it buzzes with one of the most unforgettable tailgating (pre-game) parties in American university sports.

Rowan Oak HISTORIC BUILDING
(☑ 662-234-3284; www.rowanoak.com; Old Taylor Rd; adult/child $5/free; ☺ 10am-4pm Tue-Sat, 1-4pm Sun, to 6pm Jun-Aug) Literary pilgrims head directly here, to the graceful 1840s home of William Faulkner. He authored many brilliant and dense novels set in Mississippi, and his work is celebrated in Oxford with an annual conference in July. Tours of Rowan Oak – where Faulkner lived from 1930 until his death in 1962, and which may reasonably be dubbed, to use the author's own elegant words, his 'postage stamp of native soil' – are self-guided.

University of Mississippi Museum MUSEUM
(www.museum.olemiss.edu; University Ave at 5th St; admission $5; ☺ 10am-6pm Tue-Sat) This museum has fine and folk arts and a plethora of science-related marvels, including a microscope and electromagnet from the 19th century.

Sleeping & Eating

The cheapest accommodations are chains on the outskirts of town. A number of high-quality restaurants dot the Square.

5 Twelve B&B $$
(☑ 662-234-8043; www.the5twelve.com; 512 Van Buren Ave; r $140-200, studio $200-250; P ❄ 🛜) This six-room B&B has an antebellum-style exterior and modern interior (think Tempur-Pedic beds and flat-screen TVs). Room rates include full Southern breakfast to order. It's an easy walk from shops and restaurants, and the hosts will make you feel like family.

Taylor Grocery SEAFOOD $$
(www.taylorgrocery.com; 4 County Rd 338A; dishes $9-15; ☺ 5-10pm Thu-Sat, to 9pm Sun) Be prepared to wait – and to tailgate in the parking lot – at this splendidly rusticated catfish haunt. Order fried or grilled (either way, it's amazing) and bring a marker to sign your name on the wall. It's about 7 miles from downtown Oxford, south on Old Taylor Rd.

Ravine AMERICAN $$$
(☑ 662-234-4555; www.oxfordravine.com; 53 County Rd 321; mains $19-32; ☺ 6-9pm Wed-Thu, to 10pm Fri & Sat, 10:30am-2pm & 6-9pm Sun; 🛜) About 8 miles outside Oxford, this unpretentious, cozily elegant restaurant nuzzles up to the forest. Chef Joel Miller picks and pulls much of the produce and herbs from his garden and buys locally and organically whenever possible; he's been doing it long before locavore was a buzzword. The result is simply wonderful food and a delicious experience.

JAMES MEREDITH'S MARCH

On October 1, 1962, James Meredith, accompanied by his adviser, National Association for the Advancement of Colored People state chair Medgar Evers, marched through a violent mob of segregationists to become the first African American student to register for classes at Ole Miss (the University of Mississippi). He was supposed to have registered 10 days earlier, but riots ensued and the Kennedy administration had to call in 500 federal marshals and the National Guard to ensure his safety.

Evers was eventually assassinated, and Meredith later walked across the state to raise awareness about racial violence in Mississippi. Some of Meredith's correspondence is on display at the **Center for Southern Culture** (☑ 662-915-5855; 1 Library Loop, University of Mississippi, Oxford; ☺ 8am-9pm Mon-Thu, to 4pm Fri, to 5pm Sat, 1pm-5pm Sun; 🛜) **FREE**, at the campus library.

Meredith himself went on to a career in politics, but his views were never easy to categorize. He was an active Republican who distanced himself from the Civil Rights movement, and always claimed he fought for his rights as an individual, rather than as a torchbearer for a greater movement. Regardless, Ole Miss is one of the most iconic institutions in the state, and when it was desegregated by Meredith's actions, it was inevitable the rest of Mississippi – and in some ways, the South – would follow.

City Grocery
AMERICAN $$$

(☑ 662-232-8080; www.citygroceryonline.com; 152 Courthouse Sq; mains $26-32; ☺ 11:30am-2:30pm Mon-Sat, 6-10pm Mon-Wed, to 10:30pm Thu-Sat, 11am-3pm Sun) Chef John Currance won a James Beard award and quickly set about dominating the Oxford culinary scene. City Grocery is one of his finest restaurants, offering a menu of haute Southern goodness like rice grits risotto and lard-braised hanger steak. The upstairs bar, decked out with local folk art, is a treat. Reservations recommended.

☆ Entertainment

On the last Tuesday of the month, an increasingly popular **Art Crawl** connects galleries across town with free buses carrying well-lubricated art lovers. Nibbles and wine aplenty.

Proud Larry's
LIVE MUSIC

(☑ 662-236-0050; www.proudlarrys.com; 211 S Lamar Blvd; ☺ shows 9:30pm) On the Square, this iconic music venue hosts consistently good bands, and does a nice pub-grub business at lunch and dinner before the stage lights dim.

The Lyric
LIVE MUSIC

(☑ 662-234-5333; www.thelyricoxford.com; 1006 Van Buren St) This old brickhouse, and rather intimate theater with concrete floors, exposed rafters and a mezzanine, is the place to see indie rockers and folksy crooners.

🔒 Shopping

Square Books
BOOKS

(☑ 662-236-2262; www.squarebooks.com; 160 Courthouse Sq; ☺ 9am-9pm Mon-Thu, to 10pm Fri & Sat, to 6pm Sun) Square Books, one of the South's great independent bookstores, is the epicenter of Oxford's lively literary scene and a frequent stop for traveling authors. There's a cafe and balcony upstairs, along with an immense section devoted to Faulkner. Nearby **Square Books Jr** stocks children's and young adult lit. **Off Square Books** (☑ 662-236-2828; 129 Courthouse Sq; ☺ 9am-9pm Mon-Sat, noon-5pm Sun) trades in used books.

Mississippi Delta

A long, low land of silent cotton fields bending under a severe sky, the Delta is a place of surreal, Gothic extremes. Here, in a feudal society of great manors and enslaved

---

THACKER MOUNTAIN RADIO

If you find yourself driving a lonely Mississippi back road or concrete strip of interstate on a Saturday evening at 7pm, turn your radio dial to the local NPR frequency (www.mpbonline.org/programs/radio for a listing). You'll be treated to **Thacker Mountain Radio**, a Mississippi variety show that showcases some of the region's finest authors and musicians. It's an enjoyable means of getting under the cultural skin of this state, and the music ain't half bad either. You can see the show being recorded at 6pm on Thursday nights at Off Square Books in Oxford (129 Courthouse Sq) during fall and spring.

---

servitude, songs of labor and love became American pop music. It traveled via Africa to sharecropping fields along Hwy 61, unfolding into the blues, the father of rock and roll. Tourism in this area, which still suffers some of the worst rural poverty rates in the country, largely revolves around discovering the sweat-soaked roots of this original, American art form.

Clarksdale

Clarksdale is the Delta's most useful base. It's within a couple of hours of all the blues sights, and big-name blues acts are regular weekend visitors. But this is still a poor Delta town, and it's jarring to see how many businesses find private security details a necessity after dark.

◉ Sights

The **Crossroads** of Hwys 61 and 49 is supposedly the intersection where the great Robert Johnson made his mythical deal with the devil, immortalized in his tune 'Cross Road Blues.' Now all of the implied lonely fear and dark mysticism of the space is taken up by a tacky sculpture. For what it's worth, few historians agree where the actual crossroad is located.

Delta Blues Museum
MUSEUM

(☑ 662-627-6820; www.deltabluesmuseum.org; 1 Blues Alley; adult/senior & student $7/5; ☺ 9am-5pm Mon-Sat Mar-Oct, from 10am Nov-Feb) A small but well-presented collection of memorabilia is on display here. The shrine to

MISSISSIPPI FACTS

Nickname Magnolia State

Population 3 million

Area 48,430 sq miles

Capital city Jackson (population 175,437)

Sales tax 7%

Birthplace of Author Eudora Welty (1909–2001), musicians Robert Johnson (1911–38), Muddy Waters (1913–83), BB King (1925–2015) and Elvis Presley (1935–77), activist James Meredith (b 1933) and puppeteer Jim Henson (1936–90)

Home of The blues

Politics Conservative

Famous for Cotton fields

Kitschiest souvenir Elvis lunchbox in Tupelo

Driving distances Jackson to Clarksdale 187 miles, Jackson to Ocean Springs 176 miles

Delta legend Muddy Waters includes the actual cabin where he grew up. Local art exhibits and a gift shop round out the display. Occasionally hosts live-music shows on Friday nights.

Rock & Blues Heritage Museum MUSEUM
(☑ 901-605-8662; www.blues2rock.com; 113 E Second St; admission $5; ☺ 11am-5pm Tue-Sat) A jovial Dutch transplant and blues fanatic has turned his immense personal collection of records, memorabilia and artifacts into a magic museum that traces the roots of blues and rock from the 1920s to the '70s.

Festivals & Events

Juke Joint Festival MUSIC
(www.jukejointfestival.com; tickets $15; ☺ Apr) There are more than 120 venues at this three-day festival held in joints sprinkled in and around Clarksdale.

Sunflower River Blues & Gospel Festival MUSIC
(www.sunflowerfest.org; ☺ Aug) Tends to draw bigger names than the Juke Joint Festival, and has a significant gospel component.

Sleeping & Eating

Riverside Hotel HISTORIC HOTEL $
(☑ 662-624-9163; ratfrankblues@yahoo.com; 615 Sunflower Ave; r with/without bath $75/65; ❄) Don't let a well-worn exterior put you off: this hotel, soaked in blues history – blues singer Bessie Smith died here when it was a hospital, and a festival's worth of blues artists, from Sonny Boy Williamson II to Robert Nighthawk have stayed here – offers clean and tidy rooms and sincere friendliness. It's been family-run since 1944, when it was 'the black hotel' in town. The original proprietor's son, Rat, will charm your socks off with history, hospitality and prices.

Shack Up Inn INN $
(☑ 662-624-8329; www.shackupinn.com; 001 Commisary Circle; Hwy 49; d $75-165; P ❄ ☎) At the Hopson Plantation, this self-titled 'bed and beer' allows you to stay in refurbished sharecropper cabins or the creatively renovated cotton gin. The cabins have covered porches and are filled with old furniture and musical instruments. Years of being the most storied accommodation in Clarksdale have bred complacency, however, and service can be indifferent.

Larry's Hot Tamales AMERICAN $
(☑ 662-592-4245; 947 Sunflower Ave; mains $4-12; ☺ 11am-11pm Mon-Sat) Friendly Larry's may have a small menu, but it's doing the Lord's work with what's on offer: sizzling hot Delta tamales and delicious rib tips. You'll bust your stomach way before you bust your wallet.

Yazoo Pass CAFE $$
(☑ 662-627-8686; www.yazoopass.com; 207 Yazoo Ave; lunch mains $6-10, dinner $13-26; ☺ 7am-9pm Mon-Sat; ☎) A contemporary space where you can enjoy fresh scones and croissants in the mornings, salad bar, sandwiches and soups at lunch, and pan-seared ahi, filet mignon, burgers and pastas at dinner.

Entertainment

Red's BLUES
(☑ 662-627-3166; 395 Sunflower Ave; cover $7-10; ☺ live music 9pm Fri & Sat) Clarksdale's best juke joint, with its neon-red mood lighting, plastic-bag ceiling and general soulful disintegration, is the place to see bluesmen howl. Red runs the bar, knows the acts and slings a cold beer whenever you need one.

Ground Zero   BLUES

(☑ 662-621-9009; www.groundzerobluesclub.com; 0 Blues Alley; ☺ 11am-2pm Mon & Tue, to 11pm Wed & Thu, to 2am Fri & Sat) For blues in polished environs, Morgan Freeman's Ground Zero is a huge and friendly hall with a dancefloor surrounded by tables. Bands take to the stage Wednesday to Saturday, and there's good food available.

🔒 Shopping

Cat Head Delta Blues
& Folk Art   ARTS & CRAFTS

(☑ 662-624-5992; www.cathead.biz; 252 Delta Ave; ☺ 10am-5pm Mon-Sat) Friendly St Louis carpetbagger and author Roger Stolle runs a colorful, all-purpose, blues emporium. The shelves are jammed with books, face jugs, local art and blues records. Stolle seems to be connected to everyone in the Delta, and knows when and where the bands will play.

Around Clarksdale

Down Hwy 49, **Tutwiler** is where the blues began its migration from oral tradition to popular art form. Here, WC Handy, known as the Father of the Blues, first heard a sharecropper moan his 12-bar prayer while the two waited for a train in 1903. That meeting is immortalized by a mural at the **Tutwiler Tracks** (off Hwy 49; ♿).

East of Greenville, Hwy 82 heads out of the Delta. The **Highway 61 Blues Museum** (☑ 662-686-7646; www.highway61blues.com; 307 N Broad St; ☺ 10am-5pm Mon-Sat), at the start of the route known as the 'Blues Highway,' packs a mighty wallop in a condensed, six-room space venerating local bluesmen from the Delta. Leland hosts the **Highway 61 Blues Festival** in late September or early October. **Highway 61** itself is a legendary road that traverses endless, eerie miles of flat fields, Gothic agricultural industrial facilities, one-room churches and moldering cemeteries.

Stopping in the tiny Delta town of **Indianola** is worthwhile to visit the modern **BB King Museum and Delta Interpretive Center** (☑ 662-887-9539; www.bbkingmuseum.org; 400 Second St; adult/student/child $15/5/free; ☺ 10am-5pm Tue-Sat, noon-5pm Sun-Mon, closed Mon Nov-Mar). While the museum is dedicated to the legendary bluesman, it also tackles life in the Delta as a whole. This is the best museum in the region, filled with interactive displays, video exhibits and an amazing array of artifacts, effectively communicating the history and legacy of the blues while shedding light on the soul of the Delta.

Vicksburg

Lovely Vicksburg sits atop a high bluff overlooking the Mississippi River. During the Civil War, General Ulysses S Grant besieged the city for 47 days until its surrender on July 4, 1863, at which point the North gained dominance over North America's greatest river.

⊙ Sights

The major sights are readily accessible from I-20 exit 4B (Clay St). Charming historic downtown stretches along several cobblestoned blocks of Washington St. Down by the water is a block of murals depicting the history of the area, and a **Children's Art Park**.

Vicksburg National Military Park   BATTLEFIELD

(☑ 601-636-0583; www.nps.gov/vick; Clay St; per car/individual $8/4; ☺ 8am-5pm; ♿) 🅿 Vicksburg controlled access to the Mississippi River, and its seizure was one of the turning points of the Civil War. A 16-mile driving tour passes historic markers explaining battle scenarios and key events from the city's long siege, when residents lived like moles in caverns to avoid Union shells. Plan on staying for at least 90 minutes. If you have your own bike, cycling is a fantastic way to tour the place. Locals use the scenic park for walking and running.

Lower Mississippi River Museum   MUSEUM

(☑ 601-638-9900; www.lmrm.org; 910 Washington St; ☺ 9am-4pm Wed-Sat; ♿) 🅿 **FREE** Downtown Vicksburg's pride and joy is this surprisingly interesting museum which delves into such topics as the famed 1927 flood and the Army Corps of Engineers, who have managed the river since the 18th century. Kids will enjoy the aquarium and clambering around the dry-docked research vessel, the M/V *Mississippi IV*.

🛏 Sleeping & Eating

Corners Mansion   B&B $$

(☑ 601-636-7421; www.thecorners.com; 601 Klein St; r $125-170; 🅿 ❉ 🛜) The best part of this wedding-cake 1873 B&B is looking over the Yazoo and Mississippi Rivers from your porch swing. The gardens and Southern breakfast don't hurt either.

Walnut Hills

SOUTHERN **$$**

(☑ 601-638-4910; www.walnuthillsms.net; 1214 Adams St; mains $8-25; ⊙ 11am-9pm Mon-Sat, 11am-2pm Sun) For a dining experience that takes you back in time, head to this eatery where you can enjoy rib sticking, down-home Southern food elbow-to-elbow, family-style.

🍷 Drinking & Nightlife

★ Highway 61 Coffeehouse

CAFE

(☑ 601-638-9221; www.61coffee.blogspot.com; 1101 Washington St; ⊙ 7am-5pm Mon-Fri, from 9am Sat; 🛜) ⌇ This awesome coffee shop has occasional live music on Saturday afternoons, serves Fair Trade coffee and is an energetic epicenter of artsyness, poetry readings and the like.

Jackson

Mississippi's capital and largest city mixes up stately residential areas with large swaths of blight, peppered throughout with a surprisingly funky arts-cum-hipster scene in the Fondren District. There's a slew of decent bars, good restaurants and a lot of love for live music; it's easy to have a good time in Jackson.

⊙ Sights

Mississippi Museum of Art

GALLERY

(☑ 601-960-1515; www.msmuseumart.org; 380 South Lamar St; special exhibitions $5-12; ⊙ 10am-5pm Tue-Sat, noon-5pm Sun) **FREE** This is your must-stop sight when visiting Jackson. The collection of Mississippi art – and the permanent exhibit dubbed 'The Mississippi Story' – is superb, and the surrounding grounds are nicely landscaped into a bright and quirky garden area.

Old Capitol Museum

MUSEUM

(www.mdah.state.ms.us/museum; 100 State St; ⊙ 9am-5pm Tue-Sat, 1-5pm Sun) **FREE** The state's Greek Revival capitol building from 1839 to 1903 now houses a Mississippi history museum filled with films and exhibits. You'll learn that secession was far from unanimous, and how reconstruction brought some of the harshest, presegregation 'black codes' in the South.

Eudora Welty House

HISTORIC BUILDING

(☑ 601-353-7762; www.eudorawelty.org; 1119 Pinehurst St; adult/student/child $5/3/free; ⊙ tours 9am, 11am, 1pm & 3pm Tue-Fri) Literature buffs should make a reservation to tour the Pulitzer Prize–winning author's Tudor Revival house, where she lived for more than 75 years. It's now a true historical preservation down to the most minute details. It's free on the 13th day of any month, assuming that's a normal operating day.

Smith Robertson Museum

MUSEUM

(☑ 601-960-1457; www.jacksonms.gov; 528 Bloom St; adult/child $4.50/1.50; ⊙ 9am-5pm Mon-Fri, 10am-1pm Sat) Housed in Mississippi's first public school for African American kids is the alma mater of Richard Wright, author of *Black Boy*, among many other works. It offers insight and explanation into the pain and perseverance of the African American legacy in Mississippi, and into Wright's own searing race consciousness, which framed much of the literary record of the Civil Rights movement.

Museum of Natural Science

MUSEUM

(☑ 601-576-6000; www.mdwfp.com/museum; 2148 Riverside Dr; adult/child $6/4; ⊙ 8am-5pm Mon-Fri, from 9am Sat, from 1pm Sun; 🐾) ⌇ Tucked way back in Lefleur's Bluff State Park is the Museum of Natural Science. It houses exhibits on the natural flora and fauna of Mississippi, and has aquariums inside, a tropical swamp and 2.5 miles of trails traversing 300 acres of preserved prettiness.

🛏️ Sleeping & Eating

The Fondren District is the budding artsy, boho area of town, with restaurants, art galleries and cafes dotting the happening commercial strip.

Old Capitol Inn

BOUTIQUE HOTEL **$$**

(☑ 601-359-9000; www.oldcapitolinn.com; 226 N State St; r/ste from $99/145; P❄@🛜🏊) This 24-room boutique hotel, located near museums and restaurants, is terrific. The rooftop garden includes a hot tub. A full Southern breakfast (and early-evening wine and cheese) ia included, and the rooms are all comfortable and uniquely furnished.

Big Apple Inn

AMERICAN **$**

(☑ 601-354-4549; 509 N Farish St; mains $2; ⊙ 7:30am-9pm Tue-Fri, from 8am Sat) The Big Apple basically has two items on its menu: a hot sausage sandwich and a pig's ear sandwich. Both are small, served on soft rolls, and taste delicious. The interior is hot, cramped and dingy, and the surrounding neighborhood is fading fast, but this is a true Jackson original, and the pig's ear is worth a long drive.

High Noon Cafe
VEGETARIAN $

(☑ 601-366-1513; www.rainbowcoop.org; 2807 Old Canton Rd; mains $7-10; ⏱ 11:30am-2pm Mon-Fri; 🖥☑) 🥄 Tired of fried, green, pulled-pork-covered catfish? This organic vegetarian grill, inside the Rainbow Co-op grocery store in the Fondren District, does beet burgers, portabello Reubens and other healthy delights. Stock up on organic groceries too.

Saltine
SEAFOOD $$

(☑ 601-982-2899; www.saltinerestaurant.com; 622 Duling Ave; mains $12-19; ⏱ 11am-10pm Mon-Thu, to 11pm Fri & Sat, to 9pm Sun) This playful spot takes on the delicious task of bringing oysters to the Jackson culinary world. The bivalves are served in several iterations: raw, woodfired, with Alabama white barbecue sauce and 'Nashville' (*very*) hot. Sop up some shellfish sauce with the excellent skillet cornbread, then give the grilled rainbow trout a whirl.

Walker's Drive-In
SOUTHERN $$$

(☑ 601-982-2633; www.walkersdrivein.com; 3016 N State St; mains lunch $10-17, dinner $26-36; ⏱ 11am-2pm Mon-Fri & from 5:30pm Tue-Sat) This retro masterpiece has been restored with love and infused with new Southern foodie ethos. Lunch is diner 2.0 fare with grilled redfish sandwiches, tender burgers and grilled oyster po'boys, as well as an exceptional seared, chili-crusted tuna salad, which comes with spiced calamari and seaweed.

🍸 Drinking & Entertainment

Martin's
BAR

(☑ 601-354-9712; www.martinslounge.net; 214 S State St; ⏱ 10am-1:30am Mon-Sat, to midnight Sun) This is a delightfully dirty dive, the kind of place where the bartenders know the phone numbers of their regulars in case said regulars pass out on their bar stools. Attracts a mix of old-timers, statehouse workers, slick lobbyists and lawyers plucked from a John Grisham novel. Live music and karaoke spice up weekends.

Sneaky Beans
CAFE

(☑ 601-487-6349; www.sneakybeans.tumblr.com; 2914 N State St; ⏱ 7am-9:30pm Mon-Fri, from 7:30am Sat) Every city deserves a great cafe with fast wi-fi, quirky art and an airy sense of space; Sneaky Beans, which also boasts a pretty great library, is Jackson's contribution to the genre.

The Apothecary at Brent's Drugs
COCKTAIL BAR

(www.apothecaryjackson.com; 655 Duling Ave; ⏱ 5pm-1am Tue-Thu, to 2am Fri & Sat) Tucked into the back of a '50s-style soda fountain shop is a distinctly early 21st-century craft cocktail bar, complete with bartenders sporting thick-framed glasses, customers with sleeve tattoos and a fine menu of expertly mixed libations.

F Jones Corner
BLUES

(☑ 601-983-1148; www.fjonescorner.com; 303 N Farish St; ⏱ 11am-2pm Tue-Fri, 10pm-late Thu-Sat) All shapes and sizes, colors and creeds descend on this down-home Farish St club when everywhere else closes. It hosts authentic Delta musicians who have been known to play until sunrise.

Hal & Mal's
LIVE MUSIC

(☑ 601-948-0888; www.halandmals.com; 200 Commerce St) Hal & Mal's is simply an excellent mid-sized live-music venue. The sight lines are great, it feels neither too crowded nor annoyingly expansive, bar service is quick and whoever is doing the booking is killing it, bringing in a range of acts that speak to Jackson's under-appreciated capacity for funkiness.

ℹ Information

Convention & Visitors Bureau (☑ 601-960-1891; www.visitjackson.com; 111 E Capitol St, Suite 102; ⏱ 8am-5pm Mon-Fri) Free information.

ℹ Getting There & Away

At the junction of I-20 and I-55, it's easy to get in and out of Jackson. Its international **airport** (JAN; ☑ 601-939-5631; www.jmaa.com; 100 International Dr) is 10 miles east of downtown. **Greyhound** (☑ 601-353-6342; www.greyhound.com; 300 W Capitol St) buses serve Birmingham, AL, Memphis, TN, and New Orleans, LA. Amtrak's *City of New Orleans* stops at the station.

Natchez

Some 668 antebellum homes pepper the oldest civilized settlement on the Mississippi River (beating New Orleans by two years). Natchez is also the end (or the beginning!) of the scenic 444-mile Natchez Trace Pkwy, the state's cycling and recreational jewel. Just

GRACE THE NATCHEZ TRACE

If you're driving through Mississippi, we highly recommend planning at least part of your trip around one of the oldest roads in North America: the Natchez Trace. This 444-mile trail follows a natural ridge line that was widely utilized by prehistoric animals as a grazing route; later, the area those animals trampled became a footpath and trading route utilized by Native American tribes. That route would go on to become the Natchez Trace, a major roadway into the early Western interior of the young United States, that was often plagued by roving bandits.

In 1938, 444 miles of the Trace, stretching from Pasquo, TN, southwest to Natchez, MS, was designated the federally protected **Natchez Trace Parkway** (☎662-680-4025, 800-305-7417; www.nps.gov/natr; 🛈) 🖉, administered by the National Park Service. It's a lovely, scenic drive that traverses a wide panoply of Southern landscapes: thick, dark forests, soggy wetlands, gentle hill country and long swathes of farmland. There are more than 50 access points to the Parkway and a helpful **visitor center** (☎662-680-4027, 800-305-7417; www.nps.gov/natr; Mile 266, Natchez Trace Pkwy; ⊙8am-5pm, closed Christmas; 🛈🛈) outside of Tupelo.

outside of town, along the Trace, you'll find **Emerald Mound** (☎800-305-7417; www.nps.gov/natr; Mile 10.3, Natchez Trace Pkwy; ⊙dawn-dusk; 🛈🛈), the grassy ruins of a Native American city that includes the second-largest pre-Columbian earthworks in the USA.

The **visitor and welcome center** (☎800-647-6724; www.visitnatchez.org; 640 S Canal St; tours adult/child $12/8; ⊙8:30am-5pm Mon-Sat, 9am-4pm Sun; 🛈) is a large, well-organized tourist resource. Tours of the historic downtown and antebellum mansions leave from here. During the 'pilgrimage' seasons in spring and fall, local mansions are opened to visitors.

🛏 Sleeping & Eating

Mark Twain Guesthouse GUESTHOUSE $
(☎601-446-8023; www.underthehillsaloon.com; 33 Silver St; r without bath $65-85; 🌀🛜) Mark Twain used to crash in room 1, above the bar at the current **Under the Hill Saloon** (☎601-446-8023; www.underthehillsaloon.com; 25 Silver St; ⊙9am-late), when he was a riverboat pilot passing through town. There are three rooms in all. They share one bath and laundry facilities. Check-in for the guesthouse is at the saloon.

Historic Oak Hill Inn INN $$
(☎601-446-2500; www.historicoakhill.com; 409 S Rankin St; r incl breakfast from $135; 🅿🌀🛜) Staying at this classic Natchez B&B, you'll get a taste of antebellum aristocratic living, from period furniture to china. A charmingly high-strung staff makes for an immaculate experience.

Magnolia Grill AMERICAN $$
(☎601-446-7670; www.magnoliagrill.com; 49 Silver St; mains $13-20; ⊙11am-9pm, to 10pm Fri & Sat; 🛈) Down by the riverside, this attractive wooden storefront grill with exposed rafters and outdoor patio is a good place for a pork tenderloin po'boy or a fried crawfish spinach salad.

Cotton Alley CAFE $$
(☎601-442-7452; www.cottonalleycafe.com; 208 Main St; mains $10-20; ⊙11am-2pm & 5:30-9pm Mon-Sat) This cute whitewashed dining room is chocablock with knickknacks and artistic touches and the menu borrows from local tastes. Think: grilled chicken sandwich on Texas toast or jambalaya pasta, but it does a nice chicken Caesar and a tasty grilled salmon salad, too.

Gulf Coast

The Mississippi Gulf Coast is a long, low series of breeze-swept dunes, patches of sea oats, bayside art galleries and Vegas-style casinos clustered around Biloxi. This is a popular retreat for families and military members; several important bases pepper the coast from Florida to Texas.

Charming **Bay St Louis** attracts Federal employees, including many scientists, based out at Stennis Space Center near the Louisiana border; that presence gives the town a slightly more progressive cast than you'd expect from Mississippi. Yoga studios, antique stores and galleries cluster on

Main St. The **Starfish Cafe** (☑228-229-3503; www.starfishcafebsl.com; 211 Main St; mains $8-12; ⊙11am-2pm Tue-Sat , 5-8pm Mon & Tue; ☑️🏃) ⊘ provides job training for local youth, engages in sustainable sourcing of ingredients and serves up Southern fare (with a twist of cosmopolitanism), such as fish tacos, panko-crusted tofu and blackened Gulf shrimp.

Ocean Springs remains a peaceful getaway, with a lineup of shrimp boats in the harbor alongside recreational sailing yachts, a historic downtown core, and a powdery fringe of white sand on the Gulf. The highlight is the **Walter Anderson Museum** (☑228-872-3164; www.walterandersonmuseum.org; 510 Washington St; adult/child $10/5; ⊙9:30am-4:30pm Mon-Sat, from 12:30pm Sun; 🏃) ⊘. A consummate artist and lover of Gulf Coast nature, Anderson suffered from mental illness, which spurred his monastic existence and fueled his life's work: in his own words, being one of 'those who have brought nature and art together into one thing.' After he died, the beachside shack where he lived on **Horn Island** was discovered to be painted in mind-blowing murals, which you'll see here.

Hotels line the highway as you approach downtown. Nice camping (and a visitor center) can be found at **Gulf Islands National Seashore Park** (☑228-875-9057; www.nps.gov/guis; 3500 Park Rd, Ocean Springs, MS; per person entrance $3, camping $20-30) ⊘, just out of town. Here, you'll see lumps of sugary sand dunes grown hairy with tangles of weeds and sea oats, all lapped by the calm waters of the Gulf, one of the last undeveloped stretches of the coastal South.

ARKANSAS

Forming the mountainous joint between the Midwest and the Deep South, Arkansas (ar-kan-saw) is an often overlooked treasure of swift rushing rivers, dark leafy hollows, crenellated granite outcrops and the rugged spine of the Ozark and the Ouachita (wash-ee-tah) Mountains. The entire state is blessed with exceptionally well presented state parks and tiny, empty roads crisscrossing dense forests that let out onto breathtaking vistas and gentle pastures dotted with grazing horses. Mountain towns juke between Christian fundamentalism, hippie communes and biker bars, yet all of these

divergent cultures share a love of their home state's stunning natural beauty.

ℹ️ Information

Arkansas State Parks (☑888-287-2757; www.arkansasstateparks.com) Arkansas' well-reputed park system has 52 state parks, 30 offering camping (tent and RV sites are $12 to $55, depending on amenities). A number of the parks offer lodge and cabin accommodations. Due to popularity, reservations on weekends and holidays often require multiday stays.

Little Rock

Little Rock lives up to its name; this charming state capital feels pretty petite. But this is center of urban life in Arkansas, and the angle of the urban experience this city embraces is quite cool: amid the leafy residential neighborhoods are hip bars, fresh restaurants, plenty of bike trails and a tolerant vibe. Small this town may be, but it's wonderfully situated on the Arkansas River, and as befits this state of natural wonders, you always feel as if you're within arm's reach of lush wooded river valleys.

◉ Sights

The best stroll is in the **River Market district** (www.rivermarket.info; W Markham St & President Clinton Ave), an area of shops, galleries, restaurants and pubs along the riverbank. Keep an eye out for the **Butler Center** (☑501-320-5790; www.butlercenter.org; 401 President Clinton Ave; ⊙9am-6pm Mon-Sat) **FREE**. This research institute, dedicated to promoting an understanding of the state's arts and culture, boasts a series of lovely galleries stocked with local art works.

William J Clinton Presidential Center   LIBRARY
(☑501-748-0419; www.clintonlibrary.gov; 1200 President Clinton Ave; adult/students & seniors/child $7/5/3, with audio $10/8/6; ⊙9am-5pm Mon-Sat, 1-5pm Sun) ⊘ This library houses the largest archival collection in presidential history, including 80 million pages of documents and two million photographs (although there's not a lot related to a certain intern scandal). The entire experience feels like a time travel journey to the 1990s. Peruse the full-scale replica of the Oval Office, the exhibits on all stages of Clinton's life, or gifts from visiting dignitaries. The complex is built to environmentally friendly 'green' standards.

Little Rock Central High School
HISTORIC SITE

(☑ 501-396-3001; www.nps.gov/chsc; 2125 Daisy Gatson Bates Dr; ⊙ 9:30am-4:30pm) Little Rock's most riveting attraction is the site of the 1957 desegregation crisis that changed the country forever. It was here that a group of African American students known as the Little Rock Nine were first denied entry inside the then all-white high school (despite a unanimous 1954 Supreme Court ruling forcing the integration of public schools).

Riverfront Park
PARK

(☑ 501-371-6848; LaHarpe Blvd) Just northwest of downtown, Riverfront Park rolls pleasantly along the Arkansas River and both pedestrians and cyclists take advantage of this fantastic city park. It's a truly fine integration of a landscape feature (the river) into an urban setting. You can't miss the Big Dam Bridge (www.bigdambridge.com; ⛵), a pedestrian- and cyclist-only span that connects 17 miles of multiuse trails which form a complete loop thanks to the renovation of the Clinton Presidential Park Bridge.

Arkansas Arts Center
MUSEUM

(☑ 501-372-4000; www.arkansasartscenter.org; 9th & Commerce St; ⊙ 10am-5pm Tue-Sat, from 11am Sun) FREE Little Rock's art museum features excellent visiting exhibitions and a permanent collection that includes an impressive array of contemporary crafts, an engraving by naturalist John James Audubon and several works by pointillist Paul Signac.

🛏 Sleeping & Eating

At the time of writing, work was being done on the Firehouse Hostel (☑ 501-476-0294; www.firehousehostel.org; 1201 Commerce St). The planned location, in a gorgeous 1917 Craftsman-style building that once served as a city fire station, is fantastic.

★ Capital Hotel
BOUTIQUE HOTEL $$

(☑ 501-370-7062, 877-637-0037; www.capitalhotel. com; 111 W Markham St; r $190-220; P ❄ @ 🛜) This 1872 former bank building with a cast-iron facade – a near-extinct architectural feature – is the top digs in Little Rock. There is a wonderful outdoor mezzanine for cocktails and a sense of suited, cigar-chomping posh throughout; if you want to feel like a wining, dining lobbyist, this is the place for you.

Rosemont
B&B $$

(☑ 501-374-7456; www.rosemontoflittlerock.com; 515 W 15th St; r $105-145; P ❄ 🛜) This 1880s restored farmhouse near the Governor's mansion oozes cozy Southern charm. The proprietors have also opened a bucolic historic cottage nearby (from $175).

Ottenheimer Market Hall
MARKET $

(btwn S Commerce & S Rock Sts; ⊙ 7am-6pm Mon-Sat) Trawl the stalls for some good-value breakfast or lunch – you'll find everything from fresh fruits and pastries, to sushi, burgers and barbecue.

Big Orange
AMERICAN $

(☑ 501-379-8715; www.bigorangeburger.com; 207 N University Ave; mains $9-13; ⊙ Sun-Thu 11am-10pm, til 11pm Fri & Sat; 🖊 ⛵) Sometimes you need a burger, and not just a burger, but the sort of meat between two buttered buns that leaves you in a state of post-carnivore frenzy bliss. Enter Big Orange, which serves variations on the theme ranging from a classic with American cheese, topped with white truffle for the fancy, and falafel for the vegetarians.

ARKANSAS FACTS

Nickname Natural State

Population 2.9 million

Area 52,068 sq miles

Capital city Little Rock (population 193,357)

Other cities Fayetteville (population 78,690), Bentonville (population 40,167)

Sales tax 6.5%, plus 2% visitors tax and local taxes

Birthplace of General Douglas MacArthur (1880–1964), musician Johnny Cash (1932–2003), former president Bill Clinton (b 1946), author John Grisham (b 1955), actor Billy Bob Thornton (b 1955)

Home of Walmart

Politics Like most Southern states, opposition to civil rights turned the state Republican in the 1960s

Famous for Football fans 'calling the Hogs' – Woooooooooo, Pig! Sooie!

Official state instrument Fiddle

Driving distances Little Rock to Eureka Springs 182 miles, Eureka Springs to Mountain View 123 miles

★ South on Main
AMERICAN $$

(☎501-244-9660; www.southonmain.com; 1304 S Main St; mains $16-24; ⊙11am-2:30pm Mon-Fri, 5-10pm Tue-Sat, 10am-2pm Sun) This wonderful spot is a gastronomic pet project of *The Oxford American*, the South's seminal quarterly literary magazine. It embraces the foodways of the region with a verve and dynamism that is creative and delicious; catfish comes with cornmeal pancakes, while rabbit leg is wrapped in country ham. A great bar and frequent live music round out the awesome.

♟ Drinking & Entertainment

The fun-loving pubs in the River Market district buzz at night.

White Water Tavern
LIVE MUSIC

(☎501-375-8400; www.whitewatertavern.com; 2500 W 7th St; ⊙noon-2am Mon-Fri, 6pm-1am Sat) The White Water manages to line up some excellent acts for its small stage, with bands ranging from straight-up rockers to alt country heroes to indie poppers to hip hop MCs. When the music isn't playing, this is an excellent, friendly corner pub.

ℹ Getting There & Around

Bill & Hillary Clinton National Airport (LIT; ☎501-372-3439; www.lrn-airport.com; 1 Airport Dr) lies just east of downtown. The **Greyhound station** (☎501-372-3007; www.greyhound.com; 118 E Washington St), in North Little Rock, serves Hot Springs (one to two hours), Memphis, TN (2½ hours), and New Orleans, LA (18 hours). Amtrak occupies **Union Station** (☎501-372-6841; 1400 W Markham St). **Central Arkansas Transit** (CAT; ☎501-375-6717; www.cat.org) runs local buses and the **River Rail Streetcar**, a trolley which makes a loop on W Markham and President Clinton Ave (adult/child $1/50¢).

Hot Springs

Hot Springs is a gem of a mountain town, and we're not the first to notice. The healing waters the town is named for have been attracting everyone from Native Americans to early 20th-century health nuts to a good chunk of the nation's organized crime leadership. When Hot Springs was at full throttle in the 1930s, it was a hotbed of gambling, bootlegging, prostitution and opulence. Elaborate restored bathhouses, where you can still get old-school spa treatments, line Bathhouse Row behind shady magnolias on the east side of Central Ave.

◉ Sights & Activities

A promenade runs through the park around the hillside behind **Bathhouse Row**, where some springs survive intact, and a network of trails covers Hot Springs' mountains. Many of the old bathhouses have been converted into art galleries affiliated with the National Parks Service (NPS).

NPS Visitor Center
MUSEUM

(Fordyce Bath House; ☎501-620-6715; www.nps.gov/hosp; 369 Central Ave; ⊙9am-5pm) On Bathhouse Row, set up in the 1915 Fordyce bathhouse, the NPS visitor center and museum has exhibits about the park's history, first as a Native American free-trade zone, and later as a turn-of-the-20th-century European spa. Most fascinating are the amenities and standards set forth by an early 20th-century spa; the stained glass work and Greek statues are opulent, but we could pass on the bare white walls, grout and electro-shock therapy.

Hot Springs Mountain Tower
OUTDOORS

(401 Hot Springs Mountain Rd; adult/child $7/4; ⊙9am-5pm Nov-Feb, to 6pm Mar–mid-May & Labor Day-Oct, to 9pm mid-May–Labor Day) On top of Hot Springs Mountain, the 216ft tower has spectacular views of the surrounding mountains covered with dogwood, hickory, oak and pine – lovely in the spring and fall.

Gangster Museum of America
MUSEUM

(☎501-318-1717; www.tgmoa.com; 510 Central Ave; adult/child $12/free; ⊙10am-5pm Sun-Thu, to 6pm Fri & Sat) Learn about the sinful glory days of Prohibition when this small town in the middle of nowhere turned into a hotbed of lavish wealth thanks to Chicago bootleggers like Capone, and his NYC counterparts. Highlights include original slots and a tommy gun. Entry is by guided tour, generally offered on the half-hour.

Galaxy Connection
MUSEUM

(☎501-276-4432; www.thegalaxyconnection.com; 906 Hobson Ave; admission $10; ⊙10am-5pm Mon-Sat, from noon Sun) And now for something completely different: a museum dedicated to *Star Wars*. This fantastically geeky temple is the labor of love of one particularly obsessed Arkansan, and while it may feel a little on the amateur side, it's got enough paraphernalia from life-sized Boba Fett mannequins to a Jedi dress-up area to feel awesomely nostalgic to fans.

WORTH A TRIP

ARKANSAS DELTA

Roughly 120 miles east of Little Rock, and just 20 miles from Clarksdale, Hwy 49 crosses the Mississippi River into the Arkansas Delta. **Helena**, a formerly prosperous but currently depressed mill town with a blues tradition (Sonny Boy Williamson made his name here), awakens for its annual **Arkansas Blues & Heritage Festival** (www.kingbiscuitfestival. com; tickets $45; ☉Oct) when blues musicians and their fans take over downtown for three days in early October. Year-round, blues fans and history buffs should visit the **Delta Cultural Center** (☑870-338-4350; www.deltaculturalcenter.com; 141 Cherry St; ☉9am-5pm Tue-Sat) FREE. The museum displays all manner of memorabilia such as Albert King's and Sister Rosetta Tharpe's guitars, and John Lee Hooker's signed handkerchief.

The world's longest-running blues radio program, *King Biscuit Time*, is broadcast here (12:15pm Monday to Friday), and *Delta Sounds* (1pm Monday to Friday) often hosts live musicians; both air on KFFA AM-1360. Before leaving town, make like Robert Plant and stop by the wonderfully cluttered **Bubba's Blues Corner** (☑870-338-3501; 105 Cherry St, Helena, AR; ☉9am-5pm Tue-Sat; ☝) to pick up a blues record.

The hardscrabble railroad town of **McGehee** is the home of the touching **WWII Japanese American Internment Museum** (☑870-222-9168; 100 South Railroad St; admission $5; ☉10am-5pm Tue-Sat). During World War II, Japanese Americans were rounded up and evicted from their homes and businesses and sent to live in internment camps. One of these camps took root in the delta mud just outside McGehee, and this museum is dedicated to telling the story of its inmates via personal items, art and a small collection of intimate displays.

Buckstaff Bath House　　　SPA
(☑501-623-2308; www.buckstaffbaths.com; 509 Central Ave; thermal bath $33, with massage $71; ☉8am-11am & 1:30pm Mon-Sat Mar-Nov, closed Sat afternoon Dec-Feb) Spa service Hot Springs–style was never a 'foofy' experience. Buckstaff's no-nonsense staff whip you through the baths, treatments and massages, just as in the 1930s. Wonderful.

🛏 Sleeping & Eating

Restaurants congregate along the Central Ave tourist strip and offer ho-hum food.

★ **Alpine Inn**　　　INN $
(☑501-624-9164; www.alpine-inn-hot-springs. com; 741 Park Ave/Hwy 7 N; r $65-95; P🐾🖥🛜🏊) The friendly Scottish owners of this inn, less than a mile from Bathhouse Row, have spent a few years upgrading an old motel to remarkable ends. The impeccable rooms are comfortable and include new flat-screen TVs and sumptuous beds.

Arlington Resort Hotel
& Spa　　　HISTORIC HOTEL $
(☑501-623-7771; www.arlingtonhotel.com; 239 Central Ave; s/d/ste from $99/120/194; P🐾🖥🛜🏊) This imposing historic hotel tops Bathhouse Row and constantly references its glory days, even if said days have passed. The grand lobby buzzes at night when there might be a live band. There's an in-house spa, and rooms are well-maintained, if aging. Corner rooms with a view are a steal.

Colonial Pancake House　　　DINER $
(☑501-624-9273; 111 Central Ave; mains $6-10; ☉7am-3pm; ☝) A Hot Springs classic, with turquoise booths and homey touches like quilts and doilies on the walls, this is almost like your grandma's kitchen. Except the pancakes, French toast (made with Texas toast) and malted or buckwheat waffles are better'n grandma's. Get yours with pecans inside. It does burgers and other diner grub at lunch.

McClard's　　　BARBECUE $$
(☑501-623-9665; www.mcclards.com; 505 Albert Pike; mains $4-15; ☉11am-8pm Tue-Sat) Southwest of the center, Bill Clinton's favorite boyhood BBQ is still popular for ribs, slow-cooked beans, chili and tamales. It's on the outskirts of downtown.

🍷 Drinking & Nightlife

Maxine's　　　BAR
(☑501-321-0909; www.maxineslive.com; 700 Central Ave; ☉3pm-3am Mon-Fri, to 2am Sat, noon-midnight Sun) If you're looking for some (loud) night music, head to this infamous cathouse turned live-music venue. It hosts bands out of Austin regularly.

**Superior Bathhouse
Brewery & Distillery** BREWERY
(☑501-624-2337; www.superiorbathhouse.com;
329 Central Ave; ☺11am-9pm, to 11pm Fri & Sat)
It's surprising that an outdoorsy town with
this many hikers and hipsters has lacked
a craft brewery for so long, but as the sun
rises in the east, so too does Hot Springs
now have an indie brewery. The local suds
are delicious – perfect for washing away any
health benefits your body may have mistakenly acquired in Hot Springs.

ⓘ Getting There & Away

Greyhound (☑501-623-5574; www.greyhound.
com; 100 Broadway Tce) has buses heading to
Little Rock (1½ hours, three daily).

Around Hot Springs

The wild, pretty **Ouachita National Forest** (☑501-321-5202; www.fs.usda.gov/ouachita;
welcome center 100 Reserve St; ☺8am-4:30pm)
is studded with lakes and draws hunters,
fisherfolk, mountain-bike riders and boaters. The small roads through the mountains unfailingly lead to hidden nooks and
wonderful views. The Ouachita boasts two
designated National Forest Scenic Byways:
Arkansas Scenic Hwy 7 and Talimena Scenic
Byway, navigating mountain ranges from
Arkansas into Oklahoma.

Arkansas River Valley

The Arkansas River cuts a swath across the
state from Oklahoma to Mississippi, where
folks come to fish, canoe and camp along
its banks and tributaries. The excellently
maintained trails of **Petit Jean State Park**
(☑501-727-5441; www.petitjeanstatepark.com;
1285 Petit Jean Mountain Rd, Morrilton, AR; 🐾),
west of Morrilton, wind past a lush 95ft
waterfall, romantic grottoes, expansive vistas and dense forests. There's a rustic stone
lodge, reasonable **cabins** (per night $85-185)
and campgrounds.

Another stellar state park is **Mount
Magazine** (☑479-963-8502; www.mount
magazinestatepark.com; 16878 Highway 309 S,
Paris, AR; ☺24hrs), which features 14 miles of
trails around Arkansas' highest point. Outdoor enthusiasts enjoy great hang gliding
and rock climbing here as well as hiking.

The spectacular **Highway 23/Pig Trail
Byway**, lined with wild echinacea and lilies,

climbs through **Ozark National Forest** and
into the mountains; an excellent way to reach
Eureka Springs.

Ozark Mountains

Stretching from northwest and central Arkansas into Missouri, the **Ozark Mountains**
(☑870-404-2741; www.ozarkmountainregion.com)
are an ancient range, once surrounded by
sea and now well worn by time. Verdant
mountains give way to misty fields and hard
dirt farms, while dramatic karst formations
line sparkling lakes, rivers and capillary thin
back roads. The region derives a lot of pride
from its independence and sense of place,
a zeitgeist at least partially informed by
multiple generations of familial roots and a
long history of regional poverty. For literary
company, pick up Daniel Woodrell's novel
Winter's Bone, which was adapted into a
critically acclaimed film of the same name.

Mountain View

Detour east of US 65 or along Hwy 5 to Mountain View, where an odd nexus of deeply
spiritual Christianity and hippie folk-music
culture yield a heartfelt mountain-town
warmth. Creeping commercialism is taking
its toll – the **Visitor Information Center**
(☑870-269-8068; www.yourplaceinthemountains.
com; 107 N Peabody Ave; ☺9am-4:30pm Mon-Sat)
promotes it as the 'Folk Music Capital of the
World,' but cutesy sandstone architecture
downtown, and impromptu folk, gospel
and bluegrass hootenannies (jam sessions)
by the Stone County **Court House Square**
(Washington & Franklin St) – and on porches all
around town anytime – make a visit here
rather harmonious. The music goes till about
10pm most nights. Each spring the entire
town becomes a main stage for the musical
folkways of the Ozarks during the **Arkansas
Folk Festival** (www.yourplaceinthemountains.
com/calendar/arkansas-folk-festival; ☺Apr).

◎ Sights & Actitivies

Ozark Folk Center State Park STATE PARK
(☑870-269-3851; www.ozarkfolkcenter.com; 1032
Park Ave; auditorium adult/child $12/7; ☺10am-
5pm Tue-Sat Apr-Nov) The town's top cultural
attraction, Ozark Folk Center State Park, just
north of Mountain View, hosts ongoing craft
demonstrations, a traditional herb garden,

and nightly live music that brings in an avid, older crowd.

LocoRopes
OUTDOORS

(☑ 888-669-6717, 870-269-6566; www.locoropes.com; 1025 Park Ave; per zip line $7.50; ⊙ 10am-5pm Mar 1-Nov 30) LocoRopes offers a ropes course, slack lining, a freefall, a climbing wall and three zip lines.

Blanchard Springs Caverns
OUTDOORS

(☑ 888-757-2246, 870-757-2211; www.blanchard-springs.org; NF 54, Forest Rd, off Hwy 14; Drip Stone Tour adult/child $10/5, Wild Cave Tour $75; ⊙ 10:30am-4:30pm; ⊛) The spectacular Blanchard Springs Caverns, 15 miles northwest of Mountain View, were carved by an underground river and rival those at Carlsbad. It's another little-known, mind-blowing spot in Arkansas. Three Forest Service guided tours range from disabled-accessible to adventurous three- to four-hour spelunking sessions.

🛏 Sleeping & Eating

Wildflower B&B
B&B $

(☑ 870-269-4383; www.wildflowerbb.com; 100 Washington; r $89-150; P ❋ 🕾) Set right on the Courtsquare with a rocking chair equipped wraparound porch and cool folk art on the walls. Ask for the front room upstairs; it's flooded with afternoon light, has a queen bed and a joint sitting room with TV. Booking online is best.

Tommy's Famous Pizza & BBQ
PIZZA, BARBECUE $

(☑ 870-269-3278; www.tommysfamous.com; cnr Carpenter & W Main Sts; pizza $7-26, mains $7-13; ⊙ from 3pm) Tommy's Famous Pizza & BBQ is run by the friendliest bunch of backwoods hippies you could hope to meet. The BBQ pizza marries Tommy's specialties indulgently. The affable owner, a former rocker from Memphis, plays great music, has a fun vibe, and asks just two things: no attitude and no loud kids.

Tommy's closes when the cash register hasn't opened for an hour.

Pj's Rainbow Cafe
AMERICAN $

(☑ 870-269-8633; 216 W Main St; mains $5.50-16; ⊙ 7am-8pm Tue-Sat, to 2pm Sun; 🖉⊛) This country fried cafe serves up some truly tasty diner food done with flair; think spinach-stuffed pork loin and fresh grilled rainbow trout caught in local rivers. Cash only.

Eureka Springs

Eureka Springs, near Arkansas' northwestern corner, perches in a steep valley filled with Victorian buildings, crooked streets and a crunchy, New Age–aligned local population that welcomes all – this is one of the most explicitly gay-friendly towns in the Ozarks, and mixes up an odd mash of liberal politics and rainbow flags with biker-friendly Harley bars. Hiking, cycling and horseback-riding opportunities abound. For information on LGBTQ travel in the area, log on to **Out In Eureka** (www.gayeurekasprings.com).

The **visitor center** (☑ 800-638-7352; www.eurekaspringschamber.com; 516 Village Circle, Hwy 62 E; ⊙ 9am-5pm) has information about lodging, activities, tours and local attractions, such as the rockin' **Blues Festival** (www.eurekaspringsblues.com; ⊙ Jun).

◉ Sights & Activities

1886 Crescent Hotel
HISTORIC BUILDING

(☑ 855-725-5720; www.crescent-hotel.com; 75 Prospect Ave) Built in 1886, the Crescent is a gorgeous, functioning artifact of an older age. Step into the dark-wood lobby, with its roaring fireplace and carpets, all accented by little Jazz Age flourishes, and you'll feel the need to order a cognac and berate Daisy Buchanan for ever marrying Tom Buchanan, the *cad*. Er, sorry. The Crescent sits atop a hill, and is a great place to visit for a drink, the view from its rooftop, or both.

Thorncrown Chapel
CHURCH

(☑ 479-253-7401; www.thorncrown.com; 12968 Hwy 62 W; ⊙ 9am-5pm Apr-Nov, 11am-4pm Mar & Dec) Thorncrown Chapel is a magnificent sanctuary made of glass, with its 48ft-tall wooden skeleton holding 425 windows. There's not much between your prayers and God's green earth here. It's just outside of town in the woods. Donation suggested.

Lake Leatherwood City Park
PARK

(☑ 479-253-7921; www.lakeleatherwoodcitypark.com; 1303 Co Rd 204) This expansive park includes 21 miles of hiking and biking trails that crisscross the forested mountains and surround an 85-acre lake. Located about 3.5 miles from downtown, this is the closest managed wild space to Eureka Springs.

★ Historic Loop
WALKING TOUR

This 3.5-mile ring of history through downtown and surrounding residential neighborhoods, is simply gorgeous. The route is dotted with more than 300 Victorian homes, all built before 1910, each a jaw-dropper and on par with any preserved historic district in the USA. You can access the loop via the Eureka Trolley, or just walk it – recommended if you're fit (the streets are steep!); pick up a map or buy trolley tickets at the visitor center.

Eureka Trolley TROLLEY
(🚊479-253-9572; www.eurekatrolley.org; 137 W Van Buren; day pass adult/child $6/2; ⏰10am-6pm Sun-Fri, 9am-8pm Sat May-Oct, reduced hours Nov-Apr) This old-time hop-on, hop-off trolley service plies four routes through greater Eureka Springs. Each trip takes about 20 to 30 minutes, revealing a different angle on life in this mountain town. Check website or call ahead for running times.

🛏 Sleeping & Eating

★**Treehouse Cottages** COTTAGE $$
(🚊479-253-8667; www.treehousecottages.com; 165 W Van Buren St; cottages $149-169; 🅿❄🛜) Sprinkled amid 33 acres of pine forest, these cute, kitschy and spacious stilted wooden cottages are worth finding. There's lovely accent tile in the baths, a Jacuzzi overlooking the trees, a private balcony with grill at the ready, a flat-screen TV and a fireplace.

★**FRESH** MODERN AMERICAN $
(🚊479-253-9300; www.freshanddeliciousofeureka springs.com; 179 N Main St; mains $7-13; ⏰11am-9pm Thu-Sat & Mon, to 7pm Sun; 🥗) This beautiful cafe specializes in farm-to-table cuisine, brilliant baked goods and quirky service. The openface sandwiches with shaved ham served on fresh-baked French toast are stupidly decadent, and there are vegan options ranging from salads to pesto tossed pasta.

Oscar's SANDWICHES $
(🚊479-981-1436; www.oscarseureka.com; 17 White St; mains $3-7.50; ⏰9am-3pm Tue-Fri, from 8am Sat, from 10am Sun; 🥗) This little cafe has a small menu, but what a menu: chicken, walnut and cranberry salad, prosciutto sandwiches and fresh quiche. This is bright, breezy cuisine, the sort of food that fills you up without weighing you down (rare in the South), and served in the heart of Eureka Springs' cute historic district.

Mud Street Café CAFE $$
(🚊479-253-6732; www.mudstreetcafe.com; 22G S Main St; mains $9-13; ⏰8am-3pm Thu-Mon) You'll find simple, tasty options such as gourmet sandwiches, wraps and salads. The

brilliant coffee drinks and breakfasts cultivate a devoted local following.

★**Stone House** MODERN AMERICAN $$$
(🚊479-363-6411; www.eurekastonehouse.com; 89 S Main St; cheese plates $25-47; ⏰1-10pm Thu-Sun) The Stone House has all the ingredients for a pretty perfect evening: lots of wine; a menu that focuses on cheese, bread, olives, honey and charcuterie; live music; a cute courtyard; and did we mention lots of wine? It's open until 10pm, which constitutes late-night dining in this town.

🍷 Drinking & Entertainment

Chelsea's Corner Cafe & Bar BAR
(🚊479-253-8231; www.chelseascornercafe.com; 10 Mountain St; ⏰noon-10pm Sun-Thu, to midnight Fri & Sat) Live music acts frequently take to the stage at this bar, which attracts a typically Eureka Springs blend of hippies and bikers. The kitchen is one of the few places in town open past 9pm, and even does pizza delivery.

Opera in the Ozarks OPERA
(🚊479-253-8595; www.opera.org; 16311 Hwy 62 West; tickets from $20) This much-acclaimed fine-arts program has kept opera alive and loud in the mountains. A packed performance schedule and a playhouse located just outside of town is the pride of Eureka Springs.

Buffalo National River

Yet another under-acknowledged Arkansas gem, and perhaps the best of them all, this 135-mile river flows beneath dramatic bluffs through unspoiled Ozark forest. The upriver section tends to have most of the white water, while the lower reaches ease lazily along – perfect for an easy paddle. The **Buffalo National River** (🚊870-741-5443; www.nps.gov/buff) has 10 campgrounds and three designated wilderness areas; the most accessible is through the **Tyler Bend visitor center** (🚊870-439-2502; www.nps.gov/buff; 170 Ranger Rd, St Joe, AR; ⏰8:30am-4:30pm), 11 miles north of Marshall on Hwy 65, where you can also pick up a list of approved outfitters for self-guided rafting or canoe trips, the best way to tour the park and see the gargantuan limestone bluffs. Or seek out **Buffalo Outdoor Center** (BOC; 🚊800-221-5514; www.buffaloriver.com; cnr Hwys 43 & 74; kayak/canoe per day $55/62; zip-line tour $89; ⏰8am-6pm; 🚐🐾) in Ponca. They will point you in the right direction and rent out attractive cabins in the woods, too.

WORTH A TRIP: BENTONVILLE, ARKANSAS

Bentonville was the site of Sam Walton's original five and dime corner store, which would go on to become Walmart, the world's largest company by revenue and largest private employer. Corporate headquarters is here and the distributors all maintain offices here, which means this once sleepy Arkansas town has rapidly evolved into a small city.

Bentonville includes plenty of sprawl and bland housing subdivisions, but it's anchored by a town center that is surprisingly pleasant, full of small businesses touting a locavore and 'shop local' ethos – a little ironic to say the least. But past that irony is some cool stuff.

Coolest, largest and most controversial is the **Crystal Bridges Museum of American Art** (☑ 479-418-5700; www.crystalbridges.org; 600 Museum Way; ⊙ 11am-6pm Mon & Thu, to 9pm Wed & Fri, 10am-6pm Sat & Sun; P ♿) FREE, sprawling across a series of creek ponds fed by mountain streams; the curved pavilions that house the extensive collections are connected by glass-encased tunnels, and the experience consistently filters sunlight through and across the grounds. The collections, which span the length and breadth of art in the USA, largely come from the Waltons – in particular, heiress Alice Walton – and the museum has been criticized as a tax write-off for the family's enormous wealth. Still, the space is impressive and the museum is free to the public, who seem to love the place.

The museum connects to downtown Bentonville via the **Crystal Bridges Trail** (www.crystalbridges.org/trails-and-grounds/trails) ✐, which winds past sculptures and through a series of shady woods. In Bentonville, skip the overhyped **Walmart Museum** in favor of some food; we recommend **Tusk & Trotter** (☑ 479-268-4494; www.tuskandtrotter.com; 110 SE A St; mains $13-28; ⊙ 4-9:30pm Mon, 11am-9:30pm Tue-Thu, 11am-11pm Fri, 10am-11pm Sat, 10am-9pm Sun), which serves up some amazing tail-to-snout carnivore fare, including a sinful chicken and waffles. Crash at the **21c Museum Hotel** (200 NE A St; r $179-205), where every element, from the lobby and rooms to on-site galleries, feels like an extension of the Crystal Bridges experience.

LOUISIANA

Louisiana runs deep: a French colony turned Spanish protectorate turned reluctant American purchase; a southern fringe of swampland, bayou and alligators dissolving into the Gulf of Mexico; a northern patchwork prairie of heartland farm country; and everywhere, a population tied together by a deep, unshakable appreciation for the good things in life: food and music.

New Orleans, its first city, lives and dies by these qualities, and its restaurants and music halls are second to none. But everywhere, the state shares a love for this *joie de vivre*. We're not dropping French for fun, by the way; while the language is not a cultural component of North Louisiana, near I-10 and below it is a generation removed from the household – if it has been removed at all.

History

The lower Mississippi River area was dominated by the Mississippian mound-building culture until around 1592 when Europeans arrived and decimated the Native Americans with the usual combination of disease, unfavorable treaties and outright hostility.

The land was then passed back and forth between France, Spain and England. Under the French 'Code Noir,' slaves were kept, but retained a somewhat greater degree of freedom – and thus native culture – than their counterparts in British North America.

After the American Revolution the whole area passed to the USA in the 1803 Louisiana Purchase, and Louisiana became a state in 1812. The resulting blend of American and Franco-Spanish traditions, plus the influence of Afro-Caribbean communities, gave Louisiana the unique culture it retains to this day.

Following the Civil War, Louisiana was readmitted to the Union in 1868 and the next 30 years saw political wrangling, economic stagnation and renewed discrimination against African Americans.

Hurricane Katrina (2005) and the BP Gulf Coast oil spill (2010) significantly damaged the local economy and infrastructure. Louisiana remains a bottom-rung state in terms of per capita income and education levels, yet it ranks high in national happiness scales.

ℹ Information

Sixteen welcome centers dot freeways throughout the state, or contact the **Louisiana Office of Tourism** (☑ 225-342-8100; www.louisiana travel.com).

Louisiana State Parks (☑ 877-226-7652; www. crt.state.la.us/louisiana-state-parks) Louisiana has 22 state parks that offer camping (primitive/ premium sites from $14/20). Some parks also offer lodge accommodations and cabins. Reservations can be made online, by phone or on a drop-in basis if there's availability. Camping fees rise slightly from April to September.

New Orleans

New Orleans is very much of America, but extraordinarily removed from it as well. Founded by the French and administered by the Spanish (and then the French again), New Orleans is – with its sidewalk cafes and iron balconies – the most European city in America. But, with the *vodoun* (voodoo), weekly second-line parades (essentially, neighborhood parades), Mardi Gras Indians, jazz and brass and gumbo, it's also the most African and Caribbean city in the country. New Orleans celebrates; while America is on deadline, this city is sipping a cocktail after a long lunch. But if you saw how people here rebuilt their homes after floods and storms, you'd be foolish to call the locals lazy.

Tolerating everything and learning from it is the soul of this city. When New Orleans' citizens aspire to that great Creole ideal – a mix of all influences into something better – we get: jazz; Nouveau Louisiana cuisine; storytellers from African *griots* (West African bards) to Seventh Ward rappers to Tennessee Williams; French townhouses a few blocks from Foghorn Leghorn mansions groaning under sweet myrtle and bougainvillea; Mardi Gras celebrations that mix pagan mysticism with Catholic pageantry. Just don't forget the indulgence and immersion, because that Creoleization gets watered down when folks don't live life to its intellectual and epicurean hilt.

New Orleans may take it easy, but it takes it. The whole hog. Stuffed with crawfish. Ya heard?

History

The town of Nouvelle Orléans was founded as a French outpost in 1718 by Jean-Baptiste Le Moyne de Bienville. Early settlers arrived from France, Canada and Germany, while the French imported thousands of African slaves. The city became a central port in the slave trade; due to local laws some slaves were allowed to earn their freedom and assume an established place in the Creole community as *les gens de couleur libres* (free people of color).

The Spanish were largely responsible for building the French Quarter as it still looks today after fires in 1788 and 1794 decimated the earlier French architecture. The influx of Anglo-Americans after the Louisiana Purchase led to an expansion of the city into the Central Business District (CBD), Garden District and Uptown.

New Orleans survived the Civil War intact after an early surrender to Union forces, but the economy languished with the end of the slavery-based plantations. In the early 1900s, New Orleans was the birthplace of jazz music. Many of the speakeasies and homes of the jazz originators have disappeared through neglect, but the cultural claim was canonized in 1994 when the National Park Service established the New

LOUISIANA FACTS

Nicknames Bayou State, Pelican State, Sportsman's Paradise

Population 4.6 million

Area 51,843 sq miles

Capital city Baton Rouge (population 229,426)

Other cities New Orleans (population 378,715)

Sales tax 4%, plus local city and county taxes

Birthplace of Jazz, naturalist John James Audubon (1785–1851), trumpeter Louis 'Satchmo' Armstrong (1901–71), author Truman Capote (1924–84), musician Antoine 'Fats' Domino (b 1928), pop star Britney Spears (b 1981)

Home of Tabasco sauce, chef Emeril Lagasse

Politics Republican stronghold with a very liberal large city (New Orleans)

Famous for Drive-thru margaritas

Official state reptile Alligator

Driving distances New Orleans to Lafayette 137 miles, New Orleans to St Francisville 112 miles

Orleans Jazz National Historical Park to celebrate the origins of America's most widely recognized indigenous music genre.

In 2005 Katrina, a relatively weak Category 3 hurricane, overwhelmed New Orleans' federal flood protection system in more than 50 places. Some 80% of the city was flooded, more than 1800 people lost their lives and the city was evacuated. A decade later, the population has largely returned, and the city is again one of the 50 most populous in the USA. This rebirth is not without its issues, though; gentrification has raised the cost of living, even as poverty and crime rates remain atrocious. Tourism is still the primary economic engine of the city.

◉ Sights

◎ French Quarter

Elegant, Caribbean-colonial architecture, lush gardens and wrought-iron accents are the visual norm in the French Quarter. But this is also the heart of New Orleans' tourism scene. Bourbon St generates a loutish membrane that sometimes makes the rest of the Quarter difficult to appreciate. Look past this. The Vieux Carré (Old Quarter; first laid out in 1722) is the focal point of much of this city's culture and in the quieter back lanes and alleyways there's a sense of faded time shaken and stirred with *joie de vivre*.

★ Cabildo   MUSEUM
(📞504-568-6968; http://louisianastatemuseum. org/museums/the-cabildo; 701 Chartres St; adult/ child under 12yr/student $6/free/5; ◎10am-4:30pm Tue-Sun, closed Mon; 🖑) 🖉 The former seat of government in colonial Louisiana now serves as the gateway to exploring the history of the state in general, and New Orleans in particular. It's also a magnificent building in its own right; the elegant Cabildo marries elements of Spanish colonial architecture and French urban design better than most buildings in the city. Exhibits range from Native American tools, to 'Wanted' posters for escaped slaves, to a gallery's worth of paintings of stone-faced old New Orleanians.

★ Presbytère   MUSEUM
(📞504-568-6968; http://louisianastatemuseum. org/museums/the-presbytere; 751 Chartres St; adult/student $6/5; ◎10am-4:30pm Tue-Sun, closed Mon; 🖑) 🖉 The lovely Presbytère building, designed in 1791 as a rectory for the St Louis Cathedral, serves as New Orleans' Mardi Gras museum. You'll find there's more to the city's most famous celebration than wanton debauchery – or, at least, discover the many levels of meaning behind the debauchery. There's an encyclopedia's worth of material on the krewes, secret societies, costumes and racial histories of the Mardi Gras tapestry, all intensely illuminating and easy to follow.

Jackson Square   SQUARE, PLAZA
(Decatur & St Peter Sts) Sprinkled with lazing loungers, surrounded by sketch artists, fortune-tellers and traveling performers, and watched over by cathedrals, offices and shops plucked from a Parisian fantasy, Jackson Sq is one of America's great town greens and the heart of the Quarter. The identical, block-long Pontalba Buildings overlook the scene, and the nearly identical Cabildo and Presbytère structures flank the impressive St Louis Cathedral, which fronts the square. In the middle of the park stands the Jackson monument – Clark Mills' bronze equestrian statue of the hero of the Battle of New Orleans, Andrew Jackson, which was unveiled in 1856.

The Historic New Orleans Collection   MUSEUM
(THNOC; 📞504-523-4662; www.hnoc.org; 533 Royal St; admission free, tours $5; ◎9:30am-4:30pm Tue-Sat, from 10:30am Sun) In several exquisitely restored buildings you'll find thoughtfully curated exhibits with an emphasis on archival materials, such as the original transfer documents of the Louisiana Purchase. Separate home, architecture/courtyard and history tours run at 10am, 11am, 2pm and 3pm, the home being the most interesting of them.

◎ The Tremé

The oldest African American neighborhood in the city is obviously steeped in a lot of history. Leafy Esplanade Avenue, which borders the neighborhood, is full of old-school Creole mansions, and is one of the prettiest streets in the city.

Backstreet Cultural Museum   MUSEUM
(📞504-522-4806; www.backstreetmuseum.org; 1116 Henriette Delille St/formerly St Claude Ave, per person $8; ◎10am-5pm Tue-Sat) Mardi Gras Indian suits grab the spotlight with dazzling flair – and finely crafted detail – in this informative museum, which examines the distinctive elements of African American culture in New

NEW ORLEANS IN...

Two Days

On the first day, wander Jackson Sq and the French Quarter's museums. The **Cabildo** and **Presbytère** are adjacent to each other and give a good grounding in Louisiana culture, as does the nearby **Historic New Orleans Collection**. Afterwards, stroll along the mighty Mississippi.

Grab dinner at **Bayona**, locavore base of hometown legend Susan Spicer. Enjoy drinks at **Tonique** and go see some live music at **Preservation Hall**.

Next morning, stroll along Magazine St in a state of shopping nirvana. Then walk north, pop into **Lafayette Cemetery No 1**, consider having a drink at **Commander's Palace** (☑ 504-899-8221; www.commanderspalace.com; 1403 Washington Ave, Garden Distric) – it helps to be well-dressed – and hop onto the **St Charles Avenue Streetcar**. Have a haute Southern dinner at **Boucherie**.

Four Days

On day three, join the morning Creole Neighborhoods bike tour with **Confederacy of Cruisers**. This is exceptionally easy riding, and takes in all elements of the funky Marigny and Bywater, but if you don't fancy bikes, walk past Washington Sq Park and soak up the Marigny's vibe.

Have dinner at **Bacchanal** and enjoy great wine and cheese in this musical garden. If you're feeling edgy, head to St Claude Ave where the offerings range from punk to hip-hop to bounce to '60s mod. For more traditional Nola jazz and blues, head down Frenchmen St.

The next day drive, or consider renting a bicycle, and explore around the Tremé – don't miss the **Backstreet Cultural Museum** or **Willie Mae's** fried chicken. Head up Esplanade Ave and gawk at all the gorgeous Creole mansions sitting pretty under the big live oaks. Take Esplanade all the way to **City Park** and wander around the **New Orleans Museum of Art**.

Orleans. The museum isn't terribly big – it's the former Blandin's Funeral Home – but if you have any interest in the suits and rituals of Mardi Gras Indians as well as Second Line parades and Social Aid & Pleasure Clubs (the local black community version of civic associations), you need to stop by.

Louis Armstrong Park   PARK
(701 N Rampart St; ⊘ 8am-6pm) The entrance to this massive park has got to be one of the greatest gateways in the USA, a picturesque arch that ought rightfully be the final set piece in a period drama about Jazz Age New Orleans. The original Congo Sq is here, as well as a **Louis Armstrong statue** and a **bust of Sidney Bechet**. The **Mahalia Jackson Theater** (☑ 504-525-1052, box office 504-287-0350; www.mahaliajacksontheater. com; 1419 Basin St) hosts opera and Broadway productions.

St Louis Cemetery No 1   CEMETERY
(www.noladeadspace.com; 1300 St Louis St; admission by guided tour; ⊘ 9am-3pm Mon-Sat, to noon Sun; ♿) This cemetery received the remains of most early Creoles. The shallow water table necessitated above-ground burials, with bodies placed in the family tombs you see to this day. The supposed grave of voodoo queen Marie Laveau is here, scratched with 'XXX's from spellbound devotees. By request of the family that owns the tomb, do not add to this graffiti; to do so is also technically illegal. In 2015, in response to ongoing vandalism, cemetery visitation was limited to relatives of the interred and approved guided tours.

St Augustine's Church   CHURCH
(☑ 504-525-5934; www.staugustinecatholic-church-neworleans.org; 1210 Governor Nicholls St) Open since 1841, 'St Aug's' is the second-oldest African American Catholic church in the country, a place where Creoles, émigrés from St-Domingue and free persons of color could worship shoulder to shoulder, even as separate pews were designated for slaves. The future of the church remains in question, so try to visit; more visitors increases the chance of preserving this historic landmark.

New Orleans

480 m
0.25 miles

Red's Chinese (0.4mi)
Bywater Bed & Breakfast (0.3mi)
BJ's (1mi)
Port St
Joint (0.9mi)
Crescent Park (0.4mi)
Bacchanal (1mi)
Bywater (0.4mi)

St Roch Market (0.1mi)

Franklin Ave
34
36

FAUBOURG MARIGNY

Burgundy St
Royal St
Mandeville St
Marigny St
Decatur St
N Peters St

N Rampart St
Elysian Fields Ave

Frenchmen St
Washington Sq Park
8
39 18

Touro St
Pauger St
Dauphine St
Esplanade Ave

Esplanade

N Peters St
Ursulines

Chartres St
Decatur St
27

Barracks St
Governor Nicholls St
Bourbon St
Dauphine St
23
28

Royal St
Dumaine

Presbytère
19 25

McShane Pl

Kerlerec St
Pere Antoine Alley
Rue Delille St
Treme St
Marais St
N Villere St
N Robertson St
Robertson St

Ursulines Ave
6
9

N Rampart St
35

Dumaine St
Burgundy St

Orleans Ave

FRENCH QUARTER
St Louis Cathedral
4 3
Cabildo
1 11

3
St Ann St
St Peter St
Toulouse St

Wilkinson St
Toulouse St
Woldenberg Park
Moonwalk

St Philip St
12
13

St Louis St
24
State Supreme Court

Bourbon St
Dauphine St
Burgundy St

Chartres Ave
St Charles Ave
13

St Peter St
Burgundy St
Bienville St
Iberville St

Canal St
29
22
University Pl
Baronne St

THE TREMÉ

Dumaine St
St Peter St
Basin St
17
1

37

N Claiborne Ave
Orleans Ave

St Louis Cemetery No 2

St Louis St
Conti St
Crozat St

St Ann St
Lafitte Ave
Toulouse St
N Roman St
N Prieur St
N Johnson St
N Galvez St
N Miro St

N Derbigny St
Bienville St
Iberville St

Marais St
Treme St
Saratoga St
Cleveland St
S Villere St
S Robertson St
N Robertson St

Elk Pl
La Salle St

Carousel Gardens (2.1mi);
City Park (2.1mi)

La Belle Esplanade (0.5mi);
Degas H (0.6mi)

10
10
10

Willie Mae's Scotch House (50yd)
30

India House Hostel (0.1mi)

Canal St
Tulane Ave
Twelve Mile Limit (1.3mi)

S Claiborne Ave
S Derbigny St
S Roman St
S Prieur St
Palmyra St
Tulane Ave
Gravier St
Perdido St

Delaronde St

Bienville St
N Peters St
Tchoupitoulas St

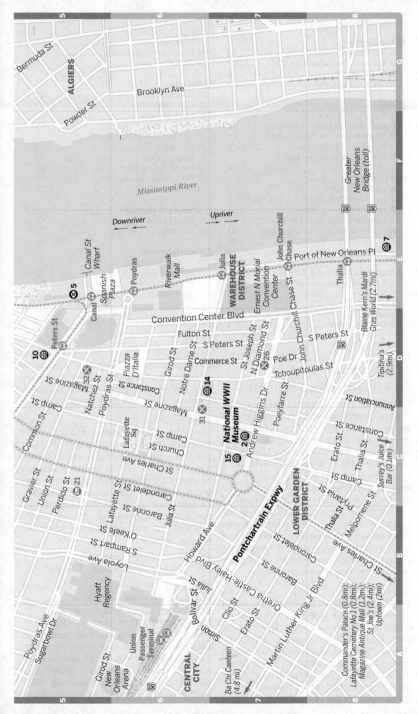

Faubourg Marigny, the Bywater & the Ninth Ward

North of the French Quarter are the Creole suburbs (*faubourgs*, which more accurately means 'neighborhoods') of the Marigny and the Bywater. **Frenchmen Street**, which runs through the center of the Marigny, is a fantastic strip of live-music goodness. It used to be known as a locals' Bourbon, but tourists are increasingly common. Nearby **St Claude Avenue** boasts a collection of non-traditional venues; folks here rock out to punk and bounce (a local style of frenetic dance music). The Bywater is a collection of candy-colored homes and an ever-expanding number of sometimes awesome, sometimes cloyingly hip, new restaurants and bars.

Crescent Park PARK
(Piety, Chartres & Mazant Sts; ☺8am-6pm, to 7pm mid-Mar–early Nov; P 🚻 🐾) 🟢 This waterfront park is our favorite spot in the city for taking in the Mississippi. Enter over the enormous arch at Piety and Chartres Sts and watch the fog blanket the nearby skyline. A promenade meanders past an angular metal and concrete conceptual 'wharf' (placed next to the burned remains of the former commer-cial wharf); one day, said path will extend to a planned performance space at Mandeville St. A dog park is located near the Mazant St entrance, which also gives disabled access.

Frenchmen Art Market MARKET
(www.facebook.com/frenchmenartmarket; 619 Frenchmen St; ☺7pm-1am Thu-Sun) 🟢 Independent artists and artisans line this alleyway market, which has built a reputation as one of the finest spots in town to find a unique gift to take home as your New Orleans souvenir. 'Art', in this case, includes clever T-shirts, hand-crafted jewelry, trinkets and, yes, a nice selection of prints and original artwork.

CBD & Warehouse District

⭐ **National WWII Museum** MUSEUM
(☎504-528-1944; www.nationalww2museum.org; 945 Magazine St; adult/child/senior $23/14/20, plus 1/2 films $5/10; ☺9am-5pm) This extensive, heart-wrenching museum presents an admirably nuanced and thorough analysis of the biggest war of the 20th century. And its exhibits, which are displayed in three grand pavilions, are amazing. Wall-sized photographs capture the confusion of

D-Day. Riveting oral histories tell remarkable stories of survival. A stroll through the snowy woods of Ardennes feels eerily cold. The experience is personal, immersive and educational. Don't miss it.

Ogden Museum of Southern Art   MUSEUM
(☑ 504-539-9650; www.ogdenmuseum.org; 925 Camp St; adult/child 5-17yr/student $10/5/8; ☺ 10am-5pm Wed-Mon, plus 5:30-8pm Thu) One of our favorite museums in the city manages to be beautiful, educational and unpretentious all at once. New Orleans entrepreneur Roger Houston Ogden has assembled one of the finest collections of Southern art anywhere, which includes huge galleries ranging from impressionist landscapes to outsider folk-art quirkiness, to contemporary installation work.

On Thursday nights, pop in for Ogden After Hours, when you can listen to great Southern musicians and sip wine with a fun-loving, arts-obsessed crowd in the midst of the masterpieces.

Blaine Kern's Mardi Gras World   MUSEUM
(☑ 504-361-7821; www.mardigrasworld.com; 1380 Port of New Orleans Pl; adult/child 2-11yr/senior $20/13/16; ☺ tours 9:30am-4:30pm; ⊞) We dare say Mardi Gras World is one of the happiest places in New Orleans by day – but at night it must turn into one of the most terrifying funhouses this side of Hell. It's all those *faces,* man, the dragons, clowns, kings and fairies, leering and dead-eyed...

That said, by day we love touring Mardi Gras World – the studio warehouse of Blaine Kern (Mr Mardi Gras) and family, who have been making parade floats since 1947. Tours last 30 to 45 minutes.

⊙ Garden District & Uptown

The main architectural division in New Orleans is between the elegant townhouses of the Creole and French northeast and the magnificent mansions of the American district, which includes the Garden District and Uptown. Magnificent oak trees arch over St Charles Ave, which cuts through the heart of this sector and where the supremely picturesque **St Charles Avenue streetcar** (per ride $1.25; ⊞) runs. The boutiques and galleries of **Magazine Street** form the best shopping strip in the city.

Lafayette Cemetery No 1   CEMETERY
(Washington Ave, at Prytania St; ☺ 7am-2:30pm Mon-Fri, to noon Sat) FREE Shaded by groves of lush greenery, this cemetery exudes a strong sense of Southern subtropical gothic. Built in 1833, it is divided by two intersecting footpaths that form a cross. Look out for the crypts built by fraternal organizations such as the Jefferson Fire Company No 22, which took care of their members and their families in large shared tombs. Some of the wealthier family tombs were built of marble, with elaborate details, but most were constructed simply of inexpensive plastered brick.

Audubon Zoological Gardens   ZOO
(☑ 504-581-4629; www.auduboninstitute.org; 6500 Magazine St; adult/child 2-12yr/senior $19/14/15; ☺ 10am-4pm Tue-Fri, to 5pm Sat & Sun Sep-Feb, 10am-5pm Mon-Fri, to 6pm Sat & Sun Mar-Aug; ⊞) This is among the country's best zoos. It contains the ultracool **Louisiana Swamp** exhibit, which is full of alligators, bobcats, foxes, bears and snapping turtles. Look for new and improved elephant and orangutan enclosures in late 2015, as well as a Lazy River water feature for kids. Open Mondays March through early September.

⊙ City Park & Mid-City

City Park   PARK
(☑ 504-482-4888; www.neworleanscitypark.com; Esplanade Ave & City Park Ave) Live oaks, Spanish moss and lazy bayous frame this masterpiece of urban planning. Three miles long and 1 mile wide, dotted with gardens, waterways and bridges, and home to a captivating art museum, City Park is bigger than Central Park in NYC, and it's New Orleans' prettiest green space. It's also a perfect expression of a local 'park,' in the sense that it is an only slightly tamed expression of the forest and Louisiana wetlands that are the natural backdrop of the city.

New Orleans Museum of Art   MUSEUM
(NOMA; ☑ 504-658-4100; www.noma.org; 1 Collins Diboll Circle; adult/child 7-17yr $10/6; ☺ 10am-6pm Tue-Thu, to 9pm Fri, 11am-5pm Sat & Sun) Inside City Park, this elegant museum was opened in 1911 and is well worth a visit both for its special exhibitions and top-floor galleries of African, Asian, Native American and Oceanic art – don't miss the outstanding Qing dynasty snuff-bottle collection. Its **sculpture garden** (☺ 10am-4:30pm Sat-Thu, to 8:45pm Fri) FREE contains a cutting-edge collection in lush, meticulously planned grounds.

THE SOUTH NEW ORLEANS

☞ Tours

The Jean Lafitte National Historic Park and Preserve Visitor Center (p443) leads free walking tours of the French Quarter at 9:30am (get tickets at 9am).

Confederacy of Cruisers CYCLING
(☑504-400-5468; www.confederacyofcruisers.com; tours from $49) Our favorite bicycle tours in New Orleans set you up on cruiser bikes that come with fat tires and padded seats for Nola's flat, pot-holed roads. The main 'Creole New Orleans' tour takes in the best architecture of the Marigny, Bywater, Esplanade Ave and the Tremé. Confederacy also does a 'History of Drinking' tour ($49; you have to be 21 or over) and a tasty culinary tour ($89).

Friends of the Cabildo WALKING TOUR
(☑504-523-3939; www.friendsofthecabildo.org; 523 St Ann St; adult/student $20/15; ⊙10am & 1:30pm Tue-Sun) 🌿 These excellent walking tours are led by knowledgeable (and often funny) docents who will give you a great primer on the history of the French Quarter, the stories behind some of the most famous streets and details of the area's many architectural styles.

Festivals & Events

New Orleans never needs an excuse to party. Just a few listings are included here; check www.neworleansonline.com for a good events calendar.

Mardi Gras CULTURAL
(www.mardigrasneworleans.com; ⊙Feb or early Mar) Fat Tuesday marks the orgasmic finale of the Carnival season.

St Joseph's Day – Super Sunday CULTURAL
(⊙Mar) March 19 and its nearest Sunday bring 'gangs' of Mardi Gras Indians out into the streets in all their feathered, drumming glory. The Super Sunday parade usually begins around noon at Bayou St John and Orleans Ave, but follows no fixed route.

French Quarter Festival MUSIC
(www.fqfi.org; ⊙2nd weekend Apr) Free music on multiple stages.

Jazz Fest MUSIC
(www.nojazzfest.com; ⊙Apr-May) The last weekend of April and the first weekend of May; a world-renowned extravaganza of music, food, crafts and good living.

🛏 Sleeping

Rates peak during Mardi Gras and Jazz Fest, and fall in the hot summer months. Book early and call or check online for special deals. Parking in the Quarter costs $15 to $30 per day.

Bywater Bed & Breakfast B&B $
(☑504-944-8438; www.bywaterbnb.com; 1026 Clouet St; r without bath $100; ❋) This is what happens when you fall through the rabbit hole and Wonderland is a B&B. This spot is popular with lesbians (it's owned by a lesbian couple), but welcomes everyone. It's about as homey and laid back as it gets. Expect to stay in what amounts to a folk-art gallery with a bit of historical heritage and a hallucinogenic vibe.

India House Hostel HOSTEL $
(☑504-821-1904; www.indiahousehostel.com; 124 S Lopez St; dm/d $20/55; @ 🛜🖨) This colorful place is larger than it looks. Half a block off Canal St in Mid-City, the hostel is a mini-complex of subtropically themed good times. The grounds include an above-ground pool, a cabana-like patio and three well-worn old houses used for sleeping. And the ambience? India House has the sort of

SWAMP TOURS

We highly recommend visiting the **Barataria Preserve** (☑504-689-3690; www.nps.gov/jela/barataria-preserve.htm; 6588 Barataria Blvd, Crown Point; ⊙visitor center 9am-5pm) FREE. If you want a boat-bound swamp tour, these can be arranged in New Orleans; there are offices along Decatur St in the French Quarter. Or find some Lost Land, as it were...

Louisiana Lost Land Tours (☑504-400-5920; http://lostlandstours.org; tours from $90) runs wonderful tours that include kayak paddles into the wetlands and a motorboat tour of Barataria Bay. Excursions focus on land loss and wildlife threats, and are led by folks who genuinely love this land. Check out their blog on environmental issues in South Louisiana, http://lostlandstours.org/category/blog/, maintained by Pulitzer Prize–winning journalist Bob Marshall.

NEW ORLEANS FOR CHILDREN

Many of New Orleans' daytime attractions are well suited for kids, including the **Audubon Zoo** (p436), **Aquarium of the Americas** (☎504-581-4629; www.auduboninstitute.org; 1 Canal St; adult/child/senior $24/18/19, with IMAX $29/23/23; ☺10am-5pm Tue-Sun; ⛵) and **Insectarium** (☎504-581-4629; www.auduboninstitute.org; 423 Canal St; adult/child $16.50/12; ☺10am-5pm; ⛵). Other great options:

Carousel Gardens Amusement Park (☎504-483-9402; www.neworleanscitypark.com; 7 Victory Ave, City Park; admission adult/children 36in & under $4/free, each ride $4; ☺10am-5pm Tue-Thu, 10am-10pm Fri, 11am-10pm Sat, 11am-6pm Sun Jun & July, Sat & Sun only spring & fall) The 1906 carousel is a gem of vintage carny-ride happiness. Other thrills include a Ferris wheel, bumper cars and a tilt-a-whirl. Buy an $18 pass for unlimited rides. Open nightly from Thanksgiving until the early new year for Celebration in the Oaks.

Louisiana Children's Museum (☎504-523-1357; www.lcm.org; 420 Julia St; admission $8.50; ☺9:30am-4:30pm Tue-Sat, noon-4:30pm Sun mid-Aug–May, 9:30am-5pm Mon-Sat, noon-5pm Sun Jun–mid-Aug) This educational museum is like a high-tech kindergarten where the wee ones can play in interactive bliss till nap time. Lots of corporate sponsorship equals lots of hands-on exhibits. The Little Port of New Orleans gallery spotlights the five types of ships found in the local port. Kids can play in a galley kitchen, or they can load cargo. Elsewhere kids can check out optical illusions, shop in a pretend grocery store or get crafty in an art studio.

Milton Latter Memorial Library (☎504-596-2625; www.neworleanspubliclibrary.org; 5120 St Charles Ave; ☺9am-8pm Mon & Wed, to 6pm Tue & Thu, 10am-5pm Sat, noon-5pm Sun) Poised elegantly above shady stands of palms, the Latter Memorial Library was once a private mansion. The Isaac family (owners 1907–12) – who installed Flemish-style carved woodwork, Dutch murals and French frescoed ceilings – passed the property to aviator Harry Williams and his silent-film-star wife, Marguerite Clark (1912–39). The couple was known for throwing grand parties. The next owner was local horse racer Robert S Eddy, followed by Mr and Mrs Harry Latter, who gave the building to the city in 1948.

free-spirited party atmosphere that got you into backpacking in the first place.

★ **La Belle Esplanade** B&B **$$**
(☎504-301-1424; www.labelleesplanade.com; 2216 Esplanade Ave; r incl breakfast $179-209; ❄🖥) A little quirky, a little saucy, and the co-owner wears a jaunty fedora – a devil-may-care touch that ties the whole colorful shebang together. Furnishings in the five themed suites vary, but look for chunky headboards, plush chairs, Gibson Girl portraits and clawfoot tubs. Bright, monochromatic walls keep it all pretention-free. Savor crawfish pie and other tasty Southern fare for breakfast.

Le Pavillon HISTORIC HOTEL **$$**
(☎504-581-3111; www.lepavillon.com; 833 Poydras Ave; r $179-279, ste from $695; 🅿❄🖥🏊) Le Pavillon exudes an old-school *joie de vivre* that's easy to love. Fluted columns support the porte cochere off the alabaster facade, and the doorman wears white gloves and a top hat (and somehow doesn't look ridiculous). Both private and public spaces are redolent with historic portraits, magnificent chandeliers, marble floors and heavy drapery.

Degas House HISTORIC HOTEL **$$**
(☎504-821-5009; www.degashouse.com; 2306 Esplanade Ave; r/ste incl breakfast from $199/300; 🅿❄🖥) Edgar Degas, the famed French Impressionist, lived in this 1852 Italianate house when visiting his mother's family in the early 1870s. Rooms recall his time here through period furnishings and reproductions of his work. The suites have balconies and fireplaces, while the less expensive garret rooms are cramped top-floor quarters that once housed the Degas family's servants.

★ **Soniat House** BOUTIQUE HOTEL **$$$**
(☎504-522-0570; www.soniathouse.com; 1133 Chartres St; r/ste from $245/425; ❄🖥) The three houses that make up this hotel in the Lower Quarter epitomize Creole elegance at its unassuming best. You enter via a cool loggia into a courtyard filled with ferns and a trickling fountain. Some rooms open onto

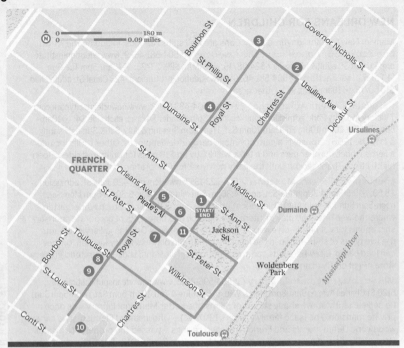

City Walk
French Quarter

START JACKSON SQ
END JACKSON SQ
LENGTH 1.1 MILES; 1½ HOURS

Begin your walk at the **1 Presbytère** (p430) on Jackson Sq and head down Chartres St to the corner of Ursulines Ave. Directly across Chartres St, at No 1113, the 1826 **2 Beauregard-Keyes House** combines Creole and American styles of design. Walk along Ursulines Ave to Royal St – the soda fountain at the **3 Royal Pharmacy** is a preserved relic from halcyon malt-shop days.

When it comes to quintessential New Orleans postcard images, Royal St takes the prize. Cast-iron galleries grace the buildings and a profusion of flowers garland the facades.

At No 915 Royal, the **4 Cornstalk Hotel** stands behind one of the most frequently photographed fences anywhere. At Orleans Ave, stately magnolia trees and lush tropical plants fill **5 St Anthony's Garden**, behind **6 St Louis Cathedral** (p430).

Alongside the garden, take the inviting Pirate's Alley and turn right down Cabildo Alley and then right up St Peter St toward Royal St. Tennessee Williams shacked up at No 632 St Peter, the **7 Avart-Peretti House**, in 1946–47 while he wrote *A Streetcar Named Desire*.

Turn left on Royal St. At the corner of Royal and Toulouse Sts stands a pair of houses built by Jean François Merieult in the 1790s. The building known as the **8 Court of Two Lions**, at 541 Royal St, opens onto Toulouse St and next door is the **9 Historic New Orleans Collection** (p430).

On the next block, the massive 1909 **10 State Supreme Court Building** was the setting for many scenes in director Oliver Stone's movie *JFK*.

Turn around and head right on Toulouse St to Decatur St and turn left. Cut across the road and walk the last stretch of this tour along the river. As Jackson Sq comes into view, cross back over to the Presbytère's near-identical twin, the **11 Cabildo** (p430).

the courtyard, while winding stairways lead to elegant upstairs quarters. Singular attention has been paid to art and antiques throughout.

Roosevelt New Orleans HOTEL $$$
(☑504-648-1200; www.therooseveltneworleans.com; 123 Baronne St; r/ste from $269/329; P ⊚ 🛜 🏊) The majestic, block-long lobby harks back to the early 20th century, a golden age of opulent hotels and grand retreats. Swish rooms have classical details, but the spa, John Besh restaurant, storied Sazerac Bar and swanky new jazz lounge are at least half the reason to stay. The rooftop pool is pretty swell, too. It's an easy walk to the French Quarter.

✕ Eating

Louisiana may have the greatest native culinary tradition in the USA – not necessarily by dint of the quality of food (although quality is very high) but from the long history that lies behind dishes that are older than most American states. While the rest of us eat to live, New Orleanians live to eat.

Just a heads up: if you're planning to head to **Cafe du Monde** (☑800-772-2927; www.cafedumonde.com; 800 Decatur St; beignets $2; ⊘24hr) for beignets (fried doughnuts), be warned the lines are obnoxious on weekends. Weekday nights are a good time to visit.

✕ French Quarter

Croissant D'Or Patisserie BAKERY $
(☑504-524-4663; www.croissantdornola.com; 617 Ursulines Ave; meals $3-5; ⊘6am-3pm Wed-Mon) On the quieter side of the French Quarter, this spotlessly clean pastry shop is where many locals start their day. Bring a paper, order coffee and a croissant – or a tart, quiche or sandwich topped with béchamel sauce – and bliss out. Check out the tiled sign on the threshold that says 'ladies entrance' – a holdover from earlier days.

Coop's Place CAJUN $
(☑504-525-9053; www.coopsplace.net; 1109 Decatur St; mains $8-17.50; ⊘11am-3am) Coop's is an authentic Cajun dive, but more rocked out. Make no mistake: it's a grotty chaotic place, the servers have attitude and the layout is annoying. But it's worth it for the food: rabbit jambalaya, chicken with shrimp

and *tasso* (smoked ham) in a cream sauce – there's no such thing as 'too heavy' here. No patrons under 21.

★ **Bayona** LOUISIANAN $$$
(☑504-525-4455; www.bayona.com; 430 Dauphine St; mains $29-38; ⊘11:30am-1:30pm Wed-Sun, 6-9:30pm Mon-Thu, 5:30-10pm Fri & Sat) Bayona is, for our money, the best splurge in the Quarter. It's rich but not overwhelming, classy but unpretentious, innovative without being precocious, and all around just a very fine spot for a meal. The menu changes regularly, but expect fresh fish, fowl and game prepared in a way that comes off as elegant and deeply cozy at the same time.

SoBou MODERN AMERICAN $$$
(☑504-552-4095; www.sobounola.com; 310 Chartres St; mains $24-38; ⊘7am-10pm) The name means 'South of Bourbon.' The food? Hard to pin, but uniformly excellent. The chefs play with a concept that mixes Louisiana indulgence with eccentricities: sweet-potato beignets slathered with duck gravy and chicory coffee glaze, and the infamous, decadent foie gras burger. The on-site bar mixes mean drinks, and there are tables with beer taps built in!

✕ The Tremé

Willie Mae's Scotch House SOUTHERN $
(2401 St Ann St; fried chicken $11; ⊘10am-5pm Mon-Sat) Willie Mae's has been dubbed some of the best fried chicken in the world by the James Beard Foundation, the Food Network and other media. It thus sees a steady flow of tourist traffic. The chicken, served in a basket, is pretty damn good, as are the butter beans.

Dooky Chase SOUTHERN, CREOLE $$
(☑504-821-0600; 2301 Orleans Ave; buffet $20, mains $16-25; ⊘11am-3pm Tue-Thu, 11am-3pm & 5-9pm Fri) Ray Charles wrote 'Early in the Morning' about Dooky's; civil rights leaders used it as informal headquarters in the 1960s; and Barack Obama ate here after his inauguration. Leah Chase's labor of love is the backbone of the Tremé, and her buffets are the stuff of legend. Top-notch gumbo and excellent fried chicken are served in a white-linen dining room to office workers and ladies who lunch.

✕ Bywater

★ Bacchanal
MODERN AMERICAN **$**

(☎504-948-9111; www.bacchanalwine.com; 600 Poland Ave; mains $8-16, cheese from $5; ⊙11am-midnight) From the outside, Bacchanal looks like a leaning Bywater shack; inside are racks of wine and stinky but sexy cheese. Musicians play in the garden, while cooks dispense delicious meals on paper plates from the kitchen in the back; on any given day you may try chorizo-stuffed dates or seared diver scallops that will blow your gastronomic mind.

★ Red's Chinese
CHINESE **$**

(☎504-304-6030; www.redschinese.com; 3048 St Claude Ave; mains $8-16; ⊙noon-3pm & 5-11pm) Red's has upped the Chinese cuisine game in New Orleans in a big way. The chefs aren't afraid to add lashings of Louisiana flavor, yet this isn't what we'd call 'fusion' cuisine. The food is grounded deeply in spicy Sichuan flavors, which pairs well with the occasional flash of cayenne. The General Lee's chicken is stupendously good.

St Roch Market
MARKET **$**

(☎504-609-3813; www.strochmarket.com; 2381 St Claude Ave; mains $9-12; ⊙9am-11pm; 🖉🍴) 🍴 Once, the St Roch Market was the seafood and produce market for a working-class neighborhood. After it was nearly destroyed by Hurricane Katrina, it was renovated into a shiny food court. The airy interior space hosts 13 restaurants serving food ranging from New Orleans classics to coffee to Nigerian cuisine.

Joint
BARBECUE **$**

(☎504-949-3232; http://alwayssmokin.com; 701 Mazant St; mains $7-17; ⊙11:30am-10pm Mon-Sat) The Joint's smoked meat has the olfactory effect of the Sirens' sweet song, pulling you, the proverbial traveling sailor, off course and into savory meat-induced blissful death (classical Greek analogies ending *now*). Knock back some ribs, pulled pork or brisket with some sweet tea in the backyard garden and learn to love life.

FROM THE MEKONG TO THE MISSISSIPPI

Following the Vietnam War, thousands of South Vietnamese fled to America, settling in Southern California, Boston, the Washington, DC area and New Orleans. If the last choice seems odd, remember that many of these refugees were Catholic and the New Orleans Catholic community – one of the largest in the country – was helping to direct refugee resettlement. In addition, the subtropical climate, rice fields and flat wetlands must have been geographically reassuring. For a Southeast Asian far from home, the Mississippi delta may have borne at least a superficial resemblance to the Mekong delta.

Probably the most pleasant way to experience local Vietnamese culture is by eating its delicious food and shopping in its markets. The following are all in the suburbs of Gretna or New Orleans East:

Dong Phuong Oriental Bakery (☎504-254-0296; www.dpbanhmi.com; 14207 Chef Menteur Hwy, New Orleans East; bakery $1.50-6, mains $7-13; ⊙8am-4pm Wed-Sun) For the best *banh mi* (Vietnamese bread rolls of sliced pork, cucumber, cilantro and other lovelies, locally called a 'Vietnamese po'boy') around and some very fine durian cake.

Tan Dinh (☎504-361-8008; 1705 Lafayette St, Gretna; mains $8-17; ⊙9:30am-9pm Mon, Wed-Fri, 9am-9pm Sat, to 8pm Sun) We'd happily contend that Tan Dinh is one of the best restaurants in greater New Orleans. The garlic butter chicken wings could be served in Heaven's pub, and the Korean short ribs are mouthwatering. Also a contender for high-quality pho (noodle soup).

Hong Kong Food Market (☎504-394-7075; 925 Behrman Hwy, Gretna; ⊙8am-8:30pm) Hong Kong Food Market is a general Asian grocery store that serves plenty of Chinese and Filipinos, but the main customer base is Vietnamese.

Vietnamese Farmers' Market (14401 Alcee Fortier Blvd, New Orleans East; ⊙6am-9am) The closest you'll come to witnessing Saigon on a Saturday morning (by the way, lots of local Vietnamese, being southern refugees, still call it 'Saigon') is the Vietnamese Farmers' Market, also known as the 'squat market' thanks to the ladies in *non la* (conical straw hats) squatting over their fresh, wonderful-smelling produce.

CBD & Warehouse District

★ Cochon Butcher SANDWICHES $
(www.cochonbutcher.com; 930 Tchoupitoulas St; mains $10-12; ⊙10am-10pm Mon-Thu, to 11pm Fri & Sat, to 4pm Sun) Tucked behind the slightly more formal Cochon, this newly expanded sandwich and meat shop calls itself a 'swine bar & deli.' We call it our favorite sandwich shop in the city, if not the entire South. From the convivial lunch crowds to the savory sandwiches to the fun-loving cocktails, this welcoming place from local restaurant maestro Donald Link encapsulates the best of New Orleans.

★ Peche Seafood Grill SEAFOOD $$
(✆504-522-1744;   www.pecherestaurant.com; 800 Magazine St; small plates $9-14, mains $14-27; ⊙11am-10pm Mon-Thu, to 11pm Fri & Sat) We're not sure why, but there is a split opinion locally about this latest venture from Donald Link. Put us firmly in the lick-the-plate and order-more category. Coastal seafood dishes are prepared simply here, but unexpected flourishes – whether from salt, spices or magic – sear the deliciousness onto your taste buds. The vibe is convivial, with a happy, stylish crowd sipping and savoring among the exposed-brick walls and wooden beams.

Domenica ITALIAN $$
(✆504-648-6020; 123 Baronne St; mains $13-30; ⊙11am-11pm; 🖉) With its wooden refectory tables, white lights and soaring ceiling, Domenica feels like a village trattoria gone posh. The 'rustic' pizza pies at this lively, often-recommended spot are loaded with nontraditional but enticing toppings – clams, prosciutto, smoked pork – and are big enough that solo diners should have a slice or two left over.

Restaurant August CREOLE $$$
(✆504-299-9777;   www.restaurantaugust.com; 301 Tchoupitoulas St; lunch $23-36, dinner $33-42; ⊙5-10pm daily, 11am-2pm Fri & Sun; 🖉) For a little romance, reserve a table at Restaurant August, the flagship of chef John Besh's nine-restaurant empire. This converted 19th-century tobacco warehouse, with its flickering candles and warm, soft shades, earns a nod for most aristocratic dining room in New Orleans, but somehow manages to be both intimate and lively. Delicious meals take you to another level of gastronomic perception.

Garden District & Uptown

★ Surrey's Juice Bar AMERICAN $
(✆504-524-3828; 1418 Magazine St; breakfast & lunch $6-13; ⊙8am-3pm) Surrey's makes a simple bacon-and-egg sandwich taste – and look – like the most delicious breakfast you've ever been served. And you know what? It probably *is* the best. Boudin biscuits; eggs scrambled with salmon; biscuits swimming in salty sausage gravy; and a shrimp, grits and bacon dish that should be illegal. And the juice, as you might guess, is blessedly fresh. Cash only.

★ Ba Chi Canteen VIETNAMESE $
(www.facebook.com/bachicanteenla; 7900 Maple St; mains $4-15; ⊙11am-2:30pm Mon-Fri, to 3:30pm Sat, 5:30-9pm Mon-Wed, 5:30-10pm Thu-Sat) Do not be skeptical of the bacos. These pillowy bundles of deliciousness – a *banh bao* crossed with a taco – successfully merge the subtle seasonings of Vietnamese fillings with the foldable convenience of a taco-shaped steamed flour bun. Pho and *banh mi* – dubbed po'boys here – round out the menu.

★ Boucherie SOUTHERN $$
(✆504-862-5514;   www.boucherie-nola.com; 1596 S Carrollton Ave; lunch $10-18, dinner $15-18; ⊙11am-3pm & 5:30-9:30pm Tue-Sat) The thick, glistening cuts of bacon on the BLT can only be the work of the devil – or chef Nathanial Zimet, whose house-cured meats and succulent Southern dishes are lauded citywide. Savor boudin balls with garlic aioli, blackened shrimp in bacon vinaigrette, and smoked Wagyu brisket with gloriously stinky garlic-Parmesan fries. The Krispy Kreme bread pudding with rum syrup is a wonder.

★ Gautreau's MODERN AMERICAN $$$
(✆504-899-7397; www.gautreausrestaurant.com; 1728 Soniat St; mains $22-42; ⊙6-10pm Mon-Sat) There's no sign outside Gautreau's, just the number 1728 discreetly marking a nondescript house in a residential neighborhood. Cross the threshold to find a refined but welcoming dining room where savvy diners, many of them New Orleanian food aficionados, dine on fresh, modern American fare. Chef Sue Zemanick has won every award a rising young star can garner in American culinary circles.

🍷 Drinking & Nightlife

New Orleans is a drinking town. Bourbon St can be fun for a night, but you need to get into the neighborhoods to experience some of the best bars in America.

Most bars open every day, often by noon, get hopping around 10pm, and can stay open all night. There's no cover charge unless there's live music. It's illegal to have open glass liquor containers in the street, so all bars dispense plastic 'go cups' when you're ready to wander.

★ Tonique   BAR
(☑504-324-6045; http://bartonique.com; 820 N Rampart St; ☺noon-2am) Tonique is a bartender's bar. Seriously: on a Sunday night, when the weekend rush is over, we've seen no less than three of the city's top bartenders arrive here to unwind. Why? Because this gem mixes some of the best drinks in the city, and it has a spirits menu as long as a Tolstoy novel to draw upon.

★ Twelve Mile Limit   BAR
(500 S Telemachus St; ☺5pm-midnight Mon-Thu, to 2am Fri & Sat, to 11pm Sun) Twelve Mile is simply a great bar. It's staffed by people who have the skill, both behind the bar and in the kitchen, to work in four-star spots, but who chose to set up shop in a neighborhood, for a neighborhood. The mixed drinks are excellent, the match of any mixologist's cocktail in Manhattan, and the vibe is super accepting.

Mimi's in the Marigny   BAR
(☑504-872-9868; 2601 Royal St; ☺6pm-2am Sun-Thu, to 4am Fri & Sat) The name of this bar could justifiably change to 'Mimi's *is* the Marigny'; we can't imagine the neighborhood without this institution. Mimi's is as attractively disheveled as Brad Pitt on a good day, all comfy furniture, pool tables, an upstairs dance hall decorated like a Creole mansion gone punk, and dim, brown lighting like a fantasy in sepia.

St Joe's   BAR
(www.stjoesbar.com; 5535 Magazine St; ☺4pm-3am Mon-Fri, noon-3am Sat, to 1am Sun) The bartender might make a face when you order a blueberry mojito – mojitos are hard to make. But dang, dude, you make 'em so good. They've been voted the best in town by New Orleanians several times. Patrons at this dark-but-inviting place are in their 20s and 30s, and friendly and chatty, as is the staff.

BJ's   BAR
(☑504-945-9256; 4301 Burgundy; ☺5pm-late) This Bywater dive attracts a neighborhood crowd seeking cheap beers, chilled-out banter and occasional live music, especially the Monday blues-rock show by King James & the Special Men, which starts around 10pm. How great is this place? Robert Plant felt the need to put on an impromptu set here the last time he visited town.

☆ Entertainment

What's New Orleans without live local music? Almost any weekend night you can find something for every taste: jazz, blues, brass band, country, Dixieland, zydeco (Cajun dance music), rock or Cajun. Free shows in the daytime abound. Check *Gambit* (www.bestof neworleans.com), *Offbeat* (www.offbeat.com) or www.nolafunguide.com for schedules.

★ Spotted Cat   LIVE MUSIC
(www.spottedcatmusicclub.com; 623 Frenchmen St; ☺4pm-2am Mon-Fri, from 3pm Sat & Sun) It's good the Spotted Cat is across the street from Snug Harbor. They're both great jazz clubs, but where the latter is a swish martini sorta spot, the former is a thumping sweatbox where drinks are served in plastic cups an ideal execution of the tiny New Orleans music club.

★ Mid-City Rock & Bowl   LIVE MUSIC
(☑504-861-1700; www.rockandbowl.com; 3000 S Carrollton Ave; ☺5pm-late) A night at the Rock & Bowl is a quintessential New Orleans experience. The venue is a strange, wonderful combination of bowling alley, deli and huge live-music and dance venue, where patrons get down to New Orleans roots music while trying to avoid that 7-10 split. The best time and place in the city to experience zydeco is the weekly Thursday-night dance party held here.

AllWays Lounge   THEATER
(☑504-218-5778; http://theallwayslounge.net; 2240 St Claude Ave; ☺6pm-midnight Sat-Wed, to 2am Thu & Fri) In a city full of funky music venues, the AllWays stands out as one of the funkiest. On any given night of the week you may see experimental guitar, local theater, thrashy rock, live comedy or a '60s-inspired shagadelic dance party. Also: the drinks are supercheap.

Tipitina's   LIVE MUSIC
(☑504-895-8477; www.tipitinas.com; 501 Napoleon Ave) 'Tips,' as locals call it, is one of New Orleans' great musical meccas. The legendary

Uptown nightclub, which takes its name from Professor Longhair's 1953 hit single, is the site of some of the city's most memorable shows, particularly when big names such as Dr John come home to roost. Outstanding music from local talent packs 'em in year-round.

Preservation Hall　　　　JAZZ
(📞504-522-2841; www.preservationhall.com; 726 St Peter St; cover $15 Sun-Thu, $20 Fri & Sat; ⊙show-times 8pm, 9pm & 10pm) Preservation Hall, housed in a former art gallery that dates back to 1803, is one of the most storied live-music venues in New Orleans. Barbara Reid and Grayson 'Ken' Mills formed the Society for the Preservation of New Orleans Jazz in 1961, at a time when Louis Armstrong's generation was already getting on in years. The resident performers, the Preservation Hall Jazz Band, are ludicrously talented, and regularly tour around the world. These white-haired musos and their tubas, trombones and cornets raise the roof every night.

🛍 Shopping

Magazine Antique Mall　　　　ANTIQUES
(📞504-896-9994;　www.magazineantiquemall. com; 3017 Magazine St; ⊙10:30am-5:30pm, from noon Sun) Scary baby dolls. Hats. Chandeliers. Coca-Cola memorabilia. Inside this overstuffed emporium, rummagers are likely to score items of interest in the dozen or so stalls, where independent dealers peddle an intriguing and varied range of antique bric-a-brac. Bargain hunters aren't likely to have much luck, though.

Maple Street Book Shop　　　　BOOKS
(www.maplestreetbookshop.com; 7523 Maple St; ⊙10am-6pm Mon-Sat, 11am-5pm Sun) This beloved Uptown shop celebrated its 50th anniversary in 2014. Founded by sisters Mary Kellogg and Rhoda Norman, it is one of the most politically progressive, well-stocked bookshops in the city. The store sells new, used and rare books in an invitingly overstuffed setting.

ℹ Information

DANGERS & ANNOYANCES
New Orleans has a high violent-crime rate, and neighborhoods go from good to ghetto very quickly. Be careful walking too far north of Faubourg Marigny and the Bywater (St Claude Ave is a good place to stop), south of Magazine St (things get dodgier past Laurel St) and too far north of Rampart St (Lakeside) from the French Quarter into the Tremé without a specific destination in mind. Stick to places that are well peopled, particularly at night, and spring for a cab to avoid dark walks. In the Quarter, street hustlers frequently approach tourists – just walk away. With all that said, don't be paranoid. Crime here, as in most of America, tends to be between people who already know each other.

INTERNET ACCESS
There's pretty good wi-fi coverage in the CBD, French Quarter, Garden and Lower Garden Districts and Uptown. Almost every coffee shop in the city has wi-fi coverage. Libraries have free internet access for cardholders.

MEDIA
Gambit Weekly (www.bestofneworleans.com) Free weekly hot sheet of music, culture, politics and classifieds.
WWOZ 90.7 FM (www.wwoz.org) Tune in here for Louisiana music and more.

MEDICAL SERVICES
Tulane University Medical Center (📞504-988-5263; www.tulanehealthcare.com; 1415 Tulane Ave; ⊙24hr) Emergency room located in the CBD.

TOURIST INFORMATION
The city's official visitor website is www.new orleansonline.com.
Jean Lafitte National Historic Park and Preserve Visitor Center (📞504-589-2636; www. nps.gov/jela; 419 Decatur St, French Quarter; ⊙9am-4:30pm Tue-Sat) Operated by the NPS, with exhibits on local history, guided walks and daily live music. There's not much in the park office itself, but educational musical programs are held on most days of the week. Many of the park rangers are musicians and knowledgeable lecturers, and their presentations discuss musical developments, cultural changes, regional styles, myths, legends and musical techniques in relation to the broad subject of jazz.
Basin St Station (📞504-293-2600; www. basinststation.com; 501 Basin St; ⊙9am-5pm) Affiliated with the New Orleans CVB, this interactive tourist info center inside the former freight administration building of the Southern Railway has loads of helpful info and maps as well as an historical overview film and a small rail museum component. It's next door to St Louis Cemetery No 1.

ℹ Getting There & Away

Louis Armstrong New Orleans International Airport (MSY; 📞504-303-7500; www.flymsy. com; 900 Airline Hwy; 🔊), 11 miles west of the city, handles primarily domestic flights.

The **Union Passenger Terminal** (☎ 504-299-1880; 1001 Loyola Ave) is home to **Greyhound** (☎ 504-525-6075; www.greyhound.com; 1001 Loyola Ave; ⊙ 5:15am-10:30am, 11:30am-1pm & 2:30-9:25pm), which has regular buses to Baton Rouge (two hours), Memphis, TN (11 hours), and Atlanta, GA (12 hours). **Amtrak** (☎ 800-872-7245, 504-528-1610; ⊙ ticketing 5:45am-10pm) trains also operate from the Union Passenger Terminal, running to Chicago, New York and Los Angeles and stops in-between.

ⓘ Getting Around

TO/FROM THE AIRPORT

There's an information booth at the airport's A&B concourse. The **Airport Shuttle** (☎ 866-596-2699; www.airportshuttleneworleans.com; one way/round-trip $20/38) runs to downtown hotels. The **Jefferson Transit** (☎ 504-364-3450; www.jeffersontransit.org; adult $2) airport route E2 picks up outside entrance 7 on the airport's upper level; it stops along Airline Hwy (Hwy 61) on its way into town (final stop Tulane and Loyola Aves). After 7pm it only goes to Tulane and Carrollton Aves in Mid-City; a solid 5 miles to get to the CBD, and from here you must transfer to a Regional Transit Authority (RTA) bus – a haphazard transfer at best, especially with luggage.

Taxis downtown cost $33 for one or two people, $14 more for each additional passenger.

PUBLIC TRANSPORTATION

The **Regional Transit Authority** (RTA; ☎ 504-248-3900; www.norta.com) runs the local bus service. Bus and streetcar fares are $1.25, plus 25¢ for transfers; express buses cost $1.50. Exact change is required.

The RTA also operates three **streetcar** lines (one-way $1.25, one-day pass $3; exact change required). The historic St Charles streetcar is running only a short loop in the CBD due to hurricane damage to the Uptown tracks. The Canal streetcar makes a long journey up Canal St to City Park, with a spur on Carrollton Ave. The Riverfront line runs 2 miles along the levee from the Old US Mint, past Canal St, to the upriver convention center and back. A **Jazzy Pass** gives you unlimited rides (one/three days $3/9); they can be bought at local Walgreen's pharmacies, or order online, but if you go the latter route, you have to wait for them to be mailed to you.

For a taxi, call **United Cabs** (☎ 504-522-9771; www.unitedcabs.com; ⊙ 24hr).

Rent bicycles at **Bicycle Michael's** (☎ 504-945-9505; www.bicyclemichaels.com; 622 Frenchmen St; per day from $35; ⊙ 10am-7pm Mon, Tue & Thu-Sat, to 5pm Sun).

Around New Orleans

Leaving colorful New Orleans behind quickly catapults you into a world of swamps, bayous, antebellum plantation homes, laid-back small communities and miles of bedroom suburbs and strip malls.

Barataria Preserve

This section of the Jean Lafitte National Historical Park & Preserve, south of New Orleans near the town of Marrero, provides the easiest access to the dense swamplands that ring New Orleans. The 8 miles of boardwalk trails are a stunning way to tread lightly through the fecund, thriving swamp, home to alligators, nutrias (big invasive river rats), tree frogs and hundreds of species of birds.

Start at the NPS Visitor Center (☎ 504-689-3690; www.nps.gov/jela; Hwy 3134; ⊙ 9am-5pm, visitor center 9:30am-4:30pm Wed-Sun; 🖈) FREE, 1 mile west of Hwy 45 off the Barataria Blvd exit, where you can pick up a map or join a guided walk or canoe trip (most Saturday mornings and monthly on full-moon nights; call to reserve a spot). To rent canoes or kayaks for a tour or an independent paddle, go to Bayou Barn (☎ 504-689-2663; www.bayoubarn.com; 7145 Barataria Blvd, canoes per person $20, single kayak $25; ⊙ 10am-6pm Thu-Sun) about 3 miles from the park entrance.

The North Shore

Bedroom communities sprawl along Lake Pontchartrain's north shore, but head north of Mandeville and you'll reach the bucolic village of Abita Springs, which was popular in the late 19th century for its curative waters. Today, the spring water still flows from a fountain in the center of the village, but the primary liquid attraction is the Abita Brew Pub (☎ 985-892-5837; www.abitabrewpub.com; 7201 Holly St; ⊙ 11am-9pm Tue-Thu & Sun, to 10pm Fri & Sat), where you can choose from the many tap beers brewed a mile west of town at the Abita Brewery Tasing Room (☎ 985-893-3143; www.abita.com; 166 Barbee Rd; tours free; ⊙ tours 2pm Wed-Fri, 11am, noon, 1pm & 2pm Sat).

The 31-mile Tammany Trace trail (☎ 985-867-9490; www.tammanytrace.org; 🖈) 🚴 connects north shore towns, beginning in Covington, passing through Abita Springs and pretty Fontainebleau State Park. In Lacombe, about 9 miles east of Mandeville, you can rent bicycles and kayaks at **Bayou Adventures** (☑985-882-9208; www.bayou adventure.com; 27725 Main St, Lacombe; bicycles per hr/day $8/25, single/double kayaks per day $35/50; ⊙6am-5pm).

River Road

Elaborate plantation homes dot the east and west banks of the Mississippi River between New Orleans and Baton Rouge. First indigo, then cotton and sugarcane, brought great wealth to the plantation owners and many plantations are open to the public. Most tours focus on the lives of the owners, the restored architecture and the ornate gardens of antebellum Louisiana.

◉ Sights

Whitney Plantation   HISTORIC SITE
(☑225-265-3300; www.whitneyplantation.com; 5099 Highway 18, Wallace; adult/student $22/15, child under 12yr free; ⊙9:30am-4:30pm Wed-Mon, tours 10am-3pm) The Whitney is the first plantation in the state to focus on the history and realities of slavery. Visitors are given a historical tour into the world of the German-American Haydel family and their slaves, but the visit emphasizes the lived experience of the latter group. Besides a tour that focuses on the appalling living conditions slaves toiled under, the property is speckled with memorials and monuments to the area's slave population.

Laura Plantation   HISTORIC SITE
(☑225-265-7690; www.lauraplantation.com; 2247 Hwy 18, Vacherie; adult/child $20/6; ⊙10am-4pm) This ever-evolving and popular plantation tour teases out the distinctions between Creole, Anglo, free and enslaved African Americans via meticulous research and the written records of the Creole women who ran the place for generations. Laura is also fascinating because it was a Creole mansion, founded and maintained by a continental European-descended elite, as opposed to Anglo-Americans; the cultural and architectural distinctions between this and other plantations is obvious and striking.

Oak Alley Plantation   HISTORIC SITE
(☑225-265-2151; www.oakalleyplantation.com; 3645 Hwy 18, Vacherie; adult/child $20/7.50; ⊙9am-5pm Mar-Oct, 9am-4:30pm Mon-Fri, to 5pm Sat & Sun Nov-Feb) The most impressive aspect of Oak Alley Plantation is its canopy of 28 majestic live oaks lining the entry to the grandiose Greek Revival–style home – even better with a fresh mint julep. The tour is relatively staid, but there are guest cottages ($145 to $200) and a restaurant on-site.

Baton Rouge

In 1699 French explorers named this area *baton rouge* (red stick) when they came upon a reddened cypress pole that Bayagoulas and Houma Native Americans had staked in the ground to mark the boundaries of their respective hunting territories. From one pole grew a lot of sprawl; Baton Rouge stretches out in an unplanned clutter in many directions. Visitors are mostly drawn to Baton Rouge for Louisiana State University (LSU) and Southern University; the latter is one of the largest historically African American universities in the country.

◉ Sights & Activities

Louisiana State Capitol   HISTORIC BUILDING
(☑225-342-7317; 900 N 3rd St; ⊙8am-4:30pm Tue-Sat) **FREE** The art-deco skyscraper looming over town was built at the height of the Great Depression to the tune of $5 million. It's the most visible leftover legacy of populist governor 'Kingfish' Huey Long. The 27th-floor observation deck (closes 4pm) offers stunning views and the ornate lobby is equally impressive. The welcome desk offers free tours of the grounds.

LSU Museum of Art   MUSEUM
(LSUMOA; ☑225-389-7200; www.lsumoa.com; 100 Lafayette St; adult/child $5/free; ⊙10am-5pm Tue-Sat, to 8pm Thu, 1-5pm Sun) The physical space this museum inhabits – the clean, geometric lines of the Shaw Center – is as impressive as the on-site galleries, which include a permanent collection of over 5000 works and curated galleries exploring regional artistic heritage and contemporary trends.

Old State Capitol   HISTORIC BUILDING
(☑225-342-0500; www.louisianaoldstatecapitol. org; 100 North Blvd; ⊙9am-4pm Tue-Sat) **FREE** The Gothic Revival, pink fairytale castle is... well, it's a pink castle. Which should tell you something about how eccentric the government of its resident state can be. Today the structure houses exhibits about the colorful political history of Louisiana.

Rural Life Museum
MUSEUM

(☑225-765-2437; http://sites01.lsu.edu/wp/
rurallife; 4560 Essen Lane; adult/child $9/8; ⊙8am-
5pm; P ♿) This outdoor museum promis-
es a trip into the architecture, occupations
and folkways of rural Louisiana. Numerous
rough-hewn buildings are scattered over the
bucolic campus, and exhibits are refresh-
ingly honest and informative, lacking any
rose-colored romanticization of the hard
country legacy that built Louisiana.

🛏 Sleeping & Eating

Stockade Bed & Breakfast
B&B $$

(☑225-769-7358; www.thestockade.com; 8860
Highland Rd; r $135-160, ste $215; P ❄ ☎) Chain
hotels line the sides of I-10. For a more inti-
mate stay, try this wonderful B&B with five
spacious, comfortable and elegant rooms
just 3.5 miles southeast of LSU and within
earshot of several standout neighborhood
restaurants. Book ahead on weekends, espe-
cially during football season.

Schlittz & Giggles
PIZZA $$

(☑225-218-4271; www.schlittzandgiggles.com; 301
3rd St; pizzas $10-22; ⊙11am-midnight Sun-Wed,
to 2am Thu-Sat; ☎) The food stands up to this
awesomely named downtown late-night bar
and pizzeria. Bubbly coeds serve up thin-
as-black-ice pizza slices ($3 to $3.50) and
fabulous panini to a student crowd, while a
gaggle of old-timer locals tend to belly up at
the bar.

Louisiana Lagniappe
CAJUN $$$

(☑225-767-9991; www.louisianalagniapperes-
taurant.com; 9900 Perkins Rd; mains $21-50;
⊙5:30pm-9pm Mon-Thu, 5-10pm Fri & Sat; P) If
you need a night out in Baton Rouge, and it
requires the presence of delicious local cui-
sine, we'll direct you to Louisiana Lagniappe
(lah-nyap). The second word means 'a little
extra' in Louisiana French, and it's a mis-
nomer, as you get a *lot* here: of fish topped
with crab meat, rib-eye steaks and shrimp
and sausage pasta.

☆ Entertainment

Varsity Theatre
LIVE MUSIC

(☑225-383-7018; www.varsitytheatre.com; 3353
Highland Rd; ⊙8pm-2am) At the gates of LSU,
there's live music here, often on weeknights.
The attached restaurant boasts an extensive
beer selection and a raucous college crowd.

ℹ Information

Visitor Center
(☑225-383-1825; www.visit
batonrouge.com; 359 3rd St; ⊙8am-5pm)
The downtown city visitor center has maps,
brochures of local attractions and festival
schedules.

Capital Park
(☑225-219-1200; www.louisiana
travel.com; 702 River Rd N; ⊙8am-4:30pm)
Near the Baton Rouge visitor center, this is the
extensive official gateway to Louisiana tourism.

ℹ Getting There & Around

Baton Rouge lies 80 miles west of New Orleans
on I-10. **Baton Rouge Metropolitan Airport**
(BTR; ☑225-355-0333; www.flybtr.com) is
north of town off I-110; it's about 1½ hours from
New Orleans, so it's a viable airport of entry if
you're renting a car. **Greyhound** (☑225-383-
3811; www.greyhound.com; 1253 Florida Blvd,
at N 12th St) has regular buses to New Orleans,
Lafayette and Atlanta, GA. **Capitol Area Transit
System** (CATS; ☑225-389-8920; www.brcats.
com; tickets $1.75) operates buses around town.

St Francisville

Lush St Francisville is the quintessential
Southern artsy small town, a blend of his-
torical homes, bohemian shops and outdoor
activities courtesy of the nearby Tunica Hills
(you read that right – hills in Louisiana).
During the antebellum decade this was
home to plantation millionaires, and much
of the architecture these aristocrats built is
still intact.

◉ Sights & Activities

In town, stroll down historic **Royal St** to
catch a glimpse of antebellum homes and
buildings-turned-homes. The visitor center
has self-guided tour brochures.

Myrtles Plantation
HISTORIC BUILDING

(☑225-635-6277; www.myrtlesplantation.com;
7747 US Hwy 61 N; tours adult/child $10/7, night
tours $12; ⊙9am-5pm, tours 6pm, 7pm & 8pm Fri &
Sat; P) Supposedly haunted, this plantation
house has night mystery tours (by reserva-
tion) on weekends. We heard secondhand
corroboration of the supernatural presence,
so it might be fun to stay overnight in the
B&B (rooms from $115) to commune with
the other world.

Oakley Plantation &
Audubon State Historic Site
HISTORIC SITE

(☑225-635-3739; www.audubonstatehistoricsite.
wordpress.com; 11788 Hwy 965; adult/student/

senior $8/4/6; ⊘ 9am-5pm Tue-Sat; P) Outside of St Francisville, Oakley Plantation & Audubon State Historic Site is where John James Audubon spent his tenure, arriving in 1821 to tutor the owner's daughter. Though his assignment lasted only four months (and his room was pretty spartan), he and his assistant finished 32 paintings of birds found in the plantation's surrounding forest.

The small West Indies–influenced house (1806) includes several original Audubon prints.

Mary Ann Brown Preserve NATURE RESERVE
(☑ 225-338-1040; www.nature.org; 13515 Hwy 965; ⊘ sunrise-sunset) Operated by the Nature Conservancy, the 110-acre Mary Ann Brown Preserve takes in some of the beech woodlands, dark wetlands and low, clay-soil hill country of the Tunica uplands. A 2-mile series of trails and boardwalks crosses the woods – the same trees that John James Audubon tramped around when he began work on *Birds of America*.

🛏 Sleeping & Eating

★**Shadetree Inn** B&B $$
(☑ 225-635-6116; www.shadetreeinn.com; cnr Royal & Ferdinand Sts; r from $145; P ❋ 🛜) Sidled up against the historic district and a bird sanctuary, this super-cozy B&B has a gorgeous flower-strewn, hammock-hung courtyard and spacious but rustic upscale rooms. A deluxe continental breakfast can be served in your room and is included along with a bottle of wine or champagne. Rates plunge if you cut out breakfast and stay midweek.

3-V Tourist Court HISTORIC INN $$
(☑ 225-721-7003; www.themagnoliacafe.net/magnolia3vtouristcourts.html; 5687 Commerce St; 1-/2-bed cabins $75/125; P ❋ 🛜) One of the oldest motor inns in the United States (started in the 1930s and now on the National Register of Historic Places), the five units take you back to simpler times. Rooms have period decorations and fixtures, though a recent renovation upgraded the beds, hardwood floors and flat-screen TVs into borderline trendy territory.

Birdman Coffee & Books CAFE $
(☑ 225-635-3665; 5687 Commerce St; mains $5-6.50; ⊘ 7am-5pm Tue-Fri, 8am-2pm Sat & Sun; 🛜) Birdman is *the* spot for a local breakfast (old-fashioned yellow grits, sweet-potato pancakes) and local art.

Magnolia Café CAFE $
(☑ 225-635-6528; www.themagnoliacafe.net; 5687 Commerce St; mains $7-13; ⊘ 10am-4pm daily, to 9pm Thu & Sat, to 10pm Fri) The nucleus of what's happening in St Francisville, the Magnolia Café was once a health-food store and VW bus repair shop. Now it's where people go to eat, socialize and, on Friday night, dance to live music. Try the cheesy shrimp po'boy.

Cajun Country

When people think of Louisiana, this (and New Orleans) is the image that comes to mind: miles of bayou, sawdust-strewn shacks, a unique take on French and lots of good food. Welcome to Cajun Country, also called Acadiana for the French settlers exiled from L'Acadie (now Nova Scotia, Canada) by the British in 1755.

Cajuns are the largest French-speaking minority in the US, and while you may not hear French spoken at the grocery store, it is still present in radio shows, church services and the sing-song lilt of local English accents. While Lafayette is the nexus of Acadiana, getting out among the waterways, villages and ramshackle roadside taverns really drops you into Cajun living. This is largely a socially conservative region, but the Cajuns also have a well-deserved reputation for hedonism. It's hard to find a bad meal here; jambalaya (a rice-based dish with tomatoes, sausage and shrimp) and crawfish étouffée (a thick Cajun stew) are prepared slowly with pride (and cayenne!), and if folks aren't fishing, they are probably dancing. Don't expect to sit on the sidelines...*allons danson* (let's dance).

LAFAYETTE

The term 'undiscovered gem' gets thrown around too much in travel writing, but Lafayette really fits the bill. First, the bad: this town is deader then a cemetery on Sundays. The rest: there's an entirely fantastic amount of good eating and lots of music venues here, plus one of the best free music festivals in the country. This is a university town so bands are rocking most any night. Heck, even those quiet Sundays have a saving grace: some famously delicious brunch options.

⊙ Sights

Vermilionville VILLAGE
(☑ 337-233-4077; www.vermilionville.org; 300 Fisher Rd; adult/student $10/6; ⊘ 10am-4pm Tue-Sun; ♿) This tranquil, re-created 19th-century

Cajun village wends along the bayou near the airport. Friendly, enthusiastic costumed docents explain Cajun, Creole and Native American history, and local bands perform on Sundays (1pm to 3pm). Guided **boat tours** (📞 337-233-4077; adult/student $12/8; ⏰ 10:30am Tue-Sat Mar-May & Sep-Nov) of Bayou Vermilion are also offered.

Acadiana Center for the Arts GALLERY
(📞 337-233-7060; www.acadianacenterforthearts. org; 101 W Vermilion St; adult/student/child $5/3/2; ⏰ 10am-5pm Mon-Sat) This arts center in the heart of downtown maintains three chic galleries and hosts dynamic theater, lectures and special events.

Acadian Cultural Center MUSEUM
(📞 337-232-0789; www.nps.gov/jela; 501 Fisher Rd; ⏰ 9am-4:30pm Tue-Fri, 8:30am-noon Sat; 🅿🚻) 🔖 This National Parks Service museum has extensive exhibits on Cajun culture.

✦ Festivals & Events

Festival International de Louisiane MUSIC
(www.festivalinternational.com; ⏰ last weekend Apr) At the fabulous Festival International de Louisiane, hundreds of local and international artists rock out for five days in the largest free music festival of its caliber in the US. Although 'Festival' avowedly celebrates Francophone music and culture, the event's remit has grown to accommodate world music in all its iterations and languages.

🛏 Sleeping & Eating

Chain hotels clump near exits 101 and 103, off I-10 (doubles from $65). Head to Jefferson St mid-downtown for a choice of bars and restaurants, from sushi to Mexican.

⭐ **Blue Moon Guest House** GUESTHOUSE $
(📞 337-234-2422; www.bluemoonpresents.com; 215 E Convent St; dm $18, r $70-90; 🅿❄@📶) This tidy home is one of Louisiana's travel gems: an upscale hostel-like hangout that's walking distance from downtown. Snag a bed and you're on the guest list for Lafayette's most popular down-home music venue, located in the backyard. The friendly owners, full kitchen and camaraderie among guests create a unique music-meets-migration environment catering to backpackers, flashpackers and those in transition (flashbackpackers?).

Prices skyrocket during festival time. Decidedly not a quiet spot.

Buchanan Lofts APARTMENTS $$
(📞 337-534-4922; www.buchananlofts.com; 403 S Buchanan; r per night/week from $110/600; 🅿❄@📶) These uber-hip lofts could be in New York City if they weren't so big. Doused in contemporary-cool art and design – all fruits of the friendly owner's globetrotting – the extra-spacious units come with kitchenettes and are awash with exposed brick and hardwoods.

⭐ **French Press** BREAKFAST $
(📞 337-233-9449; www.thefrenchpresslafayette. com; 214 E Vermillion; mains $9-15; ⏰ 7am-2pm Mon-Fri, from 9am Sat & Sun; 📶) This French-Cajun hybrid is the best culinary thing going in Lafayette. Breakfast is mind-blowing, with a sinful Cajun Benedict (*boudin* instead of ham), cheddar grits (that will kill you dead) and

CAJUNS, CREOLES AND...CREOLES

Tourists in Louisiana often use the terms 'Cajun' and 'Creole' interchangeably, but the two cultures are quite distinct. 'Creole' refers to descendants of the original European settlers of Louisiana, a blended mix of mainly French and Spanish ancestry. The Creoles tend to have urban connections to New Orleans and consider their own culture refined and urbanized.

The Cajuns can trace their lineage to the Acadians, colonists from rural France who settled Nova Scotia. After the British conquered Canada, the proud Acadians refused to kneel to the new crown and were exiled in the mid-18th century – an act known as the Grand Dérangement. Many exiles settled in South Louisiana; they knew the area was French, but the Acadians ('Cajun' is an English bastardization of the word) were often treated as country bumpkins by the Creoles. The Acadians-cum-Cajuns settled in the bayous and prairies, and to this day see themselves as a more rural, frontier-stye culture.

Adding confusion to this is the practice, standard in many post-colonial French societies, of referring to mixed-race individuals as 'Creoles'. This happens in Louisiana, but there is a cultural difference between Franco-Spanish Creoles and mixed-race Creoles, even though these two communities very likely share actual blood ancestry.

organic granola (offset the grits). Lunch ain't half bad either; the fried shrimp melt, doused in Sriracha mayo, is gorgeously decadent.

Johnson's Boucanière CAJUN $

(☑ 337-269-8878; www.johnsonsboucaniere.com; 1111 St John St; mains $3-7; ☺ 7am-3pm Tue-Fri, to 5:30pm Sat) This resurrected 70-year-old family prairie smoker business turns out detour-worthy *boudin* (Cajun-style pork and rice sausage) and an unstoppable smoked pork-brisket sandwich topped with smoked sausage.

Dwyer's DINER $

(☑ 337-235-9364; 323 Jefferson St; mains $5-12; ☺ 6am-2pm; ▣) This family-owned joint serves Cajun diner fare, finally bringing gumbo for lunch and pancakes for breakfast into one glorious culinary marriage. It's especially fun on Wednesday mornings when a French-speaking table is set up and local Cajuns shoot the breeze in their old-school dialect.

☆ Entertainment

To find out what's playing around town, pick up the free weekly *Times* (www.theadvertiser. com – check under Times of Acadiana) or *Independent* (www.theind.com).

Cajun restaurants such as **Randol's** (☑ 337-981-7080; www.randols.com; 2320 Kaliste Saloom Rd; ☺ 5-10pm Sun-Thu, to 10:30pm Fri & Sat) and **Prejean's** (☑ 337-896-3247; www. prejeans.com; 3480 NE Evangeline Thruway/I-49; ☺ 7am-10pm Sun-Thu, to 11pm Fri & Sat) feature live music on weekend nights.

Blue Moon Saloon LIVE MUSIC

(☑ 337-234-2422; www.bluemoonpresents.com; 215 E Convent St; cover $5-8; ☺ 5pm-2am Tue-Sun) This intimate venue on the back porch of the accompanying guesthouse is what Louisiana is all about: good music, good people and good beer. What's not to love? Music tends to go off Wednesday to Saturday.

Artmosphere LIVE MUSIC

(☑ 337-233-3331; www.artmosphere.co; 902 Johnston St; ☺ 10am-2am Mon-Sat, to midnight Sun) Graffiti, hookahs, hipsters and an edgy lineup of acts; it's more CBGBs then Cajun dancehall, but it's a lot of fun, and there's good Mexican food to boot.

ℹ Information

Visitor Center (☑ 337-232-3737; www. lafayettetravel.com; 1400 NW Evangeline Thruway; ☺ 8:30am-5pm Mon-Fri, 9am-5pm Sat & Sun) Information on travel, lodging and events in Lafayette and greater Acadiana (Cajun Country).

ℹ Getting There & Away

From I-10, exit 103A, the Evangeline Thruway (Hwy 167) goes to the center of town. **Greyhound** (☑ 337-235-1541; www.greyhound.com; 100 Lee Ave) operates from a hub beside the central commercial district, making several runs daily to New Orleans (3½ hours) and Baton Rouge (one hour). The **Amtrak** (100 Lee Ave) train *Sunset Limited* goes to New Orleans three times a week.

CAJUN WETLANDS

In 1755, the Grand Dérangement, the British expulsion of rural French settlers from Acadiana (now Nova Scotia, Canada), created a homeless population of Acadians who searched for decades for a place to settle. In 1785, seven boatloads of exiles arrived in New Orleans. By the early 19th century, 3000 to 4000 Acadians occupied the swamplands southwest of New Orleans. Native American tribes such as the Attakapas helped them learn to eke out a living based on fishing and trapping, and the aquatic way of life is still the backdrop to modern living.

East and south of Lafayette, the **Atchafalaya Basin** is the preternatural heart of the Cajun wetlands. Stop in at the **Atchafalaya Welcome Center** (☑ 337-228-1094; www. dnr.louisiana.gov; I-10, exit 121; ☺ 8:30am-5pm) to learn how to penetrate the dense jungle protecting these swamps, lakes and bayous from the casual visitor (incidentally, it also screens one of the most gloriously cheesy nature films in existence). They'll fill you in on camping in **Indian Bayou** and exploring the **Sherburne Wildlife Management Area**, as well as the exquisitely situated **Lake Fausse Pointe State Park**.

Eleven miles east of Lafayette in the compact, crawfish-lovin' town of **Breaux Bridge**, you'll find the utterly unexpected **Café des Amis** (☑ 337-332-5273; www.cafedesamis.com; 140 E Bridge St; mains $17-26; ☺ 11am-9pm Tue-Thu, from 7:30am Fri & Sat, 8am-2pm Sun), where you can relax amid funky local art as waiters trot out sumptuous weekend breakfasts, all set to live zydeco music on Saturday mornings. Just 3.5 miles south of Breaux Bridge, **Lake Martin** (Lake Martin Rd) is a wonderful introduction to bayou landscapes. This bird sanctuary hosts thousands of great and cattle egrets, blue heron and more than a few gators.

WORTH A TRIP

THE TAO OF FRED'S

Deep in the heart of Cajun Country, Mamou is a typical South Louisiana small town six days of the week, worth a peek and a short stop before rolling on to Eunice. But on Saturday mornings, Mamou's hometown hangout, little **Fred's Lounge** (420 6th St, Mamou; ⊙8am-2pm Sat), becomes the apotheosis of a Cajun dancehall.

OK, to be fair: Fred's is more of a dance shack than hall. It's a small bar and it gets more than a little crowded from 8:30am to 2ish in the afternoon, when the staff host a Francophone-friendly music morning, with bands, beer, cigarettes and dancing (seriously, it gets smoky in here. Fair warning). Back in the day, owner Tante (Auntie, in Cajun French) Sue herself would take to the stage to dispense wisdom and songs in Cajun French, all while taking pulls from a bottle of brown liquor she kept in a pistol holster; she has since passed, but something of her amazing, anarchic energy has been imbued into the very bricks of this place.

Check out the friendly **Tourist Center** (☑337-332-8500; www.breauxbridgelive.com; 318 E Bridge St; ⊙8am-4pm Mon-Fri, to noon Sat), whose staff can hook you up with one of numerous B&Bs in town. The wonderful **Bayou Cabins** (☑337-332-6158; www.bayoucabins.com; 100 W Mills Ave; cabins $70-150) feature 14 completely individualized cabins situated on Bayou Teche, some with 1950s retro furnishings, others decked out in regional folk art. The included breakfast is delicious, but the smoked meats may shave a few years off your lifespan. If you're in town during the first week of May, don't miss the gluttony of music, dancing and Cajun food at the **Crawfish Festival** (www.bbcrawfest.com; ⊙May).

CAJUN PRAIRIE

Think dancing cowboys! Cajun and African American settlers in the higher, drier terrain north of Lafayette developed a culture based around animal husbandry and farming, and the 10-gallon hat still rules. It's also the hotbed of Cajun and zydeco music (and thus accordions) and crawfish farming.

Opelousas squats sleepily alongside Hwy 49, and its historic downtown is home to the **Museum & Interpretive Center** (☑337-948-2589; www.cityofopelousas.com; 315 N Main St; ⊙8am-4:30pm Mon-Fri, 10am-3pm Sat) **FREE**, a grandma's attic of exhibits, artifacts and esoterica related to the town. Hit up **Slim's Y-Ki-Ki** (☑337-942-6242; www.slimsykiki.com; cnr Main St & Park St, Opelousas; ⊙9pm-late), a few miles north, for some zydeco music, and bring your dancing shoes. Zydeco shoes also often go off at the **Yambilee Building** (1939 W Landry St), which is otherwise used throughout the year as a function hall.

Plaisance, northwest of Opelousas, hosts the grassroots, fun-for-the-family **Southwest Louisiana Zydeco Festival** (www.zydeco.org; ⊙late Aug or early Sep).

In **Eunice** there's the Saturday evening 'Rendez-Vous des Cajuns' at the **Liberty Theater** (☑337-457-6577; www.eunice-la.com/index.php/things-to-do/liberty-schedule; 200 Park Ave; admission $5; ⊙6-7:30pm), which is broadcast on local radio. Visitors are welcome all day at **KBON** (☑337-546-0007; www.kbon.com; 109 S 2nd St), 101.1FM. Browse the capacious Wall of Fame, signed by visiting musicians. Two blocks away, the **Cajun Music Hall of Fame & Museum** (☑337-457-6534; www.cajunfrenchmusic.org; 230 S CC Duson Dr; ⊙9am-5pm Tue-Sat) **FREE** is a dusty collection of instruments and cultural ephemera that caters to the die-hard music buff.

The NPS runs the **Prairie Acadian Cultural Center** (☑337-457-8499; www.nps.gov/jela; 250 West Park Ave; ⊙9:30am-4:30pm Wed-Fri, to 6pm Sat) **FREE**, which has exhibits on rural life and Cajun culture and shows a variety of documentaries explaining the history of the area. Want more music? The best time to visit Eunice is on a Saturday. From 9am to noon **Savoy Music Center** (☑337-457-9563; www.savoymusiccenter.com; Hwy 190; ⊙9am-5pm Tue-Fri, 9am-noon Sat), an accordion factory and shop, hosts a Cajun-music jam session. Musician Marc Savoy and his guitarist wife, Ann, often join in.

Ruby's Café (☑337-550-7665; 123 S 2nd St; mains $9-23; ⊙6am-2pm Mon-Fri, 5-9pm Wed & Thu, to 10pm Fri & Sat) does popular plate lunches in a 1950s diner setting and **Café Mosaic** (202 S 2nd St; meals $3-4.50; ⊙6am-10pm Mon-Fri, from 7am Sat, 7am-7pm Sun; ☏) is a smart coffeehouse with waffles and grilled sandwiches. **Le Village** (☑337-457-3573; www.levillagehouse.com; 121 Seale Lane; r $115-165, 3-bed cottage $375; P ☏) is a lovely rural B&B.

Northern Louisiana

Make no mistake: the rural, oil-industry towns along the Baptist Bible-belt make Northern Louisiana as far removed from New Orleans as Paris, TX, is from Paris, France. There's a lot of optimistic tourism development, but at the end of the day, most folks come here from states like Texas and Arkansas to gamble.

Captain Henry Shreve cleared a 165-mile logjam on the Red River and founded the river-port town of Shreveport in 1839. The city boomed with oil discoveries in the early 1900s, but declined after WWII. Some revitalization came in the form of huge Vegas-sized casinos and a riverfront entertainment complex. The **visitor center** (☑ 888-458-4748; www.shreveport-bossier.org; 629 Spring St; ☺ 8am-5pm Mon-Fri, 10am-2pm Sat) is downtown. If you're a rose-lover, it would be a shame to miss the **Gardens of the American Rose Center** (☑ 318-938-5402; www.rose.org; 8877 Jefferson Paige Rd; adult/child $5/2, tours $10; ☺ 9am-5pm Mon-Sat, 1-5pm Sun), which contains more than 65 individual gardens designed to show how roses can be grown in a home garden – take exit 5 off I-20. If you're hungry, stop by **Strawn's Eat Shop** (☑ 318-868-0634; http://

strawnseatshop.com; 125 E Kings Hwy; mains under $10; ☺ 6am-8pm). This basic diner serves good, hearty Americana fare with a lot of Southern charm – think chicken-fried steak and mustard greens – but it's most notable for its delicious pies.

Shreveport boasts one of the finest, most underrated regional breweries in the nation: **Great Raft Brewing** (☑ 318-734-9881; www.greatraftbrewing.com; 1251 Dalzell St; ☺ 4-9pm Thu & Fri, noon-9pm Sat). Drop by the tasting room and give the Schwarzbier a whirl – it's a dark lager the likes of which we've not had outside of Europe.

About 50 miles northeast of Monroe on Hwy 557, near the town of Epps, the **Poverty Point State Historic Site** (☑ 318-926-5492; www.nps.gov/popo; 6859 Highway 577, Pioneer; adult/child $4/free; ☺ 9am-5pm) has a remarkable series of earthworks and mounds along what was once the Mississippi River. A two-story observation tower gives a view of the site's six concentric ridges, and a 2.6-mile hiking trail meanders through the grassy countryside. Around 1000 BC this was the hub of a civilization comprising hundreds of communities, with trading links as far north as the Great Lakes.

Florida

Why Go?

For countless visitors Florida is a place of promises: of eternal youth, sun, relaxation, clear skies, space, success, escape, prosperity and, for the kids, a chance to meet much-loved Disney characters in person.

No other state in America is as built on tourism, and tourism here comes in a thousand facets: cartoon mice, *Miami Vice,* country fried oysters, Spanish villas, gators kicking footballs, gators prowling golf courses, and of course, the beach. So. Much. Beach.

Don't think Florida is all marketing, though. This is one of the most genuinely fascinating states in the country. It's as if someone shook the nation and tipped it over, filling this sun-bleached peninsula with immigrants, country boys, Jews, Cubans, military bases, shopping malls and a subtropical wilderness laced with crystal ponds and sugary sand.

Best Places to Eat

➡ NIU Kitchen (p467)

➡ Bern's Steak House (p492)

➡ Yellow Dog Eats (p499)

➡ Tap Tap (p466)

➡ Floridian (p488)

Best Places to Stay

➡ Gale South Beach (p466)

➡ Fairbanks House (p489)

➡ Pillars (p471)

➡ Pelican Hotel (p466)

➡ Everglades International Hostel (p476)

When to Go
Miami

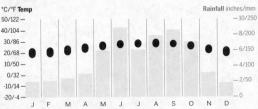

Feb–Apr Winter ends and high season begins, coinciding with spring break.

Jun–Aug The hot, humid wet months are peak season for northern Florida beaches and theme parks.

Sep–Oct The ideal shoulder season with fewer crowds, cooler temperatures and warm waters.

SOUTH FLORIDA

Once you head far enough south in Florida, you're no longer in 'the South' as a regional entity – you've slipped those bonds into South Florida, which is truly a hybrid of the USA, the Caribbean and Latin America. Miami is the area's beating urban heart, and one of the few truly international cities in the country. Wealthy oceanfront communities stretch from the Palm Beaches to Fort Lauderdale, while inland, the dreamscape of the Everglades, the state's most unique, dynamic wilderness, await. And when the state's peninsula ends, it doesn't truly end, but rather stretches into the Overseas Hwy, which leads across hundreds of mangrove islands to colorful Key West.

Miami

Miami moves to a different rhythm from anywhere else in the USA. Pastel-hued, subtropical beauty and Latin sexiness are everywhere: from the cigar-filled dance halls where Havana expats dance to *son* (a salsa-like dance that originated in Cuba) and *boleros* (a Spanish dance in triple meter) to the exclusive nightclubs where stiletto-heeled Brazilian models shake to Latin hip-hop. Whether you're meeting avant-garde gallery hipsters or passing the buffed, perfect bodies recumbent along South Beach, everyone can seem oh-so-artfully posed. Meanwhile, street vendors and restaurants dish out flavors of the Caribbean, Cuba, Argentina and Haiti. For travelers, the city can be as intoxicating as a sweaty-glassed *mojito*.

Miami is its own world, an international city whose tempos, concerns and inspira-

tions often arrive from distant shores. Over half the population is Latino and more than 60% speak predominantly Spanish. In fact, many northern Floridians don't consider immigrant-rich Miami to be part of the state, and many Miamians, particularly Cubans, feel the same way.

History

Florida has the oldest recorded history of any US state, and also the most notorious and

FLORIDA MIAMI

FLORIDA FACTS

Nickname Sunshine State

Population 19.89 million

Area 53,927 sq miles

Capital city Tallahassee (population 186,411)

Other cities Jacksonville (842,583), Miami (417,650)

Sales tax 6% (some towns add 9.5% to 11.5% to accommodations and meals)

Birthplace of Author Zora Neale Hurston (1891–1960), actor Faye Dunaway (b 1941), musician Tom Petty (b 1950), author Carl Hiaasen (b 1953)

Home of Cuban Americans, manatees, Mickey Mouse, retirees, key lime pie

Politics Sharply divided between Republicans and Democrats

Famous for Theme parks, beaches, alligators, art deco

Notable local invention Frozen concentrated orange juice (1946)

MIAMI IN...

Two Days

Focus your first day on South Beach. Bookend an afternoon of sunning and swimming with a walking tour through the **Art Deco Historic District** and a visit to **Wolfsonian-FIU**, which explains it all. That evening, sample some Haitian cuisine at **Tap Tap** and have a low-key brew at **Room**. Next morning, shop for Cuban music along Calle Ocho in **Little Havana**, followed by classic Cuban cuisine at **El Exquisito**. Go for a stroll at **Vizcaya Museum & Gardens**, cool off with a dip at the **Venetian Pool**, then end the day with dinner and cocktails at **NIU Kitchen**.

Four Days

Follow the two-day itinerary, then head to the **Everglades** on day three and jump in a kayak. For your last day, immerse yourself in art and design in **Wynwood** and the **Design District**, followed by a visit to the **Miami Art Museum** or **Museum of Contemporary Art**. In the evening, party with the hipsters at **Wood Tavern**.

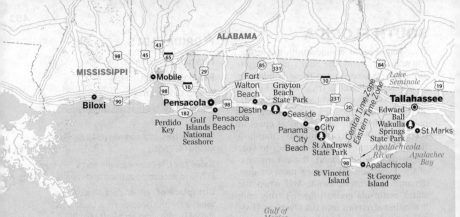

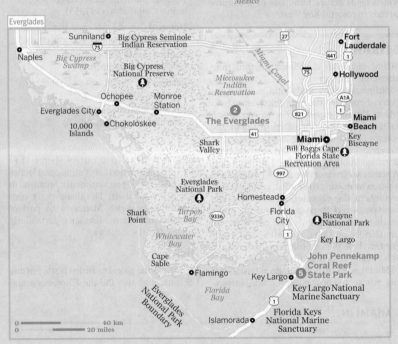

Florida Highlights

1 Joining the sunset bacchanal in Key West's **Mallory Square** (p480).

2 Paddling among alligators and sawgrass in **The Everglades** (p473).

3 Being swept up in nostalgia and thrill rides at **Walt Disney World** (p502).

4 Marveling at the murals all around **Wynwood** (p462) in Miami.

5 Snorkeling the continental USA's most extensive coral reef at **John Pennekamp Coral Reef State Park** (p478).

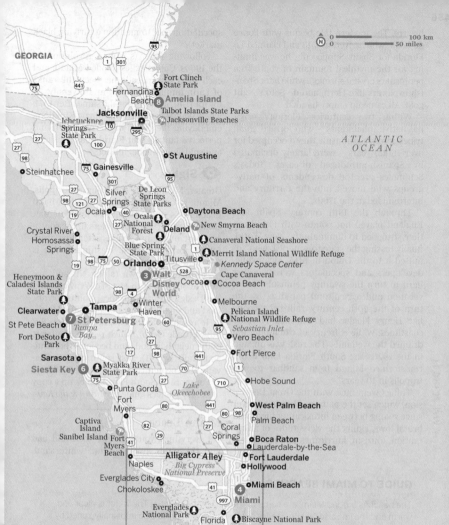

GEORGIA

ATLANTIC OCEAN

Fort Clinch State Park
Fernandina Beach **Amelia Island**
Talbot Islands State Parks
Jacksonville Jacksonville Beaches

Ichetucknee Springs State Park

St Augustine

Steinhatchee

Gainesville

Silver Springs
De Leon Springs State Parks
Ocala
Ocala National Forest
Deland New Smyrna Beach

Daytona Beach

Crystal River
Homosassa Springs
Blue Spring State Park
Orlando Titusville
Canaveral National Seashore
Merrit Island National Wildlife Refuge
Kennedy Space Center
Cape Canaveral

Heneymoon & Caladesi Islands State Park
❸ **Walt Disney World**
Cocoa Cocoa Beach

Clearwater
Tampa
Winter Haven
Melbourne
Pelican Island National Wildlife Refuge
Sebastian Inlet

❼ **St Petersburg**
St Pete Beach
Fort DeSoto Park
Tampa Bay
Vero Beach

Sarasota
Siesta Key ❻
Myakka River State Park
Fort Pierce

Punta Gorda
Lake Okeechobee

Fort Myers
Hobe Sound

Captiva Island
Sanibel Island
Fort Myers Beach
Naples
Coral Springs
West Palm Beach
Palm Beach

Boca Raton
Lauderdale-by-the-Sea
Fort Lauderdale
Hollywood

Alligator Alley
Big Cypress National Preserve

Everglades City
Chokoloskee
Miami Beach
❹ **Miami**

Everglades National Park
Florida City
Biscayne National Park
Flamingo

Dry Tortugas National Park
Florida Bay
Key Largo
See Enlargement
Islamorada

Bahia Honda State Park
Grassy Key
Marathon
Key West ❶
Big Pine Key
Florida Keys

Straits of Florida

---

❻ Relaxing on the sugar sand beaches of Sarasota's **Siesta Key** (p494).

❼ Pondering the symbolism of the Hallucinogenic Toreador at the **Salvador Dalí Museum** in St Petersburg (p494).

❽ Taking a bucolic breather amid the greenery on **Amelia Island** (p489).

bizarre. The modern tale begins with Ponce de León, who arrived in 1513 and claimed La Florida for Spain. Supposedly, he was hunting for the mythical fountain of youth (the peninsula's crystal springs), while later Spanish explorers like Hernando de Soto sought gold. All came up empty handed.

Within two centuries, Florida's original native inhabitants – who formed small tribes across a peninsula they'd occupied for over 11,000 years – were largely decimated by Spanish-introduced diseases. Today's Seminoles are the descendents of native groups who moved into the territory and intermingled in the 1700s.

Through the 18th century, Spain and England played hot potato with Florida as they struggled to dominate the New World, finally tossing the state to America, who admitted it to the Union in 1845. Meanwhile, developers and speculators were working hard to turn the swampy peninsula into a vacation and agricultural paradise. By the turn of the 20th century, railroad tycoons like Henry Flagler had unlocked Florida's coastlines, while a frenzy of canal-building drained the wetlands. The rush was on, and in the 1920s the South Florida land boom transformed Miami from sandbar to metropolis in 10 years.

Things went bust with the Great Depression, which set the pattern: Florida has ever since swung between intoxicating highs and brutal lows, riding the vicissitudes of immigration, tourism, hurricanes and real-estate speculation (not to mention a thriving black market).

Following Castro's Cuban revolution in the 1960s, Cuban exiles flooded Miami, and each successive decade has seen the ranks of Latin immigrants grow and diversify. As for tourism, it was never the same after 1971, when Walt Disney built his Magic Kingdom, embodying the vision of eternal youth and perfected fantasy that Florida has packaged and sold since the beginning.

◎ Sights

Greater Miami is a sprawling metropolis. Miami is on the mainland, while Miami Beach lies 4 miles east across Biscayne Bay. South Beach (Map p460) refers to the southern part of Miami Beach, extending from 5th St north to 21st St. Washington Ave is the main commercial artery.

North of downtown (along NE 2nd Ave from about 17th St to 41st St), Wynwood and the Design District are focal points for art, food and nightlife. Just north is Little Haiti.

To reach Little Havana, head west on SW 8th St (Calle Ocho), which pierces the heart of the neighborhood (and becomes the Tamiami Trail/Hwy 41). Just south of Little Havana are Coconut Grove and Coral Gables.

For more on South Florida, pick up a copy of Lonely Planet's guide to *Miami & the Keys*.

Miami Beach

It's everything you imagine, good and bad and ridiculous and amazing: white sand,

---

GUIDE TO MIAMI BEACHES

The beaches around Miami are some of the best in the country. The water is clear and warm and the imported white sand is relatively white. They're also informally zoned by tacit understanding into areas with their own unique crowds so that everyone can enjoy at their own speed.

Scantily clad beaches In South Beach between 5th St and 21st St; modesty is in short supply.

Family-fun beaches North of 21st St is where you'll find the more family-friendly beaches, and the beach at 53rd St has a playground and public toilets.

Nude beaches Nude bathing is legal at **Haulover Beach Park** (Map p458; ☑ 305-947-3525; www.miamidade.gov/parks/parks/haulover_park.asp; 10800 Collins Ave; per car Mon-Fri $5, Sat & Sun $7; ☺ sunrise-sunset; P) in Sunny Isles. North of the lifeguard tower is predominantly gay; south is straight.

Gay beaches All of South Beach is gay-friendly, but a special concentration seems to hover around 12th St.

Windsurfing beaches Hobie Beach, along the Rickenbacker Causeway on the way to Key Biscayne, is actually known as 'Windsurfing Beach.'

deco design, preening models and shopaholic Europeans and Latin American royalty. That movie in your head of art-deco hotels, in-line-skating models, preening young studs and cruising cars? That's Ocean Drive (from 1st to 11th Sts), with the beach merely a backdrop for strutting peacocks. This confluence of waves, sunshine and exhibitionist beauty is what made South Beach (or 'SoBe') world-famous.

Just a few blocks north, Lincoln Road (between Alton Rd and Washington Ave) becomes a pedestrian mall, or outdoor fashion runway, so all may admire SoBe's fabulously gorgeous creatures. The excellent Bass Museum of Art (Map p458; ☑ 305-673-7530; www.bassmuseum.org; 2121 Park Ave; adult/child $8/6; ☺ noon-5pm Wed, Thu, Sat & Sun, to 9pm Fri) was closed for a major expansion during writing; it is scheduled to reopen in the fall of 2016.

★ **Art Deco Historic District** AREA
(Map p460) South Beach's pastel heart is its Art Deco Historic District, which stretches from 18th St and south along Ocean Dr and Collins Ave. The smooth lines and pale color scheme of this designated historic district were ironically meant to, in the early 20th century, evoke the future and futuristic modes of transportation. Your first stop here should be the Art Deco Welcome Center (Map p460; ☑ 305-672-2014; www.mdpl.org; 1001 Ocean Dr, South Beach; ☺ 9:30am-5pm Fri-Wed, to 7pm Thu), run by the Miami Design Preservation League (MDPL).

★ **Wolfsonian-FIU** MUSEUM
(Map p460; ☑ 305-531-1001; www.wolfsonian.org; 1001 Washington Ave; adult/child 6-12yr $7/5, from 6-9pm Fri free; ☺ 10am-6pm, to 9pm Thu & Fri) A fascinating collection that spans transportation, urbanism, industrial design, advertising and political propaganda from the late 19th to mid-20th century. Visit this excellent design museum early in your stay to put the aesthetics of Miami Beach into fascinating context. By chronicling the interior evolution of everyday life, the Wolfsonian reveals how these trends were architecturally manifested in SoBe's exterior deco.

Lincoln Road Mall ROAD
(Map p460; http://lincolnroadmall.com) This outdoor pedestrian thoroughfare between Alton Rd and Washington Ave is all about seeing and being seen; there are times when Lincoln feels less like a road and more like a runway. Carl Fisher, the father of Miami

BEST BEACHES

You'll never want for shoreline in the Sunshine State. Here are a few of our favorites.

➡ Siesta Key (p494)

➡ South Beach (p456)

➡ Bahia Honda (p480)

➡ St George Island (p507)

Beach, envisioned the road as a '5th Ave of the South.' Morris Lapidus, one of the founders of the loopy, neobaroque Miami Beach style, designed much of the mall, including shady overhangs, waterfall structures and traffic barriers that look like the marbles a giant might play with.

New World Center BUILDING
(Map p460; ☑ 305-673-3330; www.newworldcenter.com; 500 17th St; tours $5; ☺ tours 4pm Tue & Thu, noon Fri & Sat) Designed by Frank Gehry, this performance hall rises majestically out of a manicured lawn just above Lincoln Rd, looking somewhat like a tissue box from the year 3000 with a glass facade; note the 'fluttering' stone waves that pop out of the exterior. The grounds form a 2.5-acre public park; performances inside the center are projected outside via a 7000-sq-ft projection wall (like you're in the classiest drive-in movie theater in the universe).

South Pointe Park PARK
(Map p460; ☑ 305-673-7779; 1 Washington Ave; ☺ sunrise-10pm; ⊕ ⊛) The very southern tip of Miami Beach has been converted into a lovely park, replete with manicured grass for lounging; views over a remarkably teal and fresh ocean; a restaurant; a refreshment stand; warm, scrubbed-stone walkways; and lots of folks who want to enjoy the great weather and views sans the South Beach strutting. That said, we saw two model photo shoots here in under an hour, so it's not all casual relaxation.

Downtown Miami

Downtown Miami is rapidly evolving, as old bazaars of cheap luggage and electronics are gentrified and replaced by art galleries, publicly designated arts space, restaurants, bars and the real-estate projects that accompany such shifts. Want to watch the water? Head to pretty Bayfront Park (Map p458; ☑ 305-358-7550; www.bayfrontparkmiami.com; 301 N Biscayne Blvd).

Greater Miami

N

0 — 5 km
0 — 2.5 miles

CAROL CITY
Palmetto Expwy
826
Fort Lauderdale (9mi)
NORTH MIAMI
Southern Memorial Park
Oleta River State Park
18
Collins Ave
11
Oleta River State Recreation Area
9
OPA-LOCKA
Palmetto Expwy
924
W 4th Ave
Griffing Blvd
909
Bal Harbour
Bay Harbor Islands
Indian Creek
NW 119th St
NE 6th Ave
15
Biscayne Blvd
Collins Ave
Little River Canal
953
HIALEAH
E 4th Ave
95
N Miami Ave
1
Pelican Harbor Park
79th St
A1A
Amtrak
9
NW 79th St
934
LITTLE HAITI
24
LIBERTY CITY
NW 27th Ave
25
NW 54th St
13
DESIGN DISTRICT
Julia Tuttle Cswy
25
27
Miami International Airport
112
NW 36th St
WYNWOOD
Wynwood Walls
NW 20th St
29
26
3
20
Biscayne Blvd
23
21
5
Sheridan Ave
MIAMI BEACH
Dolphin Expwy
NW 7th St
MIAMI
Greyhound
16
12
MacArthur Cswy
Flagler St
90
27
Máximo Gómez Park
1
28
6
SW 8th St (Calle Ocho)
SW 22nd St (Miracle Mile)
22
30
Vizcaya Museum & Gardens
Virginia Key
Fisher Island
972
Coral Way
959
8
17
LITTLE HAVANA
Coconut Grove
2
19
Hobie Island
913
826
Dinner Key Marina
Northwest Point
Biltmore Golf Course
Douglas Road
14
4
Crandon Blvd
Crandon Park Beach
874
University
South Miami
Key Biscayne
878
SW 72nd St (Sunset Dr)
KENDALL
10
7
SW 112th St (Killian Dr)
5
PINECREST
Cape Florida
Dixie Hwy
SW 152nd St
Biscayne Bay

See Miami Beach Map (p460)

ATLANTIC OCEAN

Greater Miami

Metromover MONORAIL
(☑ 305-891-3131; www.miamidade.gov/transit/metromover.asp; ☺ 5am-midnight) This elevated, electric monorail is hardly big enough to serve the mass-transit needs of the city, and has become something of a tourist attraction. Whatever its virtues as a commuting tool, the Metromover is a really great (and free!) way to see central Miami from a height (which helps, given the skyscraper-canyon nature of downtown). Because it's gratis, Metromover has a reputation as a hangout for the homeless, but commuters use it as well.

Pérez Art Museum Miami MUSEUM
(PAMM; Map p458; ☑ 305-375-3000; www.pamm.org; 1103 Biscayne Blvd; adult/senior & student $16/12; ☺ 10am-6pm Tue-Sun, to 9pm Thu, closed Mon; ℗) The Pérez can claim fine rotating exhibits that concentrate on post-WWII international art, but just as impressive are its location and exterior. This art institution inaugurated Museum Park, a patch of land that oversees the broad blue swath of Biscayne Bay. Swiss architects Herzog & de Meuron designed the structure, which integrates tropical foliage, glass and metal – a melding of

tropical vitality and fresh modernism that is a nice architectural analogy for Miami itself.

★ **Adrienne Arsht Center for the Performing Arts** BUILDING
(Map p458; ☑ 305-949-6722; www.arshtcenter.com; 1300 N Biscayne Blvd) This performing-arts center is Miami's beautiful, beloved baby. It is also a major component of downtown's urban equivalent of a face-lift and several regimens of Botox. Designed by Cesar Pelli (the man who brought you Kuala Lumpur's Petronas Towers), the center has two main components, connected by a thin pedestrian bridge. Inside the theaters there's a sense of ocean and land sculpted by wind; the rounded balconies rise up in spirals that resemble a sliced-open seashell

Little Havana

As SW 8th St heads away from downtown, it becomes **Calle Ocho** (pronounced *kah*-yeh *oh*-cho, Spanish for 'Eighth Street'). That's when you know you've arrived in Little Havana, the most prominent community of Cuban Americans in the US. Despite the cultural monuments, this is no Cuban theme

Miami Beach

0 500 m
0 0.25 miles

20th St

20th St
West Ave
19th St
18th St
Island View Park
Sheridan Ave
Belle Isle
Flamingo Way

Purdy Ave
Bay Rd
17

Alton Rd
Collins Canal
19th St
18th St
17th St

Jefferson Ave
19th St
18th St

Miami Beach Chamber of Commerce
18th St
Lincoln La N
16

Bass Museum of Art (0.2mi)
19th St
18th St
17th St

23
4
11
James Ave
12
Collins Ave

20th St
18th St
17th St
Collins Ave

Lincoln Rd
24
3
22
Lenox Ave
Lincoln Rd Mall
Lincoln Rd
8
Art Deco Historic District
1

16th St
16th St
Michigan Ave
Meridian Ave
Pennsylvania Ave
Euclid Ave
Drexel Ave
South Beach

Alton Ct
Lincoln Rd
Lincoln Ct
15th Tce
15th St
14th Tce
13th Tce
14th St

Bay Rd
Alton La S
15th St
14th St
13th St

15th St
Española Way
14th Pl
14th St

10
20
14th La

Biscayne Bay

Flamingo Park
13th St
12th St
11th St
10th St
9th St
8th St

12th St
Drexel Ave
13th St
12th St
11th St

9
12th St
Lummus Park

MIAMI BEACH
Jefferson Ave
Michigan Ave
Lenox Ave
West Ave
Alton Rd

15
Wolfsonian-FIU
2
10th St
9th St
8th St
5
6
Art Deco Welcome Center

14
Promenade

18
7th St
7th St

Downtown Miami (2.2mi); Miami International (8mi)

Miami Beach Dr (5th St)
41
19
6th St
5th St
4th St
3rd St
2nd St
1st St

6th St
5th St
4th St
13
2nd St

Euclid Ave
Washington Ave
Meridian Ave
Collins Ct
Ocean Ct
Ocean Dr

Ocean Beach Park

Causeway Island
Terminal Island
Miami Beach Marina

Pier M

Commerce St
Biscayne St

21
Pier Park

ATLANTIC OCEAN

Lummus Island

Harley St
7
Boardwalk Pier

South Pointe Park

Fisher Island

Government Cut

Biscayne Bay

Miami Beach

park. The district remains a living, breathing immigrant enclave, though one whose residents have become, admittedly, more broadly Latin American than simply Cuban. One of the best times to come is the last Friday of the month during **Viernes Culturales** (www. viernesculturales.org; ⊙ 7-11pm), or 'Cultural Fridays,' a street fair showcasing Latino artists and musicians.

★ **Máximo Gómez Park**   PARK
(Map p458; SW 8th St at SW 15th Ave; ⊙ 9am-6pm) Little Havana's most evocative reminder of Old Cuba is Máximo Gómez Park, or 'Domino Park,' where the sound of elderly men trash-talking over games of chess is harmonized by the quick clack-clack of slapping dominoes. The jarring backing track, plus the heavy smell of cigars and a sunrise-bright mural of the 1993 Summit of the Americas, combine to make Máximo Gómez one of the most sensory sites in Miami (although it's one of the most tourist-heavy as well).

Cuba Ocho   GALLERY
(Map p458; ☎ 305-285-5880; www.cubaocho.com; 1465 SW 8th St; ⊙ 11am-3am Tue-Sat) The jewel of the Little Havana Art District, Cuba Ocho functions as a community center, art gallery and research outpost for all things Cuban. The interior resembles an old Havana cigar bar, yet the walls are decked out in artwork that references both the classical past of Cuban art and its avant-garde future. Frequent music, films, drama performances, readings

and other events go off every week. The center opens during the evening for these events; check online for more information.

Cuban Memorials   MONUMENT
(Map p458; SW 13th Ave & 8-10th St) Two blocks of SW 13th Ave contain a series of monuments to Cuban and Cuban American icons. The memorials include the **Eternal Torch in Honor of the 2506th Brigade**, for the exiles who died during the Bay of Pigs Invasion; a **José Martí memorial**; and a **Madonna statue**, supposedly illuminated by a shaft of holy light every afternoon. Bursting out of the island in the center of the boulevard is a massive ceiba tree, revered by followers of Santeria.

Design District, Wynwood & Little Haiti

Proving that SoBe doesn't hold the lease on hip, these two trendy areas north of downtown – all but deserted 25 years ago – have ensconced themselves as bastions of art and design. The Design District is a mecca for interior designers, home to dozens of galleries and contemporary furniture, fixture and design showrooms. Just south of the Design District, Wynwood is a notable arts district, with myriad galleries and art studios housed in abandoned factories and warehouses.

The home of Miami's Haitian refugees, Little Haiti is defined by brightly painted homes, markets and *botanicas* (voodoo shops).

FLORIDA MIAMI

WYNWOOD GALLERIES

In Wynwood, Miami's hip proving ground for avant-garde art, 'Wipsters' (Wynwood hipsters) stock dozens of galleries with 'guerrilla' installations, new murals, graffiti and other inscrutableness. The best way to experience the scene is to attend the **Wynwood and Design District Arts Walks** (Map p458; www. artcircuits.com; ☉ 7-10pm 2nd Sat of the month) FREE, with music, food and wine.

★**Wynwood Walls**   PUBLIC ART
(Map p458; www.thewynwoodwalls.com; NW 2nd Ave btwn 25th & 26th Sts) Wynwood Walls is a collection of murals and paintings laid out over an open courtyard that invariably bowls people over with its sheer color profile and unexpected location. What's on offer tends to change with the coming and going of major arts events such as Art Basel, but it's always interesting stuff.

Little Haiti Cultural Center   GALLERY
(Map p458; ☏ 305-960-2969; http://littlehaiti culturalcenter.com; 212 NE 59th Tce; ☉ 10am-0pm Tue-Fri, 9am-4pm Sat, 11am-7pm Sun) This cultural center hosts an art gallery, dance classes, drama productions and a Caribbean-themed market on weekends (9:30am to 8pm Thursday to Saturday, to 6pm Sunday). The best time to visit is for the **Big Night in Little Haiti** (www.rhythmfoundation.com/series/ big-night-in-little-haiti), a street party held on the third Friday of every month from 6pm to 10pm. The celebration is rife with music, Caribbean food and beer, but was in need of external funding at the time of writing.

Coral Gables & Coconut Grove

For a slower pace and a more European feel, head inland. Designed as a 'model suburb' by George Merrick in the early 1920s, Coral Gables is a Mediterranean-style village that's centered around the shops and restaurants of the **Miracle Mile**, a four-block section of Coral Way between Douglas and LeJeune Rds. Coconut Grove is a trendy, student-oriented neighborhood filled with shopping, restaurants and jungly park space.

★**Vizcaya**
Museum & Gardens   HISTORIC BUILDING
(Map p458; ☏ 305-250-9133; www.vizcayamuseum. org; 3251 S Miami Ave; adult/6-12yr/student & senior $18/6/10; ☉ 9:30am-4:30pm Wed-Mon; P) They call Miami the Magic City, and if it is, this Italian villa, the housing equivalent of a Fabergé egg, is its most fairy-tale residence. In 1916 industrialist James Deering started a Miami tradition by making a ton of money and building ridiculously grandiose digs. He employed 1000 people (then 10% of the local population) and stuffed his home with 15th- to 19th-century furniture, tapestries, paintings and decorative arts; today, the grounds are used for the display of rotating contemporary-art exhibitions.

Barnacle Historic State Park   PARK
(Map p458; ☏ 305-442-6866; www.florida stateparks.org/thebarnacle; 3485 Main Hwy; admission $2, house tours adult/child $3/1; ☉ 9am-5pm Wed-Mon; ⍟) In the center of Coconut Grove is the 1891, 5-acre pioneer residence of Ralph Monroe, Miami's first honorable snowbird. The house is open for guided tours, and the park it's located on is a lovely, shady oasis for strolling. Barnacle hosts frequent (and lovely) moonlight concerts, from jazz to classical. A little way down Main Hwy, on the other side of the road, there's a small Buddhist temple shaded by large groves of banyan trees.

Biltmore Hotel   HISTORIC BUILDING
(Map p458; ☏ 855-311-6903; www.biltmorehotel. com; 1200 Anastasia Ave; ☉ tours 1:30 & 2:30pm Sun; P) The crown jewel of Coral Gables is this magnificent edifice that once housed a speakeasy run by Al Capone. Back in the day, imported gondolas transported celebrity guests such as Judy Garland and the Vanderbilts around because, of course, there was a private canal system out the back. The largest hotel pool in the continental USA, which resembles a sultan's water garden from *One Thousand & One Nights*, is still here. Catch a free tour on Sunday afternoons.

Venetian Pool   HISTORIC SITE
(Map p458; ☏ 305-460-5306; www.coralgables venetianpool.com; 2701 De Soto Blvd; adult/child $12/7; ☉ hours vary; ⍟) One of the few pools listed on the National Register of Historic Places, this is a wonderland of coral rock caves, cascading waterfalls, a palm-fringed island and Venetian-style moorings. Take a swim and follow in the footsteps (fin-steps?) of stars like Esther Williams and Johnny 'Tarzan' Weissmuller. Opening hours vary depending on the season; call or check the website for details.

MIAMI FOR CHILDREN

The best beaches for kids are in Miami Beach north of 21st St, especially at 53rd St, which has a playground and public toilets, and the dune-packed beach around 73rd St. Also head south to Matheson Hammock Park, which has calm artificial lagoons.

Miami Children's Museum (Map p458; 305-373-5437; www.miamichildrensmuseum. org; 980 MacArthur Causeway; admission $18; 10am-6pm;) On Watson Island, between downtown Miami and Miami Beach, this hands-on museum has fun music and art studios, as well as some branded 'work' experiences that make it feel a tad corporate.

Jungle Island (Map p458; 305-400-7000; www.jungleisland.com; 1111 Parrot Jungle Trail, off MacArthur Causeway; adult/child/senior $40/32/38; 10am-5pm;) Jungle Island is packed with tropical birds, alligators, orangutans, chimps and (to the delight of *Napoleon Dynamite* fans) a liger – a cross between a lion and a tiger.

Zoo Miami (Metrozoo; 305-251-0400; www.miamimetrozoo.com; 12400 SW 152nd St; adult/child $18/14; 10am-5pm Mon-Fri, 9:30am-5:30pm Sat & Sun) Miami's tropical weather makes strolling around Zoo Miami almost feel like a day in the wild. For a quick overview (and because the zoo is so big and the sun is broiling), hop on the Safari Monorail; it departs every 20 minutes.

Monkey Jungle (305-235-1611; www.monkeyjungle.com; 14805 SW 216th St; adult/child/senior $30/24/28; 9:30am-5pm, last entry 4pm;) The tagline, 'Where humans are caged and monkeys run free,' tells you all you need to know – except for the fact that it's in far south Miami.

Lowe Art Museum   MUSEUM
(Map p458; 305-284-3535; www.lowemuseum. org; 1301 Stanford Dr; adult/student $10/5; 10am-4pm Tue-Sat, noon-4pm Sun) The Lowe's tremendous collection satisfies a wide range of tastes, but it's particularly strong in Asian, African and South Pacific art and archaeology, and its pre-Columbian and Mesoamerican collection is stunning.

Greater Miami

Fairchild Tropical Garden   GARDENS
(Map p458; 305-667-1651; www.fairchildgarden. org; 10901 Old Cutler Rd; adult/child/senior $25/12/18; 7:30am-4:30pm;) If you need to escape Miami's madness, consider a green day in the country's largest tropical botanical garden. A butterfly grove, jungle biospheres, and marsh and keys habitats, plus art installations from folks like Roy Lichtenstein, are all stunning. In addition to easy-to-follow, self-guided walking tours, a free 40-minute tram tours the entire park on the hour from 10am to 3pm.

Museum of Contemporary Art North Miami   MUSEUM
(MoCA; Map p458; 305-893-6211; www.mocanomi.org; 770 NE 125th St; adult/student & senior $5/3; 11am-5pm Tue-Fri & Sun, 1-9pm Sat;)

North of downtown, MoCA has frequently changing exhibitions focusing on international, national and emerging artists.

Key Biscayne

Bill Baggs Cape Florida State Park   PARK
(Map p458; 305-361-5811; www.floridastateparks.org/capeflorida; 1200 S Crandon Blvd; per car/person $8/2; 8am-sunset;) If you don't make it to the Florida Keys, come to this park for a taste of their unique island ecosystems. The 494-acre space is a tangled clot of tropical fauna and dark mangroves, all interconnected by sandy trails and wooden boardwalks and surrounded by miles of pale ocean.

Activities

Cycling & In-Line Skating
Skating or cycling the strip along Ocean Dr in South Beach is pure Miami; also try the Rickenbacker Causeway to Key Biscayne.

DecoBike   CYCLING
(305-532-9494; www.decobike.com; 30 min/1hr/2hr/4hr/1-day rental $4/6/10/18/24) Flat, architecturally rich Miami Beach and Miami are best accessed via bicycle, and the

🏃 City Walk
Art-Deco Magic

START ART DECO WELCOME CENTER
END EDISON HOTEL
LENGTH 1-2 MILES; 30 MINUTES

There are excellent walking tours available for the Art Deco Historic District – both guided and self-guided – but if you just want to hit the highlights, follow this quick and easy path.

Start at the ❶ **Art Deco Welcome Center** (p457) at the corner of Ocean Dr and 12th St, and head inside for a taste of deco style. Next, go north on Ocean Dr. Between 12th and 14th Sts, you'll see three classic examples of deco hotels: the ❷ **Leslie**, with classic 'eyebrows' and a typically boxy shape; the ❸ **Carlyle**, which was featured in the film *The Birdcage;* and the graceful ❹ **Cardozo Hotel**, with sleek, rounded edges. At 14th St, peek inside ❺ **Winter Haven** to see its fabulous terrazzo floors.

Turn left and head along 14th St to Washington Ave, and turn left again to find the ❻ **US Post Office** at 13th St. Step inside to admire the domed ceiling and marble stamp tables, and try whispering into the domed ceiling. Two blocks down on your left is the ❼ **11th St Diner** (p466), a gleaming aluminum deco-style Pullman car where you can also stop for lunch. At 10th St, you'll find the ❽ **Wolfsonian-FIU** (p457), an excellent museum with many deco-era treasures, and across the street is the beautifully restored ❾ **Hotel Astor**.

Turn left on 8th St and head east to Collins Ave. On the corner, you'll see ❿ **The Hotel** – originally the Tiffany Hotel and still topped by a deco-style neon spire bearing that name. Continue to Ocean Dr and turn right to see the ⓫ **Colony Hotel** and its famous neon sign, then double back to find the 1935 ⓬ **Edison Hotel**, a creation of deco legend Henry Hohauser, half a block past 9th St.

easiest way of finding a bicycle is this excellent bike-sharing program.

Fritz's Skate, Bike & Surf   SKATING
(Map p460; ☑ 305-532-1954; www.fritzsmiamibeach. com; 1620 Washington Ave; bike & skate rentals per hour/day/week $10/24/69; ⊙ 10am-9pm Mon-Sat, to 8pm Sun) Sports equipment rentals and free in-line skate lessons (10:30am Sunday).

Water Sports

Blue Moon Outdoor Center   WATER SPORTS
(Map p458; ☑ 305-957-3040; http://bluemoonoutdoor.com; 3400 NE 163rd St; kayaks per 90min/3hr $23/41; ⊙ 9am-7:30pm Mon-Fri, 8am-8pm Sat & Sun) The official concessionaire for outdoor rentals in Miami area state parks.

Sailboards Miami   WATER SPORTS
(Map p458; ☑ 305-892-8992; www.sailboardsmiami. com; 1 Rickenbacker Causeway; ⊙ 10am-6pm Mon-Wed & Fri-Sun) The waters off Key Biscayne are perfect for windsurfing, kayaking and kiteboarding; get your gear and lessons here.

☞ Tours

Miami Design
Preservation League   WALKING
(Map p460; ☑ 305-672-2014; www.mdpl.org; 1001 Ocean Dr; guided tours adult/student $25/20; ⊙ 10:30am daily & 6:30pm Thu) Learn about art deco and its icons on a 90-minute walking tour departing from the Art Deco Welcome Center.

History Miami Tours   WALKING, CYCLING
(☑ 305-375-5792; www.historymiami.org/tours; tours $30-60) Historian extraordinaire Dr Paul George leads fascinating bike, boat, coach and walking tours, including those that focus on Stiltsville. Get the full menu online.

EcoAdventure Bike Tours   CYCLING
(☑ 305-365-3018; www.miamidade.gov/ecoadventures; tours from $28) The Dade County parks system leads excellent bike tours through peaceful areas of Miami and Miami Beach, including along beaches, on Key Biscayne and into the Everglades.

★☆ Festivals & Events

Calle Ocho Festival   CULTURAL
(Carnaval Miami; www.carnavalmiami.com; ⊙ Mar) This massive street party in March is the culmination of Carnaval Miami, a 10-day celebration of Latin culture.

Winter Music Conference   MUSIC
(http://wintermusicconference.com; ⊙ Mar) This festival of dance music and electronica takes place every March.

Art Basel Miami Beach   ART
(www.artbaselmiamibeach.com; ⊙ Dec) An internationally known art show held each December.

🛏 Sleeping

Miami Beach is the well-hyped mecca for stylish boutique hotels in renovated art-deco buildings. For hotel parking, expect to pay $20 to $35 a night.

South Beach

Bed & Drinks   HOSTEL $
(Map p460; ☑ 786-230-1234; http://bedsndrinks. com; 1676 James Ave; dm/d from $25/149, private 6-person dm $157) This hostel pretty shamelessly plays to the sex-appeal-seeking crowd – check the name – but hey, it's by Lincoln Rd, so the placement works. The rooms are functional and the vibe is young international folk down to party, while the staff seems a bit indifferent.

★Hotel St Augustine   BOUTIQUE HOTEL $$
(Map p460; ☑ 305-532-0570; www.hotelstaugustine. com; 347 Washington Ave; r $152-289; P❋❀≋) Wood that's blonder than Barbie and a crisp-and-clean deco theme combine to create one of South Beach's most elegant yet stunningly modern sleeps. The familiar, warm service is the cherry on top for this hip-and-homey standout, although the soothing lighting and glass showers – that turn into personal steam rooms at the flick of a switch – are pretty appealing too.

Aqua Hotel   BOUTIQUE HOTEL $$
(Map p460; ☑ 305-538-4361; www.aquamiami. com; 1530 Collins Ave; r $133-180, ste from $200; P❋❀≋) A front desk made of shiny surfboard sets the mellow tone at this former motel – the old, family kind where the rooms are set around a pool. That old-school vibe barely survives under the soft glare of aqua spotlights and an alfresco lounging area. The sleekness of the rooms is offset by quirky furniture and deep-blue-sea bathrooms.

★The Standard   BOUTIQUE HOTEL $$$
(Map p458; ☑ 305-673-1717; www.standardhotels. com/miami; 40 Island Ave; r $180-300, ste $500-965; P❋❀≋) Look for the upside-down

'Standard' sign on the old Lido building on Belle Island (between South Beach and downtown Miami) and you'll find the Standard – which is anything but. This excellent boutique blends a bevy of spa services, hipster funk and South Beach sex, and the result is a '50s motel gone glam. There are organic wooden floors, raised white beds, and gossamer curtains, which open onto a courtyard of earthly delights, including a heated hammam (Turkish bath).

★ **Gale South Beach** HOTEL $$$
(Map p460; 305-673-0199; http://galehotel.com; 1690 Collins Ave; r $160-300; P✳️🛜❄️) The Gale's exterior is an admirable re-creation of classic boxy deco aesthetic expanded to the grand dimensions of a modern SoBe super resort. This blend of classic and haute South Beach carries on indoors, where you'll find bright rooms with clean colors and sharp lines and a retro-chic vibe inspired by the mid-Century Modern movement.

★ **Pelican Hotel** BOUTIQUE HOTEL $$$
(Map p460; 305-673-3373; www.pelicanhotel.com; 826 Ocean Dr; r $198-350, ste $400-850; ✳️🛜) The owners of Diesel jeans are the minds behind this mad experiment: 30 themed rooms that come off like a fantasy-suite hotel dipped in hip. From the cowboy-hipster chic of 'High Corral, OK Chaparral' to the jungly electric tiger stripes of 'Me Tarzan, You Vain,' all the rooms are completely different fun and even come with their own 'suggested soundtrack.'

Northern Miami Beach

Freehand Miami BOUTIQUE HOTEL $$
(Map p458; 305-531-2727; http://thefreehand.com; 2727 Indian Creek Dr; dm $28-49, r $160-214; ✳️🛜❄️) The Freehand is the brilliant re-imagining of the old Indian Creek Hotel, a classic of the Miami Beach scene. Rooms are comfortably minimalist, with just the right amount of local artwork and wooden tones to strike a nice balance between warm funky and cool hip. Dorms serve the hostel crowd, and the on-site Broken Shaker (p468) is one of the best bars in town.

Coral Gables

Hotel St Michel HOTEL $$
(Map p458; 305-444-1666; www.hotelstmichel.com; 162 Alcazar Ave; r $124-225; P✳️🛜) You could conceivably think you're in Europe in

this vaulted place at Coral Gables, with inlaid floors, old-world charm and just 28 rooms.

 Eating

Florida's most international city has an international-level food scene.

South Beach

Walking up Ocean Ave, you'll find a veritable gauntlet of restaurants taking over the patios and sidewalks of almost every hotel facing the beach, all hawking lunch specials and happy-hour deals. Competition is fierce, which means you can eat inexpensively. Stroll till you find something that suits, anywhere between 5th St and 14th Pl.

Puerto Sagua CUBAN $
(Map p460; 305-673-1115; 700 Collins Ave; mains $6-20; 7:30am-2am) Pull up to the counter for authentic, tasty and inexpensive *ropa vieja* (shredded beef), black beans and *arroz con pollo* (rice with chicken) – plus some of the best Cuban coffee in town – at this beloved Cuban diner.

11th St Diner DINER $
(Map p460; 305-534-6373; www.eleventhstreetdiner.com; 1065 Washington Ave; mains $9-18; 24hr except midnight-7am Wed) This deco diner housed inside a gleaming Pullman train car sees round-the-clock activity and is especially popular with people staggering home from clubs.

★ **Tap Tap** HAITIAN $$
(Map p460; 305-672-2898; www.taptapmiamibeach.com; 819 5th St; mains $9-20; noon-9pm) In this tropi-psychedelic Haitian eatery, you dine under bright murals of Papa Legba, enjoying cuisine that's a happy marriage of West Africa, France and the Caribbean: try spicy pumpkin soup, curried goat and *mayi moulen,* a signature side of cornmeal.

★ **Pubbelly** FUSION $$
(Map p460; 305-532-7555; www.pubbellyboys.com/miami/pubbelly; 1418 20th Street; mains $11-26; 6pm-midnight Tue-Thu & Sun, to 1am Fri & Sat) Pubbelly's dining genre is hard to pinpoint. It skews between Asian, North American and Latin American, gleaning the best from all cuisines. Examples? Try duck and scallion dumplings, or the mouth-watering udon 'carbonara' with pork belly, poached eggs and parmesan. Hand-crafted cocktails wash down the dishes a treat.

Oolite
MODERN AMERICAN $$$

(Map p460; ☎ 305-907-5535; www.ooliterestaurant. com; 1661 Pennsylvania Ave; mains $20-49; ⊗4-11pm Wed-Thu, to midnight Fri & Sat, 11am-11pm Sun) Oolite has all the elements of a trendy, twenty-teens Miami Beach hot spot: a James Beard–nominated chef; gluten-free menu that focuses on local sourcing and health-conscious ingredients; a weird name. But it's also very good; a tapenade of citrus, swordfish and peppers does a hot dance on the tongue, while guava curry goat is a revelation.

Downtown Miami

Bali Cafe
INDONESIAN $

(Map p458; ☎ 305-358-5751; 109 NE 2nd Ave; mains $6-14; ⊗11am-4pm daily, 6-10pm Mon-Fri; ☑) It's odd to think of the clean flavors of sushi and the bright richness of Indonesian cuisine coming together in harmony, but they're happily married in this tropical hole-in-the-wall. Have some spicy tuna rolls for an appetizer, then follow up with *soto betawi* (beef soup cooked with coconut milk, ginger and shallots).

★NIU Kitchen
SPANISH $$

(Map p458; ☎ 786-542-5070; http://niukitchen. com; 134 NE 2nd Ave; mains $14-22; ⊗noon-3:30pm Mon-Fri, 6-10pm Sun-Thu, to 11pm Fri & Sat, 1-4pm Sat & Sun; ☑) NIU is a small living-room-sized restaurant consistently full of impossibly hip people eating impossibly good contemporary Catalan cuisine. Rarely have we had cuisine that's so compellingly different, from a poached egg with truffled potato foam to manchego and scallop pasta. Wash it all down with good wine and order multiple dishes to share.

Little Havana

★Exquisito Restaurant
CUBAN $

(Map p458; ☎ 305-643-0227; www.elexquisito-miami.com; 1510 SW 8th St; mains $7-13; ⊗7am-11pm) For great Cuban cuisine in the heart of Little Havana, this place is exquisite (ha ha). The roast pork has a tangy citrus kick and the *ropa vieja* is wonderfully rich and filling. Even standard sides like beans and rice and roasted plantains are executed with a little more care and tastiness. Prices are a steal.

Versailles
CUBAN $$

(Map p458; ☎ 305-444-0240; www.versailles-restaurant.com; 3555 SW 8th St; mains $5-26; ⊗8am-1am Mon-Thu, to 2:30am Fri, to 3:30am Sat, 9am-1am Sun) Versailles (ver-sigh-yay) is an institution, one of the mainstays of Miami's Cuban gastronomic scene. Try the ground beef in a gratin sauce or chicken breast cooked in creamy garlic sauce. Older Cubans and Miami's Latin political elite still love coming here, so you've got a real chance to rub elbows with a who's who of Miami's most prominent Latin citizens.

Design District & Wynwood

Chef Creole
HAITIAN $

(Map p458; ☎ 305-754-2223; http://chefcreole. com; 200 NW 54th St; mains $7-20; ⊗11am-11pm Mon-Sat) When you need Caribbean food on the cheap, head to the edge of Little Haiti and this excellent take-out shack. Order up fried conch, oxtail or fish, ladle rice and beans on the side, and you'll be full for a week. Enjoy the food on nearby picnic benches while Haitian music blasts out of tinny speakers – as island an experience as they come.

LATIN AMERICAN SPICE IN MIAMI

Thanks to its immigrant heritage, Miami is legendary for its authentic Cuban, Haitian, Brazilian and other Latin American cuisines. Cuban food is a mix of Caribbean, African and Latin American influences, and the fertile cross-pollination of these traditions has given rise to endlessly creative, tasty gourmet fusions, sometimes dubbed 'nuevo Latino,' 'nouvelle Floridian' or 'Floribbean' cuisine.

For a good introduction to Cuban food, sidle up to a Cuban *loncheria* (snack bar) and order a *pan cubano:* a buttered, grilled baguette stuffed with ham, roast pork, cheese, mustard and pickles. For dinner, order the classic *ropa vieja:* shredded flank steak cooked in tomatoes and peppers, and accompanied by fried plantains, black beans and yellow rice.

Other treats to look for include Haitian *griots* (marinated fried pork), Jamaican jerk chicken, Brazilian BBQ, Central American *gallo pinto* (red beans and rice) and *batidos* (a milky, refreshing Latin American fruit smoothie).

FLORIDA MIAMI

Enriqueta's
LATIN AMERICAN $

(Map p458; 305-573-4681; 186 NE 29th St; mains $5-8; 6am-4pm Mon-Fri, to 2pm Sat) Back in the day, Puerto Ricans, not installation artists, ruled Wynwood. Have a taste of those times in this perpetually packed roadhouse, where the Latin-diner ambience is as strong as the steaming shots of *cortadito* (Cuban-style coffee) served at the counter. Balance the local gallery fluff with a steak-and-potato-stick sandwich.

★ Blue Collar
AMERICAN $$

(Map p458; 305-756-0366; www.bluecollarmiami.com; 6730 Biscayne Blvd; mains $15-24; 11:30am-3:30pm Mon-Fri, 11am-3:30pm Sat & Sun, 6-10pm Sun-Thu, to 11pm Fri & Sat; P) It's not easy striking a balance between laid-back and delicious in a city like Miami, where even 'casual' eateries can feel like nightclubs, but Blue Collar has the formula nailed. Friendly staff serve all-American fare sexied the hell up, from crispy snapper to smoky ribs to a superlatively good cheeseburger. A well-curated veg board keeps noncarnivores happy.

🍷 Drinking & Nightlife

Miami truly comes alive at night. There is always something going on, and usually till the wee hours, with many bars staying open till 3am or 5am. For events calendars and gallery, bar and club reviews, check out www.cooljunkie.com and www.beachedmiami.com.

★ Wood Tavern
BAR

(Map p458; 305-748-2828; http://woodtavernmiami.com; 2531 NW 2nd Ave; 5pm-3am Tue-Sat, to 11pm Sun) Wood is a lot of things: local Miami kids who don't want a dive, but don't want the long lines and attitude of South Beach. Ergo: a cozy front bar, an outdoor space that includes picnic benches, a wooden stage complete with bleachers and giant Jenga game, and an attached art gallery with rotating exhibits.

★ Room
BAR

(Map p460; 305-531-6061; www.theotheroom.com; 100 Collins Ave; 7pm-5am) This dark, atmospheric boutique beer bar in SoBe is a gem: hip and sexy as hell but with a low-key attitude. Per the name, it's small and gets crowded.

★ Broken Shaker
BAR

(Map p458; 786-325-8974; 2727 Indian Creek Dr; 6pm-3am Mon-Fri, 2pm-3am Sat & Sun) Craft cocktails are having their moment in Miami, and if mixology is in the spotlight, you can bet Broken Shaker is sharing the glare. Expert bartenders run this spot, located in the back of the Freehand Miami hotel (p466), which takes up one closet-sized indoor niche and a sprawling outdoor courtyard of excellent drinks and beautiful people.

★ Blackbird Ordinary
BAR

(Map p458; 305-671-3307; www.blackbirdordinary.com; 729 SW 1st Ave; 3pm-5am Mon-Fri, 5pm-5am Sat & Sun) The Ordinary is almost that...well, no. It isn't ordinary at all – this is an excellent bar, with great cocktails (the London Sparrow, with gin, cayenne, lemon juice and passion fruit, goes down well) and an enormous courtyard. But it is 'ordinary' in the sense that it's a come-as-you-are joint that eschews judgment for easy camaraderie.

Kill Your Idol
BAR

(Map p460; 305-672-1852; http://killyouridol.com; 222 Española Way; 8pm-5am) This self-conscious dive aims snooty condescension at South Beach's celebrity scene with one hand (see: the name of the place) while sipping Pabst Blue Ribbon with the other. Precocious? But it does have sweet postmodern art, graffiti and undeniably cute hipsters.

Ball & Chain
LIVE MUSIC

(Map p458; www.ballandchainmiami.com; 1513 SW 8th Street; noon-midnight, to 3am Thu-Sat, 2-10pm Sun) The Ball & Chain has survived several incarnations over the years. Back in 1935, when 8th St was more Jewish than Latino, it was the sort of jazz joint Billie Holiday would croon in. That iteration closed in 1957, but the new Ball & Chain is still dedicated to music and good times – specifically, Latin music and tropical cocktails.

Bardot
CLUB

(Map p458; 305-576-5570; www.bardotmiami.com; 3456 N Miami Ave; 8pm-3am Tue & Wed, to 5am Thu-Sat) You really should see the interior of Bardot before you leave the city. It's all sexy French vintage posters and furniture seemingly plucked from a private club that serves millionaires by day, and becomes a scene of decadent excess by night. The entrance looks to be on N Miami Ave, but it's actually in a parking lot behind the building.

Hoy Como Ayer   LIVE MUSIC
(Map p458; ☑ 305-541-2631; www.hoycomoayer. us; 2212 SW 8th St; ⊘ 8:30pm-4am Thu-Sat) This Cuban hot spot – with authentic music, unstylish wood paneling and a small dance floor – is enhanced by cigar smoke and Havana transplants. Stop in nightly for *son*, *boleros* and modern Cuban beats.

☆ Entertainment

Cosmopolitan Miami attracts its fair share of creative types and wealthy patrons, and as such, has long been the seat of a thriving arts scene.

Colony Theater   PERFORMING ARTS
(Map p460; ☑ 305-674-1040; www.colonytheatre miamibeach.com; 1040 Lincoln Rd) Everything – from off-Broadway productions to ballet and movies – plays in this renovated 1934 art-deco showpiece.

Fillmore Miami Beach   PERFORMING ARTS
(Map p460; ☑ 305-673-7300; www.fillmoremb. com; 1700 Washington Ave) Miami Beach's premier showcase for Broadway shows and headliners.

🛍 Shopping

Browse for one-of-a-kind and designer items at the South Beach boutiques around Collins Ave between 6th and 9th Sts and along Lincoln Rd mall. For unique items, try Little Havana and the Design District.

Books & Books   BOOKS
(Map p460; ☑ 305-532-3222; www.booksand books.com; 927 Lincoln Rd; ⊘ 10am-11pm Sun-Thu, to midnight Fri & Sat) Best indie bookstore in South Florida; the original location is in Coral Gables at 265 Aragon Ave.

GO! Shop   ARTS, CRAFTS
(Map p458; ☑ 305-576-8205; http://thego-shop. com; 2516 NW 2nd Ave; ⊘ noon-8pm Thu-Sat) If you fancy the art at the Wynwood Walls (p462), make sure to pop into the GO! shop, located within the street-art complex. Original artwork, prints and other arts accoutrements are presented on a rotating basis; the stuff for sale is either produced by or related to the works created by the current crop of Wynwood Walls artists.

❶ Information

DANGERS & ANNOYANCES

Miami has a few areas considered dangerous at night: Little Haiti, stretches of the Miami river-front and Biscayne Blvd, and areas below 5th St in South Beach. In Downtown, use caution near the Greyhound station and shantytowns around causeways, bridges and overpasses.

EMERGENCY

Beach Patrol (☑ 305-673-7714) Lifeguards and police provide life-saving services and security in Miami Beach.

INTERNET RESOURCES

Art Circuits (www.artcircuits.com) Insider info on art events; neighborhood-by-neighborhood gallery maps.

Miami Beach 411 (www.miamibeach411.com) A great general guide for Miami Beach visitors.

Short Order (http://blogs.miaminewtimes. com/shortorder) The best local food blog.

MEDIA

Miami Herald (www.miamiherald.com) The city's major English-language daily.

Miami New Times (www.miaminewtimes.com) Edgy, alternative weekly.

MEDICAL SERVICES

Mount Sinai Medical Center (☑ 305-674-2121, emergency room 305-674-2200; www. msmc.com; 4300 Alton Rd) The area's best emergency room.

TOURIST INFORMATION

Greater Miami & the Beaches Convention & Visitors Bureau (Map p458; ☑ 305-539-3000; www.miamiandbeaches.com; 701 Brickell Ave, 27th fl; ⊘ 8:30am-6pm Mon-Fri) Located in an oddly intimidating high-rise building.

Miami Beach Chamber of Commerce (Map p460; ☑ 305-674-1300; www.miamibeach-chamber.com; 1920 Meridian Ave; ⊘ 9am-5pm Mon-Fri) Tourism and events information related to Miami Beach.

❶ Getting There & Away

Miami International Airport (MIA; Map p458; ☑ 305-876-7000; www.miami-airport.com; 2100 NW 42nd Ave) is about 6 miles west of downtown and is accessible by **SuperShuttle** (☑ 305-871-8210; www.supershuttle.com), which costs about $21 to South Beach.

Greyhound (Map p458; ☎ 800-231-2222; www.greyhound.com) serves all the major cities in Florida with three stations in Miami; check its website to see which location is best for you.

Amtrak (☎ 305-835-1222, 800-872-7245; www.amtrak.com; 8303 NW 37th Ave) has a main Miami terminal. The **Tri-Rail** (☎ 800-874-7245; www.tri-rail.com) commuter system serves Miami (with a free transfer to Miami's transit system) and MIA, Fort Lauderdale and its airport, and West Palm Beach and its airport ($11.55 round-trip).

ℹ Getting Around

Metro-Dade Transit (☎ 305-891-3131; www.miamidade.gov/transit/routes.asp; tickets $2) runs the local Metrobus and Metrorail ($2), as well as the free Metromover monorail serving downtown.

Fort Lauderdale

Spring breakers grow into suit-clad executives who still want to party in a yacht, and that's an apt analogy for a sizable chunk of Fort Lauderdale, a town once known for spring-break bacchanals that is now more recognized as an enclave of wealth and pleasure boats. Much of the tropically broiled gentry live amid a wonderfully scenic series of canals and palm fronds, but it's not all money and outboard motors here. This is a popular LGBTIQ destination that boasts a thriving arts scene, good eating, and immigrants from across Latin America and the Caribbean. Plus the beach is lovely, as always.

◉ Sights & Activities

Fort Lauderdale Beach & Promenade   BEACH
(P 🚻 🐕) Fort Lauderdale's promenade – a wide, brick, palm-tree-dotted pathway swooping along the beach and A1A – is a magnet for runners, in-line skaters, walkers and cyclists. The white-sand beach is one of the nation's cleanest and best, stretching 7 miles to Lauderdale-by-the-Sea, and there are dedicated family-, gay- and dog-friendly sections. There are pay parking lots up and down the beach.

NSU Art Museum Fort Lauderdale MUSEUM
(http://nsuartmuseum.org; 1 E Las Olas Blvd; adult/child/student $12/free/8; ⊙11am-5pm Tue-Sat, to 8pm Thu, noon-5pm Sun) A curvaceous Florida standout known for its William Glackens collection (among Glackens fans) and its exciting exhibitions (among everyone else).

Riverwalk & Las Olas Riverfront WATERFRONT
(www.goriverwalk.com) Curving along the New River, the meandering **Riverwalk** (www.goriverwalk.com) runs from Stranahan House to the Broward Center for the Performing Arts. Host to culinary tastings and other events, the walk connects a number of sights, restaurants and shops. **Las Olas Riverfront** (cnr SW 1st Ave & Las Olas Blvd) is basically a giant alfresco shopping mall with stores, restaurants and live entertainment nightly; it's also the place to catch many river cruises.

Hugh Taylor Birch State Recreation Area   PARK
(☎ 954-564-4521; www.floridastateparks.org/park/Hugh-Taylor-Birch; 3109 E Sunrise Blvd; per vehicle/bike $6/2; ⊙8am-sunset) This lusciously tropical park contains one of the last significant maritime hammocks in Broward County. There are mangroves and a freshwater lagoon system (great for birding) and several endangered plants and animals (including the golden leather fern and gopher tortoise). You can fish, picnic, stroll the short Coastal Hammock Trail or cycle the 1.9-mile park drive.

Museum of Discovery & Science MUSEUM
(☎ 954-467-6637; www.mods.org; 401 SW 2nd St; adult/child $14/12; ⊙10am-5pm Mon-Sat, noon-6pm Sun; 🎫) A 52ft kinetic-energy sculpture greets you, and fun exhibits include Gizmo City and Runways to Rockets – where it actually *is* rocket science. Plus there's an Everglades exhibit and IMAX theater.

Bonnet House   HISTORIC BUILDING
(☎ 954-563-5393; www.bonnethouse.org; 900 N Birch Rd; adult/child $20/16, grounds only $10; ⊙9am-4pm Tue-Sun) This pretty plantation-style property was once the home of artists and collectors Frederic and Evelyn Bartlett. Wandering the 35 acres of lush, subtropical gardens, you might just spot the resident Brazilian squirrel monkeys. The art-filled house is open to guided tours only.

Carrie B   BOAT TOUR
(☎ 954-642-1601; www.carriebcruises.com; 440 N New River Dr E; tours adult/child $23/13; ⊙tours 11am, 1pm & 3pm, closed Tue & Wed May-Oct) Hop aboard this replica 19th-century riverboat for a narrated 90-minute 'lifestyles of the rich and famous' tour of the ginormous mansions along the Intracoastal and New River.

Water Taxi WATER TAXI
(954-467-6677; www.watertaxi.com; all-day pass
adult/child $26/12) For a waterborne trolley
experience, hop on the water taxi, the drivers of which offer a lively narration as they
ply Fort Lauderdale's canals and waterways
from Oakland Park Boulevard to the Riverwalk Arts District. Other routes head down
the coast to Hollywood. Check online to buy
tickets and for boarding locations.

Broward BCycle BICYCLE HIRE
(754-200-5672; https://broward.bcycle.com;
first 30 min/additional 30 min $5/5) Flat Fort
Lauderdale is an easy town to traverse via
bicycle, or BCycle as the case may be. Broward County–operated bicycle-sharing stations can be found throughout town, and
provide easy access to two -wheeled exploration. Maximum daily charge is $50.

🛏 Sleeping

The area from Rio Mar St in the south to
Vistamar St in the north, and from Hwy A1A
in the east to Bayshore Dr in the west, offers
the highest concentration of accommodations in all price ranges. Check out the list of
super-small lodgings at www.sunny.org/ssl.

★ **Island Sands Inn** B&B $$
(954-990-6499; www.islandsandsinn.com; 2409
NE 7th Ave, Wilton Manors; r $129-209; P✸🛜☒)
It's hard to say whether it's the ultrathick
beach towels, the luxurious bed and bed-
ding, the thoughtful attention to detail (tis-
sues, bath products, minibar, microwave) or
the utterly unpretentious *ease* of the place
that makes Island Sands Inn so comfortable.
Certainly your charming hosts, Mike and
Jim, unobtrusively ensure that you get the
best from your stay.

Sea Club Resort MOTEL $$
(954-564-3211; www.seaclubresort.com; 619 Fort
Lauderdale Beach Blvd; r from $150; P✸🛜☒)
After extensive remodeling this funky beachfront motel, which looks to all intents and
purposes as if a spaceship has landed beach-
side, now sports fashion-forward rooms with
plum-colored accents, new carpets and even
plump pillowtop mattresses. With ocean
views, free beach towels and chairs, and a
resident parrot named Touki, it's unique.

★ **Pillars** B&B $$$
(954-467-9639; www.pillarshotel.com; 111 N
Birch Rd; r $205-569; P✸🛜☒) From the harp
in the sitting area to the private balconies

and the intimate prearranged dinners for
two, this tiny boutique B&B radiates hushed
good taste. It's a block from the beach, fac-
ing one of the best sunsets in town.

🍴 Eating

★ **Gran Forno** ITALIAN $
(954-467-2244; http://gran-forno.com; 1235 E
Las Olas Blvd; mains $6-12; ⏱7am-6pm) The best
lunch spot in downtown Fort Lauderdale is
this delightfully old-school Milanese-style
bakery and cafe: warm crusty pastries, bub-
bling pizzas, and fat golden loaves of ciabatta,
sliced and stuffed with ham, roast peppers,
pesto and other delicacies.

11th Street Annex AMERICAN $
(954-767-8306; www.twouglysisters.com; 14 SW
11th St; lunch $9; ⏱11:30am-2pm Mon-Fri, to 3pm
first Sat of the month; 🐾) In this off-the-beaten-
path peach cottage, the 'two ugly sisters'
serve whatever strikes their fancy: perhaps
brie mac 'n' cheese, chicken confit and sour
cream chocolate cake. Most of the vegetables
are grown from the cottage's garden, and
there's always a vegetarian option on the
menu. It's located a mile south of E Las Olas
Blvd, just off S Andrews Ave.

Lester's Diner DINER $
(954-525-5641; http://lestersdiner.com; 250 W
State Rd 84; mains $4-17; ⏱24hr; 🐾) Hailed en-
dearingly as a greasy spoon, campy Lester's
Diner has been keeping folks happy since
the late 1960s. Everyone makes their way
here at some point, from business types on
cell phones, to clubbers and blue-haired la-
dies with third husbands, to travel writers
needing pancakes at 4am.

★ **Green Bar & Kitchen** VEGAN $$
(954-533-7507; www.greenbarkitchen.com; 1075
SE 17th St; mains $8-14; ⏱11am-9pm Mon-Sat,
to 3pm Sun; 🐾) Discover bright flavors and
innovative dishes at this cult vegan eatery.
Instead of pasta-layered lasagna, slithers of
zucchini are layered with macadamia ricotta
and sun-dried tomatoes. Almond milk re-
places dairy in cold-pressed fruit smoothies,
and the delectable cashew cup gives Reese's
a run for its money.

Rustic Inn SEAFOOD $$
(954-584-1637; www.rusticinn.com; 4331
Ravenswood Rd; mains $9.50-30; ⏱11:30am-
10:45pm Mon-Sat, noon-9:30pm Sun) Hungry
locals at this messy, noisy crab house use
wooden mallets at long, newspaper-covered

GAY & LESBIAN FORT LAUDERDALE

Sure, Miami's South Beach is a mecca for gay travelers, but Fort Lauderdale has long been nipping at the high heels of its southern neighbor. For information on local gay life, visit www.gayftlauderdale.com. Other resources that cover South Florida include the glossy weekly *Hot Spots* (www.hotspotsmagazine.com), the insanely comprehensive www.jumponmarkslist.com, and www.sunny.org/glbt.

tables to get at the Dungeness crab, blue crab and golden crab drenched in garlic.

★**Casa D'Angelo** ITALIAN $$$
(☑ 954-564-1234; http://casa-d-angelo.com; 1201 N Federal Hwy; mains $25-50; ⊘ 5:30-10:30pm) Chef Angelo Elia presides over an impressive kitchen specializing in Tuscan and southern Italian dishes, many handed down by his mother. Seasonality and quality translate into intense flavors and delightful textures; the sunburst taste of just-ripe tomatoes, peppery arugula, silken sea bass and surprisingly spicy cinnamon gelato. The restaurant stocks one of the finest wine lists in the state.

🍷 Drinking & Entertainment

Bars generally stay open until 4am on weekends and 2am during the week. The Himmarshee area is the town's nightlife focus on weekends, when it resembles a scene from the Capital in *The Hunger Games*.

★**BREW Urban Cafe Next Door** CAFE
(☑ 954-357-3934; 537 NW 1st Ave; ⊘ 7am-7pm; 🛜) Despite an awkward, unwieldy name, Brew is the coolest thing going in Fort Lauderdale: a kick-ass cafe located in a weird, semiabandoned studio space filled with bookshelves. It looks like a British lord's library that got lost in an '80s warehouse party. Bonus: the coffee is good too.

★**Stache** COCKTAIL BAR
(☑ 954-449-1044; http://stacheftl.com; 109 SW 2nd Ave; ⊘ 7am-4am Wed-Fri, 9am-6pm & 8pm-4am Sat, 9am-3pm Sun, 7am-6pm Mon & Tue) Stache is a sexy 1920s drinking den serving crafted cocktails and rocking a crossover classic rock/funk/soul/R&B blend. At weekends there's live music, dancing and bur-

lesque. Dress up; this is where the cool cats come to play. Serves coffee during the day.

Laser Wolf BAR
(☑ 954-667-9373; www.laserwolf.com; 901 Progresso Dr, Suite 101; ⊘ 6pm-2am Mon-Thu, to 3am Fri, 8pm-3am Sat) We don't want to call Laser Wolf sophisticated, but its extensive booze menu and pop-art styling definitely attracts Fort Lauderdale's cerebral set. But they're a cerebral set that *loves* to party, so if this wolf is sophisticated, it knows how to let its hair down.

ℹ Information

For local information, head to the **visitor bureau** (☑ 954-765-4466; www.sunny.org; 101 NE 3rd Ave, Suite 100; ⊘ 8:30-5pm Mon-Fri).

ℹ Getting There & Around

The **Fort Lauderdale-Hollywood International Airport** (FLL; ☑ 954-359-1210; www.broward.org/airport; 320 Terminal Dr) is served by more than 35 airlines, some with nonstop flights from Europe. A taxi from the airport to downtown costs around $20.

The **Greyhound station** (☑ 954-764-6551; www.greyhound.com; 515 NE 3rd St) is four blocks from Broward Central Terminal, with multiple daily services. The **train station** (200 SW 21st Tce) serves **Amtrak** (☑ 800-872-7245; www.amtrak.com; 200 SW 21st Tce), and the **Tri-Rail** (☑ 954-783-6030; www.tri-rail.com; 6151 N Andrews Ave) has services to Miami and Palm Beach.

Hail a **Sun Trolley** (www.suntrolley.com; single fare/day pass $1/3) for rides between downtown, the beach, Las Olas and the Riverfront.

Palm Beach & Around

Palm Beach isn't all yachts and mansions – but just about. This is where railroad baron Henry Flagler built his winter retreat, and it's also home to Donald Trump's **Mar-a-Lago** (1100 S Ocean Blvd). In other words, if you're looking for middle-class tourism or Florida kitsch, keep driving. Contact the Palm Beach County **Convention & Visitor Bureau** (☑ 561-233-3000; www.palmbeachfl.com; 1555 Palm Beach Lakes Blvd; ⊘ 8:30am-5:30pm Mon-Fri) in West Palm Beach for area information and maps.

Palm Beach

About 30 miles north of Boca Raton are Palm Beach and West Palm Beach. The two towns have flip-flopped the traditional coastal hierarchy: Palm Beach, the beach town, is more upscale, while West Palm Beach on the mainland is younger and livelier.

Palm Beach is an enclave of the ultra-wealthy, especially during its winter 'social season,' so the main tourist activities involve gawking at oceanfront mansions and window-shopping the boutiques along the aptly named **Worth Avenue** (www.worth-avenue .com); to access the lives of the 1% on foot, trek the **Palm Beach Lake Trail** (Royal Palm Way, at the Intracoastal Waterway). You can also visit one of the country's most fascinating museums, the resplendent **Flagler Museum** (☑561-655-2833; www.flaglermuseum.us; 1 Whitehall Way; adult/child $18/10; ⏱10am-5pm Tue-Sat, noon-5pm Sun), housed in the railroad magnate's 1902 winter estate, Whitehall Mansion. The elaborate 55-room palace is an evocative immersion in Gilded Age opulence.

Flagler's opulent oceanfront 1896 hotel, the **Breakers** (☑888-273-2537; www.thebreakers. com; 1 S County Rd; r $349-590, ste $650-2050; P✳@⏺☎✉☀), is a superluxurious world unto itself, modeled after Rome's Villa Medici. It encompasses two golf courses, 10 tennis courts, a three-pool Mediterranean beach club and a trove of restaurants.

For a low-end treat, kick it Formica-style with an egg cream and a low-cal platter at the lunch counter in **Green's Pharmacy** (☑561-832-4443; 151 N County Rd; mains $4-11; ⏱8am-6pm Mon-Fri, to 4pm Sat). If you fancy something, well, fancier, but reasonably priced, try the Modern American fare cooked by James Beard–nominee Clay Conley at **Būccan** (☑561-833-3450; www. buccanpalmbeach.com; 350 S County Rd; small plates $4.50-36; ⏱4pm-midnight Mon-Thu, 5pm-1am Sat, to 10pm Sun).

West Palm Beach

Henry Flagler initially developed West Palm Beach as a working-class community to support Palm Beach, and indeed, West Palm today works harder, plays harder and is simply cooler and more relaxed. It's a groovy place to explore.

Florida's largest museum, the **Norton Museum of Art** (☑561-832-5196; www.norton. org; 1451 S Olive Ave; adult/child $12/5; ⏱10am-5pm Tue-Sat, to 9pm Thu, 11am-5pm Sun) houses an enormous collection of American and European modern masters and Impressionists, along with a large Buddha head presiding over an impressive Asian art collection. If

you like that, you'll love the outdoor **Ann Norton Sculpture Garden** (☑561-832-5328; www.ansg.org; 253 Barcelona Rd; adult/child $10/5; ⏱10am-4pm Wed-Sun). This serene collection of sculptures sprinkled among verdant gardens is a real West Palm gem.

If you have children, take them to **Lion Country Safari** (☑561-793-1084; www.lion-countrysafari.com; 2003 Lion Country Safari Rd; adult/child $31.50/23; ⏱9:30am-5:30pm; 🚗), the country's first cageless drive-through safari, where around 900 creatures roam freely around 500 acres.

Book a room at **Grandview Gardens** (☑561-833-9023; www.grandview-gardens.com; 1608 Lake Ave; r $129-215; P✳⏺☎✉) and you'll feel like a local in no time. Hidden in a tropical garden on Howard Park, the house is a period 1925 structure typical of the historic neighborhood and it sits opposite the Armory Art Center, so is perfect for longer stays for the arts-inclined.

Much of the action centers around **City-Place** (☑561-366-1000; www.cityplace.com; 700 S Rosemary Ave; ⏱10am-10pm Mon-Sat, noon-6pm Sun), a European-village-style outdoor mall with splashing fountains and a slew of dining and entertainment options. Clematis St also has several worthy bars, live-music clubs and restaurants, and every Thursday **Clematis by Night** (wpb.org/clematis-by-night; ⏱6-9:30pm Thu) hosts friendly outdoor concerts. If you're hungry, **Curbside Gourmet** (☑561-371-6565; http://curbsidegourmet.com; 2000 S Dixie Hwy) is Palm Beach's first mobile food truck dedicated to bringing good, seasonal staples to resident gourmands; they tweet their location @curbsidegourmet (or give them a call).

The Everglades

South Florida is often conflated with beauty, but her most magnificent edges reside far away from models and lounges and white-sand beaches. The real glory of this region lays in the slow trickle of freshwater percolating over a sawgrass prairie, before winding its way into an alligator- and otterrich current that snakes over mudflats and sedge basins into the turquoise explosion of Florida Bay. This is the Everglades, and it is a wilderness like no other.

Contrary to what you may have heard, the Everglades isn't a swamp. Or at least, it's not *only* a swamp. It's most accurately characterized as a wet prairie – grasslands that happen to be flooded most of the year. Nor is it stagnant. In the wet season, a horizon-wide river creeps ever so slowly beneath the rustling saw grass and around the subtly raised cypress and hardwood hammocks toward the ocean.

The scenery here is slow and timeless, which is why we feel exploring the Everglades by foot, bicycle, canoe and kayak (or camping) is more satisfying than by noisy, vibrating airboat. There is an incredible variety of wonderful creatures to see within this unique subtropical wilderness, and there are accessible entrances that, at the cost of a few hours, get you easily into the Everglades' soft heart.

The Everglades has two seasons: the summer wet season and the winter dry season. Winter – from December to April – is the prime time to visit: the weather is mild and pleasant, and the wildlife is out in abundance. In summer – May through October – it's stiflingly hot, humid and buggy, with frequent afternoon thunderstorms. In addition, as water sources spread out, so the animals disperse.

Everglades National Park

While the Everglades have a history dating back to prehistoric times, the park wasn't founded until 1947. It's considered the most endangered national park in the USA, but the Comprehensive Everglades Restoration Plan (www.evergladesplan.org) has been enacted to undo some of the damage done by draining and development.

The park has three main entrances and areas: in the south along Rte 9336 through Homestead and Florida City to Ernest Coe Visitor Center and, at road's end, Flamingo; along the Tamiami Trail/Hwy 41 in the north to Shark Valley; and on the Gulf Coast near Everglades City.

The main park entry points have visitor centers where you can get maps, camping permits and ranger information. You only need to pay the entrance fee (per car/pedestrian $10/5 for seven days) once to access all points.

Even in winter it's almost impossible to avoid mosquitoes, but they're ferocious in summer: bring *strong* repellent. Alligators are also prevalent. As obvious as it sounds, never, ever feed them: it's illegal and a sure way to provoke attacks. Four types of poisonous snakes call the Everglades home;

avoid all snakes, and wear long, thick socks and lace-up boots.

⊙ Activities

Based in Key Largo, Garl's Coastal Kayaking (p477) is an excellent outfitter that can arrange paddling tours of the Everglades backcountry.

Royal Palm Area   WALKING
(☑ 305-242-7700; Hwy 9336) Two trails, the Anhinga and Gumbo Limbo, take all of an hour to walk and put you face to face with a panoply of Everglades wildlife. Gators sun on the shoreline, anhinga spear their prey and wading birds stalk haughtily through the reeds. Come at night for a ranger walk on the boardwalk and shine a flashlight into the water to see one of the coolest sights of your life: the glittering eyes of dozens of alligators prowling the waterways.

Shark Valley   TOUR
(☑ 305-221-8776; www.nps.gov/ever/planyourvisit/svdirections.htm; 36000 SW 8th St, GPS N 25°45'27.60, W 80°46'01.01; car/cyclist $10/5; ⊙ 9:15am-5:15pm; ℗ ⋒) ⌀ One of the best places to dip your toe into the Everglades (figuratively speaking) is Shark Valley, where you can take an excellent two-hour tram tour (☑ 305-221-8455; www.sharkvalleytramtours.com; adult/child under 12yr/senior $22/19/12.75; ⊙ departures 9:30am, 11am, 2pm, 4pm May-Dec, 9am-4pm Jan-Apr every hour on the hour) along a 15-mile asphalt trail and see copious amounts of alligators in the winter months. Tours are narrated by knowledgeable park rangers who give a fascinating overview of the Everglades. Bicycles can be rented at the entrance for $7.50 per hour. Bring water.

Ernest Coe Visitor Center   WALKING, CANOEING
(☑ 305-242-7700; www.nps.gov/ever; State Rd 9336; ⊙ 9am-5pm, from 8am Dec-Apr) The main visitor center for the southern portion of the park has excellent, museum-quality exhibits and tons of activity info: the road accesses numerous short trails and lots of top-drawer canoeing opportunities. Call for a schedule of fun ranger-led programs, such as the two-hour 'slough slog.'

Flamingo Visitor Center   HIKING, CANOEING
(☑ 239-695-3101; ⊙ marina 7am-7pm, from 6am Sat & Sun) From Royal Palm, Hwy 9336 cuts through the belly of the park for 38 miles until it reaches the isolated Flamingo Visitor

A KINDER, GENTLER WILDERNESS ENCOUNTER

As you explore Florida's outdoors and encounter its wildlife, keep in mind the following guidelines.

Airboats and swamp buggies For exploring wetlands, airboats are better than big-wheeled buggies, but nonmotorized (and silent) canoes and kayaks are least damaging and disruptive.

Wild dolphins Captive dolphins are typically rescued animals already acclimated to humans. However, federal law makes it illegal to feed, pursue or touch wild dolphins in the ocean.

Manatee swims When swimming near manatees, a federally protected endangered species, look but don't touch. 'Passive observation' is the standard.

Feeding wild animals In a word, don't. Acclimating wild animals to humans usually leads to the animal's death, whether because of accidents or aggression.

Sea-turtle nesting sites It's a federal crime to approach nesting sea turtles or hatchling runs. Observe beach warning signs. If you encounter nesting turtles, keep your distance and no flash photos.

Coral-reef etiquette Never touch the coral reef. It's that simple. Coral polyps are living organisms. Touching or breaking coral creates openings for infection and disease.

Center, which has maps of canoeing and hiking trails. Call ahead about the status of facilities: the former Flamingo Lodge was wiped out by hurricanes in 2005. Flamingo Marina (☑ 239-695-3101; ⊙ store 7am-5:30pm Mon-Fri, from 6am Sat & Sun) has reopened and offers backcountry boat tours and kayak/canoe rentals for self-guided trips along the coast.

Gulf Coast Visitor Center BOATING
(☑ 239-695-2591; http://evergladesnationalpark-boattoursgulfcoast.com; 815 Oyster Bar Lane, off Hwy 29; per day canoe/single kayak/tandem kayak $24/45/55; ⊙ 9am-4:30pm mid-Apr–mid-Nov, 8am-4:30pm mid-Nov–mid-Apr; ⊞) ⊘ Those with more time should also consider visiting the northwestern edge of the Everglades, where the mangroves and waterways of the 10,000 Islands offer incredible canoeing and kayaking opportunities, and great boat tours with a chance to spot dolphins. The visitor center is next to the marina, with rentals (from $13 per hour) and various guided boat trips (from $25). Everglades City also has other private tour operators who can get you camping in the 10,000 Islands.

🛏 Sleeping

Everglades National Park has two developed campgrounds, both of which have water, toilets and grills. The best are the first-come, first-served sites at Long Pine Key (☑ 305-242-7745; www.nps.gov/ever/plan yourvisit/frontcamp; per campsite $16), just west

of Royal Palm Visitor Center; reserve ahead for campsites at Flamingo (☑ 877-444-6777; www.nps.gov/ever/planyourvisit/frontcamp; per campsite $30), which have cold-water showers and electricity. Backcountry camping (☑ 239-695-2945, 239-695-3311; www.nps.gov/ever/planyourvisit/backcamp; permit $10, plus per person per night $2) is throughout the park and includes beach sites, ground sites and chickees (covered wooden platforms above the water). A permit from the visitor center is required.

ℹ Getting There & Around

The largest subtropical wilderness in the continental USA is easily accessible from Miami. The Glades, which comprise the 80 southernmost miles of Florida, are bound by the Atlantic Ocean to the east and the Gulf of Mexico to the west. The Tamiami Trail (US Hwy 41) goes east–west, parallel to the more northern (and less interesting) Alligator Alley (I-75).

You need a car to properly enter the Everglades and once you're in, wearing a good pair of walking boots is essential to penetrate the interior. Having a canoe or kayak helps as well; these can be rented from outfits inside and outside of the park, or else you can seek out guided canoe and kayak tours. Bicycles are well suited to the flat roads of Everglades National Park, particularly in the area between Ernest Coe and Flamingo Point, but they're useless off the highway. In addition, the road shoulders in the park are dangerously small.

Around the Everglades

Coming from Miami, the gateway town of Homestead on the east side of the park can make a good base, especially if you're headed for the Keys.

Biscayne National Park

Just south of Miami (and east of Homestead), this national park is only 5% land. The 95% that's water is **Biscayne National Underwater Park** (☑305-230-1100; www.nps.gov/bisc), containing a portion of the world's third-largest coral reef, where manatees, dolphins and sea turtles highlight a vibrant, diverse ecosystem. Get general park information from **Dante Fascell Visitor Center** (☑305-230-1144; www.nps.gov/bisc; 9700 SW 328th St; ☉9am-5pm, from 10am May-Oct). The park offers canoe/kayak rentals, snorkel and dive trips, and popular three-hour glass-bottom boat tours; all require reservations.

Homestead & Florida City

Homestead and Florida City don't look like much, but they have some true Everglades highlights. Don't miss **Robert Is Here** (☑305-246-1592; www.robertishere.com; 19200 SW 344th St, Homestead; mains $3-8; ☉8am-7pm) – a kitschy Old Florida institution with a petting zoo, live music and crazy-good milk shakes.

The Homestead–Florida City area has no shortage of chain motels along Krome Ave. If you don't mind hostel living, seriously consider the **Everglades International Hostel** (☑305-248-1122; www.evergladeshostel.com; 20 SW 2nd Ave, Florida City; camping $18, dm $28, d $61-75, ste $125-225; ▣❋❀❧). Rooms are good value, the vibe is very friendly, but the back gardens – wow. It's a fantasia of natural delights, and the hostel conducts some of the best Everglades tours around, including 'wet walks' – slogs through the bog, as it were.

Tamiami Trail

The Tamiami Trail/Hwy 41 starts in Miami and beelines to Naples along the north edge of Everglades National Park. Just past the entrance to the Everglades' Shark Valley is **Miccosukee Village** (☑877-242-6464, 305-222-4600; www.miccosukee.com; Mile 70, Hwy 41; adult/child/5yr & under $12/6/free; ☉9am-5pm;

▣❧), an informative, entertaining open-air museum showcasing Miccosukee culture.

About 20 miles west of Shark Valley, you reach the **Oasis Visitor Center** (☑941-695-1201; www.nps.gov/bicy; 52105 Tamiami Trail E; ☉9am-4:30pm Mon-Fri; ❧) for 1139-sq-mile **Big Cypress National Preserve** (☑239-695-4758; www.nps.gov/bicy; 33000 Tamiami Trail E; ☉8:30am-4:30pm; ▣❧) ✿. Good exhibits and short trails bring the region's ecology to life, though the adventurous might consider tackling a portion of the **Florida National Scenic Trail** (☑850-523-8501; www.fs.usda.gov/fnst); 31 miles cut through Big Cypress.

Half a mile east of the visitor center, drop into the **Big Cypress Gallery** (☑239-695-2428; www.clydebutcher.com; Tamiami Trail; swamp walk 1½hr adult/child $50/35, 45min adult/child $35/25; ☉10am-5pm; ▣) ✿, displaying Clyde Butcher's work; his large-scale B&W landscape photographs spotlight the region's unusual beauty.

The tiny town of **Ochopee** is home to the country's smallest post office. If that's not enough to make you pull over, then stop into the eccentric **Skunk Ape Research Headquarters** (☑239-695-2275; www.skunkape.info; 40904 Tamiami Trail E; $5; ☉7am-7pm, 'zoo' closes around 4pm; ▣), dedicated to tracking Bigfoot's legendary if stinky Everglades kin. It's goofy but sincere. Based out of Skunk Ape HQ, **Everglades Adventure Tours** (EAT; ☑800-504-6554; www.evergladesadventuretours.com; tours from $89) offers knowledgeable swamp hikes and trips being poled around in a canoe or skiff.

Finally, just east of Ochopee is the quintessential 1950s-style swamp shack, **Joannie's Blue Crab Cafe** (☑239-695-2682; 39395 Tamiami Trail E; mains $9-17; ☉10:30am-5pm, closed seasonally, call to confirm), with open rafters, colorful shellacked picnic tables and a swamp dinner of gator nuggets and fritters.

Everglades City

This small town at the edge of the park makes a good base for exploring the **10,000 Islands** region. With large renovated rooms, **Everglades City Motel** (☑239-695-4224; www.evergladescitymotel.com; 310 Collier Ave; r from $89; ▣❋❀) is exceptionally good value, and the fantastically friendly staff can hook you up with any kind of tour. The same can be said for the **Ivey House Bed & Breakfast** (☑877-567-0679; www.iveyhouse.com; 107 Camellia St; inn r $99-179; ▣❋❀). Choose between basic lodge accommodations or somewhat sprucer inn rooms, then book nature trips with the on-site **Everglades Adventures** (NACT; ☑877-567-0679; www.ever gladesadventures.com; Ivey House Bed & Breakfast, 107 Camellia St; tours from $89, rentals from $35; ☺Nov–mid-Apr) 🏄. Ask about room/tour packages. For dinner, the **Camellia Street Grill** (☑239-695-2003; 202 Camellia St; mains $10-20; ☺noon-9pm) is as fancy as Everglades City gets, although the American Southern and Mediterranean food is down to earth.

Florida Keys

Laid out like a string of wacky green pearls on an asphalt string, the islands of the Florida Keys are where people go when they want to drop off the face of the earth and still have a good time doing so. Henry Flagler connected the Keys to the mainland in 1912; until then, this 126-mile-long series of islands was a pirate's den of smuggling, ship salvaging and fishing. These days there's still plenty of fishing, along with tourism, boozing, diving, snorkeling and living the most laid-back of lives.

The islands are typically divided into the Upper Keys (Key Largo to Islamorada), Middle Keys and Lower Keys (from Little Duck Key). Yet far from petering out, they crescendo at highway's end, reaching their grand finale in Key West – the Keys' gloriously unkempt, bawdy, freak-loving exclamation point.

Many addresses in the Keys are noted by their proximity to mile markers (indicated as MM), which start at MM 126 in Florida City and count down to MM 0 in Key West. They also might indicate whether they're 'oceanside' (the south side of the highway) or 'bayside' (which is north).

The **Florida Keys & Key West Visitors Bureau** (☑800-352-5397; www.fla-keys.com) has information; also check www.keysnews.com.

Key Largo

No, really, you're in the islands!

You'd be forgiven for not thinking so, though. As you drive south of Homestead, the land fringes into clumps of mangrove forest and you can't even see the water from the highway, then – bam – you're in Islamorada and water is everywhere.

Key Largo has long been romanticized in movies and song, so it can be a shock to arrive and find...no Bogart, no Bacall, no love-sick Sade. Yes, Key Largo is underwhelming, a sleepy island and town with middling views. That is, if all you do is stick to the highway and keep your head above water. On the side roads you can find some of those legendary island idiosyncracies, and dive underwater for the most amazing coral reef in the continental US.

For maps and brochures, visit the **chamber of commerce** (☑800-822-1088; www.key largochamber.org; MM 106 bayside; ☺9am-6pm), located in a yellow building just past Seashell World (not to be confused with the *other* yellow visitor center at 10624 that makes reservations and works on commission).

🏃 Activities

John Pennekamp Coral Reef State Park   PARK
(☑305-451-6300; www.pennekamppark.com; MM 102.6 oceanside; car/motorcycle/cyclist or pedestrian $8/4/2; ☺8am-sunset, aquarium to 5pm; 🅿) 🏄
The USA's first underwater park, Pennekamp contains the third-largest coral barrier reef in the world. Your options for seeing the reef are many: take a 2½-hour **glass-bottom boat tour** (☑305-451-6300; http://pennekamppark.com/glassbottom-boat; adult/child $24/17; ☺9:15am, 12:15pm & 3:15pm) on a thoroughly modern 65ft catamaran. Dive in with a **snorkeling trip** (☑305-451-6300; http://pennekamppark.com/snorkeling-tours; adult/child $30/25; ☺9am-4:30pm) or two-tank **diving trip** (☑305-451-6322; http://pennekamppark.com/scuba-tours; six-person charter $400); half-day trips leave twice daily, usually around 9am and 1pm. Or go DIY and rent a canoe, kayak (per hour single/double $12/17) or stand-up paddle board (per hour $25) and journey through a 3-mile network of water trails.

Garl's Coastal Kayaking   ECOTOUR
(☑305-393-3223; www.garlscoastalkayaking.com; tours adult half-/full day $125/150, child $95/125, kayak single/double $30/45) 🏄 Garl's is an excellent ecotour operator that gets customers into the Everglades backcountry and mangrove islets of Florida Bay via kayak and canoe. It also provides reasonable equipment rentals.

🛏 Sleeping

In addition to luxe resorts, Key Largo has loads of bright, cheery motels and camping.

John Pennekamp
Coral Reef State Park
CAMPGROUND **$**

(☎ 800-326-3521; www.pennekamppark.com; 102601 Overseas Hwy; tent & RV sites $38.50; **P**) Sleep with the – er, *near* the fishes at one of the 47 coral-reef-adjacent sites here. Camping's popular; reserve well in advance.

Hilton Key Largo Resort
HOTEL **$$**

(☎ 888-871-3437, 305-852-5553; www.keylargo resort.com; MM 102 bayside; r/ste from $179/240; **P** 🛜 ☎ ☀) This Hilton has a ton of character. Folks just seem to get all laid-back when lounging in clean, designer rooms outfitted in blues, greens and (why not?) blue-green. The grounds are enormous and include an artificial waterfall-fed pool and frontage to a rather large stretch of private white-sand beach. Book online for the best rates.

Largo Lodge
HOTEL **$$$**

(☎ 305-451-0424; www.largolodge.com; MM 102 bayside; cottages $375; **P**) These six lovely cottages with their own private beach are surrounded by palm trees, tropical flowers and lots of roaming birds. They've been appointed with sleek, modern furnishings and a Zen-esque sense of space and color design.

✗ Eating & Drinking

Key Largo Conch House
FUSION **$$**

(☎ 305-453-4844; www.keylargoconchhouse.com; MM 100.2 oceanside; lunch mains $8-16, dinner $13-30; ◷ 8am-10pm; **P** 🛜 ☀) Now *this* feels like the islands: conch architecture, tropical foliage, and crab and seafood dishes that ease you off the mainland.

Mrs Mac's Kitchen
AMERICAN **$$**

(☎ 305-451-3722; www.mrsmacskitchen.com; MM 99.4 bayside; breakfast & lunch $8-16, dinner $10-36; ◷ 7am-9:30pm Mon-Sat; **P** ☀) This cute roadside diner bedecked with rusty license plates serves classic highway food such as burgers and fish baskets. Look for a second location just half a mile south on the opposite side of the road.

Islamorada

Islamorada is actually a string of several islands, the epicenter of which is Upper Matecumbe Key. It's right around here that the view starts to open up, allowing you to fully appreciate the fact that you're surrounded by water. Several little nooks of beach are easily accessible, providing scenic rest stops. Housed in an old red caboose, the cham-ber of commerce (☎ 305-664-4503; www.isla moradachamber.com; MM 87 bayside; ◷ 9am-5pm Mon-Fri, to 4pm Sat, to 3pm Sun) has area information.

◉ Sights & Activities

Billed as 'the Sportfishing Capital of the World,' Islamorada is an angler's paradise. Indeed, most of its highlights involve getting on or in the sea.

★ Anne's Beach
BEACH

(MM 73.5 oceanside) Anne's is one of the best beaches in these parts. The small ribbon of sand opens upon a sky-bright stretch of tidal flats and a green tunnel of hammock and wetland. Nearby mudflats are a joy to get stuck in, and will be much loved by the kids.

Florida Keys
History of Diving Museum
MUSEUM

(☎ 305-664-9737; www.divingmuseum.org; MM 83; adult/child $12/6; ◷ 10am-5pm; **P** ☀) Don't miss this fantastically quirky collection of diving paraphernalia from around the world, including seemingly suicidal diving 'suits' and technology from the 19th century.

★ Robbie's Marina
MARINA

(☎ 305-664-8070; www.robbies.com; MM 77.5 bayside; kayak & SUP rentals $40-75; ◷ 9am-8pm; ☀) This marina/roadside attraction offers the buffet of boating options: fishing charters, Jet Skiing, party boats, ecotours, snorkeling trips, kayak rentals and more. Two historically significant offshore islands, Indian Key (☎ 305-664-2540; www.floridastateparks.org/indiankey; MM 78.5 oceanside; admission $2.50; ◷ 8am-sunset) and Lignumvitae Key (☎ 305-664-2540; www.florida stateparks.org/lignumvitaekey; admission/tour $2.50/2; ◷ 9am-5pm, tours 10am & 2pm Fri-Sun), are a paddle away for the moderately fit; access both via Robbie's. At a minimum, stop to feed the freakishly large tarpon from the dock ($3 per bucket, $1 to watch), and sift the flea market/tourist shop for tacky seaside trinkets.

🛏 Sleeping

Conch On Inn
MOTEL **$**

(☎ 305-852-9309; www.conchoninn.com; MM 89.5, 103 Caloosa St; apt $59-129; **P**) A simple motel popular with yearly snowbirds, Conch On Inn has basic rooms that are reliable, clean and comfortable.

Ragged Edge Resort
RESORT **$$**

(☎ 305-852-5389; www.ragged-edge.com; 243 Treasure Harbor Rd; apt $69-259; **P** ❄ 🛜 ☀) This low-key and popular efficiency and apartment complex, far from the maddening traffic jams, has 10 quiet units and friendly hosts. The larger studios have screened-in porches, and the entire vibe is happily comatose. There's no beach, but you can swim off the dock and at the pool.

Casa Morada HOTEL $$$
(☎ 305-664-0044; www.casamorada.com; 136 Madeira Rd, off MM 82.2; ste $359-659; P ❀ ☎ ☎) Come for a dash of South Beach sophistication mixed with laid-back Keys style. The slick bar is a great oceanside sunset perch.

✕ Eating

★ Midway Cafe CAFE $
(☎ 305-664-2622; http://midwaycafecoffeebar.com; 80499 Overseas Hwy; dishes $2-11; ⏰ 7am-3pm, to 2pm Sun; P ♦) Celebrate your Keys adventure with a friendly cup o' joe, a smoothie or a treat from the overflowing bakery case. The lovely folks who run this art-filled cafe roast their own beans and make destination-worthy baked goods.

The Beach Cafe at Morada Bay AMERICAN $$$
(☎ 305-664-0604; www.moradabay-restaurant.com; MM 81.6 bayside; mains $20-39; ⏰ 11:30am-10pm; P) Grab a table under a palm tree on the white-sand beach and sip a rum drink with your fresh seafood for a lovely, easy-going Caribbean experience. Don't miss the monthly full-moon party.

Marathon

Halfway between Key Largo and Key West, Marathon is the most sizable town; it's a good base and a hub for commercial fishing. Get local information at the **visitor center** (☎ 305-743-5417; www.floridakeysmarathon.com; MM 53.5 bayside; ⏰ 9am-5pm).

◉ Sights & Activities

Crane Point Museum MUSEUM
(☎ 305-743-9100; www.cranepoint.net; MM 50.5 bayside; adult/child $12.50/8.50; ⏰ 9am-5pm Mon-Sat, from noon Sun; P ♦) ✈ This is one of the nicest spots on the island to stop and smell the roses. And the pinelands. And the palm hammock – a sort of palm jungle (imagine walking under giant, organic Japanese fans) that only grows between MM 47 and MM 60. There's also Adderly House, a preserved example of a Bahamian immigrant cabin (which must have baked in summer) and 63 acres of green goodness to stomp through.

Turtle Hospital WILDLIFE RESERVE
(☎ 305-743-2552; www.theturtlehospital.org; 2396 Overseas Hwy; adult/child $18/9; ⏰ 9am-6pm; P ♦) ✈ Whether it is a victim of disease, boat-propeller strike, flipper entanglement with fishing lines or any other danger, an injured sea turtle in the Keys will hopefully end up in this motel-cum-sanctuary. We know we shouldn't anthropomorphize animals, but these turtles just seem so sweet. It's sad to see the injured and sick ones, but heartening to see them so well looked after. Tours are educational, fun and are offered on the hour from 9am until 4pm.

Pigeon Key
National Historic District ISLAND
(☎ 305-743-5999; www.pigeonkey.net; MM 47 oceanside; adult/child/under 5yr $12/9/free; ⏰ tours 10am, noon & 2pm) On the Marathon side of Seven Mile Bridge, this tiny key served as a camp for the workers who toiled to build the Overseas Hwy in the 1930s. You can tour the historic structures or just sun and snorkel on the beach. Reach it by ferry, included in admission, or walk or bike your way there on the **Old Seven Mile Bridge**, which is closed to traffic but serves as the 'World's Longest Fishing Bridge.'

Sombrero Beach BEACH
(Sombrero Beach Rd, off MM 50 oceanside; P ♦) This beautiful little white-sand beach has a playscape, shady picnic spots and big, clean bathrooms.

🛏 Sleeping & Eating

Siesta Motel MOTEL $
(☎ 305-743-5671; www.siestamotel.net; MM 51 oceanside; r $80-115; P ☎) Head here for one of the cheapest, cleanest flops in the Keys, located in a friendly cluster of cute Marathon homes – with great service, to boot.

★ Keys Fisheries SEAFOOD $$
(☎ 305-743-4353; www.keysfisheries.com; 3502 Louisa St; mains $7-22; ⏰ 11am-9pm; P ♦) Shoo the seagulls from your picnic table on the deck and dig in to fresh seafood in a down-and-dirty dockside atmosphere. The lobster Reuben is the stuff of legend.

Hurricane
AMERICAN $$

(☎305-743-2200; www.hurricaneblues.com; 4650 Overseas Hwy; mains $9-19; ⏰11am-midnight; 🅿🐾) As well as being a favorite Marathon bar, the Hurricane also serves an excellent menu of creative South Florida–inspired goodness, like snapper stuffed with crabmeat and conch sliders jerked in Caribbean seasoning.

Lower Keys

The Lower Keys (MM 46 to MM 0) are fierce bastions of conch culture in all its variety.

One of Florida's most acclaimed beaches – and certainly the best in the Keys for its shallow, warm water – is at **Bahia Honda State Park** (☎305-872-3210; www.bahiahondapark.com; MM 37; car/motorcycle/cyclist $5/4/2; ⏰8am-sunset; ♿), a 524-acre park with nature trails, ranger-led programs, water-sports rentals and some of the best coral reefs outside Key Largo.

Overnight camping at **Bahia Honda State Park** (☎800-326-3521; www.reserveamerica.com; MM 37, Bahia Honda Key; sites/cabins $38.50/122.50; 🅿) 🐾 is sublime; it'd be perfect except for the sandflies. There are also six popular waterfront cabins. Reserve far ahead for all. For a completely different experience, book one of the four cozily scrumptious rooms at **Deer Run Bed & Breakfast** (☎305-872-2015; www.deerrunfloridabb.com; 1997 Long Beach Dr, Big Pine Key, off MM 33 oceanside; r $275-460; 🅿📶🏊) 🐾. This state-certified green lodge and vegetarian B&B is a garden of quirky delights, and the owners are extremely helpful.

On Big Pine Key, stop in for a pizza, beer and ambience at **No Name Pub** (☎305-872-9115; www.nonamepub.com; N Watson Blvd, Big Pine Key, off MM 30.5 bayside; mains $7-18; ⏰11am-11pm; 🅿), right before the causeway that gets you to **No Name Key**. While you're there, staple a dollar bill to the wall to contribute to the collection of approximately $60,000 wallpapering the room.

Key West

Key West's funky, laid-back vibe has long attracted artists, renegades and free spirits. Part of that independent streak is rooted in Key West's geography: it's barely connected to the USA, and it's closer to Cuba than to the rest of the States. There's only one road in, and it's not on the way to anywhere. In other words, it's an easy place to do your own thing, which here can mean anything from piracy to smuggling to fishing to drinking to opening an art gallery. Whatever said thing may be, Key West only requires you have fun doing it.

⊙ Sights

Key West has more than its fair share of historic homes, buildings and districts (like the colorful Bahama Village); it's a walkable town that rewards exploring. Naturally, you'll snap a pic at the USA's much ballyhooed **Southernmost Point Marker**, even though it's not technically the southernmost point in the USA. (That distinction goes to a point about half a mile down the beach, but since it's part of a naval air station, it's hardly tourist friendly.)

★ **Mallory Square**
SQUARE

(♿) Sunset at Mallory Sq, at the end of Duval St, is a bizzaro attraction of the highest order. It takes all those energies, subcultures and oddities of Keys life – the hippies, the rednecks, the foreigners and the tourists – and focuses them into one torchlit, playfully edgy (but family-friendly) street party. Come for the jugglers, fire-eaters, sassy acrobats and tightrope-walking dogs, and stay for the after-dark madness.

Duval Street
AREA

Key West locals have a love–hate relationship with their island's most famous road. Duval, Old Town Key West's main drag, is a miracle mile of booze, tacky everything and awful behavior that still manages, somehow, to be fun. At the end of the night, the 'Duval Crawl' is one of the best pub crawls in the country.

Hemingway House
HOUSE

(☎305-294-1136; www.hemingwayhome.com; 907 Whitehead St; adult/child $13/6; ⏰9am-5pm) Ernest Hemingway lived in this Spanish Colonial house from 1931 to 1940 – to write, drink and fish, if not always in that order. Tours run every half-hour, and as you listen to docent-spun yarns of Papa, you'll see his studio, his unusual pool, and the descendants of his six-toed cats languishing in the sun, on furniture and pretty much wherever they feel like.

Florida Keys Eco-Discovery Center MUSEUM

(☎305-809-4750; http://eco-discovery.com/ecokw.html; 35 East Quay Rd; ⏰9am-4pm Tue-Sat; 🅿♿) 🐾 **FREE** This excellent nature center pulls together all the plants, animals and habitats that make up the Keys' unique ecosystem and presents them in fresh, accessible ways. A great place for kids and the big picture.

Key West Cemetery
CEMETERY

(www.friendsofthekeywestcemetery.com; cnr Margaret & Angela Sts; ⊗8:30am-4pm; 🚻) This dark, alluring Gothic labyrinth is in the center of town. Livening up the mausoleums are famous epitaphs like 'I told you I was sick.'

Key West Butterfly & Nature Conservatory
ANIMAL SANCTUARY

(📞305-296-2988; www.keywestbutterfly.com; 1316 Duval St; adult/4-12yr $12/8.50; ⊗9am-5pm; 🚻) Even if you have only the faintest interest in butterflies, you'll find yourself entranced by the sheer quantity flittering around you here.

🏃 Activities

Seeing as how you're out in the middle of the ocean, getting out on or in the water is one of the top activities. Charters abound for everything from fishing to snorkeling to scuba diving, including dive trips to the **USS Vandenberg**, a 522ft transport ship sunk off the coast to create the world's second-largest artificial reef.

Fort Zachary Taylor
BEACH

(📞305-292-6713; www.floridastateparks.org/fort taylor; 601 Howard England Way; per car/pedestrian $6/2; ⊗8am-sunset) Key West has three city beaches, but they aren't special; most people head to Bahia Honda. That said, Fort Zachary Taylor has the best beach on Key West, with white sand, decent swimming and some near-shore snorkeling; it's great for sunsets and picnics.

Dive Key West
DIVING

(📞305-296-3823; www.divekeywest.com; 3128 N Roosevelt Blvd; snorkel/scuba from $60/75) Everything you need for wreck-diving trips, from equipment to charters.

Jolly Rover
CRUISE

(📞305-304-2235; www.schoonerjollyrover.com; cnr Greene & Elizabeth Sts, Schooner Wharf; cruise adult/child $45/25) Set sail on a pirate-esque schooner offering daytime and sunset cruises.

👉 Tours

Both the **Conch Tour Train** (📞888-916-8687; www.conchtourtrain.com; adult/child under 13yr/senior $30/free/27; ⊗tours 9am-4:30pm; 🚻) and **Old Town Trolley** (📞855-623-8289; www. trolleytours.com/key-west; adult/child under 13yr/

senior $30/free/27; ⊗tours 9am-4:30pm; 🚻) offer tours leaving from Mallory Sq. The train offers a 90-minute narrated tour in a breezy, open car, while the hop-on/hop-off trolley makes 12 stops around town.

Original Ghost Tours
TOUR

(📞305-294-9255; www.hauntedtours.com; adult/child $18/10; ⊗8pm & 9pm) Is your guesthouse haunted? Probably. Why should you fear Robert the Doll in East Martello? You're about to find out.

✨ Festivals & Events

Key West hosts a party every sunset, but residents don't need an excuse to go crazy.

Conch Republic Independence Celebration
CULTURAL

(www.conchrepublic.com; ⊗Aug) A 10-day tribute to Conch Independence, held every April; vie for (made-up) public offices and watch a drag queens footrace.

Fantasy Fest
CULTURAL

(www.fantasyfest.net; ⊗late Oct) Room rates get hiked to the hilt for this raucous, 10-day Halloween-meets-Carnivale event in late October.

🛏 Sleeping

Key West lodging is generally pretty expensive – especially in the wintertime and even *more* especially during special events, when room rates can triple. Book ahead, or you may well end up joining the long traffic jam headed back to the mainland. Rates can be considerably reduced if booked online.

Caribbean House
GUESTHOUSE $

(📞305-296-0999; www.caribbeanhousekw.com; 226 Petronia St; r from $95; 🅿❄@) In the heart of Bahama Village, rooms are tiny, but they're clean, cozy and cheery. Add free breakfast and welcoming hosts and you get a rare find in Key West: a bargain.

⭐Key West Bed & Breakfast
B&B $$

(📞305-296-7274; www.keywestbandb.com; 415 William St; r winter $89-265, summer $89-165; ❄🛜) Sunny, airy and full of artistic touches: hand-painted pottery here, a working loom there – is that a ship's masthead in the corner? There is also a range of rooms to fit every budget.

Key Lime Inn
HOTEL $$

(📞800-549-4430; www.historickeywestinns.com; 725 Truman Ave; r from $180; 🅿🛜🚲) These

GAY & LESBIAN KEY WEST

Gay and lesbian visitors can get information at the **Gay & Lesbian Community Center** (☏ 305-292-3223; www.glcckeywest.org; 513 Truman Ave). While you'll find the entire island extraordinarily welcoming, several bars and guesthouses cater specifically to a gay clientele. Toast your arrival in town at one of the following:

801 Bourbon Bar (☏ 305-294-4737; www.801bourbon.com; 801 Duval St; ⊙9am-4am) Where boys will be boys.

Aqua (☏ 305-294-0555; www.aquakeywest.com; 711 Duval St; ⊙3pm-2am) Caters to both gays and lesbians.

cozy cottages are scattered around a tropical hardwood backdrop. Inside, the blissfully cool rooms are greener than a jade mine, with wicker furniture and tiny flat-screen TVs to keep you from ever leaving.

★ **Tropical Inn**　　　BOUTIQUE HOTEL **$$$**
(☏ 888-651-6510; www.tropicalinn.com; 812 Duval St; r/ste from $200/375; ❄ 🐾 🎈) The Tropical Inn has excellent service and a host of individualized rooms spread out over a historic-home property. Each room comes decked out in bright pastels and shades of mango, lime and sea foam. A delicious breakfast is included and can be enjoyed in the jungly courtyard next to a lovely sunken pool. Two attached cottages offer romance and privacy for couples.

Mermaid & the Alligator　　GUESTHOUSE **$$$**
(☏ 305-294-1894; www.kwmermaid.com; 729 Truman Ave; r winter $298-468, summer $168-228; P ❄ @ 🛜 🏊) Book way ahead: with only nine rooms, this place's charm exceeds its capacity. It's chock a block with treasures collected from the owners' travels, giving it a worldly flair that's simultaneously European and Zen.

Silver Palms Inn　　　BOUTIQUE HOTEL **$$$**
(☏ 305-294-8700; www.silverpalmsinn.com; 830 Truman Ave; r from $220; P ❄ 🛜 🏊) 🐾 Royal blues, sweet teals, bright limes and lemon-yellow color schemes douse the interior of this boutique property, which also boasts bicycle rentals, a saltwater swimming pool and a green certification from the Florida Department of Environmental Protection. Overall, the Silver Palms offers more of

a modern, large-hotel vibe with a candy-colored dose of Keys tropics attitude.

🍴 Eating

You aren't technically allowed to leave the island without sampling the conch fritters – like hushpuppies, but made with conch – or the key lime pie, made with key limes, sweetened condensed milk, eggs and sugar on a Graham-cracker crust.

Café　　　　　　　VEGETARIAN **$**
(☏ 305-296 5515; www.thecafekw.com; 509 Southard St; mains $7-17; ⊙11am-10pm; 🌱) The Café is the only place in Key West that exclusively caters to herbivores (OK, it has one fish dish). By day, it's a cute, sunny, earthy-crunchy luncheonette; by night, with flickering votive candles and a classy main dish (grilled, blackened tofu and polenta cakes), it's a sultry-but-healthy dining destination.

Camille's　　　　　　　FUSION **$$**
(☏ 305-296-4811; www.camilleskeywest.com; 1202 Simonton St; breakfast & lunch dishes $4-13, dinner mains $17-26; ⊙8am-3pm & 6-10pm; 🌱) Ditch Duval St and dine with the locals at Camille's; this healthy and tasty neighborhood joint is where local families go for a casual meal. Its inventive menu ranges from French toast with Godiva liqueur to tasty chicken salad.

El Siboney　　　　　　CUBAN **$$**
(☏ 305-296-4184; www.elsiboneyrestaurant.com; 900 Catherine St; mains $8-17; ⊙11am-9:30pm) Key West is only 90 miles from Cuba, so this awesome rough-and-ready corner establishment is quite literally the closest you can get to real Cuban food in the US. Cash only.

Mo's Restaurant　　　　CARIBBEAN **$$**
(☏ 305-296-8955; 1116 White St; mains $6-17; ⊙11am-10pm Mon-Sat) If the phrase 'Caribbean home cooking' causes drool to form in the corners of your mouth, don't hesitate. The dishes are mainly Haitian, and they're delicious.

Blue Heaven　　　　　AMERICAN **$$$**
(☏ 305-296-8666; http://blueheavenkw.homestead.com; 729 Thomas St; dinner mains $17-35; ⊙8am-10:30pm; 🌱) One of the island's quirkiest venues (and it's a high bar), where you dine in an outdoor courtyard with a flock of chickens. Customers gladly wait, bemusedly, for Blue Heaven's well-executed, Southern-fried interpretation of Keys cuisine.

Café Solé
FRENCH $$$

(☎305-294-0230; www.cafesole.com; 1029 Southard St; dinner $25-34; ⏰5:30-10pm) Conch carpaccio with capers? Yellowtail fillet and foie gras? Oh yes. This locally and critically acclaimed venue is known for its cozy back-porch ambience and innovative menus, the result of a French-trained chef exploring island ingredients.

Drinking & Entertainment

Hopping (or staggering) from one bar to the next – also known as the 'Duval Crawl' (p480) – is a favorite pastime here in the Conch Republic, and there are plenty of options for your drinking pleasure.

★Green Parrot
BAR

(☎305-294-6133; www.greenparrot.com; 601 Whitehead St; ⏰10am-4am) This rogue's cantina has the longest tenure of any bar on the island (since 1890). It's a fabulous dive drawing a lively mix of locals and out-of-towners, with a century's worth of strange decor. Men, don't miss the urinal.

Captain Tony's Saloon
BAR

(☎305-294-1838; www.capttonyssaloon.com; 428 Greene St; ⏰10am-2am) This former icehouse, morgue and Hemingway haunt is built around the town's old hanging tree. The eclectic decor includes emancipated bras and signed dollar bills.

Porch
BAR

(☎305-517-6358; www.theporchkw.com; 429 Caroline St; ⏰11am-4am) Escape the Duval St frat-boy bars at the Porch, where knowledgeable bartenders dispense artisan beers. It sounds civilized, and almost is, by Key West standards.

Virgilio's
JAZZ

(www.virgilioskeywest.com; 524 Duval St; ⏰7pm-3am, to 4am Thu-Sat) Thank God for a little variety. This town needs a dark, candlelit martini lounge where you can chill to jazz and salsa. Enter on Appelrouth Lane.

ℹ Information

A great trip-planning resource is www.fla-keys.com/keywest. In town, get maps and brochures at **Key West Chamber of Commerce** (☎305-294-2587; www.keywestchamber.org; 510 Greene St; ⏰8:30am-6:30pm Mon-Sat, to 6pm Sun).

ℹ Getting There & Around

The easiest way to travel around Key West and the Keys is by car, though traffic along the one major route, US 1, can be maddening during the winter high season. **Greyhound** (☎305-296-9072; www.greyhound.com; 3535 S Roosevelt Blvd) serves the Keys along US Hwy 1 from downtown Miami.

You can fly into **Key West International Airport** (EYW; ☎305-296-5439; www.keywestinternationalairport.com; 3491 S Roosevelt Blvd) with frequent flights from major cities, most going through Miami. Or, take a fast catamaran from Fort Myers or Miami; call the **Key West Express** (☎888-539-2628; www.seakeywestexpress.com; adult/child/junior/senior return $149/40/86/139, one way $89/20/60/89) for schedules and fares; discounts apply for advance booking.

Within Key West, bicycles are the preferred mode of travel (rentals along Duval St run $10 to $25 per day). **City Transit** (☎305-809-3700; www.kwtransit.com; tickets $2) runs color-coded buses through downtown and the Lower Keys.

ATLANTIC COAST

Florida's Atlantic Coast isn't all beach volleyball, surfing and lazing in the sun. It offers travelers a remarkably well-rounded experience, with something for everyone from history buffs to thrill seekers to art-lovers.

Space Coast

The Space Coast's main claim to fame (other than being the setting for the iconic 1960s TV series *I Dream of Jeannie*) is being the real-life home to the Kennedy Space Center and its massive visitor complex. Cocoa Beach is also a magnet for surfers, with Florida's best waves.

⊙ Sights

★Merritt Island National Wildlife Refuge
WILDLIFE RESERVE

(☎321-861-5601; www.fws.gov/merrittisland; off FL-406; per vehicle Black Point Wildlife Dr $5; ⏰dawn-dusk) **FREE** This unspoiled 140,000-acre refuge is one of the country's best birding spots, especially from October to May. More endangered and threatened species of wildlife inhabit the swamps, marshes and hardwood hammocks here than at any other site in the continental US.

FLORIDA SPACE COAST

DRY TORTUGAS

Seventy miles west of the Keys in the middle of the Gulf, **Dry Tortugas National Park** (☎305-242-7700; www.nps.gov/drto; adult/15yr & under $5/free) is America's most inaccessible national park. Reachable only by boat or plane, it rewards your efforts to get there with amazing snorkeling, diving, bird-watching and stargazing.

Ponce de León christened the area Tortugas (tor-*too*-guzz) after the sea turtles he found here, and the 'Dry' part was added later to warn about the absence of fresh water on the island. But this is more than just a pretty cluster of islands with no drinking water. The never-completed Civil War–era **Fort Jefferson** provides a striking hexagonal centerpiece of red brick rising up from the emerald waters on **Garden Key**, meaning along with your bottled water, you should definitely bring your camera.

So how do you get there? **Yankee Freedom** (☎800-634-0939; www.drytortugas.com; Historic Seaport; adult/child $170/125) is a fast ferry that leaves from the north end of Grinnell St in Key West; the fare includes breakfast, a picnic lunch, snorkeling gear and tour of the fort. Or, you can hop on a **Key West Seaplane** (☎305-293-9300; www.keywest seaplanecharters.com; half-day trip adult/child 3-12yr $300/239) for a half-day or full-day trip. Whichever you choose, reserve at least a week ahead.

If you really want to enjoy the isolation, stay overnight at one of Garden Key's 13 campsites (per person $3). Reserve early through the park office, and bring everything you need, because once that boat leaves, you're on your own.

Kennedy Space Center Visitor Complex   MUSEUM

(☎321-449-4444; www.kennedyspacecenter.com; adult/child $50/40, parking $10; ⊙9am-6pm) Once a working space-flight facility, Kennedy Space Center is shifting from a living museum to a historical one since the end of NASA's space-shuttle program in 2011. Devote most of your day to the **Space Shuttle Atlantis** attraction, IMAX theaters and **Rocket Garden**, featuring replicas of classic rockets towering over the complex.

Hungry space enthusiasts can add on **Lunch with an Astronaut;** (☎866-737-5235; adult/child $30/16) or the **Shuttle Launch Simulator**, which reaches a top 'speed' of 17,500mph and feels just like a space-shuttle takeoff, which you can also do alongside an astronaut; among other experiences. Book in advance!

Canaveral National Seashore   PARK

(☎386-428-3384; www.nps.gov/cana; Merritt Island; car/bike $5/1; ⊙6am-6pm) This 24 miles of pristine, windswept beaches comprise the longest stretch of undeveloped beach on Florida's east coast.

🏃 Activities

Despite all the sunshine and shoreline, Florida is no *Endless Summer*. The water around Miami tends to stay flat, and much of the Gulf Coast is too protected to get much of a swell. But the 70 miles of beaches from New Smyrna to Sebastian Inlet are surfer central. Ten-time world-champion surfer Kelly Slater was born in Cocoa Beach, which remains the epicenter of the surf community. For the local scene and surf reports, visit **Florida Surfing** (www.floridasurfing.com) and **Surf Guru** (www.surfguru.com).

Ron Jon Surf Shop   WATER SPORTS

(☎321-799-8888; www.ronjonsurfshop.com; 4151 N Atlantic Ave, Cocoa Beach; ⊙24hr) This massive, 24-hour surfing mecca rents just about anything water-related, from fat-tired beach bikes ($10 daily) to surfboards ($20 daily).

Ron Jon Surf School   SURFING

(☎321-868-1980; www.cocoabeachsurfingschool. com; 160 E Cocoa Beach Causeway, Cocoa Beach; per hour $50-65; ⊙9am-5pm) The best surf school in Cocoa Beach for all ages and levels is the state's largest, run by ex-pro surfer and Kelly Slater coach Craig Carroll. Also offers kiteboarding lessons (intro package $375) and SUP river tours (from $65).

🛏 Sleeping

Charming Cocoa Beach has the most options, as well as the most chains.

Fawlty Towers   MOTEL $

(☎321-784-3870; www.fawltytowersresort.com; 100 E Cocoa Beach Causeway, Cocoa Beach; r $99-109;) After flirtations with being a nudist resort went limp, this motel returned to its gloriously garish and extremely pink roots: straightforward rooms with an unbeatable beachside location; quiet pool and BYOB tiki hut.

★ **Beach Place Guesthouses** APARTMENT **$$$**
(☑321-783-4045; www.beachplaceguesthouses. com; 1445 S Atlantic Ave, Cocoa Beach; ste $199-399; ☐P☐☐) A slice of heavenly relaxation in Cocoa Beach's partying beach scene, this laid-back collection of guesthouses in a residential neighborhood has roomy suites with hammocks and lovely hidden patios, all just steps from the dunes and beach.

✖ Eating

Simply Delicious CAFE **$**
(☑321-783-2012; 125 N Orlando Ave, Cocoa Beach; mains $7-15; ☉8am-3pm Tue-Sat, to 2pm Sun) In a darling little yellow house on the southbound stretch of A1A, this homey Americana place packs in locals for a scrumptious menu with unusually delicious delights like mahi-mahi Reuben sandwiches and malted waffles.

★ **Fat Snook** SEAFOOD **$$$**
(☑321-784-1190; www.thefatsnook.com; 2464 S Atlantic Ave, Cocoa Beach; mains $22-33; ☉5:30-10pm) Hidden inside an uninspired building, yet sporting cool, minimalist decor, tiny Fat Snook stands out as an oasis of fine cooking. There's a distinct air of farm-to-table snobbery here; once the food arrives, you won't care.

Crush Eleven MODERN AMERICAN **$$$**
(☑321-634-1100; www.crusheleven.com/; 11 Riverside Drive, Cocoa Village; mains $18-49; ☉5.30-9pm Mon-Sat, 11am-8.30 Sun) This newcomer in noticeably charming Cocoa Village bills itself as 'rustic urban fare'; indeed, you'll see rarities like wild boar, rabbit and beef cheeks on the menu, chased with curated craft beer and cocktails.

❶ Information

Space Coast Office of Tourism (☑321-433-4470; www.visitspacecoast.com; 430 Brevard Ave, Cocoa Village; ☉9am-5pm Mon-Fri) Next to Bank of America, one block south of the Village Playhouse.

❶ Getting There & Away

From Orlando take Hwy 528 east, which connects with Hwy A1A. **Greyhound** (www.

greyhound.com) has direct services from West Palm Beach to Titusville. **Vero Beach Shuttle** (☑772-834-1060; www.verobeachshuttle. com; Melbourne/Palm Beach/Orlando airport $95/130/175) provides shuttle service from area airports. **Space Coast Area Transit** (www. ridescat.com; fare $1.25) beach trolley (Route 9) combs up and down the beaches between Cocoa Beach and Port Canaveral.

Daytona Beach

With typical Floridian hype, Daytona Beach bills itself as 'The World's Most Famous Beach.' But its fame is less about quality than the size of the parties this expansive beach has witnessed during spring break, Speed-Weeks, and motorcycle events when half a million bikers roar into town. One Daytona title no one disputes is 'Birthplace of NAS-CAR,' which started here in 1947. Its origins go back as far as 1902 to drag races held on the beach's hard-packed sands.

◉ Sights & Activities

★ **Daytona International Speedway** RACETRACK
(☑800-748-7467; www.daytonainternational speedway.com; 1801 W International Speedway Blvd; tours $16-50) Impressive and imposing, the Holy Grail of raceways is fresh off a $400-million face-lift. Ticket prices for its diverse race schedule accelerate rapidly the bigger the race, headlined by the **Daytona 500** in February.

Three first-come, first-served tram tours take in the track, pits and behind-the-scenes areas. Real fanatics can indulge in the **Richard Petty Driving Experience** (☑800-237-3889; www.drivepetty.com), where you can either ride shotgun ($69 to $135) around the track or take a day to become the driver ($549 to $2199); check schedule online.

Cici & Hyatt Brown Museum of Art MUSEUM
(www.moas.org; 352 S Nova Rd; adult/child $10.95/4.95; ☉10am-5pm Mon-Sat, from 11am Sun) Part of the **Museum of Arts & Sciences** (MOAS; ☑386-255-0285; www.moas.org; 352 S Nova Rd; adult/child $12.95/6.95; ☉10am-5pm Tue-Sat, from 11am Sun) complex, this striking must-see new museum, designed to look like a Florida Cracker house, tells the story of Florida via the largest collection of Florida-themed oil and watercolor paintings in the world.

★Ponce de Leon Inlet Lighthouse & Museum LIGHTHOUSE
(✆386-761-1821; www.ponceinlet.org; 4931 S Peninsula Dr, Ponce Inlet; adult/child $5/1.50; ⊙10am-6pm Sep-May, to 9pm Aug-Sep) It's 203 steps up to the top of Florida's tallest lighthouse.

Daytona Beach BEACH
(per car $10; ⊙beach driving 8am-7pm May-Oct, sunrise-sunset Nov-Apr) This perfectly planar stretch of sand was once the city's raceway. You can still drive sections at a strictly enforced top speed of 10mph.

🛏 Sleeping & Eating

Daytona lodging is plentiful and spans all budgets and styles. Prices soar during events; book well ahead.

Tropical Manor RESORT $
(✆386-252-4920; www.tropicalmanor.com; 2237 S Atlantic Ave, Daytona Beach Shores; r $88-135; P✳🏠🏊) This beachfront property is vintage Florida, with motel rooms, efficiencies and cottages all blanketed in a frenzy of murals and bright pastels.

Dancing Avocado Kitchen CAFE $
(✆386-947-2022; www.dancingavocadokitchen.com; 110 S Beach St; mains $7.51-13.15; ⊙8am-4:05pm Tue-Sat; ✍) Fresh, healthful, eclectic sandwiches and wraps dominate the menu at this vegetarian-leaning cafe, but the signature Dancing Avocado Melt is tops.

Aunt Catfish's on the River SOUTHERN $$
(✆386-767-4768; www.auntcatfishontheriver.com; 4009 Halifax Dr, Port Orange; mains $8-27; ⊙11:30am-9pm Mon-Sat, from 9am Sun; P🚸) Southern-style seafood lolling in butter and Cajun-spice catfish – paired with cinnamon rolls, no less! – make this place insanely popular.

🍷 Drinking

Daytona Taproom BEER HALL
(310 Seabreeze Blvd; burgers $4-13; ⊙noon-2am Sun-Tue, to 3am Wed-Sat; 📶) A bright spot among the biker and beach-bum status quo, this 'burger joint with a drinking problem' has 50 taps of regional and national microbrews and deliciously juicy, thick and creative burgers, hand-cut fries, gourmet hot dogs and waffles.

ℹ Information

Daytona Beach Area Convention & Visitors Bureau (✆386-255-0415; www.daytonabeach.

com; 126 E Orange Ave; ⊙8:30am-5pm Mon-Fri) Reluctant tourist info; pickings are slim in the office.

ℹ Getting There & Around

Daytona Beach International Airport (✆386-248-8030; www.flydaytonafirst.com; 700 Catalina Dr) is just east of the Speedway, and the **Greyhound bus station** (✆386-255-7076; www.greyhound.com; 138 S Ridgewood Ave) is the starting point for services around Florida. **Votran** (✆386-756-7496; www.votran.org; adult/child under 7yr $1.75/free) runs buses and trolleys throughout the city.

St Augustine

The first this, the oldest that…St Augustine was founded by the Spanish in 1565, which means it's chock-full of age-related superlatives. Tourists flock here to stroll the ancient streets around the National Historic Landmark District, aka the oldest permanent settlement in the US.

At times St Augustine screams, 'Hey, everyone, look how quaint we are!' but it stops just short of feeling like a historic theme park because, well, the buildings and monuments are real – many of which were given a rejuvenating face-lift for the city's 450-year anniversary in 2015 – and the narrow, cafe-strewn lanes are genuinely charming. Walk the cobblestoned streets or stand where Juan Ponce de León landed in 1513, and the historical distance occasionally collapses into present-moment chills.

👁 Sights & Activities

The town's two Henry Flagler buildings shouldn't be missed.

★Lightner Museum MUSEUM
(✆904-824-2874; www.lightnermuseum.org; 75 King St; adult/child $10/5; ⊙9am-5pm) Flagler's former Hotel Alcazar is now home to this wonderful museum, with a little bit of everything, from ornate Gilded Age furnishings to collections of marbles and cigar-box labels.

★Hotel Ponce de León HISTORIC BUILDING
(✆904-823-3378; http://legacy.flagler.edu/pages/tours; 74 King St; tours adult/child $10/1; ⊙tours hourly 10am-3pm summer, 10am & 2pm during school year) This gorgeous former hotel was built in the 1880s and is now the world's most gorgeous dormitory, belonging to Flagler College. Take a guided tour – or at least step inside to gawk at the lobby for free.

★ Castillo de San Marcos
National Monument   FORT
(☎904-829-6506; www.nps.gov/casa; 1 S Castillo
Dr; adult/child under 15yr $10/free; ⊙8:45am-
5pm; ♿) The country's oldest masonry fort,
completed by the Spanish in 1695. Park
rangers lead programs hourly and shoot off
cannons most weekends.

Colonial Quarter   HISTORIC BUILDING
(☎904-342-2857; www.colonialquarter.com; 33 St
George St; adult/child $13/7; ⊙10am-5pm) See
how they did things back in the 18th century
at this re-creation of Spanish Colonial St Augustine, complete with tour guides demonstrating blacksmithing and gunsmithing on
the scheduled tours only (10:30am, noon,
1:30pm and 3pm). It's half price after 3pm.

Pirate & Treasure Museum   MUSEUM
(☎1-877-467-5863; www.thepiratemuseum.com;
12 S Castillo Dr; adult/child $13/7; ⊙10am-7pm;
♿) A mash-up of theme park and museum,
this celebration of all things pirate has real
historical treasures (and genuine gold) as
well as animatronic pirates, blasting cannons and a kid-friendly treasure hunt.

Fountain of Youth   HISTORIC SITE
(☎904-829-3168; www.fountainofyouthflorida.
com; 11 Magnolia Ave; adult/child $15/9; ⊙9am-
6pm) As the story goes, Spanish explorer Juan
Ponce de León came ashore here in 1513, and
he considered this freshwater stream the
possible legendary Fountain of Youth. Today,
this archaeological theme park is part classic roadside attraction, part textbook history,
newly madeover to include cannon-firing
demonstrations and reconstructions of both
the original settlement and the USA's first
mission.

Anastasia State Recreation Area   PARK
(☎904-461-2033; www.floridastateparks.org/anas
tasia; 1340 Hwy A1A; car/bike $8/2; ⊙8am-sunset)
Locals escape the tourist hordes here, with a
terrific beach, a campground (campsites $28)
and rentals for all kinds of water sports.

☞ Tours

St Augustine City Walks   WALKING TOUR
(☎904-825-0087; www.staugcitywalks.com; 4
Granada St; tours $15-68; ⊙9am-8:30pm) Avoid
the tourist trolleys and join extremely fun
walking tours of all kinds.

🛏 Sleeping

St Augustine is a popular weekend escape;
expect room rates to rise about 30% to 50%
on Friday and Saturday. Inexpensive motels
and chain hotels line San Marco Ave, near
where it meets US Hwy 1, and around I-95 at
SR-16. Two dozen atmospheric B&Bs can be
found at www.staugustineinns.com.

Pirate Haus Inn   HOSTEL $
(☎904-808-1999; www.piratehaus.com; 32 Treasury St; dm $25, r from $119; P✳🛜) Yar, if ye
don't be needing anything fancy, this family-
friendly European-style guesthouse/hostel
has an unbeatable location and includes a
pirate pancake breakfast.

★ At Journey's End   B&B $$
(☎904-829-0076; www.atjourneysend.com; 89
Cedar St; r $166-279; P✳🛜🐾) Free from the
granny-ish decor that haunts many St Augustine B&Bs, this pet-friendly, kid-friendly
and gay-friendly spot, run by affable hosts,
is outfitted in a chic mix of antiques, modern furniture and new two-person steam
showers.

Casa de Solana   B&B $$
(☎904-824-3555; www.casadesolana.com; 21
Aviles St; r $179-249; P🛜) Just off pedes-
trian-only Aviles St in the oldest part of
town, this utterly charming little inn remains faithful to its early-1800s period decor. Rooms-smallish, but price and location
equal great value.

Casa Monica   HISTORIC HOTEL $$$
(☎904-827-1888; www.casamonica.com; 95 Cor-
dova St; r $219-489, ste from $399; P✳🛜🐾) 🐾
Built in 1888, this is *the* luxe hotel in town,
with turrets and fountains adding to the
Spanish-Moorish castle atmosphere. Rooms
are richly appointed, with wrought-iron
beds and velvet headboards, while the newly
madeover restaurant and expanded lounge
are equally regal.

✕ Eating & Drinking

Kookaburra   CAFE
(☎904-209-9391; www.kookaburrashop.com; 24
Cathedral Pl; coffee $2.40-4.40; ⊙7:30am-9pm
Mon-Thu, to 10pm Fri & Sat, 8am-8pm Sun; 🛜)
🍃 Ethically sourced Australian-American
coffeehouse serving real Aussie meat pies
and the best coffee in the historic quarter.

★**Floridian** MODERN AMERICAN **$$**
(☑904-829-0655; www.thefloridianstaug.com;
39 Cordova St; mains $11-24; ☺11am-3pm Wed-
Mon, 5-9pm Mon-Thu, to 10pm Fri & Sat) Oozing
hipster-locavore earnestness, this vintage-
fabulous farm-to-table restaurant serves
whimsical neo-Southern creations in an oh-
so-cool dining room.

★**Collage** INTERNATIONAL **$$$**
(☑904-829-0055; www.collagestaug.com; 60
Hypolita St; mains $28-43; ☺5:30-9pm) Classy
and upscale, with a world-class kitchen and
service, this spot feels a world away from the
bustling touristy downtown. The seafood-
heavy menu wins raves for its subtle touch
with global flavors.

★**Ice Plant** BAR
(☑904-829-6553; www.iceplantbar.com; 110 Ribe-
ria St; ☺11:30am-2am Tue-Sat, to midnight Sun-
Mon; 🔊) The hottest spot in St Augustine
flaunts exposed concrete, raw brickwork
and soaring windows surrounding a vintage, dual-facing centerpiece bar all carved
out of a former ice factory. Here coolsters
imbibe in some of Florida's finest cocktails,
coalesced by overall-clad mixologists wield-
ing hand-cut ice; and excellent farm-to-table
fare (mains from $15 to $29).

It's attached to the new St Augustine Distillery, which offers free tours and tastings.

Scarlett O'Hara's PUB
(www.scarlettoharas.net; 70 Hypolita St;
☺11am-midnight Sun-Thu, to 2am Fri-Sat; 🔊) Good
luck grabbing a rocking chair: the porch of
this pine building is packed all day, every day.
Built in 1879, Scarlett's serves regulation pub
grub, but it's got the magic ingredients – hopping happy hour, live entertainment nightly,
hardworking staff, funky bar – that draw
folks like spirits to a séance.

ℹ **Information**

Visitor Information Center (☑904-825-1000;
www.FloridasHistoricCoast.com; 10 W Castillo
Dr; ☺8:30am-5:30pm) Hosts historical exhibits in addition a wealth of tourism information.

ℹ **Getting There & Around**

Northeast Florida Regional Airport (☑904-
209-0090; www.flynf.com; 4900 US Highway 1),
5 miles north of town, began receiving limited
commercial flights in 2014.

The **Greyhound bus station** (☑904-829-
6401; www.greyhound.com; 52 San Marcos Ave)
is just a few blocks north of the Visitor's Center.

Once you're in Old Town, you can get almost
everywhere on foot.

Jacksonville

Are we there yet? Have we left yet? It's hard
to tell, because Jacksonville sprawls out over
a whopping 840 sq miles, making it the
largest city by area in the continental US
(eclipsed only by Anchorage, AK). Jacksonville Beach, known locally as 'Jax Beach,' is
about 17 miles east of the city center and is
where you'll find white sand and most of the
action. For information, peruse www.visit-
jacksonville.com.

◉ **Sights & Activities**

Atlantic and Neptune are the best beaches
in the area, located 16 miles east of downtown. Don't miss the **Downtown Artwalk**
(www.jacksonvilleartwalk.com), when artists,
musicians, food trucks and pop-up galleries
take over 16 downtown blocks on the first
Wednesday of every month.

★**Cummer Museum of**
Art & Gardens MUSEUM
(www.cummer.org; 829 Riverside Ave; adult/
student $10/6; ☺10am-9pm Tue, to 4pm Wed-Sat,
noon-4pm Sun) Jacksonville's premier cultural
space has a genuinely excellent collection of
American and European paintings, Asian
decorative art and antiquities.

Museum of Contemporary Art
Jacksonville MUSEUM
(☑904-366-6911; www.mocajacksonville.org; 333
N Laura St; adult/child $8/2.50; ☺11am-5pm Tue,
Wed, Fri & Sat, to 9pm Thu, noon-5pm Sun) The
focus of this ultramodern space extends
beyond painting: get lost among contemporary sculpture, prints, photography and
film; and refuel at the trendy Cafe Nola.

🛏 **Sleeping & Eating**

The cheapest rooms are along I-95 and I-10,
where the lower-priced chains congregate.
Beach lodging rates often rise in summer.
You'll find most of the better bars and restaurants in Jax in the atmospheric neighborhoods of Riverside, 4 miles or so southwest of
downtown, and San Marco, 3 miles southeast.

Riverdale Inn B&B **$$**
(☑904-354-5080; www.riverdaleinn.com; 1521
Riverside Ave; r $140-190, ste $220; 🅿✳🔊)
In the early 1900s this was one of 50 or so
mansions lining Riverside. Now there are

only two left. The good news is, this lovely 10-room stunner kept its full bar – the only inn in Duval County that boasts such a vital component to the traveling experience.

Clark's Fish Camp
SOUTHERN $$

(📞904-268-3474; www.clarksfishcamp.com; 12903 Hood Landing Rd; mains $10-23; ⊙4:30-9:30pm Mon-Thu, to 10pm Fri, 11:30am-10pm Sat, 11:30am-9:30pm Sun) This unforgettable swamp shack will either disgust you or you'll lap up all of its ridiculousness. Dine on Florida's Southern 'Cracker' cuisine of gator, snake, camel, kangaroo or yak (often fried) or more mainstream seafood while surrounded by the surreal animal menagerie of 'America's largest private taxidermy collection.' It's a haul south of downtown.

★Orsay
FRENCH, SOUTHERN $$$

(📞904-381-0909; www.restaurantorsay.com; 3630 Park St; mains $18-38; ⊙4-10pm Mon-Wed, to 11pm Thu, to midnight Fri, 11:30am-3:30pm & 4-10pm Sat & Sun; 📞) This minimalist bistro in Riverside merges traditional French fare with Southern intuition leading to a menu chock-full of rich and vibrant dishes, most of which are locally sourced. We may or may not have delighted ourselves silly sopping up our incredible bouillabaisse gravy with black truffle mac 'n' cheese, chased with a few of those creative and boozy cocktails.

🍷 Drinking & Entertainment

Kickbacks Gastropub
BAR

(www.kickbacksjacksonville.com; 910 King St; beers $3.45-10; ⊙7am-3am; 📞) This sprawling copper-toned, penny-lined low-brow gastropub in Riverside has 204 craft beers on tap, including several of Jacksonville's finest. It's divided between the old bar and the new bar, the latter an industrial hodgepodge of massive ceiling fans and Edison-era light bulbs.

Freebird Live
LIVE MUSIC

(📞904-246-2473; www.freebirdlive.com; 200 N 1st St, Jacksonville Beach; ⊙8pm-2am show nights) At the beach, a rocking music venue and home of the band Lynyrd Skynyrd.

ⓘ Getting There & Around

North of the city, **Jacksonville International Airport** (JAX; 📞904-741-4902; www.flyjax.com; 2400 Yankee Clipper Dr) has rental cars. **Greyhound** (📞904-356-9976; www.greyhound.com; 10 N Pearl St) serves numerous cities, and **Amtrak** (📞904-766-5110; www.amtrak.com; 3570 Clifford Lane) has trains from the north and south.

The **Jacksonville Transportation Authority** (📞904-630-3100; www.jtafla.com) runs the free Skyway monorail and city buses (fare $1.50).

Amelia Island & Around

Residents are quick to tell you: Amelia Island is just as old as that braggart St Augustine – they just can't prove it. Unfortunately, no Ponce de León, no plaque, so they have to content themselves with being a pretty little island of moss-draped Southern charm and home to **Fernandina Beach**, a shrimping village with 40 blocks of historic buildings and romantic B&Bs.

⊙ Sights & Activities

Fort Clinch State Park
PARK

(📞904-277-7274; www.floridastateparks.org/fortclinch; 2601 Atlantic Ave; park pedestrian/car $2/6; ⊙park 8am-sunset, fort 9am-5pm) Capping the north end of the island, the Spanish moss–draped Fort Clinch State Park has beaches, camping ($26), bike trails and a commanding Civil War–era fort, with reenactments taking place the first full weekend of every month.

Amelia Island Museum of History
MUSEUM

(www.ameliamuseum.org; 233 S 3rd St; adult/student $7/4; ⊙10am-4pm Mon-Sat, 1-4pm Sun) Learn about Amelia Island's intricate history, which has seen it ruled under eight different flags starting with the French in 1562. Admission includes tours at 11am and 2pm; and additional ghost and pub-crawl tours originate here as well.

Talbot Islands State Parks
PARK

(📞904-251-2320; ⊙8am-dusk) Amelia Island is part of the Talbot Islands State Parks, which includes the pristine shoreline at Little Talbot Island and the 'boneyard beach' at Big Talbot Island State Park, where silvered tree skeletons create a dramatic landscape.

Kelly Seahorse Ranch
HORSEBACK RIDING

(📞904-491-5166; www.kellyranchinc.net; 7500 1st Coast Hwy; 1hr rides adult/child $70/80; ⊙10am, noon, 2pm & 4pm, closed Mon) Offers beachfront trail rides for riders aged 13 and over. Rents beach cruisers as well.

🛏️ Sleeping

★Fairbanks House
B&B $$

(📞904-277-0500; www.fairbankshouse.com; 227 S 7th St; r/ste/cottage from $185/265/230; 🅿️❄️📶🏊) This grand, Italianate mansion has undergone a green makeover, now featuring universal and Tesla electric car charging stations. Guest rooms are so large they feel like suites; we especially like the downstairs room carved out of the house's original 1800s kitchen.

Florida House Inn HISTORIC HOTEL **$$**
(☑904-491-3322; www.floridahouseinn.com; 22 S 3rd St; r $140-200) Florida's oldest hotel features an atmospheric structure dating to 1857 that is battling real estate with an ever-expanding 400-year-old oak tree.

Hoyt House B&B **$$$**
(☑904-277-4300; www.hoythouse.com; 804 Atlantic Ave; r from $199-349; P ❄ 🐾 ☎ 🐾) This tall 1905 Victorian boasts an enchanting gazebo that begs time with a cool drink. Ten rooms each have their own stylish mix of antiques and found treasures and three-course breakfasts are served.

Elizabeth Pointe Lodge B&B **$$$**
(☑904-277-4851; www.elizabethpointelodge.com; 98 S Fletcher Ave; r/ste from $299/375; P ❄ ☎) Located right on the ocean, this 25-room lodge looks like an old Nantucket-style sea-captain's house with wraparound porches, gracious service and beautifully appointed rooms.

✕ Eating & Drinking

Gilbert's Underground Kitchen NEW SOUTHERN **$$**
(☑904-310-6374; www.undergroundkitchen.co; 510 S 8th Street; mains $13-23; ⊘6-10pm Mon & Wed-Thu, 11am-2pm & 6-10pm Fri, 10:30am-2pm & 6-10pm Sat & Sun) Celebrity *Top Chef* Kenny Gilbert's Underground Kitchen has sleepy Amelia Island abuzz with culinary glee. Feast on inventive Southern-soul hybrid dishes such as alligator BBQ ribs, noodles with collard green pesto or fried chicken with datil pepper hot sauce.

29 South SOUTHERN **$$**
(☑904-277-7919; www.29southrestaurant.com; 29 S 3rd St; mains $9-28; ⊘11:30am-2:30pm & 5:30-9:30pm Wed-Sat, 10am-2.30pm & 5:30-9:30pm Sun, 5:30-9:30pm Mon & Tue) Small plates and mains link arms happily at the tiny, stylish neo-Southern gourmet bistro.

Café Karibo & Karibrew FUSION **$$**
(☑904-277-5269; www.cafekaribo.com; 27 N 3rd St; mains $8-22; ⊘11am-3pm Mon, to 10pm Tue-Sat, to 8pm Sun; ☎) This funky side-street res-

taurant and brewery serves a large and eclectic menu in a sprawling two-story space. Live music on weekends.

★**Palace Saloon** BAR
(www.thepalacesaloon.com; 113-117 Centre St; ⊘8pm-2am) One more superlative for Fernandina: Florida's oldest bar, sporting swinging doors, draped velvet and a deadly Pirate's Punch.

ⓘ Information

Historic Downtown Visitor Center (☑904-277-0717; www.ameliaisland.com; 102 Centre St; ⊘10am-4pm) Reams of useful information and maps in the old railroad depot. A fun stop in itself.

WEST COAST

If Henry Flagler's railroad made the east coast of Florida what it is today, his lack of attention to the rest of the state similarly affected the west coast. Things are calmer here, with fewer tourist hordes and more room for nature to amuse us with shelling beaches, swamp lands and nature preserves. The west coast has front-row seats to flame-red sunsets emblazoned over the Gulf of Mexico, as well as adrenaline-pumping roller coasters, hand-rolled cigars and lip-synching mermaids.

Tampa

From the outside, Florida's third-largest city seems all business, even generically so. But Tampa surprises: its revitalized riverfront is a sparkling green swath dotted with intriguing cultural institutions, and its historic Ybor City district preserves the city's Cuban cigar-industry past while, at night, transforming into the Gulf Coast's hottest bar and nightclub scene. South Tampa, meanwhile, has a cutting-edge dining scene that's drawing food mavens from Orlando and Miami.

⊙ Sights

⊙ Downtown Tampa

Most of downtown's sights are in or along Tampa's newly completed 2.4-mile green space, **Riverwalk** (www.thetampariverwalk.com).

Tampa Museum of Art   MUSEUM

(☑ 813-274-8130; www.tampamuseum.org; 120 W Gasparilla Plaza; adult/student $15/5; ☺ 11am-7pm Mon-Thu, to 8pm Fri, to 5pm Sat & Sun) A modern, dramatically cantilevered museum with even galleries that balance Greek and Roman antiquities, contemporary photography and new media with major traveling exhibitions.

Henry B Plant Museum   MUSEUM

(☑ 813-254-1891; www.plantmuseum.com; 401 W Kennedy Blvd; adult/child $10/5; ☺ 10am-5pm Tue-Sat, from noon Sun) The silver minarets of Henry B Plant's 1891 Tampa Bay Hotel glint majestically. Now part of the University of Tampa, the audio tour re-creates the original hotel's luxurious, gilded late-Victorian world.

Tampa Bay History Center   MUSEUM

(☑ 813-228-0097; www.tampabayhistorycenter. org; 801 Old Water St; adult/child $13/8; ☺ 10am-5pm) This first-rate history museum presents the region's Seminole people, Cracker pioneers and Tampa's Cuban community and cigar industry. The on-again, off-again cartography collection dazzles.

Glazer Children's Museum   MUSEUM

(☑ 813-443-3861; www.glazermuseum.org; 110 W Gasparilla Plaza; adult/child $15/9.50; ☺ 10am-5pm Mon-Fri, to 6pm Sat, 1-6pm Sun; ⊛) Creative play spaces for kids don't get any better than this crayon-bright, inventive museum. Eager staff and tons of fun; adjacent Curtis Hixon Park is picnic-and-playground friendly.

◉ Ybor City

Like the illicit love child of Key West and Miami's Little Havana, Ybor City's cobblestoned 19th-century historic district is a redolent mix of wrought-iron balconies, globe streetlamps, immigrant history, ethnic cuisine, cigars and hip, happening nightlife. Diverse and youthful, Ybor (ee-bore) City oozes rakish, scruffy charm.

The main drag – along 7th Ave (La Septima) between 14th and 21st Sts – is packed with eats, drinks, shops and cigar stores.

Ybor City Museum State Park   MUSEUM

(☑ 813-247-6323; www.ybormuseum.org; 1818 E 9th Ave; adult/child $4/free; ☺ 9am-5pm) Join a **walking tour** (☑ 813-428-0854; online/audio tour $10/20) run by a cigar-maker with a PhD, check out the cool museum store, or delve into the old-school history museum that preserves a bygone era, with cigar-worker houses and wonderful photos.

◉ Busch Gardens & Adventure Island

No, it's not as thematically immersive as Orlando's Disney World or Universal, but Tampa's big theme park, **Busch Gardens** (☑ 888-800-5447; http://seaworldparks.com/en/buschgardens-tampa; 10165 McKinley Dr; admission 3yr & up $95, discounts online; ☺ 10am-7pm, hours vary), will satisfy your adrenaline craving with epic roller coasters and flume rides that weave through an African-theme wildlife park.

Adjacent **Adventure Island** (☑ 888-800-5447; www.adventureisland.com; 10001 McKinley Dr; admission 3yr & up $49; ☺ 10am-5pm) is a massive water park with slides and rides galore. Discounts and combination tickets are available online.

🛏 Sleeping

Chains abound along Fowler Ave and Busch Blvd (Hwy 580), near Busch Gardens.

Gram's Place Hostel   HOSTEL $

(☑ 813-221-0596; www.grams-inn-tampa.com; 3109 N Ola Ave; dm $23-26, r $50-60; ⊛ @ ☎) Gram's is a tiny, welcoming hostel for international travelers who prefer personality over perfect linens. Within a ramshackle two-home maze, it's like sleeping in a charismatic musical junkyard. Great-value private rooms.

★Epicurean Hotel   BOUTIQUE HOTEL $$

(www.epicureanhotel.com; 1207 S Howard Ave; r $159-309; P ⊛ @ ☎ ⛱) Foodies rejoice! Tampa's coolest hotel, opened in 2014, is a food-and drink-themed boutique Eden steeped in detailed design touches: vertical hydroponic lettuce and herb walls, a zinc bar, reclaimed woods from an 1820s railway station, oversized whiskers as test-kitchen door handles and so on.

Tahitian Inn   HOTEL $$

(☑ 813-877-6721; www.tahitianinn.com; 601 S Dale Mabry Hwy; r $89-109, ste $119-139; P ⊛ @ ☎ ⛱) The name is reminiscent of a tiki-theme motel, but this family-owned, full-service hotel offers fresh, boutique stylings on the cheap. Nice pool; and airport/cruise terminal transportation is included.

TAMPA BAY AREA BEACHES

The barrier islands of the Tampa Bay Area are graced with some of Florida's best beaches, whether you define 'best' as 'gorgeous untrammeled solitude' or 'family fun and thumping beach parties.' For more information, visit www.tampabaybeaches.com and www.visitstpeteclearwater.com. North to south, some highlights:

Honeymoon and Caladesi Islands Two of Florida's most beautiful beaches; unspoiled, lightly visited Caladesi Island is only reachable by ferry.

Clearwater Beach Idyllic soft white sand hosts raucous spring-break-style parties; huge resorts cater to the masses.

St Pete Beach Double-wide strand that's the epicenter of activities and all-ages fun; packed with hotels, bars and restaurants.

Pass-a-Grille Beach Most popular with city-based day-trippers; extremely long and backed by houses (not resorts); cute-as-a-button village for eats.

Fort Desoto Park and North Beach North Beach is one of Florida's finest white-sand beaches; ideal for families. Extensive park includes bike and kayak rentals, fishing piers and a cafe.

✕ Eating

At mealtime, focus on Ybor City, South Tampa's SoHo area (South Howard Ave) and Seminole Heights.

Wright's Gourmet House SANDWICHES $
(www.wrightsgourmet.com; 1200 S Dale Mabry Hwy; sandwiches & salads $6.75-11; ⊙ 7am-6pm Mon-Fri, 8am-4pm Sat) It doesn't look like much from outside (or in!) but it's been slinging sandwiches since 1963, and its unique combinations and hearty portions win it plenty of fans.

Refinery MODERN AMERICAN $$
(☑ 813-237-2000; www.thetamparefinery.com; 5137 N Florida Ave; mains $9-25; ⊙ 11am-2pm & 5-10pm Mon-Thu, 11am-2pm & 5-11pm Fri, 11am-2:30pm & 5-11pm Sat, 11am-2:30pm Sun; ⚑) ⚐ This blue-collar gourmet joint hawks playful, delicious hyperlocal cuisine that cleverly mixes a sustainability ethic with a punk attitude. Owners Michelle and Greg Baker are among a tiny number of Florida restaurateurs who are known outside the area, thanks no doubt to Greg's three James Beard nominations.

Ulele AMERICAN $$
(☑ 813-999-4952; www.ulele.com; 1810 North Highland Ave; mains $10-36; ⊙ 11am-10pm Sun-Thu, to 11pm Fri-Sat; ⚑) This former water-pumping station has been transformed into an artsy-industrial restaurant and brewery with a menu that resurrects native Flordian recipes madeover for modern times. That means liberal use of datil peppers, sides like alligator beans and okra 'fries' (amazing!), mains such as local pompano fish and desserts including guava pie.

★**Columbia Restaurant** SPANISH $$$
(☑ 813-248-4961; www.columbiarestaurant.com; 2117 E 7th Ave; mains lunch $11-26, dinner $20-31; ⊙ 11am-10pm Mon-Thu, to 11pm Fri & Sat, noon-9pm Sun) This Spanish Cuban restaurant is the oldest in Florida, dating to 1905. Occupying an entire block, it consists of 13 elegant dining rooms and romantic, fountain-centered courtyards. Many of the gloved waiters have been here a lifetime.

★**Bern's Steak House** STEAK $$$
(☑ 813-251-2421; www.bernssteakhouse.com; 1208 S Howard Ave; steaks for 1-2 people $32-105; ⊙ 5-10pm Sun-Thu, to 11pm Fri & Sat) This legendary, nationally renowned steakhouse is an event as much as a meal. Dress up, agonize over your choice of incredibly extensive on-premises dry-aged beef, ask to tour the wine cellar and kitchens, and *don't* skip dessert.

♟ Drinking & Entertainment

For nightlife, Ybor City is party central, while SoHo and Seminole Heights offer more cultured hipness. *Creative Loafing* (www.cltampa.com), Tampa Bay's alternative weekly, lists events and bars. Ybor City is also the center of Tampa's GLBT life; check out the **GaYBOR District Coalition** (www.gaybor.com) and **Tampa Bay Gay** (www.tampabaygay.com).

Cigar City Brewing
BREWERY

(☎813-348-6363; www.cigarcitybrewing.com; 3924 West Spruce St; ⊙11am-11pm Sun-Thu, to 1am Fri & Sat) This is Tampa's premier craft brewery. It has dozens of crafted brews on tap, many exclusive to the brewery. Tours are $5 (with one beer included).

ℹ Information

Tampa Bay Convention & Visitors Bureau
(☎813-223-1111; www.visittampabay.com; 615 Channelside Dr; ⊙10am-5:30pm Mon-Sat, 11am-5pm Sun) The visitor center has good free maps and lots of information. Book hotels directly through the website.

Ybor City Visitor Center (☎813-241-8838; www.ybor.org; 1600 E 8th Ave; ⊙10am-5pm Mon-Sat, from noon Sun) Get a great overview plus walking tour maps at the visitor center – itself an excellent small museum.

ℹ Getting There & Around

Tampa International Airport (TPA; ☎813-870-8700; www.tampaairport.com; 4100 George J Bean Pkwy) has car-rental agencies. **Greyhound** (☎813-229-2174; www.greyhound.com; 610 E Polk St, Tampa) has numerous services. Trains run south to Miami and north through Jacksonville from the **Amtrak station** (☎813-221-7600; www.amtrak.com; 601 N Nebraska Ave).

Hillsborough Area Regional Transit (HART; ☎813-254-4278; www.gohart.org; 1211 N Marion St; fares $2) connects downtown and Ybor City with buses, trolleys and old-style streetcars.

St Petersburg

In the bay area, St Petersburg is the more arty, youthful sibling. It also has a more compact and walkable tourist district along its attractive harbor. For a cultural city base within easy striking distance of the region's excellent beaches, St Pete is a great choice.

◎ Sights

Most of the action is around and along Central Ave, from 8th Ave to Bayshore Dr, which fronts the harbor and tourist pier.

St Petersburg Museum of Fine Arts
MUSEUM

(☎727-896-2667; www.fine-arts.org; 255 Beach Dr NE; adult/child $17/10; ⊙10am-5pm Mon-Sat, to 8pm Thu, from noon Sun) Boasts a broad collection traversing the world's antiquities and following art's progression through nearly every era.

Florida Holocaust Museum
MUSEUM

(☎727-820-0100; www.flholocaustmuseum.org; 55 5th St S; adult/student $16/8; ⊙10am-5pm) The understated exhibits of this Holocaust museum, one of the country's largest, present these mid-20th-century events with moving directness.

Chihuly Collection
GALLERY

(☎727-896-4527; www.moreanartscenter.org; 400 Beach Dr; adult/child $15/11; ⊙10am-5pm Mon-Sat, from noon Sun) A paean to Chihuly's glass artistry, with galleries designed to hold the dramatic installations.

🛏 Sleeping

★**Dickens House**
B&B $$

(☎727-822-8622; www.dickenshouse.com; 335 8th Ave NE; r $135-245; P ❄ @ 🛜) Five lushly designed rooms await in this passionately restored arts-and-crafts-style home. The gregarious, gay-friendly owner whips up a gourmet breakfast.

Ponce de Leon
BOUTIQUE HOTEL $$

(☎727-550-9300; www.poncedeleonhotel.com; 95 Central Ave; r $99-149, ste $169; ❄ @ 🛜) A boutique hotel with Spanish flair in the heart of downtown. Splashy murals, designer-cool decor, and its hot restaurant and bar, are highlights; off-site parking is not.

Birchwood Inn
BOUTIQUE HOTEL $$$

(☎727-896-1080; www.thebirchwood.com; 340 Beach Dr NE; r from $275; P ❄ 🛜) Rooms are simply gorgeous at this boutique gem: spacious, with claw-foot baths, king canopy beds and oozing vintage bordello elegance sexed up with a little South Beach sauciness. Canopy, the rooftop bar, is the hottest spot in town for cocktails.

🍴 Eating & Drinking

At night, focus anywhere on Central Ave and Beach Dr along the harborfront.

Taco Bus
MEXICAN $

(www.taco-bus.com; 2324 Central Ave; mains $6-13; ⊙11am-10pm Sun-Thu, to 4am Fri & Sat; 🛜) When this taco- and burrito-slinging food truck needed a bricks-and-mortar location, it just rolled right up next to a good-time patio and didn't skip a beat. *Cochinita pibil, carnitas* and *pollo chipotle* are highlights. A Tampa Bay institution.

Bella Brava
ITALIAN $$

(☎727-895-5515; www.bellabrava.com; 204 Beach Dr NE; mains $9-27; ⊙11:30am-10pm, to 11pm Fri

DON'T MISS

SALVADOR DALÍ MUSEUM

Of course St Petersburg was the logical place to put a museum dedicated to Salvador Dalí, the eccentric Spanish artist who painted melting clocks, grew an exaggerated handlebar mustache to look like King Philip, and once filled a Rolls Royce with cauliflower. Right? In fact, **Salvador Dalí Museum** (📞727-823-3767; www.thedali.org; 1 Dali Blvd; adult/child 6-12yr $24/10, after 5pm Thu $10; ⏱10am-5:30pm Mon-Wed, Fri & Sat, to 8pm Thu, noon-5:30pm Sun) is the largest Dalí collection outside of Spain. So how did that happen exactly?

In 1942 A Reynolds Morse and his wife Eleanor began what would become the largest private Dalí collection in the world. When it came time to find a permanent home for the collection, they had one stipulation: that the collection had to stay together. Only three cities could agree to the terms, and St Petersburg won out for its waterfront location.

The museum now has a brand-new building with a theatrical exterior that, when seen from the bay side, looks like a geodesic atrium oozing out of a shoebox. It doesn't have *the* melting clocks, but it does have *some* melting clocks, as well as an impressive collection of paintings with titles such as *The Ghost of Vermeer of Delft Which Can Be Used as a Table*.

& Sat, 1-9pm Sun; 📶) Anchoring the prime waterfront intersection, Bella Brava continues to draw a noisy young, professional crowd with its contemporary Italian cooking, pizza menu and cocktail bar. There's also sidewalk seating on Beach Dr.

Ceviche　　　　　　　　　　TAPAS $$
(www.ceviche.com; 10 Beach Dr; tapas $4-15, mains $9-20; ⏱5-11pm Mon-Fri, 8am-11pm Sat & Sun; 📶) An upbeat Spanish atmosphere and flavorful, creative, generously portioned tapas. End the evening in the sexy, cavernlike Flamenco Room below.

3 Daughters Brewing　　　　　BREWERY
(📞727-495-6002; www.3dbrewing.com; 222 22nd St S; ⏱2-9pm Mon-Tue, to 10pm Wed & Thu, to midnight Fri & Sat, 1-9pm Sun) The best brewery experience we came across in four states: a 30-barrel brewhouse with drinking games and live music *in* the brewery itself!

ℹ Information

St Petersburg Area Chamber of Commerce (📞727-8388-0686; www.stpete.com; 100 2nd Ave N; ⏱9am-5pm Mon-Fri, 10am-4pm Sat) Helpful, staffed chamber office has good maps and a driving guide.

ℹ Getting There & Around

St Petersburg-Clearwater International Airport (📞727-453-7800; www.fly2pie.com; Roosevelt Blvd & Hwy 686, Clearwater) is served by several major carriers. **Greyhound** (📞727-898-1496; www.greyhound.com; 180 Dr Martin Luther King Jr St N; ⏱8:15-10am & 2:30-6:30pm Mon-Sun) services include Tampa.

Pinellas Suncoast Transit Authority (PSTA; www.psta.net; 340 2nd Ave N; adult/student $2/1.25) operates buses citywide, as well as the Suncoast Beach Trolley that links the beaches from Clearwater to Pass-a-Grille, and the Downtown Looper trolley, which is free within a defined zone around Beach Dr.

Sarasota

Artists, writers, musicians, entertainers – artsy types have flocked to Sarasota since the 1920s, with John Ringling leading the way. He set it on this course in 1911, when he made the town the winter home of his famous circus. Today the Ringling Museum Complex is a regional highlight, and Sarasota spills over with opera, theater and art.

Another considerable boost to Sarasota's popularity is its luscious white-sand beaches. **Lido Beach** is closest and has free parking, but 5 miles away **Siesta Key** has sand like confectioner's sugar and is one of Florida's best and most popular strands; Siesta Village is also a lively, family-friendly beach town.

◉ Sights & Activities

Marie Selby Botanical Gardens　　GARDENS
(📞941-366-5731; www.selby.org; 811 S Palm Ave; adult/child 4-11yr $19/6; ⏱10am-5pm) Boasts the world's largest scientific collection of orchids and bromeliads.

Myakka Outpost　　　　　　KAYAKING
(📞941-923-1120; www.myakkaoutpost.com; 13208 SR-72; canoes/bikes $20/15; ⏱9:30am-5pm Mon-Fri, 8:30am-6pm Sat & Sun) Within the Myakka River State Park, this canoe outfitter can get you out on the Myakka River, a really cool experience among hundreds of alligators about a half-hour from downtown.

🛏 Sleeping & Eating

In addition to downtown Sarasota and Siesta Village, **St Armands Circle** on Lido Key is an evening social hub, with a proliferation of stylish shops and restaurants.

The Capri at Siesta   RESORT $$
(☑941-684-3244; www.capriinternational.com; 6782 SaraSea Circle; r $149-229, ste $189-329; P✳🔆🏊) As discerningly located – 200 steps from Siesta sands but tucked away from the hubbub – as it is well appointed, this 10-room boutique resort forgoes in-your-face tropicallia for more soothing, earth-toned decor and private refinement.

★Hotel Ranola   BOUTIQUE HOTEL $$
(☑941-951-0111; www.hotelranola.com; 118 Indian Pl; r $109-179, ste $239-269; P✳🔆) The nine rooms feel like a designer's brownstone apartment: free-spirited and effortlessly artful, but with real working kitchens. It's urban funk, walkable to downtown Sarasota.

Another Broken Egg Cafe   BREAKFAST $
(www.anotherbrokenegg.com; 140 Avenida Messina, Siesta Key; mains $5-16; ⊙7:30am-2:30pm; 👪) This chain, diner-style breakfast institution on Siesta Key is a social hub each morning. The menu is chock-full of scrumptious and creative breakfast fare (black bean Benedict with chipotle Hollandaise!).

Owen's Fish Camp   SOUTHERN $$
(☑941-951-6936; www.owensfishcamp.com; 516 Burns Lane; mains $10-28; ⊙from 4pm) This ironically hip swamp shack downtown serves upscale versions of Florida-style Southern cuisine with an emphasis on seafood.

ℹ Information

Sarasota Visitor Information Center (☑941-957-1877; www.sarasotafl.org; 14 Lemon Ave; ⊙10am-5pm Mon-Sat; 🕿) Very friendly office with tons of info; sells good maps.

Sanibel & Captiva Islands

Shaped like a fish hook trying to lure Fort Myers, these two slivers of barrier island lie across a 2-mile causeway (toll $6). Upscale but unpretentious, with a carefully managed shoreline that feels remarkably lush and undeveloped, the islands are idyllic, cushy getaways, where bikes are the preferred mode of travel and the shelling is legendary and romantic.

◉ Sights & Activities

JN 'Ding' Darling National Wildlife Refuge   WILDLIFE RESERVE
(☑239-472-1100; www.fws.gov/dingdarling; 1 Wildlife Dr; car/cyclist $5/1; ⊙9am-5pm Jan-Apr, to 4pm May-Dec) In addition to its fabulous beaches, this splendid 6300-acre refuge that is home to an abundance of seabirds and wildlife. It has an excellent nature center, a 4-mile Wildlife Drive, narrated tram tours and easy kayaking in Tarpon Bay

Bailey-Matthews National Shell Museum   MUSEUM
(☑239-395-2233; www.shellmuseum.org; 3075 Sanibel-Captiva Rd, Sanibel; adult/child 5-17yr $11/5; ⊙10am-5pm) Like a mermaid's jewel box, this fascinating museum offers a natural history of the sea, with covetous displays of shells from all over the world; and daily beach walks ($10).

FLORIDA SANIBEL & CAPTIVA ISLANDS

DON'T MISS
RINGLING COMPLEX

Who doesn't love the circus? Well, people who are afraid of clowns, perhaps, but a little coulrophobia isn't necessarily a deal-breaker at the **Ringling Museum Complex** (☑941-359-5700; www.ringling.org; 5401 Bay Shore Rd; adult/child 6-17yr $25/5; ⊙10am-5pm daily, to 8pm Thu; 👪). On the grounds of the 66-acre complex are three separate museums, all included in your admission and each one a worthy attraction on its own. Railroad, real-estate and circus baron John Ringling and his wife Mabel put down roots here, building a Venetian Gothic waterfront mansion called **Ca d'Zan**. You can wander the ground floor at your own pace, or take a $5 or $20 guided tour add-on – totally worth it – which grants you access to the upstairs bedrooms and 'private places.'

Also on the grounds, the excellent **John & Mabel Museum of Art**; and the one-of-a-kind **Museum of the Circus**, with costumes, props, posters, antique circus wagons and a humongous (3800-sq-ft!), fantastical miniature model of the big-top era in its heyday.

THE ENLIGHTENED SNOWBIRDS OF FORT MYERS

Florida's snowbirds can be easy to mock, but not this pair. Famous inventor Thomas Edison built a winter home and lab here in Fort Myers in 1885, and automaker Henry Ford became his neighbor in 1916. The **Edison & Ford Winter Estates** (☎239-334-7419; www. edisonfordwinterestates.org; 2350 McGregor Blvd; tours adult $12-25, child $5-15; ⊗9am-5:30pm) is now the city's main claim to fame. The excellent museum focuses mainly on the overwhelming scope of Edison's genius, and their homes are genteel, landscaped delights.

If you're visiting the area, 15 miles south of Fort Myers, Fort Myers Beach is 7 miles of talcum-powder-fine sand along **Estero Island**, presided over by one of Florida's quintessential activity-and-party-fueled beach towns. Families often prefer Fort Myers Beach because it's more affordable than neighboring coastal towns, and coeds like it because its bars are louder and more raucous; the area is also the gateway for the far more charming Sanibel & Captiva Islands. For town information, visit www.fortmyersbeachchamber.org.

Tarpon Bay Explorers KAYAKING
(☎239-472-8900; www.tarponbayexplorers.com; 900 Tarpon Bay Rd, Sanibel; ⊗8am-6pm) Within the Darling refuge, this outfitter rents canoes and kayaks ($25 for two hours) and SUP for easy, self-guided paddles in Tarpon Bay, a perfect place for young paddlers.

Billy's Rentals BICYCLE RENTAL
(☎239-472-5248; www.billysrentals.com; 1470 Periwinkle Way, Sanibel; bikes per 2hr/day $5/15; ⊗8:30am-6pm) Rents bikes or any other wheeled contrivance.

🛏 Sleeping & Eating

Tarpon Tale Inn COTTAGE $$
(☎239-472-0939; www.tarpontale.com; 367 Periwinkle Way, Sanibel; r $230-290; ❋@🛜) For a more personal experience, this five-room inn hides its cottages away in jungly surrounds on peaceful, hammock-strung grounds. No breakfast, though.

Over Easy Cafe CAFE $
(www.overeasycafesanibel.com; 630 Tarpon Bay Rd, Sanibel; breakfast $4-12; ⊗7am-3pm; 🛜🚸) Despite Provence-style decor, the menu offers strictly top-quality diner fare, including healthy-dose scramblers, omelets, and various style of 'Benny's' (eggs Benedict).

★Sweet Melissa's Cafe AMERICAN $$$
(☎239-472-1956; www.sweetmelissascafe.net; 1625 Periwinkle Way, Sanibel; tapas $9-16, mains $26-34; ⊗11:30am-2:30pm & 5-9pm Mon-Fri, 5-9pm Sat) From its menu to its atmosphere, Sweet Melissa's offers well-balanced, relaxed refinement.

ℹ Information

Sanibel & Captiva Islands Chamber of Commerce (☎239-472-1080; www.sanibel-captiva. org; 1159 Causeway Rd, Sanibel; ⊗9am-5pm; 🛜) One of the more helpful visitor centers around; keeps an updated hotel-vacancy list with dedicated hotel hotline.

Naples

The Gulf Coast's answer to Palm Beach, Naples is a perfectly manicured, rich town with an adult sense of self and one of the most pristine, relaxed city beaches in the state. While it is certainly family friendly, it appeals most to romance-minded travelers seeking fine art and fine dining, trendy cocktails, fashion-conscious shopping and luscious sunsets.

◉ Sights & Activities

★Baker Museum MUSEUM
(☎239-597-1900; www.artisnaples.org; 5833 Pelican Bay Blvd; adult/child $10/free; ⊗10am-4pm Tue-Sat, noon-4pm Sun) The pride of Naples, this engaging, sophisticated art museum offers a rewarding collection with cleverly designed exhibits.

Naples Nature Center NATURE RESERVE
(☎239-262-0304; www.conservancy.org/naturecenter; 1450 Merrihue Dr; adult/child 3-12yr $13/9; ⊗9:30am-4:30pm Mon-Sat, open Sun Jun-Aug) One of Florida's best nature conservancies and rehabilitation centers, with a Leadership in Energy & Enivronmental design–certified campus and fantastic exhibits. The 21-acre park offers pleasant boardwalk trails and naturalist boat rides.

🛏 Sleeping & Eating

Lemon Tree Inn MOTEL $$
(📞239-262-1414; www.lemontreeinn.com; 250 9th St S; r $152-196; 🅿✳@🛜🏊) You'll find 34 clean and brightly decorated rooms (some with passable kitchenettes and screened-in porches) forming a U around pretty, private gardens and a pool, where breakfast is served. Good value.

Inn on 5th HOTEL $$$
(📞239-403-8777; www.innonfifth.com; 699 5th Ave S; r $399, ste $599-999; 🅿✳@🛜🏊) This well-polished, Mediterranean-style luxury hotel provides an unbeatable location in the midst of 5th Ave.

The Local MODERN AMERICAN $$
(www.thelocalnaples.com; 5323 Airport Pulling Rd N; mains $12-29; ⊘11am-9pm Sun-Thu, to 10pm Fri & Sat; 🛜) 🌿 The ethics of driving 6 miles from downtown to eat local aside, this strip-mall farm-to-table bistro is worth the carbon footprint for fab sustainable fare, from ceviche tacos to grass-fed beef. Escape tourists. Eat local.

IM Tapas SPANISH $$
(📞239-403-8272; www.imtapas.com; 965 4th Ave N; tapas $5.50-18; ⊘from 5:30pm Mon-Sat) A mother-and-daughter team serving Madrid-worthy Spanish tapas.

ℹ Information

Visitor Information Center (📞239-262-6141; www.napleschamber.org; 900 5th Ave S; ⊘9am-5pm Mon-Sat, 10am-2pm Sun summer, 9am-5pm Mon-Fri, 9am-1pm Sun winter) Will help with accommodations; good maps, and acres of brochures.

CENTRAL FLORIDA

Before Disney – BD – most tourists came to Florida to see two things: the white-sand beaches and the alligator-infested Everglades. Walt Disney changed all that when he opened the Magic Kingdom in 1971. Today Orlando is the theme-park capital of the world, and Walt Disney World is Florida's number-one attraction.

Orlando

Like Las Vegas, Orlando is almost entirely given over to fantasy. It's a place to come when you want to imagine you're somewhere else: Hogwarts, perhaps, or Cinderella's Castle, or Dr Seuss' world, or an African safari. And like Vegas' casinos, Orlando's theme parks work hard to be constantly entertaining thrill rides where the only concern is your pleasure. Even outside the theme parks, Orlando can exhibit a hyper atmosphere of fiberglass-modeled, cartoon-costumed pop-culture amusement.

But if you're theme parked-out, there's a real city to explore, one with tree-shaded parks surrounding numerous lakes, art museums, orchestras, and dinners that don't involve high-fiving Goofy. And just outside the city, Florida's wilderness and wildlife, particularly its crystal springs, can be as memorably bizarre as anything Ripley ever dreamed up.

👁 Sights & Activities

🌀 Downtown & Loch Haven Park

Fashionable Thornton Park is home to several good restaurants and bars, while Loch Haven Park is home to a cluster of cultural institutions.

⭐**Orlando Museum of Art** MUSEUM
(📞407-896-4231; www.omart.org; 2416 N Mills Ave; adult/child $8/5; ⊘10am-4pm Tue-Fri, from noon Sat & Sun; ♿; 🚌Lynx 125, 🚇Florida Hospital Health Village) Spotlighting American and African art as well as unique traveling exhibits.

Mennello Museum of American Art MUSEUM
(📞407-246-4278; www.mennellomuseum.com; 900 E Princeton St, Loch Haven Park; adult/child 6-18yr $5/1; ⊘10:30am-4:30pm Tue-Sat, from noon Sun; ♿; 🚌Lynx 125, 🚇Florida Hospital Health Village) Features the bright folk art of Earl Cunningham, plus traveling exhibitions.

Orlando Science Center MUSEUM
(📞407-514-2000; www.osc.org; 777 E Princeton St, Loch Haven Park; adult/child $19/13; ⊘10am-5pm Thu-Tue; ♿; 🚌Lynx 125, 🚇Florida Hospital Health Village) Candy-coated hands-on science for the whole family.

International Drive

Like a theme park itself, International Dr (I-Dr) is shoulder to shoulder with high--energy amusements. Sprinkled among the major theme, wildlife and water parks, smaller attractions shout for attention: Ripley's Believe It or Not, the upside-down Wonder-Works and the new Orlando Eye, a 400ft tall observation Ferris wheel. Chain restaurants and hotels also crowd the thoroughfare.

★ **Universal Orlando Resort** THEME PARK
(☎ 407-363-8000; www.universalorlando.com; 1000 Universal Studios Plaza; single park 1 day/2 days $102/150, both parks $147/195, child $5-10 less; ⊙ daily, hours vary; ☒ Lynx 21, 37, 40, ☒ Universal) Universal is giving Disney a run for its money with this megacomplex that features two theme parks, five hotels and Universal City-Walk, an entertainment district that connects the two parks. But where Disney World is all happy and magical, Universal Orlando gets your adrenaline pumping with revved-up rides and entertaining shows.

The first of the two parks, Universal Studios, has a Hollywood backlot feel and simulation-heavy rides dedicated to television and the silver screen, from *The Simpsons* and *Shrek* to *Revenge of the Mummy* and *Twister*. Universal's Islands of Adventure is tops with coaster-lovers but also has plenty for the little ones in Toon Lagoon and Seuss Landing.

But the absolute highlight – and the hottest thing to hit Orlando since Cinderella's Castle – is the expanded Wizarding World of Harry Potter, which features in both parks, connected by the Hogwarts Express. Together, Universal's Islands of Adventure Hogsmeade and the brand-new Universal Studios Diagon Alley are easily the most fantastically realized themed experience in Florida. Muggles are invited to poke along the cobbled streets and impossibly crooked buildings of Hogsmeade, sip frothy Butter Beer and mail a card via Owl Post, all in the shadow of Hogwarts Castle. Dine at the Leaky Cauldron, watch a wand choose a wizard at Ollivanders Wand Shop and be gobsmacked at the spectacular multidimensional 3D thrill ride at Gringotts Bank. The detail and authenticity tickle the fancy at every turn, from the screeches of the mandrakes in the shop windows to the groans of Moaning Myrtle in the bathroom.

Review multiple ticket options online, which can include add-ons such as Express Plus line skipping and a dining plan; resort hotel guests also get nice park perks. Parking is $17.

SeaWorld THEME PARK
(☎ 888-800-5447; www.seaworldparks.com; 7007 Sea World Dr; admission $95; ⊙ 9am-8pm; ☒; ☒ Lynx 8, 38, 50, 111, ☒ I-Ride Trolley Red Line Stop 33) One of Orlando's largest and most popular theme parks, SeaWorld is an aquatic-themed park filled with marine animal shows, roller coasters and up-close sea-life encounters. However, the park's biggest draw is now its most controversial: live shows featuring trained dolphins, sea lions and killer whales.

Since the release of the 2013 documentary *Blackfish*, SeaWorld's treatment of its captive orcas has come under intense scrutiny and the company has been hit by falling visitor numbers and a catalogue of negative PR.

Discounted tickets are available online; prices vary daily.

Discovery Cove THEME PARK
(☎ 877-434-7268; www.discoverycove.com; 6000 Discovery Cove Way; admission incl SeaWorld & Aquatica from $210, SeaVenture extra $59, prices vary daily; ⊙ 8am-5:30pm, all-day experience, advance reservations required; ☒; ☒ Lynx 8, 38, 50, 111) At Discovery Cove, guests spend the day snorkeling in a fish- and ray-filled reef, floating on a lazy river through an aviary, and simply relaxing in an intimate tropical sanctuary of white-sand beaches. For an added price beyond the Resort Only package, you can swim with dolphins and walk along the sea floor. It may seem like a fun idea, but since the early 1990s, there has been a growing controversy regarding the ethics of dolphin captivity for the purposes of public display and human interaction.

Winter Park

On the northern edge of Orlando, Winter Park is the gorgeous upscale anti-Orlando built around a chain of lakes with some outstanding museums, a relaxing downtown and great cafes and restaurants.

★ **Charles Hosmer Morse Museum of American Art** MUSEUM
(☎ 407-645-5311; www.morsemuseum.org; 445 N Park Ave; adult/child $5/free; ⊙ 9:30am-4pm Tue-Sat, from 1pm Sun, to 8pm Fri Nov-Apr; ☒) Internationally famous, with the world's most comprehensive collection of Tiffany worldwide; the breathtaking centerpiece

is a chapel interior, but the stained glass throughout is stunning as well.

Scenic Boat Tour
BOAT TOUR

(✆407-644-4056; www.scenicboattours.com; 312 E Morse Blvd; adult/child $12/6; ⊙hourly 10am-4pm; ⊕) This recommended one-hour boat ride floats through 12 coastal miles of tropical canals and lakes. The enthusiastic tour guide talks about the mansions, Rollins College and other sites along the way. Boats are small pontoons, holding about 18 people each.

🛏 Sleeping

In addition to the Walt Disney World resorts, Orlando has countless lodging options. Most are clustered around I-Dr, US 192 in Kissimmee and I-4. **Reserve Orlando** (www.reserve orlando.com) is a central booking agency.

Palm Lakefront Hostel
HOSTEL $

(✆407-396-1759; www.orlandohostels.com; 4840 W Irlo Bronson/Hwy 192, Kissimmee; dm/d/q $19/36/60; P❄🐕🏊; ᮀLynx 56, 55) If you can deal with the temperamental owner, this two-story roadside-motel-styed hostel is your budget bed, with a grassy lakeside picnic and BBQ area, a quiet fishing dock and a little pool. The public bus just outside connects directly to Disney's Transportation & Ticket Center.

Barefoot'n In The Keys
MOTEL $

(✆407-589-2127; www.barefootn.com; 2754 Florida Plaza Blvd, Kissimmee; ste $76-130; P❄🐕🏊) Clean, bright and spacious suites in yellow-and-blue Key West–style bungalows. Low-key, friendly and close to Disney, this makes an excellent alternative to generic chains.

EO Inn & Spa
BOUTIQUE HOTEL $$

(✆407-481-8485; www.eoinn.com; 227 N Eola Dr, Thornton Park; r $140-250; @🐕) Sleek and understated, this downtown boutique inn overlooks Lake Eola near Thornton Park, with neutral-toned rooms that are elegant in their simplicity and were being done up with new bamboo flooring and all the fixins' when we came through.

Courtyard at Lake Lucerne
B&B $$

(✆407-648-5188; www.orlandohistoricinn.com; 211 N Lucerne Circle E; r from $130; P❄@🐕) This lovely 30-room historic inn, with enchanting gardens and genteel breakfast, has roomy art-deco suites and handsome antiques throughout. Complimentary cocktails help you forgive its location under two highway overpasses.

🍴 Eating

Orlando is no longer the culinary cesspool it once was. Though on and around I-Dr you'll find an explosion of chains, the city has learned to appreciate good food. A half-mile stretch of Sand Lake Rd has been dubbed 'restaurant row' for its upscale dining and there's a bona-fide foodie scene budding in Winter Park.

★East End Market
MARKET $

(✆231-236-3316; www.eastendmkt.com; 3201 Corrine Dr, Audubon Park; ⊙10am-7pm Tue-Sat, 11am-6pm Sun; 🐕⊕) 🍴 A revolving urban gourmet food court stocking delis, coffee, bars, bakeries and other locally sourced goodness.

Black Bean Deli
CUBAN $

(www.blackbeandeli.com; 1835 E Colonial Dr; mains $6-9; ⊙11am-9pm Mon-Thu, to 10pm Fri-Sat; 🐕) A former car dealership now wheels and deals exceptionally tasty *Cubano* specialties.

Pho 88
VIETNAMESE $

(www.pho88orlando.com; 730 N Mills Ave; mains $3.25-11; ⊙10am-10pm) A flagship in Orlando's thriving Vietnamese district (known as ViMi) just northeast of downtown, this authentic, no-frills *pho* (Vietnamese noodle soup) specialist is always packed. Cheap and tasty!

★Yellow Dog Eats
BARBECUE $$

(www.yellowdogeats.com; 1236 Hempel Ave, Windermere; mains $8-19; ⊙11am-9pm; 🐕⊕) Housed in an old, tin-roof general store, this quirky temple of dogs and barbeque is worth the haul for an incredible menu of delectable pulled-pork sandwiches in surrounds swarming with local color. Try the Fire Pig (with Gouda, pecan-smoke bacon, slaw, Sriracha and fried onions in a chipotle wrap).

★Smiling Bison
AMERICAN $$

(✆407-898-8580; www.thesmilingbison.com; 745 Bennett Rd, Audubon Park; mains $12-36; ⊙5pm-midnight Tue-Thu, to 2am Fri & Sat; 🐕) 🍴 Dive exterior and empty-lot surrounds notwithstanding, this spunky little unaffected delight is justifiably famous for its bison burger, served on an English-muffin-like bun with homemade fries; and beers are carefully curated. Live jazz most nights.

Greater Orlando & Theme Parks

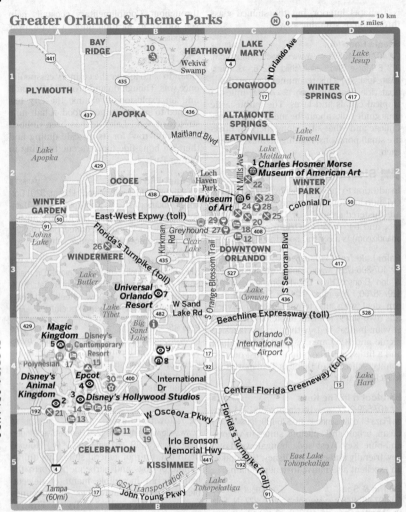

Cask & Larder

AMERICAN $$$

(☑321-280-4200; www.caskandlarder.com; 565 W Fairbanks Ave, Winter Park; mains $24-46; ⏱5-10pm Mon-Sat, 10:30am-3pm Sun) 🍃 From swampy taxidermy-meets-country-chic environs, the Cask & Larder serves an innovative menu of locally sourced Southern fare, including an extraordinary kale salad with bacon vinaigrette, charred okra and boar and dumplings. They brew their own craft beer here, and don't mess around when it comes to cocktails ($12).

🍷 Drinking & Entertainment

Orlando Weekly (www.orlandoweekly.com) is the best source for entertainment listings. There's plenty to do downtown, where there's a happening bar district around Orange Ave between Church St and Jefferson St.

Redlight, Redlight

BAR

(www.redlightredlightbeerparlour.com; 2810 Corrine Dr, Audubon Park; beers $5-9; ⏱5pm-2am; 🛜) Aficionados of the drink will love the 28 draft offerings of craft beers, cask-conditioned ales, meads and farmhouse

Greater Orlando & Theme Parks

ciders at this unassuming strip-mall beer-geek hangout housed in a former air-conditioner repair shop.

Woods COCKTAIL BAR
(☎407-203-1114; www.thewoodsorlando.com; 49 N Orange Ave, 2nd fl, Historic Rose Bldg; cocktails $12; ☉5pm-2am Mon-Fri, from 7pm Sat, 4pm-midnight Sun) It's been called Florida's best cocktail bar: a monthly changing menu of craft cocktails hidden in a cozy, smoke-free 2nd-floor setting, with exposed brick, a tree-trunk bar and not a smidgeon of mixology pretension.

Hanson's Shoe Repair COCKTAIL BAR
(☎407-476-9446; 27 E Pine St; cocktails $12; ☉8pm-2am Tue-Thu & Sat, from 7pm Fri) This downtown Orlando Prohibition-era speakeasy, complete with historically accurate cocktails and secret passwords for entry, serves classic cocktails hidden away inside another bar (NV Art Bar). To get in, call in advance, they'll text you the password if they can accommodate you.

❶ Information

Official Visitor Center (☎407-363-5872; www.visitorlando.com; 8723 International Dr; ☉8:30am-6pm) Legitimate discount attraction tickets and best source for information on theme parks, accommodations, outdoor activities, performing arts and more.

❶ Getting There & Around

Orlando International Airport (MCO; ☎407-825-8463; www.orlandoairports.net; 1 Jeff Fuqua Blvd) has buses and taxis to major tourist areas.
Mears Transportation (☎customer service 407-423-5566, reservations 855-463-2776; www.mearstransportation.com) provides shuttles for $20 to $28 per person. **Greyhound** (☎407-292-3424; www.greyhound.com; 555 N John Young Pkwy) serves numerous cities. **Amtrak** (www.amtrak.com; 1400 Sligh Blvd) has daily trains south to Miami and north to New York City.

Orlando's bus network is operated by **Lynx** (☎route info 407-841-8240; www.golynx.com; per ride/day/week $2/4.50/16, transfers free). **I-Ride Trolley** (☎407-354-5656; www.iridetrolley.com; rides adult/child 3-9yr $2/1, passes 1/3/5/7/14 days $5/7/9/12/18; ☉8am-10:30pm) buses run along I-Dr.

FLORIDA ORLANDO

When driving, note that I-4 is the main north–south connector, though it's confusingly labeled east–west. To go north, take I-4 east (toward Daytona); to go south, get on I-4 west (toward Tampa). The main east–west roads are Hwy 50 and Hwy 528 (the Bee Line Expwy), which accesses Orlando International Airport.

Walt Disney World Resort

Covering 40 sq miles, Walt Disney World (WDW) is the largest theme-park resort in the world. It includes four separate theme parks, two water parks, a sports complex, three 18-hole golf courses, more than two dozen resort hotels, over 100 restaurants and dining options and two shopping, dining and entertainment districts – proving that it's not such a small world, after all. At times it feels ridiculously crowded and corporate, but with or without kids, you won't be able to inoculate yourself against Disney's highly infectious enthusiasm and warm-hearted nostalgia. Naturally, expectations run high, and even the self-proclaimed 'happiest place on earth' doesn't always live up to its billing. Still, it always happens: Cinderella curtsies to your little Belle, your own Jedi knight vanquishes Darth Maul, or you tear up on that corny ride about our tiny planet, and suddenly you're swept up in the magic.

◎ Sights & Activities

★ Magic Kingdom   THEME PARK
(☑ 407-939-5277; www.disneyworld.disney.go.com; 1180 Seven Seas Dr; adult/child 3-10yr $105/99; ⊙9am-11pm, hours vary; ▣Disney, ⛴Disney, monorail Disney) When most people think of WDW – especially kids – it's really the Magic Kingdom they're picturing. This is where you'll find all the classic Disney experiences, such as the iconic Cinderella's Castle, rides like Space Mountain and the nighttime fireworks and light parade illuminating **Main Street, USA**. For Disney mythology, it doesn't get better.

Cinderella's Castle is at the center of the park, and from there paths lead to the different 'lands':

Tomorrowland is where Space Mountain hurtles you through the darkness of outer space. This indoor roller coaster is the most popular ride in the Magic Kingdom, so come first thing and if the line is already excruciating, get a FastPass+.

New Fantasyland is the highlight of any Disney trip for the eight-and-under crowd.

This is the land of Mickey and Minnie, Goofy and Donald Duck, Snow White and the Seven Dwarves, and many more big names. Fresh off the largest expansion in Magic Kingdom history, new rides include the gentle Under the Sea – Journey of the Little Mermaid and the Seven Dwarfs Mine Train, a family-friendly steel roller coaster.

Adventureland features pirates and jungles, magic carpets and tree houses, whimsical and silly representations of the exotic locales from storybooks and imagination.

Liberty Square is the home of the the the Haunted Mansion, a rambling, 19th-century mansion that's a Disney favorite, and **Frontierland** is Disney's answer to the Wild West.

★ Epcot   THEME PARK
(☑ 407-939-5277; www.disneyworld.disney.go.com; 200 Epcot Center Dr; adult/child 3-10yr $97/91; ⊙11am-9pm, hours vary; ▣Disney, ⛴Disney) An acronym for 'Experimental Prototype Community of Tomorrow', Epcot was Disney's vision of a high-tech city when it opened in 1982. It's divided into two halves: **Future World**, with rides and corporate-sponsored interactive exhibits, and **World Showcase**, providing an interesting toe-dip into the cultures of 11 countries.

Epcot is much more soothingly low-key than other parks, and it has some of the best food, drinks and shopping.

★ Disney's Animal Kingdom   THEME PARK
(☑ 407-939-5277; www.disneyworld.disney.go.com; 2101 Osceola Pkwy; adult/child $97/91; ⊙9am-7pm, hours vary; ▣Disney) This sometimes-surreal blend of African safari, zoo, rides, costumed characters, shows and dinosaurs establishes its own distinct tone. It's best at animal encounters and shows, with the 110-acre **Kilimanjaro Safaris** as its centerpiece. The iconic **Tree of Life** houses the fun It's Tough to Be a Bug! show, and **Expedition Everest** and **Kali River Rapids** are top thrill rides.

★ Disney's Hollywood Studios   THEME PARK
(☑ 407-939-5277; www.disneyworld.disney.go.com; 351 S Studio Dr; adult/child 3-10yr $97/91; ⊙9am-10pm, hours vary; ▣Disney, ⛴Disney) The least charming of Disney's parks is set for a major transformation: a 14-acre *Star Wars* land and an 11-acre *Toy Story* area are planned for the next few years. Until then two of WDW's most exciting rides can be found here: the unpredictable elevator in the

TIPS & TRICKS

Tickets

Consider buying a ticket that covers more days in the parks than you think you'll need. It's less expensive per day, and it gives you the freedom to break up time at the theme parks with downtime in the pool or at low-key attractions beyond theme-park gates.

You can buy single or multiday tickets, and add a Park Hopper option ($64) that allows entrance to all four parks. Check online for packages, and buy in advance to avoid lines at the gate. If you want to pick up your prepurchased tickets ahead of the day you actually enter the parks, do so at Disney Spring's Guest Relations to avoid paying the $17 parking fee you'll have to pay to access other Guest Relations inside the four parks.

For discounts, check out www.mousesavers.com and www.undercovertourist.com.

When to Go

Anytime schools are out – during summer and holidays – Walt Disney Walt will be the most crowded. The least crowded times are January to February, mid-September through October and early December. Late fall tends to have the best weather; frequent downpours accompany the hot, humid summer months.

On the actual day you go, plan on arriving early so you can see as much of the park as possible before the midday peak. Consider going back to your hotel to recharge around 2pm or 3pm when it's the hottest and most crowded, then come back a few hours later and stay till close.

FastPass+ & My Disney Experience App

For the most popular attractions, Disney replaced the old FastPass paper system in 2014 with **FastPass+** (☑ 407-828-8739; www.disneyworld.disney.go.com), which is designed to allow guests to plan their days in advance and reduce time spent waiting in line. Visitors can reserve a specific time for up to three attractions per day through My Disney Experience accessible either at www.disneyworld.disney.go.com or by downloading the free mobile app. Once you link up your tickets, the latter is an invaluable tool for on-the-go planning and managing of your entire Disney experience.

Twilight Zone Tower of Terror and the Aerosmith-themed **Rock 'n' Roller Coaster**.

🛏 Sleeping

While it's tempting to save money by staying elsewhere, the value of staying at a WDW resort lies in the conveniences they offer. WDW has more than 20 family-friendly sleeping options, from camping to deluxe resorts, and Disney guests receive great perks (extended park hours, discount dining plans, complimentary on-property transportation, airport transfers). Disney's thorough website outlines rates and amenities for every property. Don't expect the quality of the room and amenities to match the price: you're paying for WDW convenience, not for Ritz-like luxury.

Disney's Value Resorts, of which there are seven, are the least-expensive option (besides camping); quality is equivalent to basic chain hotels, and (fair warning) they are favored by school groups:

★**Disney's**
Fort Wilderness Resort   CAMPGROUND, CABIN $
(☑ 407-939-5277, 407-824-2900; www.disneyworld. disney.go.com; 4510 N Fort Wilderness Trail; tent sites $75, RV sites $109-116, 6-person cabins $359; ✳@🛜🏊; 🖥Disney, 🍴Disney) For wilderness on a budget, we love the Fort Wilderness Resort & Campground, located in a huge shaded natural preserve, with tent sites and cabins that sleep up to six people.

Disney's Art of Animation Resort   HOTEL $$
(☑ 407-939-5277, 407-938-7000; www.disneyworld. disney.go.com; 1850 Animation Way; r $109-199, ste $269-457; P✳@🛜🏊; 🖥Disney) Inspired by animated Disney classics including the *Lion King, Cars, Finding Nemo* and *The Little Mermaid*.

Disney's All-Star Movies Resort   HOTEL $$
(☑ 407-939-7000, 407-939-5277; www.disneyworld.disney.go.com; 1901 W Buena Vista Dr; r $85-192; P✳@🛜🏊; 🖥Disney) Icons from Disney movies including *Toy Story* and *101 Dalmatians*.

Disney's All-Star Music Resort
HOTEL $$

(☎ 407-939-6000, 407-939-5277; www.disneyworld.disney.go.com; 1801 W Buena Vista Dr; r $85-192; P❄🕭❄; 🖵 Disney) Family suites and motel rooms surrounded by giant instruments.

Disney's All-Star Sports Resort
HOTEL $$

(☎ 407-939-5000, 407-939-5277; www.disneyworld.disney.go.com; 1701 Buena Vista Dr; r $85-192; P❄@🕭❄; 🖵 Disney) Five pairs of three-story buildings divided thematically by sport.

Disney's Pop Century Resort
HOTEL $$

(☎ 407-939-5277, 407-938-4000; www.disneyworld.disney.go.com; 1050 Century Dr; r $95-210; P❄🕭❄; 🖵 Disney) Each section pays homage to a different decade of the late 20th century.

★ Disney's Wilderness Lodge
RESORT $$$

(☎ 407-939-5277, 407-824-3200; www.disneyworld.disney.go.com; 901 Timberline Dr; r $289-998; P❄🕭❄; 🖵 Disney, 🖳 Disney) One of our favorite deluxe resorts is the Yosemite-style Wilderness Lodge; the 'rustic opulence' theme includes erupting geysers, a lakelike swimming area and bunk beds for the kids.

✗ Eating

Theme-park food ranges from OK to awful; the most interesting is served in Epcot's World Showcase. Sit-down meals are best, but *always* make reservations; seats can be impossible to get without one. For any dining, you can call central dining reservations (☎ 407-939-3463) up to 180 days in advance; or book online Open Table–style either on the website via the My Reservations section of My Disney Experience or using the app.

Disney has two dinner shows (a luau and country-style BBQ/vaudeville show) and 15 character meals, and these are insanely popular (see website for details). Book them the minute your 180-day window opens.

★ Sci-Fi Dine-In Theater
AMERICAN $$

(☎ 407-939-3463; www.disneyworld.disney.go.com; Hollywood Studios; mains $14-32, theme park admission required; ⏱ noon-4pm & 4-9pm; 🕭🍴; 🖵 Disney, 🖳 Disney) Dine in Cadillacs, drink craft beer and watch classic sci-fi flicks.

★ Boma
BUFFET $$

(☎ 407-938-4744, 407-939-3463; www.disneyworld.disney.go.com; 2901 Osceola Pkwy, Disney's Animal Kingdom Lodge; adult/child breakfast $24.50/13, dinner $40.50/21; ⏱ 7:30-11am & 4:30-9:30pm; 🕭🍴; 🖵 Disney) African-inspired eatery with pleasant surroundings and a buffet several notches above the rest.

Cinderella's Royal Table
AMERICAN $$$

(☎ 407-934-2927; www.disneyworld.disney.go.com; Cinderella's Castle, Magic Kingdom; adult $58-73, child $36-43; ⏱ 8:05-10:40am, 11:45am-2:40pm & 3:50-9:40pm; 🕭🍴; 🖵 Disney, 🖳 Disney, 🖵 Lynx 50, 56) The most sought-after meal at Disney is inside the Magic Kingdom's castle, where you dine with Disney princesses.

California Grill
AMERICAN $$$

(☎ 407-939-3463; www.disneyworld.disney.go.com; 4600 World Dr, Disney's Contemporary Resort; mains $37-50; ⏱ 5-10pm; 🍴; 🖵 Disney, 🖳 Disney, monorail Disney) Contemporary California cuisine with two observation decks – great views of the Magic Kingdom fireworks!

Victoria & Albert's
AMERICAN $$$

(☎ 407-939-3463; www.victoria-alberts.com; 4401 Floridian Way, Disney's Grand Floridian Resort; prix fixe from $159, wine pairing extra from $65; ⏱ 5-9:20pm; 🕭; 🖵 Disney, 🖳 Disney, monorail Disney) A true jacket-and-tie, crystal-goblet, romantic gourmet restaurant – no kidding, and no kids under 10.

☆ Entertainment

In addition to theme park events like Magic Kingdom parades and fireworks and Epcot's Illuminations, Disney has two entertainment districts – the newly revamped Disney Springs and Disney's Boardwalk – with eats, bars, music, movies, shops and shows.

★ Cirque du Soleil
La Nouba
PERFORMING ARTS

(☎ 407-939-7328, 407-939-7600; www.cirquedusoleil.com; Disney Springs; adult $59-139, child $48-115; ⏱ 6pm & 9pm Tue-Sat; 🖵 Disney, 🖳 Disney, 🖵 Lynx 50) This mind-blowing acrobatic extravaganza is one of the best shows at Disney.

ℹ Getting There & Around

Most hotels in Kissimmee and Orlando – and all Disney properties – offer free transportation to WDW. Disney-owned resorts also offer free transportation from the airport. Drivers can reach all four parks via I-4 and park for $17. The Magic Kingdom lot is huge; trams or ferries get you to the entrance.

Within WDW, a complex network of monorails, boats and buses gets you between the parks, resorts and entertainment districts.

Around Orlando

Just north of Orlando await some of Florida's best outdoor adventures, particularly swimming, snorkeling and kayaking in its crystal-clear, 72°F (22°C) natural springs. Closest is **Wekiwa Springs State Park** (☑ 407-884-2009; www.floridastateparks.org/wekiwasprings; 1800 Wekiwa Circle, Apopka; admission $6, campsites per person $5, hookups $24; ⊙ 7am-dusk), with 13 miles of hiking trails, a spring-fed swimming hole, nice campground and the tranquil 'Wild and Scenic' Wekiva River; rent kayaks from **Nature Adventures** (☑ 407-884-4311; www.canoewekiva.com; 1800 Wekiwa Circle, Wekiwa Springs State Park, Apopka; 2hr canoe/kayak $17, per additional hour $3; ⊙ 8am-8pm; 🐾).

Blue Spring State Park (☑ 386-775-3663; www.floridastateparks.org/bluespring; 2100 W French Ave, Orange City; car/bike $6/2; ⊙ 8am-sunset) is a favorite of wintering manatees, and two-hour cruises ply the St John's River. Just north of Deland, **De Leon Springs State Park** (☑ 386-985-4212; www.floridastateparks.org/deleonsprings; 601 Ponce de Leon Blvd, De Leon Springs; car/bike $6/2; ⊙ 8am-sunset) has a huge swimming area, more kayaking and tours of the Ponce de León's alleged fountain of youth.

To really escape into raw wilderness, head for the **Ocala National Forest** (www.fs.usda.gov/ocala), which has dozens of campgrounds, hundreds of miles of trails and 600 lakes. The hiking, biking, canoeing and camping are some of the state's best. See the website for visitor centers and descriptions.

FLORIDA PANHANDLE

Take all the things that are great about the Deep South – friendly people, molasses-slow pace, oak-lined country roads, fried food galore – and then add several hundred miles of sugar-white beaches, dozens of gin-clear natural springs and all the fresh oysters you can suck down, and there you have it: the fantastic, highly underrated Florida Panhandle.

Tallahassee

Florida's capital, cradled between gently rising hills and beneath tree-canopied roadways, is a calm and gracious city. It's closer to Atlanta than it is to Miami – both geographically and culturally – and far more Southern than the majority of the state it administrates. Despite the city's two major universities (Florida State and Florida Agricultural and Mechanical University) and its status as a government center, there's not much to detain a visitor for more than a day or two.

◉ Sights & Activities

Be sure to take a stroll through artsy **Railroad Square** (☑ 850-224-1308; www.railroadsquare.com; 567 Industrial Dr), a former lumber yard and industrial park between downtown and Florida State University full of funky boutiques, art galleries, cafes and microbreweries.

Mission San Luis HISTORIC SITE
(☑ 850-245-6406; www.missionsanluis.org; 2100 W Tennessee St; adult/child $5/2; ⊙ 10am-4pm Tue-Sun) The 60-acre site of a 17th-century Spanish and Apalachee mission that's been wonderfully reconstructed, especially the soaring Council House. Good tours included with admission provide a fascinating taste of 300 years ago.

Museum of Florida History MUSEUM
(☑ 850-245-6400; www.museumoffloridahistory.com; 500 S Bronough St; ⊙ 9am-4:30pm Mon-Fri, from 10am Sat, from noon Sun) FREE Here it is, Florida's history splayed out in fun, crisp exhibits: from mastodon skeletons to Florida's Paleo-Indians and Spanish shipwrecks, the Civil War to 'tin-can tourism.'

Florida Capitol Buildings HISTORIC BUILDING
Old and new, side by side. The current **Florida State Capitol** (www.myfloridacapitol.com; 402 South Monroe St; ⊙ 8am-5pm Mon-Fri) FREE is, in a word, ugly, but its top-floor observation deck gives you a bird's-eye view of the city. Next door, the **Historic Capitol** (www.flhistoriccapitol.gov; 400 S Monroe St; 🐾) FREE is the more charming 1902 predecessor.

Inside, the **Historic Capitol Museum** (www.flhistoriccapitol.gov; 400 South Monroe St; ⊙ 9am-4:30pm Mon-Fri, from 10am Sat, from noon Sun) FREE has intriguing government and cultural exhibits, including one on the infamous 2000 US presidential election.

⌷ Sleeping

Chains are clumped at exits along I-10 and along Monroe St between I-10 and downtown.

Hotel Duval HOTEL $$
(☑ 850-224-6000; www.hotelduval.com; 415 N Monroe St; r $129-259; 🅿❄🛜) Tallahassee's

WAKULLA SPRINGS

Just 15 miles south of Tallahassee is the world's deepest freshwater spring at **Edward Ball Wakulla Springs State Park** (☑ 850-561-7276; www. floridastateparks.org/park/Wakulla-Springs; 465 Wakulla Park Dr; car/bike $6/2, boat tours adult/child $8/5; ☺ 8am-dusk).The springs flow from massive underwater caves that are an archaeologist's dream, with fossilized bones including a mastodon that was discovered around 1850. These days you can swim in the icy springs or enjoy them from a glass-bottom boat chasing huge manatees. The wildlife-filled Wakulla River has been used as a movie set for several Tarzan movies, as well as *The Creature from the Black Lagoon*.

slickest digs. This 117-room hotel goes in for a neo-mod look while each floor is scented differently – the 3rd floor's Bourbon Vanilla smells like Dr Pepper! A rooftop bar and lounge is open until 2am most nights.

Governor's Inn HOTEL **$$**
(☑ 850-681-6855; www.thegovinn.com; 209 S Adams St; r $219-309; [P][❋][☎]) In a stellar downtown location, this warm, inviting inn has everything from queen rooms to two-level loft suites, plus a daily cocktail hour.

✗ Eating & Drinking

Many folks drive to quaint Thomasville, Georgia for top-end dining, but Tally's scene is evolving.

Paisley Cafe CAFE **$**
(www.thepaisleycafe.com; 1123 Thomasville Rd; mains $13.50-18; ☺ 11am-2:30pm Mon-Thu, to 3pm Fri, 10am-3pm Sat & Sun; ☎) A wonderful Midtown cafe with delectable pressed sandwiches, salads and insane desserts (the slutty brownie will have your sweet tooth turning tricks in no time!).

Cypress NEW SOUTHERN **$$$**
(☑ 850-513-1100; www.cypressrestaurant.com; 320 E Tennessee St; mains $21-32; ☺ 5-10pm Mon-Sat, 10:30am-2pm Sun) This unassuming spot is the domain of local chef David Gwynn, whose regional Southern dishes outshine expectations. Start with the roasted brussels

sprout salad with poached egg and move on to souped-up classics like pork belly with pecan-fried quail or shrimp and grits with bourbon-orange-thyme jus.

Madison Social PUB
(www.madisonsocial.com; 705 South Woodward Ave; mains $9-20, beers $3-6; ☺ 11:30am-2am Sun-Thu, from 10am Fri & Sat; ☎) Never mind the trend of flipping former transmission shops into hipster locales, this trendy hot spot was built to look that way from go! It swarms with a bold and beautiful mix of locals and FSU students, downing drinks at the stellar bar or aluminum picnic tables as the sun sets over Doak Campbell football stadium, the largest continuous brick structure in the USA.

☆ Entertainment

Bradfordville Blues Club LIVE MUSIC
(☑ 850-906-0766; www.bradfordvilleblues.com; 7152 Moses Lane, off Bradfordville Rd; tickets $15-35; ☺ 10pm Fri & Sat, 8:30pm some Thu, check online) Down the end of a dirt road lit by tiki torches, you'll find a bonfire raging under the live oaks at this hidden-away juke joint that hosts excellent national blues acts.

ⓘ Information

Leon County Welcome Center (☑ 850-606-2305; www.visittallahassee.com; 106 E Jefferson St; ☺ 8am-5pm Mon-Fri) An excellent visitor information center, with brochures on walking and driving tours.

ⓘ Getting There & Around

The **Tallahassee Regional Airport** (☑ 850-891-7802; www.talgov.com/airport; 3300 Capital Circle SW) is about 5 miles southwest of downtown, off Hwy 263. The **Greyhound station** (☑ 850-222-4249; www.greyhound.com; 112 W Tennessee St) is right downtown.

Star Metro (☑ 850-891-5200; www.talgov. com/starmetro; single ride $1.25, daily unlimited $3) provides local bus service.

Apalachicola & Around

Slow, mellow and perfectly preserved, Apalachicola is one of the Panhandle's most irresistible, romantic villages. Perched on the edge of a broad bay famous for its oysters, the oak-shaded town is a hugely popular getaway, with a new wave of bistros, art galleries, eclectic boutiques and historic B&Bs.

⊙ Sights & Activities

St Vincent Island   ISLAND
(☑ 850-653-8808; www.fws.gov/saintvincent) For
nature, the pristine St Vincent Island holds
pearly dunes, pine forests and wetlands
teeming with wildlife.

St George Island State Park   PARK
(☑ 850-927-2111; www.floridastateparks.org/
stgeorgeisland; vehicle $6, tent & RV sites $24;
⊙ 8am-dusk) Offers 9 miles of glorious, undeveloped beaches. In town, seek out fishing
charters and wildlife cruises.

⨎ Sleeping & Eating

Riverwood Suites   BOUTIQUE INN $$
(☑ 850-653-3848; www.riverwoodsuites.com; 29
Ave F; r $139-169; P ❄ 🛜) The four spacious
rooms inside this formerly abandoned tin
warehouse are the newest and best in town.
Think hardwood floors, artsy headboards,
modern fixins' and tuck-your-self-away
romance.

Coombs House Inn   B&B $$
(☑ 850-653-9199; www.coombshouseinn.com; 80
6th St; r $99-189; ❄ 🛜) This stunning yellow
Victorian inn was built in 1905 and features
black-cypress wall paneling, nine fireplaces,
a carved oak staircase, leaded glass windows
and beadboard ceilings.

Owl Cafe & Tap Room   MODERN AMERICAN $$
(☑ 850-653-9888; www.owlcafeflorida.com; 15 Ave
D; mains $10-28; ⊙ 11am-3pm & 5:30-10pm Mon-
Fri, from 11am Sat, 10:30am-3pm Sun; 🛜) Every-
one is catered to in this local favorite, with
casual fine dining in the upstairs cafe and
wine room and craft beers and tap-room-
only offerings below.

❶ Information

Apalachicola Bay Visitors Center (www.
apalachicolabay.org; 122 Commerce Street)
Pick up maps and info on walking tours.

Panama City Beach

There's no mistaking Panama City Beach for
anything other than what it is: a quintessentially
Floridian, carnivalesqe beach town. Spring
breakers and summer vacationers flock here
for the beautiful white-sand beaches and
the hurdy-gurdy of amusements, while mile
after mile of high-rise condos insist on dis-
rupting the view.

⊙ Sights & Activities

Shell Island has fantastic snorkeling, and
shuttles (☑ 850-233-0504; www.shellisland-
shuttle.com; adult/child $16.95/8.95; ⊙ 9am-5pm)
depart every 30 minutes in summer.

St Andrews State Park   PARK
(☑ 850-233-5140; www.floridastateparks.org/st
andrews; 4607 State Park Lane, Panama City; vehi-
cle/pedestrian $8/2; ⊙ 8am-sunset) A peaceful
escape with nature trails, swimming beach-
es and wildlife.

Dive Locker   DIVING
(☑ 850-230-8006; www.divelocker.net; 106
Thomas Dr, Panama City Beach; ⊙ 8am-6pm
Mon-Fri, 7am-4pm Sat, to 5pm Sun) A renowned
wreck-diving site, the area around Panama
City Beach has dozens of natural, histor-
ic and artificial reefs. This well-respected
outfitter and dive school knows all the local
reefs. Basic supervised two-tank dives start
at $142, gear included.

⨎ Sleeping

PCB Bed & Breakfast   B&B $$
(☑ 850-867-0421; www.panamacitybeachbed
andbreakfast.com; 127 Toledo Pl; r $149; P ❄ 🛜)
Steps from the development-free sun-
toasted sands of pristine Laguna Beach, the
only B&B in town is a three-room affair in a
Key West–style cottage nicknamed 'Nostalgic 1950's Beach Cottage.' Luxury linens and
big Vizio TVs ensure comfort; and there are
plenty of porches and green space to while
away the time.

Wisteria Inn   MOTEL $$
(☑ 850-234-0557; www.wisteria-inn.com; 20404
Front Beach Rd; d from $119-159; P ❄ ❄ 🛜)
Every room is different at this sweet little
14-room motel – we love the colorful Carrib-
bean feel of No 8 – and there's poolside mi-
mosa hours and an 'adults only' policy that
discourages spring breakers.

✗ Eating & Drinking

Gourmet by the Bay   FAST FOOD $
(www.facebook.com/GourmetByTheBay; 284
Powell Adams Rd; mains $4-10; ⊙ noon-7:30pm
Mon-Fri & Sun, to 9:30pm Sat, to 11:30pm summer)
Hidden away inside the small Miracle Strip
Amusement Park is this wildly popular food
stall that does tremendously good mahi-
mahi or shrimp tacos on the cheap. No park
admission charge if you're just eating.

SCENIC DRIVE: THE EMERALD COAST

Along the Panhandle coast between Panama City Beach and Destin, skip the main highway (Hwy 98) in favor of one of the most enchanting drives in Florida: **Scenic Highway 30A**. This 18-mile stretch of road hugs what's referred to as the Emerald Coast for its almost fluorescent, gem-colored waters lapping brilliant white beaches of ground-quartz crystal.

Leading off Scenic Hwy 30A are wild parklands like **Grayton Beach State Park** (☑850-267-8300; www.floridastateparks.org/graytonbeach; 357 Main Park Rd, Santa Rosa Beach; vehicle $5; ⊘8am-sunset), considered one of Florida's prettiest, most pristine strands. About 15 quaint communities hug the coast, some arty and funky, and some master-planned resorts with matchy-matchy architectural perfection. Of these, the most intriguing and surreal is the little village of **Seaside** (www.seasidefl.com), a Necco Wafer–colored town that was hailed as a model of New Urbanism in the 1980s.

Seaside is such an idealized vision that, unaltered, it formed the setting for the 1998 film *The Truman Show,* about a man whose 'perfect life' is nothing but a TV show. Good online resources are www.30a.com and www.visitsouthwalton.com.

The Craft Bar BAR
(www.thecraftbarfl.com; 15600 Panama City Beach Pkwy, Pier Park North; beers $4.50-12, mains $12-35; ⊘11am-11pm Mon-Thu, to midnight Fri & Sat, to 10pm Sun) Head to this anti-PCB choice to trade pirate-themed camp and beach blanket anarchy for 30 thoughtfully sourced microbrews on tap (Mikkeller!), craft cocktails and excellent pub grub.

ℹ Information

Visitors Information Center (☑850-233-5870; www.visitpanamacitybeach.com; 17001 Panama City Beach Pkwy; ⊘8am-5pm) Come for maps, brochures and the lowdown on what's up and coming in town.

ℹ Getting There & Around

The **Panama City International Airport** (PFN; ☑850-763-6751; www.iflybeaches.com; 6300 W Bay Pkwy, Panama City) is served by a few major airlines. The **Greyhound Station** (☑850-785-6111; www.greyhound.com; 917 Harrison Ave, Panama City) is in Panama City, and the limited **Bay Town Trolley** (www.baytowntrolley.org; fare $1.50) runs only weekdays from 6am to 8pm.

Pensacola & Pensacola Beach

Neighbors with Alabama, Pensacola and its adjacent beach town welcome visitors driving in from the west. Its gorgeous snow-white beaches and tolerance of the annual spring-break bacchanal ensure Pensacola's popularity, but the city has bounced back better than others from 2004's devastating Hurricane Ivan and the 2010 Deepwater Horizon oil spill

in the Gulf of Mexico, resulting in a revitalized energy that has spawned a burgeoning foodie scene and hip cafes and bars to go with its already sultry Spanish-style downtown and wonderful preserved historic district.

◉ Sights & Activities

★**National Naval Aviation Museum** MUSEUM
(☑850-452-3604; www.navalaviationmuseum. org; 1750 Radford Blvd; ⊘9am-5pm, guided tours 9:30am, 11am, 1pm & 2:30pm; ⊕) FREE Home to a don't-miss collection of jaw-dropping military aircraft and the elite **Blue Angels** (www. blueangels.navy.mil) squadron. Shockingly, it's free, unless you sit down ($8.75 for IMAX movies, $20 for the Flight Simulators and dining). Bring ID – it's an active naval base.

Historic Pensacola Village HISTORIC BUILDING
(☑850-595-5985; www.historicpensacola.org; 205 E Zaragoza St; adult/child $6/3; ⊘10am-4pm Tue-Sat, tours 11am, 1pm & 2:30pm) Pensacola says 'take that, St Augustine!' with this village, a self-contained enclave of drop-dead-gorgeous historic homes and museums. Admission is good for one week and includes a guided tour and entrance to each building as well as admission to **TT Wentworth Florida State Museum** (www.historicpensacola.org; 330 S Jefferson St; adult/child $6/3; ⊘10am-4pm Tue-Sat) and **Pensacola Children's Museum** (☑850-595-1559; 115 E Zaragoza St; admission $3; ⊘10am-4pm Tue-Sat).

Pensacola Museum of Art MUSEUM
(☑850-432-6247; www.pensacolamuseum.org; 407 S Jefferson St; adult/student $10/8; ⊘10am-5pm Tue-Fri, from noon Sat) An impressive collection

of major 20th- and 21st-century artists, spanning cubism, realism, pop art and folk art, housed in the city's old jail (1908).

Gulf Islands National Seashore   BEACH
(☑850-934-2600; www.nps.gov/guis; 7-day pass pedestrian/cyclist/car $3/3/8; ☉sunrise-sunset) To enjoy the area's lovely white sands, head to the easy-access Pensacola Beach or the neighboring Gulf Islands National Seashore, part of a 160-mile (noncontinuous) stretch of undeveloped beach. The Pensacola portion was recently voted Florida's best beach by *USA Today*.

🛏 Sleeping

Paradise Inn   MOTEL $
(☑850-932-2319; www.paradiseinn-pb.com; 21 Via de Luna Dr; r from $89; ⓟ❄☎☀) Across from the beach, this '50s-era motel is a lively, cheery place thanks to its popular bar and grill. Rooms are small and clean, with tiled floors and brightly painted walls; and staff will cook up your fresh catches with all the fixins' for $13.

Noble Inn   B&B $$
(☑850-434-9544; www.noblemanor.com; 110 W Strong St; r/ste $160/185; ⓟ❄☎☀) This pretty 1905 mansion in the historic North Hill district is the most charming place to stay. The East Coast innkeeper, Bonnie, runs a one-woman show, from shining up those spick-and-span hardwood floors to whipping up praline French toast for breakfast.

New World Inn   HOTEL $$
(☑850-432-4111; www.newworldlanding.com; 600 S Palafax St; r from $119; ⓟ❄☎) Peek under the lid of this former box factory and you'll find surprisingly lovely rooms with luxe bedding and new hardwood flooring.

✖ Eating & Drinking

For cheap eats, check out **Al Fresco** (www.eatalfresco.com; cnr Palafox & Main Sts), a collection of five Airstream trailer food trucks on the corner of Palafax and Main Sts. Downtown's South Palafax St is lined with drinking dens.

Blue Dot   BURGERS $
(310 N De Villiers St; burgers $5.58-6.97; ☉11:30am-3pm Tue-Fri, noon-3pm Sat) The line swells with locals-in-the-know before 11am for Pensacola's best burgers – a simple, greasy and perfectly seasoned affair. Know what you want before you get to the counter and dress appropriately. You're familiar with

Seinfeld's Soup Nazi? Meet the Burger Nazi. Get here early. Cash only.

Native Café   BREAKFAST $
(www.thenativecafe.com; 45a Via de Luna Dr; mains $4.50-13; ☉7:30am-3pm; ☎) Three words: crab cakes Benedict! Locals line up at this funky breakfast and lunch spot in a colorful strip mall at the beach. Adorable staff and great service to boot.

McGuire's Irish Pub   IRISH $$
(www.mcguiresirishpub.com; 600 E Gregory St; mains $10-33; ☉11am-2am) Promising 'feasting, imbibery and debauchery,' this barnlike spot delivers all three. Stick to steaks and burgers when you order, and don't mind the animal heads or dollar-bill-adorned walls.

★Iron   NEW SOUTHERN $$$
(☑850-476-7776; www.restaurantiron.com; 22 N Palafax St; mains $18-36; ☉4:30-10pm Tue-Thu, to 1am Fri & Sat; ☎) Armed with New Orleans experience, chef Alex McPhail works his ever-changing-menu magic at downtown's Iron, the best of Pensacola's new line of vibrant, locally sourced, high-end culinary hotbeds. Extremely friendly mixologists know their craft; and McPhail's food – from beer-braised pork belly to creole-seasoned catch of the day – punches above the Emerald Coast's weight class.

★Seville Quarter   CLUB
(www.sevillequarter.com; 130 E Government St; cover $3-10; ☉7am-2:30am) Taking up an entire city block, this multivenue complex always has something going on, from breakfast through last call, in its seven separate eating, drinking and music venues.

ℹ Information

Pensacola Visitors Information Center
(☑800-874-1234; www.visitpensacola.com; 1401 E Gregory St; ☉8am-5pm Mon-Fri, 9am-4pm Sat, 10am-4pm Sun) Come to the foot of the Pensacola Bay Bridge for a bounty of tourist information and knowledgeable staff.

ℹ Getting There & Around

Five miles northeast of downtown, **Pensacola Regional Airport** (☑850-436-5000; www.flypensacola.com; 2430 Airport Blvd) is served by major airlines.

The **Greyhound station** (☑850-476-4800; www.greyhound.com; 505 W Burgess Rd) is 9 miles north of downtown.

A Downtown Pensacola–Pensacola Beach ferry is in the works for 2017; until then, bus 64 runs from Jefferson and Garden Sts downtown to the beach Friday to Sunday.

Great Lakes

Best Places to Eat

➡ New Scenic Cafe (p604)

➡ Dove's Luncheonette (p531)

➡ Tucker's (p561)

➡ Slows Bar BQ (p567)

➡ The Old Fashioned (p586)

Best Places to Stay

➡ Freehand Chicago (p527)

➡ Hotel 340 (p601)

➡ Acme Hotel (p527)

➡ Brewhouse Inn & Suites (p583)

➡ Cleveland Hostel (p551)

Why Go?

Don't be fooled by all the corn. Behind it lurks surfing beaches and Tibetan temples, car-free islands and the green-draped night-lights of the aurora borealis. The Midwest takes its knocks for being middle-of-nowhere boring; so consider the moose-filled national parks, urban five-ways and Hemingway, Dylan and Vonnegut sites to be its little secret.

Roll call for the Midwest's cities starts with Chicago, which unfurls what is arguably the country's mightiest skyline. Milwaukee keeps the beer-and-Harley flame burning, while Minneapolis shines a hipster beacon out over the fields. Detroit rocks, plain and simple.

The Great Lakes are huge, offering beaches, dunes, resort towns and lighthouse-dotted scenery. Dairy farms and orchards blanket the region – fresh pie and ice cream await road-trippers. And when the Midwest flattens out? There's always a goofball roadside attraction, like the Spam Museum or world's largest ball of twine, to revive imaginations.

When to Go

Chicago

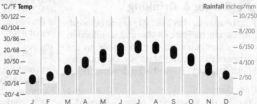

Jan & Feb Skiers and snowmobilers hit the trails.

Jul & Aug Finally, it's warm! Beer gardens hop, beaches splash, and festivals rock most weekends.

Sep & Oct Fair weather, bountiful farm and orchard harvests, and shoulder-season bargains.

History

The region's first residents included the Hopewell (around 200 BC) and Mississippi River mound builders (around AD 700). Both left behind mysterious piles of earth that were tombs for their leaders and possibly tributes to their deities. You can see remnants at Cahokia in southern Illinois, and Mound City in southeastern Ohio.

French voyageurs (fur traders) arrived in the early 17th century and established missions and forts. The British turned up soon after that, with the rivalry spilling over into the French and Indian War (Seven Years' War, 1754–61), after which Britain took control of all of the land east of the Mississippi. Following the Revolutionary War, the Great Lakes area became the new USA's Northwest Territory, which soon was divided into states and locked to the region after it developed its impressive canal and railroad network. But conflicts erupted between the newcomers and the Native Americans, including the 1811 Battle of Tippecanoe in Indiana; the bloody 1832 Black Hawk War in Wisconsin, Illinois and around, which forced indigenous people to move west of the Mississippi; and the 1862 Sioux uprising in Minnesota.

Throughout the late 19th and early 20th centuries, industries sprang up and grew quickly, fueled by resources of coal and iron, and cheap transportation on the lakes. The availability of work brought huge influxes of immigrants from Ireland, Germany, Scandinavia and southern and eastern Europe. For decades after the Civil War, a great number of African Americans also migrated to the region's urban centers from the South.

The area prospered during WWII and throughout the 1950s, but was followed by 20 years of social turmoil and economic stagnation. Manufacturing industries declined, which walloped Rust Belt cities such as Detroit and Cleveland with high unemployment and 'white flight' (white middle-class families who fled to the suburbs).

The 1980s and '90s brought urban revitalization. The region's population increased, notably with newcomers from Asia and Mexico. Growth in the service and high-tech sectors resulted in economic balance, although manufacturing industries such as car making and steel still played a big role, meaning that when the economic crisis hit in 2008, Great Lakes towns felt the pinch first and foremost.

ILLINOIS

Chicago dominates the state with its sky-high architecture and superlative museums, restaurants and music clubs. But venturing further afield reveals Hemingway's hometown of 'wide lawns and narrow minds,' scattered shrines to local hero Abe Lincoln, and a trail of corn dogs, pies and drive-in movie theaters down Route 66. A cypress swamp and a prehistoric World Heritage site make appearances in Illinois too.

❶ Information

Illinois Office of Tourism (www.enjoyillinois.com)

Illinois Highway Conditions (www.gettingaroundillinois.com)

Illinois State Park Information (www.dnr.illinois.gov) State parks are free to visit. Campsites cost $6 to $35; some accept reservations (www.reserveamerica.com; $5).

GREAT LAKES IN...

Five Days

Spend the first two days in **Chicago**. On your third day, make the 1½-hour trip to **Milwaukee** for culture, both high- and lowbrow. Take the ferry over to Michigan and spend your fourth day beaching in **Saugatuck**. Circle back via **Indiana Dunes** or **Indiana's Amish Country**.

Ten Days

After two days in **Chicago**, on day three make for **Madison** and its surrounding quirky sights. Spend your fourth and fifth days at the **Apostle Islands**, and then head into the Upper Peninsula to visit **Marquette** and **Pictured Rocks** for a few days, followed by **Sleeping Bear Dunes** and the wineries around **Traverse City**. Return via the galleries, pies and beaches of **Saugatuck**.

Great Lakes Highlights

1 Absorbing the skyscrapers, museums, festivals and foodie bounty of **Chicago** (p514).

2 Beach lounging, berry eating and surfing on **Lake Michigan's western shore** (p573).

3 Slowing down for clip-clopping horses and buggies in **Ohio's Amish Country** (p555).

4 Polka dancing at a Friday-night fish fry in **Milwaukee** (p581).

5 Paddling the **Boundary Waters** (p606) and sleeping under a blanket of stars.

6 Cycling along the river against the urban backdrop of **Detroit** (p563).

7 Taking the slowpoke, pie-filled journey through Illinois on **Route 66** (p539).

8 Being surprised by the Tibetan temples, phenomenal architecture and green hills of **Central Indiana** (p545).

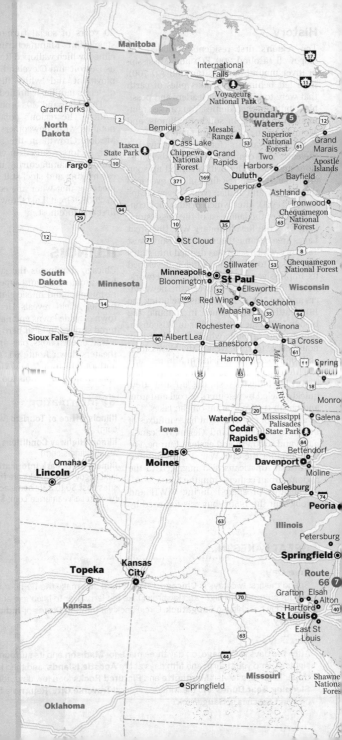

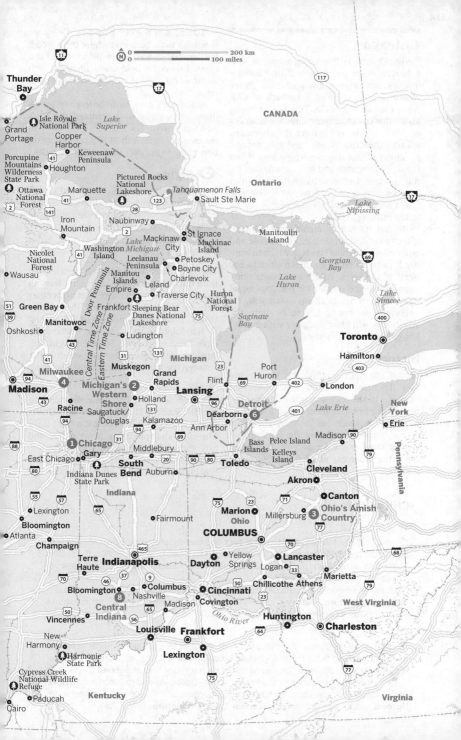

Chicago

Loving Chicago is 'like loving a woman with a broken nose: you may well find lovelier lovelies, but never a lovely so real.' Writer Nelson Algren summed it up well in *Chicago: City on the Make*. There's something about this cloud-scraping city that bewitches. Well, maybe not during the six-month winter, when the 'Windy City' gets slapped by snowy blasts; however, come May, when the weather warms and everyone dashes for the outdoor festivals, ballparks, lakefront beaches and beer gardens – ah, nowhere tops Chicago (literally: some of the world's tallest buildings are here).

Beyond its mighty architecture, Chicago is a city of Mexican, Polish, Vietnamese and other ethnic neighborhoods in which to wander. It's a city of blues, jazz and rock clubs any night of the week. And it's a chowhound's town, where the queues for hot dogs equal those at North America's top restaurants.

Forgive us, but it has to be said: the Windy City will blow you away with its low-key, cultured awesomeness.

History

In the late 17th century, the Potawatomi gave the name Checagou – meaning 'wild onions' – to the once-swampy environs. The new city's pivotal moment happened on October 8, 1871, when (so the story goes) Mrs O'Leary's cow kicked over the lantern that started the Great Chicago Fire. It torched the entire inner city and left 90,000 people homeless.

'Damn,' said the city planners. 'Guess we shouldn't have built everything from wood. It's flammable.' So they rebuilt with steel and created space for bold new structures, such as the world's first skyscraper, which popped up in 1885.

Al Capone's gang more or less ran things during the 1920s and corrupted the city's political system. Local government has had issues ever since, with 31 city council members going to jail over the last four decades.

◉ Sights

Chicago's main attractions are found mostly in or near the city center, though visits to distant neighborhoods, like Pilsen and Hyde Park, can also be rewarding.

◉ The Loop

The city center is named for the elevated train tracks that lasso its streets. It's busy all day, though not much happens at night other than in Millennium Park and the Theater District (near the intersection of N State and W Randolph Sts). Grant Park – where the city's mega-events like Blues Fest and Lollapalooza take place – forms a green buffer between the skyscrapers and Lake Michigan.

★ **Millennium Park** PARK
(Map p518; ☏ 312-742-1168; www.millenniumpark. org; 201 E Randolph St; ⊙ 6am-11pm; ⊞; Ⓜ Brown, Orange, Green, Purple, Pink Line to Randolph) FREE
The city's showpiece is a trove of free and arty sights. It includes **Pritzker Pavilion**, Frank Gehry's swooping silver band shell, hosting free concerts nightly in summer

---

CHICAGO IN...

Two Days

On your first day, take an **architectural tour** and gaze up at the city's skyscrapers. Look down from the **Willis Tower**, the city's tallest building. See 'The Bean' reflect the skyline, and splash with Crown Fountain's human gargoyles at **Millennium Park**. Chow down on a deep-dish pizza at **Giordano's**.

Make the second day a cultural one: explore the **Art Institute of Chicago** or **Field Museum of Natural History** . Grab a stylish dinner in the **West Loop**. Or listen to blues at **Buddy Guy's Legends**.

Four Days

Follow the two-day itinerary. On your third day, dip your toes in Lake Michigan at **North Avenue Beach** and saunter through leafy **Lincoln Park**. If it's baseball season, head to **Wrigley Field** (p535) for a Cubs game. In the evening yuck it up at **Second City**.

Pick a neighborhood on your fourth day: vintage boutiques and rock and roll in **Wicker Park**, murals and mole sauce in **Pilsen** (p532), pagodas and Vietnamese sandwiches in **Uptown**, or Obama sights and the **Nuclear Energy sculpture** in Hyde Park.

(6:30pm; bring a picnic and bottle of wine); Anish Kapoor's beloved silvery sculpture **Cloud Gate** (aka 'The Bean'); and Jaume Plensa's **Crown Fountain**, a de facto water park that projects video images of locals spitting water, gargoyle style.

The **McCormick Tribune Ice Rink** fills with skaters in winter (and alfresco diners in summer). The hidden **Lurie Garden** blooms with prairie flowers and tranquillity. The Gehry-designed **BP Bridge** spans Columbus Dr and offers great skyline views. And the **Nichols Bridgeway** arches from the park up to the Art Institute's small, 3rd-floor sculpture garden (free to view).

Want more? Free yoga and Pilates classes take place Saturday mornings in summer on the Great Lawn, while the Family Fun Tent provides free kids' activities daily between 10am and 2pm.

⭐**Art Institute of Chicago**   MUSEUM
(Map p518; ☎ 312-443-3600; www.artic.edu; 111 S Michigan Ave; adult/child $25/free; ⊙ 10:30am-5pm, to 8pm Thu; ♿; Ⓜ Brown, Orange, Green, Purple, Pink Line to Adams) The second-largest art museum in the country, the Art Institute's collection of impressionist and post-impressionist paintings rivals those in France, and the number of surrealist works is tremendous. Download the free app for DIY tours. It offers 50 jaunts, everything from highlights (Grant Wood's *American Gothic*, Edward Hopper's *Nighthawks*) to a 'birthday-suit tour' of naked works.

Allow two hours to browse the museum's must-sees; art buffs should allocate much longer. The main entrance is on Michigan Ave, but you can also enter via the dazzling Modern Wing on Monroe St.

⭐**Willis Tower**   TOWER
(Map p518; ☎ 312-875-9696; www.theskydeck.com; 233 S Wacker Dr; adult/child $19.50/12.50; ⊙ 9am-10pm Apr-Sep, 10am-8pm Oct-Mar; Ⓜ Brown, Orange, Purple, Pink Line to Quincy) It's Chicago's tallest building, and the 103rd-floor Skydeck puts you 1353ft into the heavens. Take the ear-popping, 70-second elevator ride to the top, then step onto one of the glass-floored ledges jutting out in mid-air for a knee-buckling perspective straight down. The entrance is on Jackson Blvd.

Queues can be up to an hour on busy days (peak times are in summer, between 11am and 4pm Friday through Sunday). A bit of history: it was the Sears Tower until insur-

ILLINOIS FACTS

Nicknames Prairie State, Land of Lincoln

Population 12.9 million

Area 57,900 sq miles

Capital city Springfield (population 117,000)

Other cities Chicago (population 2.7 million)

Sales tax 6.25%

Birthplace of Author Ernest Hemingway (1899–1961), animator Walt Disney (1901–66), jazz musician Miles Davis (1926–91), actor Bill Murray (b 1950)

Home of Cornfields, Route 66 starting point

Politics Democratic in Chicago, Republican downstate

Famous for Skyscrapers, corn dogs, Abe Lincoln sights

Official snack food Popcorn

Driving distances Chicago to Milwaukee 92 miles, Chicago to Springfield 200 miles

ance broker Willis Group Holdings bought the naming rights in 2009.

Chicago Cultural Center   BUILDING
(Map p518; ☎ 312-744-6630; www.chicagoculturalcenter.org; 78 E Washington St; ⊙ 9am-7pm Mon-Thu, to 6pm Fri & Sat, 10am-6pm Sun; Ⓜ Brown, Orange, Green, Purple, Pink Line to Randolph) **FREE** The block-long building houses ongoing art exhibitions and foreign films, as well as jazz, classical and electronic dance music concerts at lunchtime (12:15pm Monday to Friday). It also contains the world's largest Tiffany stained-glass dome and Chicago's main visitor center. Free building tours take place Wednesday, Friday and Saturday at 1:15pm; meet in the Randolph St lobby.

Maggie Daley Park   PARK
(Map p518; www.maggiedaleypark.com; 337 E Randolph St; ⊙ 6am-11pm; ♿; Ⓜ Brown, Orange, Green, Purple, Pink Line to Randolph) **FREE** Families love the park's fanciful free playgrounds in all their enchanted forest and pirate-themed glory. There's also a rock-climbing wall and 18-hole mini-golf course (which becomes an ice-skating ribbon in winter); these features have fees.

Metro Chicago Area

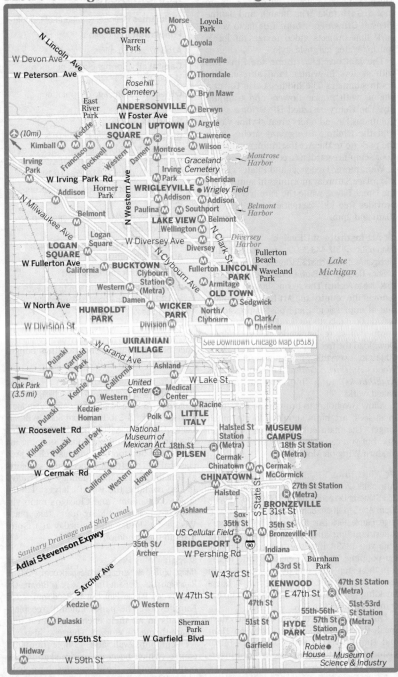

N

0 — 4 km
0 — 2 miles

ROGERS PARK

Morse
Loyola Park
Loyola
Warren Park

W Devon Ave
Granville
W Peterson Ave
Thorndale

Rosehill Cemetery
Bryn Mawr

East River Park
ANDERSONVILLE
W Foster Ave
Berwyn

(10mi)
LINCOLN SQUARE
UPTOWN
Argyle

Kimball
Lawrence

Francisco
Rockwell
Western
Damen
Montrose
Wilson

Irving Park
Graceland Cemetery
Montrose Harbor

W Irving Park Rd
Irving Park
Sheridan

Addison
Horner Park
WRIGLEYVILLE
Wrigley Field

Belmont
Addison
Addison
Belmont Harbor

Paulina
Southport

LAKE VIEW
Belmont

Logan Square
Wellington
N Clark St
Diversey Harbor

LOGAN SQUARE
W Diversey Ave
Diversey
Lake Michigan

W Fullerton Ave
BUCKTOWN
Fullerton Beach

California
Clybourn Station (Metra)
Fullerton
LINCOLN PARK
Waveland Park

Western
N Clybourn Ave
Armitage

Damen
WICKER PARK
OLD TOWN
Sedgwick

HUMBOLDT PARK
North/Clybourn
Clark/Division

W Division St
Division

UKRAINIAN VILLAGE
W Grand Ave
See Downtown Chicago Map (p518)

Pulaski
Garfield Park
Ashland

Oak Park (3.5 mi)
California
W Lake St

Kedzie
United Center
Medical Center

Western
Racine

Kedzie-Homan
Polk
LITTLE ITALY

W Roosevelt Rd
National Museum of Mexican Art
Halsted St Station (Metra)
MUSEUM CAMPUS

Kildare
Pulaski
Central Park
Kedzie
18th St
PILSEN
18th St Station (Metra)

W Cermak Rd
Cermak-Chinatown
Cermak-McCormick

California
Western
Hoyne
CHINATOWN
27th St Station (Metra)

Halsted
BRONZEVILLE

Ashland
Sox-35th St
E 31st St

US Cellular Field
35th St-Bronzeville-IIT

Sanitary Drainage and Ship Canal
Adlai Stevenson Expwy
35th St/Archer
BRIDGEPORT
W Pershing Rd
Indiana
43rd St
Burnham Park

S Archer Ave
W 43rd St

Kedzie
Western
W 47th St
47th St
KENWOOD
E 47th St
47th St Station (Metra)

Pulaski
Sherman Park
51st St
HYDE PARK
51st-53rd St Station (Metra)

Midway
W 55th St
W Garfield Blvd
Garfield
55th-56th-57th St Station (Metra)

W 59th St
Robie House
Museum of Science & Industry

FAMOUS LOOP ARCHITECTURE

Ever since it presented the world with the first skyscraper, Chicago has thought big with its architecture and pushed the envelope of modern design. The Loop is a fantastic place to roam and gawk at these ambitious structures.

The **Chicago Architecture Foundation** (p525) runs tours that explain the following buildings and more:

Chicago Board of Trade (Map p518; 141 W Jackson Blvd; Ⓜ Brown, Orange, Purple, Pink Line to LaSalle) A 1930 art-deco gem. Inside, manic traders swap futures and options. Outside, check out the giant statue of Ceres, the goddess of agriculture, that tops the building.

Rookery (Map p518; www.flwright.org; 209 S LaSalle St; ⊘ 9:30am-5:30pm Mon-Fri; Ⓜ Brown, Orange, Purple, Pink Line to Quincy) The 1888 Rookery looks fortresslike outside, but the inside is light and airy thanks to Frank Lloyd Wright's atrium overhaul. Tours ($7 to $12) are available at noon weekdays. Pigeons used to roost here, hence the name.

Monadnock Building (Map p518; www.monadnockbuilding.com; 53 W Jackson Blvd; Ⓜ Blue Line to Jackson) Architectural pilgrims get weak-kneed when they see the Monadnock Building, which is two buildings in one. The north is the older, traditional design from 1891, while the south is the newer, mod half from 1893. See the difference? The Monadnock remains true to its original purpose as an office building.

Multiple picnic tables make the park an excellent spot to relax. It connects to Millennium Park via the pedestrian BP Bridge.

Buckingham Fountain   FOUNTAIN
(Map p518; 301 S Columbus Dr; Ⓜ Red Line to Harrison) Grant Park's centerpiece is one of the world's largest squirters, with a 1.5-million-gallon capacity and a 15-story-high spray. It lets loose on the hour from 9am to 11pm mid-April to mid-October, accompanied at night by multicolored lights and music.

Route 66 Sign   HISTORIC SITE
(Map p518; E Adams St btwn S Michigan & Wabash Aves; Ⓜ Brown, Orange, Green, Purple, Pink Line to Adams) Attention Route 66 buffs: the Mother Road's starting point is here. Look for the marker on Adams St's south side as you head west toward Wabash Ave.

⊙ South Loop

The South Loop, which includes the lower ends of downtown and Grant Park, bustles with the lakefront Museum Campus and gleaming residential high-rises.

★ Field Museum of
Natural History   MUSEUM
(Map p518; ☑ 312-922-9410; www.fieldmuseum. org; 1400 S Lake Shore Dr; adult/child $18/13; ⊘ 9am-5pm; 👶; 🚌 146, 130) The mammoth museum houses everything but the kitchen sink – beetles, mummies, gemstones, Bushman the stuffed ape. The collection's rock star is Sue, the largest *Tyrannosaurus rex* yet discovered. She even gets her own gift shop. Special exhibits, like the 3D movie, cost extra.

★ Shedd Aquarium   AQUARIUM
(Map p518; ☑ 312-939-2438; www.sheddaquarium .org; 1200 S Lake Shore Dr; adult/child $31/22; ⊘ 9am-5pm Mon-Fri, to 6pm Sat & Sun Sep-May, to 6pm daily Jun-Aug; 👶; 🚌 146, 130) Top draws at the kiddie-mobbed Shedd Aquarium include the Wild Reef exhibit, where there's just 5in of Plexiglas between you and two dozen fierce-looking sharks, and the Oceanarium, with its rescued sea otters. Note the Oceanarium also keeps beluga whales and Pacific white-sided dolphins, a practice that has become increasingly controversial in recent years.

★ Adler Planetarium   MUSEUM
(Map p518; ☑ 312-922-7827; www.adlerplanetar- ium.org; 1300 S Lake Shore Dr; adult/child $12/8; ⊘ 9:30am-4pm Mon-Fri, to 4:30 Sat & Sun; 👶; 🚌 146, 130) Space enthusiasts will get a big bang (pun!) out of the Adler. There are public telescopes to view the stars, 3D lectures to learn about supernovas and the *Planet Explorers* exhibit where kids can 'launch' a rocket. The immersive digital films cost $13 extra. The Adler's front steps offer Chicago's primo skyline view.

Downtown Chicago

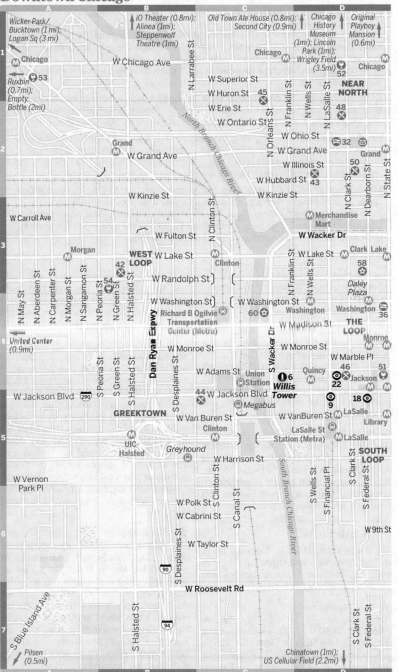

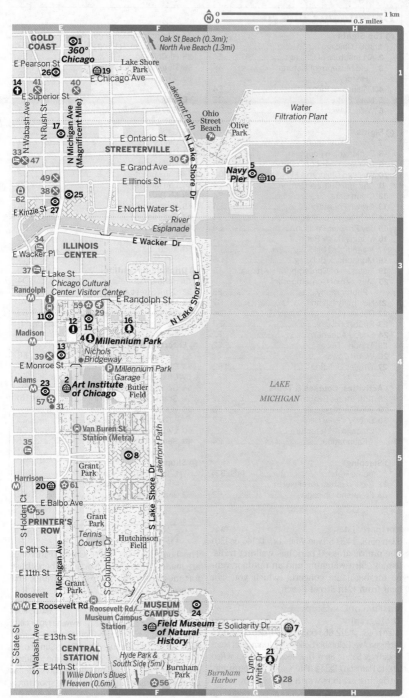

0   1 km
0   0.5 miles

GOLD COAST

●1 **360°**
   Chicago
●26
🏛19 **Lake Shore Park**
E Pearson St
14 🛈
41 ✕
      E Chicago Ave
E Superior St
40
33 🍴✕
47
17
49 ✕
38 ✕
●25
62 🏧
27
E Kinzie St

STREETERVILLE
E Ontario St
E Grand Ave
E Illinois St
30 ●
E North Water St
Navy ●5
Pier 🏛10
Ⓟ

N Michigan Ave (Magnificent Mile)
N Wabash Ave
N Rush St

Lakefront Path
N Lake Shore Dr

Ohio Street Beach
🍴
Olive Park

Water Filtration Plant

GREAT LAKES

34
37 📮
E Wacker Pl
E Lake St
Chicago Cultural
Center Visitor Center
Randolph Ⓜ
🛈
59 ✪🛈
29
11 ●
12 🛈
15
16 🛈
Madison Ⓜ
13 ●
4 🎵 **Millennium Park**
39 ✕
E Monroe St
Nichols Bridgeway
Adams Ⓜ
23 ●
2 🏛 **Art Institute**
   of Chicago
57 ✪
31 ●

ILLINOIS CENTER

River Esplanade
E Wacker Dr

E Randolph St

Millennium Park Garage Ⓟ
Butler Field

N Lake Shore Dr

LAKE MICHIGAN

35 📮

🚉 Van Buren St Station (Metra)
●8

Grant Park

Harrison Ⓜ
20 🏛
61 ✪
55 ✪
E Balbo Ave

PRINTER'S ROW
S Holden Ct
Grant Park
Tennis Courts

S Lake Shore Dr
Lakefront Path

Hutchinson Field

E 9th St
E 11th St

S Michigan Ave
S Columbus Dr

Grant Park
Roosevelt Ⓜ Ⓜ E Roosevelt Rd
S State St
S Wabash Ave
E 13th St

CENTRAL STATION
E 14th St

Roosevelt Rd/ Museum Campus Station

MUSEUM CAMPUS
●24
3 🏛 **Field Museum**
   of Natural
   History
E Solidarity Dr
🏛7

Hyde Park & South Side (5mi)
Burnham Park

S Lynn White Dr

Willie Dixon's Blues Heaven (0.6mi)
✪56

Burnham Harbor

21 🛈
●28

E   **F**   **G**   **H**

Oak St Beach (0.3mi);
North Ave Beach (1.3mi)

Downtown Chicago

Northerly Island PARK
(Map p518; 1400 S Lynn White Dr; ☐ 146 or 130)
The prairie-grassed park has walking trails,
fishing, bird-watching and an outdoor venue for big-name concerts (which you can
hear from 12th Street Beach).

**Museum of Contemporary
Photography** MUSEUM
(Map p518; ☎ 312-663-5554; www.mocp.org; 600 S
Michigan Ave, Columbia College; ◎ 10am-5pm Mon-
Wed, Fri & Sat, to 8pm Thu, noon-5pm Sun; Ⓜ Red
Line to Harrison) FREE The small museum has
intriguing exhibits worth a quick browse.

◎ Near North

The Loop may be where Chicago fortunes
are made, but the Near North is where those
fortunes are spent. Shops, restaurants and
amusements abound.

★ Navy Pier WATERFRONT
(Map p518; ☎ 312-595-7437; www.navypier.com;
600 E Grand Ave; ◎ 10am-10pm Sun-Thu, to midnight Fri & Sat Jun-Aug, 10am-8pm Sun-Thu, to
10pm Fri & Sat Sep-May; ♿; Ⓜ Red Line to Grand,
then trolley) FREE Half-mile-long Navy Pier is
Chicago's most-visited attraction, sporting a

196ft Ferris wheel and other carnival rides ($6 to $8 each), an IMAX theater, a beer garden and gimmicky chain restaurants. Locals groan over its commercialization, but its lakefront view and cool breezes can't be beat. The fireworks displays on summer Wednesdays (9:30pm) and Saturdays (10:15pm) are a treat too.

The Chicago Children's Museum (p527) is also on the pier, as are several boat-cruise operators. Try the Shoreline water taxi for a fun ride to the Museum Campus (adult/child $8/4). A renovation is bringing an ice rink and additional amusements by 2017.

Magnificent Mile   STREET
(Map p518; www.themagnificentmile.com; N Michigan Ave; M Red Line to Grand) Spanning Michigan Ave between the river and Oak St, the Mag Mile is the much-touted upscale shopping strip, where Bloomingdales, Neiman's and Saks will lighten your wallet.

Tribune Tower   ARCHITECTURE
(Map p518; 435 N Michigan Ave; M Red Line to Grand) Take a close look when passing by the Gothic tower to see chunks of the Taj Mahal, Parthenon and other famous structures embedded in the lower walls.

Wrigley Building   ARCHITECTURE
(Map p518; 400 N Michigan Ave; M Red Line to Grand) Built by the chewing-gum maker; the white exterior glows as white as the Doublemint Twins' teeth.

◉ Gold Coast

The Gold Coast has been the address of Chicago's wealthiest for more than 125 years.

★ 360° Chicago   OBSERVATORY
(Map p518; ☏ 888-875-8439; www.360chicago. com; 875 N Michigan Ave; adult/child $19/13; ◷ 9am-11pm; M Red Line to Chicago) This is the new name for the John Hancock Center Observatory. In many ways the view here surpasses the one at Willis Tower. The 94th-floor lookout has informative displays and the TILT feature (floor-to-ceiling windows that you stand in as they tip out over the ground; it costs $7 extra and is fairly cheesy). Not interested in such frivolities? Shoot straight up to the 96th-floor Signature Lounge, where the view is free if you buy a drink ($8 to $16).

Museum of Contemporary Art   MUSEUM
(MCA; Map p518; ☏ 312-280-2660; www.mca chicago.org; 220 E Chicago Ave; adult/student $12/7; ◷ 10am-8pm Tue, to 5pm Wed-Sun; M Red Line to Chicago) Consider it the Art Institute's brash, rebellious sibling, with especially strong minimalist, surrealist and conceptual photography collections. Exhibits change regularly so you never know what you'll see.

Original Playboy Mansion   BUILDING
(1340 N State Pkwy; M Red Line to Clark/Division) Hugh Hefner began wearing his all-day jammies here, when the rigors of magazine production and heavy partying prevented him from getting dressed. The building contains

GANGSTER SITES

Chicago would rather not discuss its gangster past; consequently there are no brochures or exhibits about infamous sites. So you'll need to use your imagination when visiting the following places:

St Valentine's Day Massacre Site (2122 N Clark St; 🚌 22) This is where Al Capone's goons, dressed as cops, lined up seven members of Bugs Moran's gang against the garage wall that used to be here and sprayed them with bullets. The garage was torn down in 1967; the site is now the parking lot of a retirement home.

Biograph Theater (2433 N Lincoln Ave; M Brown, Purple, Red Line to Fullerton) In 1934, the 'lady in red' betrayed 'public enemy number one' John Dillinger at the Biograph. Dillinger was shot dead by the FBI in the alley beside the venue.

Holy Name Cathedral (Map p518; www.holynamecathedral.org; 735 N State St; M Red Line to Chicago) Two murders took place near the church. In 1924 North Side boss Dion O'Banion was gunned down in his florist shop (738 N State St) after he crossed Al Capone. O'Banion's replacement, Hymie Weiss, fared no better. In 1926 he was killed on his way to church by bullets flying from a window at 740 N State St.

Green Mill (p534) The speakeasy in the basement of the glamorous jazz bar was a Capone favorite.

THE 606

New York City has the High Line, and Chicago now has The 606 (www.the606. org; ⊙6am-11pm; Ⓜ Blue Line to Damen). Opened in 2015, it converts a similar tumbledown train track into an urban-cool elevated path that runs for 2.7 miles between Wicker Park and Logan Square. Bike, run or stroll past factories, smokestacks, clattering El trains and locals' backyard affairs. It's a fascinating trek through the city's socioeconomic strata: moneyed at the east, becoming more industrial and immigrant to the west. The trail parallels Bloomingdale Ave, with access points every quarter mile. The entrance at Churchill Park (1825 N Damen Ave) is a handy place to ascend. And FYI: 606 is the zip code prefix all city neighborhoods share.

condos now, but a visit still allows you to boast that 'I've been to the Playboy Mansion.' Head east a block to Astor St and ogle more manors between the 1300 and 1500 blocks.

Water Tower

(Map p518; 108 N Michigan Ave; Ⓜ Red Line to Chicago) The 154-ft-tall, turreted tower is a defining city landmark: it was the sole downtown survivor of the 1871 Great Fire.

◉ Lincoln Park & Old Town

Lincoln Park is Chicago's largest green space, an urban oasis spanning 1200 leafy acres along the lakefront. 'Lincoln Park' is also the name for the abutting neighborhood. Both are alive day and night with people jogging, walking dogs, pushing strollers and driving in circles looking for a place to park.

Old Town rests at the southwest foot of Lincoln Park. The intersection of North Ave and Wells St is the epicenter, with saucy bars, restaurants and the Second City improv club fanning out from here.

Lincoln Park Zoo ZOO

(☑312-742-2000; www.lpzoo.org; 2200 N Cannon Dr; ⊙10am-4:30pm Nov-Mar, to 5pm Apr-Oct, to 6:30pm Sat & Sun Jun-Aug; ♿; ☐151) FREE A local family favorite, filled with gorillas, lions, tigers, snow monkeys and other exotic creatures in the shadow of downtown. Check out the Regenstein African Journey, Ape House and Nature Boardwalk for the cream of the crop.

Lincoln Park Conservatory GARDENS

(☑312-742-7736; www.lincolnparkconservancy.org; 2391 N Stockton Dr; ⊙9am-5pm; ☐151) FREE Near the zoo's north entrance, the magnificent 1891 hothouse coaxes palms, ferns and orchids to flourish. In winter, it becomes a soothing, 75°F (24°C) escape from the icy winds raging outside.

Chicago History Museum MUSEUM

(☑312-642-4600; www.chicagohistory.org; 1601 N Clark St; adult/child $14/free; ⊙9:30am-4:30pm Mon-Sat, noon-5pm Sun; ♿; ☐22) Multimedia displays cover it all, from the Great Fire to the 1968 Democratic Convention. President Lincoln's deathbed is here; so is the chance to 'become' a Chicago hot dog covered in condiments (in the kids' area, but adults are welcome for the photo op).

◉ Lake View & Wrigleyville

North of Lincoln Park, these neighborhoods can be enjoyed by ambling along Halsted St, Clark St, Belmont Ave or Southport Ave, which are well supplied with restaurants, bars and shops. The only real sight is ivy-covered Wrigley Field (www.cubs.com; 1060 W Addison St; Ⓜ Red Line to Addison), named after the chewing gum guy and home to the much-loved but hard-luck Chicago Cubs. Ninety-minute tours ($25) of the iconic, century-old ballpark are available. The area around the facility is getting a makeover with spiffed-up amenities for visitors.

◉ Andersonville & Uptown

These northern neighborhoods are good for a delicious browse. Andersonville is an old Swedish enclave centered on Clark St, where timeworn, European-tinged businesses mix with new foodie restaurants, funky boutiques, vintage shops and gay and lesbian bars. Take the CTA Red Line to the Berwyn stop, and walk west for six blocks.

A short distance south, Uptown is a whole different scene. Take the Red Line to the Argyle stop, and you're in the heart of 'Little Saigon' and its pho-serving storefronts.

◉ Wicker Park, Bucktown & Ukrainian Village

West of Lincoln Park, these three neighborhoods – once havens for working-class, central European immigrants and Bohemian writers – are hot property. Heaps of fashion boutiques, hipster record stores, thrift shops and cocktail lounges have shot up, especially near the intersection of Milwaukee and N Damen Aves. Division St is also prime wandering territory. It used to be called 'Polish Broadway' for all the polka bars that lined it, but now the requisite cafes and crafty businesses have taken over. There aren't many actual sights here, aside from **Nelson Algren's House** (1958 W Evergreen Ave; M Blue Line to Damen), where he wrote several gritty, Chicago-based novels. Alas, it's a private residence, so you can only admire it from the sidewalk.

◉ Logan Square & Humboldt Park

When artists and hipsters got priced out of Wicker Park, they moved west to the Latino communities of Logan Sq and Humboldt Park. For visitors, these are places for small, cool-cat eateries, brewpubs and music clubs. Take the CTA Blue Line to Logan Sq or California.

◉ Near West Side & Pilsen

Just west of the Loop is, well, the **West Loop**. It's akin to New York City's Meatpacking District, with chic restaurants, clubs and galleries poking out between meat-processing plants. W Randolph St and W Fulton Market are the main veins. Nearby **Greektown** runs along S Halsted St near W Jackson Blvd. The areas are about 1.25 miles west of the Loop and easily reached by taxi.

Southwest lies the enclave of Pilsen, a festive mix of art galleries, Mexican bakeries, hipster cafes and murals on the buildings. The CTA Pink Line to 18th St drops you in the midst.

National Museum of Mexican Art   MUSEUM
(☎312-738-1503; www.nationalmuseumofmexican art.org; 1852 W 19th St; ⊙10am-5pm Tue-Sun; M Pink Line to 18th St) **FREE** It's the largest Latino arts institution in the US. The museum's vivid permanent collection includes classical paintings, shining gold altars, skeleton-rich folk art and colorful beadwork.

◉ Chinatown

Chicago's small but busy Chinatown is an easy 10-minute train ride from the Loop. Take the Red Line to the Cermak-Chinatown stop, which puts you between the neighbor-

hood's two distinct parts: Chinatown Sq (an enormous bilevel strip mall) unfurls to the north along Archer Ave, while Old Chinatown (the traditional retail area) stretches along Wentworth Ave to the south. Either zone allows you to graze through bakeries, dine on steaming bowls of noodles and shop for exotic wares.

◉ Hyde Park & South Side

The South Side is the generic term applied to Chicago's myriad neighborhoods, including some of its most impoverished, that lie south of 25th St. Hyde Park and abutting Kenwood are the South Side's stars, catapulted into the spotlight by local boy Barack Obama. To get here, take the Metra Electric Line trains from Millennium Station downtown, or bus 6 from State St in the Loop. Several bicycle tours also cruise by the highlights.

University of Chicago   UNIVERSITY
(www.uchicago.edu; 5801 S Ellis Ave; ☒6, M Metra to 55th-56th-57th) The campus is worth a stroll, offering grand Gothic architecture and free art and antiquities museums. It's also where the nuclear age began: Enrico Fermi and his Manhattan Project cronies built a reactor and carried out the world's first controlled atomic reaction on December 2, 1942. The **Nuclear Energy sculpture** (S Ellis Ave btwn E 56th & E 57th Sts), by Henry Moore, marks the spot where it blew its stack.

Museum of Science & Industry   MUSEUM
(MSI; ☎773-684-1414; www.msichicago.org; 5700 S Lake Shore Dr; adult/child $18/11; ⊙9:30am-5:30pm Jun-Aug, reduced hours Sep-May; ⑩; ☒6 or 10, M Metra to 55th-56th-57th) Geek out at the largest science museum in the western hemisphere. Highlights include a WWII German U-boat nestled in an underground display ($9 extra to tour it) and the *Science Storms* exhibit with a mock tornado and tsunami. Kids will love the 'experiments' staff conduct in various galleries, like dropping things off the balcony and creating mini explosions.

Robie House   ARCHITECTURE
(☎312-994-4000; www.flwright.org; 5757 S Woodlawn Ave; adult/child $17/14; ⊙10:30am-3pm Thu-Mon; ☒6, M Metra to 55th-56th-57th) Of the numerous buildings that Frank Lloyd Wright designed around Chicago, none is more famous or influential than Robie House. The resemblance of its horizontal lines to the flat landscape of the Midwestern prairie became known as the Prairie style. Inside are

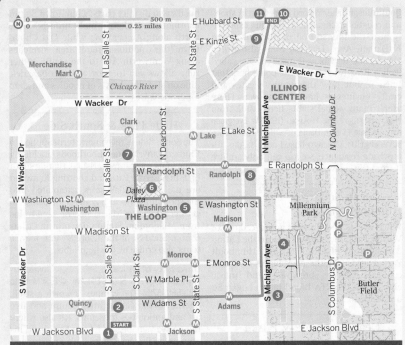

🏃 City Walk
The Loop

START CHICAGO BOARD OF TRADE
END BILLY GOAT TAVERN
LENGTH 3 MILES; ABOUT TWO HOURS

This tour swoops through the Loop, highlighting Chicago's revered art and architecture, with a visit to Al Capone's dentist thrown in for good measure.

Start at the **1 Chicago Board of Trade** (p517), where guys in Technicolor coats swap corn (or something like that) inside a cool art-deco building. Step into the nearby **2 Rookery** (p517) to see Frank Lloyd Wright's handiwork in the atrium.

Head east on Adams St to the **3 Art Institute** (p515), one of the city's most-visited attractions. The lion statues out front make a classic photo. Walk a few blocks north to avant-garde **4 Millennium Park** (p514).

Leave the park and head west on Washington St to **5 Hotel Burnham** (p528). It's housed in the Reliance Building, which was the precursor to modern skyscraper design;

Capone's dentist drilled teeth in what's now room 809. Just west, Picasso's abstract **6 Untitled** sculpture is ensconced in Daley Plaza. Baboon, dog, woman? You decide. Then go north on Clark St to Jean Dubuffet's **7 Monument with Standing Beast**, another head-scratching sculpture.

Walk east on Randolph St through the Theater District. Pop into the **8 Chicago Cultural Center** (p515) to see what free art exhibits or concerts are on. Now go north on Michigan Ave and cross the Chicago River. Just north of the bridge you'll pass the **9 Wrigley Building** (p521), shining bright and white, and the nearby Gothic, eye-popping **10 Tribune Tower** (p521).

To finish your tour, visit **11 Billy Goat Tavern** (p530), a vintage Chicago dive that spawned the Curse of the Cubs after the tavern's owner, Billy Sianis, tried to enter Wrigley Field with his pet goat. The smelly creature was denied entry, so Sianis called down a mighty curse on the baseball team in retaliation. They've pretty much stunk ever since.

LOCAL KNOWLEDGE

BLUES FANS' PILGRIMAGE

From 1957 to 1967, the humble building at 2120 S Michigan Ave was Chess Records, the seminal electric blues label. Muddy Waters, Howlin' Wolf and Bo Diddley cut tracks here, and paved the way for rock and roll with their sick licks and amped-up sound. Chuck Berry and the Rolling Stones arrived soon after. The studio is now called **Willie Dixon's Blues Heaven** (312-808-1286; www.bluesheaven.com; 2120 S Michigan Ave; tours $10; noon-4pm Mon-Fri, to 3pm Sat; Green Line to Cermak-McCormick Pl), named for the bassist who wrote most of the Chess hits. Staff give hour-long tours of the premises. It's pretty ramshackle, with few original artifacts on display. Still, when Willie's grandson hauls out the bluesman's well-worn stand-up bass and lets you take a pluck, it's pretty cool. Free blues concerts rock the side garden on summer Thursdays at 6pm. The building is near Chinatown, and about a mile south of the Museum Campus.

174 stained-glass windows and doors, which you'll see on the hour-long tours (frequency varies by season).

Obama's House BUILDING
(5046 S Greenwood Ave) Hefty security means you can't get close to the president's abode, but you can stand across the street on Hyde Park Blvd and glimpse over the barricades at the redbrick Georgian-style manor.

Activities

Tucked away among Chicago's 580 parks are public golf courses, ice rinks, swimming pools and more. Activities are free or low cost, and the necessary equipment is usually available for rent. The **Chicago Park District** (www.chicagoparkdistrict.com) runs the show.

Cycling

Riding along the 18-mile lakefront path is a fantastic way to see the city. Bike rental companies listed here also offer two- to four-hour tours ($35 to $70, including bikes) that cover themes like the lakefront, beer and pizza munching, or gangster sites. Booking online saves money.

Bike Chicago CYCLING
(Map p518; 312-729-1000; www.bikechicago.com; 239 E Randolph St; per 1/4hr from $9/30; 6:30am-10pm Mon-Fri, from 8am Sat & Sun Jun-Aug, reduced hours Sep-May; Brown, Orange, Green, Purple, Pink Line to Randolph) The company's main location – open year-round – is at Millennium Park. Other outposts include Navy Pier and the Riverwalk.

Bobby's Bike Hike CYCLING
(Map p518; 312-245-9300; www.bobbysbikehike.com; 540 N Lake Shore Dr; per 2/4hr from $20/25; 8:30am-8pm Mon-Fri, from 8am Sat & Sun Jun-Aug, 9am-7pm Sep-Nov & Mar-May; Red Line to Grand) Bobby's earns raves from riders; enter through the covered driveway.

Water Sports

Visitors often don't realize Chicago is a beach town, thanks to mammoth Lake Michigan lapping its side. There are 26 official strands of sand patrolled by lifeguards in summer. Swimming is popular, though the water is pretty damn cold. Check www.cpdbeaches.com for water-quality advice before embarking.

North Avenue Beach BEACH
(www.cpdbeaches.com; 1600 N Lake Shore Dr; ; 151) Chicago's most popular and amenity-laden stretch of sand wafts a Southern California vibe. You can rent kayaks, jet skis, stand-up paddleboards (SUPs) and lounge chairs, as well as eat and drink at the party-orientated beach house. It's 2 miles north of the Loop.

Oak Street Beach BEACH
(www.cpdbeaches.com; 1000 N Lake Shore Dr; Red Line to Chicago) Packs in bodies beautiful at the edge of downtown.

12th Street Beach BEACH
(Map p518; www.cpdbeaches.com; 1200 S Linn White Dr; 146, 130) A path runs from the Adler Planetarium to this secluded crescent of sand.

Tours

Many companies offer discounts if you book online. Outdoor-oriented tours operate from April to November only, unless otherwise specified.

Chicago Architecture Foundation BOAT TOUR
(CAF; Map p518; 312-922-3432; www.architecture.org; 224 S Michigan Ave; tours $15-50; Brown, Orange, Green, Purple, Pink Line to Adams) The gold-standard boat tours ($40) sail from

Michigan Ave's river dock. The popular Evolution of the Skyscraper walking tours ($20) leave from the downtown Michigan Ave address. Weekday lunchtime tours ($15) explore individual landmark buildings. Buy tickets online or at CAF.

Chicago by Foot   WALKING TOUR

(www.freetoursbyfoot.com/chicago) Guides for this pay-what-you-want walking tour offer engaging stories and historical details on different jaunts covering the Loop, Gold Coast, Lincoln Park's gangster sites and many more. Most takers pay around $10 per person.

Chicago Detours   WALKING, BUS TOURS

(☑ 312-350-1131; www.chicagodetours.com; tours from $26) It offers engrossing, detail-rich tours (mostly walking, but also some by bus) that take in Chicago's architecture, history and culture. The Historic Pub Crawl Tour is a popular one.

InstaGreeter   WALKING TOUR

(www.chicagogreeter.com/instagreeter; 77 E Randolph St; ⊙10am-3pm Fri & Sat, 11am-2pm Sun; Ⓜ Brown, Orange, Green, Purple, Pink Line to Randolph) FREE It provides one-hour Loop tours on the spot from the Chicago Cultural Center visitor center. In summer, free tours of Millennium Park also depart from here daily at 11:30am and 1pm.

Chicago History Museum   TOUR

(☑ 312-642-4600; www.chicagohistory.org; tours $20-55) The museum counts El (elevated/subway system) jaunts, cycling routes and cemetery walks among its excellent tour arsenal. Departure points and times vary.

Chicago Food Planet Tours   WALKING TOUR

(☑ 312-818-2170; www.chicagofoodplanet.com; 3hr tours $45-55) Go on a guided walkabout in Wicker Park, the Gold Coast or Chinatown, where you'll graze through five or more neighborhood eateries. Departure points and times vary.

Pilsen Mural Tours   WALKING TOUR

(☑ 773-342-4191; per group 1½hr tour $125) Local artists lead the highly recommended tours, during which you can learn more about this traditional art form; call to arrange an excursion.

✯✣ Festivals & Events

Chicago has a full events calendar all year, but the biggies take place in the summer.

The following events are held downtown on a weekend, unless noted otherwise.

St Patrick's Day Parade   CULTURAL

(www.chicagostpatsparade.com; ⊙mid-Mar) The local plumbers union dyes the Chicago River shamrock green; a big parade follows.

Blues Festival   MUSIC

(www.chicagobluesfestival.us; ⊙mid-Jun) The biggest free blues fest in the world, with three days of the music that made Chicago famous.

Taste of Chicago   FOOD

(www.tasteofchicago.us; ⊙mid-Jul) The free five-day bash in Grant Park includes bands and lots of food on a stick.

Pitchfork Music Festival   MUSIC

(www.pitchforkmusicfestival.com; day pass $65; ⊙mid-Jul) Indie bands strum for three days in Union Park.

Lollapalooza   MUSIC

(www.lollapalooza.com; day pass $110; ⊙early Aug) Around 130 bands spill off eight stages at Grant Park's three-day mega-gig.

Jazz Festival   MUSIC

(www.chicagojazzfestival.us; ⊙early Sep) Top names on the national jazz scene play over Labor Day weekend.

🛏 Sleeping

Chicago lodging doesn't come cheap. In summer and when the frequent big conventions trample through town, your options become much slimmer, so plan ahead to avoid unpleasant surprises. The prices we've listed are for the summer peak season. Taxes add 16.4%.

Hotels in the Loop are convenient to the museums, festival grounds and business district, but the area is pretty dead come nightfall. Accommodations in the Near North and Gold Coast are most popular, given their proximity to eating, shopping and entertainment venues. Rooms in Lincoln Park, Lake View and Wicker Park are often cheaper than rooms downtown, plus they're near swingin' nightlife. In addition, Airbnb does big business in Chicago and offers bountiful, good-value listings.

Wi-fi is free unless noted otherwise. You pay dearly for parking in Chicago: $55 to $65 per night downtown, and around $25 in outlying neighborhoods.

CHICAGO FOR CHILDREN

Chicago is a kid's kind of town. *Chicago Parent* (www.chicagoparent.com) is a dandy resource. Top choices for toddlin' times include the following:

Chicago Children's Museum (Map p518; ☑312-527-1000; www.chicagochildrensmuseum. org; 700 E Grand Ave; admission $14; ⊙10am-5pm Mon-Wed, to 8pm Thu, to 6pm Fri, to 7pm Sat & Sun; ⊞; Ⓜ Red Line to Grand, then trolley) Climb, dig and splash in this educational playland on Navy Pier; follow with an expedition down the carnival-like wharf itself, including spins on the Ferris wheel and carousel.

Chicago Children's Theatre (☑773-227-0180; www.chicagochildrenstheatre.org) See a show by one of the best kids' theater troupes in the country. Performances take place at venues around town.

American Girl Place (www.americangirl.com; 835 N Michigan Ave; ⊙10am-8pm Mon-Thu, 9am-9pm Fri & Sat, to 6pm Sun; ⊞; Ⓜ Red Line to Chicago) Young ladies sip tea and get new hair-dos with their dolls at this multistory, girl-power palace.

Chic-A-Go-Go (www.facebook.com/chicagogo) Groove at a taping of this cable-access TV show that's like a kiddie version of *Soul Train*. Check the website for dates and locations.

Other kid-friendly offerings:

Maggie Daley Park (p515)

North Avenue Beach (p525)

Field Museum of Natural History (p517)

Shedd Aquarium (p517)

Lincoln Park Zoo (p522)

Museum of Science & Industry (p523)

🛏 The Loop & Near North

Freehand Chicago HOSTEL, HOTEL $
(Map p518; ☑312-940-3699; www.thefreehand. com/chicago; 19 E Ohio St; dm $35-70, r $220-310; ❄♠; Ⓜ Red Line to Grand) This is an outpost of Miami's super-hip hostel-hotel hybrid. Rooms are small but stylish, designed in warm woods, bright tiles and Central American-tinged fabrics. Travelers are split evenly between the private rooms and eight-person, bunk-bed dorms (way spiffier than most hostels, with privacy curtains around each bed). Everyone mingles in the shaggy, totem-pole-filled common area and in the on-site Broken Shaker bar.

HI-Chicago HOSTEL $
(Map p518; ☑312-360-0300; www.hichicago. org; 24 E Congress Pkwy; dm $35-55; ℗❄@♠; Ⓜ Brown, Orange, Purple, Pink Line to Library) Chicago's most stalwart hostel is immaculate, conveniently placed in the Loop, and offers bonuses like a staffed information desk, free volunteer-led tours, free breakfast and discount passes to museums and shows. The simple dorm rooms have eight or 10 beds, and most have attached baths.

★**Acme Hotel** BOUTIQUE HOTEL $$
(Map p518; ☑312-894-0800; www.acmehotelcompany.com; 15 E Ohio St; r $179-289; ℗❄@♠; Ⓜ Red Line to Grand) Urban bohemians are loving the Acme for its indie-cool style at (usually) affordable rates. The 130 rooms mix industrial fixtures with retro lamps, mid-century furniture and funky modern art. They're wired up with free wi-fi, good speakers, smart TVs and easy connections to stream your own music and movies. Graffiti, neon and lava lights decorate the common areas.

Hampton Inn Chicago Downtown/N Loop HOTEL $$
(Map p518; ☑312-419-9014; www.hampton chicago.com; 68 E Wacker Pl; r $200-280; ℗❄♠; Ⓜ Brown, Orange, Green, Purple, Pink Line to State/ Lake) Opened in spring 2015, this unique property makes you feel like a road-tripper of yore. Set in the 1928 art-deco Chicago Motor Club Building, the lobby sports a vintage Ford and cool USA mural map from the era. The

dark-wood-paneled rooms strike the right balance of retro vibe and modern amenities. Free wi-fi and hot breakfast are included.

Best Western River North
HOTEL $$
(Map p518; 312-467-0800; www.rivernorthhotel. com; 125 W Ohio St; r $179-269; P✳@🛜🏊; M Red Line to Grand) Well-maintained rooms with maple veneer beds and desks, together with low-cost parking for the area (per night $25), an indoor pool and a sundeck overlooking the city make the Best Western good Near North value.

★ Hotel Burnham
BOUTIQUE HOTEL $$$
(Map p518; 312-782-1111; www.burnhamhotel. com; 1 W Washington St; r $239-389; P✳@🛜🏊; M Blue Line to Washington) The proprietors brag that the Burnham has the highest guest return rates in Chicago; it's easy to see why. Housed in the landmark 1890s Reliance Building (precedent for the modern skyscraper), its super-slick decor woos architecture buffs. Big windows and pops of bright, whimsical art liven up the warm wood decor. A free wine happy hour takes place each evening.

Virgin Hotel
HOTEL $$$
(Map p518; 312-940-4400; www.virginhotels. com; 203 N Wabash Ave; r $230-300; P✳@🛜🏊; M Brown, Orange, Green, Purple, Pink Line to State/ Lake) Billionaire Richard Branson transformed the 27-story, art-deco Dearborn Bank Building into the first outpost of his cheeky new hotel chain. The airy, suite-like rooms have speedy free wi-fi and low-cost minibar items, plus a bed that can double as a work desk. An app controls the thermostat, TV and other electronics. Guests receive earplugs, handy for dulling noise from nearby El trains.

Lake View, Wicker Park & Bucktown

★ Urban Holiday Lofts
HOSTEL $
(312-532-6949; www.urbanholidaylofts.com; 2014 W Wabansia Ave; dm $30-55, r from $80; ✳@🛜; M Blue Line to Damen) An international crowd fills the mix of dorms (with four to eight beds) and private rooms in this building of converted loft condos. Exposed-brick walls, hardwood floors and bunks with plump bedding are common to all 25 rooms. It's close to the El train station and in the thick of Wicker Park's nightlife. Breakfast is included.

GAY & LESBIAN CHICAGO

Chicago has a flourishing gay and lesbian scene. The *Windy City Times* (www.windycity mediagroup.com) provides the local lowdown.

The biggest concentration of bars and clubs is in Wrigleyville on N Halsted St between Belmont Ave and Grace St, an area known as Boystown. Andersonville is the other main area for GLBT nightlife; it's a more relaxed, less party-oriented scene. Top picks:

Big Chicks (www.bigchicks.com; 5024 N Sheridan Rd; 4pm-2am Mon-Fri, from 9am Sat, from 10am Sun; 🛜; M Red Line to Argyle) Despite the name, both men and women frequent Big Chicks, with its weekend DJs, art displays and next-door organic restaurant **Tweet** (www.tweet.biz; 5020 N Sheridan Rd; mains $8-14; 8:30am-3pm; 🛜) 🌱, where weekend brunch packs 'em in. Cash only.

Sidetrack (www.sidetrackchicago.com; 3349 N Halsted St; 3pm-2am Mon-Fri, from 1pm Sat & Sun; M Red, Brown, Purple Line to Belmont) Massive Sidetrack thumps dance music and show tunes and is prime for people-watching.

Hamburger Mary's (www.hamburgermarys.com/chicago; 5400 N Clark St; 11:30am-midnight Sun-Wed, to 1:30am Thu & Fri, to 2:30am Sat; M Red Line to Berwyn) Cabaret, karaoke, burgers and a booze-soaked outdoor patio make for good times at this hot spot.

Chance's Dances (www.chancesdances.org) Organizes queer dance parties at clubs around town.

Pride Parade (http://chicagopride.gopride.com; late Jun) Pride winds through Boystown and attracts around 800,000 revelers.

Northalsted Market Days (www.northalsted.com; mid-Aug) Another raucous event on the Boystown calendar, featuring a street fair and wild costumes.

Longman & Eagle INN $$
(☑ 773-276-7110; www.longmanandeagle.com; 2657 N Kedzie Ave; r $95-200; ❋ 🛜; M Blue Line to Logan Sq) Check in at the Michelin-starred gastropub downstairs, then head to your wood-floored, vintage-stylish accommodations on the floor above. The six rooms aren't particularly soundproofed, but after using your whiskey tokens in the bar, you probably won't care. From the El stop, walk a block north on Kedzie Ave.

Wicker Park Inn B&B $$
(☑ 773-486-2743; www.wickerparkinn.com; 1329 N Wicker Park Ave; r $159-225; ❋ 🛜; M Blue Line to Damen) This brick row house is steps away from rockin' restaurants and nightlife. The sunny rooms aren't huge, but have hardwood floors, pastel colors and small desk spaces. Across the street, two apartments with kitchens provide a self-contained experience. The inn is about a half-mile southeast of the El stop.

Willows Hotel BOUTIQUE HOTEL $$
(☑ 773-528-8400; www.willowshotelchicago.com; 555 W Surf St; r $159-265; P ❋ 🛜; 🚋 22) Small and stylish, the Willows wins an architectural gold star. The chic little lobby provides a swell refuge of overstuffed chairs by the fireplace, while the 55 rooms, done up in shades of peach and soft green, evoke a 19th-century French countryside feel. Continental breakfast is included. It's a block north of the commercial hub where Broadway, Clark and Diversey Sts intersect.

Days Inn Lincoln Park North HOTEL $$
(☑ 773-525-7010; www.daysinnchicago.net; 644 W Diversey Pkwy; r $130-195; P ❋ @ 🛜; 🚋 22) This well-maintained chain hotel in Lincoln Park is a favorite of both families and touring indie bands, providing good service and perks like free breakfast and health club access. It's an easy amble to the lakefront's parks and beaches, and a 15-minute bus ride to downtown. It's right at the hustle-bustle intersection of Broadway, Clark and Diversey streets.

✖ Eating

During the past decade, Chicago has become a gastronome's paradise. The beauty here is that even the buzziest restaurants are accessible: they're visionary yet traditional, pubby at the core and decently priced. You can also fork into a superb range of ethnic eats, especially if you break out of downtown and head for neighborhoods such as Pilsen or Uptown.

Need help deciding where to eat? LTH Forum (www.lthforum.com) is a great local resource.

The Loop

Most Loop eateries are geared to lunch crowds of office workers.

Cafecito CUBAN $
(Map p518; ☑ 312-922-2233; www.cafecitochicago.com; 26 E Congress Pkwy; mains $6-10; ⊙ 7am-9pm Mon-Fri, 10am-6pm Sat & Sun; 🛜; M Brown, Orange, Purple, Pink Line to Library) Attached to the HI-Chicago hostel and perfect for the hungry, thrifty traveler, Cafecito serves killer Cuban sandwiches layered with citrus-garlic-marinated roast pork and ham. Strong coffee and hearty egg sandwiches make a fine breakfast.

Native Foods Cafe VEGAN $
(Map p518; ☑ 312-332-6332; www.nativefoods.com; 218 S Clark St; mains $9-11; ⊙ 10:30am-9pm Mon-Sat, 11am-7pm Sun; ✍; M Brown, Orange, Purple, Pink Line to Quincy) ✔ If you're looking for vegan fast-casual fare downtown, Native Foods is your spot. The meatball sandwich rocks the seitan, while the scorpion burger fires up hot-spiced tempeh. Local beers and organic wines accompany the wide-ranging menu.

Gage MODERN AMERICAN $$$
(Map p518; ☑ 312-372-4243; www.thegagechicago.com; 24 S Michigan Ave; mains $17-36; ⊙ 11am-10pm Mon, to 11pm Tue-Thu, to midnight Fri & Sat, 10am-10pm Sun; M Brown, Orange, Green, Purple, Pink Line to Madison) This gastropub dishes up fanciful grub, from Gouda-topped venison burgers to mussels vindaloo to Guinness-battered fish and chips. The booze rocks, too, including a solid whiskey list and small-batch beers that pair with the food.

Near North

This is where you'll find Chicago's mother lode of restaurants.

Xoco MEXICAN $
(Map p518; www.rickbayless.com; 449 N Clark St; mains $10-14; ⊙ 8am-9pm Tue-Thu, to 10pm Fri & Sat; M Red Line to Grand) ✔ Crunch into warm *churros* (spiraled dough fritters) for breakfast, meaty *tortas* (sandwiches) for lunch and rich *caldos* (soups) for dinner at celeb chef Rick

CHICAGO'S HOLY TRINITY OF SPECIALTIES

Chicago cooks up three beloved specialties. Foremost is deep-dish pizza, a hulking mass of crust that rises two or three inches above the plate and cradles a molten pile of toppings. One gooey piece is practically a meal. Top spots:

Pizzeria Uno (Map p518; www.unos.com; 29 E Ohio St; small pizzas from $13; ☉11am-1am Mon-Fri, to 2am Sat, to 11pm Sun; Ⓜ Red Line to Grand) The deep-dish concept supposedly originated here in 1943.

Lou Malnati's (Map p518; www.loumalnatis.com; 439 N Wells St; small pizzas from $12; ☉11am-11pm Sun-Thu, to midnight Fri & Sat; Ⓜ Brown, Purple Line to Merchandise Mart) It also lays claim to inventing deep dish; famous for its butter crust.

Giordano's (Map p518; ☎312-951-0747; www.giordanos.com; 730 N Rush St; small pizzas from $15.50; ☉11am-11pm Sun-Thu, to midnight Fri & Sat; Ⓜ Red Line to Chicago) It makes 'stuffed' pizza, a bigger, doughier version of deep dish.

Gino's East (Map p518; ☎312-266-3337; www.ginoseast.com; 162 E Superior St; small pizzas from $15; ☉11am-9:30pm; Ⓜ Red Line to Chicago) Popular spot where you write on the walls while waiting for your pie.

No less iconic is the Chicago hot dog – a wiener that's been 'dragged through the garden' (ie topped with onions, tomatoes, shredded lettuce, bell peppers, pepperoncini and sweet relish, or variations thereof, but *never* ketchup), and then cushioned on a poppyseed bun. Try it at **Portillo's** (Map p518; ☎312-587-8910; www.portillos.com; 100 W Ontario St; mains $4-7; ☉10am-11pm Sun-Thu, to midnight Fri & Sat; Ⓜ Red Line to Grand).

The city is also revered for its spicy, drippy, only-in-Chicago Italian beef sandwiches. **Mr Beef** (Map p518; ☎312-337-8500; 666 N Orleans St; sandwiches $6-9; ☉9am-5pm Mon-Fri, 10am-3pm Sat, plus 10:30pm-4am Fri & Sat; Ⓜ Brown, Purple Line to Chicago) serves the gold standard.

Bayless' Mexican street-food joint. His upscale restaurants Frontera Grill and Topolobampo are next door, but you'll need reservations or a whole lot of patience to get in.

★ **Billy Goat Tavern**   BURGERS $
(Map p518; ☎312-222-1525; www.billygoattavern. com; lower level, 430 N Michigan Ave; burgers $4-6; ☉6am-2am Mon-Fri, 10am-2am Sat & Sun; Ⓜ Red Line to Grand) *Tribune* and *Sun-Times* reporters have guzzled in the subterranean Billy Goat for decades. Order a 'cheezborger' and Schlitz, then look around at the newspapered walls to get the scoop on infamous local stories, such as the Cubs Curse.

Purple Pig   MEDITERRANEAN $$
(Map p518; ☎312-464-1744; www.thepurplepig chicago.com; 500 N Michigan Ave; small plates $9-19; ☉11:30am-midnight Sun-Thu, to 1am Fri & Sat; ☏; Ⓜ Red Line to Grand) The Pig's Magnificent Mile location, wide-ranging meat and veggie menu, long list of affordable vinos and late-night serving hours make it a crowd pleaser.

Milk-braised pork shoulder is the hamtastic specialty. No reservations.

✕ Lincoln Park & Old Town

Halsted, Lincoln and Clark Sts are the main veins teeming with restaurants and bars.

Sultan's Market   MIDDLE EASTERN $
(☎312-638-9151; www.chicagofalafel.com; 2521 N Clark St; mains $4-7; ☉10am-10pm Mon-Thu, to midnight Fri & Sat, to 9pm Sun; Ⓜ Brown, Purple, Red Line to Fullerton) Neighborhood folks dig the falafel sandwiches, spinach pies and other quality Middle Eastern fare at family-run Sultan's Market. The small, homey space doesn't have many tables, but Lincoln Park is nearby for picnicking.

★ **Alinea**   MODERN AMERICAN $$$
(☎312-867-0110; www.alinearestaurant.com; 1723 N Halsted St; multicourse menu $210-265; ☉5-9:30pm Wed-Sun; Ⓜ Red Line to North/Clybourn) Widely regarded as North America's best restaurant, Alinea brings on 20 courses of

mind-bending molecular gastronomy. Dishes may emanate from a centrifuge or be pressed into a capsule, à la duck served with a 'pillow of lavender air.' There are no reservations. Instead Alinea sells tickets two to three months in advance via its website. Check the Twitter feed (@Alinea) for last-minute seats.

✖ Lake View & Wrigleyville

Clark, Halsted, Belmont and Southport are fertile grazing streets.

★Crisp   ASIAN $
(www.crisponline.com; 2940 N Broadway; mains $9-13; ⊙11:30am-9pm; Ⓜ Brown, Purple Line to Wellington) Music pours from the stereo, and cheap, delicious Korean fusions arrive from the kitchen at this cheerful cafe. The 'Bad Boy Buddha' bowl, a variation on *bi bim bop* (mixed vegetables with rice), is one of the best healthy lunches in town.

Mia Francesca   ITALIAN $$
(☎773-281-3310; www.miafrancesca.com; 3311 N Clark St; mains $16-27; ⊙5-10pm Mon-Thu, to 11pm Fri, 11:30am-11pm Sat, 10am-9pm Sun; Ⓜ Red, Brown, Purple Line to Belmont) Local chain Mia's buzzes with regulars who come for the trattoria's Italian standards, such as seafood linguine, spinach ravioli and mushroom-sauced veal medallions, all prepared with simple flair.

✖ Andersonville & Uptown

For 'Little Saigon' take the CTA Red Line to Argyle. For the European cafes in Andersonville, go one stop further to Berwyn.

Nha Hang Viet Nam   VIETNAMESE $
(☎773-878-8895; 1032 W Argyle St; mains $7-13; ⊙7am-10pm Sun-Mon; Ⓜ Red Line to Argyle) Little Nha Hang may not look like much from the outside, but it offers a huge menu of authentic, well-made dishes from the homeland. It's terrific for slurping pho and claypot catfish.

★Hopleaf   EUROPEAN $$
(☎773-334-9851; www.hopleaf.com; 5148 N Clark St; mains $12-27; ⊙noon-11pm Mon-Thu, to midnight Fri & Sat, to 10pm Sun; Ⓜ Red Line to Berwyn) A cozy, European-style tavern, Hopleaf draws crowds for its Montréal-style smoked brisket, cashew-butter-and-fig-jam sandwich and the house specialty – *frites* and ale-soaked mussels. It also pours 200 types of brew, heavy on the Belgian ales. No reservations.

✖ Wicker Park, Bucktown & Ukrainian Village

Trendy restaurants open almost every day in these 'hoods.

Dove's Luncheonette   TEX-MEX $
(☎773-645-4060; www.doveschicago.com; 1545 N Damen Ave; mains $12-15; ⊙9am-10pm Sun-Thu, to 11pm Fri & Sat; Ⓜ Blue Line to Damen) Grab a seat at the retro diner counter for plates of pork shoulder *pozole* and shrimp-stuffed sweet-corn tamales. Dessert? It's pie, of course, maybe lemon cream or peach jalapeño, depending on what they've baked that day. Soul music spins on the record player, tequila flows from the 70 bottles rattling behind the bar, and suddenly all is right in the world.

★Ruxbin   MODERN AMERICAN $$$
(☎312-624-8509; www.ruxbinchicago.com; 851 N Ashland Ave; mains $27-32; ⊙6-10pm Tue-Fri, 5:30-10pm Sat, to 9pm Sun; Ⓜ Blue Line to Division) 🍴 The passion of the brother-sister team who run Ruxbin is evident in everything from the warm decor made of found items to the artfully prepared flavors in dishes like the pork-belly salad with grapefruit, cornbread and blue cheese. It's a wee place of just 32 seats, and BYO.

✖ Logan Square & Humboldt Park

Logan Sq has become a mecca for inventive, no-pretense chefs. Eats and drinks ring the intersection of Milwaukee, Logan and Kedzie Blvds.

Kuma's Corner   BURGERS $
(☎773-604-8769; www.kumascorner.com; 2900 W Belmont Ave; mains $12-14; ⊙11:30am-midnight Mon-Wed, to 1am Thu, to 2am Fri & Sat, noon-midnight Sun; 🚌77) Ridiculously busy and head-bangingly loud, Kuma's attracts the tattooed set for its monster 10oz burgers, each named for a heavy-metal band and hefted onto a pretzel-roll bun. There's a mac 'n' cheese menu for vegetarians, and beer and bourbon for all. Expect to queue.

★Longman & Eagle   AMERICAN $$
(☎773-276-7110; www.longmanandeagle.com; 2657 N Kedzie Ave; mains $15-30; ⊙9am-2am Sun-Fri, to 3am Sat; Ⓜ Blue Line to Logan Sq) Hard to say whether this shabby-chic tavern is best for eating or drinking. Let's say eating, since

it earned a Michelin star for its beautifully cooked comfort foods such as vanilla brioche French toast for breakfast, wild-boar sloppy joes for lunch and fried chicken and duck fat biscuits for dinner. There's a whole menu of juicy small plates and whiskeys, too. No reservations.

Near West Side & Pilsen

The West Loop booms with hot-chef restaurants. Stroll along Randolph and Fulton Market Sts and take your pick. Greektown extends along S Halsted St (take the Blue Line to UIC-Halsted). The Mexican Pilsen enclave has loads of eateries around W 18th St.

★ Lou Mitchell's   BREAKFAST $

(Map p518; ☑312-939-3111; www.loumitchells restaurant.com; 565 W Jackson Blvd; mains $7-11; ⏰5:30am-3pm Mon-Fri, 7am-3pm Sat & Sun; ♿; M Blue Line to Clinton) Lou's is a relic of Route 66, where old-school waitresses deliver double-yoked eggs and thick-cut French toast just west of the Loop by Union Station. There's usually a queue, but free doughnut holes and Milk Duds help ease the wait.

Don Pedro Carnitas   MEXICAN $

(1113 W 18th St; tacos $1.50-2; ⏰8am-6pm Mon-Fri, 5am-5pm Sat, to 3pm Sun; M Pink Line to 18th) At this no-frills Pilsen meat hive, a man with a machete salutes you at the front counter. He awaits your command to hack off pork pieces, and then wraps the thick chunks with onion and cilantro in a fresh tortilla. Cash only.

★ Little Goat   DINER $$

(Map p518; ☑312-888-3455; www.littlegoat chicago.com; 820 W Randolph St; mains $10-19; ⏰7am-10pm Sun-Thu, to midnight Fri & Sat; 🛜🖋; M Green, Pink Line to Morgan) *Top Chef* winner Stephanie Izard opened this diner for the foodie masses across the street from her ever-booked main restaurant, Girl and the Goat. Sit on a vintage twirly stool and order off the all-day breakfast menu. Better yet, try lunchtime favorites such as the goat sloppy joe with mashed potato tempura or the pork belly on scallion pancakes.

Dusek's   MODERN AMERICAN $$$

(☑312-526-3851; www.dusekschicago.com; 1227 W 18th St; mains $22-30; ⏰11am-1am Mon-Fri, from 9am Sat & Sun; M Pink Line to 18th St) Pilsen's hipsters gather under the pressed tin ceiling of this gastropub to fork into an ever-changing menu of beer-inspired dishes, say beer-battered soft-shell crab or dark-lager-roasted duck. The eatery shares its historic building (modeled on Prague's opera house) with an indie band concert hall and basement cocktail bar.

🍷 Drinking & Nightlife

During the long winters, Chicagoans count on bars for warmth. The usual closing time is 2am, but some places stay open until 4am. In summer many bars boast beer gardens.

Clubs in the Near North and West Loop tend to be cavernous and luxurious (with dress codes). Clubs in Wicker Park are usually more casual.

The Loop & Near North

★ Signature Lounge   LOUNGE

(Map p518; www.signatureroom.com; 875 N Michigan Ave; ⏰11am-12:30am Sun-Thu, to 1:30am Fri & Sat; M Red Line to Chicago) Grab the elevator up to the 96th floor of the John Hancock Center (Chicago's fourth-tallest skyscraper) and order a beverage while looking out over the city. Ladies: don't miss the bathroom view.

Berghoff   BAR

(Map p518; www.theberghoff.com; 17 W Adams St; ⏰11am-9pm Mon-Sat; M Blue, Red Line to Jackson) The Berghoff was the first spot in town to serve a legal drink after Prohibition (ask to

---

DON'T MISS

MIDWESTERN BEERS

The Midwest is ready to pour you a cold one thanks to its German heritage. Yes, Budweiser and Miller are based here, but that's not what we're talking about. Far more exciting is the region's cache of craft brewers. Keep an eye on the taps for these slurpable suds-makers, available throughout the area:

➡ Bell's (Kalamazoo, MI)

➡ Capital (Middleton, WI)

➡ Founder's (Grand Rapids, MI)

➡ Great Lakes (Cleveland, OH)

➡ Lagunitas (Chicago, IL)

➡ Dark Horse (Marshall, MI)

➡ Summit (St Paul, MN)

➡ Surly (Minneapolis, MN)

➡ Three Floyds (Munster, IN)

➡ Two Brothers (Warrenville, IL)

see the liquor license stamped '#1'). Little has changed around the antique wood bar since then. Belly up for frosty mugs of the house-brand beer and order sauerbraten from the adjoining German restaurant.

★ Clark Street Ale House   BAR
(Map p518; www.clarkstreetalehouse.com; 742 N Clark St; ⊙4pm-4am Mon-Fri, from 11am Sat & Sun; Ⓜ Red Line to Chicago) Do as the retro sign advises and 'Stop & Drink Liquor.' Midwestern microbrews are the main draw; order a three-beer sampler for $7. When the weather warms, a sweet beer garden beckons out back.

Old Town & Wrigleyville

★ Old Town Ale House   BAR
(www.theoldtownalehouse.com; 219 W North Ave; ⊙3pm-4am Mon-Fri, from noon Sat & Sun; Ⓜ Brown, Purple Line to Sedgwick) This venerated dive bar lets you mingle with beautiful people and grizzled regulars, seated pint by pint under the nude-politician paintings. It's across the street from Second City. Cash only.

★ Gingerman Tavern   BAR
(3740 N Clark St; ⊙3pm-2am Mon-Fri, from noon Sat & Sun; Ⓜ Red Line to Addison) The pool tables, good beer selection and pierced-and-tattooed patrons make Gingerman wonderfully different from the surrounding Wrigleyville sports bars.

Smart Bar   CLUB
(www.smartbarchicago.com; 3730 N Clark St; ⊙10pm-4am Wed-Sun; Ⓜ Red Line to Addison) A long-standing, unpretentious favorite for dancing, attached to the Metro rock club.

Wicker Park, Bucktown & Ukrainian Village

Map Room   BAR
(www.maproom.com; 1949 N Hoyne Ave; ⊙6:30am-2am Mon-Fri, from 7:30am Sat, from 11am Sun; 🛜; Ⓜ Blue Line to Western) At this map-and-globe-filled 'traveler tavern' artsy types sip coffee by day and suds from the 200-strong beer list by night. Cash only.

Danny's   BAR
(1951 W Dickens Ave; ⊙7pm-2am; Ⓜ Blue Line to Damen) Danny's comfortably dim and dog-eared ambience is perfect for conversations over a pint early on, then DJs arrive to stoke the dance party as the evening progresses. Cash only.

HOW TO FIND A REAL CHICAGO BAR

Unfortunately, we can't list every watering hole in town, but we can give you the tools to go out and discover classic, character-filled bars on your own. Look for the following:

➡ an 'Old Style' beer sign swinging out front

➡ a well-worn dart board and/or pool table inside

➡ patrons wearing ballcaps with the logo of the Cubs, White Sox, Blackhawks or Bears

➡ bottles of brew served in buckets of ice

➡ sports on TV

Matchbox   BAR
(Map p518; 770 N Milwaukee Ave; ⊙4pm-2am Mon-Fri, from 3pm Sat & Sun; Ⓜ Blue Line to Chicago) Lawyers, artists and bums all squeeze in for retro cocktails. It's small as – you got it – a matchbox, with about 10 barstools; everyone else stands against the back wall. Matchbox sits by its lonesome northwest of downtown.

Logan Square

Revolution Brewing   BREWERY
(☎ 773-227-2739; www.revbrew.com; 2323 N Milwaukee Ave; ⊙11am-2am Mon-Fri, from 10am Sat & Sun; Ⓜ Blue Line to California) Raise your fist to Revolution, a big, industrial-chic brewpub that fills glasses with heady beers like the Eugene porter and hopped-up Anti-Hero IPA. The brewmaster here led the way for Chicago's huge craft beer scene, and his suds are top-notch.

West Loop

RM Champagne Salon   BAR
(Map p518; ☎ 312-243-1199; www.rmchampagnesalon.com; 116 N Green St; ⊙5-11pm Mon-Wed, to 2am Thu & Fri, to 3am Sat, to 11pm Sun; Ⓜ Green, Pink Line to Morgan) This West Loop spot is a twinkling-light charmer for bubbles. Score a table in the cobblestoned courtyard and you'll feel transported to Paris.

☆ Entertainment

Check the *Chicago Reader* (www.chicago reader.com) for listings.

Blues & Jazz

Blues and jazz have deep roots in Chicago.

★ Green Mill   JAZZ

(www.greenmilljazz.com; 4802 N Broadway; cover charge $5-15; ☺noon-4am Mon-Sat, from 11am Sun; Ⓜ Red Line to Lawrence) The timeless Green Mill earned its notoriety as Al Capone's favorite speakeasy. Sit in one of the leather booths and feel his ghost urging you on to another martini. Local and national jazz artists perform nightly; the venue also hosts the nationally acclaimed poetry slam on Sundays.

★ Buddy Guy's Legends   BLUES

(Map p518; www.buddyguy.com; 700 S Wabash Ave; ☺5pm-2am Mon & Tue, 11am-2am Wed-Fri, noon-3am Sat, noon-2am Sun, Ⓜ Red Line to Harrison) Top local and national acts wail on the stage of local icon Buddy Guy. Tickets cost $20 Friday and Saturday, $10 on other evenings. The man himself usually plugs in his axe for a series of shows in January. Free, all-ages acoustic performances take place from noon to 2pm Wednesday through Sunday.

Kingston Mines   BLUES

(www.kingstonmines.com; 2548 N Halsted St; cover charge $12-15; ☺8pm-4am Mon-Thu, from 7pm Fri & Sat, from 6pm Sun; Ⓜ Brown, Purple, Red Line to Fullerton) Two stages, seven nights a week, ensure somebody's always on. It's noisy, hot, sweaty, crowded and conveniently located in Lincoln Park.

BLUES   BLUES

(www.chicagobluesbar.com; 2519 N Halsted St; cover $7-10; ☺8pm-2am Wed-Sun; Ⓜ Brown, Purple, Red Line to Fullerton) This veteran club draws a slightly older crowd that soaks up every crackling, electrified moment.

Rock & World Music

★ Hideout   LIVE MUSIC

(www.hideoutchicago.com; 1354 W Wabansia Ave; ☺7pm-2am Tue, 4pm-2am Wed-Fri, 7pm-3am Sat,

varies Sun & Mon; ☒72) Hidden behind a factory at Bucktown's edge, this two-room lodge of indie rock and alt-country is well worth seeking out. The owners have nursed an outsider, underground vibe, and the place feels like the downstairs of your grandma's rumpus room. Music and other events (bingo, literary readings etc) take place nightly.

SummerDance   WORLD MUSIC

(Map p518; www.chicagosummerdance.org; 601 S Michigan Ave; ☺6-9:30pm Fri & Sat, 4-7pm Sun late Jun–mid-Sep; Ⓜ Red Line to Harrison) **FREE** Boogie at the Spirit of Music Garden in Grant Park with a multiethnic mash-up of locals. Bands play rumba, samba and other world beats preceded by fun dance lessons – all free.

Empty Bottle   LIVE MUSIC

(www.emptybottle.com; 1035 N Western Ave; ☺5pm-2am Mon-Thu, from 3pm Fri, from 11am Sat & Sun; ☒49) The scruffy, go-to club for edgy indie rock and jazz; Monday's show is often free, with cheap beer to boot.

Whistler   LIVE MUSIC

(☎773-227-3530; www.whistlerchicago.com; 2421 N Milwaukee Ave; ☺6pm-2am Mon-Thu, from 5pm Fri-Sun; Ⓜ Blue Line to California) **FREE** Indie bands and jazz trios brood at this artsy little club in Logan Sq. There's never a cover charge.

Theater

Chicago's reputation for stage drama is well deserved. Many productions export to Broadway. The Theater District is a cluster of big, neon-lit venues at State and Randolph Sts. **Broadway in Chicago** (☎800-775-2000; www.broadwayinchicago.com) handles tickets for most.

Steppenwolf Theatre   THEATER

(☎312-335-1650; www.steppenwolf.org; 1650 N Halsted St; Ⓜ Red Line to North/Clybourn) Drama club of John Malkovich, Gary Sinise and other stars; it's 2 miles north of the Loop in Lincoln Park.

Goodman Theatre   THEATER

(Map p518; ☎312-443-3800; www.goodmantheatre.org; 170 N Dearborn St; Ⓜ Brown, Orange, Green, Purple, Pink, Blue Line to Clark/Lake) The city's downtown powerhouse, known for new and classic American works.

Neo-Futurists   THEATER

(☎773-275-5255; www.neofuturists.org; 5153 N Ashland Ave; Ⓜ Red Line to Berwyn) Original works that make you ponder and laugh simultaneously; known for its manic, late-night show of 30 plays in 60 minutes. It's located in Andersonville.

Comedy

Improv comedy began in Chicago, and the city still nurtures the best in the business.

Second City
COMEDY

(☑ 312-337-3992; www.secondcity.com; 1616 N Wells St; Ⓜ Brown, Purple Line to Sedgwick) Bill Murray, Stephen Colbert, Tina Fey and many more honed their wit at this slick venue. The Mainstage and ETC stage host sketch revues (with an improv scene thrown in); they're similar in price and quality. The UP stage hosts stand-up and experimental shows. Bargain: turn up around 10pm (Friday and Saturday excluded) and watch the comics improv a set for free.

iO Theater
COMEDY

(☑ 312-929-2401; http://.ioimprov.com/chicago; 1501 N Kingsbury St; Ⓜ Red Line to North/Clybourn) Chicago's other major improv house is a bit edgier than its competition, with four stages hosting bawdy shows nightly. Two bars and a beer garden add to the fun.

Sports

Chicago Cubs
BASEBALL

(www.cubs.com; 1060 W Addison St; Ⓜ Red Line to Addison) The Cubs last won the World Series in 1908, but that doesn't stop fans from coming out to see them. Part of the draw is atmospheric, ivy-walled Wrigley Field, which dates from 1914. The bleacher seats are the most popular place to sit. No tickets? Peep through the 'knothole,' a garage-door-sized opening on Sheffield Ave, to watch the action for free.

Chicago White Sox
BASEBALL

(www.whitesox.com; 333 W 35th St; Ⓜ Red Line to Sox-35th) The Sox are the Cubs' South Side rivals and play in the more modern 'Cell,' aka US Cellular Field. Tickets are usually cheaper and easier to get than at Wrigley Field; games on Sundays and Mondays offer the best deals.

Chicago Bears
FOOTBALL

(Map p518; www.chicagobears.com; 1410 S Museum Campus Dr; ☒ 146, 128) Da Bears, Chicago's NFL team, tackle at Soldier Field, recognizable by its classical-meets-flying-saucer architecture. Expect beery tailgate parties, sleet and snow.

Chicago Bulls
BASKETBALL

(www.nba.com/bulls; 1901 W Madison St; ☒ 19, 20) Who will be the new Michael Jordan? Find out at the United Center, where the Bulls shoot hoops. It's about 2 miles west of the Loop. CTA runs special buses (No 19) on game days; it's best not to walk here.

Chicago Blackhawks
HOCKEY

(www.blackhawks.nhl.com; 1901 W Madison St; ☒ 19, 20) The Stanley Cup winners (in 2010, 2013 and 2015, most recently) skate in front of big crowds. They share the United Center with the Bulls.

Performing Arts

Grant Park Orchestra
CLASSICAL MUSIC

(Map p518; ☑ 312-742-7638; www.grantparkmusicfestival.com; Pritzker Pavilion, Millennium Park; ☺ 6:30pm Wed & Fri, 7:30pm Sat mid-Jun–mid-Aug; Ⓜ Brown, Orange, Green, Purple, Pink Line to Randolph) FREE The beloved group puts on free classical concerts in Millennium Park throughout the summer. Bring a picnic.

Chicago Symphony Orchestra
CLASSICAL MUSIC

(CSO; Map p518; ☑ 312-294-3000; www.cso.org; 220 S Michigan Ave; Ⓜ Brown, Orange, Green, Purple, Pink Line to Adams) The CSO is one of America's best symphonies; it plays in the Daniel Burnham–designed Orchestra Hall.

Lyric Opera Of Chicago
OPERA

(Map p518; ☑ 312-332-2244; www.lyricopera.org; 20 N Wacker Dr; Ⓜ Brown, Orange, Purple, Pink Line to Washington) The renowned Lyric Opera hits high Cs in a chandeliered venue a few blocks west of the Loop.

Hubbard Street Dance Chicago
DANCE

(Map p518; ☑ 312-850-9744; www.hubbardstreetdance.com; 205 E Randolph St; Ⓜ Brown, Orange, Green, Purple, Pink Line to Randolph) Chicago's pre-eminent dance company performs at the Harris Theater for Music and Dance.

🔒 Shopping

A siren song for shoppers emanates from N Michigan Ave, along the Magnificent Mile (p521). Moving onward, boutiques fill Wicker Park and Bucktown (indie and vintage), Lincoln Park (posh), Lake View (countercultural) and Andersonville (all of the above).

Chicago Architecture Foundation Shop
SOUVENIRS

(Map p518; www.architecture.org/shop; 224 S Michigan Ave; ☺ 9am-6:30pm; Ⓜ Brown, Orange, Green, Purple, Pink Line to Adams) Skyline posters, Frank Lloyd Wright note cards, skyscraper models and more for those with an edifice complex.

Strange Cargo
CLOTHING

(www.strangecargo.com; 3448 N Clark St; ⊙11am-6:45pm Mon-Sat, to 5:30pm Sun; Ⓜ Red Line to Addison) This retro store in Wrigleyville stocks kitschy iron-on T-shirts featuring Ditka, Obama and other renowned Chicagoans.

Jazz Record Mart
MUSIC

(Map p518; www.jazzmart.com; 27 E Illinois St; ⊙10am-7pm Mon-Sat, 11am-5pm Sun; Ⓜ Red Line to Grand) One-stop shop for Chicago jazz and blues CDs and vinyl.

Quimby's
BOOKS

(www.quimbys.com; 1854 W North Ave; ⊙noon-9pm Mon-Thu, to 10pm Fri & Sat, to 7pm Sun; Ⓜ Blue Line to Damen) Ground Zero for comics, zines and underground culture; in Wicker Park.

ⓘ Information

INTERNET ACCESS

Many bars and restaurants and even some beaches have free wi-fi, as does the Chicago Cultural Center.

Harold Washington Library Center (www.chipublib.org; 400 S State St; ⊙9am-9pm Mon-Thu, to 5pm Fri & Sat, 1-5pm Sun) A grand, art-filled building with free wi-fi throughout and 3rd-floor internet terminals (get a day pass at the counter).

MEDIA

Chicago Reader (www.chicagoreader.com) Free alternative newspaper with comprehensive arts and entertainment listings.

Chicago Sun-Times (www.suntimes.com) The daily, tabloid-style newspaper.

Chicago Tribune (www.chicagotribune.com) The stalwart daily newspaper; its younger, trimmed-down, freebie version is *RedEye*.

MEDICAL SERVICES

Northwestern Memorial Hospital (☎312-926-5188; www.nmh.org; 251 E Erie St; Ⓜ Red Line to Chicago) Well-respected hospital downtown.

Walgreens (☎312-664-8686; 757 N Michigan Ave; ⊙24hr; Ⓜ Red Line to Chicago) On the Magnificent Mile.

MONEY

ATMs are plentiful downtown, with many near Chicago and Michigan Aves. To change money, try Terminal 5 at O'Hare International Airport or the following places in the Loop:

Travelex (☎312-807-4941; www.travelex.com; 19 S LaSalle St; ⊙8am-5pm Mon-Fri; Ⓜ Blue Line to Monroe)

World's Money Exchange (☎312-641-2151; www.wmeinc.com; 203 N LaSalle St; ⊙8:45am-4:45pm Mon-Fri; Ⓜ Brown, Orange, Green, Purple, Pink, Blue Line to Clark/Lake)

POST

Post Office (Map p518; 540 N Dearborn St)

TOURIST INFORMATION

Chicago Cultural Center Visitor Center (Map p518; www.choosechicago.com; 77 E Randolph St; ⊙10am-5pm Mon-Sat, 11am-4pm Sun; 🛈; Ⓜ Brown, Orange, Green, Purple, Pink Line to Randolph) It's sparse, but does offer a staffed information desk and sales of discount cards for attractions. Insta-Greeter (Friday through Sunday year-round) and Millennium Park (daily in summer) tours also depart from here.

USEFUL WEBSITES

Chicagoist (www.chicagoist.com) Quirky take on food, arts and events.

Gapers Block (www.gapersblock.com) News and events site with Chicago attitude.

ONLINE TICKETS & DISCOUNT CARDS

Most major sights, including the Art Institute of Chicago and Willis Tower, allow you to buy tickets online. The advantage is that you're assured entry and you get to skip the regular ticket lines. The disadvantage is that you have to pay a service fee of $1.50 to $4 per ticket (sometimes it's just per order), and at times the prepay line is almost as long as the regular one. Our suggestion: consider buying online in summer and for big exhibits. Otherwise, there's no need.

Chicago offers a couple of discount cards that also let you skip the regular queues:

Go Chicago Card (www.smartdestinations.com/chicago) Allows you to visit an unlimited number of attractions for a flat fee; good for one, two, three or five consecutive days. The company also offers a three-choice or five-choice 'Explorer Pass' where you pick among 26 options; it's valid for 30 days.

CityPass (www.citypass.com/chicago) Gives access to five of the city's top draws, including the Art Institute, Shedd Aquarium and Willis Tower, over nine days. It's less flexible than the Go Chicago pass, but cheaper for those wanting a more leisurely sightseeing pace.

ℹ️ Getting There & Away

AIR

Chicago Midway Airport (MDW; www.fly chicago.com) The smaller airport used mostly by domestic carriers, such as Southwest; often has cheaper flights than from O'Hare.

O'Hare International Airport (ORD; www.fly chicago.com) Chicago's larger airport, and among the world's busiest. Headquarters for United Airlines and a hub for American. Most non-US airlines and international flights use Terminal 5 (except Lufthansa and flights from Canada).

BUS

Greyhound (Map p518; 🖂 312-408-5821; www. greyhound.com; 630 W Harrison St; Ⓜ Blue Line to Clinton) Buses run frequently to Cleveland (7½ hours), Detroit (seven hours) and Minneapolis (nine hours), as well as to small towns throughout the USA. Open 24 hours, the station is bit southwest of the Loop in a pretty desolate stretch of road.

Megabus (Map p518; www.megabus.com/us; Canal St & Jackson Blvd; 🛜; Ⓜ Blue Line to Clinton) Travels only to major Midwestern cities. Prices are often less, and quality and efficiency are better than Greyhound on these routes. The bus stop is adjacent to Union Station.

TRAIN

Chicago's classic **Union Station** (www.chicago unionstation.com; 225 S Canal St; Ⓜ Blue Line to Clinton) is the hub for **Amtrak** (🖂 800-872-7245; www.amtrak.com) national and regional service. Routes include the following:

Detroit (5½ hours, three trains daily)
Milwaukee (1½ hours, seven trains daily)
Minneapolis-St Paul (eight hours, one train daily)
New York (20½ hours, one train daily)
San Francisco (Emeryville; 53 hours, one train daily)
St Louis (5½ hours, five trains daily)

ℹ️ Getting Around

TO/FROM THE AIRPORT

Chicago Midway Airport Eleven miles southwest of the Loop, connected via the CTA Orange Line ($3). Trains depart every 10 minutes or so; they reach downtown in 30 minutes. Shuttle vans cost $27, taxis cost $35 to $40.

O'Hare International Airport Seventeen miles northwest of the Loop. The CTA Blue Line train ($5) runs 24/7. Trains depart every 10 minutes or so; they reach downtown in 40 minutes. Airport Express shuttle vans cost $32, taxis around $50. Taxi queues can be lengthy, and the ride can take as long as the train, depending on traffic.

BICYCLE

Chicago is a cycling-savvy city with a well-used bike-share program. **Divvy** (www.divvybikes. 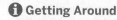 com) has 3000 sky-blue bikes at 300 stations around town. Kiosks issue 24-hour passes ($10) on the spot. Insert a credit card, get your ride code, then unlock a bike. The first 30 minutes are free; after that, rates rise fast if you don't dock the bike. Note helmets and locks are not provided.

For traditional rentals (useful for longer rides), try Bike Chicago (p525) or Bobby's Bike Hike (p525) downtown.

CAR & MOTORCYCLE

Be warned: street and garage/lot parking is expensive. If you must, try **Millennium Park Garage** (www.millenniumgarages.com; 5 S Columbus Dr; per 3/24hr $25/33). Chicago's rush-hour traffic is abysmal.

PUBLIC TRANSPORTATION

The **Chicago Transit Authority** (CTA; www. transitchicago.com) operates the city's buses and the elevated/subway train system (aka the El).

➡ Two of the eight color-coded train lines – the Red Line, and the Blue Line to O'Hare airport – operate 24 hours a day. The other lines run from 4am to 1am daily. During the day, you shouldn't have to wait more than 15 minutes for a train. Get free maps at any station.

➡ CTA buses go everywhere from early morning until late evening.

➡ The standard fare per train is $3 (except from O'Hare, where it costs $5) and includes two transfers; per bus, it is $2.25.

➡ On the train, you must use a Ventra Ticket, which is sold from vending machines at train stations. You can also buy a Ventra Card, aka a rechargeable fare card, at stations. It has a one-time $5 fee that gets refunded once you register the card. It knocks 50 to 75 cents off the cost of each ride.

➡ On buses, you can use a Ventra Card or pay the driver with exact change.

➡ Unlimited ride passes (one-/three-day pass $10/20) are also available. Get them at rail stations and drug stores.

Metra commuter trains (www.metrarail.com; fares $3.25-10.25, all-weekend pass $8) have 12 routes serving the suburbs from four terminals ringing the Loop: LaSalle St Station, Millennium Station, Union Station and Richard B Ogilvie Transportation Center (a few blocks north of Union Station).

TAXI

Cabs are plentiful in the Loop, north to Andersonville and northwest to Wicker Park and Bucktown. Flagfall is $3.25, plus $1.80 per mile and $1 per extra passenger; a 15% tip is expected. The rideshare company Uber is also popular.

Flash Cab (🖂 773-561-4444; www.flashcab.com)
Yellow Cab (🖂 312-829-4222; www.yellow-cabchicago.com)

Around Chicago

Oak Park

Located 10 miles west of the Loop and easily reached via CTA train, Oak Park has two famous sons: novelist Ernest Hemingway was born here, and architect Frank Lloyd Wright lived and worked here from 1889 to 1909.

During Wright's 20 years in Oak Park, he designed many houses. Chief among them is his own: the **Frank Lloyd Wright Home & Studio** (☑312-994-4000; www.flwright.org; 951 Chicago Ave; adult/child/camera $17/14/5; ☺10am-4pm) offers a fascinating, hour-long walk-through that reveals his distinctive style. Tour frequency varies, from every 20 minutes on summer weekends to every hour in winter. The studio also offers guided neighborhood walking tours ($15), as well as a self-guided audio version (same price). Or you can explore on the cheap by buying an architectural site map ($4.25) from the studio shop, which gives the locations of other Wright-designed abodes. Ten of them cluster nearby along Forest and Chicago Aves; gawking must be from the sidewalk since they're privately owned.

Despite Hemingway allegedly calling Oak Park a 'village of wide lawns and narrow minds,' the town still pays homage to him at the **Ernest Hemingway Museum** (☑708-848-2222; www.ehfop.org; 200 N Oak Park Ave; adult/child $15/13; ☺1-5pm Sun-Fri, from 10am Sat). Admission also includes entry to his birthplace home across the street.

From downtown Chicago, take the CTA Green Line to the Oak Park station, then walk north on Oak Park Ave. It's about a quarter mile to the Hemingway sights and a mile to the Wright home. The train traverses some bleak neighborhoods before emerging into Oak Park's wide-lawn splendor.

Evanston & North Shore

Evanston, 14 miles north of the Loop and reached via the CTA Purple Line, combines sprawling old houses with a compact downtown. It's home to Northwestern University.

Beyond are Chicago's northern lakeshore suburbs, which became popular with the wealthy in the late 19th century. A classic 30-mile drive follows Sheridan Rd through various well-off towns to the socioeconomic apex of Lake Forest. Attractions along the way include the **Baha'i House of Worship** (www.bahai.us/bahai-temple; 100 Linden Ave; ☺6am-

10pm) FREE, a glistening white architectural marvel, and the **Chicago Botanic Garden** (☑847-835-5440; www.chicagobotanic.org; 1000 Lake Cook Rd; per car weekday/weekend $25/30; ☺8am-sunset), with hiking trails, 255 bird species and weekend cooking demos by well-known chefs.

Inland lies the **Illinois Holocaust Museum** (☑847-967-4800; www.ilholocaustmuseum.org; 9603 Woods Dr; adult/child $12/6; ☺10am-5pm, to 8pm Thu). Besides its excellent videos of survivors' stories from WWII, the museum contains thought-provoking art about genocides in Armenia, Rwanda, Cambodia and elsewhere.

Galena & Northern Illinois

The highlight of this region is the hilly northwest, where cottonwood trees, grazing horses and scenic byways fill the pocket around Galena.

En route is Union, where the **Illinois Railway Museum** (☑815-923-4000; www.irm.org; US 20 to Union Rd; adult $10-14, child $7-10; ☺May-Oct, hours vary) sends trainspotters into fits of ecstasy with 200 acres of locomotives.

Galena

While it sometimes gets chided as a place for the 'newly wed and nearly dead,' thanks to all the tourist-oriented B&Bs, and fudge and antique shops, there's no denying little Galena's beauty. It spreads across wooded hillsides near the Mississippi River, amid rolling, barn-dotted farmland. Redbrick mansions in Greek Revival, Gothic Revival and Queen Anne styles fill the streets, left over from the town's heyday in the mid-1800s, when local lead mines made it rich. Throw in cool kayak trips, horseback rides and winding back-road drives, and you've got a lovely, slowpoke getaway.

⊙ Sights & Activities

When entering town on US 20, turn on Park Ave, then Bouthillier St to reach the free parking lot beside the old train depot. Most sights, shops and restaurants are walkable from here.

Ulysses S Grant Home   MUSEUM
(☑815-777-3310; www.granthome.com; 500 Bouthillier St; adult/child $5/3; ☺9am-4:45pm Wed-Sun Apr-Oct, reduced hours Nov-Mar) The 1860 abode was a gift from local Republicans to the victorious general at the Civil War's end. Grant lived here until he became the country's 18th president.

Fever River Outfitters OUTDOORS
(☑ 815-776-9425; www.feverriveroutfitters.com; 525 S Main St; ☉ 10am-5pm, closed Tue-Thu early Sep-late May) Outdoors enthusiasts should head to this shop, which rents canoes, kayaks, bicycles and snowshoes. It also offers guided tours, such as 9-mile kayak trips ($45 per person, equipment included) on the Mississippi River's backwaters.

Stagecoach Trail DRIVING TOUR
The Stagecoach Trail is a 26-mile ride on a narrow, twisty road en route to Warren. Pick it up by taking Main St northeast through downtown; at the second stop sign go right (you'll see a trail marker). And yes, it really was part of the old stagecoach route between Galena and Chicago.

Shenandoah Riding Center HORSEBACK RIDING
(☑ 815-777-9550; www.theshenandoahriding-center.com; 200 N Brodrecht Rd; 1hr ride $45) Saddle up at Shenandoah. It offers trail rides through the valley for all levels of riders. The stables are 8 miles east of Galena.

🛏 Sleeping

Galena brims with quilt-laden B&Bs. Most cost $100 to $200 nightly and fill up during weekends. Check www.galena.org for listings.

ROUTE 66: GET YOUR KICKS IN ILLINOIS

America's 'Mother Road' kicks off in Chicago on Adams St, just west of Michigan Ave. Before embarking, fuel up at Lou Mitchell's (p532) near Union Station. After all, it's 300 miles from here to the Missouri state line.

Sadly, most of the original Route 66 has been superseded by I-55 in Illinois, though the old road still exists in scattered sections often paralleling the interstate. Keep an eye out for brown 'Historic Route 66' signs, which pop up at crucial junctions to mark the way. Top stops include:

Gemini Giant (810 E Baltimore St) The first must-see rises from the cornfields 60 miles south of Chicago in Wilmington. Here the Gemini Giant – a 28ft fiberglass spaceman – stands guard outside the Launching Pad Drive In. The restaurant is now shuttered, but the green, rocket-holding statue remains a terrific photo op. To reach it, leave I-55 at exit 241, and follow Hwy 44 south a short distance to Hwy 53, which rolls into town.

Funk's Grove (☑ 309-874-3360; www.funksmaplesirup.com; ☉ 9am-5pm Mon-Fri, from 10am Sat, from noon Sun) Drive 90 miles onward to see Funk's pretty, 19th-century maple-sirup farm (yes, that's sirup with an 'i'). It's in Shirley (exit 154 off I-55). Afterward, get on Old Route 66 – a frontage road that parallels the interstate here – and in 10 miles you'll reach...

Palms Grill Cafe (☑ 217-648-2233; www.thepalmsgrillcafe.com; 110 SW Arch St; mains $5-8; ☉ 7am-7pm Tue-Sat) Pull up a chair at this diner in the throwback hamlet of Atlanta, where thick slabs of gooseberry, chocolate cream and other retro pies tempt from the glass case. Then walk across the street to snap a photo with Tall Paul, a sky-high statue of Paul Bunyan clutching a hot dog.

Cozy Dog Drive In (p541) Where the cornmeal-battered, fried hot dog on a stick was born. It's in Springfield, 50 miles down the road from Atlanta.

Ariston Cafe (☑ 217-324-2023; www.ariston-cafe.com; 413 N Old Rte 66; mains $7-20; ☉ 11am-9pm Tue-Fri, 4-10pm Sat, 11am-8pm Sun) Further south, a good section of old Route 66 parallels I-55 through Litchfield, where you can fork into chicken fried steak and red velvet cake while chatting up locals at the 1924 restaurant.

Chain of Rocks Bridge (Old Chain of Rocks Rd; ☉ 9am-sunset) Before driving into Missouri, detour off I-270 at exit 3. Follow Hwy 3 (aka Lewis and Clark Blvd) south, turn right at the first stoplight and drive west to the 1929 bridge. Open only to pedestrians and cyclists these days, the mile-long span over the Mississippi River has a 22-degree angled bend (the cause of many a crash, hence the ban on cars).

For more information, visit the **Route 66 Association of Illinois** (www.il66assoc.org) or **Illinois Route 66 Scenic Byway** (www.illinoisroute66.org). Detailed driving directions are at www.historic66.com/illinois.

Grant Hills Motel MOTEL $

(☏877-421-0924; www.granthills.com; 9372 US 20; r $80-100; ❉ 🛜 ❄) The motel is a no-frills option 1.5 miles east of town, with countryside views and a horseshoe pitch.

DeSoto House Hotel HOTEL $$

(☏815-777-0090; www.desotohouse.com; 230 S Main St; r $155-205; ❉ 🛜) 🅿 Grant and Lincoln stayed in the well-furnished rooms, and you can too. The hotel dates from 1855.

✕ Eating & Drinking

Fritz and Frites FRENCH, GERMAN $$

(☏815-777-2004; www.fritzandfrites.com; 317 N Main St; mains $17-22; ⊙11:30am-8pm Tue-Sun) This romantic little bistro serves a compact menu of both German and French classics. Dig into mussels with champagne sauce or maybe a tender schnitzel.

111 Main AMERICAN $$

(☏815-777-8030; www.oneelevenmain.com; 111 N Main St; mains $17-26; ⊙4-9pm Mon & Thu, 11am-10pm Fri & Sat, to 9pm Sun) Pot roast, pork and beans and other Midwestern favorites, using ingredients sourced from local farms.

VFW Hall BAR

(100 S Main St; ⊙10am-11pm) The VFW Hall provides an opportunity to sip cheap beer and watch TV alongside veterans of long-ago wars. Don't be shy: as the sign out front says, the public is welcome.

Quad Cities

South of Galena along a pretty stretch of the **Great River Road** (www.greatriverroad-illinois.org) is scenic **Mississippi Palisades State Park** (☏815-273-2731), a popular rock-climbing, hiking and camping area; pick up trail maps at the north entrance park office.

Further downstream, the Quad Cities (www.visitquadcities.com) – Moline and Rock Island in Illinois, and Davenport and Bettendorf across the river in Iowa – make a surprisingly good stop. Rock Island has an appealing downtown (based at 2nd Ave and 18th St), with a couple of cafes and a lively pub and music scene. On the edge of town, **Black Hawk State Historic Site** (www.blackhawkpark.org; 1510 46th Ave; ⊙sunrise-10pm) is a huge park with trails by the Rock River. Its **Hauberg Indian Museum** (☏309-788-9536; Watch Tower Lodge; ⊙9am-noon & 1-5pm Wed-Sun) FREE outlines the sorry story of Sauk leader Black Hawk and his people.

Out in the Mississippi River, the actual island of **Rock Island** once held a Civil War-era arsenal and POW camp. It now maintains the impressive **Rock Island Arsenal Museum** (www.arsenalhistoricalsociety.org; ⊙noon-4pm Tue-Sat) FREE, Civil War cemetery, national cemetery and visitor center for barge viewing. Bring photo ID as the island is still an active army facility.

Moline is the home of John Deere, the international farm machinery manufacturer. Downtown holds the **John Deere Pavilion** (www.johndeerepavilion.com; 1400 River Dr; ⊙9am-5pm Mon-Fri, 10am-5pm Sat, noon-4pm Sun; 🖝) FREE, a kiddie-beloved museum-showroom.

Springfield & Central Illinois

Abraham Lincoln and Route 66 sights are sprinkled liberally throughout central Illinois, which is otherwise farmland plain. East of Decatur, Arthur and Arcola are Amish centers.

Springfield

The small state capital has an obsession with Abraham Lincoln, who practiced law here from 1837 to 1861. Many of the attractions are walkable downtown and cost little or nothing.

◎ Sights

Lincoln Home & Visitor Center HISTORIC SITE

(☏217-492-4150; www.nps.gov/liho; 426 S 7th St; ⊙8:30am-5pm) FREE Start at the National Park Service visitor center, where you must pick up a ticket to enter Lincoln's 12-room abode, located directly across the street. You can then walk through the house where Abe and Mary Lincoln lived from 1844 until they moved to the White House in 1861; rangers are stationed throughout to provide background information and answer questions.

Lincoln Presidential Library & Museum MUSEUM

(☏217-558-8844; www.illinois.gov/alplm; 212 N 6th St; adult/child $15/6; ⊙9am-5pm; 🖝) This museum contains the most complete Lincoln collection in the world. Real-deal artifacts like Abe's shaving mirror and briefcase join whizbang exhibits and Disneyesque holograms that keep the kids agog.

Lincoln's Tomb TOMB

(www.lincolntomb.org; 1441 Monument Ave; ⊙9am-5pm Wed-Sat) FREE After his assassination,

Lincoln's body was returned to Springfield, where it lies in an impressive tomb in Oak Ridge Cemetery, 1.5 miles north of downtown. The gleam on the nose of Lincoln's bust, created by visitors' light touches, indicates the numbers of those who pay their respects here. On summer Tuesdays at 7pm, infantry re-enactors fire muskets and lower the flag outside the tomb.

Old State Capitol　　　　　HISTORIC SITE
(☑217-785-7960; cnr 6th & Adams Sts; suggested donation $5; ☺9am-5pm Wed-Sat) Chatterbox docents will take you through the building and regale you with Lincoln stories, such as how he gave his famous 'House Divided' speech here in 1858.

🛏 Sleeping & Eating

State House Inn　　　　　HOTEL $$
(☑217-528-5100; www.thestatehouseinn.com; 101 E Adams St; r $120-155; P❄@🕸) It looks concrete-drab outside, but inside the State House shows its style. Comfy beds and large baths fill the rooms; a retro bar fills the lobby.

Inn at 835　　　　　B&B $$
(☑217-523-4466; www.innat835.com; 835 S 2nd St; r $135-205; P❄🕸) The historic arts-and-crafts-style manor offers 11 rooms of the four-post bed, claw-foot bathtub variety.

Cozy Dog Drive In　　　　　AMERICAN $
(www.cozydogdrivein.com; 2935 S 6th St; mains $2-5; ☺8am-8pm Mon-Sat) This Route 66 legend – the reputed birthplace of the corn dog! – has memorabilia and souvenirs in addition to the deeply fried main course on a stick.

Norb Andy's Tabarin　　　　　PUB FOOD $
(www.norbandys.com; 518 E Capitol Ave; mains $8-10; ☺4pm-1am Tue-Sat) A favorite with locals, Norb's is a dive bar-restaurant housed in the 1837 Hickox House downtown. It piles up Springfield's best 'horseshoe,' a local sandwich of fried meat on toasted bread, mounded with french fries and smothered in melted cheese.

☆ Entertainment

Route 66 Drive In　　　　　CINEMA
(☑217-698-0066; www.route66-drivein.com; 1700 Recreation Dr; adult/child $7.50/5; ☺nightly Jun-Aug, weekends mid-Apr–May & Sep) Screens first-run flicks under the stars.

ADVANCE PLANNING

➡ Pre-book accommodations during summer, especially in resort-orientated places such as Mackinac Island in Michigan, and the North Shore in Minnesota. It's also advised for festival cities such as Milwaukee and Chicago.

➡ Pay attention to time zones: half of the Great Lakes region is on Eastern time (IN, OH, MI) and half on Central time (IL, WI, MN).

➡ Bring insect repellent, especially if you're heading to the Northwoods. The blackflies in spring and mosquitoes in summer can be brutal.

➡ Stock up on dollar bills and quarters for tollways.

❶ Information
Springfield Convention & Visitors Bureau (www.visitspringfieldillinois.com) Produces a useful visitors' guide.

❶ Getting There & Around
The downtown **Amtrak station** (☑217-753-2013; cnr 3rd & Washington Sts) has five trains daily to/from St Louis (two hours) and Chicago (3½ hours).

Petersburg
When Lincoln first arrived in Illinois in 1831, he worked variously as a clerk, storekeeper and postmaster in the frontier village of New Salem before studying law and moving to Springfield. In Petersburg, 20 miles northwest of Springfield, **Lincoln's New Salem State Historic Site** (☑217-632-4000; www.lincolnsnewsalem.com; Hwy 97; suggested donation adult/child $4/2; ☺9am-4pm Wed-Sun) reconstructs the village with building replicas, historical displays and costumed performances – a pretty informative and entertaining package.

Southern Illinois
A surprise awaits near Collinsville, 8 miles east of East St Louis: classified as a Unesco World Heritage site with the likes of Stonehenge and the Egyptian pyramids is **Cahokia Mounds State Historic Site** (☑618-346-5160; www.cahokiamounds.org; Collinsville Rd; suggested donation adult/child $7/2; ☺grounds 8am-dusk, visitor center 9am-5pm Wed-Sun) Cahokia

protects the remnants of North America's largest prehistoric city (20,000 people, with suburbs), dating from AD 1200. While the 65 earthen mounds, including the enormous Monk's Mound, are not overwhelmingly impressive in themselves, the whole site is worth seeing. If you're approaching from the north, take exit 24 off I-255 S; if approaching from St Louis, take exit 6 off I-55/70.

A short distance north in Hartford, the stellar **Lewis & Clark State Historic Site** (☑ 618-251-5811; www.campdubois.com; cnr Hwy 3 & Poag Rd; ☺ 9am-5pm Wed-Sun) FREE marks the spot where the explorers departed on their journey. The 55ft boat replica (in the visitor center), reconstructed winter camp (out on the low-slung prairie) and Mississippi River bashing by give a real feel for the scene. The nearby **Lewis & Clark Confluence Tower** (www.confluencetower.com; 435 Confluence Tower Dr; adult/child $4/2; ☺ 9:30am-5pm Mon-Sat, from noon Sun) provides sweeping views.

Continuing northwest along the water, Hwy 100 between **Alton** and **Grafton** is perhaps the most scenic 15 miles of the entire Great River Road. As you slip under windhewn bluffs, keep an eye out for the turnoff to itty-bitty **Elsah**, a hidden hamlet of 19th-century stone cottages, wood frame shops and farmhouses

An exception to the state's flat farmland is the green southernmost section, punctuated by rolling **Shawnee National Forest** (☑ 618-253-7114; www.fs.usda.gov/shawnee) and its rocky outcroppings. The area has numerous state parks and recreation areas good for hiking, climbing, swimming, fishing and canoeing, particularly around **Little Grassy Lake** and **Devil's Kitchen**. And who would think that Southern-style swampland, complete with moss-draped cypress trees and croaking bullfrogs, would be here? But it is, at **Cypress Creek National Wildlife Refuge** (☑ 618-634-2231; www.fws.gov/refuge/cypress_creek).

Union County, near the state's southern tip, has wineries and orchards. Sample the wares on the 35-mile **Shawnee Hills Wine Trail** (www.shawneewinetrail.com), which connects 12 vineyards.

INDIANA

The state revs up around the Indy 500 race, but otherwise it's about slow-paced pleasures in corn-stubbled Indiana: pie-eating in Amish Country, meditating in Bloomington's Tibetan temples and admiring the big architecture in small Columbus. For the record, folks have called Indianans 'Hoosiers' since the 1830s, but the word's origin is unknown. One theory is that early settlers knocking on a door were met with 'Who's here?' which soon became 'Hoosier.' It's certainly something to discuss with locals, perhaps over a traditional pork tenderloin sandwich.

ⓘ Information

Indiana Highway Conditions (☑ 800-261-7623; http://indot.carsprogram.org)
Indiana State Park Information (☑ 800-622-4931; www.in.gov/dnr/parklake) Park entry costs $2 per day by foot or bicycle, $9 to $12 by vehicle. Campsites cost $12 to $44; reservations accepted (☑ 866-622-6746; www.camp.in.gov).
Indiana Tourism (☑ 800-677-9800; www.visitindiana.com)

Indianapolis

Clean-cut Indy is the state capital and a perfectly pleasant place to ogle racecars and take a spin around the renowned speedway. The art museum and White River State Park have their merits, as do the Mass Ave and Broad Ripple 'hoods for eating and drinking. And Kurt Vonnegut fans are in for a treat. A well trail connects it all.

⊙ Sights & Activities

Downtown's bull's-eye is Monument Circle. White River State Park and its many attractions lie about three-quarters of a mile west.

Indianapolis Motor Speedway MUSEUM
(☑ 317-492-6784; www.indianapolismotorspeedway.com; 4790 W 16th St; adult/child $8/5; ☺ 9am-5pm Mar-Oct, 10am-4pm Nov-Feb) The Speedway, home of the Indianapolis 500 motor race, is Indy's supersight. The Hall of Fame Museum features 75 racing cars (including former winners), a 500lb Tiffany trophy and a track tour ($8 extra). OK, so you're on a bus for the latter and not even beginning to burn rubber at 37mph, but it's still fun to pretend.

The big race itself is held on the Sunday of Memorial Day weekend (late May) and attended by 450,000 crazed fans. **Tickets** (☑ 800-822-4639; www.imstix.com; $40-185) can be hard to come by. Try the pre-race trials and practices for easier access and cheaper prices. The track is about 6 miles northwest of downtown.

Dallara IndyCar Factory MUSEUM
(☑ 317-243-7171; www.indycarfactory.com; 1201 W Main St; adult/child $10/5; ☺ 10am-6pm Mon-Sat)

The shiny factory is a short walk from the Speedway. It opened in 2012 and provides a peek at how the fast cars are made. The wind tunnel models raise hairs, as do driving simulators that let you feel what it's like to tear around the track at 200mph.

White River State Park
STATE PARK

(http://inwhiteriver.wrsp.in.gov) The expansive park, located at downtown's edge, contains several worthwhile sights. The adobe **Eiteljorg Museum of American Indians & Western Art** (www.eiteljorg.org; 500 W Washington St; adult/child $12/6; ⊙10am-5pm Mon-Sat, from noon Sun) features Native American basketry, pots and masks, as well as several paintings by Frederic Remington and Georgia O'Keeffe. Other park highlights include an atmospheric **minor-league baseball stadium**, a **zoo**, a **canal walk**, **gardens**, a **science museum** and a **college sports museum**.

Indianapolis Museum of Art
MUSEUM, GARDENS

(☑317-920-2660; www.imamuseum.org; 4000 Michigan Rd; adult/child $18/10; ⊙11am-5pm Tue-Sun, to 9pm Thu) The museum has a terrific collection of European art (especially Turner and post-Impressionists), African tribal art, South Pacific art and Chinese works. The complex also includes **Oldfields – Lilly House & Gardens**, where you can tour the 22-room mansion and flowery grounds of the Lilly pharmaceutical family, and **Fairbanks Art & Nature Park**, with eye-popping mod sculptures set amid 100 acres of woodlands. Fairbanks is free – perfect for those who need an art fix but without the steep admission price.

Kurt Vonnegut Memorial Library
MUSEUM

(www.vonnegutlibrary.org; 340 N Senate Ave; ⊙11am-6pm Mon, Tue, Thu & Fri, noon-5pm Sat & Sun) FREE Author Kurt Vonnegut was born and raised in Indy, and this humble museum pays homage with displays including his Pall Mall cigarettes, droll drawings and rejection letters from publishers. The library also replicates his office, complete with checkerboard carpet, red rooster lamp and blue Coronamatic typewriter. You're welcome to sit at the desk and type Kurt a note; the library tweets the musings.

Rhythm! Discovery Center
MUSEUM

(www.rhythmdiscoverycenter.org; 110 W Washington St; adult/child $10/6; ⊙10am-5pm Mon, Tue & Thu-Sat, noon-7pm Wed, noon-5pm Sun) Bang drums, gongs, xylophones and exotic percussive instruments from around the globe at this hidden gem downtown. Kids love the interactive whomping. Adults appreciate the exhibits of famous drummers' gear and the soundproof, drum-kitted studio where you can unleash (and record) your inner Neil Peart.

Indiana Medical History Museum
MUSEUM

(☑317-635-7329; www.imhm.org; 3045 W Vermont St; adult/child $10/3; ⊙10am-3pm Thu-Sat) When you think 'horror movie insane asylum,' this century-old state psychiatric hospital is exactly what you envision. Guided tours roam the former pathology lab, from the cold-slabbed autopsy room to the eerie specimen room filled with brains in jars. Tours start on the hour. It's a few miles west of White River park.

Children's Museum of Indianapolis
MUSEUM

(☑317-334-4000; www.childrensmuseum.org; 3000 N Meridian St; adult/child $21.50/18.50; ⊙10am-5pm, closed Mon mid-Sep–Feb) It's the world's largest kids' museum, sprawled over five floors holding dinosaurs aplenty and a 43ft sculpture by Dale Chihuly that teaches tykes to blow glass (virtually!).

Cultural Trail
CYCLING, WALKING

(www.indyculturaltrail.org) The 8-mile bike and pedestrian path links cool sights and

---

INDIANA FACTS

Nickname Hoosier State

Population 6.6 million

Area 36,420 sq miles

Capital city Indianapolis (population 843,400)

Sales tax 7%

Birthplace of Author Kurt Vonnegut (1922–2007), actor James Dean (1931–55), TV host David Letterman (b 1947), rocker John Mellencamp (b 1951), King of Pop Michael Jackson (1958–2009)

Home of Farmers, corn

Politics Typically Republican

Famous for Indy 500 motor race, basketball fanaticism, pork tenderloin sandwich

Official pie Sugar cream

Driving distances Indianapolis to Chicago 185 miles, Indianapolis to Bloomington 53 miles

GREAT LAKES INDIANAPOLIS

> **ⓘ INDIANA FOODWAYS**
>
> Which restaurants serve the best pork tenderloin and sugar cream pie? Where are the local farmers markets and rib fests? What's the recipe for corn pudding? The **Indiana Foodways Alliance** (www.indianafoodways.com) is your one-stop shop for Hoosier cuisine information.

neighborhoods around Indy's center. Pacers Bikeshare stations dot the way and are handy for short jaunts.

Bicycle Garage Indy   BICYCLE RENTAL

(www.bgindy.com; 222 E Market St; rental per 2hr/day $20/40; ⊙7am-8pm Mon-Fri, 8am-4pm Sat) Rent bikes here for leisurely rides. Hop on the Cultural Trail in front of the shop; it eventually connects to the Monon Trail greenway. Rates include helmet, lock and map.

🛏 Sleeping

Hotels cost more and are usually full during race weeks in May, June, July and August. Add 17% tax to the prices listed here. Look for low-cost motels off I 465, the freeway that circles Indianapolis.

Indy Hostel   HOSTEL $

(☎317-727-1696; www.indyhostel.us; 4903 Winthrop Ave; dm/r from $28/58; 🅿❄@🛜) This small, friendly hostel has a six-bed female dorm and 12-bed coed dorm. There are also four private rooms. Got a tent? Camp in the yard for $19. The Monon Trail hiking/cycling path runs beside the property, and the hostel rents bikes (per day $10). It's located by Broad Ripple, so a bit of a haul from downtown (on bus 17).

Hilton Garden Inn   HOTEL $$

(☎317-955-9700; www.indianapolisdowntown.gardeninn.com; 10 E Market St; r $150-190; ❄@🛜❄) The century-old, neoclassical architecture, plush beds and downtown location right by Monument Circle make this a fine chainhotel choice. Valet parking is $27.

Stone Soup   B&B $$

(☎866-639-9550; www.stonesoupinn.com; 1304 N Central Ave; r $90-150; 🅿🚭❄🛜) The nine rooms fill a rambling, antique-filled house. It's a bit ramshackle, but it has its charm. The less-expensive rooms share a bath.

The Alexander   HOTEL $$

(☎317-624-8200; www.thealexander.com; 333 S Delaware St; r $170-270) The 209-room Alexander is all about art. Forty original works decorate the lobby; the Indianapolis Museum of Art curates the contemporary collection (the public is welcome to browse). The mod rooms have dark-wood floors and, of course, cool wall art. It's a block from the basketball arena, and it's where visiting teams sometimes stay. Valet parking is $29.

Eating

Massachusetts Ave (www.discovermassave. com), by downtown, is bounteous when the stomach growls. **Broad Ripple** (www.discover broadripplevillage.com), 7 miles north, has pubs, cafes and ethnic eateries.

Mug 'N' Bun   AMERICAN $

(www.mug-n-bun.com; 5211 W 10th St; mains $4-8; ⊙10am-9pm Sun-Thu, to 10pm Fri & Sat) The mugs are frosted and filled with a wonderful homebrewed root beer. The buns contain burgers, chili dogs and juicy pork tenderloins. And don't forget the fried mac 'n' cheese wedges. At this vintage drive-in near the Speedway, you are served – where else? – in your car.

Public Greens   AMERICAN $

(www.publicgreensurbankitchen.com; 900 E 64th St; mains $7-14; ⊙8am-9pm Sun-Thu, to 10pm Fri & Sat, reduced hours in winter) 🥦 The on-site micro-farm raises kale, beets, eggs and other ingredients for the eatery's homey dishes; 100% of profits are then plowed back into the community to feed at-risk children. It's a cafeteria-style set up, where you order at the counter. Located in Broad Ripple, right by the Monon Trail.

Bazbeaux   PIZZA $

(☎317-636-7662; www.bazbeaux.com; 329 Massachusetts Ave; mains $8-15; ⊙11am-10pm Sun-Thu, to 11pm Fri & Sat) A local favorite, Bazbeaux offers an eclectic pizza selection, like the 'Tchoupitoulas,' topped with Cajun shrimp and andouille sausage. Muffaletta sandwiches, stromboli and Belgian beer are some of the other offerings.

City Market   MARKET $

(www.indycm.com; 222 E Market St; ⊙7am-9pm Mon-Fri, from 8am Sat; 🛜) A smattering of food stalls fill the city's old marketplace, which dates from 1886. The 2nd-floor bar pours 16 local brews; most other vendors close by 3pm.

♟ Drinking & Entertainment

Downtown and Mass Ave have some good watering holes; Broad Ripple has several.

Bars

Sun King Brewing BREWERY
(www.sunkingbrewing.com; 135 N College Ave; ⏱ 10am-7pm Mon-Wed, to 8pm Thu & Fri, 1-6pm Sat & Sun, reduced hours in winter) FREE You never know what'll be flowing at Sun King's unvarnished downtown taproom. Indy's young and hip pile in to find out, swilling brews from a cocoa-y Baltic porter to a popcorn-tinged pilsner (made with Indiana popcorn). Flights (six 3oz samples) cost $6. Friday, when the brewery offers free samples and cheap growlers, it's packed. The outdoor patio hops in summer.

Slippery Noodle Inn BAR
(www.slipperynoodle.com; 372 S Meridian St; ⏱ 11am-3am Mon-Fri, noon-3am Sat, 4pm-12:30am Sun) Downtown's Noodle is the oldest bar in the state, and has seen action as a whorehouse, slaughterhouse, gangster hangout and Underground Railroad station; currently, it's one of the best blues clubs in the country. There's live music nightly, and it's cheap.

Rathskeller BEER HALL
(www.rathskeller.com; 401 E Michigan St; ⏱ 2pm-late Mon-Fri, from 11am Sat & Sun) Quaff German and local brews at the outdoor beer garden's picnic tables in summer, or at the deerhead-lined indoor beer hall once winter strikes. It is located in the historic Athenaeum building near Mass Ave.

Sports

The motor races aren't the only coveted spectator events. The NFL's Colts win football games under a huge retractable roof at **Lucas Oil Stadium** (☑ 317-299-4946; www.colts.com; 500 S Capitol Ave). The NBA's Pacers shoot hoops at **Bankers Life Fieldhouse** (☑ 317-917-2500; www.nba.com/pacers; 125 S Pennsylvania St).

🛍 Shopping

You could buy a speedway flag or Colts jersey as your Indy souvenir. Or you could purchase a bottle of mead made by a couple of enthusiastic former beekeepers at **New Day** (www.newdaycraft.com; 1102 E Prospect St; ⏱ 2-9pm Tue-Thu, to 10pm Fri, noon-10pm Sat, noon-6pm Sun). Sample the honeyed wares in the tasting room before making your selection. They also make cider.

ℹ Information

Indiana University Medical Center (☑ 317-274-4705; 550 N University Blvd)

Indianapolis Convention & Visitors Bureau (☑ 800-323-4639; www.visitindy.com) Download a free city app and print out coupons from the website.

Indianapolis Star (www.indystar.com) The city's daily newspaper.

Indy Rainbow Chamber (www.gayindynow.org) Provides info for gay and lesbian visitors.

Nuvo (www.nuvo.net) Free, weekly alternative paper with the arts and music low-down.

ℹ Getting There & Around

The fancy **Indianapolis International Airport** (IND; www.indianapolisairport.com; 7800 Col H Weir Cook Memorial Dr) is 16 miles southwest of town. The Washington bus (8) runs between the airport and downtown ($1.75, 50 minutes); the Go Green Airport van does it quicker ($10, 20 minutes). A cab to downtown costs about $35.

Greyhound (☑ 317-267-3074; www.greyhound.com) shares **Union Station** (350 S Illinois St) with Amtrak. Buses go frequently to Cincinnati (2½ hours) and Chicago (3½ hours). **Megabus** (www.megabus.com/us) stops at 200 E Washington St, and is often cheaper. Amtrak travels these routes but takes almost twice as long.

IndyGo (www.indygo.net; fares $1.75) runs the local buses. Bus 17 goes to Broad Ripple. Service is minimal during weekends.

Pacers Bikeshare (www.pacersbikeshare.org; 24hr pass $8) has 250 bikes at 25 stations along the Cultural Trail downtown. Additional charges apply for trips over 30 minutes.

For a taxi, call **Yellow Cab** (☑ 317-487-7777).

Bloomington & Central Indiana

Bluegrass music, architectural hot spots, Tibetan temples and James Dean all furrow into the farmland around here.

Fairmount

This small town, north on Hwy 9, is the birthplace of James Dean, one of the original icons of cool. Fans should head directly to the **Fairmount Historical Museum** (☑ 765-948-4555; www.jamesdeanartifacts.com; 203 E Washington St; ⏱ 10am-5pm Mon-Fri, from noon Sat & Sun Apr-Oct) FREE to see Dean's bongo drums, among other artifacts. This is also the place to pick up a free map that will guide you to sites like the farmhouse where Jimmy grew up and his lipstick-kissed grave

GRAY BROTHERS CAFETERIA

Cafeterias are an Indiana tradition, but most have disappeared – except for **Gray Brothers** (www.graybroscafe.com; 555 S Indiana St; mains $4-8; ⊙ 11am-8:30pm). Enter the time-warped dining room, grab a blue tray and behold a corridor of food that seems to stretch the length of a football field. Stack on plates of pan-fried chicken, meatloaf, mac 'n' cheese and sugar cream pie, then fork in with abandon. It's located in Mooresville, about 18 miles south of downtown Indianapolis en route to Bloomington.

site. The museum sells Dean posters, Zippo lighters and other memorabilia, and sponsors the annual **James Dean Festival** (⊙ late Sep), when thousands of fans pour in for four days of music and revelry. The privately owned **James Dean Gallery** (☑ 765-948-3326; www.jamesdeangallery.com; 425 N Main St; ⊙ 9am-6pm) FREE has more memorabilia a few blocks away.

Columbus

When you think of the USA's great architectural cities – Chicago, New York, Washington, DC – Columbus, Indiana, doesn't quite leap to mind, but it should. Located 40 miles south of Indianapolis on I-65, Columbus is a remarkable gallery of physical design. Since the 1940s the city and its leading corporations have commissioned some of the world's best architects, including Eero Saarinen, Richard Meier and IM Pei, to create both public and private buildings. Stop at the **visitor center** (☑ 812-378-2622; www.columbus.in.us; 506 5th St; ⊙ 9am-5pm Mon-Sat, noon-5pm Sun) to pick up a self-guided tour map ($3) or join a two-hour bus tour (adult/child $25/15); they depart at 10am Tuesday to Friday, 10am and 2pm Saturday, and 2pm Sunday. It's wise to reserve online in advance. Over 70 notable buildings and pieces of public art are spread over a wide area (car required), but about 15 diverse works can be seen on foot downtown.

Hotel Indigo (☑ 812-375-9100; www.hotelindigo.com; 400 Brown St; r $150-180; ❋ 🛜 🐾 ❋), downtown, offers the chain's trademark mod, cheery rooms, plus a fluffy white dog who works as the lobby ambassador. A few blocks away you can grab a counter stool, chat up the servers, and let the sugar buzz begin at retro, stained-glass-packed **Zaharakos** (www.zaharakos.com; 329 Washington St; ⊙ 11am-8pm), a 1909 soda fountain.

Nashville

Gentrified and antique-filled, this 19th-century town west of Columbus on Hwy 46 is now a bustling tourist center, at its busiest in fall when leaf-peepers pour in. The **visitor center** (☑ 812-988-7303; www.browncounty.com; 10 N Van Buren St; ⊙ 9am-6pm Mon-Thu, 9am-7pm Fri & Sat, 10am-5pm Sun; 🛜) provides maps and coupons.

Beyond gallery browsing, Nashville is the jump-off point to **Brown County State Park** (☑ 812-988-6406; tent & RV sites $16-33, cabins from $77), a 15,700-acre stand of oak, hickory and birch trees, where trails give hikers, mountain bikers and horseback riders access to the area's green hill country.

Among several B&Bs, central **Artists Colony Inn** (☑ 812-988-0600; www.artistscolonyinn.com; 105 S Van Buren St; r $125-180; ❋ 🛜) stands out for its spiffy, Shaker-style rooms. The **dining room** (mains $10-19; ⊙ 7:30am-8pm Sun-Thu, to 9pm Fri & Sat) offers traditional Hoosier fare, such as catfish and pork tenderloins.

As with Nashville Tennessee, Nashville Indiana enjoys country music, and bands play regularly at several venues. To shake a leg, mosey into **Mike's Music & Dance Barn** (☑ 812-988-8636; www.mikesmusicbarn.com; 2277 Hwy 46; ⊙ from 6:30pm Thu-Mon). The **Bill Monroe Museum** (☑ 812-988-6422; www.billmonroemusicpark.com; 5163 Rte 135 N; adult/child $4/free; ⊙ 9am-5pm Mon-Sat, noon-4pm Sun, closed Tue & Wed Nov-Apr), 5 miles north of town, hails the bluegrass hero; it hosts a popular, week-long bluegrass festival in mid-June.

Bloomington

Lively and lovely, limestone-clad and cycling mad, Bloomington – 53 miles south of Indianapolis via Hwy 37 – is the home of Indiana University. The town centers on Courthouse Sq, surrounded by restaurants, bars and bookshops. Nearly everything is walkable. The **Bloomington CVB** (www.visitbloomington.com) has a downloadable guide.

On the expansive university campus, the **Art Museum** (☑ 812-855-5445; https://artmuseum.indiana.edu; 1133 E 7th St; ⊙ 10am-5pm Tue-Sat, from noon Sun) FREE, designed by IM Pei, contains an excellent collection of African art and German expressionist paintings.

The colorful, prayer-flag-covered **Tibetan Mongolian Buddhist Cultural Center** (✆812-336-6807; www.tmbcc.org; 3655 Snoddy Rd; ☺sunrise-sunset) **FREE** – founded by the Dalai Lama's brother – as well as the **Dagom Gaden Tensung Ling Monastery** (✆812-339-0857; www.dgtlmonastery.org; 102 Clubhouse Dr; ☺9am-6pm) **FREE**, indicate Bloomington's significant Tibetan presence. Both have intriguing shops and offer free teachings and meditation sessions; check the websites for weekly schedules.

If you arrive in mid-April and wonder why an extra 20,000 people are hanging out in town, it's for the **Little 500** (www.iusf.indiana.edu; tickets $30). It's one of the coolest bike races you'll see, where amateurs ride one-speed Schwinns for 200 laps around a quarter-mile track.

Look for cheap lodgings along N Walnut St near Hwy 46. **Grant Street Inn** (✆800-328-4350; www.grantstinn.com; 310 N Grant St; r $159-239; @ 🖵) has 24 rooms in a Victorian house and annex near campus.

For a town of its size, Bloomington offers a mind-blowing array of ethnic eats – everything from Burmese to Eritrean to Turkish. Browse Kirkwood Ave and E 4th St. **Anyetsang's Little Tibet** (✆812-331-0122; www.anyetsangs.com; 415 E 4th St; mains $13-14; ☺11am-3pm & 5-9pm, closed Tue) offers specialties from the Himalayan homeland. Pubs on Kirkwood Ave, close to the university, cater to the student crowd. **Nick's English Hut** (www.nicksenglishhut.com; 423 E Kirkwood Ave; ☺11am-2am Mon-Sat, to midnight Sat) pours not only for students and professors, but has filled the cups of Kurt Vonnegut and Dylan Thomas, as well. On the near north side, rustic **Upland Brewing Co** (www.uplandbeer.com; 350 W 11th St; ☺11am-midnight Mon-Thu, to 1am Fri & Sat, noon-midnight Sun) makes creative suds like a seasonal persimmon lambic using local fruit.

Southern Indiana

The pretty hills, caves, rivers and utopian history of southern Indiana mark it as a completely different region from the flat and industrialized north.

Ohio River

The Indiana segment of the 981-mile Ohio River marks the state's southern border. From tiny Aurora, in the southeastern corner of the state, Hwys 56, 156, 62 and 66,

known collectively as the **Ohio River Scenic Route**, wind through a varied landscape.

Coming from the east, a perfect place to stop is little **Madison**, a well-preserved river settlement from the mid-19th century where architectural beauties beckon genteelly from the streets. At the **visitor center** (✆812-265-2956; www.visitmadison.org; 601 W First St; ☺9am-5pm Mon-Fri, to 4pm Sat, 11am-3pm Sun), pick up a walking-tour brochure, which will lead you by notable landmarks.

Madison has motels around its edges, as well as several B&Bs. Main St lines up numerous places for a bite, interspersed with antique stores. Large, wooded **Clifty Falls State Park** (✆812-273-8885; tent & RV sites $16-33), off Hwy 56 and a couple of miles west of town, has camping, hiking trails, views and waterfalls.

In Clarksville, **Falls of the Ohio State Park** (✆812-280-9970; www.fallsoftheohio.org; 201 W Riverside Dr) has only rapids, no falls, but is of interest for its 386-million-year-old fossil beds. The newly renovated **interpretive center** (adult/child $5/2; ☺9am-5pm Mon-Sat, from 1pm Sun) explains it all. Quench your thirst in adjacent New Albany, home to the **New Albanian Brewing Company Public House** (www.newalbanian.com; 3312 Plaza Dr; ☺11am-11pm Mon-Sat). Or cross the bridge to Louisville, KY, where the tonsil-singeing native bourbon awaits...

Scenic Hwy 62 heads west and leads to the Lincoln Hills and southern Indiana's limestone caves. A plunge into **Marengo Cave** (✆812-365-2705; www.marengocave.com; ☺9am-6pm Jun-Aug, to 5pm Sep-May), north on Hwy 66, is highly recommended. It offers a 40-minute tour (adult/child $15/8.50), 60-minute tour ($18/10) or combination tour ($25/14) walking past stalagmites and other ancient formations. The same group operates **Cave Country Canoes** (www.cavecountrycanoes.com; 112 W Main St; ☺May-Oct) in nearby Milltown, with half-day ($26), full-day ($30) or longer trips on the scenic Blue River; keep an eye out for river otters and rare hellbender salamanders.

Four miles south of Dale, off I-64, is the **Lincoln Boyhood National Memorial** (✆812-937-4541; www.nps.gov/libo; adult/child/family $5/free/$10; ☺8am-5pm), where young Abe lived from age seven to 21. This isolated site also includes admission to a working **pioneer farm** (☺8am-5pm May-Aug).

THE GREAT LAKES' BEST PIE

➡ **Village Inn** (p549) Mmm, rhubarb custard.

➡ **Crane's Pie Pantry** (p574) Apples and peaches picked from the surrounding orchard.

➡ **Palms Grill Cafe** (p539) Retro goodness on Route 66.

➡ **Boyd & Wurthmann Restaurant** (p556) Lots of flaky options in Amish Country.

➡ **Betty's Pies** (p605) Resistance is futile when the crunch-topping arrives.

New Harmony

In southwest Indiana, the Wabash River forms the border with Illinois. Beside it, south of I-64, captivating New Harmony is the site of two early communal-living experiments and is worth a visit. In the early 19th century a German Christian sect, the Harmonists, developed a sophisticated town here while awaiting the Second Coming. Later, the British utopian Robert Owen acquired the town. Learn more and pick up a walking-tour map at the angular **Atheneum Visitors Center** (☑ 812-682-4474; www.usi.edu/hnh; 401 N Arthur St; ☺ 9:30am-5pm, closed Jan–mid-Mar).

Today New Harmony retains an air of contemplation, if not otherworldliness, which you can experience at its newer attractions, such as the templelike Roofless Church and the Labyrinth, a maze symbolizing the spirit's quest. The town has a couple of guesthouses and camping at **Harmonie State Park** (☑ 812-682-4821; campsites $23-33). Pop into **Main Cafe** (508 Main St; mains $4-7; ☺ 5:30am-1pm Mon-Fri) for a ham, bean and cornbread lunch, but save room for the coconut cream pie.

Northern Indiana

The truck-laden I-80/I-90 tollways cut across Indiana's north. Parallel US 20 is slower and cheaper, but not much more attractive.

Indiana Dunes

Sunny beaches, rustling grasses and woodsy campgrounds are the claim to fame at **Indiana Dunes National Lakeshore** (☑ 219-926-7561; www.nps.gov/indu) FREE which stretches along 15 miles of Lake Michigan shoreline. Swimming is allowed anywhere along the expanse. A short walk away from the beaches, several hiking paths crisscross the sand and woodlands. The best are the **Bailly-Chellberg Trail** (2.5 miles) that winds by a still operating 1870s farm, and the **Heron Rookery Trail** (2 miles), where blue herons flock. Oddly, all this natural bounty lies smack-dab next to smoke-belching factories and steel mills, which you'll also see at various vantage points. Stop at the park **visitor center** (Hwy 49; ☺ 8am-6pm Jun-Aug, to 4:30pm Sep-May) for beach details and to pick up hiking, biking and birding maps.

Indiana Dunes State Park (☑ 219-926-1952; www.dnr.in.gov/parklake; per car $12) is a 2100-acre shoreside pocket within the national lakeshore; it's located at the end of Hwy 49, near Chesterton. It has more amenities, but also more regulations and more crowds (plus the vehicle entry fee). Wintertime brings out the cross-country skiers; summertime brings out the hikers. Seven trails zigzag over the landscape; No 4 up Mt Tom rewards with Chicago skyline views.

Other than a couple of beachfront snack bars, you won't find much to eat in the parks, so stop at **Great Lakes Cafe** (201 Mississippi St; mains $6-9; ☺ 5am-3pm Mon-Fri, 6am-1pm Sat; 🖥), the steelworkers' hearty favorite, at the Dunes' western edge in Gary.

The Dunes are an easy day trip from Chicago. Driving takes one hour (though parking can be a hassle). The **South Shore Metra train** (www.nictd.com) makes the journey from Millennium Station downtown, and it's about 1¼ hours to the Dune Park or Beverly Shores stops (note both stations are a 1.5-mile walk from the beach). Those who want to make a night of it can camp (national lakeshore campsites $18, state park tent and RV sites $23 to $36).

Right by the Illinois border, the steel cities of **Gary** and **East Chicago** present some of the bleakest urban landscapes anywhere. Taking the train (Amtrak or South Shore line) through here will get you up close and personal with the industrial underbelly.

South Bend

South Bend is home to the **University of Notre Dame**. You know how people in certain towns say, 'football is a religion here'? They mean it at Notre Dame, where 'Touchdown Jesus' lords over the 80,000-capacity stadium (it's a mural of the resurrected Christ with arms raised, though the pose bears a striking resemblance to a referee signaling a touchdown).

Tours of the pretty campus, with its two lakes, Gothic-style architecture and iconic Golden Dome atop the main building, start at the **visitor center** (www.nd.edu/visitors; 111 Eck Center). Less visited but worth a stop is the **Studebaker National Museum** (✆574-235-9714; www.studebakermuseum.org; 201 S Chapin St; adult/child $8/5; ◷10am-5pm Mon-Sat, from noon Sun) near downtown, where you can gaze at a gorgeous 1956 Packard and other classic beauties that used to be built in South Bend.

Indiana Amish Country

East of South Bend, around **Shipshewana** and **Middlebury**, is the USA's third-largest Amish community. Horses and buggies clip-clop by, and long-bearded men hand-plow the tidy fields. Get situated with maps from the **Elkhart County CVB** (✆800-262-8161; www.amishcountry.org). Better yet, pick a back oad between the two towns and head down it. Often you'll see families selling beeswax candles, quilts and fresh produce on their porch, which beats the often-touristy shops and restaurants on the main roads. Note that most places close on Sunday.

Village Inn (✆574-825-2043; 105 S Main St; mains $3-9; ◷5am-8pm Mon-Fri, 6am-2pm Sat; 🛜), in Middlebury, sells sublime pies, like the best-selling rhubarb custard. Bonneted women in pastel dresses come in at 4:30am to bake the flaky wares. Arrive before noon, or you'll be looking at crumbs. Across the street, **41 Degrees North** (104 S Main St; ◷11am-10:30pm Tue-Thu, to midnight Fri, 1pm-midnight Sat) pours a terrific regional beer selection. **Der Ruhe Blatz Motel** (✆260-758-0670; www.therestplace. com; 1195 S Van Buren St; r $68-105; ✳🛜) is no-frills, but has a perfect location on Shipshewana's main road to see morning buggy traffic.

Auburn

Just before reaching the Ohio border, classic car connoisseurs should dip south on I-69 to the town of Auburn, where the Cord Company produced the USA's favorite cars in the 1920s and '30s The **Auburn Cord Duesenberg Museum** (✆260-925-1444; www.automobilemuseum.org; 1600 S Wayne St; adult/child $12.50/7.50; ◷10am-7pm Mon-Fri, to 5pm Sat & Sun) has a wonderful display of early roadsters in a beautiful art-deco setting. Next

door are the vintage rigs of the **National Automotive and Truck Museum** (✆260-925-9100; www.natmus.org; 1000 Gordon Buehrig Pl; adult/child $8/4; ◷9am-5pm).

OHIO

All right, time for your Ohio quiz. In the Buckeye State you can 1) buggy-ride through the nation's largest Amish community; 2) loose your stomach on one of the world's fastest roller coasters; 3) suck down a dreamy creamy milkshake fresh from a working dairy; or 4) examine a massive, mysterious snake sculpture built into the earth. And the answer is... all of these. It hurts locals' feelings when visitors think the only thing to do here is tip over cows, so c'mon, give Ohio a chance. Besides these activities, you can partake in a five-way in Cincinnati and rock out in Cleveland.

ℹ **Information**

Ohio Division of Travel and Tourism (✆800-282-5393; www.discoverohio.com)

Ohio Highway Conditions (www.ohgo.com)

Ohio State Park Information (✆614-265-6561; http://parks.ohiodnr.gov) State parks are free to visit; some have free wi-fi. Tent and RV sites cost $19 to $39; reservations accepted (✆866-644-6727; http://ohiostateparks. reserveamerica.com; fee $8).

Cleveland

Does it or does it not rock? That is the question. Drawing from its roots as a working man's town, Cleveland has toiled hard in recent years to prove it does. Step one was to control the urban decay/river-on-fire thing – the Cuyahoga River was once so polluted that it actually burned. Step two was to bring a worthy attraction to town, say the Rock and Roll Hall of Fame. Step three was to clean up downtown's public spaces and add hip hotels and eateries. The gritty city has come a long way. Even LeBron James has deemed it happenin' enough to return to.

⊙ **Sights & Activities**

Cleveland's center is Public Sq, dominated by the conspicuous Terminal Tower and a ka-chinging casino. Most attractions are downtown on the lakefront or at University Circle (the area around Case Western Reserve University, Cleveland Clinic and other institutions).

⊙ Downtown

Rock and Roll
Hall of Fame & Museum   MUSEUM
(☏216-781-7625; www.rockhall.com; 1100 E 9th St; adult/child $22/13; ⊙10am-5:30pm, to 9pm Wed year-round, to 9pm Sat Jun-Aug) Cleveland's top attraction is like an overstuffed attic bursting with groovy finds: Jimi Hendrix' Stratocaster, Keith Moon's platform shoes, John Lennon's Sgt Pepper suit and a 1966 piece of hate mail to the Rolling Stones from a cursive-writing Fijian. It's more than memorabilia, though. Multimedia exhibits trace the history and social context of rock music and the performers who created it.

Why is the museum in Cleveland? Because this is the hometown of Alan Freed, the disk jockey who popularized the term 'rock and roll' in the early 1950s, and because the city lobbied hard and paid big. Be prepared for crowds (especially thick until 1pm or so).

Great Lakes Science Center   MUSEUM
(☏216-694-2000; www.greatscience.com; 601 Erieside Ave; adult/child $15/12; ⊙10am-5pm Mon-Sat, from noon Sun; ⛴) One of 10 museums in the country with a NASA affiliation, Great Lakes goes deep in space with rockets, moon stones and the 1973 Apollo capsule, as well as exhibits on the lakes' environmental problems.

William G Mather   MUSEUM
(☏216-694-2000; www.greatscience.com; 601 Erieside Ave; adult/child $8/6; ⊙11am-5pm Tue-Sat, from noon Sun Jun-Aug, Sat & Sun only May, Sep & Oct, closed Nov-Apr) Take a self-guided walk on this huge freighter incarnated as a steamship museum. It's docked beside the Great Lakes Science Center, which manages it.

The Flats   WATERFRONT
(www.flatseast.com) The Flats, an old industrial zone turned nightlife hub on the Cuyahoga River, has had a checkered life. After years of neglect, it's on the upswing once again. The East Bank has a waterfront boardwalk, stylish restaurants, bars and outdoor concert pavilion. The West Bank is a bit grittier and further flung, with an old garage turned brewery-winery, a skateboard park and some vintage dive bars among its assets.

⊙ Ohio City & Tremont

West Side Market   MARKET
(www.westsidemarket.org; cnr W 25th St & Lorain Ave; ⊙7am-4pm Mon & Wed, to 6pm Fri & Sat) The European-style market overflows with greengrocers and their fruit and vegetable pyramids, as well as purveyors of Hungarian sausage, Italian cannoli and Polish pierogi.

Christmas Story House & Museum   MUSEUM
(☏216-298-4919; www.achristmasstoryhouse. com; 3159 W 11th St; adult/child $10/6; ⊙10am-5pm Mon-Sat, from noon Sun) Remember the beloved 1983 film *A Christmas Story,* in which Ralphie yearns for a Red Ryder BB gun? The original house sits in Tremont, complete with leg lamp. It's for true fans only.

⊙ University Circle

Several museums and attractions are within walking distance of each other at University Circle, 5 miles east of downtown. Carless? Take the HealthLine bus to Adelbert. The neighborhood's northern stretch is known as Uptown, with student-filled cafes.

★ Cleveland Museum of Art   MUSEUM
(☏216-421-7340; www.clevelandart.org; 11150 East Blvd; ⊙10am-5pm Tue-Sun, to 9pm Wed & Fri) FREE Fresh off a whopping expansion, the art museum houses an excellent collection

---

OHIO FACTS

Nickname Buckeye State

Population 11.6 million

Area 44,825 sq miles

Capital city Columbus (population 822,500)

Other cities Cleveland (population 390,100), Cincinnati (population 297,500)

Sales tax 5.75%

Birthplace of Inventor Thomas Edison (1847–1931), author Toni Morrison (b 1931), entrepreneur Ted Turner (b 1938), filmmaker Steven Spielberg (b 1947)

Home of Cows, roller coasters, aviation pioneers the Wright Brothers

Politics Swing state

Famous for First airplane, first pro baseball team, birthplace of seven US presidents

State rock song 'Hang On Sloopy'

Driving distances Cleveland to Columbus 142 miles, Columbus to Cincinnati 108 miles

of European paintings, as well as African, Asian and American art. Head to the 2nd floor for rock-star works from Impressionists, Picasso and surrealists. Interactive touchscreens are stationed throughout the galleries and provide fun ways to learn more. Gallery One, near the entrance, holds a cool quick hit of museum highlights.

Museum of Contemporary Art Cleveland
MUSEUM

(MOCA; ☑ audio tours 216-453-3960; www.moca-cleveland.org; 11400 Euclid Ave; adult/child $8/5; ⊙11am-5pm Tue-Sun, to 9pm Thu) The shiny building impresses, with four stories of geometric black steel, though there's not a lot to see inside. Floors 2 and 4 have the galleries; exhibits focus on an artist or two and change often. Call for an audio tour of the architecture and installations.

Lake View Cemetery
CEMETERY

(☑ 216-421-2665; www.lakeviewcemetery.com; 12316 Euclid Ave; ⊙ 7:30am-7:30pm) Beyond the circle further east, don't forget this eclectic 'outdoor museum' where President James Garfield rests in an eye-poppingly enormous tower (it's especially grand for a guy who was president for only six months!). Other notables include local comic-book hero Harvey Pekar and crimefighter Eliot Ness (who happen to be side by side).

🛏 Sleeping

Prices listed are for summer, which is high season, and do not include the 16.5% tax. Several new boutique and business hotels are opening downtown as more conventions come to the city. Modest motels are southwest of Cleveland's center, near the airport. The W 150th exit off I-71 (exit 240) has several options for less than $100.

★ Cleveland Hostel
HOSTEL $

(☑ 216-394-0616; www.theclevelandhostel.com; 2090 W 25th St; dm/r from $28/71; ❋ 🛜) This newish hostel in Ohio City, steps from an RTA stop and the West Side Market, is fantastic. There are 15 rooms, a mix of dorms and private chambers. All have fluffy beds, fresh paint in soothing hues and nifty antique decor. Add in the sociable rooftop deck and free parking lot, and no wonder it's packed.

Holiday Inn Express
HOTEL $$

(☑ 216-443-1000; www.hiexpress.com; 629 Euclid Ave; r $130-190; P ❋ @ 🛜) This goes way beyond the usual chain offering and is more

like a true boutique hotel with large, nattily decorated rooms and lofty views. It's set in an old bank building that's conveniently located near the E 4th St entertainment strip. Do-it-yourself hot breakfast and evening drinks included. Parking costs $15.

Glidden House
BOUTIQUE HOTEL $$

(☑ 216-231-8900; www.gliddenhouse.com; 1901 Ford Dr; r $160-180; P ❋ 🛜) The French-Gothic-Eclectic former mansion of the Glidden family (who got rich making paint) has been carved into a graceful, 60-room hotel. The common areas are lush, while the rooms are more understated. Continental breakfast is included. Located in University Circle and walkable to the museums.

Hilton Garden Inn
HOTEL $$

(☑ 216-658-6400; www.hiltongardeninn.com; 1100 Carnegie Ave; r $110-169; P ❋ @ 🛜 ⛱) While it's nothing fancy, the Hilton's rooms are decent value with comfy beds, wi-fi-rigged workstations and mini refrigerators. It's right by the baseball park. Parking costs $16.

🍴 Eating

Downtown

E 4th St, set under twinkling lights, rolls out several great options. Off the beaten path and east of the city center, Asiatown (bounded by Payne and St Clair Aves, and E 30th and 40ths Sts) has several Chinese, Vietnamese and Korean eateries.

Noodlecat
NOODLES $

(☑ 216-589-0007; www.noodlecat.com; 234 Euclid Ave; mains $11-14; ⊙11am-10pm Sun-Thu, to 11pm

Fri & Sat) Hep-cat noodles fill bowls at this Japanese-American mash-up. Slurp mushroom udon, spicy octopus udon, beef short rib ramen and fried chicken ramen dishes. Lots of sake and craft beer help wash it down.

Lola MODERN AMERICAN $$$
(☑ 216-621-5652; www.lolabistro.com; 2058 E 4th St; mains $29-34; ⊙11:30am-2:30pm Mon-Fri, 5-10pm Mon-Thu, to 11pm Fri & Sat) Famous for his piercings, Food Channel TV appearances and multiple national awards, local boy Michael Symon put Cleveland on the foodie map with Lola. The lower-priced lunch dishes are the most fun, such as the egg-and-cheese-topped fried bologna sandwich. The glowy bar and open kitchen add a swank vibe for dinner.

✖ Ohio City & Tremont

Ohio City (especially along W 25th St) and Tremont, which straddle I-90 south of downtown, are areas with hip new establishments popping up all the time.

Barrio MEXICAN $
(☑ 216-999-7714; www.barrio-tacos.com; 806 Literary St; tacos $3-4; ⊙4pm-2am Mon-Thu, from 11am Fri-Sun) The Tremont outpost of this small chain is abuzz with young locals smitten with the build your own tacos concept. Fillings include everything from Thai chili tofu to housemade chorizo. Pear, jalapeño and other unusually flavored margaritas add to the fun.

Mitchell's Ice Cream ICE CREAM $
(☑ 216-861-2799; www.mitchellshomemade.com; 1867 W 25th St; scoops $3.50-5; ⊙11am-10pm Sun-Thu, to midnight fri & Sat; ☑) Mitchell's revamped an old movie theater into an ice-cream-making facility. Watch staff blend the rich flavors through big glass windows. The goods are super creamy, and the vegan options are brilliant. Staff are generous with samples.

✖ Little Italy & Coventry

These two neighborhoods make prime stops for refueling after hanging out in University Circle. Little Italy is closest: it's along Mayfield Rd, near Lake View Cemetery (look out for the Rte 322 sign). Alternatively, relaxed Coventry Village is a bit further east off Mayfield Rd.

Presti's Bakery BAKERY $
(☑ 216-421-3060; www.prestisbakery.com; 12101 Mayfield Rd; items $2-6; ⊙6am-9pm Mon-Thu, to 10pm Fri & Sat, to 6pm Sun) Try Presti's for its popular sandwiches, stromboli and divine pastries.

Tommy's INTERNATIONAL $
(☑ 216-321-7757; www.tommyscoventry.com; 1823 Coventry Rd; mains $8-13; ⊙9am-9pm Sun-Thu, to 10pm Fri, 7:30am-10pm Sat; ☜☑) Tofu, seitan and other old-school veggie dishes emerge from the kitchen, though carnivores have multiple options, too.

♟ Drinking & Nightlife

Tremont is chockablock with chic bars, Ohio City with breweries. Downtown has the young, testosterone-fueled Warehouse District (around W 6th St) and the resurgent Flats. Most places stay open until 2am.

Great Lakes Brewing Company BREWERY
(www.greatlakesbrewing.com; 2516 Market Ave; ⊙11:30am-midnight Mon-Thu, to 1am Fri & Sat) Great Lakes wins numerous prizes for its brewed-on-the-premises beers. Added historical bonus: Eliot Ness got into a shoot-out with criminals here; ask the bartender to show you the bullet holes.

Platform Beer Co BREWERY
(www.platformbeerco.com; 4125 Lorain Ave; ⊙3pm-midnight Mon-Thu, to 2am Fri & Sat) An all-ages, cool-cat crowd gathers around the silvery tanks in Platform's tasting room for US pints of innovative saisons, sour ales and more. The location is a bit far flung, at Ohio City's southern edge, but the brewmaster has launched a private bike-share program from the site; ask the bartender for details.

Merwin's Wharf BAR
(www.merwinswharf.com; 1785 Merwin Ave; ⊙3-10pm Tue & Wed, 11am-11pm Thu-Sat, to 9pm Sun) It's a lovely spot to sip on the riverfront patio with views of the skyline, bridges and boats gliding by; located on the Flats' West Bank.

☆ Entertainment

Gordon Square Arts District (www.gordonsquare.org) has a fun pocket of theaters, live-music venues and cafes along Detroit Ave between W 56th and W 69th Sts, a few miles west of downtown.

Live Music

Check *Scene* (www.clevescene.com) and Friday's *Plain Dealer* (www.cleveland.com) for listings.

★Happy Dog LIVE MUSIC
(www.happydogcleveland.com; 5801 Detroit Ave; ⊙4pm-12:30am Mon-Wed, 11am-2:30am Thu-Sat, to 12:30am Sun) Listen to scrappy bands while munching on a weenie, for which you can

choose from among 50 toppings, from gourmet (black truffle) to, er, less gourmet (peanut butter and jelly); in the Gordon Sq district.

Grog Shop
LIVE MUSIC
(☑216-321-5588; www.grogshop.gs; 2785 Euclid Heights Blvd) Up-and-coming rockers thrash at Coventry's long-established music house.

Beachland Ballroom
LIVE MUSIC
(www.beachlandballroom.com; 15711 Waterloo Rd) Hip young bands play at this venue east of downtown.

Sports
Cleveland is a serious jock town with three modern downtown venues.

Progressive Field
BASEBALL
(www.indians.com; 2401 Ontario St) The Indians (aka 'the Tribe') hit here; great sightlines make it a good park to see a game.

Quicken Loans Arena
BASKETBALL
(www.nba.com/cavaliers; 1 Center Ct) The Cavaliers play basketball at 'the Q,' which doubles as an entertainment venue. All is well here now that LeBron James has come home.

First Energy Stadium
FOOTBALL
(www.clevelandbrowns.com; 1085 W 3rd St) The NFL's Browns pass the football and score touchdowns on the lakefront.

Performing Arts
Severance Hall
CLASSICAL MUSIC
(☑216-231-1111; www.clevelandorchestra.com; 11001 Euclid Ave) The acclaimed Cleveland Symphony Orchestra holds its season (August to May) at Severance Hall, located by the University Circle museums.

Playhouse Square
THEATER
(☑216-771-4444; www.playhousesquare.org; 1501 Euclid Ave) Several stages comprise the elegant center, which hosts theater, opera and ballet. Check the website for $10 to $20 'Smart Seats.'

ℹ Information

INTERNET ACCESS
Many of Cleveland's public places have free wi-fi, such as Tower City and University Circle.

MEDIA
Gay People's Chronicle (www.gaypeopleschronicle.com) Free weekly publication with entertainment listings.
Plain Dealer (www.cleveland.com) The city's main newspaper.
Scene (www.clevescene.com) A weekly entertainment paper.

MEDICAL SERVICES
MetroHealth Medical Center (☑216-778-7800; 2500 MetroHealth Dr)

TOURIST INFORMATION
Cleveland Convention & Visitors Bureau (www.thisiscleveland.com) Official website, chock-full for planning.
Visitor Center (☑216-875-6680; 334 Euclid Ave; ◷9am-6pm Mon-Sat) Staff provide maps and reservation assistance; there's a sweet, arty souvenir shop attached.

USEFUL WEBSITES
Cool Cleveland (www.coolcleveland.com) Hip arts and cultural happenings.
Ohio City (www.ohiocity.org) Eats and drinks in the neighborhood.
Tremont (www.tremontwest.org) Eats, drinks and gallery hops.

ℹ Getting There & Around
Eleven miles southwest of downtown, **Cleveland Hopkins International Airport** (CLE; www.clevelandairport.com; 5300 Riverside Dr) is linked by the Red Line train ($2.25). A cab to downtown costs about $35.

From downtown, **Greyhound** (☑216-781-0520; 1465 Chester Ave) offers frequent departures to Chicago (7½ hours) and New York City (13 hours). **Megabus** (www.megabus.com/us) also goes to Chicago, often for lower fares; check the website for the departure point.

Amtrak (☑216-696-5115; 200 Cleveland Memorial Shoreway) runs once daily to Chicago (seven hours) and New York City (13 hours).

The **Regional Transit Authority** (RTA; www.riderta.com; fares $2.25) operates the Red Line train that goes to both the airport and Ohio City. It also runs the HealthLine bus that motors along Euclid Ave from downtown to University Circle's museums. Day passes are $5. Free trolleys also loop around downtown's core business and entertainment zones.

For taxis, try **Americab** (☑216-881-1111).

Around Cleveland
Sixty miles south of Cleveland, **Canton** is the birthplace of the NFL and home to the **Pro Football Hall of Fame** (☑330-456-8207; www.profootballhof.com; 2121 George Halas Dr; adult/child $24/17; ◷9am-8pm, to 5pm Sep-May). The shrine for the gridiron-obsessed has new interactive exhibits and videos even casual fans will appreciate; a hotel and entertainment complex are also being built. Look for the football-shaped tower off I-77.

West of Cleveland, attractive Oberlin is an old-fashioned college town, with noteworthy architecture by Cass Gilbert, Frank Lloyd Wright and Robert Venturi. Further west, just south of I-90, the tiny town of Milan is the birthplace of Thomas Edison. His home, restored to its 1847 likeness, is now a small museum (☑419-499-2135; www.tom edison.org; 9 Edison Dr; adult/child $7/5; ⊙10am-5pm Tue-Sat, from 1pm Sun, reduced hours winter, closed Jan) outlining his inventions, like the light bulb and phonograph.

Erie Lakeshore & Islands

In summer this good-time resort area is one of the busiest – and most expensive – places in Ohio. The season lasts from mid-May to mid-September, and then just about everything shuts down. Make sure you prebook your accommodations.

Sandusky, long a port, now serves as the jump-off point to the Erie Islands and a mighty group of roller coasters. The visitor center (☑419-625-2984; www.shoresandislands. com; 4424 Milan Rd; ⊙8am-7pm Mon-Fri, 9am-6pm Sat, 9am-4pm Sun) provides lodging and

CEDAR POINT'S RAGING ROLLER COASTERS

Cedar Point Amusement Park (☑419-627-2350; www.cedarpoint.com; adult/child $62/40; ⊙hours vary, closed Nov–mid-May) regularly wins the 'world's best amusement park' award, chosen each year by the public, which goes wild for the venue's 16 adrenaline-pumping roller coasters. Stomach-droppers include the Top Thrill Dragster, one of the globe's tallest and fastest rides. It climbs 420ft into the air before plunging and whipping around at 120mph. Meanwhile, the wing-like GateKeeper loops, corkscrews and dangles riders from the world's highest inversion (meaning you're upside down a *lot*). If those and the 14 other coasters aren't enough to keep you occupied, the surrounding area has a nice beach, a water park and a slew of old-fashioned, cotton-candy-fueled attractions. It's about 6 miles from Sandusky. Buying tickets in advance online saves money. Parking costs $15.

ferry information. Loads of chain motels line the highways heading into town.

Bass Islands

In 1812's Battle of Lake Erie, Admiral Perry met the enemy English fleet near South Bass Island. His victory ensured that all the lands south of the Great Lakes became US, not Canadian, territory. But history is all but forgotten on a summer weekend in packed Put In Bay, the island's main town and a party place full of boaters, restaurants and shops. Move beyond it, and you'll find a winery and opportunities for camping, fishing, kayaking and swimming.

A singular attraction is the 352ft Doric column known as Perry's Victory and International Peace Memorial (www.nps.gov/pevi; admission $3; ⊙10am-6pm, closed mid-Oct–mid-May). Climb to the observation deck for views of the battle site and, on a good day, Canada.

The Chamber of Commerce (☑419-285-2832; www.visitputinbay.com; 148 Delaware Ave; ⊙10am-4pm Mon-Fri, to 5pm Sat & Sun) has information on activities and lodging. Ashley's Island House (☑419-285-2844; www. ashleysislandhouse.com; 557 Catawba Ave; r $110-195; ❀ 🐾 🛜) is a 12-room B&B, where naval officers stayed in the late 1800s. The Beer Barrel Saloon (www.beerbarrelpib.com; Delaware Ave; ⊙11am-1am) has plenty of space for imbibing – its bar is 406ft long. Live bands and Jello shots are part of the package.

Cabs and tour buses serve the island, though cycling is a fine way to get around. Two ferry companies make the trip regularly from the mainland. Jet Express (☑800-245-1538; www.jet-express.com) runs passenger-only boats direct to Put In Bay from Port Clinton (one-way adult/child $18/3, 30 minutes) almost hourly. Leave your car in the lot (per day $12) at the dock. Miller Ferries (☑800-500-2421; www.millerferry.com) operates a vehicle ferry that is the cheapest option, departing from further-flung Catawba (one-way adult/child $7/1.50, car $15) every 30 minutes; the crossing takes 20 minutes. It also cruises to Middle Bass Island, a good day trip from South Bass, offering nature and quiet.

Kelleys Island

Peaceful and green, Kelleys Island is a popular weekend escape, especially for families. It has pretty 19th-century buildings, Native American pictographs, a good beach and glacial grooves raked through its landscape. Even its old limestone quarries are scenic.

The **Chamber of Commerce** (www.kelleys islandchamber.com; 240 E Lakeshore Dr; ⊙ 9:30am-4pm), by the ferry dock, has information on accommodations and activities – hiking, camping, kayaking and fishing are popular. **The Village**, the island's small commercial center, has places to eat, drink, shop and rent bicycles – the recommended way to sightsee.

Kelleys Island Ferry (☑ 419-798-9763; www.kelleysislandferry.com) departs from the wee village of Marblehead (one-way adult/child $10/6.25, car $16). The crossing takes about 20 minutes and leaves hourly (more frequently in summer). **Jet Express** (☑ 800-245-1538; www.jet-express.com) departs from Sandusky (one-way adult/child $18/4.75, no cars); the trip takes 25 minutes. It also goes onward to Put In Bay on South Bass Island (one-way adult/child $13/3, no cars).

Pelee Island

Pelee, the largest Erie island, is a ridiculously green, quiet wine-producing and birdwatching destination that belongs to Canada. **Pelee Island Transportation** (☑ 800-661-2220; www.ontarioferries.com) runs a ferry (one-way adult/child $13.75/6.75, car $30) from Sandusky to Pelee, and then onward to Ontario's mainland. Check www.pelee.com for lodging and trip-planning information.

Amish Country

Rural Wayne and Holmes counties are home to the USA's largest Amish community. They're only 80 miles south of Cleveland, but visiting here is like entering a pre-industrial time warp.

Descendants of conservative Dutch-Swiss religious factions who migrated to the USA during the 18th century, the Amish continue to follow the *ordnung* (way of life), in varying degrees. Many adhere to rules prohibiting the use of electricity, telephones and motorized vehicles. They wear traditional clothing, farm the land with plow and mule, and go to church in horse-drawn buggies. Others are not so strict.

Unfortunately, what would surely be a peaceful country scene is often disturbed by behemoth tour buses. Many Amish are happy to profit from this influx of outside dollars, but don't equate this with free photographic access – the Amish typically view photographs as taboo. Drive carefully as roads are narrow and curvy. Many places are closed Sunday.

◉ Sights & Activities

Kidron, on Rte 52, makes a good starting point. A short distance south, **Berlin** is the area's tchotchke-shop-filled core, while **Millersburg** is the region's largest town, more antique-y than Amish; US 62 connects these two 'busy' spots.

To get further off the beaten path, take Rte 557 or County Rd 70, both of which twist through the countryside to wee **Charm**, about 5 miles south of Berlin.

Lehman's   DEPARTMENT STORE
(www.lehmans.com; 4779 Kidron Rd, Kidron; ⊙ 8am-6pm Mon-Sat) Lehman's is an absolute must-see. It is the Amish community's main purveyor of modern-looking products that use no electricity, housed in a 32,000-sq-ft barn. Stroll through to ogle wind-up flashlights, wood-burning stoves and handcranked meat grinders.

Kidron Auction   MARKET
(www.kidronauction.com; 4885 Kidron Rd, Kidron; ⊙ from 10am Thu) **FREE** If it's Thursday, follow the buggy lineup down the road from Lehman's store to the livestock barn. Hay gets auctioned at 10:15am, cows at 11am and pigs at 1pm. A flea market rings the barn for folks seeking non-mooing merchandise.

Hershberger's Farm & Bakery   FARM
(☑ 330-674-6096; 5452 Hwy 557, Millersburg; ⊙ bakery 8am-5pm Mon-Sat year-round, farm from 10am mid-Apr–Oct; 🐾) Gorge on 25 kinds of pie, homemade ice-cream cones and seasonal produce from the market inside. Pet the farmyard animals (free) and take pony rides ($3) outside.

Heini's Cheese Chalet   TOUR
(☑ 800-253-6636; www.heinis.com; 6005 Hwy 77, Berlin; ⊙ 8am-6pm Mon-Sat) Heini's whips up more than 70 cheeses. Learn how Amish farmers hand-milk their cows and springcool (versus machine-refrigerate) the output before delivering it each day. Then grab abundant samples and peruse the kitschy *History of Cheesemaking* mural. To see the curd-cutting in action, come before 11am weekdays (except on Wednesday and Saturday).

Yoder's Amish Home   FARM
(☑ 330-893-2541; www.yodersamishhome.com; 6050 Rte 515, Walnut Creek; tours adult/child

$12/8; ⊙10am-5pm Mon-Sat late Apr-late Oct; 📷)
Peek into a local home and one-room school-house, and take a buggy ride through a field
at this Amish farm that's open to visitors.

🛏 Sleeping & Eating

Hotel Millersburg   HISTORIC HOTEL $$
(📞330-674-1457; www.hotelmillersburg.com; 35
W Jackson St, Millersburg; r $79-149; ❋🖐) Built
in 1847 as a stagecoach inn, the property
still provides lodging in its 26 casual rooms,
which sit above a modern dining room and
tavern (one of the few places to get a beer in
Amish Country).

Guggisberg Swiss Inn   HOTEL $$
(📞330-893-3600; www.guggisbergswissinn.com;
5025 Rte 557, Charm; r $120-150; ❋🖐) The 24
tidy, bright and compact rooms have quilts
and light-wood furnishings. A cheesemaking
facility and horseback riding stable are on
the grounds, too.

Boyd & Wurthmann Restaurant   AMERICAN $
(📞330-893-3287; www.boydandwurthmann.com;
Main St, Berlin; mains $6-12; ⊙5:30am-8pm Mon-
Sat) Hubcap-sized pancakes, 23 pie flavors,
fat sandwiches and Amish specialties such
as country-fried steak draw locals and tourists alike. Cash only.

ℹ Information

Holmes County Chamber of Commerce
(www.visitamishcountry.com)

Columbus

Ohio's capital city is like the blind date your
mom arranges – average looking, restrained
personality, but solid and affable. Better yet,
this city's easy on the wallet, an influence
from Ohio State University's 57,000-plus students (the campus is the nation's second largest). A substantial gay population has taken
up residence in Columbus in recent years.

◎ Sights & Activities

German Village   AREA
(www.germanvillage.com) The remarkably large,
all-brick German Village, a half-mile south of
downtown, is a restored 19th-century neighborhood with beer halls, cobbled streets,
arts-filled parks and Italianate and Queen
Anne architecture.

Short North   AREA
(www.shortnorth.org) Just north of downtown,
the browseworthy Short North is a redevel-

oped strip of High St that holds contemporary art galleries, restaurants and jazz bars.

Wexner Center for the Arts   ARTS CENTER
(📞614-292-3535; www.wexarts.org; 1871 N High
St; admission $8; ⊙11am-6pm Tue & Wed, to 8pm
Thu & Fri, noon-7pm Sat, to 4pm Sun) The campus
arts center offers cutting-edge art exhibits,
films and performances.

Columbus Food Tours   TOUR
(www.columbusfoodadventures.com; tours $50-60)
Foodie guides lead tours by neighborhood or
theme (ie taco trucks, desserts, coffee), some
by foot and others by van.

🛏 Sleeping & Eating

German Village and the Short North provide fertile grazing and guzzling grounds.
The **Arena District** (www.arenadistrict.com)
bursts with midrange chains and brewpubs.
Around the university and along N High St
from 15th Ave onward, you'll find everything
from Mexican to Ethiopian to sushi.

Marriott Residence Inn   HOTEL $$
(📞614-222-2610; www.marriott.com; 36 E Gay
St; r $149-229; 🅿❋@🖐) A great location
downtown, close to everything. All rooms
are suites with a full kitchen. The cute free
breakfast buffet is served in the old bank
vault each morning. Wi-fi is free; parking
is $20.

50 Lincoln-Short North B&B   B&B $$
(📞614-299-5050; www.columbus-bed-breakfast.
com; 50 E Lincoln St; r $139-159; 🅿❋🖐) The
seven well-maintained rooms are steps away
from the Short North's scene.

Schmidt's   GERMAN $
(📞614-444-6808; www.schmidthaus.com; 240 E
Kossuth St; mains $10-16; ⊙11am-10pm Sun-Thu,
to 11pm Fri & Sat) In German Village, shov-
el in Old Country staples like sausage and
schnitzel, but save room for the whopping
half-pound cream puffs. Oompah bands play
Wednesday to Saturday.

North Market   MARKET $
(www.northmarket.com; 59 Spruce St; ⊙10am-
5pm Sun-Mon, 9am-7pm Tue-Sat) Local farmers'
produce and prepared foods; seek out the
renowned Jeni's Ice Cream.

Skillet   AMERICAN $
(📞614-443-2266; www.skilletruf.com; 410 E Whit-
tier St; mains $12-16; ⊙8am-2pm Wed-Sun) 🌱
This teeny restaurant in German Village
serves rustic, locally sourced fare.

☆ Entertainment

Spectator sports rule the city.

Ohio Stadium   FOOTBALL
(☎ 800-462-8257; www.ohiostatebuckeyes.com;
411 Woody Hayes Dr) The Ohio State Buckeyes
pack a rabid crowd into legendary, horse-
shoe-shaped Ohio Stadium, held on Saturdays
in the fall. Expect 102,000 extra partiers in town.

Nationwide Arena   HOCKEY
(☎ 614-246-2000; www.bluejackets.com; 200 W
Nationwide Blvd) The pro Columbus Blue Jackets slap the puck at downtown's big arena.

Huntington Park   BASEBALL
(www.clippersbaseball.com; 330 Huntington Park
Lane) The Columbus Clippers (minor league
team of the Cleveland Indians) bats at this
stadium. Games are inexpensive and a blast.

ℹ Information

Alive (www.columbusalive.com) Free weekly
entertainment newspaper.

Columbus Convention & Visitors Bureau
(☎ 866-397-2657; www.experiencecolumbus.
com)

Columbus Dispatch (www.dispatch.com) The
daily newspaper.

ℹ Getting There & Around

The **Port Columbus Airport** (CMH; www.fly
columbus.com) is 10 miles east of town. A cab to
downtown costs about $25.

Greyhound (☎ 614-221-4642; www.greyhound.
com; 111 E Town St) buses run at least six times
daily to Cincinnati (two hours) and Cleveland (2½
hours). Often cheaper, **Megabus** (www.megabus.
com/us) runs a couple times daily to Cincinnati
and Chicago. Check the website for locations.

Athens & Southeastern Ohio

Ohio's southeastern corner cradles most of
its forested areas, as well as the rolling foothills of the Appalachian Mountains and scattered farms.

Around Lancaster, southeast of Columbus, the hills lead gently into **Hocking
County**, a region of streams and waterfalls,
sandstone cliffs and cavelike formations.
It's splendid to explore in any season, with
miles of trails for hiking and rivers for canoeing, as well as abundant campgrounds
and cabins at **Hocking Hills State Park**
(☎ 740-385-6165; www.thehockinghills.org; 20160

WORTH A TRIP

MALABAR FARM

What do Bogie, Bacall and Johnny
Appleseed have in common? They've
all spent time at **Malabar Farm State
Park** (www.malabarfarm.org). There's
a lot going on here: hiking and horse
trails; pond fishing (ask for a free rod at
the visitor center); tours of Pulitzer-
winner Louis Bromfield's home (where
Humphrey Bogart and Lauren Bacall
got married); monthly barn dances;
a farmhouse hostel (www.hiusa.org/
lucas); and a fine restaurant (open 11am
to 8pm Tuesday through Sunday) that
uses ingredients from the grounds.
Malabar is 30 miles west of Millersburg
via Hwy 39.

Hwy 664; campsites/cottages from $24/130). **Old
Man's Cave** is a scenic winner for hiking.
Hocking Hills Adventures (☎ 740-385-8685;
www.hockinghillscanoeing.com; 31251 Chieftain Dr;
2hr tours $45; ⊙ Apr-Oct) lets you paddle by
moonlight and tiki torch from nearby Logan. The town also is home to the **Columbus Washboard Company** (☎ 740-380-3828;
www.columbuswashboard.com; 14 Gallagher Ave;
adult/child $4/2; ⊙ tours 10am, noon & 2pm Mon-
Fri year-round, plus 11:30am & 1pm Sat May-Oct);
channel your jug band fantasies on a factory
tour and in the tiny museum. Continue the
hillbilly theme 12 miles east in New Straits-
ville, where a hissing, coil-laden **moonshine
distillery** (☎ 740-394-2622; www.facebook.
com/straitsvillespecialmoonshine; 105 W Main St;
⊙ noon-7pm Mon-Thu, to 8pm Fri, 10am-8pm Sat)
operates. A few sips in the tasting room will
put hair on your chest.

Athens (www.athensohio.com) makes a lovely base for seeing the region. Situated where
US 50 crosses US 33, it's set among wooded
hills and built around the Ohio University
campus (which comprises half the town).
Student cafes and pubs line Court St, Athens'
main road. The **Village Bakery & Cafe** (www.
dellazona.com; 268 E State St; mains $4-8; ⊙ 7:30am-
8pm Tue-Fri, to 6pm Sat, 9am-2pm Sun) uses organic
veggies, grass-fed meat and farmstead cheeses
in its pizzas, soups and sandwiches.

The area south of Columbus was a center
for the fascinating ancient Hopewell people,
who left behind huge geometric earthworks
and burial mounds from around 200 BC
to AD 600. For a fine introduction visit the

Hopewell Culture National Historical Park
(☑ 740-774-1126; www.nps.gov/hocu; Hwy 104 north of I-35; ☺ 8:30am-5pm) **FREE**, 3 miles north of Chillicothe. Stop in at the visitor center, and then wander about the variously shaped ceremonial mounds spread over 13-acre **Mound City**, a mysterious town of the dead. **Serpent Mound** (☑ 937-587-2796; www.ohiohistory.org; 3850 Hwy 73; per vehicle $8; ☺ 10am-4pm Mon-Thu, 9am-6pm Fri-Sun, reduced hours in winter), southwest of Chillicothe and 4 miles northwest of Locust Grove, is perhaps the most captivating site of all. The giant, uncoiling snake stretches over a quarter of a mile and is the largest effigy mound in the USA.

Dayton & Yellow Springs

Dayton has the aviation sights, but little Yellow Springs (18 miles northeast on US 68) has much more to offer in terms of accommodations and places to eat.

◉ Sights

★**National Museum
of the US Air Force** MUSEUM
(☑ 937-255-3286; www.nationalmuseum.af.mil; 1100 Spaatz St, Dayton; ☺ 9am-5pm) **FREE** Located at the Wright Patterson Air Force Base, 6 miles northeast of Dayton, the humongous museum has everything from a Wright Brothers 1909 Flyer to a Sopwith Camel (WWI biplane) and the 'Little Boy' type atomic bomb (decommissioned and rendered safe for display) dropped on Hiroshima. The hangars hold miles of planes, rockets and aviation machines. A spiffy new building adds space craft and presidential planes starting in summer 2016. Download the audio tour from the website before arriving. Plan on three or more hours here.

Wright Cycle Company HISTORIC SITE
(☑ 937-225-7705; www.nps.gov/daav; 16 S Williams St, Dayton; ☺ 9am-5pm) **FREE** Browse exhibits in the original building where Wilbur and Orville developed bikes and aviation ideas.

Huffman Prairie Flying Field HISTORIC SITE
(Gate 16A off Rte 444, Dayton; ☺ 8am-6pm) **FREE** This peaceful patch of grass looks much as it did in 1904 when the Wright Brothers tested aircraft here. A 1-mile walking trail loops around, marked with history-explaining placards. It's a 15-minute drive from the Air Force museum.

Carillon Historical Park HISTORIC SITE
(☑ 937-293-2841; www.daytonhistory.org; 1000 Carillon Blvd, Dayton; adult/child $8/5; ☺ 9:30am-5pm Mon-Sat, from noon Sun) The many heritage attractions include the 1905 Wright Flyer III biplane, a replica of the Wright workshop and an 1850s-style brewery where you can drink the wares.

🛏 Sleeping & Eating

The following are located in artsy, beatnik Yellow Springs.

Morgan House B&B $$
(☑ 937-767-1761; www.arthurmorganhouse.com; 120 W Limestone St, Yellow Springs; r $125-145; ❋ 🛜) The six comfy rooms have super-soft linens and private baths. Breakfasts are organic. It's walkable to the main business district.

★**Young's Jersey Dairy** AMERICAN $
(☑ 937-325-0629; www.youngsdairy.com; 6880 Springfield-Xenia Rd, Yellow Springs; 🛜) Young's is a working dairy farm with two restaurants: the **Golden Jersey Inn** (mains $10-17; ☺ 11am-8pm Mon-Thu, to 9pm Fri, 8am-9pm Sat, to 8pm Sun), serving dishes like buttermilk chicken; and the **Dairy Store** (sandwiches $3.60-6.60; ☺ 7am-10pm Sun-Thu, to 11pm Fri & Sat), serving sandwiches, dreamy ice cream and Ohio's best milkshakes. There's also mini-golf, batting cages, cheesemaking tours and opportunities to watch the cows get milked.

Winds Cafe AMERICAN $$$
(☑ 937-767-1144; www.windscafe.com; 215 Xenia Ave, Yellow Springs; mains $23-28; ☺ 11:30am-2pm & 5-9:30pm Tue-Sat, 10am-3pm Sun) A hippie co-op 30-plus years ago, the Winds has grown up to become a sophisticated foodie favorite plating seasonal dishes such as fig-sauced asparagus crepes and rhubarb halibut.

Cincinnati

Cincinnati splashes up the Ohio River's banks. Its prettiness surprises, as do its neon troves, its European-style neighborhoods, and the locals' unashamed ardor for a five-way. Amid all that action, don't forget to catch a baseball game, stroll the bridge-striped riverfront and visit the dummy museum.

◉ Sights & Activities

Many attractions are closed on Monday.

◉ Downtown & Over-the-Rhine

At downtown's northern edge, the historic Over-the-Rhine (OTR) neighborhood holds a whopping spread of 19th-century Italianate and Queen Anne buildings that are morphing into trendy eateries and shops. Parts of the area are edgy, but the Gateway District around 12th and Vine Sts is well trod.

National Underground
Railroad Freedom Center   MUSEUM
(☑ 513-333-7500; www.freedomcenter.org; 50 E Freedom Way; adult/child $14/10; ☺ 11am-5pm Tue-Sun Jun-Aug, closed Sun Sep-May) Cincinnati was a prominent stop on the Underground Railroad and a center for abolitionist activities led by residents such as Harriet Beecher Stowe. The Freedom Center tells their stories. Exhibits show how slaves escaped to the north, and the ways in which slavery still exists today. Download the free iPhone app for extra insight while touring.

Findlay Market   MARKET
(www.findlaymarket.org; 1801 Race St; ☺ 9am-6pm Tue-Fri, 8am-6pm Sat, 10am-4pm Sun) Indoor-outdoor Findlay Market lies deep in Over-the-Rhine, in a somewhat blighted section. The funky, wrought-iron-framed structure has been a public market since 1855. It's a good stop for fresh produce, meats, cheeses and baked goods. The Belgian waffle guy will wow your taste buds.

Contemporary Arts Center   MUSEUM
(☑ 513-345-8400; www.contemporaryartscenter.org; 44 E 6th St; adult/child $7.50/5.50, free Wed evening; ☺ 10am-4pm Mon, to 9pm Wed-Fri, to 4pm Sat & Sun) This center displays modern art in an avant-garde building designed by Iraqi architect Zaha Hadid. The structure and artworks are a pretty big deal for traditionalist Cincy. The focus is on 'art of the last five minutes.'

Fountain Square   PLAZA
(www.myfountainsquare.com; cnr 5th & Vine Sts) Fountain Sq is the city's centerpiece, a public space with a seasonal ice rink, free wi-fi, concerts (7pm Tuesday to Saturday in summer), a Reds ticket kiosk and the fancy old 'Genius of Water' fountain.

Roebling Suspension Bridge   BRIDGE
(www.roeblingbridge.org) The elegant 1876 spanner was a forerunner of John Roebling's

famous Brooklyn Bridge in New York. It's cool to walk across while passing cars make it 'sing' around you. It links to Covington, KY.

Purple People Bridge   BRIDGE
(www.purplepeoplebridge.com) This pedestrian-only bridge provides a unique crossing from Sawyer Point (a nifty park dotted by whimsical monuments and flying pigs) to Newport, KY.

◉ Covington & Newport

Covington and Newport, KY, are sort of suburbs of Cincinnati, just over the river from downtown. Newport is to the east and known for its massive **Newport on the Levee** (www.newportonthelevee.com) restaurant and shopping complex. Covington lies to the west and has the **MainStrasse** (www.mainstrasse.org) quarter, filled with funky restaurants and bars in the neighborhood's 19th-century brick row houses. Antebellum mansions fringe Riverside Dr, and old paddle-wheel boats tie up along the water's edge.

Newport Aquarium   AQUARIUM
(☑ 859-491-3467; www.newportaquarium.com; 1 Aquarium Way; adult/child $23/15; ☺ 9am-7pm Jun-Aug, 10am-6pm Sep-May; ⊡) Meet parading penguins, Sweet Pea the shark ray and lots of other razor-toothed fish at Newport's large, well-regarded facility.

◉ Mt Adams

It might be a bit of a stretch to compare Mt Adams, immediately east of downtown, to Paris' Montmartre, but this hilly 19th-century enclave of narrow, twisting streets, Victorian town houses, galleries, bars and restaurants is certainly a pleasurable surprise. Most visitors ascend for a quick look around and a drink.

To get here, follow 7th St east of downtown to Gilbert Ave, then turn right on Eden Park Dr and head up the hill to reach the lakes, paths and cultural offerings in Eden Park.

Cincinnati Art Museum MUSEUM

(☎513-721-2787; www.cincinnatiartmuseum.org; 953 Eden Park Dr; ⊙11am-5pm Tue-Sun) `FREE` The collection spans 6000 years, with an emphasis on ancient Middle Eastern art and European old masters, plus a wing devoted to local works. Parking costs $4, or get here via bus 1.

👁 West End

Cincinnati Museum Center MUSEUM

(☎513-287-7000; www.cincymuseum.org; 1301 Western Ave; adult/child $18/13; ⊙10am-5pm Mon-Sat, 11am-6pm Sun; 👪) Two miles northwest of downtown, this museum complex occupies the 1933 Union Terminal, an art-deco jewel still used by Amtrak. The interior has fantastic murals made of local Rookwood tiles. The **Museum of Natural History** is mostly geared to kids, but it does have a limestone cave with real bats inside. A history museum, children's museum and Omnimax theater round out the offerings; the admission fee provides entry to all. Parking costs $6.

VENT HAVEN VENTRILOQUIST MUSEUM

Jeepers creepers! When you first glimpse the roomful of goggle-eyed wooden heads staring mutely into space, try not to run screaming for the door. (If you've seen the film *Magic*, you know what dummies are capable of.) Local William Shakespeare Berger started the **Vent Haven Museum** (☎859-341-0461; www.venthavenmuseum.com; 33 W Maple Ave; adult/child $10/5; ⊙by appt May-Sep) after amassing a collection of some 700 dolls. Today Jacko the red-fezzed monkey, turtleneck-clad Woody DeForest and the rest of the crew sit silently throughout three buildings. A curator gives guided tours. The museum is located in Fort Mitchell, KY, about 4 miles southwest of Covington off I-71/75.

American Sign Museum MUSEUM

(☎513-541-6366; www.americansignmuseum.org; 1330 Monmouth Ave; adult/child $15/free; ⊙10am-4pm Wed-Sat, from noon Sun) This museum stocks an awesome cache of flashing, lightbulb-studded beacons in an old parachute factory. You'll burn your retinas staring at vintage neon drive-in signs, hulking genies and the Frisch's Big Boy, among other nostalgic novelties. Guides lead tours at 11am and 2pm that also visit the on-site neon-sign-making shop. It's located in the Camp Washington neighborhood (near Northside); take exit 3 off I-75.

👉 Tours

American Legacy Tours WALKING TOUR

(www.americanlegacytours.com; 1332 Vine St; 90min tours $20; ⊙Fri-Sun) Offers a variety of historical jaunts. Best is the Queen City Underground Tour, which delves into old lagering cellars deep beneath the Over-the-Rhine district.

⭐ Festivals & Events

Bockfest BEER

(www.bockfest.com; ⊙early Mar) Traditional bock beers flow in Over-the-Rhine.

Bunbury Music Festival MUSIC

(www.bunburyfestival.com; ⊙early Jun) Bigname indie bands rock the riverfront for three days; a day pass costs $79.

Oktoberfest FOOD

(www.oktoberfestzinzinnati.com; ⊙mid-Sep) German beer, brats and mania.

🛏 Sleeping

Hotel tax adds 17.25% in Cincinnati. It's only 11.3% across the river in Kentucky, where several midrange chain options line up along the water. You'll save money (less tax, free parking), but be prepared either to walk a few miles or take a short bus ride to reach downtown Cincy.

Gateway B&B B&B $$

(☎859-581-6447; www.gatewaybb.com; 326 E 6th St; r $129-169; 🅿❄🐾📶) For something different, check in to this 1878 Italianate town house in a historic neighborhood on the Kentucky side of the river. Exquisite antique oak and walnut furnishings fill the three rooms, and intriguing baseball memorabilia decorates the common area. It's a half-mile walk to Newport on the Levee's restaurants and onward over the Purple People Bridge to downtown Cincy.

Hotel 21c
HOTEL $$$

(☎ 513-578-6600; www.21cmuseumhotels.com/cincinnati; 609 Walnut St; r $289-379; P ❄ @ ☎)
The second outpost of Louisville's popular art hotel opened in 2013, next door to the Center for Contemporary Arts. The mod rooms have accoutrements such as a Nespresso machine, free wi-fi, plush bedding and, of course, original art. The lobby is a public gallery, so feel free to ogle the trippy videos and nude sculptures. The on-site restaurant and rooftop bar draw crowds. Parking costs $35.

Residence Inn
Cincinnati Downtown
HOTEL $$$

(☎ 513-651-1234; www.residenceinncincinnatidowntown.com; 506 E 4th St; r $209-299; P ❄ @ ☎)
All of the big, glistening rooms are suites with full kitchens. Continental breakfast is included. Parking costs $24.

✖ Eating

Over-the-Rhine holds several hip new eateries, especially on Vine St between 12th and 14th Sts. Restaurants also concentrate along the riverfront and in the Northside neighborhood (north of where I-74 and I-75 intersect, 5 miles north of downtown).

★ Tucker's
DINER $

(☎ 513-721-7123; 1637 Vine St; mains $4-9; ⊙ 9am-3pm Tue-Sat, 10am-2pm Sun; ☒) Located in a tough zone a few blocks from Findlay Market, family-run Tucker's has been feeding locals – African American, white, foodies, penniless – since 1946. It's an archetypal diner, serving shrimp and grits, biscuits and gravy, and other hulking breakfast dishes, along with wildly inventive vegetarian fare (like beet sliders) using ingredients sourced from the market.

Son Joe Tucker does the cookin'. Try the goetta (pronounced get-uh), a herb-spiced, pork-and-oats breakfast sausage that's found only in Cincinnati.

The Eagle OTR
AMERICAN $

(☎ 513-802-5007; www.theeagleotr.com; 1342 Vine St; mains $7-10; ⊙ 11am-midnight Mon-Sat, to 10pm Sun) A hipster magnet serving modern soul food amid reclaimed wood decor, the Eagle rustles up fantastic fried chicken (dipped in spicy honey), white cheddar grits and spoonbread (like a sweet cornbread). Expect a queue, though the doughnut shop two doors down helps take the edge off (it's open until 9pm most nights).

CHILI FIVE-WAY

Don't worry – you can keep your clothes on for this experience, though you may want to loosen your belt. A 'five-way' in Cincinnati has to do with chili, which is a local specialty. It comprises meat sauce (spiced with chocolate and cinnamon) ladled over spaghetti and beans, then garnished with cheese and onions. Although you can get it three-way (minus onions and beans) or four-way (minus onions or beans), you should go the whole way – after all, life's an adventure. **Skyline Chili** (www.skylinechili.com; 643 Vine St; items $4-7.50; ⊙ 10:30am-8pm Mon-Fri, 11am-4pm Sat) has a cultlike following devoted to its version. There are outlets throughout town; this one is downtown near Fountain Sq.

Graeter's Ice Cream
ICE CREAM $

(☎ 513-381-4191; www.graeters.com; 511 Walnut St; scoops $2.50-5; ⊙ 6:30am-11pm, reduced hours in winter) A local delicacy, with scoop shops around the city. The flavors that mix in the gargantuan, chunky chocolate chips top the list.

Terry's Turf Club
BURGERS $

(☎ 513-533-4222; 4618 Eastern Ave; mains $10-15; ⊙ 11am-11pm Wed & Thu, to midnight Fri & Sat, to 9pm Sun) This 15-table beer-and-burger joint glows inside and out with owner Terry Carter's neon stash. A giant, waving Aunt Jemima beckons you in, where so many fluorescent beer and doughnut signs shine that no other interior lighting is needed. Located 7 miles east of downtown via Columbia Pkwy.

♀ Drinking & Nightlife

Over-the-Rhine, Mt Adams and Northside are busy nightspots. The Banks, the riverfront area between the baseball and football stadiums, has several new hot spots.

★ Rhinegeist Brewery
BREWERY

(www.rhinegeist.com; 1910 Elm St, 2nd fl; ⊙ 4-11pm Mon-Thu, to midnight Fri, noon-midnight Sat, to 7pm Sun) Beer buffs pile in to Rhinegeist's hoppy clubhouse to knock back Truth IPA and 13 other brews on tap. Swig at picnic tables while watching bottles roll off the production line, or play ping-pong or foosball in the sprawling open warehouse. It sits in a forlorn patch of OTR.

Moerlein Lager House BREWERY
(www.moerleinlagerhouse.com; 115 Joe Nuxhall Way; ⊙11am-midnight Mon-Thu, to 1am Fri & Sat, to 11pm Sun) Copper kettles cook up the house beers, while the patio unfurls awesome views of the riverfront and Roebling bridge. It's a busy spot pre or post Reds game, as it sits across the street from the stadium.

Blind Lemon BAR
(www.theblindlemon.com; 936 Hatch St; ⊙5:30pm-2:30am Mon-Fri, from 3pm Sat & Sun) Head down the passageway to enter this atmospheric old speakeasy in Mt Adams. It has an outdoor courtyard in summer, with a fire pit added in winter, and there's live music nightly.

☆ Entertainment

Scope for free publications like *CityBeat* for current listings.

Sports

Great American Ballpark BASEBALL
(☑513-765-7000; www.reds.com; 100 Main St) Home to the Reds – pro baseball's first team – Cincy is a great place to catch a game thanks to its bells-and-whistles riverside ballpark. The Brewery Bar near section 117 pours loads of local beers.

Paul Brown Stadium FOOTBALL
(☑513-621-3550; www.bengals.com; 1 Paul Brown Stadium) The Bengals pro football team scrimmages a few blocks west of the ballpark.

Performing Arts

Music Hall CLASSICAL MUSIC
(☑513-721-8222; www.cincinnatiarts.org; 1241 Elm St) The acoustically pristine Music Hall is where the symphony orchestra, pops orchestra, opera and ballet hold their seasons.

Aronoff Center THEATER
(☑513-621-2787; www.cincinnatiarts.org; 650 Walnut St) The mod Aronoff hosts touring shows.

❶ Information

Cincinnati Enquirer (www.cincinnati.com) Daily newspaper.
Cincinnati USA Regional Tourism Network (☑800-543-2613; www.cincinnatiusa.com) There's a visitor center on Fountain Sq.
CityBeat (www.citybeat.com) Free alternative weekly paper with good entertainment listings.

❶ Getting There & Around

The **Cincinnati/Northern Kentucky International Airport** (CVG; www.cvgairport.com) is actually in Kentucky, 13 miles south. To get downtown, take the TANK bus ($2) from near Terminal 3; a cab costs about $35.

Greyhound (☑513-352-6012; www.greyhound.com; 1005 Gilbert Ave) buses travel daily to Columbus (two hours), Indianapolis (2½ hours) and Chicago (seven hours). Often cheaper and quicker, **Megabus** (www.megabus.com/us) travels the same routes from downtown and the University of Cincinnati; check the website for curbside locations.

Amtrak (☑513-651-3337; www.amtrak.com) choo-choos into **Union Terminal** (1301 Western Ave) thrice weekly en route to Chicago (9½ hours) and Washington, DC (14½ hours), departing in the middle of the night.

Metro (www.go-metro.com; fares $1.75) runs the local buses and links with the **Transit Authority of Northern Kentucky** (TANK; www.tankbus.org; fares $1-2). Bus 1 is useful, looping from the museum center to downtown to Mt Adams.

Red Bike (www.cincyredbike.org; 24hr pass $8) has 260 bicycles at 30 stations, mostly in downtown and Over-the-Rhine; additional charges apply for trips over 60 minutes.

MICHIGAN

More, more, more – Michigan is the Midwest state that cranks it up. It sports more beaches than the Atlantic seaboard. More than half the state is covered by forests. And more cherries and berries get shoveled into pies here than anywhere else in the USA. Plus Michigan's gritty city Detroit is the Midwest's rawest of all – and we mean that in a good way.

Michigan occupies prime real estate, surrounded by four of the five Great Lakes – Superior, Michigan, Huron and Erie. Islands – Mackinac, Manitou and Isle Royale – freckle its coast and make top touring destinations. Surfing beaches, colored sandstone cliffs and trekkable sand dunes also woo visitors.

The state consists of two parts split by water: the larger Lower Peninsula, shaped like a mitten; and the smaller, lightly populated Upper Peninsula, shaped like a slipper. They are linked by the gasp-worthy Mackinac Bridge, which spans the Straits of Mackinac (pronounced *mac*-in-aw).

ℹ️ Information

Michigan Highway Conditions (☏ 800-381-8477; www.michigan.gov/mdot)

Michigan State Park Information (☏ 800-447-2757; www.michigan.gov/stateparks) Park entry requires a vehicle permit (per day/year $9/31). Campsites cost $13 to $37; reservations accepted (www.midnrreservations.com; fee $8). Some parks have wi-fi.

Travel Michigan (☏ 800-644-2489; www.michigan.org)

Detroit

Tell any American that you're planning to visit Detroit, and then watch their eyebrows shoot up quizzically. They'll ask 'Why?' and warn you that the city is broke, with off-the-chart homicide rates, nearly 80,000 abandoned buildings and forsaken homes that sell for $1. 'Detroit's a crap-hole. You'll get killed there.'

While the city does have a bombed-out, apocalyptic vibe, it's these same qualities that fuel a raw urban energy you won't find anywhere else. Artists, entrepreneurs and young people are moving in, and a DIY spirit pervades. They're converting vacant lots into urban farms and abandoned buildings into cafes and museums. But there's a long way to go, and skeptics point out that Detroit's long-term African-American residents are not sharing equally in these new developments. How the city navigates the tricky path to recovery remains to be seen.

History

French explorer Antoine de La Mothe Cadillac founded Detroit in 1701. Sweet fortune arrived in the 1920s, when Henry Ford began churning out cars. He didn't invent the automobile, as so many mistakenly believe, but he did perfect assembly-line manufacturing and mass-production techniques. The result was the Model T, the first car the USA's middle class could afford to own.

Detroit quickly became the motor capital of the world. General Motors (GM), Chrysler and Ford were all headquartered in or near Detroit (and still are). The 1950s were the city's heyday, when the population exceeded two million and Motown music hit the airwaves. But racial tensions in 1967 and Japanese car competitors in the 1970s shook the city and its industry. Detroit entered an era of deep decline, losing about two-thirds of its population.

MICHIGAN FACTS

Nicknames Great Lakes State, Wolverine State

Population 9.9 million

Area 96,720 sq miles

Capital city Lansing (population 114,000)

Other cities Detroit (population 689,000)

Sales tax 6%

Birthplace of Industrialist Henry Ford (1863–1947), filmmaker Francis Ford Coppola (b 1939), musician Stevie Wonder (b 1950), singer Madonna (b 1958), Google co-founder Larry Page (b 1973)

Home of Auto assembly plants, freshwater beaches

Politics Leans Democratic

Famous for Cars, Cornflakes, tart cherries, Motown music

State reptile Painted turtle

Driving distances Detroit to Traverse City 255 miles, Detroit to Cleveland 168 miles

In July 2013 Detroit filed the largest municipal bankruptcy claim in US history: $18 billion. After extreme belt-tightening, it emerged from bankruptcy in December 2014.

⊙ Sights & Activities

Sights are commonly closed on Monday and Tuesday. And that's Canada across the Detroit River (Windsor, Canada, to be exact).

◉ Midtown & Cultural Center

★ **Detroit Institute of Arts** MUSEUM
(☏ 313-833-7900; www.dia.org; 5200 Woodward Ave; adult/child $8/4; ⊙ 9am-4pm Tue-Thu, to 10pm Fri, 10am-5pm Sat & Sun) The cream of the museum crop. The centerpiece is Diego Rivera's mural *Detroit Industry*, which fills an entire room and reflects the city's blue-collar labor history. Beyond it are Picassos, suits of armor, mod African American paintings and troves more.

Museum of Contemporary Art Detroit MUSEUM
(MOCAD; ☏ 313-832-6622; www.mocadetroit.org; 4454 Woodward Ave; suggested donation $5; ⊙ 11am-5pm Wed, Sat & Sun, to 8pm Thu & Fri)

Detroit

0 — 500 m
0 — 0.25 miles

Motown Historical Museum (0.7mi)

NEW CENTER

E Edsel Ford Fwy

Amtrak (0.3mi)

Ford Piquette Avenue Plant (0.2mi)

Chrysler Fwy

Russell St

Palmer Ave

Ferry St

Wayne State University

Merrick Ave

Cass Ave

3rd Ave

2nd Ave

4th Ave

Kirby St

9

Frederick

Douglass Ave

Farnsworth St

1 Detroit Institute of Arts

Warren Ave

Warren Ave

Hancock Ave

Hancock Ave

John R St

Brush St

St Antoine St

Chrysler Dr

Forest Ave

Forest Ave

Lincoln Ave

Gibson St

Lodge Fwy

Prentis Ave

10

14

Canfield Ave

Canfield Ave

Canfield St

2nd Ave

Cass Ave

15

Willis St

22

25

Alexandrine St

Selden St

13

Selden St

Selden St

MIDTOWN & CULTURAL CENTER

Chrysler Dr

Rivard St

Tolan Park

Parsens St

Brainard St

Martin Luther King Jr Blvd

Woodward Ave

Mack Ave

Erskine St

Ash St

Elm St

Peterboro St

Watson St

Edmund Pl

Wilkins St

Wilkins St

Alfred St

Charlotte Ave

3rd Ave

Temple St

Perry St

Spruce St

Temple Ave

Cass Park

Ledyard St

Alfred St

Eastern Market

2

Park Ave

Adelaide St

Detroit Hostel (0.3mi)

Grand River Ave

Henry St

Winder St

Winder St

Fisher Fwy

Slows Bar BQ (0.5mi); Michigan Central Station (0.7mi)

Montcalm St

23

Plum St

Clifford St

Cass Ave

17

Woodward Ave

18

Brush St

20

St Antoine St

Gratiot Ave

3

Elizabeth St

Adams Ave

Beacon St

5th Ave

4th Ave

Beech St

Plaza Dr

Park Pl

7

Madison St

19

Broadway Ave

Lafayette Plaisance

CORKTOWN

Labrosse St

Michigan Ave

Library Ave

Farmer St

24

Clinton St

Macomb St

Monroe St

Porter St

6th St

Abbott St

Abbott St

1st St

State St

Lafayette Blvd

GREEKTOWN

Howard St

Greyhound

8

12

11

16

Fort St

Lafayette Blvd

3rd Ave

2nd Ave

Washington Blvd

Shelby St

Griswold St

Bates St

Fort St

Green Dot Stables (0.6mi)

3rd Ave

26

Larned St

Navarre Ple

Jefferson Ave

Jefferson Ave

21

Cobo Center

Hart Plaza

3

Transit Windsor

5

Randolph St

Congress St

Woodbridge St

Franklin St

Riopelle St

Detroit River

Atwater St

Riverwalk

6

Detroit

GREAT LAKES DETROIT

MOCAD is set in an abandoned, graffiti-slathered auto dealership. Heat lamps hang from the ceiling over peculiar exhibits that change every few months. Music and literary events take place regularly. The on-site cafe/cocktail bar is uber popular.

◉ New Center

Motown Historical Museum   MUSEUM
(☑ 313-875-2264; www.motownmuseum.org; 2648 W Grand Blvd; adult $12-15, child $8; ◷10am-6pm Tue-Fri, to 8pm Sat, noon-6pm Sun Jul & Aug, to 6pm Tue-Sat Sep-Jun) In this row of modest houses Berry Gordy launched Motown Records – and the careers of Stevie Wonder, Diana Ross, Marvin Gaye and Michael Jackson – with an $800 loan in 1959. Gordy and Motown split for Los Angeles in 1972, but you can still step into humble Studio A and see where the famed names recorded their first hits.

A tour takes about 1½ hours, and consists mostly of looking at old photos and listening to guides' stories. The museum is 2 miles northwest of Midtown.

Ford Piquette Avenue Plant   MUSEUM
(☑ 313-872-8759; www.fordpiquetteaveplant.org; 461 Piquette Ave; adult/child $10/free; ◷10am-4pm Wed-Sun Apr-Oct) Henry Ford cranked out the first Model T in this landmark factory. Admission includes a detailed tour by enthusiastic docents, plus loads of shiny vehicles from 1904 onward. It's about 1 mile northeast of the Detroit Institute of Arts.

◉ Downtown & Around

Greektown (centred on Monroe St) has a stretch of restaurants, bakeries and a casino.

★**Eastern Market**   MARKET
(www.easternmarket.com; Adelaide & Russell Sts) Produce, cheese, spice and flower vendors fill the large halls on Saturday, but you also can turn up Monday through Friday to browse the specialty shops (props to the peanut roaster) and cafes that flank the halls on Russell and Market Sts. In addition, from June through October there's a scaled-down market on Tuesdays and a Sunday craft market with food trucks.

Renaissance Center   BUILDING
(RenCen; www.gmrencen.com; 330 E Jefferson Ave) GM's glossy, cloud-poking headquarters is a fine place to mooch off the free wi-fi, take a free hour-long tour (Monday through Friday at noon and 2pm) or embark on the riverfront walkway.

Hart Plaza   PLAZA
(cnr Jefferson & Woodward Aves) This is the site of many free summer weekend festivals and concerts. While there, check out the sculpture of Joe Louis' mighty fist.

People Mover   MONORAIL
(www.thepeoplemover.com; fares $0.75) As mass transit, the monorail's 3-mile loop on elevated tracks around downtown won't get you

very far. As a tourist attraction, it's a sweet ride providing great views of the city and riverfront. There are 13 stations, including one in the RenCen.

Heidelberg Project PUBLIC ART
(www.heidelberg.org; 3600 Heidelberg St; ☺sunrise-sunset) `FREE` Polka-dotted streets, houses covered in Technicolor paint blobs, strange sculptures in yards – this is no acid trip, but rather a block-spanning art installation. It's the brainchild of street artist Tyree Guyton, who wanted to beautify his run-down community. Arsonists have burned much of the project, but Guyton vows he'll keep it open and turn what remains into art once again.

It's located about 1.5 miles from Eastern Market. Take Gratiot Ave northeast to Heidelberg St. The project spans from Ellery to Mt Elliott Sts in a rough neighborhood.

Riverwalk & Dequindre Cut WALKING, CYCLING
(www.detroitriverfront.org) The city's swell riverfront path runs for 3 miles along the churning Detroit River from Hart Plaza east to Mt Elliott St, passing several parks, outdoor theaters, riverboats and fishing spots en route. Eventually it will extend all the way to beachy Belle Isle (detour onto Jefferson Ave to get there now). About halfway along the Riverwalk, near Orleans St, the 1.5-mile Dequindre Cut Greenway path juts north, offering a convenient passageway to Eastern Market.

Wheelhouse Bikes BICYCLE RENTAL
(☎313-656-2453; www.wheelhousedetroit.com; 1340 E Atwater St; per 2hr $15; ☺10am-8pm Mon-Sat, 11am-5pm Sun Jun-Aug, reduced hours Sep-May) Cycling is a great way to explore the city. Wheelhouse rents sturdy two-wheelers (helmet and lock included) on the Riverwalk at Rivard Plaza. Themed tours ($40 including bike rental) roll by various neighborhoods, architectural sites and urban farms.

☞ Tours

Preservation Detroit WALKING TOUR
(☎313-577-7674; www.preservationdetroit.org; 2hr tours $15; ☺10am Sat May-Sep) Offers architectural walking tours through downtown, Midtown and other neighborhoods; departure points vary.

☆☆ Festivals & Events

North American International Auto Show CULTURAL
(www.naias.com; tickets $13; ☺mid-Jan) It's autos galore for two weeks at the Cobo Center.

Movement Electronic Music Festival MUSIC
(www.movement.us; day pass $75; ☺late May) The world's largest electronic music festival congregates in Hart Plaza over Memorial Day weekend.

🛌 Sleeping

Add 9% to 15% tax (it varies by lodging size and location) to the rates listed here, unless stated otherwise.

Affordable motels abound in Detroit's suburbs. If you're arriving from Metro Airport, follow the signs for Merriman Rd when leaving the airport and take your pick.

Detroit Hostel HOSTEL $
(☎313-451-0333; www.hosteldetroit.com; 2700 Vermont St; dm $30-37, r $46-65; P@🛜) Volunteers rehabbed this old building, gathered up recycled materials and donations for the patchwork furnishings, and opened it to the public in 2011. There's a 10-bed dorm, a four-bed dorm and a handful of private rooms; everyone shares the four bathrooms and three kitchens. Bookings are taken online only (and must be done at least 24 hours in advance).

Bike rentals costs $20 per day. The hostel is located in Corktown on a desolate street, but near several good bars and restaurants.

★ Inn on Ferry Street INN $$
(☎313-871-6000; www.innonferrystreet.com; 84 E Ferry St; r $169-259; P✳@🛜) Forty guest rooms fill a row of Victorian mansions right by the art museum. The lower-cost rooms are small but have deliciously soft bedding; the larger rooms feature plenty of antique wood furnishings. The healthy hot breakfast and shuttle to downtown are nice touches.

Aloft HOTEL $$
(☎313-237-1700; www.aloftdetroit.com; 1 Park Ave; r $159-199; P✳@🛜🐾) The chain's new Detroit property took an exquisite 1915 neo-Renaissance skyscraper and converted it to its familiar hipster style. Mod rooms have bright pops of color and groovy city views. It's well-located near the sports venues and theaters. Parking costs $30.

Ft Shelby Doubletree Hotel HOTEL $$
($313-963-5600; http://doubletree1.hilton.com; 525 W Lafayette Blvd; r $123-189; P❋@🐕) This hotel fills a historic beaux-arts building downtown. All rooms are suites, with both the sitting area and bedroom equipped with HDTV and free wi-fi. Parking costs $27, and there's free shuttle service around downtown.

🍴 Eating

Two nearby suburbs also have caches of hip restaurants and bars: walkable, gay-oriented Ferndale at 9 Mile Rd and Woodward Ave, and Royal Oak just north of Ferndale between 12 and 13 Mile Rds.

🍴 Midtown & Cultural Center

Cass Cafe CAFE $
($313-831-1400; www.casscafe.com; 4620 Cass Ave; mains $8-15; ☺11am-11pm Mon-Thu, to 1am Fri & Sat, 5-10pm Sun; 🐕🍴) The Cass is a bohemian art gallery fused with a bar and restaurant that serves soups, sandwiches and veggie beauties, such as the lentil-walnut burger. Service can be fickle.

Selden Standard MODERN AMERICAN $$$
($313-438-5055; www.seldenstandard.com; 3921 2nd Ave; small plates $14-20; ☺11am-2:30pm & 5-10pm Mon-Fri, from 10am Sat & Sun) The city has its first upscale farm-to-table restaurant, the kind of place that cares enough to churn its own butter and hand-mold its own pasta. The menu changes, but you'll see dishes such as fresh-caught trout and celery root ravioli, plus creative cocktails.

🍴 Downtown

Lafayette Coney Island AMERICAN $
($313-964-8198; 118 Lafayette Blvd; items $2.50-5; ☺9am-3am Sun-Thu, 8am-4am Fri & Sat) The 'coney' – a hot dog smothered with chili and onions – is a Detroit specialty. When the craving strikes (and it will), take care of business at Lafayette. The minimalist menu consists of burgers, fries and beer, in addition to the signature item. Cash only.

Dime Store AMERICAN $
($313-962-9106; www.eatdimestore.com; 719 Griswold St; mains $8-13; ☺8am-3pm Mon, to 10pm Tue-Fri, 10am-3pm Sat & Sun) Take a seat in a chunky wood swivel chair in this cozy, diner-esque eatery and chow down on a duck Reuben and truffle-mayo-dipped fries, alongside a cold beer. Eggy brunch dishes are a big hit and served all day.

LOCAL KNOWLEDGE

DETROIT'S RUINS

More than 78,000 abandoned buildings blight Detroit's landscape. The city would like to demolish them, but it doesn't have the money. Many have become well-known, often-photographed sights. Top of the list is **Michigan Central Station** (2405 W Vernor Hwy), the once-grand beaux-arts rail terminal now crumbling into oblivion within eyeshot of Corktown's main drag. The **Packard Auto Plant** (E Grand Blvd at Concord St) is another. Renowned architect Albert Kahn designed the 3.5-million-sq-ft factory, and it was a thing of beauty when it opened in 1903. Now it looks like something from a zombie movie. Stay tuned though, as a developer bought the plant and has vowed to renovate it. **Detroiturbex** (www.detroiturbex.com) provides good historical information on these and other derelict structures around town.

Note that viewing the buildings has become a hot topic: some call it 'ruin porn,' as in people getting excited by urban decay. Others see it as a way to examine and take in the complex history of the city. It is illegal to enter any abandoned building.

🍴 Corktown & Mexicantown

Corktown, a bit west of downtown, shows the city's DIY spirit. Hipster joints slinging burgers, cocktails and artisanal coffee drinks line Michigan Ave. Mexicantown, along Bagley St 3 miles west of downtown, offers several inexpensive Mexican restaurants.

Green Dot Stables BURGERS $
($313-962-5588; www.greendotstables.com; 2200 W Lafayette Blvd; mains $2-3; ☺11am-midnight Mon-Wed, to 1am Thu-Sat, noon-10pm Sun) It's a bit inconveniently located between downtown, Corktown and Mexicantown, but that doesn't deter young urbanites from flocking in to munch on 20 types of gourmet mini-burgers (say, wasabi-mayo tempeh or peanut-butter kimchi) with a side of poutine.

★ Slows Bar BQ BARBECUE $$
($313-962-9828; www.slowsbarbq.com; 2138 Michigan Ave; mains $10-19; ☺11am-10pm Sun & Mon, to 11pm Tue-Thu, to midnight Fri & Sat; 🐕) Mmm, slow-cooked Southern-style barbecue

FROM MOTOWN TO ROCK CITY

Motown Records and soul music put Detroit on the map in the 1960s, while the thrashing punk rock of the Stooges and MC5 was the 1970s response to that smooth sound. By 1976, Detroit was dubbed 'Rock City' by a Kiss song (though – just Detroit's luck – the tune was eclipsed by its B-side, 'Beth'). In recent years it has been hard-edged rock – aka whiplash rock and roll – that has pushed the city to the music-scene forefront. Homegrown stars include the White Stripes, Von Bondies and Dirtbombs. Rap (thank you, Eminem) and techno are Detroit's other renowned genres. Many music aficionados say the city's blight is what produces such a beautifully angry explosion of sound, and who's to argue? Scope free publications like the *Metro Times* (www.metrotimes.com) and blogs such as Motor City Rocks (http://motorcityrocks.com) for current show and club listings.

in Corktown. Carnivores can carve into the three-meat combo plate (brisket, pulled pork and chicken). Vegetarians even have a couple of options. The taps yield 55 quality beers.

Drinking & Nightlife

★ Bronx   BAR
(4476 2nd Ave; ⊗noon-2am; �) There's not much inside Detroit's best boozer besides a pool table, dim lighting and a couple of jukeboxes filled with ballsy rock and soul. But that's the way the hipsters, slackers and rockers (the White Stripes used to hang here) like their dive bars. They're also fond of the beefy burgers served late at night and the cheap beer selection.

HopCat   PUB
(www.hopcat.com/detroit; 4265 Woodward Ave; ⊗11am-2am Mon-Sat, from 10am Sun; �) Detroit's outpost of the regional pub chain rocks: paintings of local musicians adorn the walls, and the Stooges and old Motown bang on the speakers. Around 130 beers flow from the taps, with 30 devoted to Michigan brewers. Smaller pours (5oz and 8oz glasses) are available for those who want to sample widely.

Roasting Plant   COFFEE
(www.roastingplant.com; 660 Woodward Ave; ⊗6am-7pm Mon-Fri, from 7am Sat & Sun) This slick, high-tech and super-friendly spot grinds beans fresh for each heavy-duty cup of coffee. The free gallery across the lobby usually has something cool showing. Food trucks waft their wares a few steps outside the door.

☆ Entertainment

Live Music
Cover charges hover between $5 and $15.

Majestic Theater & Populux   LIVE MUSIC
(www.majesticdetroit.com; 4120-4140 Woodward Ave) The Majestic Theater and smaller Majestic Cafe host beer-splattered rock shows, while next door club Populux brings on the electronic dance music. The entertainment complex also holds a bowling alley and pizza joint. Something cool rocks here nightly.

PJ's Lager House   LIVE MUSIC
(www.pjslagerhouse.com; 1254 Michigan Ave; ⊗11am-2am) Scrappy bands or DJs play most nights at this small Corktown club. By day it serves surprisingly good grub with a New Orleans/vegan twist (like the tempeh po'boy on gluten-free bread).

Cliff Bell's   JAZZ
(www.cliffbells.com; 2030 Park Ave; ⊗from 4pm Tue-Fri, 5pm Sat, 11am Sun) With its dark wood, candlelight and art-deco decor, Bell's evokes 1930s elegance. Local jazz bands and poetry readings attract a diverse young audience.

Performing Arts

Puppet ART/Detroit Puppet Theater   THEATER
(☎313-961-7777; www.puppetart.org; 25 E Grand River Ave; adult/child $10/5; ⊕) Soviet-trained puppeteers perform beautiful shows in this 70-person theater; a small museum displays puppets from different cultures. Shows are typically held on Saturday afternoon.

Detroit Opera House   OPERA
(☎313-237-7464; www.michiganopera.org; 1526 Broadway Ave) Gorgeous interior, top-tier company and nurturer of many renowned African American performers.

Sports

Comerica Park   BASEBALL
(www.detroittigers.com; 2100 Woodward Ave; ⊕) The Detroit Tigers play pro baseball at Comerica, one of the league's most decked-out stadiums. The park is particularly kid friendly,

with a small Ferris wheel and carousel inside (both $2 per ride).

Joe Louis Arena　　　　　　　　　HOCKEY
(www.detroitredwings.com; 600 Civic Center Dr) The much-loved Red Wings play pro ice hockey at this arena where, if you can wrangle tickets, you might witness the strange octopus-throwing custom (yes, a real octopus). A new stadium is slated to open at downtown's northern edge in late 2017.

Ford Field　　　　　　　　　　FOOTBALL
(www.detroitlions.com; 2000 Brush St) The Lions toss the pigskin at this indoor stadium next to Comerica Park.

Palace of Auburn Hills　　　　BASKETBALL
(www.nba.com/pistons; 5 Championship Dr) The Palace hosts the Pistons pro basketball team. It's about 30 miles northwest of downtown; take I-75 to exit 81.

🛍 Shopping

Pure Detroit　　　　　　　　　SOUVENIRS
(www.puredetroit.com; 500 Griswold St; ⊙10:30am-5:30pm Mon-Sat) Local artists create stylish products for Pure Detroit that celebrate the city's fast-cars-and-rock-music culture. Pick up handbags made from recycled seatbelts, groovy T-shirts and local Pewabic pottery. Located in the landmark, mosaic-strewn Guardian Building (worth a peek in its own right).

People's Records　　　　　　　　MUSIC
(www.peoplesdetroit.com; 4100 Woodward Ave; ⊙11am-7pm Mon-Sat) Calling all crate-diggers: DJ-owned People's Records is your vinyl Valhalla. Used 45s are the specialty, with more than 80,000 jazz, soul and R&B titles filling bins. The front table is loaded with flyers that tell you where the latest, greatest music events are happening.

ℹ Information

The area between the sports arenas north to around Willis Rd is pretty deserted and best avoided on foot come nighttime.

EMERGENCY & MEDICAL SERVICES
Detroit Receiving Hospital (☑313-745-3000; 4201 St Antoine St)

INTERNET ACCESS
You'll find free wi-fi in many cafes and bars, as well as the Renaissance Center lobby.

MEDIA
Between the Lines (www.pridesource.com) Free, weekly gay and lesbian paper.

Detroit Free Press (www.freep.com) Daily newspaper.

Detroit News (www.detroitnews.com) Daily newspaper.

Metro Times (www.metrotimes.com) Free alternative weekly that is the best guide to the entertainment scene.

Model D (www.modelmedia.com) Weekly e-zine about local developments and food/entertainment options, broken down by neighborhood.

TOURIST INFORMATION
Detroit Convention & Visitors Bureau (☑800-338-7648; www.visitdetroit.com)

ℹ Getting There & Around

Detroit Metro Airport (DTW; www.metroairport.com), a Delta Airlines hub, is about 20 miles southwest of Detroit. Transportation options to the city are few. Taxis cost $55 or so. The shared shuttle van **Skoot** (www.rideskoot.com) costs $20. The 125 SMART bus ($2.50) is inconvenient, unreliable and takes 1½ hours to get downtown.

Greyhound (☑313-961-8005; 1001 Howard St) runs to various cities in Michigan and beyond. **Megabus** (www.megabus.com/us) runs to/from Chicago (5½ hours) daily; departures are from downtown and Wayne State University. Check the website for exact locations.

Amtrak (☑313-873-3442; 11 W Baltimore Ave) trains go three times daily to Chicago (5½ hours). You can also head east – to New York (16½ hours) or destinations en route – but you'll first be bused to Toledo.

Transit Windsor (☑519-944-4111; www.citywindsor.ca/transitwindsor) operates the Tunnel Bus to Windsor, Canada. It costs $4.50 (American or Canadian) and departs by Mariner's Church (corner of Randolph St and Jefferson Ave) near the Detroit-Windsor Tunnel entrance, as well as other spots downtown. Bring your passport.

The **M-1 streetcar** is scheduled to start running in late 2016, providing handy transportation along Woodward Ave from Congress St downtown, past the sports venues and museums, to the Amtrak station and W Grand Blvd at the northern end. See http://m-1rail.com for updates.

For taxi service, call **Checker Cab** (☑313-963-7000).

CLASSIC CARS IN MICHIGAN

More than sand dunes, beaches and Mackinac Island fudge, Michigan is synonymous with cars. While the connection hasn't been so positive in recent years, the state commemorates its glory days via several auto museums. The following fleets are within a few hours' drive of the Motor City.

Henry Ford Museum (see below) This Dearborn museum is loaded with vintage cars, including the first one Henry Ford ever built. In adjacent Greenfield Village you can ride in a Model T that rolled off the assembly line in 1923.

Automotive Hall of Fame (313-240-4000; www.automotivehalloffame.org; 21400 Oakwood Blvd; adult/child $10/4; 9am-5pm Wed-Sun) Next door to the Henry Ford Museum, the interactive Auto Hall focuses on the people behind famed cars, such as Mr Ferdinand Porsche and Mr Soichiro Honda.

Gilmore Car Museum (269-671-5089; www.gilmorecarmuseum.org; 6865 Hickory Rd; adult/child $13/10; 9am-5pm Mon-Fri, to 6pm Sat & Sun) North of Kalamazoo along Hwy 43, this museum complex offers 22 barns filled with 120 vintage autos, including 15 Rolls-Royces dating back to a 1910 Silver Ghost.

RE Olds Transportation Museum (p572) It's a whopping garage full of shiny vintage cars that date back more than 130 years.

Around Detroit

Stunning Americana and good eatin' lie just down the road from Detroit.

Dearborn

Dearborn is 10 miles west of downtown Detroit and home to two of the USA's finest museums. The indoor **Henry Ford Museum** (313-982-6001; www.thehenryford.org; 20900 Oakwood Blvd; adult/child $20/15; 9:30am-5pm) contains a fascinating wealth of American culture, such as the chair Lincoln was sitting in when he was assassinated, the presidential limo in which Kennedy was killed, the hot-dog-shaped Oscar Mayer Wienermobile (photo op!) and the bus on which Rosa Parks refused to give up her seat. Don't worry: you'll get your vintage car fix here too. Parking is $6. The adjacent, outdoor **Greenfield Village** (adult/child $25/18.75; 9:30am-5pm daily mid-Apr–Oct, Fri-Sun Nov & Dec) features historic buildings shipped in from all over the country, reconstructed and restored, such as Thomas Edison's laboratory from Menlo Park and the Wright Brothers' airplane workshop. Plus you can add on the **Rouge Factory Tour** (adult/child $16/12; 9:30am-3pm Mon-Sat) and see F-150 trucks roll off the assembly line where Ford first perfected his self-sufficient, mass-production techniques.

The three attractions are separate, but you can get a combination ticket (adult/child $35/26.25) for Henry Ford and Greenfield Village. Plan on at least one very full day at the complex.

Dearborn has the nation's greatest concentration of people of Arab descent, so it's no surprise that the **Arab American National Museum** (313-582-2266; www.arabamericanmuseum.org; 13624 Michigan Ave; adult/child $8/4; 10am-6pm Wed-Sat, noon-5pm Sun) popped up here. It's a noble concept, located in a pretty, bright-tiled building, but it's not terribly exciting unless actor Jamie Farr's *M*A*S*H* TV-show script wows you. The Arabian eateries lining nearby Warren Ave provide a more engaging feel for the culture. Turquoise-roofed **Hamido** (www.hamidorestaurant.com; 13251 W Warren Ave; mains $6-12; 11am-midnight) serves hummus, chicken shwarma and other staples. The number of birds roasting on the spit show its popularity.

Ann Arbor

Forty-odd miles west of Detroit, liberal and bookish Ann Arbor is home to the University of Michigan. The walkable downtown, which abuts the campus, is loaded with free-trade coffee shops, bookstores and brewpubs. It's a mecca for chowhounds; follow the drool trail toward anything named 'Zingerman's.'

◎ Sights & Activities

University of Michigan
Museum of Art MUSEUM
(☑734-764-0395; www.umma.umich.edu; 525 S State St; ⊙11am-5pm Tue-Sat, from noon Sun) **FREE** The campus' bold art museum impresses with its collections of Asian ceramics, Tiffany glass and modern abstract works.

Ann Arbor Farmers Market MARKET
(www.facebook.com/a2market; 315 Detroit St; ⊙7am-3pm Wed & Sat May-Dec, Sat only Jan-Apr) Given the surrounding bounty of orchards and farms, it's no surprise this place is stuffed to the rafters with everything from spicy pickles to cider to mushroom-growing kits; located downtown near Zingerman's Deli. On Sunday an artisan market with jewelry, ceramics and textiles takes over.

Zingerman's Bakehouse COOKING COURSE
(www.bakewithzing.com; 3723 Plaza Dr) Offers popular 'bake-cations,' making bread or pastries in Ann Arbor.

✕ Eating & Drinking

Frita Batidos CUBAN $
(☑734-761-2882; www.fritabatidos.com; 117 W Washington St; mains $8-13; ⊙11am-11pm Sun-Wed, to midnight Thu-Sat) This mod take on Cuban street food is all the rage, offering burgers with tropical, citrusy toppings and booze-spiked milkshakes.

Zingerman's Delicatessen DELI $$
(☑734-663-3354; www.zingermansdeli.com; 422 Detroit St; sandwiches $13-17; ⊙7am-10pm; ▣) The shop that launched the foodie frenzy, Z's piles local, organic and specialty ingredients onto towering sandwiches in a sprawling downtown complex that also includes a coffee shop and bakery.

★ Zingerman's Roadhouse AMERICAN $$$
(☑734-663-3663; www.zingermansroadhouse. com; 2501 Jackson Ave; mains $19-33; ⊙7am-10pm Mon-Thu, to 11pm Fri, 9am-11pm Sat, to 9pm Sun) Two words: doughnut sundae. The bourbon-caramel-sauced dessert is pure genius, as are the traditional American dishes like Carolina grits, Iowa pork chops and Maryland crab cakes, all using sustainably produced ingredients. It's 2 miles west of downtown.

Jolly Pumpkin BREWERY
(www.jollypumpkin.com; 311 S Main St; ⊙from 11am Mon-Fri, from 10am Sat & Sun) Ann Arborites young and old come here for the housemade sour beers (try the Bam Biere), pizzas and truffle fries. Eat in the cozy, antique-filled downstairs, or head to the rooftop patio.

☆ Entertainment

If you happen to arrive on a fall weekend and wonder why 110,000 people – the size of Ann Arbor's entire population, more or less – are crowding into the school's stadium, the answer is football. Tickets are nearly impossible to purchase, especially when nemesis Ohio State is in town. You can try by contacting the **U of M Ticket Office** (☑734-764-0247; www.mgoblue.com/ticketoffice).

Blind Pig LIVE MUSIC
(www.blindpigmusic.com; 208 S 1st St) Everyone from John Lennon to Nirvana to the Circle Jerks has rocked the storied stage.

Ark LIVE MUSIC
(www.a2ark.org; 316 S Main St) The Ark hosts acoustic and folk-oriented tunesmiths.

❶ Information

There are several B&Bs within walking distance of downtown. Hotels tend to be about 5 miles out, with several clustered south on State St.

Ann Arbor Convention & Visitors Bureau
(www.visitannarbor.org) Accommodation information and more.

Lansing & Central Michigan

Michigan's heartland, plunked in the center of the Lower Peninsula, alternates between fertile farms and highway-crossed urban areas.

Lansing

Smallish Lansing is the state capital. A few miles east lies East Lansing, home of Michigan State University. They're worth a stop to peek into a couple of impressive museums.

◎ Sights & Activities

Broad Museum of Art MUSEUM
(www.broadmuseum.msu.edu; 547 E Circle Dr; ⊙10am-5pm Tue-Thu & Sat-Sun, noon-9pm Fri) **FREE** Renowned architect Zaha Hadid designed the wild-looking parallelogram of stainless steel and glass. It holds everything from Greek ceramics to Salvador Dalí paintings. Much of the space is devoted to avant-garde exhibitions.

RE Olds Transportation Museum   MUSEUM
(☑517-372-0529; www.reoldsmuseum.org; 240 Museum Dr; adult/child $7/5; ⊙10am-5pm Tue-Sat year-round, noon-5pm Sun Apr-Oct) The museum has a sweet collection of some 65 vintage cars that sit in the old Lansing City Bus Garage, including the first Oldsmobile, which was built in 1897. Note they're not all on display at once, but rotate regularly.

River Trail   WALKING
(www.lansingrivertrail.org) Between Lansing's downtown and the university is the 8-mile River Trail. The paved path is popular with cyclists and joggers, and links a number of attractions, including a children's museum, zoo and fish ladder.

🛏 Sleeping

Wild Goose Inn   B&B $$
(☑517-333-3334; www.wildgooseinn.com; 512 Albert St; r $139-159; 🛜) Lansing's downtown hotels feed off politicians and lobbyists, so they're fairly expensive. It's best to head to East Lansing's Wild Goose Inn, a six-room B&B one block from Michigan State's campus. All rooms have fireplaces and most have Jacuzzis.

🍴 Eating & Drinking

Golden Harvest   DINER $
(☑517-485-3663; 1625 Turner St; mains $7-9; ⊙7am-2:30pm Mon-Fri, from 8am Sat & Sun) Golden Harvest is a loud, punk-rock-meets-hippie diner serving the sausage-and-French-toast Bubba Sandwich and hearty omelets; cash only.

HopCat   PUB
(www.hopcat.com/east-lansing; 300 Grove St; ⊙11am-midnight Mon-Wed, to 2am Thu-Sat, 10am-midnight Sun) This East Lansing outpost of the regional pub chain has a bottle-cap-studded bar made from old gym bleachers, lights repurposed from a shuttered church and groovy rock-and-roll folk art. It's a treat to look at, but the 100 beers on tap (of which 20 are from Michigan) are the real draw. Beyond-the-norm burgers and sandwiches help you stay upright.

ⓘ Information

Greater Lansing CVB (www.lansing.org) Has information on East Lansing, home of Michigan State University.

Grand Rapids

The second-largest city in Michigan, Grand Rapids is known for office-furniture manufacturing and, more recently, beer tourism. Twenty craft breweries operate in the area, and that's why you're here (though some non-beer sights intrigue, as well).

⊙ Sights & Activities

Gerald R Ford Museum   MUSEUM
(☑616-254-0400; www.fordlibrarymuseum.gov; 303 Pearl St NW; adult/child $7/3; ⊙9am-5pm Mon-Sat, from noon Sun) The downtown museum is dedicated to Michigan's only president. Ford stepped into the Oval Office after Richard Nixon and his vice president, Spiro Agnew, resigned in disgrace. It's a bizarre period in US history, and the museum does an excellent job of covering it, down to displaying the burglary tools used in the Watergate break-in. Ford and wife Betty are buried on the museum's grounds.

Frederik Meijer Gardens   GARDENS
(☑616-957-1580; www.meijergardens.org; 1000 E Beltline NE; adult/child $12/6; ⊙9am-5pm Mon & Wed-Sat, to 9pm Tue, 11am-5pm Sun) The 118-acre gardens feature impressive blooms and sculptures by Auguste Rodin, Henry Moore and others. It is 5 miles east of downtown via I-196. For more on the visual theme, there's a good art museum downtown, too.

🛏 Sleeping

CityFlats Hotel   HOTEL $$
(☑866-609-2489; www.cityflatshotel.com; 83 Monroe Center St NW; r $165-235; ❄🛜) At night, tuck in under the bamboo sheets at the CityFlats Hotel downtown. The building is gold-certified by the LEED (Leadership in Energy and Environmental Design) program.

🍴 Eating & Drinking

Founders Brewing Company   BREWERY
(www.foundersbrewing.com; 235 Grandville Ave SW; ⊙11am-2am Mon-Sat, noon-midnight Sun; 🛜) If you've only got time for one stop in Grand Rapids, make it rock-and-roll Founders Brewing Company. The ruby-tinged Dirty Bastard Ale is good swillin', and there's meaty (or vegetable-y, for vegetarians) deli sandwiches to soak it up.

Brewery Vivant   BREWERY

(www.breweryvivant.com; 925 Cherry St SE; ⊙3-11pm Mon-Thu, to midnight Fri, 11am-midnight Sat, noon-10pm Sun) Set in an old chapel with stained glass and a vaulted ceiling, this atmospheric brewpub specializes in Belgian-style beers. It also serves locally sourced cheese plates and burgers at farmhouse-style communal tables.

❶ Information

Grand Rapids CVB (www.experiencegr. com) Has maps and self-guided brewery tour information online.

Lake Michigan Shore

They don't call it the Gold Coast for nothing. Michigan's 300-mile western shoreline features seemingly endless stretches of beaches, dunes, wineries, orchards and B&B-filled towns that boom during the summer – and shiver during the snow-packed winter. Note all state parks listed here take **campsite reservations** (☎800-447-2757; www.midnrreservations.com; fee $8) and require a vehicle permit ($9/31 per day/year), unless specified otherwise.

Harbor Country

Harbor Country refers to a group of eight small, lake-hugging towns just over the Michigan border (an easy day trip from Chicago). Yep, they've got your requisite beaches, wineries and antique shops; they've got a couple of big surprises too. The **Harbor Country Chamber of Commerce** (www.harborcountry.org) has the basics.

First up, surfing. Believe it, people: you can surf Lake Michigan, and the VW-bus-driving dudes at **Third Coast Surf Shop** (☎269-932-4575; www.thirdcoastsurfshop. com; 110 N Whittaker St; ⊙10am-6pm Sun-Thu, to 7pm Fri & Sat, closed Nov-Apr) will show you how. They provide wetsuits and boards for surfing and paddleboarding (rentals $20 to $35 per day). For novices, they offer two-hour private lessons ($75, including equipment) at the local beach. The shop is in New Buffalo, Harbor Country's biggest town.

Three Oaks is the only Harbor community that's inland (6 miles in, via US 12). Here Green Acres meets Greenwich Village in a funky farm-and-arts blend. By day, rent bikes at **Dewey Cannon Trading Company** (☎269-756-3361; www.applecidercentury.

com/dctc; 3 Dewey Cannon Ave; bike per day $20; ⊙9am-5pm Sun-Fri, to 8pm Sat, reduced hours Oct-Apr) and cycle lightly used rural roads past orchards and wineries. By eve, catch a provocative play or arthouse flick at Three Oaks' theaters.

Hungry? Get a wax-paper-wrapped cheeseburger, spicy curly fries and cold beer at **Redamak's** (www.redamaks.com; 616 E Buffalo St; burgers $6-12; ⊙noon-10:30pm Mar–mid-Nov) in New Buffalo. Or kick it up a notch with an organic whiskey flight at rustic **Journeyman Distillery** (www.journeyman distillery.com; 109 Generations Dr; ⊙noon-10pm Sun-Thu, to 11pm Fri & Sat) in Three Oaks.

Saugatuck & Douglas

Saugatuck is one of the Gold Coast's most popular resort areas, known for its strong arts community, numerous B&Bs and gay-friendly vibe. Douglas is its twin city a mile or so south, and they've pretty much sprawled into one.

◉ Sights & Activities

Galleries and shops proliferate downtown on Water and Butler Sts. Antiquing prevails on the Blue Star Hwy running south for 20 miles. Blueberry U-pick farms share this stretch of road and make a juicy stop, too.

Saugatuck Chain Ferry   BOAT TOUR

(end of Mary St; one way $1; ⊙9am-9pm late May-early Sep) The best thing to do in Saugatuck is also the most affordable. Jump aboard the clackety chain ferry, and the operator will pull you across the Kalamazoo River.

Mt Baldhead   WALKING

Huff up the stairs of this 200ft-high sand dune for a stellar view. Then race down the other side to Oval Beach. Get here via the chain ferry; walk right (north) from the dock.

Oval Beach
BEACH

(Oval Beach Rd; ⊙9am-10pm) Lifeguards patrol the long expanse of fine sand. There are bathrooms and concession stands, though not enough to spoil the peaceful, dune-laden scene. It costs $8 to park. Or arrive the adventurous way, via chain ferry and a trek over Mt Baldhead.

🛏 Sleeping

Several frilly B&Bs are tucked into Saugatuck's century-old Victorian homes, with most ranging from $150 to $300 per night and two-night minimum stays.

Pines Motorlodge
MOTEL $$

(📞269-857-5211; www.thepinesmotorlodge.com; 56 Blue Star Hwy; r $139-249; 🛜) Retro-cool tiki lamps, pinewood furniture and communal lawn chairs add up to a fun, social ambience amid the firs in Douglas.

Bayside Inn
INN $$

(📞269-857-4321; www.baysideinn.net; 618 Water St; r $160-260; 🛜) This former boathouse has 10 rooms on Saugatuck's waterfront.

🍴 Eating & Drinking

Crane's Pie Pantry
BAKERY $

(📞269-561-2297; www.cranespiepantry.com; 6054 124th Ave; pie slices $4.50; ⊙8am-8pm Mon-Sat, from 11am Sun May-Oct, reduced hours Nov-Apr) Buy a bulging slice, or pick apples and peaches in the surrounding orchards. Crane's is in Fennville, 3 miles south on the Blue Star Hwy, then 4 miles inland on Hwy 89.

Phil's Bar & Grille
AMERICAN $$

(📞269-857-1555; www.philsbarandgrille.com; 215 Butler St; mains $14-26; ⊙11:30am-9:30pm Sun-Thu, to 10:30pm Fri & Sat) This humming pub turns out terrific broasted (combining broiling and roasting) chicken, fish tacos, lamb lollipops and gumbo in a cozy, wood-floored room.

Saugatuck Brewing Company
BREWERY

(www.saugatuckbrewing.com; 2948 Blue Star Hwy; ⊙11am-9pm Sun-Thu, to 10pm Fri, to 11pm Sat) Locals like to hang out and sip the house-made suds.

ℹ Information

Saugatuck/Douglas CVB (www.saugatuck. com) The Saugatuck/Douglas CVB provides maps and more.

Muskegon & Ludington

These towns are jump-off points for two ferries that sail across the lake, providing a substantial shortcut over driving the Michigan-to-Wisconsin route. The **Lake Express** (📞866-914-1010; www.lake-express.com; ⊙May-Oct) crosses between Muskegon and Milwaukee (one-way adult/child/car from $86.50/30/91, 2½ hours); it's modern, faster and costs about 50% more. The **SS Badger** (📞800-841-4243; www.ssbadger.com; ⊙mid-May–mid-Oct) crosses between Ludington and Manitowoc (one-way adult/child/car from $59/24/59, four hours). The historic, coal-fired vessel is more atmospheric and cheaper, but also slower. For years it also was a polluter, though it has cleaned up its act and now meets environmental standards.

In Muskegon the **Winter Sports Complex** (📞231-744-9629; www.msports.org; 442 Scenic Dr) kicks butt with its full-on luge track (usable during summer, too) and cross-country ski trails. To the north, lakeside **Ludington State Park** (📞231-843-8671; tent & RV sites $13-33, cabins $49) is one of Michigan's largest and most popular playlots. It has a top-notch trail system, a renovated lighthouse to visit (or live in, as a volunteer lighthouse keeper) and miles of beach.

Sleeping Bear Dunes National Lakeshore

This national park stretches from north of Frankfort to just before Leland, on the Leelanau Peninsula. Stop at the park's **visitor center** (📞231-326-4700; www.nps.gov/slbe; 9922 Front St; ⊙8am-6pm Jun-Aug, 8:30am-4pm Sep-May) in Empire for information, trail maps and vehicle entry permits (week/annual $10/20).

Attractions include the famous **Dune Climb** along Hwy 109, where you trudge up the 200ft-high dune and then run or roll down. Gluttons for leg-muscle punishment can keep slogging all the way to Lake Michigan, a strenuous 1½-hour trek one way; bring water. The **Sleeping Bear Heritage Trail** (www.sleepingbeartrail.org) paves 13 pretty miles from Empire to Port Oneida, passing the Dune Climb along the way; walkers and cyclists are all over it. Short on time or stamina? Take the 7-mile, one-lane, picnic-grove-studded **Pierce Stocking Scenic Drive**, perhaps the best way to absorb the stunning lake vistas.

After you leave the park, swing into little **Leland** (www.lelandmi.com). Grab a bite at a waterfront restaurant downtown, and poke around atmospheric Fishtown with its weatherbeaten shacks-cum-shops. Boats depart from here for the Manitou Islands.

Onward near Suttons Bay, **Tandem Ciders** (www.tandemciders.com; 2055 Setterbo Rd; ☉noon-6pm Mon-Sat, to 5pm Sun) pours delicious hard ciders in its small tasting room on the family farm.

Traverse City

Michigan's 'cherry capital' is the largest city in the northern half of the Lower Peninsula. It's got a bit of urban sprawl, but it's still a happenin' base from which to see the Sleeping Bear Dunes, Mission Peninsula wineries, U-pick orchards and other area attractions.

Road tripping out to the wineries is a must. Head north from Traverse City on Hwy 37 for 20 miles to the end of the grape- and cherry-planted Old Mission Peninsula. You'll be spoiled for choice: **Chateau Grand Traverse** (www.cgtwines.com; 6-wine tasting $3; ☉10am-7pm Mon-Sat, to 6pm Sun) and **Chateau Chantal** (www.chateauchantal.com; ☉11am-8pm Mon-Sat, to 6pm Sun) pour crowd-pleasing Chardonnay and Pinot Noir. **Peninsula Cellars** (www.peninsulacellars.com; 5-wine tasting $3; ☉10am-6pm), in an old schoolhouse, makes fine whites and is often less crowded. Whatever bottle you buy, take it out to Lighthouse Park beach, at the peninsula's tip, and enjoy it with the waves chilling your toes. The wineries stay open year-round, with reduced hours in winter.

The town goes Hollywood during the **Traverse City Film Festival** (www.traversecityfilmfest.org; ☉late Jul), when founder (and native Michigander) Michael Moore comes in and unspools a six-day slate of documentaries, international flicks and 'just great movies.'

Dozens of beaches, resorts, motels and water-sports operators line US 31 around Traverse City. Lodgings are often full – and more expensive – during weekends; check www.traversecity.com for listings. Most resorts overlooking the bay cost $175 to $275 per night. The Chantal and Grand Traverse wineries also double as B&Bs and fit into this price range.

Sugar Beach Resort (☎800-509-1995; www.tcbeaches.com; 1773 US 31 N; r $150-250; ❋☎☒) has decent-value rooms right on

the water. The motels on the other side of US 31 (away from the water) are more moderately priced, such as family-owned **Mitchell Creek Inn** (☎231-947-9330; www.mitchellcreek.com; 894 Munson Ave; r/cottages from $60/125; ☎), which is near the state park beach.

After a day of fun in the sun, refresh with sandwiches at gastronome favorite **Folgarelli's** (☎231-941-7651; www.folgarellis.net; 424 W Front St; sandwiches $8-11; ☉9:30am-6:30pm Mon-Fri, to 5:30pm Sat, 11am-4pm Sun) and Belgian and Michigan craft beers at **7 Monks Taproom** (www.7monkstap.com; 128 S Union St; ☉noon-midnight), which also shakes cocktails in its basement bar.

Charlevoix & Petoskey

These two towns hold several Hemingway sights. They're also where Michigan's upper-crusters maintain summer homes. The downtown areas of both places have gourmet restaurants and high-class shops, and the marinas are filled with yachts.

In Petoskey, **Stafford's Perry Hotel** (☎231-347-4000; www.staffords.com; Bay at Lewis St; r $149-269; ❋@☎) is a grand historic place in which to stay. **Petoskey State Park** (☎231-347-2311; 2475 Hwy 119; tent & RV sites $31-33) is north along Hwy 119 and has a beautiful beach. Look for indigenous Petoskey stones, which are honeycomb-patterned fragments of ancient coral. From here, Hwy 119 – aka the **Tunnel of Trees scenic route** – dips and curves through thick forest as it rolls north along a sublime bluff, en route to the Straits of Mackinac.

> ### ℹ️ HIKING-TRAIL MAPS
>
> Plot out your walk in the woods with **Michigan Trail Maps** (www.michigan-trailmaps.com), a free resource with more than 200 trail guides. Search by city, county or activity (birding, day hikes, backpacking etc), then download and print the high-quality maps as PDFs. It covers trails statewide.

Straits of Mackinac

This region, between the Upper and Lower Peninsulas, features a long history of forts and fudge shops. Car-free Mackinac Island is Michigan's premier tourist draw.

One of the most spectacular sights in the area is the 5-mile-long **Mackinac Bridge** (known locally as 'Big Mac'), which spans the Straits of Mackinac. The $4 toll is worth it as the views from the bridge, which include two Great Lakes, two peninsulas and hundreds of islands, are second to none in Michigan.

And remember: despite the spelling, it's pronounced *mac*-in-aw.

Mackinaw City

At the south end of Mackinac Bridge, bordering I-75, is touristy Mackinaw City. It serves mainly as a jump-off point to Mackinac Island, but it does have a couple of interesting sights.

Next to the bridge (its visitor center is actually beneath the bridge) is **Colonial Michilimackinac** (☎231-436-5564; www.mackinacparks.com; adult/child $11/6.50; ☺9am-7pm Jun-Aug, to 5pm May & Sep–mid-Oct), a National Historic Landmark that features a reconstructed stockade first built in 1715 by the French. Some 3 miles southeast of the city on US 23 is **Historic Mill Creek** (☎231-436-4226; www.mackinacparks.com; adult/child $8/5; ☺9am-6pm Jun-Aug, to 5pm May & Sep–mid-Oct), which has an 18th-century sawmill, historic displays and nature trails. A combination ticket for both sights, along with the nearby Old Mackinac Point Lighthouse, is available at a discount.

If you can't find lodging on Mackinac Island – which should be your first choice – motels line I-75 and US 23 in Mackinaw City. Most cost $100-plus per night. Try the **Clarion Hotel Beachfront** (☎231-436-5539; 905 S Huron Ave; r $110-170; ⓟ❄@🛜🏊).

St Ignace

At the north end of Mackinac Bridge is St Ignace, the other departure point for Mackinac Island and the second-oldest settlement in Michigan – Père Jacques Marquette founded a mission here in 1671. As soon as you've paid your bridge toll, you'll pass a huge **visitor center** (☎906-643-6979; I-75N; ☺9am-5:30pm daily Jun-Aug, Thu-Mon rest of year) which has racks of statewide information.

Mackinac Island

From either Mackinaw City or St Ignace you can catch a ferry to Mackinac Island. The island's location in the straits between Lake Michigan and Lake Huron made it a prized port in the North American fur trade, and a site the British and Americans battled over many times.

The most important date on this 3.8-sq-mile island was 1898 – the year cars were banned in order to encourage tourism. Today all travel is by horse or bicycle; even the police use bikes to patrol the town. The crowds of tourists – called Fudgies by the islanders – can be crushing at times, particularly during summer weekends. But when the last ferry leaves in the evening and clears out the day-trippers, Mackinac's real charm emerges and you drift back into another, slower era.

The **visitor center** (☎800-454-5227; www.mackinacisland.org; Main St; ☺9am-5pm May-Oct, reduced hours Nov-Apr), by the Arnold Line ferry dock, has maps for hiking and cycling. Eighty percent of the island is state parkland. Not much stays open between November and April.

👁 Sights & Activities

Edging the island's shoreline is Hwy 185, the only Michigan highway that doesn't permit cars. The best way to view the incredible scenery along this 8-mile road is by bicycle; bring your own or rent one in town for $8 per hour at one of the many businesses. You can loop around the flat road in about an hour.

The two best attractions – **Arch Rock** (a huge limestone arch that sits 150ft above Lake Huron) and **Fort Holmes** (the island's other fort) – are both free. You can also ride past the **Grand Hotel**, which boasts a porch stretching halfway to Detroit. Unfortunately, if you're not staying at the Grand (minimum $280 per night per person), it costs $10 to stroll its long porch. Best to admire from afar.

Fort Mackinac HISTORIC SITE
(☏ 906-847-3328; www.mackinacparks.com; adult/child $12/7; ⊙ 9:30am-6pm Jun-Aug, to 5pm May & Sep–mid-Oct; ⛟) Fort Mackinac sits atop limestone cliffs near downtown. Built by the British in 1780, it's one of the best-preserved military forts in the country. Costumed interpreters and cannon and rifle firings (every half-hour) entertain the kids. Stop into the tearoom for a bite and million-dollar view of downtown and the Straits of Mackinac from the outdoor tables.

The fort admission price also allows you entry to five other museums in town along Market St, including the Dr Beaumont Museum (where the doctor performed his famous digestive tract experiments) and Benjamin Blacksmith Shop.

Mackinac Art Museum MUSEUM
(7070 Main St; adult/child $5.50/4; ⊙ 10am-5:30pm Jun-Aug, to 4pm May & Sep–mid-Oct) It houses Native American and other arts. Admission is free with a Fort Mackinac ticket.

🛏 Sleeping

Rooms are booked far in advance during summer weekends; July to mid-August is peak season. The visitor center website has lodging contacts. Camping is not permitted anywhere on the island.

Most hotels and B&Bs charge at least $210 for two people. Exceptions (all are walkable from downtown) include the following.

Bogan Lane Inn B&B $$
(☏ 906-847-3439; www.boganlaneinn.com; Bogan Lane; r $95-135) Four rooms, shared bath.

Cloghaun B&B B&B $$
(☏ 906-847-3885; www.cloghaun.com; Market St; r $114-199; ⊙ mid-May–late Oct; ☎) Eleven rooms, some with shared bath.

Hart's B&B B&B $$
(☏ 906-847-3854; www.hartsmackinac.com; Market St; r $150-205; ⊙ mid-May–late Oct; ❄) Nine rooms, all with private bath.

🍴 Eating & Drinking

Fudge shops are the island's best-known eateries; resistance is futile when they use fans to blow the aroma out onto Huron St. Hamburger and sandwich shops abound downtown.

JL Beanery Coffeehouse CAFE $
(☏ 906-847-6533; Main St; mains $6-13; ⊙ 7am-4pm; ☎) Read the newspaper, sip a steaming cup of joe and gaze at the lake at this waterside cafe. It serves dandy breakfasts, sandwiches and soups.

HEMINGWAY'S HAUNTS

A number of writers have ties to northwest Michigan, but none are as famous as Ernest Hemingway, who spent the summers of his youth at his family's cottage on Walloon Lake. Hemingway buffs often tour the area to view the places that made their way into his writing. Key sites:

Horton Bay General Store (☏ 231-582-7827; www.hortonbaygeneralstore.com; 05115 Boyne City Rd; ⊙ 8am-2pm Sun-Thu, to 2pm & 5-9pm Fri & Sat, closed mid-Oct–mid-May) As you head north on US 31, past yacht-filled Charlevoix, look for Boyne City Rd veering off to the east. It skirts Lake Charlevoix and eventually arrives at Horton Bay. Hemingway fans will recognize the store, with its 'high false front' from his short story 'Up in Michigan.' The old-time shop now sells groceries, souvenirs, sandwiches and ice cream, plus wine and tapas on weekend nights (make reservations for the latter).

Little Traverse History Museum (☏ 231-347-2620; www.petoskeymuseum.org; 100 Depot Ct; admission $3; ⊙ 10am-4pm Mon-Sat late May–mid-Oct) Further up Hwy 31 in Petoskey, stop in to see the museum's Hemingway collection, including rare first-edition books that the author autographed for a friend when he visited in 1947.

City Park Grill (☏ 231-347-0101; www.cityparkgrill.com; 432 E Lake St; ⊙ 11:30am-10pm Sun-Thu, to 1:30am Fri & Sat) A few blocks from the museum, toss back a drink at this bar where Hemingway was a regular.

Tour Hemingway's Michigan (www.mihemingwaytour.org) Provides further information for self-guided jaunts.

Horn's Bar BURGERS, MEXICAN **$$**
(✆906-847-6154; www.hornsbar.com; Main St; mains $11-19; ⊙10am-2am) Horn's saloon serves American burgers and south-of-the-border fare, and there's live entertainment nightly.

Cawthorne's Village Inn AMERICAN **$$**
(✆906-847-3542; www.grandhotel.com; Hoban St; mains $19-24; ⊙11am-10pm) Planked whitefish, pan-fried perch and other fresh-from-the-lake fish, meat and pasta dishes stuff diners at this year-round local hangout with a bar and outdoor seating. Operated by the Grand Hotel.

Pink Pony BAR
(www.pinkponybar.com; Main St; ⊙11am-2pm Mon-Sat, from noon Sun) Prepare for gloriously weird decor, as if Barbie designed an English pub in shades of her favorite color. Yes it's touristy, but it's also heaps of fun with rock bands and patio views that'll wallop your eyeballs. Operated by the Chippewa Hotel.

❶ Getting There & Around

Three ferry companies – **Arnold Line** (✆800-542-8528; www.arnoldline.com), **Shepler's** (✆800-828-6157; www.sheplersferry.com) and **Star Line** (✆800-638-9892; www.mackinac-ferry.com) – operate out of Mackinaw City and St Ignace, and charge roughly the same rates: round-trip adult/child/bicycle $25/13/9. Book online and you'll save a few bucks. The ferries run several times daily from May through October. The trip takes about 20 minutes. (Arnold Line is a bit slower and consequently, a bit cheaper.) All of the companies have free parking lots to leave your car. Once on the island, horse-drawn cabs will take you anywhere, or rent a bicycle.

Upper Peninsula

Rugged and isolated, with hardwood forests blanketing 90% of its land, the Upper Peninsula (UP) is a Midwest highlight. Only 45 miles of interstate highway slice through the trees, punctuated by a handful of cities, of which Marquette (population 21,000) is the largest. Between the small towns lie miles of undeveloped shoreline on Lakes Huron, Michigan and Superior; scenic two-lane roads; and pasties, the local meat-and-vegetable pot pies brought over by Cornish miners 150 years ago.

You'll find it's a different world up north. Residents of the UP, aka 'Yoopers,' consider themselves distinct from the rest of the state – they've even threatened to secede in the past.

Sault Ste Marie & Tahquamenon Falls

Founded in 1668, Sault Ste Marie (Sault is pronounced 'soo') is Michigan's oldest city and the third oldest in the USA. The town is best known for its locks that raise and lower 1000ft-long freighters between the different lake levels. **Soo Locks Park & Visitor Center** (312 W Portage Ave; ⊙9am-9pm mid-May–mid-Oct) FREE is on Portage Ave downtown (take exit 394 off I-75 and go left). It features displays, videos and observation decks from which you can watch the boats leap 21ft from Lake Superior to Lake Huron. Pubs and cafes line Portage Ave. The **Sault CVB** (www.saultstemarie.com) has the lowdown.

An hour's drive west of Sault Ste Marie, via Hwy 28 and Hwy 123, is eastern UP's top attraction: lovely **Tahquamenon Falls**, with tea-colored waters tinted by upstream hemlock leaves. The Upper Falls in **Tahquamenon Falls State Park** (✆906-492-3415; per vehicle $9), 200ft across with a 50ft drop, wow onlookers – including Henry Wadsworth Longfellow, who mentioned them in his *Song of Hiawatha*. The Lower Falls are a series of small cascades that swirl around an island; many visitors rent a rowboat and paddle out to it. The large state park also has camping (tent and RV sites $17 to $25), great hiking and – bonus – a brewpub near the park entrance.

North of the park, beyond the little town of Paradise, is the fascinating **Great Lakes Shipwreck Museum** (✆888-492-3747; www.shipwreckmuseum.com; 18335 N Whitefish Point Rd; adult/child $13/9; ⊙10am-6pm May–late Oct), where the intriguing displays include items trawled up from sunken ships. Dozens of vessels – including the *Edmund Fitzgerald* that Gordon Lightfoot crooned about – have sunk in the area's congested sea lanes and storm-tossed weather, earning it such nicknames as the 'Shipwreck Coast' and 'Graveyard of the Great Lakes.' The grounds also include a lighthouse President Lincoln commissioned and a bird observatory that 300 species fly by. To have the foggy place to yourself, spend the night at **Whitefish Point Light Station B&B** (✆888-492-3747; r $150; ⊙late Apr–early Nov), which offers five rooms in the old Coast Guard crew quarters on-site.

Pictured Rocks National Lakeshore

Stretching along prime Lake Superior real estate, **Pictured Rocks National Lakeshore** (www.nps.gov/piro) is a series of wild cliffs and caves where blue and green minerals have streaked the red and yellow sandstone into a kaleidoscope of color. Rte 58 (Alger County Rd) spans the park for 52 slow miles from **Grand Marais** in the east to **Munising** in the west. Top sights (from east to west) include **Au Sable Point Lighthouse** (reached via a 3-mile round-trip walk beside shipwreck skeletons), agate-strewn **Twelvemile Beach**, hike-rich **Chapel Falls** and view-worthy **Miners Castle Overlook**.

Several boat tours launch from Munising. **Pictured Rock Cruises** (☑906-387-2379; www.picturedrocks.com; 100 W City Park Dr; 2½hr tours adult/child $37/10; ☉mid-May–mid-Oct) departs from the city pier downtown and glides along the shore to Miners Castle. **Shipwreck Tours** (☑906-387-4477; www.shipwrecktours.com; 1204 Commercial St; 2hr tours adult/child $32/12; ☉late May–mid-Oct) sails in glass-bottom boats to see sunken schooners.

Grand Island (www.grandislandup.com), part of Hiawatha National Forest, is also a quick jaunt from Munising. Hop aboard the **Grand Island Ferry** (☑906-387-3503; round-trip adult/child $15/10; ☉late May–mid-Oct) to get there and rent a mountain bike ($30 per day) to zip around. There's also a three-hour bus tour (adult/child $15/5). The ferry dock is on Hwy 28, which is about 4 miles west of Munising.

Munising has lots of motels, such as tidy **Alger Falls Motel** (☑906-387-3536; www.algerfallsmotel.com; E9427 Hwy 28; r $70-105; ❄☎). **Falling Rock Cafe & Bookstore** (☑906-387-3008; www.fallingrockcafe.com; 104 E Munising Ave; mains $5-10; ☉9am-8pm Sun-Fri, to 10pm Sat; ☎) provides sandwiches and live music.

Staying in wee Grand Marais, on the park's east side, is also recommended. Turn in at **Hilltop Cabins and Motel** (☑906-494-2331; www.hilltopcabins.net; N14176 Ellen St; r & cabins $85-185; ☎) after a meal of whitefish sandwiches and brewskis at woodsy **Lake Superior Brewing Company** (☑906-494-2337; N14283 Lake Ave; mains $9-19; ☉noon-11pm).

Marquette

From Munising, Hwy 28 heads west and hugs Lake Superior. This beautiful stretch of

DA YOOPERS TOURIST TRAP

Behold Big Gus, the world's largest chainsaw. And Big Ernie, the world's largest rifle. Kitsch runs rampant at **Da Yoopers Tourist Trap and Museum** (☑906-485-5595; www.dayoopers.com; ☉9am-8pm Mon-Sat, to 6pm Sun) FREE, 15 miles west of Marquette on Hwy 28/41, past Ishpeming. Browse the store for only-in-the-UP gifts like a polyester moose tie or beer-can wind chimes.

GREAT LAKES UPPER PENINSULA

highway has lots of beaches, roadside parks and rest areas where you can pull over and enjoy the scenery. Within 45 miles you'll reach outdoorsy, oft-snowy Marquette.

Stop at the log-lodge **visitor center** (2201 US 41; ☉9am-5:30pm) as you enter the city for brochures on local hiking trails and waterfalls.

The easy **Sugarloaf Mountain Trail** and the harder, wilderness-like **Hogsback Mountain Trail** offer panoramic views. Both are reached from County Rd 550, just north of Marquette. In the city, the high bluffs of **Presque Isle Park** make a great place to catch the sunset. The **Noquemanon Trail Network** (www.noquetrails.org) is highly recommended for mountain biking and cross-country skiing. Kayaking is awesome in the area; **Down Wind Sports** (www.downwindsports.com; 514 N Third St; ☉10am-7pm Mon-Fri, to 5pm Sat, 11am-3pm Sun) has the lowdown on it, as well as fly fishing, surfing, ice climbing and other adventures.

Marquette is the perfect place to stay put for a few days to explore the central UP. Budgeteers can bunk at **Value Host Motor Inn** (☑906-225-5000; 1101 US 41 W; r $65-75; ❄☎) a few miles west of town. Downtown's **Landmark Inn** (☑906-228-2580; www.thelandmarkinn.com; 230 N Front St; r $179-229; ❄☎) fills a historic lakefront building and has a couple of resident ghosts. Check www.travelmarquettemichigan.com for more lodgings.

Sample the local meat-and-veggie pie specialty at **Jean Kay's Pasties & Subs** (www.jeankayspasties.com; 1635 Presque Isle Ave; items $5-7.50; ☉11am-9pm Mon-Fri, to 8pm Sat & Sun). In a Quonset hut at Main St's foot, **Thill's Fish House** (☑906-226-9851; 250 E Main St; items $4-9; ☉8am-5:30pm Mon-Fri, 9am-4pm Sat) is Marquette's last commercial fishing operation, and it hauls in fat catches daily; try the smoked whitefish sausage. Hop-heads and mountain bikers hang out at **Blackrocks Brewery** (www.blackrocksbrewery.com; 424 N Third St; ⊙4-11pm Mon-Thu, from noon Fri & Sun), set in a cool refurbished house downtown.

Isle Royale National Park

Totally free of vehicles and roads, **Isle Royale National Park** (www.nps.gov/isro; fee per day $4; ⊙mid-May–Oct), a 210-sq-mile island in Lake Superior, is certainly the place to go for peace and quiet. It gets fewer visitors in a year than Yellowstone National Park gets in a day, which means the 1200 moose creeping through the forest are all yours.

The island is laced with 165 miles of hiking trails that connect dozens of campgrounds along Superior and inland lakes. You must be totally prepared for this wilderness adventure, with a tent, camping stove, sleeping bags, food and water filter. Otherwise, be a softie and bunk at the **Rock Harbor Lodge** (☑906-337-4993; www.isleroyaleresort.com; r & cottages $224-256; ⊙late May-early Sep).

From the dock outside the **park headquarters** (800 E Lakeshore Dr) in Houghton, the **Ranger III** (☑906-482-0984) departs at 9am on Tuesday and Friday for the six-hour boat trip (round-trip adult/child $126/10) to Rock Harbor, at the east end of the island. **Isle Royale Seaplanes** (☑877-359-4753; www.isleroyaleseaplanes.com) offer a quicker trip, flying from Houghton County Airport to Rock Harbor in 30 minutes (round-trip $310). Or head 50 miles up the Keweenaw Peninsula to Copper Harbor (a beautiful drive) and jump on the **Isle Royale Queen** (☑906-289-4437; www.isleroyale.com) for the 8am three-hour crossing (round-trip adult/child $130/65). It usually runs daily during peak season from late July to mid-August. Bringing a kayak or canoe on the ferries costs an additional $50 round-trip; ensure you make reservations well in advance. You can also access Isle Royale from Grand Portage, MN.

Porcupine Mountains Wilderness State Park

Michigan's largest state park, with 90 miles of trails, is another UP winner, and it's a heck of a lot easier to reach than Isle Royale. 'The Porkies,' as they're called, are so rugged that loggers bypassed most of the range in the early 19th century, leaving the park with the largest tract of virgin forest between the Rocky Mountains and Adirondacks.

From Silver City, head west on Hwy 107 to reach the **Porcupine Mountains Visitor Center** (☑906-885-5275; www.michigan.gov/porkiesvc; 412 S Boundary Rd; ⊙10am-6pm mid-May–mid-Oct), where you buy vehicle entry permits ($9/31 per day/year) and backcountry permits (one to four people per night $15). Continue to the end of Hwy 107 and climb 300ft for the stunning view of **Lake of the Clouds**.

Winter is also a busy time at the Porkies, with downhill skiing (a 787ft vertical drop) and 26 miles of cross-country trails on offer; check with the **ski area** (☑906-885-5209; www.porkiesfun.com) for conditions and costs.

The park rents **rustic cabins** (☑906-885-5275; www.mi.gov/porkies; cabins $65) perfect for wilderness adventurers, as you have to hike in 1 to 4 miles, boil your own water and use a privy. **Sunshine Motel & Cabins** (☑906-884-2187; www.ontonagonmi.com; 24077 Hwy 64; r $60, cabins $68-120; 🖥🐾), 3 miles west of Ontonagon, provides another good base.

WISCONSIN

Wisconsin is cheesy and proud of it. The state pumps out 2.5 billion pounds of cheddar, Gouda and other smelly goodness – a quarter of America's hunks – from its cow-speckled farmland per year. Local license plates read 'The Dairy State' with udder dignity. Folks here even refer to themselves as 'cheeseheads' and emphasize it by wearing novelty foam rubber cheese-wedge hats for special occasions (most notably during Green Bay Packers football games).

So embrace the cheese thing, because there's a good chance you'll be here for a while. Wisconsin has heaps to offer: exploring the craggy cliffs and lighthouses of Door County, kayaking through sea caves at Apostle Islands National Lakeshore, cow chip throwing along US 12 and soaking up beer, art and festivals in Milwaukee and Madison.

❶ Information

Travel Green Wisconsin (www.travelgreenwisconsin.com) Certifies businesses as ecofriendly by grading them on waste reduction, energy efficiency and seven other categories.

Wisconsin B&B Association (www.wbba.org)

Wisconsin Department of Tourism (☑ 800-432-8747; www.travelwisconsin.com) Produces loads of free guides on subjects like bird-watching, biking, golf and rustic roads; also a free app.

Wisconsin Highway Conditions (☑ 511; www.511wi.gov)

Wisconsin Milk Marketing Board (www.eatwisconsincheese.com) Provides a free state-wide map of cheesemakers titled *A Traveler's Guide to America's Dairyland.*

Wisconsin State Park Information (☑ 608-266-2181; www.wiparks.net) Park entry requires a vehicle permit (per day/year $10/35). Campsites cost from $14 to $25; reservations (☑ 888-947-2757; www.wisconsinstateparks.reserveamerica.com; fee $10) accepted.

Milwaukee

Here's the thing about Milwaukee: it's cool, but for some reason everyone refuses to admit it. Yes, the reputation lingers as a working man's town of brewskis, bowling alleys and polka halls. But attractions like the Calatrava-designed art museum, bad-ass Harley-Davidson Museum and stylish eating and shopping 'hoods have turned Wisconsin's largest city into a surprisingly groovy place. In summertime, festivals let loose with revelry by the lake almost every weekend. And where else on the planet will you see racing sausages?

History

Milwaukee was first settled by Germans in the 1840s. Many started small breweries, but a few decades later the introduction of bulk brewing technology turned beer production into a major industry here. Milwaukee earned its 'Brew City' and 'Nation's Watering Hole' nicknames in the 1880s when Pabst, Schlitz, Blatz, Miller and 80 other breweries made suds here. Today, only Miller remains of the big brewers, though microbreweries are making a comeback.

⊙ Sights & Activities

Lake Michigan sits to the east of the city, and is rimmed by parkland. The Riverwalk path runs along both sides of the Milwaukee River downtown.

★ Harley-Davidson Museum   MUSEUM
(☑ 877-436-8738; www.h-dmuseum.com; 400 W Canal St; adult/child $20/10; ☉ 9am-6pm Fri-Wed, to 8pm Thu May-Sep, from 10am Oct-Apr) Hundreds of motorcycles show the styles through the decades, including the flashy rides of

WISCONSIN FACTS

Nicknames Badger State, America's Dairyland

Population 5.8 million

Area 65,500 sq miles

Capital city Madison (population 243,000)

Other cities Milwaukee (population 599,000)

Sales tax 5%

Birthplace of Author Laura Ingalls Wilder (1867–1957), architect Frank Lloyd Wright (1867–1959), painter Georgia O'Keeffe (1887–1986), actor Orson Welles (1915–85), guitar maker Les Paul (1915–2009)

Home of 'Cheesehead' Packer fans, dairy farms, water parks

Politics Leans Democratic

Famous for Breweries, artisanal cheese, first state to legislate gay rights

Official dance Polka

Driving distances Milwaukee to Minneapolis 336 miles, Milwaukee to Madison 80 miles

---

Elvis and Evel Knievel. You can sit in the saddle of various bikes (on the bottom floor, in the Experience Gallery) and take badass photos. Even nonbikers will enjoy the interactive exhibits and tough, leather-clad crowds.

It all started in 1903, when Milwaukee schoolmates William Harley and Arthur Davidson built and sold their first motorcycle. A century later the big bikes are a symbol of American manufacturing pride. The museum is located in a sprawling industrial building just south of downtown.

Harley-Davidson Plant   TOUR
(☑ 877-883-1450; www.harley-davidson.com/experience; W156 N9000 Pilgrim Rd; 30min tours free; ☉ 9am-2pm Mon) Hog-heads can get a fix at the plant where engines are built, in suburban Menomonee Falls. In addition to Monday's free tour, longer tours take place on Wednesday, Thursday and Friday in summer, but only as part of a package deal you buy from the museum (per person $46, including tour, museum admission, and transport between the two venues).

Milwaukee Art Museum
MUSEUM

(☑ 414-224-3200; www.mam.org; 700 N Art Museum Dr; adult/child $15/12; ⊗ 10am-5pm, to 8pm Thu, closed Mon Sep-May) You have to see this lakeside institution, which features a stunning winglike addition by Santiago Calatrava. It soars open and closed every day at 10am, noon and 5pm (8pm on Thursday), which is wild to watch (head to the suspension bridge outside for the best view). There are fabulous folk and outsider art galleries, and a sizeable collection of Georgia O'Keeffe paintings. A 2015 renovation added photography and new-media galleries to the trove.

Miller Brewing Company
BREWERY

(☑ 414-931-2337; www.millercoors.com/milwaukee-brewery-tour; 4251 W State St; ⊗ 10:30am-4:30pm Mon-Sat, to 3:30pm Sun Jun-Aug, to 3:30pm Mon-Sat only Sep-May) FREE Pabst and Schlitz have moved on, but Miller preserves Milwaukee's beer legacy. Join the legions lined up for the free tours. Though the mass-produced beer may not be your favorite, the factory impresses with its sheer scale: you'll visit the packaging plant where 2000 cans are filled each minute, and the warehouse where a half-million cases await shipment. And then there's the generous tasting session at the tour's end, where you can down three full-size samples. Don't forget your ID.

Lakefront Brewery
BREWERY

(☑ 414-372-8800; www.lakefrontbrewery.com; 1872 N Commerce St; 1hr tours $8; ⊗ 11am-8pm Mon-Thu, to 9pm Fri, 9am-9pm Sat, 10am-5pm Sun) Well-loved Lakefront Brewery, across the river from Brady St, has afternoon tours, but the swellest time to visit is on Friday nights when there's a fish fry, 16 beers to try and a polka band letting loose. Tour times vary

---

AMERICA'S BOWLING CAPITAL

You're in Milwaukee, so you probably should just do it: bowl. The city once had more than 200 bowling alleys, and many retro lanes still hide in timeworn dives. To get your game on try **Landmark Lanes** (www.landmarklanes.com; 2220 N Farwell Ave; per game $3.50-4; ⊗ 5pm-midnight Mon-Thu, noon-1am Fri & Sat, to midnight Sun; 🛜), offering 16 beat-up alleys in the historic 1927 Oriental Theater. An arcade, three bars and butt-cheap beer round out the atmosphere.

---

throughout the week, but there's usually at least a 2pm and 3pm walk-through.

Discovery World at Pier Wisconsin
MUSEUM

(☑ 414-765-9966; www.discoveryworld.org; 500 N Harbor Dr; adult/child $18/14; ⊗ 9am-4pm Mon-Fri, 10am-5pm Sat & Sun, closed Mon Sep-Mar; ♿) The city's lakefront science and technology museum is primarily a kid-pleaser, with freshwater and saltwater aquariums (where you can touch sharks and sturgeon) and a dockside, triple-masted Great Lakes schooner to ogle (two-hour sailing tours per person $40). Adults will appreciate the Les Paul exhibit, showcasing the Wisconsin native's pioneering guitars and sound equipment.

Lakefront Park
PARK

The parkland edging Lake Michigan is prime for walking, cycling and inline skating. Also here is Bradford Beach, which is good for swimming and lounging.

✦ Festivals & Events

Summerfest
MUSIC

(www.summerfest.com; day pass $19; ⊗ late Jun-early Jul) It's dubbed 'the world's largest music festival,' and indeed hundreds of rock, blues, jazz, country and alternative bands swarm its 10 stages over 11 days. The scene totally rocks; it is held at downtown's lakefront festival grounds. The headline concerts cost extra.

Other popular parties, held downtown on various summer weekends, include **PrideFest** (www.pridefest.com; ⊗ mid-Jun), **Polish Fest** (www.polishfest.org; ⊗ mid-Jun), **German Fest** (www.germanfest.com; ⊗ late Jul) and **Irish Fest** (www.irishfest.com; ⊗ mid-Aug).

🛏 Sleeping

Rates in this section are for summer, the peak season, when you should book in advance. Tax (15.1%) is not included. For cheap chain lodging, try Howell Ave, south near the airport.

County Clare Irish Inn
INN $$

(☑ 414-272-5273; www.countyclare-inn.com; 1234 N Astor St; r $129-159; P ✱ 🛜) A winner near the lakefront. Rooms have that snug Irish-cottage feel, with four-post beds, white wainscot walls and whirlpool baths. There's free parking, free breakfast and an on-site Guinness-pouring pub, of course.

★ **Brewhouse Inn & Suites**　　HOTEL **$$**
(☑ 414-810-3350; www.brewhousesuites.com; 1215 N 10th St; r $199-249; P ✳ @ 🛜) This 90-room hotel opened in 2013 in the exquisitely renovated old Pabst Brewery complex. Each of the large chambers has steampunk decor, a kitchenette and free wi-fi. Continental breakfast is included. It's at downtown's far west edge, about a half-mile walk from sausagey Old World 3rd St and a good 2 miles from the festival grounds. Parking costs $26.

Iron Horse Hotel　　HOTEL **$$$**
(☑ 888-543-4766; www.theironhorsehotel.com; 500 W Florida St; r $220-320; P ✳ 🛜) This boutique hotel near the Harley museum is geared toward motorcycle enthusiasts, with covered parking for bikes. Most of the loft-style rooms retain the post-and-beam, exposed-brick interior of what was once a bedding factory. Parking costs $30.

✖ Eating

Good places to scope for eats include Germanic Old World 3rd St downtown; hip, multiethnic Brady St by its intersection with N Farwell Ave; and the gastropub-filled Third Ward, anchored along N Milwaukee St south of I-94.

★ **Comet Cafe**　　AMERICAN **$**
(☑ 414-273-7677; www.thecometcafe.com; 1947 N Farwell Ave; mains $8-13; ⊙ 10am-10pm Mon-Fri, from 9am Sat & Sun; ✎) Students, young families, older couples and bearded, tattooed types pile in to the rock-and-roll Comet for gravy-smothered meatloaf, mac 'n' cheese, vegan gyros and hangover brunch dishes. It's a craft-beer-pouring bar on one side, and retro-boothed diner on the other. Be sure to try one of the giant cupcakes for dessert.

Milwaukee Public Market　　MARKET **$**
(☑ 414-336-1111; www.milwaukeepublicmarket.org; 400 N Water St; ⊙ 10am-8pm Mon-Fri, 8am-7pm Sat, 10am-6pm Sun; 🛜) Located in the Third Ward, it stocks mostly prepared foods – cheese, chocolate, beer, tacos, frozen custard. Take them upstairs where there are tables, free wi-fi and $1 used books.

Leon's　　ICE CREAM **$**
(☑ 414-383-1784; www.leonsfrozencustard.us; 3131 S 27th St; items $1.50-4; ⊙ 11am-midnight) This 1950s-era, neon-lit drive-in specializes in frozen custard, a local concoction that's like ice cream but smoother and richer. Cash only.

THE BRONZE FONZ

Rumor has it the **Bronze Fonz** (east side of Riverwalk), just south of Wells St downtown, is the most photographed sight in Milwaukee. The Fonz, aka Arthur Fonzarelli, was a character from the 1970s TV show *Happy Days*, which was set in the city. What do you think – do the blue pants get an 'Aaay' or 'Whoa!'?

Ardent　　MODERN AMERICAN **$$$**
(☑ 414-897-7022; www.ardentmke.com; 1751 N Farwell St; small plates $11-16; ⊙ 6-10pm Wed-Sat) Milwaukee's foodies get weak-kneed when they sniff the Beard-nominated chef's ever-changing, farm-to-table dishes. It takes at least a couple of the smallish plates to make a meal, and dinner becomes a lingering affair in the tiny glowing room. Make reservations. After 11:30pm on Friday and Saturday, the restaurant reopens as a ramen noodle purveyor, with lines around the block.

🍷 Drinking & Entertainment

Bars

Milwaukee has the second most bars per capita in the country (a hair behind New Orleans). Several pour around N Water and E State Sts downtown and in the Third Ward. Drinkeries stay open to 2am.

Best Place　　BAR
(www.bestplacemilwaukee.com; 901 W Junau Ave; ⊙ noon-6pm Mon & Wed, to 10pm Thu, 10:30am-10pm Fri & Sat, to 6pm Sun) Join the locals knocking back beers and massive whiskey pours at this small tavern in the former Pabst Brewery headquarters. A fireplace warms the cozy, dark-wood room; original murals depicting Pabst's history adorn the walls. Staff give daily tours ($8, including a 16oz Pabst or Schlitz tap brew) that explore the building.

Uber Tap Room　　BAR
(www.ubertaproom.com; 1048 N Old 3rd St; ⊙ 11am-8pm Sun-Wed, to 10pm Thu, to 11pm Fri & Sat) It's touristy, in the thick of Old World 3rd St and attached to the Wisconsin Cheese Mart, but it's a great place to sample local fare. Thirty Wisconsin beers flow from the taps, and cheese from the state's dairy bounty accompanies. Themed plates (spicy cheeses, stinky cheeses etc) cost $11 to $14.

Palm Tavern
BAR

(2989 S Kinnickinnic Ave; ⏰5pm-2am Mon-Sat, from 7pm Sun) Located in the fresh south-side neighborhood of Bay View, this warm, jazzy little bar has a mammoth selection of beer (heavy on the Belgians) and single-malt Scotches.

Kochanski's Concertina Beer Hall
BAR

(www.beer-hall.com; 1920 S 37th St; ⏰6pm-2am Wed-Sat, from 1pm Sun; 🔊) Live polka and rockabilly music rules at kitschy Kochanski's, with beers from Schlitz to Polish drafts to Wisconsin craft labels. It's 5 miles south-west of downtown.

Sports

Miller Park
BASEBALL

(www.brewers.com; 1 Brewers Way) The Brewers play baseball at fab Miller Park, which has a retractable roof, real grass and racing sausages. It's located near S 46th St.

Bradley Center
BASKETBALL

(www.nba.com/bucks; 1001 N 4th St) The NBA's Milwaukee Bucks dunk here.

ℹ Information

The East Side neighborhood near the University of Wisconsin-Milwaukee has several coffee shops with free wi-fi.

Froedtert Hospital (☎414-805-3000; 9200 W Wisconsin Ave)

Milwaukee Convention & Visitors Bureau (☎800-554-1448; www.visitmilwaukee.org) Tourist information.

Milwaukee Journal Sentinel (www.jsonline.com) The city's daily newspaper.

On Milwaukee (www.onmilwaukee.com) Online source for restaurant and entertainment news.

Quest (www.quest-online.com) GLBT entertainment magazine.

DON'T MISS

RACING SAUSAGES

It's common to see strange things after too many stadium beers. But a group of giant sausages sprinting around the perimeter of Milwaukee's Miller Park – is that for *real*? It is if it's the middle of the 6th inning. That's when the famous 'Racing Sausages' (actually five people in costumes) waddle onto the field to give the fans a thrill. If you don't know your encased meats, that's Brat, Polish, Italian, Hot Dog and Chorizo vying for supremacy.

Shepherd Express (www.expressmilwaukee.com) Free alternative weekly paper.

ℹ Getting There & Around

General Mitchell International Airport (MKE; www.mitchellairport.com) is 8 miles south of downtown. Take public bus 80 ($2.25) or a cab ($33).

The **Lake Express ferry** (☎866-914-1010; www.lake-express.com; one way per adult/child/car from $86.50/30/91; ⏰May-Oct) sails from downtown (the terminal is located a few miles south of the city center) to Muskegon, MI, providing easy access to Michigan's beach-lined Gold Coast.

Badger Bus (☎414-276-7490; www.badgerbus.com; 635 N James Lovell St) goes to Madison ($20, two hours). **Greyhound** (☎414-272-2156; 433 W St Paul Ave) and **Megabus** (www.megabus.com/us; 433 St Paul Ave) run frequent buses to Chicago (two hours) and Minneapolis (6½ to seven hours). Both use the same location; Megabus is often cheaper.

Amtrak (☎414-271-0840; www.amtrakhiawatha.com; 433 W St Paul Ave) runs the *Hiawatha* train seven times a day to/from Chicago ($24, 1½ hours); catch it downtown (where it shares the station with Greyhound/Megabus) or at the airport.

The **Milwaukee County Transit System** (www.ridemcts.com; fares $2.25) provides the local bus service. Bus 31 goes to Miller Brewery; bus 90 goes to Miller Park.

Bublr Bikes (www.bublrbikes.com; per 30min ride $3) is Milwaukee's fledgling bike-share program, with 11 or so stations downtown (including at the train/bus depot and Public Market).

For taxi service, try phoning **Yellow Cab** (☎414-271-1800).

Madison

Madison reaps a lot of kudos – most walkable city, best road-biking city, most vegetarian-friendly, gay-friendly, environmentally friendly and just plain all-round friendliest city in the USA. Ensconced on a narrow isthmus between Mendota and Monona Lakes, it's a pretty combination of small, grassy state capital and liberal, bookish college town. An impressive foodie/locavore scene has been cooking here for years.

◉ Sights & Activities

State St runs from the capitol west to the University of Wisconsin. The pedestrian-only avenue is lined with free-trade coffee shops, parked bicycles and incense-wafting stores selling hacky sacks and flowy Indian skirts.

Chazen Museum of Art MUSEUM
(www.chazen.wisc.edu; 750 University Ave; ⊘9am-5pm Tue, Wed & Fri, to 9pm Thu, 11am-5pm Sat & Sun) FREE The university's art museum is huge and fabulous, fresh off an expansion and way beyond the norm for a campus collection. The 3rd floor holds most of the genre-spanning trove: everything from the old Dutch masters to Qing Dynasty porcelain vases, Picasso sculptures and Andy Warhol pop art. Free chamber-music concerts and art-house films take place on Sundays from September to mid-May.

Monona Terrace ARCHITECTURE
(www.mononaterrace.com; 1 John Nolen Dr; ⊘8am-5pm) Frank Lloyd Wright designed the cool, white semicircular structure in 1938, though it wasn't completed until 1997. The one-hour tours ($5) explain why; they're offered daily at 1pm May through October (Friday through Monday only the rest of the year). The building serves as a community center, offering free lunchtime yoga classes and evening concerts; check the program schedule online. The rooftop garden and cafe offer sweeping lake views.

Dane County Farmers Market MARKET
(www.dcfm.org; Capitol Sq; ⊘6am-2pm Sat late Apr-early Nov) 🍃 On Saturdays, a food bazaar takes over Capitol Sq. It's one of the nation's most expansive markets, famed for its artisanal cheeses and breads. In winter it moves indoors to varying locations.

State Capitol BUILDING
(☑608-266-0382; 2 E Main St; ⊘8am-6pm Mon-Fri, to 4pm Sat & Sun) FREE The X-shaped capitol is the largest outside Washington, DC, and marks the heart of downtown. Tours are available on the hour most days, or you can go up to the observation deck on your own for a view (summer only).

Museum of Contemporary Art MUSEUM
(☑608-257-0158; www.mmoca.org; 227 State St; ⊘noon-5pm Tue-Thu, to 8pm Fri, 10am-8pm Sat, noon-5pm Sun) FREE It's worth popping into the angular glass building to see what's showing. Diego Rivera? Claes Oldenburg? Exhibits change every three months or so. The museum connects to the Overture Center for the Arts (www.overturecenter.org; 201 State St), home to jazz, opera, dance and other performing arts.

TWO-WHEELING WISCONSIN

Wisconsin has converted an impressive number of abandoned railroad lines into paved, bike-only paths. They go up hills, through old tunnels, over bridges and alongside pastures. Wherever you are in the state, there's likely a sweet ride nearby; check the **Wisconsin Biking Guide** (downloadable at www.travel-wisconsin.com, under Travel Resources, then Order Guides). The **400 State Trail** (www.400statetrail.org) and **Elroy-Sparta Trail** (www.elroy-sparta-trail.com) top the list.

Bike rentals are available in gateway towns, and you can buy trail passes ($4/20 per day/year) at area businesses or trailhead drop-boxes.

Arboretum GARDENS
(☑608-263-7888; http://uwarboretum.org; 1207 Seminole Hwy; ⊘7am-10pm) FREE The campus' 1260-acre arboretum is dense with lilac and 20 miles of trails.

Machinery Row CYCLING
(☑608-442-5974; www.machineryrowbicycles.com; 601 Williamson St; rental per day $30; ⊘10am-8pm Mon-Fri, 9am-7pm Sat, 10am-6pm Sun) It'd be a shame to leave town without taking advantage of the city's 120 miles of bike trails. Get wheels and maps at this shop, located by various trailheads. Rentals are per 24 hours only.

✦ Festivals & Events

World's Largest Brat Fest FOOD
(www.bratfest.com; ⊘late May) FREE More than 209,000 bratwursts go down the hatch; carnival rides and bands provide the backdrop.

Great Taste of the Midwest Beer Festival BEER
(www.greattaste.org; tickets $60; ⊘early Aug) Tickets sell out fast for this festival where more than 100 craft brewers pour their elixirs.

🛏 Sleeping

Moderately priced motels can be found off I-90/I-94 (about 6 miles from the town center), off Hwy 12/18 and also along Washington Ave.

HI Madison Hostel HOSTEL $
(☑608-441-0144; www.hiusa.org/madison; 141 S Butler St; dm $25 30, r from $60; P@⊛) The

brightly painted, 33-bed brick house is located on a quiet street a short walk from the State Capitol. The dorms are gender segregated; linens are free. There's a kitchen and common room with DVDs. Parking is $7.

★ Arbor House
B&B $$

(☑ 608-238-2981; www.arbor-house.com; 3402 Monroe St; r $140-230; 🛜) 🚲 Arbor House was an old tavern back in the mid-1800s. Now it's a wind-powered, vegetarian-breakfast-serving B&B equipped with energy-efficient appliances. It's located about 3 miles southwest of the State Capitol but it's accessible to public transportation. The owners will lend you mountain bikes, too.

Graduate Madison
BOUTIQUE HOTEL $$

(☑ 608-257-4391; www.graduatemadison.com; 601 Langdon St; r $149-209; P ❄ 🛜 🛁) A block from campus and right off State St's action, this 72-room newbie (opened in spring 2015) wafts a hip academic vibe with its mod-meets-plaid decor and book-themed artwork. Rooms are on the small side and can be a bit noisy, but the location rocks.

🍴 Eating & Drinking

A global smorgasbord of restaurants peppers State St amid the pizza, sandwich and cheap-beer joints; many places have inviting patios. Cruising Williamson ('Willy') St turns up cafes, dumpling bars and Lao and Thai joints. Bars stay open to 2am. **Isthmus** (www.thedailypage.com) is the free entertainment paper.

Short Stack Eats
BREAKFAST $

(www.shortstackeats.com; 301 W Johnson St; mains $7-13; ⊙ 24hr Thu-Sun) 🚲 It's all breakfast all day and all night at Short Stack. Order at the counter, then hopefully find a free table amid the cutesy, mismatched decor. Staff use old license plates as table markers to bring your locally sourced sweet potato pancakes, egg-and-bacon-filled breakfast sandwiches and enormous, spicy Bloody Marys.

Himal Chuli
ASIAN $

(☑ 608-251-9225; 318 State St; mains $8-15; ⊙ 11am-9pm Mon-Sat, noon-8pm Sun; 🌱) Cheerful and cozy Himal Chuli serves up homemade Nepalese fare, including lots of vegetarian dishes.

Food Trucks
INTERNATIONAL $

(mains $2-8; 🌱) Madison's fleet impresses. The more traditional ones, serving barbe-cue, burritos, Southwestern-style fare and Chinese food, ring the Capitol. Trucks ladling out more adventurous dishes – East African, Jamaican, Indonesian, vegan – huddle at the Library Mall (aka at foot of State St on campus).

★ The Old Fashioned
AMERICAN $$

(☑ 608-310-4545; www.theoldfashioned.com; 23 N Pinckney St; mains $9-19; ⊙ 7:30am-10:30pm Mon & Tue, to 2am Wed-Fri, 9am-2am Sat, to 10pm Sun) With its dark, woodsy decor, the Old Fashioned evokes a supper club, a type of retro eatery common in Wisconsin. The menu is all local specialties, including walleye, cheese soup and sausages. It's hard to choose among the 150 types of state-brewed suds in bottles, so opt for a sampler (four or eight little glasses) from the 30 Wisconsin tap beers.

Graze
AMERICAN $$

(☑ 608-251-2700; www.grazemadison.com; 1 S Pinckney St; mains $14-22; ⊙ 11am-10pm Mon-Thu, to 11pm Fri, 9:30am-11pm Sat, to 3pm Sun) 🌱 Set in a glassy building with floor-to-ceiling windows and Capitol views, this green, cool-cat gastropub dishes up comfort foods such as fried chicken and waffles, mussels and *frites*, and burgers. Lunch piles up fat sandwiches with vodka-battered cheese curds.

L'Etoile
MODERN AMERICAN $$$

(☑ 608-251-0500; www.letoile-restaurant.com; 1 S Pinckney St; mains $36-44; ⊙ 5:30-11pm Mon-Fri, from 5pm Sat) 🌱 L'Etoile started doing the farm-to-table thing more than three decades ago. It's still the best in the biz, offering creative meat, fish and vegetable dishes, all sourced locally and served in a casually elegant room. Reserve in advance. The gastropub Graze shares the glimmering building.

Memorial Union
PUB

(www.union.wisc.edu/venue-muterrace.htm; 800 Langdon St; ⊙ 7am-midnight Mon-Fri, 8am-1am Sat, to midnight Sun; 🛜) The campus Union is Madison's gathering spot. The festive lakeside terrace pours microbrews and hosts free live music and free Monday-night films, while the indoor ice-cream shop scoops hulking cones from the university dairy.

🔒 Shopping

Fromagination
FOOD

(☑ 608-255-2430; www.fromagination.com; 12 S Carroll St; ⊙ 10am-6pm Mon-Fri, 8am-5pm Sat, 11am-4pm Sun) The state's best cheese shop specializes in small-batch and hard-to-find

FISH FRIES & SUPPER CLUBS

Wisconsin has two dining traditions that you'll likely encounter when visiting the state:

➡ **Fish Fry** Friday is the hallowed day of the 'fish fry.' This communal meal of beer-battered cod, French fries and coleslaw came about years ago, providing locals with a cheap meal to socialize around and celebrate the workweek's end. The convention is still going strong at many bars and restaurants, including Lakefront Brewery (p582) in Milwaukee.

➡ **Supper Club** This is a type of time-warped restaurant common in the upper Midwest. Supper clubs started in the 1930s, and most retain a retro vibe. Hallmarks include a woodsy location, a radish-and-carrot-laden relish tray on the table, a surf-and-turf menu and a mile-long, unironic cocktail list. See www.wisconsinsupperclubs.net for more information. The Old Fashioned (p586) in Madison is a modern take on the venue (it's named after the quintessential, brandy-laced supper-club drink).

local hunks. Browse the basket of 'orphans' by the cash register, where you can buy small quantities for $2 to $5. The shop also sells sandwiches, beer and wine.

ⓘ Information

Madison Convention & Visitors Bureau (www.visitmadison.com)

ⓘ Getting There & Around

Badger Bus (www.badgerbus.com) uses the Chazen Museum as its pick-up/drop-off point for trips to Milwaukee ($20, two hours), as does **Megabus** (www.megabus.com/us) for trips to Chicago (four hours) and Minneapolis (five hours).

Taliesin & Southern Wisconsin

This part of Wisconsin has some of the prettiest landscapes in the state, particularly the hilly southwest. Architecture fans can be unleashed at Taliesin, the Frank Lloyd Wright ubersight, and Racine, where a handful of his other works stand. Dairies around here cut a lot of cheese.

Racine

Racine is an unremarkable industrial town 30 miles south of Milwaukee, but it has some key Frank Lloyd Wright sights. First is the **SC Johnson Administration Building & Research Tower** (✆262-260-2154; www.scjohnson.com/visit; 1525 Howe St; ⊘1-3:30pm Wed-Fri, 9am-2:30pm Sat, 11:30am-3pm Sun) FREE. Free 75- to 90-minute tours take in the magnificent, curvy, Wright-designed structures. Six miles north is **Wingspread**

(✆262-681-3353; www.scjohnson.com/visit; 33 E Four Mile Rd; ⊘9:30am-3:30pm Wed-Fri, 11:30am-3:30pm Sat, noon-2:30pm Sun) FREE, the last and largest of Wright's Prairie houses; free tours through the lakeside abode take one hour. All tours must be prebooked.

Green County

This pastoral area holds the nation's greatest concentration of cheesemakers, and **Green County Tourism** (www.greencounty.org) will introduce you to them. Monroe is a fine place to start sniffing. Follow your nose to **Roth Käse** (657 2nd St; ⊘9am-6pm Mon-Fri, 10am-5pm Sat & Sun), a store and factory where you can watch cheesemakers in action from the observation deck (weekday mornings only) and delve into the 'bargain bin' for hunks. Bite into a fresh limburger-and-raw-onion sandwich at **Baumgartner's** (www.baumgartnercheese.com; 1023 16th Ave; sandwiches $4-7; ⊘8am-11pm Sun-Thu, to midnight Fri & Sat), an old Swiss tavern on the town square. At night, catch a flick at the local drive-in movie theater, and then climb into bed at **Inn Serendipity** (✆608-329-7056; www.innserendipity.com; 7843 County Rd P; r $110-125), a two-room, wind-and-solar-powered B&B on a 5-acre organic farm in Browntown, about 10 miles west of Monroe.

For more on local dairy producers and plant tours, pick up, or download, **A Traveler's Guide to America's Dairyland** (www.eatwisconsincheese.com) map.

Spring Green

Forty miles west of Madison and 3 miles south of the small town of Spring Green, **Taliesin** was the home of Frank Lloyd Wright for most of his life and is the site of

WORTH A TRIP

ODDBALL US 12

Unusual sights huddle around US 12, all easy to experience on a northerly day trip from Madison.

National Mustard Museum (☑800-438-6878; www.mustardmuseum.com; 7477 Hubbard Ave; ⊙10am-5pm) **FREE** Heading west out of Madison (take University Ave), stop first in suburban Middleton. Born of one man's ridiculously intense passion, the museum houses 5200 mustards and kooky condiment memorabilia. Tongue-in-cheek humor abounds, especially if CMO (chief mustard officer) Barry Levenson is there to give you the shtick.

Cow Chip Throw (www.wiscowchip.com; ⊙1st weekend Sep) **FREE** About 20 miles further on US 12 is the town of Prairie du Sac. It hosts the annual Cow Chip Throw, where 800 competitors fling dried manure patties as far as the eye can see; the record is 248ft.

Dr Evermor's Sculpture Park (☑608-219-7830; www.worldofdrevermor.com; ⊙11am-5pm Mon & Thu-Sat, from noon Sun) **FREE** Seven miles onward, the doc has welded old pipes, carburetors and other salvaged metal into a hallucinatory world of futuristic birds, dragons and other bizarre structures. The crowning glory is the giant, egg-domed Forevertron, once cited by Guinness World Records as the globe's largest scrap-metal sculpture. Finding the park entrance is tricky. Look for the old Badger Army Ammunition Plant, and then a small sign leading you into a driveway across the street. The doc is in poor health and isn't around much now, but his wife Lady Eleanor usually is.

Circus World (☑608-356-8341; www.circusworldbaraboo.org; 550 Water St; adult/child summer $20/10, winter $10/5; ⊙9am-5pm summer, reduced hours in winter;) Baraboo, about 45 miles northwest of Madison, was once the winter home of the Ringling Brothers Circus. The museum preserves a nostalgic collection of wagons, posters and equipment from the touring big-top heyday. In summer, admission includes clowns, animals and acrobats doing the three-ring thing in live performances.

Wisconsin Dells (☑800-223-3557; www.wisdells.com;) Continue north another 12 miles and you'll come to the Dells, a megacenter of kitschy diversions, including 21 water parks, water-skiing thrill shows and mini-golf courses. It's a jolting contrast to the natural appeal of the area, with its scenic limestone formations carved by the Wisconsin River. To appreciate the original attraction, take a boat tour or walk the trails at nearby Mirror Lake or Devil's Lake state parks.

his architectural school. It's now a major pilgrimage destination for fans and followers. The house was built in 1903, the Hillside Home School in 1932, and the **visitor center** (☑608-588-7900; www.taliesinpreservation.org; Hwy 23; ⊙9am-5:30pm May-Oct) in 1953. A wide range of guided tours ($20 to $85) cover various parts of the complex; reserve in advance for the lengthier ones. The one-hour Hillside Tour ($20) provides a nice introduction to Wright's work.

A few miles south of Taliesin is the **House on the Rock** (☑608-935-3639; www.thehouseontherock.com; 5754 Hwy 23; adult/child $15/9; ⊙9am-6pm May-Aug, to 5pm rest of year, closed mid-Nov–mid-Mar), one of Wisconsin's busiest attractions. Alex Jordan built the structure atop a rock column in 1959 (some say as an 'up yours' to neighbor Frank Lloyd Wright). He then stuffed the house to mind-blowing proportions with wonderments, including the world's largest carousel, whirring music machines, freaky dolls and crazed folk art. The house is broken into three parts, each with its own tour. Visitors with stamina (and about four hours to kill) can experience the whole shebang for adult/child $30/16.

Spring Green has a B&B in town and six motels strung along Hwy 14, north of town. Small **Usonian Inn** (☑877-876-6426; www.usonianinn.com; E 5116 Hwy 14; r $100-135;) was designed by a Wright student.

Chomp sandwiches or inventive specials like sweet-potato stew at **Spring Green General Store** (www.springgreengeneralstore.com; 137 S Albany St; mains $5-9; ⊙8:30am-5pm Mon-Fri, 7:30am-5pm Sat, to 4pm Sun).

The **American Players Theatre** (☑608-588-2361; www.americanplayers.org) stages classical productions at an outdoor amphitheater by the Wisconsin River.

Along the Mississippi River

The Mississippi River forms most of Wisconsin's western border, and alongside it run some of the most scenic sections of the **Great River Road** (www.wigreatriverroad.org) – the designated route that follows Old Man River from Minnesota to the Gulf of Mexico.

From Madison, head west on US 18. You'll hit the River Road (aka Hwy 35) at **Prairie du Chien**. North of town, the hilly riverside wends through the scene of the final battle in the bloody Black Hawk War. Historic markers tell part of the story, which finished at the Battle of Bad Ax when Native American men, women and children were massacred trying to flee across the Mississippi.

At Genoa, Hwy 56 leads inland for 20 miles to the trout-fishing mecca of **Viroqua** (www.viroqua-wisconsin.com), a pretty little town surrounded by organic farms and distinctive round barns. Pop into **Viroqua Food Cooperative** (www.viroquafood.coop; 609 Main St; ⊘7am-9pm) to meet farmers and munch their wares.

Back riverside and 18 miles upstream, **La Crosse** (www.explorelacrosse.com) has a historic center with restaurants and pubs. Grandad Bluff offers grand views of the river. It's east of town along Main St (which becomes Bliss Rd); follow Bliss Rd up the hill and then turn right on Grandad Bluff Rd. The **World's Largest Six-Pack** (cnr 3rd St S & Mississippi St) is also in town. The 'cans' are actually storage tanks for City Brewery and hold enough beer to provide one person with a six-pack a day for 3351 years (or so the sign says).

Door County & Eastern Wisconsin

Rocky, lighthouse-dotted Door County draws crowds in summer, while Green Bay draws crazed football fans in the freakin' freezing winter.

Green Bay

Green Bay is a modest industrial town best known as the fabled 'frozen tundra' where the Green Bay Packers win Super Bowls. The franchise is unique as the only community-owned nonprofit team in the NFL; perhaps pride in ownership is what makes the fans so die-hard (and also makes them wear foam-rubber cheese wedges on their heads).

While tickets are nearly impossible to obtain, you can always get into the spirit by joining a pregame tailgate party. The generous flow of alcohol has led to Green Bay's reputation as a 'drinking town with a football problem.' On nongame days, visit the **Green Bay Packer Hall of Fame** (☑920-569-7512; www.lambeaufield.com; adult/child $11/8; ⊘9am-6pm Mon-Sat, 10am-5pm Sun) at Lambeau Field, which is indeed packed with memorabilia and movies that'll intrigue any pigskin fan. Stadium tours are also available.

The **National Railroad Museum** (☑920-437-7623; www.nationalrrmuseum.org; 2285 S Broadway; adult/child $10/7.50; ⊘9am-5pm Mon-Sat, 11am-5pm Sun, closed Mon Jan-Mar) features some of the biggest locomotives ever to haul freight into Green Bay's vast yards; train rides ($2) are offered in summer.

Tidy, bare-bones **Bay Motel** (☑920-494-3441; www.baymotelgreenbay.com; 1301 S Military Ave; r $59-77; ☏) is a mile from Lambeau Field. **Hinterland** (☑920-438-8050; www.hinterlandbeer.com; 313 Dousman St; ⊘4pm-midnight Mon-Sat) gastropub brings a touch of rustic swankiness to the beer-drinking scene.

Door County

With its rocky coastline, picturesque lighthouses, cherry orchards and small 19th-century villages, you have to admit Door County is pretty damn lovely. The area spreads across a narrow peninsula jutting 75 miles into Lake Michigan, and visitors usually loop around on the county's two highways. Hwy 57 runs beside Lake Michigan and goes through Jacksonport and Baileys Harbor; this is known as the more scenic 'quiet side.' Hwy 42 borders Green Bay and passes through (from south to north) Egg Harbor, Fish Creek, Ephraim and Sister Bay; this side is more action oriented. Only about half the businesses stay open from November to April.

◉ Sights & Activities

Parkland blankets the county. Bayside **Peninsula State Park** is the largest, with bluffside hiking and biking trails and Nicolet Beach for swimming, kayaking and sailing (equipment rentals available on-site). In winter, cross-country skiers and snowshoers take over the trails. On the lake side, secluded **Newport State Park** offers trails, backcountry camping and solitude. **Whitefish Dunes**

WASHINGTON ISLAND & ROCK ISLAND

From Door County's tip near Gills Rock, daily **ferries** (☑ 920-847-2546; www.wisferry.com; Northport Pier) go every half-hour to **Washington Island** (round-trip adult/child/bike/car $13.50/7/4/26), which has 700 Scandinavian descendants, a couple of museums, beaches, bike rentals and carefree roads for cycling. Accommodations and camping are available. More remote is lovely **Rock Island**, a state park with no cars or bikes at all. It's a wonderful place for hiking, swimming and camping. Get there via the **Karfi ferry** (www.wisferry. com), which departs Jackson Harbor on Washington Island (round-trip adult/child $11/5) every hour in summer.

State Park has sandscapes and a wide beach (beware of riptides). Adjacent **Cave Point Park** is known for its sea caves and kayaking.

Bay Shore Outfitters OUTDOORS
(☑ 920-854-9220; www.kayakdoorcounty.com; Sister Bay) Rents kayaks, stand-up paddleboards and winter gear, and offers tours.

Nor Door Sport & Cyclery OUTDOORS
(☑ 920-868-2275; www.nordoorsports.com; Fish Creek) Nor Door rents out bikes and snow shoes near the entrance to Peninsula State Park.

🛏 Sleeping & Eating

The bay side has the most lodging. Prices listed are for July and August, the peak season; many places have minimum-stay requirements. Local restaurants often host a 'fish boil,' a regional specialty started by Scandinavian lumberjacks, in which whitefish, potatoes and onions are cooked in a fiery cauldron. Finish with Door's famous cherry pie.

Julie's Park Cafe and Motel MOTEL $
(☑ 920-868-2999; www.juliesmotel.com; Fish Creek; r $85-109; ❄ 🛜) A great low-cost option located beside Peninsula State Park.

Peninsula State Park CAMPGROUND $
(☑ 920-868-3258; Fish Creek; tent & RV sites $17-25) Holds nearly 500 amenity-laden campsites.

Egg Harbor Lodge INN $$
(☑ 920-868-3115; www.eggharborlodge.com; Egg Harbor; r $165-205; ❄ 🛜 🏊) All rooms have a water view and free bike use.

Wild Tomato PIZZA $
(☑ 920-868-3095; www.wildtomatopizza.com; Fish Creek; mains $9-17; ⊙ 11am-10pm Jun-Aug, reduced hours Sep-May) Join the crowds indoors and out munching pizzas from the stone, wood-fired ovens. A lengthy list of craft beers help wash it down. It's extremely gluten-free friendly.

Village Cafe AMERICAN $
(☑ 920-868-3342; www.villagecafe-doorcounty. com; Egg Harbor; mains $7-10; ⊙ 8am-2pm, to 8pm Jul & Aug; 🛜) Delicious all-day breakfast dishes, plus sandwiches and burgers.

🛈 Information

Door County Visitors Bureau (☑ 800-527-3529; www.doorcounty.com) Special-interest brochures on art galleries, biking and lighthouses.

Apostle Islands & Northern Wisconsin

The north is a thinly populated region of forests and lakes, where folks paddle and fish in summer, and ski and snowmobile in winter. The windswept Apostle Islands steal the show.

Northwoods & Lakelands

Nicolet National Forest is a vast, wooded district ideal for outdoor activities. The simple crossroads of **Langlade** is a center for white-water river adventures. **Bear Paw Resort** (☑ 715-882-3502; www.bearpawoutdoors. com; cabins $75-95; 🛜) rents kayaks and provides full-day paddling lessons that include a trip on the river ($150 per person). It also provides cozy cabins where you can dry off, get warm and celebrate your accomplishments in the on-site pub.

North on Hwy 13, folk artist and retired lumberjack Fred Smith's **Concrete Park** (www. friendsoffredsmith.org; N8236 S Hwy 13; ⊙ sunrise-sunset) FREE in Phillips is extraordinary, with 200-plus whimsical, life-size sculptures.

West on Hwy 70, **Chequamegon National Forest** offers exceptional mountain biking with 300 miles of off-road trails. The **Chequamegon Area Mountain Bike Association** (www.cambatrails.org) has trail maps and bike rental information. The season culminates in mid-September with the **Chequamegon Fat Tire Festival** (www.cheqfattire.com), when 1700 strong-legged men and women peddle 40 grueling miles through the woods. The town of **Hayward** (www.haywardareachamber. com) makes a good base.

Apostle Islands

The 21 rugged Apostle Islands, floating in Lake Superior and freckling Wisconsin's northern tip, are a state highlight. Forested and wind-blown, trimmed with cliffs and caves, the national park gems have no facilities. Various companies offer seasonal boat trips around the islands, and kayaking and hiking are very popular. Jump off from Bayfield, a humming resort town with hilly streets, Victorian-era buildings, apple orchards and nary a fast-food restaurant in sight.

👁 Sights & Activities

Madeline Island   ISLAND
(www.madelineisland.com) Inhabited Madeline Island makes a fine day trip and is reached by a 25-minute **ferry** (☎ 715-747-2051; www. madferry.com; round-trip adult/child/bicycle/car $13.50/7/7/24.50) from Bayfield. The isle's walkable village of La Pointe has a couple of mid-priced places to stay, a smattering of eateries and a groovy 'burned down' bar (made from junk and tarps). Bike and moped rentals are available – everything is near the ferry dock.

And FYI: while Madeline is an Apostle Island, it's not part of the national park group, hence its development.

Big Bay State Park   STATE PARK
(☎ 715-747-6425; per car $10, tent sites $17-22) Big Bay is at Madeline Island's far edge, with a pretty beach and hiking trails. The well-maintained campsites are awesome and book up fast.

Apostle Islands Cruises   BOAT TOUR
(☎ 715-779-3925; www.apostleisland.com; Bayfield City Dock; ◷ mid-May–mid-Oct) The easiest way to view the Apostles is aboard these 150-person sightseeing vessels. The 'grand tour' departs at 10am for a three-hour narrated trip past sea caves and lighthouses (adult/child $40/24). A glass-bottom boat goes out to view shipwrecks at 2pm. Other trips call at islands to drop off/pick up campers and kayakers; it's possible to arrange day trips via these shuttles.

SCENIC DRIVE: HIGHWAY 13

After departing Bayfield, head north on Hwy 13. It takes a fine route around the Lake Superior shore, past the Chippewa community of **Red Cliff** and the Apostle Islands' mainland segment, which has a beach. Tiny **Cornucopia**, looking every bit like a seaside village, has great sunsets. The road runs on through a timeless countryside of forest and farm, reaching US 2 for the final miles back to civilization at Superior. See www.lake-superiorbyway.org for more.

Living Adventure   KAYAKING
(☎ 715-779-9503; www.livingadventure.com; Hwy 13; half-/full-day tours $59/99; ◷ Jun-Sep) It offers guided paddling trips to sea caves and shipwrecks; beginners are welcome.

🛏 Sleeping & Eating

Seagull Bay Motel   MOTEL $
(☎ 715-779-5558; www.seagullbay.com; 325 S 7th St; r $80-110; 🐾) Most rooms at no-frills Seagull Bay Motel have decks; ask for a lake view.

Fat Radish   AMERICAN $
(☎ 715-779-9700; http://thefatradish.weebly. com; 200 Rittenhouse Ave; sandwiches $7-9; ◷ 11am-3pm Tue & Wed, to 3pm & 5-8pm Thu-Sat) 🌱 The Radish uses quality, sustainable ingredients in its deli wares. It's located by the docks and handy for amassing snacks to take with you on the boat tours. At night the chef serves tasty pizzas and seafood dishes.

Maggie's   AMERICAN $$
(☎ 715-779-5641; www.maggies-bayfield.com; 257 Manypenny Ave; mains $11-22; ◷ 11:30am-9pm) Kitschy, flamingo-themed Maggie's is the place to sample good local lake trout and whitefish; there are pizza and burgers, too.

☆ Entertainment

Big Top Chautauqua   LIVE MUSIC
(☎ 888-244-8368; www.bigtop.org; ◷ Jun-Sep) The Chautauqua is a major regional summer event with big-name concerts and musical theater.

❶ Information

Apostle Islands National Lakeshore Visitors Center (☐ 715-779-3397; www.nps.gov/apis; 410 Washington Ave; �),8am-4:30pm late May-Sep, closed Sat & Sun rest of year) Has camping permits ($10 per night) and paddling and hiking information.

Bayfield Chamber of Commerce (www.bayfield.org) Good listings of lodgings and things to do in the area.

MINNESOTA

Is Minnesota really the land of 10,000 lakes, as it's so often advertised? You betcha. Actually, in typically modest style, the state has undermarketed itself – there are 11,842 lakes. Which is great news for travelers. Intrepid outdoorsfolk can wet their paddles in the Boundary Waters, where nighttime brings a blanket of stars and the lullaby of wolf howls. Those wanting to get further off the beaten path can journey to Voyageurs National Park, where there's more water than roadway. If that all seems too far-flung, stick to the Twin Cities of Minneapolis and St Paul, where you can't swing a moose without hitting something cool or cultural. And for those looking for middle ground – a cross between the big city and big woods – the dramatic, freighter-filled port of Duluth beckons.

❶ Information

Minnesota Highway Conditions (☐ 511; www.511mn.org)

Minnesota Office of Tourism (☐ 888-847-4866; www.exploreminnesota.com)

Minnesota State Park Information (☐ 888-646-6367; www.dnr.state.mn.us) Park entry requires a vehicle permit ($5/25 per day/year). Campsites cost $15 to $31; reservations (☐ 866-857-2757; www.stayatmnparks.com; fee $8.50) accepted.

Minneapolis

Minneapolis is the biggest and artiest town on the prairie, with all the trimmings of progressive prosperity – swank art museums, rowdy rock clubs, organic and ethnic eateries and edgy theaters. It's always happenin', even in winter. And here's the bonus: folks are attitude-free and the embodiment of 'Minnesota Nice.' Count how many times they tell you to 'Have a great day,' come rain or shine or snow.

History

Timber was the city's first boom industry, and water-powered sawmills rose along the Mississippi River in the mid-1800s. Wheat from the prairies also needed to be processed, so flour mills churned into the next big business. The population boomed in the late 19th century with mass immigration, especially from Scandinavia and Germany. Today Minneapolis' Nordic heritage is evident, whereas twin city St Paul is more German and Irish-Catholic.

◉ Sights & Activities

Most attractions are closed Monday; many stay open late on Thursday.

◉ Downtown & Loring Park

★**Walker Art Center**   MUSEUM
(☐ 612-375-7622; www.walkerart.org; 1750 Hennepin Ave; adult/child $14/free, admission free Thu evening & 1st Sat of month; ☐ 11am-5pm Tue, Wed & Fri-Sun, to 9pm Thu) The first-class center has a strong permanent collection of 20th-century art and photography, including big-name US painters and great US pop art. On Monday evenings from late July to late August, the museum hosts free movies and music across the pedestrian bridge in Loring Park that are quite the to-do.

★**Minneapolis Sculpture Garden** GARDENS
(725 Vineland Pl; ☐ 6am-midnight) **FREE** The 11-acre garden, studded with contemporary works such as the oft-photographed *Spoonbridge & Cherry* by Claes Oldenburg, sits beside the Walker Art Center. The Cowles Conservatory, abloom with exotic hothouse flowers, is also on the grounds. In summer a trippy mini-golf course amid the sculptures adds to the fun ($12 for adults, $9 for kids). Note the garden will be closed through 2016 as it gets an ecofriendly facelift.

Mary Tyler Moore statue   STATUE
(7th St S & Nicollet Mall) Mary Tyler Moore (of '70s TV fame) put Minneapolis on the pop-culture map. The spot where she threw her hat in the air during the show's opening sequence is now marked by a great, cheesy statue depicting our girl doing just that.

⊙ Riverfront District

★ Endless Bridge OBSERVATORY

(818 2nd St S; ⊘8am-8pm, to 11pm on performance days) FREE Head inside the cobalt-blue Guthrie Theater and make your way up the escalator to the Endless Bridge, a far-out cantilevered walkway overlooking the Mississippi River. You don't need a theater ticket, as it's intended as a public space. The theater's 9th floor Amber Box provides another knockout view.

Mill City Museum MUSEUM

(☑612-341-7555; www.millcitymuseum.org; 704 2nd St S; adult/child $11/6; ⊘10am-5pm Tue-Sat, noon-5pm Sun, open daily Jul & Aug) The building is indeed a former mill, and highlights include a ride inside an eight-story grain elevator (the 'Flour Tower'), Betty Crocker exhibits and a baking lab. It's not terribly exciting unless you're really into milling history, though the mill ruins in back are an atmospheric sight. A foodie-favorite farmers market takes place in the attached train shed on Saturday mornings May through September.

St Anthony Falls Heritage Trail WALKING

The 1.8-mile path provides both interesting history (placards dot the route) and the city's best access to the banks of the Mississippi River. It starts at the foot of Portland Ave and goes over the car-free Stone Arch Bridge, from which you can view cascading St Anthony Falls.

On the other side of the river, the trail goes along Main St SE, which has a stretch of redeveloped buildings housing restaurants and bars. From here you can walk down to Water Power Park and feel the river's frothy spray. Free trail maps are available at the Mill City Museum.

⊙ Northeast

Once a working-class Eastern European neighborhood, Northeast (so named because of its position to the river) is where urbanites and artists now work and play. They appreciate the dive bars pouring microbrews along with Pabst, and boutiques selling ecogifts next to companies grinding sausage. Hundreds of craftsfolk and galleries fill historic industrial buildings. They fling open their doors the first Thursday of each month when the **Northeast Minneapolis Arts Association** (www.nemaa.org) sponsors a gallery walk. Heady streets include 4th St NE and 13th Ave NE.

⊙ University Area

The **University of Minnesota**, by the river southeast of Minneapolis' center, is one of the USA's largest campuses, with some 50,000 students. Most of the campus is in the East Bank neighborhood.

Dinkytown, based at 14th Ave SE and 4th St SE, is dense with student cafes and bookshops. A small part of the university is on the West Bank of the Mississippi River, near the intersection of 4th St S and Riverside Ave. This area has a few restaurants, some student hangouts and a big Somali community.

★ Weisman Art Museum MUSEUM

(☑612-625-9494; www.wam.umn.edu; 333 E River Rd; ⊘10am-5pm Tue, Thu & Fri, to 8pm Wed, 11am-5pm Sat & Sun) FREE The Weisman, which occupies a swooping silver structure by architect Frank Gehry, is a uni (and city) highlight. The airy main galleries hold cool collections

---

MINNESOTA FACTS

Nicknames North Star State, Gopher State

Population 5.5 million

Area 86,940 sq miles

Capital city St Paul (population 295,000)

Other cities Minneapolis (population 400,100)

Sales tax 6.88%

Birthplace of Author F Scott Fitzgerald (1896–1940), songwriter Bob Dylan (b 1941), filmmakers Joel Coen (b 1954) and Ethan Coen (b 1957)

Home of Lumberjack legend Paul Bunyan, Spam, walleye fish, Hmong and Somali immigrants

Politics Leans Democratic

Famous for Niceness, funny accents, snowy weather, 10,000 lakes

Official muffin Blueberry

Driving distances Minneapolis to Duluth 153 miles, Minneapolis to Boundary Waters 245 miles

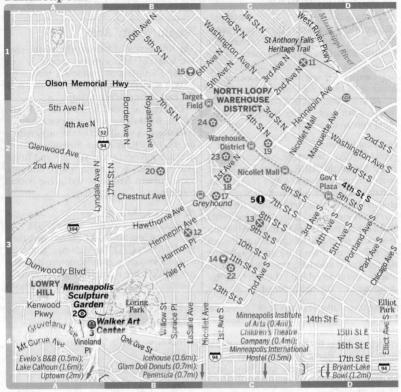

of 20th-century American art, ceramics, Korean furniture and works on paper.

Uptown, Lyn-Lake & Whittier

These three neighborhoods are south of downtown.

Uptown, based around the intersection of Hennepin Ave and Lake St, is a punk-yuppie collision of shops and restaurants that stays lively until late. Lyn-Lake abuts Uptown to the east and sports a similar urban-cool vibe; it's centered on Lyndale and Lake Sts. (Get the name?)

Uptown is a convenient jump-off point to the 'Chain of Lakes' – Lake Calhoun, Lake of the Isles, Lake Harriet, Cedar Lake and Brownie Lake. Paved cycling paths (which double as cross-country ski trails in winter) meander around the five lakes, where you

can go boating in summer or ice skating in winter.

Lake Calhoun sits at the foot of Lake St, where there are amenities galore. Further around Lake Calhoun, Thomas Beach is popular for swimming. Lake Harriet's castle-like band shell is always abuzz with free concerts.

★ **Minneapolis Institute of Arts**   MUSEUM
(☎ 612-870-3131; www.artsmia.org; 2400 3rd Ave S; ⓧ 10am-5pm Tue-Sat, to 9pm Thu, 11am-5pm Sun) **FREE** This museum is a huge trove housing a veritable history of art. The modern and contemporary collections astonish, while the Asian galleries (2nd floor) and Decorative Arts rooms (3rd floor) are also highlights. Allot at least a few hours to visit. The museum is a mile south of downtown via 3rd Ave S.

Minneapolis

MINNEAPOLIS FOR CHILDREN

Note that many of the other top sights for wee ones are in St Paul, at the Mall of America and Fort Snelling.

Minnesota Zoo (☑952-431-9500; www.mnzoo.org; 13000 Zoo Blvd; adult/child $18/12; ⊙9am-6pm summer, to 4pm winter; 🚼) You'll have to travel a way to get to the respected zoo in suburban Apple Valley, which is 20 miles south of town. It has naturalistic habitats for its 400-plus species, with an emphasis on cold-climate creatures. Parking is $7.

Valleyfair (☑952-445-7600; www.valleyfair.com; 1 Valleyfair Dr; admission $47; ⊙from 10am daily late May–early Sep, Fri-Sun only Sep & Oct, closing times vary; 🚼) If the rides at the Mall of America aren't enough, drive out to this full-scale amusement park 25 miles southwest in Shakopee. The animatronic dinosaur park ($5 extra) is a big hit. Save money by booking tickets online. Parking costs $12.

Children's Theatre Company (☑612-874-0400; www.childrenstheatre.org; 2400 3rd Ave S; 🚼) It's so good it won a Tony award for 'outstanding regional theater.'

Lake Calhoun Kiosk WATER SPORTS
(☑612-823-5765; base of Lake St; per hr $9-19; ⊙10am-8pm late May-Aug, Sat & Sun only Sep & Oct) The kiosk, at the foot of Lake St, rents kayaks, bikes, stand-up paddleboards and pedal boats. It's a busy spot as there's also a patio restaurant and sailing school here.

🎉 Festivals & Events

Art A Whirl MUSIC
(www.nemaa.org; ⊙mid-May) The Northeast's weekend-long, rock-and-roll gallery crawl heralds the arrival of spring.

Minneapolis Aquatennial CULTURAL
(www.aquatennial.com; ⊙3rd week Jul) Celebrates the ubiquitous lakes via parades, beach bashes and fireworks.

Holidazzle CULTURAL
(www.holidazzle.com; ⊙Dec) A German-style Christmas market, lights and lots of good cheer downtown throughout December.

🛏 Sleeping

B&Bs offer the best value – they've got budget prices but are solidly midrange in quality. Tax adds 13.4% to prices.

Wales House B&B $
(☑612-331-3931; www.waleshouse.com; 1115 5th St SE; r with/without shared bath $75/85; 🅿✳🛜) This cheery 10-bedroom B&B often houses scholars from the nearby University of Minnesota. Curl up with a book on the porch, or lounge by the fireplace. A two-night minimum stay is required.

Evelo's B&B B&B $
(☑612-374-9656; 2301 Bryant Ave S; r with shared bath $75-95; 🛜) Evelo's four rooms creak and charm within this polished-wood-filled Victorian home. They're close quartered, but the B&B's strategic location between the Walker Art Center and Uptown compensates.

Minneapolis International Hostel HOSTEL $
(☑612-522-5000; www.minneapolishostel.com; 2400 Stevens Ave S; dm $40-45, r from $55; ✳🛜) It's set in a cool old building with antique furniture and wood floors, and the location beside the Minneapolis Institute of Arts is excellent. But it's also not very well tended to. The rooms come in a variety of configurations, from a 15-bed male dorm to private rooms with en suite bath.

Aloft HOTEL $$
(☑612-455-8400; www.aloftminneapolis.com; 900 Washington Ave S; r $159-209; 🅿✳@🛜🏊) Aloft's efficiently designed, industrial-toned rooms draw a younger clientele. The club-by lobby has board games, a cocktail lounge and 24-hour snacks. There's a tiny pool, a decent fitness room and a bike-share station outside the front door. Parking costs $15.

🍴 Eating

Culinary magazine *Saveur* recently dubbed Minneapolis as 'America's next great food city' for its creative, sustainable, approachable and distinctively Midwestern fare.

Downtown

Hell's Kitchen   AMERICAN **$$**
(☑ 612-332-4700; www.hellskitcheninc.com; 80 9th St S; mains $12-24; ⊙ 6:30am-11pm Mon-Fri, from 7:30am Sat & Sun; 🛜) Descend the stairs to Hell's devilish lair, where spirited waitstaff bring you uniquely Minnesotan foods, like the walleye BLT sandwich, bison burger, Juicy Lucy (melted cheese in the middle of a burger) and lemon-ricotta hotcakes. Upstairs there's a delicious bakery and coffee shop.

Butcher & the Boar   AMERICAN **$$$**
(☑ 612-238-8888; www.butcherandtheboar.com; 1121 Hennepin Ave; mains $25-36; ⊙ 5-10:30pm Mon-Thu, to 11pm Fri & Sat, to 10pm Sun; 🛜) The coppery, candlelit room is carnivore nirvana. Get your carving knife ready for wild boar ham with country butter, chicken-fried veal sausage and many more house-crafted meats. Sampler plates are the way to go. The 30 taps flow with regional brews, backed up by a lengthy bourbon list (flights available). Make reservations, or opt for meaty small plates in the rockin' beer garden.

Bachelor Farmer   MODERN AMERICAN **$$$**
(☑ 612-206-3920; www.thebachelorfarmer.com; 50 2nd Ave N; mains $19-33; ⊙ 5:30-9:30pm Mon-Thu, to 10:30pm Fri & Sat, 10am-2pm & 5-9:30pm Sun) 🌿 The dishes at this fun restaurant play on the region's Scandinavian heritage: smoked fish, meatballs and cheese-and-pickled-mushroom-topped toast making frequent appearances on the ever-changing menu. The chef grows all the herbs and veggies in a rooftop garden. Marvel Bar, the restaurant's sibling, hides in the basement behind an unmarked door and is primo for cocktails. Reserve ahead.

University Area

Low-priced eateries cluster in the campus area by Washington Ave and Oak St.

Al's Breakfast   BREAKFAST **$**
(☑ 612-331-9991; 413 14th Ave SE; mains $5-9; ⊙ 6am-1pm Mon-Sat, 9am-1pm Sun) The ultimate hole in the wall: 14 stools at a tiny counter. Whenever a customer comes in, everyone picks up their plates and scoots down to make room for the newcomer. Fruit-full pancakes are the big crowd-pleaser. Cash only.

Uptown, Lyn-Lake & Whittier

Near the Minneapolis Institute of Arts, hipster eateries mingle among Vietnamese, Greek and other ethnic restaurants along Nicollet Ave S – a road known as 'Eat Street.' Lake St in Uptown is a rich vein for stylish bars and cafes.

★ **Bryant-Lake Bowl**   AMERICAN **$**
(☑ 612-825-3737; www.bryantlakebowl.com; 810 W Lake St; mains $10-15; ⊙ 8am-12:30am; 🛜🌿) A workingman's bowling alley meets epicurean food at the BLB. Biscuit-and-gravy breakfasts, artisanal cheese plates, mock duck pad thai and smoked whitefish melt in the mouth. A long list of local beers washes

---

TAPROOM BOOM

Minneapolis is all in on the local brewing trend, and most makers have taprooms. Excellent ones to try for beer fresh from the tank:

Fulton Beer (www.fultonbeer.com; 414 6th Ave N; ⊙ 3-10pm Wed & Thu, to 11pm Fri, noon-11pm Sat, noon-6pm Sun) There's usually a fab pale ale and blonde ale among the selection that you sip at communal picnic tables in the warehouse. It's a few blocks from the baseball stadium and fills up on game days. Food trucks hang out in front.

Dangerous Man Brewing (www.dangerousmanbrewing.com; 1300 2nd St NE; ⊙ 4-10pm Tue-Thu, 3pm-midnight Fri, noon-midnight Sat) Pours strong, European-style beers in hip-happenin' Northeast. You're welcome to bring in your own food (there's a choice fish-and-chips place a block east).

Surly Brewing (www.surlybrewing.com; 520 Malcolm Ave SE; ⊙ 11am-11pm Sun-Thu, to midnight Fri & Sat; ♿) Designed by the same architects who built the Guthrie Theater, Surly's sprawling, mod-industrial, family-friendly beer hall is mobbed by locals who come for the 12 rotating taps and abundant meaty snacks. It's in the Prospect Park neighborhood, next to the university and a short walk from the Prospect Park Green Line rail station.

GAY & LESBIAN MINNEAPOLIS

Minneapolis has one of the country's highest percentages of gay, lesbian, bisexual and transgender (GLBT) residents, and the city enjoys strong GLBT rights. Pick up the free, biweekly magazine *Lavender* (www.lavendermagazine.com) at coffee shops around town for info on the scene. Top picks:

Wilde Roast Cafe (www.wilderoastcafe.com; 65 Main St SE; ⊙7am-11pm) It features amazing baked goods, riverfront digs and a Victorian ambience worthy of its namesake, Oscar Wilde; it was ranked 'best cafe' by *Lavender*.

Gay Nineties (www.gay90s.com; 408 Hennepin Ave) This longstanding club has dancing, dining and drag shows that attract both a gay and straight clientele.

Pride Festival (www.tcpride.org; ⊙late Jun) It's one of the USA's largest, drawing more than 300,000 revelers.

it all down. The on-site theater always has something intriguing and odd going on, too.

Glam Doll Donuts BAKERY $
(www.glamdolldonuts.com; 2605 Nicollet Ave S; doughnuts $1.25-3; ⊙7am-9pm Mon-Thu, to 1am Fri & Sat, to 3pm Sun; 🛜📶) These tattooed ladies with bright-hued hair make seriously badass doughnuts (including many vegan ones) in their punk pink shop. Blissful kudos to the Calendar Girl (salted caramel and chocolate) and Chart Topper (peanut butter and Sriracha hot sauce). Afterward, pop into the rock and roll fashion resale shop next door.

Peninsula ASIAN $
(📶612-871-8282; www.peninsulamalaysiancuisine.com; 2608 Nicollet Ave S; mains $9-15; ⊙11am-10pm Sun-Thu, to 11pm Fri & Sat; 📶) Malaysian dishes – including red curry hot pot, spicy crab and fish in banana leaves – rock the palate in this contemporary restaurant.

🍷 Drinking & Nightlife

Bars stay open until 2am. Happy hour typically lasts from 3pm to 6pm.

Brit's Pub PUB
(www.britspub.com; 1110 Nicollet Mall; ⊙11am-2am) A lawn bowling green on the roof, plus Brit's sweeping selection of Scotch, port and beer, is sure to unleash skills you never knew you had.

Grumpy's BAR
(www.grumpys-bar.com; 2200 4th St NE; ⊙2pm-2am Mon-Fri, from 11am Sat & Sun) Grumpy's is the Northeast's classic dive, with cheap (but good local) beer and an outdoor patio. Sample the specialty 'hot dish' on Tuesdays for $1.

☆ Entertainment

With its large student population and thriving performing-arts scene, Minneapolis has an active nightlife. Check *Vita.mn* and *City Pages* for current goings on.

Live Music

Minneapolis rocks; everyone's in a band, it seems. Acts such as Prince and post-punkers Hüsker Dü and the Replacements cut their teeth here.

First Avenue & 7th St Entry LIVE MUSIC
(www.first-avenue.com; 701 1st Ave N) This is the longstanding bedrock of Minneapolis' music scene. First Avenue is the main room featuring national acts; smaller 7th St Entry is for up-and-comers. Check out the exterior stars on the building: they're all bands that have graced the stage.

Triple Rock Social Club LIVE MUSIC
(www.triplerocksocialclub.com; 629 Cedar Ave) Triple Rock is a popular punk-alternative club.

Lee's Liquor Lounge LIVE MUSIC
(www.leesliquorlounge.com; 101 Glenwood Ave) Rockabilly and country-tinged alt bands twang here.

Icehouse LIVE MUSIC
(www.icehousempls.com; 2528 Nicollet Ave S) It's a gorgeous, great-sounding venue for jazz, folk and progressive hip-hop acts. Oh, and swank cocktails, too.

Theater & Performing Arts

The city hosts a vibrant theater scene. The neon-lit **Hennepin Theater District** (www.hennepintheatretrust.org) consists of several historic venues on Hennepin Ave between 6th and 10th Sts that host big touring shows.

Guthrie Theater
THEATER

(☑612-377-2224; www.guthrietheater.org; 818 2nd St S) This is Minneapolis' top-gun theater troupe, with the jumbo facility to prove it. Unsold 'rush' tickets go on sale 30 minutes before showtime for around $25 (cash only). Download free audio tours from the website for self-guided jaunts around the funky building.

Brave New Workshop Theatre
THEATER

(☑612-332-6620; www.bravenewworkshop.com; 824 Hennepin Ave) An established venue for musical comedy, revue and satire.

Orchestra Hall
CLASSICAL MUSIC

(☑612-371-5656; www.minnesotaorchestra.org; 1111 Nicollet Mall) Superb acoustics for concerts by the acclaimed Minnesota Orchestra.

Sports

Minnesotans love their sports teams. Note that ice hockey happens in St Paul.

Target Field
BASEBALL

(www.minnesotatwins.com; 353 N 5th St) The Twins' baseball stadium is notable for beyond-the-norm, locally focused food and drink.

New Minnesota Stadium
FOOTBALL

(www.vikings.com; 900 5th St S) The NFL's Vikings begin playing in their shiny new indoor arena in fall 2016.

Target Center
BASKETBALL

(www.nba.com/timberwolves; 600 1st Ave N) This is where the Timberwolves pro basketball team plays.

ⓘ Information

City Pages (www.citypages.com) Weekly entertainment freebie.

Minneapolis Convention & Visitors Association (www.minneapolis.org) Coupons, maps, guides and bike-route info online.

Minneapolis Public Library (www.hclib.org; 300 Nicollet Mall; ☺9am-9pm Mon-Thu, to 5pm Fri & Sat, noon-5pm Sun) Mod facility with free internet and wi-fi (plus a great used bookstore).

Pioneer Press (www.twincities.com) St Paul's daily newspaper.

Star Tribune (www.startribune.com) Minneapolis' daily newspaper.

University of Minnesota Medical Center (☑612-672-6000; 2450 Riverside Ave) Well-regarded hospital near downtown.

Vita.mn (www.vita.mn) The *Star Tribune's* weekly entertainment freebie.

ⓘ Getting There & Around

AIR

The **Minneapolis-St Paul International Airport** (MSP; www.mspairport.com; ☎) is between the two cities to the south. It's a hub for Delta Airlines, which operates several direct flights to/from Europe.

The Blue Line light-rail service (regular/rush-hour fares $1.75/2.25, 25 minutes) is the cheapest way into Minneapolis. Bus 54 (regular/rush-hour fares $1.75/2.25, 25 minutes) goes to St Paul. Taxis cost around $45.

BICYCLE

Minneapolis hovers near the top of rankings for best bike city in the US. The bicycle-share program **Nice Ride** (www.niceridemn.org; ☺Apr-Nov) has 1500 lime-green bikes in 170 self-serve kiosks around the Twin Cities. Users pay a subscription fee ($6/65 per day/year) online or at the kiosk, plus a small fee per half-hour of use (with the first half-hour free). Bikes can be returned to any kiosk. Traditional rentals work better if you're riding for recreation versus transportation purposes. See the **Minneapolis Bicycle Program** (www.ci.minneapolis.mn.us/bicycles) for rental shops and trail maps.

BUS

Greyhound (☑612-371-3325; www.greyhound.com; 950 Hawthorne Ave; ☎) runs frequent buses to Milwaukee (seven hours), Chicago (nine hours) and Duluth (three hours).

Megabus (www.megabus.com/us; ☎) runs express to Milwaukee (6½ hours) and Chicago (8½ hours), often for lower fares than Greyhound. It departs from both downtown and the university; check the website for exact locations.

PUBLIC TRANSPORTATION

Metro Transit (www.metrotransit.org; regular/rush-hour fares $1.75/2.25) runs the handy Blue Line light-rail service between downtown and the Mall of America (stopping at the airport en route). The Green Line connects downtown Minneapolis to downtown St Paul. Machines at each station sell fare cards, including a day pass ($6) that also can be used on public buses.

TAXI

Call **Yellow Cab.** (☑612-888-8800; www.yellowcabmn.com)

TRAIN

Amtrak chugs in to the newly restored **Union Depot** (www.uniondepot.org; 214 E 4th St; ☎) in St Paul. Trains go daily to Chicago (eight hours) and Seattle (38 hours).

St Paul

Smaller and quieter than its twin city Minneapolis, St Paul has retained more of a historic character. Walk through F Scott Fitzgerald's old stomping grounds, trek the trails along the mighty Mississippi River, or slurp some Lao soup.

◉ Sights & Activities

Downtown and Cathedral Hill hold most of the action. The latter features eccentric shops, Gilded Age Victorian mansions and, of course, the hulking church that gives the area its name. Downtown has the museums. An insider's tip: there's a shortcut between the two areas, a footpath that starts on the Hill House's west side and drops into downtown.

F Scott Fitzgerald Sights & Summit Ave   BUILDING

The Great Gatsby author F Scott Fitzgerald is St Paul's most celebrated literary son. The Pullman-style apartment at **481 Laurel Ave** is his birthplace. Five blocks away, Fitzgerald lived in the brownstone at **599 Summit Ave** when he published *This Side of Paradise*. Both are private residences. From here stroll along Summit Ave toward the cathedral and gape at the Victorian homes rising from the street.

Literature buffs should grab the *Fitzgerald Homes and Haunts* map at the visitor center to see other footprints.

Landmark Center   MUSEUM

(www.landmarkcenter.org; 75 W 5th St; ☺8am-5pm Mon-Fri, to 8pm Thu, 10am-5pm Sat, noon-5pm Sun) Downtown's turreted 1902 Landmark Center used to be the federal courthouse, where gangsters such as Alvin 'Creepy' Karpis were tried; plaques by the various rooms show who was brought to justice here. In addition to the city's visitor center, the building also contains a couple of small museums.

On the 2nd floor the **Schubert Club Museum** (☎651-292-3267; www.schubert.org; ☺noon-4pm Sun-Fri) **FREE** has a brilliant collection of old pianos and harpsichords – some tickled by Brahms, Mendelssohn and the like – as well as old manuscripts and letters from famous composers. The club stages free chamber-music concerts Thursday at noon from October through April. A free wood-turning museum (it's a decorative form of woodworking) is also on the 2nd floor.

Science Museum of Minnesota   MUSEUM

(☎651-221-9444; www.smm.org; 120 W Kellogg Blvd; adult/child $13/10; ☺9:30am-5pm Sun, Tue & Wed, to 9pm Thu-Sat) Has the usual hands-on kids' exhibits and Omnimax theater ($8 extra). Adults will be entertained by the wacky quackery of the 4th floor's 'questionable medical devices.'

Cathedral of St Paul   CHURCH

(www.cathedralsaintpaul.org; 239 Selby Ave; ☺7am-6pm Sun-Fri, to 8pm Sat) Modeled on St Peter's Basilica in Rome, the cathedral presides over the city from its hilltop perch. Free tours are available at 1pm weekdays.

James J Hill House   HISTORIC BUILDING

(☎651-297-2555; www.mnhs.org/hillhouse; 240 Summit Ave; adult/child $9/6; ☺10am-3:30pm Wed-Sat, from 1pm Sun) Tour the palatial stone mansion of railroad magnate Hill. It's a Gilded Age beauty, with five floors and 22 fireplaces.

Harriet Island   PARK

Floating south of downtown and connected via Wabasha St, Harriet Island is a lovely place to meander. It has a river walk, paddlewheel boat cruises, concert stages and fishing docks.

★ St Paul Curling Club   SNOW SPORTS

(www.stpaulcurlingclub.org; 470 Selby Ave; ☺5-11pm mid-Oct–late May) For those uninitiated in northern ways, curling is a winter sport that involves sliding a hubcap-sized 'puck' down the ice toward a bull's-eye. The friendly folks here don't mind if you stop in to watch the action. Heck, they might invite you to share a ridiculously cheap microbrew from the upstairs bar.

Mississippi River Visitor Center   OUTDOORS

(☎651-293-0200; www.nps.gov/miss; 120 W Kellogg Blvd; ☺9:30am-5pm Sun & Tue-Thu, to 9pm Fri & Sat) **FREE** The National Park Service visitor center occupies an alcove in the science museum's lobby. Stop by to pick up trail maps and see what sort of free ranger-guided activities are going on. In summer these include short hikes to the river and bicycle rides. In winter, there are ice-fishing and snowshoeing jaunts.

Tours

Down In History Tours   WALKING TOUR

(☎651-292-1220; www.wabashastreetcaves.com; 215 S Wabasha St; 45min tours $6; ☺4pm Mon, 5pm Thu, 11am Sat & Sun) Explore St Paul's underground caves, which gangsters once used as a speakeasy. The fun ratchets up on Thursday nights, when a swing band plays in the caverns (admission $8).

✴ Festivals & Events

St Paul Winter Carnival CULTURAL
(www.wintercarnival.com; ◷ late Jan) Ten days of ice sculptures, ice skating and ice fishing.

🛏 Sleeping

You'll find a bigger selection of accommodations in Minneapolis.

★ Hotel 340 BOUTIQUE HOTEL $$
(☎ 651-280-4120; www.hotel340.com; 340 Cedar St; r $109-189; 🅿 ❄ @ 🛜) Hotel 340 delivers old-world ambience aplenty, and it's usually a great deal to boot. The 56 rooms in the stately old building have hardwood floors and plush linens. The two-story lobby stokes a grand fireplace and nifty little bar (the desk staff double as bartenders). Continental breakfast is included. Parking costs $17 per night.

Covington Inn B&B $$
(☎ 651-292-1411; www.covingtoninn.com; 100 Harriet Island Rd; r $160-250; 🅿 ❄) This four-room, Harriet Island B&B is on a tugboat floating in the Mississippi River; watch the river traffic glide by while sipping your morning coffee.

🍴 Eating & Drinking

Grand Ave between Dale St and Lexington Pkwy is a worthy browse, with cafes, foodie shops and ethnic eats in close proximity. Selby Ave by the intersection of Western Ave N also holds a quirky lineup.

Mickey's Diner DINER $
(☎ 651-222-5633; www.mickeysdiningcar.com; 36 W 7th St; mains $4-9; ◷ 24hr) Mickey's is a downtown classic, the kind of place where the friendly waitress calls you 'honey' and satisfied regulars line the bar with their coffee cups and newspapers. The food has timeless appeal, too: burgers, malts and apple pie.

Cook AMERICAN $
(☎ 651-756-1787; www.cookstp.com; 1124 Payne Ave; mains $7-12; ◷ 6:30am-2pm Mon-Fri, 7am-3pm Sat & Sun) This cute, sunny spot serves creative diner dishes (gingerbread pancakes, Asiago cheeseburgers, braised short rib sandwiches), including some with a spicy Korean twist. Cook also hosts pop-up dinners on Wednesday nights. It's located in the burgeoning East Side neighborhood, where several other foodie hot spots are sprouting on Payne Ave.

Hmongtown Marketplace ASIAN $
(www.hmongtownmarketplace.com; 217 Como Ave; mains $5-8; ◷ 8am-6:30pm) The nation's largest enclave of Hmong immigrants lives in the Twin Cities, and this market delivers their favorite Vietnamese, Lao and Thai dishes at its humble food court. Find the West Building and head to the back where vendors ladle hot-spiced papaya salad, beef ribs and curry noodle soup. Then stroll the market to buy embroidered dresses, a brass gong or lemongrass.

Happy Gnome PUB
(www.thehappygnome.com; 498 Selby Ave; ◷ 11am-midnight Mon-Wed, to 1am Thu & Fri, 10am-1am Sat, to midnight Sun; 🛜) Seventy craft beers flow from the taps, best sipped on the fireplace-warmed outdoor patio. The pub sits across the parking lot from the St Paul Curling Club.

☆ Entertainment

Fitzgerald Theater THEATER
(☎ 651-290-1221; http://fitzgeraldtheater.public radio.org; 10 E Exchange St) Where Garrison Keillor tapes his radio show *A Prairie Home Companion.*

Ordway Center for Performing Arts CLASSICAL MUSIC
(☎ 651-224-4222; www.ordway.org; 345 Washington St) Chamber music and the Minnesota Opera fill the hall here.

BIG BALL O' TWINE

Behold the **World's Largest Ball of Twine** (1st St; ◷ 24hr) FREE in Darwin, 60 miles west of Minneapolis on US 12. OK, so there are three other Midwest twine balls also claiming to be the largest. But Darwin maintains it has the 'Largest Built by One Person' – Francis A Johnson wrapped the 17,400lb whopper on his farm over the course of 29 years. Gawk at it in the town gazebo. Better yet, visit the **museum** (☎ 320-693-7544; ◷ by appointment) FREE beside it and buy your own twine-ball starter kit in the gift shop.

Xcel Energy Center
HOCKEY

(www.wild.com; 199 Kellogg Blvd) The Wild pro hockey team skates at Xcel.

Shopping

Common Good Books
BOOKS

(www.commongoodbooks.com; 38 S Snelling Ave; ⊙9am-9pm Mon-Sat, 10am-7pm Sun) Garrison Keillor owns this bright bookstore where statues of literary heroes stand guard over long shelves of tomes. It's west of downtown on the Macalester College campus.

ⓘ Information

Visitor Center (☑651-292-3225; www.visit saintpaul.com; 75 W 5th St; ⊙10am-4pm Mon-Sat, from noon Sun) In the Landmark Center; makes a good first stop for maps and DIY walking tour info.

ⓘ Getting There & Around

St Paul is served by the same transit systems as Minneapolis. Union Depot (p599) is the hub for everything: Greyhound buses, city buses, the Green Line light-rail service and Amtrak trains.

Around Minneapolis – St Paul

Mall of America
AMUSEMENT PARK

(www.mallofamerica.com; off I-494 at 24th Ave; ⊙10am-9:30pm Mon-Sat, 11am-7pm Sun; ⋒) Welcome to the USA's largest shopping center. Yes, it's just a mall, filled with the usual stores, movie theaters and eateries. But there's also a wedding chapel inside. And an 18-hole **mini-golf course** (☑952-883-8777; 3rd fl; admission $9). And a zip line. And an amusement park, aka **Nickelodeon Universe** (☑952-883-8600; www.nickelodeon universe.com), with 25 rides, including a couple of scream-inducing roller coasters. To walk through will cost you nothing; a one-day, unlimited-ride wristband is $33; or you can pay for rides individually ($3.50 to $7).

What's more, the state's largest aquarium, **Minnesota Sea Life** (☑952-883-0202; www.visitsealife.com/minnesota; adult/child $25/18) – where children can touch sharks (safe ones!) and stingrays – is in the mall too. Combination passes are available to save dough. The Blue Line light-rail runs to/from downtown Minneapolis. The mall is in suburban Bloomington, a 10-minute ride from the airport.

Fort Snelling
HISTORIC SITE

(☑612-726-1171; www.historicfortsnelling.org; cnr Hwys 5 & 55; adult/child $11/6; ⊙10am-5pm Tue-Sat & noon-5pm Sun Jun-Aug, Sat only Sep & Oct; ⋒) East of the mall, Fort Snelling is the state's oldest structure, established in 1820 as a frontier outpost in the remote Northwest Territory. Guides in period dress show restored buildings and reenact pioneer life.

Southern Minnesota

Some of the scenic southeast can be seen on short drives from the Twin Cities. Better is a loop of a few days' duration, following the rivers and stopping in some of the historic towns and state parks.

Due east of St Paul, on Hwy 36, touristy **Stillwater**, on the lower St Croix River, is an old logging town with restored 19th-century buildings, river cruises and antique stores. It's also an official 'booktown,' an honor bestowed upon a few small towns worldwide that possess an extraordinary number of antiquarian bookshops. Several classy B&Bs add to the scene. **Discover Stillwater** (www.discoverstillwater.com) has details.

Larger **Red Wing**, to the south on US 61, is a similar but less-interesting restored town, though it does offer its famous Red Wing Shoes – actually more like sturdy boots – and salt glaze pottery.

The prettiest part of the **Mississippi Valley** area begins south of here. To drive it and see the best bits, you'll need to flip-flop back and forth between Minnesota and Wisconsin on the Great River Road.

From Red Wing, cross the river on US 63. Before heading south along the water though, make a cheesy detour. Go north on US 63 in Wisconsin for 12 miles until you hit US 10. Turn right, and within a few miles you're in Ellsworth, the 'Cheese Curd Capital.' Pull into **Ellsworth Cooperative Creamery** (☑715-273-4311; www.ellsworthcheese.com; 232 N Wallace St; ⊙9am-5pm) – curd-maker for A&W and Dairy Queen – and savor squeaky goodness hot off the press (11am is prime time).

Back along the river on Wisconsin Hwy 35, a great stretch of road edges the bluffs beside **Maiden Rock**, **Stockholm** and **Pepin**. Follow your nose to local bakeries and cafes in the area.

Continuing south, cross back over the river to **Wabasha** in Minnesota, which has a historic downtown and large population of bald eagles that congregate in winter. To

learn more, visit the **National Eagle Center**
(☑ 651-565-4989; www.nationaleaglecenter.org;
50 Pembroke Ave; adult/child $8/5; ☺10am-5pm,
reduced hours Nov-Feb).

Inland and south, Bluff Country is dotted
with limestone bluffs, southeast Minnesota's
main geological feature. **Lanesboro** (www.
lanesboro.com) is a gem for rails-to-trails cycling and canoeing. Seven miles westward on
County Rd 8 (call for directions) is **Old Barn
Resort** (☑ 507-467-2512; www.barnresort.com;
dm/r/campsite/RVsite $25/50/34/46; ☺Apr–early
Nov; ☎), a pastoral hostel, campground, restaurant and outfitter. **Harmony**, south of
Lanesboro, is the center of an Amish community and another welcoming town.

Duluth & Northern Minnesota

Northern Minnesota is where you come to
'do some fishing, do some drinking,' as one
resident summed it up.

Duluth

At the Great Lakes' westernmost end, Duluth (with its neighbor, Superior, WI) is
one of the busiest ports in the country. The
town's dramatic location spliced into a cliff
makes it a fab place to see changeable Lake
Superior in action. The water, along with
the area's trails and natural splendor, has
earned Duluth a reputation as a hot spot for
outdoors junkies.

◎ Sights & Activities

The waterfront area is distinctive. Mosey
along the Lakewalk trail and around Canal
Park, where most of the sights cluster.

Aerial Lift Bridge   BRIDGE
Duluth's main landmark raises its mighty
arm to let horn-bellowing ships into port.
About 1000 vessels per year glide through.

Maritime Visitor Center   MUSEUM
(☑ 218-720-5260; www.lsmma.com; 600 S Lake
Ave; ☺10am-9pm Jun-Aug, reduced hours Sep-
May) FREE Located next to the Aerial Lift
Bridge, the center has computer screens
inside that tell what time the big ships will
be sailing through. Cool model boats and exhibits on Great Lakes shipwrecks also make
it a top stop in town.

SPAM MUSEUM

Sitting by its lonesome in Austin, near
where I-35 and I-90 intersect in southern Minnesota, lies the **Spam Museum**
(☑ 800-588-7726; www.spam.com; 400
N Main St; admission free; ☺10am-5pm
Mon-Sat, from noon Sun; ♿), an entire
institution devoted to the peculiar meat.
It educates on how the blue tins have
fed armies, become a Hawaiian food
staple and inspired legions of haiku
writers. What's more, you can chat up
the staff (aka 'spambassadors'), indulge
in free samples, and try your hand at
canning the sweet pork magic. Alas, the
museum is closed until mid-2016, when
it opens a shiny new facility downtown.

William A Irvin   MUSEUM
(☑ 218-722-7876; www.williamairvin.com; 350 Har-
bor Dr; adult/child $12/8; ☺9am-6pm Jun-Aug,
10am-4pm May & Sep) To continue the nautical
theme, tour this mighty 610ft Great Lakes
freighter.

Leif Erikson Park   PARK
(cnr London Rd & 14th Ave E) This is a lakefront
sweet spot with a rose garden, a replica of
Leif's Viking ship and free outdoor movies
each Friday night in summer. Take the Lakewalk from Canal Park (about 1½ miles) and
you can say you hiked the Superior Trail,
which traverses this stretch.

Duluth Experience   ADVENTURE TOUR
(☑ 218-464-6337; www.theduluthexperience.com;
tours from $55) It offers a range of kayaking,
cycling and brewery tours; gear and transportation provided.

Vista Fleet   BOAT TOUR
(☑ 218-722-6218; www.vistafleet.com; 323 Har-
bor Dr; adult/child $20/10; ☺mid-May–Oct) Ah,
everyone loves a boat ride. Vista's 75-minute
waterfront cruise is a favorite, departing
from the dock beside the *William A Irvin*
in Canal Park.

Spirit Mountain   SKIING
(☑ 218-628-2891; www.spiritmt.com; 9500 Spirit
Mountain Pl; per day adult/child $40/30; ☺hours
vary) Skiing and snowboarding are big pastimes come winter; in summer there's a zip
line, alpine slide and mini-golf. The mountain is 10 miles south of Duluth.

LOCAL KNOWLEDGE

DYLAN IN DULUTH

While Hibbing and the Iron Range are most often associated with Bob Dylan, he was born in Duluth. You'll see brown-and-white signs on Superior St and London Rd for **Bob Dylan Way** (www. bobdylanway.com), pointing out places associated with the legend (like the armory where he saw Buddy Holly in concert, and decided to become a musician). But you're on your own to find **Dylan's birthplace** (519 N 3rd Ave E), up a hill a few blocks northeast of downtown. Dylan lived on the top floor until age six, when his family moved inland to Hibbing. It's a private residence (and unmarked), so all you can do is stare from the street.

🛏 Sleeping

Duluth has several B&Bs; rooms cost at least $140 in the summer. Check **Duluth Historic Inns** (www.duluthbandb.com) for listings.

The town's accommodations fill up fast in summer, which may mean you'll have to try your luck across the border in Superior, WI (where it's cheaper too).

Fitger's Inn   HOTEL $$
(☎218-722-8826; www.fitgers.com; 600 E Superior St; r $169-279; @🛜) Fitger's created its 62 large rooms, each with slightly varied decor, from an old brewery. Located on the Lakewalk, the pricier rooms have great water views. Continental breakfast is included. The free shuttle to local sights is handy.

Willard Munger Inn   INN $$
(☎218-624-4814; www.mungerinn.com; 7408 Grand Ave; r incl breakfast $70-140; @🛜) Family-owned Munger Inn offers a fine variety of rooms (budget to Jacuzzi suites), along with perks for outdoor enthusiasts, such as hiking and biking trails right outside the door, free use of bikes and canoes, and a fire pit. It's near Spirit Mountain.

🍴 Eating

Most restaurants and bars reduce their hours in winter. The Canal Park waterfront area has eateries in all price ranges.

Duluth Grill   AMERICAN $
(☎218-726-1150; www.duluthgrill.com; 118 S 27th Ave W; mains $10-16; ⏱7am-9pm; 🅿🖶) 🍃 The garden in the parking lot is the tip-off that the Duluth Grill is a sustainable, hippie-vibed place. The diner-esque menu ranges from eggy breakfast skillets to curried polenta stew to bison burgers, with plenty of vegan and gluten-free options. It's a couple miles southwest of Canal Park, near the bridge to Superior, WI.

Northern Waters Smokehaus   SANDWICHES $
(☎218-724-7307; www.northernwaterssmokehaus. com; 394 S Lake Ave, DeWitt-Seitz Marketplace; sandwiches $7-10; ⏱10am-8pm Mon-Sat, to 6pm Sun) 🍃 This little spot smokes sustainably harvested salmon and whitefish; primo for picnics.

★New Scenic Cafe   MODERN AMERICAN $$
(☎218-525-6274; www.sceniccafe.com; 5461 North Shore Dr; sandwiches $10-15, mains $18-28; ⏱11am-9pm Sun-Thu, to 10pm Fri & Sat) Foodies travel from far and near to New Scenic Cafe, 8 miles beyond Duluth on Old Hwy 61. There, in a humble wood-paneled room, they fork into rustic salmon with creamed leeks or a slice of triple berry pie, served with a generous helping of lake views. Make reservations.

Pizza Luce   PIZZA $$
(☎218-727-7400; www.pizzaluce.com; 11 E Superior St; mains $10-20; ⏱10:30am-2am Mon-Fri, from 8am Sat & Sun; 🅵) 🍃 Cooks great brunches and gourmet pizzas (vegan and gluten-free versions too). It's also plugged into the local music scene and hosts bands. Fully licensed.

🍷 Drinking & Nightlife

★Thirsty Pagan   BREWERY
(www.thirstypaganbrewing.com; 1623 Broadway St; ⏱11am-10pm Mon-Thu, to 11pm Fri-Sun) This one's a bit of a trek, over the bridge in Superior, WI (a 10-minute drive), but worth it for the aggressive, spicy beers to wash down hand-tossed pizzas.

Fitger's Brewhouse   BREWERY
(www.brewhouse.net; 600 E Superior St; ⏱11am-midnight Sun & Mon, to 1am Tue-Thu, to 2am Fri & Sat) In the hotel complex, the Brewhouse rocks with live music and fresh brews. Try them via the seven-beer sampler (3oz glasses $9).

Vikre Distillery   COCKTAIL BAR
(www.vikredistillery.com; 525 S Lake Ave; ⏱5-10pm Mon, Wed & Thu, noon-10pm Fri & Sat, noon-5pm Sun) Vikre creates gin with Northwoods-foraged botanicals, as well as aquavit, a Scandinavian spirit infused with caraway and cardamom. Sample them swirled in cocktails in the Canal Park tasting room.

ℹ Information

Duluth Visitors Center (☎800-438-5884; www.visitduluth.com; Harbor Dr; ☺9:30am-7:30pm summer) Seasonal center, opposite the Vista dock.

ℹ Getting There & Away

Greyhound (☎218-722-5591; 4602 Grand Ave) has a couple of buses daily to Minneapolis (three hours).

North Shore

Hwy 61 is the main vein through the North Shore. It edges Lake Superior and passes numerous state parks, waterfalls, hiking trails and mom-and-pop towns en route to Canada. Lots of weekend, summer and fall traffic makes reservations essential.

Stop in **Two Harbors** (www.two harborschamber.com) to gawk at iron-ore freighters at the town's huge docks. **Lighthouse B&B** (☎888-832-5606; www.lighthousebb.org; r incl breakfast $135-175) is a unique place to spend the night; the four rooms in the 1892 fog-buster have sweet lake views. Two miles north of town, **Betty's Pies** (☎218-834-3367; www.bettyspies.com; 1633 Hwy 61; pie slices $4; ☺7:30am-8pm, reduced hours Oct-May) wafts racks of flaky goodness; try a fruit-filled, crunch-topping slice.

Route highlights north of Two Harbors are Gooseberry Falls, Split Rock Lighthouse and Palisade Head. About 110 miles from Duluth, artsy little **Grand Marais** (www.grandmarais.com) makes an excellent base for exploring the Boundary Waters and environs. For Boundary permits and information, visit the **Gunflint Ranger Station** (☎218-387-1750; 2020 Hwy 61; ☺8am-4:30pm May-Sep), just south of town.

Do-it-yourself enthusiasts can learn to build boats, tie flies or butcher pigs at the **North House Folk School** (☎218-387-9762; www.northhouse.org; 500 Hwy 61). The course list is phenomenal – as is the school's two-hour sailing trip aboard the Viking schooner *Hjordis* ($35 to $45 per person). Reserve in advance.

Grand Marais' lodging options include camping, resorts and motels, like the well-placed **Harbor Inn** (☎218-387-1191; www.harborinnhotel.com; 207 Wisconsin St; r $110-145; 🛜) in town or rustic, trail-encircled **Naniboujou Lodge** (☎218-387-2688; www.naniboujou.com; 20 Naniboujou Trail; r $110-150; ☺late May-late Oct), which is 14 miles northeast of town. **Sven and Ole's** (☎218-387-1713; www.svenandoles.com; 9 Wisconsin St; pizzas $10-20; ☺11am-8pm, to 9pm Thu-Sat) is a classic for sandwiches and pizza; beer flows in the attached pub. At **Dockside Fish Market** (www.docksidefishmarket.com; 418 Hwy 61; mains $7-11; ☺9am-7:30pm), the boat heads out in the morning, and by noon the freshly caught herring and whitefish have been fried into fish-and-chips at the deli counter.

Hwy 61 continues to **Grand Portage National Monument** (☎218-475-0123; www.nps.gov/grpo; ☺9am-5pm Jun–mid-Oct) FREE, beside Canada, where the early voyageurs had to carry their canoes around the Pigeon River rapids. This was the center of a far-flung trading empire, and the reconstructed 1788 trading post and Ojibwe village is well worth seeing. **Isle Royale National Park** in Lake Superior is reached by **ferries** (☎218-475-0024; www.isleroyaleboats.com; day trip adult/child $67/37) three to five times per week from June to September. (The park is also accessible from Houghton, MI.)

SCENIC DRIVE: HIGHWAY 61

Hwy 61 conjures a headful of images. Local boy Bob Dylan mythologized it in his angry 1965 album *Highway 61 Revisited*. It's the fabled 'Blues Highway' clasping the Mississippi River en route to New Orleans. And in northern Minnesota, it evokes red-tinged cliffs and forested beaches as it follows Lake Superior's shoreline.

But let's back up and get a few things straight. The Blues Highway is actually US 61, and it starts just north of the Twin Cities. Hwy 61 is a state scenic road, and it starts in Duluth. To confuse matters more, there are two 61s between Duluth and Two Harbors: a four-lane expressway and a two-lane 'Old Hwy 61' (also called North Shore Scenic Drive). Take the latter; it morphs from London Rd in Duluth and veers off to the right just past the entrance to Brighton Beach. After Two Harbors, Hwy 61 returns to one strip of pavement – a gorgeous drive that goes all the way to the Canadian border. For more information, check the North Shore Scenic Drive at www.superiorbyways.com.

SUPERIOR HIKING TRAIL

The 300-mile **Superior Hiking Trail** (www.shta.org) follows the lake-hugging ridgeline between Duluth and the Canadian border. Along the way it passes dramatic red-rock overlooks and the occasional moose and black bear. Trailheads with parking lots pop up every 5 to 10 miles, making it ideal for day hikes. The **Superior Shuttle** (☑ 218-834-5511; www.superiorhikingshuttle.com; from $15; ⊙ Fri-Sun mid-May–mid-Oct) makes life even easier, picking up trekkers from 17 stops along the route. Overnight hikers will find 86 backcountry campsites and several lodges to cushion the body come nightfall; the trail website has details. The whole footpath is free, with no reservations or permits required. The **trail office** (☑ 218-834-2700; cnr Hwy 61 & 8th St; ⊙ 9am-5pm Mon-Fri, 10am-4pm Sat, noon-4pm Sun mid-May–mid-Oct, closed Sat & Sun mid-Oct–mid-May) in Two Harbors provides maps and planning assistance.

Boundary Waters

From Two Harbors, Hwy 2 runs inland to the legendary **Boundary Waters Canoe Area Wilderness (BWCAW)**. This pristine region has more than 1000 lakes and streams in which to dip a paddle. It's possible to go just for the day, but most people opt for at least one night of camping. If you're willing to dig in and canoe for a while, you'll lose the crowds. Camping then becomes a wonderfully remote experience where it will be you, the howling wolves, the moose who's nuzzling the tent and the aurora borealis' greenish light filling the night sky. Beginners are welcome, and everyone can get set up with gear from local lodges and outfitters. Permits for **camping** (☑ 877-550-6777; www.recreation.gov; adult/child $16/8, plus $6 reservation fee) are required for overnight stays. Day permits, though free, are also required; get them at BWCAW entry-point kiosks or ranger stations. Call **Superior National Forest** (☑ 218-626-4300; www.fs.usda.gov/attmain/superior/specialplaces) for details; the website has a useful trip planning guide. Plan ahead, as permits are quota restricted and often run out.

Many argue the best BWCAW access is via the engaging town of **Ely** (www.ely.org), northeast of the Iron Range area, which has accommodations, restaurants and scores of outfitters. The **International Wolf Center** (☑ 218-365-4695; www.wolf.org; 1369 Hwy 169; adult/child $10.50/6.50; ⊙ 10am-5pm mid-May–mid-Oct, Fri-Sun only mid-Oct–mid-May) offers intriguing exhibits and wolf-viewing trips. Across the highway from the center, **Kawishiwi Ranger Station** (☑ 218-365-7600; 1393 Hwy 169; ⊙ 8am-4:30pm May-Sep) provides expert BWCAW camping and canoeing details, trip suggestions and required permits.

In winter, Ely gets mushy – it's a renowned dogsledding town. Outfitters such as **Wintergreen Dogsled Lodge** (☑ 218-365-6022; www.dogsledding.com; 4hr tours adult/child $150/100) offer numerous packages.

Iron Range District

An area of red-tinged scrubby hills rather than mountains, Minnesota's Iron Range District consists of the Mesabi and Vermilion Ranges, running north and south of Hwy 169 from roughly Grand Rapids northeast to Ely. Iron was discovered here in the 1850s, and at one time more than three-quarters of the nation's iron ore was extracted from these vast open-pit mines. Visitors can see working mines and the terrain's raw, sparse beauty all along Hwy 169.

In **Calumet**, a perfect introduction is the **Hill Annex Mine State Park** (☑ 218-247-7215; www.dnr.state.mn.us/hill_annex; 880 Gary St; tours adult/child $10/6; ⊙ 12:30pm & 3pm Fri & Sat late-May-early Sep), with its open-pit tours and exhibit center. Tours are held in summertime only, on Friday and Saturday; there's also a fossil tour both days at 10am.

An even bigger pit sprawls in **Hibbing**, where a must-see **viewpoint** (401 Penobscot Rd; ⊙ 9am-5pm mid-May–Sep) north of town overlooks the 3-mile Hull Rust Mahoning Mine. Bob Dylan lived at 2425 E 7th Ave as a boy and teenager; the **Hibbing Public Library** (☑ 218-362-5959; www.hibbing.lib.mn.us; 2020 E 5th Ave; ⊙ 10am-7pm Mon-Thu, to 5pm Fri) has well-done Dylan displays and a free walking-tour map (available online, too) that takes you past various sites, like the place where Bobby had his bar mitzvah. To snooze try the **Mitchell-Tappan House** (☑ 218-262-3862; www.mitchell-tappanhouse.com; 2125 4th Avenue E; r with shared bath $90, r with private bath $100-110; ❋ 🕏), a mining honcho's semi-frilly Victorian abode that's the best lodging around for the price.

Up in the range's northeast corner, the **Soudan Underground Mine** (www.mndnr.gov/soudan; 1379 Stuntz Bay Rd; tours adult/child $12/7; ⊙ 10am-4pm late May-late Sep) is the state's oldest and deepest pit. Wear warm clothes for the half-mile descent below ground.

Voyageurs National Park

In the 17th century, French-Canadian fur traders, or voyageurs, began exploring the Great Lakes and northern rivers by canoe. **Voyageurs National Park** (www.nps.gov/voya) FREE covers part of their customary waterway, which became the border between the USA and Canada.

It's all about water up here. Most of the park is accessible only by hiking or motorboat – the waters are mostly too wide and too rough for canoeing, though kayaks are becoming popular. A few access roads lead to campgrounds and lodges on or near Lake Superior, but these are mostly used by people putting in their own boats.

The visitor centers are car accessible and good places to begin your visit. Twelve miles east of International Falls on Hwy 11 is **Rainy Lake Visitors Center** (☑ 218-286-5258; ⊙ 9:30am-5pm late May–mid-Oct, reduced hours rest of year), the main park office. Ranger-guided walks and boat tours are available here. Seasonal visitor centers are at **Ash River** (☑ 218-374-3221; ⊙ 9:30am-5pm late May-late Sep) and **Kabetogama Lake** (☑ 218-875-2111; ⊙ 9:30am-5pm late May-late Sep). These areas have outfitters, rentals and services, plus some smaller bays for canoeing.

Houseboating is all the rage in the region. Outfitters such as **Ebel's** (☑ 888-883-2357; www.ebels.com; 10326 Ash River Trail) and **Voyagaire Houseboats** (☑ 800-882-6287; www.voyagaire.com; 7576 Gold Coast Rd) can set you up. Rentals range from $275 to $700 per day, depending on boat size. Novice boaters are welcome and receive instruction on how to operate the vessels.

Otherwise, for sleeping, your choices are pretty much camping or resorts. The 12-room, shared-bath **Kettle Falls Hotel** (☑ 218-240-1724; www.kettlefallshotel.com; r/cottage $80/180; ⊙ May-late Oct) is an exception, located inside the park and accessible only by boat; make arrangements with the owners for pick-up ($45 per person roundtrip). **Nelson's Resort** (☑ 800-433-0743; www.nelsonsresort.com; 7632 Nelson Rd; cabins from $205) at Crane Lake is a winner for hiking, fishing and relaxing under blue skies.

While this is certainly a remote and wild area, those seeking wildlife, canoeing and forest camping in all their glory are best off in the Boundary Waters.

Bemidji & Chippewa National Forest

This area is synonymous with outdoor activities and summer fun. Campsites and cottages abound; almost everybody is fishing-crazy.

Itasca State Park (☑ 218-266-2100; www.dnr.state.mn.us/itasca; off Hwy 71 N; per vehicle $5, tent & RV sites $17-31) is an area highlight. You can walk across the tiny headwaters of the mighty Mississippi River, rent canoes or bikes, hike the trails and camp. The log **HI Mississippi Headwaters Hostel** (☑ 218-266-3415; www.hiusa.org/parkrapids; 27910 Forest Lane; dm $26-28, r $90-145; ⊙ closed Apr, Nov & Dec; ❇☎) is in the park; winter hours vary, so call ahead. Or if you want a little rustic luxury, try the venerable **Douglas Lodge** (☑ 866-857-2757; r $99-145; ☎), run by the park, which also has cabins and a good restaurant.

On the western edge of the forest, about 30 miles from Itasca, tidy **Bemidji** is an old lumber town with a well-preserved downtown and a giant statue of logger Paul Bunyan and his faithful blue ox, Babe. The **visitor center** (www.visitbemidji.com; 300 Bemidji Ave N; ⊙ 8am-5pm Mon-Fri, 10am-4pm Sat, 11am-2pm Sun Jun-Aug, closed Sat & Sun Sep-May) displays Paul's toothbrush.

Understand Eastern USA

Eastern USA Today

A historic ruling by the Supreme Court legalized gay marriage – this on the heels of another high court ruling on health care, a pivotal legacy of President Obama. Meanwhile, mass shootings continue with scary regularity, prompting debates on gun control. And income inequality keeps raising its head across the landscape.

Best in Print

To Kill a Mockingbird (Harper Lee; 1960) Pulitzer winner about racism in Depression-era Alabama.

A Confederacy of Dunces (John Kennedy Toole; 1980) Pulitzer winner about a New Orleans misfit questing for a job.

Freedom (Jonathan Franzen; 2010) Follows a complex, troubled family living in modern-day Minnesota and New York City.

Redeployment (Phil Klay, 2014) National Book Award winner about soldiers and veterans dealing with the Iraq War.

Best on Film

Gone with the Wind (directed by Victor Fleming; 1939) Civil War–era saga of the South.

Mr Smith Goes to Washington (directed by Frank Capra; 1939) Jimmy Stewart gets a crash course in DC politics and corruption.

The Untouchables (directed by Brian De Palma; 1987) Eliot Ness takes down Al Capone in gangster-era Chicago.

12 Years a Slave (directed by Steve McQueen, 2013) A free African American man is kidnapped and sold into slavery in 1841.

A Rainbow Nation

No one who witnessed the Stonewall Riots – which sparked the gay liberation movement in 1969 – could have imagined that he or she would live to see the day when gay marriage would become legal in the United States. Yet on June 26, 2015, that's exactly what happened when the US Supreme Court ruled that all states must recognize same-sex marriage licenses. The historic ruling was the culmination of a long legal battle by gay rights advocates, and there was much euphoria on the streets. Major sites like the Empire State Building, Cinderella's Castle at Disney World – and even the White House – lit up their facades in rainbow colors, in proud support of the ruling. A Gallup poll after the verdict found that nearly 60% of Americans supported same-sex marriage, with some eight in 10 young adults favoring gay marriage.

Health Care for All

The ruling on same-sex marriages came just days after another important ruling. This one related to the Affordable Care Act (ACA), President Obama's program to extend health care through subsidies to millions of uninsured Americans. The court upheld key provisions of the law (the second time the Supreme Court had ruled on it), though ongoing threats to the law remain. Since 2011, Congress has tried (unsuccessfully) to repeal it more than 50 times.

Despite congressional obstructionism, the program has allowed more than 16 million uninsured Americans to obtain coverage. Republican critics of the program claim Obamacare would kill jobs and cripple the US economy – a claim Obama refuted, saying that instead of hurting the economy, the ACA had actually provided a boost. In 2015, Health and Human Services Secretary Sylvia Burwell announced that hospitals had saved

$7.4 billion in uncompensated care costs during the previous year owing to patient enrollment in the program's health insurance exchanges and Medicaid. States in the east, including Vermont and Rhode Island, are among those with the highest percentage of residents enrolled.

Income Inequality

The income gap continues to widen in the US. The top 1% of the population earns 20% of the income (up from 9% in 1976). Meanwhile, the poor are getting poorer: the median wage earner took home 11% less than in 1999. Unfortunately, it isn't just the income gap that is widening. Rich people in America are living longer than poor people: the wealthy lived 2.7 years longer than the poor in the 1980s, while they live 4.5 years longer today. And their children are outpacing their poorer peers by bigger margins (the gap in test scores between rich and poor is over 30% wider than it was two decades ago).

The split is particularly prevalent in the eastern half of the country. According to the 2013–2014 Measure of America report – which looks at well-being (including health, education and earnings) on a state-by-state basis – Connecticut, Massachusetts, Maryland and New Jersey are the nation's best for health and opportunity, while Mississippi, West Virginia and Alabama are the nation's worst.

Gun Violence

Mass shootings have been occurring with alarming frequency in recent years. Devastating incidents include the 2015 murders in Charleston, South Carolina, where a 21-year-old man attended a bible-study session at a historic African American church and killed nine people. In 2012, a heavily armed 20-year-old killed 20 young children and six adults at an elementary school in Newtown, Connecticut. On average, 32 Americans are murdered by guns every day, and another 140 wounded.

Yet despite evidence (such as a 2013 study published in the prestigious *American Journal of Medicine*) that more guns equals more murders, and the comparatively low rates of death by firearms in countries with strict gun laws, American legislators have been unwilling to enact even modest gun-control laws. After the racially motivated mass shooting in Charleston, Obama seemed resigned that nothing would ever change. The reason in part: gun lobbies such as the National Rifle Association (NRA) wield lots of power, contributing over $35 million annually to state and national political campaigns. But Americans are also enamored of their guns: a recent Pew Research poll found that 52% of Americans said it was more important to protect gun rights than to control gun ownership.

HOUSEHOLD INCOME, MARYLAND (2012–14): **$69,826**

HOUSEHOLD INCOME, MISSISSIPPI (2012–14): **$40,194**

POPULATION DENSITY, NEW YORK CITY: **27,530 PER SQ MILE**

POPULATION DENSITY, MAINE: **43 PER SQ MILE**

CHEESE PRODUCED ANNUALLY, WISCONSIN: **2.5 BILLION POUNDS**

PERCENT OF DETROIT'S BUILDINGS THAT ARE ABANDONED (2014): **30**

if USA were 100 people

65 would be white
15 would be Hispanic
13 would be African American
4 would be Asian American
3 would be other

belief systems
(% of population)

Protestant   Roman Catholic

Other   Jewish   Mormon
           2   2

population per sq mile

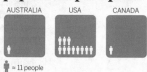

AUSTRALIA   USA   CANADA

≈ 11 people

History

From its early days as an English colony to its rise to the forefront of the world stage in the 20th century, American history has been anything but dull. War against the British, westward expansion, slavery and its abolishment, Civil War and Reconstruction, the Great Depression, the postwar boom and more recent conflicts in the 21st century – they've all played a part in shaping the nation's complicated identity.

First Inhabitants

Among North America's most significant prehistoric cultures were the Mound Builders, who inhabited the Ohio and Mississippi River valleys from around 3000 BC to AD 1200. They left behind enigmatic piles of earth that were tombs for their leaders and possibly tributes to their gods. In Illinois, Cahokia was once a metropolis of 20,000 people, the largest in pre-Columbian North America. Similar mounds rise up throughout the eastern USA, including several along the Natchez Trace in Mississippi.

By the time the first Europeans arrived, several different groups of Native Americans occupied the land, such as the Wampanoag in New England, the Calusa in southern Florida and the Shawnee in the Midwest. Two centuries later, they were all but gone. European explorers left diseases in their wake to which indigenous peoples had no immunity. More than any other factor – war, slavery or famine – disease epidemics devastated Native American populations by anywhere from 50% to 90%.

European Claims

In 1492, Italian explorer Christopher Columbus, backed by Spain, voyaged west looking for the East Indies. He found the Bahamas. With visions of gold, Spanish explorers quickly followed: Cortés conquered much of today's Mexico, Pizarro conquered Peru, and Ponce de León wandered through Florida looking for the fountain of youth. Not to be left out, the French explored Canada and the Midwest, while the Dutch and English cruised North America's eastern seaboard.

The first European-founded (and oldest continuously settled) city in North America was St Augustine, Florida, where the Spanish set up shop

Great History Museums

Henry Ford Museum/ Greenfield Village, Detroit

National Civil Rights Museum, Memphis

Nantucket Whaling Museum, Massachusetts

National Museum of the American Indian, Washington, DC

TIMELINE	7000 BC– AD 100	1492	1607
	'Archaic period' of nomadic hunter-gatherer lifestyles. By the end of this period, corn, beans and squash (the agricultural 'three sisters') and permanent settlements are well established.	Italian explorer Christopher Columbus 'discovers' America. He names the indigenous inhabitants 'Indians,' mistakenly thinking he had sailed to the East Indies.	The Jamestown settlement, the first permanent English colony in North America, is founded on marshland in present-day Virginia. The first few years are hard, with many dying from sickness and starvation.

in 1565. Up the coast in 1607, a group of English noblemen established that country's first permanent North American settlement at Jamestown. Earlier English settlements had ended badly, and Jamestown almost did, too: the noblemen chose a swamp, planted their crops late and died from disease and starvation. Local tribes provided the settlement with enough aid to survive.

For Jamestown and America, 1619 proved a pivotal year: the colony established the House of Burgesses, a representative assembly of citizens to decide local laws, and it received its first boatload of 20 African slaves. The next year was equally momentous, as a group of radically religious Puritans pulled ashore at what would become Plymouth, Massachusetts. The Pilgrims were escaping religious persecution under the 'corrupt' Church of England, and in the New World they saw a divine opportunity to create a new society that would be a religious and moral beacon. The Pilgrims signed a 'Mayflower Compact', one of the seminal texts of American democracy, to govern themselves by consensus.

Capitalism & Colonialism

For the next two centuries, European powers competed for position and territory in the New World, extending European politics into the Americas. As Britain's Royal Navy came to rule Atlantic seas, England increasingly profited from its colonies and eagerly consumed the fruits of their labors – tobacco from Virginia, sugar and coffee from the Caribbean. Over the 17th and 18th centuries, slavery in America was slowly legalized into a formal institution to support this plantation economy. By 1800, one out of every five persons was a slave.

Meanwhile, Britain mostly left the American colonists to govern themselves. Town meetings and representative assemblies, in which local citizens (that is, white men with property) debated community problems and voted on laws and taxes, became common. By the end of the Seven Years' War in 1763, Britain was feeling the strains of running an empire: it had been fighting France for a century and had colonies scattered all over the world. It was time to clean up bureaucracies and share financial burdens.

The colonies, however, resented English taxes and policies. Frustrations came to a head with the Boston Tea Party in 1773, after which Britain clamped down hard, shutting Boston's harbor and increasing its military presence. In 1774, representatives from 12 colonies convened the First Continental Congress in Philadelphia's Independence Hall to air complaints and prepare for the inevitable war ahead.

Revolution & the Republic

In April 1775, British troops skirmished with armed colonists in Massachusetts (who were prepared for the fight, thanks to Paul Revere's

Before Jamestown or Plymouth Rock, a group of 116 British men and women set up a colony at Roanoke, North Carolina in the late 1580s. When a supply ship returned three years later, the settlers had disappeared. The fate of the 'Lost Colony' remains one of America's greatest mysteries.

The New World (2005), directed by Terrence Malick, is a brutal but passionate film that retells the tragic story of the Jamestown colony and the pivotal peace-making role of Pocahontas, a Powhatan chief's daughter.

1620	1675	1773	1775
The *Mayflower* lands at Plymouth with 102 English Pilgrims, who have come to the New World to escape religious persecution. The Wampanoag tribe saves them from starvation.	For decades, the Pilgrims and local tribes live fairly cooperatively, but deadly conflict erupts in 1675. King Philip's War lasts 14 months and kills over 5000 people (mostly Native Americans).	To protest a British tax on tea, Bostonians dress as Mohawks, board East India Company ships and toss their tea overboard – later named the Boston Tea Party.	Paul Revere rides from Boston to warn colonial fighters (Minutemen) that the British are coming. The next day, the 'shot heard round the world' is fired at Lexington, starting the Revolutionary War.

famous warning), and the Revolutionary War began. George Washington, a wealthy Virginia farmer, was chosen to lead the American army. Trouble was, Washington lacked gunpowder and money (the colonists resisted taxes even for their own military), and his troops were a motley collection of poorly armed farmers, hunters and merchants, who regularly quit and returned to their farms due to lack of pay. On the other side, the British 'Redcoats' represented the world's most powerful military. The inexperienced General Washington had to improvise constantly, sometimes wisely retreating, sometimes engaging in 'ungentlemanly' sneak attacks. During the winter of 1777–78, the American army nearly starved at Valley Forge, Pennsylvania.

Meanwhile, the Second Continental Congress tried to articulate what exactly they were fighting for. In January 1776, Thomas Paine published the wildly popular *Common Sense*, which passionately argued for independence from England. Soon, independence seemed not just logical, but noble and necessary, and on July 4, 1776, the Declaration of Independence was finalized and signed. Largely written by Thomas Jefferson, it elevated the 13 colonies' particular gripes against the monarchy into a universal declaration of individual rights and republican government.

But to succeed, General Washington needed help, not just patriotic sentiment. In 1778, Benjamin Franklin persuaded France (always eager to trouble England) to ally with the revolutionaries, and they provided the troops, material and sea power that helped win the war. The British surrendered at Yorktown, Virginia, in 1781, and two years later the Treaty of Paris formally recognized the 'United States of America.' At first, the nation's loose confederation of fractious, squabbling states were hardly 'united.' So the founders gathered again in Philadelphia, and in 1787 drafted a new-and-improved Constitution: the US government was given a stronger federal center, with checks and balances between its three major branches, and to guard against the abuse of centralized power, a citizen's Bill of Rights was approved in 1791.

As radical as it was, though, the Constitution also preserved the economic and social status quo. Rich landholders kept their property, which included their slaves; Native Americans were excluded from the nation; and women were excluded from politics. These blatant discrepancies and injustices, which were widely noted, were the result of pragmatic compromise (eg to get slave-dependent Southern states on board) as well as widespread beliefs in the essential rightness of things as they were.

Louisiana Purchase & the Move West

As the 19th century dawned on the young nation, optimism was the mood of the day. Agriculture was industrialized, and US commerce surged. In 1803 Thomas Jefferson bought land from French leader

1776	1787	1791	1803–06
On July 4, colonies sign the Declaration of Independence. Creators of the document include John Hancock, Samuel Adams, John Adams, Benjamin Franklin and Thomas Jefferson.	The Constitutional Convention in Philadelphia draws up the US Constitution. Federal power is balanced between the presidency, Congress and the judiciary.	Bill of Rights is adopted as 10 constitutional amendments articulating citizens' rights, including freedom of speech, a free press and the right to bear arms.	President Thomas Jefferson sends Meriwether Lewis and William Clark west. Guided by the Shoshone tribeswoman Sacajawea, they trailblaze from St Louis, Missouri, to the Pacific Ocean and back.

THE AFRICAN AMERICAN EXPERIENCE: THE STRUGGLE FOR EQUALITY

It's impossible to grasp American history without taking into account the great struggles and hard-won victories of African Americans from all spheres of life.

Slavery

From the early 1600s until the 1800s, an estimated 600,000 slaves were brought from Africa to America. Those who survived the horrific transport on crowded ships (which sometimes had 50% mortality rates) were sold in slave markets (African males cost $27 in 1638). The majority of slaves ended up in Southern plantations where conditions were usually brutal – whipping and branding were commonplace.

All (White) Men are Created Equal

Many of the founding fathers – George Washington, Thomas Jefferson and Benjamin Franklin – owned slaves, though they privately expressed condemnation for the abominable practice. The abolition movement, however, wouldn't appear until the 1830s, long after the appearance on the Declaration of Independence of the rousing but ultimately hollow words 'all men are created equal.'

Free at Last

While some revisionist historians describe the Civil War as being about states' rights, most scholars agree that the war was really about slavery. Following the Union victory at Antietam, Lincoln drafted the Emancipation Proclamation, which freed all blacks in occupied territories. African Americans joined the Union effort, with more than 180,000 serving by war's end.

Jim Crow Laws

During Reconstruction (1865–77), federal laws provided civil rights protection for newly freed blacks. Southern bitterness, however, coupled with centuries of prejudice, fueled a backlash. By the 1890s, the Jim Crow laws (named after a derogatory character in a minstrel show) appeared. African Americans were effectively disenfranchised, and America became a deeply segregated society.

Civil Rights Movement

In the 1950s a movement was underway in African American communities to fight for equality. Rosa Parks, who refused to give up her seat to a white passenger, inspired the Montgomery bus boycott. There were sit-ins at lunch counters where blacks were excluded; massive demonstrations led by Martin Luther King Jr in Washington, DC; and harrowing journeys by 'freedom riders' aiming to end bus segregation. The work of millions paid off: in 1964 President Johnson signed the Civil Rights Act, which banned discrimination and racial segregation.

1812	1861–65	1870	1880–1920
The War of 1812 begins with battles against the British and Native Americans in the Great Lakes region. Even after the 1815 Treaty of Ghent, fighting continues along the Gulf Coast.	American Civil War erupts between North and South (delineated by the Mason–Dixon line). The war's end on April 9, 1865, is marred by President Lincoln's assassination five days later.	Freed black men are given the vote, but the South's segregationist 'Jim Crow' laws (which remain until the 1960s) effectively disenfranchise blacks from every meaningful sphere of daily life.	Millions of immigrants flood in from Europe and Asia, fueling the age of cities. New York, Chicago and Philadelphia swell in size, becoming global centers of industry and commerce.

Napoleon Bonaparte. The Louisiana Purchase included New Orleans and about 15 present-day states west of the Mississippi River. Expansion began in earnest.

Relations between the US and Britain – despite lively trade – remained tense, and in 1812, the US declared war on England again. The two-year conflict ended without much gain by either side, although the British abandoned their forts, and the US vowed to avoid Europe's 'entangling alliances.'

In the 1830s and 1840s, with growing nationalist fervor and dreams of continental expansion, many Americans came to believe it was 'Manifest Destiny' that all the land in North American should be theirs. The 1830 Indian Removal Act aimed to clear one obstacle by designating land west of the Mississippi as 'Indian territory.' Native Americans were meant to relocate themselves there, thus clearing fertile valleys in eastern states like Georgia and Alabama for white settlement. Many tribes resisted removal, including the Seminole in Florida, but the US government cajoled, threatened and bribed Native Americans to sign treaties and cooperate; when that failed, the government used guns.

Meanwhile, newly built railroads cleared another hurdle, linking Midwestern and Western lands with East Coast markets. As new states joined the USA, a troubling question loomed: would they be slave states or free states? The nation's future depended on the answer.

The Civil War

The US Constitution hadn't ended slavery, but it had given Congress the power to approve (or not) slavery in new states. Public debates raged constantly over the expansion of slavery, particularly since this shaped the balance of power between the industrial North and the agrarian South.

Since founding, Southern politicians had dominated government and defended slavery as 'natural and normal,' which an 1856 *New York Times* editorial called 'insanity.' The Southern pro-slavery lobby enraged Northern abolitionists – but even many Northern politicians feared that ending slavery with a pen-stroke would be ruinous. Limit slavery, they reasoned, and in the competition with industry and free labor, slavery would wither without inciting a violent slave revolt – a constantly feared possibility. Indeed, in 1859, radical abolitionist John Brown tried (unsuccessfully) to spark such an uprising at Harpers Ferry.

The economics of slavery were undeniable. In 1860, there were over four million slaves in the US, most held by Southern planters – who grew 75% of the world's cotton, accounting for over half of US exports. Thus, the Southern economy supported the nation's economy, and it required slaves. The 1860 presidential election became a referendum on this issue, and the election was won by a young politician from Illinois who favored limiting slavery: Abraham Lincoln.

The whaling industry thrived in New England in the 18th century, especially around Massachusetts. Buzzards Bay, Nantucket Island and New Bedford were all prominent centers. New Bedford eventually hosted a whaling fleet of over 300 ships, employing 10,000 people and earning over $12 million in profits.

1896	1908	1917	1919
In Plessy v Ferguson, the US Supreme Court rules that 'separate but equal' public facilities for blacks and whites are legal, arguing that the Constitution addresses only political, not social, equality.	The first Model T (aka 'Tin Lizzie') car is built in Detroit, MI. Assembly-line innovator Henry Ford is soon selling one million automobiles annually.	President Woodrow Wilson enters the US into WWI. The US mobilizes 4.7 million troops, and suffers around 110,000 of the war's nine million military deaths.	The temperance movement champions the 18th amendment, which bans alcohol. Prohibition is unsuccessful, leading to bootlegging and organized crime. The amendment is repealed in 1933.

In the South, even the threat of federal limits was too onerous to abide, and as President Lincoln took office, 11 states seceded from the Union and formed the Confederate States of America. Lincoln faced the nation's greatest moment of crisis. He had two choices: let the Southern states secede and dissolve the Union, or wage war to keep the Union intact. He chose the latter.

War began in April 1861, when the Confederacy attacked Fort Sumter in Charleston, South Carolina, and raged on for the next four years – in the most gruesome combat the world had ever known until that time. By the end, over 600,000 soldiers, nearly an entire generation of young men, were dead. Southern plantations and cities (most notably Atlanta) lay sacked and burned. The North's industrial might provided an advantage, but its victory was not preordained; it unfolded battle by bloody battle.

As fighting progressed, Lincoln recognized that if the war didn't end slavery outright, victory would be pointless. In 1863, his Emancipation Proclamation expanded the war's aims and freed all slaves. In April 1865, Confederate General Robert E Lee surrendered to Union General Ulysses S Grant in Appomattox, Virginia. The Union had been preserved, but at a staggering cost.

The Great Depression, the New Deal & World War II

In October 1929, investors, worried over a gloomy global economy, started selling stocks – seeing others selling, everyone panicked until they'd sold everything. The stock market crashed, and the US economy collapsed like a house of cards.

Thus began the Great Depression. Frightened banks called in their dodgy loans, people couldn't pay, and the banks folded. Millions lost their homes, farms, businesses and savings, and as much as 33% of the American workforce became unemployed. Bread lines and shanty towns sprang up in cities; New York's Central Park held one of the biggest camps. In 1932, Democrat Franklin D Roosevelt was elected president on the promise of a 'New Deal' to rescue the US from its crisis, which he did with resounding success. When war once again broke out in Europe in 1939, the isolationist mood in America was as strong as ever. However, the extremely popular President Roosevelt, elected to an unprecedented third term in 1940, understood that the US couldn't sit by and allow victory for fascist, totalitarian regimes. Roosevelt sent aid to Britain and persuaded a skittish Congress to go along with it.

Then, on December 7, 1941, Japan launched a surprise attack on Hawaii's Pearl Harbor, killing over 2000 Americans and sinking several battleships. US isolationism transformed overnight into outrage, and Roosevelt

For 100-plus years, Tecumseh's Curse loomed over presidents elected in a year ending in zero (every 20 years). Tecumseh was a Shawnee warrior whom president-to-be William Henry Harrison battled in 1811. Tecumseh hexed him as revenge. Harrison became president in 1840, but died a month later. Lincoln and Kennedy were also victims.

1920s	1933–38	1941–45	1948–51
Spurred by massive African American migration to northern cities, the Harlem Renaissance inspires an intellectual flowering of literature, art and music.	Roosevelt's New Deal establishes federal programs and legislation including Social Security, the Fair Labor Standards Act and the Civilian Conservation Corps to provide unemployment relief.	WWII: America deploys 16 million troops and suffers 400,000 deaths. (Overall, civilian deaths outpace military deaths two to one, and total 50 to 70 million people from over 50 countries.)	The US-led Marshall Plan funnels $12 billion in material and financial aid to help Europe recover from WWII. The plan also aims to contain Soviet influence and reignite America's economy.

NEW DEAL: RESCUING THE USA FROM ITS GREAT DEPRESSION

America reached its lowest point in history during the Great Depression. By 1932, nearly one third of all American workers were unemployed. National output fell by 50%, hundreds of banks were shuttered, and great swaths of the country seemed to disappear beneath enormous dust storms. Franklin Roosevelt easily won the 1932 election, and rather casually promised to give Americans a new deal. So began one of America's most progressive eras in history, under the rule of one of its most popular presidents.

Roosevelt wasted no time getting down to work. During his first 100 days, he completed the rescue of the ailing banking system with the creation of deposit insurance. He sent $500 million to states for direct relief and saved a fifth of all homeowners from foreclosure. He also sent people back to work on a grand scale. He created the Civilian Conservation Corps, which gave jobs to 250,000 young men to work in the parks and forests; they would go on to plant two billion trees. He also created the Works Progress Administration (WPA), which put another 600,000 to work on major projects across the country – building bridges, tunnels, dams, power plants, waterworks, highways, schools and town halls.

The New Deal wasn't just about infrastructure. Some 5000 artists (including famed Mexican painter Diego Rivera) were employed painting murals and creating sculptures in public buildings – many are still in existence today. Over 6000 writers were put to work crisscrossing the country, recording oral histories and folktales and compiling ethnographic studies.

---

suddenly had the support he needed. Germany also declared war on the US, and America joined the Allied fight against Hitler and the Axis powers. From that moment, the US put almost its entire will and industrial prowess into the war effort.

Fighting went on for over two years in both the Pacific and in Europe. The US finally dealt the fatal blow to Germany with its massive D-Day invasion of France on June 6, 1944. Germany surrendered in May 1945. Nevertheless, Japan continued fighting. Newly elected President Harry Truman – ostensibly worried that a US invasion of Japan would lead to unprecedented carnage – chose to drop experimental atomic bombs, created by the government's top-secret Manhattan Project, on Hiroshima and Nagasaki in August 1945. The bombs devastated both cities, killing over 200,000 people. Japan surrendered days later, and the nuclear age was born.

The Red Scare, Civil Rights & Vietnam War

The US enjoyed unprecedented prosperity in the decades after WWII but little peace. Formerly wartime allies, the communist Soviet Union and the capitalist USA soon engaged in a running competition to dominate

1954	1963	1964	1965–75
The Supreme Court rules that segregation in public schools is 'inherently unequal' and orders desegregation 'with all deliberate speed.' The fight to integrate schools spurs the Civil Rights movement.	On November 22, President John F Kennedy is publicly assassinated by Lee Harvey Oswald while riding in a motorcade through Dealey Plaza in Dallas, Texas.	Congress passes the Civil Rights Act, outlawing discrimination on the basis of race, color, religion, sex or national origin. First proposed by Kennedy, it was one of President Johnson's crowning achievements.	US involvement in the Vietnam War tears the nation apart as 58,000 Americans die, along with four million Vietnamese and 1.5 million Laotians and Cambodians.

the globe. The superpowers engaged in proxy wars – notably the Korean War (1950–53) and Vietnam War (1954–75) – with only the mutual threat of nuclear annihilation preventing direct war.

Meanwhile, with its continent unscarred and its industry bulked up by WWII, the American homeland entered an era of growing affluence. In the 1950s, masses of inner-city dwellers migrated to the suburbs, where affordable single-family homes sprang up. Americans drove cheap cars using cheap gas over brand-new interstate highways. They relaxed with the comforts of modern technology, swooned over TV, and got busy, giving birth to a 'baby boom.' Middle-class whites did, anyway. African Americans remained segregated, poor and generally unwelcome at the party. Echoing 19th-century abolitionist Frederick Douglass, the Southern Christian Leadership Coalition (SCLC), led by African American preacher Martin Luther King Jr, aimed to end segregation and 'save America's soul': to realize color-blind justice, racial equality and fairness of economic opportunity for all.

Beginning in the 1950s, King preached and organized nonviolent resistance in the form of bus boycotts, marches and sit-ins, mainly in the South. White authorities often met these protests with water hoses and police batons, and demonstrations sometimes dissolved into riots, but with the 1964 Civil Rights Act, African Americans spurred a wave of legislation that swept away racist laws and laid the groundwork for a more just and equal society.

Meanwhile, the 1960s saw further social upheavals: rock and roll spawned a youth rebellion and drugs sent Technicolor visions spinning in their heads. President John F Kennedy was assassinated in Dallas in 1963, followed by the assassinations in 1968 of his brother, Senator Robert Kennedy, and of Martin Luther King (in Memphis). Americans' faith in their leaders and government was further shocked by the bombings and brutalities of the Vietnam War, as seen on TV, which led to widespread student protests. Yet Republican President Richard Nixon, elected in 1968 partly for promising an 'honorable end to the war,' instead escalated US involvement and secretly bombed Laos and Cambodia. Then, in 1972, the Watergate scandal broke: a burglary at Democratic Party offices in Washington was, through dogged journalism, tied to 'Tricky Dick,' who in 1974 became the first US president to resign from office.

The tumultuous 1960s and '70s also witnessed the sexual revolution, women's liberation and other events challenging the status quo. Milestones included the 1969 Stonewall riots in Greenwich Village, NYC, which galvanized the gay rights movement when patrons of a gay bar called the Stonewall Inn fought back after a police raid, demanding equal rights and an end to persecution. A few months later, the Woodstock Festival defined the Vietnam era with its peace-love-and-flowers hippies swaying in the fields to rock music.

Civil Rights on Film

Selma (2014), Ava DuVernay

Malcolm X (1992), Spike Lee

Mississippi Burning (1988), Alan Parker

Ghosts of Mississippi (1996), Rob Reiner

The Long Walk Home (1990), Richard Pearce

Though the town of Woodstock, NY, lent its name to the mythic 1969 music fest, the event actually took place in the nearby hamlet of Bethel, where dairy farmer Max Yasgur rented his alfalfa field to organizers. Ticket price for the bash: $18 for a three-day pass ($24 at the gate).

1969	1973	1980s	1989
American astronauts land on the moon, fulfilling President Kennedy's unlikely 1961 promise to accomplish this feat within a decade and culminating the 'space race' between the US and USSR.	In Roe v Wade, the Supreme Court legalizes abortion. Even today this decision remains controversial and socially divisive, pitting 'right to choose' advocates against the 'right to life' anti-abortion lobby.	New Deal–era financial institutions, deregulated under President Reagan, gamble with their customers' savings and loans, and ultimately fail, leaving the government with the bill.	The 1960s-era Berlin Wall is torn down, marking the end of the Cold War between the US and the USSR (now Russia). The USA becomes the world's last remaining superpower.

Reagan, Clinton & the Bushes

In 1980, California's Republican governor and former actor Ronald Reagan campaigned for president by promising to make Americans feel good about America again. The affable Reagan won easily, and his election marked a pronounced shift to the right in US politics. Military spending and tax cuts created enormous federal deficits, which hampered the presidency of Reagan's successor, George HW Bush. Despite winning the Gulf War – liberating Kuwait in 1991 after an Iraqi invasion – Bush was soundly defeated in the 1992 presidential election by Southern Democrat Bill Clinton. Clinton had the good fortune to catch the 1990s high-tech internet boom, which seemed to augur a 'new economy' based on white-collar telecommunications. The US economy erased its deficits and ran a surplus, and Clinton presided over one of America's longest economic booms.

In 2000 and 2004, George W Bush, the eldest son of George HW Bush, won the presidential elections so narrowly that the divided results seemed to epitomize an increasingly divided nation. 'Dubya' had the misfortune of being president when the high-tech bubble burst in 2000, but he nevertheless enacted tax cuts that returned federal deficits even greater than before. He also championed the right-wing conservative 'backlash' that had been building since Reagan.

On September 11, 2001, Islamic terrorists flew hijacked planes into New York's World Trade Center and the Pentagon in Washington, DC. This catastrophic attack united Americans behind their president as he vowed to revenge and declared a 'war on terror.' Bush soon attacked Afghanistan in an unsuccessful hunt for Al-Qaeda terrorist cells, then attacked Iraq in 2003 and toppled its anti-US dictator, Saddam Hussein. Meanwhile, Iraq descended into civil war. Following scandals and failures – torture photos from the US military prison at Abu Ghraib, the federal response in the aftermath of Hurricane Katrina and the inability to bring the Iraq War to a close – Bush's approval ratings reached historic lows in the second half of his presidency.

Obama, Term One

In 2008, hungry for change, Americans elected political newcomer Barack Obama, America's first African American president. He certainly had his work cut out for him. These were, after all, unprecedented times economically, with the US in the largest financial crisis since the Great Depression. What had started as a collapse of the US housing bubble in 2007 had spread to the banking sector, with the meltdown of major financial institutions.

As Americans looked toward the future, many found it difficult to leave the past behind. This was not surprising since wars in Afghanistan and Iraq, launched a decade prior, continued to simmer on the back burner of

1990s	2001	2003	2005
The world wide web debuts in 1991. Silicon Valley, CA, leads a high-tech internet revolution, remaking communications and media; overvalued tech stocks drive the massive boom (and subsequent bust).	On September 11, Al-Qaeda terrorists hijack four commercial airplanes, flying two into NYC's twin towers and one into the Pentagon (the fourth crashes in Pennsylvania); nearly 3000 people are killed.	After citing evidence that Iraq possesses weapons of mass destruction, President George W Bush launches a preemptive war that will cost over 4000 American lives and some $3 trillion.	On August 29, Hurricane Katrina hits the Mississippi and Louisiana coasts, rupturing poorly maintained levees and flooding New Orleans. More than 1800 people die, and cost estimates exceed $110 billion.

the ever-changing news cycle. In 2011, in a subterfuge operation vetted by President Obama, Navy Seals raided Osama bin Laden's Pakistan hideout and killed the Al-Qaeda leader, bringing an end to the search for America's greatest public enemy.

Following his sober announcement describing the raid, President Obama saw his approval ratings jump by 11%. The president, for his part, certainly needed a boost. The economy remained in bad shape, and the ambitious $800-billion stimulus package passed by Congress in 2009 hadn't borne much fruit in the eyes of many Americans – even though economists estimated that the stimulus did soften the blow of the recession, which would have been much worse without it. At the end of his first term, his approval ratings were around 49%.

With lost jobs, overvalued mortgages and little relief in sight, millions of Americans found themselves adrift. This was not a recession they could spend their way out of, as Obama's predecessor had suggested. People were upset and gathered in large numbers to voice their anger. This, in turn, gave birth to the Tea Party, a wing of politically conservative Republicans who believed that Obama was leaning too far to the left, and that government handouts would destroy the economy and, thus, America. High federal spending, government bailouts (of the banking and auto industries) and especially Obama's health-care reform (derisively named 'Obamacare') particularly roused their ire.

Obama, Term Two

Despite such opposition, Obama was reelected in 2012, though he returned to office without quite the same hope that surrounded him the first time. Times had changed, and America, like much of the world, had struggled through tough years since the global economic crisis. When Obama took the oath of office in 2013, the unemployment rate, hovering around 8%, was about what it had been during his first inauguration, though economic growth seems at last to be on a solid foundation. On other fronts, Obama has had mixed success. He ended the US involvement in Iraq, but 63,000 troops still remain in Afghanistan, and the US mission there seems increasingly obscure.

The president's health-care bill could end up being his greatest legacy. Though it became law in 2010, it didn't go into effect until 2014. There were challenges by Republicans who threatened to repeal it, and two close calls by the Supreme Court (which narrowly ruled the act constitutional on both occasions). At the time of writing, Democrats point out that millions more Americans now have health insurance and say the program has helped lower costs for providers. Meanwhile, Republicans say the program is a failure, citing decreased insurance options for consumers and harsh costs for business owners. The debate continues to rage. Stay tuned...

For a heart-pounding take on national security operations, watch *Homeland*, an Emmy Award–winning cable TV series about a bipolar CIA officer (Claire Danes) playing a game of cat-and-mouse with a marine sergeant who may be an Al-Qaeda operative. It's one of President Obama's favorite shows.

2008–09	**2011**	**2012**	**2015**
Barack Obama becomes the first African American president. The stock market crashes due to mismanagement by major American financial institutions. The crisis spreads worldwide.	As unemployment remains high and household income drops, activists launch Occupy Wall Street in NYC to protest economic and social inequality. The movement spreads to cities worldwide.	Hurricane Sandy devastates the East Coast, becoming the second-costliest hurricane ($65 billion) in American history. More than 80 Americans die (plus 200 more in other countries). Obama wins re-election.	The Supreme Court makes gay marriage the law of the land. South Carolina removes the Confederate battle flag from its Capitol under pressure that it's a racist symbol that sparked mass murder in Charleston.

The Way of Life

The eastern USA is a compelling mix of accents and rhythms, big-city financiers and small-town farmers, university students and sun-seeking retirees, Yankees and Southerners.

Multiculturalism

The US holds the world's second-largest Spanish-speaking population, behind Mexico and just ahead of Spain. Latinos are also the fastest-growing minority group in the nation. In the East, Florida, Illinois, New Jersey and New York have the largest Latino populations.

From the get-go, cities in the East were 'melting pots,' with a long and proud heritage of welcoming newcomers from all over the world. So it's no surprise that the region's diversity is vast.

In the Northeast, Irish and Italian communities have been well established in the urban areas since the 19th century. In Chicago, Latinos (mostly from Mexico) comprise roughly one-quarter of the population. The upper Great Lakes states are home to the nation's biggest enclaves of Somali and Hmong immigrants, a result of the area's long tradition of resettling refugees. In Florida, Cubans lead the multicultural pack. They began arriving in Miami in the 1960s following Castro's revolution, and created a politically powerful community. Nicaraguans followed in the 1980s, fleeing war in their country, and now number over 100,000. The city's Little Haiti adds 70,000 Haitians to the mix. The South, more than any other region, is a culture unto itself, over half of all black Americans live here. These examples are just a fraction of the complex whole.

The East, like the rest of the country, can never quite decide if the continual influx of newcomers is its saving grace or what will eventually strain society to the breaking point. 'Immigration reform' has been a Washington buzzword for nearly two decades. Some people believe the nation's current system deals with illegal immigrants (there are 11.3 million of them) too leniently – that the government should deport immigrants who are here unlawfully and fine employers who hire them. Other Americans think those rules are too harsh – that immigrants who have been here for years working, contributing to society and abiding by the law deserve amnesty. Despite several attempts, Congress has not been able to pass a comprehensive package addressing illegal immigration, though it has put through various measures to beef up enforcement.

Religion

Separation of Church and State has been the law of the land ever since the Pilgrims came ashore in Massachusetts in the early 1600s. Their faith – Protestant Christianity – continues to be the main one in the East.

Protestantism covers a wide swath of denominations. They fall under two main headings: evangelical Protestants, of which Baptists form the biggest contingent; and mainline Protestants, such as Lutherans, Methodists and Presbyterians. Evangelicals have the greater number of worshippers, and that number has grown in recent years: Baptists are their powerhouse, accounting for one-third of all Protestants and close to one-fifth of the USA's total adult population. Their numbers stack up in the South. In contrast, Lutherans (who are concentrated in Minnesota and Wisconsin, as well as the Dakotas) and the other mainline denominations have experienced declining figures.

Catholicism is the East's second-most-practiced faith. In fact, New England is the country's most Catholic zone, and the numbers trickle down to the Mid-Atlantic states. Massachusetts is the most Catholic state, with 45% of residents of that faith. Baltimore is the country's oldest archdiocese, established in 1789. States with large Latino populations, such as Florida and Illinois, also support big concentrations of Catholics.

Judaism has a significant presence in the eastern USA. Jews make up roughly 12% of the population in both south Florida and the New York metro area. The latter is a major center of Orthodox Judaism and home to more Jews than anywhere outside Tel Aviv.

Also in the East: Muslim Americans cluster in the New York, Chicago and Detroit metro areas. Hindu Americans bunch in New York and New Jersey, as well as big cities like Chicago, Washington, DC and Atlanta.

Lifestyle

In general, the eastern USA has one of the world's highest standards of living, though there are some shocking variances by region. At the top end sits Maryland, with a median household income of $69,826 (based on 2012–14 census data). Mississippi dwells at the opposite end of the scale at $40,194. These amounts are the high/low not just for the region, but for the nation, upholding the pattern in which households in the Northeast earn the most, while those in the South earn the least. Wages also vary by ethnicity, with African Americans and Latinos earning less than whites and Asians ($34,600 and $41,000 respectively, versus $58,000 and $67,000).

About 86% of Americans are high-school graduates, while some 29% go on to graduate from college with a four-year bachelor's degree. The university lifestyle (ie cafes, bookshops and progressive mindsets) is especially prevalent in the Northeast, home to the eight Ivy League schools as well as the 'Little Ivies' (a self-anointed collection of a dozen elite liberal-arts colleges) and the 'Seven Sisters' (top-tier women's colleges, founded in the days when the Ivy League was still a boys-only club). More than 50 institutions of higher learning range around Boston alone.

If you peeked in a house, you'd typically find a married couple with two kids occupying it. Both parents usually work, and 28% work more than 40 hours per week. Divorce is common – 40% of first marriages break up – but both divorce and marriage rates have declined over the last three decades. Single parents head 9% of households.

While many Americans hit the gym or walk, bike or jog regularly, over 50% don't exercise at all during their free time, according to the Centers for Disease Control and Prevention (CDC). Health researchers speculate that this lack of exercise and Americans' fondness for sugary and fatty

Americans are increasingly defining their spiritual beliefs outside of organized religion. The proportion of those who say they have 'no religion' is now around 16%. Some in this catch-all category disavow religion altogether (around 4%), but the majority sustain spiritual beliefs that simply fall outside the box.

StoryCorps has collected and archived more than 50,000 interviews from people across America, which it preserves in the Library of Congress. Listen to folks tell their stories of discovery, family, identity, love and much more at www.storycorps.org.

STATES & TRAITS

Regional US stereotypes now have solid data behind them, thanks to a study titled The Geography of Personality. Researchers processed more than a half-million personality assessments collected from individual US citizens, then looked at where certain traits stacked up on the map. Turns out 'Minnesota nice' is for real – the most 'agreeable' states cluster in the Midwest, Great Plains and South. These places rank highest for friendliness and cooperation. The most neurotic states? They line up in the Northeast. But New York didn't place number one, as you might expect; that honor goes to West Virginia. Many of the most 'open' states lie out West. California, Nevada, Oregon and Washington all rate high for being receptive to new ideas – although they lag behind Washington, DC and New York.

foods have led to rising obesity and diabetes rates. The South fares the worst: Mississippi, Alabama, West Virginia, Tennessee and Louisiana lead the obesity rankings, with the condition affecting one-third of residents.

About 26% of Americans volunteer their time to help others or help a cause, especially in the Midwest, followed by the West, South and Northeast, according to the Corporation for National and Community Service. Eco-consciousness has entered the mainstream: over 75% of Americans recycle at home, and most big chain grocery stores – including Wal-Mart – now sell organic foods.

Sports

What really draws Americans together (sometimes slathered in blue body paint or with foam-rubber cheese wedges on their heads) is sports. In spring and summer there's baseball nearly every day, in fall and winter there's football, and through the long nights of winter there's plenty of basketball to keep the adrenaline going – those are the big three sports. Car racing has revved up interest, especially in the South. Major League Soccer (MLS) is attracting an ever-increasing following. Ice hockey, once favored only in northern climes, has fans throughout the area. Women's basketball and soccer also are gaining traction nationwide, with multiple teams that play in pro leagues.

Baseball

Despite high salaries and its biggest stars being dogged by steroid rumors, baseball remains America's favorite pastime. It may not command the same TV viewership (and subsequent advertising dollars) as football, but baseball has 162 games over a season versus 16 for football.

Besides, baseball is better live than on TV – being at the ballpark on a sunny day, sitting in the bleachers with a beer and hot dog, and indulging in the seventh-inning stretch, when the entire park erupts in a communal sing-along of 'Take Me Out to the Ballgame.' The playoffs, held every October, still deliver excitement and unexpected champions. The New York Yankees, Boston Red Sox and Chicago Cubs continue to be America's favorite teams, even when they're abysmal (the Cubs haven't won a World Series in more than 100 years).

Greenest Cities

Boston, MA

Minneapolis, MN

Chicago, IL

Washington, DC

Key Sports Sites

Baseball: www.mlb.com

Basketball: www.nba.com

Football: www.nfl.com

Hockey: www.nhl.com

Car racing: www.nascar.com

Soccer: www.mlssoccer.com

ICONIC SPORTING VENUES

Yankee Stadium, NYC The Bronx' fabled baseball field, steeped in history and the ghost of Babe Ruth.

Lambeau Field, Green Bay Stadium of the NFL's Packers; nicknamed 'the Frozen Tundra' for its insanely cold weather.

Fenway Park, Boston Baseball's oldest park (1912); home of the 'Green Monster' (aka the tall left-field wall).

Wrigley Field, Chicago Another vintage ballpark (1914), with ivy walls, a classic neon sign and good-time neighborhood bars all around.

Madison Square Garden, NYC Not only do the Knicks dribble at the 'mecca of basketball,' but Ali boxed here and Elvis rocked here.

Joe Louis Arena, Detroit The bad-ass rink of pro hockey's Red Wings; witness the strange octopus-throwing custom.

Churchill Downs, Louisville Home of the Kentucky Derby: fine hats, mint juleps and the 'greatest two minutes in sports.'

Indianapolis Motor Speedway, Indianapolis Race cars scream by at 170mph at the hard-partying Indy 500.

Tickets are relatively inexpensive – seats average about $25 at most stadiums – and are easy to get for most games. Minor-league baseball games cost half as much, and can be even more fun, with lots of audience participation, stray chickens and dogs running across the field, and wild throws from the pitcher's mound. For information, see www.milb.com.

Football

Football is big, physical, and rolling in dough. With the shortest season and least number of games of any of the major sports, every match takes on the emotion of an epic battle, where the results matter and an unfortunate injury can deal a lethal blow to a team's play-off chances.

It's also the toughest US sport, played in fall and winter in all manner of rain, sleet and snow – some of the most memorable matches have occurred at below-freezing temperatures. Green Bay Packers fans are in a class by themselves when it comes to severe weather. Their stadium in Wisconsin (Lambeau Field) was the site of the infamous Ice Bowl, a 1967 championship game against the Dallas Cowboys where the temperature plummeted to -13°F (-25°C) – mind you, that was with a wind-chill factor of -48°F (-44°C).

The rabidly popular Super Bowl is pro football's championship match, held in late January or early February. The other 'bowl' games (such as the Sugar Bowl in New Orleans and Orange Bowl in Miami) are college football's title matches, held on and around New Year's Day.

Basketball

The teams bringing in the most fans these days include the Chicago Bulls (thanks to the lingering Michael Jordan effect), the Cleveland Cavaliers (home of Lebron James, the league's most loved – and hated – player) and the New York Knicks (where celebrities sit courtside despite a losing team on the court in recent years).

College basketball also draws millions of fans, especially every spring when the March Madness play-offs roll around; it culminates in the Final Four, when the remaining quartet of teams competes for a spot in the championship game. The Cinderella stories and unexpected outcomes rival the pro league for excitement. The games are widely televised and bet upon – this is when Las Vegas bookies earn their keep.

The Super Bowl costs America $800 million in lost workplace productivity as employees gossip about the game, make bets and shop for new TVs online. It's still less than the $1.9 billion estimate for March Madness when many folks get caught up in the NCAA basketball tournament.

Regional Cuisine

The East's cuisine mixes myriad cultures, and each region has evolved its own unique flavor. From seafood in Maine to slow-cooked brisket in Mississippi, you're in for a treat. Tipplers will find the East to be the country's most spirited side. A booming microbrewery industry has brought artful beers to every corner of the region, while New York and Virginia give wine drinkers vintages to appreciate, and Kentucky pours on the bourbon.

Local Flavors

New York City: Foodie Heaven

They say that you could eat at a different restaurant every night of your life in New York City and not exhaust the possibilities. Considering that there are more than 20,000 restaurants in the five boroughs, with scores of new ones opening each year, it's true. Owing to its huge immigrant population and an influx of over 50 million tourists annually, New York captures the title of America's greatest restaurant city. Its diverse neighborhoods serve up authentic Italian food and thin-crust pizza, all manner of Asian food, French haute cuisine and classic Jewish deli food, from bagels to piled-high pastrami on rye. More exotic cuisines are found here as well, from Ethiopian to Scandinavian

Don't let NYC's image as expensive get to you: you can eat well here without breaking the bank, especially if you limit your cocktail intake. There may be no free lunch in New York, but compared to other world cities, eating here can be a bargain.

New England: Clambakes & Lobster Boils

New England claims to have the nation's best seafood, and who's to argue? The North Atlantic Ocean offers up clams, mussels, oysters and huge lobsters, along with shad, bluefish and cod. The bounty gets stirred into a mighty fine chowder (soup), for which every seafood shack up the coast has its own secret recipe, put to the test during summertime chowder fests and cook-offs. The clambake is another tradition, where shellfish are buried in a pit fire with foil-wrapped corn, chicken and sausages. Fried clam fritters and lobster rolls (lobster meat with mayonnaise served in a bread bun) are served throughout the region.

Vermont makes excellent cheeses, Massachusetts harvests cranberries (a Thanksgiving staple), and New England's forests drip sweet maple syrup. Still hungry? Connecticut is famed for its thin-crust New Haven–style pizza (best topped with white clams); Boston specializes in baked beans and brown bread; and Rhode Islanders pour coffee syrup into milk and embrace traditional cornmeal johnnycakes.

Mid-Atlantic: Cheesesteaks, Crab Cakes & Scrapple

From New York down through Virginia, the Mid-Atlantic states share a long coastline and a cornucopia of apple, pear and berry farms. New Jersey wins prizes for tomatoes and New York's Long Island for potatoes. Chesapeake Bay's blue crabs make diners swoon, as do Pennsylvania Dutch Country's heaped plates of chicken pot pie, noodles and meatloaf-like

---

Only three states in the nation have an official state pie, and they're all in the east: Indiana (sugar cream pie), Florida (key lime pie) and Vermont (apple pie), Illinois may soon join the ranks with pumpkin pie. In addition, Maine lists blueberry pie as its 'state dessert,' while Delaware does the same for peach pie.

Weird Regional Foods

Scrapple (rural Pennsylvania)

Lutefisk (Minnesota)

Deep-fried cheese curds (Wisconsin)

Horseshoe sandwich (Illinois)

scrapple. In Philadelphia, you can gorge on 'Philly cheese-steaks,' made with thin strips of sautéed beef, onions and melted cheese on a bun. Virginia serves its salt-cured 'country-style' ham with biscuits. New York's Finger Lakes, Hudson Valley and Long Island uncork highly regarded wines to accompany the region's well-set table.

The South: Barbecue, Biscuits & Gumbo

No region is prouder of its food culture than the South, which has a long history of mingling Anglo, French, African, Spanish and Native American foods. Slow-cooked barbecue is one of the top stokers of regional pride; there are as many meaty and saucy variations as there are towns in the South. Southern fried chicken and catfish pop out of the pan crisp on the outside and moist inside. Fluffy hot biscuits, corn bread, sweet potatoes, collard greens, and – most passionately – grits (ground corn cooked to a cereal-like consistency) accompany Southern plates, all butter-smothered. Treasured dessert recipes tend to produce big layer cakes or pies made with pecans, bananas and citrus. Sweet iced tea (nonalcoholic) or a cool mint-julep cocktail (with bourbon) help wash it down.

For the region's crème de la crème, pull up a chair at Louisiana's tables. The state stands out for its two main cuisines: Cajun food is found in the bayou country and marries native spices like sassafras and chili peppers to provincial French cooking. Creole food is more urban and centered in New Orleans, where zippy dishes like shrimp rémoulade, crabmeat *ravigote* and gumbo (a soupy stew of chicken, shellfish and/or sausage, and okra) have eaters dabbing their brow.

Midwest: Burgers, Bacon & Beer

Midwesterners eat big, and with gusto. Portions are huge – this is farm country, after all, where people need sustenance to get their work done. The region is tops for serving American classics like pot roast, meatloaf, steak and pork chops; add walleye, perch and other fresh-water fish to menus in towns near the Great Lakes. Count on a nice cold beer to complement the wares. Chicago stands tall as the region's best place to pile a plate, with hole-in-the-wall ethnic eateries cooking alongside many of the country's most acclaimed restaurants. Another great place to sample Midwestern foods is at a county fair, which offers everything from bratwurst to fried dough to grilled corn on the cob. Elsewhere at diners and family restaurants, you'll taste the varied influences of Eastern European, Scandinavian, Latino and Asian immigrants, especially in the cities.

Habits & Customs

For breakfast Americans love their eggs and bacon, waffles and hash browns, and big glasses of orange juice. Most of all, they love a steaming cup of coffee. After a mid-morning snack break, the lunch hour of most American workers affords time enough for just a sandwich, quick burger or hearty salad. While you may spot (rarely) diners drinking a glass of wine or beer with their

HARVEST TIME

January

The ice wine grape harvest takes place around the Finger Lakes, New York, and in northern Michigan. Sweet dessert drinks ensue.

March

In Vermont and Maine, it's sugaring season, when fresh maple syrup flows. Down South, crawfish ramps up: Louisiana harvests around 110 million pounds of the critters between now and May.

May

Georgia's peach harvest begins mid-month and goes until mid-August. To the north, Chesapeake Bay blue crabs hit the market through September.

July

Early in the month Michigan goes wild, picking tart cherries and hosting fruity festivities like the International Cherry Pit Spitting Championship in Eau Claire.

August

The action shifts to New England: the coast's lobster shacks and clambakes are in full swing, while Maine's wild blueberries get heaped into pies.

September & October

It's prime time to pick apples in New York and Michigan (the nation's second- and third-largest producers). Cider houses pour their wares. Meanwhile, it's cranberry season in Massachusetts and Wisconsin.

noontime meal, the days of the 'three-martini lunch' are long gone. Early in the evening, people settle in to a more substantial weeknight dinner, which, given the workload of so many two-career families, might be take-out or prepackaged dishes.

Americans tend to eat dinner early, usually between 6pm and 8pm. In smaller towns, it may be hard to find anywhere to eat after 8:30pm or so. Dinner parties usually begin around 6:30pm or 7pm, with cocktails followed by a meal. If invited to dinner, it's polite to be prompt: ideally, you should plan to arrive within 15 minutes of the designated time. Americans are notoriously informal in their dining manners, although they will usually wait until everyone is served before eating.

Cooking Courses

Many cooking schools offer courses for enthusiastic amateur chefs.

Chopping Block Cooking School (www.thechoppingblock.com) Master knife skills or learn to make deep-dish pizza in Chicago.

Kitchen Window (www.kitchenwindow.com) Hosts market tours and restaurant crawls, plus classes on baking, outdoor grilling and world cuisine in Minneapolis.

Zingerman's Bakehouse (www.bakewithzing.com; 3723 Plaza Dr) Offers popular 'bake-cations,' making bread or pastries in Ann Arbor.

Drinks

Beer

After founding the American beer industry in Milwaukee, 19th-century German immigrants developed ways to make beer in vast quantities and then deliver it all over America. Today, about 80% of domestic beer still comes from the Midwest.

Despite their ubiquity, popular brands of American beer have long been the subject of ridicule abroad due to their low alcohol content and 'light' taste. Regardless of what critics say, sales indicate that American beer is more popular than ever – and now, with the rise of microbreweries and craft beer, even beer snobs admit that American beer has reinvented itself.

Today there are more than 1900 craft and microbrewers across the USA. They generated roughly $20 billion in retail sales in 2015, and the number keeps on going up. It has become possible to 'drink local' all over the region, from urban centers to unexpected small towns. Some restaurants now have beer 'sommeliers,' while others host beer dinners, where you can experience how small-batch brews pair with different foods.

Wine

About 20% of Americans drink wine on a regular basis. The West Coast states, predominately California, produce the majority of domestic vino. In the East, New York yields the most, enough to rank third nationwide when gauged by gallons produced. The Finger Lakes region is the hot spot, awash in Riesling grapes and prime for sipping a good Chardonnay,

---

VEGETARIANS' DELIGHT

Vegetarian restaurants abound in major cities, though not always in rural areas. Here are our go-to favorites. To find more, browse www.happycow.net.

Green Elephant (p238), Portland, ME

Clover Food Lab (p180), Boston, MA

Moosewood Restaurant (p122), Ithaca, NY

Zenith (p159), Pittsburgh, PA

Angelica Kitchen (p96), New York City, NY

BEST MICROBREWERIES

Microbreweries have exploded in popularity, and you'll never be far from a finely crafted pint. Careful though: craft beers can be stronger than mass-produced brands. Look for a brewery's 'session beer' if you want a lower alcohol content. Surprising towns such as Grand Rapids, Michigan, and Asheville, North Carolina, have become particularly famed for their suds. And for the record: Vermont boasts the most microbreweries per capita in the US. As you travel around the region, keep an eye out for the following:

Three Floyds (www.3floyds.com) Munster, IN

Bell's Brewery (www.bellsbeer.com) Kalamazoo, MI

Allagash Brewing (www.allagash.com) Portland, ME

Dogfish Head (www.dogfish.com) Milton, DE

Evil Twin Brewing (eviltwin.dk) Brooklyn, NY

Gewürztraminer or ice wine. Virginia comes in number five in the US for number of wineries, with 248 within its borders, many located in the pretty hills around Charlottesville. Particularly notable is the Virginia Viognier, an exotic white grape. Michigan's west coast offers another vine-striped landscape; its winemakers are known for everything from lush Cabernet Franc to high-end sparkling wines. All of these bucolic regions have spawned entire industries of sip-tripping and bed-and-breakfast tourism.

In general, wine isn't cheap in the US, as it's considered a luxury rather than a staple (in contrast to some European countries). But it's possible to procure a perfectly drinkable bottle of American wine at a liquor or wine shop for around $10 to $12.

Spirits

The East is the cradle of the good stuff. Jack Daniels remains the most well-known brand of American whiskey around the world, and is also the oldest continually operating US distillery, going strong in Lynchburg, Tennessee, since 1870. Bourbon, made from corn, is the nation's only native spirit. Kentucky produces 95% of the world supply, most of which flows from seven distilleries in the state's central zone. The 225-mile loop between the booze-makers here is known as the Bourbon Trail, and road-tripping to visit the distilleries and sample their wares has become an offbeat version of California's Napa Valley.

Cocktails were invented in New Orleans, appropriately enough, before the Civil War. The first cocktail was the Sazerac – a mix of rye whiskey or brandy, simple syrup, bitters and a dash of absinthe. American cocktails created at bars in the late 19th and early 20th centuries include such classics as the Martini, the Manhattan and the Old-Fashioned.

The Vintage Cocktail Craze

Across US cities, it has become decidedly cool to party like it's 1929 by drinking retro cocktails from the days – less than a century ago – when alcohol was illegal. Good old Prohibition: instead of spawning a nation of teetotalers, it arguably only solidified a culture for which the forbidden became appealing – it felt good to be bad, and so-called respectable citizens congregated in secret 'speakeasies' to drink homemade moonshine and dance to hot jazz.

Fast forward to the 21st century. While Prohibition isn't in any danger of being reinstated, you'll find plenty of bars in the region where the spirit of the Roaring '20s and illicit 1930s lives on. Inspired by vintage recipes calling for natural and homemade elixirs, these cocktails are lovingly concocted by nattily dressed bartenders who regard their profession as something between an art and a science.

Best Cocktail Bars

Dead Rabbit, New York City, NY

Tonique, New Orleans, LA

Patterson House, Nashville, TN

Drink, Boston, MA

Broken Shaker, Miami, FL

Maison Premier, NYC

In many parts of the South, a 'coke' means any kind of flavored, carbonated soft drink, so you may have to specify – if you say 'I'll have a Coke,' the waiter might ask, 'What kind?'. In the Midwest, the generic term is 'pop,' while the East Coast uses 'soda.'

Arts & Architecture

New York remains the dynamic heart of the theater and art worlds, while great literature finds its voice throughout the region. Niche media networks are making edgy, must-view TV about everything from zombies in Georgia to murderers in Minnesota. In the meantime, architects in New York and Chicago keep pushing ever higher.

Literature

Several famous authors from the eastern USA wrote books that have been banned at one time or another, including Indianapolis' Kurt Vonnegut (Slaughterhouse-Five), New York's JD Salinger (The Catcher in the Rye) and Georgia born Alice Walker (The Color Purple).

The 'Great American Novel' has stirred the imagination for more than 150 years. Edgar Allan Poe told spooky short stories in the 1840s, and is credited with inventing the detective story, horror story and science fiction. Four decades later, Samuel Clemens, aka Mark Twain, also made a literary splash. Twain wrote in the vernacular, loved 'tall tales' and reveled in absurdity, which endeared him to everyday readers. His novel *Huckleberry Finn* (1884) became the quintessential American narrative: compelled by a primal moment of rebellion against his father, Huck embarks on a search for authenticity through which he discovers himself. The Mississippi River provides the backdrop.

The 'Lost Generation' brought American literature into its own in the early 20th century. These writers lived as expatriates in post-WWI Europe and described a growing sense of alienation. Plain-speaking Mid westerner Ernest Hemingway exemplified the era with his spare, stylized realism. Minnesotan F Scott Fitzgerald eviscerated East Coast society life with his fiction. Back on home turf, William Faulkner examined the South's social rifts in dense, caustic prose, and African Americans such as poet Langston Hughes and novelist Zora Neale Hurston undermined racist stereotypes during New York's Harlem Renaissance.

After WWII, American writers began depicting regional and ethnic divides, experimented with style and often bashed middle-class society's values. The 1950s Beat Generation, with Jack Kerouac, Allen Ginsberg and William S Burroughs at the center, was particularly hard core.

Great American Novels

Beloved, Toni Morrison

The Great Gatsby, F Scott Fitzgerald

The Sound and the Fury, William Faulkner

American Rust, Philipp Meyer

The Adventures of Augie March, Saul Bellow

Today's literature reflects an ever more diverse panoply of voices. Jacqueline Woodson, Junot Diaz and Sherman Alexie have all written bestsellers in the past decade and given voice to, respectively, African American, Dominican American and Native American issues. Titans of contemporary literature – all Pulitzer winners, and all from the eastern USA incidentally – include Toni Morrison (whose most recent book was *God Save the Child* in 2015), Joyce Carol Oates (who pretty much writes a book a year) and Michael Chabon (whose last sprawling novel was *Telegraph Avenue* in 2012).

Reclusive author Thomas Pynchon published *Bleeding Edge* in 2013, a bold and labyrinthine novel set in NYC during the terrorist attacks of September 11. And 89-year-old Harper Lee – who gained fame in 1960 when she wrote *To Kill a Mockingbird* and then never published another book – released *Go Set a Watchman*, the controversial sequel, in 2015.

THE GOLDEN AGE OF AMERICAN TELEVISION

For the past decade or so, cable TV and streaming networks have been targeting all manner of niche audiences and producing sophisticated, complex dramas that surpass most risk-averse Hollywood fare. The result? Some might say that the 2000s, not the 1950s, have proved to be the 'golden age' of American TV. Shows that give an eastern USA perspective include the following:

➧ *House of Cards*: A ruthless politician shows how the power game is played in Washington, DC.

➧ *The Walking Dead*: Survivors of the apocalypse must fight off zombies in Atlanta and northern Georgia.

➧ *Broad City*: A pair of 20-something slacker best friends live a life of hijinks in New York City.

➧ *Orange is the New Black*: Comedy-drama follows a large cast of characters in a women's prison in upstate New York.

➧ *Fargo*: Noirish dark comedy gives a feel for wintry, small-town Minnesota.

Film & Television

The studio system actually began in Manhattan, where Thomas Edison – inventor of the industry's earliest moving-picture technology – tried to create a monopoly with his patents. This drove many independents to move to a suburb of Los Angeles, where they could easily flee to Mexico in case of legal trouble – and ta-da, Hollywood was born.

While most of the movie magic still happens on the West Coast, New York retains its fair share of film and TV studios. ABC, CBS, NBC, CNN, MTV and HBO are among the Big Apple's big shots, and many visitors come expressly to see Jimmy Fallon *(Tonight Show)*, Stephen Colbert *(Late Show)* or their other favorite talk shows taping. Many filmmakers and actors prefer New York to the West Coast – Robert De Niro, Spike Lee and Woody Allen most famously – so keep an eye out on local streets. Other film-friendly cities include Miami, Chicago and Atlanta, and one you wouldn't normally think of: Wilmington, North Carolina, which hosts enough studios to earn the nickname 'Wilmywood' (though new state laws scrapping tax incentives may slow the scene there).

As cable TV and Netflix, Amazon and other streaming services have entered the industry, the mainstream networks have stuck to a formula of long-narrative serial dramas (like *Law & Order: SVU*, which has been on since 1999), as well as cheap-to-produce, 'unscripted' reality TV. What *Survivor* started in 2000, the contestants and 'actors' of *The Voice* and *Hell's Kitchen* keep alive today, for better or for worse.

Theater

Eugene O'Neill put American drama on the map with his trilogy *Mourning Becomes Electra* (1931), which sets a tragic Greek myth in post–Civil War New England. O'Neill was the first major US playwright, and is still widely considered to be the best.

After WWII, two playwrights dominated the stage: Arthur Miller, who famously married Marilyn Monroe and wrote about everything from middle-class male disillusionment (*Death of a Salesman*; 1949) to the mob mentality of the Salem witch trials (*The Crucible*; 1953); and Tennessee Williams, whose explosive works *The Glass Menagerie* (1945), *A Streetcar Named Desire* (1947) and *Cat on a Hot Tin Roof* (1955) dug deep into the Southern psyche.

Edward Albee gave the 1960s a healthy dose of absurdism, and David Mamet and Sam Shepard filled the '70s and '80s with rough-and-tough guys. These days Pulitzer Prize–winner Tracy Letts writes family dramas that are often compared to O'Neill, bringing the scene full circle.

Broadway is where shows get star treatment. The famed NYC district earns more than a billion dollars in revenue from ticket sales each year, with top shows pulling in a cool $2 million a week. Long-running classics like *The Lion King* and *Wicked* continue to play before sold-out houses, alongside newer hits such as the *Book of Mormon*. Meanwhile, stalwarts such as *Les Miserables* get revamped and reopen to much fanfare (as in 2014). But it's away from Broadway's bright lights, in regional theaters such as Chicago's Steppenwolf, Minneapolis' Guthrie and hundreds more, where new plays and playwrights emerge that keep the art vital.

Painting

In the wake of WWII, the USA developed its first truly original school of art: abstract expressionism. New York painters Jackson Pollock, Franz Kline, Mark Rothko and others explored freely created, nonrepresentational forms. Pollock, for example, made drip paintings by pouring and splattering pigments over large canvases.

Pop art followed, where artists drew inspiration from bright, cartoony consumer images; Andy Warhol was the king (or Pope of Pop, as he's sometimes called). Minimalism came next, and by the 1980s and '90s, the canvas was wide open – any and all styles could take their place at the arts table.

New York remains the red-hot center of the art world, and its make-or-break influence shapes tastes across the nation and around the globe. To get the pulse of contemporary art in the region, check out works by Jenny Holzer, Kara Walker, Chuck Close, Martin Puryear and Frank Stella.

Architecture

In 1885, a group of designers in Chicago shot up the pioneering skyscraper. It didn't exactly poke the clouds, but its use of steel framing launched modern architecture.

Around the same time, another Chicago architect was doing radical things closer to the ground. Frank Lloyd Wright created a building style that abandoned historical elements and references, which had long been the tradition, and instead he went organic. He designed buildings in relation to the landscape, which in the Midwest were the low-slung, horizontal lines of the surrounding prairie. An entire movement grew up around Wright's Prairie Style.

European architects absorbed Wright's ideas, and that influence bounced back when the Bauhaus school left Nazi Germany and set up in the USA. Here it became known as the International Style, an early form of modernism. Ludwig Mies van der Rohe was the main man with the plan, and his boxy, metal-and-glass behemoths rose high on urban horizons, especially in Chicago and New York City. Postmodernism followed, reintroducing color and the decorative elements of art deco, beaux arts and other earlier styles to the region's sky-high designs.

Today's architects continue to break boundaries. Recent examples of visionary designs include Jeanne Gang's rippling Aqua Tower in Chicago – the world's tallest building designed by a woman. In 2013, NYC's 1776ft-high One World Trade Center rose to become the USA's loftiest building. In 2016, David Ajaye's shimmering National Museum of African American History and Culture takes its place on the Mall in Washington, DC.

Best Modern-Art Museums

Museum of Modern Art, New York City, NY

Whitney Museum of American Art, New York City, NY

Salvador Dalí Museum, St Petersburg, FL

Andy Warhol Museum, Pittsburgh, PA

Dia Beacon, Beacon, NY

Music

Jazz, blues, country, hip-hop and rock music all were born in the eastern USA, and their beats permeate clubs and juke joints from north to south. Listen in and you'll hear the legacy of Muddy Waters' slide guitar, Hank Williams' yodel, John Coltrane's frenzied cascades and much more.

Blues

All US music starts with the blues. And the blues started in the South. That's where the genre developed out of the work songs, or 'shouts,' of black slaves and out of black spiritual songs and their call-and-response pattern, both of which were adaptations of African music.

By the 1920s, Delta blues typified the sound. Musicians from Memphis to Mississippi sung passionate, plaintive melodies accompanied by a lonely slide guitar. Traveling blues musicians, and particularly female blues singers, gained fame and employment across the South. Early pioneers included Robert Johnson, WC Handy, Ma Rainey, Huddie Ledbetter (aka Lead Belly) and Bessie Smith, who some consider the best blues singer who ever lived.

At the same time, African American Christian choral music evolved into gospel, whose greatest singer, Mahalia Jackson, came to prominence in Chicago the 1920s. She sang in the choir of the Greater Salem Baptist Church on the city's south side and was a faithful member until her death in 1972.

After WWII many musicians headed north to Chicago, which had become a hub for African American culture. And here the genre took a turn – it went electric. A new generation of players such as Muddy Waters, Buddy Guy, BB King and John Lee Hooker plugged in to amps, and their screaming guitars laid the groundwork for rock and roll.

Shrines for Music Fans

Sun Studio, Memphis, TN

Rock and Roll Hall of Fame, Cleveland, OH

Preservation Hall, New Orleans, LA

BB King Museum and Delta Interpretive Center, Indianola, MS

Jazz

Down in New Orleans, Congo Sq, where slaves gathered to sing and dance from the late 18th century onward, is considered the birthplace of jazz. There ex-slaves adapted the reed, horn and string instruments used by the city's multiracial Creoles – who themselves preferred formal European music – to play their own African-influenced music. This fertile cross-pollination produced a steady stream of innovative sound.

The first variation was ragtime, so-called because of its 'ragged,' syncopated African rhythms. Next came Dixieland jazz, centered on New Orleans' infamous Storyville red-light district. In 1917 Storyville shut down, and the musicians dispersed. Bandleader King Oliver moved to Chicago, and his star trumpet player, Louis Armstrong, soon followed. Armstrong's distinctive vocals and talented improvisations led to the solo becoming an integral part of jazz throughout much of the 20th century.

The 1920s and '30s are known as the Jazz Age, and New York City's Harlem was its hot spot. Swing – an urbane, big-band jazz style – swept the country, led by innovative bandleaders Duke Ellington and Count

Basie. Jazz singers Ella Fitzgerald and Billie Holiday combined jazz with its Southern sibling, the blues.

After WWII, bebop (aka bop) arose, reacting against the smooth melodies and confining rhythms of big-band swing. Charlie Parker, Dizzy Gillespie and Thelonious Monk led the way. In the 1950s and '60s, Miles Davis, John Coltrane and others deconstructed the sound and made up a new one that was cool, free and avant-garde. NYC, New Orleans and Chicago remain the core of the scene today.

Country

Early Scottish, Irish and English immigrants brought their own instruments and folk music to America, and what emerged over time in the secluded Appalachian Mountains was fiddle-and-banjo hillbilly, or 'country' music. In the Southwest, steel guitars and larger bands distinguished 'western' music. In the 1920s, these styles merged into 'country and western' and Nashville became its center, especially once the Grand Ole Opry began its radio broadcasts in 1925. Country musicians who are now 'classics' include Hank Williams, Johnny Cash, Willie Nelson, Patsy Cline and Loretta Lynn.

Something about the 'cry a tear in your beer' twanging clearly resonated with listeners, because country music is now big business. Singer-songwriters such as Blake Shelton, Tim McGraw and Taylor Swift have sold millions of albums. Subsequent riffs on the genre include bluegrass, rockabilly and alt-country. The South remains the genre's boot-wearin' stronghold.

Folk

The tradition of American folk music was crystallized in Woody Guthrie, who traveled the country during the Depression singing politically conscious songs. In the 1940s, New Yorker Pete Seeger emerged as a tireless preserver of America's folk heritage. Folk music experienced a revival during 1960s protest movements, but then-folkie Bob Dylan ended it almost single-handedly when he plugged in an electric guitar to shouts of 'traitor!' at the Newport Folk Festival in 1965.

Folk has seen a resurgence in the last decade. Iron and Wine's tunes channel mournful pop, blues and rock as only a Southerner can, while the Hoosier sister duo Lily & Madeleine sing ethereal, incredibly rich folk ballads.

Rock

Most say rock and roll was born in 1954 the day Elvis Presley walked into Sam Philips' Sun Studio in Memphis and recorded 'That's All Right.' Initially, radio stations weren't sure why a white country boy was singing black music, or whether they should play him. It wasn't until 1956 that Presley scored his first big breakthrough with 'Heartbreak Hotel,' and in some ways, America never recovered from the rock-and-roll aftermath.

Musically, rock was a hybrid of guitar-driven blues, black rhythm and blues (R&B), and white country-and-western music. R&B evolved in the 1940s out of swing and the blues, and was then known as 'race music.' With rock and roll, white musicians (and some African American musicians) transformed 'race music' into something that white youths could embrace freely – and boy, did they.

Rock and roll instantly abetted a social revolution even more significant than its musical one: openly sexual as it celebrated youth and dancing freely across color lines, rock scared the nation. Authorities worked diligently to control 'juvenile delinquents' and to sanitize and suppress rock and roll, which might have withered if not for the early 1960s 'British

Rock star Prince, aka Prince Rogers Nelson, was born in 1950s Minneapolis. He originally tried out for the high-school basketball team, but being too short at 5ft 2in, he was cut. His back-up hobby? He took up the guitar. He still lives in the area and throws open the doors of his abode, Paisley Park, for the occasional public concert.

invasion,' in which the Beatles and the Rolling Stones, emulating Chuck Berry, Little Richard and others, shocked rock and roll back to life.

The 1960s witnessed a full-blown youth rebellion, epitomized by the drug-inspired psychedelic sounds of the Grateful Dead and Jefferson Airplane, and the electric wails of Janis Joplin and Jimi Hendrix. Since then, rock has been about music and lifestyle, alternately torn between hedonism and seriousness, commercialism and authenticity. The Woodstock festival exemplified the scene in 1969, transforming a little patch of upstate New York into a legend.

Punk arrived in the late 1970s, led by the Ramones (the pride of Queens, NY), as did the working-class rock of Bruce Springsteen (the pride of New Jersey). As the counterculture became the culture in the 1980s, critics prematurely pronounced 'rock is dead.' Rock was saved (by the Talking Heads, REM and Sonic Youth, among other eastern US bands) as it always has been: by splintering and evolving, whether it's called new wave, heavy metal, grunge, indie rock, world beat, skate punk, hardcore, goth, emo or electronica.

Even though hip-hop has become today's outlaw sound, rock remains relevant, and it's not going anywhere. The Strokes and The Killers helped stoke a rock revival in the early 2000s. Alabama Shakes, Black Lips and Future Islands are among the bands that carry the torch currently.

Hip-Hop

From the ocean of sounds coming out of the early 1970s – funk, soul, Latin, reggae, and rock and roll – young DJs from the Bronx in NYC began to spin a groundbreaking mixture of records together in an effort to drive dance floors wild.

And so hip-hop was born. Groups such as Grandmaster Flash and the Furious Five were soon taking the party from the streets to the trendy clubs of Manhattan and mingling with punk and new wave bands including the Clash and Blondie. Break-out artists Futura 2000, Keith Haring and Jean-Michel Basquiat moved from the subways and the streets to the galleries, and soon to the worlds of fashion and advertising.

New York remained the hub into the mid-1980s. Groups like Run-DMC, Public Enemy and the Beastie Boys sold millions. And then the sounds and styles of the growing hip-hop culture started to diversify. A rivalry developed between the East Coast groups and the West Coast 'gangsta' rappers coming out of LA. Groups like Niggaz With Attitude got both accolades and bad press for their daring sounds and social commentary – which critics called battle cries for violence – on racism, drugs, sex and urban poverty.

Come the turn of the millennium, what started as raggedy gang kids playing their parents' funk records at illegal block parties had evolved into a multi-billion-dollar business. Russell Simmons and P Diddy stood atop New York–based media empires, and stars Queen Latifah (from Jersey) and Will Smith (from Philly) were Hollywood royalty. A white rapper from Detroit, Eminem, sold millions of records, and hip-hop overtook country as America's second-most-popular music behind pop rock.

Today, many view hip-hop as a vapid wasteland of commercial excess – glorifying consumerism, misogyny, homophobia, drug use and a host of other social ills. But just as the hedonistic days of arena rock and roll gave birth to the rebel child of punk, the evolving offspring of hip-hop and DJ culture are constantly breaking the rules to create something new and even more energizing. Major players of the moment include Jay-Z, Kanye West, Nicki Minaj, Common and the more experimental and feel-good hip-hop duo of Macklemore & Ryan Lewis.

Best Music Festivals

New Orleans Jazz Fest, New Orleans, LA; April

Movement Electronic Music Festival, Detroit, MI; May

Bonnaroo, Manchester, TN; June

Summerfest, Milwaukee, WI; June/July

Newport Folk Festival, Newport, RI; July

Lollapalooza, Chicago, IL; August

Landscapes & Wildlife

Whether you've come to glimpse alligators, whales, manatees or moose, the eastern USA delivers. Its coasts, mountains, swamps and forests have heaps of habitat for wildlife spotting. The national parks are prime places to take it all in.

Landscapes

The eastern USA is a land of temperate, deciduous forests and contains the ancient Appalachian Mountains, a low range that parallels the Atlantic Ocean. Between the mountains and the coast lies the country's most populated, urbanized region, particularly in the corridor between Washington, DC and Boston, MA.

To the north are the Great Lakes, which the USA shares with Canada. These five lakes, part of the Canadian Shield, are the greatest expanse of fresh water on the planet, constituting nearly 20% of the world's supply.

Going south along the East Coast, things get wetter and warmer till you reach the swamps of southern Florida and make the turn into the Gulf of Mexico, which provides the USA with a southern coastline.

West of the Appalachians are the vast interior plains, which lie flat all the way to the Rocky Mountains. The eastern plains are the nation's breadbasket, roughly divided into the northern 'corn belt' and the southern 'cotton belt.' The plains, an ancient sea bottom, are drained by the mighty Mississippi River, which together with the Missouri River forms the world's fourth-longest river system, surpassed only by the Nile, Amazon and Yangtze rivers.

Beyond the East, the Rocky Mountains and southwestern deserts eventually give way to the Pacific Ocean.

Best Landscapes off the Beaten Path

Cypress Creek National Wildlife Refuge, IL: swamplands

Ouachita National Forest, AK: spring-fed mountains

Cape Henlopen State Park, DE: dunes, wetlands

Monongahela National Forest, WV: rivers

Plants & Trees

Displays of spring wildflowers and colorful autumn foliage are a New England specialty. Great Smoky Mountains National Park contains all five eastern-forest types (spruce fir, hemlock, pine-oak, and northern and cove hardwood), which support over 100 native species of trees.

In Florida, the Everglades is the last subtropical wilderness in the US. This vital, endangered habitat is a fresh- and saltwater world of marshes, sloughs and coastal prairies that support mangroves, cypresses, sea grasses, tropical plants, pines and hardwoods.

Land Mammals

Moose

Moose nibble on shrubs throughout the northern part of the region, specifically Maine, New Hampshire, Vermont, upstate New York and the Michigan-Minnesota-Wisconsin north woods. They're part of the deer family but are far more humongous, with skinny, ballerina-like legs that support a hulking body. Males weigh up to 1200lb, all put on by a vegetarian diet of twigs and leaves. Despite their odd shape, moose can move it: they run up to 35mph, and in water they can swim as fast as two men paddling a canoe.

Males grow a spectacular rack of antlers every summer, only to discard it in November. You'll spot moose foraging near lakes and streams. They generally are not aggressive, and often will pose for photographs. They can be unpredictable, though, so don't startle them. During mating season (September) the males can become belligerent, so keep your distance.

Moose have been dying at an alarming rate in many areas. Scientists think climate change may be partly to blame. In New Hampshire a longer fall with less snow has increased the number of winter ticks, parasites that prey on moose. In Minnesota it's the same story but with brain worms as the deadly parasite. In Maine, however, the population remains robust at around 70,000 moose.

Geologists believe that roughly 460 million years ago the Appalachian Mountains were the highest mountains on earth – higher even than the Himalayas are today.

Black Bears

Despite a decline in numbers, black bears prowl most parts of the region, especially in the Adirondacks, the Great Smoky Mountains and the Midwest's north woods. Males can stand 7ft tall and weigh 550lb – but that depends on when you encounter them. In autumn they weigh up to 30% more than when they emerge from hibernation in the spring. Although they enjoy an occasional meaty snack, black bears usually fill their bellies with berries and other vegetation. They're opportunistic, adaptable and curious animals, and can survive on very small home ranges. As their forests diminish, they're occasionally seen traipsing through nearby populated areas.

Panthers

A remnant population of panthers licks its chops in Everglades National Park, Florida. Before European contact, perhaps 1500 roamed the state. The first panther bounty ($5 a scalp) was passed in 1832, and over the next 130 years they were hunted relentlessly. Though hunting was

---

INFAMOUS NATURAL DISASTERS

Earthquakes, wildfires, tornadoes, hurricanes and blizzards – the US certainly has its share of natural disasters. Following are a few of the more infamous events that have shaped the national conscience:

Hurricane Katrina August 29, 2005, is not a day easily forgotten in New Orleans. A massive hurricane swept across the Gulf of Mexico and slammed into Louisiana. As levees failed, floods inundated over 80% of the city. The death toll reached 1836, with over $100 billion in estimated damages – making it America's costliest natural disaster. Heartbreaking images of the destroyed city and anger over the government's bungled response still linger.

Hurricane Irene On August 27 and 28, 2011, a mammoth storm blew over the eastern seaboard, battering 15 states from Florida through to New England and as far inland as Pennsylvania. New York City evacuated many residents and took the unprecedented step of shutting down all public transit. More than 7.4 million homes lost electrical power, rivers ran wild, and at least 45 people died. The damage has been estimated to be $7 billion.

East Coast Earthquake On August 23, 2011, a rare earthquake rattled the eastern USA. The 5.8 magnitude tremor had its epicenter located in Mineral, Virginia, but was felt from Maine right through to South Carolina, and was the area's strongest quake since 1897. There was no serious damage, though it did crack the Washington Monument and knock three spires off the National Cathedral in Washington, DC.

Hurricane Sandy On October 29, 2012, America suffered its second-costliest hurricane in US history (after Katrina). Sandy was the largest Atlantic hurricane ever recorded, with storm winds spanning over 1000 miles. The Jersey Shore and low-lying areas of New York City (such as Staten Island) were particularly hard hit. More than 80 people died in the USA, and estimated damages amounted to more than $65 billion.

stopped in 1958, it was too late for panthers to survive on their own. Without a captive breeding program, begun in 1991, the Florida panther would now be extinct, and with only some 100 known to exist, they're not out of the swamp yet.

Wolves & Coyotes

Wolves are rare in the Eastern USA. Those that are here wander mostly in northern Minnesota, particularly the Boundary Waters. The area's cold, boreal forest is prime territory, as well as home to the International Wolf Center (www.wolfcenter.org) in Ely, Minnesota. The wolf can be every bit as fierce and cunning as is portrayed in fairy tales, although it rarely attacks humans. If you're out in the wilderness, you may hear them howling at the moon.

The coyote looks similar to the wolf but is about half the size, ranging from 15lb to 45lb. An icon of the Southwest, coyotes are found all over the eastern region too, even in cities – Chicago had one a few years ago that loped into a downtown sandwich shop during the lunchtime rush.

Deer

The white-tailed deer can be found everywhere in the region, from top to bottom. Endemic to the Florida Keys are Key deer, a Honey-I-Shrunk-the-Ungulate subspecies: less than 3ft tall and lighter than a 10-year-old boy, they live mostly on Big Pine Key.

Reptiles

Alligators & Crocodiles

American alligators slither throughout the Southeast's wetlands, mostly in Florida and Louisiana. With a snout, eyeballs and pebbled back so still they hardly dimple the water's surface, alligators have notched over the swamps for more than 200 million years.

Louisiana has close to two million gators, and Florida counts 1.5 million among the state's lakes, rivers and golf courses, mostly in the central and southern zones. The Everglades are perhaps the best place to find them lurking. Alligators are alpha predators who keep the rest of the food chain in check, and their 'gator holes' become vital water cups in the dry season and during droughts, aiding the entire wetlands ecosystem. They live about 30 years, can grow up to 14ft long and weigh 1000lb. No longer officially endangered, alligators remain protected because they resemble the still-endangered American crocodile.

South Florida is home to the only North American population of American crocodiles, around 1500 of them. They prefer saltwater, and to distinguish them from gators, check their smile – a croc's snout is more tapered and its teeth stick out.

Sea Turtles

Florida is the hot spot for sea-turtle nesting in the continental US. Three main species create over 80,000 nests annually, mostly on southern Atlantic Coast beaches, but extending to all Gulf Coast beaches, too. Loggerheads comprise the vast majority, followed by green and leatherback turtles and, historically, hawksbill and Kemp's ridley as well; all five species are endangered or threatened. The leatherback is the largest, bulking up to 10ft and 2000lb.

During the May-to-October nesting season, sea turtles deposit from 80 to 120 eggs in each nest. The eggs incubate for about two months, and then the hatchlings emerge all at once and make for the ocean. Contrary to myth, hatchlings don't need the moon to find their way.

Michigan's Isle Royale National Park hosts the world's longest-running predator-prey study, of wolves and moose. While numbers have fluctuated since research began in 1958, the biggest imbalance occurred only recently: in 2015, the wolf population dwindled to three (down from 30 wolves as recently as 2006), while moose numbers swelled to 1250. Disease, inbreeding and climate shifts are among the culprits.

Winner of the 2015 Pulitzer Prize for non-fiction, *The Sixth Extinction* by Elizabeth Kolbert looks at why species are disappearing from the planet at an alarming rate. It examines everything from the collapse in the population of golden frogs in the Panamanian rainforest and Sumatran rhinos in Southeast Asia to mass bat die-offs in Vermont, near the author's home.

EASTERN USA'S NATIONAL PARKS

NAME	STATE	FEATURES	ACTIVITIES	BEST TIME TO VISIT
Acadia National Park	ME	1530ft Cadillac Mountain, rocky coastline, islands	hiking, cycling	May-Oct
Biscayne National Park	FL	coral reefs, manatees, dolphins, sea turtles	kayaking, snorkeling, diving, glass-bottom boat tours	mid-Dec–mid-Apr
Congaree National Park	SC	moss-draped cypresses, swamp, owls	fishing, canoeing	spring & autumn
Cuyahoga Valley National Park	OH	rivers, waterfalls, canal tow path	hiking, cycling, scenic train ride	May-Oct
Dry Tortugas National Park	FL	remote islands, Civil War fort, 300 bird species, sea turtles	snorkeling, diving, bird-watching	Dec-Apr
Everglades National Park	FL	grasslands, swamp, alligators, panthers, manatees	cycling, canoeing, kayaking, hiking	Dec-Apr
Great Smoky Mountains National Park	NC, TN	mountains, woodlands, wildflowers, black bears, elk	hiking, horseback riding, fishing	mid-Apr–Oct
Hot Springs National Park	AK	thermal waters, historic buildings	spa soaking, hiking	Sep-Feb
Isle Royale National Park	MI	huge isolated island, thick forest, lakes, moose	kayaking, hiking, back-country camping	mid-May–Oct
Mammoth Cave National Park	KY	never-ending caves, underground rivers, bats	hiking, spelunking	year-round
Shenandoah National Park	VA	Blue Ridge Mountains, waterfalls, deer, bobcats	hiking, camping	Apr-Oct
Voyageurs National Park	MN	thick forest, islands, lakes, wolves, aurora borealis	boating, snowmobiling	May–late Sep

Snakes

First, here's the bad news: there are four species of rattlesnake found east of the Mississippi – the diamondback, pygmy, canebrake and timber. At 7ft long, the diamondback is the biggest and the most aggressive. Copperheads, cottonmouths and coral snakes are other poisonous types in the region. All of them slither primarily through the Mid-Atlantic and South.

Now the good news: running into a poisonous snake is uncommon. Need proof? Great Smoky Mountains National Park, with around 9.5 million visitors per year, has never recorded a snakebite fatality in its 80-plus-year history.

Marine Mammals & Fish

Whales & Dolphins

The eastern USA's top spot to whale-watch is off Massachusetts' coast at Stellwagen Bank National Marine Sanctuary, a summer feeding ground for humpbacks. These awesome creatures average 49ft and 36 tons – serious heft to be launching up and out of the water for their playful breaching. They also come surprisingly close to boats, offering great photo ops. Many of the 400 remaining North Atlantic right whales, the world's most endangered leviathan, frequent the same waters. Cruises depart from Boston, Plymouth, Provincetown and Gloucester, Massachusetts.

The waters off the coast of Florida are home to several dolphin species. By far the most common species is the bottlenose dolphin, which is highly social, extremely intelligent and frequently encountered around the entire peninsula.

Manatees

Florida's coast is home to the unusual, gentle manatee, which moves between freshwater rivers and the ocean. Around 10ft long and weighing on average 1000lb, these agile, expressive creatures don't do much, spending most of each day resting and eating 10% of their body weight. In winter they seek out Florida's warm-water springs and power-plant discharge canals. In summer, they migrate back to the ocean and can be spotted in the coastal waters of Alabama, Georgia and South Carolina, in addition to Florida.

Manatees have been under some form of protection since 1893, and they were included in the first federal endangered species list in 1967. They were once hunted for their meat – finer than filet mignon, allegedly – but collisions with boats are now a leading cause of manatee deaths, accounting for over 20% annually. Manatees number more than 5000 today.

Tropical Fish

For stunning coral reefs and vibrant tropical fish, the Florida Keys are the places to go. North America's only living coral barrier reef – and the world's third-largest such reef (after the Great Barrier Reef in Australia and the Meso-American Reef in Belize) – runs for 221 miles from Key Biscayne off Miami down to Dry Tortugas National Park, 70 miles off Key West. Both the national park and John Pennekamp Coral Reef State Park (in Key Largo) are terrific places to behold the underwater world where sea fans wave and schools of blue tangs and trumpetfish dart. The reefs are home to more than 260 types of tropical fish

Birds

The bald eagle, the USA's national symbol since 1782, is the only eagle unique to North America. Its wingspan can reach more than 6.5ft across. Good wintertime viewing sites are along the Mississippi River in Minnesota, Wisconsin and Illinois; in summer, eagles are common throughout Florida, wherever there's fish-rich water for chowing alongside tall trees for nesting. The eagle has come off the endangered species list, having made a remarkable comeback from a low of 417 breeding pairs in 1963 to almost 9800 pairs today (that's in the lower 48 states; another 30,000-plus live in Alaska).

White pelicans, which are among the region's largest birds, arrive in winter (October to April), while brown pelicans, the only kind to dive for their food, live here year-round. They're found around the Gulf Coast and throughout Florida.

In a program to introduce endangered whooping cranes to the east, naturalists use ultralight aircraft to lead young cranes from their breeding ground in central Wisconsin to a winter habitat along Florida's Gulf Coast. Once the birds learn the route, they can retrace it unaided. Follow them at www.ustream.tv/migratingcranes.

Survival Guide

Directory A–Z

Accommodations

For all but the cheapest places and the slowest seasons, reservations are advised. In high-season tourist hot spots, hotels can book up months ahead.

Seasons

➡ Peak season is summer, generally May to September, when prices are highest.

➡ Exceptions include Florida and the northern ski areas, when winter is the busiest and costliest time to visit.

Amenities

➡ Most properties offer in-room wi-fi. It's typically free in budget and midrange lodgings, while top-end hotels often charge a fee (typically $10 to $17 per day).

➡ Many smaller properties, especially B&Bs, ban smoking. Marriott and Westin hotels are 100% smoke free. All other properties have rooms set aside for nonsmokers.

➡ Air-conditioning is standard at most places.

Discounts

Check hotel websites for special online rates. If you find something cheaper on a booking site, many hotels will match it if you call and ask.

B&Bs & Inns

These accommodations vary from small, comfy houses with shared bathrooms (least expensive) to romantic, antique-filled historic homes and mansions with private baths (most expensive). Those focusing on upscale romance may discourage children. Also, inns and B&Bs often require a minimum stay of two or three days on weekends, and reservations are essential. Always call ahead to confirm policies (ie regarding kids, pets, smoking) and bathroom arrangements.

B&B agencies:

Bed & Breakfast Inns Online (www.bbonline.com)

BedandBreakfast.com (www.bedandbreakfast.com)

BnB Finder (www.bnbfinder.com)

Select Registry (www.selectregistry.com)

Camping

Campsites at national and state parks typically come in three types:

Primitive Free to $10 per night, no facilities.

Basic $10 to $20, with toilets, drinking water, fire pits and picnic tables.

Developed $20 to $50, with more amenities such as showers, barbecue grills, recreational vehicle (RV) sites with hookups etc.

Make reservations for national parks and other federal lands through **Recreation. gov** (✆877-444-6777, international ✆518-885-3639; www.recreation.gov). Camping is usually limited to 14 days and can be reserved up to six months in advance. For some state-park campgrounds, you can make bookings through **ReserveAmerica** (www.reserveamerica.com).

Most privately owned campgrounds are geared to RVs, but will also have a small section available for tent campers. Expect lots of amenities, like swimming pools, laundry facilities, convenience stores and bars. **Kampgrounds of America** (KOA; www.koa.com) is a national network of private campgrounds; their Kamping Kabins have air-con and kitchens.

Hostels

Hostelling International USA (✆240-650-2100; www.hiusa.org) runs several hostels in the eastern US. Most have gender-segregated dorms, a few private rooms, shared baths and a communal

---

BOOK YOUR STAY ONLINE

For more accommodations reviews by Lonely Planet authors, check out http://lonelyplanet.com/hotels/. You'll find independent reviews, as well as recommendations on the best places to stay. Best of all, you can book online.

kitchen. Overnight fees for dorm beds range from $25 to $45 (though in NYC, a dorm bed can cost upward of $75). You don't have to be a member to stay, but you pay a slightly higher rate. Reservations are accepted (you can book online).

The region has many independent hostels not affiliated with HI-USA. Browse listings at the following:

Hostels.com (www.hostels.com)

Hostelworld.com (www.hostelworld.com)

Hostelz.com (www.hostelz.com)

Hotels

Hotels in all categories typically include cable TV, in-room wi-fi, private baths and a simple continental breakfast. Many midrange properties provide minibars, microwaves, hair dryers and swimming pools, while top-end hotels add concierge services, fitness and business centers, spas, restaurants and bars.

POPULAR HOTEL CHAINS

Best Western (☏800-780-7234; www.bestwestern.com)

Comfort Inn (☏877-424-6423; www.comfortinn.com)

Hampton Inn (☏800-426-7866; www.hampton-inn.com)

Hilton (☏800-445-8667; www.hilton.com)

Holiday Inn (☏888-465-4329; www.holidayinn.com)

Marriott (☏888-236-2427; www.marriott.com)

Super 8 (☏800-454-3213; www.super8.com)

House & Apartment Rentals

To rent a house or apartment from locals, visit **Airbnb** (www.airbnb.com), which has thousands of listings across the country. Budget travelers can also rent a room; it's a great way to connect with locals if you don't mind sharing facilities.

Motels

Motels – distinguishable from hotels by having rooms that open onto a parking lot – tend to cluster around interstate exits and along main routes into town. Many are inexpensive 'mom-and-pop' operations; breakfast is rarely included; and amenities might top out at wi-fi and a TV (maybe with cable). Although most motel rooms won't win any style awards, they can be clean and comfortable and offer good value. Ask to see a room first if you're unsure.

Resorts

Florida, in particular, has behemoth resorts. Facilities can include all manner of fitness and sports, pools, spas, restaurants and bars, and so on. Many also have on-site babysitting services. However, some also tack an extra 'resort fee' onto rates, so always ask.

Customs Regulations

For a complete list of US customs regulations, visit the official website for **US Customs and Border Protection** (www.cbp.gov).

Duty-free allowance per person is as follows:

➡ 1L of liquor (provided you are at least 21 years old).

➡ 100 cigars and 200 cigarettes (if you are at least 18).

➡ $200 worth of gifts and purchases ($800 if a returning US citizen).

➡ If you arrive with $10,000 or more in US or foreign currency, it must be declared.

There are heavy penalties for attempting to import illegal drugs. Forbidden items include drug paraphernalia, items with fake brand names, and most goods made in Cuba, Iran, Myanmar (Burma) and Sudan. Fruit, vegetables and other food must be declared (whereby you'll undergo a time-consuming search) or left in the bins in the arrival area.

Discount Cards

The following cards can net savings (usually about 10%) on museums, accommodations and some transport (including Amtrak):

American Association of Retired Persons (www.aarp.org) For US travelers age 50 and older.

American Automobile Association (AAA; ☏877-428-2277, emergency roadside assistance 800-222-4357; www.aaa.com; annual membership from $52) For members of AAA or reciprocal clubs in Europe and Australia.

International Student Identity Card (www.isic.org) For students any age and nonstudents under age 26.

Student Advantage Card (www.studentadvantage.com) For US and foreign students aged 16 and older.

Electricity

120V/60Hz

120V/60Hz

Embassies & Consulates

In addition to the embassies in Washington, DC (see www.embassy.org for a complete list), most countries have an embassy for the UN in New York City. Some countries have consulates in other large cities.

Australian Embassy (☎202-797-3000; www.usa.embassy.gov.au; 1601 Massachusetts Ave NW; MFarragut North)

Canadian Embassy (☎202-682-1740; www.can-am.gc.ca; 501 Pennsylvania Ave NW; MArchives)

French Embassy (☎202-944-6000; www.info-france-usa.org; 4101 Reservoir Rd NW; D6)

German Embassy (☎202-298-4000; www.germany.info; 4645 Reservoir Rd NW; D6)

Irish Embassy (☎202-462-3939; www.dfa.ie/irish-embassy/USA; 2234 Massachusetts Ave NW; MDupont Circle)

Mexican Embassy (☎202-728-1600; embamex.sre.gob.mx/eua; 1911 Pennsylvania Ave NW; MFarragut West)

Netherlands Embassy (☎877-388-2443; www.the-netherlands.org; 4200 Linnean Ave NW; MVan Ness-UDC)

New Zealand Embassy (☎202-328-4800; www.nzembassy.com/usa; 37 Observatory Circle NW; MDupont Circle, then bus N2 or N4)

UK Embassy (☎202-588-6500; www.gov.uk/government/world/usa; 3100 Massachusetts Ave NW; MDupont Circle, then bus N2 or N4)

Food

See p626 for everything you need to know about eating and drinking in the region.

Gay & Lesbian Travelers

In general, the Northeast is the most tolerant region in the eastern USA, and the South the least so, though big cities in all of the regions have long-standing gay communities.

Hot Spots

Manhattan has loads of great gay bars and clubs, especially in Hell's Kitchen, Chelsea and the West Village. A few hours away (by train and ferry) is Fire Island, the sandy gay mecca on Long Island. Other East Coast cities with gay and lesbian scenes are Boston, Philadelphia, Washington, DC, Massachusetts' Provincetown (on Cape Cod) and Delaware's Rehoboth Beach. Even Maine has a gay beach destination: Ogunquit.

In the South, there's always steamy 'Hotlanta.' In Florida, Miami and the 'Conch Republic' of Key West support thriving gay communities, though Fort Lauderdale attracts bronzed boys and girls, too. Of course, everyone hits the dance floor in New Orleans. In the Midwest, seek out Chicago and Minneapolis.

Attitudes

Most major US cities have a visible and open LGBTIQ community that is easy to connect with.

The level of public acceptance varies nationwide. In some places, there is absolutely no tolerance whatsoever, and in others acceptance is predicated on LGBTIQ people not 'flaunting' their sexual orientation or identity. Be aware that bigotry still exists here. In rural areas and conservative enclaves, it's unwise to be openly out, as verbal abuse and even violence can sometimes occur. When in doubt, assume that locals follow a 'don't ask, don't tell' policy. Same-sex marriage is now legally recognized by the federal government, and 37 states (including many in the Northeast) plus DC have same-sex marriages.

Resources

The Queerest Places: A Guide to Gay and Lesbian Historic Sites, by Paula Martinac, is full of juicy details and history, and covers the country. Visit her blog at www.queerestplaces.com.

Advocate (www.advocate.com) Gay-oriented news website reports on business, politics, arts, entertainment and travel.

Damron (www.damron.com) Publishes the classic gay travel guides, but they're advertiser-driven and sometimes outdated.

Gay Travel (www.gaytravel.com) Online guides to dozens of US destinations.

National Gay & Lesbian Task Force (www.thetaskforce.org) National activist group's website covers news, politics and current issues.

Out Traveler (www.outtraveler. com) Gay-oriented travel articles.

Purple Roofs (www.purpleroofs. com) Lists gay-owned and gay-friendly B&Bs and hotels.

Health

The eastern region, like the rest of the USA, has a high level of hygiene, so infectious diseases are not a significant problem. There are no required vaccines, and tap water is safe to drink.

Bring any medications you may need in their original containers, clearly labeled. Having a signed, dated letter from your physician that describes all of your medical conditions and medications (including generic names) is also a good idea.

Health Insurance

The United States offers possibly the finest health care in the world – the problem is that it can be prohibitively expensive. It's essential to purchase travel health insurance if your home policy doesn't cover you for medical expenses abroad. Check the Insurance section of the Lonely Planet website (lonelyplanet.com/travel-insurance) for more information.

Find out in advance if your insurance plan will make payments directly to providers or reimburse you later for overseas health expenditures.

Health Care Availability

➡ If you have a medical emergency, go to the emergency room of the nearest hospital.

➡ If the problem isn't urgent, call a nearby hospital and ask for a referral to a local physician; this is usually cheaper than a trip to the emergency room.

➡ Standalone, for-profit, urgent-care centers provide good service, but can be the most expensive option.

➡ Pharmacies are abundantly supplied. However, some medications that are available over the counter in other countries require a prescription in the US.

➡ If you don't have insurance to cover the cost of prescriptions, they can be shockingly expensive.

Infectious Diseases

Most infectious diseases are acquired by mosquito or tick bites or through environmental exposure. The **Centers for Disease Control** (www.cdc.gov) has further details.

Giardiasis Intestinal infection. Avoid drinking directly from lakes, ponds, streams and rivers.

Lyme disease Occurs mostly in the Northeast. Transmitted by deer ticks in late spring and summer. Perform a tick check after you've been outdoors.

West Nile virus Mosquito-transmitted in late summer and early fall. Prevent by keeping covered (wear long sleeves, long pants, hats and shoes rather than sandals) and apply a good insect repellent, preferably one containing DEET, to exposed skin and clothing.

Environmental Hazards

Cold exposure This can be a problem, especially in the northern regions. Keep all body surfaces covered, including the head and neck. Watch out for the 'Umbles' (stumbles, mumbles, fumbles and grumbles), which are signs of impending hypothermia.

Heat exhaustion Dehydration is the main contributor. Symptoms include feeling weak, headache, nausea and sweaty skin. Lay the victim flat with their legs raised, apply cool, wet cloths to the skin, and rehydrate.

Insurance

It's expensive to get sick, crash a car or have things stolen from you in the US. Make sure to have adequate coverage before arriving. To insure yourself for items that may be stolen from your car, consult your homeowner's (or renter's) insurance policy

PRACTICALITIES

Newspapers & Magazines

➡ Regional newspapers: *Washington Post*, *Boston Globe*, *Miami Herald*, *Chicago Tribune*

➡ National newspapers: *New York Times*, *Wall Street Journal*, *USA Today*

➡ Mainstream news magazines: *Time*, *Newsweek*

Radio & TV

➡ Radio news: National Public Radio (NPR), lower end of FM dial

➡ Broadcast TV: ABC, CBS, NBC, FOX, PBS (public broadcasting)

➡ Major cable channels: CNN (news), ESPN (sports), HBO (movies), Weather Channel

Video Systems & DVDs

➡ NTSC standard (incompatible with PAL or SECAM)

➡ DVDs coded for Region 1 (US and Canada only)

Weights & Measures

➡ Weight: ounces (oz), pounds (lb), tons

➡ Liquid: oz, pints, quarts, gallons

➡ Distance: feet (ft), yards (yd), miles (mi)

Smoking

As of 2015, about half the eastern and Midwest states, and many municipalities across the region, had entirely smoke-free restaurants, bars and workplaces.

---

or consider investing in travel insurance.

Worldwide travel insurance is available at the Insurance section of the **Lonely Planet** (lonelyplanet.com/travel-insurance) website. You can buy, extend and claim online at any time – even if you're already on the road.

Internet Access

➡ Travelers will have few problems staying connected in the tech-savvy USA.

➡ Wi-fi (in-room, with decent speed) is common in lodgings across the price spectrum. Many properties also have an internet-connected computer for public use.

➡ Many restaurants, bars and cafes (such as Starbucks) offer free wi-fi. Some cities have wi-fi connected parks and plazas.

➡ If you're not packing a laptop or other web-accessible device, try the public library. Most have public terminals (though they have time limits) and wi-fi. Occasionally, out-of-state residents are charged a small fee for use.

➡ If you're not from the US, remember that you may need an AC adapter for your laptop (if it's not 110/220 dual-voltage), plus a plug adapter for US sockets; both are available at large electronics shops, such as Best Buy.

➡ For a list of wi-fi hot spots, visit www.wififreespot.com.

Legal Matters

Note that, if you are stopped by the police, there is no system of paying traffic tickets or other fines on the spot. The officer will explain your options to you; there is usually a 30-day period to pay fines by mail.

If you are arrested, never walk away from an officer. You are allowed to remain silent, and you are entitled to have access to an attorney. The legal system presumes you're innocent until proven guilty. All persons who are arrested have the right to make one phone call. If you don't have a lawyer or family member to help you, call your embassy or consulate. The police will give you the number on request.

Drugs & Alcohol

➡ In most places it's illegal to walk with an open alcoholic drink on the street. New Orleans and Memphis' Beale St are notable exceptions.

➡ Being 'carded' (ie asked to show photo ID to prove you're of legal drinking age, which is 21 years old) is standard practice everywhere.

➡ Some states, especially in the South, have 'dry' counties where liquor sales are banned altogether.

➡ In all states, the blood alcohol limit is 0.08%. Driving under the influence of alcohol or drugs is a serious offense, subject to stiff fines and even imprisonment.

➡ Twenty-three states – including most from New York on through the Northeast – treat possession of small amounts of marijuana as a misdemeanor (generally punishable with a fine of around $100 or $200 for the first offense). However, pot use is illegal in many states in the Midwest and South. It's essential to know the local laws before lighting up.

➡ Aside from marijuana, recreational drugs are prohibited by law. Possession of any illicit drug, including cocaine, ecstasy, LSD, heroin or hashish, is a felony potentially punishable by lengthy jail sentences.

Money

Most locals do not carry large amounts of cash for everyday use, relying instead on credit cards, debit cards and ATMs. Don't, however, plan to rely exclusively on credit cards, as some machines (notably at many gas stations) won't accept foreign cards. Smaller businesses may refuse to accept bills over $20.

ATMs

➡ ATMs are available 24/7 at most banks and in shopping centers, airports, grocery stores and convenience shops.

➡ Most ATMs charge a service fee of $3 or more per transaction, and your home bank may impose additional charges.

➡ For foreign visitors, ask your bank for exact information about using its cards in stateside ATMs. The exchange rate is usually as good as you'll get anywhere.

Credit Cards

Major credit cards are almost universally accepted. In fact, it's next to impossible to rent

a car or make phone reservations without one. Visa and MasterCard are the most widely accepted. Contact the issuing company for lost or stolen cards.

American Express (☑800-528-4800; www.american express.com)

MasterCard (☑800-627-8372; www.mastercard.com)

Visa (☑800-847-2911; www.visa.com)

Currency Exchange

➡ Banks are usually the best places to exchange foreign currencies. Most large city banks offer the service, but banks in rural areas may not.

➡ Currency-exchange counters at the airport and in tourist centers typically have the worst rates; ask about fees and surcharges first.

➡ **Travelex** (☑516-300-1622; www.travelex.com) is a major currency-exchange company, but **American Express** (☑800-528-4800; www.americanexpress.com) travel offices may offer better rates.

Taxes

➡ Sales tax varies by state and county, and ranges from 5% to 10%. Most prices you see advertised will exclude tax, which is calculated upon purchase.

➡ Hotel taxes vary by city from around 10% to over 18% (in NYC).

Tipping

Tipping is *not* optional; only withhold tips in cases of outrageously bad service.

Airport and hotel porters $2 per bag, minimum $5 per cart.

Bartenders 10% to 15% per round, minimum $1 per drink.

Hotel maids $2 to $5 daily, left under the card provided.

Restaurant servers 15% to 20%, unless a gratuity is already charged on the bill.

Taxi drivers 10% to 15%, rounded up to the next dollar.

Valet parking attendants At least $2 when handed back your car keys.

Opening Hours

Typical opening times are as follows:

Banks 8:30am to 4:30pm Monday to Friday (and possibly 9am to noon Saturday).

Bars 5pm to midnight Sunday to Thursday, to 2am Friday and Saturday.

Nightclubs 10pm to 3am Thursday to Saturday.

Post offices 9am to 5pm Monday to Friday.

Shopping malls 9am to 9pm.

Stores 9am to 6pm Monday to Saturday, noon to 5pm Sunday.

Supermarkets 8am to 8pm, some open 24 hours.

Post

➡ The **US Postal Service** (USPS; ☑800-275-8777; www.usps.com) is reliable and inexpensive. The postal rates for first-class mail within the USA are 49¢ for letters weighing up to 1oz (22¢ for each additional ounce) and 35¢ for postcards.

➡ International airmail rates are $1.20 for a 1oz letter or postcard.

Public Holidays

On the following national public holidays, banks, schools and government offices (including post offices) are closed, and transportation, museums and other services operate on a Sunday schedule. Holidays falling on a weekend are usually observed the following Monday.

New Year's Day January 1

Martin Luther King Jr Day Third Monday in January

Presidents' Day Third Monday in February

Memorial Day Last Monday in May

Independence Day July 4

Labor Day First Monday in September

Columbus Day Second Monday in October

Veterans' Day November 11

Thanksgiving Fourth Thursday in November

Christmas Day December 25

Safe Travel

Hurricane season along the Atlantic seaboard and Gulf of Mexico extends from June through November, but the peak season is late August through October. Relatively speaking, very few storms become East Coast hurricanes, but the devastation they wreak when they do can be enormous. Travelers should take all hurricane alerts, warnings and evacuation orders seriously.

Inland in the Midwest and South, tornado season is roughly from March to July. Again, the chances you'll encounter one are slim.

When natural disasters do threaten, listen to radio and TV news reports. For more information on storms and preparedness, contact the **National Weather Service** (www.weather.gov).

Telephone

The US phone system mixes regional service providers, competing long-distance carriers and several cell-phone companies. Overall, the system is efficient. Calls from a regular landline or cell phone are usually cheaper than a hotel phone or pay phone. Services such as **Skype** (www.skype.com) and **Google Voice** (www.google.com/voice) can make calling quite cheap. Check the websites for details.

Cell Phones

➡ Most of the USA's mobile-phone systems are incompatible with the GSM 900/1800 standard used throughout Europe and Asia (though some convertible phones will work). iPhones will work fine – but beware of roaming costs, especially for data. Check with your service provider about using your phone here.

➡ It might be cheaper to buy a prepaid SIM card for the USA, like those sold by AT&T or T-Mobile, which you can insert into your international mobile phone to get a local phone number and voicemail.

➡ You can also buy inexpensive, no-contract (prepaid) phones with a local number and a set number of minutes, which can be topped up at will. Virgin Mobile, T-Mobile, AT&T and other providers offer phones starting at $30, with a package of minutes starting at around $40 for 400 minutes.

➡ Electronics store chain **Best Buy** (www.bestbuy.com) sells prepaid phones, as well as international SIM cards. Online retailer **Telestial** (www.telestial.com) also sells SIM cards and cell phones; it rents phones, too.

➡ Rural swaths of the East, especially in the mountains and various national parklands, don't pick up a signal. Check your provider's coverage map.

Dialing Codes

All phone numbers within the USA consist of a three-digit area code followed by a seven-digit local number. Typically, if you are calling a number within the same area code, you only have to dial the seven-digit number (though if it doesn't work, try adding ☏1 + the area code at the beginning). More information on dialing:

US country code ☏1

Making international calls Dial ☏011 + country code + area code + local number

Calling other US area codes or Canada Dial ☏1 + area code + seven-digit local number

Directory assistance nationwide ☏411

Toll-free numbers ☏1 + 800 (or 888, 877, 866) + seven-digit number. Some toll-free numbers only work within the US

Pay Phones

Pay phones are an endangered species in the ever-expanding mobile-phone world. Local calls cost 35¢ to 50¢ for the first few minutes; talking longer costs more.

Phone Cards

Prepaid phone cards are a good solution for travelers on a budget. They are available from convenience stores, supermarkets and pharmacy chains. AT&T sells a reliable phone card that is widely available.

Time

The eastern region is split between the Eastern and Central time zones, which are an hour apart. The demarcation line slices through Indiana, Kentucky, Tennessee and Florida. When it's noon Eastern time, it is 11am Central time (and 5pm Greenwich Mean Time).

The region, as well as most of the country, observes Daylight Saving Time (DST). On the second Sunday in March, clocks are set one hour ahead ('spring ahead'). Then, on the first Sunday of November, clocks are turned back one hour ('fall back').

And FYI: the US date system is written as month/day/year. Thus, the 8th of June, 2016, becomes 6/8/16.

Tourist Information

The official tourism website of the USA is www.discover america.com. It has links to every US state tourism office and website, plus loads of ideas for itinerary planning.

Most cities and towns have some sort of tourist center that provides local information, typically operated by the convention and visitor bureau (CVB) or chamber of commerce. These entities tend to list only the businesses that are bureau/chamber members, so not all of the town's hotels and restaurants receive coverage – keep in mind that good, independent options may be missing.

A couple of websites to get you started:

New York State Tourism (www.iloveny.com)

Visit Florida (www.visitflorida.com)

Washington, DC (www.washington.org)

Travelers with Disabilities

Travel in the region is relatively accommodating.

➡ Most public buildings are wheelchair-accessible and have appropriate restroom facilities.

➡ All major airlines, Greyhound buses and Amtrak trains will assist travelers with disabilities; just describe your needs when making reservations at least 48 hours in advance.

➡ Some car-rental agencies, such as Budget and Hertz, offer hand-controlled vehicles and vans with wheelchair lifts at no extra charge, but you must reserve them well in advance.

➡ Most cities have taxi companies with at least one accessible van, though you'll have to call ahead.

➡ Cities with underground transport have elevators for passengers needing assistance. Washington, DC has the best network (every station has an elevator); NYC's elevators are few and far between.

➡ Many national and some state parks and recreation areas have wheelchair-accessible paved, graded dirt or boardwalk trails.

For tips on travel and thoughtful insight on traveling with a disability, check out online posts by Martin Heng, Lonely Planet's Accessible Travel Manager: twitter.com/martin_heng.

A number of organizations specialize in the needs of disabled travelers:

Flying Wheels Travel (612-381-1622; www.flyingwheels travel.com) A full-service travel agency, highly recommended for those with mobility issues or chronic illness.

Mobility International USA (541-343-1284; www.miusa.org) Advises disabled travelers on mobility issues and runs educational exchange programs.

Wheelchair Getaways (800-642-2042; www.wheelchair getaways.com) Rents accessible vans throughout the USA.

Visas

Admission requirements are subject to rapid change. The

US State Department (travel.state.gov) has the latest information, or check with a US consulate in your home country.

Visa Waiver Program & ESTA

➡ The Visa Waiver Program (VWP) allows nationals from 36 countries (including most EU countries, Japan, Australia and New Zealand) to enter the US without a visa for up to 90 days.

➡ VWP visitors require a machine-readable passport and approval under the **Electronic System For Travel Authorization** (ESTA; www.cbp.gov/esta) at least three days before arrival. There is a $14 fee for processing and authorization (payable online). Once approved, the registration is valid for two years.

➡ In essence, ESTA requires that you register specific information online (name, address, passport info etc). You will receive one of three responses: 'Authorization Approved' (this usually comes within minutes; most applicants can expect to receive this response); 'Authorization Pending' (you'll need to check the status within the next 72 hours); or 'Travel not Authorized'. If this is the case, it means you will need to apply for a visa.

➡ Those who need a visa – ie anyone staying longer than 90 days, or from a non-VWP country – should apply at the US consulate in their home country.

➡ Canadians are exempt from the process. They do not need visas, though they do need a passport or document approved by the **Western Hemisphere Travel Initiative** (www.getyouhome.gov).

Visiting Canada

It's temptingly easy to make trips across the border to Canada from the eastern

USA, but upon return, non-Americans will be subject to the full immigration procedure. Always take your passport when you cross the border.

Citizens of most Western countries will not need a visa to visit Canada, so it's really not a problem to cross to the Canadian side of Niagara Falls or detour up to Québec. Travelers entering the USA by bus from Canada may be closely scrutinized.

Volunteering

Volunteering opportunities abound in the eastern USA, providing a memorable chance to interact with locals and the land in ways you never would when just passing through.

Casual, drop-in volunteer work is plentiful in the big cities. Check weekly alternative newspapers for calendar listings or browse the free classified ads online at **Craigslist** (www.craigslist.org). The public website **United We Serve** (www.serve.gov) and private websites **Idealist** (www.idealist.org) and **Volunteer-Match** (www.volunteermatch.org) offer free searchable databases of short- and long-term volunteer opportunities nationwide.

More formal volunteer programs, especially those designed for international travelers, typically charge a fee of $250 to $1000, depending on the length of the program and what amenities are included (eg housing, meals). None cover travel expenses.

Green Project (☑504-945-0240; www.thegreenproject.org) Working to improve battered communities in New Orleans in sustainable, green ways.

Habitat for Humanity (☑800-422-4828; www.habitat.org) Focuses on building affordable housing for those in need.

Sierra Club (☑415-977-5500; www.sierraclub.org) 'Volunteer vacations' restore wilderness areas and maintain trails, including in national parks and nature preserves.

Volunteers for Peace (☑802-540-3060; www.vfp.org) Grassroots, multiweek volunteer projects emphasize manual labor and international exchange.

Wilderness Volunteers (☑928-255-1128; www.wildernessvolunteers.org) Week-long trips helping maintain national parklands and outdoor recreation areas.

World Wide Opportunities on Organic Farms USA (☑415-621-3276; www.wwoofusa.org) Represents more than 2000 organic farms in all 50 states that host volunteer workers in exchange for meals and accommodations, with opportunities for both short- and long-term stays.

Women Travelers

➡ Women traveling by themselves or in a group should encounter no particular problems unique to the eastern USA. Simply use the same common sense as you would at home.

➡ In bars and nightclubs solo women can attract a lot of attention, but if you don't want company, most men will respect a firm 'no, thank you.'

➡ Physical attack is unlikely, but if you are assaulted, consider calling a rape-crisis hotline before calling the police, unless you are in immediate danger, in which case you should call ☑911. The 24-hour **National Sexual Assault Hotline** (☑800-656-4673; https://ohl.rainn.org/online) can help.

➡ The community website www.journeywoman.com facilitates women exchanging travel tips, with links to resources. The Canadian government also publishes the booklet 'Her Own Way,' filled with useful general travel advice; click to travel.gc.ca/travelling/publications to access it.

Work

Seasonal service jobs in tourist beach towns, theme parks and ski areas are common and often easy to get, if low-paying.

If you are a foreigner in the USA with a standard non-immigrant visitors visa, you are expressly forbidden to take paid work in the USA and will be deported if you're caught working illegally. In addition, employers are required to establish the bona fides of their employees or face fines. In particular, South Florida is notorious for large numbers of foreigners working illegally, and immigration officers are vigilant.

To work legally, foreigners need to apply for a work visa before leaving home. Student exchange visitors need a J1 visa, which exchange organizations will help arrange.

For nonstudent jobs, temporary or permanent, you need to be sponsored by a US employer (who will arrange an H-category visa). These are not easy to obtain.

American Institute for Foreign Study (☑866-906-2437; www.aifs.com) Good resource for tracking down study-abroad programs.

Camp America (☑in the UK 020-7581-7373; www.campamerica.co.uk) Offers opportunities to work in a youth summer camp.

Council on International Educational Exchange (☑207-553-4000; www.ciee.org) CIEE has a wide range of programs, including internships, study-abroad programs, work-travel combos and work-exchange programs.

InterExchange (☑212-924-0446; www.interexchange.org) Camp and au-pair programs.

Transportation

GETTING THERE & AWAY

Flights, tours and rental cars can be booked online at www.lonelyplanet.com/bookings.

Entering the Country

Entering the USA is pretty straightforward.

→ If you are flying, the first airport that you land in is where you must go through immigration and customs, even if you are continuing on the flight to another destination.

→ You'll be asked to fill out the US customs declaration form, which is usually handed out on the plane. Have it completed before you approach the immigration desk. For the question, 'US Street Address,' give the address where you will spend the first night (a hotel address is fine).

→ The immigration officer will look at your customs form and passport, and have you register with the Department of Homeland Security's Office of Biometric Identity Management. This entails having your fingerprints scanned and a digital photo taken.

→ The immigration officer may ask about your plans and whether you have sufficient funds. It's a good idea to list an itinerary, produce an onward or round-trip ticket and have at least one major credit card.

→ Travelers from some countries, ie Canada and Visa Waiver Program nations (p649), can bypass the immigration desks and use self-service kiosks for automated passport control. Not all airports have this technology. See www.cbp.gov/travel for details on participating locations and for further eligibility requirements.

→ Once you go through immigration, you collect your baggage and pass through customs. If you have nothing to declare, you'll probably clear customs without a baggage search, but don't assume this.

→ The Electronic System for Travel Authorization (p649) is now required before arrival for citizens of Visa Waiver Program countries.

→ Remember: your passport should be valid for at least six months longer than your intended stay in the US.

Air

Airports

Chicago and Atlanta trade off as the busiest airport. The main international gateways in the eastern USA include the following:

CLIMATE CHANGE & TRAVEL

Every form of transport that relies on carbon-based fuel generates CO_2, the main cause of human-induced climate change. Modern travel is dependent on airplanes, which might use less fuel per kilometer per person than most cars but travel much greater distances. The altitude at which aircraft emit gases (including CO_2) and particles also contributes to their climate change impact. Many websites offer 'carbon calculators' that allow people to estimate the carbon emissions generated by their journey and, for those who wish to do so, to offset the impact of the greenhouse gases emitted with contributions to portfolios of climate-friendly initiatives throughout the world. Lonely Planet offsets the carbon footprint of all staff and author travel.

Atlanta: **Hartsfield-Jackson International** (ATL; www.atlanta-airport.com)

Boston: **Logan International** (BOS; ☎800-235-6426; www.massport.com/logan)

Charlotte: **Charlotte Douglas International** (CLT; ☎704-359-4027; www.charmeck.org/departments/airport; 5501 Josh Birmingham Pkwy)

Chicago: **O'Hare International** (ORD; www.flychicago.com)

Miami: **Miami International** (MIA; ☎305-876-7000; www.miami-airport.com; 2100 NW 42nd Ave)

Minneapolis-St Paul: **Minneapolis-St Paul International** (MSP; www.mspairport.com; ☎)

New York: **John F Kennedy International** (JFK; www.panynj.gov)

Newark: **Liberty International** (EWR; www.panynj.gov)

Orlando: **Orlando International** (MCO, ☎407-825-8463; www.orlandoairports.net; 1 Jeff Fuqua Blvd)

Washington, DC: **Dulles International** (IAD; www.metwashairports.com)

Land

Border Crossings

The eastern USA has more than 20 official border crossings with Canada, accessed via Maine, New Hampshire, Vermont, New York, Michigan and Minnesota. It is relatively easy to cross into Canada; it's crossing *back* that can pose problems if you haven't brought all your documents. **US Customs and Border Protection** (bwt.cbp.gov) tracks current wait times at the main border crossings. Some borders are open 24 hours, but most are not.

In general, waits rarely exceed 30 minutes, except during peak times (ie weekends and holidays, more so in summer). Some entry points are especially busy:

➡ Detroit, MI, to Windsor, Ontario

➡ Buffalo, NY, to Niagara Falls, Ontario

➡ Calais, ME, to St Stephen, New Brunswick

As always, have your papers in order, act polite and don't make jokes or casual conversation with US border officials.

Bus

Greyhound (☎800-231-2222, international customer service 214-849-8100; www.greyhound.com) and its Canadian equivalent, **Greyhound Canada** (☎800-661-8747; www.greyhound.ca), operate the largest bus network in North America. There are direct connections between main cities in the USA and Canada, but you usually have to transfer to a different bus at the border (where it takes a good hour for all passengers to clear customs and immigration). Most international buses have free wi-fi on board.

Megabus (☎877-462-6342; www.megabus.com) also has international routes between Toronto and eastern cities including New York City, Philadelphia and Washington, DC. They are often cheaper than Greyhound. Tickets can be purchased online only.

Car & Motorcycle

➡ To drive across the US–Canadian border, you'll need the vehicle's registration papers, proof of liability insurance and your home driver's license.

➡ Rental cars can usually be driven across the border either way, but make sure your rental agreement says so in case you are questioned by border officials.

➡ If your papers are in order, border crossing is usually fast and easy, but occasionally the authorities of either country decide to search a car *thoroughly*.

Train

Amtrak (☎800-872-7245; www.amtrak.com) and **VIA Rail Canada** (☎888-842-7245; www.viarail.ca) run daily services between Montreal and New York (11 hours), and Toronto and New York via Niagara Falls (13 hours total). Customs inspections happen at the border, not upon boarding.

Sea

Several cities on the East Coast are cruise-ship hubs, including New York City, Boston, New Orleans and Charleston, SC. Florida's ports harbor the most ships of all, particularly Miami, followed by Port Canaveral and Port Everglades (Fort Lauderdale).

You can also travel to and from the eastern USA on a freighter. These vessels usually carry between three and 12 passengers and, though considerably less luxurious than cruise ships, give a salty taste of life at sea.

GREYHOUND INTERNATIONAL BUS ROUTES & FARES

ROUTE	APPROX FARE ($)	DURATION (HR)	FREQUENCY (PER DAY)
Boston–Montréal	80	7-9½	8
Detroit–Toronto	60	5½-6½	5
New York–Montréal	90	8-9	10

For more information on the ever-changing routes:

Cruise & Freighter Travel Association (☎800-872-8584; www.travltips.com)

Maris (www.freightercruises. com)

GETTING AROUND

Air

Flying is usually more expensive than traveling by bus, train or car, but it's the way to go when you're in a hurry.

Airlines in the Eastern USA

Overall, air travel in the USA is very safe (much safer than driving out on the nation's highways). For comprehensive details by carrier, check out **Airsafe.com** (www. airsafe.com).

The main domestic carriers:

American Airlines (☎800-433-7300; www.aa.com) Nationwide service.

Delta Air Lines (☎800-221-1212; www.delta.com) Nationwide service.

Frontier Airlines (☎801-401-9000; www.flyfrontier. com) Denver-based airline with nationwide service.

JetBlue Airways (☎800-538-2583; www.jetblue.com) Nonstop connections between eastern and western US cities, plus Florida and New Orleans.

Southwest Airlines (☎800-435-9792; www.southwest. com) Service across the continental USA.

Spirit Airlines (☎801-401-2200; www.spiritair.com) Florida-based airline; serves many US gateway cities.

United Airlines (☎800-864-8331; www.united.com) Nationwide service.

US Airways (☎800-428-4322; www.usairways.com) Nationwide service.

TRAVELING TO CANADA

It's easy to journey across the border to Canada from the eastern USA and quite common to do so, especially at Niagara Falls. Here are a few things to keep in mind:

➡ You will have to show your passport. The exception is US citizens at land and sea borders, who have other options besides using a passport, such as an enhanced driver's license or passport card. See the **Western Hemisphere Travel Initiative** (www.getyouhome.gov) for approved identification documents.

➡ Citizens of the USA, most Western European nations, Australia, New Zealand and Japan do not need a visa to enter Canada for stays of up to 180 days, but some nationalities do. **Citizenship and Immigration Canada** (www.cic.gc.ca) has the details.

➡ Upon return to the USA, non-Americans will be subject to the full immigration procedure.

➡ For the lowdown on where to go, what to do and all things north of the border, check out Lonely Planet's *Canada* or *Discover Canada* guides.

Virgin America (☎877-359-8474; www.virginamerica.com) Flights between East and West Coast cities and Las Vegas.

There are also smaller regional services:

Cape Air (☎866-227-3247; www.flycapeair.com) Flights to several New England destinations, including Martha's Vineyard and Nantucket.

Isle Royale Seaplanes (☎906-483-4991; www.isleroyale seaplanes.com) Flights to Rock Harbor in Isle Royale National Park from Houghton County Airport in Michigan's Upper Peninsula.

Air Passes

International travelers who plan on doing a lot of flying might consider buying a North American air pass. Passes are normally available only to non–North American citizens, and they must be purchased in conjunction with an international ticket. Conditions and cost structures can be complicated, but all passes include a certain number of domestic flights (from two to 10) that typically must be used within a 60-day period. Two of the

biggest airline networks offering air passes are **Star Alliance** (www.staralliance. com) and **One World** (www. oneworld.com).

Bicycle

Regional bicycle touring is popular: winding back roads and scenic coastlines make for great itineraries. Many cities (including New York City, Chicago, Minneapolis and Boston) also have designated bike routes. Renting a bicycle is easy throughout the eastern USA. Some things to keep in mind:

➡ Cyclists must follow the same rules of the road as vehicles, but don't expect drivers to always respect your right of way.

➡ Helmets are mandatory for cyclists in some states and towns (though there is no federal law that requires it). It usually applies to children under age 18. The **Bicycle Helmet Safety Institute** (www.bhsi.org/mandator.htm) has a thorough, state-by-state list of local rules.

→ The **Better World Club** (📞866-238-1137; www. betterworldclub.com) provides emergency roadside assistance for cyclists. Membership costs $40 per year, plus a $12 enrollment fee, and entitles you to two free pick ups.

→ The **League of American Bicyclists** (www.bikeleague. org) offers general tips, plus lists of local bike clubs and repair shops.

Transportation

If you're bringing your own wheels, call around to check oversize luggage prices and restrictions. Bikes are considered checked luggage on airplanes, but often must be boxed and fees can be high (over $200). Amtrak trains and Greyhound buses will transport bikes within the USA, typically for much less.

Rental

Outfitters renting bicycles exist in most tourist towns. Rentals typically cost between $20 and $30 per day, including a helmet and lock. Most companies require a credit-card security deposit of $200 or so.

Purchase

Buying a bike is easy, as is reselling it before you leave. Specialist bike shops have the best selection and advice for new bikes, but general sporting-goods stores and big-box retailers may have lower prices. Better yet, buy a used bike. To sniff out the best bargains, scour garage sales and thrift shops, or browse the free classified ads at **Craigslist** (www. craigslist.org).

Boat

Several ferry services provide efficient, scenic links in the East. Most ferries transport cars, but you must make reservations well in advance.

Northeast

Bay State Cruise Company (📞877-783-3779; www. boston-ptown.com) Ferries between Boston and Provincetown, MA.

Block Island Ferry (📞401-783-4613; www.blockisland ferry.com) Ferries to Block Island from Narragansett and Newport, RI.

Lake Champlain Ferries (📞802-864-9804; www.ferries. com) Ferries between Burlington, VT, and Port Kent, NY.

Staten Island Ferry (www. siferry.com) Free commuter boats between Staten Island and Manhattan, NY.

Steamship Authority (📞508-477-8600; www.steam shipauthority.com) Ferries to Martha's Vineyard and Nantucket from Cape Cod, MA.

Great Lakes

To reach Mackinac Island, MI, three passenger ferry companies – **Arnold Line** (📞800-542-8528; www.arnoldline.com), **Shepler's** (📞800-828-6157; www.sheplersferry.com) and **Star Line** (📞800-638-9892; www.mackinacferry.com) – operate out of both Mackinaw City and St Ignace, MI.

Two ferry companies cross Lake Michigan: **Lake Express** (📞866-914-1010; www.lake-express.com; one way adult/child/car from $86.50/30/91) glides between Milwaukee, WI, and Muskegon, MI. The **SS Badger** (📞800-841-4243; www. ssbadger.com; one way adult/ child/car from $59/24/59) runs between Manitowoc, WI, and Ludington, MI.

South

Key West Express (📞888-539-2628; www.seakeywest express.com) Catamaran service between Fort Myers and Key West.

North Carolina Ferry System (📞800-293-3779; www. ncdot.gov/ferry) Runs ferries throughout the Outer Banks.

Bus

Greyhound (📞800-231-2222, international customer service 📞214-849-8100; www. greyhound.com) is the major long-distance carrier, plowing along an extensive network throughout the USA, as well as to/from Canada. As a rule, buses are reliable, clean(ish) and comfortable, with air-conditioning, barely reclining seats, on-board lavatories and a no-smoking policy. Several buses have wi-fi. While some shorter-route buses run express, most stop every 50 to 100 miles to pick up passengers, and long-distance buses stop for meal breaks and driver changes.

Other carriers (most with wi-fi and power outlets on board):

BestBus (📞202-332-2691; www.bestbus.com; 20th St & Massachusetts Ave NW; 📶) Cheap fares between the nation's capital and NYC.

BoltBus (📞877-265-8287; www.boltbus.com) Fast, cheap routes between major northeast cities, including NYC, Boston, Philadelphia, Baltimore, Newark and Washington, DC.

Go Bus (www.gobuses.com; Alewife Brook Pkwy; one way $18-34; 📶; Ⓣ Alewife) Plies the Boston-to-NYC route.

Lucky Star Bus (www.lucky starbus.com; South Station; one way $20; 📶) Also runs from Boston to NYC.

Megabus (📞877-462-6342; www.megabus.com) BoltBus' main competitor, with routes between main cities in the Northeast and also the Midwest, radiating from hubs in NYC or Chicago. Fares can be quite low; ticket bookings online only.

Peter Pan Bus Lines (📞800-343-9999; www.peterpanbus. com) Serves more than 50 destinations in the Northeast, as far north as Concord, NH, and as far south as Washington, DC.

Trailways (📞703-691-3052; www.trailways.com) Mostly in

GREYHOUND DOMESTIC BUS ROUTES & FARES

ROUTE	APPROX FARE ($)	DURATION (HR)	FREQUENCY (PER DAY)
Boston–Philadelphia	45-61	7	10
Chicago–New Orleans	96-164	24	5
New York–Chicago	70-138	18-22	6
Washington, DC–Miami	87-170	25	6

the Midwest and Mid-Atlantic states; may not be as useful as Greyhound for long trips, but fares can be competitive on shorter routes.

Costs

➜ In general, the earlier you book, the lower the fare.

➜ On BoltBus, Megabus and some of the smaller companies, the first tickets sold for a route cost $1.

➜ For lower fares on Greyhound, purchase tickets at least seven days in advance (purchasing 14 days in advance will save even more).

➜ If you're traveling with family or friends, Greyhound's companion fares let up to two additional travelers get 50% off with a minimum three-day advance purchase.

Reservations

Greyhound and BoltBus tickets can be bought over the phone or online, as well as at terminals. For Megabus, Go Bus and most of the smaller companies, tickets can only be purchased online in advance. Seating is normally first-come, first-served. Greyhound recommends arriving an hour before departure to get a seat.

Car & Motorcycle

For maximum flexibility and convenience, and to explore outside of the cities, a car is essential.

Automobile Associations

The **American Automobile Association** (AAA; ☎877-428-2277, emergency roadside assistance ☎800-222-4357; www.aaa.com; annual membership from $52) has reciprocal membership agreements with several international auto clubs (check with AAA and bring your membership card from home). For its members, AAA offers travel insurance, tour books and a wide-ranging network of regional offices. AAA advocates politically for the auto industry.

A more eco-friendly alternative, the **Better World Club** (☎866-238-1137; www.betterworldclub.com) donates 1% of revenue to assist environmental cleanup, offers ecologically sensitive choices for every service it provides and advocates politically for environmental causes.

For either organization, the primary member benefit is 24-hour emergency roadside assistance anywhere in the USA. Both also offer trip planning, free travel maps, travel-agency services, car insurance and a range of travel discounts (eg on hotels, car rentals and attractions).

Bring Your Own Vehicle

Unless you're moving to the USA, don't even think about freighting your car.

Driver's License

Foreign visitors can legally drive a car in the USA for up to 12 months using their home driver's license.

However, an International Driving Permit (IDP) will have more credibility with US traffic police, especially if your home license doesn't have a photo or isn't in English. Your automobile association at home can issue an IDP, valid for one year, for a small fee. Always carry your home license together with the IDP.

To drive a motorcycle in the USA, you will need either a valid US state motorcycle license or an IDP specially endorsed for motorcycles.

Fuel

Gas stations are ubiquitous and many are open 24 hours a day. Small-town stations may be open only from 7am to 8pm or 9pm. Plan on spending roughly $3.50 per US gallon. At many stations, you must pay before you pump.

Insurance

Insurance is legally required. Without it, you risk legal consequences and possible financial ruin if there's an accident.

➜ Car-rental agencies offer liability insurance, which covers other people and property involved in an accident.

➜ Collision Damage Waivers (CDW) reduce or eliminate the amount you'll have to reimburse the rental company if there's damage to the car itself.

➜ Paying extra for all of this insurance increases the cost of a rental car by as much as $30 a day.

➜ Some credit cards cover CDW for a certain rental

period (usually less than 15 days), if you use the card to pay for the rental, and decline the policy offered by the rental company. Always check with your card issuer to see what coverage they offer in the USA.

Car Rental

To rent a car in the USA you generally need to be at least 25 years old, hold a valid driver's license and have a major credit card.

➡ Some companies will rent to drivers between the ages of 21 and 24 for an additional charge.

➡ You should be able to get an economy-sized vehicle for about $30 to $75 per day.

➡ Child safety seats are compulsory (reserve them when you book) and cost about $13 per day.

➡ Some national companies, including Avis, Budget and Hertz, offer 'green' fleets of hybrid rental cars (eg Toyota Priuses, Honda Civics), although you'll usually have to pay a lot extra to rent a more fuel-efficient vehicle.

➡ Online, **Car Rental Express** (www.carrental express.com) rates and compares independent agencies in US cities; it's particularly useful for searching out cheaper long-term rentals.

MAJOR NATIONAL CAR-RENTAL COMPANIES

Alamo (☎877-222-9075; www. alamo.com)

Avis (☎800-633-3469; www. avis.com)

Budget (☎800-218-7992; www.budget.com)

Dollar (☎800-800-3665; www.dollar.com)

Enterprise (☎800-261-7331; www.enterprise.com)

Hertz (☎800-654-3131; www. hertz.com)

National (☎877-222-9058; www.nationalcar.com)

Rent-A-Wreck (☎877-877-0700; www.rentawreck.com) Rents cars that may have more wear and tear than your typical rental vehicle but are actually far from wrecks.

Thrifty (☎800-847-4389; www.thrifty.com)

Motorcycle & Recreational Vehicle (RV) Rental

If you dream of riding a Harley, **EagleRider** (☎310-321-3180; www.eaglerider.com) has offices in major cities nationwide and rents other kinds of adventure vehicles, too. Beware that motorcycle rental and insurance are expensive.

Companies specializing in RV and camper rentals:

Adventures on Wheels (www. wheels9.com)

Cruise America (☎800-671-8042; www.cruiseamerica.com)

Road Conditions & Hazards

Road conditions are generally very good, but keep the following in mind.

➡ Winter travel in general can be hazardous due to heavy snow and ice, which may cause roads and bridges to close periodically. The **Federal Highway Administration** (www.fhwa. dot.gov/trafficinfo/index. htm) provides links to road conditions and construction zones for each state.

➡ If you're driving in winter or in remote areas, make sure your vehicle is equipped with four-season radial or snow tires, and emergency supplies in case you're stranded.

➡ Where deer and other wild animals frequently appear roadside, you'll see signs with the silhouette of a leaping deer. Take these signs seriously, particularly at night.

Road Rules

If you're new to US roads, here are some basics:

➡ Drive on the right-hand side of the road. On highways, pass in the left-hand lane.

➡ The maximum speed limit on most interstates is 65mph or 70mph; a couple of eastern states go up to 75mph. It then drops to around 55mph in urban areas. Pay attention to the posted signs. City street speed limits vary between 15mph and 45mph.

➡ The use of seat belts and child safety seats is required in every state. In some states, motorcyclists are required to wear helmets.

➡ Unless signs prohibit it, you may turn right at a red light after first coming to a full stop (note that NYC is an exception, where it's illegal to turn right on a red).

➡ At four-way stop signs, the car that reaches the intersection first has right of way. In a tie, the car on the right when right of way.

➡ When emergency vehicles (ie police, fire or ambulance) approach from either direction, pull over safely and get out of the way.

➡ In an increasing number of states, it is illegal to talk (or text) on a handheld cell phone while driving; use a hands-free device or pull over to take your call.

➡ The blood-alcohol limit for drivers is 0.08%. Penalties are very severe for Driving Under the Influence (DUI) of alcohol and/or drugs.

➡ In some states it is illegal to carry 'open containers' of alcohol in a vehicle, even if they are empty.

Hitchhiking

Hitchhiking in the USA is potentially dangerous and definitely not recommended. Travellers who hitch should understand that they are taking a small but potentially serious risk. Indeed, drivers have heard so many lurid reports they tend to be just as afraid of those with their thumbs out. Hitchhiking on freeways is prohibited.

Local Transportation

Except in large cities, public transportation is rarely the most convenient option for travelers. However, it is usually cheap, safe and reliable. In addition, most states in the nation have adopted ♪511 as an all-purpose local-transportation help line.

Bicycle

Some cities are more friendly to bicycles than others, but most have at least a few dedicated bike lanes and paths, and bikes usually can be carried on public transportation. Many big cities – New York, Chicago, Boston, Miami and Washington, DC among them – have bike-share programs. They're also popping up in other cities such as Cincinnati, Nashville, Indianapolis and Louisville.

Bus

Most cities and larger towns have dependable local bus systems, though they are often designed for commuters and provide limited service in the evening and on weekends. Costs range from free to between $1 and $3 per ride.

Subway & Train

The largest systems are in New York, Chicago, Boston, Philadelphia and Washington, DC. Other cities may have small, one- or two-line rail systems that mainly serve downtown.

Taxi & Rideshare

Taxis are metered, with flag-fall charges of around $2.50, plus $2 to $3 per mile. They charge extra for waiting and handling baggage, and drivers expect a 10% to 15% tip. Taxis cruise the busiest areas in large cities; otherwise, it's easiest to phone and order one. Ride-share companies like **Uber** (www.uber.com) also are well used in most cities.

Tours

Hundreds of companies offer all kinds of organized tours of the USA; most focus on either cities or regions.

Backroads (♪510-527-1555; www.backroads.com) Designs a range of active, multisport and outdoor-oriented trips for all abilities and budgets.

Contiki (♪866-266-8454; www.contiki.com) Party-hardy sightseeing tour-bus vacations for 18- to 35-year-olds.

Gray Line (♪800-472-9546; www.grayline.com) For those short on time, Gray Line offers a comprehensive range of standard sightseeing tours across the country.

Green Tortoise (♪415-956-7500; www.greentortoise.com) Offering budget adventures for independent travelers, Green Tortoise is famous for its sleeping-bunk buses. Most trips leave from San Francisco, traipsing through the West and nationwide.

Road Scholar (♪800-454-5768; www.roadscholar.org) For those aged 50 and older, this venerable nonprofit organization offers 'learning adventures' in all 50 states.

Trek America (in North America ♪800-873-5872, in the UK ♪0333-999-7951; www.trekamerica.com) For active outdoor adventures; group sizes are kept small.

Train

Amtrak (♪800-872-7245; www.amtrak.com) has an extensive rail system throughout the USA, with several long-distance lines traversing the nation east to west, and even more running north to south. These link all of America's biggest cities and many of its smaller ones. In some places, Amtrak's Thruway buses provide connections to and from the rail network.

➡ Compared with other modes of travel, trains are rarely the quickest, cheapest or most convenient option, but they turn the journey into a relaxing, social and scenic all-American experience.

➡ Rail services are busiest in the northeast corridor, where high-speed Acela Express trains run from Boston, MA, to Washington, DC (via New York City, Philadelphia and Baltimore).

➡ Other busy routes include NYC to Niagara Falls, and Chicago to Milwaukee.

➡ Free wi-fi is available on many, but not all, trains. The wi-fi speed is fine for email and web browsing, but usually not suitable for streaming videos or music.

➡ Smoking is prohibited on all trains.

➡ Many big cities, such as NYC, Chicago and Miami, also have their own commuter rail networks. These trains provide faster, more frequent services on shorter routes.

Classes

➡ Coach class buys you a basic, if indeed quite comfortable, reclining seat with a headrest. On some routes you can reserve seats.

➡ Business class is available on many trains, especially on shorter routes in the Northeast. Seats are more spacious and have outlets for plugging in laptops. You also get reserved seating and access to quiet cars (no cell-phone usage etc).

➡ First class is available on Acela Express trains only, and adds an at-seat meal to the mix.

➡ Sleeper class is available on overnight routes. Sleeping cars include simple bunks (called 'roomettes'), bedrooms with ensuite facilities and suites sleeping

TRANSPORTATION TRAIN

AMTRAK SAMPLE FARES

ROUTE	ONE-WAY FARE ($)	DURATION (HR)	FREQUENCY (PER DAY)
Boston–New York	125	3½-4½	11-19
Chicago–New Orleans	127	20	1
New York–Chicago	130	19	1
Washington, DC–Miami	140	23	2

four with two bathrooms. Sleeping-car rates include meals in the dining car, which offers everyone sit-down meal service (pricey if not included).

➡ Food service on commuter lines, when it exists, consists of sandwich and snack bars. Bringing your own food and drink is recommended on all trains.

Costs

➡ Various one-way, round-trip and touring fares are available from Amtrak, with the usual discounts available to seniors (15%), students ($20 or so) and children (50% when accompanied by a paying adult). AAA members get 10% off. Web-only 'Smart Fares' offer good discounts on certain undersold routes.

➡ Generally, the earlier you book, the lower the price. To get many of the standard discounts, you need to reserve at least three days in advance. If you want to take a high-speed Acela Express train, avoid peak commute times and aim for weekends.

➡ **Amtrak Vacations** (☏800-268-7252; www. amtrakvacations.com) offers vacation packages that include rental cars, hotels, tours and attractions. Air-Rail packages let you travel by train in one direction, then return by plane in the other.

Reservations

Reservations can be made any time from 11 months in advance up to the day of departure. Space on most trains is limited, and certain routes can be crowded, especially during summer and holiday periods, so it's a good idea to book as far in advance as you can; this also gives you the best chance of fare discounts.

Train Passes

➡ Amtrak's USA Rail Pass offers coach-class travel for 15 ($460), 30 ($690) or 45 ($900) days, with travel limited to eight, 12 or 18 one-way 'segments,' respectively.

➡ A segment is *not* the same as a one-way trip. If reaching your destination requires riding more than one train (for example, getting from New York to Miami with a transfer in Washington, DC) that one-way trip will actually use two segments of your pass.

➡ Reservations should be made by phone (call ☏800-872-7245, or ☏1-215-856-7953 from outside the USA) as far in advance as possible. Each segment of the journey must be booked.

➡ Present your pass at an Amtrak office to pick up your ticket(s) for each trip.

➡ All travel must be completed within 180 days of purchasing your pass.

➡ Passes are not valid on the Acela Express, Auto Train, Thruway motorcoach connections or the Canadian portion of Amtrak routes operated jointly with Via Rail Canada.

Behind the Scenes

SEND US YOUR FEEDBACK

We love to hear from travelers – your comments keep us on our toes and help make our books better. Our well-traveled team reads every word on what you loved or loathed about this book. Although we cannot reply individually to your submissions, we always guarantee that your feedback goes straight to the appropriate authors, in time for the next edition. Each person who sends us information is thanked in the next edition – the most useful submissions are rewarded with a selection of digital PDF chapters.

Visit **lonelyplanet.com/contact** to submit your updates and suggestions or to ask for help. Our award-winning website also features inspirational travel stories, news and discussions.

Note: We may edit, reproduce and incorporate your comments in Lonely Planet products such as guidebooks, websites and digital products, so let us know if you don't want your comments reproduced or your name acknowledged. For a copy of our privacy policy visit lonelyplanet.com/privacy.

OUR READERS

Many thanks to the travelers who used the last edition and wrote to us with helpful hints, useful advice and interesting anecdotes: Michelle Gonzalez, Lukas Mohr, Manfred Mueller, Liz Ogden, Klaus Stahl, and Andrew Wieland.

AUTHOR THANKS

Karla Zimmerman

Many thanks to Kate Armstrong, Ted Bonar, Bill Brockschmidt, Joe Cimperman, Lisa DiChiera, Lea Dooley, Jim DuFresne, Ruggero Fatica, Julie Lange, Alex Leviton, Kari Lydersen, Zora O'Neill, Keith Pandolfi, Betsy Riley and Neil Anderson, Tamara Robinson, Amy Schwenkmeyer, Susan Hayes Stephan, Andrea and Greg Thomson and Karen and Don Zimmerman. Thanks most to Eric Markowitz, the world's best partner-for-life, who indulges all my hare-brained, pie-filled road trips.

Amy C Balfour

Many thanks to old friends and new friends for introducing me to the best spots in their communities. In the South, thank you Ben and Alison Kimball, Jeff Otto, Anna Schleunes, Jennifer Troch, Lavan Green, Blaire Postman, Gary Haymes, John Park, Sarah Ray Bunn and AT co-warriors Ames Shea and Lynn Neumann.

In New England, thank you Mt Monadnock madman Whit Andrews, Peaches and Genienne Hockensmith, John Shea, Amy Smereck and Amy Stone Scannell.

Adam Karlin

Thank you: the folks who put me up in many an American town, from Fort Lauderdale to Birmingham and Lafayette to Little Rock. To the waiters, bartenders, politicians, park rangers, musicians and mad folks who all gave me (and by extension, you) a tip on what to find. Thank you co-authors, especially my regional chapter homies, Kevin and Amy. Thanks Mom and Dad, who always liked to rub my itchy feet. Thanks Gizmo, for keeping me company on late-night writing jags. Thank you Rachel, my best friend and love and traveling companion extraordinaire, for pushing me to climb the next hill. And thank you Sanda, for the first of many joint explorations.

Zora O'Neill

Many thanks to: Christina Stone-Millan, Meredith Stone, Rich Tyson, Beth Kracklauer, Gabriela Gonzalez, Waverly Duck, Katie Trainor, Brandon del Pozo, Michael LoBianco, Robbi Kearns and Michael Grosberg. Also thanks to generous and kind Filona Ryan, Matt the tow-truck guy, and Bill and Melissa of Bird's Towing. And sort of thanks to the inhospitable residents of Tabernacle-Chatsworth Road: I guess that 5-mile walk was good for me.

BEHIND THE SCENES

Kevin Raub

Thanks to my wife, Adriana Schmidt Raub, who sure does get jealous of all that mac and cheese! Thanks Dora Whitaker and all my partners-in-crime. On the road thanks also to Jason and Jennifer Hatfield, David and Anysley Corbett, Katherine Roberts, Matti Bek Pauli, Ari Glantz, Cindy and Tim Moore, Erica Backus, Carey Dye Ferrara, Katherine Williams, Enma and Andrew Weber, Juliana Mesanelli, Cory O-Born and Luiza and Michael Wettrau.

Regis St Louis

I'm grateful to the many kind friends and locals who provided insight into their cities and neighborhoods. In particular, thanks to Jason and Beth Blair for fun times in Dallas and Galveston, Julien Devereux and Erik Rune in Austin, and co-author Amy C Balfour in Virginia. Big hugs to Kristie and David (and the girls) for hosting me in NY. A *grand merci* to my family: Cassandra, Magdalena and Genevieve for joining me on the road in Texas.

Mara Vorhees

What a great opportunity to explore some new parts of New England. I'm grateful for the guys at Goodyear for keeping me moving! Thanks to J, V and S for joining me on some fun outings – and for holding down the fort at the pink house when I had to go it alone.

ACKNOWLEDGMENTS

Climate map data adapted from Peel MC, Finlayson BL & McMahon TA (2007) 'Updated World Map of the Köppen-Geiger Climate Classification', *Hydrology and Earth System Sciences*, 11, 163344.

Illustrations pp76-7, pp256-7 by Javier Martinez Zarracina.

Cover photograph: Glade Creek Grist Mill, Babcock State Park, West Virginia; Danita Delimont/AWL.

THIS BOOK

This 3rd edition of Lonely Planet's *Eastern USA* guidebook was coordinated by Karla Zimmerman. The content was researched and written by Karla, along with Amy C Balfour, Adam Karlin, Zora O'Neill, Kevin Raub, Regis St Louis and Mara Vorhees. The previous edition was written by Karla Zimmerman, along with Amy C Balfour, Gregor Clark, Ned Friary, Michael Grosberg, Paula Hardy, Adam Karlin, Mariella Krause, Caroline Sieg, Adam Skolnick and Mara Vorhees. This guidebook was produced by the following:

Destination Editor Dora Whitaker

Product Editors Jenna Myers, Luna Soo

Regional Senior Cartographer Alison Lyall

Book Designer Wibowo Rusli

Assisting Editors Charlotte Orr, Monique Perrin

Cover Researcher Naomi Parker

Thanks to Victoria Harrison, Andi Jones, Karyn Noble, Kirsten Rawlings, Alison Ridgway, Angela Tinson, Tony Wheeler

Index

Map Legend

Sights

- Beach
- Bird Sanctuary
- Buddhist
- Castle/Palace
- Christian
- Confucian
- Hindu
- Islamic
- Jain
- Jewish
- Monument
- Museum/Gallery/Historic Building
- Ruin
- Shinto
- Sikh
- Taoist
- Winery/Vineyard
- Zoo/Wildlife Sanctuary
- Other Sight

Activities, Courses & Tours

- Bodysurfing
- Diving
- Canoeing/Kayaking
- Course/Tour
- Sento Hot Baths/Onsen
- Skiing
- Snorkeling
- Surfing
- Swimming/Pool
- Walking
- Windsurfing
- Other Activity

Sleeping

- Sleeping
- Camping

Eating

- Eating

Drinking & Nightlife

- Drinking & Nightlife
- Cafe

Entertainment

- Entertainment

Shopping

- Shopping

Information

- Bank
- Embassy/Consulate
- Hospital/Medical
- Internet
- Police
- Post Office
- Telephone
- Toilet
- Tourist Information
- Other Information

Geographic

- Beach
- Gate
- Hut/Shelter
- Lighthouse
- Lookout
- Mountain/Volcano
- Oasis
- Park
- Pass
- Picnic Area
- Waterfall

Population

- Capital (National)
- Capital (State/Province)
- City/Large Town
- Town/Village

Transport

- Airport
- BART station
- Border crossing
- Boston T station
- Bus
- Cable car/Funicular
- Cycling
- Ferry
- Metro/Muni station
- Monorail
- Parking
- Petrol station
- Subway/SkyTrain station
- Taxi
- Train station/Railway
- Tram
- Underground station
- Other Transport

Note: Not all symbols displayed above appear on the maps in this book

Routes

- Tollway
- Freeway
- Primary
- Secondary
- Tertiary
- Lane
- Unsealed road
- Road under construction
- Plaza/Mall
- Steps
- Tunnel
- Pedestrian overpass
- Walking Tour
- Walking Tour detour
- Path/Walking Trail

Boundaries

- International
- State/Province
- Disputed
- Regional/Suburb
- Marine Park
- Cliff
- Wall

Hydrography

- River, Creek
- Intermittent River
- Canal
- Water
- Dry/Salt/Intermittent Lake
- Reef

Areas

- Airport/Runway
- Beach/Desert
- Cemetery (Christian)
- Cemetery (Other)
- Glacier
- Mudflat
- Park/Forest
- Sight (Building)
- Sportsground
- Swamp/Mangrove

Zora O'Neill

New York, New Jersey & Pennsylvania Zora O'Neill has lived in New York City since 1998 – far from her home state of New Mexico, but very close to where, as a kid and the daughter of a New Jersey native, she spent a week nearly every summer 'down the shore,' eating pizza and fried scallops. Zora has written guidebooks since 2002; for Lonely Planet, she has covered Amsterdam, southern Spain and Egypt. She is online at www.rovinggastronome.com.

Kevin Raub

The South, Florida Kevin Raub grew up in Atlanta and started his career as a music journalist in New York, working for *Men's Journal* and *Rolling Stone* magazines. He ditched the rock 'n' roll lifestyle for travel writing and moved to Brazil. Now he lives outside the country, it's fair to say he immensely enjoyed gorging on Nashville hot chicken, Memphis BBQ, craft beer out the wazoo and various other unmentionables on his voyage through the Southern US. This is Kevin's 35th Lonely Planet guide. Follow him on Twitter (@RaubOnTheRoad).

Regis St Louis

New York, New Jersey & Pennsylvania; Washington, DC & the Capital Region A Hoosier by birth, Regis grew up in a sleepy riverside town where he dreamed of big-city intrigue. He's lived all over the US (including New York City, San Francisco, Los Angeles and New Orleans), and has crossed the country by train, bus and car while visiting remote corners of America. Favorite memories from his most recent trip include crab feasting on Maryland's eastern shore, hiking through striking state parks in west Texas, catching music jams in the Blue Ridge Mountains of Virginia and going eye-to-eye with wild horses on Assateague Island. Regis has contributed to more than 50 Lonely Planet titles, including *New York City* and *Washington, DC*.

Mara Vorhees

New England Born and raised in St Clair Shores, Michigan, Mara traveled the world (if not the universe) before finally settling in the Hub. She spent several years pushing papers and tapping keys at Harvard University, but she has since embraced the life of a full-time travel writer, covering destinations as diverse as Russia and Belize. She lives in a pink house in Somerville, Massachusetts with her husband, two kiddies and two kitties. She is often seen eating doughnuts in Union Square and pedaling her bike along the Charles River. Mara is the coordinating author of Lonely Planet's *New England* and *New England's Best Trips*, among other titles. Follow her adventures online at www.havetwinswilltravel.com.

OUR STORY

A beat-up old car, a few dollars in the pocket and a sense of adventure. In 1972 that's all Tony and Maureen Wheeler needed for the trip of a lifetime – across Europe and Asia overland to Australia. It took several months, and at the end – broke but inspired – they sat at their kitchen table writing and stapling together their first travel guide, *Across Asia on the Cheap*. Within a week they'd sold 1500 copies. Lonely Planet was born.

Today, Lonely Planet has offices in Franklin, London, Melbourne, Oakland, Beijing and Delhi, with more than 600 staff and writers. We share Tony's belief that 'a great guidebook should do three things: inform, educate and amuse'.

OUR WRITERS

Karla Zimmerman

Coordinating Author; Great Lakes, Washington, DC, Plan Your Trip, Understand, Survival Guide As a life-long Midwesterner, Karla is well versed in the region's beaches, ballparks, breweries and pie shops. When she's not home in Chicago watching the Cubs, er, writing for magazines, websites and books, she's out exploring. For this gig, she curled in Minnesota, caught a wave in Michigan, heard the curds squeak in Wisconsin and drank an embarrassing number of milkshakes in Ohio. She also covers DC, where she never fails to shake hands with Racing Abe Lincoln at Nationals Park. Karla has written for several Lonely Planet guides to the USA, Canada, Caribbean and Europe.

Read more about Karla at:
http://auth.lonelyplanet.com/profiles/karlazimmerman

Amy C Balfour

New England, The South Amy has hiked, biked and paddled her way across the US. Raised in the South, she's been visiting the Outer Banks since childhood and for this trip she backpacked along the Appalachian Trail in the Great Smokies. In New Hampshire she explored the White Mountains and tackled Mt Monadnock for the first time. She has authored 27 guidebooks for Lonely Planet and has written for *Backpacker*, *Redbook*, *Southern Living* and the *Washington Post*.

Read more about Amy at:
http://auth.lonelyplanet.com/profiles/amycbalfour

Adam Karlin

The South, Florida Adam has written around 50 guidebooks for Lonely Planet and he always enjoys exploring his native stomping grounds: the US. On this trip, he stumbled into Key West secret gardens, discovered Miami speakeasies, took shots with Birmingham bartenders, weathered tornado watches in Mississippi cotton shacks, found pizza on Arkansas mountain tops, listened to music in dozens of Louisiana bars, paddled through clear Florida mangrove channels and ate a lot of barbecue. He wants you to know that there is a lot of good light in the world, but the way it attaches to a late spring day in the South is something else.

Read more about Adam at:
http://auth.lonelyplanet.com/profiles/adamkarlin

OVER PAGE MORE WRITERS

Published by Lonely Planet Publications Pty Ltd
ABN 36 005 607 983
3rd edition – Apr 2016
ISBN 978 1 74321 863 1
© Lonely Planet 2016   Photographs © as indicated 2016
10 9 8 7 6 5 4 3 2
Printed in China

Although the authors and Lonely Planet have taken all reasonable care in preparing this book, we make no warranty about the accuracy or completeness of its content and, to the maximum extent permitted, disclaim all liability arising from its use.